WESTERN CIVILIZATION

SINCE 1300

WESTERN CIVILIZATION

SINCE 1300

JACKSON J. SPIELVOGEL
The Pennsylvania State University

WADSWORTH
CENGAGE Learning™

Australia • Brazil • Japan • Korea • Mexico • Singapore • Spain • United Kingdom • United States

WADSWORTH
CENGAGE Learning™

Western Civilization, Eighth Edition, Since 1300, AP* Edition

Jackson J. Spielvogel

Senior Publisher: Suzanne Jeans

Senior Sponsoring Editor: Nancy Blaine

Senior Development Editor: Margaret McAndrew Beasley

Assistant Editor: Lauren Floyd

Editorial Assistant: Emma Goehring

Media Editor: Robert St. Laurent

Executive Marketing Manager: Diane Wenckebach

Marketing Coordinator: Lorreen Pelletier

Senior Marketing Communications Manager: Heather Baxley

Associate Content Project Manager: Anne Finley

Senior Art Director: Cate Rickard Barr

Production Technology Analyst: Jeff Joubert

Senior Print Buyer: Judy Inouye

Senior Rights Acquisition Specialist, Text: Katie Huha

Senior Image Rights Acquisition Specialist: Jennifer Meyer Dare

Production Service: John Orr Book Services

Text Designer: Shawn Girsberger

Cover Designer: Tony Saizon

VP, Director, Advanced and Elective Products Programs: Alison Zetterquist

Editorial Coordinator, Advanced and Elective Products Programs: Jean Woy

Cover Image: Dancing, detail from copy of *Kermesse* by Brueghel, 17th century. Gianni Dagli Orti/Musee Calvet Avignon/The Art Archive

Compositor: Glyph International

For product information and technology assistance, contact us at **Cengage Learning Customer & Sales Support, 1-800-354-9706**

For permission to use material from this text or product, submit all requests online at **www.cengage.com/permissions**. Further permissions questions can be emailed to **permissionrequest@cengage.com**.

Library of Congress Control Number: 2010934327

ISBN-13: 978-0-495-91259-0
ISBN-10: 0-495-91259-X

Wadsworth
20 Channel Center Street
Boston, MA 02210
USA

Cengage Learning is a leading provider of customized learning solutions with office locations around the globe, including Singapore, the United Kingdom, Australia, Mexico, Brazil, and Japan. Locate your local office at **international.cengage.com/region**.

Cengage Learning products are represented in Canada by Nelson Education, Ltd.

For your course and learning solutions, visit **www.cengage.com**. Purchase any of our products at your local college store or at our preferred online store **www.CengageBrain.com**.

*AP and the Advanced Placement Program are registered trademarks of the College Entrance Examination Board, which was not involved in the production of, and does not endorse, this product.

Printed in the United States of America
5 6 7 14 13

ABOUT THE AUTHOR

JACKSON J. SPIELVOGEL is associate professor emeritus of history at The Pennsylvania State University. He received his Ph.D. from The Ohio State University, where he specialized in Reformation history under Harold J. Grimm. His articles and reviews have appeared in such journals as *Moreana, Journal of General Education, Catholic Historical Review, Archiv für Reformationsgeschichte,* and *American Historical Review*. He has also contributed chapters or articles to *The Social History of the Reformation, The Holy Roman Empire: A Dictionary Handbook,* the *Simon Wiesenthal Center Annual of Holocaust Studies,* and *Utopian Studies*. His work has been supported by fellowships from the Fulbright Foundation and the Foundation for Reformation Research. At Penn State, he helped inaugurate the Western civilization courses as well as a popular course on Nazi Germany. His book *Hitler and Nazi Germany* was published in 1987 (sixth edition, 2010). He is the coauthor (with William Duiker) of *World History,* first published in 1998 (sixth edition, 2010), and *The Essential World History* (third edition, 2008). Professor Spielvogel has won five major university-wide teaching awards. In 1988–1989, he held the Penn State Teaching Fellowship, the university's most prestigious teaching award. He won the Dean Arthur Ray Warnock Award for Outstanding Faculty Member in 1996 and the Schreyer Honors College Excellence in Teaching Award in 2000.

TO DIANE,
WHOSE LOVE AND SUPPORT MADE IT ALL POSSIBLE
J.J.S.

BRIEF CONTENTS

DOCUMENTS xv

MAPS xxii

FEATURES xxiv

PREFACE xxv

CORRELATION OF TOPICS FOR THE AP* EUROPEAN HISTORY COURSE xxxiii

INTRODUCTION TO STUDENTS OF WESTERN CIVILIZATION xxxvii

WESTERN CIVILIZATION TO 1300 xxxix

PREPARING FOR THE AP* EUROPEAN HISTORY EXAM xliii

TAKING THE AP* EUROPEAN HISTORY EXAM xliv

11 THE LATER MIDDLE AGES: CRISIS AND DISINTEGRATION IN THE FOURTEENTH CENTURY 306

12 RECOVERY AND REBIRTH: THE AGE OF THE RENAISSANCE 340

13 REFORMATION AND RELIGIOUS WARFARE IN THE SIXTEENTH CENTURY 376

14 EUROPE AND THE WORLD: NEW ENCOUNTERS, 1500–1800 413

15 STATE BUILDING AND THE SEARCH FOR ORDER IN THE SEVENTEENTH CENTURY 446

16 TOWARD A NEW HEAVEN AND A NEW EARTH: THE SCIENTIFIC REVOLUTION AND THE EMERGENCE OF MODERN SCIENCE 487

17 THE EIGHTEENTH CENTURY: AN AGE OF ENLIGHTENMENT 513

18 THE EIGHTEENTH CENTURY: EUROPEAN STATES, INTERNATIONAL WARS, AND SOCIAL CHANGE 542

19 A REVOLUTION IN POLITICS: THE ERA OF THE FRENCH REVOLUTION AND NAPOLEON 574

20 THE INDUSTRIAL REVOLUTION AND ITS IMPACT ON EUROPEAN SOCIETY 607

21 REACTION, REVOLUTION, AND ROMANTICISM, 1815–1850 636

22 AN AGE OF NATIONALISM AND REALISM, 1850–1871 670

23 MASS SOCIETY IN AN "AGE OF PROGRESS," 1871–1894 704

24 AN AGE OF MODERNITY, ANXIETY, AND IMPERIALISM, 1894–1914 737

25 THE BEGINNING OF THE TWENTIETH-CENTURY CRISIS: WAR AND REVOLUTION 775

26 THE FUTILE SEARCH FOR STABILITY: EUROPE BETWEEN THE WARS, 1919–1939 812

27 THE DEEPENING OF THE EUROPEAN CRISIS: WORLD WAR II 849

28 COLD WAR AND A NEW WESTERN WORLD, 1945–1965 885

29 PROTEST AND STAGNATION: THE WESTERN WORLD, 1965–1985 920

30 AFTER THE FALL: THE WESTERN WORLD IN A GLOBAL AGE (SINCE 1985) 947

GLOSSARY 981

CHAPTER NOTES 990

INDEX 996

DOCUMENT-BASED QUESTIONS (DBQs) A–1

DETAILED CONTENTS

DOCUMENTS xv

MAPS xxii

FEATURES xxiv

PREFACE xxv

CORRELATION OF TOPICS FOR THE AP* EUROPEAN HISTORY COURSE xxxiii

INTRODUCTION TO STUDENTS OF WESTERN CIVILIZATION xxxvii

WESTERN CIVILIZATION TO 1300 xxxix

PREPARING FOR THE AP* EUROPEAN HISTORY EXAM xliii

TAKING THE AP* EUROPEAN HISTORY EXAM xliv

11 THE LATER MIDDLE AGES: CRISIS AND DISINTEGRATION IN THE FOURTEENTH CENTURY 306

A Time of Troubles: Black Death and Social Crisis 307
Famine and Population 307
The Black Death: From Asia to Europe 307
The Black Death in Europe 308
OPPOSING VIEWPOINTS
CAUSES OF THE BLACK DEATH: CONTEMPORARY VIEWS 309
Economic Dislocation and Social Upheaval 312

War and Political Instability 315
Causes of the Hundred Years' War 315
Conduct and Course of the War 315
Political Instability 319
FILM & HISTORY
JOAN OF ARC (1948), THE MESSENGER: THE STORY OF JOAN OF ARC (1999) 320
The Growth of England's Political Institutions 321
The Problems of the French Kings 321
The German Monarchy 323
The States of Italy 324

The Decline of the Church 326
Boniface VIII and the Conflict with the State 326
The Papacy at Avignon (1305–1377) 326
The Great Schism 327
New Thoughts on Church and State and the Rise of Conciliarism 328
Popular Religion in an Age of Adversity 328
Changes in Theology 329

The Cultural World of the Fourteenth Century 330
The Development of Vernacular Literature 330
Art and the Black Death 332

Society in an Age of Adversity 333
Changes in Urban Life 334
New Directions in Medicine 334
IMAGES OF EVERYDAY LIFE
ENTERTAINMENT IN THE MIDDLE AGES 336
Inventions and New Patterns 336
Chapter Summary, Timeline, and Review 337
AP* Review Questions for Chapter 11 339A

12 RECOVERY AND REBIRTH: THE AGE OF THE RENAISSANCE 340

Meaning and Characteristics of the Italian Renaissance 341

The Making of Renaissance Society 341
Economic Recovery 341
Social Changes in the Renaissance 343
The Family in Renaissance Italy 345

The Italian States in the Renaissance 347
The Five Major States 347
Independent City-States 348
Warfare in Italy 349
The Birth of Modern Diplomacy 350
Machiavelli and the New Statecraft 351

The Intellectual Renaissance in Italy 352
Italian Renaissance Humanism 352
OPPOSING VIEWPOINTS
THE RENAISSANCE PRINCE: THE VIEWS OF MACHIAVELLI AND ERASMUS 353
Education in the Renaissance 355
Humanism and History 357
The Impact of Printing 358

The Artistic Renaissance 358
Art in the Early Renaissance 358
The Artistic High Renaissance 361
The Artist and Social Status 363
The Northern Artistic Renaissance 364
Music in the Renaissance 365

The European State in the Renaissance 366
The Growth of the French Monarchy 366

---

*AP and the Advanced Placement Program are registered trademarks of the College Entrance Examination Board, which was not involved in the production of, and does not endorse, this product.

England: Civil War and a New Monarchy   367

The Unification of Spain   368

The Holy Roman Empire: The Success of the
   Habsburgs   369

The Struggle for Strong Monarchy in Eastern Europe   369

The Ottoman Turks and the End of the Byzantine
   Empire   370

The Church in the Renaissance   370

The Problems of Heresy and Reform   370

The Renaissance Papacy   372

Chapter Summary, Timeline, and Review   373

💡 **AP* Review Questions for Chapter 12   375A**

13 REFORMATION AND RELIGIOUS WARFARE IN THE SIXTEENTH CENTURY   376

Prelude to Reformation   377

Christian or Northern Renaissance Humanism   377

Church and Religion on the Eve of the Reformation   379

Martin Luther and the Reformation in Germany   380

The Early Luther   380

FILM & HISTORY
***LUTHER* (2003)   383**

The Rise of Lutheranism   383

Organizing the Church   386

Germany and the Reformation: Religion and Politics   386

The Spread of the Protestant Reformation   389

Lutheranism in Scandinavia   389

The Zwinglian Reformation   389

The Radical Reformation: The Anabaptists   390

OPPOSING VIEWPOINTS
**A REFORMATION DEBATE: CONFLICT
   AT MARBURG   391**

The Reformation in England   392

John Calvin and Calvinism   394

The Social Impact of the Protestant Reformation   396

The Family   396

Education in the Reformation   397

Religious Practices and Popular Culture   398

The Catholic Reformation   398

Revival of the Old   399

The Society of Jesus   399

A Revived Papacy   401

The Council of Trent   402

Politics and the Wars of Religion in the Sixteenth Century   402

The French Wars of Religion (1562–1598)   402

Philip II and Militant Catholicism   404

Revolt of the Netherlands   405

The England of Elizabeth   407

FILM & HISTORY
***ELIZABETH* (1998)   409**

Chapter Summary, Timeline, and Review   410

💡 **AP* Review Questions for Chapter 13   412A**

14 EUROPE AND THE WORLD: NEW ENCOUNTERS, 1500–1800   413

On the Brink of a New World   414

The Motives for Expansion   414

The Means for Expansion   415

New Horizons: The Portuguese and Spanish Empires   416

The Development of a Portuguese Maritime Empire   416

IMAGES OF EVERYDAY LIFE
SPICES AND WORLD TRADE   418

Voyages to the New World   419

The Spanish Empire in the New World   420

New Rivals on the World Stage   426

Africa: The Slave Trade   426

The West in Southeast Asia   429

The French and British in India   430

OPPOSING VIEWPOINTS
**WEST MEETS EAST: AN EXCHANGE
   OF ROYAL LETTERS   431**

China   432

Japan   433

The Americas   435

The Impact of European Expansion   437

The Conquered   437

FILM & HISTORY
***THE MISSION* (1986)   439**

The Conquerors   439

Toward a World Economy   442

Economic Conditions in the Sixteenth
   Century   442

The Growth of Commercial Capitalism   442

Mercantilism   443

Overseas Trade and Colonies: Movement
   Toward Globalization   443

Chapter Summary, Timeline, and Review   444

💡 **AP* Review Questions for Chapter 14   445A**

15 STATE BUILDING AND THE SEARCH FOR ORDER IN THE SEVENTEENTH CENTURY   446

Social Crises, War, and Rebellions   447

The Witchcraft Craze   447

The Thirty Years' War   449

A Military Revolution?   452

Rebellions   454

The Practice of Absolutism: Western Europe   454
   Absolute Monarchy in France   454
   The Reign of Louis XIV (1643–1715)   456
   The Decline of Spain   461

Absolutism in Central, Eastern, and Northern Europe   462
   The German States   462
   Italy: From Spanish to Austrian Rule   464
   Russia: From Fledgling Principality to Major Power   464
   The Great Northern States   466
   The Ottoman Empire   468
   The Limits of Absolutism   469

Limited Monarchy and Republics   470
   The Weakness of the Polish Monarchy   470
   The Golden Age of the Dutch Republic   470
   England and the Emergence of Constitutional Monarchy   471
   IMAGES OF EVERYDAY LIFE
   DUTCH DOMESTICITY   472
   OPPOSING VIEWPOINTS
   OLIVER CROMWELL: THREE PERSPECTIVES   475

The Flourishing of European Culture   479
   The Changing Faces of Art   479
   A Wondrous Age of Theater   483
   Chapter Summary, Timeline, and Review   484
   💡 **AP* Review Questions for Chapter 15   486A**

16 TOWARD A NEW HEAVEN AND A NEW EARTH: THE SCIENTIFIC REVOLUTION AND THE EMERGENCE OF MODERN SCIENCE   487

Background to the Scientific Revolution   488
   Ancient Authors and Renaissance Artists   488
   Technological Innovations and Mathematics   488
   Renaissance Magic   489

Toward a New Heaven: A Revolution in Astronomy   489
   Copernicus   490
   Brahe   491
   Kepler   491
   Galileo   493
   OPPOSING VIEWPOINTS
   A NEW HEAVEN? FAITH VERSUS REASON   496
   Newton   497

Advances in Medicine and Chemistry   499
   Paracelsus   500
   Vesalius   500
   William Harvey   500
   Chemistry   501

Women in the Origins of Modern Science   501
   Margaret Cavendish   501
   Maria Merian   502
   Maria Winkelmann   502
   Debates on the Nature of Women   502

Toward a New Earth: Descartes, Rationalism, and a New View of Humankind   504

The Scientific Method and the Spread of Scientific Knowledge   505
   The Scientific Method   505
   The Spread of Scientific Knowledge   506
   Science and Religion   508
   Chapter Summary, Timeline, and Review   511
   💡 **AP* Review Questions for Chapter 16   512A**

17 THE EIGHTEENTH CENTURY: AN AGE OF ENLIGHTENMENT   513

The Enlightenment   514
   The Paths to Enlightenment   514
   The Philosophes and Their Ideas   516
   The Social Environment of the Philosophes   524
   OPPOSING VIEWPOINTS
   WOMEN IN THE AGE OF THE ENLIGHTENMENT: ROUSSEAU AND WOLLSTONECRAFT   525

Culture and Society in the Enlightenment   526
   Innovations in Art, Music, and Literature   526
   FILM & HISTORY
   AMADEUS (1984)   531
   The High Culture of the Eighteenth Century   531
   Crime and Punishment   533
   The World of Medicine   533
   Popular Culture   534

Religion and the Churches   536
   The Institutional Church   536
   Popular Religion in the Eighteenth Century   538
   Chapter Summary, Timeline, and Review   540
   💡 **AP* Review Questions for Chapter 17   541A**

18 THE EIGHTEENTH CENTURY: EUROPEAN STATES, INTERNATIONAL WARS, AND SOCIAL CHANGE   542

The European States   543
   Enlightened Absolutism?   543
   The Atlantic Seaboard States   544
   FILM & HISTORY
   MARIE ANTOINETTE (2006)   546
   Absolutism in Central and Eastern Europe   547

OPPOSING VIEWPOINTS
ENLIGHTENED ABSOLUTISM: ENLIGHTENED OR ABSOLUTE? 551
  The Mediterranean World 553
  The Scandinavian States 554
  Enlightened Absolutism Revisited 554

Wars and Diplomacy 554
  The War of the Austrian Succession (1740–1748) 554
  The Seven Years' War (1756–1763) 555
  European Armies and Warfare 557

Economic Expansion and Social Change 558
  Growth of the European Population 558
  Family, Marriage, and Birthrate Patterns 558
  An Agricultural Revolution? 561
  New Methods of Finance 562
  European Industry 563
  Mercantile Empires and Worldwide Trade 564

The Social Order of the Eighteenth Century 565
  The Peasants 566
  The Nobility 566
  IMAGES OF EVERYDAY LIFE
  THE ARISTOCRATIC WAY OF LIFE 568
  The Inhabitants of Towns and Cities 569
  Chapter Summary, Timeline, and Review 572

💡 **AP* Review Questions for Chapter 18** 573A

19 **A REVOLUTION IN POLITICS: THE ERA OF THE FRENCH REVOLUTION AND NAPOLEON** 574

The Beginning of the Revolutionary Era: The American Revolution 575
  The War for Independence 575
  Forming a New Nation 576
  Impact of the American Revolution on Europe 578

Background to the French Revolution 578
  Social Structure of the Old Regime 578
  Other Problems Facing the French Monarchy 580

The French Revolution 581
  From Estates-General to a National Assembly 581
  Destruction of the Old Regime 583
  OPPOSING VIEWPOINTS
  THE NATURAL RIGHTS OF THE FRENCH PEOPLE: TWO VIEWS 584
  The Radical Revolution 588
  Reaction and the Directory 596

The Age of Napoleon 597
  The Rise of Napoleon 597
  The Domestic Policies of Emperor Napoleon 599
  Napoleon's Empire and the European Response 601

The Fall of Napoleon 603
Chapter Summary, Timeline, and Review 604

💡 **AP* Review Questions for Chapter 19** 606A

20 **THE INDUSTRIAL REVOLUTION AND ITS IMPACT ON EUROPEAN SOCIETY** 607

The Industrial Revolution in Great Britain 608
  Origins 608
  Technological Changes and New Forms of Industrial Organization 610
  Britain's Great Exhibition of 1851 614

The Spread of Industrialization 616
  Industrialization on the Continent 616
  The Industrial Revolution in the United States 618
  Limiting the Spread of Industrialization in the Nonindustrialized World 619

The Social Impact of the Industrial Revolution 621
  Population Growth 621
  The Growth of Cities 622
  IMAGES OF EVERYDAY LIFE
  LIVING CONDITIONS OF LONDON'S POOR 624
  New Social Classes: The Industrial Middle Class 625
  OPPOSING VIEWPOINTS
  ATTITUDES OF THE INDUSTRIAL MIDDLE CLASS IN BRITAIN AND JAPAN 626
  New Social Classes: Workers in the Industrial Age 627
  Standards of Living 631
  Efforts at Change: The Workers 631
  Efforts at Change: Reformers and Government 633
  Chapter Summary, Timeline, and Review 633

💡 **AP* Review Questions for Chapter 20** 635A

21 **REACTION, REVOLUTION, AND ROMANTICISM, 1815–1850** 636

The Conservative Order (1815–1830) 637
  The Peace Settlement 637
  The Ideology of Conservatism 639
  Conservative Domination: The Concert of Europe 640
  Conservative Domination: The European States 643

The Ideologies of Change 647
  Liberalism 647
  Nationalism 649
  Early Socialism 650

Revolution and Reform (1830–1850) 651
  Another French Revolution 651
  Revolutionary Outbursts in Belgium, Poland, and Italy 652
  Reform in Great Britain 652

OPPOSING VIEWPOINTS
RESPONSE TO REVOLUTION: TWO PERSPECTIVES   653
The Revolutions of 1848   654
The Maturing of the United States   657

The Emergence of an Ordered Society   658
New Police Forces   659
Prison Reform   661

Culture in an Age of Reaction and Revolution: The Mood of Romanticism   662
The Characteristics of Romanticism   662
Romantic Poets   664
Romanticism in Art   664
Romanticism in Music   665
The Revival of Religion in the Age of Romanticism   667
Chapter Summary, Timeline, and Review   667
AP* Review Questions for Chapter 21   669A

22 AN AGE OF NATIONALISM AND REALISM, 1850–1871   670

The France of Napoleon III   671
Louis Napoleon: Toward the Second Empire   671
The Second Napoleonic Empire   671
OPPOSING VIEWPOINTS
THE PRACTICE OF *REALPOLITIK*: TWO APPROACHES   672
Foreign Policy: The Mexican Adventure   673
Foreign Policy: The Crimean War   673

National Unification: Italy and Germany   676
The Unification of Italy   676
The Unification of Germany   678

Nation Building and Reform: The National State in Midcentury   682
The Austrian Empire: Toward a Dual Monarchy   682
Imperial Russia   683
Great Britain: The Victorian Age   685
FILM & HISTORY
***THE YOUNG VICTORIA* (2009)   687**
The United States: Slavery and War   688
The Emergence of a Canadian Nation   689

Industrialization and the Marxist Response   690
Industrialization on the Continent   690
Marx and Marxism   691

Science and Culture in an Age of Realism   692
A New Age of Science   693
Charles Darwin and the Theory of Organic Evolution   694
A Revolution in Health Care   695
Science and the Study of Society   698
Realism in Literature   698
Realism in Art   698
Music: The Twilight of Romanticism   700

Chapter Summary, Timeline, and Review   701
AP* Review Questions for Chapter 22   703A

23 MASS SOCIETY IN AN "AGE OF PROGRESS," 1871–1894   704

The Growth of Industrial Prosperity   705
New Products   705
New Markets   706
New Patterns in an Industrial Economy   708
Women and Work: New Job Opportunities   710
Organizing the Working Classes   711

The Emergence of a Mass Society   714
Population Growth   714
Emigration   715
Transformation of the Urban Environment   716
Social Structure of the Mass Society   719
"The Woman Question": The Role of Women   720
OPPOSING VIEWPOINTS
ADVICE TO WOMEN: TWO VIEWS   721
IMAGES OF EVERYDAY LIFE
THE MIDDLE-CLASS FAMILY   724
Education in the Mass Society   725
Mass Leisure   727
Mass Consumption   729

The National State   729
Western Europe: The Growth of Political Democracy   729
Central and Eastern Europe: Persistence of the Old Order   731
Chapter Summary, Timeline, and Review   734
AP* Review Questions for Chapter 23   736A

24 AN AGE OF MODERNITY, ANXIETY, AND IMPERIALISM, 1894–1914   737

Toward the Modern Consciousness: Intellectual and Cultural Developments   738
Developments in the Sciences: The Emergence of a New Physics   738
Toward a New Understanding of the Irrational   739
Sigmund Freud and Psychoanalysis   740
The Impact of Darwin   741
The Attack on Christianity   742
The Culture of Modernity: Literature   743
Modernism in the Arts   744
Modernism in Music   747

Politics: New Directions and New Uncertainties   749
The Movement for Women's Rights   749
IMAGES OF EVERYDAY LIFE
THE STRUGGLE FOR THE RIGHT TO VOTE   751
Jews in the European Nation-State   752

The Transformation of Liberalism: Great Britain and
Italy   753
France: Travails of the Third Republic   755
Growing Tensions in Germany   755
Austria-Hungary: The Problem of the Nationalities   756
Industrialization and Revolution in Imperial Russia   756
The Rise of the United States   758
The Growth of Canada   758

The New Imperialism   759
Causes of the New Imperialism   759
OPPOSING VIEWPOINTS
**WHITE MAN'S BURDEN VERSUS BLACK
MAN'S BURDEN   760**
The Scramble for Africa   761
Imperialism in Asia   763
Responses to Imperialism   766
Results of the New Imperialism   768

International Rivalry and the Coming of War   769
The Bismarckian System   769
New Directions and New Crises   770
Chapter Summary, Timeline, and Review   772
💡 **AP⁕ Review Questions for Chapter 24   774A**

**25 THE BEGINNING OF THE
TWENTIETH-CENTURY CRISIS:
WAR AND REVOLUTION   775**

The Road to World War I   776
Nationalism   776
Internal Dissent   776
Militarism   777
The Outbreak of War: The Summer of 1914   777

The War   780
1914–1915: Illusions and Stalemate   780
1916–1917: The Great Slaughter   783
The Widening of the War   785
FILM & HISTORY
***PATHS OF GLORY* (1957)   787**
IMAGES OF EVERYDAY LIFE
LIFE IN THE TRENCHES   788
A New Kind of Warfare   790
The Home Front: The Impact of Total War   791

War and Revolution   797
The Russian Revolution   797
The Last Year of the War   803
Revolutionary Upheavals in Germany
and Austria-Hungary   804

The Peace Settlement   804
Peace Aims   805
OPPOSING VIEWPOINTS
THREE VOICES OF PEACEMAKING   806
The Treaty of Versailles   807
The Other Peace Treaties   807
Chapter Summary, Timeline, and Review   809
💡 **AP⁕ Review Questions for Chapter 25   811A**

**26 THE FUTILE SEARCH FOR
STABILITY: EUROPE BETWEEN
THE WARS, 1919–1939   812**

An Uncertain Peace   813
The Impact of World War I   813
The Search for Security   813
The Hopeful Years (1924–1929)   814
The Great Depression   815

The Democratic States in the West   816
Great Britain   817
France   819
The Scandinavian States   819
The United States   819
European States and the World: The Colonial Empires   820

The Authoritarian and Totalitarian States   821
The Retreat from Democracy   822
Fascist Italy   822
Hitler and Nazi Germany   826
The Soviet Union   833
Authoritarianism in Eastern Europe   836
Dictatorship in the Iberian Peninsula   836
OPPOSING VIEWPOINTS
**SPAIN DIVIDED: THE POEMS
OF TWO BROTHERS   837**

The Expansion of Mass Culture and Mass Leisure   839
Radio and Movies   839
Mass Leisure   840
FILM & HISTORY
***TRIUMPH OF THE WILL* (1934)   841**

*Cultural and Intellectual Trends in the Interwar
Years*   842
Nightmares and New Visions: Art and Music   842
The Search for the Unconscious in Literature   845
The Unconscious in Psychology: Carl Jung   845
The "Heroic Age of Physics"   846
Chapter Summary, Timeline, and Review   847
💡 **AP⁕ Review Questions for Chapter 26   848A**

**27 THE DEEPENING OF THE
EUROPEAN CRISIS: WORLD
WAR II   849**

Prelude to War (1933–1939)   850
The Role of Hitler   850
The "Diplomatic Revolution" (1933–1936)   850
The Path to War in Europe (1937–1939)   852
OPPOSING VIEWPOINTS
THE MUNICH CONFERENCE: TWO VIEWS   855
The Path to War in Asia   855

The Course of World War II   857
Victory and Stalemate   857
The War in Asia   859

The Turning Point of the War (1942–1943)   861
The Last Years of the War   864

The New Order   865

The Nazi Empire   865
Resistance Movements   867
The Holocaust   867
FILM & HISTORY
***EUROPA, EUROPA* (1990)   869**
The New Order in Asia   871

The Home Front   872

The Mobilization of Peoples   872
Front-Line Civilians: The Bombing of Cities   875

Aftermath of the War   877

The Costs of World War II   877
IMAGES OF EVERYDAY LIFE
THE IMPACT OF TOTAL WAR   878
The Allied War Conferences   879
Emergence of the Cold War   880
Chapter Summary, Timeline, and Review   882

💡 **AP* Review Questions for Chapter 27   884A**

**COLD WAR AND A NEW
WESTERN WORLD,
1945–1965   885**

Development of the Cold War   886

Confrontation of the Superpowers   886
OPPOSING VIEWPOINTS
**WHO STARTED THE COLD WAR? AMERICAN
AND SOVIET PERSPECTIVES   887**
FILM & HISTORY
***THE THIRD MAN* (1949)   889**
Globalization of the Cold War   891

Europe and the World: Decolonization   894

Africa: The Struggle for Independence   895
Conflict in the Middle East   896
Asia: Nationalism and Communism   898
Decolonization and Cold War Rivalries   900

Recovery and Renewal in Europe   900

The Soviet Union: From Stalin to Khrushchev   900
Eastern Europe: Behind the Iron Curtain   902
Western Europe: The Revival of Democracy
and the Economy   903
Western Europe: The Move Toward Unity   907

The United States and Canada: A New Era   908

American Politics and Society in the 1950s   908
Decade of Upheaval: America in the 1960s   908
The Development of Canada   909

Postwar Society and Culture in the Western World   909

The Structure of European Society   909
Creation of the Welfare State   910
IMAGES OF EVERYDAY LIFE
THE RISE OF THE SUPERMARKET   911
Women in the Postwar Western World   912

Postwar Art and Literature   913
The Philosophical Dilemma: Existentialism   915
The Attempt to Revive Religion   915
The Explosion of Popular Culture   916
Chapter Summary, Timeline, and Review   917

💡 **AP* Review Questions for Chapter 28   919A**

**PROTEST AND STAGNATION:
THE WESTERN WORLD,
1965–1985   920**

A Culture of Protest   921

A Revolt in Sexual Mores   921
Youth Protest and Student Revolt   921
IMAGES OF EVERYDAY LIFE
YOUTH CULTURE IN THE 1960S   922
The Feminist Movement   924
Antiwar Protests   925

A Divided Western World   925

Stagnation in the Soviet Union   925
Conformity in Eastern Europe   926
Repression in East Germany and Romania   927
Western Europe: The Winds of Change   927
OPPOSING VIEWPOINTS
**CZECHOSLOVAKIA, 1968: TWO FACES
OF COMMUNISM   928**
The United States: Turmoil and Tranquillity   931
Canada   932

The Cold War: The Move to Détente   932

The Second Vietnam War   932
FILM & HISTORY
***DR. STRANGELOVE, OR: HOW I LEARNED
TO STOP WORRYING AND LOVE THE BOMB*
(1964)   933**
China and the Cold War   935
The Practice of Détente   936
The Limits of Détente   937

Society and Culture in the Western World   937

The World of Science and Technology   937
The Environment and the Green
Movements   938
Postmodern Thought   939
Trends in Art, Literature, and Music   940
Popular Culture: Image and Globalization   942
Chapter Summary, Timeline, and Review   944

💡 **AP* Review Questions for Chapter 29   946A**

**AFTER THE FALL: THE WESTERN
WORLD IN A GLOBAL AGE
(SINCE 1985)   947**

Toward a New Western Order   948

The Revolutionary Era in the Soviet Union   948
Eastern Europe: The Revolutions of 1989
and the Collapse of the Communist Order   952

The Reunification of Germany   954
The Disintegration of Yugoslavia   954
Western Europe and the Search for Unity   957
FILM & HISTORY
***THE LIVES OF OTHERS* (2006)   958**
The Unification of Europe   960
The United States: Move to the Center   961
Contemporary Canada   962

After the Cold War: New World Order or Age of Terrorism?   962
The End of the Cold War   962
An Age of Terrorism?   963
Terrorist Attack on the United States   964
The West and Islam   965

New Directions and New Problems in Western Society   966
Transformation in Women's Lives   966
Guest Workers and Immigrants   967

Western Culture Today   968
Varieties of Religious Life   968
OPPOSING VIEWPOINTS
**ISLAM AND THE WEST: SECULARISM
IN FRANCE   969**

Art and Music in the Age of Commerce: The 1980s
and 1990s   970

The Digital Age   972
The Technological World   972
Music and Art in the Digital Age   973
Reality in the Digital Age   973

*Toward a Global Civilization: New Challenges
and Hopes*   974
The Global Economy   975
Globalization and the Environmental
Crisis   976
The Social Challenges of Globalization   976
New Global Movements and New Hopes   978
Chapter Summary, Timeline, and Review   979
💡 **AP⁎ Review Questions for Chapter 30   980A**

GLOSSARY   981

CHAPTER NOTES   990

INDEX   996

DOCUMENT-BASED QUESTIONS (DBQs)   A–1

DOCUMENTS

CHAPTER 11

OPPOSING VIEWPOINTS: CAUSES OF THE BLACK DEATH: CONTEMPORARY VIEWS   309

Giovanni Boccaccio, *Decameron*. From *The Decameron* by Giovanni Boccaccio, trans. by Frances Winwar, pp. xxii–xxiv, xxviii–xxix. Reprinted by permission of The Limited Editions Club.

Geoffrey de Meaux on astrological causes, On Earthquakes as the cause of plague, Herman Gigas on well-poisoning. From Rosemary Horrox, ed., *The Black Death* (Manchester: Manchester University Press, 1994), pp. 167, 169, 171, 177–178, 207.

THE CREMATION OF THE STRASBOURG JEWS   312

From *The Jew in the Medieval World* by Jacob R. Marcus. Copyright 1972 by Atheneum. Reprinted with permission of The Hebrew Union College Press.

A REVOLT OF FRENCH PEASANTS   314

From CHRONICLES by Froissart, translated by Geoffrey Brereton (Penguin Classics, 1968, Revised 1978). Translation copyright © Geoffrey Brereton, 1968. Reproduced by permission of Penguin Books, Ltd.

THE HUNDRED YEARS' WAR   317

From CHRONICLES by Froissart, translated by Geoffrey Brereton (Penguin Classics, 1968, Revised 1978). Translation copyright © Geoffrey Brereton, 1968. Reproduced by permission of Penguin Books, Ltd.

A FEMINIST HEROINE: CHRISTINE DE PIZAN ON JOAN OF ARC   322

From *The Writings of Christine de Pizan,* edited by Charity Cannon Willard. Copyright © 1994 by Persea Books, Inc. Reprinted by permission of Persea Books, Inc. (New York).

BONIFACE VIII'S DEFENSE OF PAPAL SUPREMACY   327

From *Select Historical Documents of the Middle Ages* by Ernest F. Henderson. London: George Bell & Sons, 1896.

DANTE'S VISION OF HELL   331

From THE DIVINE COMEDY by Dante Alighieri, translated by John Ciardi. Copyright 1954, 1957, 1959, 1960, 1961, 1965, 1967, 1970 by the Ciardi Family Publishing Trust. Used by permission of W. W. Norton & Company, Inc.

THE LEGAL RIGHTS OF WOMEN   335

From *Not in God's Image: Women in History from the Greeks to Victorians* by Julia O'Faolain and Lauro Martines. Copyright © 1973 by Julia O'Faolain and Lauro Martines. Reprinted by permission of the authors.

CHAPTER 12

A RENAISSANCE BANQUET   342

Reprinted from *Food in History* by Reay Tannahill, copyright © 1973, 1988 by Reay Tannahill.

MARRIAGE NEGOTIATIONS   347

From *The Society of Renaissance Florence,* edited by Gene Brucker. Copyright © 1971 by Gene Brucker.

THE LETTERS OF ISABELLA D'ESTE   350

Reuse of excerpt from The Letters of Isabella d'Este from THE BED AND THE THRONE by GEORGE R. MAREK. Copyright © 1976 by George R. Marek. Reprinted by permission of HarperCollins Publishers.

OPPOSING VIEWPOINTS: THE RENAISSANCE PRINCE: THE VIEWS OF MACHIAVELLI AND ERASMUS   353

Machiavelli, *The Prince* (1513). From *The Prince* by Machiavelli, translated by David Wootton, pp. 51–52. Copyright © 1995 by Hackett Publishing Company, Inc. Reprinted by permission of Hackett Publishing Company, Inc. All rights reserved.

Erasmas, *Education of a Christian Prince.* From *The Education of a Christian Prince*, by Erasmus, translated by L. K. Born. Copyright © 1936 by Columbia University Press. Reprinted with permission of the publisher.

PETRARCH: MOUNTAIN CLIMBING AND THE SEARCH FOR SPIRITUAL CONTENTMENT   354

From *The Renaissance Philosophy of Man* by Ernst Cassirer, Paul Kristeller, and John Randall, Jr. Copyright © 1948 by University of Chicago Press. Reprinted by permission of the publisher.

PICO DELLA MIRANDOLA AND THE DIGNITY OF MAN   356

From *The Renaissance Philosophy of Man* by Ernst Cassirer, Paul Kristeller, and John Randall, Jr. Copyright © 1948 by University of Chicago Press. Reprinted by permission of the publisher.

A WOMAN'S DEFENSE OF LEARNING   357

Laura Cereta, "Defense of the Liberal Instruction of Women," from *Her Immaculate Hand: Selected Works by and about the Women Humanists of Quattrocentro Italy,* ed. by Margaret King and Albert Rabil (Pegasus Press, Asheville, NC, 2000). Reprinted by permission.

THE GENIUS OF LEONARDO DA VINCI   364

From LIVES OF THE ARTISTS VOLUME I by Giorgio Vasari, translated by George Bull (Penguin Classics, 1965). Translation © George Bull, 1965. Reproduced by permission of Penguin Books, Ltd.

CHAPTER 13

ERASMUS: IN PRAISE OF FOLLY   379

"The Praise of Folly" from THE ESSENTIAL ERASMUS by Erasmus, translated by John P. Dolan, copyright © 1964 by John P. Dolan. Used by permission of Dutton Signet, a division of Penguin Group (USA) Inc.

LUTHER AND THE NINETY-FIVE THESES **382**

From *Martin Luther: Documents of Modern History* by
E. G. Rupp and Benjamin Drewery. Palgrave Macmillan, 1970.
Reproduced with permission of Palgrave Macmillan.

**LUTHER AND THE "ROBBING AND MURDERING
HORDES OF PEASANTS"** **385**

From *Martin Luther: Documents of Modern History* by
E. G. Rupp and Benjamin Drewery. Palgrave Macmillan, 1970.
Reproduced with permission of Palgrave Macmillan.

**OPPOSING VIEWPOINTS: A REFORMATION DEBATE:
CONFLICT AT MARBURG** **391**

"The Marburg Colloquy," from GREAT DEBATES OF THE
REFORMATION, edited by Donald Ziegler, copyright © 1969
by Donald Ziegler. Used by permission of Modern Library, a
division of Random House, Inc.

**THE ROLE OF DISCIPLINE IN THE "MOST PERFECT
SCHOOL OF CHRIST ON EARTH"** **396**

From *The Reformation: A Narrative History Related by
Contemporary Observers and Participants* by Hans J.
Hillerbrand. Copyright © 1964 by Harper & Row, Publishers.
Reprinted with permission of Hans J. Hillerbrand.

A PROTESTANT WOMAN **397**

From *Not in God's Image: Women in History from the Greeks to
Victorians* by Julia O'Faolain and Lauro Martines. Copyright
© 1973 by Julia O'Faolain and Lauro Martines. Reprinted by
permission of the authors.

**LOYOLA AND OBEDIENCE TO "OUR HOLY MOTHER,
THE HIERARCHICAL CHURCH"** **400**

Excerpt from *The Spiritual Exercises of St. Ignatius of Loyola*
translated by Louis J. Puhl, S.J. (Newman Press 1951).
Reprinted with permission of Loyola Press. To order copies of
this book, call 1-800-621-1008 or visit www.loyolabooks.org.

**QUEEN ELIZABETH ADDRESSES PARLIAMENT
(1601)** **408**

From *Elizabeth I and Her Parliaments* by John E. Neale.
London: Jonathan Cape, 1953.

CHAPTER 14

THE PORTUGUESE CONQUEST OF MALACCA **419**

From *The World of Southeast Asia: Selected Historical Readings*,
Harry J. Benda and John A. Larkin, eds. Copyright © 1967 by
Harper & Row Publishers. Used with permission of John A.
Larkin.

COLUMBUS LANDS IN THE NEW WORLD **421**

From *Letters by Christopher Columbus*, translated and
edited by R. H. Major (London: Hakluyt Society, 1843),
pp. 35–43.

**THE SPANISH CONQUISTADOR: CORTÉS AND THE
CONQUEST OF MEXICO** **423**

From *The European Reconnaissance: Selected Documents* by John
H. Parry. Copyright © 1968 by John H. Parry. Reprinted by
permission Walker & Co.

**LAS CASAS AND THE SPANISH TREATMENT OF THE
AMERICAN NATIVES** **425**

From *The Tears of the Indians*, Bartolome de Las Casas.
Copyright © 1970 by The John Lilburne Company Publishers.

THE ATLANTIC SLAVE TRADE **428**

From *European Society in the Eighteenth Century*, ed. Robert
and Elborg Forster. New York: Walker & Co., 1969. Reprinted
by permission of Walker & Co.

**OPPOSING VIEWPOINTS: WEST MEETS EAST:
AN EXCHANGE OF ROYAL LETTERS** **431**

From *The World of Southeast Asia: Selected Historical Readings*, Harry
J. Benda and John A. Larkin, eds. Copyright © 1967 by Harper &
Row Publishers. Used with permission of John A. Larkin.

AN IMPERIAL EDICT TO THE KING OF ENGLAND **434**

From *China's Response to the West: A Documentary Survey,
1839–1923* by Ssu-yu Teng and John K. Fairbank (Cambridge,
Mass.: Harvard University Press, 1982).

THE MISSION **438**

Excerpt from *Latin American Civilization* by Benjamin Keen,
ed. (Boston: Houghton Mifflin, 1974), Vol. I, pp. 223–224.
Reprinted by permission of the estate of Benjamin Keen.

CHAPTER 15

A WITCHCRAFT TRIAL IN FRANCE **448**

From *Witchcraft in Europe, 1100–1700: A Documentary History*
edited by Alan C. Kors and Edward Peters. Copyright © 1972
University of Pennsylvania Press. Reprinted with permission
of the University of Pennsylvania Press.

**THE FACE OF WAR IN THE SEVENTEENTH
CENTURY** **453**

Excerpt from *The Adventures of Simplicius Simplissimus* by Hans
Jacob Christoffel von Grimmelshausen, translated by George
Schulz-Behrend, © 1993 Camden House/Boydell & Brewer,
Rochester, New York. Reprinted with permission of Camden
House Publishers.

TRAVELS WITH THE KING **459**

From THE AGE OF MAGNIFICENCE by Sanche de Gramont,
copyright © 1964, renewed 1991 by G. P. Putnam's Sons. Used
by permission of G. P. Putnam's Sons, a division of Penguin
Group (USA), Inc.

PETER THE GREAT DEALS WITH A REBELLION **465**

From *Readings in European History*, vol. 2, by James Harvey
Robinson (Lexington, Mass.: Ginn and Co., 1906).

**OPPOSING VIEWPOINTS: OLIVER CROMWELL:
THREE PERSPECTIVES** **475**

Oliver Cromwell on the Victory at Naseby. Oliver Cromwell
on the Massacre at Drogheda. From Thomas Carlyle, ed., *The
Letters and Speeches of Oliver Cromwell*, 3 vols. (New York:
G. P. Putnam's Sons, 1904), Vol. 1, p. 204, Vol. 3, p. 15.

   Edmund Ludlow, *Memoirs*. From C. H. Firth, *The Memoirs
of Edmund Ludlow* (Oxford: Oxford University Press, 1894),
Vol. 2, pp. 10–11.

   Lord Clarendon, *The History of the Rebellion and Civil Wars
in England*. From Lord Clarendon, *The History of the Rebellion
and Civil Wars in England* (Oxford: Oxford University Press,
1839), Vol. 6, pp. 349–350.

THE BILL OF RIGHTS **478**

From *The Statutes: Revised Edition* (London: Eyre and
Spottiswoode, 1871), Vol. 2, pp. 10–12.

WILLIAM SHAKESPEARE: IN PRAISE OF ENGLAND **483**

Excerpt from *Richard II* in *Shakespeare, The Complete Works*, edited
by G. B. Harrison (New York: Harcourt Brace & World, 1952).

CHAPTER 16

**ON THE REVOLUTIONS OF THE HEAVENLY
SPHERES** **492**

From *The Collected Works* by Copernicus, translated by Edward
Rosen. Rev. ed. published 1978 by Palgrave Macmillan.
Reproduced with permission of Palgrave Macmillan.

KEPLER AND THE EMERGING SCIENTIFIC COMMUNITY   494

From *Johannes Kepler, Life and Letters* by Carola Baumgardt, copyright 1951 by the Philosophical Library. Used by permission.

THE STARRY MESSENGER   **495**

From DISCOVERIES AND OPINIONS OF GALILEO by Galileo Galilei, translated by Stillman Drake, copyright © 1957 by Stillman Drake. Used by permission of Doubleday, a division of Random House, Inc.

OPPOSING VIEWPOINTS: A NEW HEAVEN? FAITH VERSUS REASON   496

Galileo, Letter to the Grand Duchess Christina, 1614. From DISCOVERIES AND OPINIONS OF GALILEO by Galileo Galilei, translated by Stillman Drake, copyright © 1957 by Stillman Drake. Used by permission of Doubleday, a division of Random House, Inc.

Robert Bellarmine, Letter to Paolo Foscarini, 1615. From *Galileo, Science, and the Church* by Jerome J. Langford (New York: Desclee, 1966).

NEWTON'S RULES OF REASONING   498

From Isaac Newton, *The Mathematical Principles of Natural Philosophy*, 2 volumes (London, 1803), vol. 2: pp. 160–62.

THE "NATURAL" INFERIORITY OF WOMEN   503

From *A Political Treatise*, Benedict de Spinoza, copyright 1895 by George Routledge & Sons.

THE FATHER OF MODERN RATIONALISM   505

From *Descartes' Philosophical Writings,* translated by Norman Kemp Smith, copyright © 1958 by Macmillan Education. Reproduced with permission of Palgrave Macmillan.

PASCAL: "WHAT IS A MAN IN THE INFINITE?"   510

From PENSEES by Blaise Pascal, translated with an introduction by A. J. Krailsheimer (Penguin Classics, 1966). Copyright © A. J. Krailsheimer, 1966. Reproduced by permission of Penguin Books Ltd.

C H A P T E R   1 7

THE SEPARATION OF POWERS   518

From *Les Philosophes* by Norman L. Torrey, copyright © 1961 by Norman L. Torrey, G. P. Putnam's Sons, a division of Penguin Putnam, Inc.

THE ATTACK ON RELIGIOUS INTOLERANCE   520

Voltaire, *The Ignorant Philosopher.* From CANDIDE OR OPTIMISM by Voltaire, translated by John Butt (Penguin Classics, 1947). This edition copyright © John Butt, 1947. Reproduced by permission of Penguin Books, Ltd.

Voltaire, *Candide.* From CANDIDE OR OPTIMISM by Voltaire, translated by John Butt (Penguin Classics, 1947). This edition copyright © John Butt, 1947. Reproduced by permission of Penguin Books, Ltd.

DIDEROT QUESTIONS CHRISTIAN SEXUAL STANDARDS   521

From *Rameau's Nephew and Other Works* by Denis Diderot. Copyright © 1956 by Jacques Barzun and Ralph Bowen. Used by permission of Jacques Barzun.

A SOCIAL CONTRACT   524

Extract from A SOCIAL CONTRACT by Jean-Jacques Rousseau translated by Maurice Cranston (translation copyright © Estate Maurice Cranston 1968) is reproduced by permission of PFD (www.pfd.co.uk.) on behalf of the Estate of Maurice Cranston.

OPPOSING VIEWPOINTS: WOMEN IN THE AGE OF THE ENLIGHTENMENT: ROUSSEAU AND WOLLSTONECRAFT   525

Rousseau, *Emile* (1762). Copyright ©1979 Jean-Jacques Rousseau, Michael Wu. Reprinted by permission of Basic Books, a member of the Perseus Books Group.

Mary Wollstonecraft, *Vindication of the Rights of Woman (1792).* From Mary Wollstonecraft, *A Vindication of the Rights of Woman* (1792).

THE PUNISHMENT OF CRIME   533

From *Les Nuits de Paris or Nocturnal Spectator: A Selection,* trans. L. Asher and E. Fertig, pp. 7–8. New York: Knopf, 1964.

THE CONVERSION EXPERIENCE IN WESLEY'S METHODISM   539

From *The Journal of the Reverend John Wesley AM,* vol. 2. J. M. Dent & Sons Ltd., 1920.

C H A P T E R   1 8

THE FRENCH KING'S BEDTIME   545

From *Memoirs of the Comtesse de Boigne.* Ed. M. Charles Nicoullaud. New York: Heinemann, 1907.

FREDERICK THE GREAT AND HIS FATHER   550

From *Readings in European History*, vol. 2, by James Harvey Robinson (Lexington, Mass.: Ginn and Co., 1906).

OPPOSING VIEWPOINTS: ENLIGHTENED ABSOLUTISM: ENLIGHTENED OR ABSOLUTE?   551

Letter of Baron de Breteuil. From G. Vernadsky, *A Source Book for Russian History* (New Haven: Yale University Press, 1972), Vol. 2, p. 451.

Catherine II, Proposals for a New Law Code. From *Documents of Catherine the Great*, W. F. Reddaway © 1931 by Cambridge University Press. Reprinted with permission of Cambridge University Press.

Decree on Serfs. From G. Vernadsky, *A Source Book for Russian History* (New Haven: Yale University Press, 1972), Vol. 2, pp. 453–454.

BRITISH VICTORY IN INDIA   557

From *Readings in European History*, vol. 2, by James Harvey Robinson (Lexington, Mass.: Ginn and Co., 1906).

MARITAL ARRANGEMENTS   559

From *The Rivals* by Richard Sheridan (London, 1775).

PROPAGANDA FOR THE NEW AGRICULTURE   563

Arthur Young, *Travels during the Years, 1787, 1788, and 1789 ... in the Kingdom of France* (London: W. Richardson, 1794).

THE BEGINNINGS OF MECHANIZED INDUSTRY: THE ATTACK ON NEW MACHINES   565

Leeds Woolen Workers' Petition (Leeds, 1786).

POVERTY IN FRANCE   571

From *European Society in the Eighteenth Century* by Robert Forster and Elborg Forster. Copyright © 1969 by Robert and Elborg Forster. Reprinted by permission of Walker & Co.

C H A P T E R   1 9

THE ARGUMENT FOR INDEPENDENCE   577

From *The Federal and State Constitutions,* S. N. Thorpe, compiler and editor, volume 1, pp. 3–4. Washington, D.C., 1909.

THE FALL OF THE BASTILLE   583

From *The Press in the French Revolution: a selection of documents taken from the press of the Revolution for the years 1789–1794.* J. Gilchrist and W. J. Murray, eds. (London: Ginn, 1971).

OPPOSING VIEWPOINTS: THE NATURAL RIGHTS OF THE FRENCH PEOPLE: TWO VIEWS 584

Declaration of the Rights of Man and the Citizen. From *The French Revolution* by Paul H. Beik. Copyright © 1970 by Paul H. Beik. Reprinted by permission of Walker & Co.

Declaration of the Rights of Woman and the Female Citizen. From *Women in Revolutionary Paris, 1789–1795: Selected Documents Translated with Notes and Commentary*. Translated with notes and commentary by Darline Gay Levy, Harriet Branson Applewhite, and Mary Durham Johnson. Copyright 1979 by the Board of Trustees of the University of Illinois. Used with permission of the editors and the University of Illinois Press.

JUSTICE IN THE REIGN OF TERROR 592

From J. M. Thompson, *English Witness of the French Revolution* (Oxford: Blackwell, 1938).

ROBESPIERRE AND REVOLUTIONARY GOVERNMENT 593

From *Robespierre*, edited by George Rudé. Copyright © 1967 by Prentice-Hall, Inc. Reprinted by permission of the Estate of George Rudé.

DE-CHRISTIANIZATION 594

From *The French Revolution* by Paul H. Beik. Copyright © 1970 by Paul H. Beik. Reprinted by permission of Walker & Co.

NAPOLEON AND PSYCHOLOGICAL WARFARE 598

From *A Documentary Survey of the French Revolution* by John Hall Stewart. Copyright © 1951 by Macmillan Publishing Company, renewed 1979 by John Hall Stewart.

CHAPTER 20

THE TRAITS OF THE BRITISH INDUSTRIAL ENTREPRENEUR 609

From *The History of the Cotton Manufacture in Great Britain* by Edward Baines (London: Fisher, Fisher, and Jackson, 1835), pp. 195–96.

DISCIPLINE IN THE NEW FACTORIES 614

From *Documents of European Economic History*, Vol. I by Sidney Pollard & Colin Holmes. Copyright © Sidney Pollard and Colin Holmes. Reproduced with permission of Palgrave Macmillan.

"S-T-E-A-M-BOAT A-COMING!" 620

From *Life on the Mississippi* by Mark Twain. New York, Harper and Brothers, 1911.

THE GREAT IRISH FAMINE 622

From *A History of Ireland under the Union* by P. S. O'Hegarty. Copyright © 1952 by Methuen & Co.

OPPOSING VIEWPOINTS: ATTITUDES OF THE INDUSTRIAL MIDDLE CLASS IN BRITAIN AND JAPAN 626

Samuel Smiles, *Self-Help*, London, 1859.

Shibuzawa Eiichi, *The Autobiography of Shibusawa Eiichi: From Peasant to Entrepreneur*, 1927 (Tokyo: University of Tokyo Press, 1994).

CHILD LABOR: DISCIPLINE IN THE TEXTILE MILLS 628

From *Human Documents of the Industrial Revolution in Britain* by E. Royston Pike. London: Unwin & Hyman, 1966.

CHILD LABOR: THE MINES 629

From *Human Documents of the Industrial Revolution in Britain* by E. Royston Pike. London: Unwin & Hyman, 1966.

CHAPTER 21

THE VOICE OF CONSERVATISM: METTERNICH OF AUSTRIA 639

Reprinted from Klemens von Metternich, *Memoirs*, Alexander Napler, trans. (London: Richard Bentley & Sons, 1881).

UNIVERSITY STUDENTS AND GERMAN UNITY 645

From *Metternich's Europe*, Mack Walker, ed., copyright © 1968 by Mack Walker. Reprinted by permission of Walker & Co.

THE VOICE OF LIBERALISM: JOHN STUART MILL ON LIBERTY 648

From *Utilitarianism, On Liberty, and Representative Government* by John Stuart Mill. Published by Viking Press, 1914.

OPPOSING VIEWPOINTS: RESPONSE TO REVOLUTION: TWO PERSPECTIVES 653

Thomas Babington Macaulay, Speech of March 2, 1831. From *Speeches, Parliamentary and Miscellaneous* by Thomas B. Macaulay (New York: Hurst Co., 1853), vol. 1, pp. 20–21, 25–26.

Carl Schurz, *Reminiscences*. From *The Reminiscences of Carl Schurz* by Carl Schurz (New York: The McClure Co., 1907), vol. I, pp. 112–13.

THE VOICE OF ITALIAN NATIONALISM: GIUSEPPE MAZZINI AND YOUNG ITALY 659

From *Joseph Mazzini: His Life, Writings, and Political Principles* (New York: Hurd & Houghton, 1872), pp. 62–69, 71–74.

THE NEW BRITISH POLICE: "WE ARE NOT TREATED AS MEN" 660

From Clive Emsley, *Policing and Its Context, 1750–1870* (London: Palgrave Macmillan, 1983).

GOTHIC LITERATURE: EDGAR ALLAN POE 663

From *Selected Prose and Poetry*, Edgar Allan Poe. New York: Holt, Rinehart, and Winston, 1950.

CHAPTER 22

OPPOSING VIEWPOINTS: THE PRACTICE OF *REALPOLITIK*: TWO APPROACHES 672

Louis Napoleon, *Proclamation to the People* (1851). From *The Constitutions and Other Select Documents Illustrative of the History of France 1789–1907*, by Frank Maloy Anderson (Minneapolis: H. W. Wilson, 1904).

Bismarck, *Speech to the Prussian Reichstag*, 1862. From Louis L. Snyder, *Documents of German History* (Rutgers University Press, 1958), p. 202.

Bismarck, *Speech to the German Reichstag*, 1888. From Brian Tierney and Joan Scott, eds., *Western Societies: A Documentary History*, Vol. 2 (Alfred Knopf, 1984), p. 366.

GARIBALDI AND ROMANTIC NATIONALISM 678

From the *Times* of London, June 13, 1860.

EMANCIPATION: SERFS AND SLAVES 686

Tsar Alexander II, Imperial Decree, March 3, 1861. From *Annual Register* (New York: Longmans, Green, 1861), p. 207.

President Abraham Lincoln, Emancipation Proclamation, January 1, 1863. From *U. S. Statutes at Large* (Washington, D.C., Government Printing Office, 1875), vol. 12, pp. 1268–69.

THE CLASSLESS SOCIETY 693

From *The Communist Manifesto* by Karl Marx and Frederick Engels, trans. Samuel Moore, 1888.

DARWIN AND THE DESCENT OF MAN 695

From *The Descent of Man* by Charles Darwin (New York: Appleton, 1876), pp. 606–607, 619.

ANESTHESIA AND MODERN SURGERY 697

From *The History of Medicine in the United States: A Collection of Facts and Figures* by Francis Randolph Packard (Philadelphia: Lippincott, 1901).

REALISM: CHARLES DICKENS AND AN IMAGE OF HELL ON EARTH 700

From Charles Dickens, *The Old Curiosity Shop* (London: Chapman & Hall, 1841).

CHAPTER 23

THE DEPARTMENT STORE AND THE BEGINNINGS OF MASS CONSUMERISM 707

From *Documents of European Economic History,* Vol. I by Sidney Pollard & Colin Holmes. Copyright © Sidney Pollard and Colin Holmes. Reproduced with permission of Palgrave Macmillan.

THE VOICE OF EVOLUTIONARY SOCIALISM: EDUARD BERNSTEIN 713

From Eduard Bernstein, *Evolutionary Socialism*, Edith C. Harney, trans. (New York: B. W. Huebsch, 1911), pp. x–xii, xiv.

THE HOUSING VENTURE OF OCTAVIA HILL 718

From Octavia Hill, *Homes of the London Poor* (New York: Macmillan, 1875), pp. 15–16, 17–18, 23.

OPPOSING VIEWPOINTS: ADVICE TO WOMEN: TWO VIEWS 721

Elizabeth Poole Sanford, *Woman in Her Social and Domestic Character.* From Elizabeth Poole Sanford, *Woman, in Her Social and Domestic Character* (Boston: Otis, Broaders & Co., 1842), pp. 5–7, 15–16.

Henrik Ibsen, *A Doll's House.* Excerpt as appeared in *Roots of Western Civilization* by Wesley D. Camp (Wiley, 1983).

THE FIGHT SONG: SPORTS IN THE ENGLISH PUBLIC SCHOOLS 728

From *Athleticism in the Victorian and Edwardian Public School* by J. A. Mangan (Cambridge University Press, 1981).

A LEADER OF THE PARIS COMMUNE 731

From Louise Michel, THE RED VIRGIN: MEMOIRS OF LOUISE MICHEL, pp. 64, 68, trans. by Bullitt Lowry and Elizabeth Ellington Gunter (University of Alabama Press, 1981). Reprinted by permission of University of Alabama Press.

BISMARCK AND THE WELFARE OF THE WORKERS 733

From *Bismarck,* edited by Frederick B. M. Hollyday, pp. 60, 63, 65. Copyright © 1970 by Prentice-Hall, Inc.

CHAPTER 24

FREUD AND THE CONCEPT OF REPRESSION 741

From *Five Lectures on Psycho-analysis* by Sigmund Freud, translated by James Strachey. Copyright © 1961 by James Strachey. Used by permission of W. W. Norton & Company, Inc. and Sigmund Freud Copyrights Ltd.

SYMBOLIST POETRY: ART FOR ART'S SAKE 744

"The Drunken Boat" by Arthur Rimbaud from *Realism, Naturalism, Symbolism: Modes of Thought and Expression in Europe* by Roland Stromberg. English translation copyright © 1968 by Roland Stromberg. Reprinted by permission of the Estate of Roland Stromberg.

THE STRUGGLE FOR THE RIGHT TO VOTE 750

From Emmeline Pankhurst, *My Own Story* (New York: Hearst International Library, 1914).

THE VOICE OF ZIONISM: THEODOR HERZL AND THE JEWISH STATE 754

From Theodor Herzl, *The Jewish State*. Trans. Sylvia d'Avigdor. 3rd edition (New York: Federation of American Zionists, 1917), pp. 7–8, 11, 12.

BLOODY SUNDAY 757

From George Gapon, *The Story of My Life* (New York: Dutton, 1906), pp. 182–85.

OPPOSING VIEWPOINTS: WHITE MAN'S BURDEN VERSUS BLACK MAN'S BURDEN 760

Rudyard Kipling, *The White Man's Burden.* From *Rudyard Kipling's Verse* (Garden City, N.Y.: Doubleday, 1919), pp. 371–72.

Edward Morel, *The Black Man's Burden.* From E. D. Morel, *The Black Man's Burden: The White Man in Africa from the Fifteenth Century to World War I* (London: National Labour Press, 1920).

THE EMPEROR'S BIG MOUTH 770

From *The Daily Telegraph,* London, October 28, 1908.

CHAPTER 25

"YOU HAVE TO BEAR THE RESPONSIBILITY FOR WAR OR PEACE" 779

From *Diplomatic Documents Relating to the Outbreak of the European War*. Ed. James Brown Scott (New York: Oxford University Press, 1916).

THE EXCITEMENT OF WAR 781

Stefan Zweig, *The World of Yesterday.* From THE WORLD OF YESTERDAY by Stefan Zweig, translated by Helmut Ripperger, copyright 1943 by the Viking Press, Inc. Used by permission of Viking Penguin, a division of Penguin Group (USA) Inc. and by permission of Williams Verlag AG.

Robert Graves, *Goodbye to All That.* From Robert Graves, *Good-Bye to All That* (London: Jonathan Cape, 1929).

Walter Limmer, Letter to His Parents. From Jon E. Lewis, ed., *The Mammoth Book of Eyewitness: World War I* (New York: Caroll and Graf Publishers, an imprint of Avalon Publishing Group, 2003), p. 24.

THE REALITY OF WAR: TRENCH WARFARE 786

Reproduced by permission of the Estate of the Late Paulette Goddard Remarque.

THE SONGS OF WORLD WAR I 789

"Die Wacht am Rhein (The Watch on the Rhine)," Max Schneckenburger, 1840; "The Old Barbed Wire," lyrics anonymous; "Over There," George M. Cohan, 1917.

WOMEN IN THE FACTORIES 795

From "Munition Work" by Naomi Loughnan, in *Women War Workers,* edited by Gilbert Stone (London: George Harrap and Company, 1917), pp. 25, 35–38.

WAR AND THE FAMILY 796

Personal Letters of Reginald B. Mott family.

SOLDIER AND PEASANT VOICES 801

From *Voices of Revolution*, 1917 by Mark D. Steinberg. Copyright © 2001 Yale University Press. Reprinted by permission.

OPPOSING VIEWPOINTS: THREE VOICES OF PEACEMAKING 806

Georges Clemenceau, *Grandeur and Misery of Victory*. From Georges Clemenceau, *Grandeur and Misery of Victory* (New York: Harcourt, 1930), pp. 105, 107, 280.

Pan-African Congress. Excerpts from Resolution from the Pan-African Congress, Paris, 1919.

CHAPTER 26

THE GREAT DEPRESSION: UNEMPLOYED AND HOMELESS IN GERMANY 817

From *Living Age*, Vol. 344, no. 4398 (March 1933), pp. 27–31, 34–38.

THE STRUGGLES OF A DEMOCRACY: UNEMPLOYMENT AND SLUMS IN GREAT BRITAIN 818

Men Without Work: A Report to the Pilgrim Trust, 1938. From *Men without Work: A Report Made to the Pilgrim Trust* (Cambridge: Cambridge University Press, 1938).

George Orwell, "A Woman in the Slums." From George Orwell, *The Road to Wigan Pier* (London: Victor Gollancz, 1937).

THE VOICE OF ITALIAN FASCISM 825

Reprinted by permission of the publisher from *International Conciliation*, No. 306 (Washington, D.C., Carnegie Endowment for International Peace, 1935), pp. 5–17. www .carnegieendowment.org.

ADOLF HITLER'S HATRED OF THE JEWS 827

From MEIN KAMPF by Adolf Hitler, translated by Ralph Manheim. Copyright © 1943, renewed 1971 by Houghton Mifflin Company. Reprinted by permission of Houghton Mifflin Harcourt Company. All rights reserved.

PROPAGANDA AND MASS MEETINGS IN NAZI GERMANY 830

Adolf Hitler, Speech at the Nuremberg Party Rally, 1936.

A Teacher's Impression of a Hitler Rally, 1932. From Louise Solmitz, "Diary," trans. and quoted in Jeremy Noakes and Geoffrey Pridham, *Documents on Nazism, 1919–45* (New York: Viking, 1974), p. 161. Reprinted by permission of Peters Fraser and Dunlop on behalf of Jeremy Noakes and Geoffrey Pridham.

THE FORMATION OF COLLECTIVE FARMS 835

From Fedor Belov, *The History of a Soviet Collective Farm* (New York: Frederick A. Praeger, Inc., 1955). Reproduced with permission of Greenwood Publishing Group, Inc., Westport, CT.

OPPOSING VIEWPOINTS: SPAIN DIVIDED: THE POEMS OF TWO BROTHERS 837

Reprinted by permission of the publisher from ANTONIO MACHADO: SELECTED POEMS, translated by Alan S. Trueblood, pp. 263, 265, Cambridge, Mass.: Harvard University Press, Copyright © 1982 by the President and Fellows of Harvard College.

HESSE AND THE UNCONSCIOUS 846

From *Demian* by Hermann Hesse (New York: Bantam Books, 1966), p. 30.

CHAPTER 27

HITLER'S FOREIGN POLICY GOALS 851

Excerpts from *Hitler's Secret Book* by Adolf Hitler, copyright © 1961 by Grove Press, copyright renewed © 1989 by Grove Press, Inc. Used with permission of Grove/Atlantic Inc.

OPPOSING VIEWPOINTS: THE MUNICH CONFERENCE: TWO VIEWS 855

Winston Churchill, Speech to the House of Commons, October 5, 1938. From *Parliamentary Debates, House of Commons* (London: His Majesty's Stationery Office, 1938), vol. 339, pp. 361–369.

Neville Chamberlain, Speech to the House of Commons, October 6, 1938. From Neville Chamberlain, *In Search of Peace* (New York: Putnam, 1939), pp. 213–215, 217.

A GERMAN SOLDIER AT STALINGRAD 863

From Vaili Chuikov, *The Battle for Stalingrad* (Grafton Books / HarperCollins UK), 1964.

HITLER'S PLANS FOR A NEW ORDER IN THE EAST 866

From *Hitler's Secret Conversations 1941–1944* by Hugh Trevor-Roper (New York: Farrar, Straus & Young, 1953).

THE HOLOCAUST: THE CAMP COMMANDANT AND THE CAMP VICTIMS 872

From *Nazism 1919–1945: A Documentary Reader, Vol. 3: Foreign Policy, War and Racial Extermination*. Edited by J. Noakes and G. Pridham, new edition, 2001 pp. 590–592. Reprinted by permission of University of Exeter Press.

THE BOMBING OF CIVILIANS 876

From John Campbell, ed. *The Experience of World War II* (New York: Oxford University Press, 1989), p. 180.

EMERGENCE OF THE COLD WAR: CHURCHILL AND STALIN 882

From the Congressional Record, 79th Congress, 2nd Session, A (Washington, D.C.: U.S. Government Printing Office), pp. 1145–1147.

CHAPTER 28

OPPOSING VIEWPOINTS: WHO STARTED THE COLD WAR? AMERICAN AND SOVIET PERSPECTIVES 887

Origins of the Cold War: The Novikov, Kennan, and Roberts 'Long' Telegrams of 1946. (Kenneth M. Jensen, editor) Washington, DC: Endowment of the United States Institute of Peace, 1993. pp. 20–21, 28–31, 8, 16. Reprinted with permission.

THE TRUMAN DOCTRINE 888

Reprinted from the Congressional Record, 80th Congress, 1st Session (Washington, D.C.: U.S. Government Printing Office), Vol. 93, p. 1981.

THE CUBAN MISSILE CRISIS FROM KHRUSHCHEV'S PERSPECTIVE 894

From Strobe Talbot, ed., *Khrushchev Remembers*, copyright © Andrew Numberg Associates. Reprinted by permission.

FRANTZ FANON AND THE WRETCHED OF THE EARTH 897

"Colonial War and Mental Disorders, Series B" from *The Wretched of the Earth* by Frantz Fanon, copyright © 1993 by Presence Africaine. Translation copyright © 2004 by Richard Philcox. Used by permission of Grove/Atlantic, Inc.

KHRUSHCHEV DENOUNCES STALIN   901

Reprinted from the Congressional Record, 84th Congress, 2nd Session (Washington, D.C.: U.S. Government Printing Office), Vol. 102, Part 7, pp. 9389–9402.

SOVIET REPRESSION IN EASTERN EUROPE: HUNGARY, 1956   904

From the Department of State *Bulletin*, Nov. 12, 1956, pp. 746–47.

THE VOICE OF THE WOMEN'S LIBERATION MOVEMENT   913

From THE SECOND SEX by Simone de Beauvior, translated by Constance Borde and Sheila Malovany-Chevallier, translation copyright © 2009 by Constance Borde and Sheila Malovany-Chevallier. Introduction copyright © 2010 by Judith Thurman. Used by permission of Alfred A. Knopf, a division of Random House, Inc.

CHAPTER 29

"THE TIMES THEY ARE A-CHANGIN'": THE MUSIC OF YOUTHFUL PROTEST   923

Copyright © 1963; renewed 1991 by Special Rider Music. All rights reserved. International copyright secured. Reprinted by permission.

1968: THE YEAR OF STUDENT REVOLTS   924

Reprinted from *Student Protest* by Gerald F. McGuigan. Copyright © 1968 by Methuen & Co., Publishers.

OPPOSING VIEWPOINTS: CZECHOSLOVAKIA, 1968: TWO FACES OF COMMUNISM   928

Two Thousand Words Manifesto. Used with permission of Central European Press, from THE PRAGUE SPRING 1968, Jaromir Navratil, 1998; permission conveyed through Copyright Clearance Center, Inc.

A Letter to Czechoslovakia. From "A Letter to Czechoslovakia," *Moscow News*, Supplement to N. 30917 (1968), pp. 3–6.

MARGARET THATCHER: ENTERING A MAN'S WORLD   930

Pages 62–65 from THE PATH TO POWER by Margaret Thatcher. Copyright © 1995 by Margaret Thatcher. Reprinted by permission of HarperCollins Publishers and HarperCollins Publishers Ltd.

THE FURY OF THE RED GUARDS   936

From *Life and Death in Shanghai* by Nien Cheng. Copyright © 1986 by Nien Cheng. Reprinted by permission of Grove/Atlantic, Inc.

THE LIMITS OF MODERN TECHNOLOGY   939

Reuse of excerpt from SMALL IS BEAUTIFUL: ECONOMICS AS IF PEOPLE MATTERED by E.F. SCHUMACHER. Copyright © 1973 by E.F. Schumacher. Reprinted by permission of HarperCollins Publishers.

GRANDMASTER FLASH AND THE FURIOUS FIVE: "THE MESSAGE"   943

"The Message" by Clifton Chase, Edward Fletcher, Melvin Glover, and Sylvia Robinson. Performed by Grandmaster Flash and the Furious Five. Copyright © 1982 E/A Music, Inc. and Grandmaster Flash Publishing Inc. Print rights administered by Sugar Hill Music Publishing, Ltd.

CHAPTER 30

GORBACHEV AND *PERESTROIKA*   950

Pages 140–141, 253–254 from PERESTROIKA by MIKHAIL GORBACHEV. Copyright © 1987 by Mikhail Gorbachev. Reprinted by permission of HarperCollins Publishers.

VACLAV HAVEL: THE CALL FOR A NEW POLITICS   953

From *The Washington Post*, February 22, 1990, p. 28d.

A CHILD'S ACCOUNT OF THE SHELLING OF SARAJEVO   956

From *Zlata's Diary* by Zlata Filipovic, copyright © 1994 by Fixot et editions Robert Laffont. Used by permission of Viking Penguin, a division of Penguin Putnam, Inc.

OPPOSING VIEWPOINTS: ISLAM AND THE WEST: SECULARISM IN FRANCE   969

French President Jacques Chirac on Secularism in French Society. From "France's President Lays Out His Views on the Principle of Secularism in the French State—In Schools and the Public Sector," from http://news.bbc.co.uk/go/em/fr/-/2/hi/europe/3330679.stm.

North African Women in France Respond to the Headscarf Affair. Caitlin Killian, GENDER AND SOCIETY, Vol. 17, No. 4, pp. 567–590, copyright © 2003 by SAGE Publications. Reprinted by Permission of SAGE Publications.

POPE JOHN PAUL II: AN APPEAL FOR PEACE   971

From *John Paul II and the Laity,* edited by Leonard Doohan (The Jesuit Educational Center for Human Development; published by Le Jacq Publishing, Inc., 1984), pp. 48–50. Reprinted by permission of Human Development.

A WARNING TO HUMANITY   977

World Scientists' Warning to Humanity, 1992. Union of Concerned Scientists. 1992. World Scientists Warning to Humanity. Excerpt. Cambridge, MA: UCS. Online at www.ucsusa.org

Findings of the IPCC Fourth Assessment Report, 2007. Reprinted with permission from Union of Concerned Scientists. 1992. World Scientists Warning to Humanity. Excerpt. Cambridge, MA: UCS. Online at www.ucsusa.org.

MAPS

MAP 11.1   Spread of the Black Death   310

MAP 11.2   The Hundred Years' War   318

SPOT MAP   The Holy Roman Empire in the Fourteenth Century   323

SPOT MAP   The States of Italy in the Fourteenth Century   325

SPOT MAP   Avignon   327

MAP 12.1   Renaissance Italy   348

MAP 12.2   Europe in the Second Half of the Fifteenth Century   367

MAP 12.3   The Iberian Peninsula   368

MAP 12.4   The Ottoman Empire and Southeastern Europe   371

MAP 13.1   The Empire of Charles V   387

SPOT MAP   The Swiss Cantons   389

MAP 13.2   Catholics and Protestants in Europe by 1560   399

MAP 13.3   The Height of Spanish Power Under Philip II   406

MAP 14.1   Discoveries and Possessions in the Fifteenth and Sixteenth Centuries   417

SPOT MAP   The Maya   421

SPOT MAP   The Aztecs   422

SPOT MAP   The Inca   424

MAP 14.2   Triangular Trade Route in the Atlantic Economy   427

SPOT MAP   Southeast Asia, c. 1700   429

SPOT MAP   The Mughal Empire   432

SPOT MAP   The Qing Empire   433

SPOT MAP   The West Indies   435

MAP 14.3   The Columbian Exchange   440

MAP 15.1   The Thirty Years' War   450

MAP 15.2   The Wars of Louis XIV   460

MAP 15.3   The Growth of Brandenburg-Prussia   462

MAP 15.4   The Growth of the Austrian Empire   463

MAP 15.5   Russia: From Principality to Nation-State   467

SPOT MAP   Sweden in the Seventeenth Century   468

MAP 15.6   The Ottoman Empire   469

SPOT MAP   Poland in the Seventeenth Century   470

SPOT MAP   Civil War in England   473

SPOT MAP   Pacific Discoveries   515

MAP 17.1   The Enlightenment in Europe   517

MAP 17.2   Religious Populations of Eighteenth-Century Europe   537

MAP 18.1   Europe in 1763   547

SPOT MAP   Pugachev's Rebellion   552

MAP 18.2   The Partitioning of Poland   553

MAP 18.3   Battlefields of the Seven Years' War   555

MAP 19.1   North America, 1700–1803   576

SPOT MAP   Rebellion in France   589

MAP 19.2   French Expansion During the Revolutionary Wars, 1792–1799   591

SPOT MAP   Revolt in Saint-Domingue (Haiti)   595

MAP 19.3   Napoleon's Grand Empire in 1810   602

MAP 20.1   The Industrial Revolution in Britain by 1850   612

MAP 20.2   The Industrialization of Europe by 1850   617

MAP 21.1   Europe After the Congress of Vienna, 1815   638

MAP 21.2   Latin America in the First Half of the Nineteenth Century   642

SPOT MAP   The Balkans by 1830   643

SPOT MAP   Italy, 1815   644

MAP 21.3   The Distribution of Languages in Nineteenth-Century Europe   649

MAP 21.4   The Revolutions of 1848–1849   655

MAP 22.1   Decline of the Ottoman Empire   674

SPOT MAP   The Crimean War   675

MAP 22.2   The Unification of Italy   676

MAP 22.3   The Unification of Germany   680

MAP 22.4   Europe in 1871   683

MAP 22.5   Ethnic Groups in the Dual Monarchy, 1867   684

MAP 22.6   The United States: The West and the Civil War   689

MAP 23.1   The Industrial Regions of Europe at the End of the Nineteenth Century   709

MAP 23.2   Population Growth in Europe, 1820–1900   715

SPOT MAP   Palestine   753

SPOT MAP   Canada, 1871   758

SPOT MAP   The Struggle for South Africa   762

MAP 24.1   Africa in 1914   764

MAP 24.2   Asia in 1914   765

SPOT MAP   Japanese Expansion   768

SPOT MAP   The Balkans in 1878   769

MAP 24.3   The Balkans in 1913   771

MAP 25.1   Europe in 1914   777

SPOT MAP   The Schlieffen Plan   778

MAP 25.2   The Western Front, 1914–1918   782

MAP 25.3   The Eastern Front, 1914–1918   783

MAP 25.4   The Russian Revolution and Civil War   802

MAP 25.5   Europe in 1919   808

SPOT MAP   The Middle East in 1919   809

SPOT MAP   The Little Entente   814

SPOT MAP   Territory Gained by Italy   823

SPOT MAP   Eastern Europe After World War I   836

MAP 27.1   Changes in Central Europe, 1936–1939   854

MAP 27.2   World War II in Europe and North Africa   860

MAP 27.3   World War II in Asia and the Pacific   861

MAP 27.4   The Holocaust   870

MAP 27.5   Territorial Changes After World War II   881

SPOT MAP   The Berlin Air Lift   890

MAP 28.1   The New European Alliance Systems
           in the 1950s and 1960s   891

SPOT MAP   The Korean War   892

MAP 28.2   Decolonization in Africa   896

MAP 28.3   Decolonization in the Middle East   898

MAP 28.4   Decolonization in Asia   899

SPOT MAP   European Economic Community,
           1957   907

SPOT MAP   The Vietnam War   934

MAP 30.1   The New Europe   949

SPOT MAP   Chechnya   951

MAP 30.2   The Lands of the Former Yugoslavia,
           1995   957

MAP 30.3   European Union, 2007   961

SPOT MAP   Quebec   962

FEATURES

FILM & HISTORY

Joan of Arc (1948), *The Messenger: The Story of Joan of Arc* (1999)   320

Luther (2003)   383

Elizabeth (1998)   409

The Mission (1986)   439

Amadeus (1984)   531

Marie Antoinette (2006)   546

The Young Victoria (2009)   687

Paths of Glory (1957)   787

Triumph of the Will (1934)   841

Europa, Europa (1990)   869

The Third Man (1949)   889

Dr. Strangelove, Or: How I Learned to Stop Worrying and Love the Bomb (1964)   933

The Lives of Others (2006)   958

OPPOSING VIEWPOINTS

Causes of the Black Death: Contemporary Views   309

The Renaissance Prince: The Views of Machiavelli and Erasmus   353

A Reformation Debate: Conflict at Marburg   391

West Meets East: An Exchange of Royal Letters   431

Oliver Cromwell: Three Perspectives   475

A New Heaven? Faith Versus Reason   496

Women in the Age of the Enlightenment: Rousseau and Wollstonecraft   525

Enlightened Absolutism: Enlightened or Absolute?   551

The Natural Rights of the French People: Two Views   584

Attitudes of the Industrial Middle Class in Britain and Japan   626

Response to Revolution: Two Perspectives   653

The Practice of *Realpolitik:* Two Approaches   672

Advice to Women: Two Views   721

White Man's Burden Versus Black Man's Burden   760

Three Voices of Peacemaking   806

Spain Divided: The Poems of Two Brothers   837

The Munich Conference: Two Views   855

Who Started the Cold War? American and Soviet Perspectives   887

Czechoslovakia, 1968: Two Faces of Communism   928

Islam and the West: Secularism in France   969

IMAGES OF EVERYDAY LIFE

Entertainment in the Middle Ages   336

Spices and World Trade   418

Dutch Domesticity   472

The Aristocratic Way of Life   568

Living Conditions of London's Poor   624

The Middle-Class Family   724

The Struggle for the Right to Vote   751

Life in the Trenches   788

The Impact of Total War   878

The Rise of the Supermarket   911

Youth Culture in the 1960s   922

PREFACE

DURING A VISIT to Great Britain, where he studied as a young man, Mohandas Gandhi, the leader of the effort to liberate India from British colonial rule, was asked what he thought of Western civilization. "I think it would be a good idea," he replied. Gandhi's response was as correct as it was clever. Western civilization has led to great problems as well as great accomplishments, but it remains a good idea. And any complete understanding of today's world must take into account the meaning of Western civilization and the role Western civilization has played in history. Despite modern progress, we still greatly reflect our religious traditions, our political systems and theories, our economic and social structures, and our cultural heritage. I have written this history of Western civilization to assist a new generation of students in learning more about the past that has helped create them and the world in which they live.

At the same time, for the eighth edition, as in the seventh, I have added considerable new material on world history to show the impact other parts of the world have made on the West. Certainly, the ongoing struggle with terrorists since 2001 has made clear the intricate relationship between the West and the rest of the world. It is important then to show not only how Western civilization has affected the rest of the world but also how it has been influenced and even defined since its beginnings by contacts with other peoples around the world.

Another of my goals was to write a well-balanced work in which the political, economic, social, religious, intellectual, cultural, and military aspects of Western civilization have been integrated into a chronologically ordered synthesis. I have been especially aware of the need to integrate the latest research on social history and women's history into each chapter of the book rather than isolating it either in lengthy topical chapters, which confuse the student by interrupting the chronological narrative, or in separate sections that appear at periodic intervals between chapters.

Another purpose in writing this history of Western civilization has been to put the *story* back in history. That story is an exciting one; yet many textbooks fail to capture the imagination of their readers. Narrative history effectively transmits the knowledge of the past and is the form that best aids remembrance. At the same time, I have not overlooked the need for the kind of historical analysis that makes students aware that historians often disagree on their interpretations of the past.

Features of the Text

To enliven the past and let readers see for themselves the materials that historians use to create their pictures of the past, I have included in each chapter **primary sources** (boxed documents) that are keyed to the discussion in the text. The documents include examples of the religious, artistic, intellectual, social, economic, and political aspects of Western life. Such varied sources as a Renaissance banquet menu, a student fight song in nineteenth-century Britain, letters exchanged between a husband on the battle front and his wife in World War I, the Declaration of the Rights of Woman and the Female Citizen in the French Revolution, and a debate in the Reformation era all reveal in a vivid fashion what Western civilization meant to the individual men and women who shaped it by their activities. I have added questions at the end of each source to help students in analyzing the documents. In addition to the sources featured in the text, **Primary Source Icons** appear in the margins of each chapter, indicating documents that are available on the website.

Each chapter has an **introduction and an illustrated chapter summary** to help maintain the continuity of the narrative and to provide a synthesis of important themes. Anecdotes in the chapter introductions dramatically convey the major theme or themes of each chapter. **Detailed chronologies** reinforce the events discussed in the text, and a **chapter timeline** at the end of each chapter enables students to review at a glance the chief developments of an era. Many of the timelines also show parallel developments in different cultures or nations. An **annotated bibliography** at the end of each chapter reviews the most recent literature on each period and also gives references to some of the older, "classic" works in each field. New **"Upon Reflection" Chapter Review Questions and Key Terms lists** provide valuable study aids.

Updated maps and extensive illustrations serve to deepen the reader's understanding of the text. **Detailed map captions** are designed to enrich students' awareness of the importance of geography to history, and numerous **spot maps** enable readers to see at a glance the region or subject being discussed in the text. Map captions also include a **map question** to guide students' reading of the map, as well as references to **online interactive versions of the maps.** To facilitate understanding of cultural movements, illustrations of artistic works discussed in the text are placed near the discussions. Throughout the text, illustration captions have been revised and expanded to further students' understanding of the past. **Chapter outlines and focus questions, including critical thinking questions,** at the beginning of each chapter give students a useful overview and guide them to the main subjects of each chapter. The focus questions are then repeated at the beginning of each major section in the chapter. A **glossary of important terms** (boldfaced in the text when they are introduced and defined) is provided at the back of the book to maximize reader comprehension. A **guide to pronunciation** is now provided in the text in parentheses following the first mention of a complex name or term.

New to This Edition

In this new AP* edition, students will find a set of **multiple-choice review questions** in AP* format at the end of each chapter. In addition, there are fifteen **practice document-based questions** (DBQs) at the end of the text. These questions provide an opportunity for students to test their understanding of the chapter and practice answering the types of questions they will find on the AP* European History exam. The questions also provide a useful means of evaluation for teachers. The multiple-choice questions and DBQs were written by Sarah Pugh, Bentonville High School, Bentonville, Arkansas, and the DBQs were reviewed by Ane Lintvedt, McDonogh School, Owings Mills, Maryland.

At the end of this preface, there is a correlation guide that provides *Western Civilization* page references for the topics of the AP* course. With the help of teachers, these correlations will allow students to pinpoint exactly what they need to study in the textbook to make sure they are well prepared to take the exam.

As preparation for the revision of *Western Civilization*, I reexamined the entire book and analyzed the comments and reviews of many colleagues who have found the book to be a useful instrument for introducing their students to the history of Western civilization. In making revisions for the eighth edition, I sought to build on the strengths of the first seven editions and, above all, to maintain the balance, synthesis, and narrative qualities that characterized those editions. To keep up with the ever-growing body of historical scholarship, new or revised material has been added throughout the book on the following topics:

Chapter 11 new section on "The Black Death: From Asia to Europe," with a subsection on "Role of the Mongols"; revised section on "The Black Death in Europe"; new Opposing Viewpoints feature on "The Black Death: Contemporary Views."

Chapter 12 the impact of the Italian wars on Machiavelli; the *studia humanitatus;* the Spanish expulsion of the Jews and Muslims; the threat to the West posed by the Ottoman Turks; women in the home in the Italian Renaissance.

Chapter 13 Erasmus's New Testament scholarship; Thomas More; Luther and the Christian humanists; Luther and the peasants; Luther and predestination; the empire of Charles V; political motives of popes and monarchs; the Ottoman Turks; the meaning of the Catholic Reformation.

Chapter 14 new Images of Everyday Life feature on "Spices and World Trade"; revision of introduction to include a more concise road map of the chapter; viceroys in Spain's Latin American empire; impact of the slave trade on Africa; products of the Columbian Exchange, including cochineal; mercantilism.

Chapter 15 new Opposing Viewpoints feature on "Oliver Cromwell: Three Perspectives"; the causes of the Bohemian phase of the Thirty Years' War; the consequences of the Peace of Westphalia; Bishop Bossuet; the revocation of the Edict of Nantes; Colbert and the finances of Louis XIV's reign; how "Western" Russia was before Peter the Great.

Chapter 16 Antoine Lavoisier and his wife; the state and science.

Chapter 17 travel literature and the concept of race; the connection between the philosophes and the revolutionary upheaval at the end of the eighteenth century; new Film & History feature on *Amadeus*.

Chapter 18 revision of Film & History feature on *Marie Antoinette*; new Opposing Viewpoints feature on "Enlightened Absolutism: Enlightened or Absolute?"

Chapter 20 iron production, especially pig iron and wrought iron; the Crystal Palace, especially the display of handmade goods; reorganized material in newly titled section, "Industrialization on the Continent"; women in the Chartist movement; new Opposing Viewpoints feature on "Attitudes of the Industrial Middle Class in Britain and Japan"; new Images of Everyday Life feature on "Living Conditions of the London Poor."

Chapter 21 the independence movement in Latin America.

Chapter 22 nation building (in the introduction); the Crimean War; new Opposing Viewpoints feature on "The Practice of *Realpolitik:* Two Approaches"; new Film & History feature on *The Young Victoria*.

Chapter 23 the national state (in the introduction); the reconstruction of Paris; codes of masculinity in the Boy Scout movement in Great Britain; new section on "Mass Consumption," including material on masculine participation in the new consumer culture.

Chapter 24 new introduction to the chapter; Modernism in literature and the arts, including a new Cézanne illustration; revised Images of Everyday Life feature on "The Struggle for the Right to Vote"; the Dreyfus affair; David Lloyd George as chancellor of the Exchequer; imperialism, especially the impact of British rule on women in India; new section on "The Boer War"; French architecture in Southeast Asia.

Chapter 25 the outbreak of World War I, especially Austria's role; enthusiasm for the outbreak of war; the German invasion of Belgium; fighting in the African colonies; the motives of colonial subjects in fighting for their European rulers; revised material on the Turkish genocide of the Armenians; revision of the discussion of the peace settlement.

Chapter 26 the League of Nations, including protection of minorities; the Great Depression; self-rule for India; the structure and functioning of the Weimar Republic; Hitler's trial; the Enabling Act; the Soviet Union; new material on the Spanish Civil War; new Opposing Viewpoints feature on "The Spanish Civil War"; mass tourism.

Chapter 27 the prelude to World War II and the course of the war; new illustration feature (two images) on the pivotal Battle of Stalingrad.

Chapter 28 the origins of the Cold War; revision of section on "A Society of Consumers"; new Images of Everyday Life feature on "The Rise of the Supermarket"; new section on "The Attempt to Revive Religion."

Chapter 29 new Opposing Viewpoints feature on "Czechoslovakia, 1968: Two Faces of Communism"; revised document on Margaret Thatcher.

Chapter 30 Russia; Eastern Europe; the disintegration of Yugoslavia; Germany; France; Italy; the United States; the European Union; the wars in Afghanistan and Iraq; gender issues and Muslim immigrants; the arts in the section on "Art and Music in the Age of Commerce"; technology in "The Digital Age"; revision of "Reality in the Digital Age"; new section on the global financial collapse titled "End of Excess"; new Opposing Viewpoints feature on "Islam and the West: Secularism in France."

The enthusiastic response to the primary sources (boxed documents) led me to evaluate the content of each document carefully and add new documents throughout the text, including new comparative documents in the feature called **Opposing Viewpoints.** This feature, which was introduced in the seventh edition, presents a comparison of two or three primary sources in order to facilitate student analysis of historical documents. This feature has been expanded and now appears in every chapter, including such new topics as "The Black Death: Contemporary Views," "Attitudes of the Industrial Middle Class in Britain and Japan," and "Czechoslovakia, 1968: Two Faces of Communism." Focus questions are included to help students evaluate the documents.

Two additional features that were added in the seventh edition have also been expanded. **Images of Everyday Life,** which combines two or more illustrations with a lengthy caption to provide insight into various aspects of social life, can now be found in eleven chapters, including such new topics as "Spices and World Trade" and "The Rise of the Supermarket." **Film & History,** which presents a brief analysis of a film's plot as well as its historical significance, value, and accuracy, can now be found in thirteen chapters, including such additions as *Amadeus* and *The Young Victoria.*

The **Suggestions for Further Reading** at the end of each chapter have been thoroughly updated and are organized under subheadings to make them more useful. Additional reading suggestions have been included online. New illustrations were added to every chapter. **Chapter Notes** have now been placed at the end of the book rather than at the end of each chapter.

A new format has been added at the end of each chapter. The **Chapter Summary** is illustrated with thumbnail images of chapter illustrations and combined with a **Chapter Timeline.** A **Chapter Review** has been added to assist students in studying the chapter. This review includes **Upon Reflection** essay questions and a list of **Key Terms** from the chapter.

SUPPLEMENTS

Teaching and learning ancillaries include the following:

For the Teacher

Teacher's Resource Guide for the Advanced Placement Program* Prepared by Dominique Craft of Saint Stephen's Episcopal School, Bradenton, Florida. Based on the college Instructor's Manual, this manual is available printed or online, and is designed to help teachers make optimal use of *Western Civilization* in preparing for the AP* exam. The manual includes a description of the exam, advice about how to prepare students, AP* focus sections, instructional objectives, chapter outlines, glossaries, lecture and discussion topic suggestions, and suggested group work and project topics.

PowerLecture CD-ROM with ExamView® and JoinIn® This dual platform, all-in-one multimedia resource includes the Instructor's Resource Manual; Test Bank, prepared by Jason Ripper of Everett Community College (includes key term identification, multiple-choice, essay, and true/false questions); Microsoft® PowerPoint® slides of both lecture outlines and images and maps from the text that can be used as offered or customized by importing personal lecture slides or other material; and *JoinIn®* PowerPoint® slides with clicker content. Also included is ExamView, an easy-to-use assessment and tutorial system that allows teachers to create, deliver, and customize tests in minutes. Teachers can build tests with as many as 250 questions using up to twelve question types, and using ExamView's complete word-processing capabilities, they can enter an unlimited number of new questions or edit existing ones. Also available is a *PowerLecture CD-ROM with ExamView® for Since 1300 AP* Edition,* which includes both ExamView and Microsoft® Word® Test Bank files for the Since 1300 AP* Edition chapters.

AP* Test Bank This printed resource includes key term identification, multiple-choice, essay, and true/false questions. Prepared by Jason Ripper of Everett Community College.

eInstructor's Resource Manual Prepared by Richard Gianni of Westwood College–River Oaks Campus. This manual has many features, including chapter outlines and summaries, lecture suggestions, map exercises, discussion questions for the boxed primary sources, suggested research and paper topics, and suggested weblinks and resources. Available on the instructor's companion website.

CourseReader This is a new customized online reader. You simply go online to search or browse the collection of hundreds of text documents and video clips from multiple disciplines. You choose the documents to assign to your students. Each source document includes a descriptive introduction that puts it in context, and every selection is further supported by both critical thinking and multiple-choice questions; you can also add your own notes and highlighting. Ask your sales representative about pricing options.

HistoryFinder This searchable online database allows teachers to quickly and easily download thousands of assets, including art, photographs, maps, primary sources, and audio/video clips. Each asset downloads directly into a Microsoft® PowerPoint® slide, allowing teachers to easily create PowerPoint presentations for their classrooms.

WebTutor™ on Blackboard® and WebCT® With WebTutor's text-specific, pre-formatted content and total flexibility, teachers can easily create and manage their own custom course website. WebTutor's course management tool gives teachers the ability to provide virtual office hours, post syllabi, set up threaded discussions, track student progress with the quizzing material, and much more. For students, WebTutor offers real-time access to a full array of study tools, including animations and videos that bring the book's topics to life, plus chapter outlines, summaries, learning objectives, glossary flashcards (with audio), practice quizzes, and weblinks. Ask your sales representative about available discounts.

CourseMate Cengage Learning's History CourseMate brings course concepts to life with interactive learning, study, and exam preparation tools that support the printed textbook. Watch student comprehension soar as your class works with the printed textbook and the textbook-specific website. History CourseMate goes beyond the book to deliver what you need! History CourseMate includes an integrated eBook; interactive teaching and learning tools including quizzes, flashcards, videos, and more; and EngagementTracker, a first-of-its-kind tool that monitors student engagement in the course. Learn more at www.cengagebrain.com. Ask your sales representative about available discounts.

For the Student

Fast Track to a 5: Preparing for the AP* European History Exam This test-preparation manual was written by Susan Gerard, Lewis and Clark High School, Spokane, Washington; Patricia Ann Harrold, Edmond Memorial High School, Edmond, Oklahoma; and Richard Chrisler VerWiebe Jr., Onondaga Community College, Syracuse, New York. It includes an introduction for students on taking the AP* exam, a diagnostic test to help students assess their level of preparedness, chapter reviews with multiple-choice and free-response questions, and two complete practice tests in AP* format. *Fast Track to a 5* may be purchased either with or without the textbook.

AP* Study Guide Prepared by Michael P. Hipsley of Catonsville High School, Baltimore, Maryland, this printed guide contains chapter outlines, learning objectives, glossaries of names and terms, matching exercises, multiple-choice questions, fill-in-the-blank questions, chronology exercises, critical thinking questions, and exercises to practice analysis of primary source documents.

CourseMate Website for Western Civilization This website for students features a wide assortment of resources to help students master the subject matter. The website, prepared by Michael A. Sparks of Ivy Tech Community College–Central Indiana, includes a glossary, flashcards, crossword puzzles, tutorial quizzes, essay questions, critical thinking exercises, weblinks, and suggested readings. Throughout the text, icons direct students to relevant exercises and self-testing material located on the website. Ask your sales representative about available discounts.

Cengagebrain.com Save your students time and money. Direct them to www.cengagebrain.com for choice in formats and savings and a better chance to succeed in your class. *Cengagebrain.com*, Cengage Learning's online store, is a single destination for more than 10,000 new textbooks, eTextbooks, eChapters, study tools, and audio supplements.

Wadsworth Western Civilization Resource Center Wadsworth's Western Civilization Resource Center gives your students access to a "virtual reader" with hundreds of primary sources including speeches, letters, legal documents and transcripts, poems, maps, simulations, timelines, and additional images that bring history to life, along with interactive assignable exercises. A map feature including Google Earth™ coordinates and exercises will aid in student comprehension of geography and use of maps. Students can compare the traditional textbook map with an aerial view of the location today. It is an ideal resource for study, review, and research. In addition to this map feature, the resource center also provides blank maps for student review and testing. Ask your sales representative about available discounts.

Rand McNally Historical Atlas of Western Civilization, 2e This valuable resource features more than forty-five maps, including maps that highlight Classical Greece and Rome; maps documenting European civilization during the Renaissance; maps that follow events in Germany, Russia, and Italy leading up to World Wars I and II; maps that show the dissolution of communism in 1989; maps documenting language and religion in the Western world; and maps describing the unification and industrialization of Europe. Ask your sales representative about available discounts.

Writing for College History, 1e Prepared by Robert M. Frakes of Clarion University. This brief handbook for survey courses in American history, Western Civilization/European history, and world civilization guides students through the various types of writing assignments they encounter in a history class. Providing examples of student writing and candid assessments of student work, this text focuses on the rules and conventions of writing for the college history course. Ask your sales representative about available discounts.

The History Handbook, 1e   Prepared by Carol Berkin of Baruch College, City University of New York, and Betty Anderson of Boston University. This book teaches students both basic and history-specific study skills such as how to take notes, get the most out of lectures and readings, read primary sources, research historical topics, and correctly cite sources. Substantially less expensive than comparable skill-building texts, *The History Handbook* also offers tips for Internet research and evaluating online sources. Additionally, students can purchase and download the *eAudio* version of *The History Handbook* or any of its eighteen individual units at www.cengagebrain.com to listen to on the go. Ask your sales representative about available discounts.

Doing History: Research and Writing in the Digital Age, 1e Prepared by Michael J. Galgano, J. Chris Arndt, and Raymond M. Hyser of James Madison University. Whether you're starting down the path as a history major, or simply looking for a straightforward and systematic guide to writing a successful paper, you'll find this text to be an indispensable handbook to historical research. This text's "soup to nuts" approach to researching and writing about history addresses every step of the process, from locating your sources and gathering information, to writing clearly and making proper use of various citation styles to avoid plagiarism. You'll also learn how to make the most of every tool available to you—especially the technology that helps you conduct the process efficiently and effectively. Ask your sales representative about available discounts.

The Modern Researcher, 6e   Prepared by Jacques Barzun and Henry F. Graff of Columbia University. This classic introduction to the techniques of research and the art of expression is used widely in history courses, but is also appropriate for writing and research methods courses in other departments. Barzun and Graff thoroughly cover every aspect of research, from the selection of a topic through the gathering, analysis, writing, revision, and publication of findings, presenting the process not as a set of rules but through actual cases that put the subtleties of research in a useful context. Part One covers the principles and methods of research; Part Two covers writing, speaking, and getting one's work published. Ask your sales representative about available discounts.

Document Exercise Workbook   Prepared by Donna Van Raaphorst, Cuyahoga Community College. This collection of exercises is based around primary sources. Available for purchase in two volumes.

Music of Western Civilization   Available free to adopters, and for a small fee to students, this CD contains a broad sampling of many important musical pieces of Western civilization.

Reader Program   Cengage Learning publishes a number of readers, some containing exclusively primary sources, others a combination of primary and secondary sources, and some designed to guide students through the process of historical inquiry. Visit Cengage.com/history for a complete list of readers.

ACKNOWLEDGMENTS

I began to teach at age five in my family's grape arbor. By the age of ten, I wanted to know and understand everything in the world, so I set out to memorize our entire set of encyclopedia volumes. At seventeen, as editor of the high school yearbook, I chose "patterns" as its theme. With that as my early history, followed by many rich years of teaching, writing, and family nurturing, it seemed quite natural to accept the challenge of writing a history of Western civilization as I approached that period in life often described as the age of wisdom. Although I see this writing adventure as part of the natural unfolding of my life, I gratefully acknowledge that without the generosity of many others, it would not have been possible.

David Redles gave generously of his time and ideas, especially for Chapters 28 and 29. Chris Colin provided research on the history of music, while Laurie Batitto, Alex Spencer, Stephen Maloney, Shaun Mason, Peter Angelos, and Fred Schooley offered valuable editorial assistance. I deeply appreciate the valuable technical assistance provided by Dayton Coles. I am deeply grateful to John Soares for his assistance in preparing the map captions and to Charmarie Blaisdell of Northeastern University for her detailed suggestions on women's history. Daniel Haxall of Kutztown University provided valuable assistance with materials on postwar art, popular culture, Postmodern art and thought, the Digital Age, and the Film & History feature. I am especially grateful to Kathryn Spielvogel for her work as research associate for Chapters 15–30. I am also thankful to the thousands of students whose questions and responses have caused me to see many aspects of Western civilization in new ways.

My ability to undertake a project of this magnitude was in part due to the outstanding European history teachers that I had as both an undergraduate and a graduate student. These included Kent Forster (modern Europe) and Robert W. Green (early modern Europe) at The Pennsylvania State University and Franklin Pegues (medieval), Andreas Dorpalen (modern Germany), William MacDonald (ancient), and Harold J. Grimm (Renaissance and Reformation) at The Ohio State University. These teachers provided me with profound insights into Western civilization and also taught me by their examples that learning only becomes true understanding when it is accompanied by compassion, humility, and open-mindedness.

I would like to thank the many teachers and students who have used the first seven editions of my *Western Civilization*. Their enthusiastic response to a textbook that was intended to put the story back in history and capture the imagination of the reader has been very gratifying.

I especially thank the many teachers and students who made the effort to contact me personally to share their enthusiasm. Thanks to Wadsworth's comprehensive review process, many historians were asked to evaluate my manuscript and review each edition. I am grateful to the following people for their innumerable suggestions over the course of the first seven editions, which have greatly improved my work:

Anne J. Aby
  Minnesota West Community and Technical College, Worthington Campus

Paul Allen
  University of Utah

Gerald Anderson
  North Dakota State University

Susan L. H. Anderson
  Campbell University

Letizia Argenteri
  University of San Diego

Roy A. Austensen
  Illinois State University

James A. Baer
  Northern Virginia Community College–Alexandria

James T. Baker
  Western Kentucky University

Patrick Bass
  Morningside College

John F. Battick
  University of Maine

Frederic J. Baumgartner
  Virginia Polytechnic Institute

Phillip N. Bebb
  Ohio University

Anthony Bedford
  Modesto Junior College

F. E. Beemon
  Middle Tennessee State University

Leonard R. Berlanstein
  University of Virginia

Cyriaque Beurtheret
  Salt Lake Community College

Douglas T. Bisson
  Belmont University

Charmarie Blaisdell
  Northeastern University

Stephen H. Blumm
  Montgomery County Community College

John Bohstedt
  University of Tennessee–Knoxville

Hugh S. Bonar
  California State University

Werner Braatz
  University of Wisconsin–Oshkosh

Alfred S. Bradford
  University of Missouri

Janet Brantley
  Texarkana College

Maryann E. Brink
  College of William & Mary

Jerry Brookshire
  Middle Tennessee State University

Daniel Patrick Brown
  Moorpark College

Gregory S. Brown
  University of Nevada–Las Vegas

Blaine T. Browne
  Broward Community College

Kevin W. Caldwell
  Blue Ridge Community College

J. Holden Camp Jr.
  Hillyer College, University of Hartford

Jack Cargill
  Rutgers University

Martha Carlin
  University of Wisconsin–Milwaukee

Elizabeth Carney
  Clemson University

Susan Carrafiello
  Wright State University

Joseph J. Casino
  St. Joseph's University

Eric H. Cline
  Xavier University

Robert G. Clouse
  Indiana State University

Robert Cole
  Utah State University

William J. Connell
  Rutgers University

Nancy Conradt
  College of DuPage

Marc Cooper
  Southwest Missouri State

Richard A. Cosgrove
  University of Arizona

David A. Crain
  South Dakota State University

Michael A. Crane Jr. (student)
  Everett Community College

Luanne Dagley
  Pellissippi State Technical Community College

John Davies
  University of Delaware

Michael F. Doyle
  Ocean County College

Joseph J. Eble
  Burlington County College

James W. Ermatinger
  University of Nebraska–Kearney

Porter Ewing
  Los Angeles City College

Carla Falkner
  Northeast Mississippi Community College

Steven Fanning
  University of Illinois–Chicago

Ellsworth Faris
  California State University–Chico

Gary B. Ferngren
  Oregon State University

Mary Helen Finnerty
  Westchester Community College

Jennifer E. Forster
  Lakeland Community College

A. Z. Freeman
  Robinson College

Marsha Frey
  Kansas State University

Frank J. Frost
  University of California–Santa Barbara

Frank Garosi
  California State University–Sacramento

Laura Gellott
  University of Wisconsin–Parkside

Richard M. Golden
  University of North Texas

Manuel G. Gonzales
  Diablo Valley College

Amy G. Gordon
  Denison University

Richard J. Grace
  Providence College

Charlotte M. Gradie
  Sacred Heart University

Candace Gregory
  California State University–Sacramento

Katherine Gribble
  Highline Community College

Hanns Gross
  Loyola University

John F. Guilmartin
  Ohio State University

Paul Hagenloh
  The University of Alabama

Jeffrey S. Hamilton
  Gustavus Adolphus College

J. Drew Harrington
  Western Kentucky University

James Harrison
  Siena College

Doina Pasca Harsanyi
  Central Michigan University

Jay Hatheway
  Edgewood College

A. J. Heisserer
  University of Oklahoma

Betsey Hertzler
  Mesa Community College

Robert Herzstein
  University of South Carolina

Michael C. Hickey
Bloomsburg University

Shirley Hickson
North Greenville College

Martha L. Hildreth
University of Nevada

Boyd H. Hill Jr.
University of Colorado–Boulder

Michael Hofstetter
Bethany College

Donald C. Holsinger
Seattle Pacific University

Frank L. Holt
University of Houston

W. Robert Houston
University of South Alabama

Michael W. Howell
College of the Ozarks

David Hudson
California State University–Fresno

Paul J. L. Hughes
Sussex County Community College

Richard A. Jackson
University of Houston

Fred Jewell
Harding University

Nicole Jobin
University of Colorado

Jenny M. Jochens
Towson State University

William M. Johnston
University of Massachusetts

Jeffrey A. Kaufmann
Muscatine Community College

David O. Kieft
University of Minnesota

Patricia Killen
Pacific Lutheran University

Jay Kilroy
Mesa Community College

William E. Kinsella Jr.
Northern Virginia Community College–Annandale

James M. Kittelson
Ohio State University

Doug Klepper
Santa Fe Community College

Cynthia Kosso
Northern Arizona University

Ed Krzemienski
The Citadel

Paul E. Lambert
Nichols College

Clayton Miles Lehmann
University of South Dakota

Diana Chen Lin
Indiana University, Northwest

Paul Douglas Lockhart
Wright State University

Ursula W. MacAffer
Hudson Valley Community College

Harold Marcuse
University of California–Santa Barbara

Mike Markowski
Westminster College

Mavis Mate
University of Oregon

Priscilla McArthur
Troy State University–Dothan

T. Ronald Melton
Brewton Parker College

Jack Allen Meyer
University of South Carolina

Eugene W. Miller Jr.
The Pennsylvania State University–Hazleton

David B. Mock
Tallahassee Community College

John Patrick Montano
University of Delaware

Rex Morrow
Trident Technical College

Wyatt S. Moulds
Jones County Junior College

Kenneth Mouré
University of California–Santa Barbara

Thomas M. Mulhern
University of North Dakota

Pierce Mullen
Montana State University

Cliona Murphy
California State University–Bakersfield

Frederick I. Murphy
Western Kentucky University

William M. Murray
University of South Florida

Otto M. Nelson
Texas Tech University

Sam Nelson
Willmar Community College

John A. Nichols
Slippery Rock University

Lisa Nofzinger
Albuquerque Technical Vocational Institute

Chris Oldstone-Moore
Augustana College

Donald Ostrowski
Harvard University

James O. Overfield
University of Vermont

Matthew L. Panczyk
Bergen Community College

Kathleen A. Parrow
Black Hills State University

Kathleen Paul
University of South Florida

Jody Peterson
Centralia College

Carla Rahn Phillips
University of Minnesota

Keith Pickus
Wichita State University

Linda J. Piper
University of Georgia

Marjorie Plummer
Western Kentucky University

Janet Polasky
University of New Hampshire

Thomas W. Porter
Randolph-Macon College

Charles A. Povlovich
California State University–Fullerton

Penne L. Prigge
Rockingham Community College

Nancy Rachels
Hillsborough Community College

Norman G. Raiford
Greenville Technical College

Charles Rearick
University of Massachusetts–Amherst

Jerome V. Reel Jr.
Clemson University

Roger Reese
Texas A&M University

William Roba
Scott Community College

Joseph Robertson
Gadsden State Community College

Jonathan Roth
San Jose State University

Constance M. Rousseau
Providence College

Beverly J. Rowe
Texarkana College

Julius R. Ruff
Marquette University

David L. Ruffley
Pikes Peak Community College

Geraldine Ryder
Ocean County College

Richard Saller
University of Chicago

Magdalena Sanchez
Texas Christian University

Jack Schanfield
Suffolk County Community College

Roger Schlesinger
Washington State University

Joanne Schneider
Rhode Island College

Thomas C. Schunk
University of Wisconsin–Oshkosh

Kyle C. Sessions
Illinois State University

Linda Simmons
Northern Virginia Community College–Manassas

Donald V. Sippel
Rhode Island College

Stuart Smyth
University at SUNY–Albany

Glen Spann
  Asbury College

Heath A. Spencer
  Seattle University

John W. Steinberg
  Georgia Southern University

Robert P. Stephens
  Virginia Tech

Paul W. Strait
  Florida State University

James E. Straukamp
  California State University–Sacramento

Brian E. Strayer
  Andrews University

Fred Suppe
  Ball State University

Roger Tate
  Somerset Community College

Tom Taylor
  Seattle University

Emily Teipe
  Fullerton College

David Tengewall
  Anne Arundel Community College

Jack W. Thacker
  Western Kentucky University

Thomas Turley
  Santa Clara University

John G. Tuthill
  University of Guam

Maarten Ultee
  University of Alabama

Donna L. Van Raaphorst
  Cuyahoga Community College

J. Barry Vaughn
  University of Alabama

Allen M. Ward
  University of Connecticut

Richard D. Weigel
  Western Kentucky University

Michael Weiss
  Linn-Benton Community College

Arthur H. Williamson
  California State University–Sacramento

Daniel Woods
  Ferrum College

Katherine Workman
  Wright State University

Judith T. Wozniak
  Cleveland State University

Walter J. Wussow
  University of Wisconsin–Eau Claire

Edwin M. Yamauchi
  Miami University

Robert W. Young
  Carroll Community College

The following individuals contributed suggestions for the eighth edition:

Owen Bradley
  Columbia College at Coast Guard Island

Daniel Bubb
  Gonzaga University

Jane Laurel Carrington
  St. Olaf College

Elizabeth Collins
  Triton College

Michael Dolski
  Ball State University

Hugh Dubrulle
  Saint Anselm College

Carla Falkner
  Northeast Mississippi Community College

Jennifer Foray
  Purdue University

Carol Herringer
  Wright State University

Martin Menke
  Rivier College

Wyatt Moulds
  Jones County Junior College

Ted Petro
  New England College

Kevin Robbins
  Indiana University
  Purdue University–Indianapolis

Eric C. Roberson
  Wake Technical Community College

Matthew Ruane
  Florida Institute of Technology

Mark Edward Ruff
  Saint Louis University

Thomas J. Schaeper
  St. Bonaventure University

Sergei Zhuk
  Ball State University

The editors at Cengage Wadsworth have been both helpful and congenial at all times. I especially wish to thank Clark Baxter, whose clever wit, wisdom, gentle prodding, and good friendship have added much depth to our working relationship. Margaret Beasley thoughtfully, wisely, efficiently, and pleasantly guided the overall development of the eighth edition. I also thank Nancy Blaine for her suggestions and valuable insights. I also want to express my gratitude to John Orr, whose good humor, well-advised suggestions, and generous verbal support made the production process easier. Pat Lewis, a truly outstanding copy editor, continued to teach me much about the fine points of the English language. Abigail Baxter provided valuable assistance in suggesting illustrations and obtaining permissions for the illustrations.

Above all, I thank my family for their support. The gifts of love, laughter, and patience from my daughters, Jennifer and Kathryn; my sons, Eric and Christian; my daughters-in-law, Liz and Laurie; and my sons-in-law, Daniel and Eddie, were enormously appreciated. I also wish to acknowledge my grandchildren, Devyn, Bryn, Drew, Elena, Sean, Emma, and Jackson, who bring great joy to my life. My wife and best friend, Diane, contributed editorial assistance, wise counsel, good humor, and the loving support that made it possible for me to accomplish a project of this magnitude. I could not have written the book without her.

CORRELATION OF TOPICS FOR THE AP* EUROPEAN HISTORY COURSE

Topic	Correlation to pages in *Western Civilization*			
	1350–1648	**1649–1815**	**1816–1914**	**1915–Present**
Intellectual and Cultural History				
Evolution of religious and institutional thought	328–329, 383–395, 398–402, 405–406, 407, 414, 449–454	455–460, 508, 536–540, 583–596, 597–599	693, 742–743, 754–755	915–917, 939–940, 968–969
Nonspiritual thought in learning and culture	355–358, 397–398	479–483, 489–512, 514–530, 534, 583–596	698–700, 738–747	839–840, 937–943
Developments and implication of science and technology	330, 334–337, 358, 414–415, 416, 426, 437–438	488–502, 504–510, 533	563–564, 608–633, 690, 692–701, 705–713, 738–742, 790–791	813, 839, 877, 937–943, 972–973
Artistic and literary genres	330–332, 352, 358–365	479–483, 488, 514–525, 526	662–667, 698–700, 743–748	842–845, 913–915, 940–941, 970–971, 973
Impact of thought and culture on social and political life	307–312, 350–351, 402–407, 442–443, 447	471–472, 543–551, 558–564	608–633, 658–661, 690–694, 698, 705–729, 738–748	839–846, 886–916, 921–925, 937–943, 975–978
The rise and impact of political ideologies on European states	350–351, 352, 377–378, 380–395, 398–402, 414–415, 442–443, 447–448	454–469, 471, 488–510, 514–535, 536–539, 543, 560–563, 575–578, 578–596, 597–603, 608–620	639–650, 662–667, 690–691, 692–700, 738–748, 759–760, 769, 776–777	821–836, 845–847, 865, 894–900, 900–907, 915, 921–925, 937–942, 963, 968–970, 974–978
Dissemination of ideas among various European populations	330, 352–358, 396–398, 402	505–510, 526–535, 562–564, 578	647–650, 662–667, 691, 692–700, 721–726, 738–748, 766–767	842–846, 909–916, 921–925, 937–943, 968–970, 972–973, 976
Demographic trends as found in religious thought, family life, and popular culture	328–329, 333–336, 341–346, 352–365, 370, 377–397, 383–394, 396–398, 437, 447	479–483, 505–510, 514–535, 536–539, 558–560, 565–571, 575–578, 578–596, 599–600	621–633, 662–667, 692–700, 705–713, 714–729, 738–748, 749	937–943, 966–967, 968–971, 976–977
Influence of globalization on Europe	437–444	601–603, 616–620, 673, 759–768, 769–771, 777	785–796, 807–808	813–815, 852–855, 865–876, 877–881, 891–893, 894–900, 900–907, 932–937, 948–962, 974–978

*AP and the Advanced Placement Program are registered trademarks of the College Entrance Examination Board, which was not involved in the production of, and does not endorse, this product.

Topic	1350–1648	1649–1815	1816–1914	1915–Present
Political and Diplomatic History				
The development and role of the modern nation-state	366–368, 449–451	470–472, 554–557, 575–576, 597–603	639–646, 651–657, 671–681, 729–733, 749–758, 804–809	816–820, 821–836, 879–880, 886–893, 900–909, 909–912, 925–932, 936–937, 948–962
The interdependence of Europe and the rest of the world	404–408, 416–441, 443	461, 564, 575–578, 601–603	673–675, 756–757, 759–768, 785–786	857–864, 880–881, 886–893, 894–900, 900–907, 932–937, 948–961, 978
Rise of political factions and the variations of political thought and implementation	350–351	471–475, 575–578, 578–596	639–646, 647–650, 651–656, 676–681, 682–686, 691, 729–730, 749, 752–756, 776	797, 816–819, 821–836, 850, 865–867, 900–907, 925–928, 948–960
The application of political and social rights granted to, or removed from, various European groups	366–370, 402–408, 426–428, 437–441, 447, 449–451	454–461, 464–469, 470–471, 547–552, 554, 575–578, 578–596, 597–603	639–646, 647–650, 651–656, 676–681, 682–686, 729–733, 749–751, 752, 753–757, 768	797, 804, 804–807, 816–819, 821–836, 850, 865–867, 867–869, 880–882, 900–907, 912, 921–925, 925–928, 948–960
The rise and impact of nationalism on European society	366–369	581–597, 597–603	640–646, 679–650, 676–681, 682–686, 729–730, 756, 759–765, 776	821–836, 865–866, 886–893, 894–900, 900–907, 927, 948–960
Various ways in which Europeans rebelled or protested	402–408, 449–454	479–478, 547–554, 575–578, 578–604	637–650, 651–657, 671–681, 691, 753–757, 766–768, 769–771, 776–777	821–836, 850–856, 857–871, 880–881, 886–900, 900–907, 921–925, 927–928, 932–937, 948–962
The interworking of state policy and foreign policy	404–410, 414–444	449–454, 454–461, 464–466, 468, 547–557, 575–578, 578–603	637–646, 647–650, 671–681, 682–685, 756–757, 759–768, 769–770, 777–779	780–796, 804–808, 816–820, 850–856, 857–864, 865–871, 872–876, 877–880, 886–893, 894–900, 900–907, 932–937, 948–960, 962–965, 966, 975
European attempts at peace and political negotiations	402–408, 443–444, 449–452	471, 554–557, 603	637–646, 652, 769	807–808, 813, 850–855, 890, 891, 892, 905, 907, 909, 954, 956, 957
Impact of war on mass society	313–314, 366–370, 385–386, 392, 402–409, 449–454	455–461, 471–478, 454–458, 575–578, 578–596, 601–604	643–650, 651–658, 658–661, 673–676, 676–681, 682–683, 688–689, 691–692, 749–751, 755–756, 769–770, 776–777	780–804, 821–836, 850–880, 886–900, 900–907, 921–925, 927–928, 932–937, 948–960, 962–965

Topic	Correlation to pages in *Western Civilization*			
	1350–1648	**1649–1815**	**1816–1914**	**1915–Present**
Social and Economic History				
Rise and impact of agriculture on European society	443–444	561–562, 608–613, 631–633, 690–692	608–613, 631–633, 690–692, 705–711	814–815, 974–975
The impact of urbanization on European mass society	333–334	558–564, 569–572	621–632, 714–729	839–841, 974–979
The changes in European class stratification, i.e. wealth and poverty within Europe	343–346	531–535, 565–568, 578–579	656–633, 691, 710–713, 719–724, 749–751	812, 909–913, 921–924, 966–967, 976
The rise of medicine and the impact of diseases on European life	334	506–508	533–534, 558–561, 616–633, 695	910–911
The rise and influence of the new consumer society upon European social classes	334–335, 358, 414, 418–419, 426–436, 442–443	561–564	608–615, 616–619, 621–633, 690–691, 705–711, 729, 759	938, 975–976
The various perceptions and attitudes of Europeans toward other Europeans and the world	437–438, 447–448	531–532, 533, 534, 565–568	624–632, 661, 688, 694, 698, 710–713, 719–724, 741, 749–752, 759, 766–768	865–870, 894–900, 912, 921–925, 966–967, 976
The rise and impact of industrialization on society	334	563–564	608–633, 662–665, 690–691, 705–713, 712–729, 756–757, 759–760, 768	839–840, 966–967
The impact of demography on both elite and popular culture	343–346, 396–398	531–532, 558–560, 565–568	621, 625–631, 719–724, 768	824, 912, 924, 966
Gender roles and their influence on work, family, and political life	334, 396, 447	501, 503, 531–532, 558–660, 565–569, 578–596	624–632, 720–726	791–796, 872–875, 912, 916, 921–924, 966

INTRODUCTION TO STUDENTS OF WESTERN CIVILIZATION

CIVILIZATION, AS HISTORIANS define it, first emerged between five and six thousand years ago when people in different parts of the world began to live in organized communities with distinct political, military, economic, and social structures. Religious, intellectual, and artistic activities assumed important roles in these early societies. The focus of this book is on Western civilization, a civilization that many people identify with the continent of Europe.

Defining Western Civilization

Western civilization itself has evolved considerably over the centuries. Although the concept of the West did not yet exist at the time of the Mesopotamians and Egyptians, their development of writing, law codes, and different roles based on gender all eventually influenced what became Western civilization. Although the Greeks did not conceive of Western civilization as a cultural entity, their artistic, intellectual, and political contributions were crucial to the foundations of Western civilization. The Romans produced a remarkable series of accomplishments that were fundamental to the development of Western civilization, a civilization that came to consist largely of lands in Europe conquered by the Romans, in which Roman cultural and political ideals were gradually spread. Nevertheless, people in these early civilizations viewed themselves as subjects of states or empires, not as members of Western civilization.

With the rise of Christianity during the Late Roman Empire, however, peoples in Europe began to identify themselves as part of a civilization different from others, such as that of Islam, leading to a concept of a Western civilization different from other civilizations. In the fifteenth century, Renaissance intellectuals began to identify this civilization not only with Christianity but also with the intellectual and political achievements of the ancient Greeks and Romans.

Important to the development of the idea of a distinct Western civilization were encounters with other peoples. Between 700 and 1500, encounters with the world of Islam helped define the West. But after 1500, as European ships began to move into other parts of the world, encounters with peoples in Asia, Africa, and the Americas not only had an impact on the civilizations found there but also affected how people in the West defined themselves. At the same time, as they set up colonies, Europeans began to transplant a sense of Western identity to other areas of the world, especially North America and parts of Latin America, that have come to be considered part of Western civilization.

As the concept of Western civilization has evolved over the centuries, so have the values and unique features associated with that civilization. Science played a crucial role in the development of modern Western civilization. The societies of the Greeks, Romans, and medieval Europeans were based largely on a belief in the existence of a spiritual order; a dramatic departure to a natural or material view of the universe occurred in the seventeenth-century Scientific Revolution. Science and technology have been important in the growth of today's modern and largely secular Western civilization, although antecedents to scientific development also existed in Greek and medieval thought and practice, and religion remains a component of the Western world today.

Many historians have viewed the concept of political liberty, belief in the fundamental value of every individual, and a rational outlook based on a system of logical, analytical thought as unique aspects of Western civilization. Of course, the West has also witnessed horrendous negations of liberty, individualism, and reason. Racism, slavery, violence, world wars, totalitarian regimes—these, too, form part of the complex story of what constitutes Western civilization.

The Dating of Time

In our examination of Western civilization, we also need to be aware of the dating of time. In recording the past, historians try to determine the exact time when events occurred. World War II in Europe, for example, began on September 1, 1939, when Hitler sent German troops into Poland, and ended on May 7, 1945, when Germany surrendered. By using dates, historians can place events in order and try to determine the development of patterns over periods of time.

If someone asked you when you were born, you would reply with a number, such as 1993. In the United States, we would all accept that number without question because it is part of the dating system followed in the Western world (Europe and the Western Hemisphere). In this system, events are dated by counting backward or forward from the year 1. When the system was first devised, the year 1 was assumed to be the year of the birth of Jesus, and the abbreviations B.C. (before Christ) and A.D. (for the Latin words *anno Domini,* meaning "in the year of the Lord") were used to refer to the periods before and after the birth of Jesus, respectively. Historians now generally prefer to refer to the year 1 in nonreligious terms as the beginning of the "common era." The abbreviations B.C.E. (before the common era) and C.E. (common era) are used instead of B.C. and A.D., although the years are the same. Thus, an event that took place four hundred years before the year 1 would be dated 400 B.C.E. (before the common era)—or the date could be expressed as 400 B.C. Dates after the year 1 are labeled C.E. Thus, an event that took place two hundred years after the year 1 would be dated 200 C.E. (common era), or the date could be written A.D. 200. It can also be written simply as 200, just as you would not give your birth year as 1993 C.E., but simply as 1993. In keeping with the current usage by most historians, this book will use the abbreviations B.C.E. and C.E.

Historians also make use of other terms to refer to time. A *decade* is ten years, a *century* is one hundred years, and a *millennium* is one thousand years. Thus, "the fourth century B.C.E." refers to the fourth period of one hundred years counting backward from the year 1, the beginning of the common era. Since the first century B.C.E. would be the years 100 B.C.E. to 1 C.E., the fourth century B.C.E. would be the years 400 B.C.E. to 301 B.C.E. We could say, then, that an event in 350 B.C.E. took place in the fourth century B.C.E.

Similarly, "the fourth century C.E." refers to the fourth period of one hundred years after the beginning of the common era. Since the first period of one hundred years would be the years 1 to 100, the fourth period or fourth century would be the years 301 to 400. We could say, then, that an event in 350 took place in the fourth century. Likewise, the first millennium B.C.E. refers to the years 1000 B.C.E. to 1 C.E.; the second millennium C.E. refers to the years 1001 to 2000.

The dating of events can also vary from people to people. Most people in the Western world use the Western calendar, also known as the Gregorian calendar after Pope Gregory XIII, who refined it in 1582. The Hebrew calendar uses a different system in which the year 1 is the equivalent of the Western year 3760 B.C.E., considered to be the date of the creation of the world according to the Bible. Thus, the Western year 2011 is the year 5771 on the Hebrew calendar. The Islamic calendar begins year 1 on the day Muhammad fled Mecca, which is the year 622 on the Western calendar.

WESTERN CIVILIZATION TO 1300

ALTHOUGH EARLY CIVILIZATIONS emerged in different parts of the world, the foundations of Western civilization were laid by the Mesopotamians and the Egyptians. They developed cities and struggled with the problems of organized states. They developed writing to keep records and created literature. They constructed monumental archi-tecture to please their gods, symbolize their power, and preserve their culture. They developed political, military, social, and religious structures to deal with the basic problems of human existence and organization. These first literate civilizations left detailed records that allow us to view how they grappled with three of the fundamental problems that humans have pondered: the nature of human relationships, the nature of the universe, and the role of divine forces in that cosmos. Although later peoples in Western civilization would provide different answers from those of the Mesopotamians and Egyptians, it was they who first posed the questions, gave answers, and wrote them down. Human memory begins with these two civilizations.

By 1500 B.C.E., much of the creative impulse of the Mesopotamian and Egyptian civilizations was beginning to wane. The entry of new peoples known as Indo-Europeans who moved into Asia Minor and Anatolia (modern Turkey) led to the creation of a Hittite kingdom that entered into conflict with the Egyptians. The invasion of the Sea Peoples around 1200 B.C.E., however, destroyed the Hittites, severely weakened the Egyptians, and created a power vacuum that allowed a patchwork of petty kingdoms and city-states to emerge, especially in the area of Syria and Palestine. All of them were eventually overshadowed by the rise of the great empires of the Assyrians, Chaldeans, and Persians. The Assyrian Empire was the first to unite almost all of the ancient Near East. Far larger was the empire of the Great Kings of Persia. Although it owed much to the administrative organization developed by the Assyrians, the Persian Empire had its own peculiar strengths. Persian rule was tolerant as well as efficient. Conquered peoples were allowed to keep their own religions, customs, and methods of doing business. The many years of peace that the Persian Empire brought to the Near East facilitated trade and the general well-being of its peoples. Many Near Eastern peoples expressed gratitude for being subjects of the Great Kings of Persia.

The Israelites were one of these peoples. Never numerous, they created no empire and were dominated by the Assyrians, Chaldeans, and Persians. Nevertheless, they left a spiritual legacy that influenced much of the later development of Western civilization. The evolution of Hebrew monotheism (belief in a single god) created in Judaism one of the world's great religions; it influenced the development of both Christianity and Islam. When we speak of the Judeo-Christian heritage of Western civilization, we refer not only to the concept of monotheism but also to ideas of law, morality, and social justice that have become important parts of Western culture.

On the western fringes of the Persian Empire, another relatively small group of people, the Greeks, were creating cultural and political ideals that would also have an important impact on Western civilization. The first Greek civilization, known as the Mycenaean, took shape around 1600 B.C.E. and fell to new Greek-speaking invaders five hundred years later. By the eighth century B.C.E., the *polis* or city-state had become the chief focus of Greek life. Loyalty to the *polis* created a close-knit community but also divided Greece into a host of independent states. Two of them, Sparta and Athens, became the most important. They were very different, however. Sparta created a closed, highly disciplined society, while Athens moved toward an open, democratic civilization.

The Classical Age in Greece (c. 500–338 B.C.E.) began with a mighty confrontation between the Greeks and the Persian Empire. After their victory over the Persians, the Greeks began to divide into two large alliances, one headed by Sparta and the other by Athens. Athens created a naval empire and flourished during the age of Pericles, but fear of Athens led to the Great Peloponnesian War between Sparta and Athens and their allies. For all of their brilliant accomplishments, the Greeks were unable to rise above the divisions and rivalries that caused them to fight each other and undermine their own civilization.

The accomplishments of the Greeks formed the fountainhead of Western culture. Socrates, Plato, and Aristotle established the foundations of Western philosophy. Our literary forms are largely derived from Greek poetry and drama. Greek notions of harmony, proportion, and beauty have remained the touchstones for all subsequent Western art. A rational method of inquiry, so important to modern science, was conceived in ancient Greece. Many of our political terms are Greek in origin, and so are our concepts of the rights and duties of citizenship, especially as they were conceived in Athens, the first great democracy. Especially during their Classical period, the Greeks raised and debated fundamental questions about the purpose of human existence, the structure of human society, and the nature of the universe that have concerned Western thinkers ever since.

While the Greek city-states were pursuing their squabbles, to their north a new and powerful kingdom—Macedonia—emerged. Under King Philip II, the Macedonians defeated a Greek allied army in 338 B.C.E. and then consolidated their control over the Greek peninsula. Although the independent Greek city-states lost their freedom when they were conquered by the Macedonians, Greek culture did not die. Under the leadership of Alexander the Great, son of Philip II, both Macedonians and Greeks invaded and conquered the Persian Empire. In the conquered lands, Greeks and non-Greeks established a series of kingdoms (known as the Hellenistic kingdoms) and inaugurated the Hellenistic era.

The Hellenistic period was, in its own way, a vibrant one. New cities arose and flourished. New philosophical ideas captured the minds of many. Significant achievements occurred in art, literature, and science. Greek culture spread throughout the Near East and made an impact wherever it was carried. In some areas of the Hellenistic world, queens played an active role in political life, and many upper-class women found new avenues for expressing themselves. Although the Hellenistic era achieved a degree of political stability, by the late third century B.C.E., signs of decline were beginning to multiply, and the growing power of Rome would eventually endanger the Hellenistic world.

Sometime in the eighth century B.C.E., a group of Latin-speaking people built a small community called Rome on the Tiber River in Italy. Between 509 and 264 B.C.E., this city expanded and united almost all of Italy under its control. Even more dramatically, between 264 and 133 B.C.E., Rome expanded to the west and east and became master of the Mediterranean Sea.

After 133 B.C.E., however, Rome's republican institutions proved inadequate for the task of ruling an empire. In the breakdown that ensued, ambitious individuals saw

opportunities for power unparalleled in Roman history and succumbed to the temptations. After a series of bloody civil wars, peace was finally achieved when Octavian defeated Antony and Cleopatra. Octavian, who came to be known by the title of Augustus, created a new system of government that seemed to preserve the Republic while establishing the basis for a new system that would rule the empire in an orderly fashion.

After a century of internal upheaval, Augustus established a new order that began the Roman Empire, which experienced peace and prosperity between 14 and 180. During this era, trade flourished and the provinces were governed efficiently. In the course of the third century, however, the Roman Empire came near to collapse due to

invasions, civil wars, and economic decline. Although the emperors Diocletian and Constantine brought new life to the so-called Late Empire at the beginning of the fourth century, their efforts shored up the empire only temporarily. In the course of the fifth century, the empire divided into western and eastern parts.

The Roman Empire was the largest empire in antiquity. Using their practical skills, the Romans produced achievements in language, law, engineering, and government that were bequeathed to the future. The Romance languages of today (French, Italian, Spanish, Portuguese, and Romanian) are based on Latin. Western practices of impartial justice and trial by jury owe much to Roman law. As great builders, the Romans left monuments to their skills throughout Europe, some of which, such as aqueducts and roads, are still in use today. Aspects of Roman administrative practices survived in the Western world for centuries. The Romans also preserved the intellectual heritage of the ancient world.

During its last two hundred years, the Roman world underwent a slow transformation with the spread of Christianity. The rise of Christianity marked an important break with the dominant values of the Roman world. Christianity began as a small Jewish sect, but under the guidance of Paul of Tarsus it became a world religion that appealed to both Jews and non-Jews. Despite persecution by Roman authorities, Christianity grew and became widely accepted by the fourth century. At the end of that century, it was made the official state religion of the Roman Empire.

The period of late antiquity that saw the disintegration of the western part of the Roman Empire also witnessed the emergence of a new European civilization in the Early Middle Ages. This early medieval civilization was formed by the coalescence of three major elements: the Germanic peoples who moved into the western part of the empire and established new kingdoms, the continuing attraction of the Greco-Roman cultural legacy, and the Christian church. Politically, a new series of Germanic kingdoms emerged in western Europe. Each fused Roman and Germanic elements to create a new society. The Christian church (or Roman Catholic Church, as it came to be called in the west) played a crucial role in the growth of the new European civilization. The church developed an organized government under the leadership of the pope. It also assimilated the classical tradition and through its clergy brought Christianized civilization to the Germanic tribes. Especially important were the monks and nuns who led the way in converting the Germanic peoples in Europe to Christianity.

At the end of the eighth century, a new kingdom—the Carolingian Empire—came to control much of western and central Europe, especially during the reign of Charlemagne. In the long run, the creation of a western empire fostered the idea of a distinct European identity and marked a shift of power from the south to the north. Italy and the Mediterranean had been the center of the Roman Empire.

The lands north of the Alps now became the political center of Europe, and increasingly, Europe emerged as the focus and center of Western civilization.

Building on a fusion of Germanic, classical, and Christian elements, the Carolingian Empire was well governed but was held together primarily by personal loyalty to the strong king. The economy of the eighth and ninth centuries was based almost entirely on farming, which proved inadequate to maintain a large monarchical system. As a result, a new political and military order—known as fief-holding—subsequently evolved to become an integral part of the political world of the Middle Ages. Fief-holding was characterized by a decentralization of political power, in which lords exercised legal, administrative, and military power. This transferred public power into many private hands and seemed to provide security that the weak central government could not provide.

The new European civilization that had emerged in the ninth and tenth centuries began to come into its own in the eleventh and twelfth centuries, and Europeans established new patterns that reached their high point in the thirteenth century. The High Middle Ages (1000–1300) was a period of recovery and growth for Western civilization, characterized by a greater sense of security and a burst of energy and enthusiasm. Climatic improvements that produced better growing conditions, an expansion of cultivated land, and technological changes combined to enable Europe's food supply to increase significantly after 1000. This increase in agricultural production helped sustain a dramatic rise in population that was physically apparent in the expansion of towns and cities.

The development of trade and the rise of cities added a dynamic new element to the civilization of the High Middle Ages. Trading activities flourished first in northern Italy and Flanders and then spread outward from these centers. In the late tenth and eleventh centuries, this renewal of commercial life led to a revival of cities. Old Roman sites came back to life, and new towns arose at major crossroads or natural harbors favorable to trading activities. By the twelfth and thirteenth centuries, both the urban centers and the urban population of Europe were experiencing a dramatic expansion. The revival of trade, the expansion of towns and cities, and the development of a money economy did not mean the end of a predominantly rural European society, but they did open the door to new ways to make a living and new opportunities for people to expand and enrich their lives. Eventually, they created the foundations for the development of a predominantly urban industrial society.

During the High Middle Ages, European society was dominated by a landed aristocracy whose primary function was to fight. These nobles built innumerable castles that gave a distinctive look to the countryside. Although lords and vassals seemed forever mired in endless petty conflicts, over time medieval kings began to exert a centralizing authority and inaugurated the process of developing new kinds of monarchical states. By the thirteenth century, European monarchs were solidifying their governmental institutions in pursuit of greater power. The nobles, who rationalized their warlike attitudes by calling themselves the defenders of Christian society, continued to dominate the medieval world politically, economically, and socially. But quietly and surely, within this world of castles and private power, kings gradually began to extend their public powers and developed the machinery of government that would enable them to become the centers of political authority in Europe. The actions of these medieval monarchs laid the foundation for the European kingdoms that in one form or another have dominated the European political scene ever since.

During the High Middle Ages, the power of both nobles and kings was often overshadowed by the authority of the Catholic Church, perhaps the dominant institution of the High Middle Ages. In the Early Middle Ages, the Catholic Church had shared in the challenge of new growth by reforming itself and striking out on a path toward greater papal power, both within the church and over European society. The High Middle Ages witnessed a spiritual renewal that led to numerous and even divergent paths: revived papal leadership, the development of centralized administrative machinery that buttressed papal authority, and new dimensions to the religious life of the clergy and laity. A wave of religious enthusiasm in the twelfth and thirteenth centuries led to the formation of new religious orders that worked to provide for the needs of the people, especially their concern for achieving salvation.

The economic, political, and religious growth of the High Middle Ages also gave European society a new confidence that enabled it to look beyond its borders to the lands and empires of the east. Only a confident Europe could have undertaken the Crusades, a concerted military effort to recover the Holy Land of the Near East from the Muslims.

Western assurance and energy, so crucial to the Crusades, were also evident in a burst of intellectual and artistic activity. New educational institutions known as universities came into being in the twelfth century. New literature, written in the vernacular language, appealed to the growing number of people in cities or at courts who could read. The study of theology, "queen of the sciences," reached a high point in the work of Thomas Aquinas. At the same time, a religious building spree—especially evident in the great Romanesque and Gothic cathedrals of the age—left the landscape bedecked with churches that were the visible symbols of Christian Europe's vitality.

Growth and optimism seemed to characterize the High Middle Ages, but underneath the calm exterior lay seeds of discontent and change. Dissent from church teaching and practices grew in the thirteenth century, leading to a climate of fear and intolerance as the church responded with inquisitorial instruments to enforce conformity to its teachings. The breakdown of the old agricultural system and the creation of new relationships between lords and peasants led to local peasant uprisings in the late thirteenth century. The Crusades ended ignominiously with the fall of the last crusading foothold in the east in 1291. By that time, more and more signs of ominous troubles were appearing. The fourteenth century would prove to be a time of crisis for European civilization.

PREPARING FOR THE AP* EUROPEAN HISTORY EXAM

ADVANCED PLACEMENT is a challenging yet stimulating experience. Whether you are taking an AP course at your school or are working on AP independently, the stage is set for a great intellectual journey. As the school year progresses and you burrow deeper and deeper into the coursework, you will see the broad concepts, events, conflicts, resolutions, and personalities that have shaped the history of our complex world. Examining the cultural, political, and economic developments that have brought great change while acknowledging the continuities that remain throughout European history is a thrilling task. Fleshing out those forces of change and continuity in European history is exciting. Even more exciting will be your ability to recognize references to those forces in the media and to understand how history has shaped current world events.

But as spring approaches and the College Board examination looms on the horizon, Advanced Placement can seem quite intimidating, given the enormous scope and extent of the information you need to know. If you are intimidated by the College Board examination, you are certainly not alone.

The best way to approach an AP examination is to master it, not let it master you. If you manage your time effectively, you will eliminate one major obstacle—learning a considerable amount of factual material. In addition, if you can think of the AP test as a way to show off how your mind works, you have a leg up: attitude *does* help. If you are not one of those students, there is still much you can do to sideline your anxiety. Focused review and practice time will help you master the material so that you can walk into the examination with confidence and get a 5.

By February, long before the exam, you need to make sure that you are registered to take the test. Many schools take care of the paperwork and handle the fees for their AP students, but check with your teacher or the AP coordinator to ensure that you are on the registration list. (This is especially important if you have a documented disability and need test accommodations.) If you are studying AP independently, call AP Services at the College Board for the name of the local AP coordinator, who will help you through the registration process.

The evening before the exam is not a good time for cramming. If you like, look over your class notes or drift through your textbook, but concentrate on the broad outlines, not the small details, of the course. Be sure to sharpen a fistful of no. 2 pencils with good erasers for the multiple-choice section of the test; set out several black or blue ballpoint pens for the free-response questions; check your watch and turn off the alarm if it has one; and get a piece of fruit or a snack bar and a bottle of water for the break. Then relax. And get a good night's sleep. An extra hour of sleep is more valuable than an extra hour of study.

On the day of the examination, take time to eat well to provide fuel for your brain. Studies show that students who eat a good meal before testing get higher grades. Be prepared for a long afternoon: the European history exam lasts for more than three hours, with a ten-minute break between Section I and Section II. You do not want to be distracted by a growling stomach or hunger pangs. Wear comfortable clothes, and take a sweater in case the heating or air-conditioning is erratic. When you get to the testing location, make sure that you comply with all security procedures. Cell phones are not allowed, so leave yours at home or in your locker. Be careful not to drink a lot of liquids, necessitating trips to the bathroom, which take up valuable test time.

Remember, preparation is key. Best wishes on your journey to success—go get that 5.

TAKING THE AP* EUROPEAN HISTORY EXAM

THE AP EUROPEAN HISTORY exam consists of two sections: Section I has eighty multiple-choice questions that account for half of your overall exam score. Section II has three parts. Section II, Part A, is the document-based question (DBQ). Section II, Parts B and C, have three questions each; you are to write a thematic essay on one question from each part. You will have 55 minutes for the multiple-choice portion of the test. Answer sheets for Section I are then collected, and you will be given a short break. You then have a total of 130 minutes for the three essays in Section II.

There is a mandatory 15-minute period for reading all of the free-response questions. The College Board recommends that you take 45 minutes to write the DBQ essay, then spend 35 minutes on each of the two thematic essays. The three essays make up the other half of your total exam score. Your proctor will monitor the time, but you need to keep an eye on your watch and pace yourself so that you can do your best on all three essays. Remember that watch alarms are not allowed.

Here is a chart to help you visualize the breakdown of the exam.

Section	Multiple Choice	Free Response (Essay)		
Weight	50% of exam	50% of exam		
		22.5% of exam	13.75% of exam	13.75% of exam
Number of Questions	80	DBQ (document-based question)	Essay question from Part B	Essay question from Part C
Time Allowed	55 minutes	15 minutes mandated for reading all of the questions in Section II; 115 self-budgeted minutes to write 3 essays		
Suggested Pace	about 45 seconds per question	45 minutes to write	35 minutes to plan and write	35 minutes to plan and write

Strategies for the Multiple-Choice Section

Here are some rules of thumb to help you work your way through the multiple-choice questions:

- **Read the question carefully.** Pressured for time, many students make the mistake of reading the questions too quickly or merely skimming them. By reading a question carefully, you may immediately have some idea about the correct answer. You can then look for it in the responses. Careful reading is especially important in EXCEPT or NOT questions because, unlike the typical multiple-choice question, all of the answers are right except one.

- **Eliminate any answer you know is wrong.** You can write on the multiple-choice questions in the test book. As you read through the responses, draw a line through any answer you know is wrong.

- **Read all of the possible answers, then choose the most accurate response.** AP exams are written to test your precise knowledge of a subject. Sometimes there are a few probable answers, but one of them is more accurate. For example, a question dealing with the Berlin Conference of 1884–1885 may have an answer that seems correct: "It was a conference of European nations." However, there may be an even better answer, one that is more specific to the topic: "It allowed European nations to carve up Africa for their economic gain."

- **Avoid absolute responses.** These answers often include the words "always" or "never." For example, the statement "Great Britain always led in the race for industrial growth" is an overstatement because although Britain led in industrialization during the nineteenth century, it gradually gave way to the United States.

- **Mark and skip tough questions.** If you are hung up on a question, mark it in the margin of the question book and go back to it later. (Don't forget to skip that question on your answer sheet too.) But be sure to answer all of the questions before the time is up, because there is no penalty for incorrect answers.

Types of Multiple-Choice Questions

There are various kinds of multiple-choice questions. Here are some suggestions for how to approach each kind:

Classic/Best Answer Questions

This is the most common type of multiple-choice question. It requires you simply to read the question and select the most correct answer. For example:

1. The Peace of Westphalia
   (A) settled the War of the Austrian Succession.
   (B) made Calvinism legal in France.
   (C) allowed for the independence of Switzerland.
   (D) brought the Bourbons to power in Prussia.
   (E) gave the pope power over the entire Italian peninsula.

ANSWER: **C**. This is a question that has only one correct answer. The Peace of Westphalia, which ended the Thirty Years' War, included provisions for the independence of Switzerland and the recognition of Calvinism in the Holy Roman Empire.

EXCEPT Questions

In an EXCEPT question, all of the answers but one are correct. One way to approach these questions is to take out the EXCEPT and then mark the four choices that fit that new version of the question. The EXCEPT answer will be the one remaining. Another way to approach these questions is to treat them as true/false questions. Mark a T or F in the margin next to each possible answer. There should be only one false answer, and that is the one you should select. For example:

1. All of the following are true about Martin Luther EXCEPT
   (A) he disagreed with the sale of indulgences.
   (B) he became a good friend and compatriot of John Calvin.
   (C) he was a monk in the Roman Catholic Church.
   (D) he married a woman who was once a nun.
   (E) he encouraged nobles in the Holy Roman Empire to stop the German Peasants' War.

ANSWER: **B**. Luther was a monk who initially questioned the sale of indulgences by the Catholic Church. As the Protestant Reformation progressed, he married Katherina von Bora, a former nun. In response to the Peasants' War, he encouraged the nobles to quell the revolt. Luther and Calvin were not friends.

NOT Questions

NOT questions are similar to EXCEPT questions in concept; all of the answers but one are correct. You need to choose the one that is NOT true. Again, one way to approach these questions is to take out the NOT and then mark the four choices that fit your new version of the question. The NOT answer will be the one remaining. Or you can approach the questions as true/false questions, marking a T or F in the margin next to each possible answer. There should be only one false answer, and that is the one you should select. For example:

1. Which of the following was NOT a cause of World War II?
   (A) the policy of appeasement
   (B) the public's desire to avoid another world war at all costs
   (C) Hitler's invasion of Poland
   (D) Hitler's invasion of Czechoslovakia
   (E) a deeper mistrust of fascism than of communism

ANSWER: **E**. To many of the Western powers, Stalin's Communist Soviet Union posed a bigger threat than Hitler's Germany, which claimed to share similar values with the West. Because they did not trust Stalin, Britain and France did not ally themselves with the Soviet Union against Germany.

Photograph/Illustration/Cartoon Questions

These questions require you to interpret a picture in order to gain information in a different way. A good approach is to examine the picture before you read the question and possible responses. Look for symbolism in the image; symbols are especially likely to be used in cartoons and paintings. Ask yourself what the artist or photographer is trying to convey. For example:

1. Which of the following statements is the most accurate description of Rembrandt's *Syndics of the Cloth Guild,* shown above?
   (A) The painting shows the Dutch tendency to engage in cooperative control of business interests.
   (B) These Puritans are preparing to leave for the New World.
   (C) This is a portrait of six members of the Dutch Parliament.
   (D) This painting shows that Dutch women were not involved in business.
   (E) These men are the owners of textile factories in England.

ANSWER: **A**. This painting shows the leaders of a cloth guild in the Netherlands. Group business decision making was common in the Netherlands and a popular theme in Dutch portraiture. Although their dress might lead you to assume they are Puritans (English Calvinists), they are not; they are probably Dutch Reformed, another Calvinist faith.

TABLE 23.2 European Emigration, 1876–1910 (Average Annual Emigration to Non-European Countries per 100,000 Population)

	1876–1880	1881–1885	1886–1890	1891–1895	1896–1900	1901–1905	1906–1910
Europe	94	196	213	185	147	271	322
Ireland	650	1,422	1,322	988	759	743	662
Great Britain	102	174	162	119	88	127	172
Denmark	157	380	401	338	117	292	275
Norway	432	1,105	819	597	312	903	746
Sweden	301	705	759	587	249	496	347
Germany	108	379	207	163	47	50	44
Belgium	—	—	86	50	23	57	69
Netherlands	32	136	111	76	25	45	58
France	8	14	49	14	13	12	12
Spain	—	280	437	434	446	391	758
Portugal	258	356	423	609	417	464	694
Italy	396	542	754	842	974	1,706	1,938
Austria	48	90	114	182	182	355	469
Hungary	—	92	156	134	205	437	616
Russia	6	13	42	47	32	63	67

SOURCE: Robert Gildea, *Barricades and Borders: Europe, 1800–1914* (Oxford, 1987), p. 283.

Chart/Graph Questions

These questions require you to examine the data on a chart or graph. Although these questions are not difficult, spending too much time interpreting a chart or graph can slow you down. To avoid this, first read the question and all of the possible answers so that you know what you are looking for. Before you look at the chart, you may be able to eliminate some obviously incorrect responses. For example:

1. Which of the following statements does the above table best support?
   (A) The rate of emigration from northern Europe fell dramatically between 1876 and 1910.
   (B) Compared with other European nations, Russia saw the greatest growth in the rate of emigration between 1876 and 1910.
   (C) The overall number of emigrants from Germany dropped because of the impact of World War I.
   (D) Great Britain's emigration rate grew little because of the devastation caused by Napoleon's Continental System.
   (E) During the late nineteenth century, Irish emigration reflected the country's independence from Great Britain.

ANSWER: **B**. After analyzing the table, option A can be eliminated because emigration in the north actually grew during this time. Option C is incorrect because World War I did not begin until 1914, four years after the table's timeframe. Option D is incorrect because Napoleon's Continental System was in the beginning of the nineteenth century and had no impact on emigration later in the century. Option E is incorrect because during this time the Irish were fleeing restrictive British policies and waves of economic downturns caused by potato famines; Ireland did not become independent of Great Britain until the twentieth century. Because Russia's emigration rate grew by more than 1,000 percent, much more than the rate of any other country in the table, option B is the correct answer.

Interpreting a Map

For history students, maps are used to describe not just geography but social and political organization as well. Asked to interpret a map, you can pick up a lot of information just by looking at the key.

1. This map of Great Britain in 1850 shows
   (A) how poor Scotland was at that time.
   (B) that very large cities grew only where there were rich coal deposits.
   (C) that the Irish produced cotton and woolen textiles.
   (D) the dependence on coal as a fuel in the growth of industrial areas.
   (E) that iron ore was mined only in England.

ANSWER: **D**. The map shows the importance of coal as an energy source for British factories during the Industrial Revolution. As Britain shifted from water to coal as a source of power, factories no longer had to be situated along rivers and streams. Thus, factories and the towns that grew up around them could be located near the new source of power. Although some large cities were near coal deposits, they did not only develop there.

Free-Response Questions

In Section II of the AP European History exam, you are required to write essays for three free-response questions: one document-based question (DBQ) and two thematic free-response questions (FRQs). The first 15 minutes are devoted to a required reading period when you should read all of the questions. Part A presents the DBQ. Parts B and C each have three questions; you are to choose one question from each part. It is suggested that you spend 45 minutes on the DBQ and 35 minutes on each of the thematic essays.

Each of the three essays is scored on a scale of 0 to 9, with 9 the highest score. The DBQ essay is scored according to one rubric; the two FRQ essays are scored using a different rubric. The DBQ has specific requirements for meeting six basic core points. ***If and only if those six basic core points are met can your essay be considered for expanded core.*** Expanded core can earn you up to three more points. The two FRQ essays in Part B are scored holistically. The key to success on the FRQ essays is writing an analytical thesis and supporting it with solid historical evidence. The key to success on the DBQ essay is understanding the requirements of the rubric and applying them to the specific prompt you are given.

The Document-Based Question

As its name implies, the DBQ presents you with a wide variety of primary-source information in the form of ten to twelve documents. Primary sources are those that are contemporaneous with a time period or event, and they include everything from maps, political cartoons, photographs, and illustrations to speeches, essays, books, documentaries, and editorials. You might also encounter maps, statistics, or historical analyses produced at a later date.

The DBQ essay needs to be based on the documents. Your goal is to demonstrate your ability to tease out the thrust and substance of each document, and then use that information in an analytical essay. A quality DBQ essay according to the AP European History rubric does all of the following:

- **Provides an appropriate, explicitly stated thesis that directly addresses all parts of the question (1 point).** An acceptable thesis is one that makes an analytical argument that responds specifically to what the prompt is calling for you to address in the

AP Tip

For each essay in Section II, you need to take a few minutes to develop an outline. Time spent on an outline is important for a number of reasons:

- It provides you with an opportunity to brainstorm before writing.

- It allows you to determine your analytical thesis after seeing the evidence you can gather to support your argument.

- It lets you organize your thinking and helps you determine the groupings you will use in your DBQ essay.

Once you have outlined your essay, it is time to write. Remember that examination readers are looking for a clear thesis backed up with specific evidence for support. Concentrate on setting out accurate information in straightforward, concise prose. Readers can spot efforts to mask vague information with elegant prose.

DBQ. You must not simply restate the question; your thesis must reflect your analysis of the documents. A generic statement such as "There were many political, economic, and social causes of . . . ." would not be an acceptable thesis. This core point is an important one to learn: you need a solid thesis to guide your essay; further, you cannot earn a point for supporting a thesis without first earning this point.

- **Discusses a majority of the documents individually and specifically (1 point).** For the purpose of the AP exam, a majority of the documents consists of half plus one. You cannot simply list the document number in a sentence; you must talk about the document individually. For example, a weak topic sentence might say that Documents 2, 3, and 4 all illustrate a particular point. But only if you follow that statement with something specific about each of the three documents would credit be given for using three documents. You may misunderstand the documents that you use but still get the point for using them because you addressed them. You cannot earn the next two core points without earning this one.

- **Demonstrates understanding of the basic meaning of a majority of the documents (1 point).** This point considers your ability to interpret documents correctly. You can significantly misinterpret *no more than one* document. A significant misinterpretation is an incorrect analysis of the meaning of the document or one that leads to an incorrect grouping or a false conclusion. A good strategy is to use as many of the documents as you completely understand so that you meet the minimum criteria for earning this point. Exclude documents that you think you don't understand so that you will avoid significantly misinterpreting more than one document. This point cannot be earned without earning the previous point.

- **Supports the thesis with appropriate interpretations of a majority of the documents (1 point).** A thesis must be supported by strong evidence drawn from a majority of the documents. You need to demonstrate your ability to pull such evidence from each document and discuss in your own words how that evidence relates to the thesis you have written in response to the DBQ prompt. *Do not just quote the documents or summarize them in a list.* You need to analyze them and show that you can make historical connections.

- **Analyzes point of view or bias in at least THREE documents (1 point).** It is essential that historians consider how characteristics such as class, gender, nationality, profession, and the like shaped the views of a document's author. The type of document or purpose of the document can also be important in determining the point of view and the reliability of the author. For example, a diary entry might be more truthful than a public document because the diarist would not expect the entry to be subject to public scrutiny. You need to address the point of view in at least three documents. Referring to the point of view of several documents in the same sentence without addressing each of the documents individually counts as only one collective point of view. Each document must be discussed individually and specifically. It is not enough to say what point of view you see presented in a document; you must also account for why that point of view exists in the source. In addition, ask yourself how the point of view affects the document's content. A good place to begin looking for clues to the point of view is the source line of the document. The source line indicates the author of or the speaker in the document and the date of the document, which can help you place the document

in a larger historical context. Often the source line has other important pieces of information about the document as well. *Always read the source line!*

- **Analyzes documents by explicitly grouping them in at least THREE appropriate groups (1 point).** Grouping documents is an important skill because it shows your ability to recognize the relationships that exist between documents. A group consists of two or more documents. To earn this point, your essay must contain three or more groups that reflect the language and demands of the prompt. If a group is suggested by the prompt, by all means include that group in your essay. For example, if you are asked to analyze causes and impacts, one way to organize the documents would be to create a group that shows causes and a group that shows impacts. You can also group documents by the similarities and differences you see in them. Sometimes they can be grouped chronologically. Again, the key is to look at what the prompt is telling you to do and then look at the content of the documents.

If you meet all six of the basic core requirements in your DBQ essay, there are many ways that you can earn up to three additional points from the expanded core. Unlike the basic core, the expanded core is not a checklist. You will earn extra points based on the degree to which you do any or all of the items in the basic core. For example, you can offer additional groupings, analyze point of view in four or more documents, recognize and develop change over time, and bring in relevant outside historical content. You can also earn expanded core points if you shape your thesis so that your argument is comprehensive and very lucid, if you point out nuances in the documents, or if you use the documents especially persuasively.

It is important to note that the DBQ in AP European History does not require use of outside information. This is an exercise in working with documents, not in writing an essay in which you must display learned information. *Although your knowledge of the topic may help you put the documents in context, be careful not to get sidetracked writing what you know about the topic at the expense of paying attention to the documents.*

Take a look at this abbreviated DBQ, one containing six documents. (You will find full-length DBQs in the *Fast Track to a 5* and in the appendix at the end of this book.)

1. Using the documents, evaluate the responsibility of various nations for the outbreak of World War I.

Your first step is to analyze each document in order to come up with evidence to create your thesis. What is the meaning of the document? What or who is the source, and how does that affect his point of view? The source provides important clues to the position being put forth in the document. As you analyze the meaning or significance of the document, jot down margin notes—generalizations that relate to the document, the prompt, or the point of view in the document. For example:

- **Margin note for Document 1.** *Shows the alliances that existed on the eve of World War I. Did these alliances affect actions taken in the days before war broke out?*

- **Margin note for Document 2.** *Shows the German emperor attempting to maintain peace and blaming the imminent outbreak of war on Russian mobilization. He might be biased because he doesn't want Germany to be blamed for the war.*

- **Margin note for Document 3.** *Clearly blames Germany for the war—biased because it is a patriotic weekly magazine that probably would have been running articles written to muster public support for the war. Is it propaganda?*

- **Margin note for Document 4.** *Clearly blames England and Russia for the war. This document and Document 2, both German, might exhibit the hidden agenda of justifying German actions surrounding the outbreak of war.*

- **Margin note for Document 5.** *Clearly blames the war on Germany and the Triple Alliance—probably biased because it was written by the winners of the war and used to justify the reparations imposed on Germany. The winners would not have blamed themselves for the war. This document is similar to Document 3.*

- **Margin note for Document 6.** *Written a decade after the war ended, this source blames all of the great powers for the war. This author might be more unbiased because he was an American and a historian who was using hindsight to understand, not justify, the actions of the various nations.*

Once you have analyzed the documents, you should group them. Often the prompt may give you a hint to help you figure out the groups. Here the prompt suggests that one way to group the documents is to categorize

Document 1

Source: Europe in 1914.

Document 2

Source: Telegram from Emperor William II of Germany to Tsar Nicholas II of Russia, July 31, 1914.

While this action was proceeding your troops were mobilized against Austro-Hungary, my ally, thereby, as I have already pointed out to you, my mediation has been made almost illusory . . . . I now receive authentic news of serious preparations for war on my Eastern frontier. Responsibility for the safety of my empire forces preventive measures of defence upon me. In my endeavours to maintain the peace of the world I have gone to the utmost limit possible. The responsibility for the disaster which is now threatening the whole civilized world will not be laid at my door. In this moment it still lies in your power to avert it. Nobody is threatening the honour or power of Russia.

Document 3

Source: "How Germany Attacked Our Commerce," in *The Great War Magazine: The Standard History of the All-Europe Conflict,* Part 11, October 31, 1914.

The greatest war of modern times, and perhaps in the whole history of the human race, was begun by Germany using the crime of a schoolboy as an excuse.

Document 4

Source: German Chancellor Theobald von Bethmann-Hollweg in a speech to the Reichstag, August 1914.

Where the responsibility in this greatest of all wars lies is quite evident to us. Outwardly responsible are the men in Russia who planned and carried into effect the general mobilization of the Russian army. But in reality and truth the British Government is responsible. The London Cabinet could have made war impossible if they had unequivocally told Petersburg that England was not willing to let a continental war of the Great Powers result from the Austro-Hungarian conflict with Serbia. . . . Therefore, England, together with Russia (I have spoken about Russia on the 4th of August), is answerable before God and man for this catastrophe which has come over Europe and over mankind.

Document 5

Source: Article 231, The Versailles Treaty, June 28, 1919.

The Allied and Associated Governments affirm and Germany accepts the responsibility of Germany and her allies for causing all the loss and damage to which the Allied and Associated Governments and their nationals have been subjected as a consequence of the war imposed upon them by the aggression of Germany and her allies.

Document 6

Source: Sidney Bradshaw Fay, American historian, *The Origins of the World War,* 1928, revised edition 1930.

None of the Powers wanted a European War. Their governing rulers and ministers, with very few exceptions, all foresaw that it must be a frightful struggle, in which the political results were not absolutely certain. . . . Nevertheless, a European war broke out. Why? Because in each country political and military leaders did certain things, which led to mobilizations and declarations of war, or failed to do certain things which might have prevented them. In this sense, all the European countries, in a greater or lesser degree, were responsible.

them by which country or countries they blame for the war. For example, Documents 3 and 5 blame Germany, an Alliance power; Documents 2 and 4 blame England and Russia, two of the Entente powers. Each of these groups contains two logically connected documents that are relevant to the prompt, so these are appropriate groups. What should go in a third group? You have several choices. You could create a third group by connecting Documents 1 and 6. Document 6 assigns responsibility to all of the great powers; Document 1 indicates that this assumption could be true because all of the major powers had formed entangling alliances before the war. Another possibility for the third group would be to connect Document 6 with Documents 4 and 5. In this case, the assumption that all of the great powers contributed to the outbreak of war would be corroborated by the accusations made in Documents 4 and 5. Remember that usually there are many ways to group the documents; you just need to be sure that your groups are logical and explicit and appropriate to the prompt.

After grouping, you need to address point of view for a minimum of three documents. For example, you could point out that Bethmann-Hollweg, speaking before the Reichstag and probably asking the legislature for money to fight the war, could be a biased source; to convince the Reichstag that the war was necessary to maintain German honor and security, he would need to blame England and Russia for the war and paint them as threats to Germany. Just stating that Bethmann-Hollweg used his speech to blame England and Russia for the war does not demonstrate point of view. You must analyze both the particular perspective of the author *and* the reasons for that viewpoint in order to get credit for point of view. A good strategy is to analyze the point of view of as many documents as possible to ensure that you have at least three reasonable attempts.

Once you have analyzed the documents and constructed your groups, you should use this information to help you write an analytical thesis. *Make sure your thesis has an argument and does not just repeat the prompt.* For example, the thesis "Various powers were responsible for the outbreak of World War I" would not be acceptable. Here is a better one: "Various perspectives exist concerning which nations should be assigned responsibility for the outbreak of World War I. Members of the winning Triple Entente often blamed Germany and its allies, assigning blame and demanding reparations, while members of the losing Triple Alliance claimed that the war was actually perpetrated by members of the Triple Entente. Finally, from hindsight, some historians have concluded that all of the great powers shared responsibility for the catastrophe that raged across the European continent from 1914 to 1918." This thesis suggests the range of the documentary sources and provides the reader with a road map that is much more than a simple restatement of the prompt. With good planning at the beginning, your DBQ should be in great shape. The Diagnostic Test in the *Fast Track to 5* includes a full sample response to a DBQ.

Thematic Essay Questions

The AP European History exam concludes with six free-response questions divided between two parts. You will be required to choose two questions, one from Part B and one from Part C. Part B has questions that fall into the period between 1450 and the Napoleonic era. The three questions in Part C deal with the Napoleonic era to the present. Plan to devote 35 minutes to each answer.

As in the DBQ, there is no single "correct" answer for these essay questions; however, unlike the DBQ, you will not be given any documents on which to base your answer. Your essay will come from your own store of knowledge of European history.

An essential aspect of writing an effective essay is understanding the tasks required. The following is a list of terms often used in prompts. These terms have shades of meaning that suggest how to construct your essay.

- **Analyze.** Conduct an in-depth examination of an event that you have been given, and reach conclusions regarding its importance or its relationship to other events.

- **Assess.** Determine a judgment regarding a specific claim or statement, prompting you to take sides on a topic.

- **Compare and contrast.** Show the similarities between two items and then examine the differences.

- **Describe.** Give an account that presents a detailed word picture.

- **Discuss.** Present an argument that examines different sides or opinions regarding a specific topic.

- **Evaluate.** Discuss the advantages and disadvantages, or the positive and negative aspects, of a topic.

- **Explain.** Clarify a topic by presenting a cause or reason.

- **To what extent . . . .** Argue a topic in terms of "how much."

Like the DBQ, the thematic essays are graded on a scale from 0 to 9. Unlike the DBQ, the evaluation of the thematic essays is holistic rather than prescribed—that is, instead of adhering to a strict rubric, the reader decides the merit of each essay based on its overall quality. Together, the two thematic essays count for 55 percent of the total free-response score (the DBQ essay alone is worth 45 percent). Because students leave these free-response essays for last, they often give them less attention. That is a mistake; the two thematic essays account for more than 25 percent of your overall AP score. Furthermore, because so many students put less effort into their thematic essays, the essays written by diligent students will stand out and will receive better scores.

You will be given 15 minutes of reading time to look over all the free-response questions in Section II—the DBQ question and accompanying documents and the two groups of three thematic essay questions. Most of that time will be devoted to the DBQ, so you will not have much time for selecting your two thematic essay questions. The key to choosing a question is to determine how much evidence you can provide in the essay. You will need to provide at least one piece of solid evidence. Obviously, the more evidence you can supply, the higher your score.

Once you have selected your questions, keep the following in mind as you write:

- **Manage your time.** Try to split your time evenly between the two essays, allowing 35 minutes for each.

- **Address the entire prompt.** Make sure that you answer *all* parts of the question, even if you have little evidence.

- **Create a strong thesis.** A strong thesis will give you points toward your overall score. In addition, it will provide the structure for the rest of your essay.

- **When writing your introductory paragraph, do not simply restate the question.** You need to make an argument and support that argument within your essay.

- **Write legibly.** If the reader has insurmountable difficulty reading your work, you will lose points.

- **Pay attention to chronology.** If you provide a wealth of information about the wrong time period, you will not have addressed the prompt and will not receive points for your effort.

- **Organize your essay so that it flows from point to point.** Try to devote each paragraph in the body of your essay to a single idea and support that idea with relevant evidence.

Finally, remember that it's "quality, not quantity" when it comes to a good essay. Each assertion should be backed up by some evidence, and more is better. But some information presented effectively and clearly is better than a lot of information presented haphazardly.

WESTERN CIVILIZATION

SINCE 1300

A medieval illustration of Death as a reaper during the Black Death

The Later Middle Ages: Crisis and Disintegration in the Fourteenth Century

CHAPTER OUTLINE AND FOCUS QUESTIONS

A Time of Troubles: Black Death and Social Crisis

Q What impact did the Black Death have on the society and economy of Europe?

War and Political Instability

Q What major problems did European states face in the fourteenth century?

The Decline of the Church

Q How and why did the authority and prestige of the papacy decline in the fourteenth century?

The Cultural World of the Fourteenth Century

Q What were the major developments in art and literature in the fourteenth century?

Society in an Age of Adversity

Q How did the adversities of the fourteenth century affect urban life and medical practices?

CRITICAL THINKING

Q Make an argument either for or against the idea that climate and disease played a major role in producing social, economic, and political changes in the fourteenth century.

AS A RESULT OF THEIR CONQUESTS in the thirteenth and fourteenth centuries, the Mongols created a vast empire stretching from Russia in the west to China in the east. Mongol rule brought stability to the Eurasian trade routes; increased trade brought prosperity but also avenues for the spread of flea-infested rats that carried bubonic plague to both East Asia and Europe. The mid-fourteenth century witnessed one of the most destructive natural disasters in history—the Black Death. One contemporary observer named Henry Knighton, a canon of Saint Mary of the Meadow Abbey in Leicester, England, was simply overwhelmed by the magnitude of the catastrophe. Knighton began his account of the great plague with these words: "In this year [1348] and in the following one there was a general mortality of people throughout the whole world." Few were left untouched; the plague struck even isolated monasteries: "At Montpellier, there remained out of a hundred and forty friars only seven." Animals, too, were devastated: "During this same year, there was a great mortality of sheep everywhere in the kingdom; in one place and in one pasture, more than five thousand sheep died and became so putrefied that neither beast nor bird wanted to touch them." Knighton was also stunned by the economic and social consequences of the Black Death. Prices dropped: "And the price of everything was cheap, because of the fear of death; there were very few who took any care for their wealth, or for anything else." Meanwhile laborers were scarce, so their wages increased: "In the following autumn, one could not hire a reaper at a lower wage than eight pence with food, or a mower at less than twelve pence with food. Because of this, much grain rotted in the fields for lack of harvesting." So many people died that some towns were deserted and some villages disappeared altogether: "Many small villages and hamlets were completely deserted; there was not one house left in them, but all those who had lived in them were dead." Some people thought the end of the world was at hand.

Plague was not the only disaster in the fourteenth century. Signs of disintegration were everywhere: famine, economic depression, war, social upheaval, a rise in crime and violence, and a decline in the power of the universal Catholic Church. Periods of disintegration, however, are often fertile ground for change and new developments. Out of the dissolution of medieval civilization came a rebirth of culture that many historians have labeled the Renaissance.

A Time of Troubles: Black Death and Social Crisis

 Focus Question: What impact did the Black Death have on the society and economy of Europe?

Well into the thirteenth century, Europe had experienced good harvests and an expanding population. By the end of the century, however, a period of disastrous changes had begun.

Famine and Population

Toward the end of the thirteenth century, noticeable changes in weather patterns were occurring as Europe entered a period that has been called a "little ice age." A small drop in overall temperatures resulted in shortened growing seasons and disastrous weather conditions, including severe storms and constant rain. Between 1315 and 1317, heavy rains in northern Europe destroyed harvests and caused serious food shortages, resulting in extreme hunger and starvation. The great famine expanded to other parts of Europe in an all-too-familiar pattern, as is evident in this scene described by a contemporary chronicler:

> We saw a large number of both sexes, not only from nearby places but from as much as five leagues away, barefooted and maybe even, except for women, in a completely nude state, together with their priests coming in procession at the Church of the Holy Martyrs, their bones bulging out, devoutly carrying bodies of saints and other relics to be adorned hoping to get relief.[1]

Some historians estimate that famine killed 10 percent of the European population in the first half of the fourteenth century.

Europe had experienced a great increase in population in the High Middle Ages. By 1300, however, indications are that Europe had reached the upper limit of its population, not in an absolute sense, but in the number of people who could be supported by existing agricultural production and technology. Virtually all productive land was being farmed, including many marginal lands that needed intensive cultivation and proved easily susceptible to changing weather patterns.

We know that there was also a movement from overpopulated rural areas to urban locations. Eighteen percent of the people in the village of Broughton in England, for example, migrated between 1288 and 1340. There is no certainty that these migrants found better economic opportunities in urban areas. We might in fact conclude the opposite, based on the reports of increasing numbers of poor people in the cities. In 1330, for example, one chronicler estimated that of the 100,000 inhabitants of Florence, 17,000 were paupers. Moreover, evidence suggests that because of the growing population, by 1300 individual peasant holdings were shrinking in size to an acreage that could no longer support a peasant family. Europe seemed to have reached an upper limit to population growth, and the number of poor appeared to have increased noticeably.

Some historians have pointed out that famine may have led to chronic malnutrition, which in turn contributed to increased infant mortality, lower birthrates, and higher susceptibility to disease because malnourished people are less able to resist infection. This, they argue, helps explain the high mortality of the great plague known as the Black Death.

The Black Death: From Asia to Europe

In the mid-fourteenth century, the disaster known as the Black Death struck Asia, North Africa, and Europe. Although there were several types of plague, the most common and most important form in the diffusion of the Black Death was bubonic plague, which was spread by black rats infested with fleas who were host to the deadly bacterium *Yersinia pestis*.

ROLE OF THE MONGOLS This great plague originated in Asia. After disappearing from Europe and the Middle East in the Middle Ages, bubonic plague continued to haunt areas of southwestern China. In the early 1300s, rats accompanying Mongol troops spread the plague into central China and by 1331 to northeastern China. In one province near Beijing, it was reported that 90 percent of the population died. Overall, China's population may have declined from 120 million in the mid-fourteenth century to 80 million by 1400.

In the thirteenth century, the Mongols had brought much of the Eurasian landmass under a single rule, which in turn facilitated long-distance trade, particularly along the Silk Road (see Chapter 6), now dominated by Muslim merchants from Central Asia. The movement of people and goods throughout this Eurasian landmass also facilitated the spread of the plague.

In the 1330s, there were outbreaks of plague in Central Asia; by 1339, it had reached Samarkand, a caravan stop on the Silk Road. From Central Asia, trading caravans carried the plague westward, to Caffa, on the Black Sea, in 1346, and Constantinople by 1347. Its arrival in the Byzantine Empire was noted by Emperor John VI, who lost a son: "Upon arrival in Constantinople she [the empress] found Andronikos, the youngest born, dead from the invading plague, which . . . attacked almost all the seacoasts of the world and killed most of their people."[2] By 1348, the plague had spread to Egypt, Mecca, and Damascus as well as to other parts of the Middle East.

The Black Death in Europe

The **Black Death** of the mid-fourteenth century was the most devastating natural disaster in European history, ravaging Europe's population and causing economic, social, political, and cultural upheaval (see the box on p. 309). Contemporary chroniclers lamented that parents attempted to flee, abandoning their children; one related the words of a child left behind: "Oh father, why have you abandoned me? . . . Mother where have you gone?"[3] People were horrified by an evil force they could not understand and by the subsequent breakdown of all normal human relations.

Symptoms of bubonic plague included high fever, aching joints, swelling of the lymph nodes, and dark blotches caused by bleeding beneath the skin. Bubonic plague was actually the least toxic form of plague but nevertheless killed 50 to 60 percent of its victims. In pneumonic plague, the bacterial inflection spread to the lungs, resulting in severe coughing, bloody sputum, and the relatively easy spread of the bacillus from human to human by coughing.

The plague reached Europe in October 1347 when Genoese merchants brought it from Caffa to the island of Sicily off the coast of Italy. One contemporary wrote:

"As it happened, among those who escaped from Caffa by boat, there were a few sailors who had been infected with the poisonous disease. Some boats were bound for Genoa, others went to Venice and other Christian areas. When the sailors reached these places and mixed with the people there, it was as if they had brought evil spirits with them."[4] The plague spread quickly, reaching southern Italy and southern France and Spain by the end of 1347 (see Map 11.1). Usually, the diffusion of the Black Death followed commercial trade routes. In 1348, the plague spread through France and the Low Countries and into Germany. By the end of that year, it had moved to England, ravaging it in 1349. By the end of 1349, the plague had expanded to northern Europe and Scandinavia. Eastern Europe and Russia were affected by 1351, although mortality rates were never as high in eastern Europe as they were in western and central Europe.

Mortality figures for the Black Death were incredibly high. Italy was hit especially hard. As the commercial center of the Mediterranean, Italy possessed scores of ports where the plague could be introduced. Italy's crowded cities, whether large, such as Florence, Genoa, and Venice, with populations near 100,000, or small, such as Orvieto and Pistoia, suffered losses of 50 to 60 percent. France and England were also particularly devastated. In northern France, farming villages suffered mortality rates of 30 percent, while cities such as Rouen were more severely affected and experienced losses as high as 40 percent. In England and Germany, entire villages simply disappeared. In Germany, of approximately 170,000 inhabited locations, only 130,000 were left by the end of the fourteenth century.

It has been estimated that the European population declined by 25 to 50 percent between 1347 and 1351. If we accept the recent scholarly assessment of a European population of 75 million in the early fourteenth century, this means a death toll of 19 to 38 million people in four years. And the plague did not end in 1351. There were major outbreaks again in 1361–1362 and 1369 and then recurrences every five or six to ten or twelve years,

Mass Burial of Plague Victims. The Black Death had spread to northern Europe by the end of 1348. Shown here is a mass burial of victims of the plague in Tournai, located in modern Belgium. As is evident in the illustration, at this stage of the plague, there was still time to make coffins for the victims' burial. Later, as the plague intensified, the dead were thrown into open pits.

Bibliothèque Royale Albert I, Brussels//© Snark/Art Resource, NY

Causes of the Black Death: Contemporary Views

The Black Death was the most terrifying natural calamity of the Middle Ages and affected wide areas of Europe, North Africa, and Asia. People were often baffled by the plague, especially by its causes, and gave widely different explanations. The first selection is taken from the preface to the *Decameron* by the fourteenth-century Italian writer Giovanni Boccaccio. The next three selections are from contemporary treatises that offered widely different explanations for the great plague.

⇥ ⇥ ⫶⇤⇥⫶ ⇤ ⇤

Giovanni Boccaccio, *Decameron*

In the year of Our Lord 1348 the deadly plague broke out in the great city of Florence, most beautiful of Italian cities. Whether through the operation of the heavenly bodies or because of our own iniquities which the just wrath of God sought to correct, the plague had arisen in the East some years before, causing the death of countless human beings. It spread without stop from one place to another, until, unfortunately, it swept over the West. Neither knowledge nor human foresight availed against it, though the city was cleansed of much filth by chosen officers in charge and sick persons were forbidden to enter it, while advice was broadcast for the preservation of health. Nor did humble supplications serve. Not once but many times they were ordained in the form of processions and other ways for the propitiation of God by the faithful, but, in spite of everything, toward the spring of the year the plague began to show its ravages.

Geoffrey de Meaux on Astrological Causes

I have been asked by some of my friends to write something about the cause of this general pestilence, showing its natural cause, and why it affected so many countries, and why it affected some countries more than others....

Now that the basics have been discussed, you can consider the reasons for such a great mortality in so may countries, and how the illness came through the influence of the stars. Ptolemy [a second-century C.E. astronomer] in Chapter 4 of the second part of the *Quadripartitum* says: the important things are the strengths and powers of the hour, the conjunctions and oppositions, eclipses of the sun and moon, and the places the planets cross at that hour. Wherefore it has been, and is, known by all astrologers that in the year 1345 (taking the year to begin in January) there was a

total eclipse of the moon, of long duration, on 18 March. At the longitude of Oxford it began an hour after the moon rose, and at the time the two planets were in conjunction in Aquarius, and Mars was with them in the same sign, within the light of Jupiter....

You should understand, however, that I do not wish to imply that the mortality comes only from Saturn and Jupiter but rather through Mars, which was mixed with them at the time of the eclipse. And the condition which resulted from all of these will last according to the nature of the dominant planets in that configuration.

On Earthquakes as the Cause of Plague

There is a fourth opinion, which I consider more likely than the others, which is that insofar as the mortality arose from natural causes its immediate cause was a corrupt and poisonous earthy exhalation, which infected the air in various parts of the world and, when breathed in by people, suffocated them and suddenly snuffed them out....

It is a matter of scientific fact that earthquakes are caused by the exhalation of fumes enclosed in the bowels of the earth. When the fumes batter against the sides of the earth, and cannot get out, the earth is shaken and moves. I say that it is the vapor and corrupted air which has been vented—or so to speak purged—in the earthquake which occurred on St Paul's day, 1347, along with the corrupted air vented in other earthquakes and eruptions, which has infected the air above the earth and killed people in various parts of the world; and I can bring various reasons in support of this conclusion.

Herman Gigas on Well Poisoning

In 1347 there was such a great pestilence and mortality throughout almost the whole world that in the opinion of well-informed men scarcely a tenth of mankind survived.... Some say that it was brought about by the corruption of the air; others that the Jews planned to wipe out all the Christians with poison and had poisoned wells and springs everywhere. And many Jews confessed as much under torture: that they had bred spiders and toads in pots and pans, and had obtained poison from overseas; and that not every Jew knew about this wickedness, only the more powerful ones, so that it would not be betrayed. As evidence of this heinous crime, men say that the bags full of poison were

(continued)

found in many wells and springs, and as a result, in cities, towns and villages throughout Germany, and in fields and woods too, almost all the wells and springs have been blocked up or built over, so that no one can drink from them or use the water for cooking, and men have to use rain or river water instead. God, the lord of vengeance, has not suffered the malice of the Jews to go unpunished. Throughout Germany, in all but a few places, they were burnt. For fear of that punishment many accepted baptism and their lives were spared. This action was taken against the Jews in 1349, and it still continues unabated, for in a number of regions many people, noble and humble alike, have laid plans against them and their defenders which they will never abandon until the whole Jewish race has been destroyed. 🖎

Q What were the different explanations for the causes of the Black Death? How do you explain the differences, and what do these explanations tell you about the level of scientific knowledge in the Later Middle Ages? Why do you think Jews became scapegoats?

MAP 11.1 Spread of the Black Death. The plague entered Europe by way of Sicily in 1347 and within three years had killed between one-quarter and one-half of the population. Outbreaks continued into the early eighteenth century, and the European population took two hundred years to return to the level it had reached before the Black Death.

Q *Is there a general pattern between distance from Sicily and the elapsed time before a region was infected with the plague?*

📺 *View an animated version of this map or related maps on the CourseMate website.*

depending on climatic and ecological conditions, until the end of the fifteenth century. The European population thus did not begin to recover until around 1500 and took several generations after that to reattain thirteenth-century levels.

LIFE AND DEATH: REACTIONS TO THE PLAGUE

Giovanni Boccaccio, *The Decameron,* Introduction

Natural disasters of the magnitude of the great plague produce extreme psychological reactions. Knowing they could be dead in a matter of days, people began to live for the moment; some threw themselves with abandon into sexual and alcoholic orgies. The fourteenth-century Italian writer Giovanni Boccaccio (joe-VAH-nee boh-KAH-choh) gave a classic description of this kind of reaction to the plague in Florence in the preface to his famous *Decameron:*

> [Some people] held that plenty of drinking and enjoyment, singing and free living and the gratification of the appetite in every possible way, letting the devil take the hindmost, was the best preventative...; and as far as they could, they suited the action to the word. Day and night they went from one tavern to another drinking and carousing unrestrainedly. At the least inkling of something that suited them, they ran wild in other people's houses, and there was no one to prevent them, for everyone had abandoned all responsibility for his belongings as well as for himself, considering his days numbered.[5]

Wealthy and powerful people fled to their country estates, as Boccaccio recounted: "Still others... maintained that no remedy against plagues was better than to leave them miles behind. Men and women without number..., caring for nobody but themselves, abandoned the city, their houses and estates, their own flesh and blood even, and their effects, in search of a country place."[6]

The attempt to explain the Black Death and mitigate its harshness led to extreme sorts of behavior. To many people, the plague had either been sent by God as a punishment for humans' sins or been caused by the devil. Some resorted to extreme asceticism to cleanse themselves of sin and gain God's forgiveness. Such were the flagellants, whose movement became popular in 1348, especially in Germany. Groups of flagellants, both men and women, wandered from town to town, flogging themselves with whips to win the forgiveness of God, whom they believed had sent the plague to punish humans for their sinful ways. One contemporary chronicler described a flagellant procession:

> The penitents went about, coming first out of Germany. They were men who did public penance and scourged themselves with whips of hard knotted leather with little iron spikes. Some made themselves bleed very badly between the shoulder blades and some foolish women had cloths ready to catch the blood and smear it on their eyes, saying it was miraculous blood. While they were doing penance, they sang very mournful songs about the nativity and the passion of Our Lord.

The Flagellants. Reactions to the plague were extreme at times. Believing that asceticism could atone for humanity's sins and win God's forgiveness, flagellants wandered from town to town flogging themselves and each other with whips as in this illustration from a fifteenth-century German manuscript.

> The object of this penance was to put a stop to the mortality, for in that time... at least a third of all the people in the world died.[7]

The flagellants attracted attention and created mass hysteria wherever they went. The Catholic Church, however, became alarmed when flagellant groups began to kill Jews and attack clergy who opposed them. Some groups also developed a millenarian aspect, anticipating the imminent end of the world, the return of Jesus, and the establishment of a thousand-year kingdom under his governance. Pope Clement VI condemned the flagellants in October 1349 and urged the public authorities to crush them. By the end of 1350, most of the flagellant movement had been destroyed.

An outbreak of virulent anti-Semitism also accompanied the Black Death. Jews were accused of causing the plague by poisoning town wells. Although Jews were persecuted in Spain, the worst organized massacres, or **pogroms,** against this helpless minority were carried out in Germany; more than sixty major Jewish communities in Germany had been exterminated by 1351 (see the box on p. 312). Many Jews fled eastward to Russia and especially to Poland, where the king offered them protection. Eastern Europe became home to large Jewish communities.

The prevalence of death because of the plague and its recurrences affected people in profound ways. Some survivors apparently came to treat life as something cheap and transient. Violence and violent death appeared to be more common after the plague than before. Postplague Europe also demonstrated a morbid preoccupation with death. In their sermons, priests reminded parishioners that each night's sleep might be their last. Tombstones were decorated with macabre scenes of naked corpses in

The Cremation of the Strasbourg Jews

In their attempt to explain the widespread horrors of the Black Death, medieval Christian communities looked for scapegoats. As at the time of the Crusades, the Jews were blamed for poisoning wells and thereby spreading the plague. This selection by a contemporary chronicler, written in 1349, gives an account of how Christians in the town of Strasbourg in the Holy Roman Empire dealt with their Jewish community. It is apparent that financial gain was also an important motive in killing the Jews.

◆──◆⬦❖⬦◆──◆

Jacob von Königshofen, "The Cremation of the Strasbourg Jews"

In the year 1349 there occurred the greatest epidemic that ever happened. Death went from one end of the earth to the other.... And from what this epidemic came, all wise teachers and physicians could only say that it was God's will.... This epidemic also came to Strasbourg in the summer of the above-mentioned year, and it is estimated that about sixteen thousand people died.

In the matter of this plague the Jews throughout the world were reviled and accused in all lands of having caused it through the poison which they are said to have put into the water and the wells—that is what they were accused of—and for this reason the Jews were burnt all the way from the Mediterranean into Germany....

[The account then goes on to discuss the situation of the Jews in the city of Strasbourg.]

On Saturday... they burnt the Jews on a wooden platform in their cemetery. There were about two thousand people of them. Those who wanted to baptize themselves were spared. [About one thousand accepted baptism.] Many small children were taken out of the fire and baptized against the will of their fathers and mothers. And everything that was owed to the Jews was canceled, and the Jews had to surrender all pledges and notes that they had taken for debts. The council, however, took the cash that the Jews possessed and divided it among the working-men proportionately. The money was indeed the thing that killed the Jews. If they had been poor and if the lords had not been in debt to them, they would not have been burnt....

Thus were the Jews burnt at Strasbourg, and in the same year in all the cities of the Rhine, whether Free Cities or Imperial Cities or cities belonging to the lords. In some towns they burnt the Jews after a trial, in others, without a trial. In some cities the Jews themselves set fire to their houses and cremated themselves.

It was decided in Strasbourg that no Jew should enter the city for 100 years, but before 20 years had passed, the council and magistrates agreed that they ought to admit the Jews again into the city for 20 years. And so the Jews came back again to Strasbourg in the year 1368 after the birth of our Lord. ▷

Q What charges were made against the Jews in regard to the Black Death? Can it be said that these charges were economically motivated? Why or why not?

---

various stages of decomposition with snakes entwined in their bones and their innards filled with worms.

Economic Dislocation and Social Upheaval

The population collapse of the fourteenth century had dire economic and social consequences. Economic dislocation was accompanied by social upheaval. Between 1000 and 1300, Europe had been relatively stable. The division of society into the three estates of clergy (those who pray), nobility (those who fight), and laborers (those who work) had already begun to disintegrate in the thirteenth century, however. In the fourteenth century, a series of urban and rural revolts rocked European society.

NOBLE LANDLORDS AND PEASANTS Both peasants and noble landlords were affected by the demographic crisis of the fourteenth century. Most noticeably, Europe experienced a serious labor shortage that caused a dramatic rise in the price of labor. At Cuxham manor in England, for example, a farm laborer who had received two shillings a week in 1347 was paid seven in 1349 and almost eleven by 1350. At the same time, the decline in population depressed or held stable the demand for agricultural produce, resulting in stable or falling prices for output (although in England prices remained high until the 1380s). The chronicler Henry Knighton observed: "And the price of everything was cheap.... A man could buy a horse for half a mark [six shillings], which before was worth forty shillings."[8] Because landlords were having to pay more for labor at the same time that their rents or incomes were declining, they began to experience considerable adversity and lower standards of living. In England, aristocratic incomes dropped more than 20 percent between 1347 and 1353.

Aristocrats responded to adversity by seeking to lower the wage rate. The English Parliament passed the Statute of Laborers (1351), which attempted to limit wages to preplague levels and forbid the mobility of peasants as well. Although such laws proved largely unworkable, they did keep wages from rising as high as they might have in a free market. Overall, the position of landlords continued to deteriorate during the late fourteenth and early fifteenth centuries. At the same time, conditions for peasants improved, though not uniformly throughout Europe.

The decline in the number of peasants after the Black Death accelerated the process of converting labor services to rents, freeing peasants from the obligations of servile tenure and weakening the system of manorialism. But there were limits to how much the peasants could advance. Not only did they face the same economic hurdles as the lords, but the latter attempted to impose wage restrictions, reinstate old forms of labor service, and create new obligations. New governmental taxes also hurt. Peasant complaints became widespread and soon gave rise to rural revolts.

PEASANT REVOLT IN FRANCE   In 1358, a peasant revolt, known as the *Jacquerie* (zhak-REE), broke out in northern France. The destruction of normal order by the Black Death and the subsequent economic dislocation were important factors in causing the revolt, but the ravages created by the Hundred Years' War also affected the French peasantry (see "War and Political Instability" later in this chapter). Both the French and English forces followed a deliberate policy of laying waste to peasants' fields while bands of mercenaries lived off the land by taking peasants' produce as well.

Peasant anger was also exacerbated by growing class tensions. Landed nobles were eager to hold on to their politically privileged position and felt increasingly threatened in the new postplague world of higher wages and lower prices. Many aristocrats looked on peasants with utter contempt. A French tale told to upper-class audiences contained this remarkable passage:

Tell me, Lord, if you please, by what right or title does a villein [peasant] eat beef? . . . Should they eat fish? Rather let them eat thistles and briars, thorns and straw and hay on Sunday and peapods on weekdays. They should keep watch without sleep and have trouble always; that is how villeins should live. Yet each day they are full and drunk on the best wines, and in fine clothes. The great expenditures of villeins come as a high cost, for it is this that destroys and ruins the world. It is they who spoil the common welfare. From the villein comes all unhappiness. Should they eat meat? Rather should they chew grass on the heath with the horned cattle and go naked on all fours.[9]

The peasants reciprocated this contempt for their so-called social superiors.

The outburst of peasant anger led to savage confrontations. Castles were burned and nobles murdered (see the box on p. 314). Such atrocities did not go unanswered, however. The *Jacquerie* soon failed as the privileged classes closed ranks, savagely massacred the rebels, and ended the revolt.

AN ENGLISH PEASANT REVOLT   The English Peasants' Revolt of 1381 was the most prominent of all. It was a product not of desperation but of rising expectations. After the Black Death, the condition of the English peasants had improved as they enjoyed greater freedom and higher wages or lower rents. Aristocratic landlords had fought back with legislation to depress wages and attempted to reimpose old feudal dues. The most immediate cause of the revolt, however, was the monarchy's attempt to raise revenues by imposing a poll tax or a flat charge on each adult member of the population. Peasants in eastern England, the wealthiest part of the country, refused to pay the tax and expelled the collectors forcibly from their villages.

This action sparked a widespread rebellion of both peasants and townspeople led by a well-to-do peasant

Peasant Rebellion. The fourteenth century witnessed a number of revolts of the peasantry against noble landowners. Although the revolts often met with initial success, they were soon crushed. This fifteenth-century illustration shows nobles during the French *Jacquerie* of 1358 massacring the rebels in the town of Meaux, in northern France.

A Revolt of French Peasants

In 1358, French peasants rose up in a revolt known as the *Jacquerie.* The relationship between aristocrats and peasants had degenerated as a result of the social upheavals and privations caused by the Black Death and the Hundred Years' War. This excerpt from the chronicle of an aristocrat paints a horrifying picture of the barbarities that occurred during the revolt.

✦ ━ ❈⬥❈ ━ ✦

Jean Froissart, *Chronicles*

There were very strange and terrible happenings in several parts of the kingdom of France.... They began when some of the men from the country towns came together in the Beauvais region. They had no leaders and at first they numbered scarcely 100. One of them got up and said that the nobility of France, knights and squires, were disgracing and betraying the realm, and that it would be a good thing if they were all destroyed. At this they all shouted: "He's right! He's right! Shame on any man who saves the nobility from being wiped out!"

They banded together and went off, without further deliberation and unarmed except for pikes and knives, to the house of a knight who lived nearby. They broke in and killed the knight, with his lady and his children, big and small, and set fire to the house. Next they went to another castle and did much worse; for, having seized the knight and bound him securely to a post, several of them violated his wife and daughter before his eyes. Then they killed the wife, who was pregnant, and the daughter and all the other children, and finally put the knight to death with great cruelty and burned and razed the castle.

They did similar things in a number of castles and big houses, and their ranks swelled until there were a good 6,000 of them. Wherever they went their numbers grew, for all the men of the same sort joined them. The knights and squires fled before them with their families. They took their wives and daughters many miles away to put them in safety, leaving their houses open with their possessions inside. And those evil men, who had come together without leaders or arms, pillaged and burned everything and violated and killed all the ladies and girls without mercy, like mad dogs. Their barbarous acts were worse than anything that ever took place between Christians and Saracens [Muslims]. Never did men commit such vile deeds. They were such that no living creature ought to see, or even imagine or think of, and the men who committed the most were admired and had the highest places among them. I could never bring myself to write down the horrible and shameful things which they did to the ladies. But, among other brutal excesses, they killed a knight, put him on a spit, and turned him at the fire and roasted him before the lady and her children. After about a dozen of them had violated the lady, they tried to force her and the children to eat the knight's flesh before putting them cruelly to death.

Q Why did the peasants react so strongly against their aristocratic lords? Do you think this is an unbiased account? Why or why not?

---

called Wat Tyler and a preacher named John Ball. The latter preached an effective message against the noble class, as recounted by the French chronicler Jean Froissart (ZHAHNH frwah-SAR):

> Good people, things cannot go right in England and never will, until goods are held in common and there are no more villeins and gentlefolk, but we are all one and the same. In what way are those whom we call lords greater masters than ourselves? How have they deserved it? Why do they hold us in bondage? If we all spring from a single father and mother, Adam and Eve, how can they claim or prove that they are lords more than us, except by making us produce and grow the wealth which they spend?[10]

The revolt was initially successful as the rebels burned down the manor houses of aristocrats, lawyers, and government officials and murdered several important officials, including the archbishop of Canterbury. After the peasants marched on London, the young King Richard II, age fifteen, promised to accept the rebels' demands if they returned to their homes. They accepted the king's word and dispersed, but the king reneged and with the assistance of the aristocrats arrested hundreds of the rebels. The poll tax was eliminated, however, and in the end most of the rebels were pardoned.

REVOLTS IN THE CITIES Revolts also erupted in the cities. Commercial and industrial activity suffered almost immediately from the Black Death. An oversupply of goods and an immediate drop in demand led to a decline in trade after 1350. Some industries suffered greatly. Florence's woolen industry, one of the giants, produced 70,000 to 80,000 pieces of cloth in 1338; in 1378, it was yielding only 24,000 pieces. Bourgeois merchants and manufacturers responded to the decline in trade and production by attempting to restrict competition and resist the demands of the lower classes.

In urban areas, where capitalist industrialists paid low wages and managed to prevent workers from forming organizations to help themselves, industrial revolts broke out throughout Europe. Ghent experienced one in 1381, Rouen in 1382. Most famous, however, was the revolt of the *ciompi* (CHAHM-pee) in Florence in 1378. The *ciompi* were wool workers in Florence's most prominent industry. In the 1370s, not only was the woolen industry depressed, but the wool workers saw their real wages decline when the coinage in which they were paid was debased. Their revolt won them some concessions from the municipal government, including the right to form guilds and be represented in the government. But their newly won rights were short-lived; authorities ended *ciompi* participation in the government by 1382.

Although the peasant and urban revolts sometimes resulted in short-term gains for the participants, the uprisings were quickly crushed and their gains lost. Accustomed to ruling, the established classes easily formed a united front and quashed dissent. Nevertheless, the rural and urban revolts of the fourteenth century ushered in an age of social conflict that characterized much of later European history.

War and Political Instability

Q **FOCUS QUESTION:** What major problems did European states face in the fourteenth century?

Famine, plague, economic turmoil, social upheaval, and violence were not the only problems of the fourteenth century. War and political instability must also be added to the list. Of all the struggles that ensued in the fourteenth century, the Hundred Years' War was the most famous and the most violent.

Causes of the Hundred Years' War

In 1259, the English king, Henry III, had relinquished his claims to all the French territories previously held by the English monarchy except for one relatively small possession known as the duchy of Gascony. As duke of Gascony, the English king pledged loyalty as a vassal to the French king. But this territory gave rise to numerous disputes between the kings of England and France. By the thirteenth century, the Capetian monarchs had greatly increased their power over their more important vassals, the great lords of France. Royal officials interfered regularly in the affairs of the vassals' fiefs, especially in matters of justice. Although this policy irritated all the vassals, it especially annoyed the king of England, who considered himself the peer of the French king.

A dispute over the right of succession to the French throne also complicated the struggle between the French and the English. In the fourteenth century, the Capetian

CHART 11.1 Background to the Hundred Years' War: Kings of France and England

Philip III
king of France (1270–1285)

Philip IV
(1285–1314)

Charles of Valois
(d. 1325)

Louis X
(1314–1316)

Philip V
(1316–1322)

Charles IV
(1322–1328)

Isabella = Edward II
king of England
(1307–1327)

Philip VI
king of France
(1328–1350)

John I
(1316)

(daughters)

(daughters)

Edward III
king of England
(1327–1377)

John II
king of France
(1350–1364)

dynasty failed to produce a male heir for the first time in almost four hundred years. In 1328, the last son of King Philip IV died without a male heir. The closest male relative in line to the throne was King Edward III of England (1327–1377), whose mother was Isabella, the daughter of Philip IV (see Chart 11.1). Known for her strong personality (she was nicknamed the "she-wolf of France"), Isabella, with the assistance of her lover, led a revolt against her husband, King Edward II, overthrew him, and ruled England until her teenage son, Edward III, took sole control of the throne in 1330. As the son of the daughter of King Philip IV, King Edward III of England had a claim to the French throne, but the French nobles argued that the inheritance of the monarchy could not pass through the female line and chose a cousin of the Capetians, Philip, duke of Valois (val-WAH), as King Philip VI (1328–1350).

The immediate cause of the war between France and England was yet another quarrel over Gascony. In 1337, when Edward III, the king of England and duke of Gascony, refused to do homage to Philip VI for Gascony, the French king seized the duchy. Edward responded by declaring war on Philip, the "so-called king of France." There is no doubt that the personalities of the two monarchs also had much to do with the outbreak of the Hundred Years' War. Both Edward and Philip loved luxury and shared a desire for the glory and prestige that came from military engagements. Both were only too willing to use their respective nation's resources to satisfy their own desires. Moreover, for many nobles, the promise of plunder and territorial gain was an incentive to follow the disruptive path of their rulers.

Conduct and Course of the War

The Hundred Years' War began in a burst of knightly enthusiasm. Trained to be warriors, knights viewed the clash of battle as the ultimate opportunity to demonstrate

Battle of Crécy. This fifteenth-century manuscript illustration depicts the Battle of Crécy, the first of several military disasters suffered by the French in the Hundred Years' War, and shows why the English preferred the longbow to the crossbow. At the left, the French crossbowmen have to stop shooting and prime their weapons by cranking the handle, while the English archers continue to shoot their longbows (a skilled archer could launch ten arrows a minute).

© Bibliotheque Nationale, Paris/The Bridgeman Art Library

their fighting abilities. But this struggle would change the nature of warfare, for as it dragged on, the outcomes of battles were increasingly determined not by knights but by peasant foot soldiers. The French army of 1337, with its heavily armed noble cavalry, resembled its twelfth- and thirteenth-century forebears. The noble cavalrymen considered themselves the fighting elite and looked with contempt on the foot soldiers and crossbowmen, their social inferiors.

The English army, however, had evolved differently and had included peasants as paid foot soldiers since at least Anglo-Saxon times. Armed with pikes, many of these foot soldiers had also adopted the longbow, invented by the Welsh. The longbow had a more rapid speed of fire than the more powerful crossbow. Although the English made use of heavily armed cavalry, they relied even more on large numbers of foot soldiers.

EARLY PHASES OF THE WAR Edward III's early campaigns in France achieved little. When Edward renewed his efforts in 1346 with an invasion of Normandy, Philip responded by raising a large force to crush the English army and met Edward's forces at Crécy (kray-SEE), just south of Flanders. The larger French army followed no battle plan but simply attacked the English lines in a disorderly fashion. The arrows of the English archers devastated the French cavalry. As Jean Froissart described it, "The English continued to shoot [their longbows] into the thickest part of the crowd, wasting none of their arrows. They impaled or wounded horses and riders, who fell to the ground in great distress, unable to get up again [because of their heavy armor] without the help of several men."[11] It was a

Jean Froissart, "The Battle of Crécy"

stunning victory for the English. Edward followed up by capturing the French port of Calais (ka-LAY) to serve as a staging ground for future invasions.

The Battle of Crécy was not decisive, however. The English simply did not possess the resources to subjugate all of France. Truces, small-scale hostilities, and some major operations were combined in an orgy of seemingly incessant struggle. The English campaigns were waged by Edward III and his son Edward, the prince of Wales, known as the Black Prince. The Black Prince's campaigns in France were devastating (see the box on p. 317). Avoiding pitched battles, his forces deliberately ravaged the land, burning crops and entire unfortified villages and towns and stealing anything of value. For the English, such campaigns were profitable; for the French people, they meant hunger, deprivation, and death. When the army of the Black Prince was finally forced to do battle, the French, under their king, John II (1350–1364), were once again defeated. This time even the king was captured. This Battle of Poitiers (PWAH-tyay) (1356) ended the first phase of the Hundred Years' War. Under the Peace of Brétigny (bray-tee-NYEE) (1359), the French agreed to pay a large ransom for King John, the English territories in Gascony were enlarged, and Edward renounced his claims to the throne of France in return for John's promise to give up control over English lands in France. This first phase of the war made it clear that despite their victories, the English were not really strong enough to subdue all of France and make Edward III's claim to the French monarchy a reality.

Monarchs, however, could be slow learners. The Treaty of Brétigny was never really enforced. In the next phase of the war, in the capable hands of John's son Charles V (1364–1380), the French recovered what they had

The Hundred Years' War

In his account of the Hundred Years' War, the fourteenth-century French chronicler Jean Froissart described the sack of the fortified French town of Limoges by the Black Prince, Edward, the prince of Wales. It provides a vivid example of how noncombatants fared during the war.

Jean Froissart, *Chronicles*

For about a month, certainly not longer, the Prince of Wales remained before Limoges. During that time he allowed no assaults or skirmishes, but pushed on steadily with the mining. The knights inside and the townspeople, who knew what was going on, started a countermine in the hope of killing the English miners, but it was a failure. When the Prince's miners who, as they dug, were continually shoring up their tunnel, had completed their work, they said to the Prince: "My lord, whenever you like now we can bring a big piece of wall down into the moat, so that you can get into the city quite easily and safely."

The Prince was very pleased to hear this. "Excellent," he said. "At six o'clock tomorrow morning, show me what you can do."

When they knew it was the right time for it, the miners started a fire in their mine. In the morning, just as the Prince had specified, a great section of the wall collapsed, filling the moat at the place where it fell. For the English, who were armed and ready waiting, it was a welcome sight. Those on foot could enter as they liked, and did so. They rushed to the gate, cut through the bars holding it and knocked it down. They did the same with the barriers outside, meeting with no resistance. It was all done so quickly that the people in the town were taken unawares. Then the Prince, the Duke of Lancaster, the Earl of Cambridge, Sir Guichard d'Angle, with all the others and their men burst into the city, followed by pillagers on foot, all in a mood to wreak havoc and do murder, killing indiscriminately, for those were their orders. There were pitiful scenes. Men, women, and children flung themselves on their knees before the Prince, crying: "Have mercy on us, gentle sir!" But he was so inflamed with anger that he would not listen. Neither man nor woman was heeded, but all who could be found were put to the sword, including many who were in no way to blame. I do not understand how they could have failed to take pity on people who were too unimportant to have committed treason. Yet they paid for it, and paid more dearly than the leaders who had committed it.

There is no man so hard-hearted that, if he had been in Limoges on that day, and had remembered God, he would not have wept bitterly at the fearful slaughter which took place. More than 3,000 persons, men, women, and children, were dragged out to have their throats cut. May God receive their souls, for they were true martyrs.

Q What does this account reveal about the nature of late medieval warfare and its impact on civilian populations?

---

previously lost. The English returned to plundering the French countryside and avoiding pitched battles. That pleased Charles, who did not want to engage in set battles, preferring to use armed bands to reduce the English fortresses systematically.

By 1374, the French had recovered their lost lands, although France itself continued to be plagued by "free companies" of mercenaries who, no longer paid by the English, simply lived off the land by plunder and ransom. Nevertheless, for the time being, the war seemed over, especially when a twenty-year truce was negotiated in 1396.

RENEWAL OF THE WAR In 1415, however, the English king, Henry V (1413–1422), renewed the war at a time when the French were enduring civil war as the dukes of Burgundy and Orléans (or-lay-AHN) competed to control the weak French king, Charles VI (1380–1422). In the summer of 1413, Paris exploded with bloody encounters. Taking advantage of the chaos, Henry V invaded France in 1415. At the Battle of Agincourt (AH-zhen-koor) (1415), the French suffered a disastrous defeat, and 1,500 French nobles died when the heavy, armor-plated French knights attempted to attack across a field turned to mud by heavy rain. Altogether, French losses were 6,000 dead; the English lost only three hundred men.

Henry went on to reconquer Normandy and forge an alliance with the duke of Burgundy, which led Charles VI to agree to the Treaty of Troyes (TRWAH) in 1420. By this treaty, Henry V was married to Catherine, daughter of Charles VI, and recognized as the heir to the French throne. By 1420, the English were masters of northern France (see Map 11.2).

The seemingly hopeless French cause fell into the hands of Charles the dauphin (heir to the throne), the son of Charles VI, who, despite being disinherited by the Treaty of Troyes, still considered himself the real heir to the French throne. The dauphin governed the southern two-thirds of French lands from Bourges. Charles was weak and timid and was unable to rally the French against the English, who in 1428 had turned south and were besieging the city of Orléans to gain access to the valley of the Loire. The French monarch was saved, quite unexpectedly, by a French peasant woman.

MAP 11.2 **The Hundred Years' War.** This long, exhausting struggle began in 1337 and dragged on until 1453. The English initially gained substantial French territory, but in the later phases of the war, France turned the tide, eventually expelling the English from all Continental lands except the port of Calais.

Q *What gains had the English made by 1429, and how do they correlate to proximity to England and the ocean?*

View an animated version of this map or related maps on the CourseMate website.

JOAN OF ARC Joan of Arc was born in 1412 to well-to-do peasants from the village of Domrémy in Champagne. Deeply religious, Joan experienced visions and came to believe that her favorite saints had commanded her to free France and have the dauphin crowned as king. In February 1429, Joan made her way to the dauphin's court, where her sincerity and simplicity persuaded Charles to allow her to accompany a French army to Orléans. Apparently inspired by the faith of the peasant girl, the French armies found new confidence in themselves and liberated Orléans, changing the course of the war. Within a few weeks, the entire Loire valley had been freed of the English. In July 1429, fulfilling Joan's other task, the dauphin was crowned king of France and became Charles VII (1422–1461). In accomplishing the two commands of her angelic voices, Joan had brought the war to a decisive turning point.

Joan did not live to see the war concluded, however. She was captured by the Burgundian allies of the English in 1430. Wishing to eliminate the "Maid of Orléans" for

Joan of Arc. Pictured here in a suit of armor, Joan of Arc is holding aloft a banner that shows Jesus and two angels. This portrait dates from the late fifteenth century; there are no known portraits of Joan made from life.

Outbreak of hostilities	1337
Battle of Crécy	1346
Battle of Poitiers	1356
Peace of Brétigny	1359
Death of Edward III	1377
Twenty-year truce declared	1396
Henry V (1413–1422) renews the war	1415
Battle of Agincourt	1415
Treaty of Troyes	1420
French recovery under Joan of Arc	1429–1431
End of the war	1453

The Chinese had invented gunpowder in the eleventh century and devised a simple cannon by the thirteenth century. The Mongols greatly improved this technology, developing more accurate cannons and cannonballs; both spread to the Middle East by the thirteenth century and to Europe by the fourteenth.

The death of England's best commanders and the instability of the English government under King Henry VI (1422–1471) also contributed to England's defeat. By 1453, the only part of France that was left in England's hands was the coastal town of Calais, which remained English for another century.

Political Instability

The fourteenth century was a period of adversity for the internal political stability of European governments. Although government bureaucracies grew ever larger, at the same time the question of who should control the bureaucracies led to internal conflict and instability. Like the lord-serf relationship, the lord-vassal relationship based on land and military service was being replaced by a contract based on money. Especially after the Black Death, money payments called **scutage** were increasingly substituted for military service. Monarchs welcomed this development because they could now hire professional soldiers, who tended to be more reliable anyway. As lord-vassal relationships became less personal and less important, new relationships based on political advantage began to be formed, creating new avenues for political influence—and for corruption as well. Especially noticeable as the landed aristocrats suffered declining rents and social uncertainties with the new relationships was the formation of factions of nobles who looked for opportunities to advance their power and wealth at the expense of other noble factions and of their monarchs as well. Other nobles went to the royal courts, offering to serve the kings.

The kings had their own problems, however. By the mid-fifteenth century, reigning monarchs in many European countries were not the direct descendants of the

obvious political reasons, the English turned Joan over to the Inquisition on charges of witchcraft. In the fifteenth century, spiritual visions were thought to be inspired by either God or the devil. Because Joan dressed in men's clothing, it was easy for her enemies to believe that she was in league with the "prince of darkness." She was condemned to death as a heretic and burned at the stake in 1431, at the age of nineteen. To the end, as the flames rose up around her, she declared that her voices came from God and had not deceived her (see the Film & History feature on p. 320). Twenty-five years later, a church court exonerated her of these charges. To a contemporary French writer, Christine de Pizan (kris-TEEN duh pee-ZAHN) (see "Christine de Pizan" on p. 332), Joan was a feminist heroine (see the box on p. 322). In 1920, she was made a saint of the Roman Catholic Church.

The Trial of Joan of Arc (1431)

END OF THE WAR Joan of Arc's accomplishments proved decisive. Although the war dragged on for another two decades, defeats of English armies in Normandy and Aquitaine ultimately led to French victory. Important to the French success was the use of the cannon, a new weapon made possible by the invention of gunpowder.

Joan of Arc (1948)
The Messenger: The Story of Joan of Arc (1999)

Joan of Arc is one of history's best-known figures. Already by the time of her death she was a heroine, and in the nineteenth century, the French made her into an early nationalist. The Catholic Church recognized her as a saint in 1920, and a dozen films have been made about her short life. Born into a peasant family in Domrémy, France, Joan believed that, beginning at age thirteen, she had heard the voices of Saints Michael, Catherine, and Margaret telling her that she would play an important role in the liberation of France from the English invaders. Joan made her way to the court of the dauphin, the heir to the French throne, who agreed to let her accompany the royal army to Orléans, where she supposedly played a major role in the liberation of the city. In keeping with her prophecies, she then accompanied the dauphin to Reims, where he was crowned as King Charles VII. Although the king sought to end the war by negotiation, Joan continued to fight until she was captured by the Burgundians, allies of the English. Sold to the English, she was put on trial as a heretic in a French ecclesiastical court dominated by the English. Worn out by questioning, she renounced her voices but shortly afterward recanted and reaffirmed them. The English authorities then burned her at the stake as a re-lapsed heretic. Historians agree on many facts about Joan but differ in interpreting them; so too do movie producers.

Based on a play by Maxwell Anderson, the 1948 film version of Joan's story was directed by Victor Fleming. The movie follows the main historical facts that are known about Joan (Ingrid Bergman). Joan's voices are accepted as an important part of a spiritually determined young woman: "What I am commanded to do, I do." The film does deviate at times from the historical record: one member of the ecclesiastical court is shown opposing the trial, which did not happen. The dauphin (José Ferrer) is presented as a weak individual who nevertheless accepts Joan's offer of help. The movie ends in typical Hollywood fashion with a dramatic burning at the stake as Joan dies in a glorious blaze of heavenly sunbeams: "My victory is my martyrdom," she proclaims at the end.

The Messenger, directed by Luc Besson, presents a more contemporary and fictionalized approach to Joan (Milia Jovovich). The brutality of war is rendered in real-istically bloody detail. Joan's early life is reworked for the sake of the movie's theme. The movie introduces re-venge as a possible motive by having Joan witness the rape and murder of her sister by an English mercenary—she must kill the English to avenge her sister's death. After this traumatic incident, her voices become more

Joan (Ingrid Bergman) prepares for battle.

Joan (Milia Jovovich) rides into battle.

(continued)

rulers of 1300. The founders of these new dynasties had to struggle for position as factions of nobles vied to gain material advantages for themselves. As the fifteenth century began, there were two claimants to the throne of France, two aristocratic factions fighting for control of England, and three German princes struggling to be recognized as Holy Roman Emperor.

Fourteenth-century monarchs of old dynasties and new faced financial problems as well. The shift to using mercenary soldiers left monarchs perennially short of cash. Traditional revenues, especially rents from property, increasingly proved insufficient to meet their needs. Monarchs attempted to generate new sources of revenues, especially through taxes, which often meant going through parliaments. This opened the door for parliamentary bodies to gain more power by asking for favors first. Although unsuccessful in most cases, the parliaments simply added another element of uncertainty and confusion to fourteenth-century politics. Turning now to a survey of western and central European states (eastern Europe will be examined in Chapter 12), we can see how these disruptive factors worked.

The Growth of England's Political Institutions

The fifty-year reign of Edward III (1327–1377) was important for the evolution of English political institutions in the fourteenth century. Parliament increased in prominence and developed its basic structure and functions during Edward's reign. Due to his constant need for money to fight the Hundred Years' War, Edward came to rely on Parliament to levy new taxes. In return for regular grants, Edward made several concessions, including a commitment to levy no direct tax without Parliament's consent and to allow Parliament to examine the government accounts to ensure that the money was being spent properly. By the end of Edward's reign, Parliament had become an important component of the English governmental system.

During this same period, Parliament began to assume the organizational structure it has retained to this day. The Great Council of barons became the House of Lords and evolved into a body composed of the chief bishops and abbots of the realm and aristocratic peers whose position in Parliament was hereditary. The representatives of the shires and boroughs, who were considered less important than the lay and ecclesiastical lords, held collective meetings and soon came to be regarded as the House of Commons. Together, the House of Lords and House of Commons constituted Parliament. Although the House of Commons did little beyond approving measures proposed by the Lords, during Edward's reign the Commons did begin the practice of drawing up petitions, which, if accepted by the king, became law.

After Edward III's death, England began to experience the internal instability of aristocratic factionalism that was racking other European countries. The early years of the reign of Edward's grandson, Richard II (1377–1399), began inauspiciously with the peasant revolt that ended only when the king made concessions. Richard's reign was troubled by competing groups of nobles who sought to pursue their own interests. One faction, led by Henry of Lancaster, defeated the king's forces and then deposed and killed him. Henry of Lancaster became King Henry IV (1399–1413). In the fifteenth century, factional conflict would lead to a devastating series of civil wars known as the War of the Roses.

The Problems of the French Kings

At the beginning of the fourteenth century, France was the most prosperous monarchy in Europe. By the end of the century, much of its wealth had been dissipated, and rival factions of aristocrats had made effective monarchical rule virtually impossible.

The French monarchical state had always had an underlying inherent weakness that proved its undoing in difficult times. Although the Capetian monarchs had found ways to enlarge their royal domain and extend their control by developing a large and effective bureaucracy, the various territories that made up France still maintained their own princes, customs, and laws. The parliamentary institutions of France provide a good example of France's basic lack of unity. The French parliament, known as the Estates-General and composed of representatives of

A Feminist Heroine: Christine de Pizan on Joan of Arc

Christine de Pizan, France's "first woman of letters," was witness to the rescue of France from the hands of the English by the efforts of Joan of Arc and was also present at the coronation of Charles VII as king of France. Christine believed that a turning point had arrived in French history and that Joan—a woman—had been responsible for France's salvation. She wrote a poem to honor this great occasion. The following stanzas are taken from her poem.

Christine de Pizan, *The Poem of Joan of Arc,* July 31, 1429

The year of fourteen twenty-nine
The sun came out to shine again.
It brings the season new and good,
Which we had not directly seen
Too long a time, while many passed
Their lives in sorrow; I am one.
But now, no longer do I grieve
Because I see what pleases me. . . .

And you, the King of France, King Charles,
The seventh of that noble name,
Who fought a mighty war before
Good fortune came at all to you:
Do, now, observe your dignity
Exalted by the Maid, who bent
Your enemies beneath your flag
In record time (that's something new!)

And people thought that it would be
Impossible indeed for you
To ever have your country back,
For it was nearly lost; but now,
It's clearly yours; no matter who
Has done you wrong, it's yours once more,
And through the clever Maid who did
Her part therein—thanks be to God! . . .

When I reflect upon your state,
The youthful maiden that you are,
To whom God gives the force and strength
To be the champion and the one
To suckle France upon her milk
Of peace, the sweetest nourishment,
To overthrow the rebel host:
The wonder passes Nature's work!

That is, if God, through Joshua
Performed so many miracles
In conquering those places where
So many met defeat—a man
Of strength was Joshua. But she's

A woman—simple shepherdess—
More brave than ever man at Rome!
An easy thing for God to do!

But as for us, we've never heard
About a marvel quite so great
For all the heroes who have lived
In history can't measure up
In bravery against the Maid,
Who strives to rout our enemies.

It's God does that, who's guiding her
Whose courage passes that of men . . .
By miracle has she appeared,
Divine commandment sent her here.
God's angel led her in before
The king, to bring her help to him.
There's no illusion in her case
Because it's been indeed borne out
In council (in conclusion, then,
A thing is proved by its effect). . . .

What honor for the female sex!
God's love for it appears quite clear,
Because the kingdom laid to waste
By all those wretched people now
Stands safe, a woman rescued it
(A hundred thousand men could not
Do that) and killed the hostile foe!
A thing beyond belief before! . . .

While ridding France of enemies,
Retaking town and castle both.
No force was ever quite so great,
If hundreds or if thousands strong!
Among our men so brave and apt
She's captain over all; such strength
No Hector or Achilles had.
All this God does, who's guiding her. . . .

The English will be crushed through her,
And never will they rise again
For God who wills it hears the voice
Of guiltless folk they tried to harm!
The blood of those they've killed, who'll walk
No more, cries out. God wants an end
To this; instead He has resolved
To chastise them as evil men.

Q In Christine de Pizan's view, what had Joan accomplished? Why did Christine consider those accomplishments so unusual? What does Joan's career as a soldier tell you about the culture of late medieval France?

the clergy, the nobility, and the **Third Estate** (everyone else), usually represented only the north of France, not the entire kingdom. The southern provinces had their own estates, and local estates existed in other parts of France. Unlike the English Parliament, which was evolving into a crucial part of the English government, the French Estates-General was simply one of many such institutions.

When Philip VI (1328–1350) became involved in the Hundred Years' War with England, he found it necessary to devise new sources of revenue, including a tax on salt known as the *gabelle* (gah-BELL) and a hearth tax eventually called the *taille* (TY). These taxes weighed heavily on the French peasantry and middle class. Consequently, when additional taxes were needed to pay for the ransom of King John II after his capture at the Battle of Poitiers, the middle-class inhabitants of the towns tried to use the Estates-General to reform the French government and tax structure.

At the meeting of the Estates-General in 1357, under the leadership of the Parisian provost Étienne Marcel (ay-TYEN mahr-SEL), representatives of the Third Estate granted taxes in exchange for a promise from King John's son, the dauphin Charles, not to tax without the Estates-General's permission and to allow the Estates-General to meet on a regular basis and participate in important political decisions. After Marcel's movement was crushed in 1358, this attempt to make the Estates-General a functioning part of the French government collapsed. The dauphin became King Charles V (1364–1380) and went on to recover much of the land lost to the English. His military successes underscored his efforts to reestablish strong monarchical powers. He undermined the role of the Estates-General by getting it to grant him taxes with no fixed time limit. Charles's death in 1380 soon led to a new time of troubles for the French monarchy, however.

The insanity of Charles VI (1380–1422), which first became apparent in 1392, opened the door to rival factions of French nobles aspiring to power and wealth. The dukes of Burgundy and Orléans competed to control Charles and the French monarchy. Their struggles created chaos for the French government and the French people. Many nobles supported the Orléanist faction, while Paris and other towns favored the Burgundians. By the beginning of the fifteenth century, France seemed hopelessly mired in a civil war. When the English renewed the Hundred Years' War in 1415, the Burgundians supported the English cause and the English monarch's claim to the throne of France.

The German Monarchy

England and France had developed strong national monarchies in the High Middle Ages. Nevertheless, by the end of the fourteenth century, they seemed in danger of disintegrating due to dynastic problems and the pressures generated by the Hundred Years' War. In contrast, the Holy Roman Empire, whose core consisted of the lands of Germany, had already begun to fall apart in the High Middle Ages. Northern Italy, which the German emperors had tried to include in their medieval empire, had been free from any real imperial control since the end of the Hohenstaufen dynasty

The Holy Roman Empire in the Fourteenth Century

in the thirteenth century. In Germany itself, the failure of the Hohenstaufens ended any chance of centralized monarchical authority, and Germany became a land of hundreds of virtually independent states. These varied in size and power and included princely states, such as the duchies of Bavaria and Saxony; free imperial city-states (self-governing cities directly under the control of the Holy Roman Emperor rather than a German territorial prince), such as Nuremberg; modest territories of petty imperial knights; and ecclesiastical states, such as the archbishopric of Cologne, in which an ecclesiastical official, such as a bishop, archbishop, or abbot, served in a dual capacity as an administrative official of the Catholic Church and as secular lord over the territories of the state. Although all of the rulers of these different states had some obligations to the German king and Holy Roman Emperor, more and more they acted independently.

ELECTORAL NATURE OF THE GERMAN MONARCHY   Because of its unique pattern of development in the High Middle Ages, the German monarchy had become established on an elective rather than a hereditary basis. This principle of election was standardized in 1356 by the Golden Bull issued by Emperor Charles IV (1346–1378). This document stated that four lay princes (the count palatine of the Rhine, the duke of Saxony, the margrave of Brandenburg, and the king of Bohemia) and three ecclesiastical rulers (the archbishops of Mainz, Trier, and Cologne) would serve as electors with the legal power to elect the "king of the Romans and future emperor, to be ruler of the world and of the Christian people."[12] "King of the Romans" was the official title of the German king; after his imperial coronation, he would also have the title of emperor.

In the fourteenth century, the electoral principle further ensured that kings of Germany were generally weak. Their ability to exercise effective power depended on the extent of their own family possessions. At the beginning of the fifteenth century, three emperors claimed the throne. Although the dispute was quickly settled, Germany entered the fifteenth century in a condition that

Mercenaries as Looters. Mercenary soldiers, like medieval armies in general, were notorious for causing havoc by looting when they were not engaged in battle. This mid-fourteenth-century manuscript illustration shows soldiers ransacking a house in Paris.

verged on anarchy. Princes fought princes and leagues of cities. The emperors were virtually powerless to control any of them.

The States of Italy

Italy, too, had failed to develop a centralized monarchical state by the fourteenth century. Papal opposition to the rule of the Hohenstaufen emperors in northern Italy had virtually guaranteed that. Moreover, southern Italy was divided into the kingdom of Naples, ruled by the French house of Anjou, and Sicily, whose kings came from the Spanish house of Aragon. The center of the peninsula remained under the rather shaky control of the papacy. Lack of centralized authority had enabled numerous city-states in northern Italy to remain independent of any political authority.

In fourteenth-century Italy, two general tendencies can be discerned: the replacement of republican governments by tyrants and the expansion of the larger city-states at the expense of the less powerful ones. Nearly all the cities of northern Italy began their existence as free communes with republican governments. But in the fourteenth century, intense internal strife led city-states to resort to temporary expedients, allowing rule by one man with dictatorial powers. Limited rule, however, soon became long-term despotism as tyrants proved willing to use force to maintain themselves in power. Eventually, such tyrants tried to legitimize their power by purchasing titles from the emperor (still nominally the ruler of northern

Italy as Holy Roman Emperor). In this fashion, the Visconti became the dukes of Milan and the d'Este, the dukes of Ferrara.

The other change of great significance was the development of larger, regional states as the larger states conquered the smaller ones. To fight their battles, city-states came to rely on mercenary soldiers, whose leaders, called **condottieri** (kahn-duh-TYAY-ree), sold the services of their bands to the highest bidder. These mercenaries wreaked havoc on the countryside, living by blackmail and looting when they were not actively engaged in battles. Many were foreigners who flocked to Italy during the periods of truce of the Hundred Years' War. By the end of the fourteenth century, three major states came to dominate northern Italy: the despotic state of Milan and the republican states of Florence and Venice.

DUCHY OF MILAN Located in the fertile Po valley, at the intersection of the chief trade routes from Italian coastal cities to the Alpine passes, Milan was one of the richest city-states in Italy. Politically, it was also one of the most agitated until the Visconti family established themselves as the hereditary despots of Milan in 1322. Giangaleazzo Visconti (jahn-gah-lay-AH-tsoh vees-KOHN-tee), who ruled from 1385 to 1402, transformed this despotism into a hereditary duchy by purchasing the title of duke from the emperor in 1395. Under Giangaleazzo's direction, the duchy of Milan extended its power over all of Lombardy and even threatened to conquer much of northern Italy until the duke's untimely death before the gates of Florence in 1402.

REPUBLIC OF FLORENCE Florence, like the other Italian towns, was initially a free commune dominated by a patrician class of nobles known as the *grandi* (GRAHN-dee). But the rapid expansion of Florence's economy made possible the development of a wealthy merchant-industrialist class known as the *popolo grasso* (PAWP-oo-loh GRAH-soh)—literally the "fat people." In 1293, the *popolo grasso* assumed a dominant role in government by establishing a new constitution known as the Ordinances of Justice. It provided for a republican government controlled by the seven major guilds of the city, which represented the interests of the wealthier classes. Executive power was vested in the hands of a council of elected priors—the *signoria* (seen-YOR-ee-uh)—and a standard-bearer of justice called the *gonfaloniere* (gun-fah-loh-NYAY-ray), assisted by a number of councils with advisory and overlapping powers. Around the mid-fourteenth century, revolutionary activity by the *popolo minuto*, the small shopkeepers and artisans, won them a share in the government. Even greater expansion occurred briefly when the *ciompi*, or industrial wool workers, were allowed to be represented in the government after their revolt in 1378. Only four years later, however, a counterrevolution brought the "fat people" back into virtual control of the government. After 1382, the Florentine government was controlled by a small merchant oligarchy that manipulated the supposedly republican government. By that time, Florence had also been successful in a series of wars against its neighbors. It had conquered most of Tuscany and established itself as a major territorial state in northern Italy.

REPUBLIC OF VENICE The other major northern Italian state was the republic of Venice, which had grown rich from commercial activity throughout the eastern Mediterranean and into northern Europe. A large number of merchant families became extremely wealthy. In the constitution of 1297, these patricians took control of the republic. In this year, the Great Council, the source of all political power, was closed to all but the members of about two hundred families. Since all other magistrates of the city were chosen either from or by this council, these families now formed a hereditary patriciate that completely dominated the city. Although the doge (or duke) had been the executive head of the republic since the Early Middle Ages, by 1300 he had become largely a

CHRONOLOGY The States of Western and Central Europe

England	
Edward III	1327–1377
Richard II	1377–1399
Henry IV	1399–1413
France	
Philip VI	1328–1350
John II	1350–1364
Capture at Poitiers	1356
Crushing of the *Jacquerie* and Étienne Marcel	1358
Charles V	1364–1380
Charles VI	1380–1422
German Monarchy	
Golden Bull	1356
Italy	
Florence	
Ordinances of Justice	1293
Venice	
Closing of Great Council	1297
Milan	
Visconti establish themselves as rulers of Milan	1322
Giangaleazzo Visconti purchases title of duke	1395

figurehead. Actual power was vested in the hands of the Great Council and the legislative body known as the Senate, while an extraordinary body known as the Council of Ten, first formed in 1310, came to be the real executive power of the state. The Venetian government was respected by contemporaries for its stability. A sixteenth-century Italian historian noted that Venice had "the best government of any city not only in our own times but also in the classical world."[13]

In the fourteenth century, Venice also embarked on a policy of expansion. By the end of the century, it had created a commercial empire by establishing colonies and trading posts in the eastern Mediterranean and Black Sea as well as continuing its commercial monopolies in the Byzantine Empire. At the same time, Venice began to conquer the territory adjoining it in northern Italy.

The States of Italy in the Fourteenth Century

The Decline of the Church

Q **FOCUS QUESTION:** How and why did the authority and prestige of the papacy decline in the fourteenth century?

The papacy of the Roman Catholic Church reached the height of its power in the thirteenth century. Theories of papal supremacy included a doctrine of "fullness of power" as the spiritual head of Christendom and claims to universal temporal authority over all secular rulers. But papal claims of temporal supremacy were increasingly out of step with the growing secular monarchies of Europe and ultimately brought the papacy into a conflict with the territorial states that it was unable to win.

Boniface VIII and the Conflict with the State

The struggle between the papacy and the secular monarchies began during the pontificate of Pope Boniface VIII (1294–1303). One major issue appeared to be at stake between the pope and King Philip IV (1285–1314) of France. In his desire to acquire new revenues, Philip claimed the right to tax the French clergy. Boniface VIII responded that the clergy of any state could not pay taxes to their secular ruler without the pope's consent. Underlying this issue, however, was a basic conflict between the claims of the papacy to universal authority over both church and state, which necessitated complete control over the clergy, and the claims of the king that all subjects, including the clergy, were under the jurisdiction of the crown and subject to the king's authority on matters of taxation and justice. In short, the fundamental issue was the universal sovereignty of the papacy versus the royal sovereignty of the monarch.

Boniface VIII asserted his position in a series of papal bulls or letters, the most important of which was *Unam Sanctam* (OO-nam SAHNK-tahm), issued in 1302. It was the strongest statement ever made by a pope on the supremacy of the spiritual authority over the temporal authority (see the box on p. 327). When it became apparent that the pope had decided to act on his principles by excommunicating Philip IV, the latter sent a small contingent of French forces to capture Boniface and bring him back to France for trial. The pope was captured in Anagni, although Italian nobles from the surrounding countryside soon rescued him. The shock of this experience, however, soon led to the pope's death. Philip's strong-arm tactics had produced a clear victory for the national monarchy over the papacy, and no later pope has dared renew the extravagant claims of Boniface VIII.

To ensure his position and avoid any future papal threat, Philip IV brought enough pressure to bear on the college of cardinals to achieve the election of a Frenchman as pope in 1305. Using the excuse of turbulence in the city of Rome, the new pope, Clement V (1305–1314), took up residence in Avignon (ah-veen-YOHN) on the east bank of the Rhône River. Although Avignon was located in the Holy Roman Empire and was not a French possession, it lay just across the river from the territory of King Philip IV. Clement may have intended to return to Rome, but he and his successors remained in Avignon for the next seventy-two years, thereby creating yet another crisis for the church.

The Papacy at Avignon (1305–1377)

The residency of the popes in Avignon for most of the fourteenth century led to a decline in papal prestige and growing antipapal sentiment. The city of Rome was the traditional capital of the universal church. The pope was the bishop of Rome, and his position was based on being the successor to the Apostle Peter, traditionally considered the first bishop of Rome. It was unseemly that the head of the Catholic Church should reside elsewhere. In the 1330s, the popes began to construct a stately palace in Avignon, a clear indication that they intended to stay for some time.

Other factors also contributed to the decline in papal prestige during the Avignonese residency. It was widely believed that the popes at Avignon were captives of the French monarchy. Although questionable, since Avignon did not belong to the French monarchy, it was easy to believe in view of Avignon's proximity to French lands. Moreover, during the seventy-two years of the

Pope Boniface VIII. The conflict between church and state in the Middle Ages reached its height in the struggle between Pope Boniface VIII and Philip IV of France. This fourteenth-century miniature depicts Boniface VIII presiding over a gathering of cardinals.

Boniface VIII's Defense of Papal Supremacy

One of the most remarkable documents of the fourteenth century was the exaggerated statement of papal supremacy issued by Pope Boniface VIII in 1302 in the heat of his conflict with the French king Philip IV. Ironically, this strongest statement ever made of papal supremacy was issued at a time when the rising power of the secular monarchies made it increasingly difficult for the premises to be accepted.

Pope Boniface VIII, *Unam Sanctam*

We are compelled, our faith urging us, to believe and to hold—and we do firmly believe and simply confess—that there is one holy catholic and apostolic church, outside of which there is neither salvation nor remission of sins.... In this church there is one Lord, one faith and one baptism.... Therefore, of this one and only church there is one body and one head ... Christ, namely, and the vicar of Christ, St. Peter, and the successor of Peter. For the Lord himself said to Peter, feed my sheep....

We are told by the word of the gospel that in this His fold there are two swords—a spiritual, namely, and a temporal.... Both swords, the spiritual and the material, therefore, are in the power of the church; the one, indeed, to be wielded for the church, the other by the church; the one by the hand of the priest, the other by the hand of kings and knights, but at the will and sufferance of the priest. One sword, moreover, ought to be under the other, and the temporal authority to be subjected to the spiritual....

Therefore if the earthly power err it shall be judged by the spiritual power; but if the lesser spiritual power err, by the greater. But if the greatest, it can be judged by God alone, not by man, the apostle bearing witness. A spiritual man judges all things, but he himself is judged by no one. This authority, moreover, even though it is given to man and exercised through man, is not human but rather divine, being given by divine lips to Peter and founded on a rock for him and his successors through Christ himself whom he has confessed; the Lord himself saying to Peter: "Whatsoever you shall bind, etc." Whoever, therefore, resists this power thus ordained by God, resists the ordination of God....

Indeed, we declare, announce and define, that it is altogether necessary to salvation for every human creature to be subject to the Roman pontiff.

 What claims did Boniface VIII make in *Unam Sanctam*? To what extent were these claims a logical continuation of the development of the papacy in the Middle Ages? If you were a monarch, why would you object to this papal bull?

Avignon

Avignonese papacy, of the 134 new cardinals created by the popes, 113 were French. The papal residency at Avignon was also an important turning point in the church's attempt to adapt itself to the changing economic and political conditions of Europe. Like the growing monarchical states, the popes centralized their administration by developing a specialized bureaucracy. In fact, the papal bureaucracy in the fourteenth century under the leadership of the pope and college of cardinals became the most sophisticated administrative system in the medieval world.

At the same time, the popes attempted to find new sources of revenue to compensate for their loss of income from the Papal States and began to impose new taxes on the clergy. Furthermore, the splendor in which the pope and cardinals were living in Avignon led to highly vocal criticism of both clergy and papacy in the fourteenth century. Avignon had become a powerful symbol of abuses within the church, and many people began to call for the pope's return to Rome.

One of the most prominent calls came from Catherine of Siena (c. 1347–1380), whose saintly demeanor and claims of visions from God led the city of Florence to send her on a mission to Pope Gregory XI (1370–1378) in Avignon. She told the pope, "Because God has given you authority and because you have accepted it, you ought to use your virtue and power; if you do not wish to use it, it might be better for you to resign what you have accepted; it would give more honor to God and health to your soul."[14]

The Great Schism

Catherine of Siena's admonition seemed to be heeded in 1377, when at long last Pope Gregory XI, perceiving the disastrous decline in papal prestige, returned to Rome. He died soon afterward, however, in the spring of 1378. When the college of cardinals met in conclave to elect a new pope, the citizens of Rome, fearful that the French majority would choose another Frenchman who would return the papacy to Avignon, threatened that the cardinals would not leave Rome alive unless they elected a Roman or at least an Italian as pope. Indeed, the guards of the conclave warned the cardinals that they "ran the risk of being torn in pieces" if they did not choose an Italian.

Wisely, the terrified cardinals duly elected the Italian archbishop of Bari, who was subsequently crowned as Pope Urban VI (1378–1389) on Easter Sunday. Following his election, Urban VI made clear his plans to reform the papal curia and even to swamp the college of cardinals with enough new Italian cardinals to eliminate the French majority. After many of the cardinals (the French ones) withdrew from Rome in late summer and were finally free of the Roman mob, they issued a manifesto, saying that they had been coerced by the mob and that Urban's election was therefore null and void. The dissenting cardinals thereupon chose one of their number, a Frenchman, who took the title of Clement VII and promptly returned to Avignon. Since Urban remained in Rome, there were now two popes, initiating what has been called the **Great Schism** of the church.

Europe's loyalties soon became divided: France, Spain, Scotland, and southern Italy supported Clement, while England, Germany, Scandinavia, and most of Italy supported Urban. These divisions generally followed political lines and reflected the bitter division between the English and the French in the Hundred Years' War. Because the French supported the Avignonese pope, so did their allies; their enemies, particularly England and its allies, supported the Roman pope. The need for political support caused both popes to subordinate their policies to the policies of these states.

The Great Schism lasted for nearly forty years and had a baleful effect on the Catholic Church and Christendom in general. The schism greatly aggravated the financial abuses that had developed within the church during the Avignonese papacy. Two papal administrative systems (with only one-half the accustomed revenues) worked to increase taxation. At the same time, the schism badly damaged the faith of Christian believers. The pope was widely believed to be the leader of Christendom and, as Boniface VIII had pointed out, held the keys to the kingdom of heaven. Since each line of popes denounced the other as the Antichrist, such a spectacle could not help but undermine the institution that had become the very foundation of the church.

New Thoughts on Church and State and the Rise of Conciliarism

As dissatisfaction with the papacy grew, so did the calls for a revolutionary approach to solving the church's institutional problems. One of the most systematic was provided by Marsiglio of Padua (mar-SIL-yoh of PAD-juh-wuh) (c. 1270–1342), rector of the University of Paris and author of a remarkable book, *Defender of the Peace.*

Marsiglio denied that the temporal authority was subject to the spiritual authority, as popes from Innocent III to Boniface VIII had maintained. Instead, he argued that the church was only one element of society and must confine itself solely to spiritual functions. Furthermore, Marsiglio argued, the church is a community of the faithful in which all authority is ultimately derived from

CHRONOLOGY **The Decline of the Church**

Pope Boniface VIII	1294–1303
Unam Sanctam	1302
Papacy at Avignon	1305–1377
Pope Gregory XI returns to Rome	1377
Great Schism begins	1378
Pope Urban VI	1378–1389
Failure of Council of Pisa to end schism; election of Alexander V	1409
Council of Constance	1414–1418
End of schism; election of Martin V	1417

the entire community. The clergy hold no special authority from God but serve only to administer the affairs of the church on behalf of all Christians. Thus, final authority in spiritual matters must reside not with the pope but with a general church council representing all members.

THE CONCILIAR MOVEMENT The Great Schism led large numbers of churchmen to take up this theory, known as **conciliarism,** in the belief that only a general council of the church could end the schism and bring reform to the church in its "head and members." The only serious issue left to be decided was who should call the council. Church law held that only a pope could convene a council. Professors of theology argued, however, that since the competing popes would not do so, either members of the church hierarchy or even secular princes, especially the Holy Roman Emperor, could convene a council to settle all relevant issues.

In desperation, a group of cardinals from both camps finally convened a general council on their own. This Council of Pisa, which met in 1409, deposed the two popes and elected a new one, Alexander V. The council's action proved disastrous when the two deposed popes refused to step down. There were now three popes, and the church seemed more hopelessly divided than ever.

Leadership in convening a new council now passed to the Holy Roman Emperor, Sigismund. As a result of his efforts, a new ecumenical church council met at Constance from 1414 to 1418. Ending the schism proved a surprisingly easy task: after the three competing popes either resigned or were deposed, a new conclave elected Cardinal Oddone Colonna, a member of a prominent Roman family, as Pope Martin V (1417–1431). The Great Schism had finally been ended.

Popular Religion in an Age of Adversity

The seeming preoccupation of the popes and leading clerics with finances and power during the struggles of Boniface VIII, the Avignonese papacy, and the Great Schism could not help but lead to a decline in prestige and respect for the institutional church, especially the papacy.

At the same time, in the fourteenth century, the Black Death and its recurrences made an important impact on the religious life of ordinary Christians by heightening their preoccupation with death and salvation. The church often failed to provide sufficient spiritual comfort as many parish priests fled from the plague.

Christians responded in different ways to the adversities of the fourteenth century. First of all, there was a tendency to stress the performance of good works, including acts of charity, as a means of ensuring salvation. Bequests to hospitals and other charitable foundations increased. Family chapels were established, served by priests whose primary responsibility was to say Mass for the good of the souls of deceased family members. These chapels became even more significant as the importance of purgatory rose. Purgatory was defined by the church as the place where souls went after death to be purged of punishment for sins committed in life. In effect, the soul was purified in purgatory before it ascended into heaven. It was believed that like indulgences, prayers and private Masses for the dead could shorten the amount of time souls spent in purgatory.

All of these developments were part of a larger trend—a new emphasis in late medieval Christianity on a mechanical path to salvation. Chalking up good deeds to ensure salvation was done in numerous ways but was nowhere more evident than in the growing emphasis on indulgences. We should also note that pilgrimages, which became increasingly popular, and charitable contributions were good works that could be accomplished without the involvement of clerics, a reflection of the loss of faith in the institutional church and its clergy and another noticeable feature of popular religious life. At the same time, interest in Christianity itself did not decline. Indeed, people sought to play a more active role in their own salvation. This is particularly evident in the popularity of mysticism and lay piety in the fourteenth century.

MYSTICISM AND LAY PIETY The mysticism of the fourteenth century was certainly not new, for Christians throughout the Middle Ages had claimed to have had mystical experiences. Simply defined, **mysticism** is the immediate experience of oneness with God. It is this experience that characterized the teaching of Meister Eckhart (MY-stur EK-hart) (1260–1327), who sparked a mystical movement in western Germany. Eckhart was a well-educated Dominican theologian who wrote learned Latin works on theology, but he was also a popular preacher whose message on the union of the soul with God was typical of mysticism. According to Eckhart, such a union was attainable by all who pursued it wholeheartedly.

Eckhart's movement spread from Germany into the Low Countries, where it took on a new form, called the **Modern Devotion,** founded by Gerard Groote (GROH-tuh) (1340–1384). After a religious conversion, Groote entered a monastery for several years of contemplation before reentering the world. His messages were typical of a practical mysticism. To achieve true spiritual communion

with God, people must imitate Jesus and lead lives dedicated to serving the needs of their fellow human beings. Groote emphasized a simple inner piety and morality based on Scripture and an avoidance of the complexities of theology.

Eventually, Groote attracted a group of followers who came to be known as the Brothers of the Common Life. From this small beginning, a movement developed that spread through the Netherlands and back into Germany. Houses of the Brothers, as well as separate houses for women (Sisters of the Common Life), were founded in one city after another. The Sisters and Brothers of the Common Life did not constitute regular religious orders. They were laypeople who took no formal monastic vows but were nevertheless regulated by quasi-monastic rules that they imposed on their own communities. They also established schools throughout Germany and the Netherlands in which they stressed their message of imitating the life of Jesus by serving others. The Brothers and Sisters of the Common Life attest to the vitality of spiritual life among lay Christians in the fourteenth century.

UNIQUE FEMALE MYSTICAL EXPERIENCES A number of female mystics had their own unique spiritual experiences. For them, fasting and receiving the Eucharist (the communion wafer that, according to Roman Catholic doctrine, contains the body of Jesus) became the mainstay of their religious practices. Catherine of Siena, for example, gave up eating any solid food at the age of twenty-three and thereafter lived only on cold water and herbs that she sucked and then spat out. Her primary nourishment, however, came from the Eucharist. She wrote: "The immaculate lamb [Christ] is food, table, and servant.... And we who eat at that table become like the food [that is, Christ], acting not for our own utility but for the honor of God and the salvation of neighbor."[15] For Catherine and a number of other female mystics, reception of the Eucharist was their primary instrument in achieving a mystical union with God.

Changes in Theology

The fourteenth century presented challenges not only to the institutional church but also to its theological framework, especially evident in the questioning of the grand synthesis attempted by Thomas Aquinas. In the thirteenth century, Aquinas's grand synthesis of faith and reason was not widely accepted outside his own Dominican order. At the same time, differences with Aquinas were kept within a framework of commonly accepted scholastic thought. In the fourteenth century, however, the philosopher William of Occam (1285–1329) posed a severe challenge to the scholastic achievements of the High Middle Ages.

Occam posited a radical interpretation of nominalism. He asserted that all universals or general concepts were simply names and that only individual objects perceived by the senses were real. Although the mind was capable of analyzing individual objects, it could not establish any truths about the nature of external, higher reality. Reason could not be used to substantiate spiritual truths. It could not, for example, prove the statement "God exists." For William of Occam as a Christian believer, this did not mean that God did not exist, however. It simply indicated that the truths of religion could only be known by an act of faith and were not demonstrable by reason. The acceptance of Occam's nominalist philosophy at the University of Paris brought an element of uncertainty to late medieval theology by seriously weakening the synthesis of faith and reason that had characterized the theological thought of the High Middle Ages. Nevertheless, Occam's emphasis on using reason to analyze the observable phenomena of the world had an important impact on the development of physical science by creating support for rational and scientific analysis. Some late medieval theologians came to accept the compatibility of rational analysis of the material world with mystical acceptance of spiritual truths.

The Cultural World of the Fourteenth Century

Q **Focus Question**: What were the major developments in art and literature in the fourteenth century?

The cultural life of the fourteenth century was also characterized by ferment. In literature, several writers used their vernacular languages to produce notable works. In art, the Black Death and other problems of the century left their mark as many artists turned to morbid themes, but the period also produced Giotto, whose paintings expressed a new realism that would be developed further by the artists of the next century.

The Development of Vernacular Literature

Although Latin remained the language of the church liturgy and the official documents of both church and state throughout Europe, the fourteenth century witnessed the rapid growth of vernacular literature, especially in Italy. The development of an Italian vernacular literature was mostly the result of the efforts of three writers in the fourteenth century: Dante, Petrarch (PEE-trark *or* PET-trark), and Boccaccio. Their use of the Tuscan dialect common in Florence and its surrounding countryside ensured that it would prevail as the basis of the modern Italian language.

DANTE Dante Alighieri (1265–1321) came from an old Florentine noble family that had fallen on hard times. Although he had held high political office in republican Florence, factional conflict led to his exile from the city in 1302. Until the end of his life, Dante hoped to return to his beloved Florence, but his wish remained unfulfilled.

Dante's masterpiece in the Italian vernacular was the *Divine Comedy*, written between 1313 and 1321. Cast in a typical medieval framework, the *Divine Comedy* is basically the story of the soul's progression to salvation, a fundamental medieval preoccupation. The lengthy poem was divided into three major sections corresponding to the realms of the afterworld: hell, purgatory, and heaven or paradise. In the "Inferno" (see the box on p. 331), Dante is led by his guide, the Classical author Virgil, who is a symbol of human reason. But Virgil (or reason) can lead the poet only so far on his journey. At the end of "Purgatory," Beatrice (the true love of Dante's life), who represents revelation—which alone can explain the mysteries of heaven—becomes his guide into "Paradise." Here Beatrice presents Dante to Saint Bernard, a symbol of mystical contemplation. The saint turns Dante over to the Virgin Mary, since grace is necessary to achieve the final step of entering the presence of God, where one beholds "the love that moves the sun and the other stars."[16]

PETRARCH Like Dante, Francesco Petrarca, known as Petrarch (1304–1374), was a Florentine who spent much of his life outside his native city. Petrarch's role in the revival of the classics made him a seminal figure in the literary Italian Renaissance (see Chapter 12). His primary contribution to the development of the Italian vernacular was made in his sonnets. He is considered one of the greatest European lyric poets. His sonnets were inspired by his love for a married lady named Laura, whom he had met in 1327. Though honoring an idealized female figure was a long-standing medieval tradition, Laura was very human and not just an ideal. She was a real woman with whom Petrarch was involved for a long time. He poured forth his lamentations in sonnet after sonnet:

> I am as tired of thinking as my thought
> Is never tired to find itself in you,
> And of not yet leaving this life that brought
> Me the too heavy weight of signs and rue;
>
> And because to describe your hair and face
> And the fair eyes of which I always speak,
> Language and sound have not become too weak
> And day and night your name they still embrace.
>
> And tired because my feet do not yet fail
> After following you in every part,
> Wasting so many steps without avail,
>
> From whence derive the paper and the ink
> That I have filled with you; if I should sink,
> It is the fault of Love, not of my art.[17]

In analyzing every aspect of the unrequited lover's feelings, Petrarch appeared less concerned to sing his lady's praise than to immortalize his own thoughts. This interest in his own personality reveals a sense of

Dante's Vision of Hell

The *Divine Comedy* of Dante Alighieri is regarded as one of the greatest literary works of all time. Many consider it the supreme summary of medieval thought. It combines allegory with a remarkable amount of contemporary history. Indeed, forty-three of the seventy-nine people consigned to hell in the "Inferno" were Florentines. This excerpt is taken from canto 18 of the "Inferno," in which Dante and Virgil visit the eighth circle of hell, which is divided into ten trenches containing the souls of people who had committed malicious frauds on their fellow human beings.

Dante, "Inferno," *Divine Comedy*

> We had already come to where the walk
> crosses the second bank, from which it lifts
> another arch, spanning from rock to rock.
>
> Here we heard people whine in the next chasm,
> and knock and thump themselves with open palms,
> and blubber through their snouts as if in a spasm.
>
> Steaming from that pit, a vapor rose
> over the banks, crusting them with a slime
> that sickened my eyes and hammered at my nose.
>
> That chasm sinks so deep we could not sight
> its bottom anywhere until we climbed
> along the rock arch to its greatest height.
>
> Once there, I peered down; and I saw long lines
> of people in a river of excrement
> that seemed the overflow of the world's latrines.
>
> I saw among the felons of that pit
> one wraith who might or might not have been
>   tonsured—
> one could not tell, he was so smeared with shit.
>
> He bellowed: "You there, why do you stare at me
> more than at all the others in this stew?"
> And I to him: "Because if memory
>
> serves me, I knew you when your hair was dry.
> You are Alessio Interminelli da Lucca.
> That's why I pick you from this filthy fry."
>
> And he then, beating himself on his clown's head:
> "Down to this have the flatteries I sold
> the living sunk me here among the dead."
>
> And my Guide prompted then: "Lean forward a bit
> and look beyond him, there—do you see that one
> scratching herself with dungy nails, the strumpet
>
> who fidgets to her feet, then to a crouch?
> It is the whore Thäis who told her lover
> when he sent to ask her, 'Do you thank me much?'
>
> 'Much? Nay, past all believing!' And with this
> Let us turn from the sight of this abyss."

Q How does Dante's vision of hell reflect medieval religious thought? Why were there Florentines in hell? What lessons do you think this work was intended to teach its readers?

---

individuality stronger than in any previous medieval literature.

BOCCACCIO Although he too wrote poetry, Giovanni Boccaccio (1313–1375) is known primarily for his prose. Another Florentine, he also used the Tuscan dialect. While working for the Bardi banking house in Naples, he fell in love with a noble lady whom he called his Fiammetta, his Little Flame. Under her inspiration, Boccaccio began to write prose romances. His best-known work, the *Decameron*, however, was not written until after he had returned to Florence. The *Decameron* is set at the time of the Black Death. Ten young people flee to a villa outside Florence to escape the plague and decide to while away the time by telling stories. Although the stories are not new and still reflect the acceptance of basic Christian values, Boccaccio does present the society of his time from a secular point of view. It is the seducer of women, not the knight or philosopher or pious monk, who is the real hero. Perhaps, as some historians have argued, the *Decameron* reflects the immediate easygoing, cynical postplague values. Boccaccio's later work certainly became gloomier and more pessimistic; as he grew older, he even rejected his earlier work as irrelevant. He commented in a 1373 letter, "I am certainly not pleased that you have allowed the illustrious women in your house to read my trifles.... You know how much in them is less than decent and opposed to modesty, how much stimulation to wanton lust, how many things that drive to lust even those most fortified against it."[18]

CHAUCER Another leading vernacular author was Geoffrey Chaucer (c. 1340–1400), who brought a new level of sophistication to the English vernacular language in his famous *Canterbury Tales*. His beauty of expression and clear, forceful language were important in transforming his East Midland dialect into the chief ancestor of the modern English language. *The Canterbury Tales* is a collection of stories told by a group of twenty-nine pilgrims journeying from the London suburb of Southwark to the tomb of Saint Thomas à Becket at Canterbury. This format gave Chaucer the chance to portray an entire range of English society, both high- and low-born. Among

Geoffrey Chaucer, *Canterbury Tales: Prologue*

others, he presented the Knight, the Yeoman, the Prioress, the Monk, the Merchant, the Student, the Lawyer, the Carpenter, the Cook, the Doctor, the Plowman, and, of course, "A Good Wife was there from beside the city of Bath—a little deaf, which was a pity." The stories these pilgrims told to while away the time on the journey were just as varied as the storytellers themselves: knightly romances, fairy tales, saints' lives, sophisticated satires, and crude anecdotes.

Chaucer also used some of his characters to criticize the corruption of the church in the late medieval period. His portrayal of the Friar leaves no doubt of Chaucer's disdain for the corrupt practices of clerics. Of the Friar, he says:

> He knew the taverns well in every town.
> The barmaids and innkeepers pleased his mind
> Better than beggars and lepers and their kind.[19]

And yet Chaucer was still a pious Christian, never doubting basic Christian doctrines and remaining optimistic that the church could be reformed.

CHRISTINE DE PIZAN One of the extraordinary vernacular writers of the age was Christine de Pizan (c. 1364–1430). Because of her father's position at the court of Charles V of France, she received a good education. Her husband died when she was only twenty-five (they had been married for ten years), leaving her with little income and three small children and her mother to support. Christine took the unusual step of becoming a writer in order to earn her living (see the box on p. 322). Her poems were soon in demand, and by 1400 she had achieved financial security.

Christine de Pizan is best known, however, for her French prose works written in defense of women. In *The Book of the City of Ladies,* written in 1404, she denounced the many male writers who had argued that women needed to be controlled by men because women by their very nature were prone to evil, unable to learn, and easily swayed. With the help of Reason, Righteousness, and Justice, who appear to her in a vision, Christine refutes these antifeminist attacks. Women, she argues, are not evil by nature, and they could learn as well as men if they were permitted to attend the same schools: "Should I also tell you whether a woman's nature is clever and quick enough to learn speculative sciences as well as to discover them, and likewise the manual arts. I assure you that women are equally well-suited and skilled to carry them out and to put them to sophisticated use once they have learned them."[20] Much of the book includes a detailed discussion of women from the past and present who have distinguished themselves as leaders, warriors, wives, mothers, and martyrs for their religious faith. She ends by encouraging women to defend themselves against the attacks of men, who are incapable of understanding them.

Art and the Black Death

The fourteenth century produced an artistic outburst in new directions as well as a large body of morbid work influenced by the Black Death and the recurrences of the plague. The city of Florence witnessed the first dramatic break with medieval tradition in the work of Giotto (JOH-toh) (1266–1337), often considered a forerunner of Italian Renaissance painting. Born into a peasant family, Giotto acquired his painting skills in a workshop in Florence. Although he worked throughout Italy, his most famous works were done in Padua and Florence. Coming out of the formal Byzantine school, Giotto transcended it with a new kind of realism, a desire to imitate nature that Renaissance artists later identified as the basic component of Classical art. Giotto's figures were solid and rounded; placed realistically in relationship to each other and their background, they conveyed three-dimensional depth. The expressive faces and physically realistic bodies gave his sacred figures human qualities with which spectators could identify. Although Giotto had no direct successors, Florentine painting in the early fifteenth century pursued even more dramatically the new direction his work represents.

The Black Death made a visible impact on art. For one thing, it wiped out entire guilds of artists. At the same time, survivors, including the newly rich who patronized artists, were no longer so optimistic. Some were more guilty about enjoying life and more concerned about gaining salvation. Postplague art began to concentrate on pain and death. A fairly large number of artistic works

Christine de Pizan. Christine de Pizan was one of the extraordinary vernacular writers of the late fourteenth and early fifteenth centuries. In this fifteenth-century French illustration, she is shown giving instructions to an assistant from the *Works of Christine de Pizan.*

Scrovegni Chapel, Padua//© Scala/Art Resource, NY

Giotto, *Lamentation*. The work of Giotto marked the first clear innovation in fourteenth-century painting, making him a forerunner of the early Renaissance. This fresco was part of a series done on the walls of the Arena Chapel in Padua begun in 1305. Giotto painted thirty-eight scenes on three levels: the lives of Mary, the mother of Jesus, and her parents (top panel); the life and work of Jesus (middle panel); and his passion, crucifixion, and resurrection (bottom panel). Shown here from the bottom panel is the *Lamentation*. A group of Jesus's followers, including his mother and Mary Magdalene, mourn over the body of Jesus before it is placed in its tomb. The solidity of Giotto's human figures gives them a three-dimensional sense. He also captured the grief and despair felt by the mourners.

came to be based on the *ars moriendi* (AHRS moh-ree-EN-dee), the art of dying. A morbid concern with death is especially evident in Francisco Traini's fresco *The Triumph of Death* in Pisa. On the left side of the fresco, several young nobles encounter three coffins containing decomposing bodies, while on the right young aristocrats engage in pleasant pursuits but are threatened by a grim figure of Death in the form of a witch flying through the air swinging a large scythe. Beneath her lie piles of dead citizens and clergy cut down in the prime of life.

Society in an Age of Adversity

Q **FOCUS QUESTION**: How did the adversities of the fourteenth century affect urban life and medical practices?

In the midst of disaster, the fourteenth century proved creative in its own way. New inventions made an impact on daily life at the same time that the effects of the plague were felt in many areas of medieval urban life.

Camposanto, Pisa//© Alinari/Art Resource, NY

Francesco Traini, *The Triumph of Death*. The plague led to a morbid fascination with death that is visible in the art of the period. Shown here is the left side of Francesco Traini's fresco, which depicts a group of young aristocrats on a hunt encountering three decaying corpses in coffins. One of the nobles is shown gagging at the smell of the decomposing bodies.

Changes in Urban Life

One immediate by-product of the Black Death was greater regulation of urban activities by town governments. Authorities tried to keep cities cleaner by enacting new ordinances against waste products in the streets. Viewed as unhealthy places, bathhouses were closed down, leading to a noticeable decline in personal cleanliness. Efforts at regulation also affected the practice of female prostitution.

Medieval society had tolerated prostitution as a lesser evil: it was better for males to frequent prostitutes than to seduce virgins or married women. Since many males in medieval towns married late, the demand for prostitutes was high and was met by a regular supply, derived no doubt from the need of many poor girls and women to survive. The recession of the fourteenth century probably increased the supply of prostitutes, while the new hedonism prevalent after the Black Death also increased demand. As a result, cities intensified their regulation of prostitution.

By organizing brothels, city authorities could supervise as well as tax prostitutes. Officials granted charters to citizens who were allowed to set up brothels, provided they were located only in certain areas of town. Prostitutes were also expected to wear special items of clothing—such as red hats—to distinguish them from other women. It was assumed that the regulation of prostitution made it easier to supervise and hence maintained public order.

FAMILY LIFE AND GENDER ROLES IN LATE MEDIEVAL CITIES The basic unit of the late medieval town was the nuclear family of husband, wife, and children. Especially in wealthier families, there might also be servants, apprentices, and other relatives, including widowed mothers and the husband's illegitimate children.

Before the Black Death, late marriages were common for urban couples. It was not unusual for husbands to be in their late thirties or forties and wives in their early twenties. The expense of setting up a household probably necessitated the delay in marriage. But the situation changed dramatically after the plague, reflecting new economic opportunities for the survivors and a new reluctance to postpone living in the presence of so much death.

The economic difficulties of the fourteenth century also tended to strengthen the development of gender roles. Based on the authority of Aristotle, Thomas Aquinas and other scholastic theologians had advanced the belief that according to the natural order, men were active and domineering while women were passive and submissive. As more and more lawyers, doctors, and priests, who had been trained in universities where these notions were taught, entered society, these ideas about the different natures of men and women became widely accepted. This was evident in legal systems, many of which limited the legal capacity of women (see the box on p. 335). Increasingly, women were expected to give up any active functions in society and remain subject to direction from males. A fourteenth-century Parisian provost commented that among glass cutters, "no master's widow who keeps working at his craft after her husband's death may take on apprentices, for the men of the craft do not believe that a woman can master it well enough to teach a child to master it, for the craft is a very delicate one."[21] Although this statement suggests that some women were, in fact, running businesses, it also reveals that they were viewed as incapable of undertaking all of men's activities. Europeans in the fourteenth century imposed a division of labor roles between men and women that persisted until the Industrial Revolution.

In practice, however, some women in the fourteenth century benefited from the effects of the Black Death. The deaths of many male workers in cities opened up new jobs for women, such as metalworkers and stevedores. In cloth making, women were allowed to assume better-paying jobs as weavers. Brewing became an all-female profession by 1450. Widows also occasionally carried on their husbands' shops or businesses.

MEDIEVAL CHILDREN Parents in the High and Later Middle Ages invested considerable resources and affection in rearing their children. The dramatic increase in specialized roles that accompanied the spread of commerce and the growth of cities demanded a commitment to educating children in the marketable skills needed for the new occupations. Philip of Navarre noted in the twelfth century that boys ought to be taught a trade "as soon as possible. Those who early become and long remain apprentices ought to be the best masters."[22] Some cities provided schools to educate the young. A chronicler in Florence related that between 8,000 and 10,000 boys and girls between the ages of six and twelve attended the city's grammar schools, a figure that probably represented half of all school-aged children. Although grammar school completed education for girls, around 1,100 boys went on to six secondary schools that prepared them for business careers, while another 600 studied Latin and logic in four other schools that readied them for university training and a career in medicine, law, or the church. In the High Middle Ages, then, urban communities demonstrated a commitment to the training of the young.

As a result of the devastating effects of the plague and its recurrences, these same communities became concerned about investing in the survival and health of children. A number of hospitals existed in both Florence and Rome in the fourteenth century, and in the 1420s and 1430s, hospitals were established that catered only to the needs of foundlings, supporting them until boys could be taught a trade and girls could marry.

New Directions in Medicine

The medical community comprised a number of functionaries. At the top of the medical hierarchy were the physicians, usually clergymen, who received their education in the universities, where they studied ancient authorities, such as Hippocrates and Galen. As a result, physicians were highly trained in theory but had little or no clinical practice. By the

The Legal Rights of Women

During the High and Later Middle Ages, as women were increasingly viewed as weak beings who were unable to play independent roles, legal systems also began to limit the rights of women. These excerpts are taken from a variety of legal opinions in France, England, and a number of Italian cities.

— ✠ —

Excerpts from Legal Opinions

FRANCE, 1270: No married woman can go to court . . . unless someone has abused or beaten her, in which case she may go to court without her husband. If she is a tradeswoman, she can sue and defend herself in matters connected with her business, but not otherwise.

ENGLAND [probably fifteenth century]: Every Feme Covert [married woman] is a sort of infant. . . . It is seldom, almost never that a married woman can have any action to use her wit only in her own name: her husband is her stern, her prime mover, without whom she cannot do much at home, and less abroad. . . . It is a miracle that a wife should commit any suit without her husband.

ENGLAND [probably fifteenth century]: The very goods which a man gives to his wife, are still his own, her chain, her bracelets, her apparel, are all the goodman's goods. . . . A wife however gallant she be, glitters but in the riches of her husband, as the moon has no light but it is the sun's. . . . For thus it is, if before marriage the woman was possessed of horses . . . , sheep, corn, wool, money, plate and jewels, all manner of movable substance is presently . . . the husband's to sell, keep or bequeath if she die.

PESARO, ITALY [exact date unknown]: No wife can make a contract without the consent of her husband.

FLORENCE, ITALY, 1415: A married woman with children cannot draw up a last will in her own right, nor dispose of her dowry among the living to the detriment of husband and children.

LUCCA, ITALY [exact date unknown]: No married woman . . . can seal or give away [anything] unless she has the agreement of her husband and nearest [male] relative. ✑

Q Based on these documents, what socioeconomic and sociopolitical conditions in late medieval Europe do you think combined to "infantilize" women and severely limit their legal rights? Who would benefit the most from the legal disempowerment of women?

---

fourteenth century, they were educated in six chief medical schools—Salerno, Montpellier, Bologna, Oxford, Padua, and Paris. Paris was regarded as the most prestigious.

The preplague medicine of university-trained physicians was theoretically grounded in the Classical Greek theory of the "four humors," each connected to a particular organ: blood (from the heart), phlegm (from the brain), yellow bile (from the liver), and black bile (from the spleen). Because the four humors corresponded in turn to the four elemental qualities of the universe—air (blood), water (phlegm), fire (yellow bile), and earth (black bile)—a human being was a microcosm of the cosmos. Good health resulted from a perfect balance of the four humors; sickness meant that the humors were out of balance. The task of the medieval physician was to restore proper order through a number of remedies, such as rest, diet, herbal medicines, or bloodletting.

Beneath the physicians in the hierarchy of the medical profession stood the surgeons, whose activities included performing operations, setting broken bones, and bleeding patients. Their knowledge was based largely on practical experience. Below surgeons were midwives, who delivered babies, and barber-surgeons, who were less trained than surgeons and performed menial tasks such as bloodletting and setting simple bone fractures.

Barber-surgeons supplemented their income by shaving and cutting hair and pulling teeth. Apothecaries also constituted part of the medical establishment. They filled herbal prescriptions recommended by physicians and also prescribed drugs on their own authority.

All of these medical practitioners proved unable to deal with the plague. When King Philip VI of France requested the opinion of the medical faculty of the University of Paris on the plague, their advice proved worthless. This failure to understand the Black Death, however, produced a crisis in medieval medicine that resulted in some new approaches to health care.

One result was the rise of surgeons to greater prominence because of their practical knowledge. Surgeons were now recruited by universities, which placed them on an equal level with physicians and introduced a greater emphasis on practical anatomy into the university curriculum. Connected to this was a burgeoning of medical textbooks, often written in the vernacular and stressing practical, how-to approaches to medical and surgical problems.

Finally, as a result of the plague, cities, especially in Italy, gave increased attention to public health and sanitation. Public health laws were instituted, and municipal boards of health came into being. The primary concern of the latter was to prevent plague, but gradually they came to control

Entertainment in the Middle Ages

Medieval people engaged in a variety of activities for entertainment. City dwellers enjoyed feast days and holidays, when minstrels and jugglers amused people with their arts and tricks. Castle life had its courtly feasts, featuring tournaments accompanied by banquets, music, and dancing. Games were popular at all levels of society; castle dwellers played backgammon, checkers, and chess. The illustration at the left, from a fifteenth-century fresco, shows a group of ladies and gentlemen playing cards.

Like children in all ages, medieval children joined with other children in playing a variety of games. A number of writers on children saw play as a basic symbol of childhood itself. In this series of illustrations from medieval manuscripts, we see children engaged in riding hobbyhorses (undoubtedly popular in a society dependent on horses), catching butterflies and playing with a spinning top, and playing a game of blind man's bluff. ❧

almost every aspect of health and sanitation. Boards of public health, consisting of medical practitioners and public officials, were empowered to enforce sanitary conditions, report on and attempt to isolate epidemics by quarantine (rarely successful), and regulate the activities of doctors.

Inventions and New Patterns

Despite its problems, the fourteenth century witnessed a continuation of the technological innovations that had characterized the High Middle Ages.

A Medical Textbook. This illustration is taken from a fourteenth-century surgical textbook that stressed a how-to approach to surgical problems. *Top left,* a surgeon shows how to remove an arrow from a patient; *top right,* how to open a patient's chest; *bottom left,* how to deal with an injury to the intestines; *bottom right,* how to diagnose an abscess.

THE CLOCK   The most extraordinary of these inventions, and one that made a visible impact on European cities, was the clock. The mechanical clock was invented at the end of the thirteenth century but not perfected until the fourteenth. The time-telling clock was actually a by-product of a larger astronomical clock. The best-designed one was constructed by Giovanni di Dondi in the mid-fourteenth century. Dondi's clock contained the signs of the zodiac but also struck on the hour. Since clocks were expensive, they were usually installed only in the towers of churches or municipal buildings. The first clock striking equal hours was in a church in Milan; in 1335, a chronicler described it as "a wonderful clock, with a very large

clapper which strikes a bell twenty-four times according to the twenty-four hours of the day and night and thus at the first hour of the night gives one sound, at the second two strikes ... and so distinguishes one hour from another, which is of greatest use to men of every degree."[23]

Clocks introduced a wholly new conception of time into the lives of Europeans; they revolutionized how people thought about and used time. Throughout most of the Middle Ages, time was determined by natural rhythms (daybreak and nightfall) or church bells that were rung at more or less regular three-hour intervals, corresponding to the ecclesiastical offices of the church. Clocks made it possible to plan one's day and organize one's activities around the regular striking of bells. This brought a new regularity into the lives of workers and merchants, defining urban existence and enabling merchants and bankers to see the value of time in a new way.

EYEGLASSES AND PAPER   Like clocks, eyeglasses were introduced in the thirteenth century but not refined until the fourteenth. Even then they were not particularly effective by modern standards and were still extremely expensive. The high cost of parchment forced people to write in extremely small script; eyeglasses made it more readable. At the same time, a significant change in writing materials occurred in the fourteenth century when parchment was supplemented by much cheaper paper made from cotton rags. Although it was more subject to insect and water damage than parchment, medieval paper was actually superior to modern papers made of high-acid wood pulp.

GUNPOWDER AND CANNONS   Invented earlier by the Chinese, gunpowder also made its appearance in the West in the fourteenth century. The use of gunpowder eventually brought drastic changes to European warfare. Its primary use was in cannons, although early cannons were prone to blow up, making them as dangerous to the people firing them as to the enemy. Even as late as 1460, an attack on a castle using the "Lion," an enormous Flemish cannon, proved disastrous for the Scottish king James II when the "Lion" blew up, killing the king and a number of his retainers. Continued improvement in the construction of cannons, however, soon made them extremely valuable in reducing both castles and city walls. Gunpowder made castles, city walls, and armored knights obsolete.

CHAPTER SUMMARY

In the eleventh, twelfth, and thirteenth centuries, European civilization developed many of its fundamental features. Territorial states, parliaments, capitalist trade and industry, banks, cities, and vernacular literature were all products of that fertile period. During the same time, the Catholic Church under the direction of the papacy reached its apogee.

Fourteenth-century European society, however, was challenged by an overwhelming number of crises that led to the disintegration of medieval civilization. At mid-century, one of the most destructive natural disasters in history erupted—the Black Death, a devastating plague that wiped out at least one-third of the European population, with even higher mortality rates in urban areas. Reactions varied. Some people escaped into alcohol, sex, and crime. Others, such as the flagellants, believing the Black Death to be a punishment from God, attempted to atone for

people's sins through self-inflicted pain. In many areas, the Jews became scapegoats. Economic crises and social upheavals, including a decline in trade and industry, bank failures, and peasant revolts pitting the lower classes against the upper classes, followed in the wake of the Black Death.

Political stability also declined, especially during the Hundred Years' War, a long, drawn-out conflict between the English and the French. Armored knights on horseback formed the backbone of medieval armies, but English peasants using the longbow began to change the face of war. After numerous defeats, the French cause was saved by Joan of Arc,

a young peasant woman whose leadership inspired the French, who also began to rely on cannon and were victorious by 1453.

The Catholic Church, too, experienced a crisis. The confrontation between Pope Boniface VIII and Philip IV of France led to a loss of papal power and the removal of the papacy to Avignon on France's border in 1305. The absence of the popes from Rome created a new crisis, but the return of the papacy to Rome in 1377 only led to new problems with the Great Schism, which witnessed the spectacle of two competing popes condemning each other as the anti-Christ. A new conciliar movement based on the belief that church councils, not popes, should rule the church finally ended the Great Schism in 1417.

All of these crises seemed to overpower Europeans in this calamitous fourteenth century. Not surprisingly, much of the art of the period depicted the Four Horsemen of the Apocalypse described in the New Testament Book of Revelation: Death, Famine, Pestilence, and War. No doubt, to some people, the last days of the world appeared to be at hand. European society, however, proved remarkably resilient. Already in the fourteenth century new ideas and practices were beginning to emerge, as often happens in periods of crisis. As we shall see in the next chapter, the pace of

change began to quicken as Europe experienced a rebirth of Classical culture that some historians have called the Renaissance.

CHAPTER TIMELINE

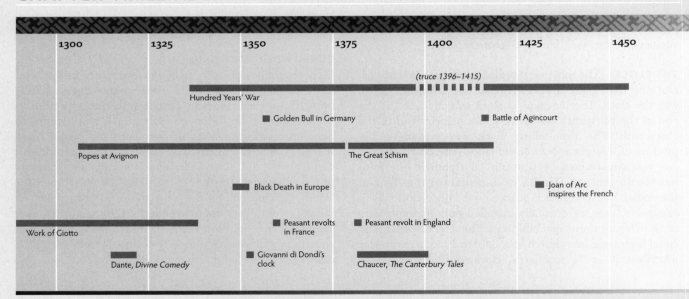

| 1300 | 1325 | 1350 | 1375 | 1400 | 1425 | 1450 |

(truce 1396–1415)

Hundred Years' War

Golden Bull in Germany

Battle of Agincourt

Popes at Avignon

The Great Schism

Black Death in Europe

Joan of Arc inspires the French

Work of Giotto

Peasant revolts in France

Peasant revolt in England

Dante, *Divine Comedy*

Giovanni di Dondi's clock

Chaucer, *The Canterbury Tales*

CHAPTER REVIEW

Upon Reflection

Q What were the chief factors that led to the urban and rural revolts of the fourteenth century?

Q What were the causes of the Hundred Years' War, and what were the results of the war in the fourteenth century for France and England?

Q What impact did the adversities of the fourteenth century have on Christian practices?

Key Terms

Black Death (p. 308)
pogroms (p. 311)
scutage (p. 319)

Third Estate (p. 323)
condottieri (p. 324)
Great Schism (p. 328)
conciliarism (p. 328)
mysticism (p. 329)
Modern Devotion (p. 329)

Suggestions for Further Reading

GENERAL WORKS   For a general introduction to the fourteenth century, see **D. P. Waley** and **P. Denley**, *Later Medieval Europe,* 3rd ed. (London, 2001); **G. Holmes**, *Europe: Hierarchy and Revolt, 1320–1450,* 2nd ed. (New York, 2000); and **J. Aberth**, *From the Brink of the Apocalypse: Confronting Famine, War, Plague, and Death in the Later Middle Ages* (London, 2001).

THE BLACK DEATH   On famine in the early fourteenth century, see **W. C. Jordan**, *The Great Famine: Northern Europe in the Early Fourteenth Century* (Princeton, N.J., 1996). On the Black Death, see **P. Ziegler**, *The Black Death* (New York, 1969); **D. Herlihy**, *The Black Death and the Transformation of the West,* ed. **S. K. Cohn Jr.** (Cambridge, Mass., 1997); and **J. Kelly**, *The Great Mortality* (New York, 2005).

HUNDRED YEARS' WAR   Good accounts of the Hundred Years' War include **A. Curry**, *The Hundred Years' War,* 2nd ed. (New York, 2004), and **R. H. Neillands**, *The Hundred Years' War,* 2nd ed. (New York, 2001). On Joan of Arc, see **M. Warner**, *Joan of Arc: The Image of Female Heroism* (New York, 1981).

POLITICAL HISTORY   On the political history of the period, see **B. Guenée**, *States and Rulers in Later Medieval Europe,* trans. **J. Vale** (Oxford, 1985). On medieval mercenaries, see **W. Urban**, *Medieval Mercenaries* (London, 2006).

CATHOLIC CHURCH   A good general study of the church in the fourteenth century can be found in **F. P. Oakley**, *The Western Church in the Later Middle Ages* (Ithaca, N.Y., 1980). On the role of food in the spiritual practices of medieval women, see **C. W. Bynum**,

Holy Feast and Holy Fast: The Religious Significance of Food to Medieval Women (Berkeley, Calif., 1987). On female mystics in the Later Middle Ages, see **D. Elliott**, *Proving Woman: A Female Spirituality and Inquisitorial Culture in the Later Middle Ages* (Princeton, N.J., 2004). On late medieval religious practices, see **R. N. Swanson**, *Religion and Devotion in Europe, c. 1215–1515* (Cambridge, 1995).

CULTURE   A classic work on the life and thought of the Later Middle Ages is **J. Huizinga**, *The Autumn of the Middle Ages,* trans. **R. J. Payton** and **U. Mammitzsch** (Chicago, 1996). On Dante, see **B. Reynolds**, *Dante: The Poet, the Political Thinker, the Man* (London, 2006). On Chaucer, see **J. Dillon**, *Geoffrey Chaucer* (New York, 1993). The best work on Christine de Pizan is by **C. C. Willard**, *Christine de Pizan: Her Life and Works* (New York, 1984).

SOCIAL HISTORY   A wealth of material on everyday life is provided in the second volume of *A History of Private Life,* edited by **G. Duby**, *Revelations of the Medieval World* (Cambridge, Mass., 1988). On women in the Later Middle Ages, see **S. Shahar**, *The Fourth Estate: A History of Women in the Middle Ages,* trans. **C. Galai**, rev. ed. (London, 2003). On childhood, see **N. Orme**, *Medieval Children* (New Haven, Conn., 2001). The subject of medieval prostitution is examined in **L. L. Otis**, *Prostitution in Medieval Society* (Chicago, 1987). Poor people are discussed in **M. Mollat**, *The Poor in the Middle Ages* (New Haven, Conn., 1986). For a general introduction to the changes in medicine, see **N. G. Siraisi**, *Medieval and Early Renaissance Medicine* (Chicago, 1990). The importance of inventions is discussed in **J. Gimpel**, *The Medieval Machine* (New York, 1976).

Visit the CourseMate website at www.cengagebrain.com for additional study tools and review materials for this chapter.

AP* REVIEW QUESTIONS FOR CHAPTER 11

1. Which of the following is true of the Black Death?

   (A) It originated in southern Europe and was spread by the invasion of the Mongols.
   (B) It was brought to Italy and the rest of Europe by crusaders returning from the Middle East.
   (C) It spread quickly among the peasants, who were more susceptible to diseases because they had already endured drought and famine.
   (D) It traveled from Asia to Genoa by way of merchant sailors, who then came in contact with other merchants on the Italian peninsula.
   (E) It was a plague sent by God to curse Europeans for their disobedience and wickedness.

2. Which of the following contributed to both the English and French peasant revolts?

   (A) growing class tensions between peasants and landlords
   (B) popular desire to end serfdom
   (C) weak rulers and incompetent armies
   (D) popular desire to increase peasant participation in the government
   (E) price inflation due to the expansion of guilds

3. In the Later Middle Ages, France, England and the Holy Roman Empire all experienced each of the following political events EXCEPT

   (A) the nobles of each country wanted more power.
   (B) representative bodies wanted more political control.
   (C) their rulers struggled with the Roman Catholic Church to gain more political influence.
   (D) they became highly centralized states, each run by a powerful monarch.
   (E) rival factions sought control of the state.

4. *Vernacular* refers to

   (A) a tax on salt.
   (B) writing in the language of the people.
   (C) a special gift given by the Catholic Church.
   (D) a new disease that emerged in the 1400s.
   (E) a new fighting technique created by the Mongols.

5. This passage from the text, "Many small villages and hamlets were completely deserted; there was not one house left in them, but all those who had lived in them were dead," is most likely describing

   (A) the aftermath of invasions of Europe by the Ottomans.
   (B) the impact of the Black Death.
   (C) the impact of the Little Ice Age.
   (D) the impact of the Hundred Years' War.
   (E) the impact of the peasant revolts in France.

6. Consequences of the population collapse in Europe in the fourteenth century included all of the following EXCEPT

   (A) peasants revolted against landowners.
   (B) a shortage of labor caused a rise in wages.
   (C) countries such as England passed new legislation to limit wages.
   (D) the population of serfs increased.
   (E) wool industries collapsed and trade declined drastically.

7. The ultimate result of the Hundred Years' War was that

   (A) England lost most of its land holdings in France.
   (B) France experienced a time of political peace and prosperity.
   (C) France created a new political alliance between the church and the state.
   (D) England and France both developed strong military leadership and dominated European affairs.
   (E) rulers no longer regarded war as a means to end political problems.

8. Which of the following is true of the political organization of the Italian states?

   (A) They were centralized under a powerful monarchy.
   (B) They were separated into groups of large, powerful city-states.
   (C) They were ruled by a powerful emperor.
   (D) They banded together as the republic of Italy.
   (E) They were ruled by a shared arrangement of power between Spain and Italy.

9. Which of the following is the most accurate description of life in the fourteenth century?

   (A) It was highly urbanized with a system of direct access to the local marketplace.
   (B) It was partly agrarian with a significant amount of the population living in urban centers.
   (C) It was highly agrarian with very little access to mass communication and social outlets.
   (D) There was significant population growth due to the expansion of the Atlantic Ocean trade and the importation of new goods and crops.
   (E) It was partially urbanized with an organized system of roads to connect the rural and urban populations.

10. The Great Schism of the Roman Catholic Church had all the following consequences EXCEPT

   (A) the common people were confused as to which pope to follow for spiritual guidance.
   (B) political support for the Catholic Church was divided.
   (C) the French gained and held control of the papacy for the next two hundred years.
   (D) the conciliar movement argued that a general council was needed to end the schism and bring reform.
   (E) it highlighted the many abuses of the church.

11. Many attempted to put an end to the Black Death by

   (A) stopping all trade with the east and looking to the west for trade.
   (B) conducting scientific studies to find medical cures for the illness.
   (C) sending envoys to the east and holding meetings with ambassadors to determine a solution.
   (D) becoming highly religious, often practicing flogging to beg for God's forgiveness.
   (E) creating new sewer systems and improving the hygiene of the common people.

12. Which of the following was NOT an underlying cause of the Hundred Years' War?

   (A) English control of lands within France
   (B) dispute over the line of succession to the French throne
   (C) Joan of Arc's leadership of the French forces
   (D) the strong personalities of King Edward and King Philip
   (E) economic disputes over the wool industries

13. Pope Boniface VIII's issuing of the bull *Unam Sanctam*

   (A) put him directly at odds with the king of England.
   (B) allowed the church to increase its authority over economic affairs.
   (C) put Europe on a path to allow more religious freedoms.
   (D) eliminated religious conflict within Europe.
   (E) placed the church in direct opposition to the secular state.

14. Which of the following authors is not correctly matched to his or her famous work?

   (A) Christine de Pizan—*The Book of the City of Ladies*
   (B) Geoffrey Chaucer—*The Canterbury Tales*
   (C) Giovanni Boccaccio—*The Decameron*
   (D) Francesco Petrarch—*Purgatory*
   (E) Dante Alighieri—*Divine Comedy*

15. The establishment of the papacy in Avignon led to

   (A) a marked increase in piety and religiosity across Europe.
   (B) French domination of the papacy and ultimately the Great Schism.
   (C) a decentralized papal bureaucracy.
   (D) widespread demonstrations of support by Catholics, especially in Italy and Spain.
   (E) greater control by the church over the state, highlighting the power of the pope.

CHAPTER 12

Sistine Chapel, Vatican Palace//© Erich Lessing/ Art Resource, NY

Michelangelo's Creation of Adam *on the Sistine Chapel ceiling*

Recovery and Rebirth: The Age of the Renaissance

CHAPTER OUTLINE AND FOCUS QUESTIONS

Meaning and Characteristics of the Italian Renaissance

Q What characteristics distinguish the Renaissance from the Middle Ages?

The Making of Renaissance Society

Q What major social changes occurred during the Renaissance?

The Italian States in the Renaissance

Q How did Machiavelli's works reflect the political realities of Renaissance Italy?

The Intellectual Renaissance in Italy

Q What was humanism, and what effect did it have on philosophy, education, attitudes toward politics, and the writing of history?

The Artistic Renaissance

Q What were the chief characteristics of Renaissance art, and how did it differ in Italy and northern Europe?

The European State in the Renaissance

Q Why do historians sometimes refer to the monarchies of the late fifteenth century as "new monarchies" or "Renaissance states"?

The Church in the Renaissance

Q What were the policies of the Renaissance popes, and what impact did those policies have on the Catholic Church?

┌─ CRITICAL THINKING ─────────────────
│ **Q** How did Renaissance art and the humanist
│ movement reflect the political, economic, and
│ social developments of the period?
└──────────────────────────────────────

WERE THE FOURTEENTH and fifteenth centuries a continuation of the Middle Ages or the beginning of a new era? Both positions can be defended. Although the disintegrative patterns of the fourteenth century continued into the fifteenth, at the same time there were elements of recovery that made the fifteenth century a period of significant political, economic, artistic, and intellectual change. The humanists or intellectuals of the age called their period (from the mid-fourteenth to the mid-sixteenth century) an age of rebirth, believing that they had restored arts and letters to new glory after they had been "neglected" or "dead" for centuries. The humanists also saw their age as one of accomplished individuals who dominated the landscape of their time. Michelangelo, the great Italian artist of the early sixteenth century, and Pope Julius II, the "warrior pope," were two such titans. The artist's temperament and the pope's temper led to many lengthy and often loud quarrels between the two. The pope had hired Michelangelo to paint the ceiling of the Sistine Chapel in Rome, a difficult task for a man long accustomed to being a sculptor. Michelangelo undertook the project but refused for a long time to allow anyone, including the pope, to see his work. Julius grew anxious, pestering Michelangelo on a regular basis about when the ceiling would be finished.

Exasperated by the pope's requests, Michelangelo once replied, according to Giorgio Vasari, his contemporary biographer, that the ceiling would be completed "when it satisfies me as an artist." The pope responded, "And we want you to satisfy us and finish it soon," and then threatened that if Michelangelo did not "finish the ceiling quickly," the pope would "have him thrown down from the scaffolding." Fearing the pope's anger, Michelangelo "lost no time in doing all that was wanted" and quickly completed the ceiling, one of the great masterpieces in the history of Western art.

The humanists' view of their age as a rebirth of the Classical civilization of the Greeks and Romans ultimately led historians to use the French word *Renaissance* to identify this age. Although recent historians have emphasized the many elements of continuity between the Middle Ages and the Renaissance, the latter age was also distinguished by its own unique characteristics.

Meaning and Characteristics of the Italian Renaissance

 FOCUS QUESTION: What characteristics distinguish the Renaissance from the Middle Ages?

Renaissance means "rebirth." Many people who lived in Italy between 1350 and 1550 believed that they had witnessed a rebirth of antiquity or Greco-Roman civilization, marking a new age. To them, the thousand or so years between the end of the Roman Empire and their own era constituted a middle period (the "Middle Ages"), characterized by darkness because of its lack of Classical culture. Historians of the nineteenth century later used similar terminology to describe this period in Italy. The Swiss historian and art critic Jacob Burckhardt (YAK-ub BOORK-hart) created the modern concept of the **Renaissance** in his celebrated book *The Civilization of the Renaissance in Italy,* published in 1860. He portrayed Italy in the fourteenth and fifteenth centuries as the birthplace of the modern world (the Italians were "the firstborn among the sons of modern Europe") and saw the revival of antiquity, the "perfecting of the individual," and secularism ("worldliness of the Italians") as its distinguishing features. Burckhardt exaggerated the individuality and secularism of the Renaissance and failed to recognize the depths of its religious sentiment; nevertheless, he established the framework for all modern interpretations of the period. Although contemporary scholars do not believe that the Renaissance represents a sudden or dramatic cultural break with the Middle Ages, as Burckhardt argued—there was, after all, much continuity in economic, political, and social life—the Renaissance can still be viewed as a distinct period of European history that manifested itself first in Italy and then spread to the rest of Europe.

Renaissance Italy was largely an urban society. As a result of its commercial preeminence and political evolution, northern Italy by the mid-fourteenth century was mostly a land of independent cities that dominated the country districts around them. These city-states became the centers of Italian political, economic, and social life. Within this new urban society, a secular spirit emerged as increasing wealth created new possibilities for the enjoyment of worldly things (see the box on p. 342).

Above all, the Renaissance was an age of recovery from the calamitous fourteenth century, a time for the slow process of recuperating from the effects of the Black Death, political disorder, and economic recession. This recovery was accompanied by a rediscovery of the culture of Classical antiquity. Increasingly aware of their own historical past, Italian intellectuals became intensely interested in the Greco-Roman culture of the ancient Mediterranean world. This revival of Classical antiquity (the Middle Ages had in fact preserved much of ancient Latin culture) affected activities as diverse as politics and art and led to new attempts to reconcile the pagan philosophy of the Greco-Roman world with Christian thought, as well as new ways of viewing human beings.

A revived emphasis on individual ability became a characteristic of the Italian Renaissance. As the fifteenth-century Florentine architect Leon Battista Alberti (al-BAYR-tee) expressed it, "Men can do all things if they will."[1] A high regard for human dignity and worth and a realization of individual potentiality created a new social ideal of the well-rounded personality or universal person—*l'uomo universale* (LWOH-moh OO-nee-ver-SAH-lay)—who was capable of achievements in many areas of life.

These general features of the Italian Renaissance were not characteristic of all Italians but were primarily the preserve of the wealthy upper classes, who constituted a small percentage of the total population. The achievements of the Italian Renaissance were the product of an elite, rather than a mass, movement. Nevertheless, indirectly it did have some impact on ordinary people, especially in the cities, where so many of the intellectual and artistic accomplishments of the period were most visible.

The Making of Renaissance Society

 FOCUS QUESTION: What major social changes occurred during the Renaissance?

After the severe economic reversals and social upheavals of the fourteenth century, the European economy gradually recovered as the volume of manufacturing and trade increased.

Economic Recovery

By the fourteenth century, Italian merchants were carrying on a flourishing commerce throughout the Mediterranean and had also expanded their lines of trade north along the Atlantic seaboard. The great galleys of the Venetian Flanders Fleet maintained a direct sea route

A Renaissance Banquet

As in Greek and Roman society, a banquet during the Renaissance was an occasion for good food, interesting conversation, music, and dancing. In Renaissance society, it was also a symbol of status and an opportunity to impress people with the power and wealth of one's family. Banquets were held to celebrate public and religious festivals, official visits, anniversaries, and weddings. The following menu lists the foods served at a grand banquet given by Pope Pius V in the sixteenth century.

⊷ ✠ ⊷

A Sixteenth-Century Banquet

First Course
Cold Delicacies from the Sideboard

Pieces of marzipan and marzipan balls
Neapolitan spice cakes
Malaga wine and Pisan biscuits
Fresh grapes
Prosciutto cooked in wine, served with capers
and grape pulp
Salted pork tongues cooked in wine, sliced
Spit-roasted songbirds, cold, with
their tongues sliced over them
Sweet mustard

Second Course
Cold Hot Foods from the Kitchen, Roasts

Fried veal sweetbreads and liver
Spit-roasted skylarks with lemon sauce
Spit-roasted quails with sliced eggplants
Stuffed spit-roasted pigeons with capers
sprinkled over them
Spit-roasted rabbits, with sauce and crushed pine nuts
Partridges larded and spit-roasted, served with lemon
Heavily seasoned poultry with lemon slices
Slices of veal, spit-roasted, with a sauce made
from the juices
Leg of goat, spit-roasted, with a sauce made
from the juices
Soup of almond paste, with the flesh of three
pigeons to each serving

Third Course
Hot Foods from the Kitchen, Boiled Meats and Stews

Stuffed fat geese, boiled Lombard style and covered
with sliced almonds
Stuffed breast of veal, boiled, garnished with flowers
Very young calf, boiled, garnished with parsley
Almonds in garlic sauce
Turkish-style rice with milk, sprinkled with cinnamon
Stewed pigeons with mortadella sausage and
whole onions
Cabbage soup with sausages
Poultry pie, two chickens to each pie
Fricasseed breast of goat dressed with fried onions
Pies filled with custard cream
Boiled calves' feet with cheese and egg

Fourth Course
Delicacies from the Sideboard

Bean tarts
Quince pastries
Pear tarts, the pears wrapped in marzipan
Parmesan cheese and Riviera cheese
Fresh almonds on vine leaves
Chestnuts roasted over the coals and served with
salt and pepper
Milk curds
Ring-shaped cakes
Wafers made from ground grain ⊱

Q What kinds of people would be present at a banquet where these foods would be served? What does this menu tell you about the material culture of the Renaissance and the association of food with social status?

from Venice to England and the Netherlands, where Italian merchants came into contact with the increasingly powerful Hanseatic League of merchants. Hard hit by the plague, the Italians lost their commercial preeminence while the Hanseatic League continued to prosper.

EXPANSION OF TRADE As early as the thirteenth century, a number of North German coastal towns had formed a commercial and military association known as the Hansa, or Hanseatic League. By 1500, more than eighty cities belonged to the League, which had established settlements and commercial bases in many cities in England and northern Europe, including the chief towns of Denmark, Norway, and Sweden. For almost two hundred years, the Hansa had a monopoly on northern European trade in timber, fish, grain, metals, honey, and wines. Its southern outlet in Flanders, the port city of Bruges, became the economic crossroads of Europe in the

Lübeck and the Hanseatic League. The Hanseatic League or Hansa was an economic and military alliance of northern European trading cities that established a monopoly on trade from the Baltic to the North Sea. The city of Lübeck in northern Germany played a major role in the founding of the Hanseatic League and became known as the "Queen of the Hansa." This colored woodcut by Michael Wohlgemut in Hartmann Schedel's *Chronicle of the World* presents a panoramic view of this prosperous German city.

fourteenth century, serving as the meeting place between Hanseatic merchants and the Flanders Fleet of Venice. In the fifteenth century, however, silting of the port caused Bruges to enter a slow decline. So did the Hanseatic League, which was increasingly unable to compete with the developing larger territorial states.

Overall, trade recovered dramatically from the economic contraction of the fourteenth century. The Italians and especially the Venetians, despite new restrictive pressures on their eastern Mediterranean trade from the Ottoman Turks (see "The Ottoman Turks and the End of the Byzantine Empire" later in this chapter), continued to maintain a wealthy commercial empire. Not until the sixteenth century, when transatlantic discoveries gave new importance to the states along the ocean, did the petty Italian city-states begin to suffer from the competitive advantages of the ever-growing and more powerful national territorial states.

INDUSTRIES OLD AND NEW The economic depression of the fourteenth century also affected patterns of manufacturing. The woolen industries of Flanders and the northern Italian cities had been particularly devastated. By the beginning of the fifteenth century, however, the Florentine woolen industry had begun to recover. At the same time, the Italian cities began to develop and expand luxury industries, especially silk, glassware, and hand-worked items in metal and precious stones.

Other new industries, especially printing, mining, and metallurgy, began to rival the textile industry in importance in the fifteenth century. New machinery and techniques for digging deeper mines and for separating metals from ore and purifying them were developed. When rulers began to transfer their titles to underground minerals to

financiers as collateral for loans, these **entrepreneurs** quickly developed large mining operations to produce copper, iron, and silver. Especially valuable were the rich mineral deposits in central Europe, Hungary, the Tyrol, Bohemia, and Saxony. Expanding iron production and new skills in metalworking in turn contributed to the development of firearms that were more effective than the crude weapons of the fourteenth century.

BANKING AND THE MEDICI The city of Florence regained its preeminence in banking in the fifteenth century, due primarily to the Medici family. The Medici had expanded from cloth production into commerce, real estate, and banking. In its best days (in the fifteenth century), the House of Medici was the greatest bank in Europe, with branches in Venice, Milan, Rome, Avignon, Bruges, London, and Lyons. Moreover, the family had controlling interests in industrial enterprises for wool, silk, and the mining of alum, used in the dyeing of textiles. Except for a brief period, the Medici were also the principal bankers for the papacy, a position that produced big profits and influence at the papal court. Despite its great success in the early and middle part of the fifteenth century, the Medici bank suffered a rather sudden decline at the end of the century due to poor leadership and a series of bad loans, especially uncollectible loans to rulers. In 1494, when the French expelled the Medici from Florence and confiscated their property, the Medici financial edifice collapsed.

Social Changes in the Renaissance

The Renaissance inherited its social structure from the Middle Ages. Society remained fundamentally divided into three **estates:** the First Estate, the clergy, whose preeminence was grounded in the belief that people should be guided to spiritual ends; the Second Estate, the nobility, whose privileges were based on the principle that the nobles provided security and justice for society; and the Third Estate, which consisted of the peasants and inhabitants of the towns and cities. This social order experienced certain adaptations in the Renaissance, which we can see by examining the Second and Third Estates (the clergy will be examined in Chapter 13).

THE NOBILITY   Throughout much of Europe, the landholding nobles faced declining real incomes during the greater part of the fourteenth and fifteenth centuries, while the expense of maintaining noble status was rising. Nevertheless, members of the old nobility survived, and new blood infused their ranks. A reconstruction of the aristocracy was well under way by 1500.

As a result, the nobles, old and new, who constituted between 2 and 3 percent of the population in most countries, managed to dominate society as they had done in the Middle Ages, serving as military officers and holding important political posts as well as advising the king. In the sixteenth century, members of the aristocracy increasingly pursued education as the means to maintain their role in government.

By 1500, certain ideals came to be expected of the aristocrat. These were best expressed in *The Book of the Courtier* by the Italian Baldassare Castiglione (bal-duh-SAH-ray ka-steel-YOH-nay) (1478–1529). First published in 1528, Castiglione's work soon became popular throughout Europe and remained a fundamental handbook for European aristocrats for centuries. In it, Castiglione described the three basic attributes of the perfect courtier. First, nobles should possess fundamental native endowments, such as impeccable character, grace, talents, and noble birth. The perfect courtier must also cultivate certain achievements. Primarily, he should participate in military and bodily exercises, because the principal profession of a courtier was bearing arms. But unlike the medieval knight, who had been required only to have military skill, the Renaissance courtier was also expected to have a Classical education and to adorn his life with the arts by playing a musical instrument, drawing, and painting. In Castiglione's hands, the Renaissance ideal of the well-developed personality became a social ideal of the aristocracy. Finally, the aristocrat was expected to follow a certain standard of conduct. Nobles were to make a good impression; while being modest, they should not hide their accomplishments but show them with grace.

What was the purpose of these courtly standards? Castiglione wrote:

> I think that the aim of the perfect Courtier, which we have not spoken of up to now, is so to win for himself, by means of the accomplishments ascribed to him by these gentlemen, the favor and mind of the prince whom he serves that he may be

able to tell him, and always will tell him, the truth about everything he needs to know, without fear or risk of displeasing him; and that when he sees the mind of his prince inclined to a wrong action, he may dare to oppose him . . . so as to dissuade him of every evil intent and bring him to the path of virtue.[2]

The aim of the perfect noble, then, was to serve his prince in an effective and honest way. Nobles would adhere to these principles for hundreds of years while they continued to dominate European life socially and politically.

PEASANTS AND TOWNSPEOPLE   Peasants made up the overwhelming mass of the Third Estate and continued to constitute 85 to 90 percent of the European population, except in the highly urbanized areas of northern Italy and Flanders. The most noticeable trend produced by the economic crisis of the fourteenth century was the decline of the manorial system and the continuing elimination of serfdom. This process had already begun in the twelfth century when the introduction of a money economy made possible the conversion of servile labor dues into rents paid in money, although they also continued to be paid in kind or labor. The contraction of the peasantry after the Black Death simply accelerated this process, since lords found it convenient to deal with the peasants by granting freedom and accepting rents. The lords' lands were then tilled by hired workers or rented out. By the end of the fifteenth century, serfdom was declining in western Europe, and more and more peasants were becoming legally free.

The remainder of the Third Estate centered around the inhabitants of towns and cities, originally the merchants and artisans who formed the bourgeoisie. The Renaissance town or city of the fifteenth century actually was home to a multitude of townspeople widely separated socially and economically.

At the top of urban society were the patricians, whose wealth from capitalistic enterprises in trade, industry, and banking enabled them to dominate their urban communities economically, socially, and politically. Below them were the petty burghers—the shopkeepers, artisans, guildmasters, and guild members, who were largely concerned with providing goods and services for local consumption. Below these two groups were the propertyless workers earning pitiful wages and the unemployed, living squalid and miserable lives; these people constituted 30 to 40 percent of the population living in cities. In many places in Europe in the late fourteenth and fifteenth centuries, urban poverty increased dramatically. One rich merchant of Florence wrote:

> Those that are lazy and indolent in a way that does harm to the city, and who can offer no just reason for their condition, should either be forced to work or expelled from the Commune. The city would thus rid itself of that most harmful part of the poorest class. . . . If the lowest order of society earn enough food to keep them going from day to day, then they have enough.[3]

But even this large group was not at the bottom of the social scale; beneath them were the slaves, especially in the Italian cities.

SLAVERY IN THE RENAISSANCE Agricultural slavery existed in the Early Middle Ages but had declined for economic reasons and been replaced by serfdom by the ninth century. Although some domestic slaves remained, slavery in European society had largely disappeared by the eleventh century. It reappeared first in Spain, where both Christians and Muslims used captured prisoners as slaves during the lengthy *Reconquista*. In the second half of the fourteenth century, the shortage of workers after the Black Death led Italians to introduce slavery on a fairly large scale. In 1363, for example, the government of Florence authorized the unlimited importation of foreign slaves.

In the Italian cities, slaves were used as skilled workers, making handcrafted goods for their masters, or as household workers. Girls served as nursemaids and boys as playmates. Fiammetta Adimari wrote to her husband in 1469: "I must remind you that when Alfonso is weaned we ought to get a little slave-girl to look after him, or else one of the black boys to keep him company."[4] Most slaves, though, were females, many of them young girls. In Florence, wealthy merchants might own two or three slaves. Often men of the household took slaves as concubines, which sometimes led to the birth of illegitimate children. In 1392, the wealthy merchant Francesco Datini fathered an illegitimate daughter by Lucia, his twenty-year-old slave. His wife, Margherita, who was unable to bear any children, reluctantly agreed to raise the girl as their own daughter. Many illegitimate children were not as fortunate.

Slaves for the Italian market were obtained primarily from the eastern Mediterranean and the Black Sea region and included Tartars, Russians, Albanians, and Dalmatians. There were also slaves from Africa, either Moors or Ethiopians, and Muslims from Spain. Because of the lucrative nature of the slave trade, Italian merchants became involved in the transportation of slaves. Between 1414 and 1423, ten thousand slaves were sold on the Venetian market.

By the end of the fifteenth century, slavery had declined dramatically in the Italian cities. Many slaves had been freed by their owners for humanitarian reasons, and the major source of slaves dried up as the Black Sea slave markets were closed to Italian traders after the Turks conquered the Byzantine Empire. Although some other sources remained, prices rose dramatically, further cutting demand. Moreover, a general feeling had arisen that slaves—the "domestic enemy," as they were called—were dangerous and not worth the effort. By the sixteenth century, slaves were in evidence only at princely courts, where they were kept as curiosities; this was especially true of black slaves.

In the fifteenth century, the Portuguese had imported increasing numbers of African slaves for southern European markets. It has been estimated that between 1444 and 1505, some 140,000 slaves were shipped from Africa. The presence of blacks in European society was not entirely new. Saint Maurice, a Christian martyr of the fourth century, was portrayed by medieval artists as a black knight and became the center of a popular cult in the twelfth and thirteenth centuries. The number of blacks in Europe was small, however, until their importation as slaves.

The Family in Renaissance Italy

The family played an important role in Renaissance Italy. Family meant, first of all, the extended household of parents, children, and servants (if the family was wealthy) and could also include grandparents, widowed mothers, and even unmarried sisters. Families that were related and bore the same surname often lived near each other and might dominate an entire urban district. Old family names— Strozzi (STRAWT-see), Rucellai (roo-CHELL-eye), Medici— conferred great status and prestige. The family bond was a source of great security in a dangerous and violent world, and its importance helps explain the vendetta in the Italian Renaissance. A crime committed by one family member fell on the entire family, ensuring that retaliation by the offended family would be a bloody affair involving large numbers of people.

MARRIAGE To maintain the family, parents gave careful attention to arranging marriages, often to strengthen business or family ties. Details were worked out well in advance, sometimes when children were only two or three years old, and reinforced by a legally binding marriage contract (see the box on p. 347). The important aspect of the contract was the size of the dowry, money presented by the wife's family to the husband upon marriage. The dowry could involve large sums and was expected of all families. The size of the dowry was an indication of whether the bride was moving upward or downward in society. With a large dowry, a daughter could marry a man of higher social status, thereby enabling her family to move up in society; if the daughter married a man of lower social status, however, her dowry would be smaller because the reputation of her family would raise the status of her husband's family.

The father-husband was the center of the Italian family. He gave it his name, was responsible for it in all legal matters, managed all finances (his wife had no share in his wealth), and made the crucial decisions that determined his children's lives. A father's authority over his children was absolute until he died or formally freed his children. In Renaissance Italy, children did not become adults on reaching a certain age; adulthood came only when the father went before a judge and formally emancipated them. The age of emancipation varied from early teens to late twenties.

CHILDREN The wife managed the household, a position that gave women a certain degree of autonomy in their

Wedding Banquet. Parents arranged marriages in Renaissance Italy to strengthen business or family ties. A legally binding marriage contract was a necessary part of the marital arrangements. So was a wedding feast. This painting by Botticelli shows the wedding banquet in Florence that celebrated the marriage of Nastagio degli Onesti and the daughter of Paulo Traversaro.

daily lives. Women of the upper and middle classes, however, were expected to remain at home, under the supervision of their father or husband. Moreover, most wives knew that their primary function was to bear children. Upper-class wives were frequently pregnant; Alessandra Strozzi of Florence, for example, who had been married at the age of sixteen, bore eight children in ten years. Poor women did not conceive at the same rate because they nursed their own babies. Wealthy women gave their infants out to wet nurses, which enabled them to become pregnant more quickly after the birth of a child.

For women in the Renaissance, childbirth was a fearful occasion. Not only was it painful, but it could be deadly; as many as 10 percent of mothers died in childbirth. In his memoirs, the Florentine merchant Gregorio Dati recalled that three of his four wives had died in childbirth. His third wife, after bearing eleven children in fifteen years, "died in childbirth after lengthy suffering, which she bore with remarkable strength and patience."[5] Nor did the tragedies end with childbirth. Surviving mothers often faced the death of their children. In Florence in the fifteenth century, for example, almost 50 percent of the children born to merchant families died before the age of twenty. Given these mortality rates, many upper-class families sought to have as many children as possible to ensure that there would be a surviving male heir to the family fortune. This concern is evident in the Florentine humanist Leon

Battista Alberti's treatise *On the Family,* where one of the characters remarks, "How many families do we see today in decadence and ruin! . . . Of all these families not only the magnificence and greatness but the very men, not only the men but the very names are shrunk away and gone. Their memory . . . is wiped out and obliterated."[6]

SEXUAL NORMS Considering that marriages were arranged, marital relationships ran the gamut from deep emotional attachments to purely formal ties. The lack of emotional attachment in arranged marriages did encourage extramarital relationships, especially among groups whose lifestyle offered special temptations. Although sexual license for males was the norm for princes and their courts, women were supposed to follow different guidelines. The first wife of Duke Filippo Maria Visconti of Milan had an affair with the court musician and was executed for it.

The great age difference between husbands and wives in Italian Renaissance marriage patterns also encouraged the tendency to seek sexual outlets outside marriage. In Florence in 1427–1428, the average difference was thirteen years. Though females married between the ages of sixteen and eighteen, factors of environment, wealth, and demographic trends favored relatively late ages for the first marriages of males, who were usually in their thirties or even early forties. The existence of large numbers of young, unmarried males encouraged extramarital sex as well as prostitution. Prostitution was viewed as a necessary

Marriage Negotiations

Marriages were so important in maintaining families in Renaissance Italy that much energy was put into arranging them. Parents made the choices for their children, most often for considerations that had little to do with the modern notion of love. This selection is taken from the letters of a Florentine matron of the illustrious Strozzi family to her son Filippo in Naples. The family's considerations were complicated by the fact that the son was in exile.

Alessandra Strozzi to Her Son Filippo in Naples

[April 20, 1464] . . . Concerning the matter of a wife [for you], it appears to me that if Francesco di Messer Tanagli wishes to give his daughter, that it would be a fine marriage. . . . Now I will speak with Marco [Parenti, Alessandra's son-in-law], to see if there are other prospects that would be better, and if there are none, then we will learn if he wishes to give her [in marriage]. . . . Francesco Tanagli has a good reputation, and he has held office, not the highest, but still he has been in office. You may ask: "Why should he give her to someone in exile?" There are three reasons. First, there aren't many young men of good family who have both virtue and property. Second, she has only a small dowry, 1,000 florins, which is the dowry of an artisan [although not a small sum, either—senior officials in the government bureaucracy earned 300 florins a year]. . . . Third, I believe that he will give her away, because he has a large family and he will need help to settle them. . . .

[July 26, 1465] . . . Francesco is a good friend of Marco and he trusts him. On S. Jacopo's day, he spoke to him discreetly and persuasively, saying that for several months he had heard that we were interested in the girl and . . . that when we had made up our minds, she will come to us willingly. [He said that] you were a

worthy man, and that his family had always made good marriages, but that he had only a small dowry to give her, and so he would prefer to send her out of Florence to someone of worth, rather than to give her to someone here, from among those who were available, with little money. . . . We have information that she is affable and competent. She is responsible for a large family (there are twelve children, six boys and six girls), and the mother is always pregnant and isn't very competent. . . .

[August 31, 1465] . . . I have recently received some very favorable information [about the Tanagli girl] from two individuals. . . . They are in agreement that whoever gets her will be content. . . . Concerning her beauty, they told me what I had already seen, that she is attractive and well-proportioned. Her face is long, but I couldn't look directly into her face, since she appeared to be aware that I was examining her . . . and so she turned away from me like the wind. . . . She reads quite well . . . and she can dance and sing. . . .

So yesterday I sent for Marco and told him what I had learned. And we talked about the matter for a while, and decided that he should say something to the father and give him a little hope, but not so much that we couldn't withdraw, and find out from him the amount of the dowry. . . . May God help us to choose what will contribute to our tranquility and to the consolation of us all.

[September 13, 1465] . . . Marco came to me and said that he had met with Francesco Tanagli, who had spoken very coldly, so that I understand that he had changed his mind. . . .

[Filippo Strozzi eventually married Fiametta di Donato Adimari in 1466.]

 Q What were the most important considerations in marriage negotiations? Why were they so important?

---

vice; since it could not be eliminated, it should be regulated. In Florence in 1415, the city fathers established communal brothels:

> Desiring to eliminate a worse evil by means of a lesser one, the lord priors . . . have decreed that the priors . . . may authorize the establishment of two public brothels in the city of Florence, in addition to the one which already exists. . . . [They are to be located] in suitable places or in places where the exercise of such scandalous activity can best be concealed, for the honor of the city and of those who live in the neighborhood in which these prostitutes must stay to hire their bodies for lucre.[7]

A prostitute in Florence was required to wear a traditional garb of "gloves on her hands and a bell on her head."

The Italian States in the Renaissance

Q **Focus Question:** How did Machiavelli's works reflect the political realities of Renaissance Italy?

By the fifteenth century, five major powers dominated the Italian peninsula: Milan, Venice, Florence, the Papal States, and Naples (see Map 12.1).

The Five Major States

Northern Italy was divided between the duchy of Milan and the republic of Venice. After the death of the last Visconti ruler of Milan in 1447, Francesco Sforza (frahn-CHESS-koh SFORT-sah), one of the leading *condottieri* of

MAP 12.1 Renaissance Italy. Italy in the late fourteenth century was a land of five major states and numerous independent city-states. Increased prosperity and a supportive intellectual climate helped create the atmosphere for the middle and upper classes to "rediscover" Greco-Roman culture. Modern diplomacy was also a product of Renaissance Italy.

Q *Could the presence of several other powers within easy marching distance make it more likely that a ruler would recognize the importance of diplomacy?*

the time (see Chapter 11), turned on his Milanese employers, conquered the city, and became its new duke. Both the Visconti and the Sforza rulers worked to create a highly centralized territorial state. They were especially successful in devising systems of taxation that generated enormous revenues for the government. The maritime republic of Venice remained an extremely stable political entity governed by a small oligarchy of merchant-aristocrats. Its commercial empire brought in enormous revenues and gave it the status of an international power. At the end of the fourteenth century, Venice embarked on the conquest of a territorial state in northern Italy to protect its food supply and its overland trade routes. Although expansion on the mainland made sense to the Venetians, it frightened Milan and Florence, which worked to curb what they perceived as the expansionary designs of the Venetians.

REPUBLIC OF FLORENCE The republic of Florence dominated the region of Tuscany. By the beginning of the fifteenth century, Florence was governed by a small merchant oligarchy that manipulated the apparently republican government. In 1434, Cosimo de' Medici took control of this oligarchy. Although the wealthy Medici family maintained republican forms of government for appearances' sake, it ran the government from behind the scenes. Through lavish patronage and careful courting of political allies, Cosimo (1434–1464), and later his grandson Lorenzo the Magnificent (1469–1492), were successful in dominating the city at a time when Florence was the center of the cultural Renaissance.

PAPAL STATES The Papal States lay in central Italy. Although these lands were nominally under the political control of the popes, papal residence in Avignon and the Great Schism had enabled individual cities and territories, such as Urbino, Bologna (buh-LOHN-yuh), and Ferrara, to become independent of papal authority. The Renaissance popes of the fifteenth century directed much of their energy toward reestablishing their control over the Papal States (see "The Renaissance Papacy" later in this chapter).

KINGDOM OF NAPLES The kingdom of Naples, which encompassed most of southern Italy and usually the island of Sicily, was fought over by the French and the Aragonese until the latter established their domination in the mid-fifteenth century. Throughout the Renaissance, the kingdom of Naples remained a backward monarchy with a population consisting largely of poverty-stricken peasants dominated by unruly nobles. It shared little in the cultural glories of the Renaissance.

Independent City-States

Besides the five major states, there were a number of independent city-states under the control of powerful

Piero della Francesca, *Duke and Duchess of Urbino.* Federigo da Montefeltro and his wife, Battista Sforza, ruled the small central Italian principality of Urbino. These profile portraits by Piero della Francesca gave a realistic rendering of the two figures. Visible in the background are the hills and valleys of Urbino.

ruling families that became brilliant centers of Renaissance culture in the fifteenth century. These included Mantua, under the enlightened rule of the Gonzaga (gun-DZAH-gah) lords; Ferrara, governed by the flamboyant d'Este (DESS-tay) family; and perhaps the most famous, Urbino, ruled by the Montefeltro dynasty.

URBINO Federigo da Montefeltro (fay-day-REE-goh dah mahn-tuh-FELL-troh), who ruled Urbino from 1444 to 1482, received a Classical education typical of the famous humanist school in Mantua run by Vittorino da Feltre (vee-tor-EE-noh dah FELL-tray) (1378–1446). He also learned the skills of fighting, since the Montefeltro family compensated for the poverty of Urbino by hiring themselves out as *condottieri*. Federigo was not only a good ruler but also a rather unusual *condottiere* by fifteenth-century standards. Although not a brilliant general, he was reliable and honest. He did not break his promises, even when urged to do so by a papal legate. At the same time, Duke Federigo was one of the greatest patrons of Renaissance culture. Under his direction, Urbino became a well-known cultural and intellectual center. Though a despot, Federigo was also benevolent. It was said of him that he could walk safely through the streets of Urbino unaccompanied by a bodyguard, a feat few Renaissance rulers dared to emulate.

THE ROLE OF WOMEN A noticeable feature of these smaller Renaissance courts was the important role played by women. Battista Sforza, niece of the ruler of Milan, was the wife of Federigo da Montefeltro. The duke called his wife "the delight of both my public and my private hours." An intelligent woman, she was well versed in both Greek and Latin and did much to foster art and letters in Urbino. As a prominent *condottiere,* Federigo was frequently absent, and like the wives of medieval lords, Battista Sforza was respected for governing the state "with firmness and good sense."

Perhaps the most famous of the Renaissance ruling women was Isabella d'Este (1474–1539), daughter of the duke of Ferrara, who married Francesco Gonzaga, marquis of Mantua. Their court was another important center of art and learning in the Renaissance. Educated at the brilliant court of Ferrara, Isabella was known for her intelligence and political wisdom. Called the "first lady of the world," she attracted artists and intellectuals to the Mantuan court and was responsible for amassing one of the finest libraries in all of Italy. Her numerous letters to friends, family, princes, and artists all over Europe reveal her political acumen as well as her good sense of humor (see the box on p. 350). Both before and after the death of her husband, she effectively ruled Mantua and won a reputation as a clever negotiator.

Warfare in Italy

The fragmented world of the Italian territorial states gave rise to a political practice that was later used on a larger scale by competing European states. This was the concept of a balance of power, designed to prevent the aggrandizement of any one state at the expense of the others. This system was especially evident after 1454 when the Italian states signed the Peace of Lodi, which ended almost a half-century of war and inaugurated a relatively peaceful forty-year era in Italy. An alliance system (Milan, Florence, and Naples versus Venice and the papacy) was then created that led to a workable balance of power within Italy. It failed, however, to establish lasting cooperation among the major powers or a common foreign policy.

The growth of powerful monarchical states (see "The European State in the Renaissance" later in this chapter) led to trouble for the Italians. Italy soon became a battlefield for the great power struggle between the French and Spanish monarchies. Italian wealth and splendor would probably have been inviting to its northern neighbors under any circumstances, but it was actually the

The Letters of Isabella d'Este

Many Italian and European rulers at the beginning of the sixteenth century regarded Isabella d'Este as an important political figure. These excerpts from her letters reveal Isabella's political skills and her fierce determination. After her husband was taken prisoner by the Venetians in 1509, she refused to accept the condition for his release—namely, that her son Federico be kept as a hostage by the Venetians or the Holy Roman Emperor. She wrote to both the emperor and her husband, refusing to do as they asked.

Letter of Isabella d'Este to the Imperial Envoy

As to the demand for our dearest first-born son Federico, besides being a cruel and almost inhuman thing for any one who knows the meaning of a mother's love, there are many reasons which render it difficult and impossible. Although we are quite sure that his person would be well cared for and protected by His Majesty [the Holy Roman Emperor], how could we wish him to run the risk of this long and difficult journey, considering the child's tender and delicate age? And you must know what comfort and solace, in his father's present unhappy condition, we find in the presence of this dear son, the hope and joy of all our people and subjects. To deprive us of him, would be to deprive us of life itself, and of all we count good and precious. If you take Federico away you might as well take away our life and state.... Once for all, we will suffer any loss rather than part from our son, and this you may take to be our deliberate and unchanging resolution.

Letter of Isabella d'Este to Her Husband, Who Had Ordered Her to Send the Boy to Venice

If in this matter Your Excellency were to despise me and deprive me of your love and grace, I would rather endure such harsh treatment, I would rather lose our State, than deprive us of our children. I am hoping that in time your own prudence and kindness will make you understand that I have acted more lovingly toward you than you have to yourself.

Have patience! You can be sure that I think continuously of your liberation and when the time comes I will not fail you, as I have not relaxed my efforts. As witness I cite the Pope, the Emperor, the King of France, and all the other reigning heads and potentates of Christendom. Yes, and the infidels as well [she had written to the Turkish sultan for help]. If it were *really* the only means of setting you free, I would not only send Federico but all the other children as well. I will do everything imaginable. Some day I hope I can make you understand....

Pardon me if this letter is badly written and worse composed, but I do not know if I am dead or alive.

Isabella, who desires the best for Your Excellency, written with her own hand

[Isabella's husband was not pleased with her response and exclaimed angrily: "That whore of my wife is the cause of it all. Send me into battle alone, do what you like with me. I have lost in one blow my state, my honor and my freedom. If she does not obey, I'll cut her vocal cords."]

Q What do these letters reveal about Isabella's character and about the attributes and strategies of expression on which noble women had to rely in order to participate effectively in high politics?

---

breakdown of the Italian balance of power that encouraged the invasions and began the Italian wars. Feeling isolated, Ludovico Sforza, the duke of Milan, foolishly invited the French to intervene in Italian politics. The French king Charles VIII (1483–1498) was eager to do so, and in 1494, with an army of 30,000 men, he advanced through Italy and occupied the kingdom of Naples. Other Italian states turned to the Spanish for help, and Ferdinand of Aragon indicated his willingness to intervene. For the next fifteen years, the French and Spanish competed to dominate Italy. After 1510, the war was continued by a new generation of rulers, Francis I of France and Charles I of Spain (see Chapter 13). This war was part of a long struggle for power throughout Europe between the Valois and Habsburg dynasties. Italy was only a pawn for the two great powers, a convenient arena for fighting battles. The terrible sack of Rome in 1527 by the armies of the Spanish king Charles I brought a temporary end to the Italian wars. Thereafter, the Spaniards dominated Italy.

Although some Italians had developed a sense of national consciousness and differentiated between Italians and "barbarians" (all foreigners), few Italians conceived of creating an alliance or confederation of states that could repel foreign invaders. Italians remained fiercely loyal to their own petty states, making invasion a fact of life in Italian history for all too long. Italy would not achieve unification and nationhood until 1870.

The Birth of Modern Diplomacy

The modern diplomatic system was a product of the Italian Renaissance. There were ambassadors in the Middle Ages, but they were used only on a temporary basis. Moreover, an ambassador, regardless of whose subject he was, regarded

CHRONOLOGY The Italian States in the Renaissance

Duchy of Milan	
The Viscontis	1311–1447
The Sforzas	1450–1494
Florence	
Cosimo de' Medici	1434–1464
Lorenzo de' Medici	1469–1492
Peace of Lodi	1454
Beginning of Italian wars—French invasion of Italy	1494
Sack of Rome	1527

© AKG/Photo Researchers, Inc.

Niccolò Machiavelli. In *The Prince,* Machiavelli gave concrete expression to the Renaissance preoccupation with political power. This slender volume remains one of the most famous and most widely read Western treatises on politics. Machiavelli is seen here in a portrait by Santi di Tito.

himself as the servant of all Christendom, not just of his particular employer. As a treatise on diplomacy stated, "An ambassador is sacred because he acts for the general welfare." Since he was the servant of all Christendom, "the business of an ambassador is peace."[8]

This concept of an ambassador changed during the Italian Renaissance because of the political situation in Italy. A large number of states existed, many so small that their security was easily threatened by their neighbors. To survive, the Italian states began to send resident diplomatic agents to each other to ferret out useful information. During the Italian wars, the practice of resident diplomats spread to the rest of Europe, and in the course of the sixteenth and seventeenth centuries, Europeans developed the diplomatic machinery still in use today, such as the rights of ambassadors in host countries and the proper procedures for conducting diplomatic business.

With the use of permanent resident agents or ambassadors, the conception of the purpose of an ambassador also changed. A Venetian diplomat attempted to define an ambassador's function in a treatise written at the end of the fifteenth century. He wrote, "The first duty of an ambassador is exactly the same as that of any other servant of a government, that is, to do, say, advise, and think whatever may best serve the preservation and aggrandizement of his own state."[9] An ambassador was now an agent only of the territorial state that sent him, not the larger body of Christendom. He could use any methods that were beneficial to the political interests of his own state. We are at the beginning of modern politics when the interests of the state supersede all other considerations.

Machiavelli and the New Statecraft

No one gave better expression to the Renaissance preoccupation with political power than Niccolò Machiavelli (nee-koh-LOH mahk-ee-uh-VEL-ee) (1469–1527). He entered the service of the Florentine republic in 1498, four years after the Medici family had been expelled from the city. As a secretary to the Florentine Council of Ten, he made numerous diplomatic missions, including trips to France and Germany, and saw the workings of statecraft at first hand. Machiavelli's political activity occurred during the period of tribulation and devastation for Italy that followed the French invasion in 1494. In 1512, French defeat and Spanish victory led to the reestablishment of Medici power in Florence. Staunch republicans, including Machiavelli, were sent into exile. Forced to give up politics, the great love of his life, Machiavelli now reflected on political power and wrote books, including *The Prince* (1513), one of the most famous treatises on political power in the Western world.

THE PRINCE Machiavelli's ideas on politics stemmed from two major sources, his knowledge of ancient Rome and his preoccupation with Italy's political problems. As a result of his experiences, Machiavelli fully realized that the small Italian states were no match for the larger monarchical states outside Italy's borders and that Italy itself had become merely a battleground for the armies of foreign states. His major concerns in *The Prince* were the acquisition and expansion of political power as the means to restore and maintain order in his time. Late medieval political theorists believed that a ruler was justified in exercising political power only if it contributed to the common good of the people he served. The ethical side of a prince's activity—how a ruler ought to behave based

Niccolò Machiavelli, *The Prince,* selected topics (1513)

on Christian moral principles—was the focus of many late medieval treatises on politics. Machiavelli bluntly contradicted this approach:

> My hope is to write a book that will be useful, at least to those who read it intelligently, and so I thought it sensible to go straight to a discussion of how things are in real life and not waste time with a discussion of an imaginary world.... For the gap between how people actually behave and how they ought to behave is so great that anyone who ignores everyday reality in order to live up to an ideal will soon discover he has been taught how to destroy himself, not how to preserve himself.[10]

Machiavelli considered his approach far more realistic than that of his medieval forebears.

In Machiavelli's view, a prince's attitude toward power must be based on an understanding of human nature, which he perceived as basically self-centered: "For of men one can, in general, say this: They are ungrateful, fickle, deceptive and deceiving, avoiders of danger, eager to gain." Political activity, therefore, could not be restricted by moral considerations. The prince acts on behalf of the state and for the sake of the state must be willing to let his conscience sleep. As Machiavelli put it:

> You need to understand this: A ruler, and particularly a ruler who is new to power, cannot conform to all those rules that men who are thought good are expected to respect, for he is often obliged, in order to hold on to power, to break his word, to be uncharitable, inhumane, and irreligious. So he must be mentally prepared to act as circumstances and changes in fortune require. As I have said, he should do what is right if he can; but he must be prepared to do wrong if necessary.[11]

Machiavelli found a good example of the new Italian ruler in Cesare Borgia, the son of Pope Alexander VI, who used ruthless measures to achieve his goal of carving out a new state in central Italy. As Machiavelli said: "So anyone who decides that the policy to follow when one has newly acquired power is to destroy one's enemies, to secure some allies, to win wars, whether by force or by fraud, to make oneself both loved and feared by one's subjects, ... cannot hope to find, in the recent past, a better model to imitate than Cesare Borgia."[12] Machiavelli was among the first to abandon morality as the basis for the analysis of political activity (see the box on p. 353).

The Intellectual Renaissance in Italy

Q FOCUS QUESTION: What was humanism, and what effect did it have on philosophy, education, attitudes toward politics, and the writing of history?

Individualism and **secularism**—two characteristics of the Italian Renaissance—were most noticeable in the intellectual and artistic realms. Italian culture had matured by the fourteenth century. For the next two centuries, Italy was the cultural leader of Europe. This new Italian culture was primarily the product of a relatively wealthy, urban lay society. The most important literary movement associated with the Renaissance was **humanism.**

Italian Renaissance Humanism

Renaissance humanism was an intellectual movement based on the study of the Classical literary works of Greece and Rome. Humanists examined the *studia humanitatis* ("the studies of humanity")—grammar, rhetoric, poetry, moral philosophy or ethics, and history—all based on the writings of ancient Greek and Roman authors. These are the subjects we call the humanities.

The central importance of literary preoccupations in Renaissance humanism is evident in the professional status or occupations of the humanists. Some of them were teachers of the humanities in secondary schools and universities, where they either gave occasional lectures or held permanent positions, often as professors of rhetoric. Others served as secretaries in the chancelleries of Italian city-states or at the courts of princes or popes. All of these occupations were largely secular, and most humanists were laymen rather than members of the clergy.

THE EMERGENCE OF HUMANISM Petrarch (1304–1374) has often been called the father of Italian Renaissance humanism (see Chapter 11 on his use of the Italian vernacular). Petrarch rejected his father's desire that he become a lawyer and took up a literary career instead. Although he lived in Avignon for a time, most of his last decades were spent in Italy as the guest of various princes and city governments. With his usual lack of modesty, Petrarch once exclaimed, "Some of the greatest kings of our time have loved me and cultivated my friendship.... When I was their guest it was more as if they were mine."[13]

Petrarch did more than any other individual in the fourteenth century to foster the development of Renaissance humanism. He was the first intellectual to characterize the Middle Ages as a period of darkness, promoting the mistaken belief that medieval culture was ignorant of Classical antiquity. Petrarch's interest in the classics led him on a quest for forgotten Latin manuscripts and set in motion a ransacking of monastic libraries throughout Europe. In his preoccupation with the classics and their secular content, Petrarch worried at times whether he was sufficiently attentive to spiritual ideals (see the box on p. 354). His qualms, however, did not prevent him from inaugurating the humanist emphasis on the use of pure Classical Latin, making it fashionable for humanists to use Cicero as a model for prose and Virgil for poetry. As Petrarch said, "Christ is my God; Cicero is the prince of the language."

HUMANISM IN FIFTEENTH-CENTURY ITALY In Florence, the humanist movement took a new direction at the beginning of the fifteenth century when it became closely tied to Florentine civic spirit and pride, giving rise to what one modern scholar has labeled **civic humanism.** Fourteenth-century humanists such as Petrarch had described the

The Renaissance Prince: The Views of Machiavelli and Erasmus

At the beginning of the sixteenth century, two writers produced very different views of political power and how a ruler should conduct affairs of state. In 1513, Niccolò Machiavelli wrote a short treatise on political power that, justly or unjustly, has given him a reputation as a political opportunist. In this selection from Chapter 17 of *The Prince*, Machiavelli analyzes whether it is better for a ruler to be loved than to be feared. Three years later the Dutch intellectual Erasmus, leader of the Christian humanists (see Chapter 13), also wrote a treatise on political power, entitled *Education of a Christian Prince*. As is evident in this excerpt from his treatise, Erasmus followed in the footsteps of medieval theorists on power by insisting that a true prince should think only of his moral obligations to the people he rules.

Machiavelli, *The Prince* (1513)

This leads us to a question that is in dispute: Is it better to be loved than feared, or vice versa? My reply is one ought to be both loved and feared; but, since it is difficult to accomplish both at the same time, I maintain it is much safer to be feared than loved, if you have to do without one of the two. For of men one can, in general, say this: They are ungrateful, fickle, deceptive and deceiving, avoiders of danger, eager to gain. As long as you serve their interests, they are devoted to you. They promise you their blood, their possessions, their lives, and their children, as I said before, so long as you seem to have no need of them. But as soon as you need help, they turn against you. Any ruler who relies simply on their promises and makes no other preparations, will be destroyed. For you will find that those whose support you buy, who do not rally to you because they admire your strength of character and nobility of soul, these are people you pay for, but they are never yours, and in the end you cannot get the benefit of your investment. Men are less nervous of offending someone who makes himself lovable, than someone who makes himself frightening. For love attaches men by ties of obligation, which, since men are wicked, they break whenever their interests are at stake. But fear restrains men because they are afraid of punishment, and this fear never leaves them. Still, a ruler should make himself feared in such a way that, if he does not inspire love, at least he does not provoke hatred. For it is perfectly possible to be feared and not hated. You will only be hated if you seize the property or the women of your subjects and citizens. Whenever you have to kill someone, make sure that you have a suitable excuse and an obvious reason; but, above all else, keep your hands off other people's property; for men are quicker to forget the death of their father than the loss of their inheritance. Moreover, there are always reasons why you might want to seize people's property; and he who begins to live by plundering others will always find an excuse for seizing other people's possessions; but there are fewer reasons for killing people, and one killing need not lead to another.

When a ruler is at the head of his army and has a vast number of soldiers under his command, then it is absolutely essential to be prepared to be thought cruel; for it is impossible to keep an army united and ready for action without acquiring a reputation for cruelty.

Erasmus, *Education of a Christian Prince* (1516)

Follow the right, do violence to no one, plunder no one, sell no public office, be corrupted by no bribes.... As you would rather stand for an injury than avenge it at great loss to the state, perchance you will lose a little something of your empire. Bear that; consider that you have gained a great deal because you have brought hurt to fewer than you would otherwise have done.... If you cannot defend your realm without violating justice, without wanton loss of human life, without great loss to religion, give up and yield to the importunities of the age!...

A good prince... is a living likeness of God, who is at once good and powerful. His goodness makes him want to help all; his power makes him able to do so. On the other hand, an evil prince, who is like a plague to his country, is the incarnation of the devil, who has great power joined with his wickedness. All his resources to the very last, he uses for the undoing of the human race....

[A good prince is one] who holds the life of each individual dearer than his own; who works and strives night and day for just one end—to be the best he can for everyone; with whom rewards are ready for all good men... for so much does he want to be of real help to his people, without thought of recompense, that if necessary he would not hesitate to look out for their welfare at great risk to himself; who considers his wealth to lie in the advantage of his country; who is ever on the watch so that everyone else may sleep deeply; who grants no leisure to himself so that he may spend his life in the peace of his country; who worries himself with continual cares so that his subjects may have peace and quiet.... He does everything and allows everything that will bring everlasting peace to his country, for he realizes that war is the source of all misfortunes to the state.

Q What does Machiavelli have to say about being loved rather than feared? How does this view contrast with that of Erasmus on the characteristics of a good ruler? Which viewpoint do you consider more modern? Why? Which viewpoint do you think is correct? Why?

Petrarch: Mountain Climbing and the Search for Spiritual Contentment

Petrarch has long been regarded as the father of Italian Renaissance humanism. One of his literary masterpieces was *The Ascent of Mount Ventoux,* a colorful description of his attempt to climb a mountain in Provence in southern France and survey the world from its top. Petrarch's primary interest is in presenting an allegory of his own soul's struggle to achieve a higher spiritual state. The work is addressed to a professor of theology in Paris who had initially encouraged Petrarch to read Augustine. The latter had experienced a dramatic conversion to Christianity almost a thousand years earlier.

—⊶ ⫸⫷ ⊷—

Petrarch, *The Ascent of Mount Ventoux*

Today I ascended the highest mountain in this region, which, not without cause, they call the Windy Peak. Nothing but the desire to see its conspicuous height was the reason for this undertaking. For many years I have been intending to make this expedition. You know that since my early childhood, as fate tossed around human affairs, I have been tossed around in these parts, and this mountain, visible far and wide from everywhere, is always in your view. So I was at last seized by the impulse to accomplish what I had always wanted to do....

[After some false starts, Petrarch finally achieves his goal and arrives at the top of Mount Ventoux.]

I was glad of the progress I had made, but I wept over my imperfection and was grieved by the fickleness of all that men do. In this manner I seemed to have somehow forgotten the place I had come to and why, until I was warned to throw off such sorrows, for which another place would be more appropriate. I had better look around and see what I had intended to see in coming here. The time to leave was approaching, they said.... Like a man aroused from sleep, I turned back and looked toward the west.... One could see most distinctly the mountains of the province of Lyons to the right and, to the left, the sea near Marseilles as well as the waves that break against Aigues-Mortes.... The Rhône River was directly under our eyes.

I admired every detail, now relishing earthly enjoyment, now lifting up my mind to higher spheres after the example of my body, and I thought it fit to look in the volume of Augustine's *Confessions* which I owe to your loving kindness and preserve carefully, keeping it always in my hands, in remembrance of the author as well as the donor.... I opened it with the intention of reading whatever might occur to me first: ... I happened to hit upon the tenth book of the work.... Where I fixed my eyes first, it was written: "And men go to admire the high mountains, the vast floods of the sea, the huge streams of the rivers, the circumference of the ocean, and the revolutions of the stars—and desert themselves." I was stunned, I confess. I bade my brother [who had accompanied him], who wanted to hear more, not to molest me, and closed the book, angry with myself that I still admired earthly things. Long since I ought to have learned, even from pagan philosophers, that "nothing is admirable besides the soul; compared to its greatness nothing is great."

I was completely satisfied with what I had seen of the mountain and turned my inner eye toward myself. From this hour nobody heard me say a word until we arrived at the bottom. These words occupied me sufficiently. I could not imagine that this had happened to me by chance: I was convinced that whatever I had read there was said to me and to nobody else. I remembered that Augustine once suspected the same regarding himself, when, while he was reading the Apostolic Epistles, the first passage that occurred to him was, as he himself relates: "Not in banqueting and drunkenness, not in chambering and wantonness, not in strife and envying; but put you on the Lord Jesus Christ, and make no provision for the flesh to fulfill your lusts." ⊱

Q   What about his own intellectual pursuits troubled Petrarch? How does the conflict within Petrarch reflect the historical debate about the nature of the Renaissance?

---

intellectual life as one of solitude. They rejected family and a life of action in the community. In the busy civic world of Florence, however, intellectuals began to take a new view of their role as intellectuals. The Classical Roman Cicero, who was both a statesman and an intellectual, became their model. Leonardo Bruni (1370–1444), a humanist, Florentine patriot, and chancellor of the city, wrote a biography of Cicero titled *The New Cicero,* in which he waxed enthusiastic about the fusion of political action and literary creation in Cicero's life. From Bruni's time on, Cicero served as the inspiration for the Renaissance ideal that it was the duty of an intellectual to live an active life for one's state. An individual only "grows to maturity—both intellectually and morally—through participation" in the life of the state. Civic humanism reflected the values of the urban society of the Italian Renaissance. Humanists came to believe that their study of the humanities should be put to the service of the state. It is no accident that humanists served the state as chancellors, councillors, and advisers.

Also evident in the humanism of the first half of the fifteenth century was a growing interest in Classical Greek civilization. One of the first Italian humanists to gain a thorough knowledge of Greek was Leonardo Bruni, who became an enthusiastic pupil of the Byzantine scholar Manuel Chrysoloras, who taught in Florence from 1396 to 1400. Humanists eagerly perused the works of Plato as well as those of Greek poets, dramatists, historians, and orators, such as Euripides, Sophocles, and Thucydides, all of whom had been ignored by the scholastics of the High Middle Ages as irrelevant to the theological questions they were examining.

By the fifteenth century, a consciousness of being humanists had emerged. This was especially evident in the career of Lorenzo Valla (1407–1457). Valla was brought up in Rome and educated in both Latin and Greek. Eventually, he achieved his chief ambition of becoming a papal secretary. Valla's major work, *The Elegances of the Latin Language,* was an effort to purify medieval Latin and restore Latin to its proper position over the vernacular. The treatise examined the proper use of Classical Latin and created a new literary standard. Early humanists had tended to take as Classical models any author (including Christians) who had written before the seventh century C.E. Valla identified different stages in the development of the Latin language and accepted only the Latin of the last century of the Roman Republic and the first century of the empire.

HUMANISM AND PHILOSOPHY In the second half of the fifteenth century, a dramatic upsurge of interest in the works of Plato occurred, especially evident among the members of an informal discussion group known as the Florentine Platonic Academy. Cosimo de' Medici, the de facto ruler of Florence, became its patron and commissioned a translation of Plato's dialogues by Marsilio Ficino (mar-SIL-yoh fee-CHEE-noh) (1433–1499), one of the academy's leaders. Ficino dedicated his life to the translation of Plato and the exposition of the Platonic philosophy known as **Neoplatonism.**

In two major works, Ficino undertook the synthesis of Christianity and Platonism into a single system. His Neoplatonism was based on two primary ideas, the Neoplatonic hierarchy of substances and a theory of spiritual love. The former postulated the idea of a hierarchy of substances, or great chain of being, from the lowest form of physical matter (plants) to the purest spirit (God), in which humans occupied a central or middle position. They were the link between the material world (through the body) and the spiritual world (through the soul), and their highest duty was to ascend toward that union with God that was the true end of human existence. Ficino's theory of spiritual or Platonic love maintained that just as all people are bound together in their common humanity by love, so too are all parts of the universe held together by bonds of sympathetic love.

RENAISSANCE HERMETICISM **Hermeticism** was another product of the Florentine intellectual environment of the late fifteenth century. At the request of Cosimo de' Medici, Ficino translated into Latin a Greek work titled *Corpus Hermeticum* (KOR-pus hur-MET-i-koom). The Hermetic manuscripts contained two kinds of writings. One type stressed the occult sciences, with an emphasis on astrology, alchemy, and magic. The other focused on theological and philosophical beliefs and speculations. Some Hermetic writings espoused **pantheism,** seeing divinity embodied in all aspects of nature and in the heavenly bodies as well as in earthly objects. As Giordano Bruno, one of the most prominent of the sixteenth-century Hermeticists, stated, "God as a whole is in all things."[14]

For Renaissance intellectuals, the Hermetic revival offered a new view of humankind. They believed that human beings had been created as divine beings endowed with divine creative power but had freely chosen to enter the material world (nature). Humans could recover their divinity, however, through a regenerative experience or purification of the soul. Thus regenerated, they became true sages or magi, as the Renaissance called them, who had knowledge of God and of truth. In regaining their original divinity, they reacquired an intimate knowledge of nature and the ability to employ the powers of nature for beneficial purposes.

In Italy, the most prominent magi in the late fifteenth century were Ficino and his friend and pupil, Giovanni Pico della Mirandola (PEE-koh DELL-uh mee-RAN-doh-lah) (1463–1494). Pico produced one of the most famous pieces of writing of the Renaissance, the *Oration on the Dignity of Man.* Pico combed diligently through the works of many philosophers of different backgrounds for the common "nuggets of universal truth" that he believed were all part of God's revelation to humanity. In the *Oration* (see the box on p. 356), Pico offered a ringing statement of unlimited human potential: "To him it is granted to have whatever he chooses, to be whatever he wills."[15] Like Ficino, Pico took an avid interest in Hermetic philosophy, accepting it as the "science of the Divine," which "embraces the deepest contemplation of the most secret things, and at last the knowledge of all nature."[16]

Education in the Renaissance

The humanist movement had a profound effect on education. Renaissance humanists believed that human beings could be dramatically changed by education. They wrote books on education and developed secondary schools based on their ideas. Most famous was the school founded in 1423 by Vittorino da Feltre at Mantua, where the ruler of that small Italian state, Gian Francesco I Gonzaga, wished to provide a humanist education for his children. Vittorino based much of his educational system on the ideas of Classical authors, particularly Cicero and Quintilian.

At the core of the academic training Vittorino offered were the "liberal studies." The Renaissance view of the value of the liberal arts was most strongly influenced by a treatise on education called *Concerning Character* by Pietro Paolo Vergerio (PYAY-troh POW-loh vur-JEER-ee-oh) (1370–1444). This work stressed the importance of liberal studies as the key to true freedom, enabling individuals to reach their full potential. According to Vergerio, "We call those studies liberal which are worthy

Pico della Mirandola and the Dignity of Man

Giovanni Pico della Mirandola was one of the foremost intellects of the Italian Renaissance. Pico boasted that he had studied all schools of philosophy, which he tried to demonstrate by drawing up nine hundred theses for public disputation at the age of twenty-four. As a preface to his theses, he wrote his famous *Oration on the Dignity of Man,* in which he proclaimed the unlimited potentiality of human beings.

Pico della Mirandola, *Oration on the Dignity of Man*

At last the best of artisans [God] ordained that that creature to whom He had been able to give nothing proper to himself should have joint possession of whatever had been peculiar to each of the different kinds of being. He therefore took man as a creature of indeterminate nature, and assigning him a place in the middle of the world, addressed him thus: "Neither a fixed abode nor a form that is yours alone nor any function peculiar to yourself have we given you, Adam, to the end that according to your longing and according to your judgment you may have and possess what abode, what form, and what functions you yourself desire. The nature of all other beings is limited and constrained within the bounds of laws prescribed by Us. You, constrained by no limits, in accordance with your own free will, in whose hand We have placed you, shall ordain for yourself the limits of your nature. We have set you at the world's center that you may from there more easily observe whatever is in the world. We have made you neither of heaven nor of earth, neither mortal nor immortal, so that with freedom of choice and with honor, as though the maker and molder of yourself, you may fashion yourself in whatever shape you shall prefer. You shall have the power to degenerate into the lower forms of life, which are brutish. You shall have the power, out of your soul's judgment, to be reborn into the higher forms, which are divine."

O supreme generosity of God the Father, O highest and most marvelous felicity of man! To him it is granted to have whatever he chooses, to be whatever he wills. Beasts as soon as they are born bring with them from their mother's womb all they will ever possess. Spiritual beings, either from the beginning or soon thereafter, become what they are to be for ever and ever. On man when he came into life the Father conferred the seeds of all kinds and the germs of every way of life. Whatever seeds each man cultivates will grow to maturity and bear in him their own fruit. If they be vegetative, he will be like a plant. If sensitive, he will become brutish. If rational, he will grow into a heavenly being. If intellectual, he will be an angel and the son of God.

 What did Pico mean by the "dignity of man"? Why would Pico be regarded as one of the Renaissance magi?

---

of a free man; those studies by which we attain and practice virtue and wisdom; that education which calls forth, trains, and develops those highest gifts of body and mind which ennoble men."[17] The liberal studies included history, moral philosophy, eloquence (rhetoric), letters (grammar and logic), poetry, mathematics, astronomy, and music. The purpose of a liberal education was thus to produce individuals who followed a path of virtue and wisdom and possessed the rhetorical skills with which to persuade others to do the same. Following the Greek precept of a sound mind in a sound body, Vittorino's school at Mantua also stressed physical education. Pupils were taught the skills of javelin throwing, archery, and dancing and encouraged to run, wrestle, hunt, and swim.

Although a small number of children from the lower classes were provided free educations, humanist schools such as Vittorino's were primarily geared for the education of an elite, the ruling classes of their communities. Also largely absent from such schools were females. Vittorino's only female pupils were the two daughters of the Gonzaga ruler of Mantua. Though these few female students studied the classics and were encouraged to know some history and to ride, dance, sing, play the lute, and appreciate poetry, they were discouraged from learning mathematics and rhetoric. In the educational treatises of the time, religion and morals were thought to "hold the first place in the education of a Christian lady."

Nevertheless, some women in Italy who were educated in the humanist fashion went on to establish their own literary careers. Isotta Nogarola (ee-ZAHT-uh NOH-guh-roll-uh), born to a noble family in Verona, mastered Latin and wrote numerous letters and treatises that brought her praise from male Italian intellectuals. Cassandra Fedele (FAY-duh-lee) of Venice, who learned both Latin and Greek from humanist tutors hired by her family, became prominent in Venice for her public recitations of orations. Laura Cereta (say-REE-tuh) was educated in Latin by her father, a physician from Brescia. Laura defended the ability of women to pursue scholarly pursuits (see the box on p. 357).

Humanist education was thought to be a practical preparation for life. Its aim was not to create great scholars but rather to produce complete citizens who could participate in the civic life of their communities. As Vittorino said, "Not everyone is obliged to excel in philosophy, medicine, or the law, nor are all equally favored by nature; but all are destined to live in society and to practice virtue."[18] Humanist schools, combining the classics and Christianity,

A Woman's Defense of Learning

As a young woman, Laura Cereta was proud of her learning but condemned by a male world that found it unseemly for women to be scholars. One monk said to her father, "She gives herself to things unworthy of her—namely, the classics." Before being silenced, Laura Cereta wrote a series of letters, including one to a male critic who had argued that her work was so good it could not have been written by a woman.

—— ━━═╪═━━ ——

Laura Cereta, *Defense of the Liberal Instruction of Women*

My ears are wearied by your carping. You brashly and publicly not merely wonder but indeed lament that I am said to possess as fine a mind as nature ever bestowed upon the most learned man. You seem to think that so learned a woman has scarcely before been seen in the world. You are wrong on both counts. . . .

I would have been silent. . . . But I cannot tolerate your having attacked my entire sex. For this reason my thirsty soul seeks revenge, my sleeping pen is aroused to literary struggle, raging anger stirs mental passions long chained by silence. With just cause I am moved to demonstrate how great a reputation for learning and virtue women have won by their inborn excellence, manifested in every age as knowledge. . . .

Only the question of the rarity of outstanding women remains to be addressed. The explanation is clear: women have been able by nature to be exceptional, but have chosen lesser goals. For some women are concerned with parting their hair correctly, adorning themselves with lovely dresses, or decorating their fingers with pearls and other gems. Others delight in mouthing carefully composed phrases, indulging in dancing, or managing spoiled puppies. Still others wish to gaze at lavish banquet tables, to rest in sleep, or, standing at mirrors, to smear their lovely faces. But those in whom a deeper integrity yearns for virtue, restrain from the start their youthful souls, reflect on higher things, harden the body with sobriety and trials, and curb their tongues, open their ears, compose their thoughts in wakeful hours, their minds in contemplation, to letters bonded to righteousness. For knowledge is not given as a gift, but [is gained] with diligence. The free mind, not shirking effort, always soars zealously toward the good, and the desire to know grows ever more wide and deep. It is because of no special holiness, therefore, that we [women] are rewarded by God the Giver with the gift of exceptional talent. Nature has generously lavished its gifts upon all people, opening to all the doors of choice through which reason sends envoys to the will, from which they learn and convey its desires. The will must choose to exercise the gift of reason. . . .

I have been praised too much; showing your contempt for women, you pretend that I alone am admirable because of the good fortune of my intellect. . . . Do you suppose, O most contemptible man on earth, that I think myself sprung [like Athena] from the head of Jove? I am a school girl, possessed of the sleeping embers of an ordinary mind. Indeed I am too hurt, and my mind, offended, too swayed by passions, sighs, tormenting itself, conscious of the obligation to defend my sex. For absolutely everything—that which is within us and that which is without—is made weak by association with my sex. 🖎

Q How did Cereta explain her intellectual interests and accomplishments? Why were Renaissance women rarely taken seriously when they sought educational opportunities and recognition for their intellectual talents? Were any of those factors unique to the Renaissance era?

---

provided the model for the basic education of the European ruling classes until the twentieth century.

Humanism and History

Humanism had a strong impact on the writing of history. Influenced by Roman and Greek historians, the humanists approached the writing of history differently from the chroniclers of the Middle Ages. The humanists' belief that Classical civilization had been followed by an age of barbarism (the Middle Ages), which had in turn been succeeded by their own age, with its rebirth of the study of the classics, enabled them to think in terms of the passage of time, of the past as past. Their division of the past into ancient world, dark ages, and their own age provided a new sense of chronology or periodization in history.

The humanists were also responsible for secularizing the writing of history. Humanist historians reduced or eliminated the role of miracles in historical interpretation, not because they were anti-Christian but because they took a new approach to sources. They wanted to use documents and exercised their newly developed critical skills in examining them. Greater attention was paid to the political events and forces that affected their city-states or larger territorial units. Thus, Leonardo Bruni wrote the *History of the Florentine People*. The new emphasis on secularization was also evident in the humanists' conception of causation in history. Medieval historical literature often portrayed historical events as being caused by God's active involvement in human affairs. Humanists de-emphasized divine intervention in favor of human motives, stressing political forces or the role of individuals in history.

GUICCIARDINI The high point of Renaissance historiography was achieved at the beginning of the sixteenth century in the works of Francesco Guicciardini (frahn-CHESS-koh gwee-char-DEE-nee) (1483–1540). He has been called by some Renaissance scholars the greatest historian between Tacitus in the first century (see Chapter 6) and Voltaire and Gibbon in the eighteenth century (see Chapter 17). His *History of Italy* and *History of Florence* represent the beginning of "modern analytical historiography." To Guicciardini, the purpose of writing history was to teach lessons, but he was so impressed by the complexity of historical events that he felt those lessons were not always obvious. From his extensive background in government and diplomatic affairs, he developed the skills that enabled him to analyze political situations precisely and critically. Emphasizing political and military history, his works relied heavily on personal examples and documentary sources.

The Impact of Printing

The Renaissance witnessed the invention of printing, one of the most important technological innovations of Western civilization. The art of printing made an immediate impact on European intellectual life and thought. Printing from hand-carved wooden blocks had been done in the West since the twelfth century and in China even before that. What was new to Europe in the fifteenth century was multiple printing with movable metal type. The development of printing from movable type was a gradual process that culminated between 1445 and 1450; Johannes Gutenberg (yoh-HAH-nuss GOO-ten-bayrk) of Mainz played an important role in bringing the process to completion. Gutenberg's Bible, completed in 1455 or 1456, was the first true book in the West produced from movable type.

The new printing spread rapidly throughout Europe in the second half of the fifteenth century. Printing presses were established throughout the Holy Roman Empire in the 1460s and within ten years had spread to Italy, England, France, the Low Countries, Spain, and eastern Europe. Especially well known as a printing center was Venice, home by 1500 to almost one hundred printers who had produced almost 2 million volumes.

By 1500, there were more than a thousand printers in Europe who had published almost 40,000 titles (between 8 million and 10 million copies). Probably 50 percent of these books were religious—Bibles and biblical commentaries, books of devotion, and sermons. Next in importance were the Latin and Greek classics, medieval grammars, legal handbooks, works on philosophy, and an ever-growing number of popular romances.

Printing became one of the largest industries in Europe, and its effects were soon felt in many areas of European life. The printing of books encouraged the development of scholarly research and the desire to attain knowledge. Moreover, printing facilitated cooperation among scholars and helped produce standardized and definitive texts. Printing also stimulated the development of an ever-expanding lay reading public, a development that had an enormous impact on European society. Indeed, without the printing press, the new religious ideas of the Reformation would never have spread as rapidly as they did in the sixteenth century.

The Artistic Renaissance

 FOCUS QUESTION: What were the chief characteristics of Renaissance art, and how did it differ in Italy and northern Europe?

Leonardo da Vinci, one of the great Italian Renaissance artists, once explained: "Hence the painter will produce pictures of small merit if he takes for his standard the pictures of others, but if he will study from natural objects he will bear good fruit. . . . Those who take for their standard any one but nature . . . weary themselves in vain."[19] Renaissance artists considered the imitation of nature their primary goal. Their search for naturalism became an end in itself: to persuade onlookers of the reality of the object or event they were portraying. At the same time, the new artistic standards reflected a new attitude of mind as well, one in which human beings became the focus of attention, the "center and measure of all things," as one artist proclaimed.

Art in the Early Renaissance

Leonardo and other Italians maintained that it was Giotto in the fourteenth century (see Chapter 11) who began the imitation of nature. But what Giotto had begun was not taken up again until the work of Masaccio (muh-ZAH-choh) (1401–1428) in Florence. Masaccio's cycle of frescoes in the Brancacci Chapel has long been regarded as the first masterpiece of Early Renaissance art. With his use of monumental figures, a more realistic relationship between figures and landscape, and visual representation of the laws of perspective, a new realistic style of painting was born. Onlookers become aware of a world of reality that appears to be a continuation of their own world. Masaccio's massive, three-dimensional human figures provided a model for later generations of Florentine artists.

This new Renaissance style was absorbed and modified by other Florentine painters in the fifteenth century. Especially important was the development of an experimental trend that took two directions. One emphasized the mathematical side of painting, the working out of the laws of perspective and the organization of outdoor space and light by geometry and perspective. In the work of Paolo Uccello (POW-loh oo-CHELL-oh) (1397–1475), figures became mere stage props to show off his mastery of the laws of perspective. The other aspect of the experimental trend involved the investigation of movement and anatomical structure. *The Martyrdom of Saint Sebastian* by Antonio Pollaiuolo (pohl-ly-WOH-loh) (c. 1432–1498) revels in Classical motifs and attempts to portray the human body under stress. Indeed, the realistic portrayal of

Masaccio, *Tribute Money*. With the frescoes of Masaccio, regarded by many as the first great works of Early Renaissance art, a new realistic style of painting was born. *Tribute Money* was one of a series of frescoes that Masaccio painted in the Brancacci Chapel of the Church of Santa Maria del Carmine in Florence. In *Tribute Money*, Masaccio illustrated the biblical story of Jesus's confrontation by a tax collector at the entrance to the town of Capernaum (seen at center). Jesus sent Peter to collect a coin from the mouth of a fish from Lake Galilee (seen at left); Peter then paid the tax collector (seen at right). In illustrating this story from the Bible, Masaccio used a rational system of perspective to create a realistic relationship between the figures and their background; the figures themselves are realistic. As one Renaissance observer said, "The works made before Masaccio's day can be said to be painted, while his are living, real, and natural."

the human nude became one of the foremost preoccupations of Italian Renaissance art. The fifteenth century, then, was a period of experimentation and technical mastery.

During the last decades of the fifteenth century, a new sense of invention emerged in Florence, especially in the circle of artists and scholars who formed part of the court of the city's leading citizen, Lorenzo the Magnificent. One of this group's prominent members was Sandro Botticelli (SAHN-droh bot-i-CHELL-ee) (1445–1510), whose interest in Greek and Roman mythology was well reflected in one of his most famous works, *Primavera* (Spring). The painting is set in the garden of Venus, a garden of eternal spring. Though Botticelli's figures are well defined, they also possess an otherworldly quality that is far removed from the realism that characterized the painting of the Early Renaissance.

The revolutionary achievements of Florentine painters in the fifteenth

Botticelli, *Primavera*. This work reflects Botticelli's strong interest in Classical antiquity. At the center of the painting is Venus, the goddess of love. At the right stands Flora, a Roman goddess of flowers and fertility, while the Three Graces dance playfully at the left. Cupid, the son of Venus, aims his arrow at the Three Graces. At the far left of the picture is Mercury, the messenger of the gods. Later in his life, Botticelli experienced a profound religious crisis, leading him to reject his earlier preoccupation with pagan gods and goddesses. He burned many of his early paintings and thereafter produced only religious works.

The Artistic Renaissance ❧ **359**

Donatello, *David*. Donatello's *David* first stood in the courtyard of the Medici Palace. On its base was an inscription praising Florentine heroism and virtue, leading art historians to believe that the statue was meant to commemorate the victory of Florence over Milan in 1428. *David*'s pose and appearance are reminiscent of the nude statues of antiquity.

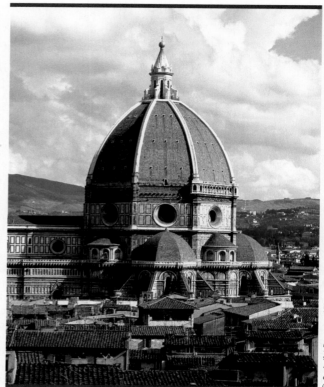

Filippo Brunelleschi, Dome of the Duomo. Brunelleschi was first commissioned to design the dome for the unfinished cathedral of Florence in 1417, but work did not begin until 1420. Although Brunelleschi would have preferred the Roman hemispheric dome, for practical reasons he was forced to elevate the center of the dome and then lessen the weight of the structure by building a thin double shell around a structure of twenty-four ribs. The most important ribs were placed on the outside of the dome (four of them are visible in this illustration).

century were matched by equally stunning advances in sculpture and architecture. Donato di Donatello (doh-NAH-toh dee doh-nuh-TELL-oh) (1386–1466) spent time in Rome studying and copying the statues of antiquity. His subsequent work in Florence reveals how well he had mastered the essence of what he saw. Among his numerous works was a statue of David, which is the first known life-size, freestanding bronze nude in European art since antiquity. With the severed head of the giant Goliath beneath David's feet, Donatello's statue may have celebrated Florentine heroism in the triumph of Florence over the Milanese in 1428. Like Donatello's other statues, *David* also radiated a simplicity and strength that reflected the dignity of humanity.

Filippo Brunelleschi (fee-LEE-poh BROO-nuh-LESS-kee) (1377–1446), a friend of Donatello's, accompanied the latter to Rome. Brunelleschi drew much inspiration from the architectural monuments of Roman antiquity, and when he returned to Florence, he poured his new insights into the creation of a new architecture. His first project involved the challenge of building a dome for the unfinished cathedral of Florence (the Duomo). The cathedral had been started in 1296, but it was Brunelleschi

who devised new building techniques and machinery to create a dome, built between 1420 and 1436, that spanned a 140-foot opening.

An even better example of Brunelleschi's new Renaissance architectural style is evident in the Church of San Lorenzo. When the Medici commissioned him to design the church, Brunelleschi, inspired by Roman models, created a church interior very different from that of the great medieval cathedrals. San Lorenzo's Classical columns, rounded arches, and coffered ceiling created an environment that did not overwhelm the worshiper materially and psychologically, as Gothic cathedrals did, but comforted as a space created to fit human, not divine, measurements. Like painters and sculptors, Renaissance architects sought to reflect a human-centered world.

The new assertion of human individuality, evident in Early Renaissance art, was also reflected in the new emphasis on portraiture. Patrons appeared in the corners of sacred pictures, and monumental tombs and portrait statues honored many of Florence's prominent citizens. By the mid-fifteenth century, artists were giving an accurate rendering of their subjects' facial features while revealing the

Brunelleschi, Interior of San Lorenzo. Cosimo de' Medici contributed massive amounts of money to the rebuilding of the Church of San Lorenzo. As seen in this view of the nave and choir of the church, Brunelleschi's architectural designs were based on the basilica plan borrowed by early Christians from pagan Rome. San Lorenzo's simplicity, evident in its rows of slender Corinthian columns, created a human-centered space.

inner qualities of their personalities. The portraits of the duke and duchess of Urbino by Piero della Francesca (c. 1410–1492) provide accurate representations as well as a sense of both the power and the wealth of the rulers of Urbino (see p. 349).

The Artistic High Renaissance

By the end of the fifteenth century, Italian painters, sculptors, and architects had created a new artistic environment. Many artists had mastered the new techniques for a scientific observation of the world around them and were now ready to move into individualistic forms of creative expression. This final stage of Renaissance art, which flourished between 1480 and 1520, is called the High Renaissance. The shift to the High Renaissance was marked by the increasing importance of Rome as a new cultural center of the Italian Renaissance.

The High Renaissance was dominated by the work of three artistic giants: Leonardo da Vinci (1452–1519), Raphael (1483–1520), and Michelangelo (1475–1564). Leonardo represents a transitional figure in the shift to

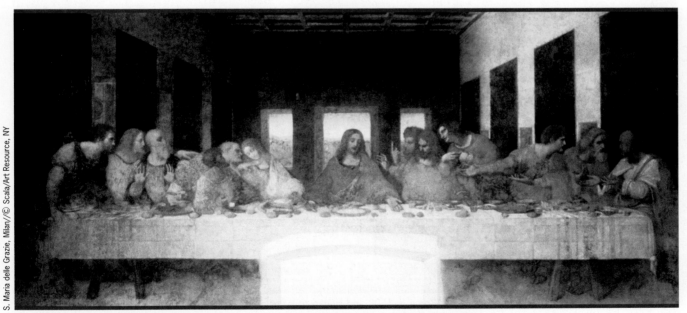

Leonardo da Vinci, *The Last Supper*. Leonardo da Vinci was the impetus behind the High Renaissance concern for the idealization of nature, moving from a realistic portrayal of the human figure to an idealized form. Evident in Leonardo's *Last Supper* is his effort to depict a person's character and inner nature by the use of gesture and movement. Unfortunately, Leonardo used an experimental technique in this fresco, which soon led to its physical deterioration.

High Renaissance principles. He carried on the fifteenth-century experimental tradition by studying everything and even dissecting human bodies to see more clearly how nature worked. But Leonardo stressed the need to advance beyond such realism and initiated the High Renaissance's preoccupation with the idealization of nature, or the attempt to generalize from realistic portrayal to an ideal form. Leonardo's *Last Supper,* painted in Milan, is a brilliant summary of fifteenth-century trends in its organization of space and use of perspective to depict subjects three-dimensionally in a two-dimensional medium. But it is also more. The figure of Philip is idealized, and the work embodies profound psychological dimensions. The words of Jesus that "one of you shall betray me" are experienced directly as each of the apostles reveals his personality and his relationship to Jesus. Through gestures and movement, Leonardo hoped to reveal a person's inner life.

Giorgio Vasari, Leonardo da Vinci (1550)

Raphael (RAFF-ee-ul) blossomed as a painter at an early age; at twenty-five, he was already regarded as one of Italy's best painters. Raphael was acclaimed for his numerous madonnas, in which he attempted to achieve an ideal of beauty far surpassing human standards. He is well known for his frescoes in the Vatican Palace; his *School of Athens* reveals a world of balance, harmony, and order—the underlying principles of the art of the Classical world of Greece and Rome.

Michelangelo (my-kuh-LAN-juh-loh), an accomplished painter, sculptor, and architect, was another giant of the High Renaissance. Fiercely driven by his desire to create, he worked with great passion and energy on a remarkable number of projects. Michelangelo was influenced by Neoplatonism, especially evident in his figures on the ceiling of the Sistine Chapel in Rome. In 1508, Pope Julius II had called Michelangelo to Rome and commissioned him to decorate the chapel ceiling. This colossal project was not completed until 1512. Michelangelo attempted to tell the story of the Fall of Man by depicting nine scenes

Stanza della Segnatura, Vatican Palace//© Erich Lessing/Art Resource, NY

Raphael, *School of Athens.* Raphael arrived in Rome in 1508 and began to paint a series of frescoes commissioned by Pope Julius II for the papal apartments at the Vatican. In *School of Athens,* painted in 1510 or 1511, Raphael created an imaginary gathering of ancient philosophers. In the center stand Plato and Aristotle. At the left is Pythagoras, showing his system of proportions on a slate. At the right is Ptolemy, holding a celestial globe.

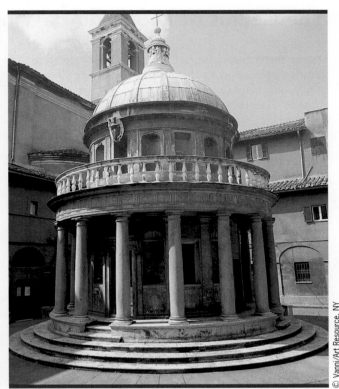

Bramante, Tempietto. Ferdinand and Isabella of Spain commissioned Donato Bramante to design a small building in Rome that would commemorate the place where Saint Peter purportedly was crucified. Completed in 1502, the temple reflected Bramante's increasing understanding of ancient Roman remains.

Michelangelo, *David*. This statue of David, cut from an 18-foot-high piece of marble, exalts the beauty of the human body and is a fitting symbol of the Italian Renaissance's affirmation of human power. Completed in 1504, *David* was moved by Florentine authorities to a special location in front of the Palazzo Vecchio, the seat of the Florentine government.

from the biblical book of Genesis. In his *Creation of Adam* (reproduced at the start of this chapter), the well-proportioned figure of Adam awaits the divine spark. Adam, like the other muscular figures on the ceiling, reveals an ideal type of human being with perfect proportions. In good Neoplatonic fashion, the beauty of these figures is meant to be a reflection of divine beauty; the more beautiful the body, the more God-like the figure.

Another manifestation of Michelangelo's search for ideal beauty was his *David*, a colossal marble statue commissioned by the Florentine government in 1501 and completed in 1504. Michelangelo maintained that the form of a statue already resided in the uncarved piece of stone: "I only take away the surplus, the statue is already there."[20] Out of a piece of marble that had remained unused for fifty years, Michelangelo created a 14-foot-high figure, the largest sculpture in Italy since the time of Rome. An awe-inspiring hero, Michelangelo's *David* proudly proclaims the beauty of the human body and the glory of human beings.

The High Renaissance was also evident in architecture, especially in the work of Donato Bramante (doh-NAH-toh brah-MAHN-tay) (1444–1514). He came from Urbino but took up residence in Rome, where he designed a small temple on the supposed site of Saint Peter's martyrdom. The Tempietto, or little temple, with its Doric columns surrounding a sanctuary enclosed by a dome, summarized the architectural ideals of the High Renaissance. Columns, dome, and sanctuary form a monumental and harmonious whole. Inspired by antiquity, Bramante had recaptured the grandeur of ancient Rome. His achievement led Pope Julius II to commission him to design a new basilica for Rome, which eventually became the magnificent Saint Peter's.

The Artist and Social Status

Early Renaissance artists began their careers as apprentices to masters in craft guilds. Apprentices with unusual talent might eventually become masters and run their own workshops. As in the Middle Ages, artists were still largely viewed as artisans. Since guilds depended on commissions for their projects, patrons played an important role in the art of the Early Renaissance. The wealthy

The Genius of Leonardo da Vinci

During the Renaissance, artists came to be viewed as creative geniuses with almost divine qualities. One individual who helped create this image was himself a painter. Giorgio Vasari was an avid admirer of Italy's great artists and wrote a series of brief biographies of them. This excerpt is taken from his account of Leonardo da Vinci.

⊷⊶✦⊰⊷

Giorgio Vasari, *Lives of the Artists*

In the normal course of events many men and women are born with various remarkable qualities and talents; but occasionally, in a way that transcends nature, a single person is marvelously endowed by heaven with beauty, grace, and talent in such abundance that he leaves other men far behind, all his actions seem inspired, and indeed everything he does clearly comes from God rather than from human art.

Everyone acknowledged that this was true of Leonardo da Vinci, an artist of outstanding physical beauty who displayed infinite grace in everything he did and who cultivated his genius so brilliantly that all problems he studied he solved with ease. He possessed great strength and dexterity; he was a man of regal spirit and tremendous breadth of mind; and his name became so famous that not only was he esteemed during his lifetime but his reputation endured and became even greater after his death. . . .

He was marvelously gifted, and he proved himself to be a first-class geometrician in his work as a sculptor and architect. In his youth Leonardo made in clay several heads of women, with smiling faces, of which plaster casts are still being made, as well as some children's heads executed as if by a mature artist. He also did many architectural drawings both of ground plans and of other elevations, and, while still young, he was the first to propose reducing the Arno River to a navigable canal between Pisa and Florence. He made designs for mills, fulling machines, and engines that could be driven by waterpower; and as he intended to be a painter by profession he carefully studied drawing from life. . . . Altogether, his genius was so wonderfully inspired by the grace of God, his powers of expression were so powerfully fed by a willing memory and intellect, and his writing conveyed his ideas so precisely, that his arguments and reasonings confounded the most formidable critics. In addition, he used to make models and plans showing how to excavate and tunnel through mountains without difficulty, so as to pass from one level to another; and he demonstrated how to lift and draw great weights by means of levers and hoists and ways of cleaning harbors and using pumps to suck up water from great depths.

Q How do you think Vasari's comments on Leonardo fostered the image of the Renaissance artist as a "creative genius with almost divine qualities"?

---

upper classes determined both the content and the purpose of the paintings and pieces of sculpture they commissioned.

By the end of the fifteenth century, a transformation in the position of the artist had occurred. Especially talented individuals, such as Leonardo, Raphael, and Michelangelo, were no longer regarded as artisans but as artistic geniuses with creative energies akin to the divine (see the box above). Artists were heroes, individuals who were praised more for their creativity than for their competence as craftspeople. Michelangelo, for example, was frequently addressed as "Il Divino"—the Divine One. As society excused their eccentricities and valued their creative genius, the artists of the High Renaissance became the first to embody the modern concept of the artist.

As respect for artists grew, so did their ability to profit economically from their work and to rise on the social scale. Now welcomed as equals into the circles of the upper classes, they mingled with the political and intellectual elite of their society and became more aware of new intellectual theories, which they then embodied in their art. The Platonic Academy and Renaissance Neoplatonism had an especially important impact on Florentine painters.

The Northern Artistic Renaissance

In trying to provide an exact portrayal of their world, the artists of the north (especially the Low Countries) and Italy took different approaches. In Italy, the human form became the primary vehicle of expression as Italian artists sought to master the technical skills that allowed them to portray humans in realistic settings. The large wall spaces of Italian churches had given rise to the art of fresco painting, but in the north, the prevalence of Gothic cathedrals with their stained-glass windows resulted in more emphasis on illuminated manuscripts and wooden panel painting for altarpieces. The space available in these works was limited, and great care was required to depict each object, leading northern painters to become masters at rendering details.

The most influential northern school of art in the fifteenth century was centered in Flanders. Jan van Eyck (YAHN vahn YK *or* van AYK) (c. 1390–1441) was among

National Gallery, London/© Erich Lessing/Art Resource, NY

Van Eyck, *Giovanni Arnolfini and His Bride*. Northern painters took great care in depicting each object and became masters at rendering details. This emphasis on a realistic portrayal is clearly evident in this oil painting, supposedly a portrait of Giovanni Arnolfini, an Italian merchant who had settled in Bruges, and his wife, Giovanna Cenami.

the first to use oil paint, a medium that enabled the artist to use a varied range of colors and create fine details. In the famous *Giovanni Arnolfini and His Bride,* van Eyck's attention to detail is staggering: precise portraits, a glittering chandelier, and a mirror reflecting the objects in the room. Although each detail was rendered as observed, it is evident that van Eyck's comprehension of perspective was still uncertain. His work is truly indicative of northern Renaissance painters, who, in their effort to imitate nature, did so not by mastery of the laws of perspective and proportion but by empirical observation of visual reality and the accurate portrayal of details. Moreover, northern painters placed great emphasis on the emotional intensity of religious feeling and created great works of devotional art, especially in their altarpieces. Michelangelo summarized the difference between northern and Italian Renaissance painting in these words:

> In Flanders, they paint, before all things, to render exactly and deceptively the outward appearance of things. The

painters choose, by preference, subjects provoking transports of piety, like the figures of saints or of prophets. But most of the time they paint what are called landscapes with plenty of figures. Though the eye is agreeably impressed, these pictures have neither choice of values nor grandeur. In short, this art is without power and without distinction; it aims at rendering minutely many things at the same time, of which a single one would have sufficed to call forth a man's whole application.[21]

By the end of the fifteenth century, however, artists from the north began to study in Italy and were visually influenced by what artists were doing there.

One northern artist of this later period who was greatly affected by the Italians was Albrecht Dürer (AHL-brekht DOO-rur) (1471–1528) from Nuremberg. Dürer made two trips to Italy and absorbed most of what the Italians could teach, as is evident in his mastery of the laws of perspective and Renaissance theories of proportion. He wrote detailed treatises on both subjects. At the same time, as in his famous *Adoration of the Magi,* Dürer did not reject the use of minute details characteristic of northern artists. He did try, however, to integrate those details more harmoniously into his works and, like the Italian artists of the High Renaissance, to achieve a standard of ideal beauty by a careful examination of the human form.

Music in the Renaissance

For much of the fifteenth century, an extraordinary cultural environment was fostered in the domains of the dukes of Burgundy in northern Europe. The court of the dukes attracted some of the best artists and musicians of the time. Among them was Guillaume Dufay (gee-YOHM doo-FAY) (c. 1400–1474), perhaps the most important composer of his era. Born in northern France, Dufay lived for a few years in Italy and was thus well suited to combine the late medieval style of France with the early Renaissance style of Italy. One of Dufay's greatest contributions was a change in the composition of the Mass. He was the first to use secular tunes to replace Gregorian chants as the fixed melody that served as the basis for the Mass. Dufay also composed a number of secular songs, an important reminder that during the Renaissance, music ceased to be used chiefly in the service of God and moved into the secular world of courts and cities. In Italy and France, the chief form of secular music was the madrigal.

The Renaissance madrigal was a poem set to music, and its origins were in the fourteenth-century Italian courts. The texts were usually twelve-line poems written in the vernacular, and their theme was emotional or erotic love. By the mid-sixteenth century, most madrigals were written for five or six voices and employed a technique called text painting, in which the music tried to portray the literal meaning of the text. Thus, the melody would rise for the word *heaven* or use a wavelike motion to represent

Dürer, *Adoration of the Magi.* By the end of the fifteenth century, northern artists had begun to study in Italy and to adopt many of the techniques used by Italian painters. As is evident in this painting, which was the central panel for an altarpiece done for Frederick the Wise in 1504, Albrecht Dürer masterfully incorporated the laws of perspective and the ideals of proportion into his works. At the same time, he did not abandon the preoccupation with detail typical of northern artists. Dürer portrayed himself in the center as the wise man with long hair.

the word *water.* By the mid-sixteenth century, the madrigal had also spread to England, where the most popular form was characterized by the *fa-la-la* refrain like that found in the English carol "Deck the Halls."

The European State in the Renaissance

 FOCUS QUESTION: Why do historians sometimes refer to the monarchies of the late fifteenth century as "new monarchies" or "Renaissance states"?

In the first half of the fifteenth century, European states continued the disintegrative patterns of the previous century. In the second half of the century, however, recovery set in, and attempts were made to reestablish the centralized power of monarchical governments. To characterize the results, some historians have used the label "Renaissance states"; others have spoken of the **"new monarchies,"** especially those of France, England, and Spain at the end of the fifteenth century (see Map 12.2). Although monarchs in western Europe succeeded to varying degrees at extending their political authority, rulers in central and eastern Europe were often weak and unable to impose their authority.

The Growth of the French Monarchy

The Hundred Years' War had left France prostrate. Depopulation, desolate farmlands, ruined commerce, and independent and unruly nobles had made it difficult for the kings to assert their authority. But the war had also developed a strong degree of French national feeling toward a common enemy that the kings could use to reestablish monarchical power. The need to prosecute the war provided an excuse to strengthen the authority of the king, already evident in the policies of Charles VII (1422–1461) after he was crowned king at Reims. With the consent of the Estates-General, Charles established a royal army composed of cavalry and archers. He received from the Estates-General the right to levy the *taille,* an annual direct tax usually on land or property, without any need for further approval from the Estates-General. Losing control of the purse meant less power for this parliamentary body.

The process of developing a French territorial state was greatly advanced by King Louis XI (1461–1483), known as the Spider because of his wily and devious ways. By retaining the *taille* as a permanent tax imposed by royal authority, Louis secured a sound, regular source of income. Louis was not, however, completely successful in repressing the French nobility, whose independence posed a threat to his own state building. A major problem was his supposed vassal, Charles the Bold, duke of Burgundy (1467–1477). Charles attempted to create a middle kingdom between France and Germany, stretching from the Low Countries to Switzerland. Louis opposed his efforts, and when Charles was killed in 1477 fighting the Swiss, Louis added part of Charles's possessions, the duchy of Burgundy, to his own lands. Three years later, the provinces of Anjou, Maine, Bar, and Provence were brought under royal control. Many historians believe that Louis created a base for the later development of a strong French monarchy.

MAP 12.2 Europe in the Second Half of the Fifteenth Century. By the second half of the fifteenth century, states in western Europe, particularly France, Spain, and England, had begun the process of modern state building. With varying success, they reined in the power of the church and nobles, increased the ability to levy taxes, and established effective government bureaucracies.

Q *What aspects of Europe's political boundaries help explain why France and the Holy Roman Empire were often at war with each other?*

View an animated version of this map or related maps on the CourseMate website.

England: Civil War and a New Monarchy

The Hundred Years' War had also strongly affected the other protagonist in that conflict. The cost of the war in its final years and the losses in manpower strained the English economy. Moreover, even greater domestic turmoil came to England when the War of the Roses broke out in the 1450s. This civil war pitted the ducal house of Lancaster, whose symbol was a red rose, against the ducal house of York, whose symbol was a white rose. Many aristocratic families of England were drawn into the conflict. Finally, in 1485, Henry Tudor, duke of Richmond, defeated the last Yorkist king, Richard III (1483–1485), at Bosworth Field and established the new Tudor dynasty.

As the first Tudor king, Henry VII (1485–1509) worked to reduce internal dissension and establish a strong monarchical government. Henry ended the private wars of the nobility by abolishing "livery and maintenance," the practice by which wealthy aristocrats maintained private armies of followers dedicated to the service of their lord. Since England, unlike France and Spain, did not possess a standing army, the king relied on special commissions to trusted nobles to raise troops for a specific campaign, after which the troops were disbanded. Henry also controlled the irresponsible activity of the nobles by establishing the Court of Star Chamber, which did not use juries and allowed torture to be used to extract confessions.

Henry VII was particularly successful in extracting income from the traditional financial resources of the

MAP 12.3 **The Iberian Peninsula.** The marriage of Isabella of Castile to Ferdinand of Aragon laid the foundation for the unification of Spain and its rise as a major European power. The two monarchs instituted military and bureaucratic reforms and forced Jews and Muslims to flee the country.

Q *What aspects of Portugal's geography help explain why it became a major seafaring nation, with little overland trade with Europe?*

English monarch, such as the crown lands, judicial fees and fines, and customs duties. By using diplomacy to avoid wars, which are always expensive, the king avoided having to call Parliament on any regular basis to grant him funds. By not overburdening the landed gentry and middle class with taxes, Henry won their favor, and they provided much support for his monarchy. Henry's policies enabled him to leave England with a stable and prosperous government and an enhanced status for the monarchy itself.

The Unification of Spain

During the Middle Ages, several independent Christian kingdoms had emerged in the course of the long reconquest of the Iberian peninsula from the Muslims. Aragon and Castile were the strongest Spanish kingdoms; in the west was the independent monarchy of Portugal; in the north, the small kingdom of Navarre, oriented toward France; and in the south, the Muslim kingdom of Granada (see Map 12.3). Few people at the beginning of the fifteenth century could have predicted the unification of the Iberian kingdoms.

A major step in that direction was taken with the marriage of Isabella of Castile (1474–1504) and Ferdinand of Aragon (1479–1516) in 1469. This was a dynastic union of two rulers, not a political union. Both kingdoms maintained their own parliaments (Cortes), courts, laws, coinage, speech, customs, and political organs. Nevertheless, the two rulers worked to strengthen royal control of government, especially in Castile. The royal council, which was supposed to supervise local administration and oversee the implementation of government policies, was stripped of aristocrats and filled primarily with middle-class lawyers. Trained in the principles of Roman law, these officials operated on the belief that the monarchy embodied the power of the state.

Seeking to replace the undisciplined feudal levies they had inherited with a more professional royal army, Ferdinand and Isabella reorganized the military forces of Spain. The development of a strong infantry force as the heart of the new Spanish army made it the best in Europe by the sixteenth century.

Because of its vast power and wealth, Ferdinand and Isabella recognized the importance of controlling the Catholic Church. They secured from the pope the right to select the most important church officials in Spain, virtually guaranteeing the creation of a Spanish Catholic Church in which the clergy became an instrument for the extension of royal power. The monarchs also used their authority over the church to institute reform. Isabella's chief minister, the able and astute Cardinal Ximenes (khee-MAY-ness), restored discipline and eliminated immorality among the monks and secular clergy.

The religious zeal exhibited in Cardinal Ximenes's reform program was also evident in the policy of strict religious uniformity pursued by Ferdinand and Isabella. Of course, it served a political purpose as well: to create unity and further bolster royal power. Spain possessed two large religious minorities, the Jews and Muslims, both of which had generally been tolerated in medieval Spain. Although anti-Semitism had become a fact of life in medieval Europe, Spain had largely remained tolerant. In some areas of Spain, Jews exercised much influence in economic and intellectual affairs. During the fourteenth century, however, increased persecution led the majority of Spanish Jews to convert to Christianity. Although many of these converted Jews came to play important roles in Spanish society, complaints that they were secretly reverting to Judaism prompted Ferdinand and Isabella to ask the pope to introduce the Inquisition into Spain in 1478. Under royal control, the Inquisition worked with cruel efficiency to guarantee the orthodoxy of the converts but had no authority over practicing Jews. Consequently, in 1492, flush with the success of their conquest of Muslim Granada, Ferdinand and Isabella took the drastic step of expelling all professed Jews from Spain. It is estimated that 150,000 out of possibly 200,000 Jews fled.

Ferdinand and Isabella also pursued a policy of battling the Muslims by attacking the kingdom of Granada. The war against this remaining Muslim kingdom lasted eleven years until the final bastion of the city of Granada fell in 1492. Muslims were now "encouraged" to convert to Christianity, and in 1502, Isabella issued a decree expelling all professed Muslims from her kingdom. To a very large degree, the "Most Catholic" monarchs had achieved their goal of absolute religious orthodoxy as a basic ingredient of the Spanish state. To be Spanish was to be Catholic, a policy of uniformity enforced by the Inquisition. It was no accident that Spain would be a staunch pillar of the Catholic Church during the era of the Reformation in the sixteenth century (see Chapter 13).

The Holy Roman Empire: The Success of the Habsburgs

Unlike France, England, and Spain, the Holy Roman Empire failed to develop a strong monarchical authority. After 1438, the position of Holy Roman Emperor remained in the hands of the Habsburg dynasty. Having gradually acquired a number of possessions along the Danube, known collectively as Austria, the house of Habsburg had become one of the wealthiest landholders in the empire and by the mid-fifteenth century began to play an important role in European affairs.

Much of the Habsburg success in the fifteenth century was due not to military success but to a well-executed policy of dynastic marriages. As the old Habsburg motto said, "Leave the waging of wars to others! But you, happy Austria, marry; for the realms which Mars [god of war] awards to others, Venus [goddess of love] transfers to you." By marrying his son Maximilian to Mary, the daughter of Duke Charles the Bold of Burgundy, Emperor Frederick III (1440–1493) gained Franche-Comté in east-central France, Luxembourg, and a large part of the Low Countries. The addition of these territories made the Habsburg dynasty an international power and brought it the undying opposition of the French monarchy because the rulers of France feared they would be surrounded by the Habsburgs.

Much was expected of the flamboyant Maximilian I (1493–1519) when he became emperor. Through the Reichstag, the imperial diet or parliament, Maximilian attempted to centralize the administration by creating new institutions common to the entire empire. Opposition from the German princes doomed these efforts, however. Maximilian's only real success lay in his marriage alliances. Philip of Burgundy, the son of Maximilian's marriage to Mary, was married to Joanna, the daughter of Ferdinand and Isabella. Philip and Joanna produced a son, Charles, who, through a series of unexpected deaths, became heir to all three lines, the Habsburg, Burgundian, and Spanish, making him the leading monarch of his age (see Chapter 13).

The Struggle for Strong Monarchy in Eastern Europe

In eastern Europe, rulers struggled to achieve the centralization of their territorial states but faced serious obstacles. Although the population was mostly Slavic, there were islands of other ethnic groups that caused untold difficulties. Religious differences also troubled the area, as Roman Catholics, Greek Orthodox Christians, and pagans confronted each other.

Much of Polish history revolved around a bitter struggle between the crown and the landed nobility until the end of the fifteenth century, when the preoccupation of Poland's rulers with problems in Bohemia and Hungary, as well as war with the Russians and Turks, enabled the aristocrats to reestablish their power. Through their control of the Sejm (SAYM) or national diet, the magnates reduced the peasantry to serfdom by 1511 and established the right to elect their kings. The Polish kings proved unable to establish a strong royal authority.

Bohemia, Poland's neighbor, was part of the Holy Roman Empire, but distrust of the Germans and close ethnic ties to the Poles and Slovaks encouraged the Czechs of Bohemia to associate with their northeastern Slavic neighbors. The Hussite wars (see "The Problems of Heresy and Reform" later in this chapter) led to further dissension and civil war. Because of a weak monarchy, the Bohemian nobles increased their authority and wealth at the expense of both crown and church.

The history of Hungary had been closely tied to that of central and western Europe by its conversion to Roman Catholicism by German missionaries. The church became a large and prosperous institution. Wealthy bishops, along with the great territorial lords, became powerful, independent political figures. For a brief while, Hungary developed into an important European state, the dominant power in eastern Europe. King Matthias Corvinus (muh-THY-uss kor-VY-nuss) (1458–1490) broke the power of the wealthy lords and created a well-organized bureaucracy. Like a typical Renaissance prince, he patronized the new humanist culture, brought Italian scholars and artists to his capital at Buda, and made his court one of the most brilliant outside Italy. After his death, however, Hungary returned to weak rule, and the work of Corvinus was largely undone.

Since the thirteenth century, Russia had been under the domination of the Mongols. Gradually, the princes of Moscow rose to prominence by using their close relationship to the Mongol khans to increase their wealth and expand their possessions. In the reign of the great prince Ivan III (1462–1505), a new Russian state—the principality of Moscow—was born. Ivan III annexed other Russian principalities and took advantage of dissension among the Mongols to throw off their yoke by 1480.

CHRONOLOGY   Europe in the Renaissance

France

Charles VII	1422–1461
Louis XI the Spider	1461–1483

England

War of the Roses	1450s–1485
Richard III	1483–1485
Henry VII	1485–1509

Spain

Isabella of Castile	1474–1504
Ferdinand of Aragon	1479–1516
Marriage of Ferdinand and Isabella	1469
Introduction of Inquisition	1478
Expulsion of the Jews	1492
Expulsion of the Muslims	1502

Holy Roman Empire

Frederick III	1440–1493
Maximilian I	1493–1519

Eastern Europe

Battle of Kosovo	1389
Hungary: Matthias Corvinus	1458–1490
Russia: Ivan III	1462–1505
Fall of Constantinople and Byzantine Empire	1453

The Ottoman Turks and the End of the Byzantine Empire

Eastern Europe was increasingly threatened by the steadily advancing Ottoman Turks (see Map 12.4). The Byzantine Empire had, of course, served as a buffer between the Muslim Middle East and the Latin West for centuries, but it had been severely weakened by the sack of Constantinople in 1204 and its occupation by the West. Although the Palaeologus dynasty (1260–1453) had tried to reestablish Byzantine power in the Balkans after the overthrow of the Latin empire, the threat from the Turks finally doomed the long-lasting empire.

Beginning in northeastern Asia Minor in the thirteenth century, the Ottoman Turks spread rapidly, seizing the lands of the Seljuk Turks and the Byzantine Empire. In 1345, they bypassed Constantinople and moved into the Balkans. Under Sultan Murad (moo-RAHD), Ottoman forces moved through Bulgaria and into the lands of the Serbians, who provided a strong center of opposition under King Lazar (lah-ZAR). But in 1389, at the Battle of Kosovo (KAWSS-suh-voh), Ottoman forces defeated the Serbs; both King Lazar and Sultan Murad perished in the battle. Kosovo became a battlefield long revered and remembered by the Serbs. Not until 1480 were Bosnia, Albania, and the rest of Serbia added to the Ottoman Empire in the Balkans.

In the meantime, in 1453, the Ottomans also completed the demise of the Byzantine Empire. With 80,000 troops ranged against only 7,000 defenders, Sultan Mehmet II (meh-MET) laid siege to Constantinople. In their attack on the city, the Turks made use of massive cannons with 26-foot barrels that could launch stone balls weighing up to 1,200 pounds each. Finally, the walls were breached; the Byzantine emperor died in the final battle. Mehmet II, standing before the palace of the emperor, paused to reflect on the passing nature of human glory.

After their conquest of Constantinople, the Ottoman Turks tried to complete their conquest of the Balkans, where they had been established since the fourteenth century. Although they were successful in taking the Romanian territory of Wallachia (wah-LAY-kee-uh) in 1476, the resistance of the Hungarians initially kept the Turks from advancing up the Danube valley. Until the end of the fifteenth century, internal problems and the need to consolidate their eastern frontiers kept the Turks from any further attacks on Europe. But at the beginning of the sixteenth century, the Ottomans would renew their offensive against the West, challenging Hungary, Austria, Bohemia, and Poland and threatening to turn the Mediterranean into a Turkish lake.

The Church in the Renaissance

 Focus Question: What were the policies of the Renaissance popes, and what impact did those policies have on the Catholic Church?

As a result of the efforts of the Council of Constance, the Great Schism had finally been brought to an end in 1417 (see Chapter 11). The ending of the schism proved to be the council's easiest task; it was much less successful in dealing with the problems of heresy and reform.

The Problems of Heresy and Reform

Heresy was not a new problem, and in the thirteenth century, the church had developed inquisitorial machinery to deal with it. But two widespread movements in the fourteenth and early fifteenth centuries—Lollardy and Hussitism—posed new threats to the church.

WYCLIF AND LOLLARDY   English Lollardy was a product of the Oxford theologian John Wyclif (WIK-lif) (c. 1328–1384), whose disgust with clerical corruption led him to make a far-ranging attack on papal authority and medieval Christian beliefs and practices. Wyclif alleged that there was no basis in Scripture for papal claims of temporal authority and advocated that the popes be stripped of their authority and their property. Believing that the Bible should be a Christian's sole authority, Wyclif urged

MAP 12.4 The Ottoman Empire and Southeastern Europe. Long a buffer between Christian Europe and the Muslim Middle East, the Byzantine Empire quickly waned in power and territory after Constantinople was sacked by crusaders in 1204. The Ottoman Turks slowly gained Byzantine territory and ended the thousand-year empire with the fall of Constantinople in 1453.

Q *Why would the Byzantine Empire have found it difficult to make alliances by 1403?*

that it be made available in the vernacular languages so that every Christian could read it. Rejecting all practices not mentioned in Scripture, Wyclif condemned pilgrimages, the veneration of saints, and a whole series of rituals and rites that had developed in the medieval church. Wyclif attracted a number of followers who came to be known as Lollards.

HUS AND THE HUSSITES A marriage between the royal families of England and Bohemia enabled Lollard ideas to spread to Bohemia, where they reinforced the ideas of a group of Czech reformers led by the chancellor of the university at Prague, John Hus (1374–1415). In his call for reform, Hus urged the elimination of the worldliness and corruption of the clergy and attacked the excessive power of the papacy within the Catholic Church. Hus's objections fell on receptive ears, for the Catholic Church, as one of the largest landowners in Bohemia, was already

widely criticized. Moreover, many clergymen were German, and the native Czechs' strong resentment of the Germans who dominated Bohemia also contributed to Hus's movement.

The Council of Constance attempted to deal with the growing problem of heresy by summoning John Hus to the council. Granted safe conduct by Emperor Sigismund, Hus went in the hope of a free hearing of his ideas. Instead he was arrested, condemned as a heretic (by a narrow vote), and burned at the stake in 1415. This action turned the unrest in Bohemia into revolutionary upheaval, and the resulting Hussite wars racked the Holy Roman Empire until a truce was arranged in 1436.

Council of Constance

REFORM OF THE CHURCH The efforts of the Council of Constance to reform the church were even less successful

The Church in the Renaissance ❧ **371**

than its attempt to eradicate heresy. The council passed two reform decrees. *Sacrosancta* (sak-roh-SANK-tuh) stated that a general council of the church received its authority from God; hence every Christian, including the pope, was subject to its authority. The decree *Frequens* (FREE-kwens) provided for the regular holding of general councils to ensure that church reform would continue. Taken together, *Sacrosancta* and *Frequens* provided for a legislative system within the church superior to the popes.

Decrees alone, however, proved insufficient to reform the church. Councils could issue decrees, but popes had to execute them, and popes would not cooperate with councils that diminished their authority. Beginning as early as Martin V in 1417, successive popes worked steadfastly for thirty years to defeat the conciliar movement. The final blow came in 1460, when Pope Pius II issued the papal bull *Execrabilis* (ek-suh-KRAB-uh-liss), condemning appeals to a council over the head of a pope as heretical.

By the mid-fifteenth century, the popes had reasserted their supremacy over the Catholic Church. No longer, however, did they have any possibility of asserting supremacy over temporal governments as the medieval papacy had. Although the papal monarchy had been maintained, it had lost much moral prestige. In the fifteenth century, the Renaissance papacy contributed to an even further decline in the moral leadership of the popes.

The Renaissance Papacy

The Renaissance papacy encompasses the line of popes from the end of the Great Schism (1417) to the beginnings of the Reformation in the early sixteenth century. The primary concern of the papacy is governing the Catholic Church as its spiritual leader. But as heads of the church, popes had temporal preoccupations as well, and the story of the Renaissance papacy is really an account of how the latter came to overshadow the popes' spiritual functions.

The manner in which Renaissance popes pursued their interests in the Papal States and Italian politics, especially their use of intrigue and even bloodshed, seemed shocking. Of all the Renaissance popes, Julius II (1503–1513) was most involved in war and politics. The fiery "warrior-pope" personally led armies against his enemies, much to the disgust of pious Christians, who viewed the pope as a spiritual leader. As one intellectual wrote, "How, O bishop standing in the room of the Apostles, dare you teach the people the things that pertain to war?"

To further their territorial aims in the Papal States, the popes needed loyal servants. Because they were not hereditary monarchs, popes could not build dynasties over several generations and came to rely on the practice of **nepotism** to promote their families' interests. Pope Sixtus IV (1471–1484), for example, made five of his

Galleria degli Uffizi, Florence//© Scala/Art Resource, NY

A Renaissance Pope: Leo X. The Renaissance popes allowed secular concerns to overshadow their spiritual duties. Shown here is the Medici pope Leo X. Raphael portrays the pope as a collector of books, looking up after examining an illuminated manuscript with a magnifying glass. At the left is the pope's cousin Guilio, a cardinal. Standing behind the pope is Luigi de' Rossi, another relative who had also been made a cardinal.

nephews cardinals and gave them an abundance of church offices to build up their finances (the word *nepotism* is in fact derived from the Latin *nepos*, meaning "nephew"). Alexander VI (1492–1503), a member of the Borgia family who was known for his debauchery and sensuality, raised one son, one nephew, and the brother of one mistress to the cardinalate. A Venetian envoy stated that Alexander, "joyous by nature, thought of nothing but the aggrandizement of his children." Alexander scandalized the church by encouraging his son Cesare to carve out a state for himself from the territories of the Papal States in central Italy.

The Renaissance popes were great patrons of Renaissance culture, and their efforts made Rome a cultural leader at the beginning of the sixteenth century. For the warrior-pope Julius II, the patronage of Renaissance culture was mostly a matter of policy as he endeavored to add to the splendor of his pontificate by tearing down the Basilica of Saint Peter, which had been built by the emperor Constantine, and beginning construction of the

CHRONOLOGY **The Church in the Renaissance**

Council of Constance	1414–1418
Burning of John Hus	1415
End of the Great Schism	1417
Pius II issues the papal bull *Execrabilis*	1460
The Renaissance papacy	
Sixtus IV	1471–1484
Alexander VI	1492–1503
Julius II	1503–1513
Leo X	1513–1521

greatest building in Christendom, the present Saint Peter's Basilica.

Julius's successor, Leo X (1513–1521), was also a patron of Renaissance culture, not as a matter of policy but as a deeply involved participant. Such might be expected of the son of Lorenzo de' Medici. Made an archbishop at the age of eight and a cardinal at thirteen, he acquired a refined taste in art, manners, and social life among the Florentine Renaissance elite. He became pope at the age of thirty-seven, reportedly remarking to the Venetian ambassador, "Let us enjoy the papacy, since God has given it to us." Raphael was commissioned to do paintings, and the construction of Saint Peter's was accelerated as Rome became the literary and artistic center of the Renaissance.

CHAPTER SUMMARY

Beginning in Italy, the Renaissance was an era that rediscovered the culture of ancient Greece and Rome. It was also a time of recovery from the difficulties of the fourteenth century as well as a period of transition that witnessed a continuation of the economic, political, and social trends that had begun in the High Middle Ages.

The Renaissance was also a movement in which intellectuals and artists proclaimed a new vision of humankind and raised fundamental questions about the value and importance of the individual. The humanists or intellectuals of the age called their period (from the mid-fourteenth to the mid-sixteenth century) an age of rebirth, believing that they had restored arts and letters to new glory. Humanism was an intellectual movement based on the study of the Classical literary works of Greece and Rome. The goal of a humanist education was to produce individuals of virtue and wisdom. Civic humanism posited that the ideal citizen was not only an intellectual but also an active participant in the life of the state.

The Renaissance is perhaps best known for its artistic brilliance. Renaissance artists in Italy sought not only

to persuade onlookers of the reality of the object they were portraying, but also to focus attention on human beings as "the center and measure of all things." This new Renaissance style was developed, above all, in Florence, but at the end of the fifteenth century, Renaissance art moved into a new phase in which Rome became the new cultural center. In the works of Leonardo da Vinci, Raphael, and

Michelangelo, the High Renaissance ideal of beauty was convincingly portrayed.

The Renaissance in Europe was also an era of "new monarchies," best seen in England, France, and Spain. Monarchs in these countries limited the private armies of the aristocracy, raised taxes, created professional armies, and in the process were able to reestablish the centralized power of monarchical governments. At the same time, the Renaissance popes became increasingly mired in political and temporal concerns that overshadowed their spiritual responsibilities.

Of course, the intellectuals and artists of the Renaissance wrote and painted for the upper classes, and the brilliant intellectual, cultural, and artistic accomplishments of the Renaissance were products of and for the elite. The ideas of the Renaissance did not have a broad base among the masses of the people. The Renaissance did, however, raise new questions about medieval traditions. In advocating a return

to the early sources of Christianity and criticizing current religious practices, the humanists raised fundamental issues about the Catholic Church, which was still an important institution. In the sixteenth century, as we shall see in the next chapter, the intellectual renaissance of the fifteenth century gave way to a religious renaissance that touched the lives of people, including the masses, in new and profound ways.

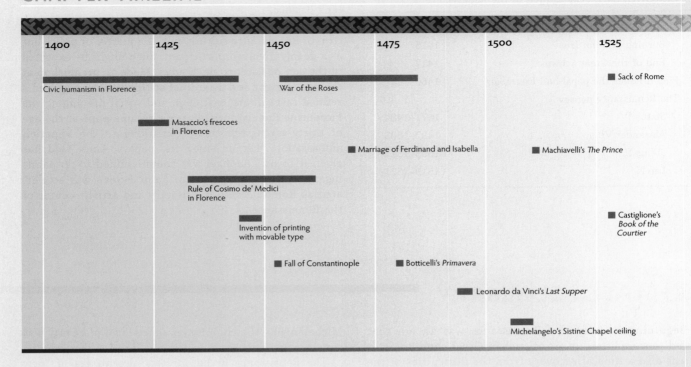

	1400	1425	1450	1475	1500	1525

Civic humanism in Florence

Masaccio's frescoes in Florence

War of the Roses

■ Sack of Rome

■ Marriage of Ferdinand and Isabella

■ Machiavelli's *The Prince*

Rule of Cosimo de' Medici in Florence

Invention of printing with movable type

■ Castiglione's *Book of the Courtier*

■ Fall of Constantinople

■ Botticelli's *Primavera*

■ Leonardo da Vinci's *Last Supper*

Michelangelo's Sistine Chapel ceiling

CHAPTER REVIEW

Upon Reflection

Q What was the pattern of political development in Renaissance Italy? What new political practices (statecraft) did the Italians contribute to Europe, and how were these new political practices reflected in the work of Machiavelli?

Q What was the relationship between Italian Renaissance humanism and Italian Renaissance art?

Q What impact did the policies of the Renaissance popes have on the Catholic Church?

Key Terms

Renaissance (p. 341)
entrepreneurs (p. 343)
estates (p. 344)
individualism (p. 352)
secularism (p. 352)
humanism (p. 352)
civic humanism (p. 352)
Neoplatonism (p. 355)
Hermeticism (p. 355)
pantheism (p. 355)
"new monarchies" (p. 366)
nepotism (p. 372)

Suggestions for Further Reading

GENERAL WORKS ON THE RENAISSANCE General works on the Renaissance in Europe include **P. Burke, *The European***

Renaissance: Centres and Peripheries (Oxford, 1998); **M. L. King, *The Renaissance in Europe*** (New York, 2005); **J. Hale, *The Civilization of Europe in the Renaissance*** (New York, 1994); and the classic work by **M. P. Gilmore, *The World of Humanism, 1453–1517*** (New York, 1962). Also valuable are **T. K. Rabb, *The Last Days of the Renaissance*** (New York, 2006), and **S. Sider, *Handbook to Life in Renaissance Europe*** (New York, 2005).

FAMILY AND MARRIAGE On family and marriage, see **C. Klapisch-Zuber, *Women, Family, and Ritual in Renaissance Italy*** (Chicago, 1985). On women, see **M. L. King, *Women of the Renaissance*** (Chicago, 1991), and **M. L. Brown** and **K. B. McBride, *Women's Roles During the Renaissance*** (New York, 2005).

ITALIAN CITY-STATES For studies of the Italian city-states, see **J. M. Najemy, *Italy in the Age of the Renaissance, 1300–1550*** (Oxford, 2004). There is an enormous literature on Renaissance Florence. A good introduction is **J. M. Najemy, *History of Florence, 1200–1575*** (London, 2006). See also **G. Brucker, *Florence: The Golden Age, 1138–1737*** (Berkeley, Calif., 1988), and **L. Martines, *April Blood: Florence and the Plot Against the Medici*** (Oxford, 2003). On the *condottieri*, see **M. Mallett, *Mercenaries and Their Masters: Warfare in Renaissance Italy*** (Totowa, N.J., 1974). Machiavelli's life can be examined in **Q. Skinner, *Machiavelli*** (Oxford, 2000).

RENAISSANCE HUMANISM A good introduction to Renaissance humanism can be found in **C. G. Nauert Jr., *Humanism and the Culture of Renaissance Europe,*** 2nd ed (Cambridge, 2006). The fundamental work on fifteenth-century civic humanism is

H. Baron, *The Crisis of the Early Italian Renaissance,* 2nd ed. (Princeton, N.J., 1966). The impact of printing is exhaustively examined in **E. Eisenstein, *The Printing Press as an Agent of Change,*** 2 vols. (New York, 1978). See also **R. Mackenny, *Renaissances: The Cultures of Italy, c. 1300–c. 1600*** (New York, 2004).

RENAISSANCE ART   Good surveys of Renaissance art include **J. T. Paoletti** and **G. M. Radke, *Art, Power, and Patronage in Renaissance Italy,*** 3rd ed. (Upper Saddle River, N.J., 2003); **C. Bucci** and **S. Buricchi, *Renaissance Art*** (New York, 2007); **R. Turner, *Renaissance Florence: The Invention of a New Art*** (New York, 1997); **P. F. Brown, *Art and Life in Renaissance Venice*** (Upper Saddle River, N.J., 1997); and **L. Murray, *The High Renaissance*** (New York, 1967).

POLITICAL DEVELOPMENTS   For general works on the political development of Europe in the Renaissance, see **R. W. Winks** and **L. P. Wandel, *Europe in a Wider World, 1350–1650*** (Oxford, 2003), and **C. Mulgan, *The Renaissance Monarchies, 1469–1558*** (Cambridge, 1998). On France, see **R. J. Knecht, *The Rise and Fall of Renaissance France, 1483–1610,*** 2nd ed. (Oxford, 2001). Early Renaissance England is examined in **J. R. Lander, *Crown and Nobility, 1450–1509*** (London, 1976). Good coverage of Renaissance Spain can be found in **J. N. Hillgarth, *The Spanish Kingdoms, 1250–1516,*** vol. 2, ***Castilian Hegemony, 1410–1516*** (New York, 1978). On the Spanish Inquisition, see **J. Perez, *The Spanish Inquisition*** (New Haven, Conn., 2005). On the Ottomans and their expansion, see **C. Imber, *The Ottoman Empire, 1300–1650: The Structure of Power*** (New York, 2004).

THE CHURCH IN THE RENAISSANCE   Aspects of the Renaissance papacy can be examined in **G. Noel, *The Renaissance Popes*** (New York, 2006), and **M. Mallett, *The Borgias*** (New York, 1969).

1. Which of the following statements best illustrates the role of women during the fifteenth century?

   (A) Dowries played significant roles in solidifying marriage arrangements between families.
   (B) Household duties were equally distributed between men and women.
   (C) Wealthy families had significantly fewer children than poor families.
   (D) Large numbers of wealthy women received a formal education.
   (E) Women were involved in both religious and political activities.

2. Which of the following was NOT a reason why the Renaissance developed first in Italy?

   (A) Italy was the center of trade in the Mediterranean Sea.
   (B) Italian city-states fostered a new urban secular society.
   (C) The Italian states were the most stable political entities in Europe.
   (D) Italian banking families used their wealth to fund new artists of the time.
   (E) Italy's Greco-Roman past inspired intellectuals to pursue greater knowledge.

3. All of the following are considered humanist thinkers EXCEPT

   (A) Lorenzo Valla.
   (B) Leonardo Bruni.
   (C) Petrarch.
   (D) Pope Leo X.
   (E) Castiglione.

4. "As I have said, he should do what is right if he can; but he must be prepared to do wrong if necessary." This statement was most likely made by

   (A) Cesare Borgia.
   (B) Niccolò Machiavelli.
   (C) Cosimo de' Medici.
   (D) Pico della Mirandola.
   (E) Giordano Bruno.

5. The Italian Renaissance brought about

   (A) great social upheaval, resulting in more social equality.
   (B) the adoption of Gothic architectural styles, especially in Florence and Rome.
   (C) new artistic techniques such as the use of perspective and shading.
   (D) a new sense of unity between the emerging humanists and the Roman Catholic Church.
   (E) widespread political reform.

6. The primary difference between Northern Renaissance artistis and Italian Renaissance artists was that

   (A) Northern Renaissance artists received financing primarily from merchants, while Italian Renaissance artists were financed only by the Roman Catholic Church.
   (B) Northern Renaissance artists focused more on wooden altarpieces and specific details in their paintings, whereas Italian Renaissance artists concentrated more on perspective and the portrayal of the nude human form.
   (C) Northern Renaissance artists worked mainly with oils and completed few sculptures, whereas Italian Renaissance artists produced oil paintings and sculptures in bronze and marble.
   (D) Northern Renaissance artists included Albrecht Dürer and Jan van Eyck, while Italian painters included Michelangelo and Dante Alighieri.
   (E) Northern Renaissance artists focused on creating works of grandeur to produce deep emotional reactions, whereas Italian artists focused on everyday subjects and landscapes.

7. The achievements of the new monarchs during the the Renaissance included all of the following EXCEPT

   (A) they increased their political authority within their own countries.
   (B) they decreased the power of the noble class.
   (C) they increased the power of the Roman Catholic Church within their countries.
   (D) they increased the power of the state military relative to noble armies.
   (E) they increased the taxes that subjects paid to the crown.

8. Compared to their counterparts in western Europe, eastern European monarchs struggled MORE with problems such as

   (A) warfare in Asia.
   (B) growth of the middle class as a result of mercantilist policies.
   (C) social unrest and constant peasant uprisings.
   (D) weak ruling families with few ties or alliances to other monarchs.
   (E) mass religious conversions of their subjects to Islam and war with the Roman Catholic Church.

9. The Roman Catholic Church of the fifteenth century could best be described as a

   (A) political entity ruled by a pope and a king who shared religious power.
   (B) religious institution with no interest in political affairs.
   (C) political entity with little or no interest in religious duties.
   (D) social institution providing relief and assistance to European peasants.
   (E) religious entity with additional interests in political and economic power.

10. The man most often credited as being the father of humanism is

    (A) Erasmus.
    (B) Cicero.
    (C) Dante.
    (D) Petrarch.
    (E) Chaucer.

11. The five most influential city-states in Italy were the

    (A) duchy of Milan, republic of Venice, kingdom of Naples, Papal States, and republic of Florence.
    (B) republic of Rome, kingdom of Lucca, state of Sicily, duchy of Siena, and Papal States.
    (C) duchy of Savoy, kingdom of Naples, republic of Parma, republic of Rome, and republic of Florence.
    (D) Papal States, republic of Venice, duchy of Siena, kingdom of Lucca, and duchy of Milan.
    (E) republic of Florence, Sicily, kingdom of Naples, duchy of Corsica, and kingdom of Naples.

12. The Peace of Lodi in 1454

    (A) sealed the defeat of Constantinople by the Ottoman Empire.
    (B) (B) introduced the concept of "balance of power" to the Italian city-states.
    (C) established a unified Italian peninsula under one monarch.
    (D) contributed to the Habsburg-Valois conflict.
    (E) contributed to the end of the Italian Renaissance.

13. Which of the following does NOT describe the humanists of the Renaissance?

    (A) They focused much of their attention on the rediscovery of ancient texts and writings.
    (B) They ignored the topic of religion in their writings.
    (C) They focused their attention on the achievements of man.
    (D) They often conveyed their teaching in the vernacular.
    (E) Some of them espoused the notion of pantheism, as seen in their writings.

14. Filippo Brunelleschi's dome of the Duomo

    (A) illustrated a shift from medieval architectural design to a more classical design reminiscent of ancient Greece and Rome.
    (B) showcased the Gothic architecture of medieval European society.
    (C) was built to glorify the supremacy of the papacy.
    (D) was a blending of architectural styles resulting from Brunelleschi's travel outside Europe.
    (E) is an example of the new humanist architecture that became prominent in northern France.

© Scala/Art Resource, NY

15. Ferdinand and Isabella were responsible for all of the following EXCEPT

    (A) the unification of Spain under the combined regions of Aragon and Castile.
    (B) pushing the Moors out of Granda in an attempt to create greater Spanish unity.
    (C) expelling Jews from the newly unified Spain and instituting the Inquisition.
    (D) the creation of a new Spanish language that highlighted regional words and phrases.
    (E) the establishment of strong unified infantry force.

A nineteenth-century engraving showing Luther before the Diet of Worms

Reformation and Religious Warfare in the Sixteenth Century

CHAPTER OUTLINE AND FOCUS QUESTIONS

Prelude to Reformation

Q What were the chief ideas of the Christian humanists, and how did they differ from the ideas of the Protestant reformers?

Martin Luther and the Reformation in Germany

Q What were Martin Luther's main disagreements with the Roman Catholic Church, and what political, economic, and social conditions help explain why the movement he began spread so quickly across Europe?

The Spread of the Protestant Reformation

Q What were the main tenets of Lutheranism, Zwinglianism, Calvinism, and Anabaptism, and how did they differ from each other and from Catholicism? What impact did political, economic, and social conditions have on the development of these four reform movements?

The Social Impact of the Protestant Reformation

Q What impact did the Protestant Reformation have on society in the sixteenth century?

The Catholic Reformation

Q What measures did the Roman Catholic Church take to reform itself and to combat Protestantism in the sixteenth century?

Politics and the Wars of Religion in the Sixteenth Century

Q What role did politics, economic and social conditions, and religion play in the European wars of the sixteenth century?

─ CRITICAL THINKING ═══════════

Q Where and how did the reform movements take hold, and how did the emergence of these reform movements affect the political and social realms where they were adopted?

ON APRIL 18, 1521, a lowly monk stood before the emperor and princes of Germany in the city of Worms. He had been called before this august gathering to answer charges of heresy, charges that could threaten his very life. The monk was confronted with a pile of his books and asked if he wished to defend them all or reject a part. Courageously, Martin Luther defended them all and asked to be shown where any part was in error on the basis of "Scripture and plain reason." The emperor was outraged by Luther's response and made his own position clear the next day: "Not only I, but you of this noble German nation, would be forever disgraced if by our negligence not only heresy but the very suspicion of heresy were to survive. After having heard yesterday the obstinate defense of Luther, I regret that I have so long delayed in proceeding against him and his false teaching. I will have no more to do with him." Luther's appearance at Worms set the stage for a serious challenge to the authority of the Catholic Church. This was by no means the first crisis in the church's fifteen-hundred-year history, but its consequences were more far-reaching than anyone at Worms in 1521 could have imagined.

Throughout the Middle Ages, the Christian church continued to assert its primacy of position. It had overcome defiance of its temporal authority by emperors and kings, and challenges to its doctrines had been crushed by the Inquisition and combated by new religious orders that carried its message of salvation to all the towns and villages of medieval Europe. The growth of the papacy had paralleled the growth of the church, but by the end of the Middle Ages, challenges to papal authority from the rising power of monarchical states had resulted in a loss of papal temporal authority. An even greater threat to papal authority and church unity arose in the sixteenth century when the unity of Christendom was shattered by the Reformation.

The movement begun by Martin Luther when he made his dramatic stand quickly spread across Europe, a clear indication of dissatisfaction with Catholic practices. Within a short time, new forms of religious practices, doctrines, and organizations, including Zwinglianism, Calvinism, Anabaptism, and Anglicanism, were attracting adherents all over Europe. Although seemingly helpless to stop the new Protestant churches, the Catholic Church also underwent a reformation and managed to revive its fortunes by the mid-sixteenth century. All too soon, the doctrinal divisions between Protestants and Catholics led to a series of religious wars that dominated the history of western Europe in the second half of the sixteenth century.

Prelude to Reformation

Q **Focus Question:** What were the chief ideas of the Christian humanists, and how did they differ from the ideas of the Protestant reformers?

Martin Luther's reform movement was by no means the first. During the second half of the fifteenth century, the new Classical learning that was part of Italian Renaissance humanism spread to northern Europe and spawned a movement called **Christian** or **northern Renaissance humanism** whose major goal was the reform of Christianity.

Christian or Northern Renaissance Humanism

Like their Italian counterparts, northern humanists cultivated a knowledge of the classics, the bond that united all humanists into a kind of international fellowship. In returning to the writings of antiquity, northern humanists (also called Christian humanists because of their profound preoccupation with religion) focused on the sources of early Christianity, the Holy Scriptures and the writings of

such church fathers as Augustine, Ambrose, and Jerome. In these early Christian writings, they discovered a simple religion that they came to feel had been distorted by the complicated theological arguments of the Middle Ages.

The most important characteristic of northern humanism was its reform program. Convinced of the ability of human beings to reason and improve themselves, the northern humanists felt that through education in the sources of Classical, and especially Christian, antiquity, they could instill a true inner piety or an inward religious feeling that would bring about a reform of the church and society. For this reason, Christian humanists supported schools, brought out new editions of the classics, and prepared new editions of the Bible and writings of the church fathers. In the preface to his edition of the Greek New Testament, the famous humanist Erasmus wrote:

I disagree very much with those who are unwilling that Holy Scripture, translated into the vulgar tongue, be read by the uneducated, as if Christ taught such intricate doctrines that they could scarcely be understood by very few theologians, or as if the strength of the Christian religion consisted in men's ignorance of it.... I would that even the lowliest women read the Gospels and the Pauline Epistles. And I would that they were translated into all languages so that they could be read and understood not only by Scots and Irish but also by Turks and Saracens.... Would that, as a result, the farmer sing some portion of them at the plow, the weaver hum some parts of them to the movement of his shuttle, the traveler lighten the weariness of the journey with stories of this kind![1]

This belief in the power of education would remain an important characteristic of European civilization. Like later intellectuals, Christian humanists believed that to change society, they must first change the human beings who compose it. Although some critics have called the Christian humanists naive, they were in fact merely optimistic. The turmoil of the Reformation, however, shattered much of this intellectual optimism, as the lives and careers of two of the most prominent Christian humanists, Desiderius Erasmus and Thomas More, illustrate.

ERASMUS The most influential of all the Christian humanists was Desiderius Erasmus (dez-i-DEER-ee-uss i-RAZZ-mus) (1466–1536), who formulated and popularized the reform program of Christian humanism. Born in Holland, Erasmus was educated at one of the schools of the Brothers of the Common Life (see Chapter 11). He wandered to France, England, Italy, Germany, and Switzerland, conversing everywhere in the Classical Latin that might be called his mother tongue. The *Handbook of the Christian Knight*, printed in 1503, reflected his preoccupation with religion. He called his conception of religion "the philosophy of Christ," by which he meant that Christianity should be a guiding philosophy for the direction of daily life rather than the system of dogmatic beliefs and practices that the medieval church seemed to stress. In other words, he emphasized inner piety and de-emphasized the external forms of religion (such as the sacraments, pilgrimages, fasts,

Louvre, Paris/© Scala/Art Resource, NY

Erasmus. Desiderius Erasmus was the most influential of the northern Renaissance humanists. He sought to restore Christianity to the early simplicity found in the teachings of Jesus. This portrait of Erasmus was painted in 1523 by Hans Holbein the Younger, who had formed a friendship with the great humanist while they were both in Basel.

veneration of saints, and relics). To return to the simplicity of the early church, people needed to understand the original meaning of the Scriptures and the writings of the early church fathers. Because Erasmus thought that the standard Latin edition of the Bible, known as the Vulgate, contained errors, he edited the Greek text of the New Testament from the earliest available manuscripts and published it, along with a new Latin translation, in 1516. Erasmus also wrote *Annotations,* a detailed commentary on the Vulgate Bible itself. In his day, Erasmus's work on the New Testament was considered his most outstanding achievement, and Martin Luther himself would use Erasmus's work as the basis for his German translation of the New Testament.

To Erasmus, the reform of the church meant spreading an understanding of the philosophy of Jesus, providing enlightened education in the sources of early Christianity, and making common-sense criticisms of the abuses in the church. This last is especially evident in *The Praise of Folly,* written in 1509, in which Erasmus engaged in humorous yet effective criticism of the most corrupt practices of his own society. He was especially harsh on the abuses within the ranks of the clergy (see the box on p. 379).

Desiderius Erasmus, *In Praise of Folly* (1509)

Erasmus's program did not achieve the reform of the church that he so desired. His moderation and his emphasis on education were quickly overwhelmed by the passions of the Reformation. Undoubtedly, though, his work helped prepare the way for the Reformation; as contemporaries proclaimed, "Erasmus laid the egg that Luther hatched." Yet Erasmus eventually disapproved of Luther and the Protestant reformers. He had no intention of destroying the unity of the medieval Christian church; rather, his whole program was based on reform within the church.

THOMAS MORE The son of a London lawyer, Thomas More (1478–1535) received the benefits of a good education. Although trained in the law, he took an avid interest in the new Classical learning and became proficient in both Latin and Greek. Like the Italian humanists, who believed in putting their learning at the service of the state, More embarked on a public career that ultimately took him to the highest reaches of power as lord chancellor of England.

His career in government service, however, did not keep More from the intellectual and spiritual interests that were so dear to him. He was well acquainted with other English humanists and became an intimate friend of Erasmus. He made translations from Greek authors and wrote both prose and poetry in Latin. A devout man, he spent many hours in prayer and private devotions. Contemporaries praised his household as a shining model of Christian family life.

More's most famous work, and one of the most controversial of his age, was *Utopia,* written in 1516. This literary masterpiece is an account of the idealistic life and institutions of the community of Utopia (Greek for "nowhere"), an imaginary island in the vicinity of the recently discovered New World. It reflects More's own concerns with the economic, social, and political problems of his day. He presented a new social system in which cooperation and reason replaced power and fame as the proper motivating agents for human society. Utopian society, therefore, was based on communal ownership rather than private property. All residents of Utopia worked nine hours a day, regardless of occupation, and were rewarded according to their needs. Possessing abundant leisure time and relieved of competition and greed, Utopians were free to lead wholesome and enriching lives.

In serving King Henry VIII, More came face to face with the abuses and corruption he had criticized in *Utopia.* But he did not allow idealism to outweigh his own ultimate realism, and in *Utopia* itself he justified his service to the king:

If you can't completely eradicate wrong ideas, or deal with inveterate vices as effectively as you could wish, that's no reason for turning your back on public life altogether.... On the other hand, it's no use attempting to put across entirely new ideas, which will obviously carry no weight with people who are prejudiced against them. You must go to work indirectly. You must handle everything as tactfully as you can, and what you can't put right you must try to make as little wrong as possible. For things will never be perfect, until human beings are perfect—which I don't expect them to be for quite a number of years.[2]

Erasmus: In Praise of Folly

The Praise of Folly is one of the most famous pieces of literature produced in the sixteenth century. Erasmus, who wrote it in a short period of time during a visit to the home of Thomas More, considered it a "little diversion" from his "serious work." Yet both contemporaries and later generations have appreciated "this laughing parody of every form and rank of human life." In this selection, Erasmus belittles one of his favorite objects of scorn, the monks. They were, however, merely one of the many groups he disparaged.

* ⋯ ⋙◆⋘ ⋯ *

Erasmus, *The Praise of Folly*

Those who are the closest to these [the theologians] in happiness are generally called "the religious" or "monks," both of which are deceiving names, since for the most part they stay as far away from religion as possible and frequent every sort of place. I cannot, however, see how any life could be more gloomy than the life of these monks if I [Folly] did not assist them in many ways. Though most people detest these men so much that accidentally meeting one is considered to be bad luck, the monks themselves believe that they are magnificent creatures. One of their chief beliefs is that to be illiterate is to be of a high state of sanctity, and so they make sure that they are not able to read. Another is that when braying out their gospels in church they are making themselves very pleasing and satisfying to God, when in fact they are uttering these psalms as a matter of repetition rather than from their hearts. . . .

Moreover, it is amusing to find that they insist that everything be done in fastidious detail, as if employing the orderliness of mathematics, a small mistake in which would be a great crime. Just so many knots must be on each shoe and the shoelace may be of only one specified color; just so much lace is allowed on each habit; the girdle must be of just the right material and width; the hood of a certain shape and capacity; their hair of just so many fingers' length; and finally they can sleep only the specified number of hours per day. Can they not understand that, because of a variety of bodies and temperaments, all this equality of restrictions is in fact very unequal? Nevertheless, because of all this detail that they employ they think that they are superior to all other people. And what is more, amid all their pretense of Apostolic charity, the members of one order will denounce the members of another order clamorously because of the way in which the habit has been belted or the slightly darker color of it. . . .

Many of them work so hard at protocol and at traditional fastidiousness that they think one heaven hardly a suitable reward for their labors; never recalling, however, that the time will come when Christ will demand a reckoning of that which he had prescribed, namely charity, and that he will hold their deeds of little account. One monk will then exhibit his belly filled with every kind of fish; another will profess a knowledge of over a hundred hymns. Still another will reveal a countless number of fasts that he has made, and will account for his large belly by explaining that his fasts have always been broken by a single large meal. Another will show a list of church ceremonies over which he has officiated so large that it would fill seven ships. ⋟

Q What are Erasmus's main criticisms of monks? What do you think he hoped to achieve by this satirical attack on monastic practices? How do you think the circulation of many printed copies of such attacks would have affected popular attitudes toward the Catholic Church?

More's religious devotion and belief in the universal Catholic Church ultimately proved even more important than his service to the king, however. While in office, More's intolerance of heresy led him to advocate persecution of those who would fundamentally change the Catholic Church. Moreover, always the man of conscience, More willingly gave up his life opposing England's break with the Roman Catholic Church over the divorce of King Henry VIII.

Church and Religion on the Eve of the Reformation

Corruption in the Catholic Church was another factor that spurred people to want reform. No doubt the failure of the Renaissance popes to provide spiritual leadership had affected the spiritual life of all Christendom. The papal court's preoccupation with finances had an especially strong impact on the clergy. So did the economic changes of the fourteenth and fifteenth centuries. The highest positions among the clergy were increasingly held by either nobles or the wealthy members of the bourgeoisie. Moreover, to increase their revenues, high church officials (bishops, archbishops, and cardinals) took over more than one church office. This so-called **pluralism** led in turn to absenteeism: church officeholders ignored their duties and hired underlings who sometimes lacked the proper qualifications. Complaints about the ignorance and ineptness of parish priests became widespread in the fifteenth century.

THE SEARCH FOR SALVATION While many of the leaders of the church were failing to meet their responsibilities, ordinary people were clamoring for meaningful religious expression and certainty of salvation. As a result, for some the salvation process became almost mechanical. As more and more people sought certainty of salvation through veneration of relics, collections of such objects grew. Frederick the Wise, elector of Saxony and Martin Luther's prince, had amassed over 19,000 relics to which were attached indulgences that could reduce one's time in purgatory by nearly 2 million years. (An indulgence, you will recall, is a remission, after death, of all or part of the punishment for sin.) Other people sought certainty of salvation in the popular mystical movement known as the Modern Devotion, which downplayed religious dogma and stressed the need to follow the teachings of Jesus. Thomas à Kempis, author of *The Imitation of Christ,* wrote that "truly, at the day of judgment we shall not be examined by what we have read, but what we have done; not how well we have spoken, but how religiously we have lived."

What is striking about the revival of religious piety in the fifteenth century—whether expressed through such external forces as the veneration of relics and the buying of indulgences or the mystical path—was its adherence to the orthodox beliefs and practices of the Catholic Church. The agitation for certainty of salvation and spiritual peace occurred within the framework of the "holy mother Church." But disillusionment grew as the devout experienced the clergy's inability to live up to their expectations. The deepening of religious life, especially in the second half of the fifteenth century, found little echo among the worldly-wise clergy, and this environment helps explain the tremendous and immediate impact of Luther's ideas.

CALLS FOR REFORM At the same time, several sources of reform were already at work within the Catholic Church at the end of the fifteenth and the beginning of the sixteenth century. Especially noticeable were the calls for reform from the religious orders of the Franciscans, Dominicans, and Augustinians. Members of these groups put particular emphasis on preaching to laypeople. One of the popular preachers was Johannes Geiler of Kaisersberg (KY-zerz-bayrk), who denounced the corruption of the clergy.

The Oratory of Divine Love, first organized in Italy in 1497, was not a religious order but an informal group of clergy and laymen who worked to foster reform by emphasizing personal spiritual development and outward acts of charity. The "philosophy of Christ," advocated by the Christian humanist Erasmus, was especially appealing to many of them. The Oratory's members included a number of cardinals who favored church reform. A Spanish archbishop, Cardinal Ximenes, was especially active in using Christian humanism to reform the church. To foster spirituality among the people, he had a number of religious writings, including Thomas à Kempis's *The Imitation of Christ,* translated into Spanish.

Martin Luther and the Reformation in Germany

 FOCUS QUESTION: What were Martin Luther's main disagreements with the Roman Catholic Church, and what political, economic, and social conditions help explain why the movement he began spread so quickly across Europe?

The Protestant Reformation began with a typical medieval question: What must I do to be saved? Martin Luther, a deeply religious man, found an answer that did not fit within the traditional teachings of the late medieval church. Ultimately, he split with that church, destroying the religious unity of western Christendom. That other people were concerned with the same question is evident in the rapid spread of the Reformation. But religion was so entangled in the social, economic, and political forces of the period that the Protestant reformers' hope of transforming the church quickly proved illusory.

The Early Luther

Martin Luther was born in Germany on November 10, 1483. His father wanted him to become a lawyer, so Luther enrolled at the University of Erfurt, where he received his bachelor's degree in 1502. Three years later, after becoming a master in the liberal arts, the young man began to study law. But Luther was not content, not in small part due to his long-standing religious inclinations. That summer, while returning to Erfurt after a brief visit home, he was caught in a ferocious thunderstorm and vowed that if he survived unscathed, he would become a monk. He then entered the monastic order of the Augustinian Hermits in Erfurt, much to his father's disgust. In the monastery, Luther focused on his major concern, the assurance of salvation. The traditional beliefs and practices of the church seemed unable to relieve his obsession with this question, especially evident in his struggle with the sacrament of penance or **confession.** The sacraments were a Catholic's chief means of receiving God's grace; confession offered the opportunity to have one's sins forgiven. Luther spent hours confessing his sins, but he was always doubtful. Had he remembered all of his sins? Even more, how could a hopeless sinner be acceptable to a totally just and all-powerful God? Luther threw himself into his monastic routine with a vengeance:

> I was indeed a good monk and kept my order so strictly that I could say that if ever a monk could get to heaven through monastic discipline, I was that monk.... And yet my conscience would not give me certainty, but I always doubted and said, "You didn't do that right. You weren't contrite enough. You left that out of your confession." The more I tried to remedy an uncertain, weak and troubled conscience with human traditions, the more I daily found it more uncertain, weaker and more troubled.[3]

Despite his herculean efforts, Luther achieved no certainty.

To help overcome his difficulties, his superiors recommended that the monk study theology. He received his doctorate in 1512 and then became a professor in the theological faculty at the University of Wittenberg (VIT-ten-bayrk), lecturing on the Bible. Sometime between 1513 and 1516, through his study of the Bible, he arrived at an answer to his problem.

Catholic doctrine had emphasized that both faith and good works were required for a Christian to achieve personal salvation. In Luther's eyes, human beings, weak and powerless in the sight of an almighty God, could never do enough good works to merit salvation. Through his study of the Bible, especially his work on Paul's Epistle to the Romans, Luther rediscovered another way of viewing this problem. To Luther, humans are saved not through their good works but through faith in the promises of God, made possible by the sacrifice of Jesus on the cross. The doctrine of salvation or justification by grace through faith alone became the primary doctrine of the Protestant Reformation (**justification** is the act by which a person is made deserving of salvation). Because Luther had arrived at this doctrine from his study of the Bible, the Bible became for Luther, as for all other Protestants, the chief guide to religious truth. Justification by faith and the Bible as the sole authority in religious affairs were the twin pillars of the Protestant Reformation.

Martin Luther. This painting by Lucas Cranach the Elder in 1533 shows Luther at the age of fifty. By this time, Luther's reforms had taken hold in many parts of Germany, and Luther himself was a happily married man with five children.

Germanisches Nationalmuseum, Nuremberg//© Scala/Art Resource, NY

THE INDULGENCE CONTROVERSY Luther did not see himself as either an innovator or a heretic, but his involvement in the indulgence controversy propelled him into an open confrontation with church officials and forced him to see the theological implications of justification by faith alone. In 1517, Pope Leo X had issued a special jubilee indulgence to finance the ongoing construction of Saint Peter's Basilica in Rome. Johann Tetzel, a rambunctious Dominican, hawked the indulgences in Germany with the slogan "As soon as the coin in the coffer rings, the soul from purgatory springs."

Luther was greatly distressed by the sale of indulgences, certain that people who relied on these pieces of paper to assure themselves of salvation were guaranteeing their eternal damnation instead. Angered, he issued his Ninety-Five Theses, although scholars are unsure whether he nailed them to a church door in Wittenberg, as is traditionally alleged, or mailed them to his ecclesiastical superior. In either case, his theses were a stunning indictment of the abuses in the sale of indulgences (see the box on p. 382). It is doubtful that Luther intended any break with the church over the issue of indulgences. If the pope had clarified the use of indulgences, as Luther wished, he would probably have been satisfied, and the controversy would have ended. But Pope Leo X did not take the issue seriously and is even reported to have said that Luther was simply "some drunken German who will amend his ways when he sobers up." Thousands of copies of a German translation of the Ninety-Five Theses were quickly printed and were received sympathetically in a Germany that had a long tradition of dissatisfaction with papal policies and power.

Martin Luther, Ninety-Five Theses (1517)

Of course, Luther was not the first theologian to criticize the powers of the papacy. As we saw in Chapter 12, John Wyclif at the end of the fourteenth century and John Hus at the beginning of the fifteenth century had attacked the excessive power of the papacy. Luther was certainly well aware of John Hus's fate at the Council of Constance, where he was burned at the stake on charges of heresy.

THE QUICKENING REBELLION The controversy reached an important turning point with the Leipzig Debate in July 1519. In Leipzig, Luther's opponent, the capable Catholic theologian Johann Eck, forced Luther to move beyond indulgences and deny the authority of popes and councils. During the debate, Eck also identified Luther's ideas with those of John Hus, the condemned heretic. Luther was now compelled to see the consequences of his new theology. At the beginning of 1520, he proclaimed: "Farewell, unhappy, hopeless, blasphemous Rome! The Wrath of God has come upon you, as you deserve. We have cared for Babylon, and she is not healed: let us then, leave her, that she may be the habitation of dragons, spectres, and witches."[4] At the same time, Luther was convinced that he was doing God's work and had to proceed regardless of the consequences.

Luther and the Ninety-Five Theses

To most historians, the publication of Luther's Ninety-Five Theses marks the beginning of the Reformation. To Luther, they were simply a response to what he considered Johann Tetzel's blatant abuses in selling indulgences. Although written in Latin, Luther's statements were soon translated into German and disseminated widely across Germany. They made an immense impression on Germans already dissatisfied with the ecclesiastical and financial policies of the papacy.

＋—＋ ⊠≣⊠ ＋—＋

Martin Luther, *Selections from the Ninety-Five Theses*

5. The Pope has neither the will nor the power to remit any penalties beyond those he has imposed either at his own discretion or by canon law.

20. Therefore the Pope, by his plenary remission of all penalties, does not mean "all" in the absolute sense, but only those imposed by himself.

21. Hence those preachers of Indulgences are wrong when they say that a man is absolved and saved from every penalty by the Pope's Indulgences.

27. It is mere human talk to preach that the soul flies out [of purgatory] immediately the money clinks in the collection-box.

28. It is certainly possible that when the money clinks in the collection-box greed and avarice can increase; but the intercession of the Church depends on the will of God alone.

50. Christians should be taught that, if the Pope knew the exactions of the preachers of Indulgences, he would rather have the basilica of St. Peter reduced to ashes than built with the skin, flesh and bones of his sheep.

81. This wanton preaching of pardons makes it difficult even for learned men to redeem respect due to the Pope from the slanders or at least the shrewd questionings of the laity.

82. For example: "Why does not the Pope empty purgatory for the sake of most holy love and the supreme need of souls? This would be the most righteous of reasons, if he can redeem innumerable souls for sordid money with which to build a basilica, the most trivial of reasons."

86. Again: "Since the Pope's wealth is larger than that of the crassest Crassi of our time, why does he not build this one basilica of St. Peter with his own money, rather than with that of the faithful poor?"

90. To suppress these most conscientious questionings of the laity by authority only, instead of refuting them by reason, is to expose the Church and the Pope to the ridicule of their enemies, and to make Christian people unhappy.

94. Christians should be exhorted to seek earnestly to follow Christ, their Head, through penalties, deaths, and hells.

95. And let them thus be more confident of entering heaven through many tribulations rather than through a false assurance of peace. ⊱

Q What were the major ideas of Luther's Ninety-Five Theses? Why did they have such a strong appeal in Germany?

In three pamphlets published in 1520, Luther moved toward a more definite break with the Catholic Church. The *Address to the Nobility of the German Nation* was a political tract written in German in which Luther called on the German princes to overthrow the papacy in Germany and establish a reformed German church. The *Babylonian Captivity of the Church,* written in Latin for theologians, attacked the sacramental system as the means by which the pope and church had held the real meaning of the Gospel captive for a thousand years. Luther called for the reform of monasticism and for the clergy to marry. Though virginity is good, he argued, marriage is better, and freedom of choice is best. *On the Freedom of a Christian Man* was a short treatise on the doctrine of salvation. It is faith alone, not good works, that justifies, frees, and brings salvation through Jesus. Being saved and freed by his faith in Jesus, however, does not free the Christian from doing good works. Rather, he performs good works out of gratitude to God.

"Good works do not make a good man, but a good man does good works."[5]

Unable to accept Luther's forcefully worded dissent from traditional Catholic teachings, the church excommunicated him in January 1521. He was also summoned to appear before the Reichstag (RYKHSS-tahk), the imperial diet of the Holy Roman Empire, in Worms, convened by the recently elected Emperor Charles V (1519–1556). Expected to recant the heretical doctrines he had espoused, Luther refused and made the famous reply that became the battle cry of the Reformation:

> Since then Your Majesty and your lordships desire a simple reply, I will answer without horns and without teeth. Unless I am convicted by Scripture and plain reason—I do not accept the authority of popes and councils, for they have contradicted each other—my conscience is captive to the Word of God. I cannot and I will not recant anything, for to go against conscience is neither right nor safe. Here I stand, I cannot do otherwise. God help me. Amen.[6]

Luther (2003)

Luther, directed by Eric Till, depicts the early life and career of Martin Luther (Joseph Fiennes), largely from a Lutheran point of view. The movie focuses on some of the major events in Luther's early life, including his years in a monastery; his trip to Rome on behalf of his religious order; his study for a doctorate in theology at the University of Wittenberg; the writing of his Ninety-Five Theses; the subsequent controversy over Luther's criticism of indulgences, including a scene showing the abuses in the sale of indulgences by Johann Tetzel (Alfred Molina); Luther's meeting with Cardinal Cajetan (Mathieu Carriere); his dramatic stand at the Diet of Worms, when he refused to recant the ideas in his writings; the meeting of the German princes with Holy Roman Emperor Charles V (Torben Liebrecht) at Augsburg in 1530; and the marriage of Luther to a former nun, Katherina von Bora (Claire Cox).

Luther (Joseph Fiennes) defends his writings at the Diet of Worms.

The movie re-creates these scenes largely based on legends about Luther, rather than on a strict adherence to the historical facts. Although Luther was visibly distressed when he celebrated his first Mass, he did not spill the wine. Historians still debate whether Luther posted his Ninety-Five Theses or mailed them to his ecclesiastical superior. Luther did travel to Rome in 1510, but it is unlikely that he encountered Pope Julius II in the streets, although it is true that Luther was appalled by the religious indifference and widespread corruption that he experienced in Rome. The meeting with Cardinal Cajetan is presented as a brief experience with a quickly frustrated cardinal, when in fact the sessions with Cajetan occurred over a number of days. Nor is Luther's doctrine of justification by faith clearly presented—not that it would be easy to present in a movie. One is left with the impression that indulgences themselves were the chief reason for Luther's stand against the Catholic Church; the movie does not show clearly that his new theological doctrine of justification by faith alone was the foundation of Luther's rebellion against the church. The Peasants' War of 1525 is handled too

quickly and too simplistically—it is never quite clear what was at stake or even why the war occurred. The scene of the princes at Augsburg in 1530 is largely fictional. Although some of the princes were no doubt adherents of Luther's new faith, the movie hardly considers the princes' political motives, especially in regard to their relationship to Charles V. We also do not know whether Luther ever had a face-to-face meeting with his prince, Frederick the Wise, the Elector of Saxony (Peter Ustinov), or whether Frederick really expressed any thoughts about Luther's German Bible. Luther's return to Wittenberg from the Wartburg Castle was done against the wishes of Frederick the Wise, not with his approval.

Above all, the greatest weakness of the movie is its failure to demonstrate what made Luther a great rebel and what enabled him to continue his rebellion in the face of almost certain martyrdom. Luther did not seek martyrdom, but he was also not that concerned about his personal safety. He was, however, determined to save the cause whose champion he had become, and to that end he was a man with a strong mind, filled with great zeal and conviction, and blessed with unstoppable persistence. ⤳

Emperor Charles was outraged at Luther's audacity and gave his opinion that "a single friar who goes counter to all Christianity for a thousand years must be wrong." By the Edict of Worms, Martin Luther was made an outlaw within the empire. His works were to be burned, and Luther himself was to be captured and delivered to the emperor. Instead, Luther's prince, the Elector of Saxony, sent him into hiding at the Wartburg (VART-bayrk)

Castle, where he remained for nearly a year (see the Film & History feature above).

The Rise of Lutheranism

At the beginning of 1522, Luther returned to Wittenberg in Electoral Saxony and began to organize a reformed church. While at the Wartburg Castle, Luther's foremost

Woodcut: Luther Versus the Pope. In the 1520s, after Luther's return to Wittenberg, his teachings began to spread rapidly, ending ultimately in a reform movement supported by state authorities. Pamphlets containing picturesque woodcuts were important in the spread of Luther's ideas. In the woodcut shown here, the crucified Jesus attends Luther's service on the left, while on the right the pope is at a table selling indulgences.

achievement was his translation of the New Testament into German. Within twelve years, his German New Testament had sold almost 200,000 copies. Lutheranism had wide appeal and spread rapidly but not primarily through the written word, since only 4 to 5 percent of people in Germany were literate. And most of these were in urban areas.

Instead, the primary means of disseminating Luther's ideas was the sermon. The preaching of evangelical sermons, based on a return to the original message of the Bible, found favor throughout Germany. In city after city, the arrival of preachers presenting Luther's teachings was soon followed by a public debate in which the new preachers proved victorious. A reform of the church was then instituted by state authorities.

Also useful to the spread of the Reformation were pamphlets illustrated with vivid woodcuts portraying the pope as a hideous Antichrist and titled with catchy phrases such as "I Wonder Why There Is No Money in the Land" (which, of course, was an attack on papal greed). Luther also insisted on the use of music as a means to teach the Gospel, and his own composition, "A Mighty Fortress Is Our God," became the battle hymn of the Reformation:

> *Standing alone are we undone, the Fiend would soon*
> *enslave us;*
> *but for us fights a mighty One whom God has sent to*
> *save us.*
> *Ask you who is this? Jesus Christ is He, Lord God*
> *of Hosts.*
> *There is no other God; He can and will uphold us.*

THE SPREAD OF LUTHER'S IDEAS Lutheranism spread to both princely and ecclesiastical states in northern and central Germany as well as to two-thirds of the free imperial cities, especially those of southern Germany, where prosperous burghers, for both religious and secular reasons, became committed to Luther's cause. Nuremberg, where an active city council led by the dynamic city secretary Lazarus Spengler (SCHPEN-ler) brought a conversion as early as 1525, was the first imperial city to convert to Lutheranism. At its outset, the Reformation in Germany was largely an urban phenomenon. Three-fourths of the early converts to the reform movement were from the clergy, many of them from the upper classes, which made it easier for them to work with the ruling elites in the cities.

A series of crises in the mid-1520s made it apparent, however, that spreading the word of God was not as easy as Luther had originally envisioned—the usual plight of most reformers. Luther experienced dissent within his own ranks in Wittenberg from people such as Andreas Carlstadt (KARL-shtaht), who wished to initiate a more radical reform by abolishing all relics, images, and the Mass. Luther had no sooner dealt with them than he began to face opposition from the Christian humanists. Many had initially supported Luther, believing that he shared their goal of reforming the abuses within the church. But when it became apparent that Luther's movement threatened the unity of Christendom, the older generation of Christian humanists, including Erasmus, broke with the reformer. A younger generation of Christian humanists, however, played a significant role in Lutheranism. When Philip Melanchthon (muh-LANK-tun)

Luther and the "Robbing and Murdering Hordes of Peasants"

The Peasants' War of 1524–1525 encompassed a series of uprisings by German peasants who were suffering from economic changes they did not comprehend. Led by radical religious leaders, the revolts quickly became entangled with the religious revolt set in motion by Luther's defiance of the church. But it was soon clear that Luther himself did not believe in any way in social revolution. This excerpt is taken from Luther's pamphlet written in May 1525 at the height of the peasants' power but not published until after their defeat.

◆━━◼◈◼━━◆

Martin Luther, *Against the Robbing and Murdering Hordes of Peasants*

The peasants have taken on themselves the burden of three terrible sins against God and man, by which they have abundantly merited death in body and soul. In the first place they have sworn to be true and faithful, submissive and obedient, to their rulers, as Christ commands, when he says, "Render unto Caesar the things that are Caesar's," and in Romans XIII, "Let everyone be subject unto the higher powers." Because they are breaking this obedience, and are setting themselves against the higher powers, willfully and with violence, they have forfeited body and soul, as faithless, perjured, lying, disobedient knaves and scoundrels are wont to do. . . .

In the second place, they are starting a rebellion, and violently robbing and plundering monasteries and castles which are not theirs, by which they have a second time deserved death in body and soul, if only as highwaymen and murderers. . . . For rebellion is not simple murder, but is like a great fire, which attacks and lays waste a whole land. . . . Therefore, let everyone who can, smite, slay and stab, secretly or openly, remembering that nothing can be more poisonous, hurtful or devilish than a rebel. . . .

In the third place, they cloak this terrible and horrible sin with the Gospel, call themselves "Christian brothers," receive oaths and homage, and compel people to hold with them to these abominations. Thus, they become the greatest of all blasphemers of God and slanderers of his holy Name, serving the devil, under the outward appearance of the Gospel, thus earning death in body and soul ten times over. . . . It does not help the peasants, when they pretend that, according to Genesis I and II, all things were created free and common, and that all of us alike have been baptized. . . . For baptism does not make men free in body and property, but in soul; and the Gospel does not make goods common. . . . Since the peasants, then, have brought both God and man down upon them and are already so many times guilty of death in body and soul, . . . I must instruct the worldly governors how they are to act in the matter with a clear conscience.

First, I will not oppose a ruler who, even though he does not tolerate the Gospel, will smite and punish these peasants without offering to submit the case to judgment. For he is within his rights, since the peasants are not contending any longer for the Gospel, but have become faithless, perjured, disobedient, rebellious murderers, robbers and blasphemers, whom even heathen rulers have the right and power to punish; nay, it is their duty to punish them, for it is just for this purpose that they bear the sword, and are "the ministers of God upon him that doeth evil." ▷

Q   What does this passage tell you about the political interests and sympathies of key religious reformers like Luther? Were the reformers really interested in bringing about massive social changes to accompany their religious innovations?

(1497–1560) arrived in Wittenberg in 1518 at the age of twenty-one to teach Greek and Hebrew, he was immediately attracted to Luther's ideas and became a staunch supporter.

THE PEASANTS' WAR   Luther's greatest challenge in the mid-1520s, however, came from the Peasants' War. Peasant dissatisfaction in Germany stemmed from several sources. Many peasants had not been touched by the gradual economic improvement of the early sixteenth century. In some areas, especially southwestern Germany, influential local lords continued to abuse their peasants, and new demands for taxes and other services caused them to wish for a return to "the good old days." Social discontent soon became entangled with religious revolt as peasants looked to Martin Luther, believing that he would

support them. It was not Luther, however, but one of his ex-followers, the radical Thomas Müntzer (MOON-tsur), himself a pastor, who inflamed the peasants against their rulers with his fiery language: "Strike while the iron is hot!" Revolt first erupted in southwestern Germany in June 1524 and spread northward and eastward.

Luther reacted quickly and vehemently against the peasants. In his pamphlet *Against the Robbing and Murdering Hordes of Peasants,* he called on the German princes to "smite, slay and stab" the stupid and stubborn peasantry (see the box above). Luther, who knew how much his reformation of the church depended on the full support of the German princes and magistrates, supported the rulers, although he also blamed them for helping to cause the rebellion by their earlier harsh treatment of the peasants. To Luther, the state and its rulers were ordained

Ninety-Five Theses	1517
Leipzig Debate	1519
Diet and Edict of Worms	1521
Peasants' War	1524–1525

by God and given the authority to maintain the peace and order necessary for the spread of the Gospel. It was the duty of princes to put down all revolts. By May 1525, the German princes had ruthlessly suppressed the peasant hordes. By this time, Luther found himself ever more dependent on state authorities for the growth and maintenance of his reformed church.

Organizing the Church

Justification by faith alone was the starting point for most of Protestantism's major doctrines. Since Luther downplayed the role of good works in salvation, the sacraments also had to be redefined. No longer regarded as merit-earning works, they were now viewed as divinely established signs signifying the promise of salvation. Based on his interpretation of scriptural authority, Luther kept only two of the Catholic Church's seven sacraments—baptism and the Lord's Supper. Baptism signified rebirth through grace. Regarding the Lord's Supper, Luther denied the Catholic doctrine of **transubstantiation,** which taught that the substance of the bread and wine consumed in the rite is miraculously transformed into the body and blood of Jesus. Yet he continued to insist on the real presence of Jesus's body and blood in the bread and wine given as a testament to God's forgiveness of sin.

Luther's emphasis on the importance of Scripture led him to reject the Catholic belief that the authority of Scripture must be supplemented by the traditions and decrees of the church. The word of God as revealed in the Bible was sufficient authority in religious affairs. A hierarchical priesthood was thus unnecessary since all Christians who followed the word of God were their own priests, constituting a "priesthood of all believers." Even though Luther thus considered the true church to be an invisible entity, the difficulties of actually establishing a reformed church led him to believe that a tangible, organized church was needed. Since the Catholic ecclesiastical hierarchy had been scrapped, Luther came to rely increasingly on the princes or state authorities to organize and guide the new Lutheran reformed churches. He had little choice. Secular authorities in Germany, as elsewhere, were soon playing an important role in church affairs. By 1530, in the German states that had converted to Lutheranism, both princes and city councils appointed officials who visited churches in their territories and regulated matters of worship. The Lutheran churches in Germany (and later in Scandinavia) quickly became territorial or state churches in which the state supervised and disciplined church members.

As part of the development of these state-dominated churches, Luther also instituted new religious services to replace the Mass. These featured a worship service consisting of a vernacular liturgy that focused on Bible reading, preaching the word of God, and song. Following his own denunciation of clerical celibacy, Luther married a former nun, Katherina von Bora (kat-uh-REE-nuh fun BOH-rah), in 1525. His union provided a model of married and family life for the new Protestant minister.

Germany and the Reformation: Religion and Politics

From its very beginning, the fate of Luther's movement was closely tied to political affairs. In 1519, Charles I, king of Spain and grandson of Emperor Maximilian (see Chart 13.1), was elected Holy Roman Emperor as Charles V. Charles ruled over an immense empire, consisting of Spain and its overseas possessions, the traditional Austrian Habsburg lands, Bohemia, Hungary, the Low Countries, and the kingdom of Naples in southern Italy (see Map 13.1). The extent of his possessions was reflected in the languages he used: "I speak Spanish to God, Italian to women, French to men, and German to my horse." Politically, Charles wanted to maintain his dynasty's control over his enormous empire; religiously, he hoped to preserve the unity of the Catholic faith throughout his empire. Despite Charles's strengths, his empire was

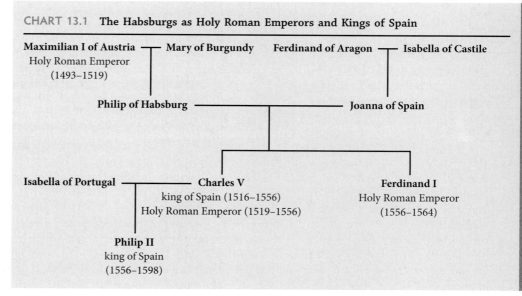

CHART 13.1   The Habsburgs as Holy Roman Emperors and Kings of Spain

Maximilian I of Austria —— Mary of Burgundy   Ferdinand of Aragon —— Isabella of Castile
Holy Roman Emperor
(1493–1519)

Philip of Habsburg ———————————————— Joanna of Spain

Isabella of Portugal ———— Charles V   Ferdinand I
king of Spain (1516–1556)   Holy Roman Emperor
Holy Roman Emperor (1519–1556)   (1556–1564)

Philip II
king of Spain
(1556–1598)

MAP 13.1 The Empire of Charles V. Charles V spent much of his reign fighting wars in Italy, against France and the Ottoman Empire, and within the borders of the Holy Roman Empire. He failed in his main goal to secure Europe for Catholicism: the 1555 Peace of Augsburg recognized the equality of Catholicism and Lutheranism and let each German prince choose his realm's religion.

Q *Why would France feel threatened by the empire of Charles V?*

overextended, and he spent a lifetime in futile pursuit of his goals. Four major problems—the French, the papacy, the Turks, and Germany's internal situation—cost him both his dream and his health. At the same time, the emperor's problems gave Luther's movement time to grow and organize before facing the concerted onslaught of the Catholic forces.

THE FRENCH AND THE PAPACY Charles V's chief political concern was his rivalry with the Valois king of France, Francis I (1515–1547). Encircled by the possessions of the Habsburg empire, Francis became embroiled in a series of conflicts with Charles over disputed territories in southern France, the Netherlands, the Rhineland, northern Spain, and Italy. These conflicts, known as the Habsburg-Valois Wars, were fought intermittently for twenty-four years (1521–1544), preventing

Charles from concentrating on the Lutheran problem in Germany.

Meanwhile, Charles faced two other enemies. The Habsburg emperor expected papal cooperation in dealing with the Lutheran heresy. Papal policy, however, was guided by political considerations, not religious ones, a clear indication that, like the Catholic king of France, a pope could act against his religious interests because of the political situation. Fearful of Charles's power in Italy, Pope Clement VII (1523–1534) joined the side of Francis I in the second Habsburg-Valois War (1527–1529), with catastrophic results. In April 1527, the Spanish-imperial army of Charles V went berserk while attacking Rome and gave the capital of Catholicism a fearful and bloody sacking. Sobered by the experience, Clement came to terms with the emperor, and by 1530, Charles V stood supreme over much of Italy.

Charles V. Charles V sought to maintain religious unity throughout his vast empire by keeping all his subjects within the bounds of the Catholic Church. Due to his conflict with Francis I of France and his difficulties with the Turks, the papacy, and the German princes, Charles was never able to check the spread of Lutheranism. This portrait by the Venetian painter Titian shows Charles at the height of his power in 1547 after the defeat of the Lutherans at the Battle of Mühlberg.

THE OTTOMAN EMPIRE   In the meantime, Charles V also faced problems in the eastern part of his empire. In the fifteenth century, the Ottoman Turks had overrun Constantinople and established control over much of the Balkans in southeastern Europe (see Chapter 12). Now, in the first decades of the sixteenth century, the Ottomans posed a new threat to Europe. Ottoman armies had taken control of much of the North African coast and captured the Christian island of Rhodes. Under their new leader, Suleiman the Magnificent (1520–1566), Ottoman forces had defeated and killed King Louis of Hungary, Charles's brother-in-law, at the Battle of Mohács (MOH-hach) in 1526. Subsequently, the Ottomans overran most of Hungary, moved into Austria, and advanced as far as Vienna, where they were finally repulsed in 1529. The emperor and much of Christian Europe breathed a sigh of relief but still remained fearful of another Ottoman attack.

POLITICS IN GERMANY   By the end of 1529, Charles was ready to deal with Germany. The second Habsburg-Valois War had ended, the Turks had been defeated temporarily, and the pope had been subdued. The internal political situation in the Holy Roman Empire was not in his favor, however. Germany was a land of several hundred territorial states: princely states, ecclesiastical principalities, and free imperial cities. Though all owed loyalty to the emperor, Germany's medieval development had enabled these states to become quite independent of imperial authority. They had no desire to have a strong emperor.

Charles's attempt to settle the Lutheran problem at the Diet of Augsburg in 1530 proved completely inadequate, and the emperor wound up demanding that the Lutherans return to the Catholic Church by April 15, 1531. In February 1531, fearful of Charles's intentions, eight princes and eleven imperial cities—all Lutheran—formed a defensive alliance known as the Schmalkaldic League. These Protestant German states vowed to assist each other "whenever any one of us is attacked on account of the Word of God and the doctrine of the Gospel." Religion was dividing the empire into two armed camps.

The renewed threat of the Turks against Vienna forced Charles once again to seek compromise instead of war with the Protestant authorities. From 1532 to 1535, Charles was forced to fight off an Ottoman, Arab, and Barbary attack on the Mediterranean coasts of Italy and Spain. Two additional Habsburg-Valois Wars (1535–1538 and 1542–1544) soon followed and kept Charles preoccupied with military campaigns in southern France and the Low Countries. Finally, Charles made peace with Francis in 1544 and the Turks in 1545. Fifteen years after the Diet of Augsburg, Charles was finally free to resolve his problem in Germany.

By the time of Luther's death in February 1546, all hopes of a peaceful compromise had faded. Charles brought a sizable imperial army of German, Dutch, Italian, and Spanish troops to do battle with the Protestants. In the first phase of the Schmalkaldic Wars (1546–1547), the emperor's forces decisively defeated the Lutherans at the Battle of Mühlberg (MOOL-bayrk). Charles V was at the zenith of his power, and the Protestant cause seemed doomed.

Appearances proved misleading, however. The Schmalkaldic League was soon reestablished, and the German Protestant princes allied themselves with the new French king, Henry II (1547–1559)—a Catholic—to revive the war in 1552. This time Charles was less fortunate and was forced to negotiate a truce. Exhausted by his efforts to maintain religious orthodoxy and the unity of his empire, Charles abandoned German affairs to his brother Ferdinand, abdicated all of his titles in 1556, and retired to his country estate in Spain to spend the remaining two years of his life in solitude.

An end to religious warfare in Germany came in 1555 with the Peace of Augsburg, which marked an important turning point in the history of the Reformation. The division of Christianity was formally acknowledged, with Lutheranism granted equal legal standing with Catholicism. Moreover, the peace settlement accepted the right of each German ruler to determine the religion of his subjects (but not the right of the subjects to choose their religion). Charles's hope for a united empire had been

First Habsburg-Valois War	1521–1525
Battle of Mohács	1526
Second Habsburg-Valois War	1527–1529
Defeat of the Turks at Vienna	1529
Diet of Augsburg	1530
Formation of Schmalkaldic League	1531
Third Habsburg-Valois War	1535–1538
Fourth Habsburg-Valois War	1542–1544
Schmalkaldic Wars	1546–1555
Peace of Augsburg	1555

completely dashed, and the ideal of medieval Christian unity was irretrievably lost. The rapid proliferation of new Protestant groups served to underscore that new reality.

The Spread of the Protestant Reformation

Q **FOCUS QUESTIONS**: What were the main tenets of Lutheranism, Zwinglianism, Calvinism, and Anabaptism, and how did they differ from each other and from Catholicism? What impact did political, economic, and social conditions have on the development of these four reform movements?

For both Catholics and Protestant reformers, Luther's heresy raised the question of what constituted the correct interpretation of the Bible. The inability to agree on this issue led not only to theological confrontations but also to bloody warfare as each Christian group was unwilling to admit that it could be wrong.

Lutheranism in Scandinavia

In 1397, the Union of Kalmar had brought about the unification of Denmark, Norway, and Sweden under the rule of one monarch, the king of Denmark. This union, however, failed to achieve any real social or political unification of the three states, particularly since the independent-minded landed nobles worked to frustrate any increase in monarchical centralization. By the beginning of the sixteenth century, the union was on the brink of disintegration. In 1520, Christian II (1513–1523) of Denmark, ruler of the three

The Swiss Cantons

Scandinavian kingdoms, was overthrown by Swedish barons led by Gustavus Vasa. Three years later, Vasa became king of an independent Sweden (1523–1560) and took the lead in establishing a Lutheran Reformation in his country. By the 1530s, the Swedish Lutheran National Church had been created.

Meanwhile, Christian II had also been deposed as the king of Denmark by the Danish nobility; he was succeeded by his uncle, who became Frederick I (1523–1533). Frederick encouraged Lutheran preachers to spread their evangelical doctrines and to introduce a Lutheran liturgy into the Danish church service. In the 1530s, under Frederick's successor, Christian III (1534–1559), a Lutheran state church was installed with the king as the supreme authority in all ecclesiastical affairs. Christian was also instrumental in spreading Lutheranism to Norway. By the 1540s, Scandinavia had become a Lutheran stronghold. Like the German princes, the Scandinavian monarchs had been the dominant force in establishing state-run churches.

The Zwinglian Reformation

In the sixteenth century, the Swiss Confederation was a loose association of thirteen self-governing states called cantons. Theoretically part of the Holy Roman Empire, they had become virtually independent in 1499. The six forest cantons were democratic republics; the seven urban cantons, which included Zürich, Bern, and Basel, were for the most part governed by city councils controlled by narrow oligarchies of wealthy citizens.

Ulrich Zwingli (OOL-rikh TSFING-lee) (1484–1531) was a product of the Swiss forest cantons. The precocious son of a relatively prosperous peasant, the young Zwingli eventually obtained both bachelor of arts and master of arts degrees. During his university education at Vienna and Basel, Zwingli was strongly influenced by Christian humanism. Ordained a priest in 1506, he accepted a parish post in rural Switzerland until his appointment as a cathedral priest in the Great Minster of Zürich in 1518. Through his preaching there, Zwingli began the Reformation in Switzerland.

Zwingli's preaching of the Gospel caused such unrest that in 1523 the city council held a public disputation or debate in the town hall. The disputation became a standard method of spreading the Reformation to many cities. It gave an advantage to reformers, since they had the power of new ideas and Catholics were not used to defending their teachings. Zwingli's party was accorded the victory, and the council declared that "Mayor, Council and Great

Zwingli. Ulrich Zwingli began the Reformation in Switzerland through his preaching in Zürich. Zwingli's theology was accepted in Zürich and soon spread to other Swiss cities. This portrait of Zwingli was done by an unknown artist in the early sixteenth century.

Council of Zürich, in order to do away with disturbance and discord, have upon due deliberation and consultation decided and resolved that Master Zwingli should continue as heretofore to proclaim the Gospel and the pure sacred Scripture."[7]

REFORMS IN ZÜRICH Over the next two years, evangelical reforms were promulgated in Zürich by a city council strongly influenced by Zwingli. Zwingli looked to the state to supervise the church. "A church without the magistrate is mutilated and incomplete," he declared. Relics and images were abolished; all paintings and decorations were removed from the churches and replaced by whitewashed walls. As Zwingli remarked, "The images are not to be endured; for all that God has forbidden, there can be no compromise."[8] The Mass was replaced by a new liturgy consisting of Scripture reading, prayer, and sermons. Music was eliminated from the service as a distraction from the pure word of God. Monasticism, pilgrimages, the veneration of saints, clerical celibacy, and the pope's authority were all abolished as remnants of papal Christianity. Zwingli's movement soon spread to other cities in Switzerland, including Bern in 1528 and Basel in 1529.

A FUTILE SEARCH FOR UNITY By 1528, Zwingli's reform movement faced a serious political problem as the forest cantons remained staunchly Catholic. Zürich feared that they would ally with the Habsburgs. To counteract this danger, Zwingli attempted to build a league of evangelical cities by seeking an agreement with Luther and the German reformers. An alliance between them seemed possible, since the Reformation had spread to the southern German cities, especially Strasbourg, where a moderate reform movement containing characteristics of both Luther's and Zwingli's movements had been instituted by Martin Bucer (1491–1551). Both the German and the Swiss reformers realized the need for unity to defend against imperial and conservative opposition.

Protestant political leaders, especially Landgrave Philip of Hesse, fearful that Charles V would take advantage of the division between the reformers, attempted to promote an alliance of the Swiss and German reformed churches by persuading the leaders of both groups to attend a colloquy (conference) at Marburg to resolve their differences. Able to agree on virtually everything else, the gathering splintered over the interpretation of the Lord's Supper (see the box on p. 391). Zwingli believed that the scriptural words "This is my body" and "This is my blood" should be taken symbolically, not literally. To Zwingli, the Lord's Supper was only a meal of remembrance, and he refused to accept Luther's insistence on the real presence of the body and blood of Jesus "in, with, and under the bread and wine." The Marburg Colloquy of 1529 produced no agreement and no evangelical alliance. It was a foretaste of the issues that would divide one reform group from another and lead to the creation of different Protestant groups.

In October 1531, war erupted between the Swiss Protestant and Catholic cantons. Zürich's army was routed, and Zwingli was found wounded on the battlefield. His enemies killed him, cut up his body, burned the pieces, and scattered the ashes. This Swiss civil war of 1531 provided an early indication of what religious passions would lead to in the sixteenth century. Unable to find peaceful ways to agree on the meaning of the Gospel, the disciples of Christianity resorted to violence and decision by force. When he heard of Zwingli's death, Martin Luther, who had not forgotten the confrontation at Marburg, is supposed to have remarked that Zwingli "got what he deserved."

The Radical Reformation: The Anabaptists

Although many reformers were ready to allow the state to play an important, if not dominant, role in church affairs, some people rejected this kind of magisterial reformation and favored a far more radical reform movement. Collectively called the Anabaptists, these radicals were actually members of a large variety of groups who shared some common characteristics. Anabaptism was especially attractive to the peasants, weavers, miners, and artisans who had been adversely affected by the economic changes of the age.

Opposing ⊰VIEWPOINTS

A Reformation Debate: Conflict at Marburg

Debates played a crucial role in the Reformation period. They were a primary instrument in introducing the Reformation into innumerable cities as well as a means of resolving differences among like-minded Protestant groups. This selection contains an excerpt from the vivacious and often brutal debate between Luther and Zwingli over the sacrament of the Lord's Supper at Marburg in 1529. The two protagonists failed to reach agreement.

The Marburg Colloquy, 1529

THE HESSIAN CHANCELLOR FEIGE: My gracious prince and lord [Landgrave Philip of Hesse] has summoned you for the express and urgent purpose of settling the dispute over the sacrament of the Lord's Supper.... Let everyone on both sides present his arguments in a spirit of moderation, as becomes such matters.... Now then, Doctor Luther, you may proceed.

LUTHER: Noble prince, gracious lord! Undoubtedly the colloquy is well intentioned.... Although I have no intention of changing my mind, which is firmly made up, I will nevertheless present the grounds of my belief and show where the others are in error.... Your basic contentions are these: In the last analysis you wish to prove that a body cannot be in two places at once, and you produce arguments about the unlimited body which are based on natural reason. I do not question how Christ can be God and man and how the two natures can be joined. For God is more powerful than all our ideas, and we must submit to his word.

Prove that Christ's body is not there where the Scripture says, "This is my body!" Rational proofs I will not listen to.... God is beyond all mathematics and the words of God are to be revered and carried out in awe. It is God who commands, "Take, eat, this is my body." I request, therefore, valid scriptural proof to the contrary. *Luther writes on the table in chalk, "This is my body," and covers the words with a velvet cloth.*

OECOLAMPADIUS [leader of the reform movement in Basel and a Zwinglian partisan]: The sixth chapter of John clarifies the other scriptural passages. Christ is not speaking there about a local presence. "The flesh is of no avail," he says. It is not my intention to employ rational, or geometrical, arguments—neither am I denying the power of God—but as long as I have the complete faith I will speak from that. For Christ is risen; he sits at the right hand of God; and so he cannot be present in the bread. Our view is neither new nor sacrilegious, but is based on faith and Scripture....

ZWINGLI: I insist that the words of the Lord's Supper must be figurative. This is ever apparent, and even required by the article of faith: "taken up into heaven, seated at the right hand of the Father." Otherwise, it would be absurd to look for him in the Lord's Supper at the same time that Christ is telling us that he is in heaven. One and the same body cannot possibly be in different places....

LUTHER: I call upon you as before: your basic contentions are shaky. Give way, and give glory to God!

ZWINGLI: And we call upon you to give glory to God and to quit begging the question! The issue at stake is this: Where is the proof of your position? I am willing to consider your words carefully—no harm meant! You're trying to outwit me. I stand by this passage in the sixth chapter of John, verse 63, and shall not be shaken from it. You'll have to sing another tune.

LUTHER: You're being obnoxious.

ZWINGLI: (*excitedly*) Don't you believe that Christ was attempting in John 6 to help those who did not understand?

LUTHER: You're trying to dominate things! You insist on passing judgment! Leave that to someone else!...It is your point that must be proved, not mine. But let us stop this sort of thing. It serves no purpose.

ZWINGLI: It certainly does! It is for you to prove that the passage in John 6 speaks of a physical repast.

LUTHER: You express yourself poorly and make about as much progress as a cane standing in a corner. You're going nowhere.

ZWINGLI: No, no, no! This is the passage that will break your neck!

LUTHER: Don't be so sure of yourself. Necks don't break this way. You're in Hesse, not Switzerland. ⊨

Q How did the positions of Zwingli and Luther on the sacrament of the Lord's Supper differ? What was the purpose of this debate? Based on this example, why do you think Reformation debates led to further hostility rather than compromise and unity between religious and sectarian opponents? What implications did this have for the future of the Protestant Reformation?

THE IDEAS OF THE ANABAPTISTS Anabaptists everywhere held certain ideas in common. All felt that the true Christian church was a voluntary association of believers who had undergone spiritual rebirth and had then been baptized into the church. Anabaptists advocated adult rather than infant baptism. No one, they believed, should be forced to accept the truth of the Bible. They also tried to return literally to the practices and spirit of early

Christianity. Adhering to the accounts of early Christian communities in the New Testament, they followed a strict sort of democracy in which all believers were considered equal. Each church chose its own minister, who might be any member of the community, since all Christians were considered priests (though women were often excluded). Those chosen as ministers had the duty to lead services, which were very simple and contained nothing not found in the early church. Like early Christians, Anabaptists, who called themselves "Christians" or "Saints," accepted that they would have to suffer for their faith. Anabaptists rejected theological speculation in favor of simple Christian living according to what they believed was the pure word of God. The Lord's Supper was interpreted as a remembrance, a meal of fellowship celebrated in the evening in private houses according to Jesus's example.

Unlike the Catholics and other Protestants, most Anabaptists believed in the complete separation of church and state. Not only was government to be excluded from the realm of religion, but it was not even supposed to exercise political jurisdiction over real Christians. Human law had no power over those whom God had saved. Anabaptists refused to hold political office or bear arms because many took the commandment "Thou shall not kill" literally, although some Anabaptist groups did become quite violent. Their political beliefs as much as their religious beliefs caused the Anabaptists to be regarded as dangerous radicals who threatened the very fabric of sixteenth-century society. Indeed, the chief thing Protestants and Catholics could agree on was the need to stamp out the Anabaptists.

VARIETIES OF ANABAPTISTS One early group of Anabaptists known as the Swiss Brethren arose in Zürich. Their ideas, especially adult baptism, frightened Zwingli, and they were expelled from the city in 1523. Because the first members of the Swiss Brethren who were baptized as adults had already been baptized as children (in the Catholic Church), their opponents labeled them Anabaptists or Rebaptists. Under Roman law, such people were subject to the death penalty.

As the teachings of the Swiss Brethren spread through southern Germany, the Austrian Habsburg lands, and Switzerland, Anabaptists suffered ruthless persecution, especially after the Peasants' War of 1524–1525, when the upper classes resorted to repression. Virtually eradicated in Germany, Anabaptist survivors emerged in Moravia and Poland, and in the Netherlands, Anabaptism took on a strange form.

In the 1530s, the city of Münster, in Westphalia in northwestern Germany near the Dutch border, was the site of an Anabaptist uprising that determined the fate of Dutch Anabaptism. Seat of a powerful Catholic prince-bishop, Münster had experienced severe economic disasters, including crop failure and plague. Although converted to Lutheranism in 1532, Münster experienced a more radical mass religious hysteria that led to legal recognition for the Anabaptists. Soon Münster became a haven for Anabaptists from the surrounding neighborhood,

especially the more wild-eyed variety known as Melchiorites, who adhered to a vivid **millenarianism.** They believed that the end of the world was at hand and that they would usher in the kingdom of God with Münster as the New Jerusalem. By the end of February 1534, these millenarian Anabaptists had taken control of the city, driven out everyone they considered godless or unbelievers, burned all books except the Bible, and proclaimed communal ownership of all property. Eventually, the leadership of this New Jerusalem fell into the hands of one man, John of Leiden, who proclaimed himself king of the New Jerusalem. As king, he would lead the elect from Münster out to cover the entire world and purify it of evil by the sword in preparation for Jesus's Second Coming and the creation of a New Age. In this new kingdom, John of Leiden believed, all goods would be held in common and the saints would live without suffering.

But it was not to be. As the Catholic prince-bishop of Münster gathered a large force and laid siege to the city, the new king repeatedly had to postpone the ushering forth from Münster. Finally, after many inhabitants had starved, a joint army of Catholics and Lutherans recaptured the city in June 1535 and executed the radical Anabaptist leaders in gruesome fashion. The New Jerusalem had ceased to exist.

Purged of its fantasies and its more extreme elements, Dutch Anabaptism reverted to its pacifist tendencies, especially evident in the work of Menno Simons (1496–1561), the man most responsible for rejuvenating Dutch Anabaptism. A popular leader, Menno dedicated his life to the spread of a peaceful, evangelical Anabaptism that stressed separation from the world in order to truly emulate the life of Jesus. Simons imposed strict discipline on his followers and banned those who refused to conform to the rules. The Mennonites, as his followers were called, spread from the Netherlands into northwestern Germany and eventually into Poland and Lithuania as well as the New World. Both the Mennonites and the Amish, who are also descended from the Anabaptists, maintain communities in the United States and Canada today.

The Reformation in England

The English Reformation was initiated by King Henry VIII (1509–1547), who wanted to divorce his first wife, Catherine of Aragon, because she had failed to produce a male heir. Furthermore, Henry had fallen in love with Anne Boleyn (BUH-lin *or* buh-LIN), a lady-in-waiting to Queen Catherine. Anne's unwillingness to be only the king's mistress and the king's desire to have a legitimate male heir made their marriage imperative, but the king's first marriage stood in the way.

Henry relied on Cardinal Wolsey, the highest-ranking English church official and lord chancellor to the king, to obtain from Pope Clement VII an annulment of the king's marriage. Normally, the pope might have been willing to oblige, but the sack of Rome in 1527 had made the pope dependent on the Holy Roman Emperor Charles V, who happened to be the nephew of Queen Catherine. Discretion dictated delay in granting the English king's request. Impatient with the process, Henry dismissed Wolsey in 1529.

Two new advisers now became the king's agents in fulfilling his wishes. These were Thomas Cranmer (1489–1556), who became archbishop of Canterbury in 1532, and Thomas Cromwell (1485–1540), the king's principal secretary after the fall of Wolsey. They advised the king to obtain an annulment of his marriage in England's own ecclesiastical courts. The most important step toward this goal was the promulgation by Parliament of an act cutting off all appeals from English church courts to Rome, a piece of legislation that essentially abolished papal authority in England. Henry no longer needed the pope to obtain his annulment. He was now in a hurry because Anne Boleyn had become pregnant and he had secretly married her in January 1533 to legitimize the expected heir. In May, as archbishop of Canterbury and head of the highest ecclesiastical court in England, Thomas Cranmer ruled that the king's marriage to Catherine was "null and absolutely void" and then validated Henry's marriage to Anne. At the beginning of June, Anne was crowned queen. Three months later, a child was born. Much to the king's disappointment, the baby was a girl, whom they named Elizabeth.

In 1534, Parliament completed the break of the Church of England with Rome by passing the Act of Supremacy, which declared that the king was "taken, accepted, and reputed the only supreme head on earth of the Church of England." This meant that the English monarch now controlled the church in all matters of doctrine, clerical appointments, and discipline. In addition, Parliament passed the Treason Act, making it punishable by death to deny that the king was the supreme head of the church.

One who challenged the new order was Thomas More, the humanist and former lord chancellor, who saw clearly to the heart of the issue: loyalty to the pope in Rome was now treason in England. More refused to support the new laws and was duly tried for treason. At his trial, he asked, rhetorically, what the effect of the actions of the king and Parliament would be: "Therefore am I not bound... to conform my conscience to the Council of one realm [England] against the general Council of Christendom?"[9] Because his conscience could not accept the victory of the national state over the church, nor would he, as a Christian, bow his head to a secular ruler in matters of faith, More was beheaded in London on July 6, 1535.

Recent research that emphasizes the strength of Catholicism in England suggests that Thomas More was not alone in his view of the new order. In fact, one historian has argued that Catholicism was vibrant in England in both the fifteenth and sixteenth centuries; in his view, the English Reformation was alien to many English people.

THE NEW ORDER Thomas Cromwell worked out the details of the Tudor government's new role in church affairs based on the centralized power exercised by the king and Parliament. Cromwell also came to his extravagant king's financial rescue with a daring plan for the dissolution of the monasteries. About four hundred religious houses were closed in 1536, and their land and possessions were confiscated by the king. Many were sold to nobles, gentry, and some merchants. The king added enormously to his treasury and also to his ranks of supporters, who now had a stake in the new Tudor order.

Although Henry VIII had broken with the papacy, little change occurred in matters of doctrine, theology, and ceremony. Some of his supporters, such as Archbishop Thomas Cranmer, wished to have a religious reformation as well as an administrative one, but Henry was unyielding. Nevertheless, some clergymen ignored Henry on the matter of priestly celibacy and secretly married.

The final decade of Henry's reign was preoccupied with foreign affairs, factional intrigue, and a continued effort to find the perfect wife. Henry soon tired of Anne Boleyn and had her beheaded in 1536 on a charge of adultery. His third wife, Jane Seymour, produced the long-awaited male heir but died twelve days later. His fourth marriage, to Anne of Cleves, a German princess, was arranged for political reasons. Henry relied on a painted portrait of Anne when he made the arrangements, but he was disappointed at her physical appearance when he saw her in person and soon divorced her. His fifth wife, Catherine Howard, was more attractive but less moral. When she committed adultery, Henry had her beheaded. His last wife was Catherine Parr, who married the king in 1543 and outlived him. Henry was succeeded by the underage and sickly Edward VI (1547–1553), the son of his third wife.

Since the new king was only nine years old at the time of his accession to the throne, real control of England passed to a council of regency. During Edward's reign, Archbishop Cranmer and others inclined toward Protestant doctrines were able to move the Church of England in a more Protestant direction. New acts of Parliament instituted the right of the clergy to marry, the elimination of images, and the creation of a revised Protestant liturgy that was elaborated in a new prayer book and liturgical guide known as the Book of Common Prayer. These rapid changes in doctrine and liturgy aroused much opposition and prepared the way for the reaction that occurred when Mary, Henry's first daughter by Catherine of Aragon, came to the throne.

REACTION UNDER MARY Mary (1553–1558) was a Catholic who fully intended to restore England to the Roman Catholic fold. But her restoration of Catholicism, achieved by joint action of the monarch and Parliament, aroused opposition. There was widespread antipathy to Mary's unfortunate marriage to Philip II, son of Charles V and the future king of Spain. Philip was strongly disliked in England, and Mary's foreign policy of alliance with Spain aroused further hostility, especially when her forces lost Calais, the last English possession in France after the Hundred Years' War. The burning of more than three hundred Protestant heretics aroused further ire against "bloody Mary." As a result of her policies, Mary managed

Henry VIII and His Successors. This allegorical painting of the Tudor succession, entitled *The Family of Henry VIII*, was done by an English artist about forty years after the death of Henry VIII. King Henry sits on his throne under the Tudor coat of arms. At the far left is the figure of a Roman soldier representing the god of war. Next is Philip II of Spain, the husband of Mary Tudor, who stands beside him. On the other side of Henry stand Edward, Elizabeth, and two female figures who represent peace and plenty.

to achieve the opposite of what she had intended: England was more Protestant by the end of her reign than it had been at the beginning. When she came to power, Protestantism had become identified with church destruction and religious anarchy. Now people identified it with English resistance to Spanish interference. Mary's death in 1558 ended the restoration of Catholicism in England.

John Calvin and Calvinism

Of the second generation of Protestant reformers, one stands out as the systematic theologian and organizer of the Protestant movement—John Calvin (1509–1564). Calvin received a remarkably diverse education in humanistic studies and law in his native France. He was also influenced by Luther's writings, which were being circulated and read by French intellectuals as early as 1523. In 1533, Calvin experienced a religious crisis that determined the rest of his life's work. He described it in these words:

> God, by a sudden conversion, subdued and brought my mind to a teachable frame, which was more hardened in such matters than might have been expected from one at my early period of life. Having thus received some taste and knowledge of true godliness, I was immediately inflamed with so intense a desire to make progress therein, although I did not leave off other studies, I yet pursued them with less ardor.[10]

Calvin's conversion was solemn and straightforward. He was so convinced of the inner guidance of God that he became the most determined of all the Protestant reformers.

After his conversion and newfound conviction, Calvin was no longer safe in Paris, since King Francis I periodically persecuted Protestants. Eventually, Calvin made his way to Basel, where in 1536 he published the first edition of the *Institutes of the Christian Religion,* a masterful synthesis of Protestant thought that immediately secured his reputation as one of the new leaders of Protestantism.

CALVIN'S IDEAS On most important doctrines, Calvin stood very close to Luther. He adhered to the doctrine of justification by faith alone to explain how humans achieved salvation. Calvin also placed much emphasis on the absolute sovereignty of God or the "power, grace, and glory of God." Thus, "God asserts his possession of omnipotence, and claims our acknowledgment of this attribute; not such as is imagined by sophists, vain, idle, and almost asleep, but vigilant, efficacious, operative and engaged in continual action."[11]

One of the ideas derived from his emphasis on the absolute sovereignty of God—**predestination**—gave a unique cast to Calvin's teachings, although Luther too believed in this principle. This "eternal decree," as Calvin called it, meant that God had predestined some people to be saved (the elect) and others to be damned (the reprobate). According to Calvin, "He has once for all determined, both whom he would admit to salvation, and

John Calvin. After a conversion experience, John Calvin abandoned his life as a humanist and became a reformer. In 1536, Calvin began working to reform the city of Geneva, where he remained until his death in 1564. This sixteenth-century portrait of Calvin pictures him near the end of his life.

Photo credit (rotated, left margin): © The Art Archive/University Library, Geneva/Gianni Dagli Orti

CHRONOLOGY New Reform Movements

The Zwinglian Reformation	
Zwingli made cathedral priest at Zürich	1518
Reform adopted in Zürich	1523
Marburg Colloquy	1529
Death of Zwingli on the battlefield	1531
The Anabaptists	
Anabaptists expelled from Zürich	1523
New Jerusalem in Münster	1534–1535
The Reformation in England	
Henry VIII	1509–1547
Act of Supremacy	1534
Execution of Thomas More	1535
Edward VI	1547–1553
Mary	1553–1558
Calvin and Calvinism	
Institutes of the Christian Religion	1536
Calvin begins ministry in Geneva	1536
Ecclesiastical Ordinances	1541

whom he would condemn to destruction."[12] Calvin identified three tests that might indicate possible salvation: an open profession of faith, a "decent and godly life," and participation in the sacraments of baptism and communion. In no instance did Calvin ever suggest that worldly success or material wealth was a sign of election. Significantly for the future of Calvinism, although Calvin himself stressed that there could be no absolute certainty of salvation, some of his followers did not always make this distinction. The practical psychological effect of predestination was to give some later Calvinists an unshakable conviction that they were doing God's work on earth. Thus, Calvinism became a dynamic and activist faith. It is no accident that Calvinism became the militant international form of Protestantism.

To Calvin, the church was a divine institution responsible for preaching the word of God and administering the sacraments. Calvin kept the same two sacraments as other Protestant reformers, baptism and the Lord's Supper. Baptism was a sign of the remission of sins. Calvin believed in the real presence of Jesus in the sacrament of the Lord's Supper, but only in a spiritual sense. Jesus's body is at the right hand of God and thus cannot be in the sacrament, but to the believer, Jesus is spiritually present in the Lord's Supper.

CALVIN'S GENEVA Before 1536, John Calvin had essentially been a scholar. But in that year, he took up a ministry in Geneva that lasted, except for a brief exile (1538–1541), until his death in 1564. Calvin achieved a major success in 1541 when the city council accepted his new church constitution, known as the Ecclesiastical Ordinances.

This document created a church government that used both clergy and laymen in the service of the church. The Consistory, a special body for enforcing moral discipline, was set up as a court to oversee the moral life and doctrinal purity of Genevans (see the box on p. 396). As its power increased, the Consistory went from "fraternal corrections" to the use of public penance and excommunication. More serious cases could be turned over to the city council for punishments greater than excommunication. During Calvin's last years, stricter laws against blasphemy were enacted and enforced with banishment and public whippings.

Calvin's success in Geneva enabled the city to become a vibrant center of Protestantism. John Knox, the Calvinist reformer of Scotland, called it "the most perfect school of Christ on earth." Following Calvin's lead, missionaries trained in Geneva were sent to all parts of Europe. Calvinism became established in France, the Netherlands, Scotland, and central and eastern Europe. By the mid-sixteenth century, Calvinism had replaced Lutheranism as the international form of Protestantism, and Calvin's Geneva stood as the fortress of the Reformation.

The Role of Discipline in the "Most Perfect School of Christ on Earth"

John Calvin had emphasized in his reform movement that the church should have the ability to enforce proper behavior. Consequently, the Ecclesiastical Ordinances of 1541, the constitution of the church in Geneva, provided for an order of elders whose function was to cooperate with the pastors in maintaining discipline, "to have oversight of the life of everyone," as Calvin expressed it. These selections from the official records of the Consistory show the nature of its work.

❖ ❖❖❖ ❖

Reports of the Genevan Consistory

Donna Jane Peterman is questioned concerning her faith and why she does not receive communion and attend worship. She confesses her faith and believes in one God and wants to come to God and the holy Church and has no other faith. She recited the Lord's Prayer in the vernacular. She said that she believes what the Church believes. Is questioned why she never participates in communion when it is celebrated in this town, but goes to other places. She answers that she goes where it seems good to her. Is placed outside the faith.

The sister of Sr. Curtet, Lucresse, to whom remonstrances have been made on account of her going with certain monies to have Masses said at Nessy by the monks of St. Claire. Questioned whether she has no scruples as to what she says. Replied that her father and mother have brought her up to obey a different law from the one now in force here. However, she does not desire the present law. Asked as to when was the festival of St. Felix, she replied that it was yesterday. Asked if she had not fasted, she replied that she fasted when it pleased her. Asked if she did not desire to pray to a single God; said that she did. Asked if she did not pray to St. Felix; said that she prayed to St. Felix and other saints who interceded for her. She is very obstinate. Decision that she be sent to some minister of her choice every sermon day and that the Lord's Supper be withheld from her.

At about this time, by resolution of the Consistory . . . the marriage contracted between the widow of Jean Archard, aged more than 70, and a servant of hers, aged about 27 or 28, was dissolved because of the too great inequality of age. The Consistory resolved further that Messieurs should be requested to make a ruling on this matter for the future. ➢

Q Based on the examples given here, what kinds of activities did the Consistory seek to root out and prevent? Why was Calvinism so determined to survey and control the personal lives of citizens?

The Social Impact of the Protestant Reformation

 Focus Question: What impact did the Protestant Reformation have on society in the sixteenth century?

Because Christianity was such an integral part of European life, it was inevitable that the Reformation would have an impact on the family, education, and popular religious practices.

The Family

For centuries, Catholicism had praised the family and sanctified its existence by making marriage a sacrament. But the Catholic Church's high regard for abstinence from sex as the surest way to holiness made the celibate state of the clergy preferable to marriage. Nevertheless, because not all men could remain chaste, marriage offered the best means to control sexual intercourse and give it a purpose, the procreation of children. To some extent, this attitude persisted among the Protestant reformers; Luther, for example, argued that sex in marriage allowed one to "make use of this sex in order to avoid sin," and Calvin advised that every man should "abstain from marriage only so long as he is fit to observe celibacy." If "his power to tame lust fails him," then he must marry.

But the Reformation did bring some change to the conception of the family. Both Catholic and Protestant clergy preached sermons advocating a more positive side to family relationships. The Protestants were especially important in developing this new view of the family. Because Protestantism had eliminated any idea of special holiness for celibacy, abolishing both monasticism and a celibate clergy, the family could be placed at the center of human life, and a new stress on "mutual love between man and wife" could be extolled. But were doctrine and reality the same? For more radical religious groups, at times they were (see the box on p. 397). One Anabaptist wrote to his wife before his execution, "My faithful helper, my loyal friend. I praise God that he gave you to me, you who have sustained me in all my trial."[13] But more often reality reflected the traditional roles of husband as the ruler and wife as the obedient servant whose chief duty was to please her husband. Luther stated it clearly:

The rule remains with the husband, and the wife is compelled to obey him by God's command. He rules the home and the

A Protestant Woman

In the initial zeal of the Protestant Reformation, women were frequently allowed to play unusual roles. Katherine Zell of Germany (c. 1497–1562) first preached beside her husband in 1527. After the deaths of her two children, she devoted the rest of her life to helping her husband and their reform faith. This selection is taken from one of her letters to a young Lutheran minister who had criticized her activities.

+—+ ⊨⫤⊨ +—+

Katherine Zell to Ludwig Rabus of Memmingen

I, Katherine Zell, wife of the late lamented Mathew Zell, who served in Strasbourg, where I was born and reared and still live, wish you peace and enhancement in God's grace....

From my earliest years I turned to the Lord, who taught and guided me, and I have at all times, in accordance with my understanding and His grace, embraced the interests of His church and earnestly sought Jesus. Even in youth this brought me the regard and affection of clergymen and others much concerned with the church, which is why the pious Mathew Zell wanted me as a companion in marriage; and I, in turn, to serve the glory of Christ, gave devotion and help to my husband, both in his ministry and in keeping his house.... Ever since I was ten years old I have been a student and a sort of church mother, much given to attending sermons. I have loved and frequented the company of learned men, and I conversed much with them, not about dancing, masquerades, and worldly pleasures but about the kingdom of God....

Consider the poor Anabaptists, who are so furiously and ferociously persecuted. Must the authorities everywhere be incited against them, as the hunter drives his dog against wild animals? Against those who acknowledge Christ the Lord in very much the same way we do and over which we broke with the papacy? Just because they cannot agree with us on lesser things, is this any reason to persecute them and in them Christ, in whom they fervently believe and have often professed in misery, in prison, and under the torments of fire and water?

Governments may punish criminals, but they should not force and govern belief, which is a matter for the heart and conscience not for temporal authorities.... When the authorities pursue one, they soon bring forth tears, and towns and villages are emptied. ⊱

 Q What new ideas did Katherine Zell bring to the Reformation? Why did people react so strongly against them?

---

state, wages war, defends his possessions, tills the soil, builds, plants, etc. The woman on the other hand is like a nail driven into the wall ... so the wife should stay at home and look after the affairs of the household, as one who has been deprived of the ability of administering those affairs that are outside and that concern the state. She does not go beyond her most personal duties.[14]

Obedience to her husband was not a wife's only role; her other important duty was to bear children. To Calvin and Luther, this function of women was part of the divine plan. God punishes women for the sins of Eve by the burdens of procreation and feeding and nurturing their children, but, said Luther, "it is a gladsome punishment if you consider the hope of eternal life and the honor of motherhood which had been left to her."[15] Although the Protestant reformers sanctified this role of woman as mother and wife, viewing it as a holy vocation, Protestantism also left few alternatives for women. Because monasticism had been destroyed, that career avenue was no longer available; for most Protestant women, family life was their only destiny. At the same time, by emphasizing the father as "ruler" and hence the center of household religion, Protestantism even removed the woman from her traditional role as controller of religion in the home.

Protestant reformers called on men and women to read the Bible and participate in religious services together. In this way, the reformers provided a stimulus for the education of girls so that they could read the Bible and other religious literature. The city council of Zwickau, for example, established a girls' school in 1525. But these schools were designed to encourage proper moral values rather than intellectual development and really did little to improve the position of women in society. Likewise, when women attempted to take more active roles in religious life, reformers—Lutheran and Calvinist alike—shrank back in horror. To them, the equality of the Gospel did not mean overthrowing the inequality of social classes or the sexes. Overall, the Protestant Reformation did not noticeably transform women's subordinate place in society.

Education in the Reformation

The Reformation had an important effect on the development of education in Europe. Renaissance humanism had significantly altered the content of education, and Protestant educators were very successful in implementing and using humanist methods in Protestant secondary schools and universities. Unlike the humanist schools, however, which had been mostly for an elite, the sons and a few daughters of the nobility and wealthier bourgeoisie, Protestant schools were aimed at a much wider audience. Protestantism created an increased need for at least a

A Sixteenth-Century Classroom. Protestants in Germany developed secondary schools that combined instruction in the liberal arts with religious education. This scene from a painting by Ambrosius Holbein shows a schoolmaster instructing a pupil in the alphabet while his wife helps a little girl.

semiliterate body of believers who could read the Bible for themselves.

While adopting the Classical emphasis of humanist schools, Protestant reformers broadened the base of the people being educated. Convinced of the need to provide the church with good Christians and good pastors as well as the state with good administrators and citizens, Martin Luther advocated that all children should have the opportunity of an education provided by the state. To that end, he urged the cities and villages of Saxony to establish schools paid for by the public. Luther's ideas were shared by his Wittenberg coworker Philip Melanchthon, whose educational efforts earned him the title of *Praecepter Germaniae* (PREE-sep-tur gayr-MAHN-ee-ee), the Teacher of Germany. In his scheme for education in Saxony, Melanchthon divided students into three classes or divisions based on their age or capabilities.

Following Melanchthon's example, the Protestants in Germany were responsible for introducing the gymnasium, or secondary school, where the humanist emphasis on the liberal arts based on instruction in Greek and Latin was combined with religious instruction. Most famous was the school in Strasbourg founded by Johannes Sturm in 1538, which served as a model for other Protestant schools. John Calvin's Genevan Academy, founded in 1559, was organized in two distinct parts. The "private school" or gymnasium was divided into seven classes for young people who were taught Latin and Greek grammar and literature as well as logic. In the "public school," students were taught philosophy, Hebrew, Greek, and theology. The Genevan Academy, which eventually became a university, came to concentrate on preparing ministers to spread the Calvinist view of the Gospel.

Religious Practices and Popular Culture

The Protestant reformers' attacks on the Catholic Church led to radical changes in religious practices. The Protestant Reformation abolished or severely curtailed such customary practices as indulgences, the veneration of relics and saints, pilgrimages, monasticism, and clerical celibacy. The elimination of saints put an end to the numerous celebrations of religious holy days and changed a community's sense of time. Thus, in Protestant communities, religious ceremonies and imagery, such as processions and statues, tended to be replaced with individual private prayer, family worship, and collective prayer and worship at the same time each week on Sunday.

In addition to abolishing saints' days and religious carnivals, some Protestant reformers even tried to eliminate customary forms of entertainment. The Puritans (as English Calvinists were called), for example, attempted to ban drinking in taverns, dramatic performances, and dancing. Dutch Calvinists denounced the tradition of giving small presents to children on the feast of Saint Nicholas, in early December. Many of these Protestant attacks on popular culture were unsuccessful, however. The importance of taverns in English social life made it impossible to eradicate them, and celebrating at Christmastime persisted in the Dutch Netherlands.

The Catholic Reformation

Q **FOCUS QUESTION:** What measures did the Roman Catholic Church take to reform itself and to combat Protestantism in the sixteenth century?

By the mid-sixteenth century, Lutheranism had become established in parts of Germany and Scandinavia, and Calvinism in parts of Switzerland, France, the Netherlands, and eastern Europe (see Map 13.2). In England, the split from Rome had resulted in the creation of a national church. The situation in Europe did not look favorable for Roman Catholicism. But constructive, positive forces for reform were at work within the Catholic Church, and by

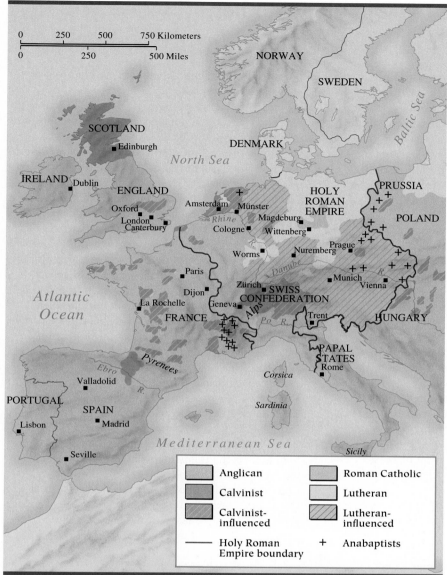

MAP 13.2 Catholics and Protestants in Europe by 1560. The Reformation continued to evolve beyond the basic split of the Lutherans from the Catholics. Several Protestant sects broke away from the teachings of Martin Luther, each with a separate creed and different ways of worship. In England, Henry VIII broke with the Catholic Church for political and dynastic reasons.

 Which areas of Europe were solidly Catholic, which were solidly Lutheran, and which were neither?

View an animated version of this map or related maps on the CourseMate website.

and practices while rejecting the principles and practices advocated by the Protestant reformers.

Revival of the Old

The Catholic Reformation revived the best features of medieval Catholicism and then adjusted them to meet new conditions, as is most apparent in the revival of mysticism and monasticism. The emergence of a new mysticism, closely tied to the traditions of Catholic piety, was especially evident in the life of the Spanish mystic Saint Teresa of Avila (1515–1582). A nun of the Carmelite order, Teresa experienced a variety of mystical visions that she claimed resulted in the ecstatic union of her soul with God. But Teresa also believed that mystical experience should lead to an active life of service on behalf of her Catholic faith. Consequently, she founded a new order of barefoot Carmelite nuns and worked to foster their mystical experiences.

The regeneration of religious orders also proved valuable to the reform of Catholicism. Old orders, such as the Benedictines and Dominicans, were reformed and renewed. The Capuchins emerged when a group of Franciscans decided to return to the simplicity and poverty of Saint Francis of Assisi, the medieval founder of the Franciscan order. In addition to caring for the sick and the poor, the Capuchins focused on preaching the Gospel directly to the people and emerged as an effective force against Protestantism.

New religious orders and brotherhoods were also created. The Theatines, founded in 1524, placed their emphasis on reforming the secular clergy and encouraging those clerics to fulfill their duties among the laity. The Theatines also founded orphanages and hospitals to care for the victims of war and plague. The Ursulines, a new order of nuns founded in Italy in 1535, focused their attention on establishing schools for the education of girls.

The Society of Jesus

Of all the new religious orders, the most important was the Society of Jesus, known as the Jesuits, who became the chief instrument of the Catholic Reformation. The

the mid-sixteenth century, they came to be directed by a revived and reformed papacy, giving the church new strength. The revival of Roman Catholicism is often called the Catholic Reformation, although some historians prefer the term Counter-Reformation, especially for those elements of the Catholic Reformation that were directly aimed at stopping the spread of Protestantism. Eventually, in the course of the Catholic Reformation, the Catholic Church reaffirmed traditional Catholic teachings

Loyola and Obedience to "Our Holy Mother, the Hierarchical Church"

In his *Spiritual Exercises,* Ignatius of Loyola developed a systematic program for "the conquest of self and the regulation of one's life" for service to the hierarchical Catholic Church. Ignatius's supreme goal was the commitment of the Christian to active service under Jesus's banner in the Church of Christ (the Catholic Church). In the final section of *The Spiritual Exercises,* Loyola explained the nature of that commitment in a series of "Rules for Thinking with the Church."

Ignatius of Loyola, "Rules for Thinking with the Church"

The following rules should be observed to foster the true attitude of mind we ought to have in the Church militant.

1. We must put aside all judgment of our own, and keep the mind ever ready and prompt to obey in all things the true Spouse of Jesus Christ, our holy Mother, the hierarchical Church.
2. We should praise sacramental confession, the yearly reception of the Most Blessed Sacrament [the Lord's Supper], and praise more highly monthly reception, and still more weekly Communion....
3. We ought to praise the frequent hearing of Mass, the singing of hymns, psalmody, and long prayers whether in the church or outside....
4. We must praise highly religious life, virginity, and continency; and matrimony ought not be praised as much as any of these.
5. We should praise vows of religion, obedience, poverty, chastity, and vows to perform other works of supererogation conducive to perfection....
6. We should show our esteem for the relics of the saints by venerating them and praying to the saints. We should praise visits to the Station Churches,

pilgrimages, indulgences, jubilees, the lighting of candles in churches.
7. We must praise the regulations of the Church, with regard to fast and abstinence, for example, in Lent, on Ember Days, Vigils, Fridays, and Saturdays.
8. We ought to praise not only the building and adornment of churches, but also images and veneration of them according to the subject they represent.
9. Finally, we must praise all the commandments of the Church, and be on the alert to find reasons to defend them, and by no means in order to criticize them.
10. We should be more ready to approve and praise the orders, recommendations, and way of acting of our superiors than to find fault with them. Though some of the orders, etc., may not have been praiseworthy, yet to speak against them, either when preaching in public or in speaking before the people, would rather be the cause of murmuring and scandal than of profit. As a consequence, the people would become angry with their superiors, whether secular or spiritual. But while it does harm in the absence of our superiors to speak evil of them before the people, it may be profitable to discuss their bad conduct with those who can apply a remedy....
13. If we wish to proceed securely in all things, we must hold fast to the following principle: What seems to me white, I will believe black if the hierarchical Church so defines. For I must be convinced that in Christ our Lord, the bridegroom, and in His spouse the Church, only one Spirit holds sway, which governs and rules for the salvation of souls.

Q What are the fundamental assumptions that inform Loyola's rules for "thinking with the church"? What do these assumptions tell you about the nature of the Catholic reform movement?

Society of Jesus was founded by a Spanish nobleman, Ignatius of Loyola (ig-NAY-shuss of loi-OH-luh) (1491–1556), whose injuries in battle cut short his military career. Loyola experienced a spiritual torment similar to Luther's but, unlike Luther, resolved his problems not by a new doctrine but by a decision to submit his will to the will of the church. Unable to be a real soldier, he vowed to be a soldier of God. Over a period of twelve years, Loyola prepared for his lifework by prayer, pilgrimages, going to school, and working out a spiritual program in his brief but powerful book, *The Spiritual Exercises.* This was a training manual for spiritual development emphasizing exercises by which the human will could be strengthened and made to follow the will of God as

manifested through his instrument, the Catholic Church (see the box above).

Loyola gathered together a small group of individuals who were eventually recognized as a religious order, the Society of Jesus, by a papal bull in 1540. The new order was grounded on the principles of absolute obedience to the papacy, a strict hierarchical order for the society, the use of education to achieve its goals, and a dedication to engage in "conflict for God." The Jesuits' organization came to resemble the structure of a military command. A two-year novitiate weeded out all but the most dedicated adherents. Executive leadership was put in the hands of a general, who nominated all-important positions in the order and was to be revered as the absolute head of

Ignatius of Loyola. The Jesuits became the most important new religious order of the Catholic Reformation. Shown here in a sixteenth-century painting by an unknown artist is Ignatius of Loyola, founder of the Society of Jesus. Loyola is seen kneeling before Pope Paul III, who officially recognized the Jesuits in 1540.

the order. Loyola served as the first general of the order until his death in 1556. A special vow of absolute obedience to the pope made the Jesuits an important instrument for papal policy.

ACTIVITIES OF THE JESUITS The Jesuits pursued three major activities. They established highly disciplined schools, borrowing freely from humanist schools for their educational methods. To the Jesuits, the thorough education of young people was crucial to combating the advance of Protestantism. In the course of the sixteenth century, the Jesuits took over the premier academic posts in Catholic universities, and by 1600, they were the most famous educators in Europe.

Another prominent Jesuit activity was the propagation of the Catholic faith among non-Christians. Francis Xavier (ZAY-vee-ur) (1506–1552), one of the original members of the Society of Jesus, carried the message of Catholic Christianity to the East. After converting tens of thousands in India, he traveled to Malacca and the Moluccas before reaching Japan in 1549. He spoke highly of the Japanese: "They are a people of excellent morals—good in general and not malicious."[16] Thousands of Japanese, especially in the southernmost islands, became Christians. In 1552, Xavier set out for China but died of a fever before he reached the mainland.

Although conversion efforts in Japan proved short-lived, Jesuit activity in China, especially that of the

Italian Matteo Ricci (ma-TAY-oh REE-chee) (1552–1610), was more long-lasting. Recognizing the Chinese pride in their own culture, the Jesuits attempted to draw parallels between Christian and Confucian concepts and to show the similarities between Christian morality and Confucian ethics. For their part, the missionaries were impressed with many aspects of Chinese civilization, and reports of their experiences heightened European curiosity about this great society on the other side of the world.

The Jesuits were also determined to carry the Catholic banner and fight Protestantism. Jesuit missionaries succeeded in restoring Catholicism to parts of Germany and eastern Europe. Poland was largely won back for the Catholic Church through Jesuit efforts.

A Revived Papacy

The involvement of the Renaissance papacy in dubious finances and Italian political and military affairs had given rise to numerous sources of corruption. The meager steps taken to control corruption left the papacy still in need of serious reform, and it took the jolt of the Protestant Reformation to bring it about.

The pontificate of Pope Paul III (1534–1549) proved to be a turning point in the reform of the papacy. Raised in the lap of Renaissance luxury, Paul III continued Renaissance papal practices by appointing his nephews as cardinals, involving himself in politics, and patronizing arts and letters on a lavish scale. Nevertheless, he perceived the need for change and expressed it decisively. Advocates of reform, such as Gasparo Contarini (GAHS-puh-roh kahn-tuh-REE-nee) and Gian Pietro Caraffa (JAHN PYAY-troh kuh-RAH-fuh), were made cardinals. In 1535, Paul took the audacious step of appointing a reform commission to study the condition of the church. The commission's report in 1537 blamed the church's problems on the corrupt policies of popes and cardinals. Paul III also formally recognized the Jesuits and summoned the Council of Trent (see the next section).

A decisive turning point in the direction of the Catholic Reformation and the nature of papal reform came in the 1540s. In 1541, a colloquy had been held at Regensburg in a final attempt to settle the religious division peacefully. Here Catholic moderates, such as Cardinal Contarini, who favored concessions to Protestants in the hope of restoring Christian unity, reached a compromise with Protestant moderates on a number of doctrinal issues. When Contarini returned to Rome with these proposals, Cardinal Caraffa and other hard-liners, who regarded all compromise with Protestant innovations as heresy, accused him of selling out to the heretics. It soon became apparent that the conservative reformers were in the ascendancy when Caraffa was able to persuade Paul III to establish the Roman Inquisition or Holy Office in 1542 to ferret out doctrinal errors. There was to be no compromise with Protestantism.

When Cardinal Caraffa was chosen pope as Paul IV (1555–1559), he so increased the power of the Inquisition that even liberal cardinals were silenced. This "first true pope of the Catholic Counter-Reformation," as he has been called, also created the Index of Forbidden Books, a list of books that Catholics were not allowed to read. It included all the works of Protestant theologians as well as authors considered "unwholesome," a category general enough to include the works of Erasmus. Rome, the capital of Catholic Christianity, was rapidly becoming Fortress Rome; any hope of restoring Christian unity by compromise was fast fading. The activities of the Council of Trent made compromise virtually impossible.

The Council of Trent

In 1542, Pope Paul III took the decisive step of calling for a general council of Christendom to resolve the religious differences created by the Protestant revolt. It was not until March 1545, however, that a group of cardinals, archbishops, bishops, abbots, and theologians met in the city of Trent on the border between Germany and Italy and initiated the Council of Trent. But a variety of problems, including an outbreak of plague, war between France and Spain, and the changing of popes, prevented the council from holding regular annual meetings. Nevertheless, the council met intermittently in three major sessions between 1545 and 1563. Moderate Catholic reformers hoped that compromises would be made in formulating doctrinal definitions that would encourage Protestants to return to the church. Conservatives, however, favored an uncompromising restatement of Catholic doctrines in strict opposition to Protestant positions. After a struggle, the latter group won.

The final doctrinal decrees of the Council of Trent reaffirmed traditional Catholic teachings in opposition to Protestant beliefs. Scripture and tradition were affirmed as equal authorities in religious matters; only the church could interpret Scripture. Both faith and good works were declared necessary for salvation. The seven sacraments, the Catholic doctrine of transubstantiation, and clerical celibacy were all upheld. Belief in purgatory and in the efficacy of indulgences was affirmed, although the hawking of indulgences was prohibited. Of the reform decrees that were passed, the most important established theological seminaries in every diocese for the training of priests.

Pope Paul III, Canons on Justification, Council of Trent (1547)

After the Council of Trent, the Roman Catholic Church possessed a clear body of doctrine and a unified church under the acknowledged supremacy of the popes, who had triumphed over bishops and councils. The Roman Catholic Church had become one Christian denomination among many with an organizational framework and doctrinal pattern that would not be significantly altered for four hundred years. With renewed confidence, the Catholic Church entered a new phase of its history.

CHRONOLOGY The Catholic Reformation

Pope Paul III	1534–1549
Papal recognition of Society of Jesus (Jesuits)	1540
Establishment of Roman Inquisition (Holy Office)	1542
Council of Trent	1545–1563
Pope Paul IV	1555–1559

Politics and the Wars of Religion in the Sixteenth Century

 FOCUS QUESTION: What role did politics, economic and social conditions, and religion play in the European wars of the sixteenth century?

By the middle of the sixteenth century, Calvinism and Catholicism had become activist religions dedicated to spreading the word of God as they interpreted it. Although this struggle for the minds and hearts of Europeans is at the heart of the religious wars of the sixteenth century, economic, social, and political forces also played an important role in these conflicts. Of the sixteenth-century religious wars, none were more momentous or shattering than the French civil wars known as the French Wars of Religion.

The French Wars of Religion (1562–1598)

Religion was the engine that drove the French civil wars of the sixteenth century. Concerned by the growth of Calvinism, the French kings tried to stop its spread by persecuting Calvinists but had little success. **Huguenots** (HYOO-guh-nots), as the French Calvinists were called, came from all levels of society: artisans and shopkeepers hurt by rising prices and a rigid guild system, merchants and lawyers in provincial towns whose local privileges were tenuous, and members of the nobility. Possibly 40 to 50 percent of the French nobility became Huguenots, including the house of Bourbon, which stood next to the Valois in the royal line of succession and ruled the southern French kingdom of Navarre (nuh-VAHR). The conversion of so many nobles made the Huguenots a potentially dangerous political threat to monarchical power. Though the Calvinists constituted only about 10 percent of the population, they were a strong-willed and well-organized minority.

The Catholic majority greatly outnumbered the Calvinist minority. The Valois monarchy was staunchly Catholic, and its control of the Catholic Church gave it little incentive to look on Protestantism favorably. When King Henry II was killed accidentally in a tournament in 1559, he was succeeded by a series of weak and neurotic sons, two of whom were dominated by their mother,

Catherine de' Medici (1519–1589). As regent for her sons, the moderate Catholic Catherine looked to religious compromise as a way to defuse the political tensions but found to her consternation that both sides possessed their share of religious fanatics unwilling to make concessions. The extreme Catholic party—known as the ultra-Catholics—favored strict opposition to the Huguenots and was led by the Guise (GEEZ) family. Possessing the loyalty of Paris and large sections of northern and northwestern France through their client-patronage system, the Guises could recruit and pay for large armies and received support abroad from the papacy and Jesuits who favored the family's uncompromising Catholic position.

But religion was not the only factor contributing to the French civil wars. Resentful of the growing power of monarchical centralization, towns and provinces were only too willing to join a revolt against the monarchy. This was also true of the nobility, and because so many of them were Calvinists, they formed an important base of opposition to the crown. The French Wars of Religion, then, presented a major constitutional crisis for France and temporarily halted the development of the French centralized territorial state. The claim of the state's ruling dynasty to a person's loyalties was temporarily superseded by loyalty to one's religious belief. For some people, the unity of France was less important than religious truth. But there also emerged in France a group of public figures who placed politics before religion and believed that no religious truth was worth the ravages of civil war. These **politiques** (puh-lee-TEEKS) ultimately prevailed, but not until both sides were exhausted by bloodshed.

COURSE OF THE STRUGGLE   The wars erupted in 1562 when the powerful duke of Guise massacred a peaceful congregation of Huguenots at Vassy. In the decade of the 1560s, the Huguenots held their own. Though too small a group to conquer France, their armies were so good at defensive campaigns that they could not be defeated either, despite the infamous Saint Bartholomew's Day massacre.

This massacre of Huguenots in August 1572 occurred at a time when the Catholic and Calvinist parties had apparently been reconciled through the marriage of the sister of the reigning Valois king, Charles IX (1560–1574), and Henry of Navarre, the Bourbon ruler of Navarre. Henry was the son of Jeanne d'Albret (ZHAHN dahl-BRAY), queen of Navarre, who had been responsible for introducing Calvinist ideas into her kingdom. Henry was also the acknowledged political leader of the Huguenots, and many Huguenots traveled to Paris for the wedding.

But the Guise family persuaded the king and his mother, Catherine de' Medici, that this gathering of Huguenots posed a threat to them. Charles and his advisers decided to eliminate the Huguenot leaders with one swift blow. According to one French military leader, Charles and his advisers believed that civil war would soon break out anyway and that "it was better to win a battle in Paris,

CHRONOLOGY The French Wars of Religion (1562–1598)	
Henry II	1547–1559
Charles IX	1560–1574
Duke of Guise massacres Huguenot congregation at Vassy	1562
Saint Bartholomew's Day massacre	1572
Henry III	1574–1589
Formation of the Holy League	1576
War of the Three Henries	1588–1589
Assassination of Henry III	1589
Coronation of Henry IV	1594
Edict of Nantes	1598

where all the leaders were, than to risk it in the field and fall into a dangerous and uncertain war."[17]

The massacre began early in the day on August 24 when the king's guards sought out and killed some prominent Huguenot leaders. These murders soon unleashed a wave of violence that gripped the city of Paris. For three days, frenzied Catholic mobs roamed the streets of Paris, killing Huguenots in an often cruel and bloodthirsty manner. According to one eyewitness account: "Then they took her [Françoise Lussault] and dragged her by the hair a long way through the streets, and spying the gold bracelets on her arms, without having the patience to unfasten them, cut off her wrists."[18] Three days of killing left three thousand Huguenots dead, although not Henry of Navarre, who saved his life by promising to turn Catholic. Thousands more were killed in provincial towns. The massacre boomeranged, however, because it discredited the Valois dynasty without ending the conflict.

The fighting continued. The Huguenots rebuilt their strength, and in 1576, the ultra-Catholics formed a "Holy League," vowing to exterminate heresy and seat a true Catholic champion—Henry, duke of Guise—on the French throne in place of the ruling king, Henry III (1574–1589), who had succeeded his brother Charles IX. The turning point in the conflict came in the War of the Three Henries in 1588–1589. Henry, duke of Guise, in the pay of Philip II of Spain, seized Paris and forced King Henry III to make him chief minister. To rid himself of Guise influence, Henry III assassinated the duke of Guise and then joined with Henry of Navarre (who meanwhile had returned to Calvinism), who was next in line to the throne, to crush the Catholic Holy League and retake the city of Paris. Although successful, Henry III was assassinated in 1589 by a monk who was repelled by the spectacle of a Catholic king cooperating with a Protestant. Henry of Navarre now claimed the throne. Realizing, however, that he would never be accepted by Catholic France, Henry took the logical way out and converted once again to Catholicism. With his coronation

The Saint Bartholomew's Day Massacre. Although the outbreak of religious war seemed unlikely in France, the collapse of the strong monarchy with the death of Henry II unleashed forces that led to a series of civil wars. Pictured here is the Saint Bartholomew's Day massacre of 1572. This contemporary painting by the Huguenot artist François Dubois vividly depicts a number of the incidents of that day when approximately three thousand Huguenots were murdered in Paris.

in 1594, the French Wars of Religion finally came to an end.

Nevertheless, the religious problem persisted until the Edict of Nantes (NAHNT) was issued in 1598. The edict acknowledged Catholicism as the official religion of France but guaranteed the Huguenots the right to worship in selected places in every district and allowed them to retain a number of fortified towns for their protection. In addition, Huguenots were allowed to enjoy all political privileges, including the holding of public offices. Although the Edict of Nantes recognized the rights of the Protestant minority and ostensibly the principle of religious toleration, it did so only out of political necessity, not out of conviction.

Philip II and Militant Catholicism

The greatest advocate of militant Catholicism in the second half of the sixteenth century was King Philip II of Spain (1556–1598), the son and heir of Charles V. Philip's reign ushered in an age of Spanish greatness, both politically and culturally.

The first major goal of Philip II was to consolidate and secure the lands he had inherited from his father. These included Spain, the Netherlands, and possessions in Italy

(see Map 13.3) and the New World. For Philip, this meant strict conformity to Catholicism, enforced by aggressive use of the Spanish Inquisition, and the establishment of strong, monarchical authority. The latter was not an easy task because Philip had inherited a governmental structure in which each of the various states and territories of his empire stood in an individual relationship to the king. Philip did manage, however, to expand royal power in Spain by making the monarchy less dependent on the traditional landed aristocracy. Philip tried to be the center of the whole government and supervised the work of all departments, even down to the smallest details. Unwilling to delegate authority, he failed to distinguish between important and trivial matters and fell weeks behind on state correspondence, where he was inclined to make marginal notes and even correct spelling. One Spanish official said, "If God used the Escorial [the royal palace where Philip worked] to deliver my death sentence, I would be immortal."

One of Philip's aims was to make Spain a dominant power in Europe. To a great extent, Spain's preeminence depended on a prosperous economy fueled by its importation of gold and silver from its New World possessions, its agriculture, its commerce, and its industry, especially in textiles, silk, and leather goods.

404 ❧ **CHAPTER 13** Reformation and Religious Warfare in the Sixteenth Century

Philip of Spain. This portrait by Titian depicts Philip II of Spain. The king's attempts to make Spain a great power led to large debts and crushing taxes, and his military actions in defense of Catholicism ended in failure and misfortune in both France and the Netherlands.

The importation of silver had detrimental effects as well, however, as it helped set off a spiraling inflation that disrupted the Spanish economy, eventually hurting both textile production and agriculture. Moreover, the expenses of war, especially after 1580, proved devastating to the Spanish economy. American gold and silver never constituted more than 20 percent of the royal revenue, leading the government to impose a crushing burden of direct and indirect taxes. Even then the government was forced to borrow. Philip repudiated his debts seven times; still, two-thirds of state income went to pay interest on the debt by the end of his reign. The attempt to make Spain a great power led to its decline after Philip's reign.

Crucial to an understanding of Philip II is the importance of Catholicism to the Spanish people and their ruler. Driven by a heritage of crusading fervor, the Spanish had little difficulty seeing themselves as a nation of people divinely chosen to save Catholic Christianity from the Protestant heretics. Philip II, the "Most Catholic King," became the champion of Catholicism throughout Europe, a role that led to spectacular victories and equally spectacular defeats for the Spanish king. Spain's leadership of a holy league against Turkish encroachments in the Mediterranean, especially the Muslim attack on the island of Cyprus, resulted in a stunning victory over the Turkish fleet in the Battle of Lepanto in 1571. Philip's greatest misfortunes came from his attempt to crush the revolt in the Netherlands and his tortured relations with Queen Elizabeth of England.

Revolt of the Netherlands

As one of the richest parts of Philip's empire, the Spanish Netherlands was of great importance to the Most Catholic King. The Netherlands consisted of seventeen provinces (the modern Netherlands, Belgium, and Luxembourg). The seven northern provinces were largely Germanic in culture and Dutch speaking, while the French- and Flemish-speaking southern provinces were closely tied to France. Situated at the commercial crossroads of northwestern Europe, the Netherlands had become prosperous through commerce and a flourishing textile industry. Because of its location, the Netherlands was open to the religious influences of the age. Though some inhabitants had adopted Lutheranism or Anabaptism, by the time of Philip II, Calvinism was also making inroads. These provinces had no real political bond holding them together except their common ruler, and that ruler was Philip II, a foreigner who was out of touch with the local situation.

Philip II hoped to strengthen his control in the Netherlands, regardless of the traditional privileges of the separate provinces. This was strongly opposed by the nobles, towns, and provincial states, which stood to lose politically if their jealously guarded privileges and freedoms were weakened. Resentment against Philip was also aroused when the residents of the Netherlands realized that the taxes they paid were being used for Spanish interests. Finally, religion became a major catalyst for rebellion when Philip attempted to crush Calvinism. Violence erupted in 1566 when Calvinists—especially nobles—began to destroy statues and stained-glass windows in Catholic churches. Philip responded by sending the duke of Alva with 10,000 veteran Spanish and Italian troops to crush the rebellion.

The repressive policies of the duke proved counterproductive. The levying of a permanent sales tax alienated many merchants and commoners, who now joined the nobles and Calvinists in the struggle against Spanish rule. A special tribunal, known as the Council of Troubles (nicknamed the Council of Blood by the Dutch),

CHRONOLOGY Philip II and Militant Catholicism

Philip II	1556–1598
Outbreak of revolt in the Netherlands	1566
Battle of Lepanto	1571
Pacification of Ghent	1576
Union of Arras	1579
Spanish armada	1588
Twelve-year truce (Spain and Netherlands)	1609
Independence of the United Provinces	1648

inaugurated a reign of terror in which even powerful aristocrats were executed. As a result, the revolt now became organized, especially in the northern provinces, where William of Nassau, the prince of Orange, also known as William the Silent, and Dutch pirates known as the "Sea Beggars" mounted growing resistance. In 1573, Philip removed the duke of Alva and shifted to a more conciliatory policy to bring an end to the costly revolt.

William of Orange wished to unify all seventeen provinces, a goal seemingly realized in 1576 with the Pacification of Ghent. This agreement stipulated that all the provinces would stand together under William's leadership, respect religious differences, and demand that the Spanish troops be withdrawn. But religious differences proved too strong for any lasting union. When the duke of Parma, the next Spanish leader, arrived in the Netherlands, he astutely played on the religious differences of the provinces and split their united front. The southern provinces formed a Catholic union—the Union of Arras—in 1579 and accepted Spanish control. To counter this, William of Orange organized the seven northern, Dutch-speaking states into a Protestant union—the Union of Utrecht—determined to oppose Spanish rule. The Netherlands was now divided along religious, geographic, and political lines into two hostile camps. The struggle dragged on until 1609, when a twelve-year truce ended the war, virtually recognizing the independence of the northern provinces. These "United Provinces" soon emerged as the Dutch Republic, although the Spanish did not formally recognize them as independent until 1648. The ten southern provinces remained a Spanish possession (see Map 13.3).

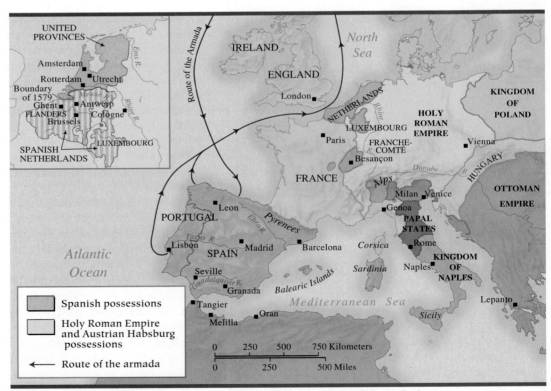

MAP 13.3   The Height of Spanish Power Under Philip II. Like his father, Charles V, Philip II, the "Most Catholic King," was a champion of the Catholic cause against Protestantism. He sought to maintain Habsburg control in the Netherlands by combating a Protestant revolt, a rebellion eventually supported by Queen Elizabeth of England. Spain's attempt to invade England in 1588 ended in disaster.

Q   *Why would England feel threatened by Spanish territory in the Netherlands?*

The England of Elizabeth

After the death of Queen Mary in 1558, her half-sister Elizabeth (1558–1603) ascended the throne of England. During Elizabeth's reign, England rose to prominence as the relatively small island kingdom became the leader of the Protestant nations of Europe, laid the foundations for a world empire, and experienced a cultural renaissance.

The daughter of King Henry VIII and Anne Boleyn, Elizabeth had had a difficult early life. During Mary's reign, she had even been imprisoned for a while and had learned early to hide her true feelings from both private and public sight. Intelligent, cautious, and self-confident, she moved quickly to solve the difficult religious problem she had inherited from Mary, who had become extremely unpopular when she tried to return England to the Catholic fold.

RELIGIOUS POLICY Elizabeth's religious policy was based on moderation and compromise. As a ruler, she wished to prevent England from being torn apart over matters of religion. Parliament cooperated with the queen in initiating the Elizabethan religious settlement in 1559. The Catholic legislation of Mary's reign was repealed, and the new Act of Supremacy designated Elizabeth as "the only supreme governor of this realm, as well in all spiritual or ecclesiastical things or causes, as temporal." She used this title rather than "supreme head of the church," which had been used by both Henry VIII and Edward VI, because she did not want to upset the Catholics, who considered the pope the supreme head, or radical Protestants, who thought that Christ alone was head of the church. The Act of Uniformity restored the church service of the Book of Common Prayer from the reign of Edward VI with some revisions to make it more acceptable to Catholics. The Thirty-Nine Articles, a new confession of faith, defined theological issues midway between Lutheranism and Calvinism. Elizabeth's religious settlement was basically Protestant, but it was a moderate Protestantism that avoided overly subtle distinctions and extremes.

The new religious settlement worked, at least to the extent that it smothered religious differences in England in the second half of the sixteenth century. Two groups, however, the Catholics and the Puritans, continued to oppose it. One of Elizabeth's greatest challenges came from her Catholic cousin, Mary, queen of Scots, who was next in line to the English throne. Mary was ousted from Scotland by rebellious Calvinist nobles in 1568 and fled for her life to England. There Elizabeth placed her under house arrest and for fourteen years tolerated her involvement in a number of ill-planned

Procession of Queen Elizabeth I. Intelligent and learned, Elizabeth Tudor was familiar with Latin and Greek and spoke several European languages. Served by able administrators, Elizabeth ruled for nearly forty-five years and generally avoided open military action against any major power. This picture, painted near the end of her reign, shows the queen in a ceremonial procession.

Queen Elizabeth Addresses Parliament (1601)

Queen Elizabeth I ruled England from 1558 to 1603 with a consummate skill that contemporaries considered unusual in a woman. Though shrewd and paternalistic, Elizabeth, like other sixteenth-century monarchs, depended for her power on the favor of her people. This selection is taken from her speech to Parliament in 1601, when she had been forced to retreat on the issue of monopolies after vehement protest by members of Parliament. Although the speech was designed to make peace with Parliament, some historians also feel that it was a sincere expression of the rapport that existed between the queen and her subjects.

⊢ ═◆═ ⊣

Queen Elizabeth I, "The Golden Speech"

I do assure you there is no prince that loves his subjects better, or whose love can countervail our love. There is no jewel, be it of never so rich a price, which I set before this jewel: I mean your love. For I do esteem it more than any treasure of riches.... And, though God has raised me high, yet this I count the glory of my crown, that I have reigned with your loves. This makes me that I do not so much rejoice that God has made me to be a Queen, as to be a Queen over so thankful a people....

Of myself I must say this: I never was any greedy, scraping grasper, nor a strait, fast-holding Prince, nor yet a waster. My heart was never set on any worldly goods, but only for my subjects' good. What you bestow on me, I will not hoard it up, but receive it to bestow on you again. Yea, mine own properties I account yours, to be expended for your good....

I have ever used to set the Last-Judgement Day before mine eyes, and so to rule as I shall be judged to answer before a higher judge, to whose judgement seat I do appeal, that never thought was cherished in my heart that tended not unto my people's good. And now, if my kingly bounties have been abused, and my grants turned to the hurt of my people, contrary to my will and meaning, and if any in authority under me neglected or perverted what I have committed to them, I hope God will not lay their culps [crimes] and offenses to my charge; who, though there were danger in repealing our grants, yet what danger would I not rather incur for your good, than I would suffer them still to continue?

There will never Queen sit in my seat with more zeal to my country, care for my subjects, and that will sooner with willingness venture her life for your good and safety, than myself. For it is my desire to live nor reign no longer than my life and reign shall be for your good. And though you have had and may have many princes more mighty and wise sitting in this seat, yet you never had nor shall have any that will be more careful and loving.

Q What qualities evident in Elizabeth's speech would have endeared her to her listeners? How was her popularity connected to the events of the late sixteenth century? Would the members of Parliament have responded differently to a king? Why or why not?

Catholic plots designed to kill Elizabeth and replace her on the throne with the Catholic Mary. Finally, in 1587, after Mary became embroiled in a far more serious plot, Elizabeth had her cousin beheaded to end the threats to her regime.

Potentially more dangerous to Anglicanism in the long run were the **Puritans.** The word *Puritan* first appeared in 1564 when it was used to refer to Protestants within the Anglican Church who, inspired by Calvinist theology, wanted to remove any trace of Catholicism from the Church of England. Elizabeth managed to keep the Puritans in check during her reign.

Elizabeth proved as adept in government and foreign policy as in religious affairs. She was well served administratively by the principal secretary of state. The talents of Sir William Cecil and Sir Francis Walsingham, who together held the office for thirty-two years, ensured much of Elizabeth's success in foreign and domestic affairs. Elizabeth also handled Parliament with much skill; it met only thirteen times during her entire reign (see the box above).

FOREIGN POLICY Caution, moderation, and expediency also dictated Elizabeth's foreign policy. Fearful of other countries' motives, Elizabeth realized that war could be disastrous for her island kingdom and her own rule. Unofficially, however, she encouraged English seamen to raid Spanish ships and colonies. Francis Drake was especially adept at plundering Spanish fleets loaded with gold and silver from Spain's New World empire. While encouraging English piracy and providing clandestine aid to French Huguenots and Dutch Calvinists to weaken France and Spain, Elizabeth pretended complete aloofness and avoided alliances that would force her into war with any major power (see the Film & History feature on p. 409).

Gradually, however, Elizabeth was drawn into more active involvement in the Netherlands. This move accelerated the already mounting friction between Spain and England. After years of resisting the idea of invading England as impractical, Philip II of Spain was finally persuaded to do so by advisers who assured him that the people of England would rise against their queen when the Spaniards arrived. Moreover, Philip was easily convinced

Elizabeth (1998)

Directed by Shekhar Kapur, *Elizabeth* opens in 1554 with a scene of three Protestant heretics being burned alive as Queen Mary (Kathy Burke) pursues her dream of restoring Catholicism to England. Mary also contemplates signing a death warrant for her Protestant half-sister Elizabeth (Cate Blanchett) but refuses to do so before dying in 1558. Elizabeth becomes queen and is portrayed in her early years of rule as an uncertain monarch who "rules from the heart instead of the mind," as one adviser tells her. Elizabeth is also threatened by foreign rulers, the duke of Norfolk (Christopher Eccleston), and others who want a Catholic on the throne of England. A plot, which supposedly includes Robert Dudley (Joseph Fiennes), her former lover, is unraveled with the help of Francis Walsingham (Geoffrey Rush), a ruthless Machiavellian adviser whose primary goal is protecting Elizabeth. The queen avoids assassination, but the attempt nevertheless convinces Elizabeth that she must be a Virgin Queen who dedicates her life to England. As she tells Lord Burghley (Richard Attenborough), her closest adviser, during the procession that ends the film: "I am now married to England."

The strength of the movie, which contains numerous historical inaccuracies, is in the performance of Cate Blanchett, who captures some of the characteristics of Queen Elizabeth I. At one point Elizabeth explains her reluctance to go to war: "I do not like wars. They have uncertain outcomes." After she rebuffs the efforts of her advisers to persuade her to marry a foreign prince for the sake of maintaining the throne, Elizabeth declares, "I will have one mistress here, and no master." Although the movie correctly emphasizes her intelligence and her clever handling of advisers and church officials, Elizabeth is shown incorrectly as weak and vacillating when she first comes to the throne. In fact, Elizabeth was already a practiced politician who knew how to use power. She was, as she reminds her advisers, her father's (Henry VIII) daughter.

In many other ways, the movie is not faithful to the historical record. The movie telescopes events that occurred over thirty years of Elizabeth's lengthy reign into the first five years of her reign and makes up other events altogether. Mary of Guise (Fanny Ardant) was not assassinated by Francis Walsingham as the movie implies. Nor was Walsingham an important figure in the early reign of Elizabeth.

Queen Elizabeth I (Cate Blanchett) and the duke of Norfolk (Christopher Eccleston).

Polygram/The Kobal Collection

Robert Dudley's marriage was well known in Elizabethan England, and there is no firm evidence that Elizabeth had a sexual relationship with him. The duke of Norfolk was not arrested until 1571. The duc d'Anjou (Vincent Cassel) never came to England nor would he, even if he had come, have addressed Elizabeth with the candid sexual words used in the film. It was the duc's younger brother, the duc d'Alençon, who was put forth as a possible husband for Elizabeth, although not until she was in her forties. And finally, Elizabeth's choice of career over family and personal happiness seems to reflect a feminist theme of our own times; it certainly was not common in the sixteenth century when women were considered unfit to rule. ✍

that the revolt in the Netherlands would never be crushed as long as England provided support for it. In any case, a successful invasion of England would mean the overthrow of heresy and the return of England to Catholicism, surely an act in accordance with the will of God. Accordingly, Philip ordered preparations for a fleet of warships that would rendezvous with the army of the duke of Parma in Flanders and escort his troops across the English Channel for the invasion.

THE SPANISH ARMADA The armada proved to be a disaster. The Spanish fleet that finally set sail had neither the ships nor the troops that Philip had planned to send. A conversation between a papal emissary and an officer of the Spanish fleet before the armada departed reveals the fundamental flaw:

> "And if you meet the English armada in the Channel, do you expect to win the battle?" "Of course," replied the Spaniard.
> "How can you be sure?" [asked the emissary].
> "It's very simple. It is well known that we fight in God's cause. So, when we meet the English, God will surely arrange matters so that we can grapple and board them, either by sending some strange freak of weather or, more likely, just by depriving the English of their wits. If we can come to close quarters, Spanish valor and Spanish steel (and the great masses of soldiers we shall have on board) will make our victory certain. But unless God helps us by a miracle the English, who have faster and handier ships than ours, and many more long-range guns, and who know their advantage just as well as we do, will never close with us at all, but stand aloof and knock us to pieces with their culverins [cannons], without our being able to do them any serious hurt. So," concluded the captain, and one fancies a grim smile, "we are sailing against England in the confident hope of a miracle."[19]

The hoped-for miracle never materialized. The Spanish fleet, battered by a number of encounters with the English, sailed back to Spain by a northward route around Scotland and Ireland, where it was further battered by storms. Although the English and Spanish would continue their war for another sixteen years, the defeat of the Spanish armada guaranteed for the time being that England would remain a Protestant country. Although Spain made up for its losses within a year and a half, the defeat was a psychological blow to the Spaniards.

CHAPTER SUMMARY

When the Augustinian monk Martin Luther burst onto the scene with a series of theses on indulgences, few people suspected that his observations would eventually split all of Europe along religious lines. But the yearning for reform of the church and meaningful religious experiences caused a seemingly simple dispute to escalate into a powerful movement.

Martin Luther established the twin pillars of the Protestant Reformation: the doctrine of justification by faith alone and the Bible as the sole authority in religious affairs. Although Luther felt that his revival of Christianity based on his interpretation of the Bible should be acceptable to all, others soon appeared who also read the Bible but interpreted it in different ways. Protestantism fragmented into different sects—Zwinglianism, Calvinism, Anglicanism, Anabaptism—which, though united in their dislike of Catholicism, were themselves divided over the interpretation of the sacraments and religious practices. As reform ideas spread, religion and politics became ever more intertwined.

Although Lutheranism was legally acknowledged in the Holy Roman Empire by the Peace of Augsburg in 1555, it had lost much of its momentum and outside of Scandinavia had scant ability to attract new supporters. Its energy was largely replaced by the new Protestant form of Calvinism, which had a clarity of doctrine and a fervor that made it attractive to a whole new generation of Europeans. But while Calvinism's activism enabled it to spread across Europe, Catholicism was also experiencing its own revival. New religious orders based on reform, a revived and reformed papacy, and the Council of Trent, which reaffirmed traditional Catholic doctrine, gave the Catholic Church a renewed vitality.

By the middle of the sixteenth century, it was apparent that the religious passions of the Reformation era had brought an end to the religious unity of medieval Europe. The religious division (Catholics versus Protestant) was instrumental in beginning a series of religious wars that were complicated by economic, social, and political forces that also played a role. The French Wars of Religion, the revolt of the Netherlands against Philip II of Spain, and the conflict between Philip II and Elizabeth of England, which led to the failed attempt of the Spanish armada to invade England, were the major struggles in the sixteenth-century religious wars.

That people who were disciples of the Apostle of Peace would kill each other over their beliefs aroused skepticism about Christianity itself. As one German writer put it, "Lutheran, popish, and Calvinistic, we've got all these beliefs here, but there is some doubt about where Christianity has got."[20] It is surely no accident that the search for a stable, secular order of politics and for order in the universe through natural laws soon came to play important roles. Before we look at this search for order in the seventeenth century, however, we need first to look at the adventures that plunged Europe into its new role in the world.

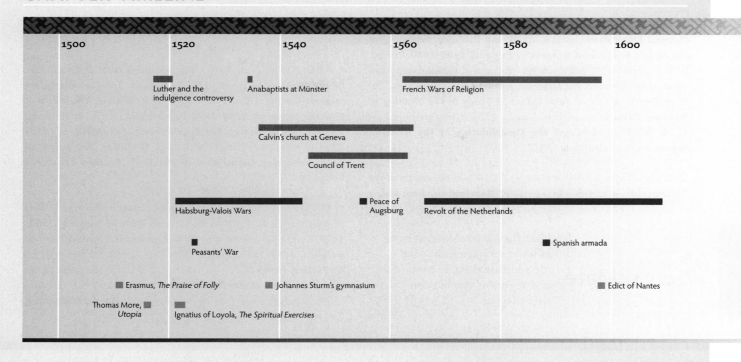

1500   1520   1540   1560   1580   1600

Luther and the indulgence controversy

Anabaptists at Münster

French Wars of Religion

Calvin's church at Geneva

Council of Trent

Habsburg-Valois Wars

Peace of Augsburg

Revolt of the Netherlands

Peasants' War

Spanish armada

Erasmus, *The Praise of Folly*

Johannes Sturm's gymnasium

Edict of Nantes

Thomas More, *Utopia*

Ignatius of Loyola, *The Spiritual Exercises*

CHAPTER REVIEW

Upon Reflection

Q If attempts at reform of the Catholic Church were unsuccessful in the fifteenth century, why did they succeed during the sixteenth-century Reformation?

Q What role did politics play in the establishment of Lutheranism and Anglicanism?

Q Elizabeth of England and Philip II of Spain were two of Europe's most famous monarchs in the second half of the sixteenth century. Compare and contrast their methods of ruling and their foreign policy. Which was a more successful ruler? Why?

Key Terms

Christian (northern Renaissance) humanism (p. 377)
pluralism (p. 379)
confession (p. 380)
justification (p. 381)
transubstantiation (p. 386)
millenarianism (p. 392)
predestination (p. 394)
Huguenots (p. 402)
politiques (p. 403)
Puritans (p. 408)

Suggestions for Further Reading

THE REFORMATION Basic surveys of the Reformation period include **J. D. Tracy, *Europe's Reformations, 1450–1650*** (Oxford,

1999); **D. MacCulloch, *The Reformation*** (New York, 2003); and **E. Cameron, *The European Reformation*** (New York, 1991). See also the brief works by **U. Rublack, *Reformation Europe*** (Cambridge, 2005), and **P. Collinson, *The Reformation: A History*** (New York, 2006). A brief but very useful introduction to the theology of the Reformation can be found in **A. McGrath, *Reformation Thought: An Introduction,*** 3rd rev. ed. (Oxford, 2001).

NORTHERN RENAISSANCE HUMANISM The development of humanism outside Italy is examined in **C. G. Nauert Jr., *Humanism and the Culture of Renaissance Europe,*** 2nd ed. (Cambridge, 2006).

LUTHER AND LUTHERANISM The classic account of Martin Luther's life is **R. Bainton, *Here I Stand: A Life of Martin Luther*** (New York, 1950). More recent works include **H. A. Oberman, *Luther*** (New York, 1992), and the brief biography by **M. Marty, *Martin Luther*** (New York, 2004). The spread of Luther's ideas in Germany can be examined in **C. S. Dixon, *The Reformation and Rural Society*** (Cambridge, 2004), on the impact of the Reformation on the countryside in Germany, and **R. W. Scribner, *For the Sake of Simple Folk: Popular Propaganda for the German Reformation*** (Oxford, 1994), on the impact of popular culture in the spread of the Reformation. On the role of Charles V, see **W. Maltby, *The Reign of Charles V*** (New York, 2002).

SPREAD OF THE PROTESTANT REFORMATION **W. P. Stephens's *Zwingli*** (Oxford, 1994) is an important study of the man's ideas. The most comprehensive account of the various groups and individuals who are called Anabaptists is **G. H. Williams, *The Radical Reformation,*** 2nd ed. (Kirksville, Mo., 1992). Worthwhile surveys of the English Reformation are **C. Haigh, *English Reformations: Religion, Politics, and Society Under the Tudors*** (Oxford, 1993); **N. L. Jones**, *English Reformation: Religion and Cultural Adaptation* (London, 2002); and **E. Duffy, *Stripping of the Altars: Traditional Religion in England, 1400–1580,*** 2nd ed. (New Haven, Conn., 2005), on the vibrancy of Catholicism in England in the fifteenth and sixteenth centuries. On John Calvin, see **A. McGrath, *A Life of John Calvin: A Study in the Shaping of Western Culture*** (Cambridge, Mass., 1990). On Calvinism, see **W. G. Naphy, *Calvin and the Consolidation of the Genevan Reformation*** (Philadelphia, 2003).

SOCIAL IMPACT OF THE REFORMATION On the impact of the Reformation on the family, see **J. F. Harrington, *Reordering**

Marriage and Society in Reformation Germany (New York, 1995). On the impact of the Reformation on women, see **L. Roper, *Women and Morals in Reformation Augsburg*** (Oxford, 1997).

CATHOLIC REFORMATION A good introduction to the Catholic Reformation can be found in **M. A. Mullett, *The Catholic Reformation*** (London, 1999). Also valuable is **R. P. Hsia, *The World of Catholic Renewal, 1540–1770*** (Cambridge, 1998). For new perspectives, see **R. Bireley, *The Refashioning of Catholicism, 1450–1700*** (Washington, D.C., 1999), and **J. O'Malley, *Trent and All That: Renaming Catholicism in the Early Modern Era*** (Cambridge, Mass., 2002).

WARS OF RELIGION For good introductions to the French Wars of Religion, see **M. P. Holt, *The French Wars of Religion, 1562–1629*** (Cambridge, 1995), and **R. J. Knecht, *The French Wars of Religion, 1559–1598,*** 2nd ed. (New York, 1996). On Philip II, see **G. Parker, *Philip II,*** 3rd ed. (Chicago, 1995). On the revolt of the Netherlands, see **G. Parker, *The Dutch Revolt,*** rev. ed. (London, 1990). Elizabeth's reign can be examined in **C. Haigh, *Elizabeth I,*** 2nd ed. (New York, 1998).

Visit the CourseMate website at www.cengagebrain.com for additional study tools and review materials for this chapter.

AP* REVIEW QUESTIONS FOR CHAPTER 13

1. Which of the following best explains the spread of pamphlets and writings across Europe in the sixteenth century?

   (A) News could be spread easily because the population was highly mobile.
   (B) There was a significant increase in literacy among the lower classes.
   (C) Social reformers secured the passage of laws protecting freedom of speech.
   (D) People were intrigued by the new intellectuals and wanted to learn more from them.
   (E) Movable type and the printing press had been developed.

2. The Huguenots were

   (A) French Catholics.
   (B) French Lutherans.
   (C) French Calvinists.
   (D) French Jews.
   (E) French Muslims.

3. In the sixteenth and seventeenth centuries, Spain experienced all of the following EXCEPT

   (A) the loss of its Mediterranean holdings to the Turks following the Battle of Lepanto.
   (B) the defeat of the Spanish Armada by England in 1588.
   (C) the loss of the Spanish Netherlands by 1648.
   (D) the decline of the Spanish economy as a result of inflation and the price revolution.
   (E) the loss of non-Catholic intellectuals and merchants to the ravages of the Inquisition.

4. Thomas More is most often recognized for writing

   (A) *The Republic.*
   (B) *Confessions.*
   (C) *The Praise of Folly.*
   (D) *The Imitation of Christ.*
   (E) *Utopia.*

5. The religious geography of Europe by the end of the seventeenth century could be described as a

   (A) Protestant north and a Catholic south.
   (B) Protestant east and a Catholic west.
   (C) Catholic north and a Protestant south.
   (D) Catholic east and a Protestant west.
   (E) Protestant north and an Orthodox west.

6. Martin Luther's complaints against the Roman Catholic Church included all of the following EXCEPT

   (A) the clergy displayed a lack of spiritual knowledge and indulged in inappropriate behavior.
   (B) baptism was an important sign of devotion to God.
   (C) the sale of indulgences was not biblical and should be stopped.
   (D) the papacy had grown exceedingly powerful and papal power needed to be limited.
   (E) salvation should be based on faith alone, not works.

7. Which of the following is true of the German Peasants' War of 1524–1525?

   (A) Martin Luther denounced the actions of the German peasants as unrighteous offenses against state authority.
   (B) Martin Luther argued for social reform and led the revolt.
   (C) German nobles and princes rallied against the peasants and looked to the Roman Catholic Church for help.
   (D) The Holy Roman Emperor Charles V enslaved the peasants as serfs.
   (E) The death count was minimal, and the rebellion's leaders were hanged in city centers.

8. Emperor Charles V's reign included all of the following EXCEPT

   (A) the Ottoman Empire's constant threat to the Holy Roman Empire as the Ottomans moved deeper into Hungarian lands.
   (B) the Habsburg-Valois wars.
   (C) uncontrollable troops and the sack of Rome in 1527.
   (D) wars with Henry VIII in England.
   (E) political and religious unrest within the German states.

9. The French Wars of Religion saw all of the following EXCEPT

   (A) political struggle between the Catholic Guise family and the Protestant Bourbon family.
   (B) assassinations of both Huguenot and Catholic political leaders.
   (C) an invasion by English forces.
   (D) the St. Bartholomew's Day massacre.
   (E) increasing monarchical control within France.

10. The primary change instituted in England by Henry VIII's religious reformation was that

   (A) religious services were held in Latin.
   (B) clerical marriage was allowed by the Church of England.
   (C) the king became the head of the Church of England.
   (D) the pope's power was reaffirmed within England.
   (E) monasteries remained open but fell under the control of the Church of England.

11. After a series of meetings, the Council of Trent agreed on all of the following EXCEPT

   (A) a reaffirmation of the traditional Roman Catholic teachings.
   (B) salvation would be based on faith alone.
   (C) clerical celibacy would be upheld.
   (D) the concept of purgatory would remain a part of church teachings.
   (E) indulgences would no longer be sold.

12. Which of the following beliefs and practices were held by Lutherans?

   (A) clerical marriage, salvation by faith alone, and the Bible written in the vernacular
   (B) the seven sacraments, salvation through faith and works, and the Bible written in Latin
   (C) adult baptism, clerical celibacy, and strict separation between church and state
   (D) predestination, transubstantiation, and the seven sacraments
   (E) recognition of the trinity, pluralism, and absenteeism

13. The Peace of Augsburg of 1555 did NOT allow for

   (A) peace between the Holy Roman Emperor and the pope.
   (B) open religious practice by Lutherans and Catholics.
   (C) the establishment of sovereignty by German rulers.
   (D) German princes to choose the religion of their subjects.
   (E) some religious peace within the German states.

14. Which of the following best describes the reign of Elizabeth I?

   (A) England experienced a golden age, as religious compromise coincided with a resurgence in literature and culture.
   (B) England was plunged into a series of wars, while Elizabeth struggled to find a husband and effective leader for England.
   (C) England began to thrive economically as its strong navy controlled the seas, and its alliance with Spain was further solidified.
   (D) England was fraught with turmoil as religious zealots attempted to overthrow the government.
   (E) England and France found peace, but Elizabeth's court was plunged deeply into debt.

15. "To be Spanish is to be Catholic" was espoused by

   (A) Pope Julius II.
   (B) Francis II (Valois).
   (C) Catherine de' Medici.
   (D) Mary I (Tudor).
   (E) Philip II.

A 1536 Mercator projection map showing the route of Ferdinand Magellan's first circumnavigation of the world

Europe and the World: New Encounters, 1500–1800

CHAPTER OUTLINE AND FOCUS QUESTIONS

On the Brink of a New World

Q Why did Europeans begin to embark on voyages of discovery and expansion at the end of the fifteenth century?

New Horizons: The Portuguese and Spanish Empires

Q How did Portugal and Spain acquire their overseas empires, and how did their empires differ?

New Rivals on the World Stage

Q How did the arrival of the Dutch, British, and French on the world scene in the seventeenth and eighteenth centuries affect Africa, India, Southeast Asia, China, and Japan? What were the main features of the African slave trade, and what effects did it have on Africa?

The Impact of European Expansion

Q How did European expansion affect both the conquerors and the conquered?

Toward a World Economy

Q What was mercantilism, and what was its relationship to colonial empires?

CRITICAL THINKING

Q What was the relationship between European overseas expansion and political, economic, and social developments in Europe?

WHILE MANY EUROPEANS were occupied with the problems of dynastic expansion and religious reform, others were taking voyages that propelled Europeans far beyond the medieval walls in which they had been enclosed for almost a thousand years. One of these adventurers was the Portuguese explorer Ferdinand Magellan. Convinced that he could find a sea passage to Asia through America, Magellan persuaded the king of Spain to finance an exploratory voyage. On August 10, 1519, Magellan set sail on the Atlantic with five ships and a Spanish crew of 277 men. After a stormy and difficult crossing of the Atlantic, Magellan's fleet moved down the coast of South America, searching for the elusive strait that would take him through. His Spanish ship captains thought he was crazy: "The fool is obsessed with his search for a strait," one remarked. "On the flame of his ambition he will crucify us all." At last, in October 1520, he found it, passing through a narrow waterway (later named the Strait of Magellan) and emerging into an unknown ocean that he called the Pacific Sea. Magellan reckoned that it would then be a short distance to the Spice Islands of the East, but he was badly mistaken. Week after week, he and his crew sailed on across the Pacific as their food supplies dwindled. According to one account, "When their last biscuit had gone, they scraped the maggots out of the casks, mashed them and served them as gruel. They made cakes out of sawdust soaked with the urine of rats—the rats themselves, as delicacies, had long since been hunted to extinction." At last they reached the islands that would later be called the Philippines (after King

Philip II of Spain), where Magellan met his death at the hands of the natives. Although only one of his original fleet of five ships survived and returned to Spain, Magellan is still remembered as the first person to circumnavigate the world.

At the beginning of the sixteenth century, European adventurers like Magellan had begun launching small fleets into the vast reaches of the Atlantic Ocean. They were hardly aware that they were beginning a new era, not only for Europe, but for the peoples of Asia, Africa, and the Americas as well. Nevertheless, the voyages of these Europeans marked the beginning of a process that led to radical changes in the political, economic, and cultural life of the entire world.

Between 1500 and 1800, European power engulfed the world. In the Americas, Europeans established colonies that spread their laws, religions, and cultures. In the island regions of Southeast Asia, Europeans firmly established their rule. In other parts of Asia and in Africa, their activities ranged from trading goods to trafficking in humans, permanently altering the lives of the local peoples. In all regions touched by European expansion, the indigenous peoples faced exposure to new diseases, alteration of their religions and customs, and the imposition of new laws.

On the Brink of a New World

 FOCUS QUESTION: Why did Europeans begin to embark on voyages of discovery and expansion at the end of the fifteenth century?

Nowhere has the dynamic and even ruthless energy of Western civilization been more apparent than in its expansion into the rest of the world. By the late sixteenth century, the Atlantic seaboard had become the center of a commercial activity that raised Portugal and Spain and later the Dutch Republic, England, and France to prominence. The age of expansion was a crucial factor in the European transition from the agrarian economy of the Middle Ages to a commercial and industrial capitalistic system. Expansion also led Europeans into new and lasting contacts with non-European peoples that inaugurated a new age of world history in the sixteenth century.

The Motives for Expansion

For almost a millennium, Catholic Europe had been confined to one geographic area. Its one major attempt to expand beyond those frontiers, the Crusades, had largely failed. Of course, Europe had never completely lost touch with the outside world: the goods of Asia and Africa made their way into medieval castles, the works of Muslim philosophers were read in medieval universities, and in the ninth and tenth centuries, the Vikings had

even made their way to the eastern fringes of North America. But in all cases, contacts with non-European civilizations remained limited until the end of the fifteenth century, when Europeans embarked on a remarkable series of overseas journeys. What caused Europeans to undertake such dangerous voyages to the ends of the earth?

FANTASTIC LANDS Europeans had long been attracted to lands outside Europe as a result of a large body of fantasy literature about "other worlds" that blossomed in the Middle Ages. In the fourteenth century, the author of *The Travels of John Mandeville* spoke of realms (which he had never seen) filled with precious stones and gold. Other lands were more frightening and considerably less appealing. In one country, "the folk be great giants of twenty-eight foot long, or thirty foot long.... And they eat more gladly man's flesh than any other flesh." Farther north was a land inhabited by "full cruel and evil women. And they have precious stones in their eyes. And they be of that kind that if they behold any man with wrath they slay him at once with the beholding."[1] Other writers, however, attracted Europeans to the lure of foreign lands with descriptions of mysterious Christian kingdoms: the magical kingdom of Prester John in Africa and a Christian community in southern India that was supposedly founded by Thomas, an apostle of Jesus.

ECONOMIC MOTIVES Although Muslim control of Central Asia cut Europe off from the countries farther east, the Mongol conquests in the thirteenth century had reopened the doors. The most famous medieval travelers to the East were the Polos of Venice. Niccolò and Maffeo, merchants from Venice, accompanied by Niccolò's son Marco, undertook the lengthy journey to the court of the great Mongol ruler Khubilai Khan (1259–1294) in 1271. An account of Marco's experiences, the *Travels,* was the most informative of all the descriptions of Asia by medieval European travelers. Others followed the Polos, but in the fourteenth century, the conquests of the Ottoman Turks and then the breakup of the Mongol Empire reduced Western traffic to the East. With the closing of the overland routes, a number of people in Europe became interested in the possibility of reaching Asia by sea to gain access to the spices and other precious items of the region. Christopher Columbus had a copy of Marco Polo's *Travels* in his possession when he began to envision his epoch-making voyage across the Atlantic Ocean.

An economic motive thus looms large in European expansion in the Renaissance. Merchants, adventurers, and government officials had high hopes of finding new areas of trade, especially more direct access to the spices of the East. These continued to come to Europe via Arab intermediaries but were outrageously expensive. In addition to the potential profits to be made from the spice trade, many European explorers and conquerors did not hesitate to express their desire for material gain in the form of gold and other precious metals. One Spanish conquistador explained the dual purpose of their mission to the New World: to "serve God and His Majesty, to give light to those who were in darkness, and to grow rich, as all men desire to do."[2]

RELIGIOUS ZEAL The conquistador's statement expressed another major reason for the overseas voyages—religious zeal. A crusading mentality was particularly strong in Portugal and Spain, where the Muslims had largely been driven out in the Middle Ages. Contemporaries of Prince Henry the Navigator of Portugal (see "The Development of a Portuguese Maritime Empire" later in this chapter) said that he was motivated by "his great desire to make increase in the faith of our Lord Jesus Christ and to bring him all the souls that should be saved." Although most scholars believe that the religious motive was secondary to economic considerations, it would be foolish to overlook the genuine desire on the part of both explorers and conquistadors, let alone missionaries, to convert the heathen to Christianity. Hernán Cortés (hayr-NAHN kor-TAYSS *or* kor-TEZ), the conqueror of Mexico, asked his Spanish rulers if it was not their duty to ensure that the native Mexicans "are introduced into and instructed in the holy Catholic faith" and predicted that if "the devotion, trust and hope which they now have in their idols turned so as to repose with the divine power of the true God . . . they would work many miracles."[3] Spiritual and secular affairs were closely intertwined in the sixteenth century. No doubt, the desire for grandeur and glory as well as plain intellectual curiosity and a spirit of adventure also played some role in European expansion.

The Means for Expansion

If "God, glory, and gold" were the primary motives, what made the voyages possible? First of all, the expansion of Europe was connected to the growth of centralized monarchies during the Renaissance. Although historians still debate the degree of that centralization, the reality is that Renaissance expansion was a state enterprise. By the second half of the fifteenth century, European monarchies had increased both their authority and their resources and were in a position to turn their energies beyond their borders. For France, that meant the invasion of Italy, but for Portugal, a state not strong enough to pursue power in Europe, it meant going abroad. The Spanish monarchy was strong enough by the sixteenth century to pursue power both in Europe and beyond.

MAPS At the same time, Europeans had achieved a level of wealth and technology that enabled them to make a regular series of voyages beyond Europe. Although the highly schematic and symbolic medieval maps were of little help to sailors, the *portolani,* or charts made by medieval navigators and mathematicians in the thirteenth and fourteenth centuries were

more useful. With details on coastal contours, distances between ports, and compass readings, these charts proved of great value for voyages in European waters. But because the *portolani* were drawn on a flat scale and took no account of the curvature of the earth, they were of little use for longer overseas voyages. Only when seafarers began to venture beyond the coast of Europe did they begin to accumulate information about the actual shape of the earth. By the end of the fifteenth century, cartography had developed to the point that Europeans possessed fairly accurate maps of the known world.

One of the most important world maps available to Europeans at the end of the fifteenth century was that of Ptolemy, an astronomer of the second century C.E. Ptolemy's work, the *Geography,* had been known to Arab geographers as early as the eighth century, but it was not until the fifteenth century that a Latin translation was made of the work. Printed editions of Ptolemy's *Geography,* which contained his world map, became available from 1477 on. Ptolemy's map (see the illustration on p. 416) showed the world as spherical with three major landmasses—Europe, Asia, and Africa—and only two oceans. In addition to showing the oceans as considerably smaller than the landmasses, Ptolemy had also drastically underestimated the circumference of the earth, which led Columbus and other adventurers to believe that it would be feasible to sail west from Europe to reach Asia.

SHIPS AND SAILING Europeans had developed remarkably seaworthy ships as well as new navigational techniques. European shipmakers had mastered the use of the axial rudder (an import from China) and had learned to combine the use of lateen sails with a square rig. With these innovations, they could construct ships mobile enough to sail against the wind and engage in naval warfare and also large enough to mount heavy cannons and carry a substantial amount of goods over long distances. Previously, sailors had used a quadrant and their knowledge of the position of the Pole Star to ascertain their latitude. Below the equator, however, this technique was useless. Only with the assistance of new navigational aids such as the compass and the astrolabe were they able to explore the high seas with confidence.

A final spur to exploration was the growing knowledge of the wind patterns in the Atlantic Ocean. The first European fleets sailing southward along the coast of West Africa had found their efforts to return hindered by the strong winds that blew steadily from the north along the coast. By the late fifteenth century, however, sailors had learned to tack out into the ocean, where they were able to catch westerly winds in the vicinity of the Azores that brought them back to the coast of western Europe. Christopher Columbus used this technique in his voyages to the Americas, and others relied on their new knowledge of the winds to round the continent of Africa in search of the Spice Islands.

Ptolemy's World Map. Contained in the Latin translation of Ptolemy's *Geography* was this world map, which did not become available to Europeans until the late fifteenth century. Scholars quickly accepted it as the most accurate map of its time. The twelve "wind faces," meant to show wind currents around the earth, were a fifteenth-century addition to the ancient map.

New Horizons: The Portuguese and Spanish Empires

Q FOCUS QUESTION: How did Portugal and Spain acquire their overseas empires, and how did their empires differ?

Portugal took the lead in the European age of expansion when it began to explore the coast of Africa under the sponsorship of Prince Henry the Navigator (1394–1460). His motives were a blend of seeking a Christian kingdom as an ally against the Muslims, acquiring trade opportunities for Portugal, and spreading Christianity.

The Development of a Portuguese Maritime Empire

In 1419, Prince Henry founded a school for navigators on the southwestern coast of Portugal. Shortly thereafter, Portuguese fleets began probing southward along the western coast of Africa in search of gold, which had been carried northward from south of the Atlas Mountains in central Morocco for centuries. In 1441, Portuguese ships reached the Senegal River, just north of Cape Verde, and brought home a cargo of black Africans, most of whom

were then sold as slaves to wealthy buyers elsewhere in Europe. Within a few years, an estimated one thousand slaves were shipped annually from the area back to Lisbon.

Through regular expeditions, the Portuguese gradually crept down the African coast, and in 1471, they discovered a new source of gold along the southern coast of the hump of West Africa (an area that would henceforth be known to Europeans as the Gold Coast). A few years later, they established contact with the state of Bakongo, near the mouth of the Zaire (Congo) River in Central Africa. To facilitate trade in gold, ivory, and slaves (some slaves were brought back to Lisbon, while others were bartered to local merchants for gold), the Portuguese leased land from local rulers and built stone forts along the coast.

THE PORTUGUESE IN INDIA Hearing reports of a route to India around the southern tip of Africa, Portuguese sea captains continued their probing. In 1488, Bartholomeu Dias (bar-toh-loh-MAY-oo DEE-ush) (c. 1450–1500) took advantage of westerly winds in the South Atlantic to round the Cape of Good Hope, but he feared a mutiny from his crew and returned (see Map 14.1). Ten years later, a fleet under the command of Vasco da Gama (VAHSH-koh dah GAHM-uh) (c. 1460–1524) rounded the cape and stopped at several ports controlled by Muslim

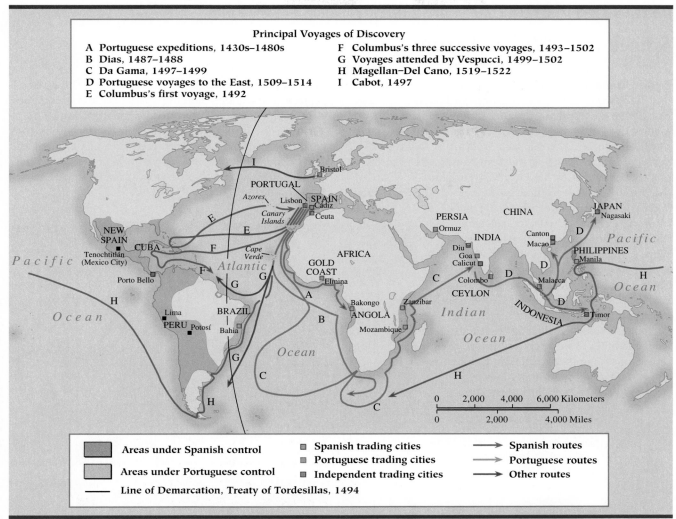

Principal Voyages of Discovery

A Portuguese expeditions, 1430s–1480s
B Dias, 1487–1488
C Da Gama, 1497–1499
D Portuguese voyages to the East, 1509–1514
E Columbus's first voyage, 1492

F Columbus's three successive voyages, 1493–1502
G Voyages attended by Vespucci, 1499–1502
H Magellan–Del Cano, 1519–1522
I Cabot, 1497

Areas under Spanish control
Areas under Portuguese control
Line of Demarcation, Treaty of Tordesillas, 1494

Spanish trading cities
Portuguese trading cities
Independent trading cities

Spanish routes
Portuguese routes
Other routes

MAP 14.1 Discoveries and Possessions in the Fifteenth and Sixteenth Centuries. Desire for wealth was the main motivation of the early explorers, though spreading Christianity was also an important factor. Portugal under Prince Henry the Navigator initiated the first voyages in the early fifteenth century; Spain's explorations began at the century's end.

Q *Which regions of the globe were primarily explored by Portugal, and which were the main focus of Spain's voyages?*

View an animated version of this map or related maps on the CourseMate website.

---

merchants along the coast of East Africa. Da Gama's fleet then crossed the Arabian Sea and reached the port of Calicut, on the southwestern coast of India, on May 18, 1498. On arriving in Calicut, da Gama announced to his surprised hosts that he had come in search of "Christians and spices." He found no Christians, but he did find the spices he sought. Although he lost two ships en route, da Gama's remaining vessels returned to Europe with their holds filled with ginger and cinnamon, a cargo that earned the investors a profit of several thousand percent.

Vasco da Gama, Round Africa to India (1497–1498)

Portuguese fleets returned annually to the area, seeking to destroy Arab shipping and establish a monopoly in the spice trade. In 1509, a Portuguese armada defeated a combined fleet of Turkish and Indian ships off the coast of India and began to impose a blockade on the entrance to the Red Sea to cut off the flow of spices to Muslim rulers in Egypt and the Ottoman Empire. The following year, seeing the need for a land base in the area, Admiral Afonso de Albuquerque (ah-FAHN-soh day AL-buh-kur-kee) (c. 1462–1515) set up port facilities at Goa, on the western coast of India south of present-day Mumbai (Bombay). Goa henceforth became the headquarters for Portuguese operations throughout the entire region. Although Indian merchants were permitted to continue their trading activities, the Portuguese conducted raids against Arab shippers, provoking the following brief report from an Arab source: "In this year the vessels of the Portuguese appeared at sea en route for India and those

New Horizons: The Portuguese and Spanish Empires   **417**

Spices and World Trade

Pepper, cinnamon, nutmeg, and other spices from the East had long been a part of European life. The illustration at the top right from a fifteenth-century French manuscript shows pepper being harvested in Malabar, in southwestern India. Europeans' interest in finding a direct route to the Spice Islands intensified after the fall of Constantinople to the Ottoman Turks in 1453 caused the price of pepper to increase thirtyfold. The Venetians had played a dominant role in the spice trade via Constantinople, as is evident in the Venetian fresco shown at the bottom right. It depicts a spice seller's shop with a wide variety of spices for sale. Vasco de Gama's success in locating a route to the East by sailing around Africa shifted much of the control over the spice trade into Portuguese hands. Following the establishment in 1518 of a fort in Ceylon, the center of cinnamon production, the Portuguese were able to dominate Europe's cinnamon trade. The third illustration

shows a portrait of da Gama from c. 1600. The artist depicted the explorer holding a large stick of cinnamon in his right hand, an indication of the significance of the spice to his legacy and its role in his expeditions. Without the desire for spices, men such as da Gama and Christopher Columbus might not have ventured around Africa or across the Atlantic Ocean, thereby opening and forever altering European trade.

Bibliothèque Nationale, Paris/© Archives Charmet/The Bridgeman Art Library

© The Art Archive/Marine Museum Lisbon/Gianni Dagli Orti

Castello d'Issogne, Val d'Aosta, Italy//© Scala/Art Resource, NY

parts. They took about seven vessels, killing those on board and making some prisoner. This was their first action, may God curse them."[4]

IN SEARCH OF SPICES The Portuguese now began to range more widely in search of the source of the spice trade (see Images of Everyday Life above). In 1511, Albuquerque sailed into the harbor of Malacca on the Malay peninsula. Malacca had been transformed by its Muslim rulers into a thriving port and a major stopping point for the spice trade. For Albuquerque, control of Malacca would serve two purposes. It could help destroy the Arab spice trade and also provide the Portuguese with a way station on the route to the Moluccas, then known as the Spice Islands (see the box on p. 419). After a short but bloody battle, the Portuguese seized the city and massacred the

The Portuguese Conquest of Malacca

In 1511, a Portuguese fleet led by Afonso de Albuquerque attacked the Muslim sultanate at Malacca, on the west coast of the Malay peninsula. Occupation of the port gave the Portuguese control over the strategic Strait of Malacca and the route to the Spice Islands. In this passage, Albuquerque tells his men the reasons for the attack. Note that he sees control of Malacca as a way to reduce the power of the Muslim world.

・⊶ ⹀⹀⹀ ⊷・

The Commentaries of the Great Afonso de Albuquerque

Although there be many reasons which I could allege in favor of our taking this city and building a fortress therein to maintain possession of it, two only will I mention to you, on this occasion. . . .

The first is the great service which we shall perform to Our Lord in casting the Muslims out of this country. . . . If we can only achieve the task before us, it will result in the Muslims resigning India altogether to our rule, for the greater part of them—or perhaps all of them—live upon the trade of this country and are become great and rich, and lords of extensive treasures.

. . . For when we were committing ourselves to the business of cruising in the Straits [of the Red Sea], where the King of Portugal had often ordered me to go (for it was there that His Highness considered we could cut down the commerce which the Muslims of Cairo, of Mecca, and of Judah carry on with these parts), Our Lord for his service thought right to lead us here, for when Malacca is taken the places on the Straits must be shut up, and the Muslims will never more be able to introduce their spices into those places.

And the other reason is the additional service which we shall render to King Manuel in taking this city, because it is the headquarters of all the spices and drugs which the Muslims carry every year hence to the Straits without our being able to prevent them from so doing; but if we deprive them of this their ancient market there, there does not remain for them a single port, nor a single situation, so commodious in the whole of these parts, where they can carry on their trade in these things. . . . I hold it as very certain that if we take this trade of Malacca away out of their hands, Cairo and Mecca are entirely ruined, and to Venice will no spices be conveyed except that which her merchants go and buy in Portugal. ⌕

 What justifications does Albuquerque give for the attack on Malacca? Which might have been the most important in the sixteenth century? Would the Muslims have responded with the same justifications? What, if anything, has changed in the twenty-first century?

---

local Arab population. This slaughter initiated a fierce and brutal struggle between the Portuguese and the Arabs. According to one account, "To enhance the terror of his name he [Albuquerque] always separated Arabs from the other inhabitants of a captured city, and cut off the right hand of the men, and the noses and ears of the women."[5]

From Malacca, the Portuguese launched expeditions farther east, to China and the Spice Islands. There they signed a treaty with a local ruler for the purchase and export of cloves to the European market. The new trading empire was now complete. Within a few years, the Portuguese had managed to seize control of the spice trade from Muslim traders and had garnered substantial profits for the Portuguese monarchy. Nevertheless, the Portuguese Empire remained limited, consisting only of trading posts on the coasts of India and China. The Portuguese lacked the power, the population, and the desire to colonize the Asian regions.

Why were the Portuguese so successful? Basically, their success was a matter of guns and seamanship. The first Portuguese fleet to arrive in Indian waters was relatively modest in size, consisting of three ships and twenty guns, a force sufficient for self-defense and intimidation but not for serious military operations. Later Portuguese fleets, which began to arrive with regularity early in the sixteenth century, were more heavily armed and were able not only to intimidate but also to inflict severe defeats if necessary on local naval and land forces. The Portuguese by no means possessed a monopoly on the use of firearms and explosives, but their effective use of naval technology, their heavy guns that could be mounted in the hulls of their sturdy vessels, and their tactics gave them military superiority over lightly armed rivals that they were able to exploit until the arrival of other European forces several decades later.

Voyages to the New World

While the Portuguese were seeking access to the spice trade of the Indies by sailing eastward through the Indian Ocean, the Spanish were attempting to reach the same destination by sailing westward across the Atlantic. Although the Spanish came to overseas discovery and exploration after the initial efforts of Henry the Navigator, their greater resources enabled them to establish a far grander overseas empire than that of the Portuguese—and one that was quite different.

THE VOYAGES OF COLUMBUS An important figure in the history of Spanish exploration was an Italian known as Christopher Columbus (1451–1506). Knowledgeable Europeans were aware that the world was round but had little

Christopher Columbus. Columbus was an Italian explorer who worked for the queen of Spain. He has become a symbol for two entirely different perspectives. To some, he was a great and heroic explorer who discovered the New World; to others, especially in Latin America, he was responsible for beginning a process of invasion that led to the destruction of an entire way of life. Because Columbus was never painted during his lifetime, the numerous portraits of him are more fanciful than accurate. The portrait shown here was probably done by the Italian painter Ridolfo Ghirlandaio.

understanding of its circumference or the extent of the continent of Asia. Convinced that the circumference of the earth was less than contemporaries believed and that Asia was larger than people thought, Columbus felt that Asia could be reached by sailing west instead of around Africa. After being rejected by the Portuguese, he persuaded Queen Isabella of Spain to finance his exploratory expedition.

With three ships, the *Santa María,* the *Niña,* and the *Pinta,* and a crew of ninety men, Columbus set sail on August 3, 1492. On October 12, he reached the Bahamas and then went on to explore the coastline of Cuba and the northern shores of Hispaniola (present-day Haiti and the Dominican Republic). Columbus believed that he had reached Asia, and in his reports to Queen Isabella and King Ferdinand upon his return to Spain, he assured them not only that he would eventually find gold but also that they had a golden opportunity to convert the natives—whom Columbus persisted in calling "Indians"—to Christianity (see the box on p. 421). In three subsequent voyages (1493, 1498, 1502), Columbus sought in vain to find a route to the Asian mainland. In his four voyages, Columbus landed on all the major islands of the Caribbean and the mainland of Central America, still convinced that he had reached the Indies in Asia.

NEW VOYAGES Although Columbus clung to his belief until his death, other explorers soon realized that he had discovered a new frontier altogether. State-sponsored explorers joined the race to the New World. A Venetian seaman, John Cabot, explored the New England coastline of the Americas under a license from King Henry VII of England. The continent of South America was discovered accidentally by the Portuguese sea captain Pedro Cabral (kuh-BRAL) in 1500. Amerigo Vespucci (ahm-ay-REE-goh vess-POO-chee), a Florentine, accompanied several voyages and wrote a series of letters describing the geography of the New World. The publication of these letters led to the use of the name "America" (after Amerigo) for the new lands.

The first two decades of the sixteenth century witnessed numerous overseas voyages that explored the eastern coasts of both North and South America. Vasco Nuñez de Balboa (VAHS-koh NOON-yez day bal-BOH-uh) (1475–1519), a Spanish explorer, led an expedition across the Isthmus of Panama and reached the Pacific Ocean in 1513. Perhaps the most dramatic of all these expeditions was the journey of Ferdinand Magellan (1480–1521) in 1519. After passing through the strait named after him at the southern tip of South America, he sailed across the Pacific Ocean and reached the Philippines, where he was killed by the natives. Although only one of his fleet of five ships completed the return voyage to Spain, Magellan's name is still associated with the first known circumnavigation of the earth.

Ferdinand Magellan's Voyage Around the World

The Europeans referred to the newly discovered territories as the New World, even though they held flourishing civilizations populated by millions of people. But the Americas were indeed new to the Europeans, who quickly saw opportunities for conquest and exploitation. The Spanish, in particular, were interested because the 1494 Treaty of Tordesillas (tor-day-SEE-yass) had divided up the newly discovered world into separate Portuguese and Spanish spheres of influence, and it turned out that most of South America (except for the eastern hump) fell within the Spanish sphere (see Map 14.1 on p. 417). Hereafter the route east around the Cape of Good Hope was to be reserved for the Portuguese while the route across the Atlantic was assigned to Spain.

The Spanish Empire in the New World

The Spanish conquerors known as **conquistadors** were hardy individuals motivated by a typical sixteenth-century blend of glory, greed, and religious crusading zeal. Although authorized by the Castilian crown, these groups were financed and outfitted privately, not by the government. Their superior weapons, organizational skills, and determination brought the conquistadors incredible success. They also benefited from rivalries among the native peoples and the decimation of the native peoples by European diseases.

EARLY CIVILIZATIONS IN MESOAMERICA Before the Spaniards arrived in the New World, Mesoamerica (modern

Columbus Lands in the New World

On returning from America, which he believed was the coast of Asia, Christopher Columbus wrote about his experience. In this passage from a letter describing his first voyage, he tells of his arrival on the island of Hispaniola (Haiti). Historians believe that Columbus wrote this letter for public consumption.

Letter to Raphael Sanchez, Treasurer to the King and Queen of Spain

Thirty-three days after my departure from Cadiz I reached the Indian sea, where I discovered many islands, thickly peopled, of which I took possession without resistance in the name of our most illustrious Monarch, by public proclamation and with unfurled banners. To the first of these islands, I gave the name of the blessed Saviour (San Salvador), relying upon whose protection I had reached this as well as the other islands; to each of these I also gave a name....

The inhabitants of both sexes in this island, and in all the others which I have seen, or of which I have received information, go always naked as they were born, with the exception of some of the women, who use the covering of a leaf, or small bough, or an apron of cotton which they prepare for that purpose. None of them are possessed of any iron, neither have they weapons, being unacquainted with, and indeed incompetent to use them, not from any deformity of body (for they are well-formed), but because they are timid and full of fear.... As soon however as they see that they are safe, and have laid aside all fear, they are very simple and honest, and exceedingly liberal with all they have; none of them refusing any thing he may possess when he is asked for it.... They also give

objects of great value for trifles, and content themselves with very little or nothing in return.

I however forbade that these trifles and articles of no value (such as pieces of dishes, plates, and glass, keys, and leather straps) should be given to them, although if they could obtain them, they imagined themselves to be possessed of the most beautiful trinkets in the world.... Thus, they bartered, like idiots, cotton and gold for fragments of bows, glasses, bottles, and jars....

In all these islands there is no difference of physiognomy, of manners, or of language, but they all clearly understand each other, a circumstance very propitious for the realization of what I conceive to be the principal wish of our most serene King, namely, the conversion of these people to the holy faith of Christ, to which indeed, as far as I can judge, they are very favorable and well-disposed....

Finally, to compress into a few words the entire summary of my voyage and speedy return, and of the advantages derivable therefrom, I promise, that with a little assistance afforded me by our most invincible sovereigns, I will procure them as much gold as they need, and as great a quantity of spices and cotton.... Let Christ rejoice on earth, as he rejoices in heaven in the prospect of the salvation of the souls of so many nations hitherto lost. Let us also rejoice as well on account of the exaltation of our faith as on account of the increase of our temporal prosperity, of which not only Spain but all Christendom will be partakers.

Q What evidence in Columbus's comments suggests that his remarks were made mainly for public consumption and not just for the Spanish court? What elements in society might have responded to his statements, and why?

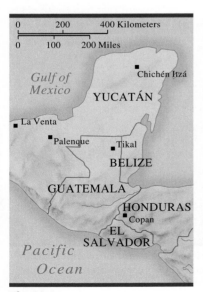

The Maya

Mexico and Central America) had already hosted a number of flourishing civilizations. Beginning around 300 C.E., on the Yucatán peninsula a people known as the Maya (MY-uh) had built one of the most sophisticated civilizations in the Americas. The Maya built splendid temples and pyramids, were accomplished artists, and developed a sophisticated calendar, as accurate as any in existence in the world at that time. The Maya were an agrarian people who cleared the dense rain forests, developed farming, and built a patchwork of city-states. Mayan civilization came to include much of Central America and southern Mexico. For unknown reasons, Mayan civilization began to decline around 800 and had collapsed less than a hundred years later.

Sometime during the early twelfth century C.E., a people known as the Aztecs began a long migration that brought them to the Valley of Mexico. They established their capital at Tenochtitlán (tay-nawch-teet-LAHN), on an island in the middle of Lake Texcoco (now the location of Mexico City). For the next hundred years, the Aztecs built their city, constructing temples, other public buildings, houses, and causeways of stone across Lake Texcoco to the north, south, and west, linking the many islands to the mainland. At the beginning of the fifteenth century, they built an aqueduct to bring fresh water from a spring 4 miles away.

The Aztecs were outstanding warriors, and while they were building their capital city, they also set out to bring the entire area around the city under their control. By the early fifteenth century, they had become the leading city-state in the lake region. For the remainder of the fifteenth century, the Aztecs consolidated their rule over much of what is modern Mexico, from the Atlantic to the Pacific Ocean and as far south as the Guatemalan border. The new kingdom was not a centralized state but a collection of semi-independent territories governed by local lords. These rulers were confirmed in their authority by the Aztec ruler in return for the payment of tribute. This loose political organization would later contribute to the downfall of the Aztec Empire.

The Aztecs

SPANISH CONQUEST OF THE AZTEC EMPIRE In 1519, a Spanish expedition under the command of Hernán Cortés (1485–1547) landed at Veracruz, on the Gulf of Mexico. He marched to the city of Tenochtitlán (see the box on p. 423) at the head of a small contingent of troops (550 soldiers and 16 horses); as he went, he made alliances with city-states that had tired of the oppressive rule of the Aztecs. Especially important was Tlaxcala (tuh-lah-SKAH-lah), a state that the Aztecs had not been able to conquer. In November, Cortés arrived at Tenochtitlán, where he received a friendly welcome from the Aztec monarch Moctezuma (mahk-tuh-ZOO-muh) (often called Montezuma). At first, Moctezuma believed that his visitor was a representative of Quetzalcoatl (KWET-sul-koh-AHT-ul), the god who had departed from his homeland centuries before and had promised that he would return. Riddled with fears, Moctezuma offered gifts of gold to the foreigners and gave them a palace to use while they were in the city.

But the Spaniards quickly wore out their welcome. They took Moctezuma hostage and proceeded to pillage the city. In the fall of 1520, one year after Cortés had arrived, the local population revolted and drove the invaders from the city. Many of the Spaniards were killed, but the Aztecs soon experienced new disasters. As one Aztec related, "At about the time that the Spaniards had fled from Mexico, there came a great sickness, a pestilence, the smallpox." With no natural immunity to the diseases of Europeans, many Aztecs fell sick and died. Meanwhile, Cortés received fresh soldiers from his new allies; the state of Tlaxcala alone provided 50,000 warriors. After four months, the city capitulated. When Cortés and his soldiers entered the city, they beheld an appalling scene, as reported by Bernal Díaz, who accompanied Cortés:

> We could not walk without treading on the bodies and heads of dead Indians. I have read about the destruction of Jerusalem, but I do not think the mortality was greater there than here in Mexico, where most of the warriors who had crowded in from all the provinces and subject towns had died. As I have said, the dry land and the stockades were piled with corpses. Indeed, the stench was so bad that no one could endure it.... Even Cortés was ill from the odors which assailed his nostrils.[6]

The devastation wrought by smallpox had won a great victory for Cortés.

The Spaniards then embarked on a new wave of destruction. The pyramids, temples, and palaces were leveled, and the stones were used to build Spanish government buildings and churches. The rivers and canals

Slaughter of the Natives. Fearful of growing Aztec resistance, the Spaniards responded by slaughtering many natives. This sixteenth-century watercolor by an unknown artist shows the massacre of the Cholula people, carried out on the orders of Cortés. The Cholula had refused to provide supplies to the forces of a Spanish expedition.

The Spanish Conquistador: Cortés and the Conquest of Mexico

Hernán Cortés was a minor Spanish nobleman who came to the New World in 1504 to seek his fortune. Contrary to his superior's orders, Cortés waged an independent campaign of conquest and overthrew the Aztec Empire in Mexico (1519–1522). Cortés wrote a series of five reports to Emperor Charles V to justify his action. The second report includes a description of Tenochtitlán, the capital of the Aztec Empire. The Spanish conquistador and his men were obviously impressed by this city, awesome in its architecture yet built by people who lacked European technology, such as wheeled vehicles and tools of hard metal.

Cortés's Description of Tenochtitlán

The great city Tenochtitlán is built in the midst of this salt lake, and it is two leagues from the heart of the city to any point on the mainland. Four causeways lead to it, all made by hand and some twelve feet wide. The city itself is as large as Seville or Córdoba. The principal streets are very broad and straight, the majority of them being of beaten earth, but a few and at least half of the smaller thoroughfares are waterways along which they pass in their canoes. Moreover, even the principal streets have openings at regular distances so that the water can freely pass from one to another, and these openings which are very broad are spanned by great bridges of huge beams, very stoutly put together, so firm indeed that over many of them ten horsemen can ride at once. Seeing that if the natives intended any treachery against us they would have every opportunity from the way in which the city is built, for by removing the bridges from the entrances and exits they could leave us to die of hunger with no possibility of getting to the mainland, I immediately set to work as soon as we entered the city on the building of four brigs, and in a short space of time had them finished so that we could ship 300 men and the horses to the mainland whenever we so desired.

The city has many open squares in which markets are continuously held and the general business of buying and selling proceeds. One square in particular is twice as big as that of Salamanca and completely surrounded by arcades where there are daily more than 60,000 folk buying and selling. Every kind of merchandise such as may be met with in every land is for sale there, whether of food and victuals, or ornaments of gold and silver, or lead, brass, copper, tin, precious stones, bones, shells, snails and feathers; limestone for building is likewise sold there, stone both rough and polished, bricks burnt and unburnt, wood of all kinds and in all stages of preparation.... There is a street of herb-sellers where there are all manner of roots and medicinal plants that are found in the land. There are houses as it were of apothecaries where they sell medicines made from these herbs, both for drinking and for use as ointments and salves. There are barbers' shops where you may have your hair washed and cut. There are other shops where you may obtain food and drink....

Finally, to avoid being wordy in telling all the wonders of this city, I will simply say that the manner of living among the people is very similar to that in Spain, and considering that this is a barbarous nation shut off from a knowledge of the true God or communication with enlightened nations, one may well marvel at the orderliness and good government which is everywhere maintained.

The actual service of Montezuma and those things which call for admiration by their greatness and state would take so long to describe that I assure your Majesty I do not know where to begin with any hope of ending. For as I have already said, what could there be more astonishing than that a barbarous monarch such as he should have reproductions made in gold, silver, precious stones, and feathers of all things to be found in his land, and so perfectly reproduced that there is no goldsmith or silversmith in the world who could better them, nor can one understand what instrument could have been used for fashioning the jewels; as for the featherwork its like is not to be seen in either wax or embroidery; it is so marvelously delicate.

 What did Cortés focus on in his description of this Aztec city? Why do you think he felt justified in overthrowing the Aztec Empire?

---

were filled in. The mighty Aztec Empire on mainland Mexico was no more. Between 1531 and 1550, the Spanish gained control of northern Mexico.

THE INCA In the late fourteenth century, the Inca were a small community in the area of Cuzco, a city located at an altitude of 10,000 feet in the mountains of southern Peru. In the 1440s, however, under the leadership of their powerful ruler Pachakuti (pah-chah-KOO-tee), the Inca launched a campaign of conquest that eventually brought the entire region under their control. Pachakuti created a highly centralized state. Cuzco, the capital, was transformed from a city of mud and thatch into an imposing city of stone. Under Pachakuti and his immediate successors, Topa Inca and Huayna Inca (the word *Inca* means "ruler"), the boundaries of the Inca Empire were extended as far as Ecuador, central Chile, and the edge of the Amazon basin. The empire included perhaps 12 million people.

Pachakuti divided his realm into four quarters, each ruled by a governor. The quarters were in turn divided into provinces, each also ruled by a governor. The individuals chosen to be governors were usually related to the royal family. Each province was supposed to contain about 10,000 residents. At the top of the entire system was the emperor, who was believed to be descended from the sun god.

The Inca were great builders. One major project was a system of 24,800 miles of roads that extended from the border of modern-day Colombia to a point south of modern-day Santiago, Chile. Two major roadways extended in a north-south direction, one through the Andes Mountains and the other along the coast, with connecting routes between them. Rest houses, located a day's walk apart, and storage depots were placed along the roads. Various types of bridges, including some of the finest examples of suspension bridges in premodern times, were built over ravines and waterways.

SPANISH CONQUEST OF THE INCA
EMPIRE The Inca Empire was still flourishing when the first Spanish expeditions arrived in the area. In December 1530, Francisco Pizarro (frahn-CHESS-koh puh-ZAHR-oh) (c. 1475–1541) landed on the Pacific coast of South America with a band of about 180 men, but like Cortés, he had steel weapons, gunpowder, and horses, none of which were familiar to his hosts. Pizarro was also lucky because the Inca Empire had already succumbed to an epidemic of smallpox. Like the Aztecs, the Inca had no immunities to European diseases, and all too soon, smallpox was devastating entire villages. In another stroke of good fortune for Pizarro, even the Inca emperor was a victim. Upon the emperor's death, two sons claimed the throne, setting off a civil war. Pizarro took advantage of the situation by seizing Atahualpa (ah-tuh-WAHL-puh), whose forces had just defeated his brother's. Armed only with stones, arrows, and light spears, Incan soldiers were no match for the charging horses of the Spanish, let alone their guns and cannons. After executing Atahualpa, Pizarro and his soldiers, aided by their Incan allies, marched on Cuzco and captured the Incan capital. By 1535, Pizarro had established a capital at Lima for a new colony of the Spanish Empire.

ADMINISTRATION OF THE SPANISH EMPIRE Spanish
policy toward the Indians of the New World was a combination of confusion, misguided paternalism, and cruel exploitation. Whereas the conquistadors made decisions based on expediency and their own interests, Queen

The Inca

Isabella declared the natives to be subjects of Castile and instituted the Spanish *encomienda* (en-koh-MYEN-dah), an economic and social system that permitted the conquering Spaniards to collect tribute from the natives and use them as laborers. In return, the holders of an *encomienda* were supposed to protect the Indians, pay them wages, and supervise their spiritual needs. In practice, this meant that the settlers were free to implement the paternalistic system of the government as they pleased. Three thousand miles from Spain, Spanish settlers largely ignored their government and brutally used the Indians to pursue their own economic interests. Indians were put to work on plantations and in the lucrative gold and silver mines. In Peru, the Spanish made use of the *mita*, a system that allowed authorities to draft native labor to work in the silver mines.

Forced labor, starvation, and especially disease took a fearful toll of Indian lives. With no natural resistance to European diseases, the Indians of America were ravaged not only by smallpox but also by the measles and typhus that came with the explorers and the conquistadors. Although scholarly estimates of native populations vary drastically, a reasonable guess is that 30 to 40 percent of the natives died. On Hispaniola alone, out of an initial population of 100,000 natives when Columbus arrived in 1493, only 300 Indians survived by 1570. The population of central Mexico, estimated at roughly 11 million in 1519, had declined to 6.5 million by 1540 and 2.5 million by the end of the sixteenth century.

Voices were raised to protest the harsh treatment of the Indians, especially by Dominican friars. In a 1510 sermon, Antón Montecino startled churchgoers in Santo Domingo by saying:

And you are heading for damnation . . . for you are destroying an innocent people. For they are God's people, these innocents,

Las Casas and the Spanish Treatment of the American Natives

Bartolomé de Las Casas (1474–1566) participated in the conquest of Cuba and received land and Indians in return for his efforts. But in 1514 he underwent a radical transformation and came to believe that the Indians had been cruelly mistreated by his fellow Spaniards. He became a Dominican friar and spent the remaining years of his life (he lived to the age of ninety-two) fighting for the Indians. This selection is taken from his most influential work, which is known to English readers as *The Tears of the Indians*. This work was largely responsible for the "black legend" of the Spanish as inherently "cruel and murderous fanatics." Most scholars feel that Las Casas may have exaggerated his account in order to shock his contemporaries into action.

→ ⇒✠⇐ →

Bartolomé de Las Casas, *The Tears of the Indians*

There is nothing more detestable or more cruel, than the tyranny which the Spaniards use toward the Indians for the getting of pearl. Surely the infernal torments cannot much exceed the anguish that they endure, by reason of that way of cruelty; for they put them under water some four or five ells [15 to 18 feet] deep, where they are forced without any liberty of respiration, to gather up the shells wherein the pearls are; sometimes they come up again with nets full of shells to take breath, but if they stay any while to rest themselves, immediately comes a hangman row'd in a little boat, who as soon as he has well beaten them, drags them again to their labor. Their food is nothing but filth, and the very same that contains the pearl, with a small portion of that bread which that country affords; in the first whereof there is little nourishment; and as for the latter, it is made with great difficulty, besides that they have not enough of that neither for sustenance; they lie upon the ground in fetters, lest they should run away; and many times they are drown'd in this labor, and are never seen again till they swim upon the top of the waves: oftentimes they also are devoured by certain sea monsters, that are frequent in those seas. Consider whether this hard usage of the poor creatures be consistent with the precepts which God commands concerning charity to our neighbor, by those that cast them so undeservedly into the dangers of a cruel death, causing them to perish without any remorse or pity, or allowing them the benefit of the sacraments, or the knowledge of religion; it being impossible for them to live any time under the water; and this death is so much the more painful, by reason that by the constricting of the breast, while the lungs strive to do their office, the vital parts are so afflicted that they die vomiting the blood out of their mouths. Their hair also, which is by nature black, is hereby changed and made of the same color with that of the sea wolves; their bodies are also so besprinkled with the froth of the sea, that they appear rather like monsters than men. ⇨

Q In what ways did this account help create the image of the Spaniards as "cruel and murderous fanatics"? What motives may have prompted Las Casas to make this critique, and how might his opinions have affected the broader standing of Spain in the global politics of the age?

---

whom you destroyed. By what right do you make them die? Mining gold for you in your mines or working for you in your fields, by what right do you unleash enslaving wars upon them? They lived in peace in this land before you came, in peace in their own homes. They did nothing to harm you to cause you to slaughter them wholesale.[7]

In 1542, largely in response to the publications of Bartolomé de Las Casas, a Dominican friar who championed the Indians (see the box above), the government abolished the *encomienda* system and provided more protection for the natives.

In the New World, the Spanish developed an administrative system based on viceroys. Spanish possessions were initially divided into two major administrative units: New Spain (Mexico, Central America, and the Caribbean islands), with its center in Mexico City, and Peru (western South America), governed by a **viceroy** in Lima. According to legislation of 1542, "the kingdoms of New Spain and Peru are to be ruled and governed by viceroys, who shall represent our royal person, hold the superior government, do and administer justice equally to all our subjects and vassals, and concern themselves with everything that will promote the calm, peace, ennoblement and pacification of those provinces."[8] Each viceroy served as the king's chief civil and military officer and was aided by advisory groups called **audiencias** (ow-dee-en-SEE-uss), which also functioned as supreme judicial bodies.

By papal agreement, the Catholic monarchs of Spain were given extensive rights over ecclesiastical affairs in the New World. They could appoint all bishops and clergy, build churches, collect fees, and supervise the various religious orders that sought to convert the heathen. Catholic missionaries—especially the Dominicans, Franciscans, and Jesuits—fanned out across the Spanish Empire, where they converted and baptized hundreds of thousands of Indians in the early years of the conquest.

The mass conversion of the Indians brought the organizational and institutional structures of Catholicism to the New World. Dioceses, parishes, cathedrals, schools, and hospitals—all the trappings of civilized European society—soon appeared in the Spanish Empire. So, too, did the Spanish Inquisition, established first in Peru in 1570 and in Mexico the following year.

New Rivals on the World Stage

 Focus Questions: How did the arrival of the Dutch, British, and French on the world scene in the seventeenth and eighteenth centuries affect Africa, India, Southeast Asia, China, and Japan? What were the main features of the African slave trade, and what effects did it have on Africa?

Portugal and Spain had been the first Atlantic nations to take advantage of the age of exploration, starting in the late fifteenth century, and both had become great colonial powers. In the seventeenth century, however, their European neighbors to the north—first the Dutch and then the French and English—moved to replace the Portuguese and Spanish and create their own colonial empires. The new rivals and their rivalry soon had an impact on much of the rest of the world—in Africa, Asia, and the Americas.

Africa: The Slave Trade

Although the primary objective of the Portuguese in sailing around Africa was to find a sea route to the Spice Islands, they soon discovered that profits could be made in Africa itself. So did other Europeans.

The Portuguese built forts on both the western and eastern coasts of Africa and tried, above all, to dominate the trade in gold. During the mid-seventeenth century, however, the Dutch seized a number of Portuguese forts along the West African coast and at the same time took control of much of the Portuguese trade across the Indian Ocean.

The Dutch East India Company, a trading company established in 1602 under government sponsorship, also set up a settlement in southern Africa, at the Cape of Good Hope, which was meant to serve as a base to provide food and other provisions to Dutch ships en route to the Spice Islands. Eventually, however, it developed into a permanent colony. Dutch farmers, known as Boers, began to settle in areas outside the city of Cape Town. The area's moderate climate and freedom from tropical diseases made it attractive for Europeans to settle there.

The European exploration of the African coastline did not affect most Africans living in the interior of the continent, but for peoples living on or near the coast, the impact was great indeed. As the trade in slaves increased during the sixteenth through the eighteenth centuries, thousands and then millions of Africans were removed from their homes and forcibly shipped to plantations in the New World.

ORIGINS OF THE SLAVE TRADE   Traffic in slaves was not new. As in other areas of the world, slavery had been practiced in Africa since ancient times. In the fifteenth century, it continued at a fairly steady level. The primary market for African slaves was the Middle East, where most were used as domestic servants. Slavery also existed in many European countries, where some slaves from Africa or war captives from the regions north of the Black Sea were used as household help or agricultural workers.

At first, the Portuguese simply replaced European slaves with African ones. During the second half of the fifteenth century, about a thousand slaves were taken to Portugal each year. Most wound up serving as domestic servants for affluent families in Europe. But the discovery of the Americas in the 1490s and the planting of sugar-cane in South America and the islands of the Caribbean changed the situation drastically.

Cane sugar had first been introduced to Europeans from the Middle East during the Crusades. At the end of the fifteenth century, the Portuguese set up sugar plantations worked by African laborers on an island off the central coast of Africa. During the sixteenth century, sugarcane plantations were set up along the eastern coast of Brazil and on several islands in the Caribbean. Because the growing of cane sugar demands both skill and large quantities of labor, the new plantations required more workers than could be provided by the small American Indian population in the New World, decimated by diseases imported from the Old World. Since the climate and soil of much of West Africa were not conducive to the cultivation of sugar, African slaves began to be shipped to Brazil and the Caribbean to work on the plantations. The first were sent from Portugal, but in 1518, a Spanish ship carried the first boatload of African slaves directly from Africa to the New World.

GROWTH OF THE SLAVE TRADE   During the next two centuries, the trade in slaves grew dramatically and became part of the **triangular trade** connecting Europe, Africa, and the American continents that characterized the new Atlantic economy (see Map 14.2). European merchant ships (primarily those of England, France, Spain, Portugal, and the Dutch Republic) carried European manufactured goods, such as guns, gin, and cloth, to Africa, where they were traded for a cargo of slaves. The slaves were then shipped to the Americas and sold. European merchants then bought tobacco, molasses, sugar, rum, coffee, and raw cotton and shipped them back to Europe to be sold in European markets.

An estimated 275,000 enslaved Africans were exported to other countries during the sixteenth century, with 2,000 going annually to the Americas alone. The total climbed to over a million in the seventeenth century and jumped to 6 million in the eighteenth century, when the trade spread from West and Central Africa to East Africa. Even during the nineteenth century, when Great Britain and other European countries tried to end the slave trade, nearly 2 million were exported. Altogether as many as 10 million African slaves were transported to the Americas between the sixteenth and nineteenth centuries. About half were transported in British ships, with the rest divided among French, Dutch, Portuguese, Danish, and later, American ships.

One reason for the astonishing numbers of slaves, of course, was the high death rate. The journey of slaves from Africa to the Americas became known as the **Middle Passage,** the middle leg of the triangular trade route. African slaves were closely packed into cargo ships, 300 to 450 per ship, and chained in holds without sanitary

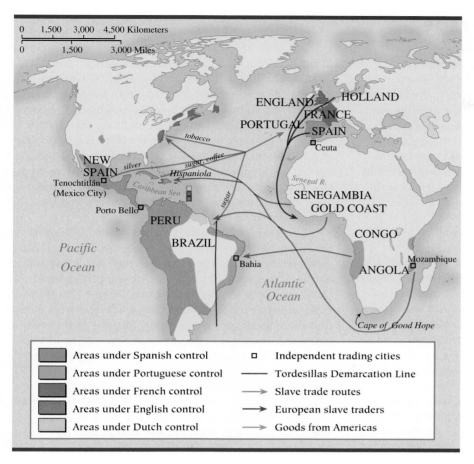

MAP 14.2 Triangular Trade Route in the Atlantic Economy. As the trade in slaves grew, it became a part of the triangular trade route that characterized the Atlantic economy, involving the exchange of goods and slaves between the western coast of Europe, the slave depots on the African coast, and the ports of North and South America.

Q *What were the important source regions for slaves, and where were most of the slaves taken?*

facilities or room to stand up; there they remained during the voyage to America, which took at least 100 days (see the box on p. 428). Mortality rates averaged 10 percent; longer journeys due to storms or adverse winds resulted in even higher death rates. The Africans who survived the journey were subject to high death rates from diseases to which they had little or no immunity. Death rates were lower for slaves born and raised in the New World: the new generation developed immunity to many of the more fatal diseases. Owners, however, rarely encouraged their slaves to have children. Many slave owners, especially in the West Indies, believed that buying a new slave was less expensive than raising a child from birth to working age at adolescence.

Before the coming of Europeans in the fifteenth century, most slaves in Africa were prisoners of war. Many served as domestic servants or as wageless workers for the local ruler. When Europeans first began to take part in the slave trade, they bought slaves from local African merchants at slave markets in return for gold, guns, or other European goods such as textiles or copper or iron utensils.

The Sale of Slaves. In the eighteenth century, the slave trade was a highly profitable commercial enterprise. This painting shows a Western slave merchant negotiating with a local African leader over slaves at Gorée, Senegal, in West Africa in the late eighteenth century.

The Atlantic Slave Trade

One of the most odious practices of early modern Western society was the Atlantic slave trade, which reached its height in the eighteenth century. Blacks were transported in densely packed cargo ships from the western coast of Africa to the Americas to work as slaves in the plantation economy. Not until late in the eighteenth century did a rising chorus of voices raise serious objections to this trade in human beings. This excerpt presents a criticism of the slave trade from an anonymous French writer.

→ ⇥⬦⇤ ⟵

Diary of a Citizen

As soon as the ships have lowered their anchors off the coast of Guinea, the price at which the captains have decided to buy the captives is announced to the Negroes who buy prisoners from various princes and sell them to Europeans. Presents are sent to the sovereign who rules over that particular part of the coast, and permission to trade is given. Immediately the slaves are brought by inhuman brokers like so many victims dragged to a sacrifice. White men who cover that portion of the human race receive them in a little house they have erected on the shore, where they have entrenched themselves with two pieces of cannon and twenty guards. As soon as the bargain is concluded, the Negro is put in chains and led aboard the vessel, where he meets his fellow sufferers. Here sinister reflections come to his mind; everything shocks and frightens him and his uncertain destiny gives rise to the greatest anxiety. . . .

The vessel sets sail for the Antilles, and the Negroes are chained in a hold of the ship, a kind of lugubrious prison where the light of day does not penetrate, but into which the air is introduced by means of a pump. Twice a day some disgusting food is distributed to them. Their consuming sorrow and the sad state to which they are reduced would make them commit suicide if they were not deprived of all the means for an attempt upon their lives. Without any kind of clothing it would be difficult to conceal from the watchful eyes of the sailors in charge any instrument apt to alleviate their despair. The fear of a revolt, such as sometimes happens on the voyage from Guinea, is the basis of a common concern and produces as many guards as there are men in the crew. The slightest noise or a secret conversation among two Negroes is punished with utmost severity. All in all, the voyage is made in a continuous state of alarm on the part of the white men, who fear a revolt, and in a cruel state of uncertainty on the part of the Negroes, who do not know the fate awaiting them.

When the vessel arrives at a port in the Antilles, they are taken to a warehouse where they are displayed, like any merchandise, to the eyes of buyers. The plantation owner pays according to the age, strength, and health of the Negro he is buying. He has him taken to his plantation, and there he is delivered to an overseer who then and there becomes his tormentor. In order to domesticate him, the Negro is granted a few days of rest in his new place, but soon he is given a hoe and a sickle and made to join a work gang. Then he ceases to wonder about his fate; he understands that only labor is demanded of him. But he does not know yet how excessive this labor will be. As a matter of fact, his work begins at dawn and does not end before nightfall; it is interrupted for only two hours at dinnertime. The food a full-grown Negro is given each week consists of two pounds of salt beef or cod and two pots of tapioca meal. . . . A Negro of twelve or thirteen years or under is given only one pot of meal and one pound of beef or cod. In place of food some planters give their Negroes the liberty of working for themselves every Saturday; others are even less generous and grant them this liberty only on Sundays and holidays. ⇥

Q What does this account reveal about the nature of the slave trade and white attitudes toward blacks in the eighteenth century?

At first, local slave traders obtained their supply from regions nearby, but as demand increased, they had to move farther inland to find their victims. In a few cases, local rulers became concerned about the impact of the slave trade on the well-being of their societies. In a letter to the king of Portugal in 1526, King Affonso of Congo (Bakongo) complained:

And we cannot reckon how great the damage is, since the mentioned merchants are taking every day our natives, sons of the land and the sons of our noblemen and vassals and our relatives, . . . and so great, Sir, is the corruption and licentiousness that our country is being completely depopulated, and Your Highness should not agree with this nor accept it as in your service.[9]

But protests from Africans were generally ignored by Europeans as well as by other Africans. As a general rule, local rulers viewed the slave trade as a source of income, and many sent raiders into defenseless villages in search of unsuspecting victims.

Historians once thought that Europeans controlled the terms of the slave trade and were able to obtain victims at bargain prices. It is now clear, however, that African middlemen—merchants, local elites, or rulers—were active in the process and were often able to dictate the price and number of slaves to European purchasers. Payment to the slave merchant was often made in goods, such as textiles, furniture, and guns.

EFFECTS OF THE SLAVE TRADE The effects of the slave trade varied from area to area. Of course, it had tragic effects on the lives of the slaves and their families. There was also an economic price as the importation of cheap manufactured goods from Europe undermined local cottage industries and forced countless families into poverty. The slave trade also led to the depopulation of some areas and deprived many African communities of their youngest and strongest men and women.

The political effects of the slave trade were also devastating. The need to maintain a constant supply of slaves led to increased warfare and violence as African chiefs and their followers, armed with guns acquired from the trade in slaves, increased their raids and wars on neighboring peoples. A few Europeans lamented what they were doing to traditional African societies. One Dutch slave trader remarked, "From us they have learned strife, quarrelling, drunkenness, trickery, theft, unbridled desire for what is not one's own, misdeeds unknown to them before, and the accursed lust for gold."[10] Nevertheless, the slave trade continued, with devastating effects for some African states. The case of Benin in West Africa is a good example. A brilliant and creative society in the sixteenth century, Benin was pulled into the slave trade. As the population declined and warfare increased, the people of Benin lost faith in their gods, their art deteriorated, and human sacrifice became more common. When the British arrived there at the end of the nineteenth century, they found it a corrupt place. It took years to discover the brilliance of the earlier culture destroyed by slavery.

Despite a rising chorus of humanitarian sentiments from European intellectuals, the use of black slaves remained largely acceptable to Western society. Europeans continued to view blacks as inferior beings fit primarily for slave labor. Not until the Society of Friends, known as the Quakers, began to criticize slavery in the 1770s and exclude from their church any member adhering to slave trafficking did European sentiment for the abolition of slavery begin to build. Even then, it was not until the radical stage of the French Revolution in the 1790s that the French abolished slavery. The British followed suit in 1807. Despite the elimination of the African source, slavery continued in the newly formed United States until the Civil War of the 1860s.

The West in Southeast Asia

Portugal's efforts to dominate the trade of Southeast Asia were never totally successful. The Portuguese lacked both the numbers and the wealth to overcome local resistance and colonize the Asian regions. Portugal's empire was simply too large and Portugal too small to maintain it. One Portuguese chronicler lamented, "My country, oh my country. Too heavy is the task that has been laid on your shoulders. Day after day I watch the ships leaving your shores filled always with your best and bravest men. And too many do not return.... Who then is left to till the fields, to harvest the grapes, to keep the enemy on our frontiers at bay?"[11] By the end of the sixteenth century, new European rivals had entered the fray.

One of them was Spain. The Spanish had established themselves in the region when Magellan had landed in the Philippines. Although he was killed there, the Spanish were able to gain control over the Philippines, which eventually became a major Spanish base in the trade across the Pacific. Spanish ships carried silk and other luxury goods to Mexico in return for silver from the mines of Mexico.

The primary threat to the Portuguese Empire in Southeast Asia, however, came with the arrival of the Dutch and the English, who were better financed than the Portuguese. The shift in power began in the early seventeenth century when the Dutch seized a Portuguese fort in the Moluccas and then gradually pushed the Portuguese out of the spice trade. During the next fifty years, the Dutch occupied most of the Portuguese coastal forts along the trade routes throughout the Indian Ocean, including the island of Ceylon (today's Sri Lanka), and seized Malacca in 1641. The aggressive Dutch drove the English traders out of the spice market as well, eventually restricting the English to a single port on the southern coast of Sumatra.

The Dutch also began to consolidate their political and military control over the entire area. On the island of Java, where they had established a fort at Batavia (modern Jakarta) in 1619, the Dutch found that it was necessary to bring the inland regions under their control to protect their position. On Java and the neighboring island of Sumatra, the Dutch East India Company established pepper plantations, which soon became the source of massive profits for Dutch merchants in Amsterdam. By the end of the eighteenth century, the Dutch had succeeded in bringing almost the entire Indonesian archipelago under their control.

The arrival of the Europeans had less impact on mainland Southeast Asia, where strong monarchies in Burma—now Myanmar (MYAN-mahr)—Thailand, and Vietnam resisted foreign encroachment. In the sixteenth century, the Portuguese established limited trade relations with several mainland states, including Thailand, Burma,

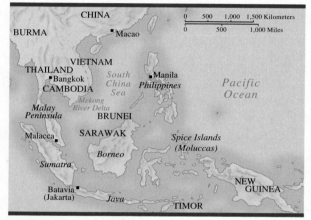

Southeast Asia, c. 1700

Europe in Asia. As Europeans began to move into parts of Asia, they reproduced many of the physical surroundings of their homeland in the port cities they built there. This is evident in comparing these two scenes. Below is a seventeenth-century view of Batavia, which the Dutch built as their headquarters on the northern coast of Java in 1619. The scene at the right is from a sixteenth-century engraving of Amsterdam. This Dutch city had become the financial and commercial capital of Europe. It was also the chief port for the ships of the Dutch East India Company, which brought the spices of the East to Europe.

Vietnam, and the remnants of the old Angkor kingdom in Cambodia. By the early seventeenth century, other nations had followed and had begun to compete actively for trade and missionary privileges. To obtain economic advantages, the Europeans soon became involved in local factional disputes. In general, however, these states were able to unite and drive the Europeans out.

In Vietnam, the arrival of Western merchants and missionaries coincided with a period of internal conflict among ruling groups in the country. Expansion had led to a civil war that temporarily divided the country into two separate states, one in the south and one in the north. After their arrival in the mid-seventeenth century, the European powers began to take sides in local politics, with the Portuguese and the Dutch supporting rival factions. The Europeans also set up trading posts for their merchants, but by the end of the seventeenth century, when it became clear that economic opportunities were limited, most of them were abandoned. French missionaries attempted to remain, but their efforts were blocked by the authorities, who viewed converts to Catholicism as a threat to the prestige of the Vietnamese emperor (see the box on p. 431).

Why were the mainland states better able to resist the European challenge than the states in the Malay world? One factor, no doubt, was the cohesive nature of these states. The mainland states in Burma, Thailand, and Vietnam had begun to define themselves as distinct political entities. The Malay states had less cohesion. Moreover, the Malay states were victims of their own resources. The spice trade was enormously profitable. European merchants and rulers were determined to gain control of the sources of the spices, and that determination led them to take direct control of the Indonesian archipelago.

The French and British in India

When a Portuguese fleet arrived at the port of Calicut in the spring of 1498, the Indian subcontinent was divided into a number of Hindu and Muslim kingdoms. But it was on the verge of a new era of unity that would be brought about by a foreign dynasty called the Mughals (MOO-guls).

THE MUGHAL EMPIRE The founders of the Mughal Empire were not natives of India but came from the

Opposing >‹VIEWPOINTS

West Meets East: An Exchange of Royal Letters

Economic gain was not the only motivation of Western rulers who wished to establish a European presence in the East. In 1681, King Louis XIV of France wrote a letter to the king of Tonkin (the Trinh family head, then acting as viceroy to the Vietnamese emperor) asking permission for Christian missionaries to proselytize in Vietnam. The king of Tonkin politely declined the request.

A Letter to the King of Tonkin from Louis XIV

Most high, most excellent, most mighty and most magnanimous Prince, our very dear and good friend, may it please God to increase your greatness with a happy end!

We hear from our subjects who were in your Realm what protection you accorded them. We appreciate this all the more since we have for you all the esteem that one can have for a prince as illustrious through his military valor as he is commendable for the justice which he exercises in his Realm. We have even been informed that you have not been satisfied to extend this general protection to our subjects but, in particular, that you gave effective proofs of it to Messrs. Deydier and de Bourges. We would have wished that they might have been able to recognize all the favors they received from you by having presents worthy of you offered you; but since the war which we have had for several years, in which all of Europe had banded together against us, prevented our vessels from going to the Indies, at the present time, when we are at peace after having gained many victories and expanded our Realm through the conquest of several important places, we have immediately given orders to the Royal Company to establish itself in your kingdom as soon as possible, and have commanded Messrs. Deydier and de Bourges to remain with you in order to maintain a good relationship between our subjects and yours, also to warn us on occasions that might present themselves when we might be able to give you proofs of our esteem and of our wish to concur with your satisfaction as well as with your best interests.

By way of initial proof, we have given orders to have brought to you some presents which we believe might be agreeable to you. But the one thing in the world which we desire most, both for you and for your Realm, would be to obtain for your subjects who have already embraced the law of the only true God of heaven and earth, the freedom to profess it, since this law is the highest, the noblest, the most sacred and especially the most suitable to have kings reign absolutely over the people.

We are even quite convinced that, if you knew the truths and the maxims which it teaches, you would give first of all to your subjects the glorious example of embracing it. We wish you this incomparable blessing together with a long and happy reign, and we pray God that it may please Him to augment your greatness with the happiest of endings.

Written at Saint-Germain-en-Laye, the 10th day of January, 1681,

> Your very dear and good friend,
> Louis

Answer from the King of Tonkin to Louis XIV

The King of Tonkin sends to the King of France a letter to express to him his best sentiments, saying that he was happy to learn that fidelity is a durable good of man and that justice is the most important of things. Consequently practicing of fidelity and justice cannot but yield good results. Indeed, though France and our Kingdom differ as to mountains, rivers, and boundaries, if fidelity and justice reign among our villages, our conduct will express all of our good feelings and contain precious gifts. Your communication, which comes from a country which is a thousand leagues away, and which proceeds from the heart as a testimony of your sincerity, merits repeated consideration and infinite praise. Politeness toward strangers is nothing unusual in our country. There is not a stranger who is not well received by us. How then could we refuse a man from France, which is the most celebrated among the kingdoms of the world and which for love of us wishes to frequent us and bring us merchandise? These feelings of fidelity and justice are truly worthy to be applauded. As regards your wish that we should cooperate in propagating your religion, we do not dare to permit it, for there is an ancient custom, introduced by edicts, which formally forbids it. Now, edicts are promulgated only to be carried out faithfully; without fidelity nothing is stable. How could we disdain a well-established custom to satisfy a private friendship? . . .

We beg you to understand well that this is our communication concerning our mutual acquaintance. This then is my letter. We send you herewith a modest gift, which we offer you with a glad heart.

This letter was written at the beginning of winter and on a beautiful day.

Q What are the underlying beliefs and approaches of these two rulers? How are they alike? How are they different? What is the significance of the way the two rulers date their letters?

The Mughal Empire

mountainous region north of the Ganges River valley. The founder of the dynasty, Babur, had an illustrious background. His father was descended from the great Asian conqueror Tamerlane; his mother, from the Mongol conqueror Genghis Khan. It was Akbar (1556–1605), Babur's grandson, however, who brought Mughal rule to most of India, creating the greatest Indian empire since the Mauryan dynasty nearly two thousand years earlier.

THE IMPACT OF THE WESTERN POWERS As we have seen, the first Europeans to arrive in India were the Portuguese. At first, Portugal dominated regional trade in the Indian Ocean, but at the end of the sixteenth century, the English and the Dutch arrived on the scene. Soon both powers were competing with Portugal, and with each other, for trading privileges in the region.

During the first half of the seventeenth century, the English presence in India steadily increased. By 1650, English trading posts had been established at Surat (a thriving port along the northwestern coast of India), Fort William (now the great city of Calcutta) near the Bay of Bengal, and Madras (now Chennai) on the southeastern coast. From Madras, English ships carried Indian-made cotton goods to the East Indies, where they were bartered for spices, which were shipped back to England.

English success in India attracted rivals, including the Dutch and the French. The Dutch abandoned their interests to concentrate on the spice trade in the middle of the seventeenth century, but the French were more persistent and established their own forts on the east coast. For a brief period, the French competed successfully with the British, even capturing the British fort at Madras.

But the British were saved by the military genius of Sir Robert Clive, an aggressive British empire-builder who eventually became the chief representative of the East India Company in India. (The East India Company had been founded as a joint-stock company in 1600—see "The Growth of Commercial Capitalism" later in this chapter.) The British were aided as well by the refusal of the French government to provide financial support for French efforts in far-off India. Eventually, the French were restricted to the fort at Pondicherry and a handful of small territories on the southeastern coast.

In the meantime, Clive began to consolidate British control in Bengal, where the local ruler had attacked Fort William and imprisoned the local British population in the "Black Hole of Calcutta" (an underground prison for holding the prisoners, many of whom died in captivity). In 1757, a small British force numbering about three thousand defeated a Mughal-led army more than ten times its size in the Battle of Plassey. As part of the spoils of victory, the British East India Company received from the now-decrepit Mughal court the authority to collect taxes from lands in the area surrounding Calcutta. During the Seven Years' War (1756–1763), the British forced the French to withdraw completely from India (see Chapter 18).

To officials of the East India Company, the expansion of their authority into the interior of the subcontinent probably seemed like a simple economic decision. It made sense to seek regular revenues that would pay for increasingly expensive military operations in India. To historians, it marks a major step in the gradual transfer of all of the Indian subcontinent to the British East India Company and later, in 1858, to the British crown as a colony (see Chapter 24).

China

In 1514, a Portuguese fleet dropped anchor off the coast of China. It was the first direct contact between the Chinese Empire and Europe since the journeys of Marco Polo two hundred years earlier. At the time, the Chinese thought little of the event. China appeared to be at the height of its power as the most magnificent civilization on earth. Its empire stretched from the steppes of Central Asia to the China Sea, from the Gobi Desert to the tropical rain forests of Southeast Asia. From the lofty perspective of the imperial throne in Beijing, the Europeans could only be seen as an unusual form of barbarian. To the Chinese ruler, the rulers of all other countries were simply "younger brothers" of the Chinese emperor, who was regarded as the Son of Heaven.

THE MING AND QING DYNASTIES By the time the Portuguese fleet arrived off the coast of China, the Ming dynasty, which ruled from 1369 to 1644, had already begun a new era of greatness in Chinese history. Under a series of strong rulers, China extended its rule into Mongolia and Central Asia. The Ming even briefly reconquered Vietnam. Along the northern frontier, they strengthened the Great Wall and made peace with the nomadic tribesmen who had troubled China for centuries.

But the days of the Ming dynasty were numbered. In the 1630s, a major epidemic devastated the population in many areas. The suffering caused by the epidemic helped spark a peasant revolt led by Li Zicheng (lee zee-CHENG). In 1644, Li and his forces occupied the capital of Beijing. The last Ming emperor committed suicide by hanging himself from a tree in the palace gardens.

The overthrow of the Ming dynasty created an opportunity for the Manchus, a farming and hunting people who lived northeast of China in the area known today as Manchuria. The Manchus conquered Beijing, and Li Zicheng's army fell. The victorious Manchus then declared the creation of a new dynasty with the reign title of the Qing ("Pure").

The Qing (CHING) were blessed with a series of strong early rulers who pacified the country, corrected the most serious social and economic ills, and restored peace and prosperity. Two Qing monarchs, Kangxi (GANG-zhee) and Qianlong (CHAN-lung), ruled China for well over a century, from the middle of the seventeenth century to the end of the eighteenth. They were responsible for much of the greatness of Manchu China.

The Qing Empire

WESTERN INROADS Although China was at the height of its power and glory in the mid-eighteenth century, the first signs of internal decay in the Manchu dynasty were beginning to appear. Qing military campaigns along the frontier were expensive and placed heavy demands on the treasury. At the same time, increasing pressure on the land because of population growth led to economic hardship for many peasants and even rebellion.

Unfortunately for China, the decline of the Qing dynasty occurred just as Europe was increasing pressure for more trade. The first conflict had come from the north, where Russian traders sought skins and furs. Formal diplomatic relations between China and Russia were established in 1689 and provided for regular trade between the two countries.

Dealing with the foreigners who arrived by sea was more difficult. By the end of the seventeenth century, the English had replaced the Portuguese as the dominant force in European trade. Operating through the East India Company, which served as both a trading unit and the administrator of English territories in Asia, the English established their first trading post at Canton in 1699.

Over the next decades, trade with China, notably the export of tea and silk to England, increased rapidly. To limit contacts between Europeans and Chinese, the Qing government confined all European traders to a small island just outside the city walls of Canton and permitted them to reside there only from October through March.

For a while, the British accepted this system, which brought considerable profit to the East India Company. But by the end of the eighteenth century, some British traders had begun to demand access to other cities along the Chinese coast and insist that the country be opened to British manufactured goods. In 1793, a British mission under Lord Macartney visited Beijing to press for liberalization of trade restrictions. But Emperor Qianlong expressed no interest in British products (see the box on p. 434). An exasperated Macartney compared the Chinese Empire to "an old, crazy, firstrate man-of-war" that had once awed its neighbors "merely by her bulk and appearance" but was now destined under incompetent leadership to be "dashed to pieces on the shore." The Chinese would later pay for their rejection of the British request (see Chapter 24).

Japan

At the end of the fifteenth century, Japan was at a point of near anarchy, but in the course of the sixteenth century, a number of powerful individuals achieved the unification of Japan. One of them, Tokugawa Ieyasu (toh-koo-GAH-wah ee-yeh-YAH-soo) (1543–1616), took the title of shogun ("general") in 1603, an act that initiated the most powerful and longest lasting of all the Japanese shogunates. The Tokugawa rulers completed the restoration of central authority and remained in power until 1868.

OPENING TO THE WEST Portuguese traders had landed on the islands of Japan in 1543, and in a few years, Portuguese ships began stopping at Japanese ports on a regular basis to take part in the regional trade between Japan, China, and Southeast Asia. The first Jesuit missionary, Francis Xavier, arrived in 1549 and had some success in converting the local population to Christianity.

Initially, the visitors were welcomed. The curious Japanese were fascinated by tobacco, clocks, eyeglasses, and other European goods, and local nobles were interested in purchasing all types of European weapons and armaments. Japanese rulers found the new firearms especially helpful in defeating their enemies and unifying the islands. The effect on Japanese military architecture was

An Imperial Edict to the King of England

In 1793, the British emissary Lord Macartney visited the Qing Empire to request the opening of trading relations between his country and China. Emperor Qianlong's reply, addressed to King George III of England, illustrates how the imperial court in Beijing viewed the world. King George cannot have been pleased.

———— ✠✦✠ ————

An Imperial Edict to the King of England

You, O King, are so inclined toward our civilization that you have sent a special envoy across the seas to bring to our Court your memorial of congratulations on the occasion of my birthday and to present your native products as an expression of your thoughtfulness. On perusing your memorial, so simply worded and sincerely conceived, I am impressed by your genuine respectfulness and friendliness and greatly pleased.

As to the request made in your memorial, O King, to send one of your nationals to stay at the Celestial Court to take care of your country's trade with China, this is not in harmony with the state system of our dynasty and will definitely not be permitted. Traditionally people of the European nations who wished to tender some service under the Celestial Court have been permitted to come to the capital. But after their arrival they are obliged to wear Chinese court costumes, are placed in a certain residence and are never allowed to return to their own countries. This is the established rule of the Celestial Dynasty with which presumably you, O King, are familiar. Now you, O King, wish to send one of your nationals to live in the capital, but he is not like the Europeans, who come to Beijing as Chinese employees, live there and never return home again, nor can he be allowed to go and come and maintain any correspondence. This is indeed a useless undertaking. . . .

The Celestial Court has pacified and possessed the territory within the four seas. Its sole aim is to do its utmost to achieve good government and to manage political affairs, attaching no value to strange jewels and precious objects. The various articles presented by you, O King, this time are accepted by my special order to the office in charge of such functions in consideration of the offerings having come from a long distance with sincere good wishes. As a matter of fact, the virtue and prestige of the Celestial Dynasty having spread far and wide, the kings of the myriad nations come by land and sea with all sorts of precious things. Consequently there is nothing we lack, as your principal envoy and others have themselves observed. We have never set much store on strange objects, nor do we need any more of your country's manufactures. ⊱

Q What reasons does Qianlong give for denying Britain's request to open diplomatic and trading relations with China? Do his comments indicate any ignorance about the West at the end of the eighteenth century? If he had known more, would his response have been different? Why or why not?

Musée des Arts Asiatiques-Guimet, Paris//
© Réunion des Musées Nationaux/Art Resource, NY

The Portuguese Arriving at Nagasaki. Portuguese traders landed accidentally in Japan in 1543. In a few years, they arrived regularly, taking part in a regional trade network involving Japan, China, and Southeast Asia. In these panels, done in black lacquer and gold leaf, we see a late-sixteenth-century Japanese interpretation of the first Portuguese landing at Nagasaki.

especially striking, as local lords began to erect castles in stone on the European model.

The success of the Catholic missionaries, however, provoked a strong reaction against the presence of Westerners. When the missionaries interfered in local politics, Tokugawa Ieyasu, newly come to power, expelled all missionaries. Japanese Christians were now persecuted. When a group of Christian peasants on the island of Kyushu revolted in 1637, they were bloodily suppressed.

The European merchants were the next to go. The government closed the two major foreign trading posts on the island of Hirado and at Nagasaki (nah-gah-SAH-kee). Only a small Dutch community in Nagasaki was allowed to remain in Japan. The Dutch, unlike the Spanish and Portuguese, had not allowed missionary activities to interfere with their trade interests. But the conditions for staying were strict. Dutch ships were allowed to dock at Nagasaki harbor just once a year and could remain for only two or three months.

The Americas

In the sixteenth century, Spain and Portugal had established large colonial empires in the Americas. Portugal continued to profit from its empire in Brazil. The Spanish also maintained an enormous South American empire, but Spain's importance as a commercial power declined rapidly in the seventeenth century because of a drop in the output of the silver mines and the poverty of the Spanish monarchy. By the beginning of the seventeenth century, both Portugal and Spain found themselves with new challenges to their American empires from the Dutch, English, and French, who increasingly sought to create their own colonial empires in the New World.

WEST INDIES Both the French and English colonial empires in the New World included large parts of the West Indies. The English held Barbados, Jamaica, and Bermuda, and the French possessed Saint-Domingue, Martinique, and Guadeloupe. On these tropical islands, both the English and the French developed plantation economies, worked by African slaves, which produced tobacco, cotton, coffee, and sugar, all products increasingly in demand in Europe.

The "sugar factories," as the sugar plantations in the Caribbean were called, played an especially prominent role. By the last two decades of the eighteenth century, the British colony of Jamaica, one of Britain's most important, was producing 50,000 tons of sugar annually with the slave labor of 200,000 blacks. The French colony of Saint-Domingue (later Haiti) had 500,000 slaves working on three thousand plantations at the same time.

The West Indies

A Sugar Mill in the West Indies. Cane sugar was one of the most valuable products produced in the West Indies. By 1700, sugar was replacing honey as a sweetener for increasing numbers of Europeans. This seventeenth-century French illustration shows the operation of a sugar mill in the French West Indies.

This colony produced 100,000 tons of sugar a year, but at the expense of a high death rate from the brutal treatment of the slaves. It is not surprising that Saint-Domingue was the site of the first successful slave uprising in 1793 (see Chapter 19).

BRITISH NORTH AMERICA Although Spain claimed all of North America as part of its American overseas empire, other nations largely ignored its claim. The British argued that "prescription without possession availeth nothing." The Dutch were among the first to establish settlements on the North American continent. Their activities began after 1609 when Henry Hudson, an English explorer hired by the Dutch, discovered the river that bears his name. Within a few years, the Dutch had established the mainland colony of New Netherland, which stretched from the mouth of the Hudson River as far north as Albany, New York. Present-day names such as Staten Island and Harlem remind us that it was the Dutch who initially settled the Hudson River valley. In the second half of the seventeenth century, competition from the English and French and years of warfare with those rivals led to the decline of the Dutch commercial empire. In 1664, the English seized the colony of New Netherland and renamed it New York; soon afterward, the Dutch West India Company went bankrupt.

In the meantime, the English had begun to establish their own colonies in North America. The first permanent English settlement in America was Jamestown, founded in 1607 in modern Virginia. It barely survived, making it evident that the colonizing of American lands was not necessarily conducive to quick profits. But the desire to practice one's own religion, combined with economic interests, could lead to successful colonization, as the Massachusetts Bay Company demonstrated. The Massachusetts colony had 4,000 settlers in its early years but by 1660 had swelled to 40,000. By the end of the seventeenth century, the English had established control over most of the eastern seaboard of the present United States.

British North America came to consist of thirteen colonies. They were thickly populated, containing about 1.5 million people by 1750, and were also prosperous. Supposedly run by the British Board of Trade, the Royal Council, and Parliament, these thirteen colonies had legislatures that tended to act independently. Merchants in such port cities as Boston, Philadelphia, New York, and Charleston resented and resisted regulation from the British government.

The British colonies in both North America and the West Indies were assigned roles in keeping with mercantilist theory (see "Mercantilism" later in this chapter). They provided raw materials for the mother country while buying the latter's manufactured goods. Navigation acts regulated what could be taken from and sold to the colonies. Theoretically, the system was supposed to provide a balance of trade favorable to the mother country.

CHRONOLOGY New Rivals on the World Stage

Portuguese traders land in Japan	1543
British East India Company formed	1600
Dutch East India Company formed	1602
English settlement at Jamestown	1607
Champlain establishes settlement at Quebec	1608
Dutch fort established at Batavia	1619
Dutch seize Malacca from the Portuguese	1641
English seize New Netherland	1664
English establish trading post at Canton	1699
Battle of Plassey	1757
French cede Canada to British	1763
British mission to China	1793

FRENCH NORTH AMERICA The French also established a colonial empire in North America. Already in 1534, the French explorer Jacques Cartier (ZHAK kar-TYAY) had discovered the Saint Lawrence River and laid claim to Canada as a French possession. It was not until 1608, however, when Samuel de Champlain established a settlement at Quebec that the French began to take a more serious interest in Canada as a colony. In 1663, Canada was made the property of the French crown and administered by a French governor like a French province.

French North America was run autocratically as a vast trading area, where valuable furs, leather, fish, and timber were acquired. The inability of the French state to get its people to emigrate to its Canadian possessions, however, left the territory thinly populated. By the mid-eighteenth century, there were only about 15,000 French Canadians, most of whom were hunters, trappers, missionaries, and explorers. The French failed to provide adequate men or money, allowing their European wars to take precedence over the conquest of the North American continent. Already in 1713, by the Treaty of Utrecht, the French began to cede some of their American possessions to their British rival. As a result of the Seven Years' War, they would surrender the rest of their Canadian lands in 1763 (see Chapter 18).

British and French rivalry was also evident in the Spanish and Portuguese colonial empires in Latin America. The decline of Spain and Portugal had led these two states to depend even more on resources from their colonies, and they imposed strict mercantilist rules to keep others out. Spain, for example, tried to limit all trade with its colonies to Spanish ships. But the British and French were too powerful to be excluded. The British cajoled the Portuguese into allowing them into the lucrative Brazilian trade. The French, however, were the first to break into the Spanish Latin American market when the French Bourbons became kings of Spain at the beginning of the eighteenth century. Britain's first entry into Spanish American markets came in 1713, when the British were granted the privilege, known as the *asiento* (ah-SYEN-toh), of transporting 4,500 slaves a year to Spanish Latin America.

The Impact of European Expansion

Q **FOCUS QUESTION:** How did European expansion affect both the conquerors and the conquered?

Between 1500 and 1800, the Atlantic nations of Europe moved into all parts of the world. The first had been Spain and Portugal, the two great colonial powers of the sixteenth century, followed by the Dutch, who built their colonial empire in the seventeenth century as Portugal and Spain declined. The Dutch were soon challenged by the British and French, who outstripped the others in the eighteenth century while becoming involved in a bitter rivalry. By the end of the eighteenth century, it appeared that Great Britain would become the great European imperial power. European expansion made a great impact on both the conquered and the conquerors.

The Conquered

Different regions experienced different effects from the European expansion. The native American civilizations, which had their own unique qualities and a degree of sophistication not much appreciated by Europeans, were virtually destroyed. In addition to devastating losses of population from European diseases, ancient social and political structures were ripped up and replaced by European institutions, religion, language, and culture. In Africa, the real demographic impact of the slave trade is uncertain due to a lack of records; however, estimates of the population in West Africa suggest that the slave trade negated any population growth, rather than causing a decline. Politically and socially, the slave trade encouraged the growth of territories in West Africa, such as Dahomey and Benin, where the leaders waged internal wars to secure more slaves to trade for guns and gunpowder. Without the slave trade, these territories became susceptible to European control in the nineteenth century. The Portuguese trading posts in the East had little direct impact on native Asian civilizations, although Dutch control of the Indonesian archipelago was more pervasive. China and Japan were still little affected by Westerners, although India was subject to ever-growing British encroachment.

In Central and South America, a new civilization arose that we have come to call Latin America. It was a multiracial society. Spanish and Portuguese settlers who arrived in the Western Hemisphere were few in number relative to the native Indians; many of the newcomers were males who not only used female natives for their sexual pleasure but married them as well. Already by 1501, Spanish rulers had authorized intermarriage between Europeans and native American Indians, whose offspring became known as mestizos (mess-TEE-zohz). Another group of people brought to Latin America were the Africans. Over a period of three centuries, possibly as many as 8 million slaves were brought to Spanish and Portuguese America to work the plantations. Africans also contributed to Latin America's multiracial character. Mulattoes (muh-LAH-tohz)—the offspring of Africans and whites—joined mestizos and descendants of whites, Africans, and native Indians to produce a unique society in Latin America. Unlike Europe, and unlike British North America, which remained a largely white offshoot of Europe, Latin America developed a multiracial society with less rigid attitudes about race.

The ecology of the conquered areas was also affected by the European presence. Europeans brought horses and cattle to the Americas, which revolutionized the life of the Indians. Cattle farming supplanted the Indian agricultural practice of growing maize, eventually leading to the development of large estates for raising cattle. South America would later become a great exporter of beef. Europeans also brought new crops, such as wheat and cane sugar, to be cultivated on large plantations by native or imported slave labor. In their trips to other parts of the world, Europeans also carried New World plants with them. Thus, Europeans introduced sweet potatoes and maize (Indian corn) to Africa in the sixteenth century.

CATHOLIC MISSIONARIES Although there were some Protestant missionaries in the world outside Europe, Catholic missionaries were far more active in spreading Christianity. From the beginning of their conquest of the New World, Spanish and Portuguese rulers were determined to Christianize the native peoples. This policy gave the Catholic Church an important role to play in the New World, one that added considerably to church power. Catholic missionaries—especially the Dominicans, Franciscans, and Jesuits—fanned out to different parts of the Spanish Empire.

To facilitate their efforts, missionaries brought Indians together into villages, where the natives could be converted, taught trades, and encouraged to grow crops. These missions enabled the missionaries to control the lives of the Indians and helped ensure that they would remain docile members of the empire (see the box on p. 438 and the Film & History feature on p. 439). Basically, missions benefited the missionaries more than the Indians. In frontier districts such as California and Texas, missions also served as military barriers to foreign encroachment.

The Catholic Church constructed hospitals, orphanages, and schools. Monastic schools instructed Indian students in the rudiments of reading, writing, and arithmetic. The Catholic Church also provided outlets for women other than marriage. Nunneries were places of prayer and quiet contemplation, but women in religious orders, many of them of aristocratic background, often lived well and worked outside their establishments by running schools and hospitals. Indeed, one of these nuns, Sor Juana Inés de la Cruz (SAWR HWAH-nuh ee-NAYSS day lah KROOZ) (1651–1695), was one of seventeenth-century Latin America's best-known literary figures. She wrote poetry and prose and promoted the education of women.

Christian missionaries also made the long voyage to China on European merchant ships. The Jesuits were among the most active and the most effective. Many of

The Mission

In 1609, two Jesuit priests embarked on a missionary calling with the Guaraní Indians in eastern Paraguay. Eventually, the Jesuits established more than thirty missions in the region. Well organized and zealous, the Jesuits transformed their missions into profitable businesses. This description of a Jesuit mission in Paraguay was written by Félix de Azara, a Spanish soldier and scientist.

<hr/>

Félix de Azara, Description and History of Paraguay and Rio de la Plata

Having spoken of the towns founded by the Jesuit fathers, and of the manner in which they were founded, I shall discuss the government which they established in them.... In each town resided two priests, a curate and a subcurate, who had certain assigned functions. The subcurate was charged with all the spiritual tasks, and the curate with every kind of temporal responsibility....

The curate allowed no one to work for personal gain; he compelled everyone, without distinction of age or sex, to work for the community, and he himself saw to it that all were equally fed and dressed. For this purpose the curates placed in storehouses all the fruits of agriculture and the products of industry, selling in the Spanish towns their surplus of cotton, cloth, tobacco, vegetables, skins, and wood, transporting them in their own boats down the nearest rivers, and returning with implements and whatever else was required.

From the foregoing one may infer that the curate disposed of the surplus funds of the Indian towns, and that no Indian could aspire to own private property. This deprived them of any incentive to use reason or talent, since the most industrious, able, and worthy person had the same food, clothing, and pleasures as the most wicked, dull, and indolent. It also follows that although this form of government was well designed to enrich the communities it also caused the Indian to work at a languid pace, since the wealth of his community was of no concern to him.

It must be said that although the Jesuit fathers were supreme in all respects, they employed their authority with a mildness and a restraint that command admiration. They supplied everyone with abundant food and clothing. They compelled the men to work only half a day, and did not drive them to produce more. Even their labor was given a festive air, for they went in procession to the fields, to the sound of music ... and the music did not cease until they had returned in the same way they had set out. They gave them many holidays, dances, and tournaments, dressing the actors and the members of the municipal councils in gold or silver tissue and the most costly European garments, but they permitted the women to act only as spectators.

They likewise forbade the women to sew; this occupation was restricted to the musicians, sacristans, and acolytes. But they made them spin cotton; and the cloth that the Indians wove, after satisfying their own needs, they sold together with the surplus cotton in the Spanish towns, as they did with the tobacco, vegetables, wood, and skins. The curate and his companion, or subcurate, had their own plain dwellings, and they never left them except to take the air in the great enclosed yard of their college. They never walked through the streets of the town or entered the house of any Indian or let themselves be seen by any woman—or indeed, by any man, except for those indispensable few through whom they issued their orders. ⯈

Q How were the missions organized to enable the missionaries to control most aspects of the Indians' lives? Why was this deemed necessary?

<hr/>

the early Jesuit missionaries to China were highly educated men who were familiar with European philosophical and scientific developments. They brought along clocks and various other instruments that impressed Chinese officials and made them more open to Western ideas.

Hsu Kuang-Chi, Memorial to Fra Matteo Ricci (1617)

The Jesuits used this openness to promote Christianity. To make it easier for the Chinese to accept Christianity, the Jesuits pointed to similarities between Christian morality and Confucian ethics. The Italian priest Matteo Ricci described the Jesuit approach:

> In order that the appearance of a new religion might not arouse suspicion among the Chinese people, the Jesuit Fathers did not speak openly about religious matters when they began to appear in public.... They did, however, try to teach this pagan people in a more direct way, namely, by virtue of their example and by the sanctity of their lives. In this way they attempted to win the good will of the people and little by little to dispose their minds to receive what they could not be persuaded to accept by word of mouth.... From the time of their entrance they wore the ordinary Chinese outer garment, which was somewhat similar to their own religious habits; a long robe reaching down to the heels and with very ample sleeves, which are much in favor with the Chinese.[12]

The efforts of the Christian missionaries reached their height in the early eighteenth century. Several hundred Chinese officials became Catholics, as did an estimated 300,000 ordinary Chinese. But ultimately the Christian effort was undermined by squabbling among the religious orders themselves. To make it easier for the Chinese to convert, the Jesuits had allowed the new Catholics to

The Mission (1986)

Directed by Roland Joffé, *The Mission* examines religion, politics, and colonialism in Europe and South America in the mid-eighteenth century. The movie begins with a flashback as Cardinal Altamirano (Ray McAnally) is dictating a letter to the pope to discuss the fate of the Jesuit missions in Paraguay. He begins by describing the establishment of a new Jesuit mission (San Carlos) in Spanish territory in the borderlands of Paraguay and Brazil. Father Gabriel (Jeremy Irons) has been able to win over the Guaraní Indians and create a community based on communal livelihood and property (private property has been abolished). The mission includes dwellings for the Guaraní and a church where they can practice their new faith by learning the Gospel and singing hymns. This small band of Jesuits is joined by Rodrigo Mendozo (Robert De Niro), who has been a slave trader dealing in Indians and now seeks to atone for killing his brother in a fit of jealous rage by joining the community at San Carlos. Won over to Father Gabriel's perspective, he also becomes a member of the Jesuit order. Cardinal Altamirano now travels to the New World, sent by a pope anxious to appease the Portuguese monarch over the activities of the Jesuits. Portuguese settlers in Brazil are eager to use the native people as slaves and to confiscate their communal lands and property. In 1750, when Spain agrees to turn over the Guaraní territory in Paraguay to Portugal, they seize their opportunity. Although the cardinal visits a number of missions, including that of San Carlos, and obviously approves of their accomplishments, his hands are tied by the Portuguese king who is threatening to disband the Jesuit order if the missions are not closed. The cardinal acquiesces, and Portuguese troops are sent to take over the missions. Although Rodrigo and the other Jesuits join the natives in fighting the Portuguese while Father Gabriel refuses to fight, all are massacred. The cardinal returns to Europe, dismayed by the murderous activities of the Portuguese

The Jesuit missionary Father Gabriel (Jeremy Irons) with the Guaraní Indians of Paraguay before their slaughter by Portuguese troops.

but hopeful that the Jesuit order will be spared. All is in vain, however, as the Catholic monarchs of Europe expel the Jesuits from their countries and pressure Pope Clement XIV into disbanding the Jesuit order in 1773.

In its approach to the destruction of the Jesuit missions, *The Mission* clearly exalts the dedication of the Jesuit order and praises its devotion to the welfare of the Indians. The movie ends with a small group of Guaraní children, now all orphans, picking up a few remnants of debris from their destroyed mission and moving off down the river back into the wilderness to escape enslavement. The final words on the screen illuminate the movie's message about the activities of the Europeans who destroyed the native civilizations in their conquest of the Americas: "The Indians of South America are still engaged in a struggle to defend their land and their culture. Many of the priests who, inspired by faith and love, continue to support the rights of the Indians, do so with their lives," a reference to the ongoing struggle in Latin America against regimes that continue to oppress the landless masses.

---

continue the practice of ancestor worship. Jealous Dominicans and Franciscans complained to the pope, who condemned the practice. Soon Chinese authorities began to suppress Christian activities throughout China.

The Jesuits also had some success in Japan, where they converted a number of local nobles. By the end of the sixteenth century, thousands of Japanese on the southernmost islands of Kyushu and Shikoku had become Christians. But the Jesuit practice of destroying local idols and shrines and turning some temples into Christian schools or churches caused a severe reaction. When a new

group of Spanish Franciscans continued the same policies, the government ordered the execution of nine missionaries and a number of their Japanese converts. When missionaries continued to interfere in local politics, Tokugawa Ieyasu expelled all missionaries. Japanese Christians were now persecuted.

The Conquerors

For some Europeans, expansion abroad brought the possibility of obtaining land, riches, and social advancement.

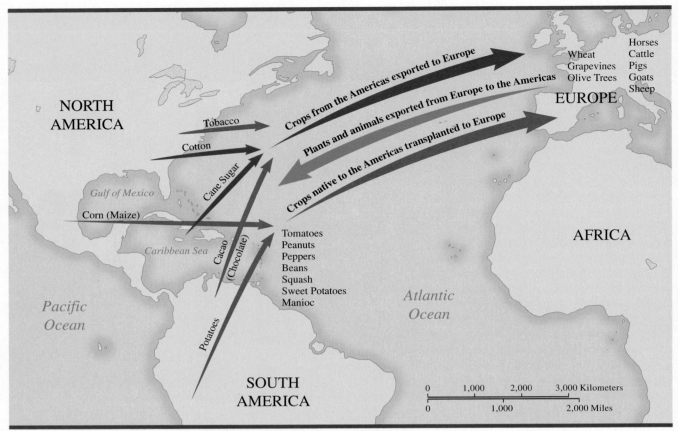

MAP 14.3   The Columbian Exchange. In addition to their diseases, which killed vast numbers of indigenous inhabitants of the Americas, Europeans transplanted many of their crops and domestic animals to the New World. Europeans also imported plants from the New World that increased food production and nutrition in Europe.

Q *Where were the main source regions for native plants imported into Europe?*

One Spaniard commented in 1572 that many "poor young men" had left Spain for Mexico, where they hoped to acquire landed estates and call themselves "gentlemen." Although some wives accompanied their husbands abroad, many ordinary European women found new opportunities for marriage in the New World because of the lack of white women. Indeed, as one commentator bluntly put it, even "a whore, if handsome, [can] make a wife for some rich planter."[13] In the violence-prone world of early Spanish America, a number of women also found themselves rich after their husbands were killed unexpectedly. In one area of Central America, women owned about 25 percent of the landed estates by 1700.

European expansion also had other economic effects on the conquerors. Wherever they went in the New World, Europeans looked for sources of gold and silver. One Aztec commented that the Spanish conquerors "longed and lusted for gold. Their bodies swelled with greed, and their hunger was ravenous; they hungered like pigs for that gold."[14] Rich silver deposits were found and exploited in Mexico and southern Peru (modern Bolivia). When the

mines at Potosí in Peru were opened in 1545, the value of precious metals imported into Europe quadrupled. Between 1503 and 1650, an estimated 16 million kilograms (more than 35 million pounds) of silver and 185,000 kilograms (407,000 pounds) of gold entered the port of Seville and set off a price revolution that affected the Spanish economy.

But gold and silver were only two of the products that became part of the exchange between the New World and the Old. Historians refer to the reciprocal importation and exportation of plants and animals between Europe and the Americas as the **Columbian Exchange** (see Map 14.3). While Europeans were bringing horses, cattle, and wheat to the New World, they were taking new agricultural products such as potatoes, chocolate, corn, tomatoes, and tobacco back to Europe. Potatoes became especially popular as a basic dietary staple in some areas of Europe. High in carbohydrates and rich in vitamins A and C, potatoes could be easily stored for winter use and soon enabled more people to survive on smaller plots of land. This improvement in nutrition was soon reflected in a

NOVA TOTIVS TERRARVM ORBIS GEOGRAPHICA AC HYDROGRAPHICA TABVLA. Auct Henr. Hondio.

A Seventeenth-Century World Map. This beautiful world map was prepared in 1630 by Henricus Hondius. The four portraits are of Caesar, the Roman statesman; Ptolemy, the second-century astronomer; Mercator, the Flemish cartographer whose map projection Hondius followed; and Hondius himself. By comparing this map with the map created by Ptolemy on p. 416, one can see how much Europeans had learned about the shape of the world by the seventeenth century.

rapid increase in population. Other products, such as cochineal, a red dye discovered in Mexico, gave European artists and artisans a "perfect red" for their paintings and cloth.

The European lifestyle was greatly affected by new products from abroad. In addition to new foods, new drinks also appeared in Europe. Chocolate, which had been brought to Spain from Aztec Mexico, became a common drink by 1700. The first coffee and tea houses opened in London in the 1650s and spread rapidly to other parts of Europe. In the eighteenth century, a craze for Chinese furniture and porcelain spread among the upper classes. Chinese ideas would also have an impact on intellectual attitudes (see Chapter 17).

European expansion, which was in part a product of European rivalries, also deepened that competition and increased the tensions among European states. Bitter conflicts arose over the cargoes coming from the New World and Asia. The Anglo-Dutch trade wars and the British-French rivalry over India and North America became part of a new pattern of worldwide warfare in the eighteenth century (see Chapter 18). Bitter rivalries also led to state-sponsored piracy in which governments authorized private captains to attack enemy shipping and keep part of the proceeds for themselves.

In the course of their expansion, Europeans also came to have a new view of the world. When the travels began in the fifteenth century, Europeans were dependent on maps that were often fanciful and inaccurate. Their explorations helped them create new maps that gave a more realistic portrayal of the world, as well as new techniques called map projections that allowed them to represent the round surface of a sphere on a flat piece of paper. The most famous of these is the Mercator projection, the work

of a Flemish cartographer, Gerardus Mercator (juh-RAHR-dus mur-KAY-tur) (1512–1594). A Mercator projection is what mapmakers call a conformal projection. It tries to show the true shape of landmasses, but only in a limited area. On the Mercator projection, the shapes of lands near the equator are quite accurate, but the farther away from the equator they lie, the more exaggerated their size becomes. For example, the island of Greenland on a Mercator projection appears to be larger than the continent of South America. In fact, Greenland is about one-ninth the size of South America. Nevertheless, the Mercator projection was valuable to ship captains. Every straight line on a Mercator projection is a line of true direction, whether north, south, east, or west. For four centuries, ship captains were very grateful to Mercator.

The psychological impact of colonization on the colonizers is awkward to evaluate but hard to deny. Europeans were initially startled by the discovery of new peoples in the Americas. Some deemed them inhuman and thus fit to be exploited for labor. Others, however, found them to be refreshingly natural and as yet untouched by European corruption. But even the latter group still believed that the Indians should be converted—if not forcefully, at least peacefully—to Christianity. Overall, the relatively easy European success in dominating native peoples (be they Africans or Indians) reinforced Christian Europe's belief in the inherent superiority of European civilization and religion. The Scientific Revolution of the seventeenth century (see Chapter 16), the Enlightenment of the eighteenth (see Chapter 17), and the imperialism of the nineteenth (see Chapter 24) would all bolster this Eurocentric perspective, which has pervaded Western civilization's relations with the rest of the world.

Toward a World Economy

Q **FOCUS QUESTION:** What was mercantilism, and what was its relationship to colonial empires?

During the High Middle Ages, Europeans had engaged in a commercial revolution that created new opportunities for townspeople in a basically agrarian economy. Although this commercial thrust was slowed by the devastating crises of the fourteenth century, the beginning of Europe's discovery of the world outside in the fifteenth century led to an even greater burst of commercial activity and the inception of a world market.

Economic Conditions in the Sixteenth Century

Inflation was a major economic problem in the sixteenth and early seventeenth centuries. This so-called **price revolution** was a Europe-wide phenomenon, although different areas were affected at different times. Though the inflation rate was probably a relatively low 2 to 3 percent a year, it was noticeable in a Europe accustomed to stable prices. Foodstuffs were most subject to price increases, especially evident in the price of wheat. An upward surge in wheat prices was first noticed in the Mediterranean area—in Spain, southern France, and Italy—and reached its peak there in the 1590s.

Although precise data are lacking, economic historians believe that as a result of the price revolution, wages failed to keep up with price increases. Wage earners, especially agricultural laborers and salaried workers in urban areas, saw their standard of living drop. At the same time, landed aristocrats, who could raise rents, managed to prosper. Commercial and industrial entrepreneurs also benefited from the price revolution because of rising prices, expanding markets, and relatively cheaper labor costs. Some historians regard this profit inflation as a valuable stimulus to investment and the growth of capitalism, helping to explain the economic expansion and prosperity of the sixteenth century. Governments were likewise affected by inflation. They borrowed heavily from bankers and imposed new tax burdens on their subjects, often stirring additional discontent.

The causes of the price revolution are a subject of much historical debate. Already in the 1560s, European intellectuals had associated the rise in prices with the great influx of precious metals from the New World. Although this view was accepted for a long time, many economic historians now believe that the increase in population in the sixteenth century played an important role in creating inflationary pressures. A growing population increased the demand for land and food and drove up prices for both.

The Growth of Commercial Capitalism

The flourishing European trade of the sixteenth century revolved around three major areas: the Mediterranean in the south, the Low Countries and the Baltic region in the north, and central Europe, whose inland trade depended on the Rhine and Danube rivers. As overseas trade expanded, however, the Atlantic seaboard began to play a more important role, linking the Mediterranean, Baltic, and central European trading areas together and making the whole of Europe into a more integrated market that was all the more vulnerable to price shifts. With their cheaper and faster ships, the Dutch came to monopolize both European and world trade, although they were increasingly challenged by the English and French in the seventeenth century.

The commercial expansion of the sixteenth and seventeenth centuries was made easier by new forms of commercial organization, especially the **joint-stock company.** Individuals bought shares in a company and received dividends on their investment while a board of directors ran the company and made the important business decisions. The return on investments could be spectacular. During its first ten years, investors received 30 percent on their money from the Dutch East India Company, which opened the Spice Islands and Southeast Asia to Dutch activity. The joint-stock company made it easier to raise large amounts of capital for world trading ventures.

Enormous profits were also being made in shipbuilding and in mining and metallurgy, where technological innovations, such as the use of pumps and new methods of extracting metals from ores, proved highly successful. The mining industry was closely tied to sixteenth-century family banking firms. In exchange for arranging large loans to Charles V, Jacob Fugger was given a monopoly over silver, copper, and mercury mines in the Habsburg possessions of central Europe that produced profits in excess of 50 percent per year. Though these close relationships between governments and entrepreneurs could lead to stunning successes, they could also be precarious. The House of Fugger went bankrupt at the end of the sixteenth century when the Habsburgs defaulted on their loans.

By the seventeenth century, the traditional family banking firms were no longer able to supply the numerous services needed for the expanding commercial capitalism. New institutions arose to take their place. The city of Amsterdam created the Bank of Amsterdam in 1609 as both a deposit and a transfer institution and the Amsterdam Bourse, or Exchange, where the trading of stocks replaced the exchange of goods. By the first half of the seventeenth century, the Amsterdam Exchange had emerged as the hub of the European business world, just as Amsterdam itself had replaced Antwerp as the greatest commercial and banking center of Europe.

Despite the growth of commercial capitalism, most of the European economy still depended on an agricultural system that had experienced few changes since the thirteenth century. At least 80 percent of Europeans still worked on the land. Almost all of the peasants of western Europe were free of serfdom, although many still owed a variety of feudal dues to the nobility. Despite the expanding

Jacob Fugger the Rich. Jacob Fugger, head of one of the wealthiest banking firms of the sixteenth century, is pictured here with his faithful secretary, Matthaus Schwartz, who painted this scene in 1516. The cabinet in the background lists the names of the cities where Fugger's firm had branch offices, including Milan, Innsbruck, Nuremberg, and Lisbon.

markets and rising prices, European peasants saw little or no improvement in their lot as they faced increased rents and fees and higher taxes imposed by the state. In eastern Europe, the peasants' position even worsened as they were increasingly tied to the land in a new serfdom enforced by powerful landowners (see Chapter 15).

Mercantilism

Mercantilism is the name historians use to identify a set of economic tendencies that came to dominate economic practices in the seventeenth century. Fundamental to mercantilism was the belief that the total volume of trade was unchangeable. Therefore, states protected their economies by following certain practices: hoarding precious metals, implementing protectionist trade policies, promoting colonial development, increasing shipbuilding, supporting trading companies, and encouraging the manufacturing of products to be used in trade.

According to the mercantilists, the prosperity of a nation depended on a plentiful supply of bullion (gold and silver).

For this reason, it was desirable to achieve a favorable balance of trade in which goods exported were of greater value than those imported, promoting an influx of gold and silver payments that would increase the quantity of bullion. Furthermore, to encourage exports, governments should stimulate and protect export industries and trade by granting trade monopolies, encouraging investment in new industries through subsidies, importing foreign artisans, and improving transportation systems by building roads, bridges, and canals. By imposing high tariffs on foreign goods, they could be kept out of the country and prevented from competing with domestic industries. Colonies were also deemed valuable as sources of raw materials and markets for finished goods.

The mercantilists also focused on the role of the state, believing that state intervention in some aspects of the economy was desirable for the sake of the national good. Government regulations to ensure the superiority of export goods, the construction of roads and canals, and the granting of subsidies to create trade companies were all predicated on government involvement in economic affairs.

Overseas Trade and Colonies: Movement Toward Globalization

Mercantilist theory on the role of colonies was matched in practice by Europe's overseas expansion. With the development of colonies and trading posts in the Americas and the East, Europeans embarked on an adventure in international commerce in the seventeenth century. Although some historians speak of a nascent world economy, we should remember that local, regional, and intra-European trade still predominated. At the end of the seventeenth century, for example, English imports totaled 360,000 tons, but only 5,000 tons came from the East Indies. About one-tenth of English and Dutch exports were shipped across the Atlantic; slightly more went to the East. What made the transoceanic trade rewarding, however, was not the volume but the value of its goods. Dutch, English, and French merchants were bringing back products that were still consumed largely by the wealthy but were beginning to make their way into the lives of artisans and merchants. Pepper and spices from the Indies, West Indian and Brazilian sugar, and Asian coffee and tea were becoming more readily available to European consumers.

Trade within Europe remained strong throughout the eighteenth century as wheat, timber, and naval stores from the Baltic, wines from France, wool and fruit from Spain, and silk from Italy were exchanged along with a host of other products. But this trade increased only slightly while overseas trade boomed. From 1716 to 1789, total French exports quadrupled; intra-European trade, which constituted 75 percent of these exports in 1716, accounted for only 50 percent of the total in 1789. This increase in overseas trade has led some historians to proclaim the emergence of a truly global economy in the eighteenth century. Trade patterns now interlocked Europe, Africa, the East, and the Americas.

CHAPTER SUMMARY

At the end of the fifteenth century, Europeans sailed out into the world in all directions. Beginning in the mid-fifteenth century with the handful of Portuguese ships that ventured southward along the West African coast, bringing back slaves and gold, the process of European expansion accelerated with the epochal voyages of Christopher Columbus to the Americas and Vasco da Gama to the Indian Ocean in the 1490s. The Portuguese Empire was based on trade; Portugal's population was too small for it to establish large colonies. But Spain had greater resources: Spanish conquistadors overthrew both the Aztec and Inca Empires, and Spain created two major administrative units in New Spain and Peru that subjected the native population to Spanish control. Catholic missionaries, under the control of the Spanish crown, brought Christianity, including cathedrals and schools.

Soon a number of other European peoples, including the Dutch, British, and French, had joined in the process of expansion, and by the end of the eighteenth century, they had created a global trade network dominated by Western ships and Western power. Although originally less prized than gold and spices, slaves became a major object of trade, and by the nineteenth century 10 million African slaves had been shipped to the Americas. Slavery was common in Africa, and the African terminus of the trade was in the hands of the Africans, but the insatiable demand for slaves led to increased warfare on that unfortunate continent. It was not until the late 1700s that slavery came under harsh criticism in Europe.

In less than three hundred years, the European age of exploration had changed the shape of the world. In some areas, such as the Americas and the Spice Islands in Asia, it led to the destruction of indigenous civilizations and the establishment of European colonies. In others, such as Africa, India, and mainland Southeast Asia, it left native regimes intact but had a strong impact on local societies and regional trade patterns. Japan and China were least affected.

At the time, many European observers viewed the process in a favorable light. They believed that it not only expanded wealth through world trade and exchanged crops and discoveries between the Old World and the New, but also introduced "heathen peoples" to the message of Jesus. No doubt, the conquest of the Americas and expansion into the rest of the world brought out the worst and some of the best of European civilization. The greedy plundering of resources and the brutal repression and enslavement were hardly balanced by attempts to create new institutions, convert the natives to Christianity, and foster the rights of the indigenous peoples. In any event, Europeans had begun to change the face of the world and increasingly saw their culture, with its religion, languages, and technology, as a coherent force to be exported to all corners of the world.

CHAPTER REVIEW

Upon Reflection

Q How did the experiences of the Spanish and Portuguese during the age of exploration differ from those of their French, Dutch, and English counterparts?

Q What role did religion play as a motivation in the age of exploration? Was it as important a motive as economics? Why or why not?

Q Why and how did Japan succeed in keeping Europeans largely away from its territory in the seventeenth century?

Key Terms

portolani (p. 415)
conquistadors (p. 420)
encomienda (p. 424)
viceroy (p. 425)
audiencias (p. 425)

triangular trade (p. 426)
Middle Passage (p. 426)
Columbian Exchange (p. 440)
price revolution (p. 442)
joint-stock company (p. 442)
mercantilism (p. 443)

Suggestions for Further Reading

GENERAL WORKS For general accounts of European discovery and expansion, see **G. V. Scammell, *The First Imperial Age: European Overseas Expansion, c. 1400–1715*** (London, 1989); **D. Arnold, *Age of Discovery*,** 2nd ed. (London, 2002); and **G. J. Ames, *The Globe Encompassed: The Age of European Discovery, 1500–1700*** (Upper Saddle River, N.J., 2007). On European perceptions of the world outside Europe, see **M. Campbell, *The Witness and the Other World: Exotic European Travel Writing, 400–1600*** (Ithaca, N.Y., 1991). On the technological aspects, see **R. C. Smith, *Vanguard of Empire: Ships of Exploration in the Age of Columbus*** (Oxford, 1993).

CHAPTER TIMELINE

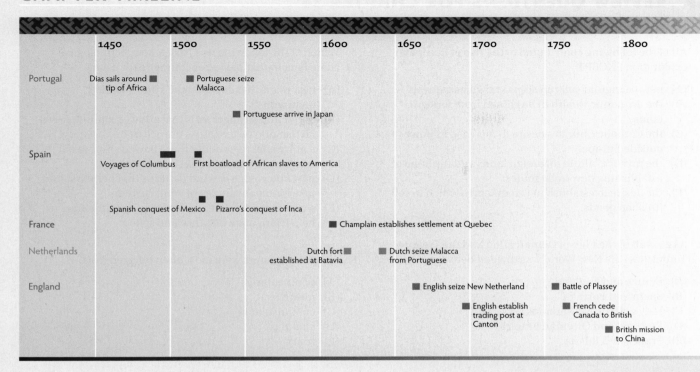

	1450	1500	1550	1600	1650	1700	1750	1800
Portugal	■ Dias sails around tip of Africa	■ Portuguese seize Malacca	■ Portuguese arrive in Japan					
Spain	■ Voyages of Columbus	■ First boatload of African slaves to America						
		■ Spanish conquest of Mexico ■ Pizarro's conquest of Inca						
France				■ Champlain establishes settlement at Quebec				
Netherlands			■ Dutch fort established at Batavia	■ Dutch seize Malacca from Portuguese				
England					■ English seize New Netherland ■ English establish trading post at Canton		■ Battle of Plassey ■ French cede Canada to British ■ British mission to China	

PORTUGUESE AND SPANISH EXPANSION On Portuguese expansion, see **M. Newitt, *A History of Portuguese Overseas Expansion*** (London, 2004). On Columbus, see **W. D. Phillips** and **C. R. Phillips, *The Worlds of Christopher Columbus*** (Cambridge, 1992). On the Spanish Empire in the New World, see **H. Kamen, *Empire: How Spain Became a World Power, 1492–1763*** (New York, 2003). For a theoretical discussion of violence and gender in America, see **R. Trexler, *Sex and Conquest: Gendered Violence, Political Order, and the European Conquest of the Americas*** (Ithaca, N.Y., 1995). On the destructive nature of the Spanish conquest of the Americas, see **D. E. Standard, *American Holocaust: Columbus and the Conquest of the New World*** (New York, 1993). For a revisionist view of the Spanish conquest of the Americas, see **M. Restall, *Seven Myths of the Spanish Conquest*** (Oxford, 2003).

MERCANTILE EMPIRES AND WORLDWIDE TRADE The subject of mercantile empires and worldwide trade is covered in **J. D. Tracy, *The Rise of Merchant Empires: Long-Distance Trade in the Early Modern World, 1350–1750*** (Cambridge, 1990); **J. H. Elliott, *Empires of the Atlantic World*** (New Haven, Conn., 2006); and **M. J. Seymour, *Transformation of the North Atlantic World, 1492–1763*** (Westport, Conn., 2004). See also **A. Grafton et al., *New Worlds, Ancient Texts: The Power of Tradition and the Shock of Discovery*** (Cambridge, Mass., 2005). On the African slave trade, see **H. Thomas, *The Slave Trade: The Story of the Atlantic Slave Trade, 1440–1870*** (New York, 1997); **M. Rediker, *The Slave Ship: A Human History*** (New York, 2007); and **J. K. Thornton, *Africa and Africans in the Making of the Atlantic World, 1400–1800*** (Cambridge, 1998).

IMPACT OF EXPANSION The impact of expansion on European consciousness is explored in **A. Pagden, *European Encounters with the New World: From Renaissance to Romanticism*** (New Haven, Conn., 1993). On the impact of disease, see **N. D. Cook, *Born to Die: Disease and the New World*** (New York, 1998). The human and ecological effects of the interaction of New World and Old World cultures are examined thoughtfully in **A. W. Crosby, *The Columbian Exchange: Biological and Cultural Consequences of 1492*** (Westport, Conn., 1972) and ***Ecological Imperialism: The Biological Expansion of Europe*** (New York, 1986). The native American female experience with the European encounter is presented in **R. Gutierrez, *When Jesus Came the Corn Mother Went Away: Marriage, Sexuality, and Power in New Mexico, 1500–1846*** (Stanford, Calif., 1991).

ECONOMIC DIMENSIONS OF EXPANSION On mercantilism, see **L. Magnusson, *Mercantilism: The Shaping of an Economic Language*** (New York, 1994). On the concept of a world economy, see **A. K. Smith, *Creating a World Economy: Merchant Capital, Colonialism, and World Trade, 1400–1825*** (Boulder, Colo., 1991). ⟩⟨

CourseMate

Visit the CourseMate website at www.cengagebrain.com for additional study tools and review materials for this chapter.

AP* REVIEW QUESTIONS FOR CHAPTER 14

1. All of the following contributed to the rise of European exploration EXCEPT

   (A) new triangular sails on ships known as caravels.
   (B) the economic wealth to be gained from foreign lands.
   (C) the Catholic Church's desire to increase its power outside Europe.
   (D) the mystical allure of foreign lands and the hope of establishing new trade routes.
   (E) the desire to establish new markets in which to sell finished goods.

2. As a result of the Line of Demarcation and the Treaty of Tordesillas, the New World was divided between

   (A) France and England.
   (B) Spain and Portugal.
   (C) Italy and the Netherlands.
   (D) Portugal and Ottoman Empire.
   (E) France and Russia.

3. Contact between Europeans and natives of the New World involved all of the following EXCEPT

   (A) Europeans brought diseases such as smallpox that eventually decimated the native populations.
   (B) the explorers pillaged and plundered gold and other treasures from the natives.
   (C) European explorers and settlers enslaved the natives.
   (D) the natives faced forced conversion to Catholicism.
   (E) Europeans brought with them new animals, such as horses, to help the natives.

4. Which of the following best illustrates the concept of mercantilism?

   (A) An individual is allowed to establish economic control over a geographic area in return for sharing any profit with the state.
   (B) A nation allows a joint-stock company to extract resources from its colonies in order to increase the wealth of both the company and the nation.
   (C) A nation's government does not intervene in the economic affairs of a colony.
   (D) A joint-stock company allows its nation's government to extract natural resources from a colony for the purpose of geopolitical dominance.
   (E) A nation supplies its colony with natural resources in order to enhance the wealth of the colony.

5. Which of the following was NOT a new technological achievement that helped encourage expansion?

   (A) new maps that depicted the known world's continents
   (B) better and stronger sails that allowed ships to travel farther and faster across the ocean
   (C) a more effective rudder that allowed ships to cut into currents more easily
   (D) new knowledge of wind patterns that helped sailors take better advantage of wind currents
   (E) a new compass that aligned maps with the stars to help triangulate distance and speed

6. Spanish explorers were most often referred to as

   (A) peninsulares.
   (B) mestizos.
   (C) conquistadors.
   (D) cholulas.
   (E) friars.

7. The statement "the Negro is put in chains and led aboard the vessel, where he meets his fellow sufferers. . . . and the Negroes are chained in a hold of the ship, a kind of lugubrious prison" most likely refers to what?

   (A) the triangular trade
   (B) the Middle Passage
   (C) the first European contact with the Africans
   (D) the establishment of trade with the New World
   (E) the African slave trade

8. All of the following were exploring countries during the sixteenth century EXCEPT

   (A) England.
   (B) France.
   (C) Italy.
   (D) the Netherlands.
   (E) Spain.

9. Under the *encomienda* system

   (A) natives were basically forced into slavery by the Spanish.
   (B) natives were granted freedom from servitude.
   (C) Africans were traded in return for supplies.
   (D) the Catholic Church was given more power over the affairs of the New World.
   (E) new governments were established to end tribal control and replace it with Spanish rulers.

10. The Columbian Exchange involved exchanges such as

(A) smallpox from North America and syphilis from Europe.
(B) native plants from North America for wheat and goats from Europe.
(C) pigs and cattle from North America for cotton and corn from Europe.
(D) slaves from Africa to the New World, and peanuts and squash from Europe.
(E) horses and wheat from North America for tobacco and sweet potatoes from Europe.

11. Jesuit missionaries spread Catholicism to

(A) India, Africa, and Latin America.
(B) Europe, the Middle East, and China.
(C) Japan, China, and the New World.
(D) Australia, Central America, and Europe.
(E) Germany, Norway, and England.

12. The price revolution that affected western Europe during the latter half of the sixteenth century is associated with

(A) the manufacture of more affordable goods for the common people.
(B) political revolutions in Spain and Portugal.
(C) a sharp decline in droughts and famines.
(D) the influx of bullion from across the Atlantic.
(E) the rise in economic prominence of France.

13. Which of the following combinations correctly matches a European colonial power with its foreign holdings?

(A) Great Britain—North America, India, Japan
(B) Spain—Central America, Africa, China
(C) Portugal—South America, East Africa, and Southeast Asia
(D) Holy Roman Empire—South Africa, Australia, Malaysia
(E) France—North America, China, South America

14. During the early decades of the fifteenth century, European technological supremacy was arguably surpassed by

(A) the African empire of Mali.
(B) the Mongols of Central Asia.
(C) Ming China.
(D) feudal Japan.
(E) indigenous societies of North America.

15. Which of the following best describes the experience of Africans in the New World during the sixteenth century?

(A) They were used for the sole purpose of developing cotton plantations in North America.
(B) They were primarily used as domestic servants in wealthy European homes.
(C) They were used as foot soldiers during colonial disputes.
(D) They were the primary source of labor for the sugar plantations in Latin America.
(E) They were brought to the New World and then shipped to Europe in the triangular trade.

Nicolas-René Jollain the Elder's portrait of Louis XIV captures the king's sense of royal grandeur.

State Building and the Search for Order in the Seventeenth Century

CHAPTER OUTLINE AND FOCUS QUESTIONS

Social Crises, War, and Rebellions

Q What economic, social, and political crises did Europe experience in the first half of the seventeenth century?

The Practice of Absolutism: Western Europe

Q What was absolutism in theory, and how did its actual practice in France reflect or differ from the theory?

Absolutism in Central, Eastern, and Northern Europe

Q What developments enabled Brandenburg-Prussia, Austria, and Russia to emerge as major powers in the seventeenth century?

Limited Monarchy and Republics

Q What were the main issues in the struggle between king and Parliament in seventeenth-century England, and how were they resolved?

The Flourishing of European Culture

Q How did the artistic and literary achievements of this era reflect the political and economic developments of the period?

CRITICAL THINKING

Q What theories of government were proposed by Jacques Bossuet, Thomas Hobbes, and John Locke, and how did their respective theories reflect concerns and problems of the seventeenth century?

BY THE END of the sixteenth century, Europe was beginning to experience a decline in religious passions and a growing secularization that affected both the political and intellectual worlds (on the intellectual effect, see Chapter 16). Some historians like to speak of the seventeenth century as a turning point in the evolution of a modern state system in Europe. The ideal of a united Christian Europe gave way to the practical realities of a system of secular states in which matters of state took precedence over the salvation of subjects' souls. By the seventeenth century, the credibility of Christianity had been so weakened through religious wars that more and more Europeans came to think of politics in secular terms.

One of the responses to the religious wars and other crises of the time was a yearning for order. As the internal social and political rebellions and revolts died down, it became apparent that the privileged classes of society—the aristocrats—remained in control, although the various states exhibited important differences in political forms. The most general trend saw an extension of monarchical power as a stabilizing force. This development, which historians have called absolute monarchy or absolutism, was most evident in France during the flamboyant reign of Louis XIV, regarded by some as the perfect embodiment of an absolute monarch. In his memoirs, the duc de Saint-Simon, who had firsthand experience of French court life, said that Louis was "the very figure of a hero, so imbued with a natural but most imposing majesty that it appeared even in his most insignificant gestures and movements." The king's natural grace gave him a special charm as well: "He was as dignified and majestic in his dressing gown as when dressed in robes of state, or on horseback at the head of his troops." He spoke well and learned quickly. He was naturally kind and "loved truth, justice, order, and reason." His life was orderly: "Nothing could be regulated with greater exactitude than were his days and hours." His self-control was impeccable: "He did not lose control of himself ten times in his whole life, and then only with inferior persons." But even absolute monarchs had imperfections, and Saint-Simon had the courage to point them out: "Louis XIV's vanity was without limit or restraint," which led to his "distaste for all merit, intelligence, education, and, most of all, for all independence of character and sentiment in others," as well as "to mistakes of judgment in matters of importance."

But absolutism was not the only response to the search for order in the seventeenth century. Other states, such as England, reacted differently to domestic crisis, and another very different system emerged in which monarchs were limited by the power of their representative assemblies. Absolute and limited monarchy were the two poles of seventeenth-century state building.

Social Crises, War, and Rebellions

 FOCUS QUESTION: What economic, social, and political crises did Europe experience in the first half of the seventeenth century?

The inflation-fueled prosperity of the sixteenth century showed signs of slackening by the beginning of the seventeenth. Economic contraction was evident in some parts of Europe in the 1620s. In the 1630s and 1640s, as imports of silver from the Americas declined, economic recession intensified, especially in the Mediterranean area. Once the industrial and financial center of Europe in the Renaissance, Italy was now becoming an economic backwater. Spain's economy was also seriously failing by the 1640s.

Population trends of the sixteenth and seventeenth centuries also reveal Europe's worsening conditions. The sixteenth century was a period of expanding population, possibly related to a warmer climate and increased food supplies. It has been estimated that the population of Europe increased from 60 million in 1500 to 85 million by 1600, the first major recovery of European population since the devastation of the Black Death in the mid-fourteenth century. Records also indicate a leveling off of the population by 1620, however, and even a decline by 1650, especially in central and southern Europe. Only the Dutch, English, and French grew in number in the first half of the seventeenth century. Europe's longtime adversaries—war, famine, and plague—continued to affect population levels. After the middle of the sixteenth century, another "little ice age," when average temperatures fell, affected harvests and caused famines. These problems created social tensions that came to a boil in the witchcraft craze.

The Witchcraft Craze

Hysteria over witchcraft affected the lives of many Europeans in the sixteenth and seventeenth centuries. Witchcraft trials were held in England, Scotland, Switzerland, Germany, some parts of France and the Low Countries, and even New England in America.

Witchcraft was not a new phenomenon. Its practice had been part of traditional village culture for centuries, but it came to be viewed as both sinister and dangerous when the medieval church began to connect witches to the activities of the devil, thereby transforming witchcraft into a heresy that had to be wiped out. After the establishment of the Inquisition in the thirteenth century, some people were accused of a variety of witchcraft practices and, following the biblical injunction "Thou shalt not suffer a witch to live," were turned over to secular authorities for burning at the stake or, in England, hanging.

THE SPREAD OF WITCHCRAFT What distinguished witchcraft in the sixteenth and seventeenth centuries from these previous developments was the increased number of trials and executions of presumed witches. Perhaps more than 100,000 people were prosecuted throughout Europe on charges of witchcraft. As more and more people were brought to trial, the fear of witches as well as the fear of being accused of witchcraft escalated to frightening proportions. Although larger cities were affected first, the trials also spread to smaller towns and rural areas as the hysteria persisted well into the seventeenth century (see the box on p. 448).

The accused witches usually confessed to a number of practices, most often after intense torture. But even when people confessed voluntarily, certain practices stand out. Many said that they had sworn allegiance to the devil and attended sabbats or nocturnal gatherings where they feasted, danced, and even copulated with the devil in sexual orgies. More common, however, were admissions of using evil incantations and special ointments and powders to wreak havoc on neighbors by killing their livestock, injuring their children, or raising storms to destroy their crops.

A number of contributing factors have been suggested to explain why the witchcraft frenzy became so widespread in the sixteenth and seventeenth centuries. Religious uncertainties clearly played some part. Many witchcraft trials occurred in areas where Protestantism had been recently victorious or in regions, such as southwestern Germany, where Protestant-Catholic controversies still raged. As religious passions became inflamed, accusations of being in league with the devil became common on both sides.

Recently, however, historians have emphasized the importance of social conditions, especially the problems of

A Witchcraft Trial in France

Persecutions for witchcraft reached their high point in the sixteenth and seventeenth centuries when tens of thousands of people were brought to trial. In this excerpt from the minutes of a trial in France in 1652, we can see why the accused witch stood little chance of exonerating herself.

⊷ ⊰≣⊱ ⊶

The Trial of Suzanne Gaudry

28 May, 1652.... Interrogation of Suzanne Gaudry, prisoner at the court of Rieux.... [During interrogations on May 28 and May 29, the prisoner confessed to a number of activities involving the devil.]

Deliberation of the Court—June 3, 1652

The undersigned advocates of the Court have seen these interrogations and answers. They say that the aforementioned Suzanne Gaudry confesses that she is a witch, that she had given herself to the devil, that she had renounced God, Lent, and baptism, that she has been marked on the shoulder, that she has cohabited with the devil and that she has been to the dances, confessing only to have cast a spell upon and caused to die a beast of Philippe Corniè....

Third Interrogation—June 27

This prisoner being led into the chamber, she was examined to know if things were not as she had said and confessed at the beginning of her imprisonment.

—Answers no, and that what she has said was done so by force.

Pressed to say the truth, that otherwise she would be subjected to torture, having pointed out to her that her aunt was burned for this same subject.

—Answers that she is not a witch....

She was placed in the hands of the officer in charge of torture, throwing herself on her knees, struggling to cry, uttering several exclamations, without being able, nevertheless to shed a tear. Saying at every moment that she is not a witch.

The Torture

On this same day, being at the place of torture.

This prisoner, before being strapped down, was admonished to maintain herself in her first confessions and to renounce her lover.

—Says that she denies everything she has said, and that she has no lover. Feeling herself being strapped down, says that she is not a witch, while struggling to cry ... and upon being asked why she confessed to being one, said that she was forced to say it.

Told that she was not forced, that on the contrary she declared herself to be a witch without any threat.

—Says that she confessed it and that she is not a witch, and being a little stretched [on the rack] screams ceaselessly that she is not a witch....

Asked if she did not confess that she had been a witch for twenty-six years.

—Says that she said it, that she retracts it, crying that she is not a witch.

Asked if she did not make Philippe Corniè's horse die, as she confessed.

—Answers no, crying Jesus-Maria, that she is not a witch.

The mark having been probed by the officer, in the presence of Doctor Bouchain, it was adjudged by the aforesaid doctor and officer truly to be the mark of the devil.

Being more tightly stretched upon the torture-rack, urged to maintain her confessions.

—Said that it was true that she is a witch and that she would maintain what she had said.

Asked how long she has been in subjugation to the devil.

—Answers that it was twenty years ago that the devil appeared to her, being in her lodgings in the form of a man dressed in a little cow-hide and black breeches....

Verdict

July 9, 1652. In the light of the interrogations, answers and investigations made into the charge against Suzanne Gaudry, ... seeing by her own confessions that she is said to have made a pact with the devil, received the mark from him, ... and that following this, she had renounced God, Lent, and baptism and had let herself be known carnally by him, in which she received satisfaction. Also, seeing that she is said to have been a part of nocturnal carols and dances.

For expiation of which the advice of the undersigned is that the office of Rieux can legitimately condemn the aforesaid Suzanne Gaudry to death, tying her to a gallows, and strangling her to death, then burning her body and burying it here in the environs of the woods. ⊱

Q Why were women, particularly older women, especially vulnerable to accusations of witchcraft? What "proofs" are offered here that Suzanne Gaudry had consorted with the devil? What does this account tell us about the spread of witchcraft accusations in the seventeenth century?

a society in turmoil, in explaining the witchcraft hysteria. At a time when the old communal values that stressed working together for the good of the community were disintegrating before the onslaught of a new economic ethic that emphasized looking out for oneself, property owners became more fearful of the growing numbers of poor in their midst and transformed them psychologically into agents of the devil. Old women were particularly susceptible to suspicion. Many of them, no longer the recipients of the local charity available in traditional society, may even have tried to survive by selling herbs, potions, or secret remedies for healing. When problems arose—and there were many in this crisis-laden period—these women were handy scapegoats.

That women should be the chief victims of witchcraft trials was hardly accidental. Nicholas Rémy, a witchcraft judge in France in the 1590s, found it "not unreasonable that this scum of humanity [witches] should be drawn chiefly from the feminine sex." To another judge, it came as no surprise that witches would confess to sexual experiences with Satan: "The Devil uses them so, because he knows that women love carnal pleasures, and he means to bind them to his allegiance by such agreeable provocations."[1] Of course, witch hunters were not the only ones who held women in such low esteem. Most theologians, lawyers, and philosophers in early modern Europe believed in the natural inferiority of women and thus would have found it plausible that women would be more susceptible to witchcraft.

DECLINE By the mid-seventeenth century, the witchcraft hysteria began to subside. The destruction caused by the religious wars had forced people to accept at least a grudging toleration, tempering religious passions. Moreover, as governments began to stabilize after the period of crisis, fewer magistrates were willing to accept the unsettling and divisive conditions generated by the trials of witches. Finally, by the turn of the eighteenth century, more and more educated people were questioning traditional attitudes toward religion and finding it contrary to reason to believe in the old view of a world haunted by evil spirits.

The Thirty Years' War

Although many Europeans responded to the upheavals of the second half of the sixteenth century with a desire for peace and order, the first fifty years of the seventeenth century continued to be plagued by crises. A devastating war that affected much of Europe and rebellions seemingly everywhere protracted the atmosphere of disorder and violence.

BACKGROUND TO THE WAR Religion, especially the struggle between militant Catholicism and militant Calvinism, played an important role in the outbreak of the Thirty Years' War (1618–1648), often called the "last of the religious wars." As the war progressed, however, it became increasingly clear that secular, dynastic-nationalist considerations were far more important. Although much of the fighting in the Thirty Years' War took place in the Germanic lands of the Holy Roman Empire, it became a Europe-wide struggle (see Map 15.1). In fact, some historians view it as part of a larger conflict for European leadership between the Bourbon dynasty of France and the Habsburg dynasties of Spain and the Holy Roman Empire and date it from 1609 to 1659.

The Peace of Augsburg in 1555 had brought an end to religious warfare between German Catholics and Lutherans. Religion, however, continued to play a divisive role in German life as Lutherans and Catholics persisted in vying for control of various principalities. In addition, although the treaty had not recognized the rights of Calvinists, a number of German states had adopted Calvinism as their state church. At the beginning of the seventeenth century, the Calvinist ruler of the Palatinate, the Elector Palatine Frederick IV, assumed the leadership in forming a league of German Protestant states called the Protestant Union. To counteract it, the Catholic League of German states was organized by Duke Maximilian of the south German state of Bavaria. By 1609, then, Germany was dividing into two armed camps in anticipation of religious war.

The religious division was exacerbated by a constitutional issue. The desire of the Habsburg emperors to consolidate their authority in the Holy Roman Empire was resisted by the princes, who fought for their "German liberties," their constitutional rights and prerogatives as individual rulers. To pursue their policies, the Habsburg emperors looked to Spain (ruled by another branch of the family) for assistance while the princes turned to the enemies of Spain, especially France, for help against the emperors. The divisions in the Holy Roman Empire and Europe made it almost inevitable that if war did erupt, it would be widespread and difficult to stop.

THE BOHEMIAN PHASE Historians have traditionally divided the Thirty Years' War into four major phases. The Bohemian phase (1618–1625) began in one of the Habsburgs' own territories. In 1617, the Bohemian Estates (primarily the nobles) accepted the Habsburg Archduke Ferdinand as their king but soon found themselves unhappy with their choice. Though many of the nobles were Calvinists, Ferdinand was a devout Catholic who began a process of re-Catholicizing Bohemia and strengthening royal power. The Protestant nobles rebelled against Ferdinand in May 1618 and proclaimed their resistance by throwing two of the Habsburg governors and a secretary out of the window of the royal castle in Prague, the seat of Bohemian government. The Catholic side claimed that their seemingly miraculous escape from death in the 70-foot fall from the castle was due to the intercession of the Virgin Mary, while Protestants pointed out that they fell into a manure pile. The Bohemian rebels now seized control of Bohemia, deposed Ferdinand, and elected as his replacement the Protestant ruler of the Palatinate, Elector Frederick V, who was also the head of the Protestant Union.

Ferdinand, who in the meantime had been elected Holy Roman Emperor, refused to accept his deposition. Realizing that the election of Frederick V, if allowed to stand, could upset the balance of religious and political power in central Europe and give the Protestant forces greater control of the Holy Roman Empire, Ferdinand sought the aid of the imposing forces of Duke Maximilian of Bavaria and the Catholic League. With their help, the imperial

MAP 15.1 The Thirty Years' War. The conflict began in the German states as Europe's major powers backed either the northern Protestant Union or the southern Catholic League. As the war progressed, religion receded in importance, replaced by a dynastic struggle between the French Bourbons and the Spanish and Austrian Habsburgs.

Q *Compare this map with Map 13.2. Which countries engaged in the war were predominantly Protestant, which were predominantly Catholic, and which were mixed?*

View an animated version of this map or related maps on the CourseMate website.

forces defeated Frederick and the Bohemian nobles at the Battle of White Mountain outside Prague on November 8, 1620. Spanish troops took advantage of Frederick's predicament by invading the Palatinate and conquering it by the end of 1622. The unfortunate Frederick fled into exile in the United Provinces. The Spanish took control of the western part of the Palatinate (to gain the access route from Italy to the Netherlands that they had wanted), and Maximilian of Bavaria took the rest of the territory. Reestablished as king of Bohemia, Emperor Ferdinand declared Bohemia a hereditary Habsburg possession, confiscated the land of the Protestant nobles, and established Catholicism as the sole religion. The Spanish renewed their attack on the Dutch, and the forces of Catholicism seemed on the road to victory. But the war was far from over.

THE DANISH PHASE The second phase of the war, the Danish phase (1625–1629), began when King Christian IV of Denmark (1588–1648), a Lutheran, intervened on behalf of the Protestant cause by leading an army into northern Germany. Christian had made an anti-Habsburg and anti-Catholic alliance with the United Provinces and England. He also wanted, however, to gain possession of some Catholic territories in northern Germany to benefit his family.

In the meantime, Ferdinand had gained a new commander for the imperial forces in Albrecht von Wallenstein (AWL-brekht fun VAHL-en-shtyn). A brilliant and enigmatic commander, Wallenstein was a Bohemian nobleman who had taken advantage of Ferdinand's victory to become the country's wealthiest landowner. Wallenstein's forces defeated a Protestant army at Dessau and then continued to operate in northern Germany. The forces of Christian IV, despite substantial aid from their allies, were defeated in 1626 by an army of the Catholic League under Count Tilly and then suffered an even more devastating loss to Wallenstein's forces the following year. Wallenstein now occupied parts of northern Germany, including the Baltic ports of Hamburg, Lübeck, and Bremen. Christian IV's defeat meant the end of Danish supremacy in the Baltic.

After the success of the imperial armies, Emperor Ferdinand II was at the height of his power and took this opportunity to issue the Edict of Restitution in March 1629. His proclamation prohibited Calvinist worship and restored to the Catholic Church all property taken by Protestant princes or cities during the past seventy-five years. But this sudden growth in the power of the Habsburg emperor frightened many German princes, who feared for their independent status and reacted by forcing the emperor to dismiss Wallenstein.

THE SWEDISH PHASE The Swedish phase (1630–1635) marked the entry of Gustavus Adolphus (goo-STAY-vus uh-DAHL-fuss), king of Sweden (1611–1632), into the war. Gustavus Adolphus was responsible for reviving Sweden and transforming it into a great Baltic power. A military genius, he brought a disciplined and well-equipped Swedish army to northern Germany. He was also a devout Lutheran who felt compelled to aid his coreligionists in Germany.

Gustavus's army swept the imperial forces out of the north and moved into the heart of Germany. In desperation, the imperial side recalled Wallenstein, who was given command of the imperial army that met Gustavus's troops near Leipzig. At the Battle of Lützen (LOOT-sun) (1632), the Swedish forces prevailed but paid a high price for the victory when the Swedish king was killed in the battle. Although the Swedish forces remained in Germany, they proved much less effective. Despite the loss of Wallenstein, who was assassinated in 1634 on the orders of Emperor Ferdinand, the imperial army decisively defeated the Swedes at the Battle of Nördlingen at the end of 1634 and drove them out of southern Germany. This imperial victory guaranteed that southern Germany would remain Catholic. The emperor used this opportunity to make peace with the German princes by agreeing to annul the Edict of Restitution of 1629. But peace failed to come to war-weary Germany. The Swedes wished to continue, while the French, under the direction of Cardinal Richelieu (REESH-uh-lyoo), the chief minister of King Louis XIII, entered the war directly, beginning the fourth and final phase of the war, the Franco-Swedish phase (1635–1648).

THE FRANCO-SWEDISH PHASE By this time, religious issues were losing their significance. The Catholic French were now supporting the Protestant Swedes against the Catholic Habsburgs of Germany and Spain. The Battle of Rocroi (roh-KRWAH) in 1643 proved decisive as the

CHRONOLOGY The Thirty Years' War

Protestant Union	1608
Catholic League	1609
Election of Habsburg Archduke Ferdinand as king of Bohemia	1617
Bohemian revolt against Ferdinand	1618
Bohemian phase	1618–1625
Battle of White Mountain	1620
Spanish conquest of Palatinate	1622
Danish phase	1625–1629
Edict of Restitution	1629
Swedish phase	1630–1635
Battle of Lützen	1632
Battle of Nördlingen	1634
Franco-Swedish phase	1635–1648
Battle of Rocroi	1643
Peace of Westphalia	1648
Peace of the Pyrenees	1659

French beat the Spanish and brought an end to Spanish military greatness. The French then moved on to victories over the imperialist-Bavarian armies in southern Germany. By this time, all parties were ready for peace, and after five years of protracted negotiations, the war in Germany was officially ended by the Peace of Westphalia in 1648. The war between France and Spain, however, continued until the Peace of the Pyrenees in 1659. By that time, Spain had become a second-class power, and France had emerged as the dominant nation in Europe.

OUTCOMES OF THE WAR What were the results of what one historian has called a "basically meaningless conflict"? The Peace of Westphalia ensured that all German states, including the Calvinist ones, were free to determine their own religion. Territorially, France gained parts of western Germany, part of Alsace, and the three cities of Metz, Toul, and Verdun, giving the French control of the Franco-German border area. While Sweden and the German states of Brandenburg and Bavaria gained some territory in Germany, the Austrian Habsburgs did not really lose any but did see their authority as rulers of Germany further diminished. The more than three hundred states that made up the Holy Roman Empire were recognized as virtually independent, since each received the power to conduct its own foreign policy. The Habsburg emperor had been reduced to a figurehead in the Holy Roman Empire. The Peace of Westphalia also made it clear that religion and politics were now separate. The pope was completely ignored in all decisions at Westphalia, and political motives became the guiding forces in public affairs as religion moved closer to becoming primarily a matter of personal conviction and individual choice. Some historians also argue that the Peace of Westphalia

The Thirty Years' War: Soldiers Plundering a Village. This 1660 painting shows a group of soldiers running amok and plundering a German village. This scene was typical of many that occurred during the Thirty Years' War, especially in Germany, where the war caused enormous destruction.

marks the beginning of a modern international order in which sovereign states began to operate as equals within a secular framework.

The economic and social effects of the Thirty Years' War on Germany are still debated. Some areas of Germany were completely devastated, but others remained relatively untouched and even experienced economic growth. The most recent work pictures a damaged economy and a population decline of 15 to 20 percent in the Holy Roman Empire. Although historians may debate the degree of devastation, many people in Germany would have understood this description by a traveler journeying along the Main River in 1636:

[We] came to a wretched little village called Neukirchen, which we found quite uninhabited yet with one house on fire. Here, since it was now late, we were obliged to stay all night, for the nearest town was four miles away; but we spent that night walking up and down with guns in our hands, and listening fearfully to the sound of shots in the woods around us.... Early next morning, His Excellency went to inspect the church and found it had been plundered and that the pictures and the altar had been desecrated. In the churchyard we saw a dead body, scraped out of the grave, while outside the churchyard we found another dead body.[2]

The Thirty Years' War was undoubtedly the most destructive conflict Europeans had yet experienced (see the box on p. 453).

A Military Revolution?

By the seventeenth century, war played an increasingly important role in European affairs. Military power was considered essential to a ruler's reputation and power; thus, the pressure to build an effective military machine was intense. Some historians believe that the changes that occurred in the science of warfare between 1560 and 1660 warrant the title of military revolution.

Medieval warfare, with its mounted knights and supplementary archers, had been transformed in the Renaissance by the employment of infantry armed with pikes and

The Face of War in the Seventeenth Century

We have a firsthand account of the face of war in Germany from a picaresque novel called *Simplicius Simplicissimus,* written by Jakob von Grimmelshausen. The author's experiences as a soldier in the Thirty Years' War give his descriptions of the effect of the war on ordinary people a certain vividness and reality. This selection describes the fate of a peasant farm, an experience all too familiar to thousands of German peasants between 1618 and 1648.

+--+ ==+== +--+

Jakob von Grimmelshausen, *Simplicius Simplicissimus*

The first thing these horsemen did in the nice back rooms of the house was to put in their horses. Then everyone took up a special job, one having to do with death and destruction. Although some began butchering, heating water, and rendering lard, as if to prepare for a banquet, others raced through the house, ransacking upstairs and down; not even the privy chamber was safe, as if the golden fleece of Jason might be hidden there. Still others bundled up big packs of cloth, household goods, and clothes, as if they wanted to hold a rummage sale somewhere. What they did not intend to take along they broke and spoiled. Some ran their swords into the hay and straw, as if there hadn't been hogs enough to stick. Some shook the feathers out of beds and put bacon slabs, hams, and other stuff in the ticking, as if they might sleep better on these. Others knocked down the hearth and broke the windows, as if announcing an everlasting summer. They flattened out copper and pewter dishes and baled the ruined goods. They burned up bedsteads, tables, chairs, and benches, though there were yards and yards of dry firewood outside the kitchen. Jars and crocks, pots and casseroles all were broken, either because they preferred their meat broiled or because they thought they'd eat only one meal with us. In the barn, the hired girl was handled so roughly that she was unable to walk away, I am ashamed to report. They stretched the hired man out flat on the ground, stuck a wooden wedge in his mouth to keep it open, and emptied a milk bucket full of stinking manure

drippings down his throat; they called it a Swedish cocktail. He didn't relish it and made a very wry face. By this means they forced him to take a raiding party to some other place where they carried off men and cattle and brought them to our farm. Among those were my father, mother, and Ursula [sister].

Then they used thumbscrews, which they cleverly made out of their pistols, to torture the peasants, as if they wanted to burn witches. Though he had confessed to nothing as yet, they put one of the captured hayseeds in the bake-oven and lighted a fire in it. They put a rope around someone else's head and tightened it like a tourniquet until blood came out of his mouth, nose, and ears. In short, every soldier had his favorite method of making life miserable for peasants, and every peasant had his own misery. My father was, as I thought, particularly lucky because he confessed with a laugh what others were forced to say in pain and martyrdom. No doubt because he was the head of the household, he was shown special consideration; they put him close to a fire, tied him by his hands and legs, and rubbed damp salt on the bottoms of his feet. Our old nanny goat had to lick it off and this so tickled my father that he could have burst laughing. This seemed so clever and entertaining to me—I had never seen or heard my father laugh so long—that I joined him in laughter, to keep him company or perhaps to cover up my ignorance. In the midst of such glee he told them the whereabouts of hidden treasure much richer in gold, pearls, and jewelry than might have been expected on a farm.

I can't say much about the captured wives, hired girls, and daughters because the soldiers didn't let me watch their doings. But I do remember hearing pitiful screams from various dark corners and I guess that my mother and our Ursula had it no better than the rest. 🖎

Q What does this document reveal about the effect of war on ordinary Europeans? Compare this description with the descriptions of the treatment of civilians in other wars. Does Grimmelshausen exaggerate, or does this description agree with the other descriptions?

---

halberds and arranged in massed rectangles known as squadrons or battalions. The use of firearms required adjustments to the size and shape of the massed infantry and made the cavalry less effective.

It was Gustavus Adolphus, the king of Sweden, who developed the first standing army of conscripts, notable for the flexibility of its tactics. The infantry brigades of Gustavus's army were composed of equal numbers of musketeers and pikemen, standing six men deep. They

employed the salvo, in which all rows of the infantry fired at once instead of row by row. These salvos of fire, which cut up the massed ranks of the opposing infantry squadrons, were followed by a pike charge, giving the infantry a primarily offensive deployment. Gustavus also used the cavalry in a more mobile fashion. After shooting a pistol volley, they charged the enemy with their swords. Additional flexibility was obtained by using lighter artillery pieces that were more easily moved during battle. All of these changes required coordination, careful training, and better discipline, forcing rulers to move away from undisciplined mercenary forces. Naturally, the success of Gustavus Adolphus led to imitation.

Some historians have questioned the use of the phrase "military revolution" to describe the military changes from 1560 to 1660, arguing instead that military developments were gradual. In any case, for the rest of the seventeenth century, warfare continued to change. Standing armies, based partly on conscription, grew ever larger and more expensive. Standing armies necessitated better-disciplined and better-trained soldiers and led to the education of officers in military schools. Armies also introduced the use of linear rather than square formations to provide greater flexibility and mobility in tactics. There was also an increased use of firearms as the musket with attached bayonet increasingly replaced the pike in the ranks of the infantry. A naval arms race in the seventeenth century led to more and bigger warships or capital ships known as "ships of the line." By the end of the seventeenth century, most of these had two or three decks and were capable of carrying between fifty and one hundred heavy cannon.

Larger armies and navies could be maintained only by levying heavier taxes, making war a greater economic burden and an ever more important part of the early modern European state. The creation of large bureaucracies to supervise the military resources of the state led to growth in the power of state governments.

Rebellions

Before, during, and after the Thirty Years' War, a series of rebellions and civil wars stemming from the discontent of both nobles and commoners rocked the domestic stability of many European governments. To strengthen their power, monarchs attempted to extend their authority at the expense of traditional powerful elements who resisted the rulers' efforts. At the same time, to fight their battles, governments increased taxes and created such hardships that common people also rose in opposition.

Between 1590 and 1640, peasant and lower-class revolts erupted in central and southern France, Austria, and Hungary. In the decades of the 1640s and 1650s, even greater unrest occurred. Portugal and Catalonia rebelled against the Spanish government in 1640. The common people in Naples and Sicily revolted against both the government and the landed nobility in 1647. Russia, too, was rocked by urban uprisings in 1641, 1645, and 1648. Nobles rebelled in France from 1648 to 1652 in an effort to halt the growth of royal power. The northern states of Sweden, Denmark, and the United Provinces were also not immune from upheavals involving clergy, nobles, and mercantile groups. The most famous and widest-ranging struggle, however, was the civil war and rebellion in England, commonly known as the English Revolution (discussed later in this chapter).

The Practice of Absolutism: Western Europe

 FOCUS QUESTION: What was absolutism in theory, and how did its actual practice in France reflect or differ from the theory?

Absolute monarchy or **absolutism** meant that the sovereign power or ultimate authority in the state rested in the hands of a king who claimed to rule by divine right. But what did sovereignty mean? The late-sixteenth-century political theorist Jean Bodin (ZHAHN boh-DAN) believed that sovereign power consisted of the authority to make laws, tax, administer justice, control the state's administrative system, and determine foreign policy. These powers made a ruler sovereign.

One of the chief theorists of **divine-right monarchy** in the seventeenth century was the French theologian and court preacher Bishop Jacques Bossuet (ZHAHK baw-SWAY) (1627–1704), who expressed his ideas in a book titled *Politics Drawn from the Very Words of Holy Scripture.* Bossuet argued first that government was divinely ordained so that humans could live in an organized society. God established kings and through them reigned over all the peoples of the world. Since kings received their power from God, their authority was absolute. They were responsible to no one (including parliaments) except God. For Bossuet, though, the last point was especially important. Because God would hold a king accountable for his actions, Bossuet believed that kings faced serious responsibilities as well as real limits on their power. There was also a large gulf between the theory of absolutism as expressed by Bossuet and the practice of absolutism. A monarch's absolute power was often limited greatly by practical realities.

Absolute Monarchy in France

France during the reign of Louis XIV (1643–1715) has traditionally been regarded as the best example of the practice of absolute monarchy in the seventeenth century. French culture, language, and manners influenced all levels of European society. French diplomacy and wars shaped the political affairs of western and central Europe. The court of Louis XIV seemed to be imitated everywhere in Europe. Of course, the stability of Louis's reign was magnified by the instability that had preceded it.

FOUNDATIONS OF FRENCH ABSOLUTISM: CARDINAL RICHELIEU The half century of French history before Louis XIV came to power was a time in which royal and ministerial governments struggled to avoid the breakdown of the state. The line between order and anarchy was often a narrow one. The situation was especially complicated by the fact that both Louis XIII (1610–1643) and Louis XIV were only boys when they succeeded to the throne in 1610 and 1643, respectively, leaving the

Cardinal Richelieu. A key figure in the emergence of a strong monarchy in France was Cardinal Richelieu, pictured here in a portrait by Philippe de Champagne. Chief minister to Louis XIII, Richelieu strengthened royal authority by eliminating the private armies and fortified cities of the Huguenots and by crushing aristocratic conspiracies.

government dependent on royal ministers. Two especially competent ministers played crucial roles in maintaining monarchical authority.

Cardinal Richelieu, Louis XIII's chief minister from 1624 to 1642, initiated policies that eventually strengthened the power of the monarchy. By eliminating the political and military rights of the Huguenots while preserving their religious ones, Richelieu transformed the Huguenots into more reliable subjects. Richelieu acted more cautiously in "humbling the pride of the great men," the important French nobility. He understood the influential role played by the nobles in the French state. The dangerous ones were those who asserted their territorial independence when they were excluded from participating in the central government. Proceeding slowly but determinedly, Richelieu developed an efficient network of spies to uncover noble plots and then crushed the conspiracies and executed the conspirators, thereby eliminating a major threat to royal authority.

Cardinal Richelieu, Political Testament (1624)

To reform and strengthen the central administration, initially for financial reasons, Richelieu sent out royal officials called **intendants** (anh-tahnh-DAHNHZ *or* in-TEN-dunts) to the provinces to execute the orders of the central government. As the functions of the *intendants* grew, they came into conflict with provincial governors. Since the *intendants* were victorious in most of these disputes, they further strengthened the power of the crown. Richelieu proved less capable in financial matters, however. Not only was the basic system of state finances corrupt, but so many people benefited from the system's inefficiency and injustice that the government faced strong resistance when it tried to institute reforms. The *taille* (an annual direct tax usually levied on land or property) was increased—in 1643 it was two and a half times what it had been in 1610—and crown lands were mortgaged again. Richelieu's foreign policy goal of confronting the growing power of the Habsburgs in the Thirty Years' War, however, led to ever-increasing expenditures, which soon outstripped the additional revenues. French debt continued its upward spiral under Richelieu.

CARDINAL MAZARIN Richelieu died in 1642, followed five months later by King Louis XIII, who was succeeded by his son Louis XIV, then but four years old. This necessitated a regency under Anne of Austria, wife of the dead king. But she allowed Cardinal Mazarin (maz-uh-RANH), Richelieu's trained successor, to dominate the government. An Italian who had come to France as a papal legate and then become naturalized, Mazarin attempted to carry on Richelieu's policies until his death in 1661.

The most important event during Mazarin's rule was a revolt known as the Fronde (FROHND). As a foreigner, Mazarin was greatly disliked by all elements of the French population. The nobles, who particularly resented the centralized administrative power being built up at the expense of the provincial nobility, temporarily allied with the members of the Parlement of Paris, who opposed the new taxes levied by the government to pay the costs of the Thirty Years' War (Mazarin continued Richelieu's anti-Habsburg policy), and with the masses of Paris, who were also angry at the additional taxes. The Parlement (par-luh-MAHNH) of Paris was the most important court in France, with jurisdiction over half of the kingdom, and its members formed the nobles of the robe, the service nobility of lawyers and administrators. These nobles of the robe led the first Fronde (1648–1649), which broke out in Paris and was ended by compromise. The second Fronde, begun in 1650, was led by the nobles of the sword, whose ancestors were medieval nobles. They were interested in overthrowing Mazarin for their own purposes: to secure their positions and increase their own power. The second Fronde was crushed by 1652, a task made easier when the nobles began fighting each other instead of Mazarin. With the end of the Fronde, the vast majority of the French concluded that the best hope for stability in France lay in the crown. When Mazarin died in 1661, the greatest of the seventeenth-century monarchs, Louis XIV, took over supreme power.

The Reign of Louis XIV (1643–1715)

The day after Cardinal Mazarin's death, Louis XIV, age twenty-three, expressed his determination to be a real king and the sole ruler of France:

> Up to this moment I have been pleased to entrust the government of my affairs to the late Cardinal. It is now time that I govern them myself. You [secretaries and ministers of state] will assist me with your counsels when I ask for them. I request and order you to seal no orders except by my command.... I order you not to sign anything, not even a passport... without my command; to render account to me personally each day and to favor no one.[3]

His mother, who was well aware of Louis's proclivity for fun and games and getting into the beds of the maids in the royal palace, laughed aloud at these words. But Louis was quite serious.

Louis proved willing to pay the price of being a strong ruler. He established a conscientious routine from which he seldom deviated, but he did not look upon his duties as drudgery since he considered his royal profession "grand, noble, and delightful." Eager for glory (in the French sense of achieving what was expected of one in an important position), Louis created a grand and majestic spectacle at the court of Versailles (vayr-SY). Consequently, Louis and his court came to set the standard for monarchies and aristocracies all over Europe. Just a few decades after the king's death, the great French writer Voltaire dubbed the period from 1661 to 1715 the "Age of Louis XIV," and historians have tended to call it that ever since.

Although Louis may have believed in the theory of absolute monarchy and consciously fostered the myth of himself as the Sun King, the source of light for all of his people, historians are quick to point out that the realities fell far short of the aspirations. Despite the centralizing efforts of Cardinals Richelieu and Mazarin, seventeenth-century France still possessed a bewildering system of overlapping authorities. Provinces had their own regional courts, their own local Estates, their own sets of laws. Members of the high nobility, with their huge estates and clients among the lesser nobility, still exercised much authority. Both towns and provinces possessed privileges and powers seemingly from time immemorial that they would not easily relinquish.

ADMINISTRATION OF THE GOVERNMENT One of the keys to Louis's power was that he was able to restructure the central policy-making machinery of government because it was part of his own court and household. The royal court located at Versailles was an elaborate structure that served different purposes: it was the personal household of the king, the location of central governmental machinery, and the place where powerful subjects came to find favors and offices for themselves and their clients as well as the main arena where rival aristocratic factions jostled for power.

The greatest danger to Louis's personal rule came from the very high nobles and princes of the blood (the royal princes), who considered it their natural function to assert the policy-making role of royal ministers. Louis eliminated this threat by removing them from the royal council, the chief administrative body of the king and overseer of the central machinery of government, and enticing them to his court, where he could keep them preoccupied with court life and out of politics. Instead of the high nobility and royal princes, Louis relied for his ministers on other nobles. His ministers were expected to be subservient; said Louis, "I had no intention of sharing my authority with them."

Louis's domination of his ministers and secretaries gave him control of the central policy-making machinery of government and thus authority over the traditional areas of monarchical power: the formulation of foreign policy, the making of war and peace, the assertion of the secular power of the crown against any religious authority, and the ability to levy taxes to fulfill these functions. Louis had considerably less success with the internal administration of the kingdom, however. The traditional groups and institutions of French society—the nobles, officials, town councils, guilds, and representative Estates in some provinces—were simply too powerful for the king to have direct control over the lives of his subjects. Consequently, control of the provinces and the people was achieved largely by bribing the individuals responsible for executing the king's policies. Nevertheless, local officials could still obstruct the execution of policies they disliked, indicating clearly that a so-called absolute monarch was not always absolute. A recent study of Louis's relationship with the **parlements,** however, asserts that he was able to exercise both political and economic control over these provincial law courts, which were responsible for registering new laws sent to them by the king.

RELIGIOUS POLICY The maintenance of religious harmony had long been considered an area of monarchical power. The desire to keep it led Louis into conflict with the French Huguenots. Louis XIV did not want to allow Protestants to practice their faith in largely Catholic France. Perhaps he was motivated by religion, but it is more likely that Louis, who believed in the motto "One king, one law, one faith," felt that the existence of this minority undermined his own political authority. In October 1685, Louis issued the Edict of Fontainebleau (fawnh-ten-BLOH). In addition to revoking the Edict of Nantes, the new edict provided for the destruction of Huguenot churches and the closing of Protestant schools. It is estimated that 200,000 Huguenots defied the prohibition against their leaving France and sought asylum in England, the United Provinces, and the German states. Although it was once believed that this exodus weakened the French economy, others maintain that an influx of English and Irish political and religious refugees into France offset the loss. Support for the expulsion of the Protestants

The Palace of Versailles as Depicted in an Eighteenth-Century Engraving. Louis XIV spent untold sums of money on the construction of a new royal residence at Versailles. The enormous palace (it was more than a quarter of a mile long) also housed the members of the king's government and served as home for thousands of French nobles. As the largest royal residence in Europe, Versailles impressed foreigners and became a source of envy for other rulers.

came from Catholic laypeople, who rejected Protestant legal rights, banned them from government meetings, and destroyed Protestant churches in an effort to regain Catholic control of heavily populated Protestant regions.

FINANCIAL ISSUES The cost of building Versailles and other palaces, maintaining his court, and pursuing his wars made finances a crucial issue for Louis XIV. He was most fortunate in having the services of Jean-Baptiste Colbert (ZHAHNH-bah-TEEST kohl-BAYR) (1619–1683) as controller general of finances. Colbert sought to increase the wealth and power of France through general adherence to mercantilism, which stressed government regulation of economic activities to benefit the state. To decrease the need for imports and increase exports, Colbert attempted to expand the quantity and improve the quality of French manufactured goods. He founded

new luxury industries, such as the royal tapestry works at Beauvais; invited Venetian glassmakers and Flemish clothmakers to France; drew up instructions regulating the quality of goods produced; oversaw the training of workers; and granted special privileges, including tax exemptions, loans, and subsidies, to individuals who established new industries. To improve communications and the transportation of goods internally, he built roads and canals. To decrease imports directly, he raised tariffs on foreign manufactured goods, especially English and Dutch cloth, and created a merchant marine to facilitate the conveyance of French goods.

Although Colbert's policies are given much credit for fostering the development of manufacturing in France, some historians are dubious about the usefulness of many of his mercantilistic policies and question whether Colbert stuck to rigid mercantilistic convictions. Regulations were

© Réunion des Musées Nationaux/Art Resource, NY

Interior of Versailles: The Hall of Mirrors. Pictured here is the exquisite Hall of Mirrors at Versailles. Located on the second floor, the hall overlooks the park below. Three hundred and fifty-seven mirrors were placed on the wall opposite the windows in order to create an illusion of even greater width. Careful planning went into every detail of the interior decoration. Even the doorknobs were specially designed to reflect the magnificence of Versailles. This photo shows the Hall of Mirrors after the restoration work that was completed in June 2007, a project that took three years, cost 12 million euros (more than $16 million), and included the restoration of the Bohemian crystal chandeliers.

often evaded, and the imposition of high tariffs brought foreign retaliation. French trading companies entered the scene too late to be really competitive with the English and the Dutch. And above all, Colbert's economic policies, which were geared to making his king more powerful, were ultimately self-defeating. The more revenue Colbert collected to enable the king to make war, the faster Louis depleted the treasury. At the same time, the burden of taxes fell increasingly on the peasants, who still constituted the overwhelming majority of the French population. Nevertheless, some historians argue that although Louis bankrupted the treasury in order to pay for his wars, the economic practices implemented under Colbert, including investment in the shipping and textile industries and improvements in transportation facilities, allowed for greater economic growth in the eighteenth century.

DAILY LIFE AT THE COURT OF VERSAILLES The court of Louis XIV at Versailles set a standard that was soon followed by other European rulers. In 1660, Louis decided to convert a hunting lodge at Versailles, not far from the capital city of Paris, into a chateau. Not until 1688, after untold sums of money had been spent and tens of thousands of workers had labored incessantly, was construction completed on the enormous palace.

Versailles served many purposes. It was the residence of the king, a reception hall for state affairs, an office building for the members of the king's government, and the home of thousands of royal officials and aristocratic courtiers. Versailles became a symbol for the French absolutist state and the power of the Sun King, Louis XIV. As a visible manifestation of France's superiority and wealth, this lavish court was intended to overawe subjects and impress foreign powers.

Versailles also served a practical political purpose. It became home to the high nobility and princes of the blood (the royal princes), those powerful figures who had aspired to hold the policy-making role of royal ministers. By keeping them involved in the myriad activities that made up daily life at the court of Versailles, Louis excluded them

Travels with the King

The duc de Saint-Simon was one of many noble courtiers who lived at Versailles and had firsthand experience of court life there. In his *Memoirs,* he left a controversial and critical account of Louis XIV and his court. In this selection, Saint-Simon describes the price court ladies paid for the "privilege" of riding with the great king.

* ⊷ ⊫ ⊰ *

Duc de Saint-Simon, *Memoirs*

The King always traveled with his carriage full of women: His mistresses, his bastard daughters, his daughters-in-law, sometimes Madame [the wife of the king's brother], and the other ladies of the court when there was room. This was the case for hunts, and trips to Fontainebleau, Chantilly, Compiègne, and the like.... In his carriage during these trips there was always an abundance and variety of things to eat: meats, pastries, and fruit. Before the carriage had gone a quarter league the King would ask who was hungry. He never ate between meals, not even a fruit, but he enjoyed watching others stuff themselves. It was mandatory to eat, with appetite and good grace, and to be gay; otherwise; he showed his displeasure by telling the guilty party she was putting on airs and trying to be coy. The same ladies or princesses who had eaten that day at the King's table were obliged to eat again as though they were weak from hunger. What is more, the women were forbidden to mention their personal needs, which in any case they could not have relieved without embarrassment, since there were guards and members of the King's household in front and in back of the carriage, and officers and equerries riding alongside the doors. The dust they kicked up choked everyone in the carriage, but the King, who loved fresh air, insisted that all the windows remain open. He would have been extremely displeased if one of the ladies had pulled a curtain to protect herself from the sun, the wind, or the cold.

He pretended not to notice his passengers' discomfort, and always traveled very fast, with the usual number of relays. Sickness in the carriage was a demerit which ruled out further invitations.... When the king had to relieve himself he did not hesitate to stop the carriage and get out; but the ladies were not allowed to budge. ⇨

Q How would you describe the king's personality? Do you think this account might be biased? Why?

---

from real power while allowing them to share in the mystique of power as companions of the king.

Life at Versailles became a court ceremony with Louis XIV at the center of it all. The king had little privacy; only when he visited his wife or mother or mistress or met with ministers was he free of the noble courtiers who swarmed about the palace. Most daily ceremonies were carefully staged, such as those attending Louis's rising from bed, dining, praying, attending Mass, and going to bed. A mob of nobles aspired to assist the king in carrying out these solemn activities. It was considered a great honor for a noble to be chosen to hand the king his shirt while dressing. But why did nobles participate in so many ceremonies, some of which were so obviously demeaning? Active involvement in the activities at Versailles was the king's prerequisite for obtaining the offices, titles, and pensions that only he could grant. This policy reduced great nobles and ecclesiastics, the "people of quality," to a plane of equality, allowing Louis to exercise control over them and prevent them from interfering in the real lines of power. To maintain their social prestige, the "people of quality" were expected to adhere to rigid standards of court etiquette appropriate to their rank.

Indeed, court etiquette became a complex matter. Nobles and royal princes were arranged in an elaborate order of seniority and expected to follow certain rules of precedence. Who could sit down and on what kind of chair was a subject of much debate. When Philip of Orléans, the king's brother, and his wife Charlotte sought to visit their daughter, the duchess of Lorraine, they encountered problems with Louis. Charlotte told why in one of her letters:

> The difficulty is that the Duke of Lorraine claims that he is entitled to sit in an armchair in the presence of Philip and myself because the Emperor gives him an armchair. To this the King [Louis] replied that the Emperor's ceremonial is one thing and the King's another, and that, for example, the Emperor gives the cardinals armchairs, whereas here they may never sit at all in the King's presence.[4]

Louis refused to compromise; the duke of Lorraine was only entitled to a stool. The duke balked, and Philip and Charlotte canceled their visit.

Daily life at Versailles also included numerous forms of entertainment. Walks through the gardens, boating trips, performances of tragedies and comedies, ballets, and concerts all provided sources of pleasure (see the box above). Three evenings a week, from seven to ten, Louis also held an *appartement* (uh-par-tuh-MAHNH) where he was "at home" to his court. The *appartement* was characterized by a formal informality. Relaxed rules of etiquette even allowed people to sit down in the presence of their superiors. The evening's entertainment began with a concert, followed by games of billiards or cards, and ended with a sumptuous buffet.

THE WARS OF LOUIS XIV Both the increase in royal power that Louis pursued and his desire for military glory

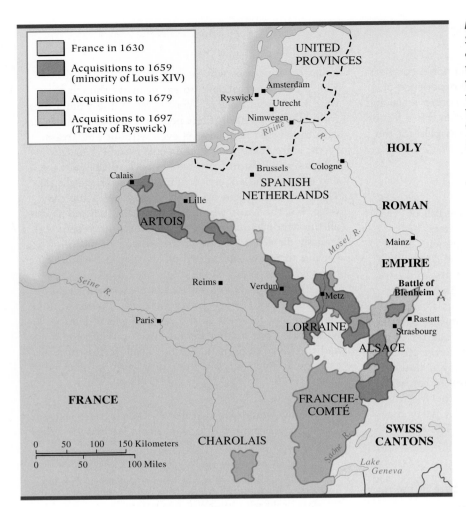

Q *Louis XIV made his territorial acquisitions primarily at the expense of what countries?*

Map legend:
- France in 1630
- Acquisitions to 1659 (minority of Louis XIV)
- Acquisitions to 1679
- Acquisitions to 1697 (Treaty of Ryswick)

led the king to wage war. Under the secretary of war, François-Michel Le Tellier (frahnh-SWAH-mee-SHEL luh tel-YAY), the marquis of Louvois (loo-VWAH), France developed a professional army numbering 100,000 men in peacetime and 400,000 in time of war. Louis made war an almost incessant activity of his reign. To achieve the prestige and military glory befitting the Sun King as well as to ensure the domination of his Bourbon dynasty over European affairs, Louis waged four wars between 1667 and 1713 (see Map 15.2).

In 1667, Louis began his first war by invading the Spanish Netherlands to his north and Franche-Comté to the east. But the Triple Alliance of the Dutch, English, and Swedes forced Louis to sue for peace in 1668 and accept a few towns in the Spanish Netherlands for his efforts. He never forgave the Dutch for arranging the Triple Alliance, and in 1672, after isolating the Dutch, France invaded the United Provinces with some initial success. But the French victories led Brandenburg, Spain, and the Holy Roman Empire to form a new coalition that forced Louis to end the Dutch War by making peace at Nimwegen (NIM-vay-gun) in 1678. While Dutch territory remained intact, France received Franche-Comté from Spain, which served merely to stimulate Louis's appetite for even more land.

This time, Louis moved eastward against the Holy Roman Empire, which he perceived from his previous war as feeble and unable to resist. The gradual annexation of the provinces of Alsace and Lorraine was followed by the occupation of the city of Strasbourg, a move that led to widespread protest and the formation of a new coalition. The creation of this League of Augsburg, consisting of Spain, the Holy Roman Empire, the United Provinces, Sweden, and England, led to Louis's third war, the War of the League of Augsburg (1689–1697). This bitterly contested eight-year struggle brought economic depression and famine to France. The Treaty of Ryswick (RYZ-wik) ending the war forced Louis to give up most of his conquests in the empire, although he was allowed to keep Strasbourg and part of Alsace. The gains were hardly worth the bloodshed and the misery he had caused the French people.

Louis's fourth war, the War of the Spanish Succession (1702–1713), was over bigger stakes, the succession to the Spanish throne. Charles II, the sickly and childless Habsburg ruler, left the throne of Spain in his will to a grandson of Louis XIV. When the latter became King Philip V of Spain after Charles's death, the suspicion that Spain and France would eventually be united in the same dynastic family caused the formation of a new coalition, determined to prevent a Bourbon hegemony that would mean the certain destruction of the European balance of power. This coalition of England, the United Provinces,

Habsburg Austria, and German states opposed France and Spain in a war that dragged on in Europe and the colonial empires in North America for eleven years. In a number of battles, including the memorable defeat of the French forces at Blenheim in 1704 by allied troops led by the English commander, John Churchill, duke of Marlborough, the coalition wore down Louis's forces. An end to the war finally came with the Peace of Utrecht in 1713 and of Rastatt in 1714. Although these peace treaties confirmed Philip V as the Spanish ruler, initiating a Spanish Bourbon dynasty that would last into the twentieth century, they also affirmed that the thrones of Spain and France were to remain separated. The Spanish Netherlands, Milan, and Naples were given to Austria, and the emerging state of Brandenburg-Prussia gained additional territories. The real winner at Utrecht, however, was England, which received Gibraltar as well as the French possessions in America of Newfoundland, Hudson Bay Territory, and Nova Scotia. Though France, by its sheer size and position, remained a great power, England had emerged as a formidable naval force.

Only two years after the treaty, the Sun King was dead, leaving France in debt and surrounded by enemies. On his deathbed, the seventy-six-year-old monarch seemed remorseful when he told his successor:

> Soon you will be King of a great kingdom. I urge you not to forget your duty to God; remember that you owe everything to Him. Try to remain at peace with your neighbors. I loved war too much. Do not follow me in that or in overspending. Take advice in everything; try to find the best course and follow it. Lighten your people's burden as soon as possible, and do what I have had the misfortune not to do myself.[5]

Did Louis mean it? Did Louis ever realize how tarnished the glory he had sought had become? Ten years before the end of his reign one of his subjects wrote: "Even the people ... who have so much loved you, and have placed such trust in you, begin to lose their love, their trust, and even their respect ... They believe you have no pity for their sorrows, that you are devoted only to your power and your glory."[6] In any event, the advice to his successor was probably not remembered; his great-grandson was only five years old.

The Decline of Spain

At the beginning of the seventeenth century, Spain possessed the most populous empire in the world, controlling almost all of South America and a number of settlements in Asia and Africa. To most Europeans, Spain still seemed the greatest power of the age, but the reality was quite different. The treasury was empty; Philip II went bankrupt in 1596 from excessive expenditures on war, and his successor, Philip III, did the same in 1607 by spending a fortune on his court. The armed forces were out-of-date, the government was inefficient, and the commercial class was weak in the midst of a suppressed peasantry, a luxury-loving class of nobles,

CHRONOLOGY Absolutism in Western Europe

France

Louis XIII	1610–1643
Cardinal Richelieu as chief minister	1624–1642
Ministry of Cardinal Mazarin	1642–1661
First Fronde	1648–1649
Second Fronde	1650–1652
Louis XIV	1643–1715
First war (versus Triple Alliance)	1667–1668
Dutch War	1672–1678
Edict of Fontainebleau	1685
War of the League of Augsburg	1689–1697
War of the Spanish Succession	1702–1713

Spain

Philip III	1598–1621
Philip IV	1621–1665

and an oversupply of priests and monks. Spain continued to play the role of a great power, but appearances were deceiving.

During the reign of Philip III (1598–1621), many of Spain's weaknesses became apparent. Interested only in court luxury or miracle-working relics, Philip III allowed his first minister, the greedy duke of Lerma, to run the country. The aristocratic Lerma's primary interest was accumulating power and wealth for himself and his family. As important offices were filled with his relatives, crucial problems went unsolved.

THE REIGN OF PHILIP IV The reign of Philip IV (1621–1665) seemed to offer hope for a revival of Spain's energies, especially in the capable hands of his chief minister, Gaspar de Guzman (gahs-PAR day goos-MAHN), the count of Olivares (oh-lee-BAH-rayss). This clever, hardworking, and power-hungry statesman dominated the king's every move and worked to revive the interests of the monarchy. A flurry of domestic reform decrees, aimed at curtailing the power of the Catholic Church and the landed aristocracy, was soon followed by a political reform program whose purpose was to further centralize the government of all Spain and its possessions in monarchical hands. All of these efforts met with little real success, however, because both the number (estimated at one-fifth of the population) and the power of the Spanish aristocrats made them too strong to curtail in any significant fashion.

At the same time, most of the efforts of Olivares and Philip were undermined by their desire to pursue Spain's imperial glory and by a series of internal revolts. Spain's involvement in the Thirty Years' War led to a series of frightfully expensive military campaigns that incited internal revolts and years of civil war. Unfortunately for Spain, the campaigns also failed to produce victory.

As Olivares wrote to King Philip IV, "God wants us to make peace; for He is depriving us visibly and absolutely of all the means of war."[7] At the Battle of Rocroi in 1643, much of the Spanish army was destroyed.

The defeats in Europe and the internal revolts of the 1640s ended any illusions about Spain's greatness. The actual extent of Spain's economic difficulties is still debated, but there is no question about its foreign losses. Dutch independence was formally recognized by the Peace of Westphalia in 1648, and the Peace of the Pyrenees with France in 1659 meant the surrender of Artois and the outlying defenses of the Spanish Netherlands as well as certain border regions that went to France.

Absolutism in Central, Eastern, and Northern Europe

Q **FOCUS QUESTION:** What developments enabled Brandenburg-Prussia, Austria, and Russia to emerge as major powers in the seventeenth century?

During the seventeenth century, a development of great importance for the modern Western world took place in central and eastern Europe, as three new powers made their appearance: Prussia, Austria, and Russia.

The German States

The Peace of Westphalia, which officially ended the Thirty Years' War in 1648, left each of the states in the Holy Roman Empire virtually autonomous and sovereign. Properly speaking, there was no longer a German state but rather more than three hundred little Germanies. Of these, two emerged as great European powers in the seventeenth and eighteenth centuries.

THE RISE OF BRANDENBURG-PRUSSIA The evolution of Brandenburg into a powerful state was largely the work of the Hohenzollern (hoh-en-TSULL-urn) dynasty, which in 1415 had come to rule the insignificant principality in northeastern Germany (see Map 15.3). In 1609, the Hohenzollerns inherited some lands in the Rhine valley in western Germany; nine years later, they received the duchy of Prussia (East Prussia). By the seventeenth century, then, the dominions of the house of Hohenzollern, now called Brandenburg-Prussia, consisted of three disconnected masses in western, central, and eastern Germany; only the person of the Hohenzollern ruler connected them.

The foundation for the Prussian state was laid by Frederick William the Great Elector (1640–1688), who came to power in the midst of the Thirty Years' War. Realizing that Brandenburg-Prussia was a small, open territory with no natural frontiers for defense, Frederick William built a competent and efficient standing army. By 1678, he possessed a force of 40,000 men that absorbed more than 50 percent of the state's revenues. To sustain the army and his own power, Frederick William established the General War Commissariat to levy taxes for the army and oversee its growth and training. The Commissariat soon evolved into an agency for civil government as well. Directly responsible to the elector, the new bureaucratic machine became his chief instrument for governing the state. Many of its officials were members of the Prussian landed aristocracy, the Junkers (YOONG-kers), who also served as officers in the all-important army.

The nobles' support for Frederick William's policies derived from the tacit agreement that he made with them. In order to eliminate the power that the members of the nobility could exercise in their provincial Estates-General, Frederick William made a deal with the nobles. In return for a free hand in running the government (in other words, for depriving the provincial Estates of their power), he gave the nobles almost unlimited power over their

Brandenburg (1415)
Prussian acquisitions to 1748
Conquest of Silesia by 1748
From Poland as result of first partition (1792)

MAP 15.3 The Growth of Brandenburg-Prussia. Frederick William the Great Elector laid the foundation for a powerful state when he increased the size and efficiency of the army, raised taxes and created an efficient bureaucracy to collect them, and gained the support of the landed aristocracy. Later rulers added more territory.

Q *Why were the acquisitions of Pomerania and West Prussia important for the continued rise in power of Brandenburg-Prussia?*

View an animated version of this map or related maps on the CourseMate website.

MAP 15.4 **The Growth of the Austrian Empire.** The Habsburgs had hoped to establish a German empire, but the results of the Thirty Years' War crushed that dream. So Austria expanded to the east and the south, primarily at the expense of the Ottoman Empire, and also gained the Spanish Netherlands and former Spanish territories in Italy.

Q *In which areas did the Austrian Empire have access to the Mediterranean Sea, and why would that potentially be important?*

View an animated version of this map or related maps on the CourseMate website.

peasants, exempted the nobles from taxation, and awarded them the highest ranks in the army and the Commissariat with the understanding that they would not challenge his political control. As for the peasants, the nobles were allowed to appropriate their land and bind them to the soil as serfs. Serfdom was not new to Brandenburg-Prussia, but Frederick William reinforced it through his concessions to the nobles.

To build Brandenburg-Prussia's economy, Frederick William followed the fashionable mercantilist policies, constructing roads and canals and using high tariffs, subsidies, and monopolies for manufacturers to stimulate domestic industry. At the same time, however, he continued to favor the interests of the nobility at the expense of the commercial and industrial middle classes in the towns.

Frederick William laid the groundwork for the Prussian state; his son Frederick III (1688–1713) made one further significant contribution: in return for aiding the Holy Roman Emperor in the War of the Spanish Succession, he was officially granted the title of king-in-Prussia. Thus was Elector Frederick III transformed into King Frederick I, ruler of an important new player on the European stage.

THE EMERGENCE OF AUSTRIA The Austrian Habsburgs had long played a significant role in European politics as Holy Roman Emperors, but by the end of the Thirty Years'

War, the Habsburg hopes of creating an empire in Germany had been dashed. In the seventeenth century, the house of Austria made an important transition; the German empire was lost, but a new empire was created in eastern and southeastern Europe.

The nucleus of the new Austrian Empire remained the traditional Austrian hereditary possessions: Lower and Upper Austria, Carinthia, Carniola, Styria, and Tyrol (see Map 15.4). To these had been added the kingdom of Bohemia and parts of northwestern Hungary in the sixteenth century.

In the seventeenth century, Leopold I (1658–1705) encouraged the eastward movement of the Austrian Empire, but he was sorely challenged by the revival of Ottoman power. Having moved into Transylvania, the Ottomans eventually pushed westward and laid siege to Vienna in 1683. A European army, led by the Austrians, counterattacked and decisively defeated the Ottomans in 1687. By the Treaty of Karlowitz (KARL-oh-vits) in 1699, Austria took control of Hungary, Transylvania, Croatia, and Slovenia, thus establishing an Austrian Empire in southeastern Europe. At the end of the War of the Spanish Succession, Austria gained possession of the Spanish Netherlands and received formal recognition of its occupation of the Spanish possessions in Italy, namely, Milan, Mantua, Sardinia, and Naples. By the beginning of the eighteenth century, the house of Austria had acquired an empire of considerable size.

The Austrian monarchy, however, never became a highly centralized, absolutist state, primarily because it included so many different national groups. The Austrian Empire remained a collection of territories held together by a personal union. The Habsburg emperor was archduke of Austria, king of Bohemia, and king of Hungary. Each of these areas had its own laws, Estates-General, and political life. The landed aristocrats throughout the empire were connected by a common bond of service to the house of Habsburg, as military officers or government bureaucrats, but no other common sentiment tied the regions together. Nevertheless, by the beginning of the eighteenth century, Austria was a populous empire in central Europe of great potential military strength.

Italy: From Spanish to Austrian Rule

By 1530, Emperor Charles V had managed to defeat the French armies in Italy and become the arbiter of Italy (see Chapter 13). Initially, he was content to establish close ties with many native Italian rulers and allowed them to rule, provided that they recognized his dominant role. But in 1540, he gave the duchy of Milan to his son Philip II and transferred all imperial rights over Italy to the Spanish monarchy.

From the beginning of Philip II's reign in 1556 until 1713, the Spanish presence was felt everywhere in Italy. Only Florence, the Papal States, and Venice managed to maintain relatively independent policies. At the same time, the influence of the papacy became oppressive in Italy as the machinery of the Catholic Counter-Reformation—the Inquisition, the Index, and the Jesuits—was used to stifle all resistance to the Catholic orthodoxy created by the Council of Trent (see Chapter 13).

At the beginning of the eighteenth century, Italy suffered further from the struggles between France and Spain. But it was Austria, not France, that benefited the most from the War of the Spanish Succession. By gaining Milan, Mantua, Sardinia, and Naples, Austria supplanted Spain as the dominant power in Italy.

Russia: From Fledgling Principality to Major Power

A new Russian state had emerged in the fifteenth century under the leadership of the principality of Moscow and its grand dukes (see Chapter 12). In the sixteenth century, Ivan IV the Terrible (1533–1584), who was the first ruler to take the title of tsar ("Caesar"), expanded the territories of Russia eastward after finding westward expansion blocked by the powerful Swedish and Polish states. Ivan also extended the autocracy of the tsar by crushing the power of the Russian nobility, known as the **boyars.** Ivan's dynasty came to an end in 1598 and was followed by a resurgence of aristocratic power in a period of anarchy known as the Time of Troubles. It did not end until the Zemsky Sobor (ZEM-skee suh-BOR), or national assembly, chose Michael Romanov (1613–1645) as the new tsar, beginning a dynasty that lasted until 1917.

In the seventeenth century, Muscovite society was highly stratified. At the top was the tsar, who claimed to be a divinely ordained autocratic ruler. Russian society was dominated by an upper class of landed aristocrats who, in the course of the seventeenth century, managed to bind their peasants to the land. An abundance of land and a shortage of peasants made serfdom desirable to the landowners. Townspeople were also controlled. Many merchants were not allowed to move from their cities without government permission or to sell their businesses to anyone outside their class. In the seventeenth century, merchant and peasant revolts as well as a schism in the Russian Orthodox Church created very unsettled conditions. In the midst of these political and religious upheavals, seventeenth-century Moscow was experiencing more frequent contacts with the West, and Western ideas were beginning to penetrate a few Russian circles. But Russia remained largely outside the framework of the West: the Renaissance, the Reformation, and the geographic discoveries of the sixteenth and seventeenth centuries made little impact on Russia. At the end of the seventeenth century, Peter the Great (1689–1725) noticeably accelerated the westernizing process.

THE REIGN OF PETER THE GREAT (1689–1725) Peter the Great was an unusual character. A strong man, towering 6 feet 9 inches tall, Peter was coarse in his tastes and

Peter the Great. Peter the Great wished to westernize Russia, especially in the realm of technical skills. His foremost goal was the creation of a strong army and navy in order to make Russia a great power. Jean Marc Nattier, a French artist, painted this portrait of the armored tsar in 1717.

Peter the Great Deals with a Rebellion

During his first visit to the West in 1697–1698, Peter received word that the Streltsy, an elite military unit stationed in Moscow, had revolted against his authority. Peter hurried home and crushed the revolt in a very savage fashion. This selection is taken from an Austrian account of how Peter dealt with the rebels.

Peter and the Streltsy

How sharp was the pain, how great the indignation, to which the tsar's Majesty was mightily moved, when he knew of the rebellion of the Streltsy, betraying openly a mind panting for vengeance! He was still tarrying at Vienna, quite full of the desire of setting out for Italy; but, fervid as was his curiosity of rambling abroad, it was, nevertheless, speedily extinguished on the announcement of the troubles that had broken out in the bowels of his realm. Going immediately to Lefort . . . , he thus indignantly broke out: "Tell me, Francis, how I can reach Moscow by the shortest way, in a brief space, so that I may wreak vengeance on this great perfidy of my people, with punishments worthy of their abominable crime. Not one of them shall escape with impunity. Around my royal city, which, with their impious efforts, they planned to destroy, I will have gibbets and gallows set upon the walls and ramparts, and each and every one of them will I put to a direful death." Nor did he long delay the plan for his justly excited wrath; he took the quick post, as his ambassador suggested, and in four weeks' time he had got over about 300 miles without

accident, and arrived the 4th of September, 1698—a monarch for the well deposed, but an avenger for the wicked.

His first anxiety after his arrival was about the rebellion—in what it consisted, what the insurgents meant, who dared to instigate such a crime. And as nobody could answer accurately upon all points, and some pleaded their own ignorance, others the obstinacy of the Streltsy, he began to have suspicions of everybody's loyalty. . . . No day, holy or profane, were the inquisitors idle; every day was deemed fit and lawful for torturing. There was as many scourges as there were accused, and every inquisitor was a butcher. . . . The whole month of October was spent in lacerating the backs of culprits with the knout and with flames; no day were those that were left alive exempt from scourging or scorching; or else they were broken upon the wheel, or driven to the gibbet, or slain with the ax. . . .

To prove to all people how holy and inviolable are those walls of the city which the Streltsy rashly meditated scaling in a sudden assault, beams were run out from all the embrasures in the walls near the gates, in each of which two rebels were hanged. This day beheld about two hundred and fifty die that death. There are few cities fortified with as many palisades as Moscow has given gibbets to her guardian Streltsy.

Q How did Peter deal with the revolt of the Streltsy? What does his approach to this problem tell us about the tsar?

---

rude in his behavior. He enjoyed a low kind of humor—belching contests, crude jokes, comical funerals—and vicious punishments including floggings, impalings, roastings, and beard burnings (see the box above). Peter gained a firsthand view of the West when he made a trip there in 1697–1698 and returned to Russia with a firm determination to westernize or Europeanize his realm. Perhaps too much has been made of Peter's desire to westernize his "backward country." Peter's policy of Europeanization was largely technical. He admired European technology and gadgets and desired to transplant these to Russia. Only this kind of modernization could give him the army and navy he needed to make Russia a great power.

As could be expected, one of his first priorities was the reorganization of the army and the creation of a navy. Employing both Russians and Europeans as officers, he conscripted peasants for twenty-five-year stints of service to build a standing army of 210,000 men. Peter has also been given credit for forming the first Russian navy.

Peter also reorganized the central government, partly along Western lines. In 1711, he created the Senate to

supervise the administrative machinery of the state while he was away on military campaigns. In time, the Senate became something like a ruling council, but its ineffectiveness caused Peter to borrow the Western institution of "colleges," or boards of administrators entrusted with specific functions, such as foreign affairs, war, and justice. To impose the rule of the central government more effectively throughout the land, Peter divided Russia into eight provinces and later, in 1719, into fifty. Although he hoped to create a "police state," by which he meant a well-ordered community governed in accordance with law, few of his bureaucrats shared his concept of honest service and duty to the state. Peter hoped for a sense of civic duty, but his own forceful personality created an atmosphere of fear that prevented it. He wrote to one administrator, "According to these orders act, act, act. I won't write more, but you will pay with your head if you interpret orders again."[8]

To further his administrative aims, Peter demanded that all members of the landholding class serve in either military or civil offices. Moreover, in 1722, Peter instituted the Table of Ranks to create opportunities for nonnobles to serve the state and join the nobility. All civil offices were ranked according to fourteen levels; a parallel list of fourteen grades was also created for all military offices. Every official was then required to begin at level one and work his way up the ranks. When a nonnoble reached the eighth rank, he acquired noble status. This attempt by Peter to create a new nobility based on merit was not carried on by his successors.

To obtain the enormous amount of money needed for an army and navy that absorbed as much as four-fifths of the state revenue, Peter adopted Western mercantilistic policies to stimulate economic growth. He tried to increase exports and develop new industries while exploiting domestic resources like the iron mines in the Urals. But his military needs were endless, and he came to rely on the old expedient of simply raising taxes, imposing additional burdens on the hapless peasants, who were becoming ever more oppressed in Peter's Russia.

Peter also sought to gain state control of the Russian Orthodox Church. In 1721, he abolished the position of patriarch and created a body called the Holy Synod to make decisions for the church. At its head stood a **procurator,** a layman who represented the interests of the tsar and assured Peter of effective domination of the church.

Shortly after his return from the West in 1698, Peter had begun to introduce Western customs, practices, and manners into Russia. He ordered the preparation of the first Russian book of etiquette to teach Western manners. Among other things, it pointed out that it was not polite to spit on the floor or to scratch oneself at dinner. Because Europeans at that time did not wear beards or traditional longskirted coats, Russian beards had to be shaved and coats shortened, a reform Peter personally enforced at court by shaving off his nobles' beards and cutting their coats at the knees with his own hands. Outside the court, barbers and tailors planted at town gates enforced the edicts by cutting the beards and cloaks of those who entered or left.

One group of Russians benefited greatly from Peter's cultural reforms—women. Having watched women mixing freely with men in Western courts, Peter shattered the seclusion of upper-class Russian women and demanded that they remove the traditional veils that covered their faces. Peter also decreed that social gatherings be held three times a week in the large houses of Saint Petersburg where men and women could mix for conversation, card games, and dancing, which Peter had learned in the West. The tsar also now insisted that women could marry of their own free will.

RUSSIA AS A MILITARY POWER The object of Peter's domestic reforms was to make Russia into a great state and a military power. His primary goal was to "open a window to the West," meaning a port easily accessible to Europe. This could only be achieved on the Baltic, but at that time the Baltic coast was controlled by Sweden, the most important power in northern Europe. Desirous of these lands, Peter, with the support of Poland and Denmark, attacked Sweden in the summer of 1700 believing that the young king of Sweden, Charles XII, could easily be defeated. Charles, however, proved to be a brilliant general. He smashed the Danes, flattened the Poles, and with a well-disciplined force of only 8,000 men, routed the Russian army of 40,000 at the Battle of Narva (1700). The Great Northern War (1701–1721) soon ensued.

But Peter fought back. He reorganized his army along Western lines and at the Battle of Poltava (pul-TAH-vuh) in 1709 defeated Charles's army decisively. Although the war dragged on for another twelve years, the Peace of Nystadt (NEE-shtaht) in 1721 gave formal recognition to what Peter had already achieved: the acquisition of Estonia, Livonia, and Karelia (see Map 15.5). Sweden had become a second-rate power, and Russia was now the great European state Peter had wanted. And he was building it a fine capital. Early in the war, in the northern marshlands along the Baltic, Peter had begun to construct a new city, Saint Petersburg, his window on the West and a symbol that Russia was looking westward to Europe. Though its construction cost the lives of thousands of peasants, the city was completed during Peter's lifetime. It remained the Russian capital until 1917.

Peter modernized and westernized Russia to the extent that it became a great military power and, by his death in 1725, an important member of the European state system. But his policies were also detrimental to Russia. Westernization was a bit of a sham, because Western culture reached only the upper classes, and the real object of the reforms, the creation of a strong military, only added more burdens to the masses of the Russian people. The forceful way in which Peter the Great imposed westernization led his people to distrust Europe and Western civilization rather than embrace them.

The Great Northern States

As the economic thoroughfare for the products of eastern Europe and the West, the Baltic Sea bestowed special importance on the lands surrounding it. In the sixteenth century, Sweden had broken its ties with Denmark and emerged as an independent state (see Chapter 13). Despite their common Lutheran religion, Denmark's and Sweden's territorial ambitions in northern Europe kept them in almost constant rivalry in the seventeenth century.

DENMARK Under Christian IV (1588–1648), Denmark seemed a likely candidate for expansion, but it met with little success. The system of electing monarchs forced the kings to share their power with the Danish nobility, who exercised strict control over the peasants who worked their lands. Danish ambitions for ruling the Baltic were severely curtailed by the losses they sustained in the Thirty Years' War and later in the so-called Northern War (1655–1660) with Sweden.

MAP 15.5 Russia: From Principality to Nation-State. Russia had swelled in size since its emergence in the fifteenth century. Peter the Great, however, modernized the country, instituting bureaucratic and taxation reforms and building up the military. He won territory on the Baltic from Sweden, giving Russia a port at Saint Petersburg.

Q *Why would the westward expansion of Russia during Peter's reign affect the international balance of power in Europe?*

View an animated version of this map or related maps on the CourseMate website.

Danish military losses led to a constitutional crisis in which a meeting of Denmark's Estates brought to pass a bloodless revolution in 1660. The power of the nobility was curtailed, a hereditary monarchy was reestablished, and a new absolutist constitution was proclaimed in 1665. Under Christian V (1670–1699), a centralized administration was instituted with the nobility as the chief officeholders.

SWEDEN Compared with Denmark, Sweden seemed a relatively poor country, and historians have had difficulty explaining why it played such a large role in European affairs in the seventeenth century. Sweden's economy was weak, and the monarchy was still locked in conflict with the powerful Swedish nobility. During the reign of Gustavus Adolphus (1611–1632), his wise and dedicated chief minister, Axel Oxenstierna (AHK-sul OOK-sen-shur-nah), persuaded the king to adopt a new policy in which the nobility formed a "First Estate" occupying the bureaucratic positions of an expanded central government. This created a stable monarchy and freed the king to raise a formidable army and participate in the Thirty Years' War, only to be killed in battle in 1632.

Sweden entered a period of severe political crisis after the death of Gustavus Adolphus. His daughter Christina (1633–1654) proved to be far more interested in philosophy

and religion than ruling. Her tendency to favor the interests of the nobility caused the other estates of the Riksdag (reeks-TAGH), Sweden's parliament—the burghers, clergy, and peasants—to protest. In 1654, tired of ruling and wishing to become a Catholic, which was forbidden in Sweden, Christina abdicated in favor of her cousin, who became King Charles X (1654–1660). His accession to the throne defused a potentially explosive peasant revolt against the nobility.

Charles X reestablished domestic order, but it was his successor, Charles XI (1660–1697), who did the painstaking work of building the Swedish monarchy along the lines of an absolute monarchy. By retaking control of the crown lands and the revenues attached to them from the nobility, Charles managed to weaken the independent power of the nobles. He built up a bureaucracy, subdued both the Riksdag and the church, improved the army and navy, and left to his son, Charles XII (1697–1718), a well-organized Swedish state that dominated northern Europe. In 1693, he and his heirs were acclaimed as "absolute, sovereign kings, responsible for their actions to no man on earth."

Charles XII was primarily interested in military affairs. Energetic and regarded as a brilliant general, his grandiose plans and strategies, which involved Sweden in conflicts with Poland, Denmark, and Russia, proved to be

Sweden in the Seventeenth Century

CHRONOLOGY Absolutism in Central, Eastern, and Northern Europe

Brandenburg-Prussia

Hohenzollerns established in Brandenburg	1415
Hohenzollerns acquire lands along the Rhine	1609
Hohenzollerns acquire East Prussia	1618
Frederick William the Great Elector	1640–1688
Elector Frederick III (King Frederick I)	1688–1713

Austrian Empire

Leopold I	1658–1705
Turkish siege of Vienna	1683
Treaty of Karlowitz	1699

Russia

Ivan IV the Terrible	1533–1584
Time of Troubles	1598–1613
Michael Romanov	1613–1645
Peter the Great	1689–1725
First trip to the West	1697–1698
Great Northern War	1701–1721
Construction of Saint Petersburg begins	1703
Battle of Poltava	1709

Denmark

Christian IV	1588–1648
"Bloodless Revolution"	1660
Christian V	1670–1699

Sweden

Gustavus Adolphus	1611–1632
Christina	1633–1654
Charles X	1654–1660
Charles XI	1660–1697
Charles XII	1697–1718

Sweden's undoing. By the time he died in 1718, Charles XII had lost much of Sweden's northern empire to Russia, and Sweden's status as a first-class northern power had ended.

The Ottoman Empire

After conquering Constantinople in 1453, the Ottoman Turks tried to complete their conquest of the Balkans, where they had been established since the fourteenth century (see Map 15.6). Although they were successful in taking the Romanian territory of Wallachia in 1476, the resistance of the Hungarians kept them from advancing up the Danube valley. From 1480 to 1520, internal problems and the need to consolidate their eastern frontiers kept the Turks from any further attacks on Europe.

The reign of Sultan Suleiman (soo-lay-MAHN) I the Magnificent (1520–1566), however, brought the Turks back to Europe's attention. Advancing up the Danube, the Turks seized Belgrade in 1521 and Hungary by 1526, although their attempts to conquer Vienna in 1529 were repulsed. At the same time, the Turks extended their power into the western Mediterranean, threatening to turn it into a Turkish lake until a large Turkish fleet was destroyed by the Spanish at Lepanto (in modern-day Greece) in 1571. Despite the defeat, the Turks continued to hold nominal control over the southern shores along the Mediterranean.

Although Europeans frequently spoke of new Christian Crusades against the "infidel" Turks, by the beginning of the seventeenth century the Ottoman Empire was being treated like just another European power by European rulers seeking alliances and trade concessions. The Ottoman Empire possessed a highly effective governmental system, especially when it was led by strong sultans or powerful grand viziers (prime ministers). The splendid capital, Constantinople, possessed a population far larger than

MAP 15.6 The Ottoman Empire. In the sixteenth and seventeenth centuries, the Ottoman Empire possessed an effective bureaucracy and military. During this period, it conquered much of the Balkans and made inroads into eastern Europe; by 1699, however, it had lost the farthest reaches of its European territory and would never again pose a serious threat to Europe.

Q *In what region did the Ottomans make the greatest territorial gains in the sixteenth century?*

View an animated version of this map or related maps on the CourseMate website.

---

that of any European city. Nevertheless, Ottoman politics periodically degenerated into bloody intrigues as factions fought each other for influence and the throne. In one particularly gruesome practice, a ruling sultan would murder his brothers to avoid challenges to his rule. Despite the periodic bouts of civil chaos, a well-trained bureaucracy of civil servants continued to administer state affairs efficiently.

A well-organized military system also added to the strength of the Ottoman Empire. Especially outstanding were the **Janissaries,** composed of Christian boys who had been taken from their parents, converted to the Muslim faith, and subjected to rigid military discipline to form an elite core of 8,000 troops personally loyal to the sultan.

In the first half of the seventeenth century, the Ottoman Empire was a "sleeping giant." Occupied by domestic bloodletting and severely threatened by a challenge from Persia, the Ottomans were content with the status quo in eastern Europe. But under a new line of grand viziers in the second half of the seventeenth century, the Ottoman Empire again took the offensive. By 1683, the Ottomans had marched through the Hungarian plain and laid siege to Vienna. Repulsed by a mixed army of Austrians, Poles, Bavarians, and Saxons, the Turks retreated and were pushed out of Hungary by a new European coalition. Although they retained the core of their empire, the Ottoman Turks would never again be a threat to Europe.

The Limits of Absolutism

In recent decades, historical studies of local institutions have challenged the traditional picture of absolute monarchs.

We now recognize that their power was far from absolute, and it is misleading to think that they actually controlled the lives of their subjects. In 1700, government for most people still meant the local institutions that affected their lives: local courts, local tax collectors, and local organizers of armed forces. Kings and ministers might determine policies and issue guidelines, but they still had to function through local agents and had no guarantee that their wishes would be carried out. A mass of urban and provincial privileges, liberties, and exemptions (including from taxation) and a whole host of corporate bodies and interest groups—provincial and national Estates, clerical officials, officeholders who had bought or inherited their positions, and provincial nobles—limited what monarchs could achieve. The most successful rulers were not those who tried to destroy the old system but rather those like Louis XIV, who knew how to use the old system to their advantage. Above all other considerations stood the landholding nobility. Everywhere in the seventeenth century, the landed aristocracy played an important role in the European monarchical system. As military officers, judges, officeholders, and landowners in control of vast, untaxed estates, their power remained immense. In some places, their strength put severe limits on how effectively even absolute monarchs could rule.

Limited Monarchy and Republics

Q FOCUS QUESTION: What were the main issues in the struggle between king and Parliament in seventeenth-century England, and how were they resolved?

Almost everywhere in Europe in the seventeenth century, kings and their ministers were in control of central governments that sought to impose order by strengthening their powers. But not all European states followed the pattern of absolute monarchy. In eastern Europe, the Polish aristocracy controlled a virtually powerless king. In western Europe, two great states—the Dutch Republic and England—successfully resisted the power of hereditary monarchs.

The Weakness of the Polish Monarchy

Much of Polish history revolved around the bitter struggle between the crown and the landed nobility. The dynastic union of Jagiello (yahg-YEL-oh), grand prince of Lithuania, with the Polish queen Jadwiga (yahd-VEE-guh) resulted in a large Lithuanian-Polish state in 1386, although it was not until 1569 that a formal merger occurred between the two crowns. The union of Poland and Lithuania under the Jagiello dynasty had created the largest kingdom in Christendom at the beginning of the fifteenth century. As a result, Poland-Lithuania played a major role in eastern Europe in the fifteenth century and also ruled

much of Ukraine by the end of the sixteenth century. Poland-Lithuania had a rather unique governmental system in that assemblies of nobles elected the king and carefully limited royal power. The power of the nobles also enabled them to keep the Polish peasantry in a state of serfdom.

In 1572, when the Jagiello dynasty came to an end, a new practice arose of choosing outsiders as kings, with the idea that they would bring in new alliances. When the throne was awarded to the Swede Sigismund III (1587–1631), the new king dreamed of creating a vast Polish empire that would include Russia and possibly Finland and Sweden. Poland not only failed to achieve this goal but by the end

Poland in the Seventeenth Century

of the seventeenth century had become a weak, decentralized state.

It was the elective nature of the Polish monarchy that reduced it to impotence. The Sejm (SAYM), or Polish diet, was a two-chamber assembly in which landowners completely dominated the few townspeople and lawyers who were also members. To be elected to the kingship, prospective monarchs had to agree to share power with the Sejm (in effect with the nobles) in matters of taxation, foreign and military policy, and the appointment of state officials and judges. The power of the Sejm had disastrous results for central monarchical authority, for the real aim of most of its members was to ensure that central authority would not affect their local interests. The acceptance of the liberum veto in 1652, whereby the meetings of the Sejm could be stopped by a single dissenting member, reduced government to virtual chaos.

Poland, then, was basically a confederation of semi-independent estates of landed nobles. By the late seventeenth century, it had also become a battleground for foreign powers, who found the nation easy to invade but difficult to rule.

The Golden Age of the Dutch Republic

The seventeenth century has often been called the golden age of the Dutch Republic as the United Provinces held center stage as one of Europe's great powers. Like France and England, the United Provinces was an Atlantic power, underlining the importance of the shift of political and economic power from the Mediterranean basin to the countries on the Atlantic seaboard. As a result of the sixteenth-century revolt of the Netherlands, the seven northern provinces, which began to call themselves the United Provinces of the Netherlands in 1581, became the core of the modern Dutch state. The new state was officially recognized by the Peace of Westphalia in 1648.

With independence came internal dissension. There were two chief centers of political power in the new state. Each province had an official known as a stadholder (STAD-hohl-dur) who was responsible for leading the army and maintaining order. Beginning with William of Orange and his heirs, the house of Orange occupied the stadholderate in most of the seven provinces and favored the development of a centralized government with themselves as hereditary monarchs. The States General, an assembly of representatives from every province, opposed the Orangist ambitions and advocated a decentralized or republican form of government. For much of the seventeenth century, the republican forces were in control. But in 1672, burdened with war against both France and England, the United Provinces turned to William III (1672–1702) of the house of Orange to establish a monarchical regime. But his death in 1702 without a direct heir enabled the republican forces to gain control once more, although the struggle persisted throughout the eighteenth century.

Underlying Dutch prominence in the seventeenth century was economic prosperity, fueled by the role of the Dutch as carriers of European trade. But warfare proved disastrous to the Dutch Republic. Wars with France and England placed heavy burdens on Dutch finances and manpower. English shipping began to challenge what had been Dutch commercial supremacy, and by 1715, the Dutch were experiencing a serious economic decline.

LIFE IN SEVENTEENTH-CENTURY AMSTERDAM By the beginning of the seventeenth century, Amsterdam had replaced Antwerp as the financial and commercial capital of Europe. In 1570, Amsterdam had 30,000 inhabitants; by 1610, that number had doubled as refugees poured in, especially from the Spanish Netherlands. In 1613, this rapid growth caused the city government to approve an "urban expansion plan" that increased the city's territory from 500 to 1,800 acres through the construction of three large concentric canals. Builders prepared plots for the tall, narrow-fronted houses that were characteristic of the city by hammering wooden columns through the mud to the firm sand underneath. The canals in turn made it possible for merchants and artisans to use the upper stories of their houses as storerooms for their goods. Wares carried by small boats were hoisted to the top windows of these dwellings by block and tackle beams fastened to the gables of the roofs. Amsterdam's physical expansion was soon matched by its population as the city grew to 200,000 by 1660.

The exuberant expansion of Amsterdam in the seventeenth century owed much to the city's role as the commercial and financial center of Europe. But what had made this possible? For one thing, Amsterdam merchants possessed vast fleets of ships, many of which were used for the lucrative North Sea herring catch. Amsterdam-based ships were also important carriers for the products of other countries. The Dutch invention of the *fluyt* (FLYT), a shallow-draft ship of large capacity, enabled the transport of enormous quantities of cereals, timber, and iron.

Amsterdam merchants unloaded their cargoes at Dam Square, where all goods weighing more than 50 pounds were recorded and tested for quality. The quantity of goods brought to Amsterdam soon made the city a crossroads for many of Europe's chief products. Amsterdam was also, of course, the chief port for the Dutch West Indian and East Indian trading companies. Moreover, city industries turned imported raw materials into finished goods, making Amsterdam an important producer of woolen cloth, refined sugar and tobacco products, glass, beer, paper, books, jewelry, and leather goods. Some of the city's great wealth came from war profits: by 1700, Amsterdam was the principal supplier of military goods in Europe; its gun foundries had customers throughout the Continent.

Another factor in Amsterdam's prosperity was its importance as a financial center. Trading profits provided large quantities of capital for investment. The city's financial role was greatly facilitated by the foundation in 1609 of the Exchange Bank of Amsterdam, long the greatest public bank in northern Europe. The city also founded the Amsterdam Stock Exchange for speculating in commodities.

At the very top of Amsterdam's society stood a select number of very prosperous manufacturers, shipyard owners, and merchants whose wealth enabled them to control the city government of Amsterdam as well as the Dutch Republic's States General. In the first half of the seventeenth century, the Calvinist background of the wealthy Amsterdam burghers led them to adopt a simple lifestyle. They wore dark clothes and lived in substantial but simply furnished houses known for their steep, narrow stairways. The oft-quoted phrase that "cleanliness is next to godliness" was literally true for these self-confident Dutch burghers. Their houses were clean and orderly (see Images of Everyday Life on p. 472); foreigners often commented that Dutch housewives always seemed to be scrubbing. But in the second half of the seventeenth century, the wealthy burghers began to reject their Calvinist heritage, a transformation that is especially evident in their more elaborate and colorful clothes.

England and the Emergence of Constitutional Monarchy

One of the most prominent examples of resistance to absolute monarchy came in seventeenth-century England, where king and Parliament struggled to determine the role each should play in governing the nation. But the struggle over this political issue was complicated by a deep and profound religious controversy. With the victory of Parliament came the foundation for constitutional monarchy by the end of the seventeenth century.

IMAGES OF EVERYDAY LIFE

Dutch Domesticity

During the golden age of the Dutch Republic, Dutch painters delighted in painting scenes of domestic life, especially the lives of the wealthy burghers who prospered from trade, finance, and manufacturing. The Dutch painter Pieter de Hooch specialized in painting pictures of Dutch interiors, as can be seen in three of his paintings. In *The Mother* (below left), de Hooch portrays a tranquil scene of a mother with her infant and small daughter. The spotless, polished floors reflect the sunlight streaming in through the open door. The rooms are both clean and in good order. Household manuals, such as *The Experienced and Knowledgeable Hollands Householder,* provided detailed outlines of the cleaning tasks that should be performed each day of the week. In *The Linen Cupboard* (below right), a Dutch mother, assisted by her daughter, is shown storing her clean sheets in an elegant cupboard in another well-polished Dutch room. The Chinese porcelain on top of the cupboard and the antique statue indicate that this is the residence of a wealthy family. In *Two Women Teach a Child to Walk* (at the right), the artist again shows a well-furnished and spotless interior. A small girl is learning to walk, assisted by a servant holding straps attached to a band around the girl's head to keep her from falling. ✄

Museum der Bildenden Kuenste, Leipzig//© Erich Lessing/Art Resource, NY

Gemaeldegalerie, Berlin//© Bildarchiv Preussischer Kulturbesitz/Art Resource, NY

Rijksmuseum, Amsterdam//© Alinari/Art Resource, NY

KING JAMES I AND PARLIAMENT Upon the death of Queen Elizabeth in 1603, the Tudor dynasty became extinct, and the Stuart line of rulers was inaugurated with the accession to the throne of Elizabeth's cousin, King James VI of Scotland (son of Mary, queen of Scots), who became James I (1603–1625) of England. Although used to royal power as king of Scotland, James understood little about the laws, institutions, and customs of the English. He espoused the divine right of kings, the belief that kings receive their power directly from God and are responsible to no one except God. This viewpoint alienated Parliament, which had grown accustomed under the Tudors to act on the premise

James I on the Divine Right of Kings (1609)

that monarch and Parliament together ruled England as a "balanced polity." Parliament expressed its displeasure with James's claims by refusing his requests for additional monies needed by the king to meet the increased cost of government. Parliament's power of the purse proved to be its trump card in its relationship with the king.

Some members of Parliament were also alienated by James's religious policy. The Puritans—Protestants in the Anglican Church inspired by Calvinist theology—wanted James to eliminate the episcopal system of church organization used in the Church of England (in which the bishop or *episcopos* played the major administrative role) in favor of a Presbyterian model (used in Scotland and patterned after Calvin's church organization in Geneva, where ministers and elders—also called presbyters—played an important governing role). James refused because he realized that the Anglican Church, with its bishops appointed by the crown, was a major support of monarchical authority. But the Puritans were not easily cowed and added to the rising chorus of opposition to the king. Many of England's **gentry,** mostly well-to-do landowners below the level of the nobility, had become Puritans, and these Puritan gentry not only formed an important and substantial part of the House of Commons, the lower house of Parliament, but also held important positions locally as justices of the peace and sheriffs. It was not wise to alienate them.

CHARLES I AND THE MOVE TOWARD REVOLUTION The conflict that had begun during the reign of James came to a head during the reign of his son, Charles I (1625–1649). In 1628, Parliament passed the Petition of Right, which the king was supposed to accept before being granted any tax revenues. This petition prohibited taxation without Parliament's consent, arbitrary imprisonment, the quartering of soldiers in private houses, and the declaration of martial law in peacetime. Although he initially accepted it, Charles later reneged on the agreement because of its limitations on royal power. In 1629, Charles decided that since he could not work with Parliament, he would not summon it to meet. From 1629 to 1640, Charles pursued a course of personal rule, which forced him to find ways to collect taxes without the cooperation of Parliament. One expedient was a tax called ship money, a levy on seacoast towns to pay for coastal defense, which was now collected annually by the king's officials throughout England and used to finance other government operations besides defense. This use of ship money aroused opposition from middle-class merchants and landed gentry, who objected to the king's attempts to tax without Parliament's consent.

The king's religious policy also proved disastrous. His marriage to Henrietta Maria, the Catholic sister of King Louis XIII of France, aroused suspicions about the king's own religious inclinations. Even more important, however, the efforts of Charles and William Laud, the archbishop of Canterbury, to introduce more ritual into the Anglican Church struck the Puritans as a return to Catholic popery. Grievances mounted. Charles might have survived unscathed if he could have avoided calling Parliament, which alone could provide a focus for the many cries of discontent throughout the land. But when the king and Archbishop Laud attempted to impose the Anglican Book of Common Prayer on the Scottish Presbyterian Church, the Scots rose up in rebellion against the king. Financially strapped and unable to raise troops to defend against the Scots, the king was forced to call Parliament into session. Eleven years of frustration welled up to create a Parliament determined to deal the king his due.

In its first session, from November 1640 to September 1641, the so-called Long Parliament (because it lasted in one form or another from 1640 to 1660) took a series of steps that placed severe limitations on royal authority. These included the abolition of arbitrary courts; the abolition of taxes that the king had collected without Parliament's consent, such as ship money; and the passage of the revolutionary Triennial Act, which specified that Parliament must meet at least once every three years, with or without the king's consent. By the end of 1641, one group in Parliament was prepared to go no further, but a group of more radical parliamentarians pushed for more change, including the elimination of bishops in the Anglican Church. When the king tried to take advantage of the split by arresting some members of the more radical faction in Parliament, a large group in Parliament led by John Pym and his fellow Puritans decided that the king had gone too far. England slipped into civil war.

CIVIL WAR IN ENGLAND Parliament proved victorious in the first phase of the English Civil War (1642–1646). Most important to Parliament's success was the creation of the New Model Army, which was composed primarily of more extreme Puritans known as the Independents, who believed they were doing battle for the Lord. It is striking to read in the military reports of Oliver Cromwell, one of the group's leaders, such statements as "Sir, this is none other but the hand of God; and to Him alone belongs the glory." We might also attribute some of the credit to Cromwell himself, since his crusaders were well disciplined and trained in the latest military tactics. Supported by the New Model Army, Parliament ended the first phase of the civil war with the capture of King Charles I in 1646.

Civil War in England

A split now occurred in the parliamentary forces. A Presbyterian majority wanted to disband the army and restore Charles I with a Presbyterian state church. The army, composed mostly of the more radical Independents, who opposed an established Presbyterian church, marched on London in 1647 and began negotiations with the king. Charles took advantage of this division to flee and seek help from the Scots. Enraged by the king's treachery, Cromwell and the army engaged in a second civil war (1648) that ended with Cromwell's victory and the capture of the king. This time, Cromwell was determined to achieve a victory for the army's point of view. The Presbyterian members of Parliament were purged, leaving a Rump Parliament of fifty-three members of the House of Commons who then tried and condemned the king on a charge of treason and adjudged that "he, the said Charles Stuart, as a tyrant, traitor, murderer, and public enemy to the good people of this nation, shall be put to death by the severing of his head from his body." On January 30, 1649, Charles was beheaded, a most uncommon act in the seventeenth century. The revolution had triumphed, and the monarchy in England had been destroyed, at least for the moment.

CROMWELL AND NEW GOVERNMENTS After the death of the king, the Rump Parliament abolished the monarchy and the House of Lords and proclaimed England a republic or commonwealth (1649–1653). This was not an easy

Oliver Cromwell. Oliver Cromwell was a dedicated Puritan who helped form the New Model Army and defeat the forces supporting King Charles I. Unable to work with Parliament, he came to rely on military force to rule England. Cromwell is pictured here in 1649, on the eve of his military campaign in Ireland.

© National Portrait Gallery, London/SuperStock

period for Cromwell. As commander in chief of the army, he had to crush a Catholic uprising in Ireland, which he accomplished with a brutality that earned him the eternal enmity of the Irish people, as well as an uprising in Scotland on behalf of the son of Charles I.

Cromwell also faced opposition at home, especially from more radically minded groups who took advantage of the upheaval in England to push their agendas. The Levellers, for example, advocated such advanced ideas as freedom of speech, religious toleration, and a democratic republic, arguing for the right to vote for all male householders over the age of twenty-one. The Levellers also called for annual Parliaments, women's equality with men, and government programs to care for the poor. As one Leveller said, "The poorest he that is in England has a life to live as the greatest he." To Cromwell, a country gentleman, only people of property had the right to participate in the affairs of state, and he warned in a fit of rage: "I tell you . . . you have no other way to deal with these men but to break them or they will break you; and make void all that work that, with so many years' industry, toil, and pains, you have done . . . I tell you again, you are necessitated to break them."[9] And break them he did; Cromwell smashed the radicals by force. More than a century would pass before their ideas of democracy and equality became fashionable.

At the same time that Cromwell was dealing with the Levellers, he also found it difficult to work with the Rump Parliament and finally dispersed it by force. As the members of Parliament departed (in April 1653), he shouted after them, "It's you that have forced me to do this, for I have sought the Lord night and day that He would slay me rather than put upon me the doing of this work." With the certainty of one who is convinced he is right, Cromwell had destroyed both king and Parliament (see the box on p. 475).

The army provided a new government when it drew up the Instrument of Government, England's first and only written constitution. Executive power was vested in the Lord Protector (a position held by Cromwell) and legislative power in a reconstituted Parliament. But the new system failed to work. Cromwell found it difficult to work with Parliament, especially when its members debated his authority and advocated once again the creation of a Presbyterian state church. In 1655, Cromwell dissolved Parliament and divided the country into eleven regions, each ruled by a major general who served virtually as a military governor. To meet the cost of military government, Cromwell levied a 10 percent land tax on all former Royalists. Unable to establish a constitutional basis for a working government, Cromwell had resorted to military force to maintain the rule of the Independents, ironically using even more arbitrary policies than those of Charles I.

Oliver Cromwell died in 1658. After floundering for eighteen months, the military establishment decided that arbitrary rule by the army was no longer feasible and reestablished the monarchy in the person of Charles II, the

Opposing >< VIEWPOINTS

Oliver Cromwell: Three Perspectives

Oliver Cromwell was a strong leader with firm religious convictions. The first selection below, taken from a letter written after the defeat of the king's forces at Naseby in 1645, reveals Cromwell's feelings about the reasons for his military victory. The next selection, also by Cromwell, is taken from his comments after his army's massacre of Catholic forces at Drogheda in Catholic Ireland. The third selection is by Edmund Ludlow, a general on Cromwell's side who broke with Cromwell after the latter had become Lord Protector. The final selection by Edward Hyde, the first earl of Clarendon, a supporter of King Charles I and later Charles II, presents a royalist view of Cromwell.

⊶ ═╬═ ⊷

Oliver Cromwell on the Victory at Naseby

Sir, this is none other but the hand of God; and to Him alone belongs the glory, wherein none are to share with Him. The general [Fairfax] served you with all faithfulness and honor: and the best commendations I can give him is, that I dare say he attributes all to God, and would rather perish than assume to himself. Which is an honest and a thriving way, and yet as much for bravery may be given to him, in this action, as to a man.

Cromwell on the Massacre at Drogheda

The next day, the other two towers were summoned, in one of which was about six or seven score; but they refused to yield themselves, and we knowing that hunger must compel them, set only good guards to secure them from running away until their stomachs were come down. From one of the said towers, notwithstanding their condition, they killed and wounded some of our men. When they submitted, their officers were knocked on the head, and every tenth man of the soldiers killed, and the rest shipped for the Barbados. The soldiers in the other tower were all spared, as to their lives only, and shipped likewise for the Barbados.

I am persuaded that this is a righteous judgment of God upon these barbarous wretches, who have imbrued their hands in so much innocent blood; and that it will tend to prevent the effusion of blood for the future, which are the satisfactory grounds to such actions, which otherwise cannot but work remorse and regret.

Edmund Ludlow, *Memoirs*

Then I drew near to the council-table, where Cromwell charged me with dispersing treasonable books in Ireland, and with endeavoring to render the officers of the army disaffected, by discoursing to them concerning new models of Government. I acknowledged that I had caused some papers to be dispersed in Ireland, but denied that they justly could be called treasonable. . . .

"You do well," said he, "to reflect on our fears. . . . I now require you to give assurance not to act against the Government." I desired to be excused in that particular, reminding him of the reasons I had formerly given him for my refusal, adding, that I was in his power, and that he might use me as he thought fit. "Pray then," said he, "what is it that you would have? May not every man be as good as he will? What can you desire more than you have?" "It were easy," said I, "to tell what we would have." "What is that, I pray?" said he. "That which we fought for," said I, "that the nation might be governed by its own consent." "I am," said he, "as much for a government by consent as any man; but where shall we find that consent? Amongst the Prelatical, Presbyterian, Independent, Anabaptist, or Leveling Parties?" I answered, "Amongst those of all sorts who had acted with fidelity and affection to the public."

Lord Clarendon, *The History of the Rebellion and Civil Wars in England*

He was one of those men, . . . whom his very enemies could not condemn without commending him at the same time: for he could never have done half that mischief without great parts of courage, industry, and judgment. He must have had a wonderful understanding in the natures and humors of men, and as great a dexterity in applying them; who, from a private and obscure birth (though of a good family), without interest or estate, alliance or friendship, could raise himself to such a height, and compound and knead such opposite and contradictory tempers, humors, and interests into a consistence, that contributed to his designs, and to their own destruction; whilst himself grew insensibly powerful enough to cut off those by whom he had climbed, in the instant that they projected to demolish their own building. What [a Roman writer] said of Cinna [a Roman politician] may very justly be said of him: he attempted those things which no good man dared have ventured on; and achieved those in which none but a valiant and great man could have succeeded. Without doubt, no man with more wickedness ever attempted any thing, or brought to pass what he

(continued)

desired more wickedly, more in the face and contempt of religion, and moral honesty; yet wickedness as great as his could never have accomplished those trophies, without the assistance of a great spirit, an admirable circumspection and sagacity, and a most magnanimous resolution. ⮑

Q What motivated Cromwell's political and military actions? What was Edmund Ludlow's criticism of Cromwell, and how did Cromwell respond? In what ways did Edward Hyde see both good and bad features in Cromwell? How do you explain the differences in these three perspectives?

---

eldest son of Charles I (see Chart 15.1 below). The restoration of the Stuart monarchy ended England's time of troubles, but it was not long before yet another constitutional crisis arose.

RESTORATION OF THE MONARCHY   After eleven years of exile, Charles II (1660–1685) returned to England. As he entered London amid the acclaim of the people, he remarked sardonically, "I never knew that I was so popular in England." The restoration of the monarchy and the House of Lords did not mean, however, that the work of the English Revolution was undone. Parliament kept much of the power it had won: its role in government was acknowledged, the necessity for its consent to taxation was accepted, and arbitrary courts were still abolished. Yet Charles continued to push his own ideas, some of which were clearly out of step with many of the English people.

A serious religious problem disturbed the tranquility of Charles II's reign. After the restoration of the monarchy, a new Parliament (the Cavalier Parliament) met in 1661 and restored the Anglican Church as the official church of England. In addition, laws were passed to force everyone, particularly Catholics and Puritan Dissenters, to conform to the Anglican Church. Charles, however, was sympathetic to and perhaps even inclined toward Catholicism. Moreover, Charles's brother James, heir to the throne, did not hide the fact that he was a Catholic. Parliament's suspicions were therefore aroused in 1672 when Charles took the audacious step of issuing the Declaration of Indulgence, which suspended the laws that Parliament had passed against Catholics and Puritans. Parliament would have none of it and induced the king to suspend the declaration. Propelled by a strong anti-Catholic sentiment, Parliament then passed the Test Act of 1673, specifying that only Anglicans could hold military and civil offices.

A purported Catholic plot to assassinate King Charles and place his brother James on the throne, though soon

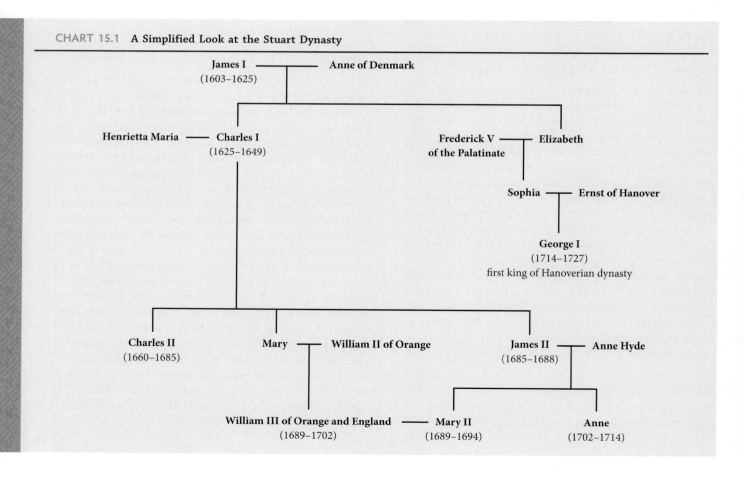

CHART 15.1   **A Simplified Look at the Stuart Dynasty**

exposed as imaginary, inflamed Parliament to attempt to pass a bill that would have barred James from the throne as a professed Catholic. Although these attempts failed, the debate over the bill created two political groupings: the Whigs, who wanted to exclude James and establish a Protestant king with toleration of Dissenters, and the Tories, who supported the king, despite their dislike of James as a Catholic, because they believed that Parliament should not tamper with the lawful succession to the throne. To foil these efforts, Charles dismissed Parliament in 1681, relying on French subsidies to rule alone. When he died in 1685, his Catholic brother came to the throne.

The accession of James II (1685–1688) virtually guaranteed a new constitutional crisis for England. An open and devout Catholic, his attempt to further Catholic interests made religion once more a primary cause of conflict between king and Parliament. Contrary to the Test Act, James named Catholics to high positions in the government, army, navy, and universities. In 1687, he issued a new Declaration of Indulgence, which suspended all laws barring Catholics and Dissenters from office. Parliamentary outcries against James's policies stopped short of rebellion because members knew that he was an old man and that his successors were his Protestant daughters Mary and Anne, born to his first wife. But on June 10, 1688, a son was born to James II's second wife, also a Catholic. Suddenly, the specter of a Catholic hereditary monarchy loomed large.

A GLORIOUS REVOLUTION A group of seven prominent English noblemen invited William of Orange, husband of James's daughter Mary, to invade England. An inveterate foe of Louis XIV, William welcomed this opportunity to fight France with England's resources. William and Mary raised an army and invaded England while James, his wife, and their infant son fled to France. With almost no bloodshed, England had embarked on a "Glorious Revolution," not over the issue of whether there would be a monarchy but rather over who would be monarch.

The events of late 1688 set the Glorious Revolution in motion. The far more important part was the Revolution Settlement, which confirmed William and Mary as monarchs. In January 1689, the Convention Parliament asserted that James had tried to subvert the constitution "by breaking the original contract between king and people" and declared the throne of England vacant. It then offered the throne to William and Mary, who accepted it along with the provisions of a declaration of rights, later enacted into law as the Bill of Rights in 1689 (see the box on p. 478). The Bill of Rights affirmed Parliament's right to make laws and levy taxes and made it impossible for kings to oppose or do without Parliament by stipulating that standing armies could be raised only with the consent of Parliament. Both elections and debates of Parliament had to be free, meaning that the king could not interfere. The rights of citizens to petition the sovereign, keep arms, have a jury trial, and not be subject to excessive bail were also confirmed. The Bill of Rights helped fashion a system of government based on the rule of law and a freely

Poland	
Merger of Poland and Lithuania	1569
Sigismund III	1587–1631
Beginning of liberum veto	1652
United Provinces	
Official recognition of United Provinces	1648
House of Orange	
William III	1672–1702
England	
James I	1603–1625
Charles I	1625–1649
Petition of Right	1628
First Civil War	1642–1646
Second Civil War	1648
Execution of Charles I	1649
Commonwealth	1649–1653
Death of Cromwell	1658
Restoration of monarchy	1660
Charles II	1660–1685
Cavalier Parliament	1661
Declaration of Indulgence	1672
Test Act	1673
James II	1685–1688
Declaration of Indulgence	1687
Glorious Revolution	1688
Bill of Rights	1689

elected Parliament, thus laying the foundation for a constitutional monarchy.

The Bill of Rights did not settle the religious questions that had played such a large role in England's troubles in the seventeenth century. The Toleration Act of 1689 granted Puritan Dissenters the right of free public worship (Catholics were still excluded), although they did not yet have full civil and political equality since the Test Act was not repealed. Although the Toleration Act did not mean complete religious freedom and equality, it marked a departure in English history: few people would ever again be persecuted for religious reasons.

Many historians have viewed the Glorious Revolution as the end of the seventeenth-century struggle between king and Parliament. By deposing one king and establishing another, Parliament had demolished the divine-right theory of kingship (William was, after all, king by grace of Parliament, not God) and confirmed its right to participate in the government. Parliament did not have complete control of the government, but it now had an unquestioned role in affairs of state. Over the next century, it would gradually prove to be the real authority in the English system of constitutional monarchy.

The Bill of Rights

In 1688, the English experienced yet another revolution, a bloodless one in which the Stuart king James II was replaced by Mary, James's daughter, and her husband, William of Orange. After William and Mary had assumed power, Parliament passed the Bill of Rights, which specified the rights of Parliament and laid the foundation for a constitutional monarchy.

✦ �ký⟩ ✦

The Bill of Rights

Whereas the said late King James II having abdicated the government, and the throne being thereby vacant, his Highness the prince of Orange (whom it has pleased Almighty God to make the glorious instrument of delivering this kingdom from popery and arbitrary power) did (by the device of the lords spiritual and temporal, and diverse principal persons of the Commons) cause letters to be written to the lords spiritual and temporal, being Protestants, and other letters to the several counties, cities, universities, boroughs, and Cinque Ports, for the choosing of such persons to represent them, as were of right to be sent to parliament, to meet and sit at Westminster upon the two and twentieth day of January, in this year 1689, in order to such an establishment as that their religion, laws, and liberties might not again be in danger of being subverted; upon which letters elections have been accordingly made.

And thereupon the said lords spiritual and temporal and Commons, pursuant to their respective letters and elections, being now assembled in a full and free representation of this nation, taking into their most serious consideration the best means for attaining the ends aforesaid, do in the first place (as their ancestors in like case have usually done), for the vindication and assertion of their ancient rights and liberties, declare:

1. That the pretended power of suspending laws, or the execution of laws, by regal authority, without consent of parliament is illegal.
2. That the pretended power of dispensing with the laws, or the execution of law by regal authority, as it has been assumed and exercised of late, is illegal.
3. That the commission for erecting the late court of commissioners for ecclesiastical causes, and all other commissions and courts of like nature, are illegal and pernicious.
4. That levying money for or to the use of the crown by pretense of prerogative, without grant of parliament, for longer time or in other manner than the same is or shall be granted, is illegal.
5. That it is the right of the subjects to petition the king, and all commitments and prosecutions for such petitioning are illegal.
6. That the raising or keeping a standing army within the kingdom in time of peace, unless it be with consent of parliament, is against law.
7. That the subjects which are Protestants may have arms for their defense suitable to their conditions, and as allowed by law.
8. That election of members of parliament ought to be free.
9. That the freedom of speech, and debates or proceedings in parliament, ought not to be impeached or questioned in any court or place out of parliament.
10. That excessive bail ought not to be required, nor excessive fines imposed, nor cruel and unusual punishments inflicted.
11. That jurors ought to be duly impaneled and returned, and jurors which pass upon men in trials for high treason ought to be freeholders.
12. That all grants and promises of fines and forfeitures of particular persons before conviction are illegal and void.
13. And that for redress of all grievances, and for the amending, strengthening, and preserving of the laws, parliament ought to be held frequently. ⟩

Q How did the Bill of Rights lay the foundation for a constitutional monarchy? What key aspects of this document testify to the exceptional nature of English state politics in the seventeenth century?

RESPONSES TO REVOLUTION The English revolutions of the seventeenth century prompted very different responses from two English political thinkers—Thomas Hobbes and John Locke. Thomas Hobbes (1588–1679), who lived during the English Civil War, was alarmed by the revolutionary upheavals in his contemporary England. Hobbes's name has since been associated with the state's claim to absolute authority over its subjects, a topic that he elaborated in his major treatise on political thought known as the *Leviathan* (luh-VY-uh-thun), published in 1651.

Hobbes claimed that in the state of nature, before society was organized, human life was "solitary, poor, nasty, brutish, and short." Humans were guided not by reason and moral ideals but by animalistic instincts and a ruthless struggle for self-preservation. To save themselves from destroying each other (the "war of every man against every man"), people contracted to form a commonwealth, which Hobbes called "that great Leviathan (or rather, to speak more reverently, that mortal god) to which we owe our peace and defense." This commonwealth placed its collective power into the hands of a sovereign authority, preferably a single ruler, who served as executor, legislator, and judge. This absolute ruler possessed unlimited power. In Hobbes's view, subjects may not rebel; if they do, they must be suppressed.

John Locke (1632–1704) viewed the exercise of political power quite differently from Hobbes and argued against

the absolute rule of one man. Locke's experience of English politics during the Glorious Revolution was incorporated into a political work called *Two Treatises of Government*. Like Hobbes, Locke began with the state of nature before human existence became organized socially. But unlike Hobbes, Locke believed that humans lived then in a state of equality and freedom rather than a state of war. In this state of nature, humans had certain inalienable natural rights—to life, liberty, and property. Like Hobbes, Locke did not believe all was well in the state of nature. Since there was no impartial judge in the state of nature, people found it difficult to protect these rights. So they mutually agreed to establish a government to ensure the protection of their rights. This agreement established mutual obligations: government would protect the rights of the people while the people would act reasonably toward government. But if a government broke this agreement—for example, if a monarch failed to live up to his obligation to protect the people's rights or claimed absolute authority and made laws without the consent of the community—the people might form a new government. For Locke, however, the community of people was primarily the landholding aristocracy

who were represented in Parliament, not the landless masses. Locke was hardly an advocate of political democracy, but his ideas proved important to both the Americans and the French in the eighteenth century and were used to support demands for constitutional government, the rule of law, and the protection of rights.

The Flourishing of European Culture

 Focus Question: How did the artistic and literary achievements of this era reflect the political and economic developments of the period?

In the midst of religious wars and the growth of absolutism, European culture continued to flourish. The era was blessed with a number of prominent artists and writers.

The Changing Faces of Art

After the Renaissance, European art passed through a number of stylistic stages. The artistic Renaissance came to an end when a new movement called Mannerism emerged in Italy in the 1520s and 1530s.

MANNERISM The Reformation's revival of religious values brought much political turmoil. Especially in Italy, the worldly enthusiasm of the Renaissance gave way to anxiety, uncertainty, suffering, and a yearning for spiritual experience. **Mannerism** reflected this environment in its

El Greco, *Laocoön*. Mannerism reached its height of expression in the work of El Greco. Born in Crete, trained in Venice and Rome, and settling finally in Spain, El Greco worked as a church painter in Toledo. Pictured here is his version of the *Laocoön*, a Hellenistic sculpture discovered in Rome in 1506. The elongated, contorted bodies project a world of suffering while the somber background scene of the city of Toledo and the threatening sky add a sense of terror and doom.

deliberate attempt to break down the High Renaissance principles of balance, harmony, and moderation (the term *Mannerism* derives from critics who considered their contemporary artists to be second-rate imitators, painting "in the manner of" Michelangelo's late style). Italian Mannerist painters deliberately distorted the rules of proportion by portraying elongated figures that conveyed a sense of suffering and a strong emotional atmosphere filled with anxiety and confusion.

Mannerism spread from Italy to other parts of Europe and perhaps reached its apogee in the work of El Greco (1541–1614). Doménikos Theotocópoulos (called "the Greek"—El Greco) was from Crete, but after studying in Venice and Rome, he moved in the 1570s to Spain, where he became a church painter in Toledo. El Greco's elongated and contorted figures, portrayed in unusual shades of yellow and green against an eerie background of turbulent grays, reflect the artist's desire to create a world of intense emotion.

THE BAROQUE PERIOD   Mannerism was eventually replaced by a new movement—the **Baroque**—that began in Italy in the last quarter of the sixteenth century and spread to the rest of Europe. The style was most wholeheartedly embraced by the Catholic reform movement, as is evident at the Catholic courts, especially those of the Habsburgs in Madrid, Prague, Vienna, and Brussels. Although it was resisted in France, England, and the Netherlands, eventually the Baroque style spread to all of Europe and to Latin America.

Baroque artists sought to bring together the Classical ideals of Renaissance art with the spiritual feelings of the sixteenth-century religious revival. The Baroque painting style was known for its use of dramatic effects to arouse the emotions. In large part, though, Baroque art and architecture reflected the search for power that was such a large part of the seventeenth-century ethos. Baroque churches and palaces were magnificent and richly detailed. Kings and princes wanted other kings and princes as well as their subjects to be in awe of their power.

Baroque painting was known for its use of dramatic effects to heighten emotional intensity. This style was especially evident in the works of the Flemish master Peter Paul Rubens (1577–1640), a prolific artist and an important figure in the spread of the Baroque from Italy to other parts of Europe. In his artistic masterpieces, bodies in violent motion, heavily fleshed nudes, a dramatic use of light and shadow, and rich, sensuous pigments converge to express intense emotions. The restless forms and constant movement blend together into a dynamic unity.

Perhaps the greatest figure of the Baroque was the Italian architect and sculptor Gian Lorenzo Bernini (ZHAHN loh-RENT-zoh bur-NEE-nee) (1598–1680), who completed Saint Peter's Basilica at the Vatican and designed the vast colonnade enclosing the piazza in front of it. Action, exuberance, profusion, and dramatic effects mark the work of Bernini in the interior of Saint Peter's, where his *Throne of Saint Peter* hovers in midair, held by

Peter Paul Rubens, *The Landing of Marie de' Medici at Marseilles.* Peter Paul Rubens played a key role in spreading the Baroque style from Italy to other parts of Europe. In *The Landing of Marie de' Medici at Marseilles,* Rubens made dramatic use of light and color, bodies in motion, and luxurious nudes to heighten the emotional intensity of the scene. This was one of a cycle of twenty-one paintings dedicated to the queen mother of France.

the hands of the four great doctors of the Catholic Church. Above the chair, rays of golden light drive a mass of clouds and angels toward the spectator. In his most striking sculptural work, the *Ecstasy of Saint Theresa,* Bernini depicts a moment of mystical experience in the life of the sixteenth-century Spanish saint. The elegant draperies and the expression on her face create a sensuously real portrayal of physical ecstasy.

Less well known than the male artists who dominated the art world of seventeenth-century Italy but prominent in her own right was Artemisia Gentileschi (ar-tuh-MEE-zhuh jen-tuh-LESS-kee) (1593–1653). Born in Rome, she studied painting under her father's direction. In 1616, she moved to Florence and began a successful career as a painter. At the age of twenty-three, she became the first woman to be elected to the Florentine Academy of Design. Although she was known internationally in her day as a portrait painter, her fame now rests on a series of pictures of heroines from the Old Testament. Most famous is *Judith Beheading Holofernes,* a dramatic rendering of the biblical scene in which Judith slays the Assyrian general Holofernes to save her besieged town from the Assyrian army.

Gian Lorenzo Bernini, *Ecstasy of Saint Theresa.* One of the great artists of the Baroque period was the Italian sculptor and architect Gian Lorenzo Bernini. The *Ecstasy of Saint Theresa*, created for the Cornaro Chapel in the Church of Santa Maria della Vittoria in Rome, was one of Bernini's most famous sculptures. Bernini sought to convey visually Theresa's mystical experience when, according to her description, an angel pierced her heart repeatedly with a golden arrow.

FRENCH CLASSICISM In the second half of the seventeenth century, France replaced Italy as the cultural leader of Europe. Rejecting the Baroque style as overly showy and impassioned, the French remained committed to the Classical values of the High Renaissance. French late Classicism, with its emphasis on clarity, simplicity, balance, and harmony of design, was, however, a rather austere version of the High Renaissance style. Its triumph reflected the shift in seventeenth-century French society from chaos to order. Though it rejected the emotionalism and high drama of the Baroque, French Classicism continued the Baroque's conception of grandeur in the portrayal of noble subjects, especially those from Classical antiquity. Nicolas Poussin (NEE-koh-lah poo-SANH) (1594–1665) exemplified these principles in his paintings. His choice of scenes from Classical mythology, the orderliness of his landscapes, the postures of his figures copied from the sculptures of antiquity, and his use of brown tones all reflect French Classicism of the late seventeenth century.

DUTCH REALISM The supremacy of Dutch commerce in the seventeenth century was paralleled by a brilliant flowering of Dutch painting. Wealthy patricians and burghers of

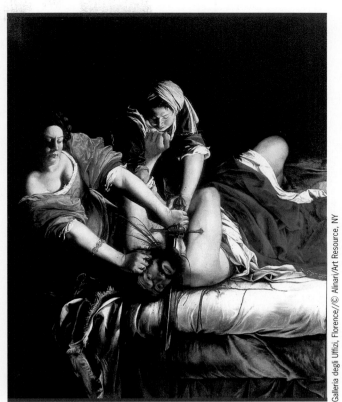

Artemisia Gentileschi, *Judith Beheading Holofernes.*
Artemisia Gentileschi painted a series of pictures portraying scenes from the lives of courageous Old Testament women. In this painting, a determined Judith, armed with her victim's sword, struggles to saw off the head of Holofernes. Gentileschi realistically and dramatically shows the gruesome nature of Judith's act.

Dutch urban society commissioned works of art for their guild halls, town halls, and private dwellings. The interests of this burgher society were reflected in the subject matter of many Dutch paintings: portraits of themselves, group portraits of their military companies and guilds, landscapes, seascapes, genre scenes, still lifes, and the interiors of their residences. Neither classical nor Baroque, Dutch painters were primarily interested in the realistic portrayal of secular everyday life.

This interest in painting scenes of everyday life is evident in the work of Judith Leyster (LESS-tur) (c. 1609–1660), who established her own independent painting career, a remarkable occurrence in seventeenth-century Europe. Leyster became the first female member of the painting Guild of Saint Luke in Haarlem, which enabled her to set up her own workshop and take on three male pupils. Musicians playing their instruments, women sewing, children laughing while playing games, and actors performing all form the subject matter of Leyster's paintings of everyday Dutch life.

The finest product of the golden age of Dutch painting was Rembrandt van Rijn (REM-brant vahn RYN) (1606–1669). During his early career, Rembrandt painted opulent portraits and grandiose scenes that were often quite colorful. He was prolific and successful, but he turned away

Judith Leyster, *Laughing Children with a Cat.* Although Judith Leyster was a well-known artist to her Dutch contemporaries, her fame diminished soon after her death. In the late nineteenth century, a Dutch art historian rediscovered her work. In *Laughing Children with a Cat*, painted in 1629, she shows two children laughing as one tickles the other, a scene repeated throughout history.

Rembrandt van Rijn, *Syndics of the Cloth Guild.* The Dutch experienced a golden age of painting during the seventeenth century. The burghers and patricians of Dutch urban society commissioned works of art, and these quite naturally reflected the burghers' interests, as this painting by Rembrandt illustrates.

William Shakespeare: In Praise of England

William Shakespeare is one of the most famous play-wrights of the Western world. He was a universal genius, outclassing all others in his psychological insights, depth of characterization, imaginative skills, and versatility. His historical plays reflected the patriotic enthusiasm of the English in the Elizabethan era, as this excerpt from *Richard II* illustrates.

William Shakespeare, *Richard II*

This royal throne of kings, this sceptered isle,
This earth of majesty, this seat of Mars,
This other Eden, demi-Paradise,
This fortress built by Nature for herself
Against infection and the hand of war,
This happy breed of men, this little world,
This precious stone set in the silver sea,
Which serves it in the office of a wall
Or as a moat defensive to a house
Against the envy of less happier lands—
This blessed plot, this earth, this realm, this
England,
This nurse, this teeming womb of royal kings,
Feared by their breed and famous by their birth,

Renowned for their deeds as far from home,
For Christian service and true chivalry,
As is the sepulcher in stubborn Jewry [the Holy
Sepulcher in Jerusalem]
Of the world's ransom, blessed Mary's Son—
This land of such dear souls, this dear dear land,
Dear for her reputation through the world,
Is now leased out, I die pronouncing it,
Like a tenement or pelting farm.
England, bound in with the triumphant sea,
Whose rocky shore beats back the envious siege
Of watery Neptune, is now bound in with shame,
With inky blots and rotten parchment bonds.
That England, what was wont to conquer others,
Hath made a shamful conquest of itself.
Ah, would the scandal vanish with my life,
How happy then were my ensuing death!

Q Why is William Shakespeare aptly described as not merely a playwright, but a "complete man of the theater"? Which countries might Shakespeare have meant by the phrase "the envy of less happier lands"?

---

from materialistic success to follow his own artistic path; in the process, he lost public support and died bankrupt.

Although Rembrandt shared the Dutch predilection for realistic portraits, he became more introspective as he grew older. He refused to follow his contemporaries, whose pictures were largely secular; half of his own paintings depicted scenes from biblical tales. Since the Protestant tradition of hostility to religious pictures had discouraged artistic expression, Rembrandt stands out as the one great Protestant painter of the seventeenth century.

A Wondrous Age of Theater

In England and Spain, writing reached new heights between 1580 and 1640. All of these impressive new works were written in the vernacular. Except for academic fields, such as theology, philosophy, jurisprudence, and the sciences, Latin was no longer a universal literary language.

The greatest age of English literature is often called the Elizabethan era because much of the English cultural flowering of the late sixteenth and early seventeenth centuries occurred during the reign of Queen Elizabeth I. Elizabethan literature exhibits the exuberance and pride associated with England's international exploits at the time. Of all the forms of Elizabethan literature, none expressed the energy and intellectual versatility of the era better than drama. And of all the dramatists, none is more famous than William Shakespeare (1564–1616).

WILLIAM SHAKESPEARE Shakespeare was the son of a prosperous glovemaker from Stratford-upon-Avon. When he appeared in London in 1592, Elizabethans were already addicted to the stage. In Greater London, as many as six theaters were open six afternoons a week. London theaters ranged from the Globe, which was a circular unroofed structure holding three thousand spectators, to the Blackfriars, which was roofed and held only five hundred. In the former, an admission charge of a penny or two enabled even the lower classes to attend; the higher prices in the latter ensured an audience of the well-to-do. Elizabethan audiences varied greatly, putting pressure on playwrights to write works that pleased nobles, lawyers, merchants, and even vagabonds.

William Shakespeare was a "complete man of the theater." Although best known for writing plays, he was also an actor and shareholder in the chief company of the time, the Lord Chamberlain's Company, which played in theaters as diverse as the Globe and the Blackfriars. Shakespeare has long been recognized as a universal genius. A master of the English language, he was instrumental in codifying a language that was still in transition. His technical proficiency, however, was matched by an incredible insight into human psychology. In tragedies as well as comedies, Shakespeare exhibited a remarkable understanding of the human condition (see the box above).

SPAIN'S GOLDEN CENTURY The theater was also one of the most creative forms of expression during Spain's golden century. The first professional theaters established in Seville and Madrid in the 1570s were run by actors' companies, as in England. Soon a public playhouse could be found in every large town, including Mexico City in the New World. Touring companies brought the latest Spanish plays to all parts of the Spanish Empire.

Beginning in the 1580s, the agenda for playwrights was set by Lope de Vega (LOH-pay day VAY-guh) (1562–1635). Like Shakespeare, he was from a middle-class background. He was an incredibly prolific writer; almost one-third of his fifteen hundred plays survive. They have been characterized as witty, charming, action packed, and realistic. Lope de Vega made no apologies for the fact that he wrote his plays to please his audiences. In a treatise on drama written in 1609, he stated that the foremost duty of the playwright was to satisfy public demand. Shakespeare undoubtedly believed the same thing, since his livelihood depended on public approval, but Lope de Vega was considerably more cynical about it: he remarked that if anyone thought he had written his plays for fame, "undeceive him and tell him that I wrote them for money."

FRENCH DRAMA As the great age of theater in England and Spain was drawing to a close around 1630, a new dramatic era began to dawn in France that lasted into the 1680s. Unlike Shakespeare in England and Lope de Vega in Spain, French playwrights wrote more for an elite audience and were forced to depend on royal patronage. Louis XIV used theater as he did art and architecture—to attract attention to his monarchy.

French dramatists cultivated a style that emphasized the clever, polished, and correct over the emotional and imaginative. Many of the French works of the period derived both their themes and their plots from Classical Greek and Roman sources, especially evident in the works of Jean-Baptiste Racine (ZHAHNH-bah-TEEST ra-SEEN) (1639–1699). In *Phèdre,* which has been called his best play, Racine followed closely the plot of *Hippolytus* by the Greek tragedian Euripides. Like the ancient tragedians, Racine, who perfected the French neoclassical tragic style, focused on conflicts, such as between love and honor or inclination and duty, that characterized and revealed the tragic dimensions of life.

Jean-Baptiste Molière (ZHAHNH-bah-TEEST mohl-YAYR) (1622–1673) enjoyed the favor of the French court and benefited from the patronage of King Louis XIV. Molière wrote, produced, and acted in a series of comedies that often satirized the religious and social world of his time. In *Tartuffe,* he ridiculed religious hypocrisy. His satires, however, sometimes got him into trouble. The Paris clergy did not find *Tartuffe* funny and had it banned for five years. Only the protection of the king saved Molière from more severe harassment.

CHAPTER SUMMARY

To many historians, the seventeenth century has assumed extraordinary proportions. The divisive effects of the Reformation had been assimilated and the concept of a united Christendom, held as an ideal since the Middle Ages, had been irrevocably destroyed by the religious wars, making possible the emergence of a system of nation-states in which power politics took on an increasing significance. The growth of political thought focusing on the secular origins of state power reflected the changes that were going on in seventeenth-century society.

Within those states, there slowly emerged some of the machinery that made possible a growing centralization of power. In those states called absolutist, strong monarchs

with the assistance of their aristocracies took the lead in providing the leadership for greater centralization. In this so-called age of absolutism, Louis XIV, the Sun King of France, was the model for other rulers. His palace of Versailles, where the aristocracy was entertained and controlled by ceremony and etiquette, symbolized his

authority. Louis revoked his grandfather's Edict of Nantes, and he fought four costly wars, mainly to acquire lands on France's eastern borders. Strong monarchy also prevailed in central and eastern Europe, where three new powers made their appearance: Prussia, Austria, and Russia. Peter the Great attempted to westernize Russia, especially militarily, and built St. Petersburg, a new capital city, as his window on the west.

But not all European states followed the pattern of absolute monarchy. Especially important were developments in England, where a series of struggles between king and Parliament took place in the seventeenth century. The conflict between the Stuart kings, who were advocates of divine-right monarchy, and Parliament led to civil war and the creation of a republic and then a military dictatorship under Oliver Cromwell. After his death, the Stuart monarchy was restored, but a new conflict led to the overthrow of James II and the establishment of a new order. The landed aristocracy gained power at the expense of the monarchs, thus laying the foundations for a constitutional government in which Parliament provided the focus for the institutions of centralized power. In all the major European states, a growing concern for power and dynamic expansion led to larger armies and greater conflict. War remained an endemic feature of Western civilization.

But the search for order and harmony continued, evident in art and literature. At the same time, religious preoccupations and values were losing ground to secular considerations. The seventeenth century was a period of transition toward the more secular spirit that has characterized modern Western civilization to the present. No stronger foundation for this spirit could be found than in the new view of the universe that was ushered in by the Scientific Revolution of the seventeenth century, and it is to that story that we turn in the next chapter.

CHAPTER TIMELINE

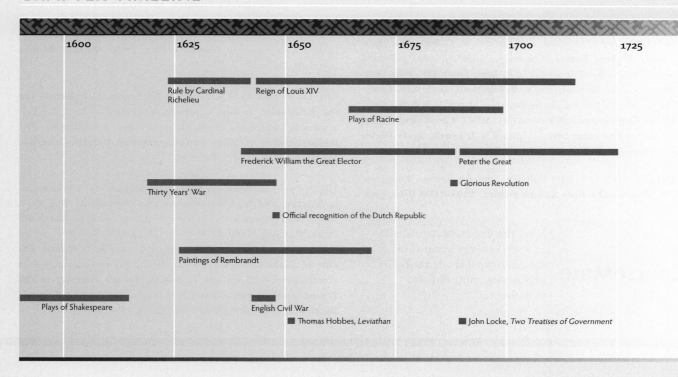

| 1600 | 1625 | 1650 | 1675 | 1700 | 1725 |

Rule by Cardinal Richelieu

Reign of Louis XIV

Plays of Racine

Frederick William the Great Elector

Peter the Great

Glorious Revolution

Thirty Years' War

Official recognition of the Dutch Republic

Paintings of Rembrandt

Plays of Shakespeare

English Civil War

Thomas Hobbes, *Leviathan*

John Locke, *Two Treatises of Government*

CHAPTER REVIEW

Upon Reflection

Q What does the witchcraft craze tell us about European society in the sixteenth and seventeenth centuries?

Q What did Louis XIV hope to accomplish in his domestic and foreign policies? To what extent did he succeed?

Q What role did the nobility play in Poland and England?

Key Terms

absolutism (p. 454)
divine-right monarchy (p. 454)
intendants (p. 455)
parlements (p. 456)
boyars (p. 464)
procurator (p. 466)
Janissaries (p. 469)
gentry (p. 473)
Mannerism (p. 479)
Baroque (p. 480)

Suggestions for Further Reading

GENERAL WORKS For general works on the seventeenth century, see **T. Munck, *Seventeenth-Century Europe, 1598–1700,*** 2nd ed. (London, 2005); **Q. Deakin, *Expansion, War, and Rebellion, 1598–1661*** (Cambridge, 2000); and **J. Bergin, *Seventeenth-Century Europe, 1598–1715*** (Oxford, 2001).

WITCHCRAFT CRAZE The story of the witchcraft craze can be examined in **J. Klaits, *Servants of Satan: The Age of the Witch Hunts*** (Bloomington, Ind., 1985). See also **R. Briggs, *Witches and***

Neighbors: The Social and Cultural Context of European Witchcraft, 2nd ed. (Oxford, 2002).

THIRTY YEARS' WAR The fundamental study of the Thirty Years' War is now **P. H. Wilson, *The Thirty Years War: Europe's Tragedy*** (Cambridge, Mass., 2009). For a brief study, see **R. Bonney, *The Thirty Years' War, 1618–1648*** (Oxford, 2002).

THE MILITARY REVOLUTION On the military revolution, see **G. Parker, *The Military Revolution: Military Innovation and the Rise of the West, 1500–1800,*** 3rd ed. (Cambridge, 1995), and **J. M. Black, *A Military Revolution? Military Change and European Society*** (London, 1991).

FRANCE AND SPAIN For succinct accounts of seventeenth-century French history, see **R. Briggs, *Early Modern France, 1560–1715,*** 2nd ed. (Oxford, 1998), and **J. B. Collins, *The State in Early Modern France*** (Cambridge, 1995). A solid and very readable biography of Louis XIV is **A. Levi, *Louis XIV*** (New York, 2004). For a shorter study, see **P. R. Campbell, *Louis XIV, 1661–1715*** (London, 1993). See also the collection of articles in **P. Sonnino, ed., *The Reign of Louis XIV*** (New York, 1990). A good general work on seventeenth-century Spanish history is **J. Lynch, *Spain Under the Habsburgs,*** 2nd ed. (New York, 1981).

CENTRAL AND EASTERN EUROPE On the German states, see **P. H. Wilson, *The Holy Roman Empire, 1495–1806*** (New York,

1999). On the creation of Austria, see **C. Ingrao, *The Habsburg Monarchy, 1618–1815*** (Cambridge, 1994), and **P. S. Fichtner, *The Habsburg Monarchy, 1490–1848*** (New York, 2003). On Austria and Prussia, see **P. H. Wilson, *Absolutism in Central Europe*** (New York, 2000). On Frederick William the Great Elector, see **D. McKay, *The Great Elector*** (Essex, 2001).

RUSSIA Works on Peter the Great include **L. Hughes, *Russia in the Age of Peter the Great*** (New Haven, Conn., 1998), and **P. Bushkovitz, *Peter the Great*** (Oxford, 2001).

ENGLISH REVOLUTIONS On the period of the English Revolutions, see **M. A. Kishlansky, *A Monarchy Transformed*** (London, 1996), and **D. Purkiss, *The English Civil War*** (New York, 2006). On Oliver Cromwell, see **P. Gaunt, *Oliver Cromwell*** (Cambridge, Mass., 1996). For a general survey of the post-Cromwellian era, see **T. Harris, *Politics Under the Late Stuarts*** (London, 1993).

UNITED PROVINCES On the United Provinces, **J. Israel, *The Dutch Republic: Its Rise, Greatness, and Fall*** (New York, 1995), is a valuable but lengthy study. Of much value is **S. Schama, *The Embarrassment of Riches: An Interpretation of Dutch Culture in the Golden Age*** (New York, 1987).

EUROPEAN CULTURE A brief, readable guide to Mannerism is **L. Murray, *The High Renaissance and Mannerism*** (New York, 1985). For a general survey of Baroque culture, see **F. C. Marchetti et al., *Baroque, 1600–1770*** (New York, 2005). The literature on Shakespeare is enormous. For a biography, see **A. L. Rowse, *The Life of Shakespeare*** (New York, 1963). For an examination of French and Dutch art, see **A. Merot, *French Painting in the Seventeenth Century*** (New Haven, Conn., 1995), and **S. Slive, *Dutch Painting, 1600–1800*** (New Haven, Conn., 1993).

Visit the CourseMate website at www.cengagebrain.com for additional study tools and review materials for this chapter.

1. The Baroque style

   (A) represents an artistic spiritual element that was brought about by the Protestant Reformation.
   (B) invoked an element of grandeur and opulence that glorified the political leadership of European monarchs.
   (C) originated in western Europe due to the emphasis on nature and the revival of Classical architecture that was taking place there.
   (D) was heavily influenced by the Islamic architecture that was dominant in southern Spain.
   (E) was brought about by the artistic changes of the Italian Renaissance.

2. The Thirty Years' War resulted in all of the following EXCEPT

   (A) expanded religious toleration for Lutherans, Catholics, and Calvinists.
   (B) the revival of the economies and populations in many German states.
   (C) the expansion of France's territorial holdings.
   (D) a decline in the power of the Habsburgs as the Holy Roman Emperor lost prestige and power.
   (E) greater independence for 300 German states.

3. The seventeenth century in Europe could best be characterized as

   (A) plagued by wars, peasant uprisings, and noble unrest.
   (B) a period of rejuvenation and rebirth as art and culture flourished.
   (C) a time of political repression and social upheaval as movements such as nationalism spurred revolutions.
   (D) a period of political and economic liberalism as seen in the writings of French intellectuals.
   (E) a time of academic renewal when peasants sought greater knowledge of their surroundings.

4. Which of the following correctly pairs a European king with his adviser?

   (A) Henry II—Colbert
   (B) Louis XV—Mazarin
   (C) Louis XIV—Sully
   (D) Louis XIII—Richelieu
   (E) Henry III—Necker

5. Peter the Great accomplished all of the following EXCEPT

   (A) gaining a warm-water port for Russia.
   (B) limiting the power of the Russian Orthodox Church.
   (C) building a new capital city of St. Petersburg.
   (D) sealing an agreement to share power with the boyars.
   (E) establishing a shipbuilding industry in Russia.

6. As a result of Louis XIV's reign, France

   (A) doubled the size of its borders and became financially stable.
   (B) pacified its nobles and formed an alliance between Protestants and Catholics.
   (C) was left with a great amount of debt and little effective leadership to guide the country.
   (D) saw the power of the nobles increase as the country moved closer to becoming a constitutional monarchy.
   (E) emerged as the intellectual and technological leader of western Europe.

7. The primary unifying force for the noncontiguous Prussian state was

   (A) its sense of history and its multiethnic populations.
   (B) the building of a new state army.
   (C) an alliance between the Junkers and the king.
   (D) the feeling of nationalism within the country.
   (E) the love and admiration for its leader, Frederick William the Great Elector.

8. By 1650, the Austrian state faced all of the following EXCEPT

   (A) constant invasions by the Ottoman Empire.
   (B) differences among the multiple nationalities within the country.
   (C) an inability to become highly centralized.
   (D) a strong group of Magyar landowners in the Hungarian territories.
   (E) a choice not to expand its borders within eastern Europe.

9. In *Leviathan* (1651), Thomas Hobbes said that life in the state of nature was "solitary, poor, nasty, brutish, and short." With which form of political thought is this quotation most closely associated?

   (A) divine right
   (B) absolutism
   (C) oligarchy
   (D) constitutional monarchy
   (E) republicanism

10. Which of the following marked the reigns of both James I and Charles I?

   (A) Puritan unrest, Parliament's control of the purse, and belief in the divine right of kings
   (B) wars with the German states, uprisings of Catholics, and noble attacks
   (C) civil peace, religious harmony, and an English Renaissance
   (D) Catholic uprisings, Irish rebellion, and French attacks
   (E) mass emigration, famine, and civil war

11. The Levellers hoped to achieve which of the following?

   (A) freedom of religion
   (B) freedom of speech
   (C) a democratic republic
   (D) universal male suffrage
   (E) All of the options are correct.

12. Under Lord Protector Oliver Cromwell,

   (A) England intervened in the Thirty Years' War on behalf of German Protestants.
   (B) the state enacted divine right as the official dogma of the Church of England.
   (C) the Irish faced heavy persecution.
   (D) many Calvinists sought to return to England from the North American colonies.
   (E) the English army fell into disrepair as Cromwell practiced antiquated military tactics and style.

13. What was the political impact of the Glorious Revolution of 1688?

   (A) It established a new monarchical state of absolute rule.
   (B) It forged a union between the nobility and the church.
   (C) It created a limited government and ensured a bill of rights for the people.
   (D) It formed a new revolutionary state in England under a republican government.
   (E) It forced out the Stuarts and brought in the Hanovers to begin a new dynasty.

14. Which of the following factors best explains the growth and expansion of the hysteria over witchcraft during the sixteenth and seventeenth centuries?

   (A) increasing tension within villages across gender and class divisions
   (B) rapid growth in the practice of infanticide
   (C) the decline of civil and religious conflict
   (D) widespread dissemination of literature due to the use of the printing press
   (E) the increasing number of women holding political positions

A nineteenth-century painting of Galileo before the Holy Office in the Vatican in 1633

Louvre, Paris//© Erich Lessing/Art Resource, NY

Toward a New Heaven and a New Earth: The Scientific Revolution and the Emergence of Modern Science

CHAPTER OUTLINE AND FOCUS QUESTIONS

Background to the Scientific Revolution

Q What developments during the Middle Ages and the Renaissance contributed to the Scientific Revolution of the seventeenth century?

Toward a New Heaven: A Revolution in Astronomy

Q What did Copernicus, Kepler, Galileo, and Newton contribute to a new vision of the universe, and how did it differ from the Ptolemaic conception of the universe?

Advances in Medicine and Chemistry

Q What did Paracelsus, Vesalius, and Harvey contribute to a scientific view of medicine?

Women in the Origins of Modern Science

Q What role did women play in the Scientific Revolution?

Toward a New Earth: Descartes, Rationalism, and a New View of Humankind

Q Why is Descartes considered the "founder of modern rationalism"?

The Scientific Method and the Spread of Scientific Knowledge

Q How were the ideas of the Scientific Revolution spread, and what impact did they have on society and religion?

CRITICAL THINKING

Q In what ways were the intellectual, political, social, and religious developments of the seventeenth century related?

IN ADDITION TO the political, economic, social, and international crises of the seventeenth century, we need to add an intellectual one. The Scientific Revolution questioned and ultimately challenged conceptions and beliefs about the nature of the external world and reality that had crystallized into a rather strict orthodoxy by the Later Middle Ages. Derived from the works of ancient Greeks and Romans and grounded in Christian thought, the medieval worldview had become formidable. But the breakdown of Christian unity during the Reformation and the subsequent religious wars had created an environment in which Europeans became more comfortable with challenging both the ecclesiastical and political realms. Should it surprise us that a challenge to intellectual authority soon followed?

The Scientific Revolution taught Europeans to view the universe and their place in it in a new way. The shift from an earth-centered to a sun-centered cosmos had an emotional as well as an intellectual effect on the people who understood it. Thus, the Scientific Revolution, popularized in the eighteenth-century Enlightenment, stands as the major force in the transition to the largely secular, rational, and materialistic perspective that has defined the modern Western mentality since its full acceptance in the nineteenth and twentieth centuries.

The transition to a new worldview, however, was far from easy. In the seventeenth century, the Italian scientist Galileo Galilei (gal-li-LAY-oh GAL-li-lay), an outspoken advocate of the new worldview, found that his ideas were strongly opposed by the authorities of the Catholic Church. Galileo's position was clear: "I hold the sun to be situated motionless in the center of the revolution of the celestial bodies, while the earth rotates on its axis and revolves about the sun." Moreover, "nothing physical that sense-experience sets before our eyes . . . ought to be called in question (much less condemned) upon the testimony of Biblical passages." But the church had a different view, and in 1633, Galileo, now sixty-eight and in ill health, was called before the dreaded Inquisition in Rome. He was kept waiting for two months before he was tried and found guilty of heresy and disobedience. Completely shattered by the experience, he denounced his errors: "With a sincere heart and unfeigned faith I curse and detest the said errors and heresies contrary to the Holy Church." Legend holds that when he left the trial room, Galileo muttered to himself: "And yet it does move!" Galileo had been silenced, but his writings remained, and they spread through Europe. The Inquisition had failed to stop the new ideas of the Scientific Revolution.

In one sense, the Scientific Revolution was not a revolution. It was not characterized by the explosive change and rapid overthrow of traditional authority that we normally associate with the word *revolution*. The Scientific Revolution did overturn centuries of authority, but only in a gradual and piecemeal fashion. Nevertheless, its results were truly revolutionary. The Scientific Revolution was a key factor in setting Western civilization along its modern secular and materialistic path.

Background to the Scientific Revolution

 FOCUS QUESTION: What developments during the Middle Ages and the Renaissance contributed to the Scientific Revolution of the seventeenth century?

To say that the **Scientific Revolution** brought about a dissolution of the medieval worldview is not to say that the Middle Ages was a period of scientific ignorance. Many educated Europeans took an intense interest in the world around them since it was, after all, "God's handiwork" and therefore an appropriate subject for study. Late medieval scholastic philosophers had advanced mathematical and physical thinking in many ways, but the subjection of these thinkers to a strict theological framework and their unquestioning reliance on a few ancient authorities, especially Aristotle and Galen, limited where they could go. Many "natural philosophers," as medieval scientists were called, preferred refined logical analysis to systematic observations of the natural world. A number of changes and advances in the fifteenth and sixteenth centuries may have played a major role in helping "natural philosophers" abandon their old views and develop new ones.

Ancient Authors and Renaissance Artists

Whereas medieval scholars had made use of Aristotle, Galen, and Ptolemy in Latin translations to develop many of their positions in the fields of physics, medicine, and astronomy, the Renaissance humanists had mastered Greek and made available new works of Galen, Ptolemy, and Archimedes as well as Plato and the pre-Socratics. These writings made it apparent that even the unquestioned authorities of the Middle Ages, Aristotle and Galen, had been contradicted by other thinkers. The desire to discover which school of thought was correct stimulated new scientific work that sometimes led to a complete rejection of the Classical authorities.

Renaissance artists have also been credited with making an impact on scientific study. Their desire to imitate nature led them to rely on a close observation of nature. Their accurate renderings of rocks, plants, animals, and human anatomy established new standards for the study of natural phenomena. At the same time, the "scientific" study of the problems of perspective and correct anatomical proportions led to new insights. "No painter," one Renaissance artist declared, "can paint well without a thorough knowledge of geometry."[1] Renaissance artists were frequently called on to be practicing mathematicians as well. Leonardo da Vinci devised "war machines," and Albrecht Dürer made designs for the fortifications of cities.

Technological Innovations and Mathematics

Technical problems such as accurately calculating the tonnage of ships also stimulated scientific activity because they required careful observation and precise measurements. The fifteenth and sixteenth centuries witnessed a proliferation of books dedicated to machines and technology, all of which espoused the belief that innovation in techniques was necessary. The relationship between technology and the Scientific Revolution was not a simple one, however, for many technological experts did not believe in abstract or academic learning. Indeed, many of the technical innovations of the Middle Ages and the Renaissance were accomplished outside the universities by people who emphasized practical rather than theoretical knowledge. In any case, the invention of new instruments and machines, such as the telescope and the microscope, often made new scientific discoveries possible. The printing press had an indirect but crucial role in spreading innovative ideas quickly and easily.

Mathematics, so fundamental to the scientific achievements of the sixteenth and seventeenth centuries, was promoted in the Renaissance by the rediscovery of the works of ancient mathematicians and the influence of Plato, who had emphasized the importance of mathematics in explaining the universe. While mathematics was applauded as the key to navigation, military science, and geography, the Renaissance also held the widespread belief that mathematics was the key to understanding the nature of things. According to Leonardo da Vinci, since God eternally geometrizes, nature is inherently mathematical: "Proportion is not only found in numbers and measurements but also in sounds, weights, times, positions, and in whatsoever power there may be."[2] Moreover, mathematical reasoning was seen as promoting a degree of certainty that was otherwise impossible. In the words of Leonardo da Vinci: "There is no certainty where one can neither apply any of the mathematical sciences nor any of those which are based upon the mathematical sciences."[3] Copernicus, Kepler, Galileo, and Newton were all great mathematicians who believed that the secrets of nature were written in the language of mathematics.

Renaissance Magic

Another factor in the origins of the Scientific Revolution may have been magic. Renaissance magic was the preserve of an intellectual elite from all of Europe. By the end of the sixteenth century, Hermetic magic had become fused with alchemical thought into a single intellectual framework. This tradition believed that the world was a living embodiment of divinity. Humans, who it was believed also had that spark of divinity within, could use magic, especially mathematical magic, to understand and dominate the world of nature or employ the powers of nature for beneficial purposes. Was it Hermeticism, then, that inaugurated the shift in consciousness that made the Scientific Revolution possible, since the desire to control and dominate the natural world was a crucial motivating force in the Scientific Revolution? One scholar has argued:

> It is a movement of the will which really originates an intellectual movement. A new center of interest arises, surrounded by emotional excitement; the mind turns where the will has directed it and new attitudes, new discoveries follow. Behind the emergence of modern science there was a new direction of the will toward the world, its marvels, and mysterious workings, a new longing and determination to understand those workings and to operate with them.[4]

"This time," the author continues, "the return to the occult [Hermetic tradition] stimulates the genuine science."[5] Scholars debate the issue, but histories of the Scientific Revolution frequently overlook the fact that the great names we associate with the revolution in cosmology—Copernicus, Kepler, Galileo, and Newton—all had a serious interest in Hermetic ideas and the fields of astrology and alchemy. The mention of these names also reminds us

of one final consideration in the origins of the Scientific Revolution: it largely resulted from the work of a handful of great intellectuals.

Toward a New Heaven: A Revolution in Astronomy

 Focus Question: What did Copernicus, Kepler, Galileo, and Newton contribute to a new vision of the universe, and how did it differ from the Ptolemaic conception of the universe?

The greatest achievements in the Scientific Revolution of the sixteenth and seventeenth centuries came in the fields most dominated by the ideas of the Greeks—astronomy, mechanics, and medicine. The cosmological views of the Later Middle Ages had been built on a synthesis of the ideas of Aristotle, Ptolemy (the greatest astronomer of antiquity, who lived in the second century C.E.), and Christian theology. In the resulting Ptolemaic (tahl-uh-MAY-ik) or **geocentric conception,** the universe was seen as a series of concentric spheres with a fixed or motionless earth at its center. Composed of the material substances of earth, air, fire, and water, the earth was imperfect and constantly changing. The spheres that surrounded the earth were made of a crystalline, transparent substance and moved in circular orbits around the earth. Circular movement, according to Aristotle, was the most "perfect" kind of motion and hence appropriate for the "perfect" heavenly bodies thought to consist of a nonmaterial, incorruptible "quintessence." These heavenly bodies, pure orbs of light, were embedded in the moving, concentric spheres, which in 1500 were believed to number ten. Working outward from the earth, eight spheres contained the moon, Mercury, Venus, the sun, Mars, Jupiter, Saturn, and the fixed stars. The ninth sphere imparted to the eighth sphere of the fixed stars its motion, and the tenth sphere was frequently described as the prime mover that moved itself and imparted motion to the other spheres. Beyond the tenth sphere was the Empyrean Heaven—the location of God and all the saved souls. This Christianized Ptolemaic universe, then, was finite. It had a fixed outer boundary in harmony with Christian thought and expectations. God and the saved souls were at one end of the universe, and humans were at the center. They had been given power over the earth, but their real purpose was to achieve salvation.

This conception of the universe, however, did not satisfy professional astronomers, who wished to ascertain the precise paths of the heavenly bodies across the sky. Finding that their observations did not always correspond to the accepted scheme, astronomers tried to "save appearances" by developing an elaborate system of devices. They proposed, for example, that the planetary bodies traveled on epicycles, concentric spheres within spheres, that would enable the paths of the planets to correspond

Medieval Conception of the Universe. As this sixteenth-century illustration shows, the medieval cosmological view placed the earth at the center of the universe, surrounded by a series of concentric spheres. The earth was imperfect and constantly changing, whereas the heavenly bodies that surrounded it were perfect and incorruptible. Beyond the tenth and final sphere was heaven, where God and all the saved souls were located. (The circles read, from the center outward: 1. Moon, 2. Mercury, 3. Venus, 4. Sun, 5. Mars, 6. Jupiter, 7. Saturn, 8. Firmament (of the Stars), 9. Crystalline Sphere, 10. Prime Mover; and around the outside, Empyrean Heaven—Home of God and All the Elect, that is, saved souls.)

more precisely to observations while adhering to Aristotle's ideas of circular planetary movement.

Copernicus

Nicolaus Copernicus (nee-koh-LOW-uss kuh-PURR-nuh-kuss) (1473–1543) had studied both mathematics and astronomy first at Krakow in his native Poland and later at the Italian universities of Bologna and Padua. Before he left Italy in 1506, he had become aware of ancient views that contradicted the Ptolemaic, earth-centered conception of the universe. Between 1506 and 1530, he completed the manuscript of his famous book, *On the Revolutions of the Heavenly Spheres,* but his own timidity and fear of ridicule from fellow astronomers kept him from publishing it until May 1543, shortly before his death.

Copernicus was not an accomplished observational astronomer and relied for his data on the records of his predecessors. But he was a mathematician who felt that Ptolemy's geocentric system was too complicated and failed to accord with the observed motions of the heavenly bodies (see the box on p. 492). Copernicus hoped that his **heliocentric** or sun-centered **conception** would offer a simpler and more accurate explanation.

Copernicus argued that the universe consisted of eight spheres with the sun motionless at the center and the sphere of the fixed stars at rest in the eighth sphere. The planets revolved around the sun in the order of Mercury, Venus, the earth, Mars, Jupiter, and Saturn. The moon,

however, revolved around the earth. Moreover, according to Copernicus, what appeared to be the movement of the sun and the fixed stars around the earth was really explained by the daily rotation of the earth on its axis and the journey of the earth around the sun each year.

Copernicus, however, was basically conservative. He did not reject Aristotle's principle of the existence of heavenly spheres moving in circular orbits. As a result, when he put forth the calculations to prove his new theory, he retained about half of Ptolemy's epicycles and wound up with a system somewhat simpler than that of the Alexandrian astronomer but still extremely complicated.

Nevertheless, the shift from an earth-centered to a sun-centered system was significant and raised serious questions about Aristotle's astronomy and physics despite Copernicus's own adherence to Aristotle. It also seemed to create uncertainty about the human role in the universe as well as God's location. Protestant reformers, adhering to a literal interpretation of Scripture, were the first to attack the new ideas. Martin Luther thundered against "the new astrologer who wants to prove that the earth moves and goes round. . . . The fool wants to turn the whole art of astronomy upside down. As Holy Scripture tells us, so did Joshua bid the sun stand still and not the earth." Luther's cohort at Wittenberg, Philip Melanchthon, condemned Copernicus as well:

The eyes are witness that the heavens revolve in the space of twenty-four hours. But certain men, either from the love of novelty, or to make a display of ingenuity, have concluded

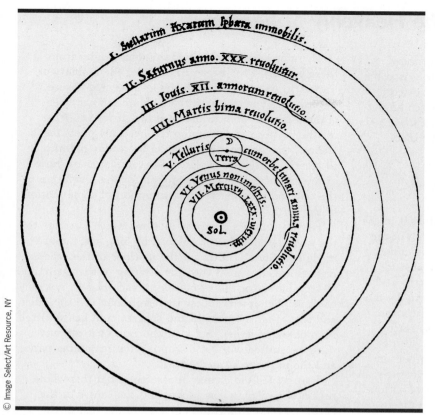

The Copernican System. The Copernican system was presented in *On the Revolutions of the Heavenly Spheres,* published shortly before Copernicus's death. As shown in this illustration from the first edition of the book, Copernicus maintained that the sun was the center of the universe and that the planets, including the earth, revolved around it. Moreover, the earth rotated daily on its axis. (The circles read, from the inside out: 1. Sun; 2. Mercury, orbit of 80 days; 3. Venus; 4. Earth, with the moon, orbit of one year; 5. Mars, orbit of 2 years; 6. Jupiter, orbit of 12 years; 7. Saturn, orbit of 30 years; 8. Immobile Sphere of the Fixed Stars.)

that the earth moves, and they maintain that neither the eighth sphere [of the fixed stars] nor the sun revolves.... Now it is a want of honesty and decency to assert such notions publicly, and the example is pernicious. It is the part of a good mind to accept the truth as revealed by God and to acquiesce in it.[6]

The Catholic Church remained silent for the time being; it did not denounce Copernicus until the work of Galileo appeared. The denunciation came at a time when an increasing number of astronomers were being attracted to Copernicus's ideas.

Brahe

Copernicus did not have a great impact immediately, but doubts about the Ptolemaic system were growing. The next step in destroying the geocentric conception and supporting the Copernican system was taken by Johannes Kepler. It has been argued, however, that Kepler's work would not have occurred without the material provided by Tycho Brahe (TY-koh BRAH).

A Danish nobleman, Tycho Brahe (1546–1601) was granted possession of an island near Copenhagen by King Frederick II. On it, Brahe built the elaborate Uraniborg Castle, which he outfitted with a library, observatories, and instruments he had designed for more precise astronomical observations. For twenty years, Brahe patiently concentrated on compiling a detailed record of his observations of the positions and movements of the stars

and planets, a series of observations described as the most accurate up to that time. This body of data led him to reject the Aristotelian-Ptolemaic system, but at the same time he was unable to accept Copernicus's suggestion that the earth actually moved. Brahe's last years were spent in Prague as imperial mathematician to Emperor Rudolf II, who took a keen interest in astronomy, astrology, and the Hermetic tradition. While he was in Prague, Brahe took on an assistant by the name of Johannes Kepler.

Kepler

Johannes Kepler (1571–1630) had been destined by his parents for a career as a Lutheran minister. While studying theology at the university at Tübingen (TOO-bing-un), however, he fell under the influence of Michael Mästlin (MEST-lin), Germany's best-known astronomer, and spent much time pursuing his real interests, mathematics and astronomy. He abandoned theology and became a teacher of mathematics and astronomy at Graz in Austria.

Kepler's work illustrates well the narrow line that often separated magic and science in the early Scientific Revolution. An avid astrologer, Kepler possessed a keen interest in Hermetic mathematical magic. In a book written in 1596, he elaborated on his theory that the universe was constructed on the basis of geometric figures, such as the pyramid and the cube. Believing that the harmony of the human soul (a divine attribute) was mirrored in the

On the Revolutions of the Heavenly Spheres

Nicolaus Copernicus began a revolution in astronomy when he argued that the sun and not the earth was at the center of the universe. Expecting controversy and scorn, Copernicus hesitated to publish the work in which he put forth his heliocentric theory. He finally relented, however, and managed to see a copy of it just before he died.

✦ ⊫⊨ ✦

Nicolaus Copernicus, *On the Revolutions of the Heavenly Spheres*

For a long time, then, I reflected on this confusion in the astronomical traditions concerning the derivation of the motions of the universe's spheres. I began to be annoyed that the movements of the world machine, created for our sake by the best and most systematic Artisan of all [God], were not understood with greater certainty by the philosophers, who otherwise examined so precisely the most insignificant trifles of this world. For this reason I undertook the task of rereading the works of all the philosophers which I could obtain to learn whether anyone had ever proposed other motions of the universe's spheres than those expounded by the teachers of astronomy in the schools. And in fact first I found in Cicero that Hicetas supposed the earth to move. Later I also discovered in Plutarch that certain others were of this opinion. I have decided to set his words down here, so that they may be available to everybody:

> Some think that the earth remains at rest. But Philolaus the Pythagorean believes that, like the sun and moon, it revolves around the fire in an oblique circle. Heraclides of Pontus and Ecphantus the Pythagorean make the earth move, not in a progressive motion, but like a wheel in a rotation from the west to east about its own center.

Therefore, having obtained the opportunity from these sources, I too began to consider the mobility of the earth. And even though the idea seemed absurd, nevertheless I knew that others before me had been granted the freedom to imagine any circles whatever for the purpose of explaining the heavenly phenomena. Hence I thought that I too would be readily permitted to ascertain whether explanations sounder than those of my predecessors could be found for the revolution of the celestial spheres on the assumption of some motion of the earth.

Having thus assumed the motions which I ascribe to the earth later on in the volume, by long and intense study I finally found that if the motions of the other planets are correlated with the orbiting of the earth, and are computed for the revolution of each planet, not only do their phenomena follow therefrom but also the order and size of all the planets and spheres, and heaven itself is so linked together that in no portion of it can anything be shifted without disrupting the remaining parts and the universe as a whole. . . .

Hence I feel no shame in asserting that this whole region engirdled by the moon, and the center of the earth, traverse this grand circle amid the rest of the planets in an annual revolution around the sun. Near the sun is the center of the universe. Moreover, since the sun remains stationary, whatever appears as a motion of the sun is really due rather to the motion of the earth. ⊱

Q What major new ideas did Copernicus discuss in this excerpt? What was the source of these ideas? Why might one say that European astronomers finally destroyed the Middle Ages?

---

numerical relationships existing between the planets, he focused much of his attention on discovering the "music of the spheres." Kepler was also a brilliant mathematician and astronomer and, after Brahe's death, succeeded him as imperial mathematician to Rudolf II. There he gained possession of Brahe's detailed astronomical data and, using them, arrived at his three laws of planetary motion. These laws may have confirmed Kepler's interest in the "music of the spheres," but more important, they confirmed Copernicus's heliocentric theory while modifying it in some ways. Above all, they drove another nail into the coffin of the Aristotelian-Ptolemaic system.

Kepler published his first two laws of planetary motion in 1609. Although at Tübingen he had accepted Copernicus's heliocentric ideas, in his first law he rejected Copernicus by showing that the orbits of the planets around the sun were not circular but elliptical, with the sun at one focus of the ellipse rather than at the center. In his

second law, he demonstrated that the speed of a planet is greater when it is closer to the sun and decreases as its distance from the sun increases. This proposition destroyed a fundamental Aristotelian tenet that Copernicus had shared—that the motion of the planets was steady and unchanging. Published ten years later, Kepler's third law established that the square of a planet's period of revolution is proportional to the cube of its average distance from the sun. In other words, planets with larger orbits revolve at a slower average velocity than those with smaller orbits.

Kepler's three laws effectively eliminated the idea of uniform circular motion as well as the idea of crystalline spheres revolving in circular orbits. The basic structure of the traditional Ptolemaic system had been disproved, and people had been freed to think in new ways about the actual paths of planets revolving around the sun in elliptical orbits. By the end of Kepler's life, the Ptolemaic

Johannes Kepler. Abandoning theology in favor of mathematics and astrology, Kepler became a key figure in the rise of the new astronomy. Building on Tycho Brahe's vast store of astronomical data, Kepler discovered the three laws of planetary motion that both confirmed and modified the Copernican theory. They also eliminated the Ptolemaic-Aristotelian ideas of uniform circular motion and crystalline spheres moving in circular orbits. This portrait was done by an unknown painter three years before Kepler's death.

system was rapidly losing ground to the new ideas (see the box on p. 494). Important questions remained unanswered, however: What were the planets made of? And how could motion in the universe be explained? It was an Italian scientist who achieved the next important breakthrough to a new cosmology by answering the first question and making important strides toward answering the second.

Galileo

Galileo Galilei (1564–1642) taught mathematics, first at Pisa and later at Padua, one of the most prestigious universities in Europe. Galileo was the first European to make systematic observations of the heavens by means of a telescope, thereby inaugurating a new age in astronomy. He had heard of a Flemish lens grinder who had created a "spyglass" that magnified objects seen at a distance and soon constructed his own after reading about it. Instead of peering at terrestrial objects, Galileo turned his telescope to the skies and made a remarkable series of discoveries: mountains and craters on the moon,

The Telescope. The invention of the telescope enabled Europeans to inaugurate a new age in astronomy. Shown here is Johannes Hevelius, an eminent German-Polish astrologer (1611–1697), making an observation with his telescope. Hevelius's observations were highly regarded. He located his telescope on the roof of his own house, and by the 1660s, his celestial observatory was considered one of the best in Europe.

four moons revolving around Jupiter, the phases of Venus, and sunspots. Galileo's observations demolished yet another aspect of the traditional cosmology in that the universe seemed to be composed of material substance similar to that of the earth rather than ethereal or perfect and unchanging substance.

Galileo's revelations, published in *The Starry Messenger* in 1610 (see the box on p. 495), stunned his contemporaries and probably did more to make Europeans aware of the new picture of the universe than the mathematical theories of Copernicus and Kepler did. The English ambassador in Venice wrote to the chief minister of King James I in 1610:

> I send herewith unto His Majesty the strangest piece of news . . . that he has ever yet received from any part of the world; which is the annexed book of the Mathematical Professor at Padua [Galileo], who by the help of an optical instrument . . . has discovered four new planets rolling about the sphere of Jupiter. . . . So upon the whole subject he has first overthrown all former astronomy. . . . By the next ship your Lordship shall receive from me one of the above instruments [a telescope], as it is bettered by this man.[7]

During a trip to Rome, Galileo was received by scholars as a conquering hero. Grand Duke Cosimo II of Florence offered him a new position as his court mathematician, which Galileo readily accepted. But even in the midst of

Kepler and the Emerging Scientific Community

The exchange of letters between intellectuals was an important avenue for scientific communication. After receiving a copy of Johannes Kepler's first major work, the Italian Galileo Galilei wrote to Kepler, inaugurating a correspondence between them. This selection contains samples of their letters to each other.

Galileo to Kepler, Padua, August 4, 1597

Your book, highly learned gentleman, which you sent me through Paulus Amberger, reached me not days ago but only a few hours ago, and as this Paulus just informed me of his return to Germany, I should think myself indeed ungrateful if I should not express to you my thanks by this letter. I thank you especially for having deemed me worthy of such a proof of your friendship.... So far I have read only the introduction, but have learned from it in some measure your intentions and congratulate myself on the good fortune of having found such a man as a companion in the exploration of truth. For it is deplorable that there are so few who seek the truth and do not pursue a wrong method of philosophizing. But this is not the place to mourn about the misery of our century but to rejoice with you about such beautiful ideas proving the truth.... I would certainly dare to approach the public with my ways of thinking if there were more people of your mind. As this is not the case, I shall refrain from doing so....
I shall always be at your service. Farewell, and do not neglect to give me further good news of yourself.
Yours in sincere friendship,
Galilaeus Galilaeus
Mathematician at the Academy of Padua

Kepler to Galileo, Graz, October 13, 1597

I received your letter of August 4 on September 1. It was a double pleasure to me. First because I became friends with you, the Italian, and second because of the agreement in which we find ourselves concerning Copernican cosmography. As you invite me kindly at the end of your letter to enter into correspondence with you, and I myself feel greatly tempted to do so, I will not let pass the occasion of sending you a letter with the present young nobleman. For I am sure, if your time has allowed it, you have meanwhile obtained a closer knowledge of my book. And so a great desire has taken hold of me, to learn your judgment. For this is my way, to urge all those to whom I have written to express their candid opinion. Believe me, the sharpest criticism of one single understanding man means much more to me than the thoughtless applause of the great masses.

I would, however, have wished that you who have such a keen insight into everything would choose another way to reach your practical aims. By the strength of your personal example you advise us, in a cleverly veiled manner, to go out of the way of general ignorance and warn us against exposing ourselves to the furious attacks of the scholarly crowd.... But after the beginning of a tremendous enterprise has been made in our time, and furthered by so many learned mathematicians, and after the statement that the earth moves can no longer be regarded as something new, would it not be better to pull the rolling wagon to its destination with united effort?... For it is not only you Italians who do not believe that they move unless they feel it, but we in Germany, too, in no way make ourselves popular with this idea. Yet there are ways in which we protect ourselves against these difficulties.... Be of good cheer, Galileo, and appear in public. If I am not mistaken there are only a few among the distinguished mathematicians of Europe who would dissociate themselves from us. So great is the power of truth. If Italy seems less suitable for your publication and if you have to expect difficulties there, perhaps Germany will offer us more freedom. But enough of this. Please let me know, at least privately if you do not want to do so publicly, what you have discovered in favor of Copernicus. ⊱

Q What does the correspondence between Galileo and Kepler reveal about an emerging spirit of scientific inquiry? What other notable achievements must European society have reached even to make this exchange of letters possible? What aspects of European material culture made the work of these scientists easier?

---

his newfound acclaim, Galileo found himself increasingly suspect by the authorities of the Catholic Church.

GALILEO AND THE INQUISITION   In *The Starry Messenger,* Galileo had revealed himself as a firm proponent of Copernicus's heliocentric system. The Roman Inquisition (or Holy Office) of the Catholic Church condemned Copernicanism and ordered Galileo to reject the Copernican thesis. As one cardinal commented, "The intention of the Holy Spirit is to teach us not how the heavens go, but how to go to heaven." The report of the Inquisition ran:

> That the doctrine that the sun was the center of the world and immovable was false and absurd, formally heretical and contrary to Scripture, whereas the doctrine that the earth was not the center of the world but moved, and has further a daily motion, was philosophically false and absurd and theologically at least erroneous.[8]

The Starry Messenger

The Italian Galileo Galilei was the first European to use a telescope to make systematic observations of the heavens. His observations, as reported in *The Starry Messenger* in 1610, stunned European intellectuals by revealing that the celestial bodies were not perfect and immutable but composed of material substance similar to that of the earth. In this selection, Galileo describes how he devised a telescope and what he saw with it.

Galileo Galilei, *The Starry Messenger*

About ten months ago a report reached my ears that a certain Fleming had constructed a spyglass by means of which visible objects, though very distant from the eye of the observer, were distinctly seen as if nearby. Of this truly remarkable effect several experiences were related, to which some persons gave credence while others denied them. A few days later the report was confirmed to me in a letter from a noble Frenchman at Paris, Jacques Badovere, which caused me to apply myself wholeheartedly to inquire into the means by which I might arrive at the invention of a similar instrument. This I did shortly afterwards, my basis being the theory of refraction. First I prepared a tube of lead, at the ends of which I fitted two glass lenses, both plane on one side while on the other side one was spherically convex and the other concave. Then placing my eye near the concave lens I perceived objects satisfactorily large and near, for they appeared three times closer and nine times larger than when seen with the naked eye alone. Next I constructed another one, more accurate, which represented objects as enlarged more than sixty times. Finally, sparing neither labor nor expense, I succeeded in constructing for myself so excellent an instrument that objects seen by means of it appeared nearly one thousand times larger and over thirty times closer than when regarded without natural vision.

It would be superfluous to enumerate the number and importance of the advantages of such an instrument at sea as well as on land. But forsaking terrestrial observations, I turned to celestial ones, and first I saw the moon from as near at hand as if it were scarcely two terrestrial radii. After that I observed often with wondering delight both the planets and the fixed stars, and since I saw these latter to be very crowded, I began to seek (and eventually found) a method by which I might measure their distances apart. . . .

Now let us review the observations made during the past two months, once more inviting the attention of all who are eager for true philosophy to the first steps of such important contemplations. Let us speak first of that surface of the moon which faces us. For greater clarity I distinguish two parts of this surface, a lighter and a darker; the lighter part seems to surround and to pervade the whole hemisphere, while the darker part discolors the moon's surface like a kind of cloud, and makes it appear covered with spots. . . . From observation of these spots repeated many times I have been led to the opinion and conviction that the surface of the moon is not smooth, uniform, and precisely spherical as a great number of philosophers believe it (and the other heavenly bodies) to be, but is uneven, rough, and full of cavities and prominences, being not unlike the face of the earth, relieved by chains of mountains and deep valleys.

Q What was the significance of Galileo's invention? What impressions did he receive of the moon? Why were his visual discoveries so stunning, and how did he go about publicizing them?

Galileo was told, however, that he could continue to discuss Copernicanism as long as he maintained that it was not a fact but a mathematical supposition. It is apparent from the Inquisition's response that the church attacked the Copernican system because it threatened not only Scripture but also an entire conception of the universe (see the box on p. 496). The heavens were no longer a spiritual world but a world of matter. Humans were no longer at the center, and God was no longer in a specific place. The new system raised such uncertainties that it seemed prudent simply to condemn it.

Galileo, however, never really accepted his condemnation. In 1632, he published his most famous work, *Dialogue on the Two Chief World Systems: Ptolemaic and Copernican*. Unlike most scholarly treatises, it was written in Italian rather than Latin, making it more widely available to the public, which no doubt alarmed the church authorities.

The work took the form of a dialogue among Simplicio, a congenial but somewhat stupid supporter of Aristotle and Ptolemy; Sagredo, an open-minded layman; and Salviati, a proponent of Copernicus's ideas. There is no question who wins the argument, and the *Dialogue* was quickly perceived as a defense of the Copernican system. Galileo was dragged once more before the Inquisition in 1633, found guilty of teaching the condemned Copernican system, and forced to recant his errors. Placed under house arrest on his estate near Florence, he spent the remaining eight years of his life studying mechanics, a field in which he made significant contributions.

GALILEO AND THE PROBLEM OF MOTION One of the problems that fell under the heading of mechanics was the principle of motion. The Aristotelian conception, which dominated the late medieval world, held that an object

Opposing ❯VIEWPOINTS

A New Heaven? Faith Versus Reason

In 1614, Galileo wrote a letter to the Grand Duchess Christina of Tuscany in which he explained why his theory that the earth rotated around the sun was not necessarily contrary to Scripture. To Galileo, it made little sense for the church to determine the nature of physical reality on the basis of biblical texts that were subject to different interpretations. One year later, Cardinal Robert Bellarmine, a Jesuit and now a member of the church's Inquisition, wrote a letter to one of Galileo's followers that laid out the Catholic Church's approach to the issue of Galileo's theory.

⊹ ⚌⬩⚌ ⊹

Galileo, Letter to the Grand Duchess Christina, 1614

Some years ago, as Your Serene Highness well knows, I discovered in the heavens many things that had not been seen before our own age. The novelty of these things, as well as some consequences which followed from them in contradiction to the physical notions commonly held among academic philosophers, stirred up against me no small number of professors—as if I had placed these things in the sky with my own hands in order to upset nature and overturn the sciences....

Contrary to the sense of the Bible and the intention of the holy Fathers, if I am not mistaken, they would extend such authorities until even in purely physical matters—where faith is not involved—they would have us altogether abandon reason and the evidence of our senses in favor of some biblical passage, though under the surface meaning of its words this passage may contain a different sense....

The reason produced for condemning the opinion that the earth moves and the sun stands still is that in many places in the Bible one may read that the sun moves and the earth stands still. Since the Bible cannot err, it follows as a necessary consequence that anyone takes an erroneous and heretical position who maintains that the sun is inherently motionless and the earth movable.

With regard to this argument, I think in the first place that it is very pious to say and prudent to affirm that the holy Bible can never speak untruth—whenever its true meaning is understood. But I believe nobody will deny that it is often very abstruse, and may say things which are quite different from what its bare words signify. Hence, in expounding the Bible if one were always to confine oneself to the unadorned grammatical meaning, one might fall into error. Not only

contradictions and propositions far from true might thus be made to appear in the Bible, but even grave heresies and follies. Thus, it would be necessary to assign to God feet, hands, and eyes, as well as corporeal and human affections, such as anger, repentance, hatred, and sometimes even the forgetting of things past and ignorance of those to come. These propositions uttered by the Holy Ghost were set down in that manner by the sacred scribes in order to accommodate them to the capacities of the common people, who are rude and unlearned. For the sake of those who deserve to be separated from the herd, it is necessary that wise expositors should produce the true senses of such passages, together with the special reasons for which they were set down in these words....

This being granted, I think that in discussions of physical problems we ought to begin not from the authority of scriptural passages, but from sense-experiences and necessary demonstrations; for the holy Bible and the phenomena of nature proceed alike from the divine Word.... For that reason it appears that nothing physical which sense-experience sets before our eyes, or which necessary demonstrations prove to us, ought to be called in question (much less condemned) upon the testimony of biblical passages which may have some different meaning beneath their words.

Robert Bellarmine, Letter to Paolo Foscarini, 1615

First. I say that it seems to me that Your Reverence and Galileo did prudently to content yourself with speaking hypothetically, and not absolutely, as I have always believed that Copernicus spoke. For to say that, assuming the earth moves and the sun stands still, all the appearances are saved better than with eccentrics and epicycles, is to speak well; there is no danger in this, and it is sufficient for mathematicians. But to want to affirm that the sun really is fixed in the center of the heavens and only revolves around itself (i.e., turns upon its axis) without traveling from east to west, and that the earth is situated in the third sphere and revolves with great speed around the sun, is a very dangerous thing, not only by irritating all the philosophers and scholastic theologians, but also by injuring our holy faith and rendering the Holy Scriptures false. For Your Reverence has demonstrated many ways of explaining Holy Scripture, but you have not applied them in particular, and without a doubt you would have found it most difficult if

(continued)

you had attempted to explain all the passages which you yourself have cited.

Second. I say that, as you know, the Council [of Trent] prohibits expounding the Scriptures contrary to the common agreement of the holy Fathers. And if Your Reverence would read not only the Fathers but also the commentaries of modern writers on Genesis, Psalms, Ecclesiastes and Josue, you would find that all agree in explaining literally (*ad litteram*) that the sun is in the heavens and moves swiftly around the earth, and that the earth is far from the heavens and stands immobile in the center of the universe. Now consider whether in all prudence the Church could encourage giving to Scripture a sense contrary to the holy Fathers and all the Latin and Greek commentators. Nor may it be answered that this is not a matter of faith, for if it is not a matter of faith from the point of view of the subject matter, it is on the part of the ones who have spoken. . . .

Third. I say that if there were a true demonstration that the sun was in the center of the universe and the earth in the third sphere, and that the sun did not travel around the earth but the earth circled the sun,

then it would be necessary to proceed with great caution in explaining the passages of Scripture which seemed contrary, and we would rather have to say that we did not understand them than to say that something was false which has been demonstrated. But I do not believe that there is any such demonstration; none has been shown to me. It is not the same thing to show that the appearances are saved by assuming that the sun really is in the center and the earth in the heavens. I believe that the first demonstration might exist, but I have grave doubts about the second, and in a case of doubt, one may not depart from the Scriptures as explained by the holy Fathers.

Q What does Galileo think is the difference between knowledge about the natural world and knowledge about the spiritual world? What does Galileo suggest that his opponents should do before dismissing his ideas? In what ways does Cardinal Bellarmine attempt to refute Galileo's ideas? Why did Galileo's ideas represent a threat to the Catholic Church?

---

remained at rest unless a force was applied against it. If a force was constantly exerted, then the object moved at a constant rate, but if it was removed, then the object stopped. This conception encountered some difficulties, especially with a projectile thrown out of a cannon. Late medieval theorists had solved this problem by arguing that the rush of air behind the projectile kept it in motion. The Aristotelian principle of motion also raised problems in the new Copernican system. In the Ptolemaic system, the concentric spheres surrounding the earth were weightless, but in the Copernican system, if a constant force had to be applied to objects to cause movement, then what power or force kept the heavy earth and other planets in motion?

Galileo made two contributions to the problem of motion. First, he demonstrated by experiments that if a uniform force was applied to an object, it would move at an accelerated speed rather than a constant speed. Moreover, Galileo discovered the principle of inertia when he argued that a body in motion continues in motion forever unless deflected by an external force. Thus, a state of uniform motion is just as natural as a state of rest. Before Galileo, natural philosophers had tried to explain motion; now their task was to explain changes in motion.

The condemnation of Galileo by the Inquisition, coming at a time of economic decline, seriously undermined further scientific work in Italy, which had been at the forefront of scientific innovation. Leadership in science now passed to the northern countries, especially England, France, and the Dutch Netherlands. By the 1630s and 1640s, no reasonable astronomer could overlook that Galileo's discoveries, combined with Kepler's mathematical laws, had made nonsense of the Ptolemaic-Aristotelian

world system and clearly established the reasonableness of the Copernican model. Nevertheless, the problem of explaining motion in the universe and tying together the ideas of Copernicus, Galileo, and Kepler had not yet been solved. This would be the work of an Englishman who has long been considered the greatest genius of the Scientific Revolution.

Newton

Born in the English village of Woolsthorpe in 1642, Isaac Newton was an unremarkable young man until he attended Cambridge University. His first great burst of creative energy came in 1666, when the fear of plague closed Cambridge and forced him to return to Woolsthorpe for eighteen months. There Newton discovered his creative talents: "In those days I was in the prime of my life for invention and minded mathematics and philosophy more than at any time since."[9] During this period, he invented the calculus, a mathematical means of calculating rates of change; began his investigations into the composition of light; and inaugurated his work on the law of universal gravitation. Two years after his return to Cambridge, in 1669, he accepted a chair in mathematics at the university. During a second intense period of creativity from 1684 to 1686, he wrote his famous *Principia* (prin-SIP-ee-uh) (see the box on p. 498). After a nervous breakdown in 1693, he sought and received an administrative post as warden of the royal mint and was advanced to master of the mint by 1699, a post he held until his death in 1727. Made president of the Royal Society (see "The Scientific Societies" later in this chapter) in 1703 and knighted in

Newton's Rules of Reasoning

In 1687, Isaac Newton published his masterpiece, the *Mathematical Principles of Natural Philosophy*, or *Principia*. In this work, Newton demonstrated the mathematical proofs for his universal law of gravitation and completed the new cosmology begun by Copernicus, Kepler, and Galileo. He also described the rules of reasoning by which he arrived at his universal law.

Isaac Newton, Rules of Reasoning in Philosophy

Rule 1

We are to admit no more causes of natural things than such as are both true and sufficient to explain their appearances.

To this purpose the philosophers say that Nature does nothing in vain, and more is in vain when less will serve; for Nature is pleased with simplicity, and affects not the pomp of superfluous causes.

Rule 2

Therefore to the same natural effects we must, as far as possible, assign the same causes.

As to respiration in a man and in a beast; the descent of stones in Europe and in America; the light of our culinary fire and of the sun; the reflection of light in the earth and in the planets.

Rule 3

The qualities of bodies, which admit neither intensification nor remission of degrees, and which are found to belong to all bodies within the reach of our experiments, are to be esteemed the universal qualities of all bodies whatsoever.

For since qualities of bodies are only known to us by experiments, we are to hold for universal all such as universally agree with experiments; and such as are not liable to diminution can never be quite taken away.

Rule 4

In experimental philosophy we are to look upon propositions inferred by general induction from phenomena as accurately or very nearly true, notwithstanding any contrary hypotheses that may be imagined, till such time as other phenomena occur, by which they may either be made more accurate, or liable to exceptions.

This rule we must follow, that the argument of induction may not be evaded by hypotheses.

Q What are Newton's rules of reasoning? How important were they to the development of the Scientific Revolution? How would following these rules change a person's view of the world, of European religious traditions, and of ancient "science"?

1705 for his great achievements, Sir Isaac Newton is to this day the only English scientist to be buried in Westminster Abbey.

NEWTON AND THE OCCULT Although Newton occupies a very special place in the history of modern science, we need to remember that he, too, remained extremely interested in aspects of the occult world. He left behind hundreds of manuscript pages of his studies of alchemy, and in fact, his alchemical experiments were a major feature of his life until he moved to London in 1696 to become warden of the royal mint. The British economist John Maynard Keynes said of Newton after examining his manuscripts in 1936:

> Newton was not the first of the age of reason. He was the last of the magicians.... He looked on the whole universe and all that is in it as a riddle, as a secret which could be read by applying pure thought to certain evidence, certain mystic

Isaac Newton. With a single law, that of universal gravitation, Isaac Newton was able to explain all motion in the universe. His great synthesis of the work of his predecessors created a new picture of the universe, one in which the universe was viewed as a great machine operating according to natural laws. Enoch Seeman painted this portrait of Newton one year before his death.

© National Portrait Gallery, London/The Bridgeman Art Library clues which God had laid about the world to allow a sort of philosopher's treasure hunt to the esoteric brotherhood. He believed that these clues were to be found partly in the evidence of the heavens and in the constitution of elements, . . . but also partly in certain papers and traditions handed down by the brethren in an unknown chain back to the original cryptic revelation in Babylonia.[10]

Although Newton may have considered himself a representative of the Hermetic tradition, he chose, it has been recently argued, for both political and psychological reasons to repress that part of his being, and it is as the "symbol of Western science" that Newton came to be viewed.

UNIVERSAL LAW OF GRAVITATION Newton's major work, the "hinge point of modern scientific thought," was his *Mathematical Principles of Natural Philosophy,* known simply as the *Principia,* the first word of its Latin title. In this work, the last highly influential book in Europe to be written in Latin, Newton spelled out the mathematical proofs demonstrating his universal law of gravitation. Newton's work was the culmination of the theories of Copernicus, Kepler, and Galileo. Though each had undermined some part of the Ptolemaic-Aristotelian cosmology, until Newton no one had pieced together a coherent synthesis for a new cosmology.

In the first book of the *Principia,* Newton defined the basic concepts of mechanics by elaborating the three laws of motion: every object continues in a state of rest or uniform motion in a straight line unless deflected by a force, the rate of change of motion of an object is proportional to the force acting on it, and to every action there is always an equal and opposite reaction. In book 3, Newton applied his theories of mechanics to the problems of astronomy by demonstrating that these three laws of motion govern the planetary bodies as well as terrestrial objects. Integral to his whole argument was the universal law of gravitation, which explained why the planetary bodies did not go off in straight lines but continued in elliptical orbits about the sun. In mathematical terms, Newton explained that every object in the universe was attracted to every other object with a force (gravity) that is directly proportional to the product of their masses and inversely proportional to the square of the distances between them.

The implications of Newton's universal law of gravitation were enormous, even though another century would pass before they were widely recognized. Newton had demonstrated that one universal law, mathematically proved, could explain all motion in the universe, from the movements of the planets in the celestial world to an apple falling from a tree in the terrestrial world. The secrets of the natural world could be known by human investigations. At the same time, the Newtonian synthesis created a new cosmology in which the world was seen largely in mechanistic terms. The universe was one huge, regulated, and uniform machine that operated according to natural laws in absolute time, space, and motion. Although Newton believed that God was "everywhere present" and acted as the force that moved all bodies on the basis of the laws he had

discovered, later generations dropped his spiritual assumptions. Newton's **world-machine,** conceived as operating absolutely in time, space, and motion, dominated the Western worldview until the twentieth century, when the Einsteinian revolution, based on the concept of relativity, superseded the Newtonian mechanistic concept.

Newton's ideas were soon accepted in England, possibly out of national pride and conviction and, as has been argued recently, for political reasons (see "Science and Society" later in this chapter). Natural philosophers on the Continent resisted Newton's ideas, and it took much of the eighteenth century before they were generally accepted everywhere in Europe. They were also reinforced by developments in other fields, especially medicine.

Advances in Medicine and Chemistry

 FOCUS QUESTION: What did Paracelsus, Vesalius, and Harvey contribute to a scientific view of medicine?

Although the Scientific Revolution of the sixteenth and seventeenth centuries is associated primarily with the dramatic changes in astronomy and mechanics that precipitated a new perception of the universe, a third field that had been dominated by Greek thought in the Later Middle Ages, that of medicine, also experienced a transformation. Late medieval medicine was dominated not by the teachings of Aristotle but by those of the Greek physician Galen, who had lived in the second century C.E.

Galen's influence on the medieval medical world was pervasive in anatomy, physiology, and disease. Galen had relied on animal, rather than human, dissection to arrive at a picture of human anatomy that was quite inaccurate in many instances. Even when Europeans began to practice human dissection in the Later Middle Ages, instruction in anatomy still relied on Galen. While a professor read a text of Galen, an assistant dissected a cadaver for illustrative purposes. Physiology, or the functioning of the body, was also dominated by Galenic hypotheses, including the belief that there were two separate blood systems. One controlled muscular activities and contained bright red blood moving upward and downward through the arteries; the other governed the digestive functions and contained dark red blood that ebbed and flowed in the veins.

Treatment of disease was highly influenced by Galen's doctrine of four bodily humors: blood, considered warm and moist; yellow bile, warm and dry; phlegm, cold and moist; and black bile, cold and dry. Since disease was supposedly the result of an imbalance of humors that could be discerned from the quantity and color of urine, the examination of a patient's urine became the chief diagnostic tool. Although purging and bleeding to remedy the imbalance were often harmful to patients, treatment with traditional herbal medicines sometimes proved beneficial.

Paracelsus

Three figures are associated with the changes in medicine in the sixteenth and seventeenth centuries: Paracelsus (par-uh-SELL-suss), Andreas Vesalius (ahn-DRAY-uss vuh-SAY-lee-uss), and William Harvey. Philippus Aureolus von Hohenheim (1493–1541), who renamed himself Paracelsus ("greater than Celsus," an ancient physician), was born in a small town near Zürich. After leaving home at the age of fourteen, Paracelsus traveled widely and may have been awarded a medical degree from the University of Ferrara. He achieved a moment of glory when he was appointed city physician and professor of medicine at Basel in 1527. But this, like so many other appointments, proved short-lived due to his vanity and quick temper. He could never disguise his contempt for universities and physicians who did not agree with his new ideas:

> I am *monarcha medicorum,* monarch of physicians, and I can prove to you what you cannot prove.... It was not the constellations that made me a physician: God made me.... I need not don a coat of mail or a buckler against you, for you are not learned or experienced enough to refute even one word of mine.... Let me tell you this: every little hair on my neck knows more than you and all your scribes, and my shoebuckles are more learned than your Galen and Avicenna, and my beard has more experience than all your high colleges.[11]

Paracelsus was not easy to get along with, and he was forced to wander from one town to another until his death in 1541.

Paracelsus rejected the work of both Aristotle and Galen and attacked the universities as centers of their moribund philosophy. He and his followers hoped to replace the traditional system with a new chemical philosophy that was based on a new understanding of nature derived from fresh observation and experiment. This chemical philosophy was in turn closely connected to a view of the universe based on the macrocosm-microcosm analogy. According to this view, a human being was a small replica (microcosm) of the larger world (macrocosm). All parts of the universe were represented within each person. As Paracelsus said, "For the sun and the moon and all planets, as well as the stars and the whole chaos, are in man.... For what is outside is also inside; and what is not outside man is not inside. The outer and the inner are one thing."[12] In accordance with the macrocosmic-microcosmic principle, Paracelsus believed that the chemical reactions of the universe as a whole were reproduced in human beings on a smaller scale. Disease, then, was not caused by an imbalance of the four humors, as Galen had argued, but was due to chemical imbalances that were localized in specific organs and could be treated by chemical remedies.

Although others had used chemical remedies, Paracelsus and his followers differed from them in giving careful attention to the proper dosage of their chemically prepared metals and minerals. Paracelsus had turned against the Galenic principle that "contraries cure" in favor of the ancient Germanic folk principle that "like cures like." The poison that caused a disease would be its cure if used in proper form and quantity. This use of toxic substances to cure patients was, despite its apparent effectiveness (Paracelsus did have a strong reputation for actually curing his patients), viewed by Paracelsus's opponents as the practice of a "homicide physician." Later generations came to view Paracelsus more favorably, and historians who have stressed Paracelsus's concept of disease and recognition of "new drugs" for medicine have viewed him as a father of modern medicine. Others have argued that his macrocosmic-microcosmic philosophy and use of "like cures like" drugs make him the forerunner of both homeopathy and the holistic medicine of the postmodern era.

Vesalius

Historians usually associate the name of Paracelsus with the diagnosis and treatment of disease. The new anatomy of the sixteenth century, however, was the work of Andreas Vesalius (1514–1564). His study of medicine at Paris involved him in the works of Galen. Especially important to him was a recently discovered text of Galen, *On Anatomical Procedures,* that led Vesalius to emphasize practical research as the principal avenue for understanding human anatomy. After receiving a doctorate in medicine at the University of Padua in 1536, he accepted a position there as professor of surgery. In 1543, he published his masterpiece, *On the Fabric of the Human Body.*

This book was based on his Paduan lectures, in which he deviated from traditional practice by personally dissecting a body to illustrate what he was discussing. Vesalius's anatomical treatise presented a careful examination of the individual organs and general structure of the human body. The book would not have been feasible without both the artistic advances of the Renaissance and technical developments in the art of printing. Together, they made possible the creation of illustrations superior to any hitherto produced.

Vesalius's hands-on approach to teaching anatomy enabled him to rectify some of Galen's most glaring errors. He did not hesitate, for example, to correct Galen's assertion that the great blood vessels originated from the liver since his own observations made it apparent that they came from the heart. Nevertheless, Vesalius still clung to a number of Galen's erroneous assertions, including the Greek physician's ideas on the ebb and flow of two kinds of blood in the veins and arteries. It was not until William Harvey's work on the circulation of the blood nearly a century later that this Galenic misperception was corrected.

William Harvey

William Harvey (1578–1657) attended Cambridge University and later Padua, where he received a doctorate of medicine in 1602. His reputation rests on his book *On the Motion of the Heart and Blood,* published in 1628. Although

CHRONOLOGY   **Important Works of the Scientific Revolution**

Copernicus, *On the Revolutions of the Heavenly Spheres*	1543
Vesalius, *On the Fabric of the Human Body*	1543
Galileo, *The Starry Messenger*	1610
Harvey, *On the Motion of the Heart and Blood*	1628
Galileo, *Dialogue on the Two Chief World Systems*	1632
Cavendish, *Grounds of Natural Philosophy*	1668
Newton, *Principia*	1687

questions had been raised in the sixteenth century about Galen's physiological principles, no major break from his

William Harvey, "On the Circulation of the Blood" (1628)

system had occurred. Harvey's work, which was based on meticulous observations and experiments, led him to demolish the ancient Greek's erroneous contentions. Harvey demonstrated that the heart and not the liver was the beginning point of the circulation of blood in the body, that the same blood flows in both veins and arteries, and most important, that the blood makes a complete circuit as it passes through the body. Although Harvey's work dealt a severe blow to Galen's theories, his ideas did not begin to achieve general recognition until the 1660s, when capillaries, which explained how the blood passed from the arteries to the veins, were discovered. Harvey's theory of the circulation of the blood laid the foundation for modern physiology.

Chemistry

We have already examined the new chemical philosophy that Paracelsus proposed in the sixteenth century, but it was not until the seventeenth and eighteenth centuries that a science of chemistry arose. Robert Boyle (1627–1691) was one of the first scientists to conduct controlled experiments. His pioneering work on the properties of gases led to Boyle's law, which states that the volume of a gas varies with the pressure exerted on it. Boyle also rejected the medieval belief that all matter consisted of the same components in favor of the view that matter is composed of atoms, which he called "little particles of all shapes and sizes" and which would later be known as the chemical elements.

In the eighteenth century, Antoine Lavoisier (AHN-twahn lah-vwah-ZYAY) (1743–1794) invented a system of naming the chemical elements, much of which is still used today. In helping to show that water is a compound of oxygen and hydrogen, he demonstrated the fundamental rules of chemical combination. He is regarded by many as the founder of modern chemistry. Lavoisier's wife, Marie-Anne, was her husband's scientific collaborator. She learned English in order to translate the work of British chemists for her husband and made engravings to illustrate

his scientific experiments. Marie-Anne Lavoisier is a reminder that women too played a role in the Scientific Revolution.

Women in the Origins of Modern Science

 FOCUS QUESTION: What role did women play in the Scientific Revolution?

During the Middle Ages, except for members of religious orders, women who sought a life of learning were severely hampered by the traditional attitude that a woman's proper role was as a daughter, wife, and mother. But in the late fourteenth and early fifteenth centuries, new opportunities for elite women emerged as enthusiasm for the new secular learning called humanism encouraged Europe's privileged and learned men to encourage women to read and study Classical and Christian texts. The ideal of a humanist education for some of the daughters of Europe's elite persisted into the seventeenth century, but only for some privileged women.

Margaret Cavendish

Much as they were drawn to humanism, women were also attracted to the Scientific Revolution. Unlike females educated formally in humanist schools, women interested in science had to obtain a largely informal education. European nobles had the leisure and resources that gave them easy access to the world of learning. This door was also open to noblewomen who could participate in the informal scientific networks of their fathers and brothers. One of the most prominent female scientists of the seventeenth century, Margaret Cavendish (KAV-un-dish) (1623–1673), came from an aristocratic background. Cavendish was not a popularizer of science for women but a participant in the crucial scientific debates of her time. Despite her achievements, however, she was excluded from membership in the Royal Society (see "The Scientific Societies" later in this chapter), although she was once allowed to attend a meeting. She wrote a number of works on scientific matters, including *Observations upon Experimental Philosophy* and *Grounds of Natural Philosophy*. In these works, she did not hesitate to attack what she considered the defects of the rationalist and empiricist approaches to scientific knowledge and was especially critical of the growing belief that through science, humans would be masters of nature: "We have no power at all over natural causes and effects . . . for man is but a small part. . . . His powers are but particular actions of Nature, and he cannot have a supreme and absolute power."[13]

As an aristocrat, Cavendish was a good example of the women in France and England who worked in science. In Germany, women interested in science came from a different background. There the tradition of female participation in craft production enabled some women to

Margaret Cavendish. Shown in this portrait is Margaret Cavendish, the duchess of Newcastle. Her husband, who was thirty years her senior, encouraged her to pursue her literary interests. In addition to scientific works, she wrote plays, an autobiography, and a biography of her husband titled *The Life of the Thrice Noble, High and Puissant Prince William Cavendish, Duke, Marquess and Earl of Newcastle.* The autobiography and biography led one male literary critic to call her "a mad, conceited and ridiculous woman."

become involved in observational science, especially entomology and astronomy. Between 1650 and 1710, one of every seven German astronomers was a woman.

Maria Merian

A good example of female involvement in the Scientific Revolution stemming from the craft tradition was Maria Sibylla Merian (MAY-ree-un) (1647–1717), who had established a reputation as an important entomologist by the beginning of the eighteenth century. Merian's training came from working in her father's workshop, where she learned the art of illustration, a training of great importance since her exact observation of insects and plants was demonstrated through the superb illustrations she made. In 1699, she undertook an expedition into the wilds of the Dutch colony of Surinam in South America to collect and draw samples of plants and insect life. This led to her major scientific work, the *Metamorphosis of the Insects of Surinam,* in which she used sixty illustrations to show the reproductive and developmental cycles of Surinam's insect life.

Maria Winkelmann

The craft organization of astronomy also gave women opportunities to become involved in science. Those who did worked in family observatories; hence, daughters and wives received training as apprentices to fathers or husbands. The most famous of the female astronomers in Germany was Maria Winkelmann (VINK-ul-mahn) (1670–1720). She was educated by her father and uncle and received advanced training in astronomy from a nearby self-taught astronomer. When she married Gottfried Kirch, Germany's foremost astronomer, she became his assistant at the astronomical observatory operated in Berlin by the Academy of Science. She made some original contributions, including a hitherto undiscovered comet, as her husband related:

> Early in the morning (about 2:00 A.M.) the sky was clear and starry. Some nights before, I had observed a variable star, and my wife (as I slept) wanted to find and see it for herself. In so doing, she found a comet in the sky. At which time she woke me, and I found that it was indeed a comet.... I was surprised that I had not seen it the night before.[14]

Moreover, Winkelmann corresponded with the famous scientist Gottfried Leibniz (who invented the calculus independently of Newton), who praised her effusively as "a most learned woman who could pass as a rarity." When her husband died in 1710, she applied for a position as assistant astronomer for which she was highly qualified. As a woman—with no university degree—she was denied the post by the Berlin Academy, which feared that it would establish a precedent by hiring a woman ("mouths would gape").

Winkelmann's difficulties with the Berlin Academy reflect the obstacles women faced in being accepted in scientific work, which was considered a male preserve. Although no formal statutes excluded women from membership in the new scientific societies, no woman was invited to join either the Royal Society of England or the French Academy of Sciences until the twentieth century. All of these women scientists were exceptional, since a life devoted to any kind of scholarship was still viewed as being at odds with the domestic duties women were expected to perform.

Debates on the Nature of Women

The nature and value of women had been the subject of an ongoing, centuries-long debate known as the ***querelles des femmes*** (keh-REL day FAHM)—arguments about women. Male opinions in the debate were largely a carryover from medieval times and were not favorable. Women were portrayed as inherently base, prone to vice, easily swayed, and "sexually insatiable." Hence, men needed to control them. Learned women were viewed as having overcome female liabilities to become like men. One man in praise of a woman scholar remarked that her writings were so good that you "would hardly believe they were done by a woman at all."

The "Natural" Inferiority of Women

Despite the shattering of old views and the emergence of a new worldview in the Scientific Revolution of the seventeenth century, attitudes toward women remained tied to traditional perspectives. In this selection, the philosopher Benedict de Spinoza argues for the "natural" inferiority of women to men.

Benedict de Spinoza, *A Political Treatise*

But, perhaps, someone will ask, whether women are under men's authority by nature or institution? For if it has been by mere institution, then we had no reason compelling us to exclude women from government. But if we consult experience itself, we shall find that the origin of it is in their weakness. For there has never been a case of men and women reigning together, but wherever on the earth men are found, there we see that men rule, and women are ruled, and that on this plan, both sexes live in harmony. But on the other hand, the Amazons, who are reported to have held rule of old, did not suffer men to stop in their country, but reared only their female children, killing males to whom they gave birth. But if by nature women were equal to men, and were equally distinguished by force of character and ability, in which human power and therefore human right chiefly consist; surely among nations so many and different some would be found, where both sexes rule alike, and others, where men are ruled by women, and so brought up, that they can make less use of their abilities. And since this is nowhere the case, one may assert with perfect propriety, that women have not by nature equal right with men: but that they necessarily give way to men, and that thus it cannot happen, that both sexes should rule alike, much less that men should be ruled by women. But if we further reflect upon human passions, how men, in fact, generally love women merely from the passion of lust, and esteem their cleverness and wisdom in proportion to the excellence of their beauty, and also how very ill-disposed men are to suffer the women they love to show any sort of favor to others, and other facts of this kind, we shall easily see that men and women cannot rule alike without great hurt to peace.

Q What arguments did Spinoza use to support the idea of female inferiority? What was the effect of this line of reasoning on the roles women could play?

In the early modern era, women joined this debate by arguing against these male images of women. They argued that women also had rational minds and could grow from education. Further, since most women were pious, chaste, and temperate, there was no need for male authority over them. These female defenders of women emphasized education as the key to women's ability to move into the world. How, then, did the era of the Scientific Revolution affect this debate over the nature of women? As an era of intellectual revolution in which traditional authorities were being overthrown, we might expect significant change in men's views of women. But by and large, instead of becoming an instrument for liberation, science was used to find new support for the old, stereotypical views about a woman's place in the scheme of things.

An important project in the new anatomy of the sixteenth and seventeenth centuries was the attempt to illustrate the human body and skeleton. For Vesalius, the portrayal of physical differences between males and females was limited to external bodily form (the outlines of the body) and the sexual organs. Vesalius saw no difference in skeletons and portrayed them as the same for men and women. It was not until the eighteenth century, in fact, that a new anatomy finally prevailed. Drawings of female skeletons between 1730 and 1790 varied, but females tended to have a larger pelvic area, and, in some instances, female skulls were portrayed as smaller than those of males. Eighteenth-century studies on the anatomy and physiology of sexual differences provided "scientific evidence" to reaffirm the traditional inferiority of women. The larger pelvic area "proved" that women were meant to be childbearers, and the larger skull "demonstrated" the superiority of the male mind. Male-dominated science had been used to "prove" male social dominance.

At the same time, during the seventeenth and eighteenth centuries, women even lost the traditional spheres of influence they had possessed, especially in the science-related art of midwifery. Women serving as midwives had traditionally been responsible for birthing. Similar to barber-surgeons or apothecaries (see Chapter 17), midwives had acquired their skills through apprenticeship. But the impact of the Scientific Revolution caused traditional crafts to be upgraded and then even professionalized as males took over. When medical men entered this arena, they also began to use devices and techniques derived from the study of anatomy. These were increasingly used to justify the male takeover of the traditional role of midwives. By the end of the eighteenth century, midwives were simply accessories to the art they had once controlled, except among the poor. Since little money was to be made in serving the lower classes, midwives were allowed to continue to practice their traditional art among them.

Overall, the Scientific Revolution reaffirmed traditional ideas about women. Male scientists used the new science to spread the view that women were inferior by nature, subordinate to men, and suited by nature to play a domestic role as nurturing mothers (see the box above). The widespread distribution of books ensured the continuation of these ideas. Jean de La Bruyère (ZHAHNH duh lah broo-YARE), the seventeenth-century French moralist, was typical when he remarked that an educated woman was like a gun that was a collector's item, "which one shows to the curious, but which has no use at all, any more than a carousel horse."[15]

Toward a New Earth: Descartes, Rationalism, and a New View of Humankind

Q FOCUS QUESTION: Why is Descartes considered the "founder of modern rationalism"?

The fundamentally new conception of the universe contained in the cosmological revolution of the sixteenth and seventeenth centuries inevitably had an impact on the Western view of humankind. Nowhere is this more evident than in the work of René Descartes (ruh-NAY day-KART) (1596–1650), an extremely important figure in Western history. Descartes began by reflecting the doubt and uncertainty that seemed pervasive in the confusion of the seventeenth century and ended with a philosophy that dominated Western thought until the twentieth century.

Descartes. René Descartes was one of the primary figures in the Scientific Revolution. Claiming to use reason as his sole guide to truth, Descartes posited a sharp distinction between mind and matter. He is shown here in a portrait by Frans Hals, one of the painters of the Dutch golden age who was famous for his portraits, especially that of Descartes.

Descartes was born into a family of the French lower nobility. After a Jesuit education, he studied law at Poitiers but traveled to Paris to study by himself. In 1618, at the beginning of the Thirty Years' War, Descartes volunteered for service in the army of Maurice of Nassau, but his motives seem to have been guided less by the desire for military action than for travel and leisure time to think. On the night of November 10, 1619, Descartes underwent what one historian has called an experience comparable to the "ecstatic illumination of the mystic." Having perceived in one night the outlines of a new rational-mathematical system, with a sense of divine approval he made a new commitment to mind, mathematics, and a mechanical universe. For the rest of his life, Descartes worked out the details of his vision.

René Descartes, *Discourse on Method* (1637)

The starting point for Descartes's new system was doubt, as he explained at the beginning of his most famous work, the *Discourse on Method*, written in 1637:

> From my childhood I have been familiar with letters; and as I was given to believe that by their means a clear and assured knowledge can be acquired of all that is useful in life, I was extremely eager for instruction in them. As soon, however, as I had completed the course of study, at the close of which it is customary to be admitted into the order of the learned, I entirely changed my opinion. For I found myself entangled in so many doubts and errors that, as it seemed to me, the endeavor to instruct myself had served only to disclose to me more and more of my ignorance.[16]

Descartes decided to set aside all that he had learned and begin again. One fact seemed beyond doubt—his own existence:

> But I immediately became aware that while I was thus disposed to think that all was false, it was absolutely necessary that I who thus thought should be something; and noting that this truth, *I think, therefore I am,* was so steadfast and so assured that the suppositions of the skeptics, to whatever extreme they might all be carried, could not avail to shake it, I concluded that I might without scruple accept it as being the first principle of the philosophy I was seeking.[17]

With this emphasis on the mind, Descartes asserted that he would accept only those things that his reason said were true.

From his first postulate, Descartes deduced an additional principle, the separation of mind and matter. Descartes argued that since "the mind cannot be doubted but the body and material world can, the two must be radically different." From this came an absolute duality between mind and body that has been called **Cartesian dualism.** Using mind or human reason, the path to certain knowledge, and its best instrument, mathematics, humans can understand the material world because it is pure mechanism, a machine that is governed by its own physical laws because it was created by God, the great geometrician.

Descartes's conclusions about the nature of the universe and human beings had important implications. His separation of mind and matter allowed scientists to view matter as dead or inert, as something that was totally

The Father of Modern Rationalism

René Descartes has long been viewed as the founder of modern rationalism and modern philosophy because he believed that human beings could understand the world—itself a mechanical system—by the same rational principles inherent in mathematical thinking. In his *Discourse on Method,* he elaborated on his approach to discovering truth.

━━━ ⋯⋙✦⋘⋯ ━━━

René Descartes, *Discourse on Method*

In place of the numerous precepts which have gone to constitute logic, I came to believe that the four following rules would be found sufficient, always provided I took the firm and unswerving resolve never in a single instance to fail in observing them.

The first was to accept nothing as true which I did not evidently know to be such, that is to say, scrupulously to avoid precipitance and prejudice, and in the judgments I passed to include nothing additional to what had presented itself to my mind so clearly and so distinctly that I could have no occasion for doubting it.

The second, to divide each of the difficulties I examined into as many parts as may be required for its adequate solution.

The third, to arrange my thoughts in order, beginning with things the simplest and easiest to know, so that I may then ascend little by little, as it were step by step, to the knowledge of the more complex, and in doing so, to assign an order of thought even to those objects which are not of themselves in any such order of precedence.

And the last, in all cases to make enumerations so complete, and reviews so general, that I should be assured of omitting nothing.

Those long chains of reasonings, each step simple and easy, which geometers are wont to employ in arriving even at the most difficult of their demonstrations, have led me to surmise that all the things we human beings are competent to know are interconnected in the same manner, and that none are so remote as to be beyond our reach or so hidden that we cannot discover them—that is, provided we abstain from accepting as true what is not thus related, i.e., keep always to the order required for their deduction one from another. And I had no great difficulty in determining what the objects are with which I should begin, for that I already knew, namely, that it was with the simplest and easiest. Bearing in mind, too, that of all those who in time past have sought for truth in the sciences, the mathematicians alone have been able to find any demonstrations, that is to say, any reasons which are certain and evident, I had no doubt that it must have been by a procedure of this kind that they had obtained them.

Q Describe Descartes's principles of inquiry and compare them with Newton's rules of reasoning. What are the main similarities between these systems of thinking?

---

separate from themselves and could be investigated independently by reason. The split between mind and body led Westerners to equate their identity with mind and reason rather than with the whole organism. Descartes has rightly been called the father of modern **rationalism** (see the box above). His books were placed on the papal Index of Forbidden Books and condemned by many Protestant theologians. The radical Cartesian split between mind and matter, and between mind and body, had devastating implications not only for traditional religious views of the universe but also for how Westerners viewed themselves.

The Scientific Method and the Spread of Scientific Knowledge

Q **Focus Question:** How were the ideas of the Scientific Revolution spread, and what impact did they have on society and religion?

During the seventeenth century, scientific learning and investigation began to increase dramatically. Major universities in Europe established new chairs of science, especially in medicine. Royal and princely patronage of individual scientists became an international phenomenon. Even in the late sixteenth century, the king of Denmark had constructed an astronomical observatory for Tycho Brahe; later Emperor Rudolf II hired Brahe and Kepler as imperial mathematicians, and the grand duke of Tuscany appointed Galileo to a similar post.

The Scientific Method

Of great importance to the work of science was establishing the proper means to examine and understand the physical realm. This development of a **scientific method** was crucial to the evolution of science in the modern world.

FRANCIS BACON Curiously enough, it was an Englishman with few scientific credentials who attempted to put forth a new method of acquiring knowledge that made an impact on the Royal Society in England in the seventeenth century and other European scientists in the eighteenth century. Francis Bacon (1561–1626), a lawyer and lord chancellor, rejected Copernicus and Kepler and misunderstood Galileo. And yet in his unfinished work, *The Great Instauration,* he called for his contemporaries "to commence a total reconstruction of sciences, arts, and all human knowledge, raised upon the proper foundations." Bacon did not doubt humans' ability to know the natural world, but he believed that they had proceeded incorrectly: "The entire fabric of human reason which we employ in the inquisition of nature is badly put together and built up, and like some magnificent structure without foundation."

Bacon's new foundation—a correct scientific method—was to be built on inductive principles. Rather than beginning with assumed first principles from which logical conclusions could be deduced, he urged scientists to proceed from the particular to the general. From carefully organized experiments and thorough, systematic observations, correct generalizations could be developed.

Bacon was clear about what he believed his method could accomplish. His concern was more for practical than for pure science. He stated that "the true and lawful goal of the sciences is none other than this: that human life be endowed with new discoveries and power." He wanted science to contribute to the "mechanical arts" by creating devices that would benefit industry, agriculture, and trade. Bacon was prophetic when he said that he was "laboring to lay the foundation, not of any sect or doctrine, but of human utility and power." And how would this "human power" be used? To "conquer nature in action."[18] The control and domination of nature became a central proposition of modern science and the technology that accompanied it. Only in the twentieth century did some scientists begin to ask whether this assumption might not be at the heart of the earth's ecological crisis.

DESCARTES Descartes proposed a different approach to scientific methodology by emphasizing deduction and mathematical logic. As Descartes explained in the *Discourse on Method,* each step in an argument should be as sharp and well founded as a mathematical proof:

> Those long chains of reasonings, each step simple and easy, which geometers are wont to employ in arriving even at the most difficult of their demonstrations, have led me to surmise that all the things we human beings are competent to know are interconnected in the same manner, and that none are so remote as to be beyond our reach or so hidden that we cannot discover them—that is, provided we abstain from accepting as true what is not thus related, i.e., keep always to the order required for their deduction one from another.[19]

Descartes believed, then, that one could start with self-evident truths, comparable to geometric axioms, and deduce more complex conclusions. His emphasis on deduction and mathematical order complemented

Bacon's stress on experiment and induction. It was Sir Isaac Newton who synthesized them into a single scientific methodology by uniting Bacon's **empiricism** with Descartes's rationalism. This scientific method began with systematic observations and experiments, which were used to arrive at general concepts. New deductions derived from these general concepts could then be tested and verified by precise experiments.

The scientific method, of course, was valuable in answering the question of *how* something works, and its success in doing this gave others much confidence in the method. It did not attempt to deal with the question of *why* something happens or the purpose and meaning behind the world of nature. This allowed religion to retain its central importance in the seventeenth century (see "Science and Religion" later in this chapter).

The Spread of Scientific Knowledge

Also important to the work of science was the emergence of new learned societies and journals that enabled the new scientists to communicate their ideas to each other and to disseminate them to a wider, literate public.

THE SCIENTIFIC SOCIETIES The first of these scientific societies appeared in Italy, but those of England and France were ultimately of greater significance. The English Royal Society evolved out of informal gatherings of scientists at London and Oxford in the 1640s, although it did not

Louis XIV and Colbert Visit the Academy of Sciences. In the seventeenth century, individual scientists received royal and princely patronage, and a number of learned societies were established. In France, Louis XIV, urged on by his controller general, Jean-Baptiste Colbert, gave formal recognition to the French Academy in 1666. In this painting by Henri Testelin, Louis XIV is shown seated, surrounded by Colbert and members of the French Royal Academy of Sciences.

Chateaux de Versailles et de Trianon, Versailles// © Réunion des Musées Nationaux/Art Resource, NY

The Royal Observatory at Greenwich. To facilitate their astronomical investigations, both the English and the French constructed observatories such as the one pictured here, which was built at Greenwich, England, in 1675. Here the royal astronomer works at the table while his two assistants make observations.

receive a formal charter from King Charles II until 1662. The French Royal Academy of Sciences also arose out of informal scientific meetings in Paris during the 1650s. In 1666, Louis XIV formally recognized the group. The French Academy received abundant state support and remained under government control; its members were appointed and paid salaries by the state. In contrast, the Royal Society of England received little government encouragement, and its fellows simply co-opted new members.

Early on, both the English and the French scientific societies formally emphasized the practical value of scientific research. The Royal Society created a committee to investigate technological improvements for industry; the French Academy collected tools and machines. This concern with the practical benefits of science proved short-lived, however, as both societies came to focus their primary interest on theoretical work in mechanics and astronomy. The construction of observatories at Paris in 1667 and at Greenwich, England, in 1675 greatly facilitated research in astronomy by both groups. The French Academy, however, since it was controlled by the state, was forced by the war minister of France, the marquis de Louvois, to continue its practical work to benefit both "the king and the state." The French example was especially important as a model for the scientific societies established in neighboring Germany. German princes and city governments encouraged the foundation of small-scale scientific societies of their own. Most of them were sponsored by governments and were mainly devoted to the betterment of the state. Although both the English and the French societies made useful contributions to scientific knowledge in the second half of the seventeenth century, their true significance was

that they demonstrated the benefits of science proceeding as a cooperative venture.

Scientific journals furthered this concept of cooperation. The French *Journal des Savants* (zhoor-NAHL day sah-VAHNH), published weekly beginning in 1665, printed results of experiments as well as general scientific knowledge. Its format appealed to both scientists and the educated public interested in the new science. In contrast, the *Philosophical Transactions* of the Royal Society, also initiated in 1665, published papers of its members and learned correspondence and was aimed at practicing scientists. It became a prototype for the scholarly journals of later learned and academic societies and a crucial instrument for circulating news of scientific and academic activities.

SCIENCE AND SOCIETY The importance of science in the history of modern Western civilization is usually taken for granted. No doubt the Industrial Revolution of the nineteenth century provided tangible proof of the effectiveness of science and ensured its victory over Western minds. But how did science become such an integral part of Western culture in the seventeenth and eighteenth centuries? Recent research has stressed that one cannot simply assert that people perceived that science was a rationally superior system. Several factors, however, might explain the relatively rapid acceptance of the new science.

It has been argued that the literate mercantile and propertied elites of Europe were attracted to the new science because it offered new ways to exploit resources for profit. Some of the early scientists made it easier for these groups to accept the new ideas by showing how they could be applied directly to specific industrial and technological needs. Galileo, for example, consciously sought an alliance between science and the material interests of the educated elite when he assured his listeners that the science of mechanics would be quite useful "when it becomes necessary to build bridges or other structures over water, something occurring mainly in affairs of great importance." At the same time, Galileo stressed that science was fit for the "minds of the wise" and not for "the shallow minds of the common people." This made science part of the high culture of Europe's wealthy elites at a time when that culture was being increasingly separated from the popular culture of the lower classes (see Chapter 17).

It has also been argued that political interests used the new scientific conception of the natural world to bolster social stability. One scholar has argued that "no single event in the history of early modern Europe more profoundly shaped the integration of the new science into Western culture than did the English Revolution (1640–1660)."[20] Fed by their millenarian expectations that the end of the world would come and usher in a thousand-year reign of the saints, Puritan reformers felt it was important to reform and renew their society. They seized on the new science as a socially useful instrument to accomplish this goal. The Puritan Revolution's role in the acceptance of science, however, stemmed even more from the reaction to the radicalism spawned by the revolutionary ferment. The upheavals of the Puritan Revolution gave rise to groups, such as the Levellers, Diggers, and Ranters, who advocated not only radical political ideas but also a new radical science based on Paracelsus and the natural magic associated with the Hermetic tradition. The chaplain of the New Model Army said that the radicals wanted "the philosophy of Hermes, revived by the Paracelsian schools." The propertied and educated elites responded vigorously to these challenges to the established order by supporting the new mechanistic science and appealing to the material benefits of science. Hence, the founders of the Royal Society were men who wanted to pursue an experimental science that would remain detached from radical reforms of church and state. Although willing to make changes, they now viewed those changes in terms of an increase in food production and commerce. By the eighteenth century, the Newtonian world-machine had been readily accepted, and Newtonian science would soon be applied to trade and industry by a mercantile and landed elite that believed that they "could retain a social order that primarily rewarded and enriched themselves while still improving the human condition."

At the same time, princes and kings who were providing patronage for scientists were doing so not only for prestige but also for practical reasons, especially the military applications of the mathematical sciences. The use of gunpowder, for example, gave new importance to ballistics and metallurgy. Rulers, especially absolute ones, were also concerned about matters of belief in their realms and recognized the need to control and manage the scientific body of knowledge, as we have seen in the French Academy. In appointing its members and paying their salaries, Louis XIV was also ensuring that the members and their work would be under his control.

Science and Religion

In Galileo's struggle with the inquisitorial Holy Office of the Catholic Church, we see the beginning of the conflict between science and religion that has marked the history of modern Western civilization. Since time immemorial, theology had seemed to be the queen of the sciences. It was natural that the churches would continue to believe that religion was the final measure of all things. To the emerging scientists, however, it often seemed that theologians knew not of what they spoke. These "natural philosophers" then tried to draw lines between the knowledge of religion and the knowledge of "natural philosophy" or nature. Galileo had clearly felt that it was unnecessary to pit science against religion when he wrote:

In discussions of physical problems we ought to begin not from the authority of scriptural passages, but from sense-experiences and necessary demonstrations; for the holy Bible and the phenomena of nature proceed alike from the divine word, the former as the dictate of the Holy Ghost and the latter as the observant executrix of God's commands. It is necessary for the Bible, in order to be accommodated to the understanding of every man, to speak many things which appear to differ from the absolute truth so far as the bare meaning of the words is concerned. But Nature, on the other hand, is inexorable and immutable; she never transgresses the laws imposed upon her, or cares a whit whether her abstruse reasons and methods of operation are understandable to men.[21]

To Galileo, it made little sense for the church to determine the nature of physical reality on the basis of biblical texts that were subject to radically divergent interpretations. The church, however, decided otherwise in Galileo's case and lent its great authority to one scientific theory, the Ptolemaic-Aristotelian cosmology, no doubt because it fit so well with its own philosophical views of reality. But the church's decision had tremendous consequences, just as the rejection of Darwin's ideas did in the nineteenth century. For educated individuals, it established a dichotomy between scientific investigations and religious beliefs. As the scientific beliefs triumphed, it became almost inevitable that religious beliefs would suffer, leading to a growing secularization in European intellectual life—precisely what the church had hoped to combat by opposing Copernicanism. Many seventeenth-century intellectuals were both religious and scientific and believed that the implications of this split would be tragic. Some believed that the split was largely unnecessary, while others felt the need to combine God, humans, and a mechanistic universe into a new philosophical synthesis. Two individuals—Spinoza and Pascal—illustrate the wide diversity in the response of European intellectuals to the implications of the cosmological revolution of the seventeenth century.

SPINOZA Benedict de Spinoza (spi-NOH-zuh) (1632–1677) was a philosopher who grew up in the relatively tolerant atmosphere of Amsterdam. He was excommunicated from the Amsterdam synagogue at the age of twenty-four for rejecting the tenets of Judaism. Ostracized by the local Jewish community and major Christian churches alike, Spinoza lived a quiet, independent life, earning a living by grinding optical lenses and refusing to accept an academic position in philosophy at the University of Heidelberg for fear of compromising his freedom of thought. Spinoza read a great deal of the new scientific literature and was influenced by Descartes.

Spinoza was unwilling to accept the implications of Descartes's ideas, especially the separation of mind and matter and the apparent separation of an infinite God from the finite world of matter. God was not simply the creator of the universe; he was the universe. All that is is in God, and nothing can be apart from God. This philosophy of pantheism (or monism) was set out in Spinoza's book *Ethics Demonstrated in the Geometrical Manner*, which was not published until after his death.

To Spinoza, human beings are not "situated in nature as a kingdom within a kingdom" but are as much a part of God or nature or the universal order as other natural objects. The failure to understand God had led to many misconceptions—for one, that nature exists only for one's use:

> As they find in themselves and outside themselves many means which assist them not a little in their search for what is useful, for instance, eyes for seeing, teeth for chewing, herbs and animals for yielding food, the sun for giving light, the sea for breeding fish, they come to look on the whole of nature as a means for obtaining such conveniences.[22]

Furthermore, unable to find any other cause for the existence of these things, they attributed them to a creator-God who must be worshiped to gain their ends: "Hence also it follows, that everyone thought out for himself, according to his abilities, a different way of worshiping God, so that God might love him more than his fellows, and direct the whole course of nature for the satisfaction of his blind cupidity and insatiable avarice." Then, when nature appeared unfriendly in the form of storms, earthquakes, and diseases, "they declared that such things happen, because the gods are angry at some wrong done them by men, or at some fault committed in their worship," rather than realizing "that good and evil fortunes fall to the lot of pious and impious alike."[23] Likewise, human beings made moral condemnations of others because they failed to understand that human emotions, "passions of hatred, anger, envy and so, considered in themselves, follow from the same necessity and efficacy of nature" and "nothing comes to pass in nature in contravention to her universal laws." To explain human emotions, like everything else, we need to analyze them as we would the movements of planets: "I shall, therefore, treat of the nature and strength of my emotions according to the same method as I employed heretofore in my investigations concerning God and the mind. I shall consider human actions and desires in exactly the same manner as though I were concerned with lines, planes, and solids."[24] Everything has a rational explanation, and humans are capable of finding it. In using reason, people can find true happiness. Their real freedom comes when they understand the order and necessity of nature and achieve detachment from passing interests.

PASCAL Blaise Pascal (BLEZ pass-KAHL) (1623–1662) was a French scientist who sought to keep science and religion united. He had a brief but checkered career. An accomplished scientist and a brilliant mathematician, he excelled at both the practical, by inventing a calculating machine, and the abstract, by devising a theory of chance or probability and doing work on conic sections.

Bacon, *The Great Instauration*	1620
Descartes, *Discourse on Method*	1637
Pascal, *Pensées*	1669
Spinoza, *Ethics Demonstrated in the Geometrical Manner*	1677

After a profound mystical vision on the night of November 23, 1654, which assured him that God cared for the human soul, he devoted the rest of his life to religious matters. He planned to write an "apology for the Christian religion" but died before he could do so. He did leave a set of notes for the larger work, however, which in published form became known as the *Pensées* (pahn-SAY) (*Thoughts*).

In the *Pensées*, Pascal tried to convert rationalists to Christianity by appealing to both their reason and their emotions. Humans were, he argued, frail creatures, often deceived by their senses, misled by reason, and battered by their emotions. And yet they were beings whose very nature involved thinking: "Man is but a reed, the weakest in nature; but he is a thinking reed."[25]

Blaise Pascal. Blaise Pascal was a brilliant scientist and mathematician who hoped to keep science and Christianity united. In his *Pensées,* he made a passionate argument on behalf of the Christian religion. He is pictured here in a portrait by Philippe de Champaigne, a well-known French portrait painter of the Baroque period.

© Giraudon/The Bridgeman Art Library

Pascal: "What Is a Man in the Infinite?"

Perhaps no intellectual in the seventeenth century gave greater expression to the uncertainties generated by the cosmological revolution than Blaise Pascal, himself a scientist. Pascal's work, the *Pensées,* consisted of notes for a large unfinished work justifying the Christian religion. In this selection, Pascal presents his musings on the human place in an infinite world.

⊷ ≕✦≕ ⊶

Blaise Pascal, *Pensées*

Let man then contemplate the whole of nature in her full and exalted majesty. Let him turn his eyes from the lowly objects which surround him. Let him gaze on that brilliant light set like an eternal lamp to illumine the Universe; let the earth seem to him a dot compared with the vast orbit described by the sun, and let him wonder at the fact that this vast orbit itself is not more than a very small dot compared with that described by the stars in their revolutions around the firmament. But if our vision stops here, let the imagination pass one; it will exhaust its powers of thinking long before nature ceases to supply it with material for thought. All this visible world is no more than an imperceptible speck in nature's ample bosom. No idea approaches it. We may extend our conceptions beyond all imaginable space; yet produce only atoms in comparison with the reality of things. It is an infinite sphere, the center of which is everywhere, the circumference nowhere. In short, it is the greatest perceptible mark of God's almighty power that our imagination should lose itself in that thought.

Returning to himself, let man consider what he is compared with all existence; let him think of himself as lost in his remote corner of nature; and from this little dungeon in which he finds himself lodged—I mean the Universe—let him learn to set a true value on the earth, its kingdoms, and cities, and upon himself. What is a man in the infinite? . . .

For, after all, what is a man in nature? A nothing in comparison with the infinite, an absolute in comparison with nothing, a central point between nothing and all. Infinitely far from understanding these extremes, the end of things and their beginning are hopelessly hidden from him in an impenetrable secret. He is equally incapable of seeing the nothingness from which he came, and the infinite in which he is engulfed. What else then will he perceive but some appearance in the middle of things, in an eternal despair of knowing either their principle or their purpose? All things emerge from nothing and are borne onward to infinity. Who can follow this marvelous process? The Author of these wonders understands them. None but He can.

Q Why did Pascal question whether human beings could achieve scientific certainty? What is the significance of Pascal's thoughts for modern science?

Pascal was determined to show that the Christian religion was not contrary to reason: "If we violate the principles of reason, our religion will be absurd, and it will be laughed at." Christianity, he felt, was the only religion that recognized people's true state of being as both vulnerable and great. To a Christian, a human being was both fallen and at the same time God's special creation. But it was not necessary to emphasize one at the expense of the other—to view humans as only rational or only hopeless. Pascal even had an answer for skeptics in his famous wager. God is a reasonable bet; it is worthwhile to assume that God exists. If he does, then we win all; if he does not, we lose nothing.

Despite his own background as a scientist and mathematician, Pascal refused to rely on the scientist's world of order and rationality to attract people to God: "If we submit everything to reason, there will be no mystery and no supernatural element in our religion." In the new cosmology of the seventeenth century, "finite man," Pascal believed, was lost in the new infinite world, a realization that frightened him: "The eternal silence of those infinite spaces strikes me with terror" (see the box above). The world of nature, then, could never reveal God: "Because they have failed to contemplate these infinites, men have rashly plunged into the examination of nature, as though they bore some proportion to her. . . . Their assumption is as infinite as their object." A Christian could only rely on a God who through Jesus cared for human beings. In the final analysis, after providing reasonable arguments for Christianity, Pascal came to rest on faith. Reason, he believed, could take people only so far: "The heart has its reasons of which the reason knows nothing." As a Christian, faith was the final step: "The heart feels God, not the reason. This is what constitutes faith: God experienced by the heart, not by the reason."[26]

In retrospect, it is obvious that Pascal failed to achieve his goal of uniting Christianity and science. Increasingly, the gap between science and traditional religion grew wider as Europe continued along its path of secularization. Of course, traditional religions were not eliminated, nor is there any evidence that churches had yet lost their followers. That would happen later. Nevertheless, more and more of the intellectual, social, and political elites began to act on the basis of secular rather than religious assumptions.

CHAPTER SUMMARY

The Scientific Revolution represents a major turning point in modern Western civilization. In the Scientific Revolution, the Western world overthrew the medieval, Ptolemaic-Aristotelian worldview and geocentric universe and arrived at a new conception of the universe: the sun at the center, the planets as material bodies revolving around the sun in elliptical orbits, and an infinite rather than finite world. This new conception of the heavens was the work of a number of brilliant individuals: Nicolaus Copernicus, who theorized a heliocentric, or sun-centered, universe; Johannes Kepler, who discovered that planetary orbits were elliptical; Galileo Galilei, who, by using a telescope and observing the moon and sunspots, discovered that the universe seemed to be composed of material substance; and Isaac Newton, who tied together all of these ideas with his universal law of gravitation. The contributions of each individual built on the work of the others, thus establishing one of the basic principles of the new science—cooperation in the pursuit of new knowledge.

With the changes in the conception of "heaven" came changes in the conception of "earth." The work of Bacon and Descartes left Europeans with the separation of mind and matter and the belief that by using only reason they could in fact understand and dominate the world of nature. The development of a scientific methodology furthered the work of the scientists, and the creation of scientific societies and learned journals spread its results. The Scientific Revolution was more than merely intellectual theories. It also appealed to nonscientific elites because of its practical implications for economic progress and for maintaining the social order, including the waging of war.

Although traditional churches stubbornly resisted the new ideas and a few intellectuals pointed to some inherent flaws, nothing was able to halt the supplanting of the traditional ways of thinking by new ways of thinking that created a more fundamental break with the past than that represented by the breakup of Christian unity in the Reformation.

The Scientific Revolution forced Europeans to change their conception of themselves. At first, some were appalled and even frightened by its implications. Formerly, humans on earth had viewed themselves as being at the center of the universe. Now the earth was only a tiny planet revolving around a sun that was itself only a speck in a boundless universe. Most people remained optimistic despite the apparent blow to human dignity. After all, had Newton not demonstrated that the universe was a great machine governed by natural laws? Newton had found one—the universal law of gravitation. Could others not find other laws? Were there not natural laws governing every aspect of human endeavor that could be found by the new scientific method? Thus, as we shall see in the next chapter, the Scientific Revolution leads us logically to the Enlightenment in the eighteenth century.

CHAPTER REVIEW

Upon Reflection

Q How do you explain the emergence of the Scientific Revolution?

Q What do we mean by the "Newtonian world-machine," and what is its significance?

Q Compare the methods used by Bacon and Descartes. Would Pascal agree with the methods and interests of these men? Why or why not?

Key Terms

Scientific Revolution (p. 488)
geocentric conception (p. 489)
heliocentric conception (p. 490)
world-machine (p. 499)
querelles des femmes (p. 502)

Cartesian dualism (p. 504)
rationalism (p. 505)
scientific method (p. 505)
empiricism (p. 506)

Suggestions for Further Reading

GENERAL WORKS General surveys of the entire Scientific Revolution include **J. Henry, *The Scientific Revolution and the Origins of Modern Science,*** 2nd ed. (London, 2002), and **J. R. Jacob, *The Scientific Revolution: Aspirations and Achievements, 1500–1700*** (Atlantic Highlands, N.J., 1998). For a revisionist perspective, see **S. Shapin, *The Scientific Revolution*** (Chicago, 1996). See also the collections of articles in **R. Porter, ed., *Scientific Revolution in National Context*** (Cambridge, 2007), and **P. Dear, *Revolutionizing the Sciences: European Knowledge and Its Ambitions, 1500–1700*** (Princeton, N.J., 2001). On the relationship of magic to the beginnings of the Scientific Revolution, see the pioneering works by **F. Yates,**

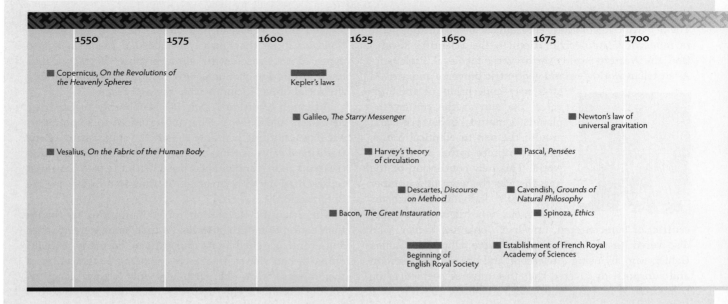

1550   1575   1600   1625   1650   1675   1700

- Copernicus, *On the Revolutions of the Heavenly Spheres*
- Kepler's laws
- Galileo, *The Starry Messenger*
- Newton's law of universal gravitation
- Vesalius, *On the Fabric of the Human Body*
- Harvey's theory of circulation
- Pascal, *Pensées*
- Descartes, *Discourse on Method*
- Cavendish, *Grounds of Natural Philosophy*
- Bacon, *The Great Instauration*
- Spinoza, *Ethics*
- Beginning of English Royal Society
- Establishment of French Royal Academy of Sciences

Giordano Bruno and the Hermetic Tradition (New York, 1964) and *The Rosicrucian Enlightenment* (London, 1975). On the importance of mathematics, see **P. Dear, *Discipline and Experience: The Mathematical Way in the Scientific Revolution*** (Chicago, 1995). On the relationship between Renaissance artists and the Scientific Revolution, see **P. H. Smith, *Body of the Artisan: Art and Experience in the Scientific Revolution*** (Chicago, 2006).

A REVOLUTION IN ASTRONOMY On the important figures of the revolution in astronomy, see **E. Rosen, *Copernicus and the Scientific Revolution*** (New York, 1984); **H. Margolis, *It Started with Copernicus: How Turning the World Inside Out Led to the Scientific Revolution*** (New York, 2002); **M. Sharratt, *Galileo: Decisive Innovator*** (Oxford, 1994); **S. Drake, *Galileo, Pioneer Scientist*** (Toronto, 1990); **M. Casper, *Johannes Kepler,*** trans. C. D. Hellman (London, 1959), the standard biography; **R. S. Westfall, *The Life of Isaac Newton*** (New York, 1993); and **P. Fara, *Newton: The Making of Genius*** (New York, 2004). On Newton's relationship to alchemy, see **M. White, *Isaac Newton: The Last Sorcerer*** (Reading, Mass., 1997).

Visit the CourseMate website at www.cengagebrain.com for additional study tools and review materials for this chapter.

ADVANCES IN MEDICINE The worldview of Paracelsus can be examined in **P. Ball, *The Devil's Doctor: Paracelsus and the World of Renaissance Magic and Science*** (New York, 2006). The standard biography of Vesalius is **C. D. O'Malley, *Andreas Vesalius of Brussels, 1514–1564*** (Berkeley, Calif., 1964). The work of Harvey is discussed in **G. Whitteridge, *William Harvey and the Circulation of the Blood*** (London, 1971).

IMPACT OF SCIENCE The importance of Francis Bacon in the early development of science is underscored in **P. Zagorin, *Francis Bacon*** (Princeton, N.J., 1998). A good introduction to the work of Descartes can be found in **G. Radis-Lewis, *Descartes: A Biography*** (Ithaca, N.Y., 1998). The standard biography of Spinoza in English is **S. Hampshire, *Spinoza*** (New York, 1961).

WOMEN AND SCIENCE On the subject of women and early modern science, see the comprehensive and highly informative work by **L. Schiebinger, *The Mind Has No Sex? Women in the Origins of Modern Science*** (Cambridge, Mass., 1989). See also **C. Merchant, *The Death of Nature: Women, Ecology, and the Scientific Revolution*** (San Francisco, 1980).

SCIENCE AND SOCIETY The social and political context for the triumph of science in the seventeenth and eighteenth centuries is examined in **M. Jacobs, *The Cultural Meaning of the Scientific Revolution*** (New York, 1988) and ***The Newtonians and the English Revolution, 1689–1720*** (Ithaca, N.Y., 1976). ⇨

1. All of the following contributed to the Scientific Revolution EXCEPT

    (A) Renaissance humanist thinking.
    (B) the development of new technology that aided in scientific discovery.
    (C) the influence of Classical thinkers like Ptolemy.
    (D) encouragement by the church to question God's power.
    (E) new advances in the field of mathematics.

2. In *On the Revolutions of the Heavenly Spheres,* Copernicus asserted that

    (A) the earth is at the center of the universe and all planets revolve around it.
    (B) the sun is at the center of universe and the planets move in concentric circles around it.
    (C) the heavens are at the center of the universe and the planets move around the heavens.
    (D) the sun is at the center of the universe and the planets move in elliptical orbits around it.
    (E) the earth is at the center of the universe and all planets move in conjunction with the moon.

3. The Dutch painting below

Louvre, Paris/© Giraudon/The Bridgeman Art Library

    (A) is an example of new scientific painting techniques.
    (B) embodies the Puritan ideal that science and God were not inherently at odds.
    (C) reflects an attempt to spread the knowledge of science to the New World.
    (D) was condemned by the Catholic Church because the church was in opposition to Dutch painters.
    (E) reflects mass popular culture and the response of the poorer classes to the subtleties of style.

4. When René Descartes wrote "I think, therefore I am," he did so to demonstrate the concept of

    (A) the power of the human mind.
    (B) deductive reasoning.
    (C) the new emerging agnostics.
    (D) inductive reasoning.
    (E) the humanists' ability to control the mind.

5. During the seventeenth century, European society generally saw women as

    (A) nurturers who were essential to the survival of the family.
    (B) deserving of limited education and some political freedoms.
    (C) worthy of being encouraged to participate in academic endeavors and venues such as royal societies.
    (D) valuable autonomous voices in community forums and church leadership meetings.
    (E) the superior sex because they had the ability to bring new life.

6. Vesalius and Harvey both made advances in the field of

    (A) astronomy.
    (B) medicine.
    (C) philosophy.
    (D) alchemy.
    (E) religion.

7. When Pascal said, "Man is but a reed, the weakest in nature, but he is a thinking reed," he was trying to convey that

    (A) man needs God and that science is unnecessary within God's realm.
    (B) God was like a clockmaker; he created man and then allowed him to function as an individual needing little spiritual intervention.
    (C) man and nature are connected; as the two can work together, so can God and man combine reason and religion.
    (D) man is alone in the world and only through reason can he find his way.
    (E) man is merely a small piece of the universe and he must cooperate with his fellow men in order to live in the complex society that they have built.

8. The Catholic Church chose to denounce Galileo because

   (A) he posed a political threat to authorities like the pope.
   (B) the church leaders wanted to start their own scientific revolution.
   (C) he was a social leader that many of the peasants followed, and the church feared a peasant uprising.
   (D) the church leaders were convinced that Galileo's scientific ideas would cause people to leave the church or to embrace the new reform religions.
   (E) many of the leading scientists at the time had proved him wrong, and he had given an unconvincing explanation for the movement of the planets.

9. Galileo Galilei is NOT credited with which of the following?

   (A) discovering the laws of inertia
   (B) naming the moons of Jupiter
   (C) developing an optical lens to view the heavens
   (D) using a telescope to view the heavens
   (E) writing *The Starry Messenger*

10. During the seventeenth century, women often lost jobs as midwives to men because

    (A) men convinced pregnant women that their scientific expertise made them better suited than women to deliver children.
    (B) women chose to leave the profession to spend more time with their families.
    (C) women lost interest in the field of medicine and felt they were not able to perform their duties as well as men could.
    (D) the church decreed that women should not be involved in birth, as it was a holy experience that only learned men could attend.
    (E) pregnant women feared other women would harm their infants, and found solace in the presence of a man during childbirth.

11. Science became part of elite culture because

    (A) peasants lost interest in their own mundane lives and turned to science for academic fulfillment.
    (B) the wealthy elites were more religious and were therefore more willing to accept science.
    (C) the new universities allowed the poor to attend classes, which spread an interest in science across society.
    (D) scientists saw their craft as fit for only the best members of society, and the elite were the embodiment of that concept.
    (E) it allowed both men and women to aspire to scientific accomplishments.

12. The scientific societies throughout Europe

    (A) were primarily based in Italy because the church led the way in associating science with religion.
    (B) were open to much of the public and became a valuable outlet for women to produce and highlight their new scientific work.
    (C) varied by country, with the governments of some states (like France) sponsoring societies, and other governments exerting little direct control over them.
    (D) primarily worked in isolation and failed to create any meaningful connections with other societies.
    (E) were primarily engaged in theory and failed to produce any meaningful accomplishments.

13. Which of the following is true of Benedict Spinoza's philosophical writings?

    (A) They were accepted by many, especially the Catholic Church, as he suggested that all are part of God's kingdom.
    (B) They caused him to be excommunicated by the Catholic Church and ostracized by many of his fellow scientists.
    (C) They caused him to be banned from all royal societies and many royal courts.
    (D) They proved him to be diametrically opposite in thought from Galileo and Pascal.
    (E) They proposed the rationalization of universal laws that are developed by God and that humans could formulate rational explanations about the world and nature.

14. All of the following arguments were used to explain the status of women EXCEPT

    (A) that women were content with their station and did not seek change.
    (B) that women were irrational and could not benefit from education.
    (C) that women's skulls were smaller than men's skulls, thereby proving natural male superiority.
    (D) that women were naturally more prone to sin or easily swayed.
    (E) that women were similar to sheep and needed the guidance of men to keep them from going astray.

The Parisian salon of Madame Geoffrin (third figure from the right in the first row)

The Eighteenth Century: An Age of Enlightenment

CHAPTER OUTLINE AND FOCUS QUESTIONS

The Enlightenment

Q What intellectual developments led to the emergence of the Enlightenment? Who were the leading figures of the Enlightenment, and what were their main contributions? In what type of social environment did the philosophes thrive, and what role did women play in that environment?

Culture and Society in the Enlightenment

Q What innovations in art, music, and literature occurred in the eighteenth century? How did popular culture differ from high culture in the eighteenth century?

Religion and the Churches

Q How did popular religion differ from institutional religion in the eighteenth century?

┌─ CRITICAL THINKING ══════════
Q What was the relationship between the Scientific Revolution and the Enlightenment?
└──────────────────────

THE EARTH-SHATTERING WORK of the "natural philosophers" in the Scientific Revolution had affected only a relatively small number of Europe's educated elite. In the eighteenth century, this changed dramatically as a group of intellectuals known as the philosophes popularized the ideas of the Scientific Revolution and used them to undertake a dramatic reexamination of all aspects of life. In Paris, the cultural capital of Europe, women took the lead in bringing together groups of men and women to discuss the new ideas of the philosophes. At her fashionable home in the Rue Saint-Honoré, Marie-Thérèse de Geoffrin (ma-REE-tay-RAYZ duh zhoh-FRANH), the wife of a wealthy merchant, held sway over gatherings that became the talk of France and even Europe. Distinguished foreigners, including a future king of Sweden and a future king of Poland, competed to receive invitations. When Madame Geoffrin made a visit to Vienna, she was so well received that she exclaimed, "I am better known here than a couple of yards from my own house." Madame Geoffrin was an amiable but firm hostess who allowed wide-ranging discussions as long as they remained in good taste. When she found that artists and philosophers did not mix particularly well (the artists were high-strung and the philosophers talked too much), she set up separate meetings. Artists were invited only on Mondays, philosophers, on Wednesdays. These gatherings were among the many avenues for the spread of the ideas of the philosophes. And those ideas had such a widespread impact on their society that historians ever since have called the eighteenth century the Age of Enlightenment.

For most of the philosophes, "enlightenment" included the rejection of traditional Christianity. The religious wars and intolerance of the sixteenth and seventeenth centuries had so alienated intellectuals that they were open and even eager to embrace the new ideas of the Scientific Revolution. Whereas the great scientists of the seventeenth century believed that their work exalted God, the intellectuals of the eighteenth century read those scientific conclusions a different way and increasingly turned their backs on Christian orthodoxy. Consequently, European intellectual life in the eighteenth century was marked by the emergence of the secularization that has characterized the modern Western mentality ever since. Ironically, at the same time that reason and materialism were beginning to replace faith and worship, a great outburst of religious sensibility manifested itself in music and art. Clearly, the growing secularization of the eighteenth century had not yet captured the hearts and minds of all European intellectuals and artists.

The Enlightenment

Q **FOCUS QUESTIONS:** What intellectual developments led to the emergence of the Enlightenment? Who were the leading figures of the Enlightenment, and what were their main contributions? In what type of social environment did the philosophes thrive, and what role did women play in that environment?

Immanuel Kant, *What Is Enlightenment?*

In 1784, the German philosopher Immanuel Kant (i-MAHN-yoo-el KAHNT) defined the **Enlightenment** as "man's leaving his self-caused immaturity." Whereas earlier periods had been handicapped by the inability to "use one's intelligence without the guidance of another," Kant proclaimed as the motto of the Enlightenment: "Dare to know! Have the courage to use your own intelligence!" The eighteenth-century Enlightenment was a movement of intellectuals who dared to know. They were greatly impressed with the accomplishments of the Scientific Revolution, and when they used the word *reason*—one of their favorite words—they were advocating the application of the scientific method to the understanding of all life. All institutions and all systems of thought were subject to the rational, scientific way of thinking if only people would free themselves from the shackles of old, worthless traditions, especially religious ones. If Isaac Newton could discover the natural laws regulating the world of nature, they too, by using reason, could find the laws that governed human society. This belief in turn led them to hope that they could make progress toward a better society than the one they had inherited. *Reason, natural law, hope, progress*—these were the buzz words in the heady atmosphere of the eighteenth century.

The Paths to Enlightenment

The intellectuals of the eighteenth century were especially influenced by the revolutionary thinkers of the seventeenth century. What were the major intellectual changes that culminated in the intellectual movement of the Enlightenment?

THE POPULARIZATION OF SCIENCE Although the intellectuals of the eighteenth century were much influenced by the scientific ideas of the seventeenth, they did not always acquire this knowledge directly from the original sources. Newton's *Principia* was not an easy book to read or comprehend. Scientific ideas were spread to ever-widening circles of educated Europeans not so much by scientists themselves as by popularizers. Especially important as the direct link between the Scientific Revolution of the seventeenth century and the philosophes of the eighteenth was Bernard de Fontenelle (bayr-NAHR duh fawnt-NELL) (1657–1757), secretary of the French Royal Academy of Science from 1691 to 1741.

Although Fontenelle performed no scientific experiments and made no scientific discoveries, he possessed a deep knowledge of all the scientific work of earlier centuries and his own time. Moreover, he was able to communicate that body of scientific knowledge in a clear and even witty fashion that appealed to his upper-class audiences in a meaningful way. One of his most successful books, *Plurality of Worlds,* was actually presented in the form of an intimate conversation between a lady aristocrat and her lover who are engaged in conversation under the stars. What are they discussing? "Tell me," she exclaims, "about these stars of yours." Her lover proceeds to tell her of the tremendous advances in cosmology after the foolish errors of their forebears:

> There came on the scene a certain German, one Copernicus, who made short work of all those various circles, all those solid skies, which the ancients had pictured to themselves. The former he abolished; the latter, he broke in pieces. Fired with the noble zeal of a true astronomer, he took the earth and spun it very far away from the center of the universe, where it had been installed, and in that center he put the sun, which had a far better title to the honor.[1]

In the course of two evenings under the stars, the lady learned the basic fundamentals of the new mechanistic universe. So too did scores of the educated elite of Europe. What bliss it was to learn the "truth" in such lighthearted fashion.

Thanks to Fontenelle, science was no longer the monopoly of experts but part of literature. He was especially fond of downplaying the religious backgrounds of the seventeenth-century scientists. Himself a skeptic, Fontenelle contributed to the growing **skepticism** toward religion at the end of the seventeenth century by portraying the churches as enemies of scientific progress.

A NEW SKEPTICISM The great scientists of the seventeenth century, including Kepler, Galileo, and Newton, had pursued their work in a spirit of exalting God, not

The Popularization of Science in the Age of the Enlightenment. During the Enlightenment, the ideas of the *Scientific Revolution* were spread and popularized in a variety of ways. Scientific societies funded by royal and princely patronage were especially valuable in providing outlets for the spread of new scientific ideas. This illustration shows the German prince Frederick Christian visiting his Academy of Sciences in 1739. Note the many instruments of the new science around the rooms—human skeletons, globes, microscopes, telescopes, and orreries (mechanical models of the solar system).

undermining Christianity. But as scientific knowledge spread, more and more educated men and women began to question religious truths and values. Skepticism about religion and a growing secularization of thought were especially evident in the work of Pierre Bayle (PYAYR BELL) (1647–1706), who remained a Protestant while becoming a leading critic of traditional religious attitudes. Bayle attacked superstition, religious intolerance, and dogmatism. In his view, compelling people to believe a particular set of religious ideas (as Louis XIV was doing at the time in Bayle's France) was wrong. It simply created hypocrites and in itself was contrary to what religion should be about. Individual conscience should determine one's actions. Bayle argued for complete religious toleration, maintaining that the existence of many religions would benefit rather than harm the state.

Bayle was one of a number of intellectuals who believed that the new rational principles of textual criticism should be applied to the Bible as well as secular documents. In his most famous work, the *Historical and Critical Dictionary*, Bayle demonstrated the results of his own efforts with a famous article on the Israelite King David. Undermining the traditional picture of the heroic David, he portrayed the king as a sensual, treacherous, cruel, and basically evil man. Bayle's *Dictionary*, which attacked traditional religious practices and heroes, was well known to eighteenth-century philosophes. One critic regarded it as the "Bible of the eighteenth century."

THE IMPACT OF TRAVEL LITERATURE Skepticism about both Christianity and European culture itself was nourished by travel reports. As we saw in Chapter 14, Europeans had embarked on voyages of discovery to other

Pacific Discoveries

parts of the world in the late fifteenth and sixteenth centuries. In the course of the seventeenth century, traders, missionaries, medical practitioners, and explorers began to publish an increasing number of travel books that gave accounts of many different cultures. Then, too, the new geographic adventures of the eighteenth century, especially the discovery of the Pacific island of Tahiti and of New Zealand and Australia by James Cook, aroused much enthusiasm. Cook's *Travels*, an account of his journey, became a best seller. Educated Europeans responded to these accounts of lands abroad in different ways.

For some intellectuals, the existence of exotic peoples, such as the natives of Tahiti, presented an image of a "natural man" who was far happier than many Europeans. One intellectual wrote:

> The life of savages is so simple, and our societies are such complicated machines! The Tahitian is close to the origin of the world, while the European is closer to its old age. . . . [The Tahitians] understand nothing about our manners or our laws, and they are bound to see in them nothing but shackles disguised in a hundred different ways. Those shackles could only provoke the indignation and scorn of creatures in whom the most profound feeling is a love of liberty.[2]

The idea of the "noble savage" would play an important role in the political work of some philosophes.

The travel literature of the seventeenth and eighteenth centuries also led to the realization that there were highly developed civilizations with different customs in other parts of the world. China was especially singled out. One German university professor praised Confucian morality as superior to the intolerant attitudes of Christianity. Some European intellectuals began to evaluate their own civilization relative to others. Practices that had seemed to be grounded in reason now appeared to be merely matters of custom. Certainties about European practices gave way to **cultural relativism.**

Cultural relativism was accompanied by religious skepticism. As these travel accounts made clear, the Christian perception of God was merely one of many. Some people were devastated by this revelation: "Some complete their demoralization by extensive travel, and lose whatever shreds of religion remained to them. Every day they see a new religion, new customs, new rites."[3]

As Europeans were exposed to growing numbers of people around the world who were different from themselves, some intellectuals also began to classify people into racial groups. One group espoused polygenesis, or the belief in separate human species; others argued for monogenesis, or the belief in one human species characterized by racial variations. Both groups were especially unsympathetic to Africans and placed them in the lowest rank of humankind. In his *Encyclopedia,* the intellectual Denis Diderot (see "Diderot and the *Encyclopedia*" later in this chapter) maintained that all Africans were black and characterized the Negro as a "new species of mankind."

THE LEGACY OF LOCKE AND NEWTON   The intellectual inspiration for the Enlightenment came primarily from two Englishmen, Isaac Newton and John Locke, acknowledged by the philosophes as great minds. Newton was frequently singled out for praise as the "greatest and rarest genius that ever rose for the ornament and instruction of the species." One English poet declared: "Nature and Nature's Laws lay hid in Night; God said, 'Let Newton be,' and all was Light." Enchanted by the grand design of the Newtonian world-machine, the intellectuals of the Enlightenment were convinced that by following Newton's rules of reasoning, they could discover the natural laws that governed politics, economics, justice, religion, and the arts.

John Locke,
An Essay Concerning Human Understanding (1690)

John Locke's theory of knowledge especially influenced the philosophes. In his *Essay Concerning Human Understanding,* written in 1690, Locke denied Descartes's belief in innate ideas. Instead, argued Locke, every person was born with a *tabula rasa,* a blank mind:

> Let us then suppose the mind to be, as we say, white paper, void of all characters, without any ideas. How comes it to be furnished? Whence comes it by that vast store which the busy and boundless fancy of man has painted on it with an almost endless variety? Whence has it all the materials of reason and knowledge? To this I answer, in one word, from experience.... Our observation, employed either about external sensible objects or about the internal operations of our minds perceived and reflected on by ourselves, is that which supplies our understanding with all the materials of thinking.[4]

Our knowledge, then, is derived from our environment, not from heredity; from reason, not from faith. Locke's philosophy implied that people were molded by their environment, by the experiences that they received through their senses from their surrounding world. By changing the environment and subjecting people to proper influences, they could be changed and a new society created. And how should the environment be changed? Newton had already paved the way by showing how reason enabled enlightened people to discover the natural laws to which all institutions should conform. No wonder the philosophes were enamored of Newton and Locke. Taken together, their ideas seemed to offer the hope of a "brave new world" built on reason.

The Philosophes and Their Ideas

The intellectuals of the Enlightenment were known by the French term *philosophe* (fee-loh-ZAWF), although not all of them were French and few were actually philosophers. The **philosophes** were literary people, professors, journalists, statesmen, economists, political scientists, and above all, social reformers. They came from both the nobility and the middle class, and a few even stemmed from lower origins. Although it was a truly international and **cosmopolitan** movement, the Enlightenment also enhanced the dominant role being played by French culture. Paris was its recognized capital, and most of the leaders of the Enlightenment were French (see Map 17.1). The French philosophes in turn affected intellectuals elsewhere and created a movement that engulfed the entire Western world, including the British and Spanish colonies in America.

Although the philosophes faced different political circumstances depending on the country in which they lived, they shared common bonds as part of a truly international movement. Although they were called philosophers, what did philosophy mean to them? The role of philosophy was to change the world, not just discuss it. As one writer said, the philosophe is one who "applies himself to the study of society with the purpose of making his kind better and happier." To the philosophes, rationalism did not mean the creation of a grandiose system of thought to explain all things. Reason was scientific method, an appeal to facts and experience. A spirit of rational criticism was to be applied to everything, including religion and politics.

The philosophes' call for freedom of expression is a reminder that their work was done in an atmosphere of censorship. The philosophes were not free to write whatever they chose. State censors decided what could be published, and protests from any number of government bodies could result in the seizure of books and the imprisonment of their authors, publishers, and sellers.

The philosophes found ways to get around state censorship. Some published under pseudonyms or anonymously or abroad, especially in Holland. The use of double meanings, such as talking about the Persians when they meant the French, became standard procedure for many. Books were also published and circulated secretly or in manuscript form to avoid the censors. As frequently happens when censorship is attempted, the government's announcement that a book had been burned often made the book more popular.

MAP 17.1 **The Enlightenment in Europe.** "Have the courage to use your own intelligence!" Kant's words epitomize the role of the individual in using reason to understand all aspects of life—the natural world and the sphere of human nature, behavior, and institutions.

Q *Which countries or regions were at the center of the Enlightenment, and what could account for peripheral regions being less involved?*

Although the philosophes constituted a kind of "family circle" bound together by common intellectual bonds, they often disagreed. Spanning almost a century, the Enlightenment evolved over time, with each succeeding generation becoming more radical as it built on the contributions of the previous one. A few people, however, dominated the landscape completely, and we might best begin our survey of the ideas of the philosophes by looking at three French giants—Montesquieu, Voltaire, and Diderot.

MONTESQUIEU AND POLITICAL THOUGHT Charles de Secondat, the baron de Montesquieu (MOHN-tess-kyoo) (1689–1755), came from the French nobility. He received a Classical education and then studied law. In his first work, the *Persian Letters,* published in 1721, he used the format

of two Persians supposedly traveling in western Europe and sending their impressions back home to enable him to criticize French institutions, especially the Catholic Church and the French monarchy. Much of the program of the French Enlightenment is contained in this work: the attack on traditional religion, the advocacy of religious toleration, the denunciation of slavery, and the use of reason to liberate human beings from their prejudices.

Montesquieu's most famous work, *The Spirit of the Laws,* was published in 1748. This treatise was a comparative study of governments in which Montesquieu attempted to apply the scientific method to the social and political arena to ascertain the "natural laws" governing the social relationships of human beings. Montesquieu distinguished three basic kinds of governments: republics,

The Separation of Powers

The Enlightenment affected the new world of America as much as it did the old world of Europe. American philosophes were well aware of the ideas of European Enlightenment thinkers. This selection from Montesquieu's *Spirit of the Laws* enunciates the "separation of powers" doctrine.

Montesquieu, "Of the Constitution of England"

In every government there are three sorts of power: the legislative; the executive in respect to things dependent on the law of nations; and the executive in regard to matters that depend on the civil law.

By virtue of the first, the prince or magistrate enacts temporary or perpetual laws, and amends or abrogates those that have been already enacted. By the second, he makes peace or war, sends or receives embassies, establishes the public security, and provides against invasions. By the third, he punishes criminals, or determines the disputes that arise between individuals. The latter we shall call the judiciary power, and the other simply the executive power of the state.

The political liberty of the subject is a tranquillity of mind arising from the opinion each person has of his safety. In order to have this liberty, it is requisite the government be so constituted as one man need not be afraid of another.

When the legislative and executive powers are united in the same person, or in the same body of magistrates, there can be no liberty; because apprehensions may arise, lest the same monarch or senate should enact tyrannical laws, to execute them in a tyrannical manner.

Again, there is no liberty, if the judiciary power be not separated from the legislative and executive. Were it joined with the legislative, the life and liberty of the subject would be exposed to arbitrary control; for the judge would be then the legislator. Were it joined to the executive power, the judge might behave with violence and oppression.

There would be an end of everything, were the same man or the same body, whether of the nobles or of the people, to exercise those three powers, that of enacting laws, that of executing the public resolutions, and of trying the causes of individuals.

Q As seen in this excerpt, what is Montesquieu's doctrine of the separation of powers? What are the underlying moral and political justifications for this system of government? How was this doctrine incorporated into the U.S. Constitution?

---

suitable for small states and based on citizen involvement; monarchy, appropriate for middle-sized states and grounded in the ruling class's adherence to law; and despotism, apt for large empires and dependent on fear to inspire obedience. Montesquieu used England as an example of the second category, and it was his praise and analysis of England's constitution that led to his most far-reaching and lasting contribution to political thought—the importance of checks and balances created by means of a **separation of powers** (see the box above). He believed that England's system, with its separate executive, legislative, and judicial powers that served to limit and control each other, provided the greatest freedom and security for a state. In large part, Montesquieu misread the English situation and insisted on a separation of powers because he wanted the nobility of France (of which he was a member) to play an active role in running the French government. The translation of his work into English two years after publication ensured that it would be read by American philosophes, such as Benjamin Franklin, James Madison, John Adams, Alexander Hamilton, and Thomas Jefferson, who incorporated its principles into the U.S. Constitution (see Chapter 19).

VOLTAIRE AND THE ENLIGHTENMENT The greatest figure of the Enlightenment was François-Marie Arouet, known simply as Voltaire (vohl-TAYR) (1694–1778). Son of a prosperous middle-class family from Paris, Voltaire received a Classical education in Jesuit schools. Although he studied law, he wished to be a writer and achieved his first success as a playwright. By his mid-twenties, Voltaire had been hailed as the successor to Racine (see Chapter 15) for his tragedy *Œdipe* and his epic *Henriade* on his favorite king, Henry IV. His wit made him a darling of the Parisian intellectuals but also involved him in a quarrel with a dissolute nobleman that forced him to flee France and live in England for almost two years.

Well received in English literary and social circles, the young playwright was much impressed by England. His *Philosophic Letters on the English,* written in 1733, expressed a deep admiration of English life, especially its freedom of the press, its political freedom, and its religious toleration. In judging the English religious situation, he made the famous remark that "if there were just one religion in England, despotism would threaten; if there were two religions, they would cut each other's throats; but there are thirty religions, and they live together peacefully and happily." Although he clearly exaggerated the freedoms England possessed, in a roundabout way Voltaire had managed to criticize many of the ills oppressing France, especially royal absolutism and the lack of religious toleration and freedom of thought. The criticism of absolute monarchy by Voltaire and other philosophes reflected the broader dissatisfaction of middle-class

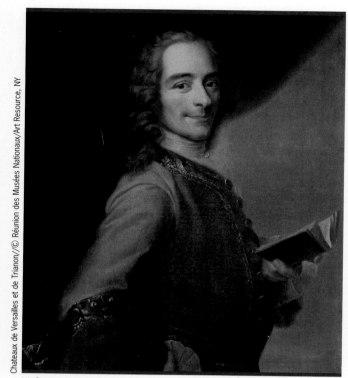

Voltaire. François-Marie Arouet, better known as Voltaire, achieved his first success as a playwright. A philosophe, Voltaire was well known for his criticism of traditional religion and his support of religious toleration. Maurice-Quentin de La Tour painted this portrait of Voltaire holding one of his books in 1736.

individuals with their society. In the course of the eighteenth century, this would help lead to revolutionary upheavals in France and other countries (see Chapter 19).

On his return to France, Voltaire's reputation as the author of the *Philosophic Letters* made it necessary for him to retire to Cirey, near France's eastern border, where he lived in semiseclusion on the estate of his mistress, the marquise du Châtelet (mahr-KEEZ duh shat-LAY) (1706–1749). Herself an early philosophe, the marquise was one of the first intellectuals to adopt the ideas of Isaac Newton and in 1759 published her own translation of Newton's famous *Principia*. While Voltaire lived with her at her château at Cirey, the two collaborated on a book about the natural philosophy of Newton.

Voltaire eventually settled on a magnificent estate at Ferney. Located in France near the Swiss border, Ferney gave Voltaire the freedom to write what he wished. By this time, through his writings, inheritance, and clever investments, Voltaire had become wealthy and now had the leisure to write an almost endless stream of pamphlets, novels, plays, letters, and histories.

Although he touched on all of the themes of importance to the philosophes, Voltaire was especially well known for his criticism of traditional religion and his strong attachment to the ideal of religious toleration (see the box on p. 520). He lent his prestige and skills as a polemicist to fighting cases of intolerance in France. The most famous incident was the Calas affair. Jean Calas (ZHAHNH ka-LAH)

was a Protestant from Toulouse who was accused of murdering his own son to stop him from becoming a Catholic. Tortured to confess his guilt, Calas died shortly thereafter. An angry and indignant Voltaire published devastating broadsides that aroused public opinion and forced a retrial in which Calas was exonerated when it was proved that his son had actually committed suicide. The family was paid an indemnity, and Voltaire's appeals for toleration appeared all the more reasonable. In 1763, he penned his *Treatise on Toleration,* in which he argued that religious toleration had created no problems for England and Holland and reminded governments that "all men are brothers under God." As he grew older, Voltaire became ever more strident in his denunciations. "Crush the infamous thing," he thundered repeatedly—the infamous thing being religious fanaticism, intolerance, and superstition.

Throughout his life, Voltaire championed not only religious tolerance but also **deism,** a religious outlook shared by most other philosophes. Deism was built on the Newtonian world-machine, which suggested the existence of a mechanic (God) who had created the universe. Voltaire said, "In the opinion that there is a God, there are difficulties, but in the contrary opinion there are absurdities." To Voltaire and most other philosophes, God had no direct involvement in the world he had created and allowed it to run according to its own natural laws. God did not extend grace or answer prayers as Christians liked to believe. Jesus might be a "good fellow," as Voltaire called him, but he was not divine, as Christianity claimed.

DIDEROT AND THE *ENCYCLOPEDIA* Denis Diderot (duh-NEE DEE-droh) (1713–1784), the son of a skilled craftsman

Denis Diderot. Editor of the monumental *Encyclopedia,* Diderot was a major figure in propagating the ideas of the French philosophes. He had diverse interests and penned an incredible variety of literary works. He is shown here in a portrait by Jean-Honoré Fragonard.

The Attack on Religious Intolerance

Voltaire's lucid prose, biting satire, and clever wit caused his works to be widely read and all the more influential. These two selections present different sides of Voltaire's attack on religious intolerance. The first is from a straightforward treatise, *The Ignorant Philosopher*, and the second is from his only real literary masterpiece, the novel *Candide*, where he used humor to make the same fundamental point about religious intolerance.

——— ✦✧✦ ———

Voltaire, *The Ignorant Philosopher*

The contagion of fanaticism then still subsists. . . . The author of the *Treatise upon Toleration* has not mentioned the shocking executions wherein so many unhappy victims perished in the valleys of Piedmont. He has passed over in silence the massacre of six hundred inhabitants of Valtelina, men, women, and children, who were murdered by the Catholics in the month of September, 1620. I will not say it was with the consent and assistance of the archbishop of Milan, Charles Borome, who was made a saint. Some passionate writers have averred this fact, which I am very far from believing; but I say, there is scarce any city or borough in Europe, where blood has not been spilt for religious quarrels; I say, that the human species has been perceptibly diminished, because women and girls were massacred as well as men; I say, that Europe would have had a third larger population, if there had been no theological disputes. In fine, I say, that so far from forgetting these abominable times, we should frequently take a view of them, to inspire an eternal horror for them; and that it is for our age to make reparation by toleration, for this long collection of crimes, which has taken place through the want of toleration, during sixteen barbarous centuries.

Let it not then be said, that there are no traces left of that shocking fanaticism, of the want of toleration; they are still everywhere to be met with, even in those countries that are esteemed the most humane. The Lutheran and Calvinist preachers, were they masters, would, perhaps, be as little inclined to pity, as obdurate, as insolent as they upbraid their antagonists with being.

Voltaire, *Candide*

At last he [Candide] approached a man who had just been addressing a big audience for a whole hour on the subject of charity. The orator peered at him and said:

"What is your business here? Do you support the Good Old Cause?"

"There is not effect without a cause," replied Candide modestly. "All things are necessarily connected and arranged for the best. It was my fate to be driven from Lady Cunégonde's presence and made to run the gantlet, and now I have to beg my bread until I can earn it. Things should not have happened otherwise."

"Do you believe that the Pope is Antichrist, my friend?" said the minister.

"I have never heard anyone say so," replied Candide; "but whether he is or he isn't, I want some food."

"You don't deserve to eat," said the other. "Be off with you, you villain, you wretch! Don't come near me again or you'll suffer for it."

The minister's wife looked out of the window at that moment, and seeing a man who was not sure that the Pope was Antichrist, emptied over his head a chamber pot, which shows to what lengths ladies are driven by religious zeal. ✍

Q Compare the two approaches that Voltaire uses to address the problem of religious intolerance. Do you think one is more effective? Why?

---

from eastern France, became a freelance writer so that he could study many subjects and read in many languages. One of his favorite topics was Christianity, which he condemned as fanatical and unreasonable. As he grew older, his literary attacks on Christianity grew more vicious. Of all religions, he maintained, Christianity was the worst, "the most absurd and the most atrocious in its dogma" (see the box on p. 521). Near the end of his life, he argued for an essentially materialistic conception of life: "This world is only a mass of molecules."

Diderot's most famous contribution to the Enlightenment was the twenty-eight-volume *Encyclopedia, or Classified Dictionary of the Sciences, Arts, and Trades,* that he edited and called the "great work of his life." Its purpose, according to Diderot, was to "change the general way of thinking." It did precisely that in becoming a major weapon of the philosophes' crusade against the old French society. The contributors included many philosophes who expressed their major concerns. They attacked religious superstition and advocated toleration as well as a program for social, legal, and political improvements that would lead to a society that was more cosmopolitan, more tolerant, more humane, and more reasonable. In later editions, the price of the *Encyclopedia* was drastically reduced, dramatically increasing its sales and making it available to doctors, clergy, teachers, lawyers, and even military officers. The ideas of the Enlightenment were spread even further as a result.

THE NEW "SCIENCE OF MAN" The Enlightenment belief that Newton's scientific methods could be used to discover the natural laws underlying all areas of human

Diderot Questions Christian Sexual Standards

Denis Diderot was one of the boldest thinkers of the Enlightenment. In his *Supplement to the Voyage of Bougainville,* he constructed a dialogue between Orou, a Tahitian who symbolizes the wisdom of a philosophe, and a chaplain who defends Christian sexual mores. The dialogue gave Diderot the opportunity to criticize the practice of sexual chastity and monogamy.

→ ⊶⊷ ←

Denis Diderot, *Supplement to the Voyage of Bougainville*

[Orou, speaking to the Chaplain.] "You are young and healthy and you have just had a good supper. He who sleeps alone sleeps badly; at night a man needs a woman at his side. Here is my wife and here are my daughters. Choose whichever one pleases you most, but if you would like to do me a favor, you will give your preference to my youngest girl, who has not yet had any children. . . ."

The chaplain replied that his religion, his holy orders, his moral standards and his sense of decency all prevented him from accepting Orou's invitation.

Orou answered: "I don't know what this thing is that you call religion, but I can only have a low opinion of it because it forbids you to partake of an innocent pleasure to which Nature, the sovereign mistress of us all, invites everybody. It seems to prevent you from bringing one of your fellow creatures into the world, from doing a favor asked of by a father, a mother and their children, from repaying the kindness of a host, and from enriching a nation by giving it an additional citizen. . . . Look at the distress you have caused to appear on the faces of these four women—they are afraid you have noticed some defect in them that arouses your distaste. . . . "

The Chaplain: "You don't understand—it's not that. They are all four of them equally beautiful. But there is

my religion! My holy orders! . . . [God] spoke to our ancestors and gave them laws; he prescribed to them the way in which he wishes to be honored; he ordained that certain actions are good and others he forbade them to do as being evil."

Orou: "I see. And one of these evil actions which he has forbidden is that of a man who goes to bed with a woman or girl. But in that case, why did he make two sexes?"

The Chaplain: "In order that they might come together—but only when certain conditions are satisfied and only after certain initial ceremonies one man belongs to one woman and only to her; one woman belongs to one man and only to him."

Orou: "For their whole lives?"

The Chaplain: "For their whole lives. . . ."

Orou: "I find these strange precepts contrary to nature, and contrary to reason. . . . Furthermore, your laws seem to me to be contrary to the general order of things. For in truth is there anything so senseless as a precept that forbids us to heed the changing impulses that are inherent in our being, or commands that require a degree of constancy which is not possible, that violate the liberty of both male and female by chaining them perpetually to one another? . . . I don't know what your great workman [God] is, but I am very happy that he never spoke to our forefathers, and I hope that he never speaks to our children, for if he does, he may tell them the same foolishness, and they may be foolish enough to believe it." ⊱

Q What attack does Diderot make on Christian sexual standards? What does this passage say about enlightened conceptions of nature and the place of physical pleasure in healthy human life?

---

life led to the emergence in the eighteenth century of what the philosophes called the "science of man," or what we would call the social sciences. In a number of areas, philosophes arrived at natural laws that they believed governed human actions. If these "natural laws" seem less than universal to us, it reminds us how much the philosophes were people of their times reacting to the conditions they faced. Nevertheless, their efforts did at least lay the foundations for the modern social sciences.

That a science of man was possible was a strong belief of the Scottish philosopher David Hume (1711–1776). An important figure in the history of philosophy, Hume has also been called "a pioneering social scientist." In his *Treatise on Human Nature,* which he subtitled "An Attempt to Introduce the Experimental Method of Reasoning into Moral Subjects," Hume argued that observation

and reflection, grounded in "systematized common sense," made conceivable a "science of man." Careful examination of the experiences that constituted human life would lead to the knowledge of human nature that would make this science possible.

The Physiocrats and Adam Smith have been viewed as founders of the modern discipline of economics. The leader of the Physiocrats was François Quesnay (frahnn-SWAH keh-NAY) (1694–1774), a highly successful French court physician. Quesnay and the Physiocrats claimed they would discover the natural economic laws that governed human society. Their first principle was that land constituted the only source of wealth and that wealth itself could be increased only by agriculture because all other economic activities were unproductive and sterile. Even the state's revenues should come from a single tax on the land rather than the hodgepodge of inequitable taxes and privileges currently in place. In stressing the economic primacy of agricultural production, the Physiocrats were rejecting the mercantilist emphasis on the significance of money—that is, gold and silver—as the primary determinants of wealth (see Chapter 14).

Their second major "natural law" of economics also represented a repudiation of mercantilism, specifically, its emphasis on a controlled economy for the benefit of the state. Instead, the Physiocrats stressed that the existence of the natural economic forces of supply and demand made it imperative that individuals should be left free to pursue their own economic self-interest. In doing so, all of society would ultimately benefit. Consequently, they argued that the state should in no way interrupt the free play of natural economic forces by government regulation of the economy but rather should just leave it alone, a doctrine that subsequently became known by its French name, **laissez-faire** (less-ay-FAYR) (noninterference; literally, "let people do as they choose").

The best statement of *laissez-faire* was made in 1776 by a Scottish philosopher, Adam Smith (1723–1790), in his

Adam Smith, *The Wealth of Nations*, selected topics (1776)

Inquiry into the Nature and Causes of the Wealth of Nations, known simply as *The Wealth of Nations*. In the process of enunciating three basic principles of economics, Smith presented a strong attack on mercantilism. First, he condemned the mercantilist use of tariffs to protect home industries. If one country can supply another country with a product cheaper than the latter can make it, it is better to purchase than to produce it. To Smith, free trade was a fundamental economic principle. Smith's second principle was his labor theory of value. Like the Physiocrats, he claimed that gold and silver were not the source of a nation's true wealth, but unlike the Physiocrats, he did not believe that soil was either. Rather labor—the labor of individual farmers, artisans, and merchants—constituted the true wealth of a nation. Finally, like the Physiocrats, Smith believed that the state should not interfere in economic matters; indeed, he assigned to government only three basic functions: to protect society from invasion (army), defend individuals from injustice and oppression (police), and keep up certain public works, such as roads and canals, that private individuals could not afford. Thus, in Smith's view, the state should stay out of the lives of individuals. In emphasizing the economic liberty of the individual, the Physiocrats and Adam Smith laid the foundation for what became known in the nineteenth century as **economic liberalism.**

THE LATER ENLIGHTENMENT By the late 1760s, a new generation of philosophes who had grown up with the worldview of the Enlightenment began to move beyond their predecessors' beliefs. Baron Paul d'Holbach (dawl-BAHK) (1723–1789), a wealthy German aristocrat who settled in Paris, preached a doctrine of strict atheism and

materialism. In his *System of Nature,* written in 1770, he argued that everything in the universe consisted of matter in motion. Human beings were simply machines; God was a product of the human mind and was unnecessary for leading a moral life. People needed only reason to live in this world: "Let us persuade men to be just, beneficent, moderate, sociable; not because the gods demand it, but because they must please men. Let us advise them to abstain from vice and crimes; not because they will be punished in the other world, but because they will suffer for it in this."[5] Holbach shocked almost all of his fellow philosophes with his uncompromising atheism. Most intellectuals remained more comfortable with deism and feared the effect of atheism on society.

Marie-Jean de Condorcet (muh-REE-ZHAHNH duh kohn-dor-SAY) (1743–1794), another French philosophe, made an exaggerated claim for progress. Condorcet was a victim of the turmoil of the French Revolution and wrote his chief work, *The Progress of the Human Mind,* while in hiding during the Reign of Terror (see Chapter 19). His survey of human history convinced him that humans had progressed through nine stages of history. Now, with the spread of science and reason, humans were about to enter the tenth stage, one of perfection, in which they will see that "there is no limit to the perfecting of the powers of man; that human perfectibility is in reality indefinite, that the progress of this perfectibility . . . has no other limit than the duration of the globe upon which nature has placed us." Shortly after composing this work, the prophet of humankind's perfection died in a French revolutionary prison.

ROUSSEAU AND THE SOCIAL CONTRACT No one was more critical of the work of his predecessors than Jean-Jacques Rousseau (ZHAHNH-ZHAHK roo-SOH) (1712–1778). Born in Geneva, he spent his youth wandering about France and Italy holding various jobs. He went back to school for a while to study music and the classics (he could afford to do so after becoming the paid lover of an older woman). Eventually, he made his way to Paris, where he was introduced into the circles of the philosophes. He never really liked the social life of the cities, however, and frequently withdrew into long periods of solitude.

Rousseau's political beliefs were presented in two major works. In his *Discourse on the Origins of the Inequality of Mankind,* Rousseau began with humans in their primitive condition (or state of nature—see Chapter 15), where they were happy. There were no laws, no judges; all people were equal. But what had gone wrong?

The first man who, having enclosed a piece of ground, thought of saying, This is mine, and found people simple enough to believe him, was the true founder of civil society. How many crimes, wars, murders; how much misery and horror the human race would have been spared if someone had pulled up the stakes and filled in the ditch, and cried to his fellow men: "Beware of listening to this impostor. You are lost if you forget that the fruits of the earth belong to everyone and that the earth itself belongs to no one!"[6]

Jean-Jacques Rousseau. By the late 1760s, a new generation of philosophes arose who began to move beyond and even to question the beliefs of their predecessors. Of the philosophes of the late Enlightenment, Rousseau was perhaps the most critical of his predecessors. Shown here is a portrait of Rousseau by Maurice-Quentin de La Tour.

To preserve their private property, people adopted laws and governors. In so doing, they rushed headlong not to liberty but into chains. "What then is to be done? Must societies be totally abolished? . . . Must we return again to the forest to live among bears?" No, civilized humans could "no longer subsist on plants or acorns or live without laws and magistrates." Government was an evil, but a necessary one.

In his celebrated treatise *The Social Contract,* published in 1762, Rousseau tried to harmonize individual liberty with governmental authority (see the box on p. 524). The social contract was basically an agreement on the part of an entire society to be governed by its general will. If any individual wished to follow his own self-interest, he should be compelled to abide by the general will. "This means nothing less than that he will be forced to be free," said Rousseau, because the general will represented a community's highest aspirations, whatever was best for the entire community. Thus, liberty was achieved through being forced to follow what was best for all people because, he believed, what was best for all was best for each individual. True freedom is adherence to laws that one has imposed on oneself. To Rousseau, because everybody was responsible for framing the general will, the creation

of laws could never be delegated to a parliamentary institution:

> Thus, the people's deputies are not and could not be its representatives; they are merely its agents; and they cannot decide anything finally. Any law which the people has not ratified in person is void; it is not law at all. The English people believes itself to be free; it is gravely mistaken; it is free only during the election of Members of Parliament; as soon as the Members are elected, the people is enslaved; it is nothing.[7]

This is an extreme and idealistic statement, but it is the ultimate statement of participatory democracy.

Another influential treatise by Rousseau also appeared in 1762. Titled *Émile,* it is one of the Enlightenment's most important works on education. Written in the form of a novel, the work is really a general treatise "on the education of the natural man." Rousseau's fundamental concern was that education should foster rather than restrict children's natural instincts. Life's experiences had shown Rousseau the importance of the promptings of the heart, and what he sought was a balance between heart and mind, between sentiment and reason. This emphasis on heart and sentiment made him a precursor of the intellectual movement called **Romanticism** that dominated Europe at the beginning of the nineteenth century.

But Rousseau did not necessarily practice what he preached. His own children were sent to foundling homes, where many children died young. Rousseau also viewed women as "naturally" different from men: "To fulfill [a woman's] functions, an appropriate physical constitution is necessary to her. . . . She needs a soft sedentary life to suckle her babies. How much care and tenderness does she need to hold her family together." In *Émile,* Sophie, who was Émile's intended wife, was educated for her role as wife and mother by learning obedience and the nurturing skills that would enable her to provide loving care for her husband and children. Not everyone in the eighteenth century agreed with Rousseau, however, making ideas of gender an important issue in the Enlightenment.

THE "WOMAN'S QUESTION" IN THE ENLIGHTENMENT For centuries, men had dominated the debate about the nature and value of women. In general, many male intellectuals had argued that the base nature of women made them inferior to men and made male domination of women necessary (see Chapter 16). In the seventeenth and eighteenth centuries, many male thinkers reinforced this view by arguing that it was based on "natural" biological differences between men and women. Like Rousseau, they argued that the female constitution made women mothers. Male writers, in particular, were critical of the attempts of some women in the Enlightenment to write on intellectual issues, arguing that women were by nature intellectually inferior to men. Nevertheless, some Enlightenment thinkers offered more positive views of women. Diderot, for example, maintained that men and women were not all that different, and Voltaire asserted

A Social Contract

Although Jean-Jacques Rousseau was one of the French philosophes, he has also been called "the father of Romanticism." His political ideas have proved extremely controversial. Though some people have hailed him as the prophet of democracy, others have labeled him an apologist for totalitarianism. This selection is taken from one of his most famous books, *The Social Contract*.

Jean-Jacques Rousseau, *The Social Contract*

Book 1, Chapter 6: "The Social Pact"

"How to find a form of association which will defend the person and goods of each member with the collective force of all, and under which each individual, while uniting himself with the others, obeys no one but himself, and remains as free as before." This is the fundamental problem to which the social contract holds the solution. . . .

Book 1, Chapter 7: "The Sovereign"

Despite their common interest, subjects will not be bound by their commitment unless means are found to guarantee their fidelity.

For every individual as a man may have a private will contrary to, or different from, the general will that he has as a citizen. His private interest may speak with a very different voice from that of the public interest; his absolute and naturally independent existence may make him regard what he owes to the common cause as a gratuitous contribution, the loss of which would be less painful for others than the payment is onerous for him; and fancying that the artificial person which constitutes the state is a mere rational entity, he might seek to enjoy the rights of a citizen without doing the duties of a subject. The growth of this kind of injustice would bring about the ruin of the body politic.

Hence, in order that the social pact shall not be an empty formula, it is tacitly implied in that commitment—which alone can give force to all others—that whoever refused to obey the general will shall be constrained to do so by the whole body, which means nothing other than that he shall be forced to be free; for this is the condition which, by giving each citizen to the nation, secures him against all personal dependence, it is the condition which shapes both the design and the working of the political machine, and which alone bestows justice on civil contracts—without it, such contracts would be absurd, tyrannical and liable to the grossest abuse.

Q What was Rousseau's concept of the social contract? What implications did it have for political thought, especially in regard to the development of democratic ideals?

---

that "women are capable of all that men are" in intellectual affairs.

It was women thinkers, however, who added new perspectives to the "woman's question" by making specific suggestions for improving the condition of women. Mary Astell (AST-ul) (1666–1731), daughter of a wealthy English coal merchant, argued in 1697 in *A Serious Proposal to the Ladies* that women needed to become better educated. Men, she believed, would resent her proposal, "but they must excuse me, if I be as partial to my own sex as they are to theirs, and think women as capable of learning as men are, and that it becomes them as well."[8] In a later work titled *Some Reflections upon Marriage,* Astell argued for the equality of the sexes in marriage: "If absolute sovereignty be not necessary in a state, how comes it to be so in a family . . . ? For if arbitrary power is evil in itself, and an improper method of governing rational and free agents, it ought not be practiced anywhere. . . . If all men are born free, how is it that all women are born slaves?"[9]

The strongest statement for the rights of women in the eighteenth century was advanced by the English writer Mary Wollstonecraft (WULL-stun-kraft) (1759–1797), viewed by many as the founder of modern European **feminism.** In *Vindication of the Rights of Woman,* written in 1792, Wollstonecraft pointed out two contradictions in the views of women held by such Enlightenment thinkers as Rousseau. To argue that women must obey men, she said, was contrary to the beliefs of the same individuals that a system based on the arbitrary power of monarchs over their subjects or slave owners over their slaves was wrong. The subjection of women to men was equally wrong. In addition, she argued, the Enlightenment was based on the ideal that reason is innate in all human beings. If women have reason, then they are entitled to the same rights that men have. Women, Wollstonecraft declared, should have equal rights with men in education and in economic and political life as well (see the box on p. 525).

Mary Wollstonecraft, *Vindication of the Rights of Woman,* selected topics (1792)

The Social Environment of the Philosophes

The social background of the philosophes varied considerably, from the aristocratic Montesquieu to the lower-middle-class Diderot and Rousseau. The Enlightenment was not the preserve of any one class, although obviously its greatest appeal was to the aristocracy and upper middle classes of the major cities. The common

Opposing ><VIEWPOINTS

Women in the Age of the Enlightenment: Rousseau and Wollstonecraft

The "woman's question"—the debate about the nature and value of women—continued to be discussed in the eighteenth century. In *Émile*, Jean-Jacques Rousseau reflected the view of many male thinkers when he argued that there were natural biological differences between men and women that made women mothers rather than intellectuals. Some women thinkers, however, presented new perspectives.

Mary Wollstonecraft responded to an unhappy childhood in a large family by seeking to lead an independent life. Few occupations were available for middle-class women in her day, but she survived by working as a teacher, chaperone, and governess to aristocratic children. All the while, she wrote and developed her ideas on the rights of women. The selection below is taken from her *Vindication of the Rights of Woman,* the work that led to her reputation as the foremost British feminist thinker of the eighteenth century.

—— ⊷⊷ ——

Rousseau, *Émile* (1762)

It follows that woman is made specially to please men. If man ought to please her in turn, it is due to a less direct necessity. His merit is in his power; he pleases by the sole fact of his strength. . . .

The strictness of the relative duties of the two sexes is not and cannot be the same. When woman complains on this score about unjust man-made inequality, she is wrong. This inequality is not a human institution—or, at least, it is the work not of prejudice but of reason. It is up to the sex that nature has charged with the bearing of children to be responsible for them to the other sex. Doubtless it is not permitted to anyone to violate his faith, and every unfaithful husband who deprives his wife of the only reward of the austere duties of sex is an unjust and barbarous man. But the unfaithful woman does more; she dissolves the family and breaks all the bonds of nature. . . .

The good constitution of children initially depends on that of their mothers. The first education of men depends on the care of women. . . . Thus, the whole education of women ought to relate to men. To please men, to be useful to them, to make herself loved and honored by them, to raise them when young, to care for them when grown, to counsel them, to console them, to make their lives agreeable and sweet—these are the duties of

women at all times, and they ought to be taught from childhood. . . .

The quest for abstract and speculative truths, principles, and axioms in the sciences, for everything that tends to generalize ideas, is not within the competence of women. All their studies ought to be related to practice. . . . Nor do women have sufficient precision and attention to succeed at the exact sciences. And as for the physical sciences, they are for the sex which is more active, gets around more, and sees more objects, the sex which has more strength and uses it more to judge the relations of sensible beings and the laws of nature. Woman, who is weak and who sees nothing outside the house, estimates and judges the forces she can put to work to make up for her weakness.

Mary Wollstonecraft, *Vindication of the Rights of Woman* (1792)

It is a melancholy truth—yet such is the blessed effect of civilization—the most respectable women are the most oppressed; and, unless they have understandings far superior to the common run of understandings, taking in both sexes, they must, from being treated like contemptible beings, become contemptible. How many women thus waste life away the prey of discontent, who might have practiced as physicians, regulated a farm, managed a shop, and stood erect, supported by their own industry, instead of hanging their heads surcharged with the dew of sensibility, that consumes the beauty to which it at first gave luster. . . .

Proud of their weakness, however, [women] must always be protected, guarded from care, and all the rough toils that dignify the mind. If this be the fiat of fate, if they will make themselves insignificant and contemptible, sweetly to waste "life away," let them not expect to be valued when their beauty fades, for it is the fate of the fairest flowers to be admired and pulled to pieces by the careless hand that plucked them. In how many ways do I wish, from the purest benevolence, to impress this truth on my sex; yet I fear that they will not listen to a truth that dear-bought experience has brought home to many an agitated bosom, nor willingly resign the privileges of rank and sex for the privileges of humanity, to which those have no claim who do not discharge its duties. . . .

Would men but generously snap our chains, and be content with the rational fellowship instead of slavish

(continued)

(Opposing Viewpoints continued)

obedience, they would find us more observant daughters, more affectionate sisters, more faithful wives, and more reasonable mothers—in a word, better citizens. We should then love them with true affection, because we should learn to respect ourselves; and the peace of mind of a worthy man would not be interrupted by the idle vanity of his wife.

Q What did Rousseau believe was the role of women, and how did he think they should be educated? What arguments did Mary Wollstonecraft make on behalf of the rights of women? What picture did she paint of the women of her day? Why did Wollstonecraft suggest that both women and men were at fault for the "slavish" situation of women?

CHRONOLOGY Works of the Philosophes

Montesquieu, *Persian Letters*	1721
Voltaire, *Philosophic Letters on the English*	1733
Hume, *Treatise on Human Nature*	1739–1740
Montesquieu, *The Spirit of the Laws*	1748
Voltaire, *The Age of Louis XIV*	1751
Diderot, *Encyclopedia*	1751–1765
Rousseau, *The Social Contract; Émile*	1762
Voltaire, *Treatise on Toleration*	1763
Beccaria, *On Crimes and Punishments*	1764
Holbach, *System of Nature*	1770
Smith, *The Wealth of Nations*	1776
Gibbon, *The Decline and Fall of the Roman Empire*	1776–1788
Wollstonecraft, *Vindication of the Rights of Woman*	1792
Condorcet, *The Progress of the Human Mind*	1794

people, especially the peasants, were little affected by the Enlightenment.

Of great importance to the Enlightenment was the spread of its ideas to the literate elite of European society. Although the publication and sale of books and treatises were crucial to this process, the salon was also a factor. **Salons** came into being in the seventeenth century but rose to new heights in the eighteenth. These were the elegant drawing rooms in the urban houses of the wealthy where invited philosophes and guests gathered to engage in witty, sparkling conversations that often centered on the ideas of the philosophes. In France's rigid hierarchical society, the salons were important in bringing together writers and artists with aristocrats, government officials, and wealthy bourgeoisie.

As hostesses of the salons, women found themselves in a position to affect the decisions of kings, sway political opinion, and influence literary and artistic taste. Salons provided havens for people and views unwelcome in the royal court. When the *Encyclopedia* was suppressed by the French authorities, Marie-Thérèse de Geoffrin (1699–1777), a wealthy bourgeois widow whose father had been a valet, welcomed the encyclopedists to her salon and offered financial assistance to complete the work in secret.

Madame Geoffrin was not without rivals, however. The marquise du Deffand (mar-KEEZ duh duh-FAHNH) (1697–1780) had abandoned her husband in the provinces and established herself in Paris, where her ornate drawing room attracted many of the Enlightenment's great figures, including Montesquieu, Hume, and Voltaire.

Although the salons were run by women, the reputation of a salon depended on the stature of the males a hostess was able to attract. Despite this male domination, however, both French and foreign observers complained that females exerted undue influence in French political affairs. Though exaggerated, this perception led to the decline of salons during the French Revolution.

The salon served an important role in promoting conversation and sociability between upper-class men and women as well as spreading the ideas of the Enlightenment. But other means of spreading Enlightenment ideas were also available. Coffeehouses, cafés, reading clubs, and public lending libraries established by the state were gathering places for the exchange of ideas. Learned societies were formed in cities throughout Europe and America. At such gatherings as the Select Society of Edinburgh, Scotland, and the American Philosophical Society in Philadelphia, lawyers, doctors, and local officials gathered to discuss enlightened ideas. Secret societies also developed. The most famous was the Freemasons, established in London in 1717, France and Italy in 1726, and Prussia in 1744. It was no secret that the Freemasons were sympathetic to the ideas of the philosophes.

Culture and Society in the Enlightenment

Q FOCUS QUESTIONS: What innovations in art, music, and literature occurred in the eighteenth century? How did popular culture differ from high culture in the eighteenth century?

The intellectual adventure fostered by the philosophes was accompanied by both traditional practices and important changes in eighteenth-century culture and society.

Innovations in Art, Music, and Literature

Although the Baroque and Neoclassical styles that had dominated the seventeenth century continued into the

Antoine Watteau, *Return from Cythera*. Antoine Watteau was one of the most gifted painters in eighteenth-century France. His portrayal of aristocratic life reveals a world of elegance, wealth, and pleasure. In this painting, which is considered his masterpiece, Watteau depicts a group of aristocratic lovers about to depart from the island of Cythera, where they have paid homage to Venus, the goddess of love. Luxuriously dressed, they move from the woodlands to a golden barge that is waiting to take them from the island.

eighteenth century, by the 1730s a new style known as **Rococo** (ruh-KOH-koh) had begun to affect decoration and architecture all over Europe. Unlike the Baroque, which stressed majesty, power, and movement, Rococo emphasized grace and gentle action. Rococo rejected strict geometrical patterns and had a fondness for curves; it liked to follow the wandering lines of natural objects, such as seashells and flowers. It made much use of interlaced designs colored in gold with delicate contours and graceful curves. Highly secular, its lightness and charm spoke of the pursuit of pleasure, happiness, and love.

Some of Rococo's appeal is evident already in the work of Antoine Watteau (AHN-twahn wah-TOH) (1684–1721), whose lyrical views of aristocratic life—refined, sensual, civilized, with gentlemen and ladies in elegant dress—reflected a world of upper-class pleasure and joy. Underneath that exterior, however, was an element of sadness as the artist revealed the fragility and transitory nature of pleasure, love, and life.

Another aspect of Rococo was that its decorative work could easily be used with Baroque architecture. The palace of Versailles had made an enormous impact on Europe. "Keeping up with the Bourbons" became important as the Austrian emperor, the Swedish king, German princes and prince-bishops, Italian princes, and even a Russian tsar built grandiose palaces. While emulating Versailles's size, they were modeled less after the French classical style of Versailles than after the seventeenth-century Italian Baroque, as modified by a series of brilliant German and Austrian

sculptor-architects. This Baroque-Rococo architectural style of the eighteenth century was used in both palaces and churches, and often the same architects designed both. This is evident in the work of one of the greatest architects of the eighteenth century, Balthasar Neumann (BAHL-tuh-zahr NOI-mahn) (1687–1753).

Neumann's two masterpieces are the pilgrimage church of the Vierzehnheiligen (feer-tsayn-HY-li-gen) (Fourteen Saints) in southern Germany and the Bishop's Palace, known as the Residenz, the residential palace of the Schönborn (SHURN-bawn) prince-bishop of Würzburg (VOORTS-boork). Secular and spiritual become easily interchangeable in both buildings as the visitor is greeted by lavish and fanciful ornament; light, bright colors; and elaborate, rich detail.

Despite the popularity of the Rococo style, **Neoclassicism** continued to maintain a strong appeal and in the late eighteenth century emerged in France as an established movement. Neoclassical artists wanted to recapture the dignity and simplicity of the Classical style of ancient Greece and Rome. Some were especially influenced by the recent excavations of the ancient Roman cities of Herculaneum and Pompeii. Classical elements are evident in the work of Jacques-Louis David (ZHAHK-LWEE dah-VEED) (1748–1825). In the *Oath of the Horatii,* he re-created a scene from Roman history in which the three Horatius brothers swore an oath before their father, proclaiming their willingness to sacrifice their lives for their country. David's Neoclassical style, with its moral seriousness and

Vierzehnheiligen, Exterior View. Balthasar Neumann, one of the most prominent architects of the eighteenth century, used the Baroque-Rococo style of architecture to design some of the most beautiful buildings of the century. Pictured here is the exterior of his pilgrimage church of the Vierzehnheiligen (Fourteen Saints), located in southern Germany.

Vierzehnheiligen, Interior View. Pictured here is the interior of the Vierzehnheiligen, the pilgrimage church designed by Balthasar Neumann. Elaborate detail, blazing light, rich colors, and opulent decoration were blended together to create a work of stunning beauty. The pilgrim in search of holiness is struck by an incredible richness of detail. Persuaded by joy rather than fear, the believer is lifted toward heaven on a cloud of rapture.

its emphasis on honor and patriotism, made him extremely popular during the French Revolution.

THE DEVELOPMENT OF MUSIC The seventeenth and eighteenth centuries were the formative years of classical music and saw the rise of the opera and oratorio, the sonata, the concerto, and the symphony. The Italians were the first to develop these genres but were soon followed by the Germans, Austrians, and English. As in previous centuries, most musicians depended on a patron—a prince, a well-endowed ecclesiastic, or an aristocrat. The many individual princes, archbishops, and bishops, each with his own court, provided the patronage that made Italy and Germany the musical leaders of Europe.

Many of the techniques of the Baroque musical style, which dominated Europe between 1600 and 1750, were perfected by two composers—Bach and Handel—who stand out as musical geniuses. Johann Sebastian Bach (yoh-HAHN suh-BASS-chun BAKH) (1685–1750) came from a family of musicians. Bach held the post of organist and music director at a number of small German courts

before becoming director of church music at the Church of Saint Thomas in Leipzig in 1723. There Bach composed his Mass in B Minor, his *Saint Matthew's Passion,* and the cantatas and motets that have established his reputation as one of the greatest composers of all time. For Bach, music was above all a means to worship God; in his own words, his task in life was to make "well-ordered music in the honor of God."

The other great musical giant of the early eighteenth century, George Frederick Handel (HAN-dul) (1685–1759), was, like Bach, born in Saxony in Germany and in the same year. In contrast to Bach's quiet provincial life, however, Handel experienced a stormy international career and was profoundly secular in temperament. After studying in Italy, where he began his career by writing operas in the Italian manner, in 1712 he moved to England, where he spent most of his adult life attempting to run an opera company. Although patronized by the English royal court, Handel wrote music for large public audiences and was not averse to writing huge, unusual-sounding pieces.

Jacques-Louis David, *Oath of the Horatii*. The Frenchman David was one of the most famous Neoclassical artists of the late eighteenth century. To immerse himself in the world of Classical antiquity, he painted the *Oath of the Horatii* in Rome. Thanks to its emphasis on patriotic duty, the work became an instant hit in both Paris and Rome.

The band for his *Fireworks Music,* for example, was supposed to be accompanied by 101 cannons. Although he wrote more than forty operas and much other secular music, the worldly Handel is, ironically, probably best known for his religious music. His *Messiah* has been called "one of those rare works that appeal immediately to everyone, and yet is indisputably a masterpiece of the highest order."[10]

Although Bach and Handel composed many instrumental suites and concerti, orchestral music did not come to the fore until the second half of the eighteenth century, when new instruments such as the piano appeared. A new musical period, the classical era (1750–1830), also emerged, represented by two great innovators—Haydn and Mozart. Their renown caused the musical center of Europe to shift from Italy and Germany to the Austrian Empire.

Franz Joseph Haydn (FRAHNTS YO-zef HY-dun) (1732–1809) spent most of his adult life as musical director for the wealthy Hungarian princes, the Esterhazy brothers. Haydn was incredibly prolific, composing 104 symphonies in addition to string quartets, concerti, songs, oratorios, and Masses. His visits to England in 1790 and 1794 introduced him to another world, where musicians wrote for public concerts rather than princely patrons. This "liberty," as he called it, induced him to write his two great oratorios, *The Creation* and *The Seasons,* both of which were dedicated to the common people.

The concerto, symphony, and opera all reached their zenith in the works of Wolfgang Amadeus Mozart (VULF-gahng ah-muh-DAY-uss MOH-tsart) (1756–1791), a child prodigy who gave his first harpsichord concert at six and wrote his first opera at twelve. He, too, sought a patron, but his discontent with the overly demanding archbishop of Salzburg forced him to move to Vienna, where his failure to find a permanent patron made his life miserable. Nevertheless, he wrote music prolifically and passionately until he died a debt-ridden pauper at thirty-five (see the Film & History feature on p. 531). Mozart carried the tradition of Italian comic opera to new heights with *The Marriage of Figaro,* based on a Parisian play of the 1780s in which a valet outwits and outsings his noble employers, and *Don Giovanni,* a "black comedy" about the havoc Don Giovanni wrought on earth before he descended into hell. *The Marriage of Figaro, The Magic Flute,* and *Don Giovanni* are three of the world's greatest operas. Mozart composed with an ease of melody and a blend of grace, precision, and emotion that arguably no one has ever excelled. Haydn remarked to Mozart's father that "your son is the greatest composer known to me either in person or by reputation."

THE DEVELOPMENT OF THE NOVEL The eighteenth century was also decisive in the development of the novel. The novel was not a completely new literary genre but grew out of the medieval romances and the picaresque stories of the sixteenth century. The English are credited with establishing the modern novel as the chief vehicle for

Mozart as Child Prodigy. This painting, done in Paris in 1763 or 1764, shows the seven-year-old Mozart playing at the harpsichord while his composer father, Leopold, plays the violin and his sister, Nannerl, sings. Crowds greeted the young Mozart enthusiastically throughout the family's three-year tour of northern Europe.

fiction writing. With no established rules, the novel was open to much experimentation. It also proved especially attractive to women readers and women writers.

Samuel Richardson (1689–1761) was a printer by trade and did not turn to writing until his fifties. His first novel, *Pamela: or, Virtue Rewarded,* focused on a servant girl's resistance to numerous seduction attempts by her master. Finally, by reading the girl's letters describing her feelings about his efforts, the master realizes that she has a good mind as well as an attractive body and marries her. Virtue is rewarded. *Pamela* won Richardson a large audience as he appealed to the growing cult of sensibility in the eighteenth century—the taste for the sentimental and emotional. Samuel Johnson, another great English writer of the century and an even greater wit, remarked, "If you were to read Richardson for the story . . . you would hang yourself. But you must read him for the sentiment."

Reacting against the moral seriousness of Richardson, Henry Fielding (1707–1754) wrote novels about people without scruples who survived by their wits. His best work was *The History of Tom Jones, a Foundling,* a lengthy novel about the numerous adventures of a young scoundrel. Fielding presented scenes of English life from the hovels of London to the country houses of the aristocracy. In a number of hilarious episodes, he described characters akin to real types in English society. Although he emphasized action rather than inner feeling, Fielding did his own moralizing by attacking the hypocrisy of his age.

THE WRITING OF HISTORY The philosophes were responsible for creating a revolution in the writing of history. Their secular orientation caused them to eliminate

the role of God in history and freed them to concentrate on events themselves and search for causal relationships in the natural world. Earlier, the humanist historians of the Renaissance had also placed their histories in purely secular settings, but not with the same intensity and complete removal of God.

The philosophe-historians also broadened the scope of history from the humanists' preoccupation with politics. Politics still predominated in the work of Enlightenment historians, but they also paid attention to economic, social, intellectual, and cultural developments. As Voltaire explained in his masterpiece, *The Age of Louis XIV:* "It is not merely the life of Louis XIV that we propose to write; we have a wider aim in view. We shall endeavor to depict for posterity, not the actions of a single man, but the spirit of men in the most enlightened age the world has ever seen."[11] In seeking to describe the "totality of past human experience," Voltaire initiated the modern ideal of social history.

The weaknesses of these philosophe-historians stemmed from their preoccupations as philosophes. Following the ideals of the classics that dominated their minds, the philosophes sought to instruct as well as entertain. Their goal was to help civilize their age, and history could play a role by revealing its lessons according to their vision. Their emphasis on science and reason and their dislike of Christianity made them less than sympathetic to the period we call the Middle Ages. This is particularly noticeable in the other great masterpiece of eighteenth-century historiography, the six-volume *Decline and Fall of the Roman Empire* by Edward Gibbon (1737–1794). Although Gibbon thought that the decline of Rome had many causes, he portrayed the growth of Christianity as a major reason for Rome's eventual collapse. Like some

Amadeus (1984)

Directed by Milos Forman (who won the Academy Award for Best Director), *Amadeus* is a visually stunning Academy Award–winning film based on the relationship of two eighteenth-century composers, Antonio Salieri and Wolfgang Amadeus Mozart. The movie is also the story of Mozart's musical genius. Written by Peter Shaffer, the movie is based on Shaffer's stage play of the same name.

A fictional account of the relationship between Salieri and Mozart, the story is told by Salieri to a priest through a series of flashbacks. Salieri (played by F. Murray Abraham, who won an Academy Award as Best Actor for his performance) was the court composer to Joseph II (Jeffrey Jones), the Austrian emperor, but he was also a man who dedicated his life to serving God through music. Salieri becomes insanely jealous of the young Mozart (Tom Hulce), who impresses everyone with his musical genius. Salieri, however, is dismayed by Mozart's lewd, irreverent, and foolish behavior. In hearing Mozart's music, he believes he is hearing the voice of God ("God is singing through this little man to all the world"), but he cannot fathom why God would speak through such a common person and comes to believe that God is laughing at Salieri's own musical mediocrity through Mozart's genius. As Mozart suffers through a series of trials and rejections by people who have little appreciation of his genius, Salieri plots the downfall of Amadeus (literally "God's beloved") as a way of defeating God. He secretly commissions Mozart to write a Requiem Mass, which he plans to pass off as his own work of genius after he has killed Mozart. As his financial worries increase, however, Mozart becomes increasingly weakened by drink and illness and dies before the Requiem is completed. Salieri now believes that God killed Mozart so that Salieri could not be recognized as a musical genius.

Amadeus is a brilliant film about brilliance—the musical genius of Mozart. While the movie is accurate in

Mozart (Tom Hulce) meets with Salieri (F. Murray Abraham).

© Warner Bros./Courtesy Everett Collection

presenting Mozart as a child prodigy and a great composer who died at the young age of thirty-five, the story of the rivalry between Salieri and Mozart is mostly fictional. There was indeed some antipathy between these two composers who vied for royal commissions and teaching jobs. Nevertheless, there is also evidence that the two men respected each other, and there is certainly no evidence that Salieri was instrumental in bringing about Mozart's downfall and death. Musical scholars also reject the view of Mozart as a giggling fool, subject to the outbursts of laughter that Tom Hulce used so effectively in his portrayal of Mozart. The film's depiction of Mozart writing out perfect manuscripts of what he had already composed in his head is also questionable. Mozart himself said once, "People make a mistake who think that my art has come easily to me. Nobody has devoted so much time and thought to composition as I." Despite the lack of historical accuracy, however, *Amadeus* beautifully conveys the genius of Mozart and gives viewers a sense of why he is regarded as one of the world's greatest composers. ⇨

of the philosophes, Gibbon believed in the idea of progress and, in reflecting on the decline and fall of Rome, expressed his optimism about the future of European civilization and the ability of Europeans to avoid the fate of the Romans.

The High Culture of the Eighteenth Century

Historians and cultural anthropologists have grown accustomed to distinguishing between a civilization's high culture and its popular culture. **High culture** usually means the literary and artistic world of the educated and wealthy ruling classes; **popular culture** refers to the written and unwritten lore of the masses, most of which is passed down orally. By the eighteenth century, European high culture consisted of a learned world of theologians, scientists, philosophers, intellectuals, poets, and dramatists, for whom Latin remained a truly international language. Their work was supported by a wealthy and literate lay group, the most important of whom were the landed aristocracy and the wealthier upper classes in the cities.

A London Coffeehouse.
Coffeehouses first appeared in Venice and Constantinople but quickly spread throughout Europe by the beginning of the eighteenth century. In addition to drinking coffee, patrons of coffeehouses could read magazines and newspapers, exchange ideas, play chess, smoke, and engage in business transactions. In this scene from a London coffeehouse of 1705, well-attired gentlemen make bids on commodities.

Especially noticeable in the eighteenth century was an expansion of both the reading public and publishing. One study revealed that French publishers were issuing about sixteen hundred titles yearly in the 1780s, up from three hundred titles in 1750. Though many of these titles were still aimed at small groups of the educated elite, many were also directed to the new reading public of the middle classes, which included women and even urban artisans. The growth of publishing houses made it possible for authors to make money from their works and be less dependent on wealthy patrons.

An important aspect of the growth of publishing and reading in the eighteenth century was the development of magazines for the general public. Great Britain, an important center for the new magazines, saw 25 periodicals published in 1700, 103 in 1760, and 158 in 1780. Although short-lived, the best known was Joseph Addison and Richard Steele's *Spectator,* begun in 1711. Its goal was "to enliven Morality with wit, and to temper Wit with Morality.... To bring Philosophy out of the closets and libraries, schools and colleges, to dwell in clubs and assemblies, at tea-tables and coffeehouses." In keeping with one of the chief intellectual goals of the philosophes, the *Spectator* wished to instruct and entertain at the same time. With its praise of family, marriage, and courtesy, the *Spectator* also had a strong appeal to women. Some of the new magazines were aimed specifically at women, such as *The Female Spectator* in England, which was also edited by a woman, Eliza Haywood, and featured articles by female writers.

Along with magazines came daily newspapers. The first was printed in London in 1702, but by 1780, thirty-seven other English towns had their own newspapers. Filled with news and special features, they were relatively cheap and were provided free in coffeehouses. Books, too, received wider circulation through the development of public libraries in the cities as well as private circulating libraries, which offered books for rent.

EDUCATION AND UNIVERSITIES By the eighteenth century, Europe was home to a large number of privately endowed secondary schools, such as the grammar and public schools in England, the gymnasiums in German-speaking lands, and the *collèges* in France and Spain. These schools tended to be elitist, designed to meet the needs of the children of the upper classes of society. Basically, European secondary schools perpetuated the class hierarchy of Europe rather than creating avenues for social mobility. In fact, most of the philosophes reinforced the belief that education should function to keep people in their own social class. Baron d'Holbach said, "Education should teach princes to reign, the ruling classes to distinguish themselves by their merit and virtue, the rich to use their riches well, the poor to live by honest industry."

The curriculum of these secondary schools still largely concentrated on the Greek and Latin classics with little attention paid to mathematics, the sciences, and modern languages. Complaints from philosophe-reformers, as well as from merchants and other middle-class people who wanted their sons to have a more practical education, led to the development of new schools designed to provide a broader education. In Germany, the first *Realschule* (ray-AHL-shoo-luh) was opened in Berlin in 1747 and offered modern languages, geography, and bookkeeping to prepare boys for careers in business. New schools of this kind were also created for upper-class girls, although they focused primarily on religion and domestic skills.

The Punishment of Crime

Torture and capital punishment remained common features of European judicial systems well into the eighteenth century. Public spectacles were especially gruesome, as this excerpt from the *Nocturnal Spectator* of Restif de la Bretonne demonstrates.

———— ✦≡✦ ————

Restif de la Bretonne, "The Broken Man"

I went home by way of rue Saint-Antoine and the Place de Grève. Three murderers had been broken on the wheel there, the day before. I had not expected to see any such spectacle, one that I had never dared to witness. But as I crossed the square I caught sight of a poor wretch, pale, half dead, wracked by the pains of the interrogation inflicted on him twenty hours earlier; he was stumbling down from the Hôtel de Ville supported by the executioner and the confessor. These two men, so completely different, inspired an inexpressible emotion in me! I watched the latter embrace a miserable man consumed by fever, filthy as the dungeons he came from, swarming with vermin! And I said to myself, "O Religion, here is your greatest glory!..."

I saw a horrible sight, even though the torture had been mitigated.... The wretch had revealed his accomplices. He was garroted before he was put to the wheel. A winch set under the scaffold tightened a noose around the victim's neck and he was strangled; for a long while the confessor and the hangman felt his heart to see whether the artery still pulsed, and the hideous blows were dealt only after it beat no longer.... I left, with my hair standing on end in horror. ⊱

 What does this selection reveal about the punishment of crime in the eighteenth century? What impact did such descriptions have on the philosophes' attitudes toward the administration of justice as it was carried out by their respective monarchical states?

The most common complaint about universities, especially from the philosophes, was the old-fashioned curriculum that emphasized the classics and Aristotelian philosophy and provided no training in the sciences or modern languages. Before the end of the century, this criticism led to reforms that introduced new ideas in the areas of physics, astronomy, and even mathematics into the universities. It is significant, however, that very few of the important scientific discoveries of the eighteenth century occurred in the universities.

Crime and Punishment

By the eighteenth century, most European states had developed a hierarchy of courts to deal with crimes. Except in England, judicial torture remained an important means of obtaining evidence before a trial. Courts used the rack, thumbscrews, and other instruments to obtain confessions in criminal cases. Punishments for crimes were often cruel and even spectacular. Public executions were a basic part of traditional punishment and were regarded as a necessary means of deterring potential offenders in an age when a state's police forces were too weak to ensure the capture of criminals. Although nobles were executed by simple beheading, lower-class criminals condemned to death were tortured, broken on the wheel, or drawn and quartered (see the box above). The death penalty was still commonly used for property crimes as well as for violent offenses. By 1800, more than two hundred crimes were subject to the death penalty in England. In addition to executions, European states resorted to forced labor in mines, forts, and navies. England also sent criminals as indentured servants to colonies in the New World and, after the American Revolution, to Australia.

Appalled by the unjust laws and brutal punishments of their times, some philosophes sought to create a new approach to justice. The most notable effort was made by an Italian philosophe, Cesare Beccaria (CHAY-zuh-ray buh-KAH-ree-uh) (1738–1794). In his essay *On Crimes and Punishments,* written in 1764, Beccaria argued that punishments should serve only as deterrents, not as exercises in brutality: "Such punishments...ought to be chosen as will make the strongest and most lasting impressions on the minds of others, with the least torment to the body of the criminal."[12] Beccaria was also opposed to the use of capital punishment. It was spectacular, but it failed to stop others from committing crimes. Imprisonment—the deprivation of freedom—made a far more lasting impression. Moreover, capital punishment was harmful to society because it set an example of barbarism: "Is it not absurd that the laws, which detest and punish homicide, should, in order to prevent murder, publicly commit murder themselves?"

By the end of the eighteenth century, a growing sentiment against executions and torture led to a decline in both corporal and capital punishment. A new type of prison, in which criminals were placed in cells and subjected to discipline and regular work to rehabilitate them, began to replace the public spectacle of barbarous punishments.

The World of Medicine

In the eighteenth century, medicine was practiced by a hierarchy of practitioners. At the top stood the physicians, who were university graduates and enjoyed a high social status. Despite the scientific advances of the seventeenth and eighteenth centuries, however, university medical education was still largely conducted in Latin and was based primarily on Galen's work. New methods emphasizing clinical experience did begin to be introduced at the University of Leiden, which replaced Padua as the foremost medical school of Europe in the first half of the seventeenth century, only to be surpassed in the second half of that century by Vienna. A graduate with a doctorate in medicine from a university needed to receive a license before he could be a practicing member of the physicians' elite corporate body. In England, the Royal College of Physicians licensed only one hundred physicians in the early eighteenth century. Only officially licensed physicians could hold regular medical consultations with patients and receive payments, already regarded in the eighteenth century as outrageously high.

Below the physicians were the surgeons, who were still known as barber-surgeons well into the eighteenth century from their original dual occupation. Their primary functions were to bleed patients and perform surgery; the latter was often done crudely, without painkillers and in filthy conditions, because there was no understanding of anesthesia or infection. Bleeding was widely believed to be beneficial in reducing fevers and combating a variety of illnesses.

The surgeons underwent significant changes in the course of the eighteenth century. In the 1740s, they began to separate themselves from the barbers and organize their own guilds. At the same time, they started to undergo additional training by dissecting corpses and studying anatomy more systematically. As they became more effective, the distinction between physicians and surgeons began to break down, and surgeons were examining patients in a fashion similar to physicians by the end of the century. Moreover, surgeons also began to be licensed. In England, the Royal College of Surgeons required clinical experience before granting the license.

Other medical practitioners, such as apothecaries, midwives, and faith healers, primarily served the common people in the eighteenth century. Although their main function was to provide herbs and potions as recommended by physicians, apothecaries or pharmacists also acted independently in diagnosing illnesses and selling remedies. In the course of the eighteenth century, male doctors increasingly supplanted midwives in delivering babies. At the same time, the tradition of faith healing, so prominent in medieval medicine, continued to be practiced, especially in the rural areas of Europe.

Hospitals in the eighteenth century seemed more a problem than an aid in dealing with disease and illness. That conditions were bad is evident in this description by the philosophe Denis Diderot, who characterized the Hôtel-Dieu in Paris, France's "biggest, roomiest, and richest" hospital, in these words:

> Imagine a long series of communicating wards filled with sufferers of every kind of disease who are sometimes packed three, four, five or even six into a bed, the living alongside the dead and dying, the air polluted by this mass of unhealthy bodies, passing pestilential germs of their afflictions from one to the other, and the spectacle of suffering and agony on every hand. That is the Hôtel-Dieu. The result is that many of these poor wretches come out with diseases they did not have when they went in, and often pass them on to the people they go back to live with.[13]

Despite appeals, efforts at hospital reform in the eighteenth century remained ineffectual.

Popular Culture

Popular culture refers to the written and unwritten literature and the social activities and pursuits that are fundamental to the lives of most people. The distinguishing characteristic of popular culture is its collective and public nature. Group activity was especially evident in the festival, a broad name used to cover a variety of celebrations: community festivals in Catholic Europe that celebrated the feast day of the local patron saint; annual festivals, such as Christmas and Easter, that went back to medieval Christianity; and Carnival, the most spectacular form of festival, which was celebrated in Spain, Italy, France, Germany, and Austria. All of these festivals were special occasions when people ate, drank, and celebrated to excess. In traditional societies, festival was a time for relaxation and enjoyment because much of the rest of the year was a time of unrelieved work. As the poet Thomas Gray said of Carnival in Turin in 1739: "This Carnival lasts only from Christmas to Lent; one half of the remaining part of the year is passed in remembering the last, the other in expecting the future Carnival."[14]

CARNIVAL Carnival was celebrated in the weeks leading up to the beginning of Lent, the forty-day period of fasting and purification preceding Easter. Carnival was, understandably, a time of great indulgence, just the reverse of Lent, when people were expected to abstain from meat, sex, and most recreations. Hearty consumption of food, especially meat and other delicacies, and heavy drinking were the norm during Carnival; so was intense sexual activity. Songs with double meanings that would be considered offensive at other times could be sung publicly at this time of year. A float of Florentine "key-makers," for example, sang this ditty to the ladies: "Our tools are fine, new and useful; We always carry them with us; They are good for anything; If you want to touch them, you can."[15] Finally, Carnival was a time of aggression, a time to release pent-up feelings. Most often this took the form of verbal aggression, since people were allowed to openly insult other people and even criticize their social superiors and authorities. Certain acts of physical violence were also permitted. People pelted each other with apples, eggs, flour, and pig's bladders filled with water.

TAVERNS AND ALCOHOL The same sense of community evident in festival was also present in the chief gathering places of the common people, the local taverns or cabarets. Taverns functioned as regular gathering places for neighborhood men to talk, play games, conduct small business matters, and drink. In some countries, the favorite drinks of poor people, such as gin in England and vodka in Russia, proved devastating as poor people regularly drank themselves into oblivion. Gin was cheap; the classic sign in English taverns, "Drunk for a penny, dead drunk for two pence," was literally true. In England, the

Popular Culture: Carnival. Pictured here in a painting by Giovanni Signorini is a scene from the celebration of Carnival on the Piazza Santa Croce in Florence, Italy. Carnival was a period of festivities before Lent, celebrated in most Roman Catholic countries. Carnival became an occasion for indulgence in food, drink, games, practical jokes, and merriment, all of which are evident here.

consumption of gin rose from 2 million to 5 million gallons between 1714 and 1733 and declined only when complaints finally led to laws restricting sales in the 1750s. Of course, the rich drank too. Samuel Johnson once remarked, "All the decent people in Lichfield got drunk every night and were not the worse thought of." But unlike the poor, the rich drank port and brandy, usually in large quantities.

This difference in drinking habits between rich and poor reminds us of the ever-widening separation between the elite and the poor in the eighteenth century. In 1500, popular culture was for everyone; a second culture for the elite, it was the only culture for the rest of society. But between 1500 and 1800, the nobility, clergy, and bourgeoisie had abandoned popular culture to the lower classes. This was, of course, a gradual process, and in abandoning the popular festivals, the upper classes were also abandoning the popular worldview as well. The new scientific outlook had brought a new mental world for the upper classes, and they now viewed such things as witchcraft, faith healing, fortune telling, and prophecy as the beliefs of those who were, as one writer said, "of the weakest judgment and reason, as women, children, and ignorant and superstitious persons."

LITERACY AND PRIMARY EDUCATION Popular culture had always included a vast array of traditional songs and stories that were passed down from generation to generation. But popular culture was not entirely based on an oral tradition; a popular literature existed as well. So-called chapbooks, printed on cheap paper, were short brochures sold by itinerant peddlers to the lower classes. They contained both spiritual and secular material: lives of saints and inspirational stories competed with crude satires and adventure stories.

It is apparent from the chapbooks that popular culture did not have to remain primarily oral. Its ability to change was dependent on the growth of literacy. Studies in France indicate that literacy rates for men increased from 29 percent in the late seventeenth century to 47 percent in the late eighteenth century; for women, the increase was from 14 to 27 percent during the same period. Of course, certain groups were more likely to be literate than others. Upper-class elites and the upper middle classes in the cities were mostly all literate. Nevertheless, the figures also indicate dramatic increases for lower-middle-class artisans in urban areas. Recent research in the city of Marseilles, for example, indicates that literacy of male artisans and workers increased from 28 percent in 1710 to 85 percent in 1789, though the rate for women remained at 15 percent. Peasants, who constituted as much as 75 percent of the French population, remained largely illiterate.

The spread of literacy was closely connected to primary education. In Catholic Europe, primary education was largely a matter of local community effort, leading to little real growth. Only in the Habsburg Austrian Empire was a system of state-supported primary schools—*Volkschulen* (FULK-shoo-lun)—established, although only one in four school-age children actually attended.

The emphasis of the Protestant reformers on reading the Bible had led Protestant states to take a greater interest in primary education. Some places, especially the

Swiss cantons, Scotland, and the German states of Saxony and Prussia, witnessed the emergence of universal primary schools that provided a modicum of education for the masses. But effective systems of primary education were hindered by the attitudes of the ruling classes, who feared the consequences of teaching the lower classes anything beyond the virtues of hard work and deference to their superiors. Hannah More, an English writer who set up a network of Sunday schools, made clear the philosophy of her charity school for poor children: "My plan of instruction is extremely simple and limited. They learn on weekdays such coarse work as may fit them for servants. I allow of no writing for the poor. My object is to train up the lower classes in habits of industry and piety."

Religion and the Churches

 FOCUS QUESTION: How did popular religion differ from institutional religion in the eighteenth century?

The music of Bach and the pilgrimage and monastic churches of southern Germany and Austria make us aware of a curious fact. Though much of the great art and music of the time was religious, the thought of the time was antireligious as life became increasingly secularized and men of reason attacked the established churches. And yet most Europeans were still Christians. Even many of those most critical of the churches accepted that society could not function without religious faith.

The Institutional Church

In the eighteenth century, the established Catholic and Protestant churches were basically conservative institutions that upheld society's hierarchical structure, privileged classes, and traditions. Although churches experienced change because of new state policies, they did not sustain any dramatic internal changes. In both Catholic and Protestant countries, the parish church run by a priest or pastor remained the center of religious practice. In addition to providing religious services, the parish church kept records of births, deaths, and marriages; provided charity for the poor; supervised whatever primary education there was; and cared for orphans.

CHURCH-STATE RELATIONS Early on, the Protestant Reformation had solved the problem of the relationship between church and state by establishing the principle of state control over the churches. In the eighteenth century, Protestant state churches flourished throughout Europe: Lutheranism in Scandinavia and the north German states; Anglicanism in England; and Calvinism (or Reformed churches) in Scotland, the United Provinces, and some of the Swiss cantons and German states (see Map 17.2). There were also Protestant minorities in other European countries.

In 1700, the Catholic Church still exercised much power in Catholic European states: Spain, Portugal, France, Italy, the Habsburg Empire, Poland, and most of southern Germany. The church also continued to possess enormous wealth. In Spain, three thousand monastic institutions housing 100,000 men and women controlled enormous landed estates.

The Catholic Church remained hierarchically structured. In most Catholic countries, the highest clerics, such as bishops, archbishops, abbots, and abbesses, were members of the upper class, especially the landed nobility, and received enormous revenues from their landed estates and tithes from the faithful. A wide gulf existed between the upper and lower clergy. While the French bishop of Strasbourg, for example, received 100,000 livres a year, parish priests were paid only 500.

In the eighteenth century, the governments of many Catholic states began to seek greater authority over the churches in their countries. This "nationalization" of the Catholic Church meant controlling the papacy and in turn the chief papal agents, the Society of Jesus. The Jesuits had proved extremely successful, perhaps too successful for their own good. They had created special enclaves, virtually states within states, in the French, Spanish, and Portuguese colonies in the New World. As advisers to Catholic rulers, the Jesuits exercised considerable political influence. But the high profile they achieved through their successes attracted a wide range of enemies, and a series of actions soon undermined Jesuit power. The Portuguese monarch destroyed the powerful Jesuit state in Paraguay and then in 1759 expelled the Jesuits from Portugal and confiscated their property. In 1764, they were expelled from France and three years later from Spain and the Spanish colonies. In 1773, when Spain and France demanded that the entire society be dissolved, Pope Clement XIV reluctantly complied. The dissolution of the Jesuit order, one important pillar of Catholic strength, was yet another victory for Catholic governments determined to win control over their churches.

The end of the Jesuits was paralleled by a decline in papal power. Already by the mid-eighteenth century, the papacy played only a minor role in diplomacy and international affairs. The nationalization of the churches by the states meant the loss of the papacy's power to appoint high clerical officials.

TOLERATION AND RELIGIOUS MINORITIES One of the chief battle cries of the philosophes was a call for religious toleration. Out of political necessity, a certain level of tolerance of different creeds had occurred in the seventeenth century, but many rulers still found it difficult to accept. Louis XIV had turned back the clock in France at the end of the seventeenth century, insisting on religious uniformity and suppressing the rights of the Huguenots (see Chapter 15). Many rulers continued to believe that there was only one path to salvation; it was the true duty of a ruler not to allow subjects to be condemned to hell by being heretics. Hence, persecution of heretics continued; the last burning of a heretic took place in 1781.

Nevertheless, some progress was made toward religious toleration. No ruler was more interested in the philosophes'

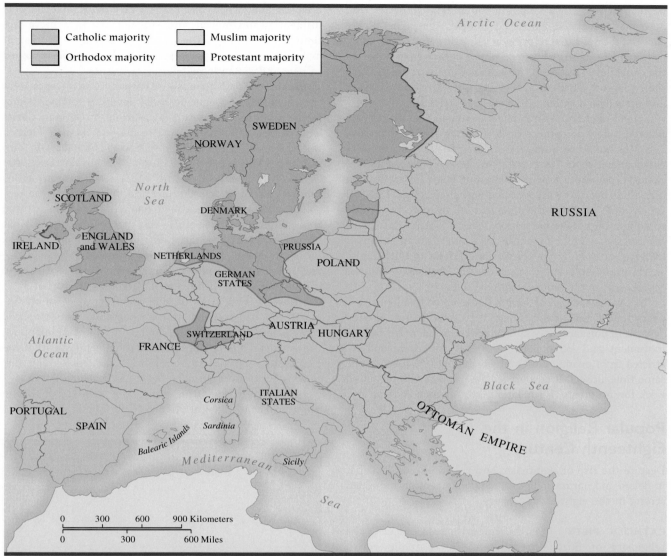

MAP 17.2 Religious Populations of Eighteenth-Century Europe. Christianity was still a dominant force in eighteenth-century Europe—even many of the philosophes remained Christians while attacking the authority and power of the established Catholic and Protestant churches. By the end of the century, however, most monarchs had increased royal power at the expense of religious institutions.

Q *To what extent were religious majorities geographically concentrated in certain areas, and what accounted for this?*

call for religious toleration than Joseph II of Austria. His Toleration Patent of 1781, while recognizing Catholicism's public practice, granted Lutherans, Calvinists, and Greek Orthodox the right to worship privately. In all other ways, all subjects were now equal: "Non-Catholics are in future admitted under dispensation to buy houses and real property, to practice as master craftsmen, to take up academic appointments and posts in public service, and are not to be required to take the oath in any form contrary to their religious tenets."[16]

TOLERATION AND THE JEWS The Jews remained the despised religious minority of Europe. The largest number

of Jews (known as the Ashkenazic Jews) lived in eastern Europe. Except in relatively tolerant Poland, Jews were restricted in their movements, forbidden to own land or hold many jobs, forced to pay burdensome special taxes, and also subject to periodic outbursts of popular wrath. The resulting **pogroms,** in which Jewish communities were looted and massacred, made Jewish existence precarious and dependent on the favor of their territorial rulers.

Another major group was the Sephardic Jews, who had been expelled from Spain in the fifteenth century. Although many had migrated to Turkish lands, some of them had settled in cities, such as Amsterdam, Venice, London, and Frankfurt, where they were relatively free to participate in the banking and commercial activities that Jews had practiced since the Middle Ages. The highly successful ones came to provide valuable services to rulers, especially in central Europe, where they were known as the court Jews. But even these Jews were insecure because their religion set them apart from the Christian majority and served as a catalyst to social resentment.

Some Enlightenment thinkers in the eighteenth century favored a new acceptance of Jews. They argued that Jews and Muslims were human and deserved the full rights of citizenship despite their religion. Many philosophes denounced persecution of the Jews but made no attempt to hide their hostility and ridiculed Jewish customs. Diderot, for example, said that the Jews had "all the defects peculiar to an ignorant and superstitious nation." Many Europeans favored the assimilation of the Jews into the mainstream of society, but only by the conversion of Jews to Christianity as the basic solution to the "Jewish problem." This, of course, was not acceptable to most Jews.

The Austrian emperor Joseph II attempted to adopt a new policy toward the Jews, although it too was limited. It freed Jews from nuisance taxes and allowed them more freedom of movement and job opportunities, but they were still restricted from owning land and worshiping in public. At the same time, Joseph II encouraged Jews to learn German and work toward greater assimilation into Austrian society.

Popular Religion in the Eighteenth Century

Despite the rise of skepticism and the intellectuals' belief in deism and natural religion, religious devotion remained strong in the eighteenth century.

CATHOLIC PIETY   It is difficult to assess precisely the religiosity of Europe's Catholics. The Catholic parish church remained an important center of life for the entire community. How many people went to church regularly cannot be known exactly, but it has been established that 90 to 95 percent of Catholic populations did go to Mass on Easter Sunday, one of the church's most special celebrations.

Catholic religiosity proved highly selective, however. Despite the Reformation, much popular devotion was still directed to an externalized form of worship focusing on prayers to saints, pilgrimages, and devotion to relics and images. This bothered many clergymen, who felt that their parishioners were "more superstitious than devout," as one Catholic priest put it. Many common people continued to fear witches and relied on the intervention of the saints and the Virgin Mary to save them from personal disasters caused by the devil.

PROTESTANT REVIVALISM: PIETISM   After the initial century of religious fervor that created Protestantism in the sixteenth century, Protestant churches in the seventeenth century had settled down into well-established patterns controlled by state authorities and served by a well-educated clergy. Protestant churches became bureaucratized and bereft of religious enthusiasm. In Germany

and England, where rationalism and deism had become influential and moved some theologians to a more "rational" Christianity, the desire of ordinary Protestant churchgoers for greater depths of religious experience led to new and dynamic religious movements.

Pietism (PY-uh-tiz-um) in Germany was a response to this desire for a deeper personal devotion to God. Begun in the seventeenth century by a group of German clerics who wished their religion to be more personal, Pietism was spread by the teachings of Count Nikolaus von Zinzendorf (NEE-koh-LOWSS fun TSIN-sin-dorf) (1700–1760). To Zinzendorf and his Moravian Brethren, as his sect was called, it was the mystical dimensions—the personal experience of God—in one's life that constituted true religious experience. He was utterly opposed to what he perceived as the rationalistic approach of orthodox Lutheran clergy, who were being educated in new "rational" ideas. As Zinzendorf commented, "He who wishes to comprehend God with his mind becomes an atheist."

After the civil wars of the seventeenth century, England too had arrived at a respectable, uniform, and complacent state church. A pillar of the establishment, the Anglican Church seemed to offer little spiritual excitement, especially to the masses of people. The dissenting Protestant groups—Puritans, Quakers, Baptists— were relatively subdued, while the growth of deism seemed to challenge Christianity itself. The desire for deep

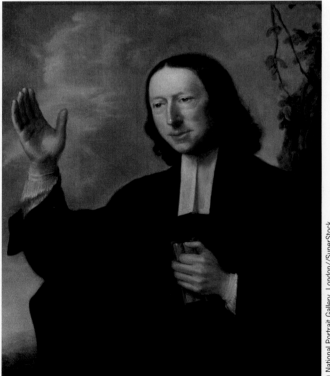

John Wesley. In leading a deep spiritual revival in Britain, John Wesley founded a religious movement that came to be known as Methodism. He loved to preach to the masses, and this 1766 portrait by Nathaniel Hope shows him as he might have appeared before a crowd of people.

© National Portrait Gallery, London//SuperStock

The Conversion Experience in Wesley's Methodism

After his own conversion experience, John Wesley traveled extensively to bring the "glad tidings" of Jesus to other people. It has been estimated that he preached more than 40,000 sermons, some of them to audiences numbering 20,000 listeners. Wesley gave his message wherever people gathered—in the streets, hospitals, private houses, and even pubs. In this selection from his journal, Wesley describes how emotional and even violent conversion experiences could be.

⤙ ⧊⧊ ⤚

The Journal of the Reverend John Wesley

Sunday, May 20 [1759], being with Mr. B——ll at Everton, I was much fatigued, and did not rise: but Mr. B. did, and observed several fainting and crying out, while Mr. Berridge was preaching: afterwards at Church, I heard many cry out, especially children, whose agonies were amazing: one of the eldest, a girl of ten or twelve years old, was full in my view, in violent contortions of body, and weeping aloud, I think incessantly, during the whole service.... The Church was equally crowded in the afternoon, the windows being filled within and without, and even the outside of the pulpit to the very top; so that Mr. B. seemed almost stifled by their breath; yet feeble and sickly as he is, he was continually strengthened, and his voice, for the most part, distinguishable; in the midst of all the outcries. I believe there were present three times more men than women, a great part of whom came from far; thirty of them having set out at two in the morning, from a place thirteen miles off. The text was, *Having a form of godliness, but denying the power thereof.* When the power of religion began to be spoken of, the presence of God really filled the place: and while poor sinners felt the sentence of death in their souls, what sounds of distress did I hear! The greatest number of them who cried or fell, were men: but some women, and several children, felt the power of the same almighty Spirit, and seemed just sinking into hell. This occasioned a mixture of several sounds; some shrieking, some roaring aloud. The most general was a loud breathing, like that of people half strangled and gasping for life: and indeed almost all the cries were like those of human creatures, dying in bitter anguish. Great numbers wept without any noise: others fell down as death: some sinking in silence; some with extreme noise and violent agitation. I stood on the pew-seat, as did a young man in the opposite pew, an able-bodied, fresh, healthy countryman: but in a moment, while he seemed to think of nothing less, down he dropped with a violence inconceivable. The adjoining pews seemed to shake with his fall: I heard afterwards the stamping of his feet; ready to break the boards, as he lay in strong convulsions, at the bottom of the pew. Among several that were struck down in the next pew, was a girl, who was as violently seized as he.... Among the children who felt the arrows of the Almighty, I saw a sturdy boy, about eight years old, who roared above his fellows, and seemed in his agony to struggle with the strength of a grown man. His face was as red as scarlet: and almost all on whom God laid his hand, turned either very red or almost black....

The violent struggling of many in the above-mentioned churches, has broken several pews and benches. Yet it is common for people to remain unaffected there, and afterwards to drop down on their way home. Some have been found lying as dead on the road: others, in Mr. B.'s garden; not being able to walk from the Church to his house, though it is not two hundred yards. ⤜

Q What was a conversion experience? How does the emotionalism of this passage relate to enlightened thinkers' fascination with the passions and the workings of human reason?

spiritual experience seemed unmet until the advent of John Wesley.

WESLEY AND METHODISM An ordained Anglican minister, John Wesley (1703–1791) experienced a deep spiritual crisis and underwent a mystical experience: "I felt I did trust in Christ alone for salvation; and an assurance was given me, that He had taken away my sins, even mine, and saved me from the law of sin and death. I felt my heart strangely warmed." To Wesley, "the gift of God's grace" assured him of salvation and led him to become a missionary to the English people, bringing the "glad tidings" of salvation to all people, despite opposition from the Anglican Church, which criticized this emotional mysticism or religious enthusiasm as superstitious nonsense. To Wesley, all could be saved by experiencing God and opening the doors to his grace.

In taking the Gospel to the people, Wesley preached to the masses in open fields, appealing especially to the lower classes neglected by the socially elitist Anglican Church. He tried, he said, "to lower religion to the level of the lowest people's capacities." Wesley's charismatic preaching often provoked highly charged and even violent conversion experiences (see the box above). Afterward, converts were organized into so-called Methodist societies or chapels in which they could aid each other in doing the good works that Wesley considered a component of salvation. Although Wesley sought to keep Methodism within the Anglican Church, after his death it became a separate and independent sect. Methodism was an important revival of Christianity and proved that the need for spiritual experience had not been expunged by the eighteenth-century search for reason.

CHAPTER SUMMARY

The eighteenth century was a time of change but also of tradition. The popularization of the ideas of the Scientific Revolution, the impact of travel literature, a new skepticism, and the ideas of Locke and Newton led to what historians call the Age of Enlightenment. Its leading figures were the intellectuals known as philosophes who hoped that they could create a new society by using reason to discover the natural laws that governed it. Like the Christian humanists of the fifteenth and sixteenth centuries, they believed that education could create better human beings and a better human society. Such philosophes as Montesquieu, Voltaire, Diderot, Hume, Quesnay, Smith, Beccaria, Condorcet, and Rousseau attacked traditional religion as the enemy, advocated religious toleration and freedom of thought, criticized their oppressive societies, and created a new "science of man" in economics, politics, and education. In doing so, the philosophes laid the foundation for a modern worldview based on rationalism and secularism.

 Although many of the philosophes continued to hold traditional views about women, female intellectuals like Mary Astell and Mary Wollstonecraft began to argue for the equality of the sexes and the right of women to be educated. The Enlightenment appealed largely to the urban middle classes and some members of the nobility, and its ideas were discussed in salons, coffeehouses, reading clubs, lending libraries, and societies like the Freemasons.

Innovation in the arts also characterized the eighteenth century. The cultural fertility of the age is evident in Rococo painting and architecture; the achievements of Bach, Handel, Haydn, and Mozart in music; the birth of the novel in literature; and new directions in education and historical writing.

Although the philosophes attacked the established Christian churches, many Europeans continued to practice their traditional faith. Moreover, a new wave of piety swept both Catholic and Protestant churches, especially noticeable in Protestant Europe with the advent of Pietism in Germany and John Wesley and Methodism in England.

Thus, despite the secular thought and secular ideas that began to pervade the mental world of the ruling elites, most people in eighteenth-century Europe still lived by seemingly eternal verities and practices—God, religious worship, and farming. The most brilliant architecture and music of the age were religious. And yet the forces of secularization were too strong to stop. In the midst of intellectual change, economic, political, and social transformations of great purport were taking shape and would lead, as we shall see in the next two chapters, to both political and social upheavals and even revolution before the century's end.

CHAPTER TIMELINE

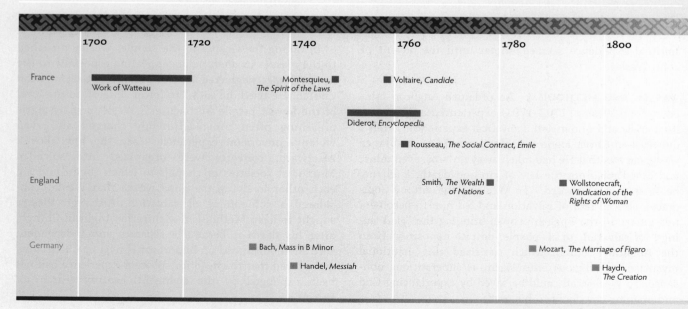

	1700	1720	1740	1760	1780	1800
France	Work of Watteau		Montesquieu, ■ *The Spirit of the Laws*	■ Voltaire, *Candide* Diderot, *Encyclopedia* ■ Rousseau, *The Social Contract, Émile*		
England				Smith, *The Wealth* ■ *of Nations*	■ Wollstonecraft, *Vindication of the Rights of Woman*	
Germany			■ Bach, Mass in B Minor ■ Handel, *Messiah*		■ Mozart, *The Marriage of Figaro* ■ Haydn, *The Creation*	

CHAPTER REVIEW

Upon Reflection

Q What contributions did Montesquieu, Voltaire, Diderot, and Rousseau make to the Enlightenment? What did they have in common? How did they differ?

Q What is popular culture, and how was it expressed in the eighteenth century?

Q What kinds of experiences do you associate with popular religion in the eighteenth century? How do you explain the continuing growth of popular religious devotion?

Key Terms

Enlightenment (p. 514)
skepticism (p. 514)
cultural relativism (p. 516)
philosophes (p. 516)
cosmopolitan (p. 516)
separation of powers (p. 518)
deism (p. 519)
laissez-faire (p. 522)
economic liberalism (p. 522)
Romanticism (p. 523)
feminism (p. 524)
salons (p. 526)
Rococo (p. 527)
Neoclassicism (p. 527)
high culture (p. 531)
popular culture (p. 531)
pogroms (p. 537)
Pietism (p. 538)

Suggestions for Further Reading

EIGHTEENTH-CENTURY EUROPE Surveys of eighteenth-century Europe include **I. Woloch, *Eighteenth-Century Europe*** (New York, 1986); **M. S. Anderson, *Europe in the Eighteenth Century,*** 4th ed. (London, 2000); **R. Birn, *Crisis, Absolutism, Revolution: Europe, 1648–1789,*** 3rd ed. (Fort Worth, Tex., 2005); and **T. C. W. Blanning, ed., *The Eighteenth Century: Europe, 1689–1815*** (Oxford, 2000).

THE ENLIGHTENMENT Good introductions to the Enlightenment can be found in **U. Im Hof, *The Enlightenment*** (Oxford, 1994); **D. Goodman, *The Republic of Letters: A Cultural History of the French Enlightenment*** (Ithaca, N.Y., 1994); and **D. Outram, *The Enlightenment,*** 2nd ed. (Cambridge, 2005). A more detailed synthesis can be found in **P. Gay, *The Enlightenment: An Interpretation,*** 2 vols. (New York, 1966–69). See also **P. H. Reill** and **E. J. Wilson, eds., *Encyclopedia of the Enlightenment,*** rev. ed. (New York, 2004); the beautifully illustrated work by **D. Outram,**

Panorama of the Enlightenment (Los Angeles, 2006); and **M. Fitzpatrick et al., *The Enlightenment World*** (New York, 2004). On the social history of the Enlightenment, see **T. Munck, *The Enlightenment: A Comparative Social History, 1721–1794*** (London, 2000). Studies of the major Enlightenment intellectuals include **J. Sklar, *Montesquieu*** (Oxford, 1987); **R. Pearson, *Voltaire Almighty: A Life in Pursuit of Freedom*** (New York, 2005); **P. N. Furbank, *Diderot: A Critical Biography*** (New York, 1992); and **L. Damrosch, *Jean-Jacques Rousseau: Restless Genius*** (Boston, 2005). On women in the eighteenth century, see **N. Z. Davis** and **A. Farge, eds., *A History of Women: Renaissance and Enlightenment Paradoxes*** (Cambridge, Mass., 1993); **C. Lougee, *Le Paradis des Femmes: Women, Salons, and Social Stratification*** (Princeton, N.J., 1976); **O. Hufton, *The Prospect Before Her: A History of Women in Western Europe, 1500–1800*** (New York, 1998); and **M. E. Wiesner-Hanks, *Women and Gender in Early Modern Europe*** (Cambridge, 2000).

CULTURE AND SOCIETY Two general surveys on the arts are **E. Gesine** and **J. F. Walther, *Rococo*** (New York, 2007), and **D. Irwin, *Neoclassicism*** (London, 1997). On the eighteenth-century novel, see **G. J. Barker-Benfield, *The Culture of Sensibility: Sex and Society in the Eighteenth-Century English Novel*** (Chicago, 1992). On Gibbon, see **W. B. Carnuchan, *Gibbon's Solitude: The Inward World of the Historian*** (London, 1987). On the growth of literacy, see **R. A. Houston, *Literacy in Early Modern Europe: Culture and Education, 1500–1800*** (New York, 1988). The impact of the Enlightenment on modern views of the body can be examined in **R. Porter, *Flesh in the Age of Reason*** (New York, 2004).

POPULAR CULTURE Important studies on popular culture include **P. Burke, *Popular Culture in Early Modern Europe*** (New York, 1978); **J. Mullan, ed., *Eighteenth-Century Popular Culture*** (Oxford, 2000); and **R. Darnton, *The Great Cat Massacre and Other Episodes in French Cultural History*** (New York, 1984).

EIGHTEENTH-CENTURY RELIGIOUS HISTORY A good introduction to the religious history of the eighteenth century can be found in **G. R. Cragg, *The Church and the Age of Reason, 1648–1789,*** rev. ed. (London, 1990). On Pietism, see **R. Gawthrop, *Pietism and the Making of Eighteenth-Century Prussia*** (New York, 1993). On John Wesley, see **H. Rack, *Reasonable Enthusiast: John Wesley and the Rise of Methodism,*** 3rd ed. (New York, 2002).

 Visit the CourseMate website at www.cengagebrain.com for additional study tools and review materials for this chapter.

AP* REVIEW QUESTIONS FOR CHAPTER 17

1. Western European society experienced which of the following during the eighteenth century?

   (A) Widespread fear that population growth would cause shortages of the resources needed for survival.
   (B) Popular movements to make the right to vote more inclusive.
   (C) Social campaigns that called on peasants to refrain from alcohol and live more moral lives.
   (D) Widespread adoption of state-sponsored schools for the masses.
   (E) The closing of most foundling hospitals due to a rise in infant mortality.

2. Which of the following authors is NOT correctly matched to his work?

   (A) Denis Diderot—*Encyclopedia*
   (B) Voltaire—*Candide*
   (C) John Locke—*Nature*
   (D) Montesquieu—*The Spirit of the Laws*
   (E) Adam Smith—*The Wealth of Nations*

3. All of the following contributed to the rise of the Enlightenment EXCEPT

   (A) continued interest in scientific knowledge.
   (B) the desire to apply reason to society.
   (C) the influence of philosophers such as John Locke and Thomas Hobbes.
   (D) a rise of religiosity within Europe.
   (E) European recognition of other developed civilizations throughout the world.

4. The new Christian denomination of Methodism

   (A) was not widely accepted, as it appealed only to the most devout.
   (B) brought about a radical reaction by the Catholic Church known as Mannerism that condemned the basic tenets of Methodism.
   (C) often appealed to those who found traditional religion to be cold and formal.
   (D) aligned with the Anabaptists to create a new religion that held a broader appeal to eastern Europeans.
   (E) split from Calvinism and carried Calvin's ideas to new lands in the east.

5. Which of the following was NOT argued by most of the philosophes?

   (A) Capital punishment should be eliminated.
   (B) Education should be used to keep society stratified.
   (C) History should be broadened to include matters beyond politics and God.
   (D) Women should be given social and political equality.
   (E) God has little to no direct involvement in daily life.

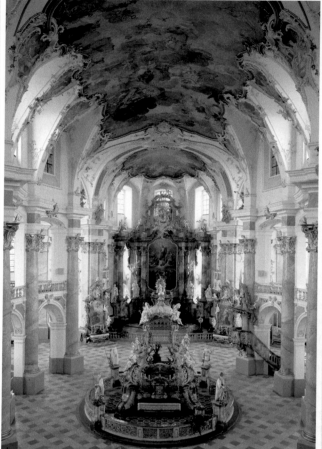

Vierzehnheiligen, Germany//© Erich Lessing/Art Resource, NY

6. The interior pictured above embodies the concepts of

   (A) fluidity, love of nature, and simplicity.
   (B) realism, classical lines, and stoicism.
   (C) Renaissance renewal, religious emotion, and nationalism.
   (D) virtue, opulence, and power.
   (E) restraint, gentleness, and understated elegance.

7. Which of the following was NOT a feature of eighteenth-century popular culture?

   (A) drinking in local taverns
   (B) participating in festivals, especially Carnival
   (C) circulation of chapbooks containing spiritual and secular material
   (D) broadening of class divisions between the ruling class and the poor
   (E) acceptance of the importance and necessity of literacy

8. Which of the following movements and ideas are most associated with the philosophes?

   (A) constitutionalism, Romanticism, equality
   (B) feminism, pietism, submission
   (C) tolerance, reason, deism
   (D) intolerance, conservatism, criticism
   (E) religiosity, humanism, nationalism

9. Seventeenth- and eighteenth-century Protestant leaders often encouraged literacy more than Catholic leaders did because

   (A) Protestants wanted all people to become literate and to aspire to lead more virtuous lives.
   (B) Catholics saw knowledge of mathematics as more important than literacy.
   (C) Protestants believed the ability to read was necessary to understand the Bible.
   (D) Catholics believed reading was necessary, but not as important as speaking Latin.
   (E) Protestants were better able to afford the cost of educating their children than were Catholics.

10. "Despite their common interest, subjects will not be bound by their commitment unless means are found to guarantee their fidelity." Which of the following would NOT support this concept?

    (A) John Locke
    (B) Thomas Hobbes
    (C) David Hume
    (D) Jean-Jacques Rousseau
    (E) Voltaire

11. Many European countries remained Catholic after the Protestant Reformation. Which of the following best describes the religious affiliations within Europe?

    (A) Russia and the Ottoman Empire both supported Protestantism within their countries.
    (B) Southern Europe remained Catholic, while the German states and Scandinavian countries supported Protestantism.
    (C) Older European countries like Italy and Greece held on to their Catholic traditions, while the newer states like France more openly accepted the new reform religions.
    (D) As the Ottoman Empire retreated from eastern Europe, its Muslim traditions remained in the countries it vacated.
    (E) Both the English and the Spanish sought the guidance and stability that the Catholic Church afforded them.

12. Which of the following best describes the contributions of women to the Enlightenment?

    (A) They published significant writings on Enlightenment subjects.
    (B) They established and ran salons, where they made some intellectual contributions.
    (C) They created their own societies that allowed them to seek their own philosophical truths.
    (D) They wrote and spoke as equal partners to men, because the philosophes believed in gender equality.
    (E) They provided financial support for the philosophes.

13. John Locke's theory of the *tabula rasa*

    (A) helped justify the division of the sexes.
    (B) was quickly proved incorrect by theologians who believed it diminished God's importance.
    (C) became the starting point for modern political theory.
    (D) was widely accepted by most Europeans of his time.
    (E) became an argument for the necessity of fixing the social ills of the day.

14. The Physiocrats

    (A) saw mercantilism as the economic theory that best embodied an ideal economy that would benefit all members of society.
    (B) moved beyond deism to openly espouse atheism.
    (C) suggested that the laws of nature could also be used to establish new economic theories.
    (D) were widely seen as the ones who brought the concepts of the Enlightenment down to the common people.
    (E) were new rulers that attempted to apply reason and rational thought to their rule.

15. John Locke, Thomas Hobbes, and Jean-Jacques Rousseau favored a social contract theory that

    (A) suggested that humans originated in a state of nature and that government came about in order to prevent anarchy.
    (B) suggested the best society is one that exists in absolute anarchy.
    (C) suggested that a divine entity had defined the laws of nature and promoted ruling elites to secure such laws.
    (D) suggested a righteous society is one dedicated to the premise of theocracy.
    (E) sought to fulfill the individual desires of the common man and woman.

© Hermitage, St. Petersburg, Russia/The Bridgeman Art Library

A 1793 portrait of Catherine the Great of Russia by Johann Lampi

The Eighteenth Century: European States, International Wars, and Social Change

CHAPTER OUTLINE AND FOCUS QUESTIONS

The European States

Q What were the main developments in France, Great Britain, the Dutch Republic, the Mediterranean states, and the Scandinavian monarchies in the eighteenth century? What do historians mean by the term *enlightened absolutism,* and to what degree did eighteenth-century Prussia, Austria, and Russia exhibit its characteristics?

Wars and Diplomacy

Q How did the concepts of "balance of power" and "reason of state" influence international relations in the eighteenth century? What were the causes and results of the Seven Years' War?

Economic Expansion and Social Change

Q What changes occurred in agriculture, finance, industry, and trade during the eighteenth century?

The Social Order of the Eighteenth Century

Q Who were the main groups making up the European social order in the eighteenth century, and how did the conditions in which they lived differ both between groups and between different parts of Europe?

CRITICAL THINKING

Q What was the relationship among intellectual, political, economic, and social changes in the eighteenth century?

HISTORIANS OFTEN DEFINE the eighteenth century as the years from 1715 to 1789. Politically, this makes sense since 1715 marks the end of the age of Louis XIV and 1789 was the year in which the French Revolution erupted. This period has often been portrayed as the final phase of Europe's old order, before the violent upheaval and reordering of society associated with the French Revolution. Europe's old order—still largely agrarian, dominated by kings and landed aristocrats, and grounded in privileges for nobles, clergy, towns, and provinces—seemed to continue a basic pattern that had prevailed in Europe since medieval times. But new ideas and new practices were also beginning to emerge. Just as a new intellectual order based on rationalism and secularism was evolving from the Scientific Revolution and the Enlightenment, demographic, economic, and social patterns were beginning to change in ways that reflected a modern new order.

The ideas of the Enlightenment seemed to proclaim a new political age as well. Catherine the Great, who ruled Russia from 1762 to 1796, wrote to Voltaire, "Since 1746 I have been under the greatest obligations to you. Before that period I read nothing but romances, but by chance your works fell into my hands, and ever since then I have never ceased to read them, and have no desire for books less well written than yours, or less instructive." The empress of Russia also invited Diderot to Russia and, when he arrived, urged him to speak frankly "as man to man." Diderot did, offering her advice for a far-ranging program of political and financial reform. But Catherine's apparent eagerness to make enlightened reforms was tempered by skepticism. She said of Diderot, "If I had believed him everything would have been turned upside down in my kingdom; legislation, administration, finance—all would have been turned topsy-turvy to make room for impractical theories." For Catherine, enlightened reform remained more a dream than a reality, and in the end, the waging of wars to gain more power was more important.

In the eighteenth century, the process of centralization that had characterized the growth of states since the Middle Ages continued as most European states enlarged their bureaucratic machinery and consolidated their governments in order to collect the revenues and build the armies they needed to compete militarily with the other European states. International competition continued to be the favorite pastime of eighteenth-century rulers. Within the European state system, the nations that would dominate Europe until World War I—Britain, France, Austria, Prussia, and Russia—emerged as the five great powers of Europe. Their rivalries led to major wars, which some have called the first world wars because they were fought outside as well as inside Europe. In the midst of this state building and war making, dramatic demographic, economic, and social changes heralded the emergence of a radical transformation in the way Europeans would raise food and produce goods.

The European States

Q FOCUS QUESTIONS: What were the main developments in France, Great Britain, the Dutch Republic, the Mediterranean states, and the Scandinavian monarchies in the eighteenth century? What do historians mean by the term *enlightened absolutism,* and to what degree did eighteenth-century Prussia, Austria, and Russia exhibit its characteristics?

Most European states in the eighteenth century were ruled by monarchs. Although the justifications of the previous century for strong monarchy continued to hold sway, divine-right assumptions were gradually superseded by influential utilitarian arguments as Europe became increasingly secularized. The Prussian king Frederick II expressed this new thinking well when explaining the services a monarch must provide for his people:

> These services consisted in the maintenance of the laws; a strict execution of justice; an employment of his whole powers to prevent any corruption of manners; and defending the state against its enemies. It is the duty of this magistrate to pay attention to agriculture; it should be his care that provisions for the nation should be in abundance, and that commerce and industry should be encouraged. He is a perpetual sentinel, who must watch the acts and the

conduct of the enemies of the state. . . . If he be the first general, the first minister of the realm, it is not that he should remain the shadow of authority, but that he should fulfill the duties of such titles. He is only the first servant of the state.[1]

This utilitarian argument was reinforced by the praises of the philosophes.

Enlightened Absolutism?

There is no doubt that Enlightenment thought had some impact on the political development of European states in the eighteenth century. Closely related to the Enlightenment idea of **natural laws** was the belief in **natural rights,** which were thought to be inalterable privileges that ought not to be withheld from any person. These natural rights included equality before the law, freedom of religious worship, freedom of speech and press, and the right to assemble, hold property, and seek happiness. The American Declaration of Independence summarized the Enlightenment concept of natural rights in its opening paragraph: "We hold these truths to be self-evident, that all men are created equal; that they are endowed by their creator with certain unalienable rights; that among these are life, liberty and the pursuit of happiness."

But how were these natural rights to be established and preserved? In the opinion of most philosophes, most people needed the direction provided by an enlightened ruler. What made rulers enlightened? They must allow religious toleration, freedom of speech and press, and the right to hold private property. They must foster the arts, sciences, and education. Above all, they must not be arbitrary in their rule; they must obey the laws and enforce them fairly for all subjects. Only strong monarchs seemed capable of overcoming vested interests and effecting the reforms society needed. Reforms then should come from above—from the rulers rather than from the people. Distrustful of the masses, the philosophes believed that absolute rulers, swayed by enlightened principles, were the best hope of reforming their societies.

The extent to which rulers actually did so is frequently discussed in the political analyses of Europe in the eighteenth century. Many historians once asserted that a new type of monarchy emerged in the late eighteenth century, which they called enlightened despotism or **enlightened absolutism.** Monarchs such as Frederick II of Prussia, Catherine the Great of Russia, and Joseph II of Austria supposedly followed the advice of the philosophes and ruled by enlightened principles, establishing a path to modern nationhood. Recent scholarship, however, has questioned the usefulness of the concept of enlightened absolutism. We can best determine the extent to which it can be applied by surveying the development of the European states in the eighteenth century and then making a judgment about the enlightened absolutism of the century's later years.

The Atlantic Seaboard States

As a result of the overseas voyages of the sixteenth century, the European economic axis began to shift from the Mediterranean to the Atlantic seaboard. In the seventeenth century, the English and Dutch expanded as Spain and Portugal declined. By the eighteenth century, Dutch power had waned, and it was left to the English and French to build the commercial empires that created a true global economy.

FRANCE: THE PROBLEMS OF THE FRENCH MONARCHS In the eighteenth century, France experienced an economic revival as the Enlightenment gained strength. The French monarchy, however, was not overly influenced by the philosophes and resisted reforms even as the French aristocracy grew stronger.

Louis XIV had left France with enlarged territories, an enormous debt, an unhappy populace, and a five-year-old great-grandson as his successor. The governing of France fell into the hands first of the regent, the duke of Orléans, whose good intentions were thwarted by his drunken and immoral behavior, and later of Cardinal Fleury (floo-REE), the king's minister. France pulled back from foreign adventures while commerce and trade expanded and the government promoted the growth of industry, especially in coal and textiles. The budget was even balanced for a while. When Fleury died in 1743, Louis XV (1715–1774) decided to rule alone. But Louis was both lazy and weak, and ministers and mistresses soon began to influence the king, control the affairs of state, and undermine the prestige of the monarchy. One mistress—probably the most famous of eighteenth-century Europe—was Madame de Pompadour (ma-DAM duh POM-puh-door). An intelligent and beautiful woman, she charmed Louis XV and gained both wealth and power, often making important government decisions and giving advice on appointments and foreign policy. The loss of an empire in the Seven Years' War,

accompanied by burdensome taxes, an ever-mounting public debt, more hungry people, and a court life at Versailles that remained frivolous and carefree, forced even Louis to recognize the growing disgust with his monarchy.

Perhaps all might not have been in vain if Louis had been succeeded by a competent king. But the new king, Louis's twenty-year-old grandson who became Louis XVI (1774–1792), knew little about the operations of the French government and lacked the energy to deal decisively with state affairs (see the box on p. 545). His wife, Marie Antoinette (ma-REE ahn-twahn-NET), was a spoiled Austrian princess who devoted much of her time to court intrigues (see the Film & History feature on p. 546). As France's financial crises worsened, neither Louis nor his queen seemed able to fathom the depths of despair and discontent that soon led to violent revolution (see Chapter 19).

GREAT BRITAIN: KING AND PARLIAMENT The success of the Glorious Revolution in England had prevented absolutism without clearly inaugurating constitutional monarchy. The eighteenth-century British political system was characterized by a sharing of power between king and Parliament, with Parliament gradually gaining the upper hand. (The United Kingdom of Great Britain came into existence in 1707 when the governments of England and Scotland were united; the term *British* came to refer to both English and Scots.) The king chose ministers responsible to himself who set policy and guided Parliament; Parliament had the power to make laws, levy taxes, pass the budget, and indirectly influence the king's ministers. The eighteenth-century British Parliament was dominated by a landed aristocracy that historians usually divide into two groups: the peers, who sat for life in the House of Lords, and the landed gentry, who sat in the House of Commons and served as justices of the peace in the counties. The two groups had much in common: both were landowners with similar economic interests, and they frequently intermarried.

The British House of Commons. A sharing of power between king and Parliament characterized the British political system in the eighteenth century. Parliament was divided into the House of Lords and the House of Commons. This painting shows the House of Commons in session in 1793 during a debate over the possibility of war with France. William Pitt the Younger is addressing the House.

The French King's Bedtime

Louis XIV had used court etiquette to magnify the dignity of kingship. During the reign of Louis XVI (1774–1792), however, court etiquette degenerated to ludicrous depths. This excerpt from the *Memoirs of the Comtesse de Boigne* describes the king's *coucher,* the formal ceremony in which the king retired for the night.

Comtesse de Boigne, *Memoirs*

The king [Louis XVI] went to his *coucher.* The so-called *coucher* took place every evening at half past nine. The gentlemen of the court assembled in the bedroom of Louis XVI (but Louis XVI did not sleep there). I believe that all those who had been presented at court were permitted to attend.

The king came in from an adjoining room, followed by his domestic staff. His hair was in curlers, and he was not wearing his decorations. Without paying attention to anybody, he stepped behind the handrail surrounding the bed, and the chaplain on duty was given the prayer book and a tall taperstand with two candles by one of the valets. He then joined the king behind the handrail, handed him the book, and held the taperstand during the king's prayer, which was short. The king then went to the part of the room where the courtiers were, and the chaplain gave the taperstand back to the first valet who, in turn, took it over to a person indicated by the king. This person held it as long as the *coucher* lasted. This distinction was very much sought after....

The king had his coat, vest and finally shirt removed. He was naked to the waist, scratching and rubbing himself as if alone, though he was in the presence of the whole court and often a number of distinguished foreigners.

The first valet handed the nightshirt to the most qualified person.... If it was a person with whom the king was on familiar terms, he often played little tricks before donning it, missed it, passed it, and ran away, accompanying this charming nonsense with hearty laughter, making those who were sincerely attached to him suffer. Having donned the nightshirt, he put on his robe and three valets unfastened the belt and the knee buckles of his trousers, which fell down to his feet. Thus attired, hardly able to walk so absurdly encumbered, he began to make the round of the circle.

The duration of this reception was by no means fixed; sometimes it lasted only a few minutes, sometimes almost an hour; it depended on who was there.... When the king had enough, he dragged himself backward to an easy chair which had been pushed to the middle of the room and fell heavily into it, raising both legs. Two pages on their knees seized his shoes, took them off, and dropped them on the floor with a thump, which was part of the etiquette. When he heard it, the doorman opened the door and said, "This way, gentlemen." Everybody left, and the ceremony was over. However, the person who held the taperstand was permitted to stay if he had anything special to say to the king. This explains the high price attached to this strange favor.

Q What does this account reveal about the condition of the French monarchy and the high French aristocracy during the reign of Louis XVI?

The deputies to the House of Commons were chosen from the boroughs and counties, but not by popular voting. Who was eligible to vote in the boroughs varied wildly, enabling wealthy landed aristocrats to gain support by **patronage** and bribery; the result was a number of "pocket boroughs" controlled by a single person (hence "in his pocket"). The duke of Newcastle, for example, controlled the representatives from seven boroughs. It has been estimated that out of 405 borough deputies, 293 were chosen by fewer than 500 voters. This aristocratic control also extended to the county delegates, two from each of England's forty counties. Although all holders of property worth at least 40 shillings a year could vote, members of the leading landed gentry families were elected over and over again.

In 1714, a new dynasty—the Hanoverians—was established. When the last Stuart ruler, Queen Anne, died without an heir, the crown was offered to the Protestant rulers of the German state of Hanover. Because the first Hanoverian king, George I (1714–1727), did not speak English and neither he nor George II (1727–1760) had much familiarity with the British system, their chief ministers were allowed to handle Parliament. Many historians believe that this exercise of ministerial power was an important step in the development of the modern cabinet system in British government.

Robert Walpole served as prime minister from 1721 to 1742 and pursued a peaceful foreign policy to avoid new land taxes. But new forces were emerging in eighteenth-century England as growing trade and industry led an ever-increasing middle class to favor expansion of trade and world empire. The exponents of empire found a spokesman in William Pitt the Elder, who became prime minister in 1757 and furthered imperial ambitions by acquiring Canada and India in the Seven Years' War.

Despite his successes, Pitt the Elder was dismissed in 1761 by the new king, George III (1760–1820), and replaced by the king's favorite, Lord Bute. Discontent over the electoral system, however, and the loss of the American colonies (see Chapter 19) led to public criticism of the king. In 1780, the House of Commons affirmed

Marie Antoinette (2006)

The film *Marie Antoinette* (2006), directed by Sofia Coppola, is based on Antonia Fraser's interpretation of the early life of Marie Antoinette in her book, *Marie Antoinette: A Journey* (2001). The film begins with the marriage of Marie Antoinette (Kirsten Dunst), the daughter of Empress Maria Theresa of Austria (Marianne Faithful), to the dauphin Louis (Jason Schwartzman), the heir to the French throne. Four years later, in 1774, Marie Antoinette became queen of France; in 1793, she went to the guillotine. Although the Revolution and financial troubles of the monarchy briefly enter the film toward the end, the majority of the film focuses on the experiences of a young woman thrust into the court of Versailles where she faces increasing suspicion, frustration, and isolation.

Marie Antoinette (Kirsten Dunst) at Versailles.

Perhaps the best part of the film is the portrayal of court life at Versailles. The film depicts days filled with courtly ceremonies, daily mass, and attendance of the public at meals. Under intense scrutiny due to her Austrian heritage and unfamiliar with the protocol of life at Versailles, Marie Antoinette makes several early missteps. She refuses to speak to Louis XV's mistress, the comtesse du Barry (Asia Argento), because the comtesse threatens Marie Antoinette's position as the highest-ranking woman at court. Ignoring the king's mistress, however, places the young dauphine in the precarious position of appearing to insult the king.

In addition to her troubles at court, Marie Antoinette faces an even greater challenge: the need to secure her place by producing an heir to the French throne. But her young husband, whose interests include hunting, lock making, and reading, creates problems for the young couple. Their marriage is not consummated for seven years. During these years, Marie Antoinette faces increasing pressure from her mother, who has produced sixteen children while ruling the Austrian Empire. Bored but aware that she must remain chaste, the young dauphine turns to frivolous pursuits including games, plays, outings in Paris, decorating, gambling, and above all, purchasing clothes. Marie Antoinette's desire for elaborate gowns is encouraged by her role as the taste maker for the French court. In 1782, she

commissions ninety-three gowns made of silk and other expensive fabrics. The scene of Marie Antoinette's twenty-first birthday is particularly effective in conveying how her frustration and boredom have led her to a life of frivolity and luxury. Sitting in her finery, she plays cards and eats sweets until the early hours of the morning.

After the birth of her children, the first in 1777, Marie Antoinette begins to withdraw from the scrutiny of the court. In 1783, she is given the keys to the Petit Trianon, a small palace on the grounds of Versailles, where she spends most of her days. Although she is spending more time with her children and less on the frivolity of her earlier days at Versailles, her increasing estrangement from the court only worsens her reputation with the French public.

Filmed at Versailles, the film captures the grandeur and splendor of eighteenth-century royal life. But the movie did not receive favorable reviews when it opened in France, in part because of its use of contemporary music by artists such as The Cure and The Strokes and the inclusion of modern products such as Converse sneakers. Although the flurry of costumes and music can be distracting, they also convey the rebelliousness of a young woman, frustrated and bored, isolated, and yet always on display.

that "the influence of the crown has increased, is increasing, and ought to be diminished." King George III managed to avoid drastic change by appointing William Pitt the Younger (1759–1806), son of William Pitt the Elder, as prime minister in 1783. Supported by the merchants, industrial classes, and the king, Pitt managed

to stay in power. George III, however, remained an uncertain supporter because of periodic bouts of insanity (he once mistook a tree in Windsor Park for the king of Prussia). Nevertheless, thanks to Pitt's successes, serious reform of the corrupt parliamentary system was avoided for another generation.

France	
Louis XV	1715–1774
Louis XVI	1774–1792
Great Britain	
George I	1714–1727
George II	1727–1760
Robert Walpole	1721–1742
William Pitt the Elder	1757–1761
George III	1760–1820
William Pitt the Younger	1783–1801

THE DECLINE OF THE DUTCH REPUBLIC   After its century in the sun, the Dutch Republic or United Netherlands suffered a decline in economic prosperity. Both local and national political affairs were dominated by the oligarchies that governed the Dutch Republic's towns. In the eighteenth century, the struggle continued between these oligarchs (or regents, as they were called, from their governing positions) and the house of Orange, who as stadholders headed the executive branch of government. The regents sought to reduce the power of the Orangists but soon became divided when Dutch burghers who called themselves the Patriots (artisans, merchants, and shopkeepers) began to agitate for democratic reforms that would open up the municipal councils to greater participation than that of the oligarchs. The success of the Patriots, however, led to foreign interference when the Prussian king sent troops to protect his sister, the wife of the Orangist stadholder. The Patriots were crushed, and both Orangists and regents reestablished the old system. The intervention by Prussia serves to remind us of the growing power of the central European states.

Absolutism in Central and Eastern Europe

Of the five major European states, three were located in central and eastern Europe and came to play an increasingly important role in European international politics (see Map 18.1).

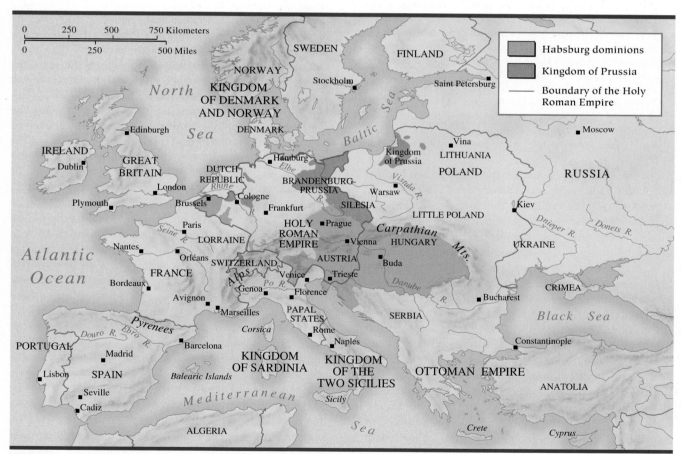

MAP 18.1   Europe in 1763. By the middle of the eighteenth century, five major powers dominated Europe—Prussia, Austria, Russia, Britain, and France. Each sought to enhance its power both domestically, through a bureaucracy that collected taxes and ran the military, and internationally, by capturing territory or preventing other powers from doing so.

Q *Given the distribution of Prussian and Habsburg holdings, in what areas of Europe were they most likely to compete for land and power?*

PRUSSIA: THE ARMY AND THE BUREAUCRACY Two able Prussian kings in the eighteenth century, Frederick William I and Frederick II, further developed the two major institutions—the army and the bureaucracy—that were the backbone of Prussia. Frederick William I (1713–1740) promoted the evolution of Prussia's highly efficient civil bureaucracy by establishing the General Directory. It served as the chief administrative agent of the central government, supervising military, police, economic, and financial affairs. Frederick William strove to maintain a highly efficient bureaucracy of civil service workers. It had its own code, in which the supreme values were obedience, honor, and service to the king as the highest duty. As Frederick William asserted, "One must serve the king with life and limb, with goods and chattels, with honor and conscience, and surrender everything except salvation. The latter is reserved for God. But everything else must be mine."[2] For his part, Frederick William personally kept a close watch over his officials to ensure that they performed their duties. As the Saxon minister at Berlin related:

> Every day His Majesty gives new proofs of his justice. Walking recently at Potsdam at six in the morning, he saw a post-coach arrive with several passengers who knocked for a long time at the post-house which was still closed. The King, seeing that no one opened the door, joined them in knocking and even knocked in some window-panes. The master of the post then opened the door and scolded the travelers, for no one recognized the King. But His Majesty let himself be known by giving the official some good blows of his cane and drove him from his house and his job after apologizing to the travelers for his laziness. Examples of this sort, of which I could relate several others, make everybody alert and exact.[3]

Close personal supervision of the bureaucracy became a hallmark of the eighteenth-century Prussian rulers.

Under Frederick William I, the rigid class stratification that had emerged in seventeenth-century Brandenburg-Prussia persisted. The nobility or landed aristocracy known as Junkers, who owned large estates with many serfs, still played a dominating role in the Prussian state. The Junkers held a complete monopoly over the officer corps of the Prussian army, which Frederick William passionately continued to expand. By the end of his reign, the army had grown from 45,000 to 83,000 men. Though tenth in geographic area and thirteenth in population among the European states, Prussia had the fourth largest army, after France, Russia, and Austria.

By using nobles as officers, Frederick William ensured a close bond between the nobility and the army and, in turn, the loyalty of the nobility to the absolute monarch. As officers, the Junker nobility became imbued with a sense of service to the king or state. All the virtues of the Prussian nobility were, in effect, military virtues: duty, obedience, sacrifice. At the same time, because of its size and reputation as one of the best armies in Europe, the Prussian army was the most important institution in the state. "Prussian militarism" became synonymous with the extreme exaltation of military virtues. Indeed, one

Prussian minister around 1800 remarked that "Prussia was not a country with an army, but an army with a country which served as headquarters and food magazine."[4]

The remaining classes in Prussia were considerably less important than the nobility. The peasants were born on their lords' estates and spent most of the rest of their lives there or in the army. They had few real rights and even needed their Junker's permission to marry. For the middle class, the only opportunity for any social prestige was in the Prussian civil service, where the ideal of loyal service to the state became a hallmark of the middle-class official. Frederick William allowed and even encouraged men of nonnoble birth to serve in important administrative posts. When he died in 1740, only three of his eighteen privy councillors were nobles.

Frederick II, known as the Great (1740–1786), was one of the best-educated and most cultured monarchs in the eighteenth century. He was well versed in Enlightenment thought and even invited Voltaire to live at his court for several years. His intellectual interests were despised by his father, who forced his intelligent son to prepare for a career in ruling (see the box on p. 550). A believer in the king as the "first servant of the state," Frederick the Great became a conscientious ruler who made few innovations in the administration of the state. His diligence in overseeing its operation, however, made the Prussian bureaucracy well known for both its efficiency and its honesty.

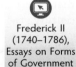

Frederick II (1740–1786), Essays on Forms of Government

For a time, Frederick seemed quite willing to follow the philosophes' recommendations for reform. He established a single code of laws for his territories that eliminated the use of torture except in treason and murder cases. He also granted limited freedom of speech and press as well as complete religious toleration—no difficult task since he had no strong religious convictions. Although Frederick was well aware of the philosophes' condemnation of serfdom, he was too dependent on the Prussian nobility to interfere with it or with the hierarchical structure of Prussian society. In fact, Frederick was a social conservative who made Prussian society even more aristocratic than it had been before. Frederick reversed his father's policy of allowing commoners to rise to power in the civil service and reserved the higher positions in the bureaucracy for members of the nobility. The upper ranks of the bureaucracy came close to constituting a hereditary caste over time.

Like his predecessors, Frederick the Great took a great interest in military affairs and enlarged the Prussian army (to 200,000 men). Unlike his predecessors, he had no objection to using it. Frederick did not hesitate to take advantage of a succession crisis in the Habsburg monarchy to seize the Austrian province of Silesia for Prussia. This act aroused Austria's bitter hostility and embroiled Frederick in two major wars, the War of the Austrian Succession and the Seven Years' War (see "Wars and Diplomacy" later in this chapter). Although the latter war left his country exhausted, Frederick succeeded in keeping Silesia.

After the wars, the first partition of Poland with Austria and Russia in 1772 gave him the Polish territory between Prussia and Brandenburg, bringing greater unity to the scattered lands of Prussia. By the end of his reign, Prussia was recognized as a great European power.

THE AUSTRIAN EMPIRE OF THE HABSBURGS The Austrian Empire had become one of the great European states by the beginning of the eighteenth century. The city of Vienna, center of the Habsburg monarchy, was filled with magnificent palaces and churches built in the Baroque style and became the music capital of Europe. And yet Austria, a sprawling empire composed of many different nationalities, languages, religions, and cultures, found it difficult to provide common laws and a centralized administration for its people.

Empress Maria Theresa (1740–1780), however, stunned by the loss of Austrian Silesia to Prussia in the War of the Austrian Succession, resolved to reform her empire in preparation for the seemingly inevitable next conflict with rival Prussia. Maria Theresa curtailed the role of the diets or provincial assemblies in taxation and local administration. Now clergy and nobles were forced to pay property and income taxes to royal officials rather than the diets. The Austrian and Bohemian lands were divided into ten provinces and subdivided into districts, all administered by royal officials rather than representatives of the diets, making part of the Austrian Empire more centralized and more bureaucratic. But these administrative reforms were done for practical reasons—to strengthen the power of the Habsburg state—and were accompanied by an enlargement and modernization of the armed forces.

Maria Theresa remained staunchly Catholic and conservative and was not open to the wider reform calls of the philosophes. But her successor was.

Joseph II (1780–1790) was determined to make changes; at the same time, he carried on his mother's chief goal of enhancing Habsburg power within the monarchy and Europe. Joseph was an earnest man who believed in the need to sweep away anything standing in the path of reason. As he expressed it, "I have made philosophy the lawmaker of my empire; her logical applications are going to transform Austria."

Joseph's reform program was far-reaching. He abolished serfdom and tried to give the peasants hereditary rights to their holdings. A new penal code was instituted that abrogated the death penalty and established the principle of equality of all before the law. Joseph introduced drastic religious reforms as well, including complete religious toleration and restrictions on the Catholic Church. Altogether, Joseph II issued 6,000 decrees and 11,000 laws in his effort to transform Austria.

Frederick II at Sans-Souci. Frederick II was one of the most cultured and best-educated European monarchs. In this painting, he is shown (holding a walking stick) visiting the building site of his residential retreat, Sans-Souci, at Potsdam, accompanied by the marquis of Argens.

Maria Theresa and Her Family. Maria Theresa governed the vast possessions of the Austrian Empire from 1740 to 1780. Of her ten surviving children, Joseph II (shown here in red standing beside his mother) succeeded her; Leopold became grand-duke of Tuscany and the ruler of Austria after Joseph's death; Ferdinand was made duke of Modena; and Marie Antoinette became the bride of King Louis XVI of France.

Frederick the Great and His Father

As a young man, the future Frederick the Great was quite different from his strict and austere father, Frederick William I. Possessing a high regard for French culture, poetry, and flute playing, Frederick resisted his father's wishes that he immerse himself in governmental and military affairs. Eventually, Frederick capitulated to his father's will and accepted the need to master affairs of state. These letters, written when Frederick was sixteen, illustrate the difficulties in their relationship.

⊷ ⬥⬥ ⊷

Frederick to His Father, Frederick William I (September 11, 1728)

I have not ventured for a long time to present myself before my dear papa, partly because I was advised against it, but chiefly because I anticipated an even worse reception than usual and feared to vex my dear papa still further by the favor I have now to ask; so I have preferred to put it in writing.

I beg my dear papa that he will be kindly disposed toward me. I do assure him that after long examination of my conscience I do not find the slightest thing with which to reproach myself; but if, against my wish and will, I have vexed my dear papa, I hereby beg most humbly for forgiveness, and hope that my dear papa will give over the fearful hate which has appeared so plainly in his whole behavior and to which I cannot accustom myself. I have always thought hitherto that I had a kind father, but now I see the contrary. However, I will take courage and hope that my dear papa will think this all over and take me again into his favor. Meantime I assure him that I will never, my life long, willingly fail him, and in spite of his disfavor I am

still, with most dutiful and childlike respect, my dear papa's

> Most obedient and faithful servant and son,
> Frederick

Frederick William to His Son Frederick

A bad, obstinate boy, who does not love his father; for when one does one's best, and especially when one loves one's father, one does what he wishes not only when he is standing by but when he is not there to see. Moreover you know very well that I cannot stand an effeminate fellow who has no manly tastes, who cannot ride or shoot (to his shame be it said!), is untidy about his person, and wears his hair curled like a fool instead of cutting it; and that I have condemned all these things a thousand times, and yet there is no sign of improvement. For the rest, haughty, offish as a country lout, conversing with none but a favored few instead of being affable and popular, grimacing like a fool, and never following my wishes out of love for me but only when forced into it, caring for nothing but to have his own way, and thinking nothing else is of any importance. This is my answer. ⇗

> Frederick William

Q Based on these documents, why was the relationship between Frederick II and his father such a difficult one? What does this troubled relationship tell you about the effects of rulership on the great kings of Europe and their families? What new duties and concerns of monarchs (like Frederick William) may have reshaped relations between kings and sons?

Joseph's reform program proved overwhelming for Austria, however. He alienated the nobility by freeing the serfs and alienated the church by his attacks on the monastic establishment. Even the serfs were unhappy, unable to comprehend the drastic changes inherent in Joseph's policies. His attempt to rationalize the administration of the empire by imposing German as the official bureaucratic language alienated the non-German nationalities. As Joseph complained, there were not enough people for the kind of bureaucracy he needed. His deep sense of failure is revealed in the epitaph he wrote for his gravestone: "Here lies Joseph II, who was unfortunate in everything that he undertook." His successors undid many of his reform efforts.

RUSSIA UNDER CATHERINE THE GREAT The six successors to Peter the Great of Russia all fell under the thumb of the palace guard. The last of these six was Peter III, whose German wife, Catherine, learned Russian and won the favor of the guard. When Peter was murdered by

a faction of nobles, Catherine II the Great (1762–1796) emerged as autocrat of all Russia.

Catherine was an intelligent woman who was familiar with the works of the philosophes. She claimed that she wished to reform Russia along the lines of Enlightenment ideas, but she was always shrewd enough to realize that her success depended on the support of the palace guard and the gentry class from which it stemmed. She could not afford to alienate the Russian nobility (see the box on p. 551).

Initially, Catherine seemed eager to pursue reform. She called for the election of an assembly in 1767 to debate the details of a new law code. In her *Instruction*, written as a guide to the deliberations, Catherine questioned the institutions of serfdom, torture, and capital punishment and even advocated the principle of the equality of all people in the eyes of the law. But a year and a half of negotiation produced little real change.

In fact, Catherine's subsequent policies had the effect of strengthening the landholding class at the expense of

Enlightened Absolutism: Enlightened or Absolute?

Although historians have used the term *enlightened absolutism* to describe a new type of monarchy in the eighteenth century, scholars have recently questioned the usefulness of the concept. The three selections below offer an opportunity to evaluate one so-called enlightened monarch, Catherine the Great of Russia. The first selection is from a letter written by the baron de Breteuil, the French ambassador to Russia, giving his impressions of Catherine. In 1767, Catherine convened a legislative commission to prepare a new code of laws for Russia. In her *Instruction,* parts of which form the second selection, she gave the delegates a detailed guide to the principles they should follow. Although the guidelines were culled from the liberal ideas of the philosophes, the commission itself accomplished nothing. The third selection, from a Decree on Serfs (also issued in 1767), reveals Catherine's authoritarian nature.

Letter of the Baron de Breteuil

[Catherine] seems to combine every kind of ambition in her person. Everything that may add luster to her reign will have some attraction for her. Science and the arts will be encouraged to flourish in the empire, projects useful for the domestic economy will be undertaken. She will endeavor to reform the administration of justice and to invigorate the laws; but her policies will be based on Machiavellianism; and I should not be surprised if in this field she rivals the king of Prussia. She will adopt the prejudices of her entourage regarding the superiority of her power and will endeavor to win respect not by the sincerity and probity of her actions but also by an ostentatious display of her strength. Haughty as she is, she will stubbornly pursue her undertakings and will rarely retrace a false step. Cunning and falsity appear to be vices in her character; woe to him who puts too much trust in her.

Catherine II, Proposals for a New Law Code

13. What is the true End of Monarchy? Not to deprive People of their natural Liberty; but to correct their Actions, in order to attain the supreme good....

33. The Laws ought to be so framed, as to secure the Safety of every Citizen as much as possible.

34. The Equality of the Citizens consists in this; that they should all be subject to the same Laws....

123. The Usage of Torture is contrary to all the Dictates of Nature and Reason; even Mankind itself cries out against it, and demands loudly the total Abolition of it....

180. That Law, therefore, is highly beneficial to the Community where it is established, which ordains that every Man be judged by his Peers and Equals. For when the Fate of a Citizen is in Question, all Prejudices arising from the Difference of Rank or Fortune should be stifled; because they ought to have no Influence between the Judges and the Parties accused....

194. No Man ought to be looked upon as guilty, before he has received his judicial Sentence; nor can the Laws deprive him of their Protection, before it is proved that he has forfeited all Right to it. What Right therefore can Power give to any to inflict Punishment upon a Citizen at a Time, when it is yet dubious, whether he is Innocent or guilty?

Catherine II, Decree on Serfs

The Governing Senate . . . has deemed it necessary to make known that the landlords' serfs and peasants . . . owe their landlords proper submission and absolute obedience in all matters, according to the laws that have been enacted from time immemorial by the autocratic forefathers of Her Imperial Majesty and which have not been repealed, and which provide that all persons who dare to incite serfs and peasants to disobey their landlords shall be arrested and taken to the nearest government office, there to be punished forthwith as disturbers of the public tranquillity, according to the laws and without leniency. And should it so happen that even after the publication of the present decree of Her Imperial Majesty any serfs and peasants should cease to give the proper obedience to their landlords . . . and should make bold to submit unlawful petitions complaining of their landlords, and especially to petition Her Imperial Majesty personally, then both those who make the complaints and those who write up the petitions shall be punished by the knout and forthwith deported to Nerchinsk to penal servitude for life and shall be counted as part of the quota of recruits which their landlords must furnish to the army. ⮞

Q What impressions of Catherine do you get from the letter by the French ambassador to Russia? To what extent were the ideas expressed in the proposals for a new law code taken from the writings of the philosophes? What does the decree on serfs reveal about Catherine's view of power? Based on these documents, was Catherine an enlightened monarch? Why or why not?

all others, especially the Russian serfs. To reorganize local government, Catherine divided Russia into fifty provinces, each of which was in turn subdivided into districts ruled by officials chosen by the nobles. In this way, the local nobility became responsible for the day-to-day governing of Russia. Moreover, the gentry were now formed into corporate groups with special legal privileges, including the right to trial by peers and exemption from personal taxation and corporal punishment. The Charter of the Nobility formalized these rights in 1785.

Catherine's policy of favoring the landed nobility led to even worse conditions for the Russian peasantry. The government's attempt to impose restrictions on free peasants in the border districts of the Russian Empire soon led to a full-scale revolt that spread to the Volga valley. It was intensified by the support of the Cossacks, independent tribes of fierce warriors who had at times fought for the Russians against the Turks but now resisted the government's attempt to absorb them into the empire.

An illiterate Cossack, Emelyan Pugachev (yim-yil-YAHN poo-guh-CHAWF), succeeded in welding the disparate elements of discontent into a mass revolt. Beginning in 1773, Pugachev's rebellion spread across southern Russia from the Urals to the Volga River. Initially successful, Pugachev won the support of many peasants when he issued a manifesto in July 1774 freeing all peasants from oppressive taxes and military service. Encouraged by Pugachev to seize their landlords' estates, the peasants responded by killing more than fifteen hundred estate owners and their families. The rebellion soon faltered, however, as government forces rallied and became more effective. Betrayed by his own subordinates, Pugachev was captured, tortured, and executed. The rebellion collapsed completely, and Catherine responded with even greater repression of the peasantry. All rural reform was halted, and serfdom was expanded into newer parts of the empire.

Pugachev's Rebellion

Catherine proved a worthy successor to Peter the Great by expanding Russia's territory westward into Poland and southward to the Black Sea. Russia spread southward by defeating the Ottoman Turks. In the Treaty of Kuchuk-Kainarji (koo-CHOOK-ky-NAR-jee) in 1774, the Russians gained some land and the privilege of protecting Greek Orthodox Christians in the Ottoman Empire. Russian expansion westward occurred at the expense of neighboring Poland. In the three partitions of Poland, Russia gained about 50 percent of Polish territory.

THE DESTRUCTION OF POLAND Poland was an excellent example of why a strong monarchy was needed in early

CHRONOLOGY Central and Eastern Europe

Prussia	
Frederick William I	1713–1740
Frederick II the Great	1740–1786
Austrian Empire	
Maria Theresa	1740–1780
Joseph II	1780–1790
Russia	
Catherine II the Great	1762–1796
Pugachev's rebellion	1773–1775
Charter of the Nobility	1785
Poland	
First partition	1772
Second partition	1793
Third partition	1795

modern Europe. The Polish king was elected by the Polish nobles and forced to accept drastic restrictions on his power, including limited revenues, a small bureaucracy, and a standing army of no more than 20,000 soldiers. For Polish nobles, these limitations eliminated an absolute king; for Poland's powerful neighbors, they were an invitation to meddle in its affairs.

The total destruction of the Polish state in the eighteenth century resulted from the rivalries of its three great neighbors, Austria, Russia, and Prussia. To avoid war, the leaders of these powers decided to compensate themselves by dividing Poland. To maintain the balance of power in central and eastern Europe, the three great powers cynically agreed to the acquisition of roughly equal territories at Poland's expense.

In 1772, Poland lost about 30 percent of its land and 50 percent of its population (see Map 18.2). Austria gained the agriculturally rich district of Galicia, Russia took the largest slice of land in eastern Poland, and Prussia acquired West Prussia, the smallest but most valuable territory because it united two of the chief sections of Prussia.

The remaining Polish state was supposedly independent; in truth, it was dominated by the Russians, who even kept troops on Polish territory. After the Poles attempted to establish a stronger state under a hereditary monarchy in 1791, the Russians gained the support of Austria and Prussia and intervened militarily in May 1792. In the following year, Russia and Prussia undertook a second partition of Polish territory. Finally, after a heroic but hopeless rebellion in 1794–1795 under General Thaddeus Kosciuszko (tah-DAY-oosh kaw-SHOOS-koh), the remaining Polish state was obliterated by Austria, Prussia, and Russia in the third partition of Poland (1795). Many historians have pointed to Poland's demise as a cogent example of why building a strong, absolutist state was essential to survival in the seventeenth and eighteenth centuries.

The Mediterranean World

At the beginning of the eighteenth century, Spain experienced a change of dynasties from the Habsburgs to the Bourbons. Bourbon rule temporarily rejuvenated Spain and at least provided an opportunity to centralize the institutions of the state. Under Philip V (1700–1746), the laws, administrative institutions, and language of Castile were established in the other Spanish kingdoms, making the king of Castile truly the king of Spain. Moreover, French-style ministries replaced the old conciliar system of government, and officials similar to French *intendants* were introduced into the various Spanish provinces.

Since the Treaty of Utrecht in 1713 had taken the Italian territories and the Netherlands away from Spain, the latter now had fewer administrative problems and less drain on its already overtaxed economic resources. In the second half of the eighteenth century, especially during the reign of Charles III (1759–1788), the Catholic Church was also brought under royal control when the king banished the

CHRONOLOGY The Mediterranean World and Scandinavia

Spain	
Philip V, the first Bourbon king	1700–1746
Charles III	1759–1788
Portugal	
Marquis of Pombal	1750–1777
Sweden	
Charles XII	1697–1718
Gustavus III	1771–1792
Denmark	
Christian VII	1766–1808

Jesuits and circumscribed the activities of the Inquisition. The landed aristocracy continued to exercise substantial power throughout the eighteenth century, however.

PORTUGAL Portugal had experienced decline since the glorious days of empire in the sixteenth century. Nevertheless, during the long ministry of the marquis of Pombal (mar-KEE duh pum-BAHL) (1750–1777), who served as chief minister to a series of Portuguese kings, the nobility and Catholic Church were curtailed and the Portuguese Empire temporarily revived. After Pombal was removed from office, the nobility and church regained much of their power.

THE ITALIAN STATES After the Treaty of Utrecht, Austria had replaced Spain as the dominant force in Italy in the eighteenth century. The duchy of Milan, Sardinia, and the kingdom of Naples were all surrendered to the Habsburg emperors, and Sicily was given to the northern Italian state of Savoy, which was slowly emerging as a state with an appetite for territorial expansion. In 1734, the Bourbons of Spain reestablished control over Naples and Sicily. Though some Italian states, such as Venice and Genoa, remained independent, they grew increasingly impotent in international affairs.

MAP 18.2 The Partitioning of Poland. Crowded by three great powers, Poland lay primarily on a plain with few easily defensible borders. This fact, combined with a weak and ineffectual monarchy, set the stage for Poland's destruction. By 1795, Austria, Prussia (Germany in 1870), and Russia had long borders with each other, a situation that would contribute to the outbreak of World War I in 1914.

Q *Which country gained the most territory at the expense of Poland?*

The Scandinavian States

In the seventeenth century, Sweden had become the dominant power in northern Europe, but after the Battle of Poltava in 1709, Swedish power declined rapidly. Following the death of the powerful Charles XII in 1718, the Swedish nobility, using the Swedish diet as its instrument, gained control of public life and reduced the monarchy to puppet status. But the division of the nobility into pro-French and pro-Russian factions eventually enabled King Gustavus III (1771–1792) to reassert the power of the monarchy. Gustavus proved to be one of the most enlightened monarchs of his age. By decree, he established freedom of religion, speech, and press and instituted a new code of justice that eliminated the use of torture. Moreover, his economic reforms smacked of *laissez-faire:* he reduced tariffs, abolished tolls, and encouraged trade and agriculture. In 1792, however, a group of nobles, incensed at these reforms and their loss of power, assassinated the king, but they proved unable to fully restore the rule of the aristocracy.

Denmark also saw an attempt at enlightened reforms by King Christian VII (1766–1808) and his chief minister, John Frederick Struensee (SHTROO-un-zay). Aristocratic opposition stymied their efforts, however, and led to Struensee's death in 1772.

Enlightened Absolutism Revisited

Of the three major rulers traditionally associated most closely with enlightened absolutism—Joseph II, Frederick II, and Catherine the Great—only Joseph II sought truly radical changes based on Enlightenment ideas. Both Frederick and Catherine liked to be cast as disciples of the Enlightenment, expressed interest in enlightened reforms, and even attempted some, but the policies of neither seemed seriously affected by Enlightenment thought. Necessities of state and maintenance of the existing system took precedence over reform. Indeed, many historians feel that Joseph, Frederick, and Catherine were all guided primarily by a concern for the power and well-being of their states and that their policies were not all that different from those of their predecessors. In the final analysis, heightened state power was used to amass armies and wage wars to gain more power. Nevertheless, in their desire to build stronger state systems, these rulers did pursue such enlightened practices as legal reform, religious toleration, and the extension of education because these served to create more satisfied subjects and strengthened the state in significant ways.

It would be foolish, however, to overlook the fact that not only military but also political and social realities limited the ability of enlightened rulers to make reforms. Everywhere in Europe, the hereditary aristocracy still held the most power in society. Enlightened reforms were often limited to changes in the administrative and judicial systems that did not seriously undermine the powerful interests of the European nobility. Although aristocrats might join the populace in opposing monarchical extension of centralizing power, as the chief beneficiaries of a system based on traditional rights and privileges for their class, they were certainly not willing to support a political ideology that trumpeted the principle of equal rights for all.

Wars and Diplomacy

 FOCUS QUESTIONS: How did the concepts of "balance of power" and "reason of state" influence international relations in the eighteenth century? What were the causes and results of the Seven Years' War?

The philosophes condemned war as a foolish waste of life and resources in stupid quarrels of no value to humankind. Rulers, however, paid little attention to these comments and continued their costly struggles. By the eighteenth century, the European system of self-governing, individual states was grounded largely in the principle of self-interest. Because international relations were based on considerations of power, the eighteenth-century concept of a **balance of power** was predicated on how to counterbalance the power of one state by another to prevent any one state from dominating the others. This balance of power, however, did not imply a desire for peace. Large armies created to defend a state's security were often used for offensive purposes as well. As Frederick the Great of Prussia remarked, "The fundamental rule of governments is the principle of extending their territories." Nevertheless, the regular use of diplomacy served at times to lead to compromise.

The diplomacy of the eighteenth century still focused primarily on dynastic interests, or the desire of ruling families to provide for their dependents and extend their dynastic holdings. But the eighteenth century also saw the emergence of the concept of **reason of state,** on the basis of which a ruler such as Frederick II and a minister such as William Pitt the Elder looked beyond dynastic interests to the long-term future of their states.

International rivalry and the continuing centralization of the European states were closely related. The need for money to support the new standing armies, navies, and weapons of war that had originated in the seventeenth century created its own imperative for more efficient and effective control of power in the hands of bureaucrats who could collect taxes and organize states for the task of winning wars. At the same time, the development of large standing armies ensured that political disputes would periodically be resolved by armed conflict rather than diplomacy. Between 1715 and 1740, it had seemed that Europe preferred peace. But in 1740, a major conflict erupted over the succession to the Austrian throne.

The War of the Austrian Succession (1740–1748)

Unable to produce a male heir to the Austrian throne, the Habsburg emperor Charles VI (1711–1740) so feared the consequences of the succession of his daughter Maria Theresa that he spent much of his reign negotiating the Pragmatic Sanction, by which different European powers agreed to recognize his daughter as his legal heir.

After Charles's death, however, the Pragmatic Sanction was conveniently pushed aside, especially by Frederick II, who had just succeeded to the throne of Prussia. The new Prussian ruler took advantage of the new empress to invade Austrian Silesia. The vulnerability of Maria Theresa encouraged France to enter the war against its traditional enemy Austria; in turn, Maria Theresa made an alliance with Great Britain, which feared French hegemony over Continental affairs. All too quickly, the Austrian succession had set off a worldwide conflagration. The war was fought not only in Europe, where Prussia seized Silesia and France occupied the Austrian Netherlands, but in the East, where France took Madras (now Chennai) in India from the British, and in North America, where the British captured the French fortress of Louisbourg at the entrance to the Saint Lawrence River. By 1748, all parties were exhausted and agreed to stop. The peace treaty of Aix-la-Chapelle (ex-lah-shah-PELL) promised the return of all occupied territories except Silesia to their original owners. Prussia's refusal to return Silesia guaranteed another war, at least between the two hostile central European powers of Prussia and Austria.

The Seven Years' War (1756–1763)

Maria Theresa refused to accept the loss of Silesia and prepared for its return by rebuilding her army while working diplomatically through her able foreign minister, Count Wenzel von Kaunitz (VENT-sul fun KOW-nits), to separate Prussia from its chief ally, France. In 1756, Austria achieved what was soon labeled a diplomatic revolution. Bourbon-Habsburg rivalry had been a fact of European diplomacy since the late sixteenth century. But two new rivalries made this old one seem superfluous: Britain and France over colonial empires, and Austria and Prussia over Silesia. France now abandoned Prussia and allied with Austria. Russia, which saw Prussia as a major hindrance to Russian goals in central Europe, joined the new alliance. In turn, Great Britain allied with Prussia. This diplomatic revolution of 1756 now led to another war, with three major areas of conflict: Europe, India, and North America (see Map 18.3). Indeed, the Seven Years' War could be seen, as some historians have argued, as the first world war.

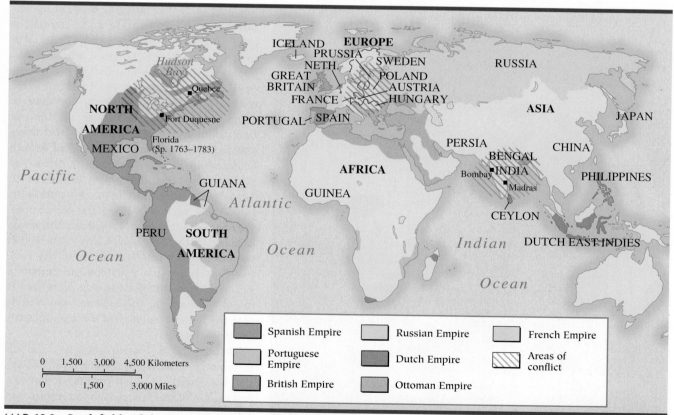

MAP 18.3 **Battlefields of the Seven Years' War.** A major struggle among the five great powers, the Seven Years' War was truly a worldwide conflict. In central Europe, Prussia survived against the combined forces of France, Austria, and Russia, while Britain emerged victorious against France in the struggle for empire, gaining control of French North America and India.

Q *Why were naval strength and ability important in the conflict between Britain and France?*

CONFLICT IN EUROPE Europe witnessed the clash of the two major alliances: the British and Prussians against the Austrians, Russians, and French. With his superb army and military prowess, Frederick the Great was able for some time to defeat the Austrian, French, and Russian armies. He won a spectacular victory at the Battle of Rossbach (RAWSS-bahkh) in Saxony (1757) over combined French-Austrian forces that far outnumbered his own troops. Under attack from three different directions, however, the forces of Frederick II were gradually worn down and faced utter defeat when they were saved by the death of Tsarina Elizabeth of Russia (1741–1762), which brought her nephew Peter III to power. A great admirer of Frederick the Great, Peter withdrew the Russian troops from the conflict and from the Prussian lands that they had occupied. His withdrawal guaranteed a stalemate and led to a desire for peace. The European conflict was ended by the Peace of Hubertusburg in 1763. All occupied territories were returned, and Austria officially recognized Prussia's permanent control of Silesia.

WAR IN INDIA The Anglo-French struggle in the rest of the world had more decisive results. Known as the Great

CHRONOLOGY The Mid-Century Wars

War of the Austrian Succession	1740–1748
Peace of Aix-la-Chapelle	1748
Seven Years' War	1756–1763
Diplomatic revolution	1756
Battle of Rossbach	1757
British capture of Forts Duquesne and Louisbourg	1758
Battle of Quebec	1759
Peace of Hubertusburg	1763
Treaty of Paris	1763

War for Empire, it was fought in India and North America. The French had returned Madras to Britain after the War of the Austrian Succession, but jockeying for power continued as the French and British supported opposing native Indian princes. The British under Robert Clive (1725–1774) ultimately won out, not because they had better forces but because they were more persistent (see the box on p. 557). By the Treaty of Paris in 1763, the French withdrew and left India to the British.

THE FRENCH AND INDIAN WAR By far the greatest conflicts of the Seven Years' War took place in North America, where it was known as the French and Indian War. There were two primary areas of contention. One consisted of the waterways of the Gulf of Saint Lawrence, guarded by the fortress of Louisbourg and by forts near the Great Lakes and Lake Champlain that protected French Quebec and French traders. The other was the unsettled Ohio River valley. As the French moved south from the Great Lakes and north from their garrisons along the Mississippi, they began to establish forts from the Appalachians to the Mississippi River. To British settlers in the thirteen colonies to the east, this French activity threatened to cut off a vast area from British expansion. The French found allies among the Indians, who considered the French traders less threatening than the British settlers.

Despite initial French successes, British fortunes were revived by the efforts of William Pitt the Elder, who was convinced that the destruction of the French colonial empire was a necessary prerequisite for the creation of Britain's own colonial empire. Accordingly, Pitt decided to make a minimal effort in Europe while concentrating resources, especially the British navy, on the colonial war. Although French troops were greater in number, the ability of the French to use them in the New

British Library, London//© Erich Lessing/Art Resource, NY

Robert Clive in India. Robert Clive was the leader of the army of the British East India Company. He had been commanded to fight the ruler of Bengal in order to gain trading privileges. After the Battle of Plassey in 1757, Clive and the East India Company took control of Bengal. In this painting by Edward Penny, Clive is shown receiving a grant of money for his injured soldiers from the local nabob or governor of Bengal.

British Victory in India

The success of the British against the French in India was due to Robert Clive, who, in this excerpt from one of his letters, describes his famous victory at Plassey, north of Calcutta, on June 23, 1757. This battle demonstrated the inability of native Indian soldiers to compete with Europeans and signified the beginning of British control in Bengal. Clive claimed to have a thousand Europeans, two thousand sepoys (local soldiers), and eight cannons available for this battle.

Robert Clive's Account of His Victory at Plassey

At daybreak we discovered the [governor's army] moving toward us, consisting, as we since found, of about fifteen thousand horse and thirty-five thousand foot, with upwards of forty pieces of cannon. They approached apace, and by six began to attack with a number of heavy cannon, supported by the whole army, and continued to play on us very briskly for several hours, during which our situation was of the utmost service to us, being lodged in a large grove with good mud banks. To succeed in an attempt on their cannon was next to impossible, as they were planted in a manner round us and at considerable distances from each other. We therefore remained quiet in our post, in expectation of a successful attack upon their camp at night. About noon the enemy drew off their artillery and retired to their camp....

On finding them make no great effort to dislodge us, we proceeded to take possession of one or two more eminences lying very near an angle of their camp, from whence, and an adjacent eminence in their possession, they kept a smart fire of musketry upon us. They made several attempts to bring out their cannon, but our advanced fieldpieces played so warmly and so well upon them that they were always driven back. Their horse exposing themselves a good deal on this occasion, many of them were killed, and among the rest four or five officers of the first distinction; by which the whole army being visibly dispirited and thrown into some confusion, we were encouraged to storm both the eminence and the angle of their camp, which were carried at the same instant, with little or no loss; though the latter was defended (exclusively of blacks) by forty French and two pieces of cannon; and the former by a large body of blacks, both horse and foot. On this a general rout ensued, and we pursued the enemy six miles, passing upwards of forty pieces of cannon they had abandoned, with an infinite number of carts and carriages filled with baggage of all kinds.... It is computed there are killed of the enemy about five hundred. Our loss amounted to only twenty-two killed and fifty wounded, and those chiefly blacks.

Q In what ways, if any, would Clive's account likely have been different if the Battle of Plassey had occurred in Europe? According to the letter, what role did native Indians seemingly play in the battle? Why does Clive give them such little mention?

World was contingent on naval support. The defeat of French fleets in major naval battles in 1759 gave the British an advantage since the French could no longer easily reinforce their garrisons. A series of British victories soon followed. Already in 1758, Forts Louisbourg and Duquesne had been captured. Then, on the night of September 13, 1759, British forces led by General James Wolfe scaled the heights outside Quebec and defeated the French under General Louis-Joseph Montcalm on the Plains of Abraham. Both generals died in the battle. The British went on to seize Montreal, the Great Lakes area, and the Ohio valley. The French were forced to make peace. By the Treaty of Paris, they ceded Canada and the lands east of the Mississippi to Britain. Their ally Spain transferred Spanish Florida to British control; in return, the French gave their Louisiana territory to the Spanish. By 1763, Great Britain had become the world's greatest colonial power.

Treaty of Paris (1763)

European Armies and Warfare

The professional standing army, initiated in the seventeenth century, became a standard feature of eighteenth-century Europe. Especially noticeable was the increase in the size of armies, which paralleled the development of absolutist states. Between 1740 and 1780, the French army grew from 190,000 to 300,000 men; the Prussian, from 83,000 to 200,000; the Austrian, from 108,000 to 282,000; and the Russian, from 130,000 to 290,000.

COMPOSITION OF ARMIES The composition of these armies reflected the hierarchical structure of European society and the great chasm that separated the upper and lower classes. Officers were primarily from the landed aristocracy, which had for centuries regarded military activity as one of its major functions. Middle-class individuals were largely kept out of the higher ranks of the officer corps while being admitted to the middle ranks.

Rank-and-file soldiers came mostly from the lower classes of society. Some states, such as Prussia and Russia, conscripted able-bodied peasants. But many states realized that this was counterproductive since they could not afford to waste their farmers. For that reason, eighteenth-century armies were partly composed of foreign troops, many from Switzerland or the petty German states. Of the great powers, Britain alone had no regular standing army and relied on mercenaries, evident in its use of German troops in America. Most troops in European armies, especially the French and Austrian, were natives who enlisted voluntarily for six-year terms. Some were not exactly volunteers; often vagabonds and the unemployed were pressed into service. Most, however, came from the lower classes—peasants and also artisans from the cities—who saw the military as an opportunity to escape from hard times or personal problems.

The maritime powers, such as Britain and the Dutch Republic, regarded navies as more important than armies. In the second half of the eighteenth century, the British possessed 174 warships manned by 80,000 sailors. Conditions on these ships were often poor. Diseases such as scurvy and yellow fever were rampant, and crews were frequently press-ganged into duty.

THE NATURE OF WARFARE The dramatic increase in the size of armies and navies did not necessarily result in more destructive warfare in eighteenth-century Europe. For one thing, war was no longer driven by ideology as the religious conflicts of the sixteenth and seventeenth centuries had been. By their very nature, ideological wars are often violent and destructive. Moreover, since the larger armies depended on increased tax revenues, rulers regarded the wanton destruction of civilian taxpayers as foolish. Finally, the costliness of eighteenth-century armies as well as the technology and tactical traditions of the age created a system of warfare based on limited objectives.

Since generals were extremely reluctant to risk the destruction of their armies in pitched battles, clever and elaborate maneuvers, rather than direct confrontation, became fashionable. A system of formalities accepted by all sides allowed defeated opponents to withdraw without being captured or destroyed. This mentality also encouraged the construction of vast fortresses to secure major roads and the enormous quantities of supplies needed by eighteenth-century armies. With its own set patterns of tactics, siege warfare often became, as one French critic said disgustedly, "the art of surrendering strongholds honorably after certain conventional formalities." Nevertheless, despite the maneuvering and the sieges, European warfare in the eighteenth century also involved many battles and considerable risk.

Economic Expansion and Social Change

Q **FOCUS QUESTION**: What changes occurred in agriculture, finance, industry, and trade during the eighteenth century?

The depressed economic conditions of the seventeenth century began to improve in the early eighteenth century. Rapid population growth, expansion in banking and trade, an agricultural revolution (at least in Britain), the stirrings

of industrialization, and an increase in worldwide trade characterized the economic patterns of the eighteenth century.

Growth of the European Population

Europe's population began to grow around 1750 and experienced a slow but steady rise, with some regional variations. It has been estimated that the total European population was around 120 million in 1700, expanded to 140 million by 1750, and grew to 190 million by 1790; thus, the growth rate in the second half of the century was double that of the first half. Individual states also experienced rapid growth between 1700 and 1790: Russia's population went from 14 million to 28 million (much of it due to territorial expansion); France's, from 20 to 26 or 27 million; Spain's, from 6 to 10 million; Brandenburg-Prussia's, from 1.5 to 5.5 million (over half of this came from territorial acquisition); and Britain's, from 5 or 6 to 9 million. These increases occurred during the same time that several million Europeans were going abroad as colonists.

Perhaps the most important cause of population growth was a decline in the death rate, thanks, no doubt, to more plentiful food and better transportation of food supplies, which led to improved diets and some relief from devastating famines. The introduction of new crops from the Americas, such as corn and potatoes, played an important role in creating a more bountiful and nutritious food supply (see "An Agricultural Revolution?" later in this chapter). Some historians have estimated that at the beginning of the eighteenth century, farmers were producing about 20 to 30 percent more food than they needed to sustain themselves; by 1750, the surplus reached 50 percent.

But an increase in food supply was not the only factor in the population growth. Also of great significance was the end of the bubonic plague: the last great outbreak in western Europe occurred in 1720 in southern France. In England, a significant factor in population growth may have been the change in the number of women who remained unmarried during their childbearing years. It has been estimated that this number fell from 15 to 7 percent between 1700 and 1800.

Nevertheless, death was still a ubiquitous feature of everyday life. Diseases such as typhus, smallpox, influenza, and dysentery were rampant, especially since hygienic conditions remained poor—little bathing, dirty clothes, and no systematic elimination of human wastes. Despite the improved transportation, famine and hunger could still be devastating.

Family, Marriage, and Birthrate Patterns

The family, rather than the individual, was still at the heart of Europe's social organization. For the most part, people still thought of the family in traditional terms, as a patriarchal institution with the husband dominating his

Marital Arrangements

In the eighteenth century, upper-class parents continued to choose marriage partners for their children. This practice and the turmoil it could cause are evident in this selection from *The Rivals,* a play written in 1775 by Richard Sheridan. Sheridan was an Irish playwright who quit writing plays in order to pursue a political career. In this scene from *The Rivals,* a father, Sir Anthony Absolute, informs his son, Captain Jack Absolute, of the arrangements he has made for his son's marriage. Jack, in love with another woman, is dumbfounded by his father's plans.

＋—＝◆＝—＋

Richard Sheridan, *The Rivals*

ABSOLUTE: Now, Jack, I am sensible that the income of your commission, and what I have hitherto allowed you, is but a small pittance for a lad of your spirit.

CAPTAIN JACK: Sir, you are very good.

ABSOLUTE: And it is my wish, while yet I live, to have my boy make some figure in the world. I have resolved, therefore, to fix you at once in a noble independence.

CAPTAIN JACK: Sir, your kindness overpowers me—such generosity makes the gratitude of reason more lively than the sensations even of filial affection.

ABSOLUTE: I am so glad you are so sensible of my attention—and you shall be master of a large estate in a few weeks.

CAPTAIN JACK: Let my future life, sir, speak my gratitude; I cannot express the sense I have of your munificence.—Yet, sir, I presume you would not wish me to quit the army?

ABSOLUTE: Oh, that shall be as your wife chooses.

CAPTAIN JACK: My wife, sir!

ABSOLUTE: Ay, ay, settle that between you—settle that between you.

CAPTAIN JACK: A wife, sir, did you say?

ABSOLUTE: Ay, a wife—why, did I not mention her before?

CAPTAIN JACK: Not a word of her, sir.

ABSOLUTE: Odd, so! I mus'n't forget her though.—Yes, Jack, the independence I was talking of is by marriage—the fortune is saddled with a wife—but I suppose that makes no difference.

CAPTAIN JACK: Sir! Sir! You amaze me!

ABSOLUTE: Why, what the devil's the matter with you, fool? Just now you were all gratitude and duty.

CAPTAIN JACK: I was, sir—you talked of independence and a fortune, but not a word of a wife!

ABSOLUTE: Why—what difference does that make? Odds life, sir! If you had an estate, you must take it with the live stock on it, as it stands!

CAPTAIN JACK: If my happiness is to be the price, I must beg leave to decline the purchase. Pray, sir, who is the lady?

ABSOLUTE: What's that to you, sir? Come, give me your promise to love, and to marry her directly.

CAPTAIN JACK: Sure, sir, this is not very reasonable. . . . You must excuse me, sir, if I tell you, once for all, that in this point I cannot obey you. . . .

ABSOLUTE: Sir, I won't hear a word—not one word! . . .

CAPTAIN JACK: What, sir, promise to link myself to some mass of ugliness!

ABSOLUTE: Zounds! Sirrah! The lady shall be as ugly as I choose: she shall have a hump on each shoulder; she shall be as crooked as the crescent; her one eye shall roll like the bull's in Cox's Museum; she shall have a skin like a mummy, and the beard of a Jew—she shall be all this, sirrah! Yet I will make you ogle her all day, and sit up all night to write sonnets on her beauty. ⊱

Q What does Sheridan suggest about marriage among the upper classes in the eighteenth century? What social, political, and economic considerations were significant in eighteenth-century marriages? Could he be overstating the issue? Why or why not?

---

wife and children. The upper classes in particular were still concerned for the family as a "house," an association whose collective interests were more important than those of its individual members. In all social classes, parents, especially the fathers, still generally selected marriage partners for their children, based on the interests of the family (see the box above). One French noble responded to his son's inquiry about his upcoming marriage: "Mind your own business."

CHILD CARE   At the beginning of the eighteenth century, traditional attitudes also prevailed in the care of children. Generally, lower-class women breast-fed their own children because it provided the best nourishment. Moreover, since there were strong taboos in various parts of Europe against sexual intercourse while one was breast-feeding, mothers might also avoid another immediate pregnancy; if the infant died, they could then have another child. Lower-class women, however, also served as wet nurses for children of the aristocratic and upper middle classes. Mothers from these higher social strata considered breast-feeding undignified and hired wet nurses instead. Even urban mothers, the wives of artisans, for economic reasons sent their babies to wet nurses in the countryside if they could, making the practice widespread in the eighteenth century.

In the second half of the eighteenth century, traditional attitudes began to alter, especially in western Europe. The impact of Enlightenment thought, such as Rousseau's *Émile,* and the increasing survival of more infants led to new attitudes toward children. Childhood was more and more viewed as a phase in human development. One result was a shift to dressing children in more comfortable clothes appropriate to their age rather than dressing them in clothes modeled after adult styles. Shops for children's clothes appeared for the first time. **Primogeniture,** the practice of treating the first son as the favorite, also came under attack. All children, it was argued, deserve their parents' attention. Appeals for women to breast-feed their own children rather than use wet nurses soon followed. In England, games and toys specifically for children now appeared. The jigsaw puzzle was invented in the 1760s, and books, such as *Little Pretty Pocket-Book* (1744), aimed to please as well as teach children. These changes, however, were limited mostly to the upper classes of western European society and did not extend to the peasants. For most Europeans, children were still a source of considerable anxiety. They represented a health risk to the mothers who bore them and more mouths to feed if they survived. In times of economic crisis, children proved such a burden to some families that they resorted to **infanticide** or abandoned their children at foundling homes.

Despite being punishable by death, infanticide remained a solution to the problem of too many children. So many children were being "accidentally" suffocated while in their parents' bed that in Austria in 1784 a law was enacted that forbade parents to place children under five years old in bed with them. More common than infanticide was simply leaving unwanted children at foundling homes or hospitals, which became a favorite charity of the rich in eighteenth-century Europe. The largest of its kind, located in Saint Petersburg, Russia, was founded by members of the nobility. By the end of the century, it was taking in 5,000 new babies a year and caring for 25,000 children at one time.

But severe problems arose as the system became overburdened. One historian has estimated that in the 1770s, one-third of all babies born in Paris were taken to foundling institutions by parents or desperate unmarried mothers, creating serious overcrowding. Foundling institutions often proved fatal for infants. Mortality rates ranged from 50 percent to as high as 90 percent (in a sense making foundling homes a legalized form of infanticide). Children who survived were usually sent to miserable jobs. The suffering of poor children was one of the blackest pages of eighteenth-century European history.

MARRIAGE AND BIRTHRATES In most of Europe, newly married couples established their own households independent of their parents. This nuclear family, which had its beginning in the Middle Ages, had become a common pattern, especially in northwestern Europe. In order to save up what they needed to establish their own households,

Children of the Upper Classes. This painting of John Bacon and his family illustrates an important feature of upper-class family life in Great Britain in the first half of the eighteenth century. The children appear as miniature adults, dressed in clothes modeled after the styles of their parents' clothes.

© Yale Center for British Art/The Bridgeman Art Library

both men and women (outside the aristocracy) married quite late; the average age for men in northwestern Europe was between twenty-seven and twenty-eight; for women, between twenty-five and twenty-seven.

Late marriages imposed limits on the birthrate; in fact, they might be viewed as a natural form of birth control. But was this limitation offset by the number of babies born illegitimately? From the low illegitimacy rate of 1 percent in some places in France and 5 percent in some English parishes, it would appear that it was not, at least in the first half of the eighteenth century. After 1750, however, illegitimacy appears to have increased. Studies in Germany, for example, show that rates of illegitimacy increased from 2 percent in 1700 to 5 percent in 1760 and to 10 percent in 1800, followed by an even more dramatic increase in the early nineteenth century.

For married couples, the first child usually appeared within one year of marriage, and additional children came at intervals of two or three years, producing an average of five births per family. It would appear, then, that the birthrate had the potential of causing a significant increase in population. This possibility was restricted, however, because 40 to 60 percent of European women of childbearing age (between fifteen and forty-four) were not married at any given time. Moreover, by the end of the eighteenth century, especially among the upper classes in France and Britain, birth control techniques were being used to limit the number of children. Figures for the French aristocracy indicate that the average number of children declined from six in the period between 1650 and 1700 to three between 1700 and 1750 and to two between 1750 and 1780. These figures are even more significant when one considers that aristocrats married at younger ages than the rest of the population. Coitus interruptus remained the most commonly used form of birth control.

Among the working classes, whether peasants or urban workers, the contributions of women and children to the "family economy" were often crucial. In urban areas, both male and female children either helped in the handicraft manufacturing done in the home or were sent out to work as household servants. In rural areas, children worked on the land or helped in the activities of cottage industry. Married women grew vegetables in small plots, tended livestock, and sold eggs, vegetables, and milk. Wives of propertyless agricultural workers labored in the fields or as textile workers, spinning or knitting. In the cities, wives of artisans helped their husbands at their crafts or worked as seamstresses. The wives of unskilled workers labored as laundresses and cleaners for the rich or as peddlers of food or used clothing to the lower classes. But the family economy was often precarious. Bad harvests in the countryside or a downturn in employment in the cities often reduced people to utter poverty and a life of begging.

An Agricultural Revolution?

Did improvements in agricultural practices and methods in the eighteenth century lead to an **agricultural revolution**?

The topic is much debated. Some historians have noted the beginning of agrarian changes already in the seventeenth century, especially in the Low Countries. Others, however, have questioned the use of the term, arguing that significant changes occurred only in England and noting that even there the upward trend in agricultural production was not maintained after 1750.

Eighteenth-century agriculture was characterized by increases in food production that can be attributed to four interrelated factors: more farmland, increased yields per acre, healthier and more abundant livestock, and an improved climate. Climatologists believe that the "little ice age" of the seventeenth century declined in the eighteenth, especially evident in moderate summers that provided more ideal growing conditions.

The amount of land under cultivation was increased by abandoning the old open-field system, in which part of the land was allowed to lie fallow to renew it. The formerly empty fields were now planted with new crops, such as alfalfa, turnips, and clover, which stored nitrogen in their roots and thereby restored the soil's fertility. They also provided winter fodder for livestock, enabling landlords to maintain an ever-larger number of animals.

The more numerous livestock increased the amount of meat in the European diet and enhanced food production by making available more animal manure, which was used to fertilize fields and produce better yields per acre. Increased yields were also encouraged by landed aristocrats, who shared in the scientific experimentation of the age. In England, Jethro Tull (1674–1741) discovered that using a hoe to keep the soil loose allowed air and moisture to reach plants and enabled them to grow better. He also used a drill to plant seeds in rows instead of scattering them by hand, a method that had lost much seed to the birds.

The eighteenth century witnessed greater yields of vegetables, including two important American crops, the potato and maize (Indian corn). Although they were not grown in quantity until after 1700, both had been brought to Europe from America in the sixteenth century. The potato became a staple in Germany, the Low Countries, and especially Ireland, where repression by English landlords forced large numbers of poor peasants to survive on small plots of marginal land. The potato took relatively little effort to produce in large quantities. High in carbohydrates and calories, rich in vitamins A and C, it could be easily stored for winter use.

The new agricultural techniques were considered best suited to large-scale farms. Consequently, a change in landholding accompanied the increase in food production. Large landowners or yeomen farmers enclosed the old open fields, combining many small holdings into larger units. The end of the open-field system led to the demise of the cooperative farming of the village community. In England, where small landholders resisted this process, Parliament, dominated by the landed aristocracy, enacted legislation allowing agricultural lands to be legally enclosed. As a result of these enclosure acts,

Jethro Tull and the Seed Drill. A major innovation in the new agricultural practices of the eighteenth century was the development of seed drills that enabled farmers to plant seeds in rows and prevent them from being picked up by birds. The seed drill pictured here was invented by Jethro Tull (left), one of the many landed aristocrats who participated in the scientific experimentation of the age.

England gradually became a land of large estates, and many small farmers were forced to become wage laborers or tenant farmers working farms of 100 to 500 acres. The enclosure movement and new agricultural practices largely destroyed the traditional patterns of English village life.

In the eighteenth century, the English were the leaders in adopting the new techniques behind the agricultural revolution (see the box on p. 563). This early modernization of English agriculture, with its noticeable increase in productivity, made possible the feeding of an expanding population about to enter a new world of industrialization and urbanization.

New Methods of Finance

A decline in the supply of gold and silver in the seventeenth century had created a chronic shortage of money that undermined the efforts of governments to meet their needs. The establishment of new public and private banks and the acceptance of paper notes made possible an expansion of credit in the eighteenth century.

Perhaps the best example of this process can be observed in England, where the Bank of England was founded in 1694. Unlike other banks accustomed to receiving deposits and exchanging foreign currencies, the Bank of England also made loans. In return for lending money to the government, the bank was allowed to issue paper "banknotes" backed by its credit. These soon became negotiable and provided a paper substitute for gold and silver currency. In addition, the issuance of government bonds paying regular interest, backed by the Bank of England and the London financial community, created the notion of a public or "national debt" distinct from the monarch's personal debts. This process meant that capital for financing larger armies and other government undertakings could be raised in ever-greater quantities.

These new financial institutions and methods were not risk-free, however. In both Britain and France in the early eighteenth century, speculators provided opportunities for people to invest in colonial trading companies. The French company under John Law was also tied to his attempt to create a national bank and paper currency for France. When people went overboard and drove the price of the stock to incredibly high levels, the bubble burst. Law's company and bank went bankrupt, leading to a loss of confidence in paper money that prevented the formation of a French national bank. Consequently, French public finance developed slowly in the eighteenth century.

This was not the case in Britain, however. Despite crises, public confidence in the new financial institutions enabled the British government to borrow large sums of money at relatively low rates of interest, giving it a distinct advantage in the struggle with France. According to a contemporary observer, Britain's public credit was "the permanent miracle of her policy, which has inspired both astonishment and fear in the States of Europe."[5] Despite Britain's growing importance in finance, however, the Dutch Republic remained the leader in Europe's financial life, and Amsterdam continued to be the center of

Propaganda for the New Agriculture

Enthusiastic supporters of the new English agricultural practices went to the Continent to examine less efficient kinds of farming. One of these Englishmen, Arthur Young, wrote an account of his travels in which he blamed the low yields of French farmers on the old system of allowing part of the land to lie fallow and the small size of the farms. The latter factor was especially important to English aristocratic landholders, who wished to justify the enclosure movement. This selection is taken from Young's account.

✦━✦◆✦━✦

Arthur Young, *Travels During the Years 1787, 1788, and 1789 . . . in the Kingdom of France*

The Englishman, in eleven years, gets three bushels more of wheat than the Frenchman. He gets three crops of barley, tares [vetches grown for fodder], or beans, which produce nearly twice as many bushels per acre, as what the three French crops of spring corn [grain] produce. And he farther gets, at the same time, three crops of turnips, and two of clover, the turnips worth 40 s. the acre, and the clover 60 s. That is 121 for both. What an enormous superiority. More wheat; almost double of the spring corn; and above 20 s. per acre per annum in turnips and clover. But farther; the Englishman's land, by means of the manure arising from the consumption of the turnips and clover is in a constant state of improvement, while the Frenchman's farm is stationary.

The great populousness of France, I attribute very much to the division of the lands into small properties, which takes place in that country to a degree of which we have in England but little conception. . . . It has been said to me in France, "Would you leave uncultivated lands wastes, rather than let them be cultivated in small portions, through a fear of population?" I certainly would not: I would, on the contrary, encourage their culture; but I would prohibit the division of small farms, which is as mischievous to cultivation, as it is sure to be distressing to the people. . . . Go to districts where the properties are minutely divided, and you will find (at least I have done it) universally, great distress, and even misery, and probably very bad agriculture. Go to others, where such subdivision has not taken place, and you will find a better cultivation, and infinitely less misery. When you are engaged in this political tour, finish it by seeing England, and I will show you a set of peasants well clothed, well nourished, and tolerably drunken from superfluity, well-lodged, and at their ease.

Q In Young's eyes, how did French agricultural practices compare with those of the English? Was this an unbiased account? Why or why not?

---

international finance until London replaced it in the nineteenth century. One observer noted in 1769:

> If ten or twelve businessmen of Amsterdam of the first rank meet for a banking operation, they can in a moment send circulating throughout Europe over two hundred million florins in paper money, which is preferred to cash. There is no Sovereign who could do as much. . . . This credit is a power which the ten or twelve businessmen will be able to exert over all the States of Europe, in complete independence of any authority.[6]

The decline of Dutch trade, industry, and power meant that Dutch capitalists were inclined to lend money abroad because they had fewer opportunities at home.

European Industry

The most important product of European industry in the eighteenth century was textiles. Woolen cloth made up 75 percent of Britain's exports in the early part of the century. France, too, was a leader in the production of woolen cloth, and other major states emulated both France and Britain by encouraging the development of their own textile industries.

COTTAGE INDUSTRY Most textiles were still produced by traditional methods. In cities that were textile centers, master artisans used timeworn methods to turn out finished goods in their guild workshops. But by the eighteenth century, textile production was beginning to shift to the countryside in parts of Europe. In the countryside, textiles were produced by the "putting-out" or "domestic" system, in which a merchant-capitalist entrepreneur bought the raw materials, mostly wool and flax, and "put them out" to rural workers, who spun the raw material into yarn and then wove it into cloth on simple looms. Capitalist entrepreneurs sold the finished product, made a profit, and used it to manufacture more. This system became known as the **cottage industry** because spinners and weavers did their work in their own cottages. The cottage industry was truly a family enterprise: women and children could spin while men wove on the looms, enabling rural people to earn incomes that supplemented their pitiful wages as agricultural laborers.

NEW METHODS AND NEW MACHINES The cottage system employed traditional methods of manufacturing and spread to many areas of rural Europe in the eighteenth century. But significant changes in industrial production also began to occur in the second half of the century, pushed along by the introduction of cotton, originally imported from India. The importation of

Cottage Industry. One important source of textile production in the eighteenth century was the cottage industry, truly a family enterprise. Shown here is a family at work producing knitwear. It was customary in the cottage industry for women to spin and wind the yarn and for men to weave the yarn into cloth on looms.

raw cotton from slave plantations encouraged the production of cotton cloth in Europe, where a profitable market developed because of the growing demand for lightweight cotton clothes that were less expensive than linens and woolens. But the traditional methods of the cottage industry proved incapable of keeping up with the growing demand, leading English cloth entrepreneurs to develop new methods and new machines. The flying shuttle sped up the process of weaving on a loom, thereby increasing the need for large quantities of yarn. In response, Richard Arkwright (1732–1792) invented a "water frame," powered by horse or water, which turned out yarn much faster than cottage spinning wheels. This abundance of yarn, in turn, led to the development of mechanized looms, invented in the 1780s but not widely adopted until the early nineteenth century. By that time, Britain was in the throes of the Industrial Revolution (see Chapter 20), but already at the end of the eighteenth century, rural workers, perceiving that the new machines threatened their traditional livelihood, had begun to call for the machines' destruction (see the box on p. 565).

Mercantile Empires and Worldwide Trade

As we saw in Chapter 14, the growth of commercial capitalism led to integrated markets, joint-stock trading companies, and banking and stock exchange facilities.

Mercantilist theory had posited that a nation should acquire as much gold and silver as possible; that it should maintain a favorable balance of trade, or more exports than imports; and that the state should provide subsidies to manufacturers, grant monopolies to traders, build roads and canals, and impose high tariffs to limit imports. Colonies were also seen as valuable sources of raw materials and markets for finished goods. Mercantilist theory on the role of colonies was matched in practice by Europe's overseas expansion. With the development of colonies and trading posts in the Americas, Asia, and Africa, Europeans embarked on an adventure in international commerce. This increase in overseas trade has led some historians to speak of the emergence of a truly global economy in the eighteenth century.

Although trade within Europe still dominated total trade figures, overseas trade boomed in the eighteenth century. As we saw in Chapter 14, of all the goods traded in the eighteenth century, perhaps the most profitable were African slaves. The African slave trade and the plantation economy in the Americas that depended on it were an integral part of the new Atlantic economy, which enabled the nations of western Europe to experience greater prosperity than the states in central and eastern Europe.

During the eighteenth century, trade between European states and their colonies increased dramatically. In 1715, 19 percent of Britain's trade was with its American colonies; by 1785, that figure had risen to 34 percent. The growing trade of Europe with the Americas, Africa, and Asia was also visible in the expansion of merchant fleets. The British, for example, had 3,300 merchant ships carrying 260,000 tons in 1700; by 1775, those numbers had increased to 9,400 ships carrying 695,000 tons.

Flourishing trade also had a significant impact on the European economy, especially visible in the growth of towns and cities. The rise of the Atlantic trade led to great prosperity for such port cities as Bordeaux, Nantes, and Marseilles in France; Bristol and Liverpool in Britain; and Lisbon and Oporto in Portugal. Trade also led to the growth of related industries, such as textile manufacturing, sugar refining, and tobacco processing, and to an increase in dock workers, building tradesmen, servants, and numerous service people. Visitors' accounts of their visits to prosperous port cities

The Beginnings of Mechanized Industry: The Attack on New Machines

Already by the end of the eighteenth century, mechanization was bringing changes to the traditional cottage industry of textile manufacturing. Rural workers who depended on the extra wages earned in their own homes often reacted by attacking the machinery that threatened their livelihoods. This selection is a petition that English woolen workers published in their local newspapers asking that machines no longer be used to prepare wool for spinning.

The Leeds Woolen Workers' Petition (1786)

To the Merchants, Clothiers and all such as wish well to the Staple Manufactory of this Nation.

The Humble ADDRESS and PETITION of Thousands, who labor in the Cloth Manufactory.

The Scribbling-Machines have thrown thousands of your petitioners out of employ, whereby they are brought into great distress, and are not able to procure a maintenance for their families, and deprived them of the opportunity of bringing up their children to labor: We have therefore to request, that prejudice and self-interest may be laid aside, and that you may pay that attention to the following facts, which the nature of the case requires.

The number of Scribbling-Machines extending about seventeen miles southwest of LEEDS, exceed all belief, being no less than *one hundred and seventy!* and as each machine will do as much work in twelve hours, as ten men can in that time do by hand (speaking within bounds) and they working night and day, one machine will do as much work in one day as would otherwise employ twenty men.

As we do not mean to assert any thing but what we can prove to be true, we allow four men to be employed at each machine twelve hours, working night and day, will take eight men in twenty-four hours; so that, upon a moderate computation twelve men are thrown out of employ for every single machine used in scribbling; and as it

may be supposed the number of machines in all the other quarters together, nearly equal those in the South-West, full four thousand men are left to shift for a living how they can, and must of course fall to the Parish, if not time relieved. Allowing one boy to be bound apprentice from each family out of work, eight thousand hands are deprived of the opportunity of getting a livelihood.

We therefore hope, that the feelings of humanity will lead those who have it in their power to prevent the use of those machines, to give every discouragement they can to what has a tendency so prejudicial to their fellow-creatures....

We wish to propose a few queries to those who would plead for the further continuance of these machines:

How are those men, thus thrown out of employ to provide for their families; and what are they to put their children apprentice to, that the rising generation may have something to keep them at work, in order that they may not be like vagabonds strolling about in idleness? Some say, Begin and learn some other business.—Suppose we do, who will maintain our families, whilst we undertake the arduous task; and when we have learned it, how do we know we shall be any better for all our pains; for by the time we have served our second apprenticeship, another machine may arise, which may take away that business also....

But what are our children to do; are they to be brought up in idleness? Indeed as things are, it is no wonder to hear of so many executions; for our parts, though we may be thought illiterate men, our conceptions are, that bringing children up to industry, and keeping them employed, is the way to keep them from falling into those crimes, which an idle habit naturally leads to.

Q What arguments did the Leeds woolen workers use against the new machines? What does the petition reveal about the concept of "progress" at the end of the eighteenth century?

---

detail the elegant buildings and affluent lifestyle they encountered.

The Social Order of the Eighteenth Century

 FOCUS QUESTION: Who were the main groups making up the European social order in the eighteenth century, and how did the conditions in which they lived differ both between groups and between different parts of Europe?

The pattern of Europe's social organization, first established in the Middle Ages, continued well into the eighteenth

century. Social status was still largely determined not by wealth and economic standing but by the division into the traditional "orders" or "estates" determined by heredity. This divinely sanctioned division of society into traditional orders was supported by Christian teaching, which emphasized the need to fulfill the responsibilities of one's estate. Although Enlightenment intellectuals attacked these traditional distinctions, they did not die easily. In the Prussian law code of 1794, marriage between noble males and middle-class females was forbidden without a government dispensation. Even without government regulation, however, different social groups remained easily distinguished everywhere in Europe by the distinctive, traditional clothes they wore.

Nevertheless, some forces of change were at work in this traditional society. The ideas of the Enlightenment made headway as reformers argued that the concept of an unchanging social order based on privilege was hostile to the progress of society. Not until the revolutionary upheavals at the end of the eighteenth century, however, did the old order finally begin to crumble.

The Peasants

Because society was still mostly rural in the eighteenth century, the peasantry constituted the largest social group, making up as much as 85 percent of Europe's population. There were rather large differences, however, between peasants from area to area. The most important distinction, at least legally, was between the free peasant and the serf. Peasants in Britain, northern Italy, the Low Countries, Spain, most of France, and some areas of western Germany were legally free, though not exempt from burdens. Some free peasants in Andalusia in Spain, southern Italy, Sicily, and Portugal lived in a poverty more desperate than that of many serfs in Russia and eastern Germany. In France, 40 percent of free peasants owned little or no land by 1789.

Small peasant proprietors or tenant farmers in western Europe were also not free from compulsory services. Most owed **tithes,** often one-third of their crops. Although tithes were intended for parish priests, in France only 10 percent of the priests received them. Instead the tithes wound up in the hands of towns and aristocratic landowners. Moreover, peasants could still owe a variety of dues and fees. Local aristocrats claimed hunting rights on peasant land and had monopolies over the flour mills, community ovens, and wine and oil presses needed by the peasants. Hunting rights, dues, fees, and tithes were all deeply resented.

Eastern Europe continued to be dominated by large landed estates owned by powerful lords and worked by serfs. Serfdom had come late to the east, having largely been imposed in the sixteenth and seventeenth centuries. Peasants in eastern Germany were bound to the lord's estate, had to perform labor services on the lord's land, and could not marry or move without permission and payment of a tax. By the eighteenth century, landlords also possessed legal jurisdiction, giving them control over the administration of justice. Only in the Habsburg empire had a ruler attempted to improve the lot of the peasants through a series of reforms. With the exception of the clergy and a small merchant class, eighteenth-century Russia, unlike the rest of Europe, was still largely a society of landlords and serfs. Russian peasants were not attached to the land but to the landlord and thus existed in a condition approaching slavery.

THE VILLAGE   The local villages in which they dwelt remained the centers of peasants' social lives. The village, especially in western Europe, maintained public order; provided poor relief, a village church, and sometimes a schoolmaster; collected taxes for the central government; maintained roads and bridges; and established common procedures for sowing, plowing, and harvesting crops. But villages were often dominated by the wealthiest peasants and proved highly resistant to innovations, such as new agricultural practices.

THE PEASANT DIET   The diet of the peasants in the eighteenth century had not changed much since the Middle Ages. Dark bread, made of roughly ground wheat and rye flour, remained the basic staple. It was quite nourishing and high in vitamins, minerals, and even proteins, since the bran and germ were not ground out. Peasants drank water, wine, and beer and ate soups and gruel made of grains and vegetables. The new foods of the eighteenth century, potatoes and American corn, added important elements to the peasant diet. Of course, when harvests were bad, hunger and famine became the peasants' lot in life, making them even more susceptible to the ravages of disease.

The Nobility

The nobles, who constituted only 2 to 3 percent of the European population, played a dominating role in society. Being born a noble automatically guaranteed a place at the top of the social order, with all the attendant special privileges and rights. The legal privileges of the nobility included judgment by their peers, immunity from severe punishment, and exemption from many forms of taxation. Especially in central and eastern Europe, the rights of landlords over their serfs were overwhelming. In Poland until 1768, the nobility even possessed the right of life or death over their serfs.

In many countries, nobles were self-conscious about their unique lifestyle, which set them apart from the rest of society. This did not mean, however, that they were unwilling to bend the conventions of that lifestyle if there were profits to be made. For example, by convention, nobles were expected to live off the yields of their estates. But although nobles almost everywhere talked about trade being beneath their dignity, many were not averse to mercantile endeavors. Many were also all too eager to profit from industries based on the exploitation of raw materials found on their estates; as a result, many nobles were involved in mining, metallurgy, and glassmaking. Their diet also set them off from the rest of society. Aristocrats consumed enormous quantities of meat and fish accompanied by cheeses, nuts, and a variety of sweets.

Nobles also played important roles in military and government affairs. Since medieval times, landed aristocrats had served as military officers. Although monarchs found it impossible to exclude commoners from the ranks of officers, tradition maintained that nobles made the most natural and hence the best officers. Moreover, the eighteenth-century nobility played a significant role in the administrative machinery of state. In some countries, such as Prussia, the entire bureaucracy reflected aristocratic values. Moreover, in most of Europe, landholding nobles controlled much of the local government in their districts.

The nobility or landowning class was not a homogeneous social group. Landlords in England leased their land to tenant farmers, while those in eastern Europe used the labor services of serfs. Nobles in Russia and Prussia served the state, but those in Spain and Italy had few official functions. Differences in wealth, education, and political power also led to differences within countries as well. The gap between rich and poor nobles could be enormous. As the century progressed, poor nobles sometimes sank into the ranks of the unprivileged masses of the population. It has been estimated that the number of European nobles declined by one-third between 1750 and 1815.

Although the nobles clung to their privileged status and struggled to keep others out, almost everywhere a person with money found it possible to enter the ranks of the nobility. Rights of nobility were frequently attached to certain lands, so purchasing the lands made one a noble; the acquisition of government offices also often conferred noble status.

THE ARISTOCRATIC WAY OF LIFE: THE COUNTRY HOUSE One aristocrat who survived the French Revolution commented that "no one who did not live before the Revolution" could know the real sweetness of living. Of course, he spoke not for the peasants whose labor maintained the system but for the landed aristocrats. For them, the eighteenth century was a final century of "sweetness" before the Industrial Revolution and bourgeois society diminished their privileged way of life.

In so many ways, the court of Louis XIV had provided a model for other European monarchs, who built palaces and encouraged the development of a court society as a center of culture. As at Versailles, these courts were peopled by members of the aristocracy whose income from rents or officeholding enabled them to participate in this lifestyle. This court society, whether in France, Spain, or Germany, manifested common characteristics: participation in intrigues for the king's or prince's favor, serene walks in formal gardens, and duels to maintain one's honor.

The majority of aristocratic landowners, however, remained on their country estates and did not participate in court society; their large houses continued to give witness to their domination of the surrounding countryside. This was especially true in England, where the court of the Hanoverian kings (Georges I–III, from 1714 to 1820) made little impact on the behavior of upper-class society. English landed aristocrats invested much time, energy, and money in their rural estates, giving the English country house an important role in English social life. One American observer remarked, "Scarcely any persons who hold a leading place in the circles of their society live in London. They have houses in London, in which they stay while Parliament sits, and occasionally visit at other seasons; but their homes are in the country."[7]

Although there was much variety in country houses, many in the eighteenth century were built in the Georgian style (named after the Hanoverian kings). This style was greatly influenced by the classical serenity and sedateness of the sixteenth-century Venetian architect Andrea Palladio, who had specialized in the design of country villas. The Georgian country house combined elegance with domesticity, and its interior was often described as combining visual delight and utility while offering the comfort of a home.

The country house also fulfilled a new desire for greater privacy that was reflected in the growing separation between the lower and upper floors. The lower floors were devoted to public activities—dining, entertaining, and leisure (see Images of Everyday Life on p. 568). A central entrance hall provided the setting for the ceremonial arrival and departure of guests on formal occasions. From the hall, guests could proceed to a series of downstairs common rooms. The largest was the drawing room (larger houses possessed two), which contained musical instruments and was used for dances or card games, a favorite pastime. Other common rooms included a formal dining room, informal breakfast room, library, study, gallery, billiard room, and conservatory. The entrance hall also featured a large staircase that led to the upstairs rooms, which consisted of bedrooms for husbands and wives, sons, and daughters. These rooms were used not only for sleeping but also for private activities, such as playing for the children and sewing, writing, and reading for wives. "Going upstairs" literally meant leaving the company of others in the downstairs common rooms to be alone in the privacy of one's bedroom. This eighteenth-century desire for privacy also meant keeping servants at a distance. They were now housed in their own wing of rooms and alerted to their employers' desire for assistance by a new invention—long cords connected to bells in the servants' quarters.

Although the arrangement of the eighteenth-century Georgian house originally reflected male interests, the influence of women was increasingly evident by the second half of the century. Already in the seventeenth century, it had become customary for the sexes to separate after dinner; while the men preoccupied themselves with brandy and cigars in the dining room, women would exit to a "withdrawing room" for their own conversation. In the course of the eighteenth century, the drawing room became a larger, more feminine room with comfortable pieces of furniture grouped casually in front of fireplaces to create a cozy atmosphere.

Aristocratic landowners, especially in Britain, also sought to expand the open space around their country houses to separate themselves from the lower classes in the villages and to remove farmland from their view. Often these open spaces were then enclosed by walls to create parks (as they were called in England) to provide even more privacy. Sometimes entire villages were destroyed to create a park, causing one English poet to lament the social cost:

> The man of wealth and pride
> Takes up the space that many poor supplied;
> Space for his lake, his park's extended bounds,
> Space for his horses, equipage and hounds.[8]

The Aristocratic Way of Life

© Collection Earl of Pembroke, Wilton House, UK/The Bridgeman Art Library

Louvre, Paris//© Scala/Art Resource, NY

Alnwick Castle, Northumberland//© Erich Lessing/Art Resource, NY

Staatliche Schloesser und Gaerten, Karlsruhe//© Erich Lessing/Art Resource, NY

The eighteenth-century country house in Britain fulfilled the desire of aristocrats for both elegance and greater privacy. The painting above at the left, by Richard Wilson, shows a typical English country house of the eighteenth century surrounded by a simple, serene landscape.

Thomas Gainsborough's *Conversation in the Park,* above right, captures the relaxed life of two aristocrats in the park of their country estate. The illustration at the left below shows the formal dining room of a great British country house. In the course of the eighteenth century, upper-class country houses came to be furnished with upholstered furniture and elaborate carpets

(continued)

as aristocrats sought greater comfort. Cabinets with glass windows also became fashionable as a way to display fine china and other objects. Especially desirable were objects from the East as vast amounts of Chinese and Japanese ceramics were imported into Europe in the eighteenth century. The illustration at the right below shows Chinese cups without handles, which became extremely fashionable. As seen in the painting, it was even acceptable to pour tea into the saucer in order to cool it.

Along with a sense of privacy, parks gave landed aristocrats the ability to reshape their property to meet their leisure needs.

THE ARISTOCRATIC WAY OF LIFE: THE GRAND TOUR

One characteristic of the high culture of the Enlightenment was its cosmopolitanism, reinforced by education in the Latin classics and the use of French as an international language. Travel was another manifestation of the Enlightenment's sophistication and interest in new vistas. One important aspect of eighteenth-century travel was the grand tour, in which the sons of aristocrats completed their education by making a tour of Europe's major cities. The English aristocracy in particular regarded the grand tour as crucial to their education. The great-aunt of Thomas Coke wrote to him upon his completion of school: "Sir, I understand you have left Eton and probably intend to go to one of those Schools of Vice, the Universities. If, however, you choose to travel I will give you 500 pounds [about $12,500] per annum."[9] Coke was no fool and went on the grand tour, along with many others. In one peak year alone, 40,000 Englishmen were traveling in Europe.

Travel was not easy in the eighteenth century. Crossing the English Channel could be difficult in rough seas and might take anywhere from three to twelve hours. The trip from France to Italy could be made by sea, where the traveler faced the danger of pirates, or overland by sedan chair over the Alps, where narrow passes made travel an adventure in terror. Inns, especially in Germany, were populated by thieves and the ubiquitous bedbugs. The English in particular were known for spending vast sums of money during their travels; as one observer recounted, "The French usually travel to save money, so that they sometimes leave the places where they sojourn worse off than they found them. The English, on the other hand, come over with plenty of cash, plenty of gear, and servants to wait on them. They throw their money about like lords."[10]

Since the trip was intended to be educational, young Englishmen in particular were usually accompanied by a tutor who ensured that his charges spent time looking at museum collections of natural history and antiquities. But tutors were not able to stop young men from also pursuing wine, women, and song. After crossing the Channel, English visitors went to Paris for a cram course on how to act sophisticated. They then went on to Italy, where their favorite destinations were Florence, Venice, and Rome. In Florence, the studious and ambitious studied art in the Uffizi Gallery. The less ambitious followed a less vigorous routine; according to the poet Thomas Gray, they "get up at twelve o'clock, breakfast till three, dine till five, sleep till six, drink cooling liquors till eight, go to the bridge till ten, sup till two, and so sleep till twelve again." In Venice, where sophisticated prostitutes had flourished since Renaissance times, women were the chief attraction for young English males. As Samuel Johnson remarked, "If a young man is wild, and must run after women and bad company, it is better this should be done abroad." Rome was another "great object of our pilgrimage," where travelers visited the "modern" sights, such as Saint Peter's and, above all, the ancient ruins. To a generation raised on a Classical education, souvenirs of ruins and Piranesi's etchings of Classical ruins were required purchases. After the accidental rediscovery of the ancient Roman towns of Herculaneum and Pompeii, they became a popular eighteenth-century tourist attraction.

The Inhabitants of Towns and Cities

Townspeople were still a distinct minority of the total population, except in the Dutch Republic, Britain, and parts of Italy. At the end of the eighteenth century, about one-sixth of the French population lived in towns of 2,000 people or more. The biggest city in Europe was London, with 1 million inhabitants, while Paris numbered between 550,000 and 600,000. Altogether, Europe had at least twenty cities in twelve countries with populations over 100,000, including Naples, Lisbon, Moscow, Saint Petersburg, Vienna, Amsterdam, Berlin, Rome, and Madrid.

Although urban dwellers were vastly outnumbered by rural inhabitants, towns played an important role in Western culture. The contrasts between a large city, with its education, culture, and material consumption, and the surrounding, often poverty-stricken countryside were striking, evident in this British traveler's account of Russia's Saint Petersburg in 1741:

> The country about Petersburg has full as wild and desert a look as any in the Indies; you need not go above 200 paces out of the town to find yourself in a wild wood of firs, and such a low, marshy, boggy country that you would think God when he created the rest of the world for the use of mankind had created this for an inaccessible retreat for all sorts of wild beasts.[11]

Peasants often resented the prosperity of towns and their exploitation of the countryside to serve urban interests. Palermo in Sicily used one-third of the island's food production while paying only one-tenth of the taxes. Towns lived off the countryside not by buying peasant produce but by acquiring it through tithes, rents, and dues.

A Market Square in Naples. Below the wealthy patrician elites who dominated the towns and cities were a number of social groups with a wide range of incomes and occupations. This remarkable diversity is evident in this eighteenth-century painting by Angelo Costa, which shows a fair being held in the chief market square of the Italian city of Naples.

Many cities in western and even central Europe had a long tradition of patrician oligarchies that continued to control their communities by dominating town and city councils. Despite their domination, patricians constituted only a small minority of the urban population. Just below the patricians stood an upper crust of the middle classes: nonnoble officeholders, financiers and bankers, merchants, wealthy rentiers who lived off their investments, and important professionals, including lawyers. Another large urban group was the petty bourgeoisie or lower middle class, made up of master artisans, shopkeepers, and small traders. Below them were the laborers or working classes. Much urban industry was still carried on in small guild workshops by masters, journeymen, and apprentices. Apprentices who acquired the proper skills became journeymen before entering the ranks of the masters, but increasingly in the eighteenth century, guilds became closed oligarchies as membership was restricted to the relatives of masters. Many skilled artisans were then often forced to become low-paid workers. Urban communities also had a large group of unskilled workers who served as servants, maids, and cooks at pitifully low wages.

Despite an end to the ravages of plague, eighteenth-century cities still experienced high death rates, especially among children, because of unsanitary living conditions, polluted water, and a lack of sewerage facilities. One observer compared the stench of Hamburg to an open sewer that could be smelled for miles around. Overcrowding also exacerbated urban problems as cities continued to grow from an influx of rural immigrants. But cities proved no paradise for them as unskilled workers found few employment opportunities. The result was a serious problem of poverty in the eighteenth century.

THE PROBLEM OF POVERTY Poverty was a highly visible problem in the eighteenth century, both in cities and in the countryside (see the box on p. 571). In Venice, licensed beggars made up 3 to 5 percent of the population, and unlicensed beggars may have constituted as much as 13 to 15 percent. Beggars in Bologna were estimated at 25 percent of the population; in Mainz, figures indicate that 30 percent of the people were beggars or prostitutes. Prostitution was often an alternative to begging. In France and Britain by the end of the century, an estimated 10 percent of the people depended on charity or begging for their food.

Earlier in Europe, the poor had been viewed as blessed children of God; assisting them was a Christian duty. A change of attitude that had begun in the latter part of

Poverty in France

Unlike the British, who had a system of public-supported poor relief, the French responded to poverty with ad hoc policies when conditions became acute. This selection is taken from an *intendant's* report to the controller general at Paris describing his suggestions for a program to relieve the grain shortages expected for the winter months.

———— ✦✦ ————

M. de la Bourdonnaye, Intendant of Bordeaux, to the Controller General, September 30, 1708

Having searched for the means of helping the people of Agen in this cruel situation and having conferred with His Eminence, the Bishop, it seems to us that three things are absolutely necessary if the people are not to starve during the winter.

Most of the inhabitants do not have seed to plant their fields. However, we decided that we would be going too far if we furnished it, because those who have seed would also apply [for more]. Moreover, we are persuaded that all the inhabitants will make strenuous efforts to find some seed, since they have every reason to expect prices to remain high next year. . . .

But this project will come to nothing if the collectors of the taille continue to be as strict in the exercise of their functions as they have been of late and continue to employ troops [to force collection]. Those inhabitants who have seed grain would sell it to be freed from an oppressive garrison, while those who must buy seed, since they have none left from their harvest and have scraped together a little money for this purchase, would prefer to give up that money [for taxes] when put under police constraint. To avoid this, I feel it is absolutely necessary that you order the receivers-general to reduce their operations during this winter, at least with respect to the poor. . . .

We are planning to import wheat for this region from Languedoc and Quercy, and we are confident that there will be enough. But there are two things to be feared: one is the greed of the merchants. When they see that general misery has put them in control of prices, they will raise them to the point where the calamity is almost as great as if there were no provisions at all. The other fear is that the artisans and the lowest classes, when they find themselves at the mercy of the merchants, will cause disorders and riots. As a protective measure, it would seem wise to establish two small storehouses. Ten thousand ecus [30,000 livres] would be sufficient for each. . . .

A third point demanding our attention is the support of beggars among the poor, as well as of those who have no other resources than their wages. Since there will be very little work, these people will soon be reduced to starvation. We should establish public workshops to provide work as was done in 1693 and 1694. I should choose the most useful kind of work, located where there are the greatest number of poor. In this manner, we should rid ourselves of those who do not want to work and assure the others a moderate subsistence. For these workshops, we would need about 40,000 livres, or altogether 100,000 livres. The receiver-general of the taille of Agen could advance this sum. The 60,000 livres for the storehouses he would get back very soon. I shall await your orders on all of the above.

Marginal Comments by the Controller General

Operations for the collection of the taille are to be suspended. The two storehouses are to be established; great care must be taken to put them to good use. The interest on the advances will be paid by the king. His Majesty has agreed to the establishment of the public workshops for the able-bodied poor and is willing to spend up to 40,000 livres on them this winter. ▷

Q What does this document reveal about the nature of poverty in France in the eighteenth century? How would the growing ranks of the poor in Europe further destabilize this society?

the sixteenth century became even more apparent in the eighteenth century. Charity to poor beggars, it was argued, simply encouraged their idleness and led them to vice and crime. A French official stated, "Beggary is the apprenticeship of crime; it begins by creating a love of idleness which will always be the greatest political and moral evil. In this state the beggar does not long resist the temptation to steal."[12] Although private charitable institutions such as the religious Order of Saint Vincent de Paul and the Sisters of Charity had been founded to help such people, they were soon overwhelmed by the increased numbers of indigent in the eighteenth century.

Although some "enlightened" officials argued that the state should become involved in the problem, mixed feelings prevented concerted action. Since the sixteenth century, vagrancy and begging had been considered crimes. In the eighteenth century, French authorities attempted to round up vagrants and beggars and incarcerate them for eighteen months to act as a deterrent. This effort accomplished little, however, since the basic problem was socioeconomic. These people had no work. In the 1770s, the French tried to use public works projects, such as road building, to give people jobs, but not enough funds were available to accomplish much. The problem of poverty remained another serious blemish on the quality of eighteenth-century life.

CHAPTER SUMMARY

Everywhere in Europe at the beginning of the eighteenth century, the old order remained strong. Nobles, clerics, towns, and provinces all had privileges, some medieval in origin, others the result of the attempt of monarchies in the sixteenth and seventeenth centuries to gain financial support from their subjects. Everywhere in the eighteenth century, monarchs sought to enlarge their bureaucracies to raise taxes to support the new large standing armies that had originated in the seventeenth century. During the eighteenth century, royal authority was often justified by the service the monarch could give to the state and its people rather than by divine right, creating a form of monarchy that some have labeled "enlightened absolutism." Three rulers, Frederick II of Prussia, Joseph II of Austria, and Catherine the Great of Russia, are traditionally associated with the concept of enlightened absolutism, although only Joseph II truly sought radical change based on Enlightenment ideas. Joseph abolished serfdom, reformed the laws, and granted religious toleration, but his reforms did not outlast his reign. Frederick and Catherine expressed interest in enlightened reforms, but maintenance of the existing political system took precedence over reform. Indeed, many historians believe that Frederick, Catherine, and Joseph were all guided by a policy of using state power to amass armies and wage wars to gain more power.

The existence of these armies made wars more likely. The emergence of five great powers, two of them (France and Britain) in conflict in the East and North America,

initiated a new scale of confrontation. The mid-century War of the Austrian Succession and the Seven Years' War were fought not only in Europe but also in North America and India. Frederick the Great was the instigator, desiring Austrian Silesia, but Great Britain was the true victor, driving France from Canada and India. Britain emerged with a worldwide empire and became the world's greatest naval and colonial power. Standing armies became the norm, and everywhere in Europe, increased demands for taxes to support these conflicts led to attacks on the privileged orders and a desire for change not met by the ruling monarchs.

At the same time, the population grew, mainly as a result of a declining death rate and improvements in agriculture; paper money began to compensate for gold and silver; institutions such as the Bank of England mobilized the wealth of the nation through credit; and the beginnings of an industrial revolution emerged in the textile industry. This growth in population, along with dramatic changes in finance, trade, and industry and an increase in poverty, created tensions that undermined the traditional foundations of European society. The inability of the old order to deal meaningfully with these changes led to a revolutionary outburst at the end of the eighteenth century that marked the beginning of the end for that old order.

CHAPTER REVIEW

Upon Reflection

Q If you were a philosophe serving Joseph II of Austria or Catherine the Great of Russia, what advice would you give the monarch on the best way to rule his or her country?

Q What were the characteristics of war and diplomacy in the eighteenth century, and how would you compare the nature of war and diplomacy in the eighteenth century with that of the seventeenth century?

Q How and why did the nobility play a dominating role in the European society of the eighteenth century?

Key Terms

natural laws (p. 543)
natural rights (p. 543)
enlightened absolutism (p. 543)
patronage (p. 545)

balance of power (p. 554)
reason of state (p. 554)
primogeniture (p. 560)
infanticide (p. 560)
agricultural revolution (p. 561)
cottage industry (p. 563)
tithes (p. 566)

Suggestions for Further Reading

GENERAL WORKS For a good introduction to the political history of the eighteenth century, see the relevant chapters in the general works by **Woloch, Anderson, Birn,** and **Blanning** listed in Chapter 17. See also **G. Treasure, *The Making of Modern Europe, 1648–1780,*** rev. ed. (London, 2003); **O. Hufton, *Europe: Privilege and Protest, 1730–1789,*** 2nd ed. (London, 2001); and **W. Doyle, *The Old European Order, 1500–1800*** (New York, 1996). On enlightened absolutism, see **H. M. Scott, ed., *Enlightened Absolutism: Reform and Reformers in Later Eighteenth-Century Europe*** (Ann Arbor, Mich., 1990), and **D. Beales, *Enlightenment and***

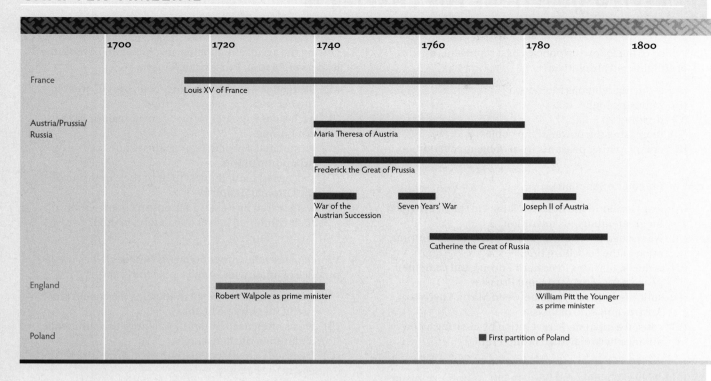

	1700	1720	1740	1760	1780	1800
France		Louis XV of France				
Austria/Prussia/Russia			Maria Theresa of Austria			
			Frederick the Great of Prussia			
			War of the Austrian Succession	Seven Years' War	Joseph II of Austria	
				Catherine the Great of Russia		
England		Robert Walpole as prime minister			William Pitt the Younger as prime minister	
Poland				First partition of Poland		

Reform in Eighteenth-Century Europe (New York, 2005). Good studies of individual states include **J. Black, *Eighteenth-Century Britain, 1688–1783*** (New York, 2001); **P. R. Campbell, *The Ancien Régime in France*** (Oxford, 1988); **E. Wangermann, *The Austrian Achievement, 1700–1800*** (London, 1973); **J. Gagliardo, *Germany Under the Old Regime*** (London, 1995); **J. Lynch, *Bourbon Spain, 1700–1808*** (Oxford, 1989); **C. Clark, *Iron Kingdom: The Rise and Downfall of Prussia, 1600–1947*** (Cambridge, Mass., 2006); **P. Dukes, *The Making of Russian Absolutism, 1613–1801,*** 2nd ed. (London, 1990); and **D. Kirby, *Northern Europe in the Early Modern Period*** (London, 1991). Good biographies of some of Europe's monarchs include **G. MacDonough, *Frederick the Great*** (New York, 2001); **I. De Madariaga, *Catherine the Great: A Short History,*** 2nd ed. (New Haven, Conn., 2002); **V. Rounding, *Catherine the Great: Love, Sex, and Power*** (New York, 2007); **T. C. W. Blanning, *Joseph II*** (New York, 1994); and **J. Black, *George III: America's Last King*** (New Haven, Conn., 2006).

EIGHTEENTH-CENTURY WARFARE The warfare of this period is examined in **M. S. Anderson, *War and Society in Europe of the Old Regime, 1615–1789*** (New York, 1998).

ECONOMIC AND SOCIAL CHANGE A good introduction to European population can be found in **M. W. Flinn, *The European Demographic System, 1500–1820*** (Brighton, 1981). One of the best works on family and marriage patterns is **L. Stone, *The Family, Sex, and Marriage in England, 1500–1800*** (New York, 1977). On wet nurses and infanticide, see **G. Sussman, *Selling Mother's Milk: The Wet-Nursing Business*** (Bloomington, Ind.,

1982), and **M. Jackson, *Newborn Child Murder: Women, Illegitimacy, and the Courts in Eighteenth-Century England*** (New York, 1996). On England's agricultural revolution, see **M. Overton, *Agricultural Revolution in England*** (Cambridge, 1996). Eighteenth-century cottage industry and the beginnings of industrialization are examined in **M. Berg, *The Age of Manufactures: Industry, Innovation, and Work in Britain, 1700–1820*** (Oxford, 1985).

THE SOCIAL ORDER On the European nobility, see **J. Dewald, *The European Nobility, 1400–1800,*** 2nd ed. (Cambridge, 2004), and **H. M. Scott, *The European Nobility in the Seventeenth and Eighteenth Centuries*** (London, 1995). On the peasantry, see **J. Blum, *The End of the Old Order in Rural Europe*** (Princeton, N.J., 1978), and **R. Evans, ed., *The German Peasantry*** (New York, 1986). On European cities, see **J. de Vries, *European Urbanization, 1500–1800*** (Cambridge, Mass., 1984). On the lower urban classes, see **R. M. Schwartz, *Policing the Poor in Eighteenth-Century France*** (Chapel Hill, N.C., 1988). There is no better work on the problem of poverty than **O. Hufton, *The Poor of Eighteenth-Century France*** (Oxford, 1974).

 CourseMate

Visit the CourseMate website at www.cengagebrain.com for additional study tools and review materials for this chapter.

AP❋ REVIEW QUESTIONS FOR CHAPTER 18

1. Which of the following policies best represents an ideal of enlightened absolutism?

   (A) reducing religious freedoms
   (B) imposing higher taxes
   (C) dividing up Poland
   (D) increasing the power of the nobles
   (E) emancipating peasants from obligatory servitude

2. The Pragmatic Sanction

   (A) was similar to the Edict of Nantes in that it provided for greater religious toleration.
   (B) was issued to ensure a successful dynastic continuation of the Habsburg line.
   (C) reduced tensions in eastern Europe and cemented peace between Austria and Prussia.
   (D) solidified the marriage between Maria Theresa of Austria and Paul of Russia.
   (E) caused a diplomatic revolution by creating a new alliance between Austria and France.

3. Both Robert Walpole and William Pitt, as prime ministers in Great Britain,

   (A) struggled to keep the British economy healthy under the rule of the Hanovers.
   (B) actively sought to decrease the power of the prime minister as they felt that one person should not be allowed to have so much power over the monarch.
   (C) were widely resented for questioning the principle of a strong and uninfluenced monarch.
   (D) were instrumental in decreasing the power of the British monarchy and developing a strong cabinet system.
   (E) were never fully allowed to exercise power and became puppets of the Hanover monarchs.

4. Pugachev's rebellion

   (A) was an attempt by the peasants to increase their involvement in government.
   (B) awakened Catherine the Great to the plight of the peasants and prompted her to use her power to help the people of her country.
   (C) was successful as the Russian peasants forced the nobles to finally grant them their freedoms.
   (D) was the quintessential seventeenth-century event that launched eastern European states into a period of revolutions.
   (E) led Catherine the Great to make a philosophical break from her Enlightenment ideals.

5. During the age of enlightened absolutism in Europe, the leaders of Austria, Prussia, and Russia

   (A) pledged peace between their countries in order to further stabilize eastern Europe.
   (B) each sought greater influence over regions in eastern Europe.
   (C) formulated a pact to fight against Louis XIV's ever-expanding power.
   (D) succeeded in their quest to limit the expansion of the Ottoman Empire.
   (E) were feared by western European countries for their combined power and determination.

6. Which of the following statements best describes the practice of infanticide in the eighteenth century?

   (A) It is the most likely explanation for the concurrent rise in illegitimate births.
   (B) It was often used by families to limit the number of children in the household.
   (C) It ceased to exist as a method of birth control by the end of the century.
   (D) It was officially recognized by the state and the church.
   (E) It occurred more often in middle-class and upper-class families because they wanted to be able to provide more for their older children.

7. Which of the following best describes warfare in the eighteenth century?

   (A) Wars were rare as European states sought to make greater use of diplomacy.
   (B) Military technology underwent great advances, and Spain reemerged as a military power.
   (C) Many wars were sparked by the desire of some European monarchs to dominate the Atlantic Ocean trade.
   (D) Wars were largely confined to central and eastern Europe.
   (E) Wars became increasingly centered on the religious beliefs of European rulers.

8. The western European cottage industry

   (A) allowed families to participate in a form of commercial enterprise within their own homes.
   (B) was dominated by men, as women were not allowed to participate.
   (C) failed as demand for textiles decreased.
   (D) began to develop only after the start of the Industrial Revolution.
   (E) was driven by entrepreneurs and capitalists who sought to elevate the status of working peasants.

9. The agricultural revolution of the eighteenth century allowed for all of the following EXCEPT

   (A) an increase in crop production.
   (B) more efficient use of farmlands by rotating crops.
   (C) freedom for the serfs throughout Europe.
   (D) further experimentation with fertilizers and selective breeding.
   (E) fewer peasants to be directly involved in the farming process.

10. Joseph II of Austria is best described as

   (A) the "Father of the Enlightenment," as his enlightened reforms were widely accepted and celebrated within Austria as great achievements.
   (B) the most enlightened ruler, though his reforms were relatively short-lived and put him in conflict with the Austrian nobility.
   (C) a disinterested ruler who spent most of his time studying the arts and sciences.
   (D) an expansionist who annexed parts of Poland in order to expand the Austrian state.
   (E) a "new economic monarch," as he implemented a tariff on the ruling classes in an effort to centralize his power.

11. Public health improved during the eighteenth century due to

   (A) a significant increase in the availability and consumption of staple foods.
   (B) a price revolution that helped more people afford basic necessities.
   (C) new antiseptics that helped prevent the spread of bacteria.
   (D) major advances in smallpox inoculation.
   (E) a rise in urbanization that provided better living conditions for greater numbers of people.

12. During the eighteenth century, the nobles

   (A) enjoyed increasing political autonomy throughout western Europe.
   (B) sought to enhance their power in eastern Europe through land reforms.
   (C) were challenged by the middle class to share their power and wealth.
   (D) of England looked to join the nobles of France in a solidarity movement.
   (E) witnessed their political and economic power come under attack as reformers argued that social order based on privilege was hostile to the progress of society.

13. Which of the following best describes eighteenth-century attitudes toward poverty?

   (A) It was believed that those living in poverty deserved their condition.
   (B) Poverty was seen as an unavoidable effect of the Industrial Revolution.
   (C) Poverty was seen as a state problem that should be corrected by the government.
   (D) It was believed that nothing could be done to ease poverty, so charitable organizations ceased to participate in the affairs of the poor.
   (E) Views of poverty were generally negative, as the church often preached against helping the poor.

14. All of the following areas were involved in the wars of the eighteenth century EXCEPT

   (A) North America.
   (B) eastern Europe.
   (C) India.
   (D) North Africa.
   (E) northern Europe.

© The Art Archive/Marc Charmet

The storming of the Bastille

A Revolution in Politics: The Era of the French Revolution and Napoleon

CHAPTER OUTLINE AND FOCUS QUESTIONS

The Beginning of the Revolutionary Era: The American Revolution

Q What were the causes and results of the American Revolution, and what impact did it have on Europe?

Background to the French Revolution

Q What were the long-range and immediate causes of the French Revolution?

The French Revolution

Q What were the main events of the French Revolution between 1789 and 1799? What role did each of the following play in the French Revolution: lawyers, peasants, women, the clergy, the Jacobins, the sansculottes, the French revolutionary army, and the Committee of Public Safety?

The Age of Napoleon

Q Which aspects of the French Revolution did Napoleon preserve, and which did he destroy?

⌐ CRITICAL THINKING ═══════════

Q In what ways were the French Revolution, the American Revolution, and the seventeenth-century English revolutions alike? In what ways were they different?

ON THE MORNING OF JULY 14, 1789, a Parisian mob of eight thousand people in search of weapons streamed toward the Bastille (bass-STEEL), a royal armory filled with arms and ammunition. The Bastille was also a state prison, and although it now held only seven prisoners, in the eyes of these angry Parisians, it was a glaring symbol of the government's despotic policies. The armory was defended by the marquis de Launay (mar-KEE duh loh-NAY) and a small garrison of 114 men. The attack began in earnest in the early afternoon, and after three hours of fighting, de Launay and the garrison surrendered. Angered by the loss of ninety-eight of their members, the victorious mob beat de Launay to death, cut off his head, and carried it aloft in triumph through the streets of Paris. When King Louis XVI was told the news of the fall of the Bastille by the duc de La Rochefoucauld-Liancourt (dook duh lah-RUSH-foo-koh-lee-ahnh-KOOR), he exclaimed, "Why, this is a revolt." "No, Sire," replied the duc, "it is a revolution."

Historians have long assumed that the modern history of Europe began with two major transformations—the French Revolution (discussed in this chapter) and the Industrial Revolution (see Chapter 20). Accordingly, the French Revolution has been portrayed as the major turning point in European political and social history, when the institutions of the "old regime" were destroyed and a new order was created based on individual rights, representative institutions, and a concept of loyalty to the nation rather than the monarch. This perspective does have certain limitations, however.

France was only one of a number of areas in the Western world where the assumptions of the old order were challenged. Although some historians have called the upheavals of the eighteenth and early nineteenth centuries a "democratic revolution," it is probably more appropriate to speak of a liberal movement to extend political rights and power to the bourgeoisie in possession of capital—citizens besides the aristocracy who were literate and had become wealthy through capitalist enterprises in trade, industry, and finance. The years preceding and accompanying the French Revolution included attempts at reform and revolt in the North American colonies, Britain, the Dutch Republic, some Swiss cities, and the Austrian Netherlands. The success of the American and French Revolutions makes them the center of attention for this chapter.

Not all of the decadent privileges that characterized the old European regime were destroyed in 1789, however. The revolutionary upheaval of the era, especially in France, did create new liberal and national political ideals, summarized in the French revolutionary slogan, "Liberty, Equality, Fraternity," that transformed France and were then spread to other European countries through the conquests of Napoleon. After Napoleon's defeat, however, the forces of reaction did their best to restore the old order and resist pressures for reform.

The Beginning of the Revolutionary Era: The American Revolution

 Focus Question: What were the causes and results of the American Revolution, and what impact did it have on Europe?

At the end of the Seven Years' War in 1763, Great Britain had become the world's greatest colonial power. In North America, Britain controlled Canada and the lands east of the Mississippi (see Map 19.1). After the Seven Years' War, British policy makers sought to obtain new revenues from the thirteen American colonies to pay for expenses the British army incurred in defending the colonists. An attempt to levy new taxes by a stamp act in 1765 led to riots and the law's quick repeal.

The Americans and the British had different conceptions of empire. The British envisioned a single empire with Parliament as the supreme authority throughout. Only Parliament could make laws for all the people in the empire, including the American colonists. The Americans, in contrast, had their own representative assemblies. They believed that neither the king nor Parliament had any right to interfere in their internal affairs and that no tax could be levied without the consent of an assembly whose members actually represented the people.

Crisis followed crisis in the 1770s until 1776, when the colonists decided to declare their independence from the British Empire. On July 4, 1776, the Second Continental Congress approved a declaration of independence written by Thomas Jefferson (1743–1826) (see the box on p. 577). A stirring political document, the declaration affirmed the Enlightenment's natural rights of "life, liberty, and the pursuit of happiness" and declared the colonies to be "free and independent states absolved from all allegiance to the British crown." The war for American independence had formally begun.

The War for Independence

The war against Great Britain was a great gamble. Britain was a strong European military power with enormous financial resources. The Second Continental Congress had authorized the formation of a Continental Army under George Washington (1732–1799) as commander in chief. Washington, who had had political experience in Virginia and military experience in the French and Indian War, was a good choice for the job. As a southerner, he brought balance to an effort that to that point had been led by New Englanders. Nevertheless, compared with the British forces, the Continental Army consisted of undisciplined amateurs whose terms of service were usually very brief.

Complicating the war effort were the internal divisions within the colonies. Fought for independence, the Revolutionary War was also a civil war, pitting family members and neighbors against one another. The Loyalists, between 15 and 30 percent of the population, questioned whether British policies justified the rebellion. The Loyalists were strongest in New York and Pennsylvania and tended to be wealthy, older, and politically moderate.

Since probably half the colonial population was apathetic at the beginning of the struggle, the patriots, like the Loyalists, constituted a minority of the population. The patriots, however, managed to win over many of the uncommitted, either by persuasion or by force. There were patriots among the rich as well as Loyalists; George Washington owned an estate with 15,000 acres and 150 slaves. But the rich patriots joined an extensive coalition that included farmers and artisans. The wide social spectrum in this coalition had an impact on representative governments in the states after the war. The right to vote was often broadened; Pennsylvania, for example, dropped all property qualifications for voting.

Of great importance to the colonies' cause was the assistance provided by foreign countries that were eager to gain revenge for earlier defeats at the hands of the British. The French supplied arms and money to the rebels from the beginning of the war, and French officers and soldiers also served in Washington's Continental Army. When the British army of General Cornwallis was forced to surrender to a combined American and French army and French fleet under Washington at Yorktown in 1781, the British government decided to call it quits. The Treaty of Paris, signed in 1783, recognized the independence of the American colonies and granted the Americans control of

MAP 19.1 **North America, 1700–1803.** The Seven Years' War gained Britain much territory in eastern North America, but asking the American colonies to help pay for the war sparked the American Revolution. The 1803 Louisiana Purchase nearly doubled the size of the United States and spurred westward expansion to the Pacific Ocean.

Q *In what periods was the Mississippi River a national boundary, and why was control of the river important for the United States?*

View an animated version of this map or related maps on the CourseMate website.

the western territory from the Appalachians to the Mississippi River.

Forming a New Nation

The thirteen American colonies had gained their independence as the United States of America, but a fear of concentrated power and concern for their own interests caused them to have little enthusiasm for establishing a united nation with a strong central government. The Articles of Confederation, ratified in 1781, did little to provide for a strong central government. A movement for a different form of national government soon arose. In the summer of 1787, fifty-five delegates attended a convention in Philadelphia to revise the Articles of Confederation. The convention's delegates—wealthy, politically experienced, well educated—rejected revision and decided to devise a new constitution.

The proposed constitution created a central government distinct from and superior to the governments of the individual states. The national government was given the power to levy taxes, raise a national army, regulate domestic and foreign trade, and create a national currency. The central or federal government was divided into three branches, each with some power to check the functioning of the others. A president would serve as the chief executive with the power to execute laws, veto the legislature's acts, supervise foreign affairs, and direct military forces.

The Argument for Independence

On July 2, 1776, the Second Continental Congress adopted a resolution declaring the independence of the American colonies. Two days later, the delegates approved the Declaration of Independence, which gave the reasons for their action. Its principal author was Thomas Jefferson, who basically restated John Locke's theory of revolution (see Chapter 15).

—— ✦≡✦ ——

The Declaration of Independence

When in the course of human events it becomes necessary for one people to dissolve the political bands which have connected them with another, and to assume among the Powers of the earth, the separate and equal station to which the Laws of Nature and of Nature's God entitle them, a decent respect to the opinions of mankind requires that they should declare the causes which impel them to the separation.

We hold these truths to be self-evident, that all men are created equal, that they are endowed by their Creator with certain unalienable Rights, that among these are Life, Liberty and the pursuit of Happiness. That to secure these rights, Governments are instituted among Men, deriving their just powers from the consent of the governed, That whenever any Form of Government becomes destructive of these ends, it is the Right of the People to alter or to abolish it and to institute new Government, laying its foundation on such principles and organizing its powers in such form, as to them shall seem most likely to effect their Safety and Happiness. Prudence, indeed, will dictate that Governments long established should not be changed for light and transient causes; and accordingly all experience has shown, that mankind are more disposed to suffer, while evils are sufferable, than to right themselves by abolishing the forms to which they are accustomed. But when a long train of abuses and usurpations, pursuing invariably the same Object evinces a design to reduce them under absolute Despotism, it is their right, it is their duty, to throw off such Government, and to provide new Guards for their future security.— Such has been the patient sufferance of these Colonies; and such is now the necessity which constrains them to alter their former Systems of government. The history of the present King of Great Britain is a history of repeated injuries and usurpations, all having in direct object the establishment of an absolute Tyranny over these States.

Q What influence did John Locke's theory of revolution have on the American Declaration of Independence? How would a member of the British Parliament have responded to this declaration?

© Yale University Art Gallery/Art Resource, NY

The Declaration of Independence. The Declaration of Independence, approved on July 4, 1776, by the Second Continental Congress, opened the door to the war for American independence. John Trumbull's famous painting, *The Signing of the Declaration,* shows the members of the committee responsible for the Declaration of Independence (from left to right, John Adams, Roger Sherman, Robert Livingston, Thomas Jefferson, and Benjamin Franklin) standing before John Hancock, president of the Second Continental Congress.

Legislative power was vested in the second branch of government, a bicameral legislature composed of the Senate, elected by the state legislatures, and the House of Representatives, elected directly by the people. The Supreme Court and other courts "as deemed necessary" by Congress served as the third branch of government. They would enforce the Constitution as the "supreme law of the land."

The United States Constitution was approved by the states—by a slim margin—in 1788. Important to its success was a promise to add a bill of rights to it as the new government's first piece of business. Accordingly, in March 1789, the new Congress proposed twelve amendments to the Constitution; the ten that were ratified by the states have been known ever since as the Bill of Rights. These guaranteed freedom of religion, speech, press, petition, and assembly, as well as the right to bear arms, protection against unreasonable searches and arrests, trial by jury, due process of law, and protection of property rights. Many of these rights were derived from the natural rights philosophy of the eighteenth-century philosophes, which was popular among the American colonists. Is it any wonder that many European intellectuals saw the American Revolution as the embodiment of the Enlightenment's political dreams?

Impact of the American Revolution on Europe

The year 1789 witnessed two far-reaching events, the beginning of a new United States of America and the eruption of the French Revolution. Was there a connection between the two great revolutions of the late eighteenth century?

There is no doubt that the American Revolution had an important impact on Europeans. Books, newspapers, and magazines provided the newly developing reading public with numerous accounts of American events. To many in Europe, it seemed to portend an era of significant changes, including new arrangements in international politics. The Venetian ambassador to Paris astutely observed in 1783 that "if only the union of the [American] provinces is preserved, it is reasonable to expect that, with the favorable effects of time, and of European arts and sciences, it will become the most formidable power in the world."[1] But the American Revolution also meant far more than that. It proved to many Europeans that the liberal political ideas of the Enlightenment were not the vapid utterances of intellectuals. The rights of man, ideas of liberty and equality, popular sovereignty, the separation of powers, and freedom of religion, thought, and press were not utopian ideals. The Americans had created a new social contract, embodied it in a written constitution, and made concepts of liberty and representative government a reality. The premises of the Enlightenment seemed confirmed; a new age and a better world could be achieved. As a Swiss philosophe expressed it, "I am tempted to believe that North America is the country where reason and humanity will develop more rapidly than anywhere else."[2]

Europeans obtained much of their information about America from returning soldiers, especially the hundreds of French officers who had served in the American war. One of them, the aristocratic marquis de Lafayette (mar-KEE duh lah-fay-ET), had volunteered for service in America in order to "strike a blow against England," France's old enemy. Closely associated with George Washington, Lafayette returned to France with ideas of individual liberties and notions of republicanism and popular sovereignty. He became a member of the Society of Thirty, a club composed of people from the Paris salons. These "lovers of liberty" were influential in the early stages of the French Revolution. The Declaration of the Rights of Man and the Citizen (see "Destruction of the Old Regime" later in this chapter) showed unmistakable signs of the influence of the American Declaration of Independence as well as the American state constitutions. Yet for all of its obvious impact, the American Revolution proved in the long run to be far less important to Europe than the French Revolution. The French Revolution was more complex, more violent, and far more radical in its attempt to construct both a new political order and a new social order. The French Revolution provided a model of revolution for Europe and much of the rest of the world; to many analysts, it remains the political movement that truly inaugurated the modern political world.

Background to the French Revolution

 FOCUS QUESTION: What were the long-range and immediate causes of the French Revolution?

Although we associate events like the French Revolution with sudden changes, the causes of such events involve long-range problems as well as immediate precipitating forces. **Revolutions,** as has been repeatedly shown, are not necessarily the result of economic collapse and masses of impoverished people hungering for change. In fact, in the fifty years before 1789, France had experienced a period of economic growth due to an expansion of foreign trade and an increase in industrial production, although many people, especially peasants, failed to share in the prosperity. Thus, the causes of the French Revolution must be found in a multifaceted examination of French society and its problems in the late eighteenth century.

Social Structure of the Old Regime

The long-range or indirect causes of the French Revolution must first be sought in the condition of French society. Before the Revolution, French society was grounded in the inequality of rights or the idea of privilege. The population of 27 million was divided, as it had been since the Middle Ages, into legal categories known as the three orders or estates.

THE FIRST ESTATE The First Estate consisted of the clergy and numbered about 130,000 people. The church owned approximately 10 percent of the land. Clergy were exempt from the *taille*, France's chief tax, although the church had agreed to pay a "voluntary" contribution every five years to the state. Clergy were also radically divided, since the higher clergy, stemming from aristocratic families, shared the interests of the nobility while the parish priests were often poor commoners.

THE SECOND ESTATE   The Second Estate was the nobility, composed of no more than 350,000 people who nevertheless owned about 25 to 30 percent of the land. Under Louis XV and Louis XVI, the nobility had continued to play an important and even crucial role in French society, holding many of the leading positions in the government, the military, the law courts, and the higher church offices. Much heavy industry in France was controlled by nobles, either through investment or by ownership of mining and metallurgical enterprises. The French nobility was also divided. The nobility of the robe derived their status from officeholding, a pathway that had often enabled commoners to attain noble rank. These nobles now dominated the royal law courts and important administrative offices. The nobility of the sword claimed to be descendants of the original medieval nobility. As a group, the nobles sought to expand their privileges at the expense of the monarchy—to defend liberty by resisting the arbitrary actions of monarchy, as some nobles asserted—and to maintain their monopolistic control over positions in the military, church, and government. In 1781, in reaction to the ambitions of aristocrats newly arrived from the bourgeoisie, the Ségur (say-GOO-uh) Law attempted to limit the sale of military officerships to fourth-generation nobles, thus excluding newly enrolled members of the nobility.

Although there were many poor nobles, on the whole the fortunes of the wealthy aristocrats outstripped those of most others in French society. Generally, the nobles tended to marry within their own ranks, making the nobility a fairly closed group. Although their privileges varied from region to region, the very possession of privileges remained a hallmark of the nobility. Common to all were tax exemptions, especially from the *taille*.

THE THIRD ESTATE   The Third Estate, the commoners of society, constituted the overwhelming majority of the French population. They were divided by vast differences in occupation, level of education, and wealth. The peasants, who alone constituted 75 to 80 percent of the total population, were by far the largest segment of the Third Estate. They owned about 35 to 40 percent of the land, although their landholdings varied from area to area and more than half had no or little land on which to survive. Serfdom no longer existed on any large scale in France, but French peasants still had obligations to their local landlords that they deeply resented. These relics of feudalism included the

The Three Estates. This French political cartoon from 1789 reveals a critical view of France's privileged orders. Shown in the cartoon is a naked common man held in chains and being ridden by an aristocrat, a clergyman, and a judge. The message is clear: most ordinary French people (the Third Estate) are suffering horribly as a result of the privileges of the First and Second Estates.

payment of fees for the use of village facilities, such as the flour mill, community oven, and winepress, as well as tithes to the clergy. The nobility also maintained the right to hunt on peasants' land.

Another part of the Third Estate consisted of skilled artisans, shopkeepers, and other wage earners in the cities. Although the eighteenth century had been a period of rapid urban growth, 90 percent of French towns had fewer than 10,000 inhabitants; only nine cities had more than 50,000. In the eighteenth century, consumer prices rose faster than wages, with the result that these urban groups experienced a decline in purchasing power. In Paris, for example, income lagged behind food prices and especially behind a 140 percent rise in rents for working people in skilled and unskilled trades. The economic discontent of this segment of the Third Estate—and often simply their struggle for survival—led them to play an important role in the Revolution, especially in the city of Paris. Insubordination, one observer noted, "has been visible among the people for some years now and above all among craftsmen." One historian has charted the ups and downs of revolutionary riots in Paris by showing their correlation with changes in bread prices. Ordinary people spent one-third to one-half of their income on bread, which constituted three-fourths of their diet, so sudden increases in the price of bread immediately affected public order. People expected bread prices to be controlled. They grew desperate when prices rose, and their only recourse was mob action to try to change the situation. The towns and cities were also home to large groups of unskilled and often unemployed workers. One magistrate complained that "misery . . . has thrown into the towns people who overburden them with their uselessness, and who find nothing to do, because there is not enough for the people who live there."[3]

About 8 percent, or 2.3 million people, constituted the bourgeoisie or middle class, who owned about 20 to 25 percent of the land. This group included the merchants, industrialists, and bankers who controlled the resources of trade, manufacturing, and finance and benefited from the economic prosperity after 1730. The bourgeoisie also included professional people—lawyers, holders of public offices, doctors, and writers. Many members of the bourgeoisie sought security and status through the purchase of land. They had their own set of grievances because they were often excluded from the social and political privileges monopolized by the nobles. These resentments of the middle class were for a long time assumed to be a major cause of the French Revolution. But although these tensions existed, the situation was not a simple case of a unified bourgeoisie against a unified noble class. As is evident, neither group was monolithic. Nobles were separated by vast differences in wealth and importance. A similar gulf separated wealthy financiers from local lawyers in French provincial towns.

Remarkable similarities existed at the upper levels of society between the wealthier bourgeoisie and the nobility. It was still possible for wealthy middle-class individuals to enter the ranks of the nobility by obtaining public offices and entering the nobility of the robe. In fact, between 1774 and 1789, the not insignificant number of 2,500 wealthy bourgeoisie entered the ranks of the nobility. Over the century as a whole, 6,500 new noble families were created. In addition, as we saw in Chapter 18, the aristocrats were also engaging in capitalist activities on their landed estates, such as mining, metallurgy, and glassmaking, and were even investing in foreign trade. Viewed in terms of economic function, many members of the bourgeoisie and nobility formed a single class. Finally, the new and critical ideas of the Enlightenment proved attractive to both aristocrats and bourgeoisie. Members of both groups shared a common world of liberal political thought. The old view that the French Revolution was the result of the conflict between two rigid orders, the bourgeoisie and the nobility, has been enlarged and revised. Both aristocratic and bourgeois elites, long accustomed to a new socioeconomic reality based on wealth and economic achievement, were increasingly frustrated by a monarchical system resting on privileges and on an old and rigid social order based on the concept of estates. The opposition of these elites to the **old order** ultimately led them to take drastic action against the monarchical regime, although they soon split over the question of how far to proceed in eliminating traditional privileges. In a real sense, the Revolution had its origins in political grievances.

Other Problems Facing the French Monarchy

Although the long-range causes of the French Revolution can thus be found in part in the growing frustration at the monarchy's inability to deal with new social realities and problems, other factors were also present. The failure of the French monarchy was exacerbated by specific problems in the 1780s. Although the country had enjoyed fifty years of growth overall, periodic economic crises still occurred. Bad harvests in 1787 and 1788 and the beginnings of a manufacturing depression resulted in food shortages, rising prices for food and other necessities, and unemployment in the cities. The number of poor, estimated by some at almost one-third of the population, reached crisis proportions on the eve of the Revolution. An English traveler noted the misery of the poor in the countryside: "All the country girls and women are without shoes or stockings; and the plowmen at their work have neither sabots nor stockings to their feet. This is a poverty that strikes at the root of national prosperity."[4]

IDEAS OF THE PHILOSOPHES Increased criticism of existing privileges as well as social and political institutions also characterized the eighteenth century. Although the philosophes did not advocate revolution, their ideas were widely circulated among the literate bourgeois and noble elites of France. The actual influence of the ideas of the philosophes is difficult to prove, but once the Revolution began, the revolutionary leaders frequently quoted Enlightenment writers, especially Rousseau.

FAILURE TO MAKE REFORMS The French Parlements often frustrated efforts at reform. These thirteen law courts, which were responsible for registering royal decrees, could block royal edicts by not registering them. Although Louis XIV had forced them into submission, the Parlements had gained new strength in the eighteenth century as they and their noble judges assumed the role of defenders of "liberty" against the arbitrary power of the monarchy. As noble defenders, however, they often pushed their own interests as well, especially by blocking new taxes. This last point reminds us that one of the fundamental problems facing the monarchy was financial.

FINANCIAL CRISIS The immediate cause of the French Revolution was the near collapse of government finances. At a time when France was experiencing economic crises, the government was drastically short of money. Yet French governmental expenditures continued to grow due to costly wars and royal extravagance. The government responded by borrowing; in the budget of 1788, the interest on the debt alone constituted half of government spending. Total debt had reached 4 billion livres (roughly $40 billion). Financial lenders, fearful they would never be repaid, were refusing to lend additional amounts.

The king's finance ministry wrestled with the problem but met with resistance. In 1786, Charles de Calonne

(SHAHRL duh ka-LUNN), the controller general of finance, finding himself unable to borrow any more, proposed a complete revamping of the fiscal and administrative system of the state. To gain support, Calonne convened an "assembly of notables" early in 1787. This gathering of nobles, prelates, and magistrates refused to cooperate, and the government's attempt to go it alone brought further disaster. On the verge of a complete financial collapse, the government was finally forced to call a meeting of the Estates-General, the French parliamentary body that had not met since 1614. By calling the Estates-General, the government was virtually admitting that the consent of the nation was required to raise taxes.

The French Revolution

Q **FOCUS QUESTIONS:** What were the main events of the French Revolution between 1789 and 1799? What role did each of the following play in the French Revolution: lawyers, peasants, women, the clergy, the Jacobins, the sans-culottes, the French revolutionary army, and the Committee of Public Safety?

In summoning the Estates-General, the government was merely looking for a way to solve the immediate financial crisis. The monarchy had no wish for a major reform of the government, nor did the delegates who arrived at Versailles come with plans for the revolutionary changes that ultimately emerged. Yet over the next years, through the interplay of the deputies meeting in various legislative assemblies, the common people in the streets of Paris and other cities, and the peasants in the countryside, much of the old regime would be destroyed, and Europe would have a new model for political and social change.

From Estates-General to a National Assembly

The Estates-General consisted of representatives from the three orders of French society. In the elections for the Estates-General, the government had ruled that the Third Estate should get double representation (it did, after all, constitute 97 percent of the population). Consequently, while both the First Estate (the clergy) and the Second (the nobility) had about 300 delegates each, the commoners had almost 600 representatives. Two-thirds of the latter were people with legal training, and three-fourths were from towns with more than two thousand inhabitants, giving the Third Estate a particularly strong legal and urban representation. Of the 282 representatives of the nobility, about 90 were liberal minded, urban oriented, and interested in the enlightened ideas of the century; half of them were under forty years of age. The activists of the Third Estate and the reform-minded individuals among the First and Second Estates had

common ties in their youth, urban background, and hostility to privilege. The *cahiers de doléances* (ka-YAY duh doh-lay-AHNSS), or statements of local grievances, which were drafted throughout France during the elections to the Estates-General, advocated a regular constitutional government that would abolish the fiscal privileges of the church and nobility as the major way to regenerate the country.

Cahiers de doléances (1789)

The Estates-General opened at Versailles on May 5, 1789. It was divided from the start over the question of whether voting should be by order or by head (each delegate having one vote). The Parlement of Paris, consisting of nobles of the robe, had advocated voting by order according to the form used in 1614. Each order would vote separately; each would have veto power over the other two, thus guaranteeing aristocratic control over reforms. But opposition to the Parlement's proposal arose from a group of reformers calling themselves patriots or "lovers of liberty." Although they claimed to represent the nation, they consisted primarily of bourgeoisie and nobles. One group of patriots known as the Society of Thirty drew most of its members from the salons of Paris. Some of this largely noble group had been directly influenced by the American Revolution, but all had been affected by the ideas of the Enlightenment and favored reforms made in the light of reason and utility.

THE NATIONAL ASSEMBLY The failure of the government to assume the leadership at the opening of the Estates-General created an opportunity for the Third Estate to push its demands for voting by head. Since it had double representation, with the assistance of liberal nobles and clerics, it could turn the three estates into a single-chamber legislature that would reform France in its own way. One representative, the Abbé Sieyès (ab-BAY syay-YESS), issued a pamphlet in which he asked, "What is the Third Estate? Everything. What has it been thus far in the political order? Nothing. What does it demand? To become something." Sieyès's sentiment, however, was not representative of the general feeling in 1789. Most delegates still wanted to make changes within a framework of respect for the authority of the king; revival or reform did not mean the overthrow of traditional institutions. When the First Estate declared in favor of voting by order, the Third Estate felt compelled to respond in a significant fashion. On June 17, 1789, the Third Estate voted to constitute itself a "National Assembly" and decided to draw up a constitution. Three days later, on June 20, the deputies of the Third Estate arrived at their meeting place only to find the doors locked; thereupon they moved to a nearby indoor tennis court and swore (in what has come to be known as the Tennis Court Oath) that they would continue to meet until they had produced a French constitution. These actions of June 17 and June 20 constituted the first step in the French Revolution, since the Third Estate had no legal right to act as the National Assembly. This revolution, largely the work of the lawyers

The Tennis Court Oath. Finding themselves locked out of their regular meeting place on June 20, 1789, the deputies of the Third Estate met instead in the nearby tennis courts of the Jeu de Paume and committed themselves to continue to meet until they established a new constitution for France. In this painting, the Neoclassical artist Jacques-Louis David presents a dramatic rendering of the Tennis Court Oath.

of the Third Estate, was soon in jeopardy, however, as the king sided with the First Estate and threatened to dissolve the Estates-General. Louis XVI now prepared to use force. The revolution of the lawyers appeared doomed.

INTERVENTION OF THE COMMON PEOPLE The common people, however, in a series of urban and rural uprisings in July and August 1789, saved the Third Estate from the king's attempt to stop the Revolution. From now on, the common people would be mobilized by both revolutionary and counterrevolutionary politicians and used to support their interests. The common people had their own interests as well and would use the name of the Third Estate to wage a war on the rich, claiming that the aristocrats were plotting to destroy the Estates-General and retain its privileges. This war was not what the deputies of the Third Estate had planned.

The most famous of the urban risings was the fall of the Bastille (see the box on p. 583). The king's attempt to take defensive measures by increasing the number of troops at the arsenals in Paris and along the roads to Versailles served not to intimidate but rather to inflame public opinion. Increased mob activity in Paris led Parisian leaders to form the so-called Permanent Committee to keep order. Needing arms, they organized a popular force to capture the Invalides, a royal armory, and on July 14 attacked the Bastille, another royal armory. The Bastille had also been a state prison but now held only seven prisoners (five forgers and two insane persons). There were few weapons there except those in the hands of the small group of defenders. The Bastille was an imposing fortress with eight towers connected by 9-foot-thick walls. It was easily defended, but its commander, the marquis de Launay, was more inclined to negotiate. Although fighting erupted, de Launay refused to open fire with his cannon, and the garrison soon surrendered. In the minds of the

Parisians who fought there, the fall of the Bastille was a great victory, and it quickly became a popular symbol of triumph over despotism.

Paris was abandoned to the insurgents, and Louis XVI was soon informed that the royal troops were unreliable. Louis's acceptance of that reality signaled the collapse of royal authority; the king could no longer enforce his will. Louis then confirmed the appointment of the marquis de Lafayette as commander of a newly created citizens' militia known as the National Guard.

At the same time, independently of what was going on in Paris, popular revolutions broke out in numerous cities. In Nantes, permanent committees and national guards were created to maintain order after crowds had seized the chief citadels. This collapse of royal authority in the cities was paralleled by peasant revolutions in the countryside.

PEASANT REBELLIONS AND THE GREAT FEAR A growing resentment of the entire seigneurial system, with its fees and obligations, greatly exacerbated by the economic and fiscal activities of the great estate holders—whether noble or bourgeois—in the difficult decade of the 1780s, created the conditions for a popular uprising. The fall of the Bastille and the king's apparent capitulation to the demands of the Third Estate now encouraged peasants to take matters into their own hands. From July 19 to August 3, peasant rebellions occurred in five major areas of France. Patterns varied. In some places, peasants simply forced their lay and ecclesiastical lords to renounce dues and tithes; elsewhere they burned charters listing their obligations. The peasants were not acting in blind fury; they knew what they were doing. Many also believed that the king supported their actions. As a contemporary chronicler wrote, "For several weeks, news went from village to village. They announced that the Estates-General was going to abolish tithes, quitrents and dues, that the

The Fall of the Bastille

On July 14, 1789, Parisian crowds in search of weapons attacked and captured the royal armory known as the Bastille. It had also been a state prison, and its fall marked the triumph of "liberty" over despotism. This intervention of the Parisian populace saved the Third Estate from Louis XVI's attempted counterrevolution.

⇥ ▰▰ ⇤

A Parisian Newspaper Account of the Fall of the Bastille

First, the people tried to enter this fortress by the Rue St.-Antoine, this fortress, which no one has even penetrated against the wishes of this frightful despotism and where the monster still resided. The treacherous governor had put out a flag of peace. So a confident advance was made; a detachment of French Guards, with perhaps five to six thousand armed bourgeois, penetrated the Bastille's outer courtyards, but as soon as some six hundred persons had passed over the first drawbridge, the bridge was raised and artillery fire mowed down several French Guards and some soldiers; the cannon fired on the town, and the people took fright; a large number of individuals were killed or wounded; but then they rallied and took shelter from the fire.... Meanwhile, they tried to locate some cannon; they attacked from the water's edge through the gardens of the arsenal, and from there made an orderly siege; they advanced from various directions, beneath a ceaseless round of fire. It was a terrible scene.... The fighting grew steadily more intense; the citizens had become hardened to the fire; from all directions they clambered onto the roofs or broke into the rooms; as soon as an enemy appeared among the turrets on the tower, he was fixed in the sights of a hundred guns and mown down in an instant; meanwhile cannon fire was hurriedly directed against the second drawbridge, which it pierced, breaking the chains; in vain did the cannon on the tower reply, for most people were sheltered from it; the fury was at its height; people bravely faced death and every danger; women, in their eagerness, helped us to the utmost; even the children, after the discharge of fire from the fortress, ran here and there picking up the bullets and shot; [and so the Bastille fell and the governor, de Launay, was captured].... Serene and blessed liberty, for the first time, has at last been introduced into this abode of horrors, this frightful refuge of monstrous despotism and its crimes.

Meanwhile, they get ready to march; they leave amidst an enormous crowd; the applause, the outbursts of joy, the insults, the oaths hurled at the treacherous prisoners of war; everything is confused; cries of vengeance and of pleasure issue from every heart; the conquerors, glorious and covered in honor, carry their arms and the spoils of the conquered, the flags of victory, the militia mingling with the soldiers of the fatherland, the victory laurels offered them from every side, all this created a frightening and splendid spectacle. On arriving at the square, the people, anxious to avenge themselves, allowed neither de Launay nor the other officers to reach the place of trial; they seized them from the hands of their conquerors, and trampled them underfoot one after the other. De Launay was struck by a thousand blows, his head was cut off and hoisted on the end of a pike with blood streaming down all sides.... This glorious day must amaze our enemies, and finally usher in for us the triumph of justice and liberty. In the evening, there were celebrations.

Q Why did the fall of the Bastille come to mark the triumph of French "liberty" over despotism? Do you think this Parisian newspaper account might be biased? Why or why not?

King agreed but that the peasants had to support the public authorities by going themselves to demand the destruction of titles."[5]

The agrarian revolts served as a backdrop to the Great Fear, a vast panic that spread like wildfire through France between July 20 and August 6. Fear of invasion by foreign troops, aided by a supposed aristocratic plot, encouraged the formation of more citizens' militias and permanent committees. The greatest impact of the agrarian revolts and the Great Fear was on the National Assembly meeting in Versailles. We will now examine its attempt to reform France.

Destruction of the Old Regime

One of the first acts of the National Assembly (also called the Constituent Assembly because from 1789 to 1791 it was writing a new constitution) was to destroy the relics of feudalism or aristocratic privileges. To some deputies, this measure was necessary to calm the peasants and restore order in the countryside, although many urban bourgeois were willing to abolish feudalism as a matter of principle. On the night of August 4, 1789, the National Assembly in an astonishing session voted to abolish seigneurial rights as well as the fiscal privileges of nobles, clergy, towns, and provinces.

THE DECLARATION OF THE RIGHTS OF MAN AND THE CITIZEN On August 26, the assembly provided the ideological foundation for its actions and an educational device for the nation by adopting the Declaration of the Rights of Man and the Citizen (see the box on p. 584). This charter of basic liberties reflected the ideas of the

The Natural Rights of the French People: Two Views

One of the important documents of the French Revolution, the Declaration of the Rights of Man and the Citizen was adopted in August 1789 by the National Assembly. The declaration affirmed that "men are born and remain free and equal in rights," that government must protect these natural rights, and that political power is derived from the people.

Olympe de Gouges (the pen name used by Marie Gouze) was a butcher's daughter who wrote plays and pamphlets. She argued that the Declaration of the Rights of Man and the Citizen did not apply to women and composed her own Declaration of the Rights of Woman and the Female Citizen in 1791.

Declaration of the Rights of Man and the Citizen

The representatives of the French people, organized as a national assembly, considering that ignorance, neglect, and scorn of the rights of man are the sole causes of public misfortunes and of corruption of governments, have resolved to display in a solemn declaration the natural, inalienable, and sacred rights of man, so that this declaration, constantly in the presence of all members of society, will continually remind them of their rights and their duties.... Consequently, the National Assembly recognizes and declares, in the presence and under the auspices of the Supreme Being, the following rights of man and citizen:

1. Men are born and remain free and equal in rights; social distinctions can be established only for the common benefit.
2. The aim of every political association is the conservation of the natural and imprescriptible rights of man; these rights are liberty, property, security, and resistance to oppression.
3. The source of all sovereignty is located in essence in the nation; no body, no individual can exercise authority which does not emanate from it expressly.
4. Liberty consists in being able to do anything that does not harm another person....
6. The law is the expression of the general will; all citizens have the right to concur personally or through their representatives in its formation; it must be the same for all, whether it protects or punishes. All citizens being equal in its eyes are equally admissible to all honors, positions, and public employments, according to their capabilities and without other distinctions than those of their virtues and talents.

7. No man can be accused, arrested, or detained except in cases determined by the law, and according to the forms which it has prescribed....
10. No one may be disturbed because of his opinions, even religious, provided that their public demonstration does not disturb the public order established by law.
11. The free communication of thoughts and opinions is one of the most precious rights of man: every citizen can therefore freely speak, write, and print....
12. The guaranteeing of the rights of man and citizen necessitates a public force; this force is therefore instituted for the advantage of all, and not for the private use of those to whom it is entrusted....
14. Citizens have the right to determine for themselves or through their representatives the need for taxation of the public, to consent to it freely, to investigate its use, and to determine its rate, basis, collection, and duration.
15. Society has the right to demand an accounting of his administration from every public agent.
16. Any society in which guarantees of rights are not assured nor the separation of powers determined has no constitution.
17. Property being an inviolable and sacred right, no one may be deprived of it unless public necessity, legally determined, clearly requires such action, and then only on condition of a just and prior indemnity.

Declaration of the Rights of Woman and the Female Citizen

... Mothers, daughters, sisters and representatives of the nation demand to be constituted into a national assembly. Believing that ignorance, omission, or scorn for the rights of woman are the only causes of public misfortunes and of the corruption of governments, the women have resolved to set forth in a solemn declaration the natural, inalienable, and sacred rights of woman in order that this declaration, constantly exposed before all the members of the society, will ceaselessly remind them of their rights and duties....

Consequently, the sex that is as superior in beauty as it is in courage during the sufferings of maternity recognizes and declares in the presence and under the auspices of the Supreme Being, the following Rights of Woman and of Female Citizens.

1. Woman is born free and lives equal to man in her rights. Social distinctions can be based only on the common utility.

(continued)

2. The purpose of any political association is the conservation of the natural and imprescriptible rights of woman and man; these rights are liberty, property, security, and especially resistance to oppression.

3. The principle of all sovereignty rests essentially with the nation, which is nothing but the union of woman and man; no body and no individual can exercise any authority which does not come expressly from it [the nation].

4. Liberty and justice consist of restoring all that belongs to others; thus, the only limits on the exercise of the natural rights of woman are perpetual male tyranny; these limits are to be reformed by the laws of nature and reason....

6. The law must be the expression of the general will; all female and male citizens must contribute either personally or through their representatives to its formation; it must be the same for all: male and female citizens, being equal in the eyes of the law, must be equally admitted to all honors, positions, and public employment according to their capacity and without other distinctions besides those of their virtues and talents.

7. No woman is an exception; she is accused, arrested, and detained in cases determined by law. Women, like men, obey this rigorous law....

10. No one is to be disquieted for his very basic opinions; woman has the right to mount the scaffold; she must equally have the right to mount the rostrum, provided that her demonstrations do not disturb the legally established public order.

11. The free communication of thought and opinions is one of the most precious rights of woman, since that liberty assured the recognition of children by their fathers....

12. The guarantee of the rights of woman and the female citizen implies a major benefit; this guarantee must be instituted for the advantage of all, and not for the particular benefit of those to whom it is entrusted....

14. Female and male citizens have the right to verify, either by themselves or through their representatives, the necessity of the public contribution. This can only apply to women if they are granted an equal share, not only of wealth, but also of public administration, and in the determination of the proportion, the base, the collection, and the duration of the tax.

15. The collectivity of women, joined for tax purposes to the aggregate of men, has the right to demand an accounting of his administration from any public agent.

16. No society has a constitution without the guarantee of rights and the separation of powers; the constitution is null if the majority of individuals comprising the nation have not cooperated in drafting it.

17. Property belongs to both sexes whether united or separate; for each it is an inviolable and sacred right; no one can be deprived of it, since it is the true patrimony of nature, unless the legally determined public need obviously dictates it, and then only with a just and prior indemnity.

Q What "natural rights" does the first document proclaim? To what extent was this document influenced by the writings of the philosophes? What rights for women does the second document enunciate? Given the nature and scope of the arguments in favor of natural rights and women's rights in these two documents, what key effects on European society would you attribute to the French Revolution?

---

major philosophes of the French Enlightenment and also owed much to the American Declaration of Independence and American state constitutions. The declaration began with a ringing affirmation of "the natural and imprescriptible rights of man" to "liberty, property, security, and resistance to oppression." It went on to affirm the destruction of aristocratic privileges by proclaiming an end to exemptions from taxation, freedom and equal rights for all men, and access to public office based on talent. The monarchy was restricted, and all citizens were to have the right to take part in the legislative process. Freedom of speech and press were coupled with the outlawing of arbitrary arrests.

The declaration also raised another important issue. Did the proclamation's ideal of equal rights for "all men" include women? Many deputies insisted that it did, at least in terms of civil liberties, provided that, as one said, "women do not aspire to exercise political rights and functions." Olympe de Gouges (oh-LAMP duh GOOZH), a playwright and pamphleteer, refused to accept this exclusion of women from political rights. Echoing the words of the official declaration, she penned a Declaration of the Rights of Woman and the Female Citizen in which she insisted that women should have all the same rights as men (see the box on p. 584). The National Assembly ignored her demands.

THE WOMEN'S MARCH TO VERSAILLES In the meantime, Louis XVI had remained inactive at Versailles. He did refuse, however, to promulgate the decrees on the abolition of feudalism and the declaration of rights, but an unexpected turn of events soon forced the king to change his mind. On October 5, after marching to the Hôtel de Ville, the city hall, to demand bread, crowds of Parisian women numbering in the thousands set off for Versailles, 12 miles away, to confront the king and the National Assembly. One eyewitness was amazed at the sight of "detachments of women coming up from every direction,

Depart des Heroines de Paris pour Versailles le 5 Octobre 1789.

The Women's March to Versailles. On October 5, 1789, thousands of Parisian women marched to Versailles to confront King Louis XVI and to demand bread for their starving children. This contemporary print shows a group of dedicated marchers, some armed with pikes and other weapons while others pull an artillery piece. The aristocratic woman at the far right does not appear to be very enthusiastic about joining the march.

armed with broomsticks, lances, pitchforks, swords, pistols and muskets." After meeting with a delegation of these women, who tearfully described how their children were starving for lack of bread, Louis XVI promised them grain supplies for Paris, thinking that this would end the protest. But the women's action had forced the Paris National Guard under Lafayette to follow their lead and march to Versailles. The crowd now insisted that the royal family return to Paris. On October 6, the king complied. As a goodwill gesture, he brought along wagonloads of flour from the palace stores. All were escorted by women armed with pikes (some of which held the severed heads of the king's guards), singing, "We are bringing back the baker, the baker's wife, and the baker's boy" (the king, queen, and their son). The king now accepted the National Assembly's decrees; it was neither the first nor the last occasion when Parisian crowds would affect national politics. The king was virtually a prisoner in Paris, and the National Assembly, now meeting in Paris, would also feel the influence of Parisian insurrectionary politics.

THE CATHOLIC CHURCH The Catholic Church was viewed as an important pillar of the old order, and it soon also felt the impact of reform. Because of the need for money, most of the lands of the church were confiscated, and *assignats* (ah-see-NYAH), a form of paper money, were issued based on the collateral of the newly nationalized church property. The church was also secularized. In July 1790, the new Civil Constitution of the Clergy was put into effect. Both bishops and priests of the Catholic Church were to be elected by the people and paid by the state. All clergy were also required to swear an oath of allegiance to the Civil Constitution. Since the pope forbade it, only 54 percent of the French parish clergy took the oath, and the majority of bishops refused. This was a critical

Civil Constitution of the Clergy (1790)

development because the Catholic Church, still an important institution in the life of the French people, now became an enemy of the Revolution. The Civil Constitution has often been viewed as a serious tactical blunder on the part of the National Assembly, for by arousing the opposition of the church, it gave counterrevolution a popular base from which to operate.

A NEW CONSTITUTION By 1791, the National Assembly had completed a new constitution that established a limited constitutional monarchy. There was still a monarch (now called "king of the French"), but he enjoyed few powers not subject to review by the new Legislative Assembly. The assembly, in which sovereign power was vested, was to sit for two years and consist of 745 representatives chosen by an indirect system of election that preserved power in the hands of the more affluent members of society. A distinction was drawn between active and passive citizens. Although all had the same civil rights, only active citizens (men over the age of twenty-five paying taxes equivalent in value to three days' unskilled labor) could vote. The active citizens probably numbered 4.3 million in 1790. These citizens did not elect the members of the Legislative Assembly directly but voted for electors (men paying taxes equal in value to ten days' labor). This relatively small group of 50,000 electors chose the deputies. To qualify as a deputy, one had to pay at least a "silver mark" in taxes, an amount equivalent to fifty-four days' labor.

The National Assembly also undertook an administrative restructuring of France. In 1789, it abolished all the old local and provincial divisions and divided France into eighty-three departments, roughly equal in size and population. Departments were in turn divided into districts and communes, all supervised by elected councils and officials who oversaw financial, administrative, judicial, and ecclesiastical institutions within their domains.

Although both bourgeois and aristocrats were eligible for offices based on property qualifications, few nobles were elected, leaving local and departmental governments in the hands of the bourgeoisie, especially lawyers of various types.

OPPOSITION FROM WITHIN By 1791, France had moved into a vast reordering of the old regime that had been achieved by a revolutionary consensus that was largely the work of the wealthier members of the bourgeoisie. By mid-1791, however, this consensus faced growing opposition from clerics angered by the Civil Constitution of the Clergy, lower classes hurt by the rise in the cost of living resulting from the inflation of the *assignats*, peasants who remained opposed to dues that had still not been abandoned, and political clubs offering more radical solutions to the nation's problems. The most famous were the Jacobins (JAK-uh-binz), who first emerged as a gathering of more radical deputies at the beginning of the Revolution, especially during the events of the night of August 4, 1789. After October 1789, they occupied the former Jacobin convent in Paris. Jacobin clubs also formed in the provinces, where they served primarily as discussion groups. Eventually, they joined together in an extensive correspondence network and by spring 1790 were seeking affiliation with the Parisian club. One year later, there were nine hundred Jacobin clubs in France associated with the Parisian center. Members were usually the elite of their local societies, but they also included artisans and tradespeople.

In addition, by mid-1791, the government was still facing severe financial difficulties due to massive tax evasion. Despite all of their problems, however, the bourgeois politicians in charge remained relatively unified on the basis of their trust in the king. But Louis XVI disastrously undercut them. Quite upset with the whole turn of revolutionary events, he sought to flee France in June 1791 and almost succeeded before being recognized, captured at Varennes, and brought back to Paris. Though radicals called for the king to be deposed, the members of the National Assembly, fearful of the popular forces in Paris calling for a republic, chose to ignore the king's flight and pretended that he had been kidnapped. In this unsettled situation, with a discredited and seemingly disloyal monarch, the new Legislative Assembly held its first session in October 1791.

Because the National Assembly had passed a "self-denying ordinance" that prohibited the reelection of its members, the composition of the Legislative Assembly tended to be quite different from that of the National Assembly. The clerics and nobles were largely gone. Most of the representatives were men of property; many were lawyers. Although lacking national reputations, most had gained experience in the new revolutionary politics and prominence in their local areas through the National Guard, the Jacobin clubs, and the many elective offices spawned by the administrative reordering of France. The king made what seemed to be a genuine effort to work with the new Legislative Assembly, but France's relations with the rest of Europe soon led to Louis's downfall.

OPPOSITION FROM ABROAD By this time, some European countries had become concerned about the French example and feared that revolution would spread to their countries. On August 27, 1791, Emperor Leopold II of Austria and King Frederick William II of Prussia issued the Declaration of Pillnitz, which invited other European monarchs to take "the most effectual means . . . to put the king of France in a state to strengthen, in the most perfect liberty, the bases of a monarchical government equally becoming to the rights of sovereigns and to the well-being of the French Nation."[6] But European monarchs were too suspicious of each other to undertake such a plan, and in any case, French enthusiasm for war led the Legislative Assembly to declare war on Austria on April 20, 1792. Why take such a step in view of its obvious dangers? Many people in France wanted war. Reactionaries hoped that a preoccupation with war would cool off the Revolution; French defeat, which seemed likely in view of the army's disintegration, might even lead to the restoration of the old regime. Leftists hoped that war would consolidate the Revolution at home and spread it to all of Europe.

The French fared badly in the initial fighting. A French army invaded the Austrian Netherlands (Belgium) but was routed, and Paris now feared invasion. In fact, if the Austrians and Prussians had cooperated, they might have seized Paris in May or June. Alarmed by the turn of events, the Legislative Assembly called for 20,000 National Guardsmen from the provinces to come and defend Paris. One such group came from Marseilles singing a rousing war song, soon known as the "Marseillaise," that three years later was made the French national anthem:

> Arise children of the motherland
> The day of glory has arrived.
> Against us, tyranny's
> Bloody flag is raised.
> Don't you hear in our countryside
> The roar of their ferocious soldiers?
> They are coming into your homes
> To butcher your sons and your companions.
> To arm, citizens! Form your battalions!
> We march, we march!
> Let their impure blood water our fields.

As fears of invasion grew, a frantic search for scapegoats began; as one observer noted, "Everywhere you hear the cry that the king is betraying us, the generals are betraying us, that nobody is to be trusted; . . . that Paris will be taken in six weeks by the Austrians. . . . We are on a volcano ready to spout flames."[7] Defeats in war coupled with economic shortages in the spring reinvigorated popular groups that had been dormant since the previous summer and led to renewed political demonstrations, especially against the king. Radical Parisian political groups, declaring themselves an insurrectionary commune, organized a mob attack on the royal palace and Legislative Assembly in August 1792, took the king captive, and forced the Legislative Assembly to suspend the monarchy and call for a national convention, chosen on the basis of universal male suffrage, to decide on the future form of government. The French Revolution was about to enter a more radical stage as power passed from the assembly to the new Paris Commune, composed of many who proudly called themselves the **sans-culottes** (sahn-koo-LUT *or* sanz-koo-LAHTSS), ordinary patriots without fine clothes. Although it has become customary to equate the more radical sans-culottes with working people or the poor, many were merchants and better-off artisans who were often the elite of their neighborhoods and trades.

The Radical Revolution

Before the National Convention met, the Paris Commune dominated the political scene. Led by the newly appointed minister of justice, Georges Danton (ZHORZH dahn-TAWNH) (1759–1794), the sans-culottes sought revenge on those who had aided the king and resisted the popular will. Fears of treachery were intensified by the advance of a Prussian army on Paris. Thousands of presumed traitors were arrested and then massacred as ordinary Parisian tradespeople and artisans solved the problem of overcrowded prisons by mass executions of their inmates. In September 1792, the newly elected National Convention began its sessions. Although it was called to draft a new constitution, it also acted as the sovereign ruling body of France.

Socially, the composition of the National Convention was similar to that of its predecessors. Dominated by lawyers, professionals, and property owners, it also included for the first time a handful of artisans. Two-thirds of the deputies were under age forty-five, and almost all had had political experience as a result of the Revolution. Almost all were also intensely distrustful of the king and his activities. It was therefore no surprise that the convention's first major step on September 21 was to abolish the monarchy and establish a republic. But that was about as far as members of the convention could agree, and the National Convention soon split into factions over the fate of the king. The two most important were the **Girondins** (juh-RAHN-dinz) (so-called because their leaders came from the department of Gironde, located in southwestern France) and the **Mountain** (so-called because its members' seats were on the side of the convention hall where the floor slanted upward). Both were members of the Jacobin club.

DOMESTIC CRISES Representing primarily the provinces, the Girondins came to fear the radical mobs in Paris and were disposed to keep the king alive as a hedge against future eventualities. The Mountain represented the interests of the city of Paris and owed much of its strength to the radical and popular elements in the city,

Execution of the King. At the beginning of 1793, the National Convention decreed the death of the king, and on January 21 of that year, Louis XVI was executed. As seen in this engraving by Carnavalet, the execution of the king was accomplished by a new revolutionary device, the guillotine.

although the members of the Mountain themselves were middle class. The Mountain won out at the beginning of 1793 when the National Convention found the king guilty of treason and sentenced him to death. On January 21, 1793, the king was executed, and the destruction of the old regime was complete. Now there could be no turning back. But the execution of the king produced further challenges by creating new enemies for the Revolution both at home and abroad while strengthening those who were already its enemies.

Factional disputes between the Girondins and the Mountain were only one aspect of France's domestic crisis in 1792 and 1793. In Paris, the local government was controlled by the Commune, which drew a number of its leaders from the city's artisans and shopkeepers. The Commune favored radical change and put constant pressure on the National Convention, pushing it to ever more radical positions. As one man warned his fellow deputies, "Never forget that you were sent here by the sans-culottes."[8] At the end of May and the beginning of June 1793, the Commune organized a demonstration, invaded the National Convention, and forced the arrest and execution of the leading Girondins, thereby leaving the Mountain in control of the convention. The National Convention itself still did not rule all of France.

Rebellion in France

The authority of the convention was repudiated in western France, particularly in the department of the Vendée (vahnh-DAY), by peasants who revolted against the new military draft (see "A Nation in Arms" later in this chapter). The Vendéan rebellion soon escalated into a full-blown counterrevolutionary appeal: "Long live the king and our good priests. We want our king, our priests and the old regime." Some of France's major provincial cities, including Lyons (LYOHNH) and Marseilles (mar-SAY), also began to break away from the central authority. Arguing as Marseilles did that "it is time for the anarchy of a few men of blood to stop,"[9] these cities favored a decentralized republic to free themselves from the ascendancy of Paris. In no way did they favor breaking up the "indivisible republic."

FOREIGN CRISIS Domestic turmoil was paralleled by a foreign crisis. Early in 1793, after Louis XVI had been executed, much of Europe—an informal coalition of Austria, Prussia, Spain, Portugal, Britain, and the Dutch Republic—was pitted against France. Carried away by initial successes and their own rhetoric, the French welcomed the struggle. Danton exclaimed to the convention, "They threaten you with kings! You have thrown down your gauntlet to them, and this gauntlet is a king's head, the signal of their coming death."[10] Grossly overextended, the French armies began to experience reverses, and by late spring some members of the anti-French coalition were poised for an invasion of France. If they succeeded, both the Revolution and the revolutionaries would be destroyed and the old regime reestablished. The Revolution had reached a decisive moment.

To meet these crises, the program of the National Convention became one of curbing anarchy and counter-revolution at home while attempting to win the war by a vigorous mobilization of the people. To administer the government, the convention gave broad powers to an executive committee known as the Committee of Public Safety, which was dominated initially by Danton. For the next twelve months, virtually the same twelve members were reelected and gave the country the leadership it needed to weather the domestic and foreign crises of 1793. One of the most important members was Maximilien Robespierre (mak-see-meel-YENH ROHBZ-pyayr) (1758–1794), a small-town lawyer who had moved to Paris as a member of the Estates-General. Politics was his life, and he was dedicated to using power to benefit the people, whom he loved in the abstract though not on a one-to-one basis.

A NATION IN ARMS To meet the foreign crisis and save the Republic from its foreign enemies, the Committee of Public Safety decreed a universal mobilization of the nation on August 23, 1793:

> Young men will fight, young men are called to conquer. Married men will forge arms, transport military baggage and guns and will prepare food supplies. Women, who at long last are to take their rightful place in the revolution and follow their true destiny, will forget their futile tasks: their delicate hands will work at making clothes for soldiers; they will make tents and they will extend their tender care to shelters where the defenders of the Patrie [nation] will receive the help that their wounds require. Children will make lint of old cloth. It is for them that we are fighting: children, those beings destined to gather all the fruits of the revolution, will raise their pure hands toward the skies. And old men, performing their missions again, as of yore, will be guided to the public squares of the cities where they will kindle the courage of young warriors and preach the doctrines of hate for kings and the unity of the Republic.[11]

In less than a year, the French revolutionary government had raised an army of 650,000; by September 1794, it numbered 1,169,000. The Republic's army—a **nation in arms**—was the largest ever seen in European history. It now pushed the allies back across the Rhine and even conquered the Austrian Netherlands (see Map 19.2). By May 1795, the anti-French coalition of 1793 was breaking up.

Historians have focused on the importance of the French revolutionary army in the creation of modern nationalism. Previously, wars had been fought between governments or ruling dynasties by relatively small armies of professional soldiers. The new French army, however, was the creation of a "people's" government; its wars were now "people's" wars. The entire nation was to be involved in the war. But when dynastic wars became people's wars, warfare increased in ferocity and lack of restraint. Although innocent civilians had suffered in the earlier struggles, now the carnage became appalling at times. The wars of the French revolutionary era opened the door to the total war of the modern world.

THE COMMITTEE OF PUBLIC SAFETY AND THE REIGN OF TERROR To meet the domestic crisis, the National Convention and the Committee of Public Safety established the "Reign of Terror." Revolutionary courts were organized to protect the Republic from its internal enemies, "who either by their conduct, their contacts, their words or their writings, showed themselves to be supporters of tyranny or enemies of liberty" or "who have not constantly manifested their attachment to the revolution."[12] Victims of the Terror ranged from royalists, such as Queen Marie Antoinette, to former revolutionary Girondins, including Olympe de Gouges, the chief advocate for political rights for women, and even included thousands of peasants. Many victims were persons who had opposed the radical activities of the

Citizens in the New French Army. To save the Republic from its foreign enemies, the National Convention created a revolutionary army of unprecedented size. The illustration above, from a book of paintings on the French Revolution by the Lesueur brothers, shows three citizens learning to drill, while a young volunteer is being armed and outfitted by his family. The illustration at the left, also by the Lesueur brothers, shows two volunteers joyfully going off to fight.

Public Safety decided to make an example of it. By April 1794, some 1,880 citizens of Lyons had been executed. When guillotining proved too slow, cannon fire and grapeshot were used to blow condemned men into open graves. A German observed:

> Whole ranges of houses, always the most handsome, [were] burnt. The churches, convents, and all the dwellings of the former patricians were in ruins. When I came to the guillotine, the blood of those who had been executed a few hours beforehand was still running in the street.... I said to a group of sans-culottes that it would be decent to clear away all this human blood. Why should it be cleared? one of them said to me. It's the blood of aristocrats and rebels. The dogs should lick it up.[13]

In the Vendée, revolutionary armies were also brutal in defeating the rebel armies. After destroying one army on December 12, the commander of the revolutionary army ordered that no quarter be given: "The road to Laval is strewn with corpses. Women, priests, monks, children, all have been put to death. I have spared nobody." The Terror was at its most destructive in the Vendée. Forty-two percent of the death sentences during the Terror were passed in territories affected by the Vendée rebellion. Perhaps the most notorious act of violence occurred in Nantes, where victims were executed by sinking them in barges in the Loire River.

To a great extent, the Terror demonstrated little class prejudice. Estimates are that the nobles constituted 8 percent of its victims; the middle classes, 25 percent; the clergy, 6; and the peasant and laboring classes, 60. To the Committee of Public Safety, this bloodletting was only a

sans-culottes. In the course of nine months, 16,000 people were officially killed under the blade of the guillotine, a revolutionary device for the quick and efficient separation of heads from bodies. But the true number of the Terror's victims was probably closer to 50,000 (see the box on p. 592). The bulk of the Terror's executions took place in the Vendée and in cities such as Lyons and Marseilles, places that had been in open rebellion against the authority of the National Convention.

Military force in the form of revolutionary armies was used to bring recalcitrant cities and districts back under the control of the National Convention. Marseilles fell to a revolutionary army in August. Starving Lyons surrendered early in October after two months of bombardment and resistance. Since Lyons was France's second city after Paris and had defied the National Convention during a time when the Republic was in peril, the Committee of

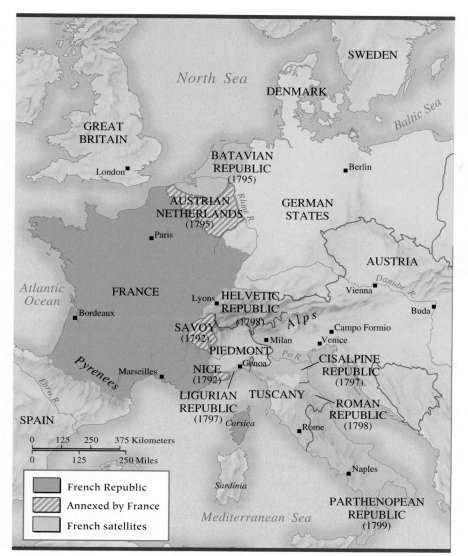

MAP 19.2   French Expansion During the Revolutionary Wars, 1792–1799. The conservative rulers of Europe, appalled at the republican character of the French Revolution, took up arms to restore the power of the Bourbon monarchy. The French responded with a people's army, the largest ever seen, which pushed the invaders out of France, annexed the Austrian Netherlands and some Italian territory, and created a number of French satellite states.

Q *Why would Austria desire cooperation from the German states if it wanted to wage war on France?*

View an animated version of this map or related maps on the CourseMate website.

temporary expedient. Once the war and domestic emergency were over, "the republic of virtue" would ensue, and the Declaration of the Rights of Man and the Citizen would be fully established. Although theoretically a republic, the French government during the Terror was led by a group of twelve men who ordered the execution of people as national enemies. But how did they justify this? Louis Saint-Just (sanh-ZHOOST), one of the younger members of the Committee of Public Safety, explained their rationalization in a speech to the convention: "Since the French people has manifested its will, everything opposed to it is outside the sovereign. Whatever is outside the sovereign is an enemy."[14] Clearly, Saint-Just was referring to Rousseau's concept of the general will, but it is equally apparent that these twelve men, in the name of the Republic, had taken upon themselves the right to ascertain the sovereign will of the French people (see the box on p. 593) and to kill their enemies as "outside the sovereign."

THE "REPUBLIC OF VIRTUE"   Along with the Terror, the Committee of Public Safety took other steps both to control

France and to create a new republican order and new republican citizens. By spring 1793, the committee was sending "representatives on mission" as agents of the central government to all departments to explain the war emergency measures and to implement the laws dealing with the wartime emergency.

The committee also attempted to provide some economic controls, especially since members of the more radical working class were advocating them. It established a system of requisitioning food supplies for the cities enforced by the forays of revolutionary armies into the countryside. The Law of the General Maximum established price controls on goods declared of first necessity, ranging from food and drink to fuel and clothing. The controls failed to work very well because the government lacked the machinery to enforce them.

THE ROLE OF WOMEN   Women continued to play an active role in this radical phase of the French Revolution. As spectators at sessions of revolutionary clubs and the National Convention, women made the members and deputies aware of their demands. When on Sunday, February 25,

Justice in the Reign of Terror

The Reign of Terror created a repressive environment in which revolutionary courts often acted quickly to condemn traitors to the revolutionary cause. In this account, an English visitor describes the court, the procession to the scene of execution, and the final execution procedure.

J. G. Milligen, *The Revolutionary Tribunal* (Paris, October 1793)

In the center of the hall, under a statue of Justice, holding scales in one hand, and a sword in the other, sat Dumas, the President, with the other judges. Under them were seated the public accuser, Fourquier-Tinville, and his scribes.... To the right were benches on which the accused were placed in several rows, and *gendarmes* with carbines and fixed bayonets by their sides. To the left was the jury.

Never can I forget the mournful appearance of these funeral processions to the place of execution. The march was opened by a detachment of mounted *gendarmes*—the carts followed; they were the same carts as those that are used in Paris for carrying wood; four boards were placed across them for seats, and on each board sat two, and sometimes three victims; their hands were tied behind their backs, and the constant jolting of the cart made them nod their heads up and down, to the great amusement of the spectators. On the front of the cart stood Samson, the executioner, or one of his sons or assistants; *gendarmes* on foot marched by the side; then followed a hackney, in which was the reporting clerk, whose duty it was to witness the execution, and then return to the public accuser's office to report the execution of what they called the law.

The process of execution was also a sad and heart-rending spectacle. In the middle of the Place de la Revolution was erected a guillotine, in front of a colossal statue of Liberty, represented seated on a rock, a cap on her head, a spear in her hand, the other reposing on a shield. On one side of the scaffold were drawn out a sufficient number of carts, with large baskets painted red, to receive the heads and bodies of the victims. Those bearing the condemned moved on slowly to the foot of the guillotine; the culprits were led out in turn, and if necessary, supported by two of the executioner's assistants, but their assistance was rarely required. Most of these unfortunates ascended the scaffold with a determined step—many of them looked up firmly on the menacing instrument of death, beholding for the last time the rays of the glorious sun, beaming on the polished axe: and I have seen some young men actually dance a few steps before they went up to be strapped to the perpendicular plane, which was then tilted to a horizontal plane in a moment, and ran on the grooves until the neck was secured and closed in by a moving board, when the head passed through what was called, in derision, "the republican toilet seat"; the weighty knife was then dropped with a heavy fall; and, with incredible dexterity and rapidity, two executioners tossed the body into the basket, while another threw the head after it.

Q How were the condemned taken to the executioner? How did this serve to inflame the crowds? How were people executed? Why?

1793, a group of women appealed formally to the National Convention for lower bread prices, the convention reacted by adjourning until Tuesday. The women responded bitterly by accosting the deputies: "We are adjourned until Tuesday; but as for us, we adjourn ourselves until Monday. When our children ask us for milk, we don't adjourn them until the day after tomorrow."[15] In 1793, two women—an actress and a chocolate manufacturer—founded the Society for Revolutionary Republican Women. Composed largely of working-class women, this Parisian group viewed itself as a "family of sisters" and vowed "to rush to the defense of the Fatherland."

Despite the importance of women to the revolutionary cause, male revolutionaries reacted disdainfully to female participation in political activity. In the radical phase of the Revolution, the Paris Commune outlawed women's clubs and forbade women to be present at its meetings. One of its members explained why:

It is horrible, it is contrary to all laws of nature for a woman to want to make herself a man. The Council must recall that some time ago these denatured women, these viragos, wandered through the markets with the red cap to sully that badge of liberty and wanted to force all women to take off the modest headdress that is appropriate for them [the bonnet].... Is it the place of women to propose motions? Is it the place of women to place themselves at the head of our armies?[16]

Most men—radical or conservative—agreed that a woman's place was in the home and not in military or political affairs. As one man asked, "Since when is it considered normal for a woman to abandon the pious care of her home, the cradle of her children, to listen to speeches in the public forum?"[17]

DE-CHRISTIANIZATION AND THE NEW CALENDAR In its attempt to create a new order, the National Convention also pursued a policy of **de-Christianization.** The word *saint* was removed from street names, churches were pillaged and closed by revolutionary armies, and priests were encouraged to marry. In Paris, the cathedral of

Robespierre and Revolutionary Government

In its time of troubles, the National Convention, under the direction of the Committee of Public Safety, instituted the Reign of Terror to preserve the Revolution from its internal enemies. In this selection, Maximilien Robespierre, one of the committee's leading members, tries to justify the violence to which these believers in republican liberty resorted.

+ ⸙ +

Robespierre, Speech on Revolutionary Government

The theory of revolutionary government is as new as the Revolution that created it. It is as pointless to seek its origins in the books of the political theorists, who failed to foresee this revolution, as in the laws of the tyrants, who are happy enough to abuse their exercise of authority without seeking out its legal justification. And so this phrase is for the aristocracy a mere subject of terror or a term of slander, for tyrants an outrage and for many an enigma. It behooves us to explain it to all in order that we may rally good citizens, at least, in support of the principles governing the public interest.

It is the function of government to guide the moral and physical energies of the nation toward the purposes for which it was established.

The object of constitutional government is to preserve the Republic; the object of the revolutionary government is to establish it.

Revolution is the war waged by liberty against its enemies; a constitution is that which crowns the edifice of freedom once victory has been won and the nation is at peace.

The revolutionary government has to summon extraordinary activity to its aid precisely because it is at war. It is subjected to less binding and less uniform regulations, because the circumstances in which it finds itself are tempestuous and shifting above all because it is compelled to deploy, swiftly and incessantly, new resources to meet new and pressing dangers.

The principal concern of constitutional government is civil liberty; that of revolutionary government, public liberty. Under a constitutional government little more is required than to protect the individual against abuses by the state, whereas revolutionary government is obliged to defend the state itself against the factions that assail it from every quarter.

To good citizens revolutionary government owes the full protection of the state; to the enemies of the people it owes only death. ⸙

Q How did Robespierre justify the violent activities of the French revolutionaries? In your opinion, do his explanations justify his actions? How does this document glorify the state and advance preservation of the state as the highest goal of modern politicians and policy makers?

Musée de la Ville de Paris//© Giraudon/Art Resource, NY

Women Patriots. Women played a variety of roles in the events of the French Revolution. This picture shows a middle-class women's patriotic club discussing the decrees of the National Convention, an indication that some women had become highly politicized by the upheavals of the Revolution. The women are also giving coins to create a fund for impoverished families.

De-Christianization

The phenomenon of de-Christianization produced some unusual spectacles during the radical stage of the French Revolution. This selection from the minutes of the National Convention describes how the cathedral of Notre Dame was put to new use as the Temple of Reason.

The Temple of Reason

A member puts in the form of a motion the demand of the citizens of Paris that the metropolitan cathedral [Notre Dame] be henceforth the Temple of Reason.

A member requests that the goddess of Reason place herself at the side of the president.

The attorney of the Commune conducts her to the desk. The president and the secretaries give her the fraternal kiss in the midst of applause.

She sits at the side of the president.

A member demands that the National Convention march in a body, in the midst of the People, to the Temple of Reason to sing the hymn of Liberty there.

This proposal is passed.

The Convention marches with the People to the Temple of Reason in the midst of general enthusiasm and joyful acclamations.

Having entered the Temple of Reason, they sing the following hymn:

Descend, O Liberty, daughter of Nature:
The People have recaptured their immortal power;
Over the pompous remains of age-old imposture
Their hands raise thine altar.
Come, vanquisher of kings, Europe gazes upon you;
Come, vanquish the false gods.
Thou, holy Liberty, come dwell in this temple;
Be the goddess of the French.
Thy countenance rejoices the most savage mountain,
Amid the rocks harvests grow:
Embellished by thy hands, the harshest coast,
Embedded in ice, smiles.
Thou doublest pleasures, virtues, genius;
Under thy holy standards, man is always victorious;
Before knowing thee he does not know life;
He is created by thy glance.
All kings make war on the sovereign People;
Let them henceforth fall at thy feet, O goddess;
Soon on the coffins of the world's tyrants
the world's peoples will swear peace.
Warrior liberators, powerful, brave race,
Armed with a human sword, sanctify terror;
Brought down by your blows, may the last slave
Follow the last king to the grave. ⇛

Q What was the purpose of de-Christianization? Based on the ceremony described here, how effective do you think it was?

Notre-Dame was designated the Temple of Reason (see the box above). In November 1793, a public ceremony dedicated to the worship of reason was held in the former cathedral; patriotic maidens adorned in white dresses paraded before a temple of reason where the high altar once stood. At the end of the ceremony, a female figure personifying Liberty rose out of the temple. As Robespierre came to realize, de-Christianization backfired because France was still overwhelmingly Catholic. In fact, de-Christianization created more enemies than friends.

Yet another manifestation of de-Christianization was the adoption of a new republican calendar on October 5, 1793. Years would no longer be numbered from the birth of Jesus but from September 22, 1792, the day the French Republic was proclaimed. Thus, at the time the calendar was adopted, the French were already living in year II. The calendar contained twelve months; each month consisted of three ten-day weeks called *décades* (day-KAD) with the tenth day of each week a rest day (*décadi*). This eliminated Sundays and Sunday worship services and put an end to the ordering of French lives by a Christian calendar that emphasized Sundays, saints' days, and church holidays and festivals. Religious celebrations were to be replaced by revolutionary festivals. Especially important were the five

days (six in leap years) left over in the calendar at the end of the year. These days were to form a half-week of festivals to celebrate the revolutionary virtues—Virtue, Intelligence, Labor, Opinion, and Rewards. The sixth extra day in a leap year would be a special festival day when French citizens would "come from all parts of the Republic to celebrate liberty and equality, to cement by their embraces the national fraternity." Of course, ending church holidays also reduced the number of nonworking holidays from fifty-six to thirty-two, a goal long recommended by eighteenth-century economic theorists.

The calendar's anti-Christian purpose was also apparent in the renaming of the months of the year. The months were given names that were supposed to evoke the seasons, the temperature, or the state of the vegetation: Vendémiaire (vahnh-duh-MYAYR) (harvest—the first month of thirty days beginning September 22), Brumaire (broo-MAYR) (mist), Frimaire (free-MAYR) (frost), Nivôse (nee-VOHZ) (snow), Pluviôse (ploo-VYOHZ) (rain), Ventôse (vahnh-TOHZ) (wind), Germinal (jayr-mee-NAHL) (seeding), Floréal (floh-ray-AHL) (flowering), Prairial (pray-RYAL) (meadows), Messidor (MESS-i-dor) (wheat harvest), Thermidor (TAYR-mi-dor) (heat), and Fructidor (FROOK-ti-dor) (ripening).

The new calendar faced intense popular opposition, and the revolutionary government relied primarily on coercion to win its acceptance. Journalists, for example, were commanded to use republican dates in their newspaper articles. But many people refused to give up the old calendar, as one official reported:

> Sundays and Catholic holidays, even if there are ten in a row, have for some time been celebrated with as much pomp and splendor as before. The same cannot be said of *décadi*, which is observed by only a small handful of citizens. The first to disobey the law are the wives of public officials, who dress up on the holidays of the old calendar and abstain from work more religiously than anyone else.[18]

The government could hardly expect peasants to follow the new calendar when government officials were ignoring it. Napoleon later perceived that the revolutionary calendar was politically unpopular, and he simply abandoned it on January 1, 1806 (11 Nivôse XIV).

In addition to its anti-Christian function, the revolutionary calendar had also served to mark the Revolution as a new historical beginning, a radical break in time. Revolutionary upheavals often project millenarian expectations, the hope that a new age is dawning. The revolutionary dream of a new order presupposed the creation of a new human being freed from the old order and its symbols, a new citizen surrounded by a framework of new habits. Restructuring time itself offered the opportunity to forge new habits and create a lasting new order.

EQUALITY AND SLAVERY Early in the French Revolution, the desire for equality led to a discussion of what to do about slavery. A club called Friends of the Blacks advocated the abolition of slavery, which was achieved in France in September 1791. Nevertheless, French planters in the West Indies, who profited greatly from the use of slaves on their sugar plantations, opposed the abolition of slavery in the French colonies. When the National Convention came into power, the issue was revisited, and on February 4, 1794, guided by ideals of equality, the government abolished slavery in the colonies.

In one French colony, slaves had already rebelled for their freedom. In 1791, black slaves in the French sugar colony of Saint-Domingue (the western third of the island of Hispaniola), inspired by the ideals of the revolution occurring in France, revolted against French plantation owners. Slaves attacked, killing plantation owners and their families and burning their buildings. White planters retaliated with equal brutality. One wealthy French settler reported, "How can we stay in a country where slaves have raised their hands against their masters?"

Revolt in Saint-Domingue (Haiti)

Eventually, leadership of the revolt was taken over by Toussaint L'Ouverture (too-SANH loo-vayr-TOOR) (1746–1803), a son of African slaves, who seized control of all of Hispaniola by 1801. Although Napoleon had accepted the revolutionary ideal of equality, he did not deny the reports of white planters that the massacres of white planters by slaves demonstrated the savage nature of blacks. In 1802, he reinstated slavery in the French West Indian colonies and sent an army that captured L'Ouverture, who died in a French dungeon within a year. But the French soldiers, weakened by disease, soon succumbed to the slave forces. On January 1, 1804, the western part of Hispaniola, now called Haiti, announced its freedom and became the first independent state in Latin America. Despite Napoleon's efforts to the contrary, one of the French revolutionary ideals had triumphed abroad.

DECLINE OF THE COMMITTEE OF PUBLIC SAFETY Maintaining the revolutionary ideals in France proved not to be easy. By the Law of 14 Frimaire (passed on December 4, 1793), the Committee of Public Safety sought to centralize the administration of France more effectively and to exercise greater control in order to check the excesses of the Reign of Terror. The activities of both the representatives on mission and the revolutionary armies were scrutinized more carefully, and the campaign against Christianity was also dampened. Finally, in 1794, the Committee of Public Safety turned against its radical Parisian supporters, executed the leaders of the revolutionary Paris Commune, and turned it into a docile tool. This might have been a good idea for the sake of order, but in suppressing the people who had been its chief supporters, the National Convention alienated an important group. At the same time, the French had been successful against their foreign foes. The military successes meant that the Terror no longer served much purpose. But the Terror continued because Robespierre, now its dominant figure, had become obsessed with purifying the body politic of all the corrupt. Only then could the Republic of Virtue follow. Many deputies in the National Convention, however, feared that they were not safe while Robespierre was free to act. An anti-Robespierre coalition in the National Convention, eager now to destroy Robespierre before he destroyed them, gathered enough votes to condemn him. Robespierre was guillotined on July 28, 1794, beginning a reaction that brought an end to this radical stage of the French Revolution.

The National Convention and its Committee of Public Safety had accomplished a great deal. By creating a nation in arms, they preserved the French Revolution and prevented it from being destroyed by its foreign enemies, who, if they had succeeded, would have reestablished the old monarchical order. Domestically, the Revolution had also been saved from the forces of counterrevolution. The committee's tactics, however, provided an example for the use of violence in domestic politics that has continued to bedevil the Western world to this day.

Robespierre. Maximilien Robespierre eventually came to exercise much control over the Committee of Public Safety. Robespierre and the committee worked to centralize the administration of France and curb the excesses of the Reign of Terror. Fear of Robespierre, however, led many in the National Convention to condemn him, and on July 28, 1794, he was executed.

Musée de la Ville de Paris//© Giraudon/Art Resource, NY

CHRONOLOGY The French Revolution

Assembly of notables	1787
National Assembly (Constituent Assembly)	*1789–1791*
Meeting of Estates-General	May 5, 1789
Formation of National Assembly	June 17, 1789
Tennis Court Oath	June 20, 1789
Fall of the Bastille	July 14, 1789
Great Fear	Summer 1789
Abolition of feudalism	August 4, 1789
Declaration of the Rights of Man and the Citizen	August 26, 1789
Women's march to Versailles; king's return to Paris	October 5–6, 1789
Civil Constitution of the Clergy	July 12, 1790
Flight of the king	June 20–21, 1791
Declaration of Pillnitz	August 27, 1791
Legislative Assembly	*1791–1792*
France declares war on Austria	April 20, 1792
Attack on the royal palace	August 10, 1792
National Convention	*1792–1795*
Abolition of the monarchy	September 21, 1792
Execution of the king	January 21, 1793
Universal mobilization of the nation	August 23, 1793
Execution of Robespierre	July 28, 1794
Directory	*1795–1799*
Constitution of 1795 is adopted	August 22, 1795

Reaction and the Directory

After the execution of Robespierre, revolutionary fervor began to give way to the Thermidorean Reaction, named after the month of Thermidor. The Terror began to abate. The National Convention curtailed the power of the Committee of Public Safety, shut down the Jacobin club, and attempted to provide better protection for its deputies against the Parisian mobs. Churches were allowed to reopen for public worship, and a decree of February 21, 1795, gave freedom of worship to all cults. Economic regulation was dropped in favor of *laissez-faire* policies, another clear indication that moderate forces were regaining control of the Revolution. In addition, a new constitution was written in August 1795 that reflected this more conservative republicanism or a desire for a stability that did not sacrifice the ideals of 1789.

To avoid the dangers of another single legislative assembly, the Constitution of 1795 established a national legislative assembly consisting of two chambers: a lower house, known as the Council of 500, whose function was to initiate legislation, and an upper house of 250 members, the Council of Elders, composed of married or widowed members over age forty, which would accept or reject the proposed laws. The 750 members of the two legislative bodies were chosen by electors who had to be owners or renters of property worth between one hundred and two hundred days' labor, a requirement that limited their number to 30,000, an even smaller base than the Constitution of 1791 had provided. The electors were chosen by the active citizens, now defined as all male taxpayers over the age of twenty-one. The executive authority or Directory consisted of five directors elected by the Council of Elders from a list presented by the Council of 500. To ensure some continuity from the old order to the new, the members of the National Convention ruled that two-thirds of the new members of the National Assembly must be chosen from their ranks. This decision produced disturbances in Paris and an insurrection at the beginning of October that was dispersed after fierce combat by an army contingent under the artillery general Napoleon Bonaparte. This would be the last time in the great French Revolution that the city of Paris would attempt to impose its wishes on the central government. Even more significant and ominous was this use of the army, which made it clear that the Directory from the beginning had to rely on the military for survival.

The period of the Directory was an era of materialistic reaction to the suffering and sacrifices that had been demanded in the Reign of Terror and the Republic of Virtue.

Speculators made fortunes in property by taking advantage of the government's severe monetary problems. Elaborate fashions, which had gone out of style because of their identification with the nobility, were worn again. Gambling and roulette became popular once more. Groups of "gilded youth"—sons of the wealthy, with long hair and rumpled clothes—took to the streets to insult former supporters of the Revolution.

The government of the Directory had to contend with political enemies from both ends of the political spectrum. On the right, royalists who dreamed of restoring the monarchy continued their agitation; some still toyed with violent means. On the left, Jacobin hopes of power were revived by continuing economic problems, especially the total collapse in the value of the *assignats*. Some radicals even went beyond earlier goals, especially Gracchus Babeuf (GRAK-uss bah-BUFF), who sneered, "What is the French Revolution? An open war between patricians and plebeians, between rich and poor." Babeuf, who was appalled at the misery of the common people, wanted to abolish private property and eliminate private enterprise. His Conspiracy of Equals was crushed in 1796, and he was executed in 1797.

New elections in 1797 created even more uncertainty and instability. Battered by the left and right, unable to find a definitive solution to the country's economic problems, and still carrying on the wars left from the Committee of Public Safety, the Directory increasingly relied on the military to maintain its power. This led to a coup d'état in 1799 in which the successful and popular general Napoleon Bonaparte was able to seize power.

The Age of Napoleon

 FOCUS QUESTION: Which aspects of the French Revolution did Napoleon preserve, and which did he destroy?

Napoleon (1769–1821) dominated both French and European history from 1799 to 1815. The coup that brought him to power occurred exactly ten years after the outbreak of the French Revolution. In a sense, Napoleon brought the Revolution to an end, but he was also its child; he even called himself the Son of the Revolution. The French Revolution had made possible his rise first in the military and then to supreme power in France. Even beyond this, Napoleon had once said, "I am the Revolution," and he never ceased to remind the French that they owed to him the preservation of all that was beneficial in the revolutionary program.

The Rise of Napoleon

Napoleon was born in Corsica in 1769, only a few months after France had annexed the island. The son of an Italian lawyer whose family stemmed from the Florentine nobility, Napoleone Buonaparte (to use his birth name) grew up in the countryside of Corsica, a willful and demanding child who nevertheless developed discipline, thriftiness,

and loyalty to his family. His father's connections in France enabled him to study first at a school in the French town of Autun, where he learned to speak French, and then to obtain a royal scholarship to study at a military school. At that time, he changed his first name to the more French-sounding Napoleon (he did not change his last name to Bonaparte until 1796).

Napoleon's military education led to his commission in 1785 as a lieutenant, although he was not well liked by his fellow officers because he was short, spoke with an Italian accent, and had little money. For the next seven years, Napoleon spent much of his time reading the works of the philosophes, especially Rousseau, and educating himself in military matters by studying the campaigns of great military leaders from the past, including Alexander the Great, Charlemagne, and Frederick the Great. The French Revolution and the European war that followed broadened his sights and presented him with new opportunities.

NAPOLEON'S MILITARY CAREER   Napoleon rose quickly through the ranks. In 1792, he became a captain and in the following year performed so well as an artillery commander in the capture of Toulon that he was promoted to the rank of brigadier general in 1794, when he was only twenty-five. In October 1795, he saved the National Convention from the Parisian mob, for which he was promoted to the rank of major general.

By this time, Napoleon had become a hero in some Parisian social circles, where he met Josephine de Beauharnais (zhoh-seff-FEEN duh boh-ar-NAY), widow of a guillotined general. Six years older than Napoleon, she lived a life of luxury, thanks to gifts from her influential male lovers. Napoleon fell deeply in love with her, married her in 1796, and remained committed to her for many years, despite her well-known affairs with other men.

Soon after his marriage, Napoleon was made commander of the French army in Italy (see the box on p. 598). There he turned a group of ill-disciplined soldiers into an effective fighting force and in a series of stunning victories defeated the Austrians and dictated peace to them in 1797.

Throughout his Italian campaign, Napoleon won the confidence of his men by his energy, charm, and ability to comprehend complex issues quickly and make decisions rapidly. He was tough with his officers and drove them relentlessly. With rank-and-file soldiers, he took a different approach. He ate with them, provided good food and clothing, and charmed them with his words. "They knew I was their patron," Napoleon once remarked. Throughout the rest of his life, these qualities, combined with his keen intelligence, ease with words, and supreme confidence in himself, enabled Napoleon to influence people and win their firm support. Napoleon liked to see himself as a man of destiny and a great man who mastered luck. He once said:

A consecutive series of great actions never is the result of chance and luck, it always is the product of planning and genius. Great men are rarely known to fail in their most perilous enterprises.... Is it because they are lucky that they

Napoleon and Psychological Warfare

In 1796, at the age of twenty-seven, Napoleon Bonaparte was given command of the French army in Italy, where he won a series of stunning victories. His use of speed, deception, and surprise to overwhelm his opponents is well known. In this selection from a proclamation to his troops in Italy, Napoleon also appears to be a master of psychological warfare.

+ ⊷ ≣ ⊶ +

Napoleon Bonaparte, Proclamation to the French Troops in Italy (April 26, 1796)

Soldiers:

In a fortnight you have won six victories, taken twenty-one standards, fifty-five pieces of artillery, several strong positions, and conquered the richest part of Piedmont [in northern Italy]; you have captured 15,000 prisoners and killed or wounded more than 10,000 men.... You have won battles without cannon, crossed rivers without bridges, made forced marches without shoes, camped without brandy and often without bread. Soldiers of liberty, only republican troops could have endured what you have endured. Soldiers, you have our thanks! The grateful Patrie [nation] will owe its prosperity to you....

The two armies which but recently attacked you with audacity are fleeing before you in terror; the wicked men who laughed at your misery and rejoiced at the thought of the triumphs of your enemies are confounded and trembling.

But, soldiers, as yet you have done nothing compared with what remains to be done.... Undoubtedly the greatest obstacles have been overcome; but you still have battles to fight, cities to capture, rivers to cross. Is there one among you whose courage is abating? No.... All of you are consumed with a desire to extend the glory of the French people; all of you long to humiliate those arrogant kings who dare to contemplate placing us in fetters; all of you desire to dictate a glorious peace, one which will indemnify the Patrie for the immense sacrifices it has made; all of you wish to be able to say with pride as you return to your villages, "I was with the victorious army of Italy!"

Q What themes did Napoleon use to play on the emotions of his troops and inspire them to greater efforts? Do you think Napoleon believed these words? Why or why not?

---

become great? No, but being great, they have been able to master luck.[19]

Napoleon also saw himself as a military genius who had a "touch for leading, which could not be learned from books, nor by practice."

In 1797, Napoleon returned to France as a conquering hero and was given command of an army training to invade England. Believing that the French were unready for such an invasion, he proposed instead to strike indirectly at Britain by taking Egypt and threatening India, a major source of British wealth. But the British controlled the seas and by 1799 had cut off supplies from Napoleon's army in Egypt. Seeing no future in certain defeat, Napoleon did not hesitate to abandon his army and return to Paris, where he participated in the coup d'état that ultimately led to his virtual dictatorship of France. He was only thirty years old at the time.

NAPOLEON IN CONTROL With the coup of 1799, a new form of the Republic was proclaimed with a constitution that established a bicameral legislative assembly elected indirectly to reduce the role of elections. Executive power

Napoleon as a Young Officer. Napoleon rose quickly through the military ranks, being promoted to the rank of brigadier general at the age of twenty-five. This painting of Napoleon by the Romantic painter Baron Gros presents an idealized, heroic image of the young leader.

The Coronation of Napoleon. In 1804, Napoleon restored monarchy to France when he crowned himself emperor. In the coronation scene painted by Jacques-Louis David, Napoleon is shown crowning the empress Josephine while the pope looks on. Shown seated in the box in the background is Napoleon's mother, even though she was not at the ceremony.

in the new government was vested in the hands of three consuls, although, as Article 42 of the constitution said, "the decision of the First Consul shall suffice." As first consul, Napoleon directly controlled the entire executive authority of government. He had overwhelming influence over the legislature, appointed members of the bureaucracy, controlled the army, and conducted foreign affairs. In 1802, Napoleon was made consul for life, and in 1804 he returned France to monarchy when he crowned himself Emperor Napoleon I. This step undoubtedly satisfied his enormous ego but also stabilized the regime and provided a permanence not possible in the consulate. The revolutionary era that had begun with an attempt to limit arbitrary government had ended with a government far more autocratic than the monarchy of the old regime. As his reign progressed and the demands of war increased, Napoleon's regime became ever more dictatorial

The Domestic Policies of Emperor Napoleon

Napoleon often claimed that he had preserved the gains of the Revolution for the French people. The ideal of republican liberty had, of course, been destroyed by Napoleon's thinly disguised autocracy. But were revolutionary ideals maintained in other ways? An examination of his domestic policies will enable us to judge the truth or falsehood of Napoleon's assertion.

NAPOLEON AND THE CATHOLIC CHURCH In 1801, Napoleon made peace with the oldest and most implacable enemy of the Revolution, the Catholic Church. Napoleon himself was devoid of any personal faith; he was an eighteenth-century rationalist who regarded religion at most as a convenience. In Egypt, he called himself a Muslim; in France, a Catholic. But Napoleon saw the necessity to come to terms with the Catholic Church in order to stabilize his regime. In 1800, he had declared to the clergy of Milan: "It is my firm intention that the Christian, Catholic, and Roman religion shall be preserved in its entirety.... No society can exist without morality; there is no good morality without religion. It is religion alone, therefore, that gives to the State a firm and durable support."[20] Soon after making this statement, Napoleon opened negotiations with Pope Pius VII to reestablish the Catholic Church in France.

Both sides gained from the Concordat that Napoleon arranged with the pope in 1801. Although the pope gained the right to depose French bishops, this gave him little real control over the French Catholic Church, since the state retained the right to nominate bishops. The Catholic Church was also permitted to hold processions again and reopen the seminaries. But Napoleon gained more than the pope. Just by signing the Concordat, the pope acknowledged the accomplishments of the Revolution. Moreover, the pope agreed not to raise the question of the church lands confiscated during the Revolution. Contrary to the pope's wishes, Catholicism was not reestablished as the state religion; Napoleon was only willing to recognize Catholicism as the religion of a majority of the French people. The clergy would be paid by the state, but to avoid the appearance of a state church, Protestant ministers were also put on the state payroll. As a result of the Concordat, the Catholic Church was no longer an enemy of the French government. At the same time, the agreement reassured those who had acquired church lands during the Revolution that they would not be stripped of them, an assurance that obviously made them supporters of the Napoleonic regime.

A NEW CODE OF LAWS Before the Revolution, France did not have a single set of laws but rather some three hundred different legal systems. Efforts were made during the Revolution to codify laws for the entire nation, but it remained for Napoleon to bring the work to completion in seven codes, the most important of which was the Civil Code (also known as the Code Napoléon). This preserved most of the revolutionary gains by recognizing the principle of the equality of all citizens before the law, the right of individuals to choose their professions, religious toleration, and the abolition of serfdom and feudalism. Property rights continued to be carefully protected, while the interests of employers were safeguarded by outlawing trade unions and strikes. The Civil Code clearly reflected the revolutionary aspirations for a uniform legal system, legal equality, and protection of property and individuals.

But the rights of some people were strictly curtailed by the Civil Code. During the radical phase of the French Revolution, new laws had made divorce an easy process for both husbands and wives, restricted the rights of fathers over their children (they could no longer have their children put in prison arbitrarily), and allowed all children (including daughters) to inherit property equally. Napoleon's Civil Code undid most of this legislation. The control of fathers over their families was restored. Divorce was still allowed but was made more difficult for women to obtain. A wife caught in adultery, for example, could be divorced by her husband and even imprisoned. A husband, however, could only be accused of adultery if he moved his mistress into his home. Women were now "less equal than men" in other ways as well. When they married, their property was brought under the control of their husbands. In lawsuits, they were treated as minors, and their testimony was regarded as less reliable than that of men.

THE FRENCH BUREAUCRACY Napoleon also worked on rationalizing the bureaucratic structure of France by developing a powerful centralized administrative machine. During the Revolution, the National Assembly had divided France into eighty-three departments and replaced the provincial estates, nobles, and *intendants* with self-governing assemblies. Napoleon kept the departments but eliminated the locally elected assemblies and instituted new officials, the most important of which were the **prefects.** As the central government's agents, appointed by the first consul (Napoleon), the prefects were responsible for supervising all aspects of local government. Yet they were not local men, and their careers depended on the central government.

As part of Napoleon's overhaul of the administrative system, tax collection became systematic and efficient (which it had never been under the old regime). Taxes were now collected by professional collectors employed by the state who dealt directly with each individual taxpayer. No tax exemptions due to birth, status, or special arrangement were granted. In principle, these changes had been introduced in 1789, but not until Napoleon did they actually work. In 1802, the first consul proclaimed a balanced budget.

Administrative centralization required a bureaucracy of capable officials, and Napoleon worked hard to develop one. Early on, the regime showed its preference for experts and cared little whether that expertise had been acquired in royal or revolutionary bureaucracies. Promotion in civil or military offices was to be based not on rank or birth but only on demonstrated abilities. This was, of course, what many bourgeois had wanted before the Revolution. Napoleon, however, also created a new aristocracy based on merit in the state service. Napoleon created 3,263 nobles between 1808 and 1814; nearly 60 percent were military officers, and the remainder came from the upper ranks of the civil service or were other state and local officials. Socially, only 22 percent of Napoleon's aristocracy came from the nobility of the old regime; almost 60 percent were of bourgeois origin.

NAPOLEON'S GROWING DESPOTISM In his domestic policies, then, Napoleon both destroyed and preserved aspects of the Revolution. Although equality was preserved in the law code and the opening of careers to talent, the creation of a new aristocracy, the strong protection accorded to property rights, and the use of conscription for the military make it clear that much equality had been lost. Liberty had been replaced by an initially benevolent despotism that grew increasingly arbitrary. Napoleon shut down sixty of France's seventy-three newspapers and insisted that all manuscripts be subjected to government scrutiny before they were published. Even the mail was opened by government police.

One prominent writer, Germaine de Staël (zhayr-MEN duh STAHL) (1766–1817), refused to accept Napoleon's growing despotism. Educated in Enlightenment ideas, she set up a salon in Paris that was a prominent intellectual center by 1800. She wrote novels and political works that denounced Napoleon's rule as tyrannical. Napoleon banned her books in France and exiled her to the German states, where she continued to write, although not without considerable anguish at being absent from France. "The universe is in France," she once wrote; "outside it there is nothing." After the overthrow of Napoleon, Germaine de Staël returned to her beloved Paris, where she died two years later.

Napoleon's Empire and the European Response

When Napoleon became consul in 1799, France was at war with a second European coalition of Russia, Great Britain, and Austria. Napoleon realized the need for a pause. He remarked to a Prussian diplomat "that the French Revolution is not finished so long as the scourge of war lasts.... I want peace, as much to settle the present French government as to save the world from chaos."[21] The peace he sought was achieved at Amiens in March 1802 and left France with new frontiers and a number of client territories from the North Sea to the Adriatic. But the peace did not last because the British and French both regarded it as temporary and had little intention of adhering to its terms.

In 1803, war was renewed with Britain, which was soon joined by Austria and Russia in the Third Coalition. At the Battle of Ulm in southern Germany in 1805, Napoleon surrounded an Austrian army, which quickly surrendered. Proceeding eastward from Ulm, Napoleon faced a large Russian army under Tsar Alexander I and some Austrian troops at Austerlitz (AWSS-tur-litz). The combined allied forces outnumbered Napoleon's forces, but the tsar chose poor terrain for the battle, and Napoleon devastated the allied forces. Austria sued for peace, and Tsar Alexander took his remaining forces back to Russia.

At first, Prussia had refused to join the Third Coalition, but after Napoleon began to reorganize the German states, Prussia reversed course. Acting quickly, Napoleon crushed the Prussian forces in two battles at Jena (YAY-nuh) and Auerstadt (OW-urr-shtaht) in October 1806 and then moved on to defeat the Russians, who had decided to reenter the fray, at Eylau (Y-low) and Friedland (FREET-lahnt) in June 1807. Napoleon's Grand Army had defeated the Continental members of the coalition, giving him the opportunity to create a new European order.

NAPOLEON'S GRAND EMPIRE The Grand Empire was composed of three major parts: the French empire, a series of dependent states, and allied states (see Map 19.3). The French empire, the inner core of the Grand Empire, consisted of an enlarged France extending to the Rhine in the east and including the western half of Italy north of Rome. Dependent states included Spain, the Netherlands, the kingdom of Italy, the Swiss Republic, the Grand Duchy of Warsaw, and the Confederation of the Rhine (a union of all German states except Austria and Prussia). Allied states were those defeated by Napoleon and forced to join his struggle against Britain; they included Prussia, Austria, and Russia. Although the internal structure of the Grand Empire varied outside its inner core, Napoleon considered himself the leader of the whole: "Europe cannot be at rest except under a single head who will have kings for his officers, who will distribute his kingdom to his lieutenants."

Within his empire, Napoleon demanded obedience, in part because he needed a common front against the British and in part because his growing egotism required obedience to his will. But as a child of the Enlightenment and the Revolution, Napoleon also sought acceptance everywhere of certain revolutionary principles, including legal equality, religious toleration, and economic freedom. As he explained to his brother Jerome, shortly after making him king of the new German state of Westphalia:

> What the peoples of Germany desire most impatiently is that talented commoners should have the same right to your esteem and to public employments as the nobles, that any trace of serfdom and of an intermediate hierarchy between the sovereign and the lowest class of the people should be completely abolished. The benefits of the Code Napoléon, the publicity of judicial procedure, the creation of juries must be so many distinguishing marks of your monarchy.... What nation would wish to return under the arbitrary Prussian government once it had tasted the benefits of a wise and liberal administration? The peoples of Germany, the peoples of France, of Italy, of Spain all desire equality and liberal ideas. I have guided the affairs of Europe for many years now, and I have had occasion to convince myself that the buzzing of the privileged classes is contrary to the general opinion. Be a constitutional king.[22]

In the inner core and dependent states of his Grand Empire, Napoleon tried to destroy the old order. Nobility and clergy everywhere in these states lost their special privileges. He decreed equality of opportunity with offices open to talent, equality before the law, and religious toleration. This spread of French revolutionary principles was an important factor in the development of liberal traditions in these countries. These reforms have led some historians to view Napoleon as the last of the enlightened absolutists.

THE PROBLEM OF GREAT BRITAIN Like Hitler 130 years later, Napoleon hoped that his Grand Empire would last for centuries; like Hitler's empire, it collapsed almost as rapidly as it had been formed. Two major reasons help explain this: the survival of Great Britain and the force of nationalism. Britain's survival was due primarily to its seapower. As long as Britain ruled the waves, it was almost invulnerable to military attack. Although Napoleon contemplated an invasion of England and even collected ships for it, he could not overcome the British navy's decisive defeat of a combined French-Spanish fleet at Trafalgar in 1805. Napoleon then turned to his **Continental System** to defeat Britain. Put into effect between 1806 and 1807, it attempted to prevent British goods from reaching the European continent in order to weaken Britain economically and destroy its capacity to wage war. But the

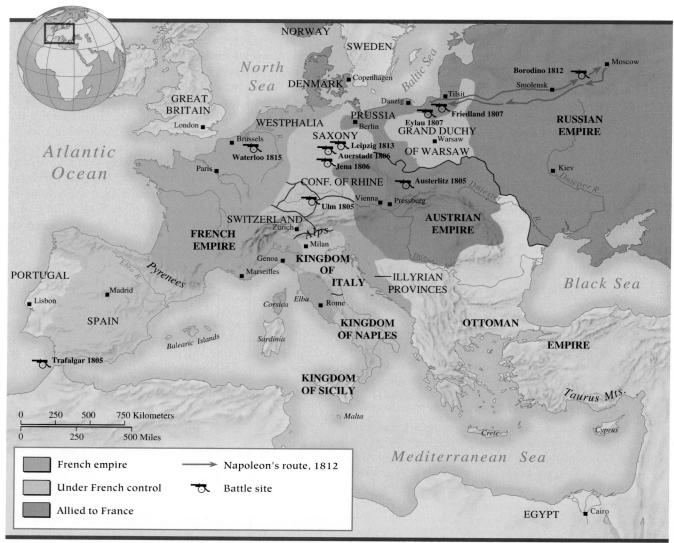

MAP 19.3 Napoleon's Grand Empire in 1810. Napoleon's Grand Army won a series of victories against Austria, Prussia, and Russia that gave the French emperor full or partial control over much of Europe by 1807.

Q   *On the Continent, what is the overall relationship between distance from France and degree of French control, and how can you account for this?*

Continental System failed. Allied states resented the ever-tightening French economic hegemony; some began to cheat and others to resist, thereby opening the door to British collaboration. New markets in the eastern Mediterranean and in Latin America also provided compensation for the British. Indeed, by 1810, British overseas exports were approaching record highs.

NATIONALISM   A second important factor in the defeat of Napoleon was **nationalism.** This political creed had arisen during the French Revolution in the French people's emphasis on brotherhood (*fraternité*) and solidarity against other peoples. Nationalism involved the unique cultural identity of a people based on a common language, religion, and national symbols. The spirit of French nationalism had made possible the mass armies of the revolutionary and Napoleonic eras. But in spreading the principles of the French Revolution beyond France, Napoleon inadvertently brought about a spread of nationalism as well. The French aroused nationalism in two ways: by making themselves hated oppressors, and thus arousing the patriotism of others in opposition to French nationalism, and by showing the people of Europe what nationalism was and what a nation in arms could do. The lesson was not lost on other peoples and rulers. A Spanish uprising against Napoleon's rule, aided by British support, kept a French force of 200,000 pinned down for years.

Nationalist movements also arose in the German states, where a number of intellectuals advocated a cultural nationalism based on the unity of the German people. The philosopher Johann Gottlieb Fichte (yoh-HAHN got-LEEP FIKH-tuh) (1762–1814), who had at first welcomed the French Revolution for freeing the human spirit, soon became a proponent of a German national spirit radically

Francisco Goya, *The Third of May 1808.* After Napoleon imposed his brother Joseph on Spain as its king, the Spanish people revolted against his authority, and a series of riots broke out in Madrid. This painting by Francisco Goya shows the French response—a deliberate execution of Spanish citizens to frighten people into submission. Goya portrays the French troops as a firing squad, killing people (including a monk) reacting in terror. The peasant in the middle throws out his arms in a gesture reminiscent of crucifixion. Goya painted many scenes depicting the horrors of war in Napoleonic Spain.

different from that of France. Although philosophical voices like Fichte's did little to overthrow the French, they did awaken a dream of German nationalism that would bear fruit later in the nineteenth century.

In Prussia, feeling against Napoleon led to a serious reform of the old order that had been so easily crushed by the French emperor. As one Prussian officer put it, the Prussians must learn from the French example and "place their entire national energies in opposition to the enemy." Under the direction of Baron Heinrich von Stein (HYN-rikh fun SHYTN) and later Prince Karl von Hardenberg (KARL fun HAR-den-berk), Prussia embarked on a series of political and military reforms, including the abolition of serfdom, election of city councils, and creation of a larger standing army. Prussia's reforms, instituted as a response to Napoleon, enabled it to again play an important role in European affairs.

The Fall of Napoleon

Napoleon once said, "If I had experienced pleasure, I might have rested; but the peril was always in front of me, and the day's victory was always forgotten in the pre-occupation with the necessity of winning a new victory on the morrow."[23] Never at rest, Napoleon decided in 1812 to invade Russia. It was the beginning of his downfall, but Russia's defection from the Continental System had left him with little choice. Although aware of the risks in invading such a large country, Napoleon also knew that if the Russians were allowed to challenge the Continental System unopposed, others would soon follow suit. In June 1812, Napoleon's Grand Army of more than 600,000 men entered Russia. Napoleon's hopes for victory depended on quickly meeting and defeating the Russian armies, but the Russian forces refused to give battle and retreated hundreds of miles while torching their own villages and countryside to prevent Napoleon's army from finding food and forage. Heat and disease also took their toll of the army, and the vast space of Russian territory led many troops to desert. When the Russians did stop to fight at Borodino, Napoleon's forces won an indecisive and costly victory. Forty-five thousand Russian troops were killed; the French lost 30,000 men, but they had no replacements nearby. When the remaining troops of the Grand Army arrived in Moscow, they found the city ablaze. Lacking food and supplies, Napoleon abandoned Moscow late in October and made the "Great Retreat" across Russia in terrible winter conditions. Only 40,000 troops managed to straggle back to Poland in January 1813. This military disaster then led to a war of liberation all over Europe, culminating in Napoleon's defeat in April 1814.

CHRONOLOGY The Napoleonic Era, 1799–1815

Napoleon as first consul	1799–1804
Concordat with Catholic Church	1801
Peace of Amiens	1802
Emperor Napoleon I	1804–1815
Battle of Ulm (defeat of Austria)	1805
Battle of Austerlitz (defeat of Russia)	1805
Battle of Trafalgar (naval defeat of Napoleon's forces)	1805
Battles of Jena and Auerstadt (defeat of Prussia)	1806
Continental System established	1806
Battles of Eylau and Friedland (defeat of Russia)	1807
Invasion of Russia	1812
War of liberation	1813–1814
Exile to Elba	1814
Battle of Waterloo; exile to Saint Helena	1815
Death of Napoleon	1821

The defeated emperor of the French was allowed to play ruler on the island of Elba, off the coast of Tuscany, while the Bourbon monarchy was restored to France in the person of Louis XVIII, brother of the executed king. But the new king had little support, and Napoleon, bored on Elba, slipped back into France. When troops were sent to capture him, Napoleon opened his coat and addressed them: "Soldiers of the fifth regiment, I am your Emperor.... If there is a man among you would kill his Emperor, here I am!" No one fired a shot. Shouting "Vive l'Empéreur! Vive l'Empéreur," the troops went over to his side, and Napoleon entered Paris in triumph on March 20, 1815.

The powers that had defeated him pledged once more to fight this person they called the "Enemy and Disturber of the Tranquility of the World." Having decided to strike first at his enemies, Napoleon raised yet another army and moved to attack the nearest allied forces stationed in Belgium. At Waterloo on June 18, Napoleon met a combined British and Prussian army under the duke of Wellington and suffered a bloody defeat. This time, the victorious allies exiled him to Saint Helena, a small, forsaken island in the South Atlantic. Only Napoleon's memory would continue to haunt French political life.

CHAPTER SUMMARY

The late eighteenth century was a time of dramatic political transformation. Revolutionary upheavals, beginning in North America and continuing in France, produced movements for political liberty and equality. The documents created by these revolutions, the Declaration of Independence and the Declaration of the Rights of Man and the Citizen, embodied the fundamental ideas of the Enlightenment and set forth a liberal political agenda based on a belief in popular sovereignty—the people as the source of political power—and the principles of liberty and equality. Liberty meant, in theory, freedom from arbitrary power as well as the freedom to think, write, and worship as one chose. Equality meant equality in rights and equality of opportunity based on talent rather than birth. In practice, equality remained limited; men who owned property had great opportunities for voting and officeholding, and there was certainly no equality between men and women.

The leaders of France's liberal revolution during the National and Legislative Assemblies between 1789 and 1791 were men of property, both bourgeois and noble, but they were assisted by commoners, both sans-culottes and peasants. In this first phase of the revolution, the old order was demolished as a new constitution established a limited constitutional monarchy. Yet, despite the hopes of the men of property, the liberal revolution was not the end of the revolution. The decision of the revolutionaries to go to war with European monarchs who opposed the revolution "revolutionized the revolution," opening the door to a more radical, democratic, and violent stage between 1792 and 1795 under the National Convention led by the Committee of Public Safety. During this phase, revolutionary courts persecuted those not sufficiently supportive of the revolutionary cause, creating the infamous Reign of Terror. The excesses of the Reign of Terror, however, led to a reaction and a government headed by a five-member Directory, which governed from 1795 to 1799. But it satisfied neither the radicals nor the royalists. In 1799, Napoleon Bonaparte overthrew this government and established first the Consulate and then a new monarchy with himself as emperor. Napoleon, while diminishing freedom by establishing order and centralizing the government, shrewdly preserved equality of rights and the opening of careers to talent and integrated the bourgeoisie and old nobility into a new elite of property owners.

The French Revolution defined the modern revolutionary concept. No one had foreseen or consciously planned the upheaval that began in 1789, but after 1789, "revolutionaries" knew that mass uprisings could succeed in overthrowing unwanted governments. The French Revolution became the classic political and social model for revolution. At the same time, the liberal and national political ideals created by the Revolution and spread through Europe by Napoleon's conquests dominated the political landscape of the nineteenth and early twentieth centuries.

CHAPTER TIMELINE

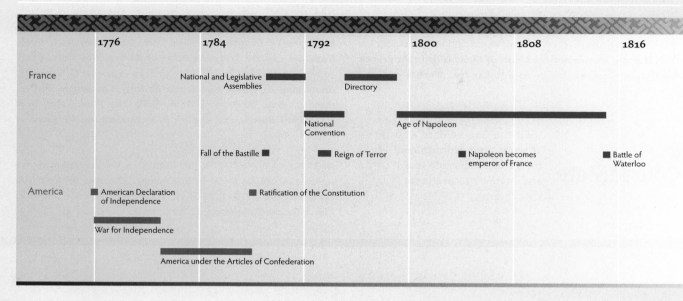

CHAPTER REVIEW

Upon Reflection

Q How was France changed by the revolutionary events of 1789 to 1792, and who benefited the most from these changes?

Q Why did the French Revolution enter a radical phase, and what did that radical phase accomplish?

Q In what ways did Napoleon's policies reject the accomplishments of the French Revolution? In what ways did his policies strengthen the Revolution's accomplishments?

Key Terms

revolution (p. 578)
old order (p. 580)
sans-culottes (p. 588)
Girondins (p. 588)
Mountain (p. 588)
nation in arms (p. 589)
de-Christianization (p. 592)
prefects (p. 600)
Continental system (p. 601)
nationalism (p. 602)

Suggestions for Further Reading

GENERAL WORKS A well-written introduction to the French Revolution can be found in **W. Doyle, The Oxford History of the French Revolution,** 2nd ed. (Oxford, 2003). On the entire revolutionary and Napoleonic eras, see **O. Connelly, The French Revolution and Napoleonic Era,** 3rd ed. (Fort Worth, Tex., 2000). A brief work is **J. D. Popkin et al., A Short History of the French Revolution,** 4th ed. (Upper Saddle River, N.J., 2005). Two comprehensive reference works are **S. F. Scott** and **B. Rothaus, eds., Historical Dictionary of the French Revolution,** 2 vols. (Westport, Conn., 1985), and **F. Furet** and **M. Ozouf, A Critical Dictionary of the French Revolution,** trans. **A. Goldhammer** (Cambridge, Mass., 1989). See also **G. Kates, ed., The French Revolution,** 2nd ed. (London, 2006).

EARLY YEARS OF THE REVOLUTION The origins of the French Revolution are examined in **W. Doyle, Origins of the French Revolution,** 3rd ed. (Oxford, 1999), and **P. R. Cambell, ed., Origins of the French Revolution** (New York, 2006), a collection of essays. On the early years of the Revolution, see **M. Kennedy, The Jacobin Clubs in the French Revolution: The First Years** (Princeton, N.J., 1982); **N. Hampson, Prelude to Terror** (Oxford, 1988); and **T. Tackett, Becoming a Revolutionary** (Princeton, N.J., 1996), on the deputies to the National Assembly. For interesting insight into Louis XVI and French society, see **T. Tackett, When the King Took Flight** (Cambridge, Mass., 2003).

RADICAL REVOLUTION Important works on the radical stage of the French Revolution include **D. Andress, The Terror: The Merciless War for Freedom in Revolutionary France** (New York, 2005);

R. R. Palmer, *Twelve Who Ruled* (New York, 1965), a classic; and R. Cobb, *The People's Armies* (London, 1987). For a biography of Robespierre, one of the leading figures of this period, see **R. Scurr, Fatal Purity: Robespierre and the French Revolution** (New York, 2006). The importance of the revolutionary wars in the radical stage of the Revolution is underscored in **T. C. W. Blanning, The French Revolutionary Wars, 1787–1802** (New York, 1996). On the Directory, see **M. Lyons, France Under the Directory** (Cambridge, 1975).

WOMEN   On the role of women in revolutionary France, see **O. J. Hufton, Women and the Limits of Citizenship in the French Revolution** (Toronto, 1992), and **J. Landes, Women and the Public Sphere in the Age of the French Revolution** (Ithaca, N.Y., 1988).

NAPOLEON   The best biography of Napoleon is **S. Englund, Napoleon: A Political Life** (New York, 2004). Also valuable are **G. J. Ellis, Napoleon** (New York, 1997); **M. Lyons, Napoleon Bonaparte and the Legacy of the French Revolution** (New York, 1994); and the massive biographies by **F. J. McLynn, Napoleon: A Biography** (London, 1997), and **A. Schom, Napoleon Bonaparte** (New York, 1997). See also **I. Woloch, Napoleon and His Collaborators: The Making of a Dictatorship** (New York, 2002), and **A. I. Grab, Napoleon and the Transformation of Europe** (New York, 2003), on Napoleon's Grand Empire. On Napoleon's wars, see **O. Connelly, Blundering to Glory: Napoleon's Military Campaigns,** 3rd ed. (Lanham, Md., 2006), and **D. A. Bell, The First Total War: Napoleon's Europe and the Birth of Warfare as We Know It** (Boston, 2007).

AMERICAN REVOLUTION   A history of the revolutionary era in America can be found in **S. Conway, The War of American Independence, 1775–1783** (New York, 1995), and **C. Bonwick, The American Revolution** (Charlottesville, Va., 1991).

Visit the CourseMate website at www.cengagebrain.com for additional study tools and review materials for this chapter.

CourseMate

1. "We hold these truths to be self-evident . . . that [all men] are endowed by their creator with certain unalienable rights, that among these are life, liberty and the pursuit of happiness." This statement most closely reflects the thoughts of

   (A) Thomas Hobbes.
   (B) George Washington.
   (C) John Locke.
   (D) Baron de Montesquieu.
   (E) Voltaire.

2. As a result of the Great Fear,

   (A) the First and Second Estates remained untaxed.
   (B) the Bastille was destroyed.
   (C) Louis XVI and Marie Antoinette were killed.
   (D) nobles were forced to give up their titles and aristocratic privileges.
   (E) women marched on Versailles and demanded a reduction in bread prices.

3. The French experienced all of the following problems during the late eighteenth century EXCEPT

   (A) high bread prices.
   (B) high taxes for all three Estates.
   (C) an increase in the national debt.
   (D) a weak, indecisive king.
   (E) food shortages due to bad harvests.

4. The political cartoon below depicts

   (A) Napoleon fighting with the rest of the European leaders as he attempts to rule all of Europe.
   (B) Louis XVI successfully leading his country into prosperity.
   (C) a peasant carrying the physical and financial burdens of the other Estates of France.
   (D) a Spanish peasant being controlled by Napoleon and his advisers as they rule Spain.
   (E) the clergy controlling the king, nobles, and peasants.

5. Napoleon successfully accomplished which of the following?

   (A) an economic and military blockade against England
   (B) the reestablishment of the Holy Roman Empire
   (C) invasion and subjugation of Russia.
   (D) the elimination of primogeniture and peace with the Roman Catholic Church
   (E) the creation of a new peacekeeping body known as the Congress of Vienna

6. The summoning of the Estates-General

   (A) allowed the First and Second Estates to willingly permit themselves to be taxed.
   (B) was Louis XVI's last attempt to fix the problems with France's economy.
   (C) was intended to negotiate peace between the king and his subjects.
   (D) was the primary cause of Louis XVI's beheading.
   (E) was Napoleon's attempt to stage a coup d'état and gain power.

7. Who is most likely to have invited others to take "the most effectual means . . . to put the king of France in a state to strengthen . . . the bases of a monarchical government"?

   (A) a concerned European monarch
   (B) a French Jacobin
   (C) the leader of the Reign of Terror
   (D) an American who sympathized with the French revolutionary cause
   (E) a member of the sans-culottes

8. Which of the following is the correct order of events in the French Revolution?

   (A) Tennis Court Oath, death of the king, Directory, Reign of Terror
   (B) Declaration of the Rights of Man, National Assembly, Directory, Reign of Terror
   (C) Great Fear, storming of the Bastille, Republic of Virtue, Declaration of the Rights of Man
   (D) calling of the Estates-General, creation of the National Assembly, Tennis Court Oath, Constitution of 1791, death of the king
   (E) creation of the Estates-General, Reign of Terror, Directory, Great Fear

9. The American Revolution

   (A) resulted in a complete social and political change for the colonists.
   (B) was an economic defeat for the Americans as they attempted to gain control over the Atlantic Ocean trade.
   (C) was spurred by the French Revolution and the agitation of Enlightenment thinkers.
   (D) culminated in a complete British military defeat that hastened Britain's political decline.
   (E) was a military victory for the colonists as they singlehandedly defeated their mother country.

10. During the late eighteenth century, France's economic problems worsened because

    (A) the country became embroiled in an economic boycott against Russia.
    (B) the Roman Catholic Church increased its taxation of France, sending it into bankruptcy.
    (C) Louis XIV had modified the tax structure to pacify the nobles, thereby exempting them from taxation and starving the state of revenue.
    (D) Louis XVI did not attempt to alter the tax system of the state.
    (E) the Third Estate was destitute and no one within the class held any financial assets.

11. The creation of the United States

    (A) embodied the philosophies of thinkers such as Locke and Montesquieu.
    (B) established the first effective republic in the west since ancient Athens.
    (C) signified a dramatic social shift as social classes and economic divisions were eliminated.
    (D) instituted a constitutional monarchy with an unrestricted ruler.
    (E) was the primary cause of the revolts within France.

12. France's social structure

    (A) contained two main social groups, those who were educated and wealthy and those who were uneducated and poor.
    (B) consisted of Estates that found relative peace and harmony between their apportioned social divisions.
    (C) consisted of a relatively satisfied Second Estate, but a clash of ideas within the Third Estate.
    (D) allowed the Second Estate to include both the nobles and all educated professionals.
    (E) allowed for a relatively equal apportionment of land among the three Estates.

13. Women during the French Revolution

    (A) were unable to provide emotional and financial support for their fellow revolutionaries.
    (B) won greater freedoms, such as freedom of speech and the right to vote.
    (C) often were the instigators of revolutionary action against the monarchy.
    (D) mostly attempted to avoid association with the Revolution or the revolutionaries.
    (E) gained political equality with men and served in the Directory.

14. Napoleon Bonaparte

    (A) succeeded in bringing an end to the violence within France; however, he plunged France further into despair with his continental wars and limitations on speech and the press.
    (B) revitalized France by expanding its borders and bringing financial recovery to its empire.
    (C) continued in the path set by the philosophes by granting further rights to citizens and ending existing feudalism in many parts of the empire.
    (D) was a revolutionary in his vision for the Grand Empire and successfully placated those he ruled.
    (E) was a military genius who effectively brought peace to the continent.

Power looms in an English textile factory

CHAPTER 20

The Industrial Revolution and Its Impact on European Society

CHAPTER OUTLINE AND FOCUS QUESTIONS

The Industrial Revolution in Great Britain

Q Why was Great Britain the first state to have an Industrial Revolution? Why did it happen in Britain when it did? What were the basic features of the new industrial system created by the Industrial Revolution?

The Spread of Industrialization

Q How did the Industrial Revolution spread from Great Britain to the Continent and the United States, and how did industrialization in those areas differ from British industrialization?

The Social Impact of the Industrial Revolution

Q What effects did the Industrial Revolution have on urban life, social classes, family life, and standards of living? What were working conditions like in the early decades of the Industrial Revolution, and what efforts were made to improve them?

┌─ CRITICAL THINKING ═══════════════

Q What role did government and trade unions play in the industrial development of the Western world? Who helped the workers the most?

THE FRENCH REVOLUTION dramatically and quickly altered the political structure of France, and the Napoleonic conquests spread many of the revolutionary principles in an equally rapid and stunning fashion to other parts of Europe. During the late eighteenth and early nineteenth centuries, another revolution—an industrial one—was transforming the economic and social structure of Europe, although more slowly and less dramatically.

The Industrial Revolution caused a quantum leap in industrial production. New sources of energy and power, especially coal and steam, replaced wind and water to build and run machines that dramatically decreased the use of human and animal labor and at the same time increased productivity. This in turn called for new ways of organizing human labor to maximize the benefits and profits from the new machines; factories replaced workshops and home workrooms. Many early factories were dreadful places with difficult working conditions. Reformers, appalled at these conditions, were especially critical of the treatment of married women. One reported, "We have repeatedly seen married females, in the last stage of pregnancy, slaving from morning to night beside these never-tiring machines, and when . . . they were obliged to sit down to take a moment's ease, and being seen by the manager, were fined for the offense." But there were also examples of well-run factories. William Cobbett described one in Manchester in 1830: "In this room, which is lighted in the most convenient and beautiful manner, there were five hundred pairs of looms at work, and five hundred persons attending those looms; and, owing to the goodness of the masters, the whole looking healthy and well-dressed."

During the Industrial Revolution, Europe experienced a shift from a traditional, labor-intensive economy based on farming and handicrafts to a more capital-intensive economy based on manufacturing by machines, specialized labor, and industrial factories. Although the Industrial Revolution took decades to spread, it was truly revolutionary in the way it fundamentally changed Europeans, their society, and their relationship to the rest of the world. The development of large factories encouraged mass movements of people from the countryside to urban areas, where impersonal coexistence replaced the traditional intimacy of rural life. Higher levels of productivity led to a search for new sources of raw materials, new consumption patterns, and a revolution in transportation that allowed raw materials and finished products to be moved quickly around the world. The creation of a wealthy industrial middle class and a huge industrial working class (or proletariat) substantially transformed traditional social relationships.

The Industrial Revolution in Great Britain

 Focus Questions: Why was Great Britain the first state to have an Industrial Revolution? Why did it happen in Britain when it did? What were the basic features of the new industrial system created by the Industrial Revolution?

Although the Industrial Revolution evolved over a long period of time, historians generally agree that it began in Britain sometime after 1750. By 1850, the Industrial Revolution had made Great Britain the wealthiest country in the world; it had also spread to the European continent and the New World. In another fifty years, both Germany and the United States would surpass Britain in industrial production.

Origins

A number of factors or conditions coalesced in Britain to produce the first Industrial Revolution. One of these was the **agricultural revolution** of the eighteenth century. The changes in the methods of farming and stock breeding that characterized this agricultural transformation led to a significant increase in food production. British agriculture could now feed more people at lower prices with less labor. Unlike people in the rest of Europe, even ordinary British families did not have to use most of their income to buy food, giving them the potential to purchase manufactured goods. At the same time, rapid population growth in the second half of the eighteenth century provided a pool of surplus labor for the new factories of the emerging

British industry. Rural workers in cottage industries also provided a potential labor force for industrial enterprises.

SUPPLY OF CAPITAL Britain had a ready supply of **capital** for investment in the new industrial machines and the factories that were needed to house them. In addition to profits from trade and cottage industry, Britain possessed an effective central bank and well-developed, flexible credit facilities. Nowhere in Europe were people so accustomed to using paper instruments to facilitate capital transactions. Many early factory owners were merchants and entrepreneurs who had profited from the eighteenth-century cottage industry. Of 110 cotton-spinning mills in operation in the area known as the Midlands between 1769 and 1800, fully 62 were established by hosiers, drapers, mercers, and others involved in some fashion in the cottage textile industry.

EARLY INDUSTRIAL ENTREPRENEURS But capital is only part of the story. Britain had a fair number of individuals who were interested in making profits if the opportunity presented itself (see the box on p. 609). The British were a people, as one historian has said, "fascinated by wealth and commerce, collectively and individually." No doubt the English revolutions of the seventeenth century had helped create an environment in Britain, unlike that of the absolutist states on the Continent, where political power rested in the hands of a progressive group of people who favored innovation in economic matters.

Nevertheless, these early industrial entrepreneurs faced considerable financial hazards. Fortunes were made quickly and lost just as quickly. The structure of early firms was fluid. An individual or family proprietorship was the usual mode of operation, but entrepreneurs also brought in friends to help—and just as easily jettisoned them. John Marshall, who made money in flax spinning, threw his partners out: "As they could neither of them be of any further use, I released them from the firm and took the whole upon myself."[1]

MINERAL RESOURCES Britain had ample supplies of important mineral resources, such as coal and iron ore, needed in the manufacturing process. Britain was also small, so the resources needed to be transported only relatively short distances. In addition to nature's provision of abundant rivers, from the mid-seventeenth century onward, both private and public investment poured into the construction of new roads, bridges, and, beginning in the 1750s and 1760s, canals. By 1780, roads, rivers, and canals linked the major industrial centers of the North, the Midlands, London, and the Atlantic. Unlike the Continental countries, Britain had no internal customs barriers to hinder domestic trade.

ROLE OF GOVERNMENT Britain's government also played a significant role in the process of industrialization. Parliament contributed to the favorable business climate by providing a stable government and passing laws that

The Traits of the British Industrial Entrepreneur

Richard Arkwright (1732–1792), inventor of a spinning frame and founder of cotton factories, was a good example of the successful entrepreneur in the early Industrial Revolution in Britain. In this selection, Edward Baines, writing in 1835, discusses the traits that explain the success of Arkwright and presumably other British entrepreneurs.

Edward Baines, *The History of the Cotton Manufacture in Great Britain*

Richard Arkwright rose by the force of his natural talents from a very humble condition in society. He was born at Preston on the 23rd of December, 1732, of poor parents: being the youngest of thirteen children, his parents could only afford to give him an education of the humblest kind, and he was scarcely able to write. He was brought up to the trade of a barber at Kirkham and Preston, and established himself in that business at Bolton in the year 1760. Having become possessed of a chemical process for dyeing human hair, which in that day (when wigs were universal) was of considerable value, he traveled about collecting hair, and again disposing of it when dyed. In 1761, he married a wife from Leigh, and the connections he thus formed in that town are supposed to have afterwards brought him acquainted with Highs's experiments in making spinning machines. He himself manifested a strong bent for experiments in mathematics, which he is stated to have followed with so much devotedness as to have neglected his business and injured his circumstances. His natural disposition was ardent, enterprising, and stubbornly persevering: his mind was as coarse as it was bold and active, and his manners were rough and unpleasing. . . .

The most marked traits in the character of Arkwright were his wonderful ardor, energy, and perseverance. He commonly labored in his multifarious concerns from five o'clock in the morning till nine at night; and when considerably more than fifty years of age,—feeling that the defects of his education placed him under great difficulty and inconvenience in conducting his correspondence, and in the general management of his business,—he encroached upon his sleep, in order to gain an hour each day to learn English grammar, and another hour to improve his writing and orthography [spelling]! He was impatient of whatever interfered with his favorite pursuits; and the fact is too strikingly characteristic not to be mentioned, that he separated from his wife not many years after their marriage, because she, convinced that he would starve his family [because of the impractical nature of his schemes], broke some of his experimental models of machinery. Arkwright was a severe economist of time; and, that he might not waste a moment, he generally traveled with four horses, and at a very rapid speed. His concerns in Derbyshire, Lancashire, and Scotland were so extensive and numerous, as to [show] at once his astonishing power of transacting business and his all grasping spirit. In many of these he had partners, but he generally managed in such a way, that, whoever lost, he himself was a gainer.

Q As seen in the life of Richard Arkwright, what traits did Edward Baines think were crucial to being a successful entrepreneur? To what extent are these still considered the necessary traits for a successful entrepreneur?

---

protected private property. Moreover, Britain was remarkable for the freedom it provided for private enterprise. It placed fewer restrictions on private entrepreneurs than any other European state.

MARKETS Finally, a supply of markets gave British industrialists a ready outlet for their manufactured goods. British exports quadrupled between 1660 and 1760. In the course of its eighteenth-century wars and conquests, Great Britain had developed a vast colonial empire at the expense of its leading Continental rivals, the Dutch Republic and France. Britain also possessed a well-developed merchant marine that was able to transport goods anywhere in the world. A crucial factor in Britain's successful industrialization was the ability to produce cheaply the articles most in demand abroad. And the best markets abroad were not in Europe, where countries protected their own incipient industries, but in the Americas, Africa, and the East, where people wanted sturdy, inexpensive clothes rather than costly,

highly finished luxury items. Britain's machine-produced textiles fulfilled that demand. Nor should we overlook the British domestic market. Britain had the highest standard of living in Europe and a rapidly growing population. As Daniel Defoe noted already in 1728:

> For the rest, we see their Houses and Lodgings tolerably furnished, at least stuff'd well with useful and necessary household Goods: Even those we call poor People, Journeymen, working and Pains-taking People do thus; they lye warm, live in Plenty, work hard, and know no Want. These are the People that carry off the Gross of your Consumption; 'tis for these your Markets are kept open late on Saturday nights; because they usually receive their Week's Wages late. . . . In a Word, these are the Life of our whole Commerce, and all by their Multitude: Their Numbers are not Hundreds or Thousands, or Hundreds of Thousands, but Millions; . . . by their Wages they are able to live plentifully, and it is by their expensive, generous, free way of living, that the Home Consumption is rais'd to such a Bulk, as well of our own, as of foreign Production.[2]

This demand from both domestic and foreign markets and the inability of the old system to fulfill it led entrepreneurs to seek and adopt the new methods of manufacturing that a series of inventions provided. In so doing, these individuals initiated the Industrial Revolution.

Technological Changes and New Forms of Industrial Organization

In the 1770s and 1780s, the cotton textile industry took the first major step toward the Industrial Revolution with the creation of the modern factory.

THE COTTON INDUSTRY Already in the eighteenth century, Great Britain had surged ahead in the production of cheap cotton goods using the traditional methods of the cottage industry. The development of the flying shuttle had sped the process of weaving on a loom, enabling weavers to double their output. This caused shortages of yarn, however, until James Hargreaves's spinning jenny, perfected by 1768, enabled spinners to produce yarn in greater quantities. Richard Arkwright's water frame spinning machine, powered by water or horse, and Samuel

William Radcliffe, On Power Looms (1828)

Crompton's so-called mule, which combined aspects of the water frame and the spinning jenny, increased yarn production even more. Edmund Cartwright's power loom, invented in 1787, allowed the weaving of cloth to catch up with the spinning of yarn. Even then, early power looms were grossly inefficient, enabling home-based hand-loom weavers to continue to prosper, at least until the mid-1820s. After that, they were gradually replaced by the new machines. In 1813, there were 2,400 power looms in operation in Great Britain; they numbered 14,150 in 1820, 100,000 in 1833, and 250,000 by 1850. In the 1820s, there were still 250,000 hand-loom weavers in Britain; by 1860, only 3,000 were left.

The water frame, Crompton's mule, and power looms presented new opportunities to entrepreneurs. It was much more efficient to bring workers to the machines and organize their labor collectively in factories located next to rivers and streams, the sources of power for many of these early machines, than to leave the workers dispersed in their cottages. The concentration of labor in the new factories also brought the laborers and their families to live in the new towns that rapidly grew up around the factories.

The early devices used to speed up the processes of spinning and weaving were the products of weavers and spinners—in effect, of artisan tinkerers.

But the subsequent expansion of the cotton industry and the ongoing demand for even more cotton goods created additional pressure for new and more complicated technology. The invention that pushed the cotton industry to even greater heights of productivity was the steam engine.

THE STEAM ENGINE The steam engine revolutionized the production of cotton goods and allowed the factory system to spread to other areas of production, thereby securing whole new industries. The steam engine thus ensured the triumph of the Industrial Revolution.

In the 1760s, a Scottish engineer, James Watt (1736–1819), created an engine powered by steam that could pump water from mines three times as quickly as previous engines. In 1782, Watt enlarged the possibilities of the steam engine when he developed a rotary engine that could turn a shaft and thus drive machinery. Steam power could now be applied to spinning and weaving cotton, and before long, cotton mills using steam engines were multiplying across Britain. Because steam engines were fired by coal, they did not need to be located near rivers; entrepreneurs now had greater flexibility in their choice of location.

The new boost given to cotton textile production by technological changes became readily apparent. In 1760, Britain had imported 2.5 million pounds of raw cotton, which was farmed out to cottage industries. In 1787, the British imported 22 million pounds of cotton; most of it was spun on machines, some powered by water in large mills. By 1840, fully 366 million pounds of cotton—now Britain's most important product in value—were imported. By this time, most cotton industry employees worked in factories. The cheapest labor in India could not compete in quality or quantity with Britain. British cotton goods sold everywhere in the world. And in Britain itself, cheap cotton cloth made it possible for millions of poor

A Boulton and Watt Steam Engine. Encouraged by his business partner, Matthew Boulton, James Watt developed the first genuine steam engine. Pictured here is a typical Boulton and Watt engine. Steam pressure in the cylinder on the left drives the beam upward and sets the flywheel in motion.

people to wear undergarments, long a luxury of the rich, who could afford expensive linen cloth. Cotton clothing was tough, comfortable, cheap, and easily washable.

The steam engine proved indispensable. Unlike horses, the steam engine was a tireless source of power and depended for fuel on a substance—coal—that seemed unlimited in quantity. The popular saying that "steam is an Englishman" had real significance by 1850. The success of the steam engine led to a need for more coal and an expansion in coal production; between 1815 and 1850, the output of coal quadrupled. In turn, new processes using coal furthered the development of the iron industry.

THE IRON INDUSTRY The British iron industry was radically transformed during the Industrial Revolution. Britain had large resources of iron ore, but at the beginning of the eighteenth century, the basic process of producing iron had changed little since the Middle Ages and still depended heavily on charcoal. In the early eighteenth century, new methods of smelting iron ore to produce cast iron were devised, based on the use of coke or "courke" that was made by slowly burning coal. Coke could heat iron ore at a faster rate than charcoal, thus yielding higher amounts. Still, a better quality of iron was not possible until the 1780s, when Henry Cort developed a process called puddling in which coke was used to burn away impurities in **pig iron** (the product of smelting iron ore with coke) to produce an iron of high quality called **wrought iron.** Wrought iron, with its lower carbon content, was malleable and able to withstand strain. A boom then ensued in the British iron industry. In 1740, Britain produced 17,000 tons of iron; in the 1780s, almost 70,000 tons; by the 1840s, more than 2 million tons; and by 1852, almost 3 million tons, more than the rest of the world combined.

The development of the iron industry was in many ways a response to the demand for the new machines. The high-quality wrought iron produced by the Cort process made it the most widely used metal until the production of cheaper steel in the 1860s. The growing supply of less costly metal encouraged the use of machinery in other industries, most noticeably in new means of transportation.

A REVOLUTION IN TRANSPORTATION The eighteenth century had witnessed an expansion of transportation facilities in Britain as entrepreneurs realized the need for more efficient means of moving resources and goods. Turnpike trusts constructed new roads, and between 1760 and 1830, a network of canals was built. But both roads and canals were soon overtaken by a new form of transportation that dazzled people with its promise. To many economic historians, railroads were the "most important single factor in promoting European economic progress in the 1830s and 1840s." Again, Britain was the leader in the revolution.

The railways got their start in mining operations in Germany as early as 1500 and in British coal mines after 1600, where small handcarts filled with coal were pushed along parallel wooden rails. The rails reduced friction, enabling horses to haul more substantial loads. By 1700, some entrepreneurs began to replace wooden rails with cast-iron rails, and by the early nineteenth century, railways—still dependent on horsepower—were common in British mining and industrial districts. The development of the steam engine led to a radical transformation of the railways.

In 1804, Richard Trevithick (TREV-uh-thik) pioneered the first steam-powered locomotive on an industrial rail line in southern Wales. It pulled 10 tons of ore and seventy people at 5 miles per hour. Better locomotives soon followed. The engines built by George Stephenson and his son proved superior, and it was in their workshops in Newcastle-upon-Tyne that the locomotives for the first modern railways in Britain were built. George Stephenson's *Rocket* was used on the first public railway line,

Railroad Line from Liverpool to Manchester. The railroad line from Liverpool to Manchester, opened in 1830, relied on steam locomotives. As is evident in this illustration, carrying passengers was the railroad's main business. First-class passengers rode in covered cars; second- and third-class passengers, in open cars.

The Industrial Revolution in Great Britain ❧ **611**

MAP 20.1   The Industrial Revolution in Britain by 1850.
The Industrial Revolution began in the mid-1700s. Increased food production, rapid population growth, higher incomes, plentiful capital, solid banking and financial institutions, an abundance of mineral resources, and easy transport all furthered the process, making Britain the world's wealthiest country by 1850.

Q *How well did the railroad system connect important British industrial areas?*

which opened in 1830, extending 32 miles from Liverpool to Manchester. *Rocket* sped along at 16 miles per hour. Within twenty years, locomotives had reached 50 miles per hour, an incredible speed to contemporary passengers. During the same period, new companies were formed to build additional railroads as the infant industry proved successful not only technically but also financially. In 1840, Britain had almost 2,000 miles of railroads; by 1850, 6,000 miles of railroad track crisscrossed much of the country (see Map 20.1).

The railroad contributed significantly to the maturing of the Industrial Revolution. The railroad's demands for coal and iron furthered the growth of those industries. British supremacy in civil and mechanical engineering, so evident after 1840, was in large part based on the skills acquired in railway building. The huge capital demands necessary for railway construction encouraged a whole new group of middle-class investors to invest their money in joint-stock companies (see "Industrialization on the Continent" later in this chapter). Railway construction created new job opportunities, especially for farm laborers and peasants, who had long been accustomed to finding work outside their local villages. Perhaps most important, a cheaper and faster means of transportation had a rippling effect on the growth of an industrial economy. By reducing the price of goods, larger markets were created; increased sales necessitated more factories and more machinery, thereby reinforcing the self-sustaining nature of the Industrial Revolution, which marked a fundamental break with the traditional European economy. The great productivity of the Industrial Revolution enabled entrepreneurs to reinvest their profits in new capital equipment, further expanding the productive capacity of the economy. Continuous, even rapid, self-sustaining economic growth came to be seen as a fundamental characteristic of the new industrial economy.

The railroad was the perfect symbol of this aspect of the Industrial Revolution. The ability to transport goods and people at dramatic speeds also provided visible confirmation of a new sense of power. When railway engineers penetrated mountains with tunnels and spanned chasms with breathtaking bridges, contemporaries experienced a sense of power over nature not felt before in Western civilization.

THE INDUSTRIAL FACTORY   Initially the product of the cotton industry, the factory became the chief means of organizing labor for the new machines. As the workplace shifted from the artisan's shop and the peasant's cottage to the factory, the latter was not viewed as just a larger work unit. Employers hired workers who no longer owned the means of production but were simply paid wages to run the machines.

From its beginning, the factory system demanded a new type of discipline from its employees. Factory owners could not afford to let their expensive machinery stand idle. Workers were forced to work regular hours and in shifts to keep the machines producing at a steady pace for maximum output. This represented a massive adjustment for early factory laborers.

Preindustrial workers were not accustomed to a timed format. Agricultural laborers had always kept irregular hours; hectic work at harvest time might be followed by weeks of inactivity. Even in the burgeoning cottage industry of the eighteenth century, weavers and spinners who worked at home might fulfill their weekly quotas by working around the clock for two or three days and then

Opening of the Royal Albert Bridge. This painting by Thomas Robins shows the ceremonies attending the official opening of the Royal Albert Bridge. I. K. Brunel, one of Britain's great engineers, designed this bridge, which carried a railroad line across the Tamar River into Cornwall. As is evident in the picture, the bridge was high enough to allow ships to pass underneath.

proceeding at a leisurely pace until the next week's demands forced another work spurt.

Factory owners therefore faced a formidable task. They had to create a system of time-work discipline that would accustom employees to working regular, unvarying hours during which they performed a set number of tasks over and over again as efficiently as possible. One early industrialist said that his aim was "to make such machines of the men as cannot err." Such work, of course, tended to be repetitive and boring, and factory owners

resorted to tough methods to accomplish their goals. Factory regulations were minute and detailed (see the box on p. 614). Adult workers were fined for a wide variety of minor infractions, such as being a few minutes late for work, and dismissed for more serious misdoings, especially drunkenness. Drunkenness was viewed as particularly offensive because it set a bad example for younger workers and also courted disaster amid dangerous machinery. Employers found that dismissals and fines worked well for adult employees; in a time when

A British Textile Factory. The development of the factory changed the relationship between workers and employers as workers were encouraged to adjust to a new system of discipline that forced them to work regular hours under close supervision. This 1851 illustration shows women working in a British textile factory.

Discipline in the New Factories

Workers in the new factories of the Industrial Revolution had been accustomed to a lifestyle free of overseers. Unlike the cottages, where workers spun thread and wove cloth in their own rhythm and time, the factories demanded a new, rigorous discipline geared to the requirements of the machines. This selection is taken from a set of rules for a factory in Berlin in 1844. They were typical of company rules everywhere the factory system had been established.

Factory Rules, Foundry and Engineering Works of the Royal Overseas Trading Company, Berlin

In every large works, and in the co-ordination of any large number of workmen, good order and harmony must be looked upon as the fundamentals of success, and therefore the following rules shall be strictly observed.

1. The normal working day begins at all seasons at 6 A.M. precisely and ends, after the usual break of half an hour for breakfast, an hour for dinner and half an hour for tea, at 7 P.M., and it shall be strictly observed.... Workers arriving 2 minutes late shall lose half an hour's wages; whoever is more than 2 minutes late may not start work until after the next break; or at least shall lose his wages until then. Any disputes about the correct time shall be settled by the clock mounted above the gatekeeper's lodge....

3. No workman, whether employed by time or piece, may leave before the end of the working day, without having first received permission from the overseer and having given his name to the gatekeeper. Omission of these two actions shall lead to a fine of ten silver groschen [pennies] payable to the sick fund.

4. Repeated irregular arrival at work shall lead to dismissal. This shall also apply to those who are found idling by an official or overseer, and refused to obey their order to resume work....

6. No worker may leave his place of work otherwise than for reasons connected with his work.

7. All conversation with fellow-workers is prohibited; if any worker requires information about his work, he must turn to the overseer, or to the particular fellow-worker designated for the purpose.

8. Smoking in the workshops or in the yard is prohibited during working hours; anyone caught smoking shall be fined five silver groschen for the sick fund for every such offense....

10. Natural functions must be performed at the appropriate places, and whoever is found soiling walls, fences, squares, etc., and similarly, whoever is found washing his face and hands in the workshop and not in the places assigned for the purpose, shall be fined five silver groschen for the sick fund....

12. It goes without saying that all overseers and officials of the firm shall be obeyed without question, and shall be treated with due deference. Disobedience will be punished by dismissal.

13. Immediate dismissal shall also be the fate of anyone found drunk in any of the workshops....

14. Every workman is obliged to report to his superiors any acts of dishonesty or embezzlement on the part of his fellow workmen. If he omits to do so, and it is shown after subsequent discovery of a misdemeanor that he knew about it at the time, he shall be liable to be taken to court as an accessory after the fact and the wage due to him shall be retained as punishment.

Q What impact did factories have on the lives of workers? To what extent have such "rules" determined much of modern industrial life?

---

great population growth had produced large numbers of unskilled workers, dismissal could be disastrous. Children were less likely to understand the implications of dismissal, so they were sometimes disciplined more directly—by beating.

The efforts of factory owners in the early Industrial Revolution to impose a new set of values were frequently reinforced by the new evangelical churches. Methodism, in particular, emphasized that people "reborn in Jesus" must forgo immoderation and follow a disciplined path. Laziness and wasteful habits were sinful. The acceptance of hardship in this life paved the way for the joys of the next. Evangelical values paralleled the efforts of the new factory owners to instill laborers with their own middle-class values of hard work, discipline, and thrift. In one crucial sense, the early industrialists proved successful. As the nineteenth century progressed, the second and third generations of workers came to view a regular working week as a natural way of life. It was, of course, an attitude that made possible Britain's incredible economic growth in that century.

Britain's Great Exhibition of 1851

In 1851, the British organized the world's first industrial fair. It was housed at Kensington in London in the Crystal Palace, an enormous structure made entirely of glass and iron, a tribute to British engineering skills. Covering

The Great Exhibition of 1851. The Great Exhibition of 1851 was a symbol of the success of Great Britain, which had become the world's first industrial nation and its richest. More than 100,000 exhibits were housed in the Crystal Palace, a giant structure of cast iron and glass. The first illustration shows the front of the palace and some of its numerous visitors. The second shows the opening day ceremonies. Queen Victoria is seen at the center with her family, surrounded by visitors from all over the world. Note the large tree inside the building, providing a visible symbol of how the Industrial Revolution had supposedly achieved human domination over nature.

19 acres, the Crystal Palace contained 100,000 exhibits that showed the wide variety of products created by the Industrial Revolution. Six million people visited the fair in six months. Though most of them were Britons who had traveled to London by train, foreign visitors were also prominent. The Great Exhibition displayed Britain's wealth to the world; it was a gigantic symbol of British success. Even trees were brought inside the Crystal Palace as a visible symbol of how the Industrial Revolution had achieved human domination over nature. Prince Albert, Queen Victoria's husband, expressed the sentiments of the age when he described the exhibition as a sign that "man is approaching

a more complete fulfillment of that great and sacred mission which he has to perform in this world . . . to conquer nature to his use." Not content with that, he also linked British success to divine will: "In promoting [the progress of the human race], we are accomplishing the will of the great and blessed God."[3]

In addition to demonstrating Britain's enormous industrial growth, the Crystal Palace exhibition also represented British imperial power. Goods from India were a highlight of the exhibition, and the East India Company drew attention to its role in India with exhibits of cotton, tea, and flax. But it was the display of Indian silks, jewels, shawls, and an elephant canopy that captured the attention of the British press and visitors. Despite the public interest in the ornate and intricate works from India, many British commentators, such as the scientist William Whewell, were less complimentary. They characterized the Indian handmade goods as typical of a system in which "tens of thousands" worked for a few despots. Moreover, these goods were examples of the "wasteful and ridiculous excess" of the labor-intensive production practices in the East, which could not compare to enlightened British labor practices.[4]

By the year of the Great Exhibition, Great Britain had become the world's first industrial nation and its wealthiest. Britain was the "workshop, banker, and trader of the world." It produced one-half of the world's coal and manufactured goods; its cotton industry alone in 1851 was equal in size to the industries of all other European countries combined. The quantity of goods produced was growing at three times the rate in 1780. Britain's certainty about its mission in the world in the nineteenth century was grounded in its incredible material success.

The Spread of Industrialization

 FOCUS QUESTION: How did the Industrial Revolution spread from Great Britain to the Continent and the United States, and how did industrialization in those areas differ from British industrialization?

Beginning first in Great Britain, industrialization spread to the Continental countries of Europe and the United States at different times and speeds during the nineteenth century. First to be industrialized on the Continent were Belgium, France, and the German states; the first in North America was the new United States. Not until after 1850 did the Industrial Revolution spread to the rest of Europe and other parts of the world.

Industrialization on the Continent

In 1815, the Low Countries, France, and the German states were still largely agrarian. During the eighteenth century, some of the Continental countries had experienced developments similar to those of Britain. They, too,

had achieved population growth, made agricultural improvements, expanded their cottage industries, and witnessed growth in foreign trade. But whereas Britain's economy began to move in new industrial directions in the 1770s and 1780s, Continental countries lagged behind because they did not share some of the advantages that had made Britain's Industrial Revolution possible. Lack of good roads and problems with river transit made transportation difficult. Toll stations on important rivers and customs barriers along state boundaries increased the costs and prices of goods. Guild restrictions were also more prevalent, creating impediments that pioneer industrialists in Britain did not have to face. Finally, Continental entrepreneurs were generally less enterprising than their British counterparts and tended to adhere to traditional business attitudes, such as a dislike of competition, a high regard for family security coupled with an unwillingness to take risks in investment, and an excessive worship of thriftiness. Thus, industrialization on the Continent faced numerous hurdles, and as it proceeded in earnest after 1815, it did so along lines that were somewhat different from Britain's.

BORROWING TECHNIQUES AND PRACTICES Lack of technical knowledge was initially a major obstacle to industrialization. But the Continental countries possessed an advantage here; they could simply borrow British techniques and practices. Of course, the British tried to prevent that. Until 1825, British artisans were prohibited from leaving the country; until 1842, the export of important machinery and machine parts, especially for textile production, was forbidden. Nevertheless, the British were not able to control this situation by legislation. Already by 1825, there were at least two thousand skilled British mechanics on the Continent, and British equipment was also being sold abroad, legally or illegally.

Gradually, the Continent achieved technological independence as local people learned all the skills their British teachers had to offer. By the 1840s, new generations of skilled mechanics from Belgium and France were spreading their knowledge east and south, playing the same role that the British had earlier. Even more important, however, Continental countries, especially France and the German states, began to establish a wide range of technical schools to train engineers and mechanics.

ROLE OF GOVERNMENT That government played an important role in this regard brings us to another difference between British and Continental industrialization. Governments in most of the Continental countries were accustomed to playing a significant role in economic affairs. Furthering the development of industrialization was a logical extension of that attitude. Hence, governments provided for the costs of technical education, awarded grants to inventors and foreign entrepreneurs, exempted foreign industrial equipment from import duties, and in some places even financed factories. Of equal if not

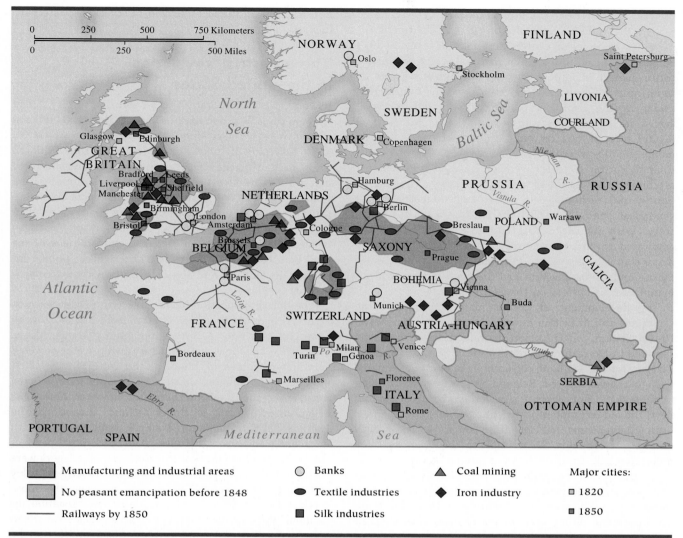

MAP 20.2   The Industrialization of Europe by 1850. Great Britain was Europe's first industrialized country; however, by the middle of the nineteenth century, several regions on the Continent, especially in Belgium, France, and the German states, had made significant advances in industrialization.

Q *What reasons could explain why coal mining and iron industries are densely clustered in manufacturing and industrial areas?*

View an animated version of this map or related maps on the CourseMate website.

greater importance in the long run, governments actively bore much of the cost of building roads and canals, deepening and widening river channels, and constructing railroads. By 1850, a network of iron rails had spread across Europe, although only Germany and Belgium had completed major parts of their systems by that time (see Map 20.2).

Governments on the Continent also used **tariffs** to further industrialization. After 1815, cheap British goods flooded Continental markets. The French responded with high tariffs to protect their fledgling industries. The most systematic argument for the use of tariffs, however, was made by a German writer, Friedrich List (FREED-rikh LIST) (1789–1846), who emigrated to America and returned to Germany as a U.S. consul. In his *National System of Political Economy,* written in 1844, List advocated a rapid and large-scale program of industrialization as the surest path to develop a nation's strength. To assure that path to industrialization, he felt that a nation must use protective tariffs. If countries followed the British policy of free trade, then cheaper British goods would inundate national markets and destroy infant industries before they had a chance to grow. Germany, he insisted, could not compete with Britain without protective tariffs.

CENTERS OF CONTINENTAL INDUSTRIALIZATION As noted earlier, the Industrial Revolution on the Continent occurred in three major centers between 1815 and 1850—Belgium, France, and the German states. As in Britain, cotton played an important role, although it was not as significant as heavy industry. France was the Continental leader in the manufacture of cotton goods but still lagged far behind Great Britain. In 1849, France used 64,000 tons of raw cotton, Belgium, 11,000, and Germany, 20,000, whereas Britain used 286,000 tons. Continental cotton factories were older, used less efficient machines, and had less productive labor. In general, Continental technology in the cotton industry was a generation behind Great Britain. But that is not the whole story. With its cheap coal and scarce water, Belgium gravitated toward the use of the steam engine as the major source of power and invested in the new machines. By the mid-1840s, Belgium had the most modern cotton-manufacturing system on the Continent.

The development of cotton manufacturing on the Continent and in Britain differed in two significant ways. Unlike Britain, where cotton manufacturing was mostly centered in Lancashire (in northwestern England) and the Glasgow area of Scotland, cotton mills in France, Germany, and, to a lesser degree, Belgium were dispersed through many regions. Noticeable, too, was the mixture of old and new. The old techniques of the cottage system, such as the use of hand looms, held on much longer. In the French district of Normandy, for example, in 1849, eighty-three mills were still driven by hand or animal power.

As traditional methods persisted alongside the new methods in cotton manufacturing, the new steam engine came to be used primarily in mining and metallurgy on the Continent rather than in textile manufacturing. At first, almost all of the steam engines on the Continent came from Britain; not until the 1820s was a domestic machine industry developed.

In Britain, the Industrial Revolution had been built on the cotton industry; on the Continent, the iron and coal of heavy industry led the way. As in textiles, however, heavy industry on the Continent before 1850 was a mixture of old and new. The adoption of new techniques, such as coke-smelted iron and puddling furnaces, coincided with the expansion of old-type charcoal blast furnaces. Before 1850, Germany lagged significantly behind both Belgium and France in heavy industry, and most German iron manufacturing was still based on old techniques. Not until the 1840s was coke-blast iron produced in the Rhineland. At that time, no one had yet realized the treasure of coal buried in the Ruhr valley. A German official wrote in 1852 that "it is clearly not to be expected that Germany will ever be able to reach the level of production of coal and iron currently attained in England. This is implicit in our far more limited resource endowment." Little did he realize that although the industrial development of Continental Europe was about a generation behind Britain at midcentury, after 1850 an incredibly rapid growth in Continental industry would demonstrate that Britain was not, after all, destined to remain the world's greatest industrial nation.

The Industrial Revolution in the United States

In 1800, the United States was an agrarian society. There were no cities with populations of more than 100,000, and six out of every seven American workers were farmers. By 1860, however, the population had grown from 5 million to 30 million people, larger than Great Britain's. Almost half of them lived west of the Appalachian Mountains. The number of states had more than doubled, from sixteen to thirty-four, and nine American cities had more than 100,000 in population. Only 50 percent of American workers were farmers. Between 1800 and the eve of the Civil War, the United States had experienced its own Industrial Revolution and the urbanization that accompanied it.

The initial application of machinery to production was accomplished, as in Continental Europe, by borrowing from Great Britain. A British immigrant, Samuel Slater, established the first textile factory using water-powered spinning machines in Rhode Island in 1790. By 1813, factories were being established with power looms copied from British models. Soon thereafter, however, Americans began to equal or surpass British technical inventions. The Harpers Ferry arsenal, for example, built muskets with interchangeable parts. Because all the individual parts of the muskets were identical (for example, all triggers were the same), the final product could be put together quickly and easily; this enabled Americans to avoid the more costly system in which skilled workers fitted together individual parts made separately. The so-called American system reduced costs and revolutionized production by saving labor, important to a society that had few skilled artisans.

THE NEED FOR TRANSPORTATION Unlike Britain, the United States was a large country. The lack of a good system of internal transportation seemed to limit American economic development by making the transport of goods prohibitively expensive. This deficiency was gradually remedied by the introduction of the steamboat and the railroad as well as the contruction of roads and canals. Thousands of miles of roads and canals were built linking east and west. The steamboat facilitated transportation on the Great Lakes, Atlantic coastal waters, and rivers. It was especially important to the Mississippi valley; by 1860, one thousand steamboats plied that river (see the box on p. 620). Most important of all in the development of the American transportation system was the railroad. Beginning with 100 miles in 1830, by 1860 more than 27,000 miles of railroad track covered the United States. This transportation revolution turned the United States into a single massive market for the manufactured goods of the Northeast, the early center of American industrialization.

The Steamboat. The steamboat was an important means of transportation for American products and markets. Steamboats like the one shown in this illustration regularly plied the Mississippi River, moving the farm products of the Midwest and the southern plantations to markets in New Orleans. After the American Civil War, railroads began to replace steamboats on many routes.

THE LABOR FORCE Labor for the growing number of factories came primarily from rural areas. The United States did not possess a large number of craftspeople, but it did have a rapidly expanding farm population; its size in the Northeast soon outstripped the available farmland. While some of this excess population, especially men, went west, others, mostly women, found work in the new textile and shoe factories of New England. Indeed, women made up more than 80 percent of the laboring force in the large textile factories. In Massachusetts mill towns, company boarding houses provided rooms for large numbers of young women who worked for several years before marriage. Outside Massachusetts, factory owners sought entire families, including children, to work in their mills; one mill owner ran this advertisement in a newspaper in Utica, New York: "Wanted: A few sober and industrious families of at least five children each, over the age of eight years, are wanted at the Cotton Factory in Whitestown. Widows with large families would do well to attend this notice." When a decline in rural births threatened to dry up this labor pool in the 1830s and 1840s, European immigrants, especially poor and unskilled Irish, English, Scots, and Welsh, appeared in large numbers to replace American women and children in the factories.

Women, children, and these immigrants had one thing in common as employees: they were largely unskilled laborers. Unskilled labor pushed American industrialization into a capital-intensive pattern. Factory owners invested heavily in machines that could produce in quantity at the hands of untrained workers. In Britain, the pace of mechanization was never as rapid because Britain's supply of skilled artisans made it more profitable to pursue a labor-intensive economy.

By 1860, the United States was well on its way to being an industrial nation. In the Northeast, the most industrialized section of the country, per capita income was 40 percent higher than the national average. Diets, it has been argued, were better and more varied; machine-made clothing was more abundant. Industrialization did not necessarily lessen economic disparities, however. Despite a growing belief in a myth of social mobility based on equality of economic opportunity, the reality was that the richest 10 percent of the population in the cities held 70 to 80 percent of the wealth, compared to 50 percent in 1800. Nevertheless, American historians generally argue that while the rich got richer, the poor, thanks to an increase in their purchasing power, did not get poorer.

Limiting the Spread of Industrialization in the Nonindustrialized World

Before 1870, the industrialization that had developed in western and central Europe and the United States did not extend in any significant way to the rest of the world. Even in eastern Europe, industrialization lagged far behind. Russia, for example, remained largely rural and

"S-t-e-a-m-boat A-coming!"

Steamboats and railroads were crucial elements in a transportation revolution that enabled industrialists to expand markets by shipping goods cheaply and efficiently. At the same time, these marvels of technology aroused a sense of power and excitement that was an important aspect of the triumph of industrialization. The American novelist Mark Twain captured this sense of excitement in this selection from *Life on the Mississippi*.

Mark Twain, *Life on the Mississippi*

After all these years I can picture that old time to myself now, just as it was then: the white town drowsing in the sunshine of a summer's morning; the streets empty, or pretty nearly so; one or two clerks sitting in front of the Water street stores, with their splint-bottomed chairs tilted back against the walls, chins on breasts, hats slouched over their faces, asleep; . . . two or three lonely little freight piles scattered about the "levee"; a pile of "skids" on the slope of the stone-paved wharf, and the fragrant town drunkard asleep in the shadow of them; . . . the great Mississippi, the majestic, the magnificent Mississippi, rolling its mile-wide along, shining in the sun; the dense forest away on the other side; the "point" above the town, and the "point" below, bounding the river glimpse and turning it into a sort of sea, and withal a very still and brilliant and lonely one. Presently a film of dark smoke appears above on those remote "points"; instantly a negro drayman, famous for his quick eye and prodigious voice, lifts up to cry, "S-t-e-a-m-boat a-coming!" and the scene changes! The town drunkard stirs, the clerks wake up, a furious clatter of drays follows, every house and store pours out a human contribution, and all in a twinkling the dead town [Hannibal, Missouri] is alive and moving. Drays, carts, men, boys, all go hurrying from many quarters to a common center, the wharf. Assembled there, the people fasten their eyes upon the coming boat as upon a wonder they are seeing for the first time. And the boat is rather a handsome sight, too. She is long and sharp and trim and pretty; she has two tall, fancy-topped chimneys, with a gilded device of some kind swung between them; a fanciful pilot-house, all glass and "ginger bread," perched on top of the "texas" deck behind them; the paddle-boxes are gorgeous with a picture or with gilded rays above the boat's name; the boiler deck, the hurricane deck, and the texas deck are fenced and ornamented with clean white railings; there is a flag gallantly flying from the jack-staff; the furnace doors are open and the fires glaring bravely; the upper decks are black with passengers; the captain stands by the big bell, calm, imposing, the envy of all; great volumes of the blackest smoke are rolling and tumbling out of the chimneys—a husbanded grandeur created with a bit of pitch pine just before arriving at a town; the crew are grouped on the forecastle; the broad stage is run far out over the port bow, and an envied deck-hand stands picturesquely on the end of it with a coil of rope in his hand; the pent steam is screaming through the gauge-cocks; the captain lifts his hand, a bell rings, the wheels stop; then they turn back, churning the water to foam, and the steam is at rest. Then such a scramble as there is to get aboard, and to get ashore, and to take in freight and discharge freight, all at one and the same time; and such a yelling and cursing as the mates facilitate it all with! Ten minutes later the steamer is under way again, with no flag on the jack-staff and no black smoke issuing from the chimneys. After ten more minutes the town is dead again, and the town drunkard asleep by the skids once more.

Q In what ways does Twain's description illustrate the impact of the transportation revolution on daily life in the United States?

---

agricultural, and its autocratic rulers kept the peasants in serfdom. There was not much of a middle class, and the tsarist regime, fearful of change, preferred to import industrial goods in return for the export of raw materials, such as grain and timber. Russia would not have its Industrial Revolution until the end of the nineteenth century.

THE EXAMPLE OF INDIA In other parts of the world where they had established control, newly industrialized European states pursued a deliberate policy of preventing the growth of mechanized industry. A good example is India. In the eighteenth century, India had become one of the world's greatest exporters of cotton cloth produced by hand labor. In the first half of the nineteenth century, much of India fell under the control of the British East India Company (see Chapter 24). With British control came inexpensive British factory-produced textiles, and soon thousands of Indian spinners and hand-loom weavers were unemployed. British policy encouraged Indians to export their raw materials while buying British-made goods. Although some limited forms of industrial factories for making textiles and jute (used in making rope) were opened in India in the 1850s, a lack of local capital and the advantages given to British imports limited the growth of new manufacturing operations. India, then, provides an excellent example of how some of the rapidly industrializing nations of Europe worked to deliberately thwart the spread of the Industrial Revolution to their colonial dominions.

The Social Impact of the Industrial Revolution

Q **Focus Questions:** What effects did the Industrial Revolution have on urban life, social classes, family life, and standards of living? What were working conditions like in the early decades of the Industrial Revolution, and what efforts were made to improve them?

Eventually, the Industrial Revolution radically altered the social life of Europe and the world. Although much of Europe remained bound by its traditional ways, already in the first half of the nineteenth century, the social impact of the Industrial Revolution was being felt, and future avenues of growth were becoming apparent. Vast changes in the number of people and where they lived were already dramatically evident.

Population Growth

Population increases had already begun in the eighteenth century, but they accelerated dramatically in the nineteenth. They were also easier to discern because record keeping became more accurate. In the nineteenth century, governments began to take periodic censuses and systematically collect precise data on births, deaths, and marriages. In Britain, for example, the first census was taken in 1801, and a systematic registration of births, deaths, and marriages was begun in 1836. In 1750, the total European population stood at an estimated 140 million; by 1800, it had increased to 187 million and by 1850 to 266 million, almost twice its 1750 level.

This population explosion cannot be explained by a higher birthrate, for birthrates were declining after 1790. Between 1790 and 1850, Germany's birthrate dropped from 40 per 1,000 to 36.1; Great Britain's, from 35.4 to 32.6; and France's, from 32.5 to 26.7. The key to the expansion of population was the decline in death rates evident throughout Europe. Historians now believe that two major causes explain this decline. There was a drop in the number of deaths from famines, epidemics, and war. Major epidemic diseases, such as plague and smallpox, declined noticeably, although small-scale epidemics broke out now and then. The ordinary death rate also declined as a general increase in the food supply, already evident in the agricultural revolution of Britain in the late eighteenth century, spread to more areas. More food enabled a greater number of people to be better fed and therefore more resistant to disease. Famine largely disappeared from western Europe, although there were dramatic exceptions in isolated areas, Ireland being the most significant.

Although industrialization itself did not cause population growth, industrialized areas did experience a change in the composition of the population. By 1850, the proportion of the population actively involved in manufacturing, mining, or building had risen to 48 percent in Britain, 37 percent in Belgium, and 27 percent in France. But the actual pockets of industrialization in 1850 were small and decentralized; one author characterized them as "islands in an agricultural sea."

This minimal industrialization in light of the growing population meant severe congestion in the countryside, where ever-larger numbers of people divided the same amount of land into ever-smaller plots, and also gave rise to an ever-increasing mass of landless peasants. Overpopulation, especially noticeable in parts of France, northern Spain, southern Germany, Sweden, and Ireland, magnified the already existing problem of rural poverty. In Ireland, it produced the century's greatest catastrophe.

THE GREAT HUNGER Ireland was one of the most oppressed areas in western Europe. The predominantly Catholic peasant population rented land from mostly absentee British Protestant landlords whose primary concern was collecting their rents. Irish peasants lived in mud hovels in desperate poverty. The cultivation of the potato, a nutritious and relatively easy food to grow that produced three times as much food per acre as grain, gave Irish peasants a basic staple that enabled them to survive and even expand in numbers. As only an acre or two of potatoes was sufficient to feed a family, Irish men and women married earlier than elsewhere and started having children earlier as well. This led to significant growth in the population. Between 1781 and 1845, the Irish population doubled from 4 million to 8 million. Probably half of this population depended on the potato for survival. In the summer of 1845, the potato crop in Ireland was struck by blight due to a fungus that turned the potatoes black. Between 1845 and 1851, the Great Famine decimated the Irish population (see the box on p. 622). More than a million died of starvation and disease, and almost 2 million emigrated to the United States and Britain. Of all the European nations, only Ireland had a declining population in the nineteenth century. But other countries, too, faced problems of dire poverty and declining standards of living as their populations exploded.

EMIGRATION The flight of so many Irish to America reminds us that the traditional safety valve for overpopulation has always been emigration. Between 1821 and 1850, the number of emigrants from Europe averaged about 110,000 a year. Most of these emigrants came from places like Ireland and southern Germany, where peasant life had been reduced to marginal existence. Times of agrarian crisis resulted in great waves of emigration. Bad harvests in Europe in 1846–1847 (such as the catastrophe in Ireland) produced massive numbers of emigrants. In addition to the estimated 1.6 million from Ireland, for example, 935,000 people left Germany between 1847 and 1854. More often than emigrating, however, the rural masses sought a solution to their poverty by moving to towns and cities within their own countries to find work. It should not astonish us, then, that the first half of the nineteenth century was a period of rapid urbanization.

The Great Irish Famine

The Great Irish Famine caused by the potato blight was one of the nineteenth century's worst natural catastrophes, resulting in the decimation of the Irish population. In this selection, an Irish nationalist reported what he had witnessed in Galway in 1847.

⊷ ⊞ ⊷

John Mitchel, *The Last Conquest of Ireland*

In the depth of winter we traveled to Galway, through the very center of that fertile island, and saw sights that will never wholly leave the eyes that beheld them—cowering wretches, almost naked in the savage weather, prowling in turnip-fields, and endeavoring to grub up roots which had been left, but running to hide as the mail-coach rolled by;—very large fields where small farms had been "consolidated," showing dark bars of fresh mold running through them where the ditches had been leveled;—groups and families, sitting or wandering on the high-road, with failing steps and dim patient eyes, gazing hopelessly into infinite darkness; before them, around them, above them, nothing but darkness and despair—parties of tall brawny men, once the flower of Meath and Galway, stalking by with a fierce but vacant scowl; as if they knew that all this ought not to be, but knew not whom to blame, saw none whom they could rend in their wrath.... Around those farmhouses which were still inhabited were to be seen hardly any stacks of grain; the poor-rate collector, the rent agent, the county-cess collector had carried it off; and sometimes I could see in front of the cottages little children leaning against a fence when the sun shone out—for they could not stand—their limbs fleshless, their bodies half naked, their faces bloated yet wrinkled, and of a pale greenish hue,—children who would never, it was too plain, grow up to be men and women. ⊱

Q What was the impact of the Great Irish Famine on the Irish people and on the broader Atlantic world? How were the industrial revolutions of other nations affected by this disaster?

The Growth of Cities

Although the Western world would not become a predominantly urban society until the twentieth century, cities and towns had already grown dramatically in the first half of the nineteenth century, a phenomenon related to industrialization. Cities had traditionally been centers for princely courts, government and military offices, churches, and commerce. By 1850, especially in Great Britain and Belgium, cities were rapidly becoming places for manufacturing and industry. With the steam engine, entrepreneurs could locate their manufacturing plants in urban centers where they had ready access to transportation facilities and unemployed people from the country looking for work.

In 1800, Great Britain had one major city, London, with a population of one million, and six cities between 50,000 and 100,000. Fifty years later, London's population had swelled to 2,363,000, and there were nine cities over 100,000 and eighteen cities with populations between 50,000 and 100,000. All together, these twenty-eight cities accounted for 5.7 million residents, or one-fifth of the total British population. When the populations of cities under 50,000 are added to this total, we realize that more

© Oxford Science Archive, Oxford/HIP/Art Resource, NY

A New Industrial Town. Cities and towns grew dramatically in Britain in the first half of the nineteenth century, largely as a result of industrialization. Pictured here is Saltaire, a model textile factory and town founded near Bradford by Titus Salt in 1851. To facilitate the transportation of goods, the town was built on the Leeds and Liverpool canals.

than 50 percent of the British population lived in towns and cities by 1850. Britain was forced to become a food importer rather than an exporter as the number of people involved in agriculture declined to 20 percent of the population.

Urban populations also grew on the Continent, but less dramatically. Paris had 547,000 inhabitants in 1800, but only two other French cities had populations of 100,000: Lyons and Marseilles. In 1851, Paris had grown to a million while Lyons and Marseilles were still under 200,000. German and Austrian lands had only three cities with more than 100,000 inhabitants (Vienna had 247,000) in 1800; fifty years later, there were only five, but Vienna had grown to 440,000. As these figures show, urbanization did not proceed as rapidly here as in Britain; of course, neither had industrialization. Even in Belgium, the most heavily industrialized country on the Continent, almost 50 percent of the male workforce was still engaged in agriculture at midcentury.

URBAN LIVING CONDITIONS IN THE EARLY INDUSTRIAL REVOLUTION The dramatic growth of cities in the first half of the nineteenth century produced miserable living conditions for many of the inhabitants. Of course, this had been true for centuries for many people in European cities, but the rapid urbanization associated with the Industrial Revolution intensified the problems and made these wretched conditions all the more apparent. Wealthy, middle-class inhabitants, as usual, insulated themselves as best they could, often living in suburbs or the outer ring of the city, where they could have individual houses and gardens. In the inner ring of the city stood the small row houses, some with gardens, of the artisans and the lower middle class. Finally, located in the center of most industrial towns were the row houses of the industrial workers (see Images of Everyday Life on p. 624). This report on working-class housing in the British city of Birmingham in 1843 gives an idea of the conditions they faced:

> The courts [of working-class row houses] are extremely numerous; . . . a very large portion of the poorer classes of the inhabitants reside in them. . . . The courts vary in the number of the houses which they contain, from four to twenty, and most of these houses are three stories high, and built, as it is termed, back to back. There is a wash-house, an ash-pit, and a privy at the end, or on one side of the court, and not unfrequently one or more pigsties and heaps of manure. Generally speaking, the privies in the old courts are in a most filthy condition. Many which we have inspected were in a state which renders it impossible for us to conceive how they could be used; they were without doors and overflowing with filth.[5]

Rooms were not large and were frequently overcrowded, as this government report of 1838 revealed: "I entered several of the tenements. In one of them, on the ground floor, I found six persons occupying a very small room, two in bed, ill with fever. In the room above this were two more persons in one bed ill with fever."[6] Another report said, "There were 63 families where there were at least five

persons to one bed; and there were some in which even six were packed in one bed, lying at the top and bottom—children and adults."[7]

Sanitary conditions in these towns were appalling. Due to the lack of municipal direction, city streets were often used as sewers and open drains: "In the center of this street is a gutter, into which potato parings, the refuse of animal and vegetable matters of all kinds, the dirty water from the washing of clothes and of the houses, are all poured, and there they stagnate and putrefy."[8] Unable to deal with human excrement, cities in the new industrial era smelled horrible and were extraordinarily unhealthy. The burning of coal blackened towns and cities with soot, as Charles Dickens described in one of his novels: "A long suburb of red brick houses—some with patches of garden ground, where coal-dust and factory smoke darkened the shrinking leaves, and coarse rank flowers; and where the struggling vegetation sickened and sank under the hot breath of kiln and furnace."[9] Towns and cities were fundamentally death traps. As deaths outnumbered births in most large cities in the first half of the nineteenth century, only a constant influx of people from the countryside kept them alive and growing.

Adding to the deterioration of urban life was the adulteration of food. Consumers were defrauded in a variety of ways: alum was added to make bread look white and hence more expensive; beer and milk were watered down; and red lead, despite its poisonous qualities, was substituted for pepper. The government refused to intervene; a parliamentary committee stated that "more benefit is likely to result from the effects of a free competition . . . than can be expected to result from any regulations." It was not until 1875 that an effective food and drug act was passed in Britain.

Our knowledge of the pathetic conditions in the early industrial cities is largely derived from an abundance of social investigations. Such investigations began in France in the 1820s. In Britain, the Poor Law Commission produced detailed reports. The investigators were often struck by the physically and morally debilitating effects of urban industrial life on the poor. They observed, for example, that young working-class men were considerably shorter and scrawnier than the sons of middle-class families and much more subject to disease. They were especially alarmed by what they considered the moral consequences of such living conditions: prostitution, crime, and sexual immorality, all of which they saw as effects of living in such squalor.

URBAN REFORMERS To many of the well-to-do, this situation presented a clear danger to society. Were not these masses of workers, sunk in crime, disease, and immorality, a potential threat to their own well-being? Might not the masses be organized and used by unscrupulous demagogues to overthrow the established order? One of the most eloquent British reformers of the 1830s and 1840s, James Kay-Shuttleworth, described them as "volcanic elements, by whose explosive violence the

Living Conditions of London's Poor

Although some environmental hazards existed before industrialization, others intensified in early industrial Britain, with a dramatic impact on living conditions. Burning coal filled the air with ash and soot, metal smelting gave off pungent fumes, and industrial plants belched clouds of smoke from the fires stoked in the steam engines. Water pollution was another problem as slaughterhouses dumped their refuse into the streams and human waste found its way there as well due to a lack of proper sewerage. Consequently, working-class tenants in London found themselves living in crowded rooms surrounded by filth and putrid smells. Many of the houses for the poor were built back to back, leaving little room for sanitation. Despite efforts to improve conditions, the plight of London's workers remained dire. In 1869, an English writer, Blanchard Jerrold, commissioned the French illustrator Gustave Doré to create illustrations for a guide to London called *London: A Pilgrimage*. The book was published in 1872 with Doré's illustrations accompanying Jerrold's textual descriptions of the living conditions of London's poor. Doré's most haunting images are of tenement housing and its inhabitants in areas such as Whitechapel. In the first illustration, Doré shows a London slum district overshadowed by rail viaducts. The second image depicts an open air market on Drury Lane, where men, women, and children are attempting to sell their wares. In the image at the right, children in ragged clothes play in the street. ✍

© British Museum, London/Art Resource, NY

Bibliothèque des Arts Decoratifs, Paris/© Archives Charmet/The Bridgeman Art Library

© The Art Archive/John Meek

structure of society may be destroyed." Another observer spoke more contemptuously in 1850:

> They live precisely like brutes, to gratify . . . the appetites of their uncultivated bodies, and then die, to go they have never thought, cared, or wondered whither. . . . Brought up in the darkness of barbarism, they have no idea that it is possible for them to attain any higher condition; they are not even sentient enough to desire to change their situation. . . . They eat, drink, breed, work and die; and . . . the richer and more intelligent classes are obliged to guard them with police.[10]

Some observers were less arrogant, however, and wondered if the workers should be held responsible for their fate.

One of the best of a new breed of urban reformers was Edwin Chadwick (1800–1890). With a background in law, Chadwick became obsessed with eliminating the poverty and squalor of the metropolitan areas. He became a civil servant and was soon appointed to a number of government investigatory commissions. As secretary of the Poor Law Commission, he initiated a passionate search for detailed facts about the living conditions of the working classes. After three years of investigation, Chadwick summarized the results in his *Report on the Condition of the Labouring Population of Great Britain,* published in 1842. In it, he concluded that "the various forms of epidemic, endemic, and other disease" were directly caused by the "atmospheric impurities produced by decomposing animal and vegetable substances, by damp and filth, and close overcrowded dwellings [prevailing] amongst the population in every part of the kingdom." Such conditions, he argued, could be eliminated. As to the means: "The primary and most important measures, and at the same time the most practicable, and within the recognized province of public administration, are drainage, the removal of all refuse of habitations, streets, and roads, and the improvement of the supplies of water."[11] In other words, Chadwick was advocating a system of modern sanitary reforms consisting of efficient sewers and a supply of piped water. Six years after his report and largely due to his efforts, Britain's first Public Health Act created the National Board of Health, empowered to form local boards that would establish modern sanitary systems.

Many middle-class citizens were quite willing to support the public health reforms of men like Chadwick because of their fear of **cholera.** Outbreaks of this deadly disease had ravaged Europe in the early 1830s and late 1840s and were especially rampant in the overcrowded cities. As city authorities and wealthier residents became convinced that filthy conditions helped spread the disease, they began to support the call for new public health measures.

New Social Classes: The Industrial Middle Class

The rise of industrial capitalism produced a new middle-class group. The bourgeoisie or middle class was not new; it had existed since the emergence of cities in the Middle Ages. Originally, the bourgeois was the burgher or town dweller, active as a merchant, official, artisan, lawyer, or scholar, who enjoyed a special set of rights from the charter of the town. As wealthy townspeople bought land, the original meaning of the word *bourgeois* became lost, and the term came to include people involved in commerce, industry, and banking as well as professionals, such as lawyers, teachers, physicians, and government officials at various levels. At the lower end of the economic scale were master craftspeople and shopkeepers.

THE NEW INDUSTRIAL ENTREPRENEURS Lest we make the industrial middle class too much of an abstraction, we need to look at who the new industrial entrepreneurs actually were. These were the people who constructed the factories, purchased the machines, and figured out where the markets were (see the box on p. 626). Their qualities included resourcefulness, single-mindedness, resolution, initiative, vision, ambition, and often, of course, greed. As Jedediah Strutt, the cotton manufacturer, said, the "getting of money . . . is the main business of the life of men."

But this was not an easy task. The early industrial entrepreneurs were called on to superintend an enormous array of functions that are handled today by teams of managers; they raised capital, determined markets, set company objectives, organized the factory and its labor, and trained supervisors who could act for them. The opportunities for making money were great, but the risks were also tremendous. The cotton trade, for example, which was so important to the early Industrial Revolution, was intensely competitive. Only through constant expansion could one feel secure, so early entrepreneurs reinvested most of their initial profits. Fear of bankruptcy was constant, especially among small firms. Furthermore, most early industrial enterprises were small. Even by the 1840s, only 10 percent of British industrial firms employed more than five thousand workers; 43 percent had fewer than one hundred. As entrepreneurs went bankrupt, new people could enter the race for profits, especially since the initial outlay required was not gigantic. In 1816, only one mill in five in the important industrial city of Manchester was in the hands of its original owner.

The new industrial entrepreneurs were from incredibly diverse social origins. Many of the most successful came from a mercantile background. Three London merchants, for example, founded a successful ironworks in Wales that owned eight steam engines and employed five thousand men. In Britain, land and domestic industry were often interdependent. Joshua Fielden, for example, acquired sufficient capital to establish a factory by running a family sheep farm while working looms in the farmhouse. Intelligent, clever, and ambitious apprentices who had learned their trades well could also strike it rich. William Radcliffe's family engaged in agriculture and spinning and weaving at home; he learned quickly how to succeed:

> Availing myself of the improvements that came out while I was in my teens . . . with my little savings and a practical knowledge of every process from the cotton bag to the piece of cloth . . . I was

Attitudes of the Industrial Middle Class in Britain and Japan

In the nineteenth century, a new industrial middle class in Great Britain took the lead in creating the Industrial Revolution. Japan did not begin to industrialize until after 1870. There, too, an industrial middle class emerged, although there were important differences in the attitudes of business leaders in Britain and Japan. Some of these differences can be seen in these documents. The first is an excerpt from the book *Self-Help*, first published in 1859, by Samuel Smiles, who espoused the belief that people succeed through "individual industry, energy, and uprightness." The other two selections are by Shibuzawa Eiichi, a Japanese industrialist who supervised textile factories. Although he began his business career in 1873, he did not write his autobiography, the source of his first excerpt, until 1927.

✦ ▦ ✦

Samuel Smiles, *Self-Help*

"Heaven helps those who help themselves" is a well-worn maxim, embodying in a small compass the results of vast human experience. The spirit of self-help is the root of all genuine growth in the individual; and, exhibited in the lives of many, it constitutes the true source of national vigor and strength. Help from without is often enfeebling in its effects, but help from within invariably invigorates. Whatever is done for men or classes, to a certain extent takes away the stimulus and necessity of doing for themselves; and where men are subjected to overguidance and overgovernment, the inevitable tendency is to render them comparatively helpless....

National progress is the sum of individual industry, energy, and uprightness, as national decay is of individual idleness, selfishness, and vice. What we are accustomed to decry as great social evils, will, for the most part, be found to be only the outgrowth of our own perverted life; and though we may endeavor to cut them down and extirpate them by means of law, they will only spring up again with fresh luxuriance in some other form, unless the individual conditions of human life and character are radically improved. If this view be correct, then it follows that the highest patriotism and philanthrophy consist, not so much in altering laws and modifying institutions as in helping and stimulating men to elevate and improve themselves by their own free and independent action as individuals....

Many popular books have been written for the purpose of communicating to the public the grand secret of making money. But there is no secret whatever about it, as the proverbs of every nation abundantly testify.... "A penny saved is a penny gained."—"Diligence is the mother of good-luck."—"No pains, no gains."—"No sweat, no sweet."—"Sloth, the Key of poverty."—"Work, and thou shalt have."—"He who will not work, neither shall he eat."—"The world his, who has patience and industry."

Shibuzawa Eiichi, *Autobiography*

I ... felt that it was necessary to raise the social standing of those who engaged in commerce and industry. By way of setting an example, I began studying and practicing the teachings of the *Analects* of Confucius. It contains teachings first enunciated more than twenty-four hundred years ago. Yet it supplies the ultimate in practical ethics for all of us to follow in our daily living. It has many golden rules for businessmen. For example, there is a saying: "Wealth and respect are what men desire, but unless a right way is followed, they cannot be obtained; poverty and lowly position are what men despise, but unless a right way is found, one cannot leave that status once reaching it." It shows very clearly how a businessman must act in this world.

Shibuzawa Eiichi on Progress

One must beware of the tendency of some to argue that it is through individualism or egoism that the State and society can progress most rapidly. They claim that under individualism, each individual competes with the others, and progress results from this competition. But this is to see merely the advantages and ignore the disadvantages, and I cannot support such a theory. Society exists, and a State has been founded. Although people desire to rise to positions of wealth and honor, the social order and the tranquility of the State will be disrupted if this is done egoistically. Men should not do battle in competition with their fellow men. Therefore, I believe that in order to get along together in society and serve the State, we must by all means abandon this idea of independence and self-reliance and reject egoism completely. ▷

Q What are the major similarities and differences between the attitudes toward business of Samuel Smiles and Shibuzawa Eiichi? How do you explain the differences, and what are their implications?

ready to commence business for myself and by the year 1789 I was well established and employed many hands both in spinning and weaving as a master manufacturer.[12]

By 1801, Radcliffe was operating a factory employing a thousand workers.

Members of dissenting religious minorities were often prominent among the early industrial leaders of Britain. The Darbys and Lloyds, who were iron manufacturers; the Barclays and Lloyds, who were bankers; and the Trumans and Perkins, who were brewers, were all Quakers. These were expensive trades and depended on the financial support that coreligionists in religious minorities provided for each other. Most historians believe that a major reason members of these religious minorities were so prominent in business was that they lacked other opportunities. Legally excluded from many public offices, they directed their ambitions into the new industrial capitalism.

It is interesting to note that in Britain in particular, aristocrats also became entrepreneurs. The Lambtons in Northumberland, the Curwens in Cumberland, the Norfolks in Yorkshire, and the Dudleys in Staffordshire all invested in mining enterprises. This close relationship between land and industry helped Britain assume the leadership role in the early Industrial Revolution.

SIGNIFICANCE OF THE INDUSTRIAL ENTREPRENEURS By 1850, in Britain at least, the kind of traditional entrepreneurship that had created the Industrial Revolution was declining and was being replaced by a new business aristocracy. This new generation of entrepreneurs stemmed from the professional and industrial middle classes, especially as sons inherited the successful businesses established by their fathers. It must not be forgotten, however, that even after 1850, a large number of small businesses existed in Britain, and some were still being founded by people from humble backgrounds. Indeed, the age of large-scale corporate capitalism did not begin until the 1890s (see Chapter 23).

Increasingly, the new industrial entrepreneurs—the bankers and owners of factories and mines—came to amass much wealth and play an important role alongside the traditional landed elites of their societies. The Industrial Revolution began at a time when the preindustrial agrarian world was still largely dominated by landed elites. As the new bourgeois bought great estates and acquired social respectability, they also sought political power, and in the course of the nineteenth century, their wealthiest members would merge with those old elites.

New Social Classes: Workers in the Industrial Age

At the same time that the members of the industrial middle class were seeking to reduce the barriers between themselves and the landed elite, they also were trying to separate themselves from the laboring classes below them. The working class was actually a mixture of groups in the first half of the nineteenth century. Factory workers would eventually form an industrial proletariat, but in the first half of the century, they did not constitute a majority of the working class in any major city, even in Britain. According to the 1851 census in Britain, there were 1.8 million agricultural laborers and 1 million domestic servants but only 811,000 workers in the cotton and woolen industries. And one-third of these were still working in small workshops or at home.

In the cities, artisans or craftspeople remained the largest group of urban workers during the first half of the nineteenth century. They worked in numerous small industries, such as shoemaking, glovemaking, bookbinding, printing, and bricklaying. Some craftspeople, especially those employed in such luxury trades as coach building and clock making, formed a kind of aristocracy of labor and earned higher wages than others. Artisans were not factory workers; they were traditionally organized in guilds, where they passed on their skills to apprentices. But guilds were increasingly losing their power, especially in industrialized countries. Fearful of losing out to the new factories that could produce goods more cheaply, artisans tended to support movements against industrialization. Industrialists welcomed the decline of skilled craftspeople, as one perceptive old tailor realized in telling his life story:

> It is upwards of 30 years since I first went to work at the tailoring trade in London.... I continued working for the honorable trade and belonging to the Society [for tailors] for about 15 years. My weekly earnings then averaged £1 16s. a week while I was at work, and for several years I was seldom out of work.... No one could have been happier than I was.... But then, with my sight defective...I could get no employment at the honorable trade, and that was the ruin of me entirely; for working there, of course, I got "scratched" from the trade society, and so lost all hope of being provided for by them in my helplessness. The workshop...was about seven feet square, and so low, that as you [sat] on the floor you could touch the ceiling with the tip of your finger. In this place seven of us worked. [The master] paid little more than half the regular wages, and employed such men as myself—only those who couldn't get anything better to do.... I don't think my wages there averaged above 12s. a week.... I am convinced I lost my eyesight by working in that cheap shop.... It is by the ruin of such men as me that these masters are enabled to undersell the better shops.... That's the way, sir, the cheap clothes is produced, by making blind beggars of the workmen, like myself, and throwing us on [the benevolence of] the parish [church] in our old age.[13]

Servants also formed another large group of urban workers, especially in major cities like London and Paris. Many were women from the countryside who became utterly dependent on their upper- and middle-class employers.

WORKING CONDITIONS FOR THE INDUSTRIAL WORKING CLASS Workers in the new industrial factories also faced wretched working conditions. We have already observed the psychological traumas workers experienced

Child Labor: Discipline in the Textile Mills

Child labor was not new, but in the early Industrial Revolution, it was exploited more systematically. These selections are taken from the Report of Sadler's Committee, a report that was commissioned by the government in 1832 to inquire into the condition of child factory workers.

———— ❦❖❦ ————

Keeping the Children Awake

It is a very frequent thing at Mr. Marshall's [at Shrewsbury] where the least children were employed (for there were plenty working at six years of age), for Mr. Horseman to start the mill earlier in the morning than he formerly did; and provided a child should be drowsy, the overlooker walks round the room with a stick in his hand, and he touches that child on the shoulder, and says, "Come here." In a corner of the room there is an iron cistern; it is filled with water; he takes this boy, and takes him up by the legs, and dips him over head in the cistern, and sends him to work for the remainder of the day. . . .

What means were taken to keep the children to their work?—Sometimes they would tap them over the head, or nip them over the nose, or give them a pinch of snuff, or throw water in their faces, or pull them off where they were, and job them about to keep them waking.

The Sadistic Overlooker

Samuel Downe, age 29, factory worker living near Leeds; at the age of about ten began work at Mr. Marshall's mills at Shrewsbury, where the customary hours when work was brisk were generally 5 A.M. to 8 P.M., sometimes from 5:30 A.M. to 8 or 9.

What means were taken to keep the children awake and vigilant, especially at the termination of such a day's labor as you have described?—There was generally a blow or a box, or a tap with a strap, or sometimes the hand.

Have you yourself been strapped?—Yes, most severely, till I could not bear to sit upon a chair without having pillows, and through that I left. I was strapped both on my own legs, and then I was put upon a man's back, and then strapped and buckled with two straps to an iron pillar, and flogged, and all by one overlooker; after that he took a piece of tow, and twisted it in the shape of a cord, and put it in my mouth, and tied it behind my head.

He gagged you?—Yes; and then he orders me to run round a part of the machinery where he was overlooker, and he stood at one end, and every time I came there he struck me with a stick, which I believe was an ash plant, and which he generally carried in his hand, and sometimes he hit me, and sometimes he did not; and one of the men in the room came and begged me off, and that he let me go, and not beat me any more, and consequently he did.

You have been beaten with extraordinary severity?—Yes, I was beaten so that I had not power to cry at all, or hardly speak at one time. What age were you at that time?—Between 10 and 11. ❧

 What kind of working conditions did children face in the textile mills during the early Industrial Revolution? Why were they beaten?

from their employers' efforts to break old preindustrial work patterns and create a well-disciplined labor force. But what were the physical conditions of the factories?

Unquestionably, in the early decades of the Industrial Revolution, "places of work," as early factories were called, were dreadful. Work hours ranged from twelve to sixteen hours a day, six days a week, with a half hour for lunch and for dinner. There was no security of employment and no minimum wage. The worst conditions were in the cotton mills, where temperatures were especially debilitating. One report noted that "in the cotton-spinning work, these creatures are kept, fourteen hours in each day, locked up, summer and winter, in a heat of from eighty to eighty-four degrees." Mills were also dirty, dusty, and unhealthy:

> Not only is there not a breath of sweet air in these truly infernal scenes, but . . . there is the abominable and pernicious stink of the gas to assist in the murderous effects of the heat. In addition to the noxious effluvia of the gas, mixed with the steam, there are the dust, and what is called cotton-flyings or fuz, which the unfortunate creatures have to inhale; and . . . the notorious fact is that well constituted men are rendered old and past labor at forty years of age, and that children are rendered decrepit and deformed, and thousands upon thousands of them slaughtered by consumptions [lung diseases], before they arrive at the age of sixteen.[14]

Thus ran a report on working conditions in the cotton industry in 1824.

Conditions in the coal mines were also harsh. The introduction of steam power meant only that steam-powered engines mechanically lifted coal to the top. Inside the mines, men still bore the burden of digging the coal out while horses, mules, women, and children hauled coal carts on rails to the lift. Dangers abounded in coal mines; cave-ins, explosions, and gas fumes (called "bad air") were a way of life. The cramped conditions—tunnels often did not exceed 3 or 4 feet in height—and constant dampness in the mines resulted in deformed bodies and ruined lungs.

Child Labor: The Mines

After examining conditions in British coal mines, a government official commented that "the hardest labor in the worst room in the worst-conducted factory is less hard, less cruel and less demoralizing than the labor in the best of coal-mines." Yet it was not until 1842 that legislation was passed eliminating the labor of boys under ten from the mines. This selection is taken from a government report on the mines in Lancashire.

✦ ✦ ✦

The Black Holes of Worsley

Examination of Thomas Gibson and George Bryan, witnesses from the coal mines at Worsley:

Have you worked from a boy in a coal mine?—(Both) Yes.

What had you to do then?—Thrutching the basket and drawing. It is done by little boys; one draws the basket and the other pushes it behind. Is that hard labor?—Yes, very hard labor.

For how many hours a day did you work?—Nearly nine hours regularly; sometimes twelve; I have worked about thirteen. We used to go in at six in the morning, and took a bit of bread and cheese in our pocket, and stopped two or three minutes; and some days nothing at all to eat.

How was it that sometimes you had nothing to eat?—We were over-burdened. I had only a mother, and she had nothing to give me. I was sometimes half starved. . . .

Do they work in the same way now exactly?—Yes, they do; they have nothing more than a bit of bread and cheese in their pocket, and sometimes can't eat it all, owing to the dust and damp and badness of air; and sometimes it is as hot as an oven; sometimes I have seen it so hot as to melt a candle.

What are the usual wages of a boy of eight?—They used to get 3d or 4d a day. Now a man's wages is divided into eight eighths; and when a boy is eight years old he gets one of those eighths; at eleven, two eighths; at thirteen, three eighths; at fifteen, four eighths; at twenty, man's wages.

What are the wages of a man?—About 15s if he is in full employment, but often not more than 10s, and out of that he has to get his tools and candles. He consumes about four candles in nine hours' work, in some places six; 6d per pound, and twenty-four candles to the pound.

Were you ever beaten as a child?—Yes, many a score of times; both kicks and thumps.

Are many girls employed in the pits?—Yes, a vast of those. They do the same kind of work as the boys till they get about 14 years of age, when they get the wages of half a man, and never get more, and continue at the same work for many years.

Did they ever fight together?—Yes, many days together. Both boys and girls; sometimes they are very loving with one another. ✒

 What kind of working conditions did children face in the mines during the early Industrial Revolution? Why did entrepreneurs permit such conditions and such treatment of children?

Both children and women were employed in large numbers in early factories and mines. Children had been an important part of the family economy in preindustrial times, working in the fields or carding and spinning wool at home with the growth of the cottage industry. In the Industrial Revolution, however, child labor was exploited more than ever and in a considerably more systematic fashion (see the boxes on pp. 628–629). The owners of cotton factories appreciated certain features of child labor. Children had an especially delicate touch as spinners of cotton. Their smaller size made it easier for them to crawl under machines to gather loose cotton. Moreover, children were more easily broken to factory work. Above all, children represented a cheap supply of labor. In 1821, just about half of the British population was under twenty years of age. Hence, children made up a particularly abundant supply of labor, and they were paid only about one-sixth to one-third of what a man was paid. In the cotton factories in 1838, children under eighteen made up 29 percent of the total workforce; children as young as seven worked twelve to fifteen hours per day, six days a week, in cotton mills.

Especially terrible in the early Industrial Revolution was the use of so-called pauper apprentices. These were orphans or children abandoned by their parents who had wound up in the care of local parishes. To save on their upkeep, parish officials found it convenient to apprentice them to factory owners looking for a cheap source of labor. These children worked long hours under strict discipline and received inadequate food and recreation; many became deformed from being kept too long in contorted positions. Although economic liberals and some industrialists were against all state intervention in economic matters, Parliament eventually remedied some of the worst ills of child abuse in factories and mines (see "Efforts at Change: Reformers and Government" later in this chapter). The legislation of the 1830s and 1840s, however, primarily affected child labor in textile factories and mines. It did not touch the use of children in small workshops or the nonfactory trades that were not protected. As these trades were in competition with the new factories, conditions there were often even worse. Pottery works, for example, were not investigated until the 1860s, when it

Women and Children in the Mines. Women and children were often employed in the factories and mines of the early nineteenth century. These illustrations are from the Report of the Children's Employment Commission in Great Britain in 1842. The top image shows a woman dragging a cart loaded with coal. The image below shows a boy walking backwards in a mine, pulling a cart also filled with coal. Both images show the trying conditions under which both women and children worked in the early Industrial Revolution. In 1842, the Coal Mines Act forbade the use of boys younger than ten and women in the mines.

was found that 17 percent of the workers were under eleven years of age. One investigator reported what he found:

> The boys were kept in constant motion throughout the day, each carrying from thirty to fifty dozen of molds into the stoves, and remaining... long enough to take the dried earthenware away. The distance thus run by a boy in the course of a day... was estimated at seven miles. From the very nature of this exhausting occupation children were rendered pale, weak and unhealthy. In the depth of winter, with the thermometer in the open air sometimes below zero, boys, with little clothing but rags, might be seen running to and fro on errands or to their dinners with the perspiration on their foreheads, "after laboring for hours like little slaves." The inevitable result of such transitions of temperature were consumption, asthma and acute inflammation.[15]

Little wonder that child labor legislation enacted in 1864 included pottery works.

By 1830, women and children made up two-thirds of the cotton industry's labor. As the number of children employed declined under the Factory Act of 1833, however, their places were taken by women, who came to dominate the labor forces of the early factories. Women made up 50 percent of the labor force in textile (cotton and woolen) factories before 1870. They were mostly unskilled labor and were paid half or less of what men received. Excessive working hours for women were outlawed in 1844, but only in textile factories and mines; not until 1867 were they outlawed in craft workshops.

The employment of children and women in large part represents a continuation of a preindustrial kinship pattern. The cottage industry had always involved the efforts of the entire family, and it seemed perfectly natural to continue this pattern. Men migrating from the countryside to industrial towns and cities took their wives and children with them into the factory or into the mines. Of 136 employees in Robert Peel's factory at Bury in 1801, 95 were members of the same twenty-six families. The impetus for this family work often came from the family itself. The factory owner Jedediah Strutt was opposed to child labor under age ten but was forced by parents to take children as young as seven.

The employment of large numbers of women in factories did not significantly transform female working patterns, as was once assumed. Studies of urban households in France and Britain, for example, have revealed that throughout the nineteenth century, traditional types of female labor still predominated in the women's work world. In 1851, fully 40 percent of the female workforce in Britain consisted of domestic servants. In France, the largest group of female workers, 40 percent, worked in agriculture. In addition, only 20 percent of female workers in Britain labored in factories, and only 10 percent did so in France. Regional and local studies have also found that most of the workers were single women. Few married women worked outside the home.

The factory acts that limited the work hours of children and women also began to break up the traditional kinship pattern of work and led to a new pattern based on a separation of work and home. Men came to be regarded as responsible for the primary work obligations as women assumed daily control of the family and performed low-paying jobs such as laundry work that could be done in the home. Domestic industry made it possible for women to continue their contributions to family survival.

Historians have also reminded us that if the treatment of children in the mines and factories seems particularly cruel and harsh, contemporary treatment of children in general was often brutal. Beatings, for example, had long been regarded, even by dedicated churchmen and churchwomen, as the best way to discipline children.

The problem of poverty among the working classes was also addressed in Britain by government action in the form of the Poor Law Act of 1834, which established workhouses where jobless poor people were forced to live. The intent of this policy, based on the assumption that the poor were responsible for their own pitiful conditions, was "to make the workhouses as like prisons as possible . . . to establish therein a discipline so severe and repulsive as to make them a terror to the poor." Within a few years, despite sporadic opposition, more than 200,000 poor people were locked up in workhouses, where family members were separated, forced to live in dormitories, given work assignments, and fed dreadful food. Children were often recruited from parish workhouses as cheap labor in factories.

Standards of Living

One of the most heated debates on the Industrial Revolution concerns the standard of living. Most historians assume that in the long run, the Industrial Revolution improved living standards dramatically in the form of higher per capita incomes and greater consumer choices. But did the first generation of industrial workers experience a decline in their living standards and suffer unnecessarily? Some historians have argued that early industrialization required huge profits to be reinvested in new and ever more expensive equipment; thus, to make the requisite profits, industrialists had to keep wages low. Others have questioned that argument, pointing out that initial investments in early machinery were not necessarily large, nor did they need to be. What certainly did occur in the first half of the nineteenth century was a widening gap between rich and poor. One estimate, based on income tax returns in Britain, is that the wealthiest 1 percent of the population increased its share of the national product from 25 percent in 1801 to 35 percent in 1848.

Wages, prices, and consumption patterns are some of the criteria used for measuring the standard of living. Between 1780 and 1850, as far as we can determine from the available evidence, both wages and prices fluctuated widely. Most historians believe that during the Napoleonic wars, the increase in prices outstripped wages. Between 1815 and 1830, a drop in prices was accompanied by a slight increase in wages. From 1830 to the late 1840s, real wages seem to have improved, although regional variations make generalizations difficult.

When we look at consumption patterns, we find, on the one hand, that in Britain in 1850, tea, sugar, and coffee were still semiluxuries consumed primarily by the upper and middle classes and better-off artisans. Meat consumption per capita was less in 1840 than in 1780. On the other hand, a mass market had developed in the cheap cotton goods so important to the Industrial Revolution. As a final note on the issue of the standard of living, some historians who take a positive view of the early Industrial Revolution have questioned what would have happened to Britain's growing population without the Industrial Revolution. Would it have gone the way of Ireland's in the Great Hunger of the mid-nineteenth century? No one really knows.

No doubt the periodic crises of overproduction that haunted industrialization from its beginnings caused even further economic hardship. Short-term economic depressions brought high unemployment and increased social tensions. Unemployment figures could be astronomical. During one of these economic depressions in 1842, for example, 60 percent of the factory employees in Bolton were laid off. Cyclical depressions were particularly devastating in towns whose prosperity rested on one industry.

Overall we can say that some evidence exists for an increase in real wages for the working classes between 1790 and 1850, especially in the 1840s. But can standards of living be assessed only in terms of prices, wages, and consumption patterns? No doubt those meant little to people who faced dreadful housing, adulterated food, public health hazards, and the physical and psychological traumas of work life. The real gainers in the early Industrial Revolution were members of the middle class—and some skilled workers whose jobs were not eliminated by the new machines. But industrial workers themselves would have to wait until the second half of the nineteenth century to reap the benefits of industrialization.

Efforts at Change: The Workers

Before long, workers looked to the formation of labor organizations to gain decent wages and working conditions. The British government, reacting against the radicalism of the French revolutionary working classes, had passed the Combination Acts in 1799 and 1800 outlawing associations of workers. The legislation failed to prevent the formation of **trade unions,** however. Similar to the craft societies of earlier times, these new associations were formed by skilled workers in a number of new industries, including the cotton spinners, ironworkers, coal miners, and shipwrights. These unions served two purposes. One was to preserve their own workers' position by limiting entry into their trade; the other was to gain benefits from the employers. These early trade unions had limited goals. They favored a working-class struggle against employers, but only to win improvements for the members of their own trades.

THE TRADE UNION MOVEMENT Some trade unions were even willing to strike to attain their goals. Bitter strikes were carried out by hand-loom weavers in Glasgow in 1813, cotton spinners in Manchester in 1818, and miners in Northumberland and Durham in 1810. Such blatant illegal activity caused Parliament to repeal the Combination Acts in 1824, accepting the argument of some members that the acts themselves had so alienated workers that they had formed unions. Unions were now tolerated, but other legislation enabled authorities to keep close watch over their activities.

In the 1820s and 1830s, the union movement began to focus on the creation of national unions. One of the leaders in this effort was a well-known cotton magnate

and social reformer, Robert Owen (1771–1858). Owen came to believe in the creation of voluntary associations that would demonstrate to others the benefits of cooperative rather than competitive living (see Chapter 21). Although Owen's program was not directed specifically to trade unionists, his ideas had great appeal to some of their leaders. Under Owen's direction, plans emerged for the Grand National Consolidated Trades Union, which was formed in February 1834. As a national federation of trade unions, its primary purpose was to coordinate a general strike for the eight-hour working day. Rhetoric, however, soon outpaced reality, and by the summer of that year, the lack of real working-class support led to the federation's total collapse, and the union movement reverted to trade unions for individual crafts. The largest and most successful of these unions was the Amalgamated Society of Engineers, formed in 1850. Its provision of generous unemployment benefits in return for a small weekly payment was precisely the kind of practical gains these trade unions sought. Larger goals would have to wait.

LUDDITES Trade unionism was not the only type of collective action by workers in the early decades of the Industrial Revolution. The Luddites were skilled craftspeople in the Midlands and northern England who in 1812 attacked the machines that they believed threatened their livelihoods. These attacks failed to stop the industrial mechanization of Britain and have been viewed as utterly naive. Some historians, however, have also seen them as an intense eruption of feeling against unrestrained industrial capitalism. The inability of 12,000 troops to find the culprits provides stunning evidence of the local support they received in their areas.

CHARTISM A much more meaningful expression of the attempts of British workers to improve their condition developed in the movement known as Chartism—the "first important political movement of working men organized during the nineteenth century." Its aim was to achieve political democracy. Chartism took its name from the People's Charter, a document drawn up in 1838 by the London Working Men's Association. The charter demanded universal male suffrage, payment for members of Parliament, the elimination of property qualifications for members of Parliament, and annual sessions of Parliament. Women, too, joined in the movement. Chartist groups in many large towns often had female sections. Although some women were quite active in the movement, they were fighting to win political rights for their husbands, not for themselves, as the Chartist platform did not include the right to vote for women.

Two national petitions incorporating the Chartist demands gained millions of signatures and were presented to Parliament in 1839 and 1842. Chartism attempted to encourage change through peaceful, constitutional means, although there was an underlying threat of force, as is evident in the Chartist slogan, "Peacefully if we can, forcibly if

A Trade Union Membership Card. Skilled workers in a number of new industries formed trade unions in an attempt to gain higher wages, better working conditions, and special benefits. The scenes at the bottom of this membership card for the Associated Shipwrights Society illustrate some of the medical and social benefits it provided for its members.

© Trades Union Congress, London/The Bridgeman Art Library

we must." In 1842, Chartist activists organized a general strike on behalf of their goals, but it had little success.

Despite the pressures exerted by the Chartists, both national petitions were rejected by the members of Parliament, who were not at all ready for political democracy. As one member said, universal male suffrage would be "fatal to all the purposes for which government exists" and was "utterly incompatible with the very existence of civilization." After 1848, Chartism as a movement had largely played itself out. It had never really posed a serious threat to the British establishment, but it had not been a total failure either. Its true significance stemmed from its ability to arouse and organize millions of working-class men and women, to give them a sense of working-class consciousness that they had not really possessed before. This political education of working people was important to the ultimate acceptance of all the points of the People's Charter in the future.

Efforts at Change: Reformers and Government

Efforts to improve the worst conditions of the industrial factory system also came from outside the ranks of the working classes. From its beginning, the Industrial Revolution had drawn much criticism. Romantic poets like William Wordsworth (see Chapter 21) decried the destruction of the natural world:

> I grieve, when on the darker side
> Of this great change I look; and there behold
> Such outrage done to nature as compels
> The indignant power to justify herself.

Reform-minded individuals, be they factory owners who felt twinges of conscience or social reformers in Parliament, campaigned against the evils of the industrial factory, especially condemning the abuse of children. One

hoped for the day "that these little ones should once more see the rising and setting of the sun."

GOVERNMENT ACTION   As it became apparent that the increase in wealth generated by the Industrial Revolution was accompanied by ever-increasing numbers of poor people, more and more efforts were made to document and deal with the problems. As reports from civic-minded citizens and parliamentary commissions intensified and demonstrated the extent of poverty, degradation, and suffering, the reform efforts began to succeed.

Their first success was a series of factory acts passed between 1802 and 1819 that limited labor for children between the ages of nine and sixteen to twelve hours a day; the employment of children under nine years old was forbidden. Moreover, the laws stipulated that children were to receive instruction in reading and arithmetic during working hours. But these acts applied only to cotton mills, not to factories or mines where some of the worst abuses were taking place. Just as important, no provision was made for enforcing the acts through a system of inspection.

In the reform-minded decades of the 1830s and 1840s, new legislation was passed. The Factory Act of 1833 strengthened earlier labor legislation. All textile factories were now included. Children between the ages of nine and thirteen could work only eight hours a day; those between thirteen and eighteen, twelve hours. Factory inspectors were appointed with the power to fine those who broke the law. Another piece of legislation in 1833 required that children between nine and thirteen have at least two hours of elementary education during the working day. In 1847, the Ten Hours Act reduced the workday for children between thirteen and eighteen to ten hours. Women were also now included in the ten-hour limit. In 1842, the Coal Mines Act eliminated the employment of boys under ten and women in mines. Eventually, men too would benefit from the move to restrict factory hours.

CHAPTER SUMMARY

The Industrial Revolution was one of the major forces of change in the nineteenth century as it led Western civilization into the machine-dependent modern world. It

began in Britain, which had an agricultural revolution that increased the quantity of foodstuffs, a population increase that created a supply of labor, capital for investment, a good supply of coal and iron ore, and a transportation revolution that created a system of canals, roads, and bridges. As the world's leading colonial power, Britain also had access to overseas markets. The cotton industry led the way as new

machines such as the spinning jenny and power loom enabled the British to produce cheap cotton goods. Most important was the steam engine, which led to factories and a system of steam-powered railroads that moved people and goods efficiently. The Great Exhibition of 1851 in London showed the world the achievements of Britain's Industrial Revolution. Industrialization also spread to the Continent, and by 1860, the United States was also well along that road. In the non-Western world, industrial development was much slower, in large part because European colonial powers deliberately pursued a policy of preventing the growth of mechanized industry, thus keeping the colonies as purchasers of industrial products.

The Industrial Revolution also transformed the social world of Europe. The creation of an industrial proletariat produced a whole new force for change. The work environment, especially in the new factories and mines, was dreadful, characterized by long hours, unsafe conditions, monotonous labor, and the use of child labor. Eventually, laws were passed to improve working conditions, especially for women and children. Labor unions were also formed to improve wages and conditions but met with limited success. Workers sometimes protested by destroying the factories and machines, as did the Luddites. The Chartist movement petitioned Parliament, calling for the right to vote and other reforms, but the members of Parliament refused their demands. The development of a wealthy industrial middle class presented a challenge to the long-term hegemony of landed wealth. Though that wealth had been threatened by the fortunes of commerce, it had never been overturned. But the new bourgeoisie became more demanding, as we shall see in the next chapter.

The Industrial Revolution seemed to prove to Europeans the underlying assumption of the Scientific Revolution of the seventeenth century— that human beings were capable of dominating nature. By rationally manipulating the material environment for human benefit, people could attain new levels of material prosperity and produce ma- chines not dreamed of in their wildest imaginings. Lost in the excitement of the Industrial Revolution were the voices that pointed to the dehumanization of the workforce and the alienation from one's work, one's associates, oneself, and the natural world.

CHAPTER TIMELINE

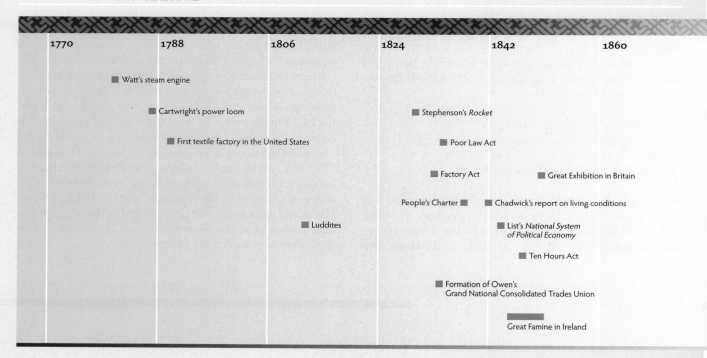

1770	1788	1806	1824	1842	1860

■ Watt's steam engine

■ Cartwright's power loom

■ First textile factory in the United States

■ Stephenson's *Rocket*

■ Poor Law Act

■ Factory Act ■ Great Exhibition in Britain

People's Charter ■ ■ Chadwick's report on living conditions

■ Luddites

■ List's *National System of Political Economy*

■ Ten Hours Act

■ Formation of Owen's Grand National Consolidated Trades Union

■ Great Famine in Ireland

CHAPTER REVIEW

Upon Reflection

Q What made the factory system possible, and why was it such an important part of the early industrial system? What impact did it have on the lives of workers?

Q How are changes in population growth and the increase in urbanization related to the Industrial Revolution?

Q What efforts did workers make to ameliorate the harsh working conditions of the early Industrial Revolution?

Key Terms

agricultural revolution (p. 608)
capital (p. 608)
pig iron (p. 611)
wrought iron (p. 611)
tariffs (p. 617)
cholera (p. 625)
trade unions (p. 631)

Suggestions for Further Reading

GENERAL WORKS The well-written work by **D. Landes, *The Unbound Prometheus: Technological Change and Industrial Development in Western Europe from 1750 to the Present*** (Cambridge, 1969), is a good introduction to the Industrial Revolution, but see also **J. Horn, *The Industrial Revolution*** (Westport, Conn., 2007), and **D. Fisher, *The Industrial Revolution*** (New York, 1992). On the "makers" of the Industrial Revolution, see **G. Weightman, *The Industrial Revolutionaries: The Making of the Modern World, 1776–1914*** (New York, 2007). For a broader perspective, see **P. Stearns, *The Industrial Revolution in World History*** (Boulder, Colo., 1993). On the Industrial Revolution in Britain, see **K. Morgan, *The Birth of Industrial Britain: Social Change, 1750–1850*** (New York, 2004); **P. Mathias, *The First Industrial Nation: An Economic History of Britain, 1700–1914,*** 3rd ed. (New York, 2001); and **R. Brown, *Society and Economy in Modern Britain, 1700–1850*** (London, 1991). On the Crystal Palace, see **J. A. Auerbach, *The Great Exhibition of 1851: A Nation on Display*** (New Haven, Conn., 1999), and **L. Kriegel, *Grand Designs: Labor, Empire, and the Museum in Victorian Culture*** (Durham, N.C., 2007). On the spread of industrialization to the Continent, see **T. Kemp, *Industrialization in Nineteenth-Century Europe,*** 2nd ed. (London, 1985).

INDUSTRIALIZATION IN THE UNITED STATES The early industrialization of the United States is examined in **B. Hindle** and **S. Lubar, *Engines of Change: The American Industrial Revolution, 1790–1860*** (Washington, D.C., 1986). On the economic ties between Great Britain and the United States, see **D. Jeremy, *Transatlantic Industrial Revolution: The Diffusion of Textile Technology Between Britain and America, 1790–1830*** (Cambridge, Mass., 1981).

SOCIAL IMPACT OF INDUSTRIALIZATION For an examination of urban growth, see the classic work of **A. F. Weber, *The Growth of Cities in the Nineteenth Century: A Study in Statistics*** (Ithaca, N.Y., 1963); **J. G. Williamson, *Coping with City Growth During the British Industrial Revolution*** (Cambridge, 2002); and **L. D. Schwarz, *London in the Age of Industrialization*** (New York, 1992). **C. Kinealy, *A Death-Dealing Famine: The Great Hunger in Ireland*** (Chicago, 1997), is a good account of the great Irish tragedy, but see also **J. S. Donnelly, *The Great Irish Potato Famine*** (London, 2001). Many of the works cited here have much information on the social impact of the Industrial Revolution, but additional material is available in **F. Crouzet, *The First Industrialists: The Problems of Origins*** (Cambridge, 1985), on British entrepreneurs; **J. Merriman, *The Margins of City Life*** (New York, 1991), on French cities; **P. Pilbeam, *The Middle Classes in Europe, 1789–1914*** (Basingstoke, England, 1990); and **T. Koditschek, *Class Formation and Urban Industrial Society*** (New York, 1990). **G. Himmelfarb, *The Idea of Poverty: England in the Early Industrial Age*** (New York, 1984), traces the concepts of poverty and the poor from the mid-eighteenth century to the mid-nineteenth century. **M. J. Maynes, *Taking the Hard Road*** (Chapel Hill, N.C., 1995), offers a glimpse into the lives of workers. A classic work on female labor patterns is **L. A. Tilly** and **J. W. Scott, *Women, Work, and Family*** (New York, 1978). See also **J. Lown, *Women and Industrialization: Gender at Work in Nineteenth-Century England*** (Minneapolis, Minn., 1990); **J. Rendall, *Women in an Industrializing Society: England, 1750–1880*** (Oxford, 2002); and **K. Honeyman, *Women, Gender, and Industrialization in England, 1700–1870*** (New York, 2000).

AP* REVIEW QUESTIONS FOR CHAPTER 20

1. "As they could neither of them be of any further use, I released them from the firm and took the whole upon myself. " This statement most likely describes which group of people?

   (A) socialists
   (B) industrial entrepreneurs
   (C) Marxists
   (D) English nobles
   (E) new urban workers

2. The Industrial Revolution began in England for all of the following reasons EXCEPT

   (A) it had many navigable rivers allowing for easy transportation of goods.
   (B) it had readily available capital as a result of a strong economy and an effective banking system.
   (C) it had a mobile population free from traditional servitudes.
   (D) it had support from the government in the form of parliamentary legislation.
   (E) it had a larger population than other European countries.

3. An important factor that led to the Industrial Revolution in Great Britain was

   (A) the agricultural revolution.
   (B) the French Revolution.
   (C) the growth of the urban population.
   (D) Britain's increased colonial holdings in North America.
   (E) the influence of the Enlightenment thinkers.

4. The legislation that had the greatest impact in limiting child labor in England's factories was

   (A) the Factory Act of 1833.
   (B) the Reform Act of 1832.
   (C) the Ten Hours Act of 1847.
   (D) the Coal Mines Act of 1842.
   (E) the Trade Union Act of 1824.

5. Though their movement ultimately failed, the Chartists attempted to achieve

   (A) an expansion of the franchise and political equality for women.
   (B) effective reform in the area of child labor.
   (C) social justice for those losing land to the enclosure movements.
   (D) equality amongt workers in the industrial system.
   (E) universal suffrage and payment for members of Parliament.

6. The First Industrial Revolution was concentrated mainly in the areas of

   (A) gas lamps, coal production, and shipping.
   (B) textiles, steam engines, and iron.
   (C) petroleum, steel, and automobiles.
   (D) farm equipment, railroads, and electricity.
   (E) crop fertilizers, textiles, and heavy industry.

7. The eighteenth-century population explosion is mainly attributed to

   (A) an increase in the birthrate after 1750.
   (B) the rise of industrial production, which put less physical stress on workers.
   (C) the end of the potato blight and the Great Irish Famine.
   (D) a decline in the death rate due to greater food production and fewer wars.
   (E) widespread inoculation against disease and cleaner cities.

8. The industrial workers of the mid-nineteenth century were often

   (A) skilled men working in new factory towns.
   (B) women who were paid half or less of what men received.
   (C) unskilled, uneducated children.
   (D) immigrants fleeing oppressive regimes in the countries of their birth.
   (E) isolated colonists in the New World.

9. James Kay-Shuttleworth and Edwin Chadwick were reformers concerned with

   (A) eradicating the Luddites from society.
   (B) the emergence of new wealthy classes that rivaled the power of England's nobles.
   (C) the unsanitary and miserable living conditions of the working class that could potentially lead to violence.
   (D) the resurgence of the bubonic plague in crowded industrial cities.
   (E) increasing political representation of the working class in England.

10. The Combination Acts in England were enacted in an attempt to

   (A) suppress workers' trade unions.
   (B) prohibit trade with the Ottoman Empire.
   (C) prevent women from taking jobs that traditionally belonged to men.
   (D) limit Irish immigration into England or France.
   (E) prevent the establishment of secular schools.

11. The English laws that allowed common lands to be partitioned and sold off were known as the

   (A) Factory Acts.
   (B) English poor laws.
   (C) enclosure acts.
   (D) industrialization acts.
   (E) property laws.

12. Which statement best describes continental Europe's experience in the Industrial Revolution?

   (A) Great Britain's output of coal and iron was surpassed by the United States by the early nineteenth century.
   (B) Though eastern Europe was late to industrialize, its textile output rivaled western Europe's by 1870.
   (C) Whereas industrialization in Great Britain was based on textile production, on the Continent the iron and coal of heavy industry played the leading role.
   (D) India, under the guiding hand of Great Britain, was able to rival British cotton production and thus became Great Britain's greatest competitor in textiles.
   (E) Spain and Portugal united with Italy to create a Southern Industrial League that focused on building railroads and steam engines.

13. The Great Exhibition of 1851 was designed to

   (A) showcase British military superiority.
   (B) promote nationalism in England.
   (C) serve as a haven for intellectuals.
   (D) promote the social welfare of British citizens.
   (E) illustrate the industrial might and technological capabilities of Great Britain.

14. Which of the following best exemplifies urban living conditions in the early nineteenth century?

   (A) There was a sharp decline in diseases as doctors and medical care became more readily accessible to the masses.
   (B) Governments played a proactive role in improving living conditions by upholding strict standards in housing and imposing steep fines on abusers.
   (C) Urban living space was at a premium as the population continued to increase.
   (D) Urban families enjoyed the rise of theater districts and readily available outdoor entertainment.
   (E) Due to the great number of churches found in urban centers, urbanites tended to be more religious than those living in the countryside.

© The Art Archive/Museo del Risorgimento Brescia/Gianni Dagli Orti

A meeting of the Congress of Vienna

CHAPTER

21

Reaction, Revolution, and Romanticism, 1815–1850

CHAPTER OUTLINE AND FOCUS QUESTIONS

The Conservative Order (1815–1830)

Q What were the goals of the Congress of Vienna and the Concert of Europe, and how successful were they in achieving those goals?

The Ideologies of Change

Q What were the main tenets of conservatism, liberalism, nationalism, and utopian socialism, and what role did each ideology play in Europe in the first half of the nineteenth century?

Revolution and Reform (1830–1850)

Q What forces for change were present in France and Great Britain between 1830 and 1848, and how did each nation respond? What were the causes of the revolutions of 1848, and why did the revolutions fail?

The Emergence of an Ordered Society

Q How did Europe respond to the need for order in society in the first half of the nineteenth century?

Culture in an Age of Reaction and Revolution: The Mood of Romanticism

Q What were the characteristics of Romanticism, and how were they reflected in literature, art, and music?

CRITICAL THINKING

Q In what ways were intellectual and artistic developments related to the political and social forces of the age?

IN SEPTEMBER 1814, hundreds of foreigners began to converge on Vienna, the capital city of the Austrian Empire. Many were members of European royalty—kings, archdukes, princes, and their wives—accompanied by their diplomatic advisers and scores of servants. Their congenial host was the Austrian emperor, Francis I, who never tired of regaling Vienna's guests with concerts, glittering balls, sumptuous feasts, and countless hunting parties. One participant remembered, "Eating, fireworks, public illuminations. For eight or ten days, I haven't been able to work at all. What a life!" Of course, not every waking hour was spent in pleasure during this gathering of notables, known to history as the Congress of Vienna. These people were also representatives of all the states that had fought Napoleon, and their real business was to arrange a final peace settlement after almost a decade of war. On June 8, 1815, they finally completed their task.

The forces of upheaval unleashed during the French revolutionary and Napoleonic wars were temporarily quieted in 1815 as rulers sought to restore stability by reestablishing much of the old order to a Europe ravaged by war. Kings, landed aristocrats, and bureaucratic elites regained their control over domestic governments, and internationally the forces of conservatism tried to maintain the new status quo; some states even used military force to intervene in the internal affairs of other countries in their desire to crush revolutions.

But the Western world had been changed, and it would not readily go back to the old system. New ideologies, especially liberalism and nationalism, both products of the revolutionary upheaval initiated in France, had become too powerful to be contained. Not content with the status quo, the forces of change gave rise first to the revolts and revolutions that periodically shook Europe in the 1820s and 1830s and then to the widespread revolutions of 1848. Some of the revolutions and revolutionaries were successful; most were not. Although the old order usually appeared to have prevailed, by 1850 it was apparent that its days were numbered. This perception was reinforced by the changes wrought by the Industrial Revolution. Together the forces unleashed by the dual revolutions—the French Revolution and the Industrial Revolution—made it impossible to return to prerevolutionary Europe. Nevertheless, although these events ushered in what historians like to call the modern European world, remnants of the old remained amid the new.

The Conservative Order (1815–1830)

Q **Focus Question:** What were the goals of the Congress of Vienna and the Concert of Europe, and how successful were they in achieving those goals?

The immediate response to the defeat of Napoleon was the desire to contain revolution and the revolutionary forces by restoring much of the old order.

The Peace Settlement

In March 1814, even before Napoleon had been defeated, his four major enemies—Great Britain, Austria, Prussia, and Russia—had agreed to remain united, not only to defeat France but also to ensure peace after the war. After Napoleon's defeat, this Quadruple Alliance restored the Bourbon monarchy to France in the person of Louis XVIII and agreed to meet at a congress in Vienna in September 1814 to arrange a final peace settlement.

The leader of the Congress of Vienna was the Austrian foreign minister, Prince Klemens von Metternich (KLAY-menss fun MET-ayr-nikh) (1773–1859). An experienced diplomat who was also conceited and self-assured, Metternich described himself in his memoirs in 1819: "There is a wide sweep about my mind. I am always above and beyond the preoccupation of most public men; I cover a ground much vaster than they can see. I cannot keep myself from saying about twenty times a day: 'How right I am, and how wrong they are.'"[1]

Klemens von Metternich, *Memoirs*, excerpts (1815–1829)

THE PRINCIPLE OF LEGITIMACY Metternich claimed that he was guided at Vienna by the **principle of legitimacy.** To reestablish peace and stability in Europe, he considered it necessary to restore the legitimate monarchs who would preserve traditional institutions. This had already been done in France and Spain with the restoration of the Bourbons, as well as in a number of the Italian states where rulers had been returned to their thrones. Elsewhere, however, the principle of legitimacy was largely ignored and completely overshadowed by more practical considerations of power. The congress's treatment of Poland, to which Russia, Austria, and Prussia all laid claim, illustrates this approach. Prussia and Austria were allowed to keep some Polish territory. A new, nominally independent Polish kingdom, about three-quarters of the size

Metternich and the Congress of Vienna. Prince Klemens von Metternich, the foreign minister of Austria, played a major role at the Congress of Vienna as the chief exponent of the principle of legitimacy. This painting by Engelbert Seibertz shows a group of the statesmen who participated in the discussions at Vienna. From left to right, they are Talleyrand, the French representative; Montgelas, the Bavarian minister; Hardenberg, the Prussian minister; Metternich, who appears to be the focus of attention in the group; and von Gentz, a German political theorist.

MAP 21.1 Europe After the Congress of Vienna, 1815. The Congress of Vienna imposed order on Europe based on the principles of monarchical government and a balance of power. Monarchs were restored in France, Spain, and other states recently under Napoleon's control, and much territory changed hands, often at the expense of small, weak states.

Q *How did Europe's major powers manipulate territory to decrease the probability that France could again threaten the Continent's stability?*

View an animated version of this map or related maps on the CourseMate website.

of the duchy of Warsaw, was established, with the Romanov dynasty of Russia as its hereditary monarchs. Although Poland was guaranteed its independence, the kingdom's foreign policy (and the kingdom itself) remained under Russian control. As compensation for the Polish lands it lost, Prussia received two-fifths of Saxony, the Napoleonic German kingdom of Westphalia, and the left bank of the Rhine. Austria was compensated for its loss of the Austrian Netherlands by being given control of two northern Italian provinces, Lombardy and Venetia (vuh-NEE-shuh) (see Map 21.1).

A NEW BALANCE OF POWER In making these territorial rearrangements, the diplomats at Vienna believed they were forming a new **balance of power** that would prevent any one country from dominating Europe. For example, to balance Russian gains, Prussia and Austria had been strengthened. According to Metternich, this arrangement had clearly avoided a great danger: "Prussia and Austria are completing their systems of defense; united, the two monarchies form an unconquerable barrier against the enterprises of any conquering prince who might perhaps once again occupy the throne of France or that of Russia."[2]

Considerations of the balance of power also dictated the allied treatment of France. France had not been significantly weakened; it remained a great power. The fear that France might again upset the European peace remained so strong that the conferees attempted to establish major defensive barriers against possible French expansion. To the north of France, they created a new enlarged kingdom of the Netherlands composed of the former Dutch Republic and the Austrian Netherlands (Belgium) under a new ruler, King William I of the house of Orange. To the southeast, Piedmont (officially part of the kingdom of Sardinia) was enlarged. On France's eastern frontier, Prussia was strengthened by giving it control of the territory along the east bank of the Rhine. The British at least expected Prussia to be the major bulwark against French expansion in central Europe, but the Congress of Vienna also created a new league of German states, the Germanic Confederation, to replace the Napoleonic Confederation of the Rhine.

Napoleon's escape from Elba and his return to France for one hundred days in the midst of the Congress of Vienna delayed the negotiations but did not significantly alter the overall agreement. It was decided, however, to punish the French people for their enthusiastic response

The Voice of Conservatism: Metternich of Austria

There was no greater symbol of conservatism in the first half of the nineteenth century than Prince Klemens von Metternich of Austria. Metternich played a crucial role at the Congress of Vienna and worked tirelessly for thirty years to repress the "revolutionary seed," as he called it, that had been spread to Europe by the "military despotism of Bonaparte."

Klemens von Metternich, *Memoirs*

We are convinced that society can no longer be saved without strong and vigorous resolutions on the part of the Governments still free in their opinions and actions.

We are also convinced that this may be, if the Governments face the truth, if they free themselves from all illusion, if they join their ranks and take their stand on a line of correct, unambiguous, and frankly announced principles.

By this course the monarchs will fulfill the duties imposed upon them by Him who, by entrusting them with power, has charged them to watch over the maintenance of justice, and the rights of all, to avoid the paths of error, and tread firmly in the way of truth. . . .

If the same elements of destruction which are now throwing society into convulsions have existed in all ages—for every age has seen immoral and ambitious men, hypocrites, men of heated imaginations, wrong motives, and wild projects—yet ours, by the single fact of the liberty of the press, possesses more than any preceding age the means of contact, seduction, and attraction whereby to act on these different classes of men.

We are certainly not alone in questioning if society can exist with the liberty of the press, a scourge unknown to the world before the latter half of the seventeenth century, and restrained until the end of the eighteenth, with

scarcely any expectations but England—a part of Europe separated from the continent by the sea, as well as by her language and by her peculiar manners.

The first principle to be followed by the monarchs, united as they are by the coincidence of their desires and opinions, should be that of maintaining the stability of political institutions against the disorganized excitement which has taken possession of men's minds; the immutability of principles against the madness of their interpretation; and respect for laws actually in force against a desire for their destruction. . . .

The first and greatest concern for the immense majority of every nation is the stability of the laws, and their uninterrupted action—never their change. Therefore, let the Governments govern, let them maintain the groundwork of their institutions, both ancient and modern; for if it is at all times dangerous to touch them, it certainly would not now, in the general confusion, be wise to do so. . . .

Let them maintain religious principles in all their purity, and not allow the faith to be attacked and morality interpreted according to the social contract or the visions of foolish sectarians.

Let them suppress Secret Societies, that gangrene of society. . . .

To every great State determined to survive the storm there still remain many chances of salvation, and a strong union between the States on the principles we have announced will overcome the storm itself.

Q Based on Metternich's discussion, how would you define conservatism? What experiences conditioned Metternich's ideas? Based on this selection, what policies do you think Metternich would have wanted his government to pursue?

---

to Napoleon's return. France's borders were pushed back to those of 1790, and the nation was forced to pay an indemnity and accept an army of occupation for five years. The order established by the Congress of Vienna managed to avoid a general European conflict for almost a century.

The Ideology of Conservatism

The peace arrangements of 1815 were the beginning of a conservative reaction determined to contain the liberal and nationalist forces unleashed by the French Revolution. Metternich and his kind were representatives of the **ideology** known as **conservatism** (see the box above). As a modern political philosophy, conservatism dates from 1790 when Edmund Burke (1729–1797) wrote his *Reflections on the Revolution in France* in reaction to the

French Revolution, especially its radical republican and democratic ideas. Burke maintained that society was a contract, but "the state ought not to be considered as nothing better than a partnership agreement in a trade of pepper and coffee, to be taken up for a temporary interest and to be dissolved by the fancy of the parties." The state was a partnership but one "not only between those who are living, but between those who are living, those who are dead and those who are to be born."[3] No one generation has the right to destroy this partnership; each generation has the duty to preserve and transmit it to the next. Burke advised against the violent overthrow of a government by revolution, but he did not reject all change. Sudden change was unacceptable but that did not mean that there should never be gradual or evolutionary improvements.

Burke's conservatism, however, was not the only kind. The Frenchman Joseph de Maistre (MESS-truh)

(1753–1821) was the most influential spokesman for a counterrevolutionary and authoritarian conservatism. De Maistre espoused the restoration of hereditary monarchy, which he regarded as a divinely sanctioned institution. Only absolute monarchy could guarantee "order in society" and avoid the chaos generated by movements like the French Revolution.

Despite their differences, most conservatives held to a general body of beliefs. They favored obedience to political authority, believed that organized religion was crucial to social order, hated revolutionary upheavals, and were unwilling to accept either the liberal demands for civil liberties and representative governments or the nationalistic aspirations generated by the French revolutionary era. The community took precedence over individual rights; society must be organized and ordered, and tradition remained the best guide for order. After 1815, the political philosophy of conservatism was supported by hereditary monarchs, government bureaucracies, landowning aristocracies, and revived churches, be they Protestant or Catholic. The conservative forces appeared dominant after 1815, both internationally and domestically.

Conservative Domination: The Concert of Europe

The European powers' fear of revolution and war led them to develop the Concert of Europe as a means to maintain the new status quo they had constructed. This accord grew out of the reaffirmation of the Quadruple Alliance in November 1815. Great Britain, Russia, Prussia, and Austria renewed their commitment against any attempted restoration of Bonapartist power and agreed to meet periodically in conferences to discuss their common interests and examine measures that "will be judged most salutary for the repose and prosperity of peoples, and for the maintenance of peace in Europe."

In accordance with the agreement for periodic meetings, four congresses were held between 1818 and 1822. The first, held in 1818 at Aix-la-Chapelle, was by far the most congenial. "Never have I known a prettier little congress," said Metternich. The four great powers agreed to withdraw their army of occupation from France and to add France to the Concert of Europe. The Quadruple Alliance became a quintuple alliance.

The next congress proved far less pleasant. This session, at Troppau, was called in the autumn of 1820 to deal with the outbreak of revolution in Spain and Italy. The revolt in Spain was directed against Ferdinand VII, the Bourbon king who had been restored to the throne in 1814. In southern Italy, the restoration of another Bourbon, Ferdinand I, as king of Naples and Sicily sparked a rebellion that soon spread to Piedmont in northern Italy.

THE PRINCIPLE OF INTERVENTION Metternich was especially disturbed by the revolts in Italy because he saw them as a threat to Austria's domination of the peninsula.

At Troppau, he proposed a protocol that established the **principle of intervention.** It read:

> States which have undergone a change of Government due to revolution, the results of which threaten other states, *ipso facto* cease to be members of the European Alliance, and remain excluded from it until their situation gives guarantees for legal order and stability. If, owing to such situations, immediate danger threatens other states, the Powers bind themselves, by peaceful means, or if need be by arms, to bring back the guilty state into the bosom of the Great Alliance.[4]

The principle of intervention meant that the great powers of Europe had the right to send armies into countries where there were revolutions to restore legitimate monarchs to their thrones. Britain refused to agree to the principle, arguing that it had never been the intention of the Quadruple Alliance to interfere in the internal affairs of other states, except in France. Ignoring the British response, Austria, Prussia, and Russia met in a third congress at Laibach in January 1821 and authorized the sending of Austrian troops to Naples. These forces crushed the revolt, restored Ferdinand I to the throne, and then moved north to suppress the rebels in Piedmont. At the fourth postwar conference, held at Verona in October 1822, the same three powers authorized France to invade Spain to crush the revolt against Ferdinand VII. In the spring of 1823, French forces restored the Bourbon monarch.

The success of this policy of intervention came at a price, however. The Concert of Europe had broken down when the British rejected Metternich's principle of intervention. And although the British had failed to thwart allied intervention in Spain and Italy, they were successful in keeping the Continental powers from interfering with the revolutions in Latin America.

THE REVOLT OF LATIN AMERICA Although much of North America had been freed of European domination in the eighteenth century by the American Revolution, Latin America remained in the hands of the Spanish and Portuguese. By the end of the eighteenth century, the ideas of the Enlightenment and the new political ideals stemming from the successful revolution in North America were beginning to influence the creole elites (descendants of Europeans who became permanent inhabitants of Latin America). The principles of the equality of all people in the eyes of the law, free trade, and a free press proved very attractive. Sons of creoles, such as Simón Bolívar (see-MOHN buh-LEE-var) (1783–1830) of Venezuela and José de San Martín (hoh-SAY day san mar-TEEN) (1778–1850) of Argentina, who became the leaders of the independence movement, even attended European universities, where they imbibed the ideas of the Enlightenment. These Latin American elites, joined by a growing class of merchants, especially resented the domination of their trade by Spain and Portugal. At the beginning of the nineteenth century, Napoleon's continental wars provided the creoles with an opportunity for change. When Bonaparte toppled the monarchies of Spain and Portugal, the authority of the Spaniards and Portuguese in their colonial empires was weakened, and between 1807 and 1824, a series of revolts enabled most of Latin America to become independent.

Simón Bolívar has long been regarded as the George Washington of Latin America. Born into a wealthy Venezuelan family, he was introduced as a young man to the ideas of the Enlightenment. While in Rome to witness the coronation of Napoleon as king of Italy in 1805, he committed himself to free his people from Spanish control. When he returned to South America, Bolívar began to lead the bitter struggle for independence in Venezuela as well as other parts of northern South America. Although he was acclaimed as the "liberator" of Venezuela in 1813 by the people, it was not until 1821 that he definitively defeated Spanish forces there. He went on to liberate Colombia, Ecuador, and Peru. Already in 1819, he had become president of Venezuela, at the time part of a federation that included Colombia and Ecuador.

While Bolívar was busy liberating northern South America from the Spanish, José de San Martín was concentrating his efforts on the southern part of the continent. Son of a Spanish army officer in Argentina, San Martín went to Spain and pursued a military career in the Spanish army. In 1811, after serving twenty-two years, he learned of the liberation movement in his native Argentina, abandoned his military career in Spain, and returned to his homeland in March 1812. Argentina had already been freed from Spanish control, but San Martín believed that the Spaniards must be removed from all of South America if any nation was to remain free. In January 1817, he led his forces over the high Andes Mountains, an amazing feat in itself. Two-thirds of his pack mules and horses died during the difficult journey. Many of the soldiers suffered from lack of oxygen and severe cold while crossing mountain passes more than 2 miles above sea level. The arrival of San Martín's troops in Chile surprised the Spaniards, whose forces were routed at the Battle of Chacabuco on February 12, 1817.

In 1821, San Martín moved on to Lima, Peru, the center of Spanish authority. Convinced that he was unable to complete the liberation of all of Peru, San Martín welcomed the arrival of Bolívar and his forces. As he wrote to Bolívar, "For me it would have been the height of happiness to end the war of independence under the orders of a general to whom [South] America owes its freedom. Destiny orders it otherwise, and one must resign oneself to it."[5] Highly

The Liberators of South America. José de San Martín of Argentina and Simón Bolívar are hailed as the leaders of the Latin American independence movement. In the painting on the left, by Theodore Géricault, a French Romantic artist, San Martín is shown leading his troops at the Battle of Chacabuco in Chile in 1817. His forces liberated Argentina, Chile, and Peru from Spanish authority. The painting on the right shows Bolívar leading his troops across the Andes in 1823 to fight in Peru. This depiction of impeccably uniformed troops moving in perfect formation through the snow of the Andes, by the Chilean artist Franco Gomez, is, of course, highly unrealistic.

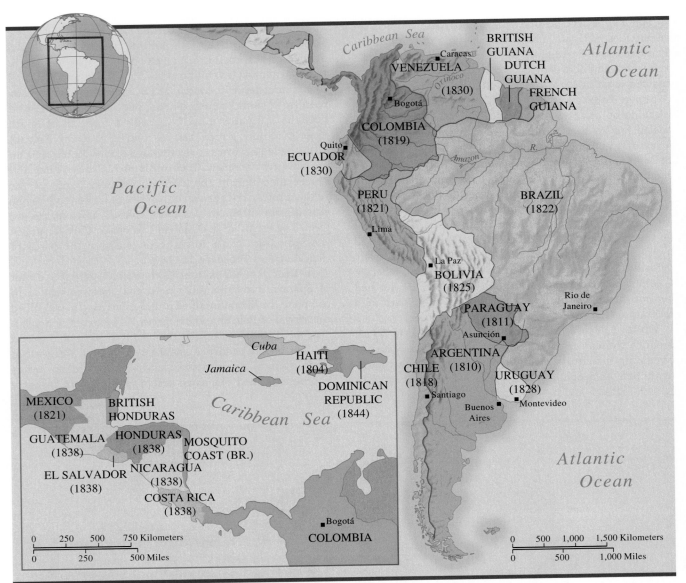

MAP 21.2 **Latin America in the First Half of the Nineteenth Century.** Latin American colonies took advantage of Spain's weakness during the Napoleonic wars to fight for independence, beginning with Argentina in 1810 and spreading throughout the region over the next decade with the help of leaders like Simón Bolívar and José de San Martín. The dates in parentheses show the years in which the countries received formal recognition.

Q *How many South American countries are sources of rivers that feed the Amazon, and roughly what percentage of the continent is contained within the Amazon's watershed?*

disappointed, San Martin left South America for Europe, where he remained until his death outside Paris in 1850. Meanwhile, Bolívar took on the task of crushing the last significant Spanish army at Ayacucho on December 9, 1824. By then, Peru, Uruguay, Paraguay, Colombia, Venezuela, Argentina, Bolivia, and Chile had all become free states (see Map 21.2). In 1823, the Central American states became independent and in 1838–1839 divided into five republics (Guatemala, El Salvador, Honduras, Costa Rica, and Nicaragua). Earlier, in 1822, the prince regent of Brazil had declared Brazil's independence from Portugal.

The Continental powers, however, flushed by their success in crushing the rebellions in Spain and Italy, favored the use of troops to restore Spanish control in Latin America. This time, British opposition to intervention prevailed. Eager to gain access to an entire continent for investment and trade, the British proposed joint action with the United States against European interference in Latin America. Distrustful of British motives, President James Monroe acted alone in 1823, guaranteeing the independence of the new Latin American nations and warning against any further European intervention in the

Congress of Vienna	1814–1815
Reaffirmation of the Quadruple Alliance	1815
Congress of Aix-la-Chapelle	1818
Revolutions win independence for Latin America	1819–1824
Congress of Troppau	1820
Congress of Laibach	1821
Crushing of revolt in southern Italy	1821
Greek revolt against the Ottoman Empire	1821
Congress of Verona	1822
Crushing of revolt in Spain	1823
Monroe Doctrine	1823
Treaty of Adrianople	1829
Independence of Greece and Belgium	1830

In 1827, a combined British and French fleet went to Greece and defeated a large Ottoman armada. A year later, Russia declared war on the Ottoman Empire and invaded its European provinces of Moldavia and Wallachia. By the Treaty of Adrianople in 1829, which ended the Russian-Turkish war, the Russians received a protectorate over the two provinces. By the same treaty, the Ottoman Empire agreed to allow Russia, France, and Britain to decide the fate of Greece. In 1830, the three powers declared Greece an independent kingdom, and two years later, a new royal dynasty was established. The revolution had been successful only because the great powers themselves supported it. Until 1830, the Greek revolt was the only successful one in Europe; the conservative domination was still largely intact.

The Balkans by 1830

New World in the famous Monroe Doctrine. Actually, British ships were more important to Latin American independence than American words. Britain's navy stood between Latin America and any European invasion force, and the Continental powers were extremely reluctant to challenge British naval power.

Although political independence brought economic independence to Latin America, old patterns were quickly reestablished. Instead of Spain and Portugal, Great Britain now dominated the Latin American economy. British merchants moved in in large numbers, while British investors poured in funds, especially in the mining industry. Old trade patterns soon reemerged. Because Latin America served as a source of raw materials and foodstuffs for the industrializing nations of Europe and the United States, exports—especially of wheat, tobacco, wool, sugar, coffee, and hides—to the North Atlantic countries increased noticeably. At the same time, finished consumer goods, especially textiles, were imported in increasing quantities, causing a decline in industrial production in Latin America. The emphasis on exporting raw materials and importing finished products ensured the ongoing domination of the Latin American economy by foreigners.

THE GREEK REVOLT The principle of intervention proved to be a double-edged sword. Designed to prevent revolution, it could also be used to support revolution if the great powers found it in their interest to do so. In 1821, the Greeks revolted against their Ottoman Turkish masters. Although subject to Muslim control for four hundred years, the Greeks had been allowed to maintain their language and their Greek Orthodox faith. A revival of Greek national sentiment at the beginning of the nineteenth century added to the growing desire for liberation "from the terrible yoke of Turkish oppression." The Greek revolt was soon transformed into a noble cause by an outpouring of European sentiment for the Greeks' struggle.

Conservative Domination: The European States

Between 1815 and 1830, the conservative domination of Europe evident in the Concert of Europe was also apparent in domestic affairs as conservative governments throughout Europe worked to maintain the old order.

GREAT BRITAIN: RULE OF THE TORIES In 1815, Great Britain was governed by the aristocratic landowning classes that dominated both houses of Parliament. Suffrage for elections to the House of Commons, controlled by the landed gentry, was restricted and unequal, especially in light of the changing distribution of the British population due to the Industrial Revolution. Large new industrial cities such as Birmingham and Manchester had no representatives, while landowners used pocket and rotten boroughs (see Chapter 18) to control seats in the House of Commons. Although the monarchy was not yet powerless, in practice the power of the crown was largely in the hands of the ruling party in Parliament.

There were two political factions in Parliament, the Tories and the Whigs. Both were still dominated by members of the landed classes, although the Whigs were beginning to receive support from the new industrial middle class. Tory ministers largely dominated the government until 1830 and had little desire to change the existing political and electoral system.

Popular discontent grew after 1815 because of severe economic difficulties. The Tory government's response to falling agricultural prices was the Corn Law of 1815, a measure that imposed extraordinarily high tariffs on foreign grain. Though the tariffs benefited the landowners, the price of bread rose substantially, making conditions for the working classes more difficult. Mass protest meetings took a nasty turn when a squadron of cavalry attacked a crowd of 60,000 demonstrators at Saint Peter's Fields in Manchester in 1819. The deaths of eleven people, called the Peterloo Massacre by government detractors, led Parliament to take even more repressive measures. The government restricted large public meetings and the dissemination of pamphlets among the poor. At the same time, by making minor reforms in the 1820s, the Tories managed to avoid meeting the demands for electoral reforms—at least until 1830 (see "Reform in Great Britain" later in this chapter).

RESTORATION IN FRANCE In 1814, the Bourbon family was restored to the throne of France in the person of Louis XVIII (1814–1824). Louis understood the need to accept some of the changes brought to France by the revolutionary and Napoleonic eras. He accepted Napoleon's Civil Code with its recognition of the principle of equality before the law (see Chapter 19). The property rights of those who had purchased confiscated lands during the Revolution were preserved. A bicameral (two-house) legislature was established, consisting of the Chamber of Peers, chosen by the king, and the Chamber of Deputies, chosen by an electorate restricted to slightly fewer than 100,000 wealthy people.

Louis's grudging moderation, however, was opposed by liberals eager to extend the revolutionary reforms and by a group of **ultraroyalists** who criticized the king's willingness to compromise and retain so many features of the Napoleonic era. The ultras hoped to return to a monarchical system dominated by a privileged landed aristocracy and to restore the Catholic Church to its former position of influence.

The initiative passed to the ultraroyalists in 1824 when Louis XVIII died and was succeeded by his brother, the count of Artois (ar-TWAH), who became Charles X (1824–1830). In 1825, Charles granted an indemnity to aristocrats whose lands had been confiscated during the Revolution. Moreover, the king pursued a religious policy that encouraged the Catholic Church to reestablish control over the French educational system. Public outrage, fed by liberal newspapers, forced the king to compromise in 1827 and even to accept the principle of **ministerial responsibility**—that the ministers of the king were responsible to the legislature. But in 1829, he violated his commitment. A protest by the deputies led the king to dissolve the legislature in 1830 and call for new elections. France was on the brink of another revolution.

INTERVENTION IN THE ITALIAN STATES AND SPAIN The Congress of Vienna had established nine states in

Italy, 1815

Italy, including Piedmont (part of the kingdom of Sardinia) in the north, ruled by the house of Savoy; the kingdom of the Two Sicilies (Naples and Sicily); the Papal States; a handful of small duchies ruled by relatives of the Austrian emperor; and the important northern provinces of Lombardy and Venetia, which were now part of the Austrian Empire. Much of Italy was under Austrian domination, and all the states had extremely reactionary governments eager to smother any liberal or nationalist sentiment. Nevertheless, secret societies motivated by nationalistic dreams and known as the Carbonari (kar-buh-NAH-ree) ("charcoal burners") continued to conspire and plan for revolution.

In Spain, another Bourbon dynasty had been restored in the person of Ferdinand VII in 1814. Ferdinand (1814–1833) had agreed to observe the liberal constitution of 1812, which allowed for the functioning of an elected parliamentary assembly known as the Cortes. But the king soon reneged on his promises, tore up the constitution, dissolved the Cortes, and persecuted its members, which led a combined group of army officers, upper-middle-class merchants, and liberal intellectuals to revolt. The king capitulated in March 1820 and promised once again to restore the constitution and the Cortes. But Metternich's policy of intervention came to Ferdinand's rescue. In April 1823, a French army moved into Spain and forced the revolutionary government to flee Madrid. By August of that year, the king had been restored to his throne.

REPRESSION IN CENTRAL EUROPE After 1815, the forces of reaction were particularly successful in central Europe. The Habsburg empire and its chief agent, Prince Klemens von Metternich, played an important role. Metternich boasted, "You see in me the chief Minister of Police in Europe. I keep an eye on everything. My contacts are such that nothing escapes me."[6] Metternich's spies were everywhere, searching for evidence of liberal or nationalist plots. Although both liberalism and nationalism emerged in the German states and the Austrian Empire, they were initially weak as central Europe tended to remain under the domination of aristocratic landowning classes and autocratic, centralized monarchies.

The Vienna settlement in 1815 had recognized the existence of thirty-eight sovereign states in what had once been the Holy Roman Empire. Austria and Prussia were the two great powers; the other states varied considerably in size. Together these states formed the Germanic Confederation, but the confederation had little power.

University Students and German Unity

In the early nineteenth century, university students and professors were the chief supporters of German nationalism. Especially important were the *Burschenschaften,* student societies that espoused the cause of German unity. In this selection, the liberal Heinrich von Gagern explains the purpose of the *Burschenschaften* to his father.

＋—◆—＋

Heinrich von Gagern, Letter to His Father

It is very hard to explain the spirit of the student movement to you, but I shall try, even though I can only give you a few characteristics.... It speaks to the better youth, the man of heart and spirit and love for all this good, and gives him nourishment and being. For the average student of the past, the university years were a time to enjoy life, and to make a sharp break with his own background in defiance of the philistine world, which seemed to him somehow to foreshadow the tomb. Their pleasures, their organizations, and their talk were determined by their *status* as students, and their university obligation was only to avoid failing the examination and scraping by adequately—bread-and-butter learning. They were satisfied with themselves if they thought they could pass the examination. There are still many of those nowadays, indeed the majority overall. But at several universities, and especially here, another group—in my eyes a better one—has managed to get the upper hand in the sense that it sets the mood. I prefer really not to call it a mood; rather, it is something that presses hard and tried to spread its ideas....

Those who share in this spirit have then quite another tendency in their student life, Love of Fatherland is their guiding principle. Their purpose is to make a better future for the Fatherland, each as best he can, to spread national consciousness, or to use the much ridiculed and maligned Germanic expression, more folkishness, and to work for better constitutions....

We want more sense of community among the several states of Germany, greater unity in their policies and in their principles of government; no separate policy for each state, but the nearest possible relations with one another; above all, we want Germany to be considered *one* land and the German people *one* people. In the forms of our student comradeship we show how we want to approach this as nearly as possible in the real world. Regional fraternities are forbidden, and we live in a German comradeship, one people in spirit, as we want it for all Germany in reality. We give our selves the freest of constitutions, just as we should like Germany to have the freest possible one, insofar as that is suitable for the German people. We want a constitution for the people that fits in with the spirit of the times and with the people's own level of enlightenment, rather than what each prince gives his people according to what he likes and what serves his private interest. Above all, we want the princes to understand and to follow the principle that they exist for the country and not the country for them. In fact, the prevailing view is that the constitution should not come from the individual states at all. The main principles of the German constitution should apply to all states in common, and should be expressed by the German federal assembly. This constitution should deal not only with the absolute necessities, like fiscal administration and justice, general administration and church and military affairs and so on; this constitution ought to be extended to the education of the young, at least at the upper age levels, and to many other such things. ▷

Q Would you call Heinrich von Gagern a nationalist? Why or why not? Based on this selection, why do you think the forces of nationalism and liberalism were allies during the first half of the nineteenth century?

It had no real executive, and its only central organ was the federal diet, which needed the consent of all member states to take action, making it virtually powerless. Nevertheless, it also came to serve as Metternich's instrument to repress revolutionary movements within the German states.

Initially, Germans who favored liberal principles and German unity looked to Prussia for leadership. During the Napoleonic era, King Frederick William III (1797–1840), following the advice of his two chief ministers, Baron Heinrich von Stein and Prince Karl von Hardenberg, instituted political and institutional reforms in response to Prussia's defeat at the hands of Napoleon. The reforms included the abolition of serfdom, municipal self-government through town councils, the expansion of primary and secondary schools, and universal military conscription to form a national army. The reforms, however, did not include the creation of a legislative assembly or representative government as Stein and Hardenberg wished. After 1815, Frederick William grew more reactionary and was content to follow Metternich's lead. Though reforms had made Prussia strong, it remained largely an absolutist state with little interest in German unity.

Liberal and national movements in the German states seemed largely limited to university professors and students. The latter began to organize **Burschenschaften** (BOOR-shun-shahf-tuhn), student societies dedicated to fostering the goal of a free, united Germany (see the box above). Their ideas and their motto, "Honor, Liberty, Fatherland," were in part inspired by Friedrich Ludwig

Jahn (FREED-rikh LOOD-vik YAHN), who had organized gymnastic societies during the Napoleonic wars to promote the regeneration of German youth. Jahn encouraged Germans to pursue their Germanic heritage and urged his followers to disrupt the lectures of professors whose views were not nationalistic.

From 1817 to 1819, the *Burschenschaften* pursued a variety of activities that alarmed German governments. At an assembly held at the Wartburg Castle in 1817, marking the three hundredth anniversary of Luther's Ninety-Five Theses, the crowd burned books written by conservative authors. When a deranged student assassinated a reactionary playwright, Metternich had the diet of the Germanic Confederation draw up the Karlsbad (KARLSS-baht) Decrees of 1819. These closed the *Burschenschaften,* provided for censorship of the press, and placed the universities under close supervision and control. Thereafter, except for a minor flurry of activity from 1830 to 1832, Metternich and the cooperative German rulers maintained the conservative status quo.

The Austrian Empire was a multinational state, a collection of different peoples under the Habsburg emperor, who provided a common bond. The empire contained eleven peoples of different national origin, including Germans, Czechs, Magyars (Hungarians), Slovaks, Romanians, Slovenes, Poles, Serbians, and Italians. The Germans, though only a quarter of the population, were economically the most advanced and played a leading role in governing Austria. Essentially, the Austrian Empire was held together by the dynasty, the imperial civil service, the imperial army, and the Catholic Church. But its national groups, especially the Hungarians, with their increasing desire for autonomy, acted as forces to break the empire apart.

Still Metternich managed to hold it all together. His antipathy to liberalism and nationalism was understandably grounded in the realization that these forces threatened to tear the empire apart. The growing liberal belief that each national group had the right to its own system of government could only mean disaster for the multinational Austrian Empire. While the forces of liberalism and nationalism grew, the Austrian Empire largely stagnated.

RUSSIA: AUTOCRACY OF THE TSARS   At the beginning of the nineteenth century, Russia was overwhelmingly rural, agricultural, and autocratic. The Russian tsar was still regarded as a divine-right monarch. Alexander I (1801–1825) had been raised in the ideas of the Enlightenment and initially seemed willing to make reforms. With the aid of his liberal adviser Michael Speransky (spyuh-RAHN-skee), he relaxed censorship, freed political prisoners, and reformed the educational system. He refused, however, to grant a constitution or free the serfs in the face of opposition from the nobility. After the defeat of Napoleon, Alexander became a reactionary, and his government reverted to strict and arbitrary censorship. Soon opposition to Alexander arose from a group of secret societies.

One of these societies, known as the Northern Union, was composed of young aristocrats who had served in the Napoleonic wars and had become aware of the world outside Russia as well as intellectuals alienated by the censorship and lack of academic freedom in Russian universities. The Northern Union favored the establishment of a constitutional monarchy and the abolition of serfdom. The sudden death of Alexander in 1825 offered them their opportunity.

Although Alexander's brother Constantine was the legal heir to the throne, he had renounced his claims in favor of his brother Nicholas. Constantine's abdication had not been made public, however, and during the ensuing confusion in December 1825, the military leaders of the Northern Union rebelled against the accession of Nicholas. This so-called Decembrist Revolt was soon crushed by troops loyal to Nicholas, and its leaders were executed.

The revolt transformed Nicholas I (1825–1855) from a conservative into a reactionary determined to avoid another rebellion. He strengthened both the bureaucracy and the secret police. The political police, known as the Third Section of the tsar's chancellery, were given sweeping powers over much of Russian life. They deported suspicious or dangerous persons, maintained close surveillance of foreigners in Russia, and reported regularly to the tsar on public opinion.

Portrait of Nicholas I. Tsar Nicholas I was a reactionary ruler who sought to prevent rebellion in Russia by strengthening the government bureaucracy, increasing censorship, and suppressing individual freedom by the use of political police. One of his enemies remarked about his facial characteristics: "The sharply retreating forehead and the lower jaw were expressive of iron will and feeble intelligence."

Matching Nicholas's fear of revolution at home was his fear of revolution abroad. There would be no revolution in Russia during the rest of his reign; if he could help it, there would be none in Europe either. Contemporaries called him the Policeman of Europe because of his willingness to use Russian troops to crush revolutions.

The Ideologies of Change

 Focus Question: What were the main tenets of conservatism, liberalism, nationalism, and utopian socialism, and what role did each ideology play in Europe in the first half of the nineteenth century?

Although the conservative forces were in the ascendancy from 1815 to 1830, powerful movements for change were also at work. These depended on ideas embodied in a series of political philosophies or ideologies that came into their own in the first half of the nineteenth century.

Liberalism

One of these ideologies was **liberalism,** which owed much to the Enlightenment of the eighteenth century and to the American and French Revolutions at the end of that century. In addition, liberalism became even more significant as the Industrial Revolution made rapid strides because the developing industrial middle class largely adopted the doctrine as its own. There were divergences of opinion among people classified as liberals, but all began with the belief that people should be as free from restraint as possible. This opinion is evident in both economic and political liberalism.

ECONOMIC LIBERALISM Also called classical economics, economic liberalism had as its primary tenet the concept of *laissez-faire,* the belief that the state should not interrupt the free play of natural economic forces, especially supply and demand. Government should not restrain the economic liberty of the individual and should restrict itself to only three primary functions: defense of the country, police protection of individuals, and the construction and maintenance of public works too expensive for individuals to undertake. If individuals were allowed economic liberty, ultimately they would bring about the maximum good for the maximum number and benefit the general welfare of society.

The case against government interference in economic matters was greatly enhanced by Thomas Malthus (MAWL-thuss) (1766–1834). In his major work, *Essay on the Principles of Population,* Malthus argued that population, when unchecked, increases at a geometric rate while the food supply correspondingly increases at a much slower arithmetic rate. The result will be severe overpopulation and ultimately starvation for the human race if this growth is not held in check. According to Malthus,

nature imposes a major restraint: "Unwholesome occupations, severe labor and exposure to the seasons, extreme poverty, bad nursing of children, great towns, excesses of all kinds, the whole train of common disease, and epidemics, wars, plague and famine." Thus, misery and poverty were simply the inevitable result of the law of nature; no government or individual should interfere with its operation.

Malthus's ideas were further developed by David Ricardo (1772–1823). In *Principles of Political Economy,* written in 1817, Ricardo developed his famous "iron law of wages." Following Malthus, Ricardo argued that an increase in population means more workers; more workers in turn cause wages to fall below the subsistence level. The result is misery and starvation, which then reduce the population. Consequently, the number of workers declines, and wages rise above the subsistence level again, which in turn encourages workers to have larger families as the cycle is repeated. According to Ricardo, raising wages arbitrarily would be pointless since it would accomplish little but perpetuate this vicious circle.

David Ricardo, *The Principles of Political Economy* (1817)

POLITICAL LIBERALISM Politically, liberals came to hold a common set of beliefs. Chief among them was the protection of civil liberties or the basic rights of all people, which included equality before the law; freedom of assembly, speech, and press; and freedom from arbitrary arrest. All of these freedoms should be guaranteed by a written document, such as the American Bill of Rights or the French Declaration of the Rights of Man and the Citizen. In addition to religious toleration for all, most liberals advocated separation of church and state. The right of peaceful opposition to the government in and out of parliament and the making of laws by a representative assembly (legislature) elected by qualified voters constituted two other liberal demands. Many liberals believed, then, in a constitutional monarchy or constitutional state with limits on the powers of government to prevent despotism and in written constitutions that would help guarantee these rights.

Many liberals also advocated ministerial responsibility, which would give the legislative branch a check on the power of the executive because the king's ministers would answer to the legislature rather than to the king. Liberals in the first half of the nineteenth century also believed in a limited suffrage. Although all people were entitled to equal civil rights, they should not have equal political rights. The right to vote and hold office would be open only to men who met certain property qualifications. As a political philosophy, liberalism was tied to middle-class men, especially industrial middle-class men who favored the extension of voting rights so that they could share power with the landowning classes. They had little desire to let the lower classes share that power. Liberals were not democrats.

One of the most prominent advocates of liberalism in the nineteenth century was the English philosopher John

The Voice of Liberalism: John Stuart Mill on Liberty

John Stuart Mill was one of Britain's most famous philosophers of liberalism. Mill's essay *On Liberty* is viewed as a classic statement of the liberal belief in the unfettered freedom of the individual. In this excerpt, Mill defends freedom of opinion from both government and the coercion of the majority.

John Stuart Mill, *On Liberty*

The object of this Essay is to assert one very simple principle, as entitled to govern absolutely the dealings of society with the individual in the way of compulsion and control, whether the means used be physical force in the form of legal penalties, or the moral coercion of public opinion. That principle is, that the sole end for which mankind are warranted, individually or collectively, interfering with the liberty of action of any of their number, is self-protection. That the only purpose for which power can be rightfully exercised over any member of a civilized community, against his will, is to prevent harm to others. His own good, either physical or moral, is not a sufficient warrant.... These are good reasons for remonstrating with him, or reasoning with him, or persuading him, or entreating him, but not for compelling him, or visiting him with any evil in case he do otherwise. To justify that, the conduct from which it is desired to deter him, must be calculated to produce evil to some one else. The only part of the conduct of any one, for which he is amenable to society, is that which concerns others. In the part which merely concerns himself, his independence is, of right, absolute. Over himself, over his own body and mind, the individual is sovereign....

Society can and does execute its own mandates: and if it issues wrong mandates instead of right, or any mandates at all in things with which it ought not to meddle, it practices a social tyranny more formidable than many kinds of political oppression, since, though not usually upheld by such extreme penalties, it leaves fewer means of escape, penetrating more deeply into the details of life, and enslaving the soul itself. Protection, therefore, against the tyranny of the magistrate is not enough: there needs protection also against the tyranny of prevailing opinion and feeling, against the tendency of society to impose, by other means than civil penalties, its own ideas and practices as rules of conduct on those who dissent from them....

But there is a sphere of action in which society, as distinguished from the individual has, if any, only an indirect interest; comprehending all that portion of a person's life and conduct which affects only himself, or if it also affects others, only with their free, voluntary and undeceived consent and participation.... This then is the appropriate region of human liberty. It comprises, first, the inward domain of consciousness; demanding liberty of conscience in the most comprehensive sense; liberty of thought and feeling; absolute freedom of opinion and sentiment on all subjects, practical or speculative, scientific, moral, or theological....

Let us suppose, therefore, that the government is entirely at one with the people, and never thinks of exerting any power of coercion unless in agreement with what it conceives to be their voice. But I deny the right of the people to exercise such coercion, either by themselves or by their government. The power itself is illegitimate. The best government has no more title to it than the worst. It is as noxious, or more noxious, when exerted in accordance with public opinion, than when in opposition to it. If all mankind minus one were of one opinion, and only one person were of the contrary opinion, mankind would be no more justified in silencing that one person, than he, if he had the power, would be justified in silencing mankind.... The peculiar evil of silencing the expression of an opinion is, that it is robbing the human race; posterity as well as the existing generation; those who dissent from the opinion, still more than those who hold it. If the opinion is right, they are deprived of the opportunity of exchanging error for truth: if wrong, they lose, what is almost as great a benefit, the clearer perception and livelier impression of truth, produced by its collision with error.

Q Based on the principles outlined here, how would you define liberalism? How do Mill's ideas fit into the concept of democracy? Which is more important in his thought: the individual or society?

Stuart Mill (1806–1873). *On Liberty,* his most famous work, published in 1859, has long been regarded as a classic statement on the liberty of the individual (see the box above). Mill argued for an "absolute freedom of opinion and sentiment on all subjects" that needed to be protected from both government censorship and the tyranny of the majority.

Mill was also instrumental in expanding the meaning of liberalism by becoming an enthusiastic supporter of women's rights. When his attempt to include women in the voting reform bill of 1867 failed, Mill published an essay titled *On the Subjection of Women,* which he had written earlier with his wife, Harriet Taylor. He argued that "the legal subordination of one sex to the other" was wrong. Differences between women and men, he claimed, were due not to different natures but simply to social practices. With equal education, women could achieve as much as men. *On the Subjection of Women* would become

MAP 21.3 **The Distribution of Languages in Nineteenth-Century Europe.** Numerous languages were spoken in Europe. People who used the same language often had a shared history and culture, which laid the seeds for growing nationalism in the nineteenth century. Such nationalism eventually led to unification for Germany and Italy but spelled trouble for the polyglot Habsburg empire.

Q *Look at the distribution of Germanic, Latin, and Slavic languages. What patterns emerge, and how can you explain them?*

an important work in the nineteenth-century movement for women's rights.

Nationalism

Nationalism was an even more powerful ideology for change in the nineteenth century. Nationalism arose out of an awareness of being part of a community that has common institutions, traditions, language, and customs. This community constitutes a "nation," and it, rather than a dynasty, city-state, or other political unit, becomes the focus of the individual's primary political loyalty.

Nationalism did not become a popular force for change until the French Revolution. From then on, nationalists came to believe that each nationality should have its own government. Thus, a divided people such as the Germans wanted national unity in a German nation-state with one central government. Subject peoples, such as the Hungarians, wanted national self-determination, or the right to establish their own autonomy rather than be subject to a German minority in a multinational empire.

Nationalism threatened to upset the existing political order, both internationally and nationally (see Map 21.3). A united Germany or united Italy would upset the balance of power established in 1815. By the same token, an independent Hungarian state would mean the breakup of the Austrian Empire. Because many European states were multinational, conservatives tried hard to repress the radical threat of nationalism.

At the same time, in the first half of the nineteenth century, nationalism and liberalism became strong allies. Most liberals believed that liberty could be realized only by peoples who ruled themselves. One British liberal said, "It is in general a necessary condition of free institutions that the boundaries of governments should coincide in the main with those of nationalities." Many nationalists believed that once each people obtained its own state, all nations could be linked together into a broader community of all humanity.

Early Socialism

In the first half of the nineteenth century, the pitiful conditions found in the slums, mines, and factories of the Industrial Revolution gave rise to another ideology for change known as **socialism.** The term eventually became associated with a Marxist analysis of human society (see Chapter 22), but early socialism was largely the product of political theorists or intellectuals who wanted to introduce equality into social conditions and believed that human cooperation was superior to the competition that characterized early industrial capitalism. To later Marxists, such ideas were impractical dreams, and they contemptuously labeled the theorists **utopian socialists.** The term has endured to this day.

The utopian socialists were against private property and the competitive spirit of early industrial capitalism. By eliminating these things and creating new systems of social organization, they thought that a better environment for

humanity could be achieved. Early socialists proposed a variety of ways to accomplish that task.

FOURIER One group of early socialists sought to create voluntary associations that would demonstrate the advantages of cooperative living. Charles Fourier (SHAHRL foo-RYAY) (1772–1838) proposed the creation of small model communities called phalansteries. These were self-contained cooperatives, each consisting ideally of 1,620 people. Communally housed, the inhabitants of the **phalanstery** (fuh-LAN-stuh-ree) would live and work together for their mutual benefit. Work assignments would be rotated frequently to relieve workers of undesirable tasks. Fourier was unable to gain financial backing for his phalansteries, however, and his plan remained untested.

OWEN Robert Owen (1771–1858), the British cotton manufacturer, also believed that humans would reveal their true natural goodness if they lived in a cooperative environment. At New Lanark in Scotland, he was successful in transforming a squalid factory town into a flourishing, healthy community. But when he attempted to create a self-contained cooperative community at New Harmony, Indiana, in the United States in the 1820s, bickering within the community eventually destroyed his dream. One of Owen's disciples, a wealthy woman named Frances Wright, bought slaves in order to set up a model community at Nashoba, Tennessee. The community failed, but Wright continued to work for women's rights.

BLANC The Frenchman Louis Blanc (LWEE BLAHNH) (1813–1882) offered yet another early socialist approach to a better society. In *The Organization of Work*, he maintained that social problems could be solved by government assistance. Denouncing competition as the main cause of

Children at New Lanark. Robert Owen created an early experiment in utopian socialism by establishing a model industrial community at New Lanark, Scotland. In this illustration, the children of factory workers are shown dancing the quadrille.

the economic evils of his day, he called for the establishment of workshops that would manufacture goods for public sale. The state would finance these workshops, but the workers would own and operate them.

FEMALE SUPPORTERS With their plans for the reconstruction of society, utopian socialists attracted a number of female supporters who believed that only a reordering of society would help women. Zoé Gatti de Gamond (zoh-AY gah-TEE duh gah-MOHNH), a Belgian follower of Fourier, established her own phalanstery, which was supposed to provide men and women with the same educational and job opportunities. As part of collective living, men and women were to share responsibilities for child care and housecleaning. The ideas of the comte de Saint-Simon, which combined Christian values, scientific thought, and socialist utopianism, proved especially attractive to a number of women who participated in the growing activism of women in politics that had been set in motion during the French Revolution. Saint-Simon's ideal cooperative society recognized the principle of equality between men and women, and a number of working-class women, including Suzanne Voilquin (soo-ZAHN vwahl-KANH), Claire Démar (DAY-mar), and Reine Guindorf (RY-nuh GWIN-dorf), published a newspaper dedicated to the emancipation of women.

TRISTAN One female utopian socialist, Flora Tristan (TRISS-tun) (1803–1844), even attempted to foster a "utopian synthesis of socialism and feminism." She traveled through France preaching the need for the liberation of women. Her *Worker's Union*, published in 1843, advocated the application of Fourier's ideas to reconstruct both family and work:

> Workers, be sure of it. If you have enough equity and justice to inscribe into your Charter the few points I have just outlined, this declaration of the rights of women will soon pass into custom, from custom into law, and before twenty-five years pass you will then see inscribed in front of the book of laws which will govern French society: THE ABSOLUTE EQUALITY of man and woman. Then, my brothers, and only then, will human unity be constituted.[7]

She envisioned this absolute equality as the only hope to free the working class and transform civilization.

Flora Tristan, like the other utopian socialists, was largely ignored by her contemporaries. Although criticized for their impracticality, the utopian socialists at least laid the groundwork for later attacks on capitalism that would

have a far-reaching result. In the first half of the nineteenth century, however, socialism remained a fringe movement largely overshadowed by liberalism and nationalism.

Revolution and Reform (1830–1850)

Q FOCUS QUESTIONS: What forces for change were present in France and Great Britain between 1830 and 1848, and how did each nation respond? What were the causes of the revolutions of 1848, and why did the revolutions fail?

Beginning in 1830, the forces of change began to break through the conservative domination of Europe, more successfully in some places than in others. Finally, in 1848, a wave of revolutionary fervor moved through Europe, causing liberals and nationalists everywhere to think that they were on the verge of creating a new order.

Another French Revolution

The new elections Charles X had called in 1830 produced another victory for the French liberals; at this point, the king decided to seize the initiative. On July 26, 1830, Charles issued a set of edicts (the July Ordinances) that imposed rigid censorship on the press, dissolved the legislative assembly, and reduced the electorate in preparation

The Revolution of 1830. In 1830, the forces of change began to undo the conservative domination of Europe. In France, the reactionary Charles X was overthrown and replaced by the constitutional monarch Louis-Philippe, a liberal and former revolutionary soldier. In this painting by Gustave Wappers, Louis-Philippe is seen riding to the Hôtel de Ville, the city hall, preceded by a man holding the French revolutionary tricolor flag, which had not been seen in France since 1815.

for new elections. Charles's actions produced an immediate rebellion—the July Revolution. Barricades went up in Paris as a provisional government led by a group of moderate, propertied liberals was hastily formed and appealed to Louis-Philippe, the duke of Orléans, a cousin of Charles X, to become the constitutional king of France. Charles X fled to Britain; a new monarchy had been born.

Louis-Philippe (1830–1848) was soon called the bourgeois monarch because political support for his rule came from the upper middle class. Louis-Philippe even dressed like a member of the middle class in business suits and hats. Constitutional changes that favored the interests of the upper bourgeoisie were instituted. Financial qualifications for voting were reduced yet remained sufficiently high that the number of voters increased only from 100,000 to barely 200,000, guaranteeing that only the wealthiest people would vote.

To the upper middle class, the bourgeois monarchy represented the stopping place for political progress. To the lesser bourgeoisie and the Parisian working class, who had helped overthrow Charles X in 1830, it was a severe disappointment because they had been completely excluded from political power. The rapid expansion of French industry in the 1830s and 1840s gave rise to an industrial working class concentrated in certain urban areas. Terrible working and living conditions and the periodic economic crises that created high levels of unemployment led to worker unrest and sporadic outbursts of violence.

Even in the legislature—the Chamber of Deputies—there were differences of opinion about the bourgeois monarchy and the direction it should take. Two groups rapidly emerged, both composed of upper-middle-class representatives. The Party of Movement, led by Adolphe Thiers (a-DAWLF TYAYR), favored ministerial responsibility, the pursuit of an active foreign policy, and limited expansion of the franchise. The Party of Resistance was led by François Guizot (frahnh-SWAH gee-ZOH), who believed that France had finally reached the "perfect form" of government and needed no further institutional changes. After 1840, the Party of Resistance dominated the Chamber of Deputies. Guizot cooperated with Louis-Philippe in suppressing ministerial responsibility and pursuing a policy favoring the interests of the wealthier manufacturers and tradespeople.

Revolutionary Outbursts in Belgium, Poland, and Italy

Supporters of liberalism played a primary role in the July Revolution in France, but nationalism was the crucial force in three other revolutionary outbursts in 1830. In an effort to create a stronger, larger state on France's northern border, the Congress of Vienna had added the area once known as the Austrian Netherlands (Belgium) to the Dutch Republic. The merger of Catholic Belgium into the Protestant Dutch Republic never sat well with the Belgians, however, and in 1830, they rose up against the

Dutch and succeeded in convincing the major European powers to accept their independence. Leopold of Saxe-Coburg, a minor German prince, was designated to be the new king, and a Belgian national congress established a constitutional monarchy for the new state.

The revolutionary scenarios in Italy and Poland were much less successful. Metternich sent Austrian troops to crush revolts in three Italian states. Poland, too, had a nationalist uprising in 1830 when revolutionaries tried to end Russian control of their country. But the Polish insurgents failed to get hoped-for support from France and Britain, and by September 1831, the Russians had crushed the revolt and established an oppressive military dictatorship over Poland.

Reform in Great Britain

In 1830, new parliamentary elections brought the Whigs to power in Britain. At the same time, the successful July Revolution in France served to catalyze change in Britain. The Industrial Revolution had led to an expanding group of industrial leaders who objected to the corrupt British electoral system, which excluded them from political power. The Whigs, though also members of the landed classes, realized that concessions to reform were superior to revolution; the demands of the wealthy industrial middle class could no longer be ignored. In 1830, the Whigs introduced an election reform bill that was enacted in 1832 after an intense struggle (see the box on p. 653).

THE REFORM ACT OF 1832 The Reform Act gave explicit recognition to the changes wrought in British life by the Industrial Revolution. It disenfranchised fifty-six rotten boroughs and enfranchised forty-two new towns and cities and reapportioned others. This gave the new industrial urban communities some voice in government. A property qualification (of £10 annual rent) for voting was retained, however, so the number of voters increased only from 478,000 to 814,000, a figure that still meant that only one in every thirty people was represented in Parliament. Thus, the Reform Act of 1832 primarily benefited the upper middle class; the lower middle class, artisans, and industrial workers still had no vote. Moreover, the change did not significantly alter the composition of the House of Commons. One political leader noted that the Commons chosen in the first election after the Reform Act seemed "to be very much like every other Parliament." Nevertheless, a significant step had been taken. The industrial middle class had been joined to the landed interests in ruling Britain.

NEW REFORM LEGISLATION The 1830s and 1840s witnessed considerable reform legislation. The aristocratic landowning class was usually (but not always) the driving force for legislation that halted some of the worst abuses in the industrial system by instituting government regulation of working conditions in the factories

Opposing ><VIEWPOINTS
Response to Revolution: Two Perspectives

Based on their political beliefs, Europeans responded differently to the specter of revolution that haunted Europe in the first half of the nineteenth century. The first excerpt is taken from a speech given by Thomas Babington Macaulay (1800–1859), a historian and a Whig member of Parliament. Macaulay spoke in Parliament on behalf of the Reform Act of 1832, which extended the right to vote to the industrial middle classes of Britain. The Revolution of 1830 in France had influenced his belief that it was better to reform than to have a political revolution.

The second excerpt is taken from the *Reminiscences* of Carl Schurz (1829–1906). Like many liberals and nationalists in Germany, Schurz received the news of the February Revolution of 1848 in France with much excitement and great expectations for revolutionary change in the German states. After the failure of the German revolution, Schurz made his way to the United States and eventually became a U.S. senator.

—✦——

Thomas Babington Macaulay, Speech of March 2, 1831

My hon. friend the member of the University of Oxford tells us that, if we pass this law, England will soon be a Republic. The reformed House of Commons will, according to him, before it has sat ten years, depose the King, and expel the Lords from their House. Sir, if my hon. friend could prove this, he would have succeeded in bringing an argument for democracy infinitely stronger than any that is to be found in the works of Paine. His proposition is, in fact, this—that our monarchical and aristocratical institutions have no hold on the public mind of England; that these institutions are regarded with aversion by a decided majority of the middle class.... Now, sir, if I were convinced that the great body of the middle class in England look with aversion on monarchy and aristocracy, I should be forced, much against my will, to come to this conclusion, that monarchical and aristocratical institutions are unsuited to this country. Monarchy and aristocracy, valuable and useful as I think them, are still valuable and useful as means, and not as ends. The end of government is the happiness of the people; and I do not conceive that, in a country like this, the happiness of the people can be promoted by a form of government in which the middle classes place no confidence, and which exists only because the middle classes have no organ by which to make their sentiments known. But, sir, I am fully convinced that the middle classes sincerely wish to uphold the royal prerogatives, and the constitutional rights of the Peers....

But let us know our interest and our duty better. Turn where we may—within, around—the voice of great events is proclaiming to us, "Reform, that you may preserve." Now, therefore, while everything at home and abroad forebodes ruin to those who persist in a hopeless struggle against the spirit of the age; now, while the crash of the proudest throne of the Continent is still resounding in our ears; ... now, while the heart of England is still sound; now, while the old feelings and the old associations retain a power and a charm which may too soon pass away; now, in this your accepted time; now, in this your day of salvation, take counsel, not of prejudice, not of party spirit, not of the ignominious pride of a fatal consistency, but of history, of reason, of the ages which are past, of the signs of this most portentous time. Pronounce in a manner worthy of the expectation with which this great debate has been anticipated, and of the long remembrance which it will leave behind. Renew the youth of the State. Save property divided against itself. Save the multitude, endangered by their own ungovernable passions. Save the aristocracy, endangered by its own unpopular power. Save the greatest, and fairest, and most highly civilized community that ever existed, from calamities which may in a few days sweep away all the rich heritage of so many ages of wisdom and glory. The danger is terrible. The time is short. If this Bill should be rejected, I pray to God that none of those who concur in rejecting it may ever remember their votes with unavailing regret, amidst the wreck of laws, the confusion of ranks, the spoliation of property, and the dissolution of social order.

Carl Schurz, *Reminiscences*

One morning, toward the end of February, 1848, I sat quietly in my attic-chamber, working hard at my tragedy of "Ulrich von Hutten" [a sixteenth-century German knight] when suddenly a friend rushed breathlessly into the room, exclaiming: "What, you sitting here! Do you not know what has happened?"

"No; what?"

"The French have driven away Louis Philippe and proclaimed the republic."

I threw down my pen—and that was the end of "Ulrich von Hutten." I never touched the manuscript again. We tore down the stairs, into the street, to the market-square, the accustomed meeting-place for all the student societies after their midday dinner. Although it

(continued)

was still forenoon, the market was already crowded with young men talking excitedly. There was no shouting, no noise, only agitated conversation. What did we want there? This probably no one knew. But since the French had driven away Louis Philippe and proclaimed the republic, something of course must happen here, too. . . . We were dominated by a vague feeling as if a great outbreak of elemental forces had begun, as if an earthquake was impending of which we had felt the first shock, and we instinctively crowded together. . . .

The next morning there were the usual lectures to be attended. But how profitless! The voice of the professor sounded like a monotonous drone coming from far away. What he had to say did not seem to concern us. The pen that should have taken notes remained idle. At last we closed with a sigh the notebook and went away, impelled by a feeling that now we had something more important to do—to devote ourselves to the affairs of the fatherland. And this we did by seeking as quickly as possible again the company of our friends, in order to discuss what had happened and what was to come. In these conversations, excited as they were, certain ideas and catchwords worked themselves to the surface, which expressed more or less the feelings of the people. Now had arrived in Germany the day for the establishment of "German Unity," and the founding of a great, powerful national German Empire. In the first line the convocation of a national parliament. Then the demands for civil rights and liberties, free speech, free press, the right of free assembly, equality before the law, a freely elected representation of the people with legislative

power, responsibility of ministers, self-government of the communes, the right of the people to carry arms, the formation of a civic guard with elective officers, and so on—in short, that which was called a "constitutional form of government on a broad democratic basis." Republican ideas were at first only sparingly expressed. But the word democracy was soon on all tongues, and many, too, thought it a matter of course that if the princes should try to withhold from the people the rights and liberties demanded, force would take the place of mere petition. Of course the regeneration of the fatherland must, if possible, be accomplished by peaceable means. . . . Like many of my friends, I was dominated by the feeling that at last the great opportunity had arrived for giving to the German people the liberty which was their birthright and to the German fatherland its unity and greatness, and that it was now the first duty of every German to do and to sacrifice everything for this sacred object. ⮥

Q What arguments did Macaulay use to support the Reform Bill of 1832? Was he correct? Why or why not? Why was Carl Schurz so excited when he heard the news about the revolution in France? Do you think being a university student helps to explain his reaction? Why or why not? What differences do you see in the approaches of these two writers? What do these selections tell you about the development of politics in the German states and Britain in the nineteenth century?

and mines. The industrialists and manufacturers now in Parliament opposed such legislation and were usually (but not always) the driving forces behind legislation that favored the principles of economic liberalism. The Poor Law of 1834 was based on the theory that giving aid to the poor and unemployed only encouraged laziness and increased the number of paupers. The Poor Law tried to remedy this by making paupers so wretched they would choose to work. Those unable to support themselves were crowded together in workhouses where living and working conditions were intentionally miserable so that people would be encouraged to find profitable employment.

Another piece of liberal legislation involved the repeal of the Corn Laws. This was primarily the work of the manufacturers Richard Cobden and John Bright, who formed the Anti–Corn Law League in 1838 to help workers by lowering bread prices. But abolishing the Corn Laws would also aid the industrial middle classes, who, as economic liberals, favored the principles of free trade. Repeal came in 1846 when Robert Peel (1788–1850), leader of the Tories, persuaded some of his associates to support free trade principles and abandon the Corn Laws.

While most of Europe experienced revolutions in 1848, the year ended without a major crisis in Britain. On the Continent, middle-class liberals and nationalists were at the forefront of the revolutionary forces. In Britain, however, the middle class had been largely satisfied by the Reform Act of 1832 and the repeal of the Corn Laws in 1846.

The Revolutions of 1848

Despite the successes of revolutions in France, Belgium, and Greece, the conservative order remained in control of much of Europe. But liberalism and nationalism continued to grow. In 1848, these forces of change erupted once more. Yet again, revolution in France provided the spark for other countries, and soon most of central and southern Europe was ablaze with revolutionary fires (see Map 21.4). Tsar Nicholas I of Russia lamented to Queen Victoria in April 1848, "What remains standing in Europe? Great Britain and Russia."

YET ANOTHER FRENCH REVOLUTION A severe industrial and agricultural depression beginning in 1846 brought great hardship to the French lower middle class, workers,

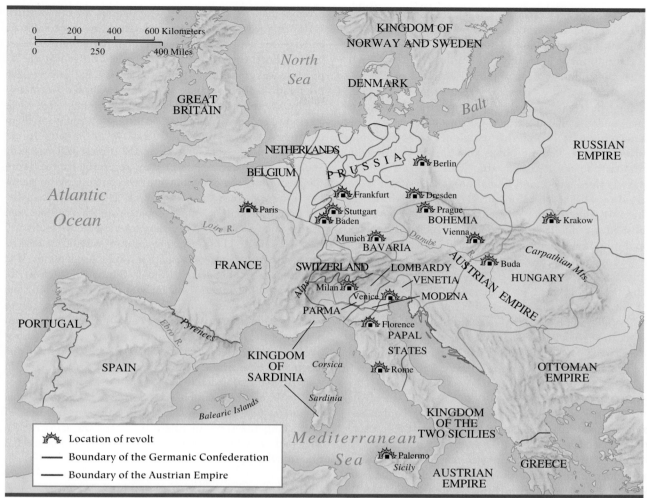

MAP 21.4 **The Revolutions of 1848–1849.** Beginning in Paris, revolutionary fervor fueled by liberalism and nationalism spread to the east and the south. After initial successes, the revolutionaries failed to maintain unity: propertied classes feared the working masses, and nationalists such as the Hungarians could not agree that all national groups deserved self-determination. The old order rallied its troops and prevailed.

Q *Which regions saw a great deal of revolutionary activity in 1848–1849, and which did not?*

and peasants. One-third of the workers in Paris were unemployed by the end of 1847. Scandals, graft, and corruption were rife, and the government's persistent refusal to extend the suffrage angered the disenfranchised members of the middle class.

As Louis-Philippe's government continued to refuse to make changes, opposition grew. Radical republicans and socialists, joined by the upper middle class under the leadership of Adolphe Thiers, agitated for the dismissal of Guizot. Since they were forbidden by law to stage political rallies, they used the political banquet to call for reforms. Almost seventy such banquets were held in France during the winter of 1847–1848; a grand culminating banquet was planned for Paris on February 22. When the government forbade it, people came anyway; students and workers threw up barricades in Paris. Although Louis-Philippe now proposed reform, he was unable to form

another ministry and abdicated on February 24 and fled to Britain. A provisional government was established by a group of moderate and radical republicans; the latter even included the socialist Louis Blanc. The provisional government ordered that representatives for a constituent assembly convened to draw up a new constitution be elected by universal manhood suffrage.

The provisional government also established national workshops under the influence of Louis Blanc. As Blanc envisioned them, the workshops were to be cooperative factories run by the workers. In fact, the workshops primarily provided unskilled jobs, such as leaf raking and ditch digging, for unemployed workers. The cost of the program became increasingly burdensome to the government.

The result was a growing split between the moderate republicans, who had the support of most of France, and the radical republicans, whose main support came from the Parisian working class. In the elections for the National Assembly, five hundred seats went to moderate republicans and three hundred to avowed monarchists, while the radicals gained only one hundred. From March to June, the number of unemployed enrolled in the national workshops rose from 10,000 to almost 120,000, emptying the treasury and frightening the moderates, who responded by closing the workshops on June 23. The workers refused to accept this decision and poured into the streets. Four days of bitter and bloody fighting by government forces crushed the working-class revolt. Thousands were killed, and four thousand prisoners were deported to the French colony of Algeria in North Africa.

The new constitution, ratified on November 4, 1848, established a republic (the Second Republic) with a uni-cameral (one-house) legislature of 750 elected by universal male suffrage for three years and a president, also elected by universal male suffrage, for four years. In the elections for the presidency held in December 1848, four republicans who had been associated with the early months of the Second Republic were resoundingly defeated by Charles Louis Napoleon Bonaparte, the nephew of Napoleon Bonaparte. Within four years, President Napoleon would become Emperor Napoleon (see Chapter 22).

REVOLUTION IN THE GERMANIC STATES News of the revolution in Paris in February 1848 triggered upheavals in central Europe as well (see the box on p. 653). Revolutionary cries for change caused many German rulers to promise constitutions, a free press, jury trials, and other liberal reforms. In Prussia, concessions were also made to appease the revolutionaries. King Frederick William IV (1840–1861) agreed to abolish censorship, establish a new constitution, and work for a united Germany. This last promise had its counterpart throughout all the German states as governments allowed elections by universal male suffrage for deputies to an all-German parliament to meet in Frankfurt, the seat of the Germanic Confederation. Its purpose was to fulfill a liberal and nationalist dream—the preparation of a constitution for a new united Germany.

This Frankfurt Assembly was dominated by well-educated, articulate, middle-class delegates, many of them professors, lawyers, and bureaucrats. When it came to nationalism, many were ahead of the times and certainly ahead of the governments of their respective states. From the beginning, the assembly aroused controversy by claiming to be the government for all of Germany. Then it became embroiled in a sticky debate over the composition of the new German state. Supporters of a *Grossdeutsch* (GROHS-doich) ("Big German") solution wanted to include the German province of Austria, while proponents of a *Kleindeutsch* (KLYN-doich) ("Small German") solution favored excluding Austria and making the Prussian king the emperor of the new German state. The problem was solved when the Austrians withdrew, leaving the field to the supporters of the *Kleindeutsch* solution. Their victory was short-lived, however, as Frederick William IV gruffly refused the assembly's offer of the title of "emperor of the Germans" in March 1849 and ordered the Prussian delegates home.

The Frankfurt Assembly soon disbanded. Although some members spoke of using force, they had no real means of compelling the German rulers to accept the constitution they had drawn up. The attempt of the German liberals at Frankfurt to create a German state had failed.

UPHEAVAL IN THE AUSTRIAN EMPIRE The Austrian Empire also had its social, political, and nationalist grievances and needed only the news of the revolution in Paris

Austrian Students in the Revolutionary Civil Guard. In 1848, revolutionary fervor swept the European continent and toppled governments in France, central Europe, and Italy. In the Austrian Empire, students joined the revolutionary civil guard in taking control of Vienna and forcing the Austrian emperor to call a constituent assembly to draft a liberal constitution.

Wien Museum Karlsplatz, Vienna//© Erich Lessing/Art Resource, NY to encourage it to erupt in flames in March 1848. The Hungarian liberals under Louis Kossuth (KAWSS-uth *or* KAW-shoot) agitated for "commonwealth" status; they were willing to keep the Habsburg monarch but wanted their own legislature. In March, demonstrations in Buda, Prague, and Vienna led to Metternich's dismissal, and the archsymbol of the conservative order fled abroad. In Vienna, revolutionary forces, carefully guided by the educated and propertied classes, took control of the capital and insisted that a constituent assembly be summoned to draw up a liberal constitution. Hungary was granted its wish for its own legislature, a separate national army, and control over its foreign policy and budget. Allegiance to the Habsburg dynasty was now Hungary's only tie to the Austrian Empire. In Bohemia, the Czechs began to demand their own government as well.

Although Emperor Ferdinand I (1835–1848) and Austrian officials had made concessions to appease the revolutionaries, they awaited an opportunity to reestablish their firm control. As in the German states, the conservatives were increasingly encouraged by the divisions between radical and moderate revolutionaries and played on the middle-class fear of a working-class social revolution. Their first success came in June 1848 when a military force under General Alfred Windischgrätz (VIN-dish-grets) ruthlessly suppressed the Czech rebels in Prague. In October, the death of the minister for war at the hands of a Viennese mob gave Windischgrätz the pretext for an attack on Vienna. By the end of the month, the radical rebels there had been crushed. In December, the feebleminded Ferdinand I agreed to abdicate in favor of his nephew, Francis Joseph I (1848–1916), who worked vigorously to restore the imperial government in Hungary. The Austrian armies, however, were unable to defeat Kossuth's forces, and it was only through the intervention of Nicholas I, who sent a Russian army of 140,000 men to aid the Austrians, that the Hungarian revolution was finally crushed in 1849. The revolutions in Austria had also failed. Autocratic government was restored; emperor and propertied classes remained in control, and the numerous nationalities were still subject to the Austrian government.

REVOLTS IN THE ITALIAN STATES The failure of revolutionary uprisings in Italy in 1830–1831 had encouraged the Italian movement for unification to take a new direction. The leadership of Italy's *risorgimento* (ree-SOR-jee-men-toh) ("resurgence") passed into the hands of Giuseppe Mazzini (joo-ZEP-pay maht-SEE-nee) (1805–1872), a dedicated Italian nationalist who founded an organization known as Young Italy in 1831 (see the box on p. 659). This group set as its goal the creation of a united Italian republic. In *The Duties of Man*, Mazzini urged Italians to dedicate their lives to the Italian nation: "O my Brother! Love your Country. Our Country is our home." A number of Italian women also took up Mazzini's call. Especially notable was Cristina Belgioioso (bell-joh-YOH-soh), a wealthy aristocrat who worked to bring about Italian

Giuseppe Mazzini, *The Duties of Man*, selected topics (1844–1858)

unification. Pursued by the Austrian authorities, she fled to Paris and started a newspaper espousing the Italian cause.

The dreams of Mazzini and Belgioioso seemed on the verge of fulfillment when a number of Italian states rose in revolt in 1848. Beginning in Sicily, rebellions spread northward as ruler after ruler granted a constitution to his people. Citizens in Lombardy and Venetia also rebelled against their Austrian overlords. The Venetians declared a republic in Venice. The king of the northern Italian state of Piedmont, Charles Albert (1831–1849), took up the call and assumed the leadership for a war of liberation from Austrian domination. His invasion of Lombardy proved unsuccessful, however, and by 1849, the Austrians had reestablished complete control over Lombardy and Venetia. Counterrevolutionary forces also prevailed throughout Italy. French forces helped Pope Pius IX regain control of Rome. Elsewhere Italian rulers managed to recover power on their own. Only Piedmont was able to keep its liberal constitution.

THE FAILURES OF 1848 Throughout Europe in 1848, popular revolts had initiated revolutionary upheavals that had led to the formation of liberal constitutions and liberal governments. But how could so many immediate successes in 1848 be followed by so many disasters only months later? Two reasons stand out. The unity of the revolutionaries had made the revolutions possible, but divisions soon shattered their ranks. Except in France, moderate liberals from the propertied classes failed to extend suffrage to the working classes who had helped achieve the revolutions. But as radicals pushed for universal male suffrage, liberals everywhere pulled back. Concerned about their property and security, they rallied to the old ruling classes for the sake of order and out of fear of social revolution by the working classes. All too soon, established governments were back in power.

In 1848, nationalities everywhere had also revolted in pursuit of self-government. But here too, frightfully little was achieved as divisions among nationalities proved utterly disastrous. Though the Hungarians demanded autonomy from the Austrians, at the same time they refused the same to their minorities—the Slovenes, Croats, and Serbs. Instead of joining together against the old empire, minorities fought each other. No wonder that one Czech could remark in April 1848, "If the Austrian state had not already existed for so long, it would have been in the interests of Europe, indeed of humanity itself, to endeavor to create it as soon as possible."[8] The Austrians' efforts to recover the Hungarian provinces met with little success until they began to play off Hungary's rebellious minority nationalities against the Hungarians.

The Maturing of the United States

The U.S. Constitution, ratified in 1789, committed the United States to two of the major forces of the first half of the nineteenth century, liberalism and nationalism. Initially, this constitutional commitment to national unity

Great Britain

Peterloo Massacre	1819
Reform Act	1832
Poor Law	1834
Repeal of Corn Laws	1846

France

Louis XVIII	1814–1824
Charles X	1824–1830
July Revolution	1830
Louis-Philippe	1830–1848
Abdication of Louis-Philippe; formation of provisional government	1848 (February 22–24)
June Days: workers' revolt in Paris	1848 (June)
Establishment of Second Republic	1848 (November)
Election of Louis Napoleon as French president	1848 (December)

Low Countries

Union of Netherlands and Belgium	1815
Belgian independence	1830

German States

Frederick William III of Prussia	1797–1840
Germanic Confederation established	1815
Karlsbad Decrees	1819
Frederick William IV of Prussia	1840–1861
Revolution in Germany	1848
Frankfurt Assembly	1848–1849

Austrian Empire

Emperor Ferdinand I	1835–1848
Revolt in Austrian Empire; Metternich dismissed	1848 (March)
Austrian forces under General Windischgrätz crush Czech rebels	1848 (June)
Viennese rebels crushed	1848 (October)
Francis Joseph I	1848–1916
Defeat of Hungarians with help of Russian troops	1849

Italian States

Revolts in southern Italy and Sardinia crushed	1821
King Charles Albert of Piedmont	1831–1849
Revolutions in Italy	1848
Charles Albert attacks Austrians	1848
Austrians reestablish control in Lombardy and Venetia	1849

Russia

Tsar Alexander I	1801–1825
Decembrist Revolt	1825
Tsar Nicholas I	1825–1855
Polish uprising	1830
Suppression of Polish revolt	1831

was challenged by divisions over the power of the federal government vis-à-vis the individual states. Bitter conflict erupted between the Federalists and the Republicans. Led by Alexander Hamilton (1757–1804), the Federalists favored a financial program that would establish a strong central government. The Republicans, guided by Thomas Jefferson (1743–1826) and James Madison (1751–1836), feared centralization and its consequences for popular liberties. These divisions were intensified by European rivalries because the Federalists were pro-British and the Republicans pro-French. The successful conclusion of the War of 1812 brought an end to the Federalists, who had opposed the war, while the surge of national feeling generated by the war served to heal the nation's divisions.

Another strong force for national unity came from the Supreme Court while John Marshall (1755–1835) was chief justice from 1801 to 1835. Marshall made the Supreme Court into an important national institution by asserting the right of the Court to overrule an act of Congress if the Court found it to be in violation of the Constitution. Under Marshall, the Supreme Court contributed further to establishing the supremacy of the national government by curbing the actions of state courts and legislatures.

The election of Andrew Jackson (1767–1845) as president in 1828 opened a new era in American politics, the era of mass democracy. The electorate was expanded by dropping traditional property qualifications; by the 1830s, suffrage had been extended to almost all adult white males. During the period from 1815 to 1850, the traditional liberal belief in the improvement of human beings was also given concrete expression. Americans developed detention schools for juvenile delinquents and new penal institutions, both motivated by the liberal belief that the right kind of environment would rehabilitate those in need of it.

The Emergence of an Ordered Society

 FOCUS QUESTION: How did Europe respond to the need for order in society in the first half of the nineteenth century?

Everywhere in Europe, the revolutionary upheavals of the late eighteenth and early nineteenth centuries made the ruling elite nervous about social disorder and the potential dangers to their lives and property. At the same time, the influx of large numbers of people from the countryside into rapidly growing cities had led to horrible living conditions, poverty, unemployment, and great social dissatisfaction. The first half of the nineteenth century witnessed a significant increase in crime, especially against property, in Britain, France, and Germany. The rise in property crimes caused a severe reaction among middle-class urban inhabitants, who feared that the urban poor posed a threat to their security and possessions. New police forces soon appeared to defend the propertied classes from criminals and social misfits.

The Voice of Italian Nationalism: Giuseppe Mazzini and Young Italy

After the failure of the uprisings in Italy in 1830–1831, Giuseppe Mazzini emerged as the leader of the Italian *risorgimento*—the movement for Italian nationhood. In 1831, he founded an organization known as Young Italy whose goal was the creation of a united Italian republic. This selection is from the oath that the members of Young Italy were required to take.

Giuseppe Mazzini, *The Young Italy Oath*

Young Italy is a brotherhood of Italians who believe in a law of Progress and Duty, and are convinced that Italy is destined to become one nation,—convinced also that she possesses sufficient strength within herself to become one, and that the ill success of her former efforts is to be attributed not to the weakness, but to the misdirection of the revolutionary elements within her,— that the secret of force lies in constancy and unity of effort. They join this association in the firm intent of consecrating both thought and action to the great aim of reconstituting Italy as one independent sovereign nation of free men and equals....

Each member will, upon his initiation into the association of Young Italy, pronounce the following form of oath, in the presence of the initiator: In the name of God and of Italy;

In the name of all the martyrs of the holy Italian cause who have fallen beneath foreign and domestic tyranny;

By the duties which bind me to the land wherein God has placed me, and to the brothers whom God has given me;

By the love—innate in all men—I bear to the country that gave my mother birth, and will be the home of my children....

By the sufferings of the millions,—

I, ... believing in the mission intrusted by God to Italy, and the duty of every Italian to strive to attempt its fulfillment; convinced that where God has ordained that a nation shall be, He has given the requisite power to create it; that the people are the depositaries of that power, and that in its right direction for the people, and by the people, lies the secret of victory; convinced that virtue consists in action and sacrifice, and strength in union and constancy of purpose: I give my name to Young Italy, an association of men holding the same faith, and swear:

To dedicate myself wholly and forever to the endeavor with them to constitute Italy one free, independent, republican nation; to promote by every means in my power—whether by written or spoken word, or by action—the education of my Italian brothers toward the aim of Young Italy; toward association, the sole means of its accomplishment, and to virtue, which alone can render the conquest lasting; to abstain from enrolling myself in any other association from this time forth; to obey all the instructions, in conformity with the spirit of Young Italy, given me by those who represent with me the union of my Italian brothers; and to keep the secret of these instructions, even at the cost of my life; to assist my brothers of the association both by action and counsel—NOW AND FOREVER.

Q Based on the principles outlined here, define nationalism. Why have some called nationalism a "secular religion"?

New Police Forces

The first major contribution of the nineteenth century to the development of a disciplined or ordered society in Europe was a regular system of police. A number of European states established civilian police forces—groups of well-trained law enforcement officers who were to preserve property and lives, maintain domestic order, investigate crime, and arrest offenders. It was hoped that their very presence would prevent crime. That the new police existed to protect citizens eventually made them acceptable, and by the end of the nineteenth century, many Europeans viewed them approvingly.

FRENCH POLICE This new approach to policing made its first appearance in France in 1828 when Louis-Maurice Debelleyme (LWEE-moh-REESS duh-buh-LAYM), the prefect of Paris, proclaimed, "The essential object of our municipal police is the safety of the inhabitants of Paris. Safety by day and night, free traffic movement, clean streets, the supervision of and precaution against accidents, the maintenance of order in public places, the seeking out of offenses and their perpetrators."[9] In March 1829, the new police, known as *serjents,* became visible on Paris streets. They were dressed in blue uniforms to make them easily recognizable by all citizens. They were also lightly armed with a white cane during the day and a saber at night, underscoring the fact that they were a civilian, not a military, body. Initially, there were not many of the new police officers. Paris had eighty-five by August 1829 and only five hundred in 1850. Before the end of the century, their number had increased to four thousand.

BRITISH BOBBIES The British, fearful of the powers exercised by military or secret police in authoritarian Continental states, had long resisted the creation of a

The New British Police: "We Are Not Treated as Men"

The new British police forces, organized first in London in 1829, were well established throughout much of Britain by the 1840s. As professionalism rose in the ranks of the forces, so did demands for better pay and treatment. In these two selections, police constables make clear their demands and complaints.

✦ ✠ ✦

Petition for Higher Pay by a Group of Third-Class Constables (1848)

Men joining the Police service as 3rd Class Constables and having a wife and 3 children to support on joining, are not able properly to do so on the pay of 16/8d. Most of the married men on joining are somewhat in debt, and are unable to extricate themselves on account of rent to pay and articles to buy which are necessary for support of wife and children. We beg leave to state that a married man having a wife and 2 children to support on joining, that it is as much as he can do upon 16/8d per week, and having to remain upon that sum for the first 12 to 18 months.

Complaints from Constables of D Division of the London Metropolitan Police

We are not treated as men but as slaves we englishmen do not like to be terrorized by a set of Irish Sergeants who are only lenient to their own countrymen we the D division of Paddington are nearly all ruled by these Irish Sergeants after we have done our night-Duty may we not have the privilege of going to Church or staying at home to Suit our own inclination when we are ordered by the Superintendent to go to church in our uniform on wednesday we do not object to the going to church we like to go but we do not like to be ordered there and when we go on Sunday nights we are asked like so many schoolboys have we been to church should we say no let reason be what it may it does not matter we are forthwith ordered from Paddington to Marylebone lane the next night—about 2 hours before we go to Duty that is 2 miles from many of our homes being tired with our walk there and back we must either loiter about the streets or in some public house and there we do not want to go for we cannot spare our trifling wages to spend them there but there is no other choice left—for us to make our time out to go on Duty at proper time on Day we are ordered there for that offense another Man may faultlessly commit—the crime of sitting 4 minutes during the night—then we must be ordered there another to Shew his old clothes before they are given in even we must go to the expense of having them put in repair we have indeed for all these frightful crimes to walk 3 or 4 miles and then be wasting our time that makes our night 3 hours longer than they ought to be another thing we want to know who has the money that is deducted out of our wages for fines and many of us will be obliged to give up the duty unless we can have fair play as to the stationing of us on our beats why cannot we follow round that may all and each of us go over every beat and not for the Sergeants to put their favorites on the good beats and the others kept back their favorites are not the best policemen but those that will spend the most with them at the public house there are a great many of these things to try our temper. ✤

Q What were the complaints of the British constables? What was the main issue that the complaints raised? Why might it be said that the development of police forces is a defining characteristic of Western civilization in modern times?

---

professional police force. Instead, Britain depended on a system of unpaid constables recruited by local authorities. Often these local constables were incapable of keeping order, preventing crimes, or apprehending criminals. Such jobs could also be dangerous and involve incidents like the one reported by a man passing by a local pub in 1827:

> I saw Thomas Franklin [constable of the village of Leighton Buzzard] coming out backwards. John Brandon . . . was opposite and close to the constable. I saw the said John Brandon strike the said constable twice "bang full in the face" the blows knocked the constable down on his back. John Brandon fell down with him. Sarah Adams . . . got on top of the constable and jostled his head against the ground. . . . The constable appeared very much hurt and his face was all over blood.[10]

The failure of the local constables led to a new approach. Between September 1829 and May 1830, three thousand uniformed police officers appeared on the streets of London. They came to be known as bobbies after Sir Robert Peel, who had introduced the legislation that created the force.

As is evident from the first instruction book for the new British police, their primary goal was to prevent crime: "Officers and police constables should endeavour to distinguish themselves by such vigilance and activity as may render it impossible for any one to commit a crime within that portion of the town under their charge."[11] The municipal authorities soon found, however, that the police were also useful for imposing order on working-class urban inhabitants. On Sundays, they were called on to clean up after Saturday night's drinking bouts. As demands for better pay and treatment led to improved working conditions, British police began to develop a sense of professionalism (see the box above).

The London Police. One response to the revolutionary upheavals of the late eighteenth and early nineteenth centuries was the development of civilian police forces that would be responsible for preserving property, arresting criminals, and maintaining domestic order. This early photograph shows a group of London policemen, who came to be known as bobbies after Sir Robert Peel, the man responsible for introducing the legislation that initiated the London police force.

SPREAD OF POLICE SYSTEMS Police systems were organized throughout the Western world during the nineteenth century. After the revolutions of 1848 in Germany, a state-financed police force called the *Schutzmannschaft* (SHOOTS-mun-shahft), modeled after the London police, was established for the city of Berlin. The *Schutzmannschaft* began as a civilian body, but already by 1851, the force had become organized more along military lines and was used for political purposes. Its military nature was reinforced by the force's weaponry, which included swords, pistols, and brass knuckles. One observer noted that "a German policeman on patrol is armed as if for war."[12]

OTHER APPROACHES TO THE CRIME PROBLEM Although the new police alleviated some of the fears about the increase in crime, contemporary reformers approached the problem in other ways. Some of them believed that the increase in crime was related to the dramatic increase in poverty. As one commented in 1816, "Poverty, misery are the parents of crime." Strongly influenced by the middle-class belief that unemployment was the result of sheer laziness, European states passed poor laws that attempted to force paupers to either find work on their own or enter workhouses designed to make people so utterly uncomfortable that they would choose to reenter the labor market.

Meanwhile, another group of reformers was arguing that poor laws failed to address the real problem, which was that poverty was a result of the moral degeneracy of the lower classes, increasingly labeled the "dangerous classes" because of the perceived threat they posed to middle-class society. This belief led one group of secular reformers to form institutes to instruct the working classes in the applied sciences in order to make them more productive members of society. The London Mechanics' Institute, established in Britain, and the Society for the Diffusion of Useful Knowledge in the Field of Natural Sciences, Technical Science, and Political Economy, founded in Germany, are but two examples of this approach to the "dangerous classes."

Organized religion took a different approach. British evangelicals set up Sunday schools to improve the morals of working children, and in Germany, evangelical Protestants established nurseries for orphans and homeless children, women's societies to care for the sick and poor, and prison societies that prepared women to work in prisons. The Catholic Church attempted the same kind of work through a revival of its religious orders; dedicated priests and nuns used spiritual instruction and recreation to turn young male workers away from the moral vices of gambling and drinking and female workers from lives of prostitution.

Prison Reform

The increase in crime led to a rise in arrests. By the 1820s in most countries, the indiscriminate use of capital punishment, even for crimes against property, was increasingly being viewed as ineffective and was replaced by imprisonment. Although the British had shipped people convicted of serious offenses to their colonial territory of Australia, that practice began to slow down in the late 1830s when the colonists loudly objected. Incarceration, then, was the only alternative. Prisons served to isolate criminals from society, but a growing number of reformers questioned their purpose and effectiveness, especially when prisoners were subjected to harsh and even humiliating work as punishment. By the 1830s, European governments were seeking ways to reform their penal systems. Motivated by the desire not just to punish but to rehabilitate and transform criminals into new persons, the British and French sent missions to the United States in the early 1830s to examine how the two different systems then used in American prisons accomplished this goal. At the Auburn Prison in New York, for example, prisoners were separated at night but worked together in the same workshop during the day. At Walnut Street Prison in Philadelphia, prisoners were separated into individual cells.

After examining the American prisons, both the French and the British constructed prisons on the Walnut Street model with separate cells that isolated prisoners from one another. At Petite Roquette (puh-TEET raw-KET) in France and Pentonville in Britain, prisoners wore leather masks while they exercised and sat in separate stalls when in chapel. Solitary confinement, it was believed, forced prisoners to examine their consciences, led to greater remorse, and increased the possibility that they would change their evil ways. One supporter of the separate-cell system noted:

> A few months in the solitary cell renders a prisoner strangely impressible. The chaplain can then make the brawny navvy cry like a child; he can work on his feelings in almost any way he pleases; he can, so to speak, photograph his thoughts, wishes and opinions on his patient's mind, and fill his mouth with his own phrases and language.[13]

As prison populations increased, however, solitary confinement proved expensive and less feasible. The French even returned to their custom of sending prisoners to French Guiana to handle the overload.

Prison reform and police forces were geared toward one primary end, the creation of a more disciplined society. Disturbed by the upheavals associated with revolutions and the social discontent wrought by industrialization and urbanization, the ruling elites sought to impose some order on society.

Culture in an Age of Reaction and Revolution: The Mood of Romanticism

 Focus Question: What were the characteristics of Romanticism, and how were they reflected in literature, art, and music?

At the end of the eighteenth century, a new intellectual movement known as Romanticism emerged to challenge the Enlightenment's preoccupation with reason in discovering truth. The Romantics tried to balance the use of reason by stressing the importance of intuition, feeling,

emotion, and imagination as sources of knowing. As one German Romantic put it, "It was my heart that counseled me to do it, and my heart cannot err."

The Characteristics of Romanticism

Romantic writers emphasized emotion, sentiment, and inner feelings in their works. An important model for Romantics was the tragic figure in *The Sorrows of the Young Werther,* a novel by the great German writer Johann Wolfgang von Goethe (yoh-HAHN VULF-gahnk fun GUR-tuh) (1749–1832), who later rejected Romanticism in favor of Classicism. Werther was a Romantic figure who sought freedom in order to fulfill himself. Misunderstood and rejected by society, he continued to believe in his own worth through his inner feelings, but his deep love for a girl who did not love him finally led him to commit suicide. After Goethe's *Sorrows of the Young Werther,* numerous novels and plays appeared whose plots revolved around young maidens tragically carried off at an early age (twenty-three was most common) by disease (usually tuberculosis, at that time a protracted disease that was usually fatal) to the sorrow and despair of their male lovers.

Another important characteristic of Romanticism was **individualism,** an interest in the unique traits of each person. The Romantics' desire to follow their inner drives led them to rebel against middle-class conventions. Long hair, beards, and outrageous clothes served to reinforce the individualism that young Romantics were trying to express.

Sentiment and individualism came together in the Romantics' stress on the heroic. The Romantic hero was a solitary genius who was ready to defy the world and sacrifice his life for a great cause. In the hands of the British writer Thomas Carlyle (1795–1881), however, the Romantic hero did not destroy himself in ineffective protests against society but transformed society instead. In his historical works, Carlyle stressed that historical events were largely determined by the deeds of such heroes.

Many Romantics possessed a passionate interest in the past. This historical focus was manifested in many ways. In Germany, the Grimm brothers collected and published local fairy tales, as did Hans Christian Andersen in Denmark. The revival of medieval Gothic architecture left European countrysides adorned with pseudo-medieval castles and cities bedecked with grandiose neo-Gothic cathedrals, city halls, parliamentary buildings, and even railway stations. Literature, too, reflected this historical consciousness. The novels of Walter Scott (1771–1832) became European best sellers in the first half of the nineteenth century. *Ivanhoe,* in which Scott tried to evoke the clash between Saxon and Norman knights in medieval England, became one of his most popular works.

To the history-mindedness of the Romantics could be added an attraction to the bizarre and unusual. In an exaggerated form, this preoccupation gave rise to so-called **Gothic literature** (see the box on p. 663), chillingly evident in the short stories of horror by the American Edgar

Gothic Literature: Edgar Allan Poe

American writers and poets made significant contributions to Romanticism. Although Edgar Allan Poe (1809–1849) was influenced by the German Romantic school of mystery and horror, many literary historians give him the credit for pioneering the modern short story. This selection from the conclusion of "The Fall of the House of Usher" gives a sense of the nature of so-called Gothic literature.

Edgar Allan Poe, "The Fall of the House of Usher"

No sooner had these syllables passed my lips, than—as if a shield of brass had indeed, at the moment, fallen heavily upon a floor of silver—I became aware of a distinct, hollow, metallic, and clangorous, yet apparently muffled, reverberation. Completely unnerved, I leaped to my feet; but the measured rocking movement of Usher was undisturbed. I rushed to the chair in which he sat. His eyes were bent fixedly before him, and throughout his whole countenance there reigned a stony rigidity. But, as I placed my hand upon his shoulder, there came a strong shudder over his whole person; a sickly smile quivered about his lips and I saw that he spoke in a low, hurried, and gibbering murmur, as if unconscious of my presence. Bending closely over him, I at length drank in the hideous import of his words.

"Not hear it?—yes, I hear it, and *have* heard it. Long-long-long-many minutes, many hours, many days, have I heard it—yet I dared not—oh, pity me, miserable wretch that I am!—I dared not—I *dared* not speak! *We have put her living in the tomb!* Said I not that my senses were acute? I now tell you that I heard her first feeble movements in the hollow coffin. I heard them—many, many days ago—yet I dared not—I *dared not speak!* And now—tonight . . . the rending of her coffin, and the grating of the iron hinges of her prison, and her struggles within the coppered archway of the vault! Oh whither shall I fly? Will she not be here anon? Is she not hurrying to upbraid me for my haste? Have I not heard her footstep on the stair? Do I not distinguish that heavy and horrible beating of her heart? MADMAN!"—here he sprang furiously to his feet, and shrieked out his syllables, as if in the effort he were giving up his soul— "MADMAN! I TELL YOU THAT SHE NOW STANDS WITHOUT THE DOOR!"

As if in the superhuman energy of his utterance there had been found the potency of a spell, the huge antique panels to which the speaker pointed threw slowly back, upon the instant, their ponderous and ebony jaws. It was the work of the rushing gust—but then without those doors there DID stand the lofty and enshrouded figure of the lady Madeline of Usher. There was blood upon her white robes, and the evidence of some bitter struggle upon every portion of her emaciated frame. For a moment she remained trembling and reeling to and fro upon the threshold, then, with a low moaning cry, fell heavily inward upon the person of her brother, and in her violent and now final death-agonies, bore him to the floor a corpse, and a victim to the terrors he had anticipated. ⮊

Q What characteristics of Romanticism are revealed in Poe's tale? In what ways did Romanticism offer alternatives to the reigning influences of rationalism and industrialization?

Neo-Gothic Revival: British Houses of Parliament. The Romantic movement of the first half of the nineteenth century led, among other things, to a revival of medieval Gothic architecture that left European cities bedecked with neo-Gothic buildings. After the Houses of Parliament in London burned down in 1834, they were replaced with new buildings of neo-Gothic design, as seen in this photograph.

Allan Poe (1808–1849) and in *Frankenstein* by Mary Shelley (1797–1851). Shelley's novel was the story of a mad scientist who brings into being a humanlike monster who goes berserk. Some Romantics even sought the unusual in their own lives by pursuing extraordinary states of experience in dreams, nightmares, frenzies, and suicidal depression or by experimenting with cocaine, opium, and hashish to produce altered states of consciousness.

Romantic Poets

To the Romantics, poetry ranked above all other literary forms because they believed it was the direct expression of one's soul. The Romantic poets were viewed as seers who could reveal the invisible world to others. Their incredible sense of drama made some of them the most colorful figures of their era, living intense but short lives. Percy Bysshe Shelley (1792–1822), expelled from school for advocating atheism, set out to reform the world. His *Prometheus Unbound,* completed in 1820, is a portrait of the revolt of human beings against the laws and customs that oppress them. He drowned in a storm in the Mediterranean. Lord Byron (1788–1824) dramatized himself as the melancholy Romantic hero that he had described in his work, *Childe Harold's Pilgrimage.* He participated in the movement for Greek independence and died in Greece fighting the Ottomans.

LOVE OF NATURE Romantic poetry gave full expression to one of the most important characteristics of Romanticism: love of nature, especially evident in the works of William Wordsworth (1770–1850). His experience of nature was almost mystical as he claimed to receive "authentic tidings of invisible things":

> One impulse from a vernal wood
> May teach you more of man,
> Of Moral Evil and of good,
> Than all the sages can.[14]

To Wordsworth, nature contained a mysterious force that the poet could perceive and learn from. Nature served as a mirror into which humans could look to learn about themselves. Nature was, in fact, alive and sacred:

> To every natural form, rock, fruit or flower,
> Even the loose stones that cover the high-way,
> I gave a moral life, I saw them feel,
> Or link'd them to some feeling: the great mass
> Lay bedded in a quickening soul, and all
> That I beheld, respired with inward meaning.[15]

Other Romantics carried this worship of nature further into **pantheism** by identifying the great force in nature with God. The Romantics would have nothing to do with the deist God of the Enlightenment, the remote creator of the world-machine. As the German Romantic poet Friedrich Novalis (FREED-rikh noh-VAH-lis) said, "Anyone seeking God will find him anywhere."

CRITIQUE OF SCIENCE The worship of nature also led Wordsworth and other Romantic poets to critique the mechanistic materialism of eighteenth-century science, which, they believed, had reduced nature to a cold object of study. Against that view of the natural world, Wordsworth offered his own vivid and concrete experience. To him, the scientists' dry, mathematical approach left no room for the imagination or for the human soul. The poet who left to the world "one single moral precept, one single affecting sentiment," Wordsworth said, did more for the world than scientists who were soon forgotten. The monster created by Frankenstein in Mary Shelley's Gothic novel symbolized well the danger of science when it tries to conquer nature. Many Romantics were convinced that the emerging industrialization would cause people to become alienated from their inner selves and the natural world around them.

Romanticism in Art

Like the literary arts, the visual arts were also deeply affected by Romanticism. Although their works varied widely, Romantic artists shared at least two fundamental characteristics. All artistic expression to them was a reflection of the artist's inner feelings; a painting should mirror the artist's vision of the world and be the instrument of his own imagination. Moreover, Romantic artists deliberately rejected the principles of Classicism. Beauty was not a timeless thing; its expression depended on one's culture and one's age. The Romantics abandoned classical restraint for warmth, emotion, and movement. Through an examination of three painters, we can see how Romanticism influenced the visual arts.

FRIEDRICH The early life experiences of the German painter Caspar David Friedrich (kass-PAR dah-VEET FREED-rikh) (1774–1840) left him with a lifelong preoccupation with God and nature. Friedrich painted landscapes with an interest that transcended the mere presentation of natural details. His portrayal of mountains shrouded in mist, gnarled trees bathed in moonlight, and the stark ruins of monasteries surrounded by withered trees all conveyed a feeling of mystery and mysticism. For Friedrich, nature was a manifestation of divine life, as is evident in *Man and Woman Gazing at the Moon.* To Friedrich, the artistic process depended on one's inner vision. He advised artists, "Shut your physical eye and look first at your picture with your spiritual eye; then bring to the light of day what you have seen in the darkness."

TURNER Another artist who dwelt on nature and made landscape his major subject was the Englishman Joseph Malford William Turner (1775–1851). Turner was an incredibly prolific artist who produced more than 20,000

Caspar David Friedrich, *Man and Woman Gazing at the Moon.* The German artist Caspar David Friedrich sought to express in painting his own mystical view of nature. "The divine is everywhere," he once wrote, "even in a grain of sand." In this painting, two solitary wanderers are shown from the back gazing at the moon. Overwhelmed by the all-pervasive presence of nature, the two figures express the human longing for infinity.

paintings, drawings, and watercolors. Turner's concern with nature manifested itself in innumerable landscapes and seascapes, sunrises and sunsets. He did not idealize nature or reproduce it with realistic accuracy, however. He sought instead to convey its moods by using a skilled interplay of light and color to suggest natural effects. In allowing his objects to melt into their surroundings, he anticipated the Impressionist painters of the second half of the nineteenth century (see Chapter 24). John Constable, a contemporary English Romantic painter, described Turner's paintings as "airy visions, painted with tinted steam."

DELACROIX Eugène Delacroix (oo-ZHEN duh-lah-KRWAH) (1798–1863) was the most famous French Romantic artist.

Largely self-taught, he was fascinated by the exotic and had a passion for color. Both characteristics are visible in *The Death of Sardanapalus.* Significant for its use of light and its patches of interrelated color, this portrayal of the world of the last Assyrian king was criticized at the time for its garishness. Delacroix rejoiced in combining theatricality and movement with a daring use of color. Many of his works reflect his own belief that "a painting should be a feast to the eye."

Romanticism in Music

To many Romantics, music was the most Romantic of the arts because it enabled the composer to probe deeply into

J. M. W. Turner, *Rain, Steam, and Speed—The Great Western Railway.* Although Turner began his artistic career by painting accurate representations of the natural world, he increasingly sought to create an atmosphere through the skillful use of light and color. In this painting, Turner eliminates specific details and uses general fields of color to convey the impression of a locomotive rushing toward the viewer.

Eugène Delacroix, *The Death of Sardanapalus.* Delacroix's *Death of Sardanapalus* was based on Lord Byron's verse account of the dramatic last moments of the decadent Assyrian king. Besieged by enemy troops and with little hope of survival, Sardanapalus orders that his harem women and prized horses go to their death with him. At the right, a guard stabs one of the women as the king looks on.

human emotions. One Romantic writer noted, "It has been rightly said that the object of music is the awakening of emotion. No other art can so sublimely arouse human sentiments in the innermost heart of man."[16] Although music historians have called the eighteenth century the age of Classicism and the nineteenth the era of Romanticism, there was much carryover of classical forms from one century to the next. One of the greatest composers of all time, Ludwig van Beethoven, served as a bridge between Classicism and Romanticism.

BEETHOVEN Beethoven (1770–1827) is one of the few composers to singlehandedly transform the art of music. Set ablaze by the events in France, a revolutionary mood burned brightly across Europe, and Beethoven, like other creative personalities, yearned to communicate his cherished beliefs. He said, "I *must* write, for what weighs on my heart, I *must* express." For Beethoven, music had to reflect his deepest inner feelings.

Born in Bonn, Beethoven came from a family of musicians who worked for the electors of Cologne. He became an assistant organist at the court by the age of thirteen and soon made his way to Vienna, the musical capital of Europe, where he studied briefly under Haydn. Beginning in 1792, this city became his permanent residence.

During his first major period of composing (1792–1800), his work was largely within the classical framework of the eighteenth century, and the influences of Haydn and Mozart are apparent. But with the composition of the Third Symphony (1804), also called the *Eroica,* which was originally intended for Napoleon, Beethoven broke through to the elements of Romanticism in his use of uncontrolled rhythms to create dramatic struggle and

uplifted resolutions. E. T. A. Hoffman, a contemporary composer and writer, said, "Beethoven's music opens the flood gates of fear, of terror, of horror, of pain, and arouses that longing for the eternal which is the essence of Romanticism. He is thus a pure Romantic composer."[17] Beethoven went on to write a vast quantity of works, but in the midst of this productivity and growing fame, he was more and more burdened by his growing deafness. One of the most moving pieces of music of all time, the chorale finale of his Ninth Symphony, was composed when Beethoven was totally deaf.

BERLIOZ Beethoven served as a bridge from the classical era to Romanticism; after him came a number of musical geniuses who composed in the Romantic style. The Frenchman Hector Berlioz (ek-TOR BAYR-lee-ohz) (1803–1869) was one of the most outstanding. His father, a doctor in Grenoble, intended that his son should also study medicine. The young Berlioz eventually rebelled, however, maintaining to his father's disgust that he would be "no doctor or apothecary but a great composer." Berlioz managed to fulfill his own expectations, achieving fame in Germany, Russia, and Britain, although the originality of his work kept him from receiving much recognition in his native France.

Berlioz was one of the founders of program music, which was an attempt to use the moods and sound effects of instrumental music to depict the actions and emotions inherent in a story, an event, or even a personal experience. This development of program music was evident in his most famous piece, the first complete program symphony, known as the *Symphonie Fantastique.* In this work, Berlioz used music to evoke the passionate emotions of a tortured love affair, including a fifth movement in which he musically creates an opium-induced nightmare of a witches' gathering.

The Revival of Religion in the Age of Romanticism

After 1815, Christianity experienced a revival. In the eighteenth century, Catholicism had lost its attraction for many of the educated elite as even the European nobility flirted with the ideas of the Enlightenment. The restoration of the nobility brought a new appreciation for the Catholic faith as a force for order in society. This appreciation was greatly reinforced by the Romantic movement. The Romantics' attraction to the Middle Ages and their emphasis on emotion led them to their own widespread revival of Christianity.

CATHOLICISM Catholicism, in particular, benefited from this Romantic enthusiasm for religion. Especially among German Romantics, there were many conversions to the Catholic faith. One of the most popular expressions of this Romantic revival of Catholicism was found in the work of the Frenchman François-René de Chateaubriand (frahnh-SWAH-ruh-NAY duh shah-TOH-bree-AHNH) (1768–1848). His book *Genius of Christianity,* published in 1802, was soon

labeled the "Bible of Romanticism." His defense of Catholicism was based not on historical, theological, or even rational grounds but largely on Romantic sentiment. As a faith, Catholicism echoed the harmony of all things. Its cathedrals brought one into the very presence of God; according to Chateaubriand, "You could not enter a Gothic church without feeling a kind of awe and a vague sentiment of the Divinity.... Every thing in a Gothic church reminds you of the labyrinths of a wood; every thing excites a feeling of religious awe, of mystery, and of the Divinity."[18]

PROTESTANTISM Protestantism also experienced a revival. That "awakening," as it was called, had already begun in the eighteenth century with the enthusiastic emotional experiences of Methodism in Britain and Pietism in Germany (see Chapter 17). Methodist missionaries from England and Scotland carried their messages of sin and redemption to liberal Protestant churches in France and Switzerland, winning converts to their strongly evangelical message. Germany, too, witnessed a Protestant awakening as enthusiastic evangelical preachers found that their messages of hellfire and their methods of emotional conversion evoked a ready response among people alienated by the highly educated establishment clergy of the state churches.

CHAPTER SUMMARY

In 1815, a conservative order was reestablished throughout Europe at the Congress of Vienna, which made peace at the end of the Napoleonic wars and tried to restore Europe's "legitimate" rulers. The great powers, whose cooperation

was embodied in the Concert of Europe, attempted to ensure the durability of the new conservative order by intervening to uphold conservative governments. Great Britain, however, seeking new markets, opposed intervention when the Latin American colonies of Spain and Portugal declared their independence. Within the European countries, conservative rulers worked to reestablish the old order.

But the revolutionary waves of the 1820s and 1830s made it clear that the ideologies of liberalism and nationalism, first unleashed by the French Revolution and now reinforced by the spread of the Industrial Revolution, were still alive and active. Liberalism favored freedom both in politics and in economics. Natural rights and representative government were essential, but most liberals favored limiting the right to vote to male property owners. Nationalism, with its belief in a community with

common traditions, language, and customs, threatened the status quo in divided Germany and Italy and the multiethnic Austrian Empire.

The forces of liberalism and nationalism, however, faced enormous difficulties as failed revolutions in Poland, Russia, Italy, and Germany all testify. At the same time, reform legislation in Britain and successful revolutions in Greece, France, and Belgium demonstrated the continuing strength of these forces for change. In 1848, they erupted once more as revolutions broke out all across Europe. A republic with universal manhood suffrage was established in France, but conflict emerged between socialist demands and the republican political agenda. The Frankfurt Assembly worked to create a unified Germany, but it also failed. In Austria, the liberal demands of Hungarians and other nationalities were eventually put down. In Italy, too, uprisings against Austrian rule failed when conservatives regained control. Although they failed, both liberalism and nationalism would succeed in the second half of the nineteenth century but in ways not foreseen by the idealistic liberals and nationalists. The disorder of the age also led European states to create civilian police forces.

Efforts at reform had a cultural side as well in the movement of Romanticism. Romantics reacted against what they viewed as the Enlightenment's excessive emphasis on reason. They favored intuition, feeling, and emotion, which became evident in the medieval fantasies of Walter Scott, the poetry of William Wordsworth and Percy Bysshe Shelley, the Gothic literature of Mary Shelley and Edgar Allan Poe, the paintings of Caspar David Friedrich and Eugène Delacroix, and the music of Ludwig van Beethoven and Hector Berlioz. Romanticism also brought a revival of religion evident in a renewed interest in Catholicism's medieval heritage and in a Protestant "awakening."

CHAPTER TIMELINE

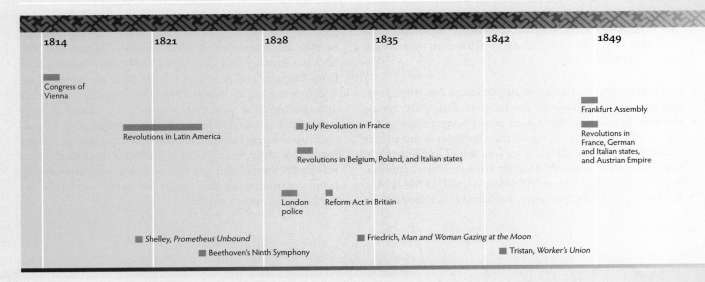

1814	1821	1828	1835	1842	1849

Congress of Vienna

Revolutions in Latin America

July Revolution in France

Revolutions in Belgium, Poland, and Italian states

London police

Reform Act in Britain

Frankfurt Assembly

Revolutions in France, German and Italian states, and Austrian Empire

Shelley, *Prometheus Unbound*

Beethoven's Ninth Symphony

Friedrich, *Man and Woman Gazing at the Moon*

Tristan, *Worker's Union*

CHAPTER REVIEW

Upon Reflection

Q What were the chief ideas associated with the ideology of conservatism, and how were these ideas put into practice in the first half of the nineteenth century?

Q What were the chief ideas associated with the ideologies of liberalism and nationalism, and how were these ideas put into practice in the first half of the nineteenth century?

Q How was Great Britain able to avoid revolution in the 1830s and the 1840s?

Key Terms

principle of legitimacy (p. 637)
balance of power (p. 638)
ideology (p. 639)
conservatism (p. 639)
principle of intervention (p. 640)
ultraroyalists (p. 644)
ministerial responsibility (p. 644)
Burschenschaften (p. 645)
liberalism (p. 647)

socialism (p. 650)
utopian socialists (p. 650)
phalanstery (p. 650)
risorgimento (p. 657)
individualism (p. 662)
Gothic literature (p. 662)
pantheism (p. 664)

Suggestions for Further Reading

GENERAL WORKS For a good survey of the entire nineteenth century, see **R. Gildea, *Barricades and Borders: Europe, 1800–1914,*** 3rd ed. (Oxford, 2003). Also valuable is **T. C. W. Blanning, ed., *Nineteenth Century: Europe 1789–1914*** (Oxford, 2000). For surveys of the period covered in this chapter, see **M. Broers, *Europe After Napoleon: Revolution, Reaction, and Romanticism, 1814–1848*** (New York, 1996); **M. Lyons, *Postrevolutionary Europe 1815–1856*** (New York, 2006); and **C. Breunig** and **M. Levinger, *The Age of Revolution and Reaction, 1789–1850,*** 3rd ed. (New York, 2002).

There are also some useful books on individual countries that cover more than the subject of this chapter. These include **R. Magraw, *France, 1815–1914: The Bourgeois Century,*** rev. ed.

(Oxford, 2006); **D. Saunders, *Russia in the Age of Reaction and Reform, 1801–1881*** (London, 1992); **D. Blackbourn, *The Long Nineteenth Century: A History of Germany, 1789–1918*** (New York, 1998); **A. Sked, *The Decline and Fall of the Habsburg Empire, 1815–1918,*** 2nd ed. (London, 2001); **J. A. David, *Italy in the Nineteenth Century: 1796–1900*** (Oxford, 2001); and **N. McCord, *British History, 1815–1906*** (New York, 1991).

EUROPE, 1815–1830   On the peace settlement of 1814–1815, see **T. Chapman, *The Congress of Vienna*** (London, 1998). A concise summary of the international events of the entire nineteenth century can be found in **R. Bullen** and **F. R. Bridge, *The Great Powers and the European States System, 1815–1914,*** rev. ed. (London, 2004). On the man whose conservative policies dominated this era, see the brief but good biography by **A. Palmer, *Metternich*** (New York, 1972). On the revolutions in Europe in 1830, see **C. Church, *Europe in 1830: Revolution and Political Change*** (Chapel Hill, N.C., 1983). On Great Britain's reform legislation, see **E. J. Evans, *Great Reform Act of 1832,*** 2nd ed. (London, 1994). The Greek revolt is examined in detail in **D. Brewer, *Greek War of Independence*** (New York, 2001).

REVOLUTIONS OF 1848   The best introduction to the revolutions of 1848 is **J. Sperber, *The European Revolutions, 1848–1851,*** 2nd ed. (New York, 2005). On Mazzini, see **D. M. Smith, *Mazzini*** (New Haven, Conn., 1994). On the ideologies connected to the revolutions of 1848, see **J. Gray, *Liberalism*** (Minneapolis, Minn., 1995), and **T. Baycroft, *Nationalism in Europe, 1789–1945*** (Cambridge, 1998).

AN ORDERED SOCIETY   On changes in the treatment of crime and punishment, see **M. Foucault, *Discipline and Punish: The Birth of the Prison*** (New York, 1977). The new police forces are examined in **C. Emsley, *Policing and Its Context, 1750–1870*** (New York, 1984), and **C. Emsley, *Crime and Society in England, 1750–1900,*** 3rd ed. (London, 2005).

ROMANTICISM   On the ideas of the Romantics, see **M. Cranston, *The Romantic Movement*** (Oxford, 1994). On Wordsworth and English Romanticism, see **S. Hebron, *William Wordsworth*** (New York, 2000). For an introduction to the arts, see **W. Vaughan, *Romanticism and Art*** (New York, 1994), and **I. Ciseri, *Romanticism 1780–1860: The Birth of a New Sensibility*** (New York, 2003).

 CourseMate

Visit the CourseMate website at www.cengagebrain.com for additional study tools and review materials for this chapter.

AP❖ REVIEW QUESTIONS FOR CHAPTER 21

1. Which country was NOT part of the Quadruple Alliance?

   (A) Great Britain
   (B) Austria
   (C) Prussia
   (D) Spain
   (E) Russia

2. The Reform Act of 1832 in Great Britain

   (A) extended the right to vote to the lower classes.
   (B) was a liberal-supported movement to extend the franchise to the industrial middle class.
   (C) removed property qualifications for voting.
   (D) limited child labor in an attempt to rectify problems created by the Industrial Revolution.
   (E) created a new police force to quell the uprisings of the utopian socialists.

3. Metternich's principle of legitimacy guided him

   (A) in aiding Italy's unification process.
   (B) in giving Poland its legitimate independence.
   (C) in creating new colonial holdings for Great Britain.
   (D) in establishing conservative monarchs on the thrones of Europe.
   (E) in occupying France for two years and limiting the size of its military.

4. Both Ricardo and Malthus

   (A) sought to explain the basis of political liberalism and attempted to convince the members of the middle class to try to obtain the rights they deserved.
   (B) sought to increase the influence of the early utopian socialists and to convince the government to provide additional benefits to the people.
   (C) agreed with Marx and Engels that the class struggle is the basis for all revolutions.
   (D) were economic liberals who suggested that wage increases ultimately have a negative impact on the economy and that government should not intervene in the economy.
   (E) suggested that anarchism is a better option than any of the other governments available to the people.

5. By 1848, all of the following South and Central American countries had gained their independence from European states EXCEPT

   (A) Brazil.
   (B) Argentina.
   (C) Mexico.
   (D) British Guiana.
   (E) Colombia.

6. Which of the following occurred in Great Britain during the early nineteenth century?

   (A) The people sought increased government control of society, as they were fearful of the revolutions that roiled the Continent.
   (B) The push for further economic reforms and liberal changes in the government led to a violent clash between the government and the people.
   (C) The Tories and the Whigs battled for the people's political support as they sought to expand the electorate.
   (D) The enactment of the Corn Laws symbolized a movement away from aristocratic privilege and toward more equitable economic legislation.
   (E) Metternich quickly intervened to put down the Peterloo revolutionaries for fear that unrest would spread to Continental Europe.

7. In both Italy and Spain, reformers argued for new constitutions based on the ideals of

   (A) nationalism.
   (B) conservatism.
   (C) liberalism.
   (D) absolutism.
   (E) royalism.

8. After the reestablishment of the Bourbon monarchy in France,

   (A) the people were content to see the traditional monarchy in control, and were satisfied with their political rights.
   (B) some considered the monarch's reforms too liberal while others considered them too conservative, causing unhappiness across the entire political spectrum.
   (C) the king sought support from Metternich's army to suppress any further rebellion by the populace.
   (D) subversive groups attempted to assassinate Louis XVIII for failing to live up to the expectations of the royalists.
   (E) the balance of power within Europe was upset as Louis XVIII attempted to regain much of the land lost after Napoleon's defeat.

9. All of the following factors contributed to Metternich's concept of a balance of power EXCEPT

   (A) his desire to strengthen Prussia and Austria to balance Russian gains.
   (B) his desire to increase the defensive power of the countries surrounding France in order to prevent the emergence of another dictator like Napoleon.
   (C) his desire to ensure that Austria would remain the strongest and most influential state in central Europe.
   (D) the desire of many countries subjugated by Napoleon to divide France and deny its sovereignty.
   (E) his fear that the growing power of the United States would upset the power currently held by the European states.

10. Dynastic conflict within Russia

(A) allowed for a liberal uprising inspired by the revolutions in France.

(B) signified a weakening of the Russian monarchy and prompted Metternich's intervention.

(C) brought about new reforms like the end of serfdom and extension of the franchise.

(D) led to uprisings throughout eastern Europe and the Ottoman Empire.

(E) brought about a true reformer in Nicholas I who wanted to put an end to peasant unrest.

11. During the early nineteenth century, liberals in Spain, Italy, and Austria all sought

(A) independence from monarchical control by rising up in revolutions.

(B) economic reforms to solidify the power they had gained as a result of the Industrial Revolution.

(C) to achieve liberal ideals such as a constitution that extended political rights to the populace.

(D) radical changes to the government including the creation of republics with the help of the United States.

(E) to make peace with Metternich and establish a balance between liberals and conservatives within their countries.

12. The revolutions of the early 1800s differed from those of 1848 in that

(A) the revolutions of the early 1800s were generally more successful than those of 1848.

(B) Metternich's power had waned by 1848, making him impotent against the later revolutionaries.

(C) the earlier revolutions were more violent and more widespread than the revolutions of 1848.

(D) the earlier revolutions were largely led by nationalists whereas the revolutions of 1848 were mainly led by liberals.

(E) the early revolutions focused on a single demand for political independence, whereas the later revolutions had various goals.

13. In the painting which follows, the artist J.M.W. Turner attempted to portray

(A) the business of life and the inability of humans to compete with machines.

(B) the positive impact that industry had had on landscapes as new bridges and buildings were erected.

(C) the progress of new industries as they made a physical mark on nature.

(D) the importance of humans as they celebrated their achievements.

(E) the basic values of the Realists as they confronted the ills of society.

14. "To dedicate myself wholly and forever to the endeavor with them to constitute Italy one free, independent, republican nation." This statement by Giuseppe Mazzini

(A) is the embodiment of the ideals of the utopian socialists.

(B) exemplifies his militaristic desire to conquer and control Italy.

(C) was the impetus that led Metternich to invade Italy countless times.

(D) embodies the nationalist sentiment of the day.

(E) coupled with the Catholic Church's overt support of Mazzini inflamed fears that the pope would attempt to upset the balance of power.

15. The French Revolution of 1848

(A) caused widespread fear of France and prompted Metternich's forces to occupy the country for two years in order to suppress further unrest.

(B) established a stronger, more limited monarchy that could counterbalance the revolutionary tendencies of the French people.

(C) ultimately failed to make any lasting changes to the country as the king was reestablished on the throne.

(D) finally solved the problems of both the liberals and the conservatives and realized peace within the state.

(E) established an effective republic that was later overthrown by a dictatorship.

Proclamation of the German Empire in the Hall of Mirrors in the palace of Versailles

An Age of Nationalism and Realism, 1850–1871

CHAPTER OUTLINE AND FOCUS QUESTIONS

The France of Napoleon III

Q What were the characteristics of Napoleon III's government, and how did his foreign policy contribute to the unification of Italy and Germany?

National Unification: Italy and Germany

Q What actions did Cavour and Bismarck take to bring about unification in Italy and Germany, respectively, and what role did war play in their efforts?

Nation Building and Reform: The National State in Midcentury

Q What efforts for reform occurred in the Austrian Empire, Russia, and Great Britain between 1850 and 1870, and how successful were they in alleviating each nation's problems?

Industrialization and the Marxist Response

Q What were the main ideas of Karl Marx?

Science and Culture in an Age of Realism

Q How did the belief that the world should be viewed realistically manifest itself in science, art, and literature in the second half of the nineteenth century?

┌─ CRITICAL THINKING ═══════════════

Q What was the relationship between nationalism and reform between 1850 and 1871?

└──────────────────────────────────

ACROSS THE EUROPEAN continent, the revolutions of 1848 had failed. The forces of liberalism and nationalism appeared to have been decisively defeated as authoritarian governments reestablished their control almost everywhere in Europe by 1850. And yet within twenty-five years, many of the goals sought by the liberals and nationalists during the first half of the nineteenth century seemed to have been achieved. National unity became a reality in Italy and Germany, and many European states were governed by constitutional monarchies, even though the constitutional-parliamentary features were frequently facades.

All the same, these goals were not achieved by liberal and nationalist leaders but by a new generation of conservative leaders who were proud of being practitioners of *Realpolitik* (ray-AHL-poh-lee-teek), the "politics of reality." One reaction to the failure of the revolutions of 1848 had been a new toughness of mind as people prided themselves on being realistic in their handling of power. The new conservative leaders used armies and power politics to achieve their foreign policy goals. And they did not hesitate to manipulate liberal means to achieve conservative ends at home. Nationalism had failed as a revolutionary movement in 1848–1849, but between 1850 and 1871, these new leaders found a variety of ways to pursue nation building. Winning wars was, however, only one means of nation building as rulers sought to improve the economy and foster cultural policies that led the citizens of their states to a greater sense of national identity.

One of the most successful of these new conservative leaders was the Prussian Otto von Bismarck, who used both astute diplomacy and war to achieve the unification of Germany. On January 18, 1871, Bismarck and six hundred German princes, nobles, and generals filled the Hall of Mirrors in the palace of Versailles, outside Paris. The Prussian army had defeated the French, and the assembled notables were gathered for the proclamation of the Prussian king as the new emperor of a united German state. When the words "Long live His Imperial Majesty, the Emperor William!" rang out, the assembled guests took up the cry. One participant wrote, "A thundering cheer, repeated at least six times, thrilled through the room while the flags and standards waved over the head of the new emperor of Germany." European rulers who feared the power of the new German state were not so cheerful. "The balance of power has been entirely destroyed," declared the British prime minister.

The France of Napoleon III

Q **Focus Question:** What were the characteristics of Napoleon III's government, and how did his foreign policy contribute to the unification of Italy and Germany?

After 1850, a new generation of conservative leaders came to power in Europe. Foremost among them was Napoleon III (1852–1870) of France, who taught his contemporaries how authoritarian governments could use liberal and nationalistic forces to bolster their own power. It was a lesson others quickly learned.

Louis Napoleon: Toward the Second Empire

Even after his election as the president of the French Republic, many of his contemporaries dismissed "Napoleon the Small" as a nonentity whose success was due only to his name. But Louis Napoleon was a clever politician who was especially astute at understanding the popular forces of his day. After his election, he was clear about his desire to have personal power. He wrote, "I shall never submit to any attempt to influence me.... I follow only the promptings of my mind and heart.... Nothing, nothing shall trouble the clear vision of my judgment or the strength of my resolution."[1]

Louis Napoleon was a patient man. For three years, he persevered in winning the support of the French people, and when the National Assembly rejected his wish to revise the constitution and be allowed to stand for reelection, Louis used troops to seize control of the government on December 1, 1851. After restoring universal male suffrage, Louis Napoleon asked the French people to restructure the government by electing him president for ten years (see the box on p. 672). By an overwhelming majority, 7.5 million yes votes to 640,000 no votes, they agreed. A year later, on November 21, 1852, Louis Napoleon returned to the people to ask for the restoration of the empire. This time, 97 percent responded affirmatively, and on December 2, 1852, Louis Napoleon assumed the title of Napoleon III (the first Napoleon had abdicated in favor of his son, Napoleon II, on April 6, 1814). The Second Empire had begun.

The Second Napoleonic Empire

The government of Napoleon III was clearly authoritarian in a Bonapartist sense. Louis Napoleon had asked, "Since France has carried on for fifty years only by virtue of the administrative, military, judicial, religious and financial organization of the Consulate and Empire, why should she not also adopt the political institutions of that period?"[2] As chief of state, Napoleon III controlled the armed forces, police, and civil service. Only he could introduce legislation and declare war. The Legislative Corps gave an appearance

Emperor Napoleon III. On December 2, 1852, Louis Napoleon took the title of Napoleon III and then proceeded to create an authoritarian monarchy. As opposition to his policies intensified in the 1860s, Napoleon III began to liberalize his government. A disastrous military defeat at the hands of Prussia in 1870–1871, however, brought the collapse of his regime.

The Practice of *Realpolitik:* Two Approaches

During the mid-nineteenth century, a new generation of conservative leaders emerged who were proud of being practitioners of *Realpolitik,* the "politics of reality." Two of the most prominent were Louis Napoleon of France and Otto von Bismarck of Prussia. The first selection is taken from Louis Napoleon's proclamation to the French people in 1851, asking them to approve his actions after his coup d'état on December 1, 1851. The second and third selections are excerpts from Bismarck's famous "iron and blood" speech to a committee of the Prussian Reichstag and his 1888 speech to the German Reichstag on Germany's need for military preparation.

⟶ ⟶

Louis Napoleon, Proclamation to the People, 1851

Frenchmen! The present situation cannot last much longer. Each passing day increases the danger to the country. The [National] Assembly, which ought to be the firmest supporter of order, has become a center of conspiracies.... It attacks the authority that I hold directly from the people; it encourages all evil passions; it jeopardizes the peace of France: I have dissolved it and I make the whole people judge between it and me....

I therefore make a loyal appeal to the whole nation, and I say to you: If you wish to continue this state of uneasiness which degrades us and makes our future uncertain, choose another in my place, for I no longer wish an authority which is powerless to do good, makes me responsible for acts I cannot prevent, and chains me to the helm when I see the vessel speeding toward the abyss....

Persuaded that the instability of authority and the preponderance of a single Assembly are permanent causes of trouble and discord, I submit to you the following fundamental bases of a constitution which the Assemblies will develop later.

1. A responsible chief elected for ten years.
2. Ministers dependent upon the executive power alone.
3. A Council of State composed of the most distinguished men to prepare the laws and discuss them before the legislative body.
4. A legislative body to discuss and vote the laws, elected by universal [male] suffrage....

This system, created by the First Consul [Napoleon I] at the beginning of the century, has already given France calm and prosperity; it will guarantee them to her again.

Such is my profound conviction. If you share it, declare that fact by your votes. If, on the contrary, you prefer a government without force, monarchical or republican, borrowed from I know not what past or from which chimerical future, reply in the negative....

If I do not obtain a majority of your votes, I shall then convoke a new assembly, and I shall resign to it the mandate that I received from you. But if you believe that the cause of which my name is the symbol, that is, France regenerated by the revolution of 1789 and organized by the Emperor, is forever yours, proclaim it by sanctioning the powers that I ask from you. Then France and Europe will be saved from anarchy, obstacles will be removed, rivalries will disappear, for all will respect the decree of Providence in the decision of the people.

Bismarck, Speech to the Prussian Reichstag, 1862

...It is true that we can hardly escape complications in Germany, although we do not seek them. Germany does not look to Prussia's liberalism, but to her power. The south German States—Bavaria, Württemberg, and Baden—would like to indulge in liberalism, and because of that no one will assign Prussia's role to them! Prussia must collect her forces and hold them in reserve for an opportune moment, which has already come and gone several times. Since the Treaty of Vienna, our frontiers have not been favorably designed for a healthy body politic. Not by speeches and majorities will the great questions of the day be decided—that was the mistake of 1848 and 1849—but by iron and blood.

Bismarck, Speech to the German Reichstag, 1888

When I say that it is our duty to endeavor to be ready at all times and for all emergencies, I imply that we must make greater exertions than other people for the same purpose, because of our geographical position. We are situated in the heart of Europe, and have at least three fronts open to an attack. France has only her eastern, and Russia only her western frontier where they may be attacked. We are also more exposed to the dangers of a coalition than any other nation, as is proved by the whole development of history, by our geographical position, and the lesser degree of cohesiveness, which until now has characterized the German nation

(continued)

in comparison with others. God has placed us where we are prevented, thanks to our neighbors, from growing lazy and dull. He has placed by our side the most war-like and restless of all nations, the French, and He has permitted warlike inclinations to grow strong in Russia, where formerly they existed to a lesser degree. Thus we are given the spur, so to speak, from both sides, and are compelled to exertions which we should perhaps not be making otherwise. ▷

Q Why did Louis Napoleon's argument to the French people have such a strong popular appeal? What are the similarities in the practice of *Realpolitik* by these two leaders? What are the noticeable differences in their approaches? Are the similarities more important than the differences? Why or why not? What can you learn about *Realpolitik* from these three selections?

of representative government since its members were elected by universal male suffrage for six-year terms. But they could neither initiate legislation nor affect the budget.

EARLY DOMESTIC POLICIES The first five years of Napoleon III's reign were a spectacular success as he reaped the benefits of worldwide economic prosperity as well as of some of his own economic policies. Napoleon believed in using the resources of government to stimulate the national economy and took many steps to encourage industrial growth. Government subsidies were used to foster the construction of railroads, harbors, roads, and canals. The major French railway lines were completed during Napoleon's reign, and industrial expansion was evident in the tripling of iron production. In his concern to reduce tensions and improve the social welfare of the nation, Napoleon provided hospitals and free medicine for the workers and advocated better housing for the working class.

In the midst of this economic expansion, Napoleon III undertook a vast reconstruction of the city of Paris. Under the direction of Baron Haussmann (HOWSS-mun), the medieval Paris of narrow streets and old city walls was destroyed and replaced by a modern Paris of broad boulevards, spacious buildings, circular plazas, public squares, an underground sewage system, a new public water supply, and gaslights. The new Paris served a military as well as an aesthetic purpose: broad streets made it more difficult for would-be insurrectionists to throw up barricades and easier for troops to move rapidly through the city to put down revolts.

LIBERALIZATION OF THE REGIME In the 1860s, as opposition to some of the emperor's policies began to mount, Napoleon III liberalized his regime. He reached out to the working class by legalizing trade unions and granting them the right to strike. He also began to liberalize the political process. The Legislative Corps had been closely controlled during the 1850s. In the 1860s, opposition candidates were allowed greater freedom to campaign, and the Legislative Corps was permitted more say in affairs of state, including debate over the budget. Napoleon's liberalization policies did serve initially to strengthen the hand of the government. In a plebiscite in May 1870 on whether to accept a new constitution that might have inaugurated a

parliamentary regime, the French people gave Napoleon another resounding victory. This triumph was short-lived, however. Foreign policy failures led to growing criticism, and war with Prussia in 1870 turned out to be the death blow for Napoleon III's regime (see "The Franco-Prussian War" later in this chapter).

Foreign Policy: The Mexican Adventure

Napoleon III was considerably less accomplished at dealing with foreign policy, especially his imperialistic adventure in Mexico. Seeking to dominate Mexican markets for French goods, the emperor sent French troops to Mexico in 1861 to join British and Spanish forces in protecting their interests in the midst of the upheaval caused by a struggle between liberal and conservative Mexican factions. Although the British and Spanish withdrew their troops after order had been restored, French forces remained, and in 1864, Napoleon III installed Archduke Maximilian of Austria, his handpicked choice, as the new emperor of Mexico. When the French troops were needed in Europe, Maximilian became an emperor without an army. He surrendered to liberal Mexican forces in May 1867 and was executed in June. His execution was a blow to the prestige of the French emperor.

Foreign Policy: The Crimean War

Napoleon III's participation in the Crimean War (1854–1856) had been more rewarding. As heir to the Napoleonic empire, Napoleon III was motivated by the desire to free France from the restrictions of the peace settlements of 1814–1815 and to make France the chief arbiter of Europe. In the decline of the Ottoman Empire, he saw an opportunity to take steps toward these goals.

THE OTTOMAN EMPIRE The Crimean War was yet another attempt to answer the Eastern Question: Who would be the chief beneficiaries of the disintegration of the Ottoman Empire? In the seventeenth century, the Ottoman Empire had controlled southeastern Europe, but in 1699 it had lost Hungary, Transylvania, Croatia, and Slovenia to the expanding Austrian Empire. The Russian Empire to its north also encroached on the Ottoman

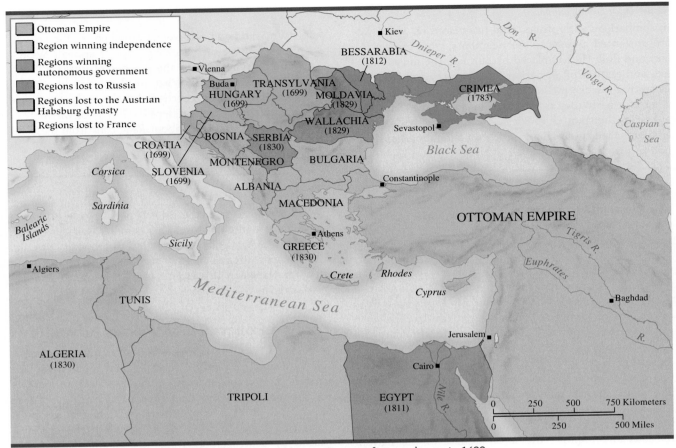

Legend:
- Ottoman Empire
- Region winning independence
- Regions winning autonomous government
- Regions lost to Russia
- Regions lost to the Austrian Habsburg dynasty
- Regions lost to France

MAP 22.1 Decline of the Ottoman Empire. The decline in Ottoman fortunes began in 1699 with major losses to the Austrian Empire. The slide accelerated in the nineteenth century with nationalist revolts in the European provinces and defeat in the Crimean War. Being on the losing side in World War I would complete its destruction.

Q *What is the relationship between distance from Constantinople and date of independence, and how can you explain it?*

View an animated version of this map or related maps on the CourseMate website.

Empire by seizing the Crimea in 1783 and Bessarabia in 1812 (see Map 22.1).

By the beginning of the nineteenth century, the Ottoman Empire had entered a fresh period of decline. A nationalist revolt had gained independence for Greece in 1830. Serbia claimed autonomy in 1827, which was recognized by the Ottoman Empire in 1830. The Russians had obtained a protectorate over the Danubian provinces of Moldavia and Wallachia in 1829.

As Ottoman authority over the outlying territories in southeastern Europe waned, European governments began to take an active interest in the empire's apparent demise. Russia's proximity to the Ottoman Empire and the religious bonds between the Russians and the Greek Orthodox Christians in Ottoman-dominated southeastern Europe naturally gave it special opportunities to enlarge its sphere of influence. Other European powers not only feared Russian ambitions but also had objectives of their own in the area. Austria craved more land in the Balkans, a desire that inevitably meant conflict with Russia, and

France and Britain were interested in commercial opportunities and naval bases in the eastern Mediterranean.

WAR IN THE CRIMEA War erupted between Russia and the Ottoman Empire in 1853 when the Russians demanded the right to protect Christian shrines in Palestine, a privilege that had already been extended to the French. When the Ottomans refused, the Russians occupied Moldavia and Wallachia. Failure to resolve the dispute by negotiations led the Ottoman Empire to declare war on Russia on October 4, 1853. The following year, on March 28, Great Britain and France declared war on Russia.

Why did Britain and France take that step? Concern over the prospect of an upset in the balance of power was clearly one reason. The British in particular feared that an aggressive Russia would try to profit from the obvious weakness of the Ottoman government by seizing Ottoman territory or the long-coveted Dardanelles. Such a move would make Russia the major power in eastern Europe and would enable the Russians to challenge British naval

Florence Nightingale. Florence Nightingale is shown caring for wounded British soldiers in the military hospital at Scutari during the Crimean War. After a British journalist, W. H. Russell, issued a scathing denunciation of the quality of medical care afforded to wounded British soldiers, the British government allowed Nightingale to take a group of nurses to the Crimean warfront. Through her efforts in the Crimean War, Nightingale helped make nursing an admirable profession for middle-class women. At the right is a photograph of Nightingale.

control of the eastern Mediterranean. Napoleon III felt that the Russians had insulted France, first at the Congress of Vienna and now by their insistence on replacing the French as the protectors of Christians living in the Ottoman Empire. The French also feared the collapse of the Ottoman Empire and the growth of Russian influence there. Although the Russians assumed that they could count on support from the Austrians (since Russian troops had saved the Austrian government in 1849), the Austrian prime minister blithely observed, "We will astonish the world by our ingratitude," and Austria remained neutral. Since the Austrians had perceived that it was not in their best interest to intervene, Russia had to fight alone.

Poorly planned and poorly fought, the Crimean War is perhaps best remembered for the suicidal charge of the British Light Brigade at the Battle of Balaklava. Britain and France decided to attack Russia's Crimean peninsula in the Black Sea. After a long siege and at a terrible cost in manpower for both sides, the main Russian fortress of Sevastopol fell in September 1855, six months after the death of Tsar Nicholas I. His successor, Alexander II, soon sued for peace. By the Treaty of Paris, signed in March 1856, Russia was forced to give up Bessarabia at the mouth of the Danube and accept the neutrality of the Black Sea. In addition, the principalities of Moldavia and Wallachia were placed under the protection of all five great powers.

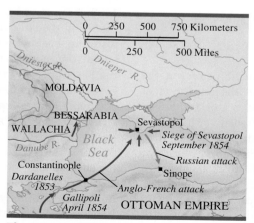

The Crimean War

The Crimean War proved costly to both sides. More than 250,000 soldiers died in the war, with 60 percent of the deaths coming from disease (especially cholera). Even more would have died on the British side if it had not been for the efforts of Florence Nightingale (1820–1910). Her insistence on strict sanitary conditions saved many lives and helped make nursing a profession of trained, middle-class women.

The Crimean War broke up long-standing European power relationships and effectively destroyed the Concert of Europe. Austria and Russia, the two chief powers maintaining the status quo in the first half of the nineteenth century, were now enemies because of Austria's unwillingness to support Russia in the war. Russia, defeated, humiliated, and weakened by the obvious failure of its serf-armies, withdrew from European affairs for the next two decades to set its house in order. Great Britain, disillusioned by its role in the war, also pulled back from Continental affairs. Austria, paying the price for its neutrality, was now without friends among the great powers. Not until the 1870s were new combinations formed to replace those that had disappeared, and in the meantime, the European international situation remained fluid. Leaders who were willing to pursue the "politics of reality" found themselves in a situation rife with opportunity. It was this new international situation that made possible the unification of Italy and Germany.

MAP 22.2 The Unification of Italy. Piedmont under the able guidance of Count Camillo di Cavour provided the nucleus for Italian unification. Alliances with France and Prussia, combined with the military actions of republican nationalists like Giuseppe Garibaldi, led to complete unification in 1870.

Q *Taking geographic factors and size of population into account, which of the countries shown on this map would likely have posed the greatest military threat to the new Italian state?*

View an animated version of this map or related maps on the CourseMate website.

National Unification: Italy and Germany

Q FOCUS QUESTION: What actions did Cavour and Bismarck take to bring about unification in Italy and Germany, respectively, and what role did war play in their efforts?

The breakdown of the Concert of Europe opened the way for the Italians and the Germans to establish national states. Their successful unifications transformed the power structure of the European continent. Europe would be dealing with the consequences well into the twentieth century.

The Unification of Italy

In 1850, Austria was still the dominant power on the Italian peninsula. After the failure of the revolution of 1848–1849, a growing number of advocates for Italian unification focused on the northern Italian state of Piedmont as their best hope to achieve their goal. The royal house of Savoy ruled the kingdom of Piedmont, which also included the island of Sardinia (see Map 22.2). Although soundly defeated by the Austrians in 1848–1849, Piedmont under King Charles Albert had made a valiant effort; it seemed reasonable that Piedmont would now assume the leading role in the cause of national unity. The little state

seemed unlikely to supply the needed leadership, however, until the new king, Victor Emmanuel II (1849–1878), named Count Camillo di Cavour (kuh-MEEL-oh dee kuh-VOOR) (1810–1861) as his prime minister in 1852.

THE LEADERSHIP OF CAVOUR Cavour was a liberal-minded nobleman who had made a fortune in agriculture and went on to make even more money in banking, railroads, and shipping. Cavour was a moderate who favored constitutional government. He was a consummate politician with the ability to persuade others of the rightness of his own convictions. After becoming prime minister in 1852, he pursued a policy of economic expansion, encouraging the building of roads, canals, and railroads and fostering business enterprise by expanding credit and stimulating investment in new industries. The growth in the Piedmontese economy and the subsequent increase in government revenues enabled Cavour to pour money into equipping a large army.

Cavour had no illusions about Piedmont's military strength and was well aware that he could not challenge Austria directly. He would need the French. In 1858, Cavour came to an agreement with Napoleon III. The emperor agreed to ally with Piedmont in driving the Austrians out of Italy. Once the Austrians were driven out, Italy would be reorganized. Piedmont would be extended into the kingdom of Upper Italy by adding Lombardy,

Venetia, Parma, Modena, and part of the Papal States to its territory. In compensation for its efforts, France would receive the Piedmontese provinces of Nice and Savoy. A kingdom of Central Italy would be created for Napoleon III's cousin, Prince Napoleon, who would be married to the younger daughter of King Victor Emmanuel. This agreement between Napoleon and Cavour seemed to assure the French ruler of the opportunity to control Italy. Confident that the plan would work, Cavour provoked the Austrians into invading Piedmont in April 1859.

In the initial stages of fighting, it was the French who were largely responsible for defeating the Austrians in two major battles at Magenta and Solferino. It was also the French who made peace with Austria on July 11, 1859, without informing their Italian ally. Why did Napoleon withdraw so hastily? For one thing, he realized that despite two losses, the Austrian army had not yet been defeated; the struggle might be longer and more costly than he had anticipated. Moreover, the Prussians were mobilizing in support of Austria, and Napoleon III had no desire to take on two enemies at once. As a result of Napoleon's peace with Austria, Piedmont received only Lombardy; Venetia remained under Austrian control. Cavour was furious at the French perfidy, but events in northern Italy now turned in his favor. Soon after the war with Austria had begun, some northern Italian states, namely, Parma, Modena, Tuscany, and part of the Papal States, had been taken over by nationalists. In plebiscites held in 1860, these states agreed to join Piedmont. Napoleon agreed to the annexations in return for Nice and Savoy.

THE EFFORTS OF GARIBALDI Meanwhile, in southern Italy, a new leader of Italian unification had come to the fore. Giuseppe Garibaldi (joo-ZEP-pay gar-uh-BAHL-dee) (1807–1882), a dedicated Italian patriot who had supported Mazzini and the republican cause of Young Italy, raised an army of a thousand Red Shirts, as his volunteers were called because of their distinctive dress, and on May 11, 1860, landed in Sicily, where a revolt had broken out against the Bourbon king of the Two Sicilies.

Although his forces were greatly outnumbered, Garibaldi's daring tactics won the day (see the box on p. 678). By the end of July 1860, most of Sicily had been pacified under Garibaldi's control. In August, Garibaldi and his forces crossed over to the mainland and began a victorious march up the Italian peninsula. Naples and the Two Sicilies fell in early September. At this point, Cavour reentered the scene. Aware that Garibaldi planned to march on Rome, Cavour feared that such a move would bring war with France as the defender of papal interests. Moreover, Garibaldi and his men favored a democratic republicanism; Cavour did not and acted quickly to preempt Garibaldi. The Piedmontese army invaded the Papal States and, bypassing Rome, moved into the kingdom of Naples. Ever the patriot, Garibaldi chose to yield to Cavour's fait accompli rather than provoke a civil war and retired to his farm. Plebiscites in the Papal States and the Two Sicilies resulted in overwhelming support for union with

Piedmont. On March 17, 1861, the new kingdom of Italy was proclaimed under a centralized government subordinated to the control of Piedmont and King Victor Emmanuel II (1861–1878) of the house of Savoy. Worn out by his efforts, Cavour died three months later.

Despite the proclamation of the new kingdom, the task of unification was not yet complete since Venetia in the

Garibaldi Arrives in Sicily. The Italian nationalists' dream of a united Italian state finally became a reality by 1870. An important figure in the cause of unification was Giuseppe Garibaldi, a determined Italian patriot. Garibaldi is shown here in his red shirt in a portrait done by Silvestro Lega.

© The Art Archive/Museo Civico, Modigliana/Alfredo Dagli Orti

Garibaldi and Romantic Nationalism

Giuseppe Garibaldi was one of the most colorful figures involved in the unification of Italy. Accompanied by only one thousand of his famous Red Shirts, the Italian soldier of fortune left Genoa on the night of May 5, 1860, for an invasion of the kingdom of the Two Sicilies. The ragged band entered Palermo, the chief city on the island of Sicily, on May 31. This selection is taken from an account by a correspondent for the *Times* of London, the Hungarian-born Nandor Eber.

✦ ═◆═ ✦

London Times, June 13, 1860

PALERMO, May 31—Anyone in search of violent emotions cannot do better than set off at once for Palermo. However blasé he may be, or however milk-and-water his blood, I promise it will be stirred up. He will be carried away by the tide of popular feeling....

In the afternoon Garibaldi made a tour of inspection round the town. I was there, but find it really impossible to give you a faint idea of the manner in which he was received everywhere. It was one of those triumphs which seem to be almost too much for a man.... The popular idol, Garibaldi, in his red flannel shirt, with a loose colored handkerchief around his neck, and his worn "wide-awake" [a soft-brimmed felt hat], was walking on foot among those cheering, laughing, crying, mad thousands; and all his few followers could do was to prevent him from being bodily carried off the ground. The people threw themselves forward to kiss his hands, or, at least, to touch the hem of his garment, as if it contained the panacea for all their past and perhaps coming suffering. Children were brought up, and mothers asked on their knees for his blessing; and all this while the object of this idolatry was calm and smiling as when in the deadliest fire, taking up the children and kissing them, trying to quiet the crowd, stopping at every moment to hear a long complaint of houses burned and property sacked by the retreating soldiers, giving good advice, comforting, and promising that all damages should be paid for....

One might write volumes of horrors on the vandalism already committed, for every one of the hundred ruins has its story of brutality and inhumanity.... In these small houses a dense population is crowded together even in ordinary times. A shell falling on one, and crushing and burying the inmates, was sufficient to make people abandon the neighboring one and take refuge a little further on, shutting themselves up in the cellars. When the Royalists retired they set fire to those of the houses which had escaped the shells, and numbers were thus burned alive in their hiding places....

If you can stand the exhalation, try and go inside the ruins, for it is only there that you will see what the thing means and you will not have to search long before you stumble over the remains of a human body, a leg sticking out here, an arm there, a black face staring at you a little further on. You are startled by a rustle. You look round and see half a dozen gorged rats scampering off in all directions, or you see a dog trying to make his escape over the ruins.... I only wonder that the sight of these scenes does not convert every man in the town into a tiger and every woman into a fury. But these people have been so long ground down and demoralized that their nature seems to have lost the power of reaction. ⊨

Q Why did Garibaldi become such a hero to the Italian people? How does Garibaldi's comportment as a political and military leader prefigure the conduct of later revolutionary military leaders and activists?

---

north was still held by Austria and Rome was under papal control, supported by French troops. To attack either one meant war with a major European state, which the Italian army was not prepared to handle. It was the Prussian army that indirectly completed the task of Italian unification. In the Austro-Prussian War of 1866, the new Italian state became an ally of Prussia. Although the Italian army was defeated by the Austrians, Prussia's victory left the Italians with Venetia. In 1870, the Franco-Prussian War resulted in the withdrawal of French troops from Rome. The Italian army then annexed the city on September 20, 1870, and Rome became the new capital of the united Italian state.

The Unification of Germany

After the failure of the Frankfurt Assembly to achieve German unification in 1848–1849, German nationalists focused on Austria and Prussia as the only two states powerful enough to dominate German affairs. Austria had long controlled the existing Germanic Confederation, but Prussian power had grown, strongly reinforced by economic expansion in the 1850s. Prussia had formed the **Zollverein** (TSOHL-fuh-ryn), a German customs union, in 1834. By eliminating tolls on rivers and roads among member states, the *Zollverein* had stimulated trade and added to the prosperity of its member states. By 1853, all the German states except Austria had joined the Prussian-dominated customs union. A number of middle-class liberals now began to see Prussia in a new light; some even looked openly to Prussia to bring about the unification of Germany.

In 1848, Prussia had framed a constitution that at least had the appearance of constitutional monarchy in that it had established a bicameral legislature with the lower house elected by universal male suffrage. The voting population, however, was divided into three classes determined by the amount of taxes they paid, a system that allowed the biggest taxpayers to gain the most seats. Unintentionally, by 1859, this system had allowed control of the lower house to fall largely into the hands of the rising middle classes, whose numbers were growing as a result of continuing industrialization. Their desire was to have a real parliamentary system, but the king's executive power remained too strong; royal ministers answered for their actions only to the king, not the parliament. Nevertheless, the parliament had been granted important legislative and taxation powers on which it could build.

In 1861, King Frederick William IV died and was succeeded by his brother. King William I (1861–1888) had definite ideas about the Prussian army because of his own military training. He and his advisers believed that the army was in dire need of change if Prussia was to remain a great power. The king planned to double the size of the army and institute three years of compulsory military service for all young men.

Middle-class liberals in the parliament, while willing to have reform, feared compulsory military service because they believed the government would use it to inculcate obedience to the monarchy and strengthen the influence of the conservative-military clique in Prussia. When the Prussian legislature rejected the new military budget submitted to parliament in March 1862, William I appointed a new prime minister, Count Otto von Bismarck (1815–1898). Bismarck, regarded even by the king as too conservative, came to determine the course of modern German history. Until 1890, he dominated both German and European politics.

BISMARCK

Otto von Bismarck was born into the Junker class, the traditional, landowning aristocracy of Prussia, and remained loyal to it throughout his life. "I was born and raised as an aristocrat," he once said. As a university student, Bismarck indulged heartily in wine, women, and song yet managed to read widely in German history. After earning a law degree, he embarked on a career in the Prussian civil service but soon tired of bureaucratic, administrative routine and retired to manage his country estates. Comparing the civil servant to a musician in an orchestra, he responded, "I want to play the tune the way it sounds good to me or not at all. . . . My pride bids me command rather than obey."[3] In 1847, desirous of more excitement and power than he could find in the country, he reentered public life. Four years later, he began to build a base of diplomatic experience as the Prussian delegate to the parliament of the Germanic Confederation. This, combined with his experience as Prussian ambassador to Russia and later to France, gave him opportunities to acquire a wide knowledge of European affairs and to learn how to assess the character of rulers.

Because Bismarck succeeded in guiding Prussia's unification of Germany, it is often assumed that he had determined on a course of action that led precisely to that goal. That is hardly the case. Bismarck was a consummate politician and opportunist. He was not a political gambler

Otto von Bismarck. Otto von Bismarck played a major role in leading Prussia to achieve the unification of the German states into a new German Empire, proclaimed on January 18, 1871. Bismarck then became chancellor of the new Germany. This photograph of Bismarck was taken in 1874, when he was at the height of his power and prestige.

but a moderate who waged war only when all other diplomatic alternatives had been exhausted and when he was reasonably sure that all the military and diplomatic advantages were on his side. Bismarck has often been portrayed as the ultimate realist, the foremost nineteenth-century practitioner of **_Realpolitik._** He was also quite open about his strong dislike of anyone who opposed him. He said one morning to his wife, "I could not sleep the whole night; I hated throughout the whole night."

In 1862, Bismarck resubmitted the army appropriations bill to parliament along with a passionate appeal to his liberal opponents: "Germany does not look to Prussia's liberalism, but to her power. . . . Not by speeches and majorities will the great questions of the day be decided—that was the mistake of 1848–1849—but by iron and blood"[4] (see the box on p. 672). His opponents were not impressed and rejected the bill once again. Bismarck went ahead, collected the taxes, and reorganized the army anyway, blaming the liberals for causing the breakdown of constitutional government. From 1862 to 1866, Bismarck governed Prussia by largely ignoring parliament. Unwilling to revolt, parliament did nothing. In the meantime,

MAP 22.3 **The Unification of Germany.** Count Otto von Bismarck, the Prussian prime minister, skillfully combined domestic policies with wars with Denmark, Austria, and France to achieve the creation of the German Empire in 1871.

Q *From the perspective of Prussia's increasing its military power and ability to rule all parts of its lands, which was more important: formation of the North German Confederation or absorption of the South German Confederation?*

View an animated version of this map or related maps on the CourseMate website.

opposition to his domestic policy determined Bismarck on an active foreign policy, which in 1864 led to his first war.

THE DANISH WAR (1864) In the three wars that he waged, Bismarck's victories were as much diplomatic and political as they were military. Before war was declared, Bismarck always saw to it that Prussia would be fighting only one power and that that opponent was isolated diplomatically.

The Danish War arose over the duchies of Schleswig (SHLESS-vik) and Holstein (HOHL-shtyn). In 1863, contrary to international treaty, the Danish government moved to incorporate the two duchies into Denmark. German nationalists were outraged since both duchies had large German populations and were regarded as German

states. The diet of the Germanic Confederation urged its member states to send troops against Denmark, but Bismarck did not care to subject Prussian policy to the Austrian-dominated German parliament. Instead, he persuaded the Austrians to join Prussia in declaring war on Denmark on February 1, 1864. The Danes were quickly defeated and surrendered Schleswig and Holstein to the victors (see Map 22.3). Austria and Prussia then agreed to divide the administration of the two duchies; Prussia took Schleswig while Austria administered Holstein. The plan was Bismarck's. By this time, Bismarck had come to the realization that for Prussia to expand its power by dominating the northern, largely Protestant part of the Germanic Confederation, Austria would have to be excluded from German affairs or, less likely, be willing to accept Prussian domination of Germany. The joint administration of the two duchies offered plenty of opportunities to create friction with Austria and provide a reason for war if it came to that. While he pursued negotiations with Austria, he also laid the foundations for the isolation of Austria.

THE AUSTRO-PRUSSIAN WAR (1866) Bismarck had no problem gaining Russia's agreement to remain neutral in the event of an Austro-Prussian war because Prussia had been the only great power to support Russia's repression of a Polish revolt in 1863. Napoleon III was a thornier problem, but Bismarck was able to buy his neutrality with vague promises of territory in the Rhineland. Finally, Bismarck made an alliance with the new Italian state and promised it Venetia in the event of Austrian defeat.

With the Austrians isolated, Bismarck used the joint occupation of Schleswig-Holstein to goad the Austrians into a war on June 14, 1866. Many Europeans, including Napoleon III, expected a quick Austrian victory, but they overlooked the effectiveness of the Prussian military reforms of the 1860s. The Prussian breech-loading needle gun had a much faster rate of fire than the Austrian muzzleloader, and a superior network of railroads enabled the Prussians to mass troops quickly. At Königgrätz (kur-nig-GRETS) (Sadowa) on July 3, the Austrian army was defeated. Looking ahead, Bismarck refused to create a hostile enemy by burdening Austria with a harsh peace as the Prussian king wanted. Austria lost no territory except Venetia to Italy but was excluded from German affairs. The German states north of the Main River were organized into the North German Confederation, controlled by Prussia. The southern German states, largely Catholic, remained independent but were coerced into signing military agreements with Prussia. In addition to Schleswig and Holstein, Prussia annexed Hanover and Hesse-Cassel because they had openly sided with Austria.

The Austrian war was a turning point in Prussian domestic affairs. After the war, Bismarck asked the Prussian parliament to pass a bill of indemnity, retroactively legalizing the taxes he had collected illegally since 1862. Even most of the liberals voted in favor of the bill because they had been won over by Bismarck's successful use of military power. With his victory over Austria and the creation of the North German Confederation, Bismarck had proved Napoleon III's dictum that nationalism and authoritarian government could be combined. In using nationalism to win support from liberals and prevent governmental reform, Bismarck showed that liberalism and nationalism, the two major forces of change in the early nineteenth century, could be separated.

He showed the same flexibility in the creation of a new constitution for the North German Confederation. Each German state kept its own local government, but the king of Prussia was head of the confederation, and the chancellor (Bismarck) was responsible directly to the king. Both the army and foreign policy remained in the hands of the king and his chancellor. Parliament consisted of two bodies: the Bundesrat (BOON-duhs-raht), or federal council, composed of delegates nominated by the states, and a lower house, the Reichstag, elected by universal male suffrage. Like Napoleon, Bismarck believed that the peasants and artisans who made up most of the population were conservative at heart and could be used to overcome the advantages of the liberals.

THE FRANCO-PRUSSIAN WAR (1870–1871) Bismarck and William I had achieved a major goal by 1866. Prussia now dominated all of northern Germany, and Austria had been excluded from any significant role in German affairs. Nevertheless, unsettled business led to new international complications and further change. Bismarck realized that France would never be content with a strong German state to its east because of the potential threat to French security. At the same time, after a series of setbacks, Napoleon III needed a diplomatic triumph to offset his serious domestic problems. The French were not happy with the turn of events in Germany and looked for opportunities to humiliate the Prussians.

After a successful revolution had deposed Queen Isabella II, the throne of Spain was offered to Prince Leopold of Hohenzollern-Sigmaringen (hoh-en-TSULL-urn-zig-mah-RING-un), a distant relative of the Hohenzollern king of Prussia. Bismarck welcomed this possibility for the same reason that the French objected to it. If Leopold were placed on the throne of Spain, France would be virtually encircled by members of the Hohenzollern dynasty. French objections caused King William I to force his relative to withdraw his candidacy. Bismarck was disappointed with the king's actions, but at this point, the French overreached. Not content with their diplomatic victory, they pushed William I to make a formal apology to France and promise never to allow Leopold to be a candidate again. When Bismarck received a telegram from the king informing him of the French request, Bismarck edited it to make it appear even more insulting to the French, knowing that the French would be angry and declare war. The French reacted as Bismarck expected they would and declared war on Prussia on July 15, 1870. The French prime minister remarked, "We go to war with a light heart."

Unfortunately for the French, a "light heart" was not enough. They proved no match for the better-led and better-organized Prussian forces. The southern German states honored their military alliances with Prussia and joined the war effort against the French. The Prussian armies advanced into France, and at Sedan on September 2, 1870, an entire French army and Napoleon III himself were captured. The Second French Empire collapsed, but the war was not yet over. After four months of bitter resistance, Paris finally capitulated on January 28, 1871, and an official peace treaty was signed in May. France had to pay an indemnity of 5 billion francs (about $1 billion) and give up the provinces of Alsace and Lorraine to the new German state, a loss that angered the French and left them burning for revenge.

Otto von Bismarck, Letter on the Capture of Napoleon III (1870)

King William I of Prussia	1861–1888
Bismarck becomes minister-president of Prussia	1862
Danish War	1864
Austro-Prussian War	1866
Battle of Königgrätz	1866 (July 3)
Franco-Prussian War	1870–1871
Battle of Sedan	1870 (September 2)
Fall of Paris	1871 (January 28)
German Empire is proclaimed	1871 (January 18)

Even before the war had ended, the southern German states had agreed to enter the North German Confederation. On January 18, 1871, in the Hall of Mirrors in Louis XIV's palace at Versailles, William I, with Bismarck standing at the foot of the throne, was proclaimed kaiser or emperor of the Second German Empire (the first was the medieval Holy Roman Empire). German unity had been achieved by the Prussian monarchy and the Prussian army. In a real sense, Germany had been merged into Prussia, not Prussia into Germany. German liberals also rejoiced. They had dreamed of unity and freedom, but the achievement of unity now seemed much more important. One old liberal proclaimed:

> I cannot shake off the impression of this hour. I am no devotee of Mars; I feel more attached to the goddess of beauty and the mother of graces than to the powerful god of war, but the trophies of war exercise a magic charm even upon the child of peace. One's view is involuntarily chained and one's spirit goes along with the boundless row of men who acclaim the god of the moment—success.[5]

The Prussian leadership of German unification meant the triumph of authoritarian, militaristic values over liberal, constitutional sentiments in the development of the new German state. With its industrial resources and military might, the new state had become the strongest power on the Continent. A new European balance of power was at hand.

Nation Building and Reform: The National State in Midcentury

 FOCUS QUESTION: What efforts for reform occurred in the Austrian Empire, Russia, and Great Britain between 1850 and 1870, and how successful were they in alleviating each nation's problems?

While European affairs were dominated by the unification of Italy and Germany, other states were also undergoing transformations (see Map 22.4). War, civil war, and changing political alignments served as catalysts for domestic reforms.

The Austrian Empire: Toward a Dual Monarchy

After the Habsburgs had crushed the revolutions of 1848–1849, they restored centralized, autocratic government to the empire. What seemed to be the only lasting result of the revolution of 1848 was the act of emancipation of September 7, 1848, that freed the serfs and eliminated all compulsory labor services. Nevertheless, the development of industrialization after 1850, especially in Vienna and the provinces of Bohemia and Galicia, served to bring economic and social change to the empire in the form of an urban proletariat, labor unrest, and a new industrial middle class.

In 1851, the revolutionary constitutions were abolished, and a system of centralized autocracy was imposed on the empire. Under the leadership of Alexander von Bach (1813–1893), local privileges were subordinated to a unified system of administration, law, and taxation implemented by German-speaking officials. Hungary was subjected to the rule of military officers, and the Catholic Church was declared the state church and given control of education. Economic troubles and war, however, soon brought change. After Austria's defeat in the Italian war in 1859, the Emperor Francis Joseph (1848–1916) attempted to establish an imperial parliament—the Reichsrat (RYKHSS-raht)—with a nominated upper house and an elected lower house of representatives. Although the system was supposed to provide representation for the nationalities of the empire, the complicated formula used for elections ensured the election of a German-speaking majority and thus served once again to alienate the ethnic minorities, particularly the Hungarians.

THE *AUSGLEICH* OF 1867 Only when military disaster struck again in the Austro-Prussian War did the Austrians deal with the fiercely nationalistic Hungarians. The result was the negotiated **Ausgleich** (OWSS-glykh), or Compromise, of 1867, which created the Dual Monarchy of Austria-Hungary. Each part of the empire now had a constitution, its own bicameral legislature, its own governmental machinery for domestic affairs, and its own capital (Vienna for Austria and Buda—soon to be united with Pest, across the river—for Hungary). Holding the two states together were a single monarch (Francis Joseph was emperor of Austria and king of Hungary) and a common army, foreign policy, and system of finances. In domestic affairs, the Hungarians had become an independent nation. The *Ausgleich* did not, however, satisfy the other nationalities that made up the multinational Austro-Hungarian Empire (see Map 22.5). The Dual Monarchy simply enabled the German-speaking Austrians and Hungarian Magyars to dominate the minorities,

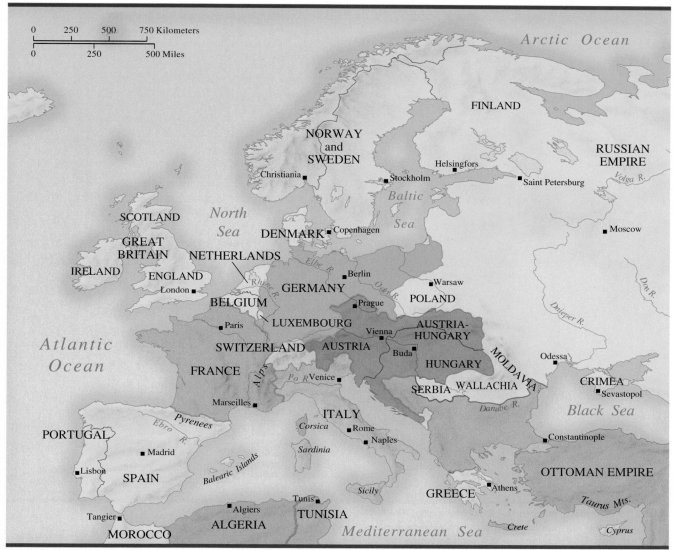

MAP 22.4 Europe in 1871. By 1871, most of the small states of Europe had been absorbed into larger ones, leaving the major powers uncomfortably rubbing shoulders with one another. Meanwhile, the power equation was shifting: the German Empire increased in power while Austria-Hungary and the Ottoman Empire declined.

 Of the great powers, which had the greatest overall exposure to the others in terms of shared borders and sea access?

especially the Slavic peoples (Poles, Croats, Czechs, Serbs, Slovaks, Slovenes, and Little Russians), in their respective states. As the Hungarian nationalist Louis Kossuth remarked, "Dualism is the alliance of the conservative, reactionary and any apparently liberal elements in Hungary with those of the Austrian Germans who despise liberty, for the oppression of the other nationalities and races."[6] The nationalities problem persisted until the demise of the empire at the end of World War I.

Imperial Russia

Russia's defeat in the Crimean War at the hands of the British and French revealed the blatant deficiencies behind the facade of absolute power and made it clear even to staunch conservatives that Russia was falling hopelessly behind the western European powers. Tsar Alexander II (1855–1881), who came to power in the midst of the Crimean War, turned his energies to a serious overhaul of the Russian system.

Serfdom was the most burdensome problem in tsarist Russia. The continuing subjugation of millions of peasants to the land and their landlords was an obviously corrupt and failing system. Reduced to antiquated methods of production based on serf labor, Russian landowners were economically pressed and unable to compete with foreign agriculture. The serfs, who formed the backbone of the Russian infantry, were uneducated and consequently

MAP 22.5   Ethnic Groups in the Dual Monarchy, 1867. Nationalism continued to be a problem in the Austrian Empire after the suppression of the 1848–1849 revolutions. Military defeats led Emperor Francis Joseph to create the Dual Monarchy, giving Hungary power over its domestic affairs. The demands of other ethnic minorities went largely unmet, however.

Q *Which ethnic group was most widely dispersed throughout the Dual Monarchy?*

increasingly unable to deal with the more complex machines and weapons of war. Then, too, peasant dissatisfaction still led to local peasant revolts that disrupted the countryside. Alexander II seemed to recognize the inevitable: "The existing order of serfdom," he told a group of Moscow nobles, "cannot remain unchanged. It is better to abolish serfdom from above than to wait until it is abolished from below."

ABOLITION OF SERFDOM   On March 3, 1861, Alexander issued his emancipation edict (see the box on p. 686). Peasants could now own property, marry as they chose, and bring suits in the law courts. Nevertheless, the benefits of emancipation were limited. The government provided land for the peasants by purchasing it from the

landowners, but the landowners often chose to keep the best lands. The Russian peasants soon found that they had inadequate amounts of good arable land to support themselves, a situation that worsened as the peasant population increased rapidly in the second half of the nineteenth century.

Nor were the peasants completely free. The state compensated the landowners for the land given to the peasants, but the peasants were expected to repay the state in long-term installments. To ensure that the payments were made, peasants were subjected to the authority of their **mir,** or village commune, which was collectively responsible for the land payments to the government. In a very real sense, then, the village commune, not the individual peasants, owned the land the peasants were purchasing.

Emancipation of the Serfs. On March 3, 1861, Tsar Alexander II issued an edict emancipating the Russia serfs. This watercolor by Alexei Kivshenko shows the tsar proclaiming the emancipation.

And since the village communes were responsible for the payments, they were reluctant to allow peasants to leave their land. Emancipation, then, led not to a free, land-owning peasantry along the Western model but to an unhappy, land-starved peasantry that largely followed the old ways of farming.

OTHER REFORMS Alexander II also attempted other reforms. In 1864, he instituted a system of **zemstvos** (ZEMPST-vohz), or local assemblies, that provided a moderate degree of self-government. Representatives to the zemstvos were to be elected from the noble land-owners, townspeople, and peasants, but the property-based system of voting gave a distinct advantage to the nobles. Zemstvos were given a limited power to provide public services, such as education, famine relief, and road and bridge maintenance. They could levy taxes to pay for these services, but their efforts were frequently disrupted by bureaucrats, who feared any hint of self-government. The hope of liberal nobles and other social reformers that the zemstvos would be expanded into a national parliament remained unfulfilled. The legal reforms of 1864, which created a regular system of local and provincial courts and a judicial code that accepted the principle of equality before the law, proved successful, however.

Even the autocratic tsar was unable to control the forces he unleashed by his reform program. Reformers wanted more and rapid change; conservatives opposed what they perceived as the tsar's attempts to undermine the basic institutions of Russian society. By 1870, Russia was witnessing an increasing number of reform movements. One

of the most popular stemmed from the radical writings of Alexander Herzen (HAYRT-sun) (1812–1870), a Russian exile living in London, whose slogan "Land and Freedom" epitomized his belief that the Russian peasant must be the chief instrument for social reform. Herzen believed that the peasant village commune could serve as an independent, self-governing body that would form the basis of a new Russia. Russian students and intellectuals who followed Herzen's ideas formed a movement called **populism** whose aim was to create a new society through the revolutionary acts of the peasants. The peasants' lack of interest in these revolutionary ideas, however, led some of the populists to resort to violent means to overthrow tsarist autocracy. One who advocated the use of violence to counteract the violent repression of the tsarist regime was Vera Zasulich (tsah-SOO-likh) (1849–1919). Daughter of a poor nobleman, she worked as a clerk before joining Land and Freedom, an underground populist organization advocating radical reform. In 1878, Zasulich shot and wounded the governor-general of Saint Petersburg. Put on trial, she was acquitted by a sympathetic jury.

Encouraged by Zasulich's successful use of violence against the tsarist regime, another group of radicals, known as the People's Will, succeeded in assassinating Alexander II in 1881. His son and successor, Alexander III (1881–1894), turned against reform and returned to the traditional methods of repression.

Great Britain: The Victorian Age

Like Russia, Britain was not troubled by revolutionary disturbances during 1848, although for quite different reasons. The Reform Act of 1832 had opened the door to political representation for the industrial middle class, and in the 1860s, Britain's liberal parliamentary system demonstrated once more its ability to make both social and political reforms that enabled the country to remain stable and prosperous.

One of the reasons for Britain's stability was its continuing economic growth. After 1850, middle-class prosperity was at last coupled with some improvements for the working classes. Real wages for laborers increased more than 25 percent between 1850 and 1870. The British feeling of national pride was well reflected in Queen Victoria, whose reign from 1837 to 1901 was the longest in English history. Her sense of duty and moral respectability reflected the attitudes of her age, which has ever since

Emancipation: Serfs and Slaves

Although overall their histories have been quite different, Russia and the United States shared a common feature in the 1860s. They were the only states in the Western world that still had large enslaved populations (the Russian serfs were virtually slaves). The leaders of both countries issued emancipation proclamations within two years of each other. The first excerpt is taken from the Imperial Decree of March 3, 1861, which freed the Russian serfs. The second excerpt is from Abraham Lincoln's Emancipation Proclamation, issued on January 1, 1863.

⊷ ⩥⩦ ⊶

Tsar Alexander II, Imperial Decree, March 3, 1861

By the grace of God, we, Alexander II, Emperor and Autocrat of all the Russias, King of Poland, Grand Duke of Finland, etc., to all our faithful subjects, make known:

Called by Divine Providence and by the sacred right of inheritance to the throne of our ancestors, we took a vow in our innermost heart to respond to the mission which is intrusted to us as to surround with our affection and our Imperial solicitude all our faithful subjects of every rank and of every condition, from the warrior, who nobly bears arms for the defense of the country to the humble artisan devoted to the works of industry; from the official in the career of the high offices of the State to the laborer whose plow furrows the soil. . . .

We thus came to the conviction that the work of a serious improvement of the condition of the peasants was a sacred inheritance bequeathed to us by our ancestors, a mission which, in the course of events, Divine providence called upon us to fulfill. . . .

In virtue of the new dispositions above mentioned, the peasants attached to the soil will be invested within a term fixed by the law with all the rights of free cultivators. . . .

At the same time, they are granted the right of purchasing their close, and, with the consent of the proprietors, they may acquire in full property the arable lands and other appurtenances which are allotted to them as a permanent holding. By the acquisition in full property of the quantity of land fixed, the peasants are free from their obligations toward the proprietors for land thus purchased, and they enter definitely into the condition of free peasants–landholders.

President Abraham Lincoln, Emancipation Proclamation, January 1, 1863

Now therefore, I, Abraham Lincoln, President of the United States, by virtue of the power in me vested as Commander-in-Chief of the Army and Navy of the United States in time of actual armed rebellion against the authority and government of the United States, and as a fit and necessary war measure for suppressing such rebellion, do, on this 1st day of January, A.D. 1863, and in accordance with my purpose to do so, . . . order and designate as the States and parts of States wherein the people thereof, respectively, are this day in rebellion against the United States the following, to wit:

Arkansas, Texas, Louisiana, . . . Mississippi, Alabama, Florida, Georgia, South Carolina, North Carolina, and Virginia. . . .

And by virtue of the power for the purpose aforesaid, I do order and declare that all persons held as slaves within said designated States and parts of States are, and henceforward shall be free; and that the Executive Government of the United States, including the military and naval authorities thereof, will recognize and maintain the freedom of said persons. ▷

Q What changes did Tsar Alexander's emancipation of the serfs initiate in Russia? What effect did Lincoln's Emancipation Proclamation have on the southern "armed rebellion"? What reason did each leader give for his action? Were their actions equally effective?

---

been known as the Victorian Age (see the Film & History feature on p. 687).

Politically, this was an era of uneasy stability as the aristocratic and upper-middle-class representatives who dominated Parliament blurred party lines by their internal strife and shifting positions. One political figure who stood out was Henry John Temple, Lord Palmerston (1784–1865), who was prime minister for most of the period from 1855 to 1865. Although a Whig, Palmerston was without strong party loyalty and found it easy to make political compromises. He was not a reformer, however, and opposed expanding the franchise. He said, "We should by such an arrangement increase the number of Bribeable Electors and overpower Intelligence and Property by Ignorance and Poverty."

DISRAELI AND THE REFORM ACT OF 1867 After Palmerston's death in 1865, the movement for the extension of the franchise only intensified. Although the Whigs (now called the Liberals), who had been responsible for the Reform Act of 1832, talked about passing additional reform legislation, it was actually the Tories (now called the Conservatives) who carried it through. The Tory leader in Parliament, Benjamin Disraeli (diz-RAY-lee) (1804–1881), was apparently motivated by the desire to win over the newly enfranchised groups to the Conservative

The Young Victoria (2009)

Directed by Jean-Marc Vallée, *The Young Victoria* is an imaginative and yet relatively realistic portrayal of the early struggles of the young woman who became Britain's longest-reigning monarch. The film begins in 1836 when the seventeen-year-old Victoria (Emily Blunt) is the heir to the throne. Her controlling mother, the duchess of Kent (Miranda Richardson), schemes to prevent her daughter from ascending the throne by trying to create a regency for herself and her close adviser and paramour, Sir John Conroy (Mark Strong). Conroy is accurately shown trying to force the young Victoria to sign a paper establishing a regency. The mother and Conroy fail, and Victoria succeeds to the throne after the death of her uncle, King William IV (Jim Broadbent), on June 20, 1837, about one month after Victoria turned eighteen. The movie also shows the impact that Lord Melbourne (Paul Bettany), the prime minister, had on the young queen as her private secretary and adviser. Indeed, Victoria's attachment to Melbourne led to considerable discontent among her subjects. Central to the film, however, is the romantic portrayal of the wooing of Victoria by her young German cousin, Prince Albert of Saxe-Coburg-Gotha (Rupert Friend), the nephew of the king of Belgium. The film accurately conveys the close bond and the deep and abiding love that developed between Victoria and Albert.

The film is a visual treat, re-creating the life of the young Victoria in a number of castle and cathedral settings. As a romantic dramatization of some of the main events before and after the coronation of Victoria, the film also contains some noticeable flaws. Victoria is shown painting with her right hand, although she was actually left-handed. The facts are also embellished at times in

The coronation of Victoria (Emily Blunt) as the queen of England.

GK Films/The Kobal Collection

order to dramatize the story. Although there was an assassination attempt on the queen, Prince Albert was not shot while trying to protect her. Both shots fired by Edward Oxford, her would-be assassin, went wide of the mark. The character of Victoria's other uncle, King Leopold I of Belgium (Thomas Kretschmann), is also not quite accurate. He was not as selfish as he is portrayed in pushing Albert to marry Victoria. The banquet scene in which King William IV insults the duchess of Kent is quite accurate (it actually uses many of the exact words the king uttered), but its consequences are not. The duchess did not leave the room, and Victoria did not remain calm, but broke into tears. Finally, except for a passing reference to Victoria's concern for workers' housing conditions, this romantic movie makes no attempt to understand the political and social issues that troubled the British Empire of Victoria's time. ⌦

Party. The Reform Act of 1867 was an important step toward the democratization of Britain. By lowering the monetary requirements for voting (taxes paid or income earned), it by and large enfranchised many male urban workers. The number of voters increased from about 1 million to slightly over 2 million (see Table 22.1). Although Disraeli believed that this would benefit the Conservatives, industrial workers helped produce a huge Liberal victory in 1868.

The extension of the right to vote had an important by-product as it forced the Liberal and Conservative Parties to organize carefully in order to manipulate the electorate. Party discipline intensified, and the rivalry between the Liberals and Conservatives became a regular feature of

parliamentary life. In large part this was due to the personal and political opposition of the two leaders of these parties, William Gladstone (1809–1898) and Disraeli.

THE LIBERAL POLICIES OF GLADSTONE   The first Liberal administration of William Gladstone, from 1868 to 1874, was responsible for a series of impressive reforms. Legislation and government orders opened civil service positions to competitive exams rather than patronage, introduced the secret ballot for voting, and abolished the practice of purchasing military commissions. The Education Act of 1870 attempted to make elementary schools available for all children (see Chapter 24). These reforms were typically liberal. By eliminating abuses and enabling

Queen Victoria and Her Family.
Queen Victoria, who ruled Britain from 1837 to 1901, married her German first cousin, Prince Albert of Saxe-Coburg-Gotha, in 1840 and subsequently gave birth to four sons and five daughters, who married into a number of European royal families. When she died at age eighty-one, she had thirty-seven great-grandchildren. Victoria is seated at the center of this 1881 photograph, surrounded by members of her family.

people with talent to compete fairly, they sought to strengthen the nation and its institutions.

The United States: Slavery and War

By the mid-nineteenth century, American national unity was increasingly threatened by the issue of slavery. Both North and South had grown dramatically in population during the first half of the nineteenth century. But their development was quite different. The cotton economy and social structure of the South were based on the exploitation of enslaved black Africans and their descendants. The importance of cotton is evident from production figures. In 1810, the South produced a raw cotton crop of 178,000 bales worth $10 million. By 1860, it was generating 4.5 million bales of cotton with a value of $249 million. Fully 93 percent of southern cotton in 1850 was produced by a slave population that had grown dramatically in fifty years. Although new slave imports had been barred in 1808, there were 4 million Afro-American slaves in the South by 1860—four times the number sixty years earlier. The cotton economy and plantation-based slavery were

intimately related, and the attempt to maintain them in the course of the first half of the nineteenth century led the South to become increasingly defensive, monolithic, and isolated. At the same time, the rise of an abolitionist movement in the North challenged the southern order and created an "emotional chain reaction" that led to civil war.

By the 1850s, the slavery question had caused the Whig Party to become defunct and the Democrats to split along North-South lines. The Kansas-Nebraska Act of 1854, which allowed slavery in the Kansas and Nebraska territories to be determined by popular sovereignty, created a firestorm in the North and led to the creation of a new sectional party. The Republicans were united by antislavery principles and were especially driven by the fear that the "slave power" of the South would attempt to spread the slave system throughout the country.

As polarization over the issue of slavery intensified, compromise became less feasible. When Abraham Lincoln, the man who had said in a speech in Illinois in 1858 that "this government cannot endure permanently half slave and half free," was elected president in November 1860, the die was cast. Lincoln carried only 2 of the 1,109 counties in the South; the Republicans were not even on the ballot in ten southern states. On December 20, 1860, a South Carolina convention voted to repeal the state's ratification of the U.S. Constitution. In February 1861, six more southern states did the same, and a rival nation—the Confederate States of America—was formed (see Map 22.6). In April, fighting erupted between North and South.

THE CIVIL WAR The American Civil War (1861–1865) was an extraordinarily bloody struggle, a foretaste of the total war to come in the twentieth century. More than 600,000 soldiers died, either in battle or from deadly infectious diseases spawned by filthy camp conditions. Over a period of four years, the Union states of the North mobilized their superior assets and gradually wore down the Confederate forces of the South. As the war dragged

TABLE 22.1 Expansion of the British Electorate

Year	Number of Voters	Percentage of Total Population
1831 (Reform Act of 1832)	516,000	2.1
1833	812,000	3.4
1866 (Reform Act of 1867)	1,364,000	4.7
1868	2,418,000	8.4
1883 (Reform Act of 1884)	3,152,000	9.0
1885	5,669,000	16.3

SOURCE: Chris Cook and Brendan Keith, *British Historical Facts, 1830–1900* (London, 1975), pp. 115, 232–233.

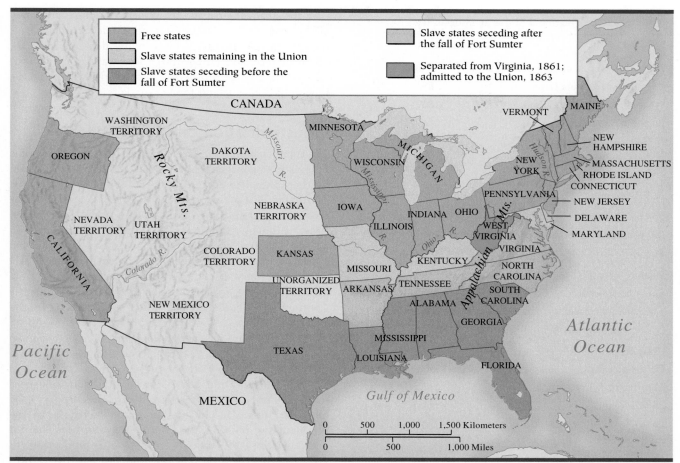

MAP 22.6   **The United States: The West and the Civil War.** By 1860, the North had developed an economy based on industry and commerce, whereas the South had remained a primarily agrarian economy based on black slave labor. The question of the continuance of slavery itself and the expansion of slavery into western territories led to the Civil War, in which the South sought to create an independent country.

 Why would its inhabitants want to create a separate state of West Virginia?

 View an animated version of this map or related maps on the CourseMate website.

on, it had the effect of radicalizing public opinion in the North. What began as a war to save the Union became a war against slavery. On January 1, 1863, Lincoln's Emancipation Proclamation made most of the nation's slaves "forever free" (see the box on p. 686). The increasingly effective Union blockade of the South, combined with a shortage of fighting men, made the Confederate cause desperate by the end of 1864. The final push of Union troops under General Ulysses S. Grant forced General Robert E. Lee's Confederate Army to surrender on April 9, 1865. Although problems lay ahead, the Union victory confirmed that the United States would be "one nation, indivisible."

The Emergence of a Canadian Nation

North of the United States, the process of nation building was also making progress. By the Treaty of Paris in 1763,

Canada—or New France, as it was called—passed into the hands of the British. By 1800, most Canadians favored more autonomy, although the colonists disagreed on the form this autonomy should take. Upper Canada (now Ontario) was predominantly English-speaking, whereas Lower Canada (now Quebec) was dominated by French Canadians. A dramatic increase in immigration to Canada from Great Britain (almost one million immigrants between 1815 and 1850) also fueled the desire for self-government.

In 1837, a number of Canadian groups rose in rebellion against British authority. Rebels in Lower Canada demanded separation from Britain, creation of a republic, universal male suffrage, and freedom of the press. Although the rebellions were crushed by the following year, the British government now began to seek ways to satisfy some of the Canadian demands. The American Civil War proved to be a turning point. Fearful of American designs on Canada during the war and eager to reduce the costs of

CHRONOLOGY National States at Midcentury

France

Louis Napoleon is elected president	1848
Coup d'état by Louis Napoleon	1851
Creation of the Second Empire	1852
Emperor Napoleon III	1852–1870
"Authoritarian empire"	1852–1860
Crimean War	1854–1856
Treaty of Paris	1856
"Liberal empire"	1860–1870

Austrian Empire

Establishment of imperial parliament	1859
Ausgleich, Dual Monarchy	1867

Russia

Tsar Alexander II	1855–1881
Emancipation edict	1861 (March 3)
Creation of zemstvos and legal reforms	1864

Great Britain

Queen Victoria	1837–1901
Ministry of Palmerston	1855–1865
Reform Act	1867
First Liberal ministry of William Gladstone	1868–1874

United States

Kansas-Nebraska Act	1854
Election of Lincoln and secession of South Carolina	1860
Outbreak of Civil War	1861
Surrender of Lee	1865 (April 9)

Canada

Formation of the Dominion of Canada	1867

maintaining the colonies, the British government finally capitulated to Canadian demands. In 1867, Parliament established the Canadian nation—the Dominion of Canada—with its own constitution. Canada now possessed a parliamentary system and ruled itself, although foreign affairs still remained under the control of the British government.

Industrialization and the Marxist Response

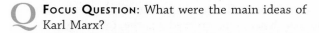

Q **FOCUS QUESTION:** What were the main ideas of Karl Marx?

Between 1850 and 1871, Continental industrialization came of age. The innovations of the British Industrial Revolution—mechanized factory production, the use of

coal, the steam engine, and the transportation revolution—all became regular features of economic expansion. Although marred periodically by economic depression (1857–1858) or recession (1866–1867), this was an age of considerable economic prosperity, particularly evident in the growth of domestic and foreign markets.

Industrialization on the Continent

The transformation of textile production from hand looms to power looms had largely been completed in Britain by the 1850s (for cotton) and 1860s (for wool). On the Continent, the period from 1850 to 1870 witnessed increased mechanization of the cotton and textile industries, although Continental countries still remained behind Britain. By 1870, hand looms had virtually disappeared in Britain, whereas in France there were still 200,000 of them, along with 80,000 power looms. Nevertheless, this period of industrial expansion on the Continent was fueled not so much by textiles as by the growth of railroads. Between 1850 and 1870, European railroad track mileage increased from 14,500 to almost 70,000. The railroads, in turn, stimulated growth in both the iron and coal industries.

Between 1850 and 1870, Continental iron industries made the transition from charcoal iron smelting to coke blast smelting. Despite the dramatic increases in the production of pig iron, the Continental countries had not yet come close to surpassing British iron production. In 1870, the British iron industry produced half the world's pig iron—four times as much as Germany and five times as much as France. In the middle decades of the nineteenth century, the textile, mining, and metallurgical industries on the Continent also rapidly converted to the use of the steam engine.

An important factor in the expansion of markets was the elimination of barriers to international trade. Essential international waterways were opened up by the elimination of restrictive tolls. The Danube River in 1857 and the Rhine in 1861, for example, were declared freeways for all ships. The negotiation of trade treaties in the 1860s reduced or eliminated protective tariffs throughout much of western Europe.

Governments also played a role in first allowing and then encouraging the formation of **joint-stock investment banks.** These banks were crucial to Continental industrial development because they mobilized enormous capital resources for investment. In the 1850s and 1860s, they were very important in the promotion of railway construction, although railroads were not always a safe investment. During a trip to Spain to examine possibilities for railroad construction, the locomotive manufacturer George Stephenson reported, "I have been a month in the country, but have not seen during the whole of that time enough people of the right sort to fill a single train."[7] His misgivings proved to be well founded. In 1864, the Spanish banking system, which depended largely on investments in railway shares, collapsed.

Opening of the Suez Canal. Between 1850 and 1871, Continental Europeans built railways, bridges, and canals as part of the ever-spreading process of industrialization. A French diplomat, Ferdinand de Lesseps, was the guiding force behind the construction of the Suez Canal, which provided a link between the Mediterranean and Red seas. Work on the canal began in 1859 and was completed ten years later. As seen here, an elaborate ceremony marked the opening of the canal. A French vessel led the first convoy of ships through the canal. The banks are lined with curious local inhabitants.

Before 1870, capitalist factory owners remained largely free to hire labor on their own terms based on market forces. Although workers formed trade unions in an effort to fight for improved working conditions and reasonable wages, the unions tended to represent only a small part of the industrial working class and proved largely ineffective. Real change for the industrial proletariat would come only with the development of socialist parties and socialist trade unions. These emerged after 1870, but the theory that made them possible had already been developed by midcentury in the work of Karl Marx.

Marx and Marxism

The beginnings of Marxism can be traced to the 1848 publication of *The Communist Manifesto,* a short treatise written by two Germans, Karl Marx (1818– 1883) and Friedrich Engels (1820–1895). Marx was born into a relatively prosperous middle-class family in Trier in western Germany. He descended from a long line of rabbis, although his father, a lawyer, had become a Protestant to keep his job. Marx enrolled at the University of Bonn in 1835, but his carefree student ways soon led his father to send him to the more serious-minded University of Berlin, where he encountered the ideas of the German philosopher Georg Wilhelm Friedrich Hegel. After receiving a Ph.D. in philosophy, Marx planned to teach at a university. Unable to obtain a position because of his professed atheism, Marx decided on a career in journalism and eventually became the editor of a liberal bourgeois newspaper in Cologne in 1842. After the newspaper was suppressed because of his radical views, Marx moved to Paris. There he met Friedrich Engels, who became his lifelong friend and financial patron.

Engels, the son of a wealthy German cotton manufacturer, had worked in Britain at one of his father's factories

Friedrich Engels & Karl Marx, *The Communist Manifesto* (1848)

in Manchester. There he had acquired a firsthand knowledge of what he came to call the "wage slavery" of the British working classes, which he detailed in *The Conditions of the Working Class in England,* a damning

Karl Marx. Karl Marx was a radical journalist who joined with Friedrich Engels to write *The Communist Manifesto,* which proclaimed the ideas of a revolutionary socialism. After the failure of the 1848 revolution in Germany, Marx fled to Britain, where he continued to write and became involved in the work of the first International Working Men's Association.

indictment of industrial life written in 1844. Engels would contribute his knowledge of actual working conditions as well as monetary assistance to the financially strapped Marx.

In 1847, Marx and Engels joined a tiny group of primarily German socialist revolutionaries known as the Communist League. By this time, both Marx and Engels were enthusiastic advocates of the radical working-class movement and agreed to draft a statement of their ideas for the league. The resulting *Communist Manifesto,* published in German in January 1848, appeared on the eve of the revolutions of 1848. One would think from the opening lines of the preface that the pamphlet alone had caused this revolutionary upheaval: "A spectre is haunting Europe—the spectre of Communism. All the Powers of Old Europe have entered into a holy alliance to exorcise this spectre: Pope and Czar, Metternich and Guizot, French Radicals and German police spies."[8] In fact, *The Communist Manifesto* was known to only a few of Marx's friends. Although its closing words—"The proletarians have nothing to lose but their chains. They have a world to win. WORKING MEN OF ALL COUNTRIES, UNITE!"— were clearly intended to rouse the working classes to action, they passed unnoticed in 1848. The work, however, became one of the most influential political treatises in modern European history.

According to Engels, Marx's ideas were partly a synthesis of French and German thought. The French provided Marx with ample documentation for his assertion that a revolution could totally restructure society. They also provided him with several examples of socialism. From the German idealistic philosophers such as Hegel, Marx took the idea of dialectic: everything evolves, and all change in history is the result of conflicts between antagonistic elements. Marx was particularly impressed by Hegel, but he disagreed with Hegel's belief that history is determined by ideas manifesting themselves in historical forces. Instead, said Marx, the course of history is determined by material forces.

IDEAS OF *THE COMMUNIST MANIFESTO* Marx and Engels began the *Manifesto* with the statement that "the history of all hitherto existing society is the history of class struggles." Throughout history, oppressed and oppressor have "stood in constant opposition to one another." In an earlier struggle, the feudal classes of the Middle Ages were forced to accede to the emerging middle class or bourgeoisie. As the bourgeoisie took control in turn, its ideas became the dominant views of the era, and government became its instrument. Marx and Engels declared, "The executive of the modern State is but a committee for managing the common affairs of the whole bourgeoisie."[9] In other words, the government of the state reflected and defended the interests of the industrial middle class and its allies.

Although bourgeois society had emerged victorious out of the ruins of feudalism, Marx and Engels insisted that it had not triumphed completely. Now once again the members of the bourgeoisie were antagonists in an emerging class struggle, but this time they faced the **proletariat,** or the industrial working class. The struggle would be fierce, but eventually, so Marx and Engels predicted, the workers would overthrow their bourgeois masters. After this victory, the proletariat would form a dictatorship to reorganize the means of production. Then a classless society would emerge, and the state—itself an instrument of the bourgeoisie—would wither away since it no longer represented the interests of a particular class. Class struggles would then be over (see the box on p. 693). Marx believed that the emergence of a classless society would lead to progress in science, technology, and industry and to greater wealth for all.

After the failure of the revolutions of 1848, Marx went to London, where he spent the rest of his life. He continued his writing on political economy, especially his famous work, *Das Kapital* (*Capital*), only one volume of which he completed. After his death, the remaining volumes were edited by his friend Engels.

ORGANIZING THE WORKING CLASS One of the reasons *Das Kapital* was not finished was Marx's own preoccupation with organizing the working-class movement. In *The Communist Manifesto,* Marx had defined the communists as "the most advanced and resolute section of the working-class parties of every country." Their advantage was their ability to understand "the line of march, the conditions, and the ultimate general results of the proletarian movement." Marx saw his role in this light and participated enthusiastically in the activities of the International Working Men's Association. Formed in 1864 by British and French trade unionists, this "First International" served as an umbrella organization for working-class interests. Marx was the dominant personality on the organization's General Council and devoted much time to its activities. Internal dissension within the ranks soon damaged the organization, and it failed in 1872. Although it would be revived in 1889, the fate of socialism by that time was in the hands of national socialist parties.

Science and Culture in an Age of Realism

 FOCUS QUESTION: How did the belief that the world should be viewed realistically manifest itself in science, art, and literature in the second half of the nineteenth century?

Between 1850 and 1870, two major intellectual developments are evident: the growth of scientific knowledge, with its rapidly increasing impact on the Western worldview, and the shift from Romanticism and its focus on the

The Classless Society

In *The Communist Manifesto,* Karl Marx and Friedrich Engels projected the creation of a classless society as the end product of the struggle between the bourgeoisie and the proletariat. In this selection, they discuss the steps by which that classless society would be reached.

⊷ ⊷≡⊷ ⊷

Karl Marx and Friedrich Engels, *The Communist Manifesto*

We have seen . . . that the first step in the revolution by the working class is to raise the proletariat to the position of ruling class. . . . The proletariat will use its political supremacy to wrest, by degrees, all capital from the bourgeoisie, to centralize all instruments of production in the hands of the State, i.e., of the proletariat organized as the ruling class; and to increase the total of productive forces as rapidly as possible.

Of course, in the beginning, this cannot be effected except by means of despotic inroads on the rights of property, and on the conditions of bourgeois production; by means of measures, therefore, which appear economically insufficient and untenable, but which, in the course of the movement, outstrip themselves, necessitate further inroads upon the old social order, and are unavoidable as a means of entirely revolutionizing the mode of production.

These measures will of course be different in different countries.

Nevertheless, in the most advanced countries, the following will be pretty generally applicable:

1. Abolition of property in land and application of all rents of land to public purposes.
2. A heavy progressive or graduated income tax.
3. Abolition of all right of inheritance. . . .
5. Centralization of credit in the hands of the State, by means of a national bank with State capital and an exclusive monopoly.
6. Centralization of the means of communication and transport in the hands of the State.
7. Extension of factories and instruments of production owned by the State. . . .
8. Equal liability of all to labor. Establishment of industrial armies, especially for agriculture.
9. Combination of agriculture with manufacturing industries; gradual abolition of the distinction between town and country, by a more equable distribution of the population over the country.
10. Free education for all children in public schools. Abolition of children's factory labor in its present form. . . .

When, in the course of development, class distinctions have disappeared, and all production has been concentrated in the whole nation, the public power will lose its political character. Political power, properly so called, is merely the organized power of one class for oppressing another. If the proletariat during its contest with the bourgeoisie is compelled, by the force of circumstances, to organize itself as a class, if, by means of a revolution, it makes itself the ruling class, and, as such, sweeps away by force the old conditions of production, then it will, along with these conditions, have swept away the conditions for the existence of class antagonisms and of classes generally, and will thereby have abolished its own supremacy as a class.

In place of the old bourgeois society, with its classes and class antagonisms, we shall have an association, in which the free development of each is the condition for the free development of all. ⊱

Q How did Marx and Engels define the proletariat? The bourgeoisie? Why did Marxists come to believe that this distinction was paramount for understanding history? What steps did Marx and Engels believe would lead to a classless society? Considering that Marx criticized early socialists as utopian and regarded his own socialism as scientific, do you think that his socialism was also utopian? Why or why not?

---

inner world of reality to Realism and its turning toward the outer, material world.

A New Age of Science

By the mid-nineteenth century, science was having an ever-greater impact on European life. The Scientific Revolution of the sixteenth and seventeenth centuries had fundamentally transformed the Western worldview and led to a modern, rational approach to the study of the natural world. Even in the eighteenth century, however, these intellectual developments had remained the preserve of an educated elite and resulted in few practical benefits. Moreover, the technical advances of the early Industrial Revolution had depended little on pure science and much more on the practical experiments of technologically oriented amateur inventors. Advances in industrial technology, however, fed an interest in basic scientific research, which in the 1830s and afterward resulted in a rash of basic scientific discoveries that were soon converted into technological improvements that affected everybody.

The development of the steam engine was important in encouraging scientists to work out its theoretical foundations, a preoccupation that led to thermodynamics, the science of the relationship between heat and mechanical energy. The laws of thermodynamics were at the core of nineteenth-century physics. In biology, the Frenchman Louis Pasteur (LWEE pas-TOOR) formulated the germ theory of disease, which had enormous practical applications in the development of modern scientific medical practices (see "A Revolution in Health Care" later in this chapter). In chemistry, in the 1860s, the Russian Dmitri Mendeleyev (di-MEE-tree men-duh-LAY-ef) (1834–1907) classified all the material elements then known on the basis of their atomic weights and provided the systematic foundation for the periodic law. The Englishman Michael Faraday (1791–1867) discovered the phenomenon of electromagnetic induction and put together a primitive generator that laid the foundation for the use of electricity, although economically efficient generators were not built until the 1870s.

The steadily increasing and often dramatic material gains generated by science and technology led to a growing faith in the benefits of science. The popularity of scientific and technological achievement produced a widespread acceptance of the scientific method, based on observation, experiment, and logical analysis, as the only path to objective truth and objective reality. This in turn undermined the faith of many people in religious revelation and truth. It is no accident that the nineteenth century was an age of increasing secularization, particularly evident in the growth of **materialism,** the belief that everything mental, spiritual, or ideal was simply a result of physical forces. Truth was to be found in the concrete material existence of human beings and not, as the Romantics imagined, in revelations gained by feeling or intuitive flashes. The importance of materialism was strikingly evident in the most important scientific event of the nineteenth century, the development of the theory of organic evolution according to natural selection. On the theories of Charles Darwin could be built a picture of humans as material beings that were simply part of the natural world.

Charles Darwin and the Theory of Organic Evolution

Charles Darwin (1809–1882), like many of the great scientists of the nineteenth century, was a scientific amateur. Born into an upper-middle-class family, he studied theology at Cambridge University while pursuing an intense side interest in geology and biology. In 1831, at the age of twenty-two, his hobby became his vocation when he accepted an appointment as a naturalist to study animals and plants on an official Royal Navy scientific expedition aboard the H.M.S. *Beagle.* Its purpose was to survey and study the landmasses of South America and the South Pacific. Darwin's specific job was to study the structure of various forms of plant and animal life. He was able to

observe animals on islands virtually untouched by external influence and compare them with animals on the mainland. As a result, Darwin came to discard the notion of a special creation and to believe that animals evolved over time and in response to their environment. When he returned to Britain, he eventually formulated an explanation for evolution in the principle of **natural selection,** a theory that he presented in 1859 in his celebrated book, *On the Origin of Species by Means of Natural Selection.*

Charles Darwin, *On the Origin of Species,* Chapters 1–5 (1859)

THE THEORY OF EVOLUTION The basic idea of Darwin's book was that all plants and animals had evolved over a long period of time from earlier and simpler forms of life, a principle known as **organic evolution.** Darwin was important in explaining how this natural process worked. He took the first step from Thomas Malthus's theory of population: in every species, "many more individuals of each species are born than can possibly survive." This results in a "struggle for existence." Darwin believed that "as more individuals are produced than can possibly survive, there must in every case be a struggle for existence, either one individual with another of the same species, or with the individuals of distinct species, or with the physical conditions of life." Those who succeeded in this struggle for existence had adapted better to their environment, a process made possible by the appearance of "variants." Chance variations that occurred in the process of inheritance enabled some organisms to be more adaptable to the environment than others, a process that Darwin called natural selection: "Owing to this struggle [for existence], variations, however slight, . . . if they be in any degree profitable to the individuals of a species, in their infinitely complex relations to other organic beings and to their physical conditions of life, will tend to the preservation of such individuals, and will generally be inherited by the offspring."[10] Those that were naturally selected for survival ("survival of the fit") survived. The unfit did not and became extinct. The fit who survived propagated and passed on the variations that enabled them to survive until, from Darwin's point of view, a new separate species emerged.

In *On the Origin of Species,* Darwin discussed plant and animal species only. He was not concerned with humans themselves and only later applied his theory of natural selection to humans. In *The Descent of Man,* published in 1871, he argued for the animal origins of human beings: "man is the co-descendant with other mammals of a common progenitor." Humans were not an exception to the rule governing other species (see the box on p. 695).

Darwin's ideas were highly controversial at first. Some people fretted that Darwin's theory made human beings ordinary products of nature rather than unique beings. Others were disturbed by the implications of life as a struggle for survival, of "nature red in tooth and claw." Was there a place in the Darwinian world for moral values? For those who believed in a rational order in the

Darwin and the Descent of Man

Darwin published his theory of organic evolution in 1859, followed twelve years later by *The Descent of Man,* in which he argued that human beings, like other animals, evolved from lower forms of life. The theory provoked a firestorm of criticism, especially from the clergy. One critic described Darwin's theory as a "brutal philosophy—to wit, there is no God, and the ape is our Adam."

━━━━━✠═━━━━━

Charles Darwin, *The Descent of Man*

The main conclusion here arrived at, and now held by many naturalists, who are well competent to form a sound judgment, is that man is descended from some less highly organized form. The grounds upon which this conclusion rests will never be shaken, for the close similarity between man and the lower animals in embryonic development, as well as in innumerable points of structure and constitution, both of high and of the most trifling importance,—the rudiments which he retains, and the abnormal reversions to which he is occasionally liable,—are facts which cannot be disputed. They have long been known, but until recently they told us nothing with respect to the origin of man. Now when viewed by the light of our knowledge of the whole organic world, their meaning is unmistakable. The great principle of evolution stands up clear and firm, when these groups of facts are considered in connection with others, such as the mutual affinities of the members of the same group, their geographical distribution in past and present times, and their geological succession. It is incredible that all these facts should speak falsely. He who is not content to look, like a savage, at the phenomena of nature as disconnected, cannot any longer believe that man is the work of a separate act of creation. He will be forced to admit that the close resemblance of the embryo of man to that, for instance, of a dog—the construction of his skull, limbs and whole frame on the same plan with that of other mammals, independently of the uses to which the parts may be put—the occasional reappearance of various structures, for instance of several muscles, which man does not normally possess . . . —and a crowd of analogous facts—all point in the plainest manner to the conclusion that man is the co-descendant with other mammals of a common progenitor. . . .

Man may be excused for feeling some pride at having risen, though not through his own exertions, to the very summit of the organic scale; and the fact of his having thus risen, instead of having been aboriginally placed there, may give him hope for a still higher destiny in the distant future. But we are not here concerned with hopes or fears, only with the truth as far as our reason permits us to discover it; and I have given the evidence to the best of my ability. We must, however, acknowledge, as it seems to me, that man with all his noble qualities, with sympathy which feels for the most debased, with benevolence which extends not only to other men but to the humblest living creature, with his god-like intellect which has penetrated into the movements and constitution of the solar system—with all these exalted powers—Man still bears in his bodily frame the indelible stamp of his lowly origin.

Q What was Darwin's basic argument in *The Descent of Man*? Why did so many object to it? What forces in nineteenth-century European society do you think came together to stimulate Darwin's thinking and publications on this subject?

---

world, Darwin's theory seemed to eliminate purpose and design from the universe. Gradually, however, Darwin's theory was accepted by scientists and other intellectuals. In the process of accepting Darwin's ideas, some people even tried to apply them to society, yet another example of science's increasing prestige.

A Revolution in Health Care

The application of natural science to the field of medicine in the nineteenth century led to revolutionary breakthroughs in health care. The first steps toward a more scientific basis for medicine were taken in Paris hospitals during the first half of the nineteenth century. Clinical observation, consisting of an active physical examination of patients, was combined with the knowledge gained from detailed autopsies to create a new clinical medicine.

PASTEUR AND GERMS The major breakthrough toward a scientific medicine occurred with the discovery of microorganisms, or germs, as the agents causing disease. The germ theory of disease was largely the work of Louis Pasteur (1822–1895). Pasteur was not a doctor but a chemist who approached medical problems in a scientific fashion. In 1857, Pasteur went to Paris as director of scientific studies at the École Normale, where experiments he conducted proved that microorganisms of various kinds were responsible for the process of fermentation, thereby launching the science of bacteriology.

Government and private industry soon perceived the inherent practical value of Pasteur's work. His examination of a disease threatening the wine industry led to the development in 1863 of a process—subsequently known as **pasteurization**—for heating a product to destroy the organisms causing spoilage. In 1877, Pasteur turned his attention to human diseases. His desire to do more than simply identify disease-producing organisms led him in 1885 to a preventive vaccination against rabies. In the 1890s, the principle of vaccination was extended to diphtheria, typhoid fever, cholera, and plague, creating a modern immunological science.

The work of Pasteur and the others who followed him in isolating the specific bacteriological causes of numerous diseases had a far-reaching impact. By providing a rational means of treating and preventing infectious diseases, they transformed the medical world. Both the practice of surgery and public health experienced a renaissance.

NEW SURGICAL PRACTICES Surgeons had already achieved a new professionalism by the end of the eighteenth century (see Chapter 17), but the discovery of germs and the introduction of anesthesia created a new environment for surgical operations. Surgeons had traditionally set broken bones, treated wounds, and amputated limbs, usually as a result of injuries in war. One major obstacle to more successful surgery was the inevitable postoperative infection, which was especially rampant in hospitals.

Joseph Lister (1827–1912), who developed the antiseptic principle, was one of the first people to deal with

© Jefferson College, Philadelphia/The Bridgeman Art Library

Thomas Eakins, *The Gross Clinic.* This painting, completed in 1875, shows Dr. Samuel Gross, one of the foremost surgeons in the United States, scalpel in hand, pausing midway in surgery on a young man's leg to discuss the operation with his students in the amphitheater of the Jefferson Medical College. Various tasks are performed by assistant doctors, including the anesthetist, who holds his cloth over the youth's face. Eakins's painting is a realistic portrayal of the new medical science at work.

this problem. Following the work of Pasteur, Lister perceived that bacteria might enter a wound and cause infection. His use of carbolic acid, a newly discovered disinfectant, proved remarkably effective in eliminating infections during surgery. Lister's discoveries dramatically transformed surgery wards as patients no longer succumbed regularly to what was called "hospital gangrene."

The second great barrier to large-scale surgery stemmed from the inability to lessen the pain of the patient. Alcohol and opiates had been used for centuries during surgical operations, but even their use did not allow unhurried operative maneuvers. After experiments with numerous agents, sulfuric ether was first used successfully in an operation at the Massachusetts General Hospital in 1846 (see the box on p. 697). Within a year, chloroform began to rival ether as an anesthetic agent.

NEW PUBLIC HEALTH MEASURES Although the great discoveries of bacteriology came after the emergence of the first public health movement, they significantly furthered its development. Based on the principle of preventive rather than curative medicine, the urban public health movement of the 1840s and 1850s was largely a response to the cholera epidemic (see Chapter 23). One medical man, in fact, called cholera "our best ally" in furthering public hygiene. The prebacteriological hygiene movement focused on providing clean water, adequate sewage disposal, and less crowded housing conditions. Bacterial discoveries led to greater emphasis on preventive measures, such as the pasteurization of milk, improved purification of water supplies, immunization against disease, and control of waterborne diseases. The public health movement also resulted in the government's hiring medical doctors not just to treat people but to deal with issues of public health as well.

NEW MEDICAL SCHOOLS The new scientific developments also had an important impact on the training of doctors for professional careers in health care. Although there were a few medical schools at the beginning of the nineteenth century, most medical instruction was still done by a system of apprenticeship. In the course of the nineteenth century, virtually every Western country founded new medical schools, but attempts to impose uniform standards on them through certifying bodies met considerable resistance. Entrance requirements were virtually nonexistent, and degrees were granted after several months of lectures. Professional organizations founded around midcentury, such as the British Medical Association in 1832, the American Medical Association in 1847, and the German Doctors' Society in 1872, attempted to elevate professional standards but achieved little until the end of the century. The establishment of the Johns Hopkins University School of Medicine in 1893, with its four-year graded curriculum, clinical training for advanced students, and use of laboratories for teaching purposes, provided a new model for medical training that finally became standard practice in the twentieth century.

Anesthesia and Modern Surgery

Modern scientific medicine became established in the nineteenth century. Important to the emergence of modern surgery was the development of anesthetic agents that would block the patient's pain and enable surgeons to complete their surgery without the haste that had characterized earlier operations. This document is an eyewitness account of the first successful use of ether anesthesia, which took place at the Massachusetts General Hospital in 1846.

The First Public Demonstration of Ether Anesthesia, October 16, 1846

The day arrived; the time appointed was noted on the dial, when the patient was led into the operating-room, and Dr. Warren and a board of the most eminent surgeons in the State were gathered around the sufferer. "All is ready—the stillness oppressive." It had been announced "that a test of some preparation was to be made for which the astonishing claim had been made that it would render the person operated upon free from pain." These are the words of Dr. Warren that broke the stillness.

Those present were incredulous, and, as Dr. Morton had not arrived at the time appointed and fifteen minutes had passed, Dr. Warren said, with significant meaning, "I presume he is otherwise engaged." This was followed with a "derisive laugh," and Dr. Warren grasped his knife and was about to proceed with the operation. At that moment Dr. Morton entered a side door, when Dr. Warren turned to him and in a strong voice said, "Well, sir, your patient is ready." In a few minutes he was ready for the surgeon's knife, when Dr. Morton said, "Your patient is ready, sir."

Here the most sublime scene ever witnessed in the operating-room was presented, when the patient placed himself voluntarily upon the table, which was to become the altar of future fame. Not that he did so for the purpose of advancing the science of medicine, nor for the good of his fellow-men, for the act itself was purely a personal and selfish one. He was about to assist in solving a new and important problem of therapeutics, whose benefits were to be given to the whole civilized world, yet wholly unconscious of the sublimity of the occasion or the art he was taking.

That was a supreme moment for a most wonderful discovery, and, had the patient died upon the operation, science would have waited long to discover the hypnotic effects of some other remedy of equal potency and safety, and it may be properly questioned whether chloroform would have come into use as it has at the present time.

The heroic bravery of the man who voluntarily placed himself upon the table, a subject for the surgeon's knife, should be recorded and his name enrolled upon parchment, which should be hung upon the walls of the surgical amphitheater in which the operation was performed. His name was Gilbert Abbott.

The operation was for a congenital tumor on the left side of the neck, extending along the jaw to the maxillary gland and into the mouth, embracing a margin of the tongue. The operation was successful; and when the patient recovered he declared he had suffered no pain. Dr. Warren turned to those present and said, "Gentlemen, this is no humbug." ▷

Q In what ways does this account demonstrate the impact that modern science had made on Western society by the middle of the nineteenth century? What forces conjoined to encourage the practical application and refinement of new scientific discoveries?

WOMEN AND MEDICAL SCHOOLS During most of the nineteenth century, medical schools in Europe and the United States were closed to female students. When Harriet Hunt applied to Harvard Medical School, the male students drew up resolutions that prevented her admission:

> Resolved, that no woman of true delicacy would be willing in the presence of men to listen to the discussion of subjects that necessarily come under consideration of the students of medicine.
>
> Resolved, that we object to having the company of any female forced upon us, who is disposed to unsex herself, and to sacrifice her modesty by appearing with men in the lecture room.[11]

Elizabeth Blackwell (1821–1910) achieved the first major breakthrough for women in medicine. Although she had been admitted to the Geneva College of Medicine in New York by mistake, Blackwell's perseverance and intelligence won her the respect of her fellow male students. She received her M.D. degree in 1849 and eventually established a clinic in New York City.

European women experienced difficulties similar to Blackwell's. In Britain, Elizabeth Garret and Sophia Jex-Blake had to struggle for years before they were finally admitted to the practice of medicine. The unwillingness of medical schools to open their doors to women led to the formation of separate medical schools for women. The Female Medical College of Pennsylvania, established in 1850, was the first in the United States, and the London School of Medicine for Women was founded in 1874. But even after graduation from such institutions, women faced obstacles when they tried to practice as doctors. Many were denied licenses, and hospitals often closed their doors to them. In Britain, Parliament finally capitulated to pressure and passed a bill in 1876 giving women the right to take qualifying examinations. Soon women were entering medical schools in ever-larger numbers. By the 1890s, universities in Great Britain, Sweden, Denmark, Norway, Finland, Russia, and Belgium were admitting women to medical training and practice. Germany and Austria did not do so until after 1900. Even then, medical associations refused to accept women as equals in the medical profession. Women were not given full membership in the American Medical Association until 1915.

Science and the Study of Society

The importance of science in the nineteenth century perhaps made it inevitable that a scientific approach would be applied to the realm of human activity. The attempt to apply the methods of science systematically to the study of society was perhaps most evident in the work of the Frenchman Auguste Comte (ow-GOOST KOHNT) (1798–1857). His major work, *System of Positive Philosophy,* was published between 1837 and 1842 but had its real impact after 1850.

Comte created a system of "positive knowledge" based on a hierarchy of all the sciences. Mathematics was the foundation on which the physical sciences, earth sciences, and biological sciences were built. At the top was sociology, the science of human society, which for Comte incorporated economics, anthropology, history, and social psychology. Comte saw sociology's task as a difficult one. The discovery of the general laws of society would have to be based on the collection and analysis of data on humans and their social environment. Although his schemes were often complex and dense, Comte played an important role in the growing popularity of science and materialism in the mid-nineteenth century.

Realism in Literature

The belief that the world should be viewed realistically, frequently expressed after 1850, was closely related to the materialistic outlook. The term **Realism** was first employed in 1850 to describe a new style of painting and soon spread to literature.

The literary Realists of the mid-nineteenth century were distinguished by their deliberate rejection of Romanticism. The literary Realists wanted to deal with ordinary characters from real life rather than Romantic heroes in unusual settings. They also sought to avoid flowery and sentimental language by using careful observation and accurate description, an approach that led them to eschew poetry in favor of prose and the novel. Realists often combined their interest in everyday life with a searching examination of social questions.

The leading novelist of the 1850s and 1860s, the Frenchman Gustave Flaubert (goo-STAHV floh-BAYR) (1821–1880), perfected the Realist novel. His *Madame*

Bovary (1857) was a straightforward description of barren and sordid small-town life in France. Emma Bovary, a woman of some vitality, is trapped in a marriage to a drab provincial doctor. Impelled by the images of romantic love she has read about in novels, she seeks the same thing for herself in adulterous affairs. Unfulfilled, she is ultimately driven to suicide, unrepentant to the end for her lifestyle. Flaubert's contempt for bourgeois society was evident in his portrayal of middle-class hypocrisy and smugness.

William Thackeray (1811–1863) wrote Britain's prototypical Realist novel, *Vanity Fair: A Novel Without a Hero,* in 1848. Thackeray deliberately flouted the Romantic conventions. A novel, Thackeray said, should "convey as strongly as possible the sentiment of reality as opposed to a tragedy or poem, which may be heroical." Perhaps the greatest of the Victorian novelists was Charles Dickens (1812–1870), whose realistic novels focusing on the lower and middle classes in Britain's early industrial age became extraordinarily successful. His descriptions of the urban poor and the brutalization of human life were vividly realistic (see the box on p. 700).

Realism in Art

In the first half of the nineteenth century, Romanticism in art had been paralleled by the classical school of painting, but both were superseded by the new mood of the mid-nineteenth century. In art, too, Realism became dominant after 1850, although Romanticism was by no means dead. Among the most important characteristics of Realism were a desire to depict the everyday life of ordinary people, be they peasants, workers, or prostitutes; an attempt at photographic realism; and an interest in the natural environment. The French became leaders in Realist painting.

COURBET Gustave Courbet (goo-STAHV koor-BAY) (1819–1877) was the most famous artist of the Realist school. In fact, the word *Realism* was first coined in 1850 to describe one of his paintings. Courbet reveled in a realistic portrayal of everyday life. His subjects were factory workers, peasants, and the wives of saloon keepers. "I have never seen either angels or goddesses, so I am not interested in painting them," he exclaimed. One of his famous works, *The Stonebreakers,* painted in 1849, shows two road workers engaged in the deadening work of breaking stones to build a road. This representation of human misery was a scandal to those who objected to his "cult of ugliness." To Courbet, no subject was too ordinary, too harsh, or too ugly to interest him.

MILLET Jean-François Millet (ZHAHNH-frahnh-SWAH mi-YEH) (1814–1875) was preoccupied with scenes from rural life, especially peasants laboring in the fields, although his Realism still contained an element of Romantic sentimentality. In *The Gleaners,* his most famous work, three peasant women gather grain in a field, a centuries-old practice that for Millet showed the symbiotic relationship between humans and nature. Millet made landscape and

Gustave Courbet, *The Stonebreakers.* Realism, largely developed by French painters, aimed at a lifelike portrayal of the daily activities of ordinary people. Gustave Courbet was the most famous of the Realist artists. As is evident in *The Stonebreakers*, he sought to portray things as they really appear. He shows an old road builder and his young assistant in their tattered clothes, engrossed in their dreary work of breaking stones to construct a road. The use of browns and grays helps communicate the drudgery of their task.

Jean-François Millet, *The Gleaners.* Jean-François Millet, another prominent French Realist painter, took a special interest in the daily activities of French peasants, although he tended to transform his peasants into heroic figures who dominated their environment. In *The Gleaners*, for example, the three peasant women engaged in the backbreaking work of gathering grain left after the harvest still appear as powerful figures, symbolizing the union of humans with the earth.

Realism: Charles Dickens and an Image of Hell on Earth

Charles Dickens was one of Britain's greatest novelists. Though he realistically portrayed the material, social, and psychological milieu of his time, an element of Romanticism still pervaded his novels. This is evident in this selection from *The Old Curiosity Shop* in which his description of the English mill town of Birmingham takes on the imagery of Dante's Hell.

Charles Dickens, *The Old Curiosity Shop*

A long suburb of red brick houses,—some with patches of garden ground, where coal-dust and factory smoke darkened the shrinking leaves, and coarse rank flowers; and where the struggling vegetation sickened and sank under the hot breath of kiln and furnace, making them by its presence seem yet more blighting and unwholesome than in the town itself,—a long, flat, straggling suburb passed, they came by slow degrees upon a cheerless region, where not a blade of grass was seen to grow; where not a bud put forth its promise in the spring; where nothing green could live but on the surface of the stagnant pools, which here and there lay idly sweltering by the black roadside.

Advancing more and more into the shadow of this mournful place, its dark depressing influence stole upon their spirits, and filled them with a dismal gloom. On every side, and as far as the eye could see into the heavy distance, tall chimneys, crowding on each other, and presenting that endless repetition of the same dull, ugly form, which is the horror of oppressive dreams, poured out their plague of smoke, obscured the light, and made foul the melancholy air. On mounds of ashes by the wayside, sheltered only by a few rough boards, or rotten pent-house roofs, strange engines spun and writhed like tortured creatures; clanking their iron chains, shrieking in their rapid whirl from time to time as though in torment unendurable, and making the ground tremble with their agonies. Dismantled houses here and there appeared, tottering to the earth, propped up by fragments of others that had fallen down, unroofed, windowless, blackened, desolate, but yet inhabited. Men, women, children, wan in their looks and ragged in attire, tended the engines, fed their tributary fires, begged upon the road, or scowled half-naked from the doorless houses. Then came more of the wrathful monsters, whose like they almost seemed to be in their wildness and their untamed air, screeching and turning to the right and left, with the same interminable perspective of brick towers, never ceasing in their black vomit, blasting all things living or inanimate, shutting out the face of day, and closing in on all these horrors with a dense dark cloud.

But night-time in this dreadful spot!—night, when the smoke was changed to fire; when every chimney spurted up its flame; and places, that had been dark vaults all day, now shone red-hot, with figures moving to and fro within their blazing jaws, and calling to one another with hoarse cries—night, when the noise of every strange machine was aggravated by the darkness; when the people near them looked wilder and more savage; when bands of unemployed laborers paraded in the roads, or clustered by torchlight round their leaders, who told them in stern language of their wrongs, and urged them on by frightful cries and threats; when maddened men, armed with sword and firebrand, spurning the tears and prayers of women who would restrain them, rushed forth on errands of terror and destruction, to work no ruin half so surely as their own—night, when carts came rumbling by, filled with rude coffins (for contagious disease and death had been busy with the living crops); or when orphans cried, and distracted women shrieked and followed in their wake—night, when some called for bread, and some for drink to drown their cares; and some with tears, and some with staggering feet, and so with bloodshot eyes, went brooding home—night, which, unlike the night that Heaven sends on earth, brought with it no peace, nor quiet, nor signs of blessed sleep—who shall tell the terrors of the night to that young wandering child! ⊱

Q What image of Birmingham do you get from this selection by Dickens? Why is it so powerful? What does the passage reveal about Dickens himself and the roles European writers played in the reform of nineteenth-century society?

---

country life an important subject matter for French artists, but he, too, was criticized by his contemporaries for crude subject matter and unorthodox technique.

Music: The Twilight of Romanticism

The mid-nineteenth century witnessed the development of a new group of musicians known as the New German School. They emphasized emotional content rather than abstract form and championed new methods of using music to express literary or pictorial ideas.

LISZT The Hungarian-born composer Franz Liszt (FRAHNTS LIST) (1811–1886) best exemplifies the achievements of the New German School. A child prodigy, he established himself as an outstanding concert artist by the age of twelve. Liszt's performances and his dazzling personality made him the most highly esteemed virtuoso of his age. He has been called the greatest pianist of all time and has been credited with introducing the concept of the modern piano recital.

Liszt's compositions consist mainly of piano pieces, although he composed in other genres as well, including sacred music. He invented the term *symphonic poem* to refer to his orchestral works, which did not strictly obey traditional forms and were generally based on a literary or pictorial idea. Under the guidance of Liszt and the New German School, Romantic music reached its peak.

WAGNER Although Liszt was an influential mentor to a number of young composers, he was most closely associated with his eventual son-in-law Richard Wagner (RIKH-art VAHG-nur) (1813–1883). Building on the advances made by Liszt and the New German School, Wagner ultimately realized the German desire for a truly national opera. Wagner was not only a composer but also a propagandist and writer in support of his unique conception of dramatic music. Called both the culmination of the Romantic era and the beginning of the avant-garde, Wagner's music may be described as a monumental development in classical music.

Believing that opera is the best form of artistic expression, Wagner transformed opera into "music drama" through his *Gesamtkunstwerk* (guh-ZAHMT-koonst-vayrk) ("total art work"), a musical composition for the theater in which music, acting, dance, poetry, and scenic design are synthesized into a harmonious whole. He abandoned the traditional divisions of opera, which interrupted the dramatic line of the work, and instead used a device called a leitmotiv, a recurring musical theme in which the human voice combined with the line of the orchestra instead of rising above it. His operas incorporate literally hundreds of leitmotivs in order to convey the story. For his themes, Wagner looked to myth and epic tales from the past. His most ambitious work was *The Ring of the Nibelung,* a series of four music dramas dealing with the mythical gods of the ancient German epic.

CHAPTER SUMMARY

Between 1850 and 1871, the national state became the focus of people's loyalty, and the nations of Europe spent their energies in achieving unification or reform. France attempted to relive its memories of Napoleonic greatness through the election of Louis Napoleon, Napoleon's nephew, as president and later Emperor Napoleon III. Louis Napoleon was one of a new generation of conservative political leaders who were practitioners of *Realpolitik.*

Unification to achieve a national state preoccupied leaders in Italy and Germany. The dreams of Mazzini became a reality when the combined activities of Count Cavour and Giuseppe Garibaldi finally led to the unification of Italy in 1870. Under the guidance of Otto von Bismarck, Prussia engaged in wars with Denmark, Austria, and France before it finally achieved the goal of national unification in 1871.

Reform characterized developments in other Western states. Austria compromised with Hungarian nationalists and created the Dual Monarchy of Austria-Hungary. Russia's defeat in the Crimean War led to reforms under Alexander II, which included the freeing of the Russian serfs. In Great Britain, the pressures of industrialization led to a series of reforms that made the realm of Queen Victoria more democratic. The American Civil War ended with the union of the states preserved and slavery abolished. Canada achieved dominion status from Britain, which included the right to rule itself in domestic affairs.

Political nationalism had emerged during the French revolutionary era and had become a powerful force for change during the first half of the nineteenth century, but its triumph came only after 1850. Associated initially with middle-class liberals, it would have great appeal to the broad masses as well by the end of the century as people created their national "imagined communities." In 1871, however, the political transformations stimulated by the force of nationalism were by no means complete. Significantly large minorities, especially in the multiethnic empires controlled by the Austrians, Turks, and Russians, had not achieved the goal of their own national states. Moreover, the nationalism that had triumphed by 1871 was no longer the nationalism that had been closely identified with liberalism. Liberal nationalists had believed that unified nation-states would preserve individual rights and lead to a greater community of European peoples. Rather than unifying people, however, the new, loud, chauvinistic nationalism of the late nineteenth century divided them as the new national states became embroiled in bitter competition after 1871.

The period between 1850 and 1871 was also characterized by the emergence of Marxian socialism, new advances in science including the laws of thermodynamics, a germ theory of disease, and Darwin's theory of evolution. In the arts, Realism prevailed, evident in the writers and artists who were only too willing to portray realistically the grim world in which they lived.

CHAPTER TIMELINE

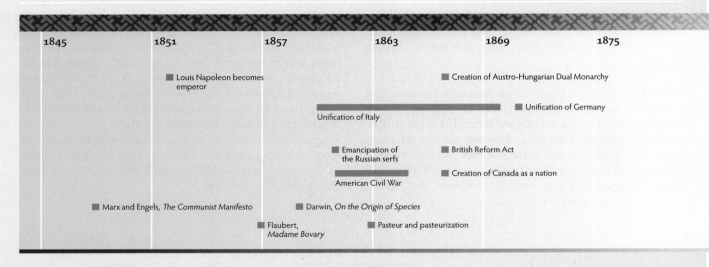

1845	1851	1857	1863	1869	1875

- Louis Napoleon becomes emperor
- Creation of Austro-Hungarian Dual Monarchy
- Unification of Germany
- Unification of Italy
- Emancipation of the Russian serfs
- British Reform Act
- American Civil War
- Creation of Canada as a nation
- Marx and Engels, *The Communist Manifesto*
- Darwin, *On the Origin of Species*
- Flaubert, *Madame Bovary*
- Pasteur and pasteurization

CHAPTER REVIEW

Upon Reflection

Q To what extent is it true to say that the forces of liberalism and nationalism triumphed in the Austrian Empire, Russia, and Great Britain between 1850 and 1871?

Q Despite Marx's claim for its scientific basis, can Marxism be viewed primarily as a product of its age? Why or why not?

Q How did Realism differ from Romanticism, and how did Realism reflect the economic and social realities of Europe during the middle decades of the nineteenth century?

Key Terms

Zollverein (p. 678)
Realpolitik (p. 679)
Ausgleich (p. 682)
mir (p. 684)
zemstvos (p. 685)
populism (p. 685)
joint-stock investment bank (p. 690)
proletariat (p. 692)
materialism (p. 694)
natural selection (p. 694)
organic evolution (p. 694)
pasteurization (p. 695)
Realism (p. 698)

Suggestions for Further Reading

GENERAL WORKS In addition to the general works on nineteenth-century Europe cited in Chapter 21, see three general surveys of the midcentury decades: **N. Rich, *The Age of Nationalism and Reform, 1850–1890,*** 2nd ed. (New York, 1980); **E. Hobsbawm, *The Age of Capital, 1845–1875*** (London, 1975); and **J. A. S. Grenville, *Europe Reshaped, 1848–1878,*** 2nd ed. (London, 2000).

THE FRENCH SECOND EMPIRE For a good introduction to the French Second Empire, see **A. Plessis, *The Rise and Fall of the Second Empire, 1852–1871,*** trans. **J. Mandelbaum** (New York, 1985). Napoleon III's role can be examined in **J. F. McMillan, *Napoleon III*** (New York, 1991). The Crimean War and its impact are examined in **C. Ponting, *The Crimean War*** (New York, 2004).

UNIFICATION OF ITALY AND GERMANY The unification of Italy can be examined in **F. Coppa, *The Origins of the Italian Wars of Independence*** (New York, 1992); **B. Derek** and **E. F. Biagini, *The Risorgimento and the Unification of Italy,*** 2nd ed. (London, 2002); **D. M. Smith, *Cavour*** (London, 1985); and **H. Hearder, *Cavour*** (New York, 1994). The unification of Germany can be pursued first in **W. Carr, *The Origins of the Wars of German Unification*** (New York, 1991), and in two good biographies of Bismarck, **E. Crankshaw, *Bismarck*** (New York, 1981), and **E. Feuchtwanger, *Bismarck*** (London, 2002). See also the brief study by **B. Waller, *Bismarck,*** 2nd ed. (Oxford, 1997). On the Franco-Prussian War, see **G. Wawro, *The Franco-Prussian War*** (Cambridge, 2003).

THE NATIONAL STATE For a background discussion of the impact and character of nationalism, see **B. Anderson, *Imagined Communities: Reflections on the Origins and Spread of Nationalism,*** rev. ed. (New York, 2006). On the Austrian Empire, see **R. Okey, *The Habsburg Monarchy*** (New York, 2001). Imperial Russia is covered in **T. Chapman, *Imperial Russia, 1801–1905*** (London, 2001). On Victorian Britain, see **W. L. Arnstein, *Queen Victoria*** (New York, 2005), and **I. Machlin, *Disraeli*** (London, 1995). The definitive one-volume history of the American Civil War is **J. M. McPherson, *Battle Cry of Freedom: The Civil War Era*** in the Oxford History of the United States series (New York, 2003).

ECONOMIC DEVELOPMENTS AND THOUGHT In addition to the general works on economic development listed in Chapters 20 and 21, some specialized works on this period are worthwhile. These include **W. O. Henderson, *The Rise of German Industrial Power, 1834–1914*** (Berkeley, Calif., 1975), and **F. Crouzet, *The Victorian Economy*** (London, 1982). On Marx, a standard work is **D. McLellan, *Karl Marx: A Biography,*** 4th ed. (New York, 2006). See also **F. Wheen, *Karl Marx: A Life*** (New York, 2001), but it can be supplemented by the interesting and comprehensive work by **L. Kolakowski, *Main Currents of Marxism,*** 3 vols. (Oxford, 1978).

SCIENCE AND CULTURE For an introduction to the intellectual changes of the nineteenth century, see **O. Chadwick, *The Secularization of the European Mind in the Nineteenth Century*** (Cambridge, 1975). A detailed biography of Darwin can be found in **J. Bowlby, *Charles Darwin: A Biography*** (London, 1990). For an introduction to the transformation of medical practices in the nineteenth century, see the appropriate chapters in **L. N. Magner, *A History of Medicine*** (New York, 1992). On Realism, **J. Malpas, *Realism*** (Cambridge, 1997), is a good introduction. ⮞

Visit the CourseMate website at www.cengagebrain.com for additional study tools and review materials for this chapter.

1. Which of the following best describes the Victorian era in Great Britain?

   (A) Queen Victoria led English society into a time of moral ambiguity and acceptance of newer, less strict moral codes.
   (B) Though Britain lagged behind Europe economically, the people's love for the queen soothed any dissatisfaction they felt over this imbalance.
   (C) Voting restrictions were greatly reduced, and the working class enjoyed economic prosperity.
   (D) Britain was constantly involved in external conflicts, both with Ireland and on the Continent.
   (E) Britain struggled to redefine its identity without its colonies.

2. Emperor Napoleon III of France achieved all of the following during his reign EXCEPT

   (A) the construction of an extensive railroad network.
   (B) the reconstruction and modernization of Paris.
   (C) industrial expansion that tripled the country's iron production.
   (D) strong economic growth.
   (E) the creation of a new military organization.

3. The unification both of Germany and of Italy can be best described as

   (A) a campaign completed by liberal leaders.
   (B) a process dominated by conservative military leaders.
   (C) a movement supported by other European monarchs.
   (D) a peaceful process driven by a sense of collective nationalism.
   (E) a slow process that drew the two countries into war with each other.

4. Which of the following took place in the German states in the mid-nineteenth century?

   (A) Austria became much more powerful than Prussia, as its government enjoyed wide popular support and the Habsburgs provided strong leadership to the nation.
   (B) The *Zollverein* was established as a customs union that stimulated trade under the leadership of the Prussian state.
   (C) The new Prussian monarch, Frederick William IV, became bored with governing, leaving the Prussian state virtually powerless and without any firm direction.
   (D) Many of the German states sought to increase their power by allying with Great Britain.
   (E) Nationalists and liberals made repeated attempts to unify the German states under Bavarian leadership.

5. The Crimean War

   (A) showed that the Ottoman Empire was still a viable threat to central Europe.
   (B) culminated in a new political alliance between Austria and France.
   (C) highlighted the military dominance of Russia.
   (D) marked an end to the peace that had been maintained by the Concert of Europe.
   (E) saw Piedmont emerge as a legitimate threat to the balance of power.

6. The Eastern Question refers to the region of

   (A) Poland.
   (B) the Ottoman Empire.
   (C) Russia.
   (D) the Mediterranean islands.
   (E) the Balkans.

7. The results of the Danish War, the Austro-Prussian War, and the Franco-Prussian War

   (A) demonstrated the advances in European military weaponry and tactics.
   (B) showed that Britain desired to gain more power in western Europe.
   (C) enabled the German states to successfully eliminate foreigners from their lands.
   (D) enabled the Austrians to increase their power within central Europe.
   (E) shifted the balance of power by creating an alliance between Denmark and France.

8. The *Ausgleich* of 1867

   (A) was championed by Austrian nationalists and resulted in a compromise that added Serbia to the Austrian Empire.
   (B) embodied the desire of the German states to unify.
   (C) sowed further conflict between Austria and Russia.
   (D) helped prevent the multiethnic Austrian Empire from fragmenting into smaller, less powerful states.
   (E) allowed Joseph II of Austria to free the serfs within his empire.

9. "The history of all hitherto existing society is the history of class struggle." This statement is most closely associated with

   (A) liberalism.
   (B) nationalism.
   (C) Marxism.
   (D) conservatism.
   (E) socialism.

10. Which of the following best describes Otto von Bismarck's pursuit of German unification?

   (A) He rallied liberal activists in pursuit of a constitution to unify the German people.
   (B) He hoped, above all, to achieve a new peace in Europe by establishing an equal balance of power.
   (C) He practiced *realpolitik*, recognizing the importance of military and diplomatic action.
   (D) He agitated for a Marxist revolution in Germany.
   (E) He used his powers as the Prussian monarch to increase Prussian central power.

11. Alexander II accomplished all of the following EXCEPT

   (A) creating a system of zemstvos.
   (B) allowing peasants to bring lawsuits before the courts.
   (C) allowing peasants to own property and marry as they chose.
   (D) emancipating the serfs and granting them free land.
   (E) instituting legal reform of the judicial courts.

12. Charles Darwin's greatest scientific achievement was

   (A) to spread the idea that science and nature are not static but always changing.
   (B) to contribute to the new intellectual movement of Realism.
   (C) to develop a practice known as pasteurization.
   (D) to help contribute to a cure for cholera.
   (E) to apply Marxist principles to science.

13. Which of the following artists is most closely identified with German nationalism?

   (A) Johann Sebastian Bach
   (B) Fyodor Dostoevsky
   (C) Charles Dickens
   (D) Richard Wagner
   (E) Franz Liszt

14. The Realists

   (A) sought to engage the reader in appreciating the simple things in nature and life.
   (B) rarely received much acclaim for their works as they did not seek widespread attention or distribution.
   (C) often highlighted and discussed important social issues, yet did not offer solutions to these problems.
   (D) wanted to glorify human accomplishments and celebrate progress.
   (E) tended to separate their protagonists from the social issues of the day and created a world of innocence for their characters.

15. During the reign of Napoleon III,

   (A) he seized more power and became highly conservative, causing the people of France to quickly regret electing him emperor.
   (B) France enjoyed internal peace and relative prosperity as Louis Napoleon worked to provide liberal reforms to the people.
   (C) the rest of Europe, fearing that he would invade other lands, organized a coalition against France.
   (D) the country's attempts at liberal reform were quickly undone by Louis Napoleon's swing toward conservatism in his later years.
   (E) France remained peaceful, as Napoleon III avoided all wars and concentrated on improving his state.

© Museum of the City of New York/Getty Images

Coney Island fun: a Ferris wheel and onlookers

Mass Society in an "Age of Progress," 1871–1894

CHAPTER OUTLINE AND FOCUS QUESTIONS

The Growth of Industrial Prosperity

Q What was the Second Industrial Revolution, and what effects did it have on European economic and social life? What roles did socialist parties and trade unions play in improving conditions for the working classes?

The Emergence of a Mass Society

Q What is a mass society, and what were its main characteristics? What role were women expected to play in society and family life in the latter half of the nineteenth century, and how closely did patterns of family life correspond to this ideal?

The National State

Q What general political trends were evident in the nations of western Europe in the last decades of the nineteenth century, and how did these trends differ from the policies pursued in Germany, Austria-Hungary, and Russia?

CRITICAL THINKING

Q What was the relationship among economic, social, and political developments between 1871 and 1894?

IN THE LATE 1800S, Europe entered a dynamic period of material prosperity. Bringing with it new industries, new sources of energy, and new goods, a second Industrial Revolution transformed the human environment, dazzled Europeans, and led them to believe that their material progress meant human progress. Scientific and technological achievements, many naively believed, would improve humanity's condition and solve all human problems. The doctrine of progress became an article of great faith.

The new urban and industrial world created by the rapid economic changes of the nineteenth century led to the emergence of a mass society by the late nineteenth century. Mass society meant improvements for the lower classes, who benefited from the extension of voting rights, a better standard of living, and education. It also brought mass leisure. New work patterns established the "weekend" as a distinct time of recreation and fun, and new forms of mass transportation—railroads and streetcars—enabled even ordinary workers to make excursions to amusement parks. Coney Island was only 8 miles from central New York City; Blackpool in England was a short train ride from nearby industrial towns. With their Ferris wheels and other daring rides that threw young men and women together, amusement parks offered a whole new world of entertainment. Thanks to the railroad, seaside resorts, once the preserve of the wealthy, became accessible to more people for weekend visits, much to the disgust of one upper-class regular, who complained about the new "day-trippers": "They swarm upon the beach, wandering listlessly about with apparently no other aim than to get a mouthful of fresh air." Enterprising entrepreneurs in resorts like Blackpool welcomed the masses of new visitors, however, and built piers laden with food, drink, and entertainment to serve them.

The coming of mass society also created new roles for the governments of Europe's nation-states. In the early nineteenth century, "nations" functioned as communities of people bound together by common language, traditions, customs, and institutions. By the mid-nineteenth century, however, the "state"—the organized institutions of government—had come to dominate European lives. By 1871, the national states promoted economic growth and mass education, amassed national armies by conscription, and took more responsibility for public health and housing in their cities. By taking these steps, the governments of the national states hoped to foster national unity and national loyalty.

Within many of these national states, the growth of the middle class had led to the triumph of liberal practices: constitutional governments, parliaments, and principles of equality. The period after 1871 also witnessed the growth of political democracy as the right to vote was extended to all adult males; women, though, would still have to fight for the same political rights. With political democracy came a new mass politics and a new mass press. Both would become regular features of the twentieth century.

The Growth of Industrial Prosperity

 FOCUS QUESTIONS: What was the Second Industrial Revolution, and what effects did it have on European economic and social life? What roles did socialist parties and trade unions play in improving conditions for the working classes?

At the heart of Europeans' belief in progress after 1871 was the stunning material growth produced by what historians have called the Second Industrial Revolution. The First Industrial Revolution had given rise to textiles, railroads, iron, and coal. In the second revolution, steel, chemicals, electricity, and petroleum led the way to new industrial frontiers.

New Products

The first major change in industrial development after 1870 was the substitution of steel for iron. New methods of rolling and shaping steel made it useful in the construction of lighter, smaller, and faster machines and engines, as well as railways, ships, and armaments. In 1860, Great Britain, France, Germany, and Belgium together produced 125,000 tons of steel; by 1913, the total was 32 million tons. Whereas in the early 1870s Britain had produced twice as much steel as Germany, by 1910, German production was double that of Great Britain. Both had been surpassed by the United States in 1890.

CHEMICALS Great Britain also fell behind in the new chemical industry. A change in the method of making soda enabled France and Germany to take the lead in producing the alkalies used in the textile, soap, and paper industries. German laboratories soon overtook the British in the development of new organic chemical compounds, such as artificial dyes. By 1900, German firms had cornered 90 percent of the market for dyestuffs and also led in the development of photographic plates and film.

ELECTRICITY Electricity was a major new form of energy that proved to be of great value since it could be easily converted into other forms of energy, such as heat, light, and motion, and moved relatively effortlessly through space over wires. In the 1870s, the first commercially practical generators of electrical current were developed. By 1881, Britain had its first public power station. By 1910, hydroelectric power stations and coal-fired steam-generating plants enabled entire districts to be tied in to a single power distribution system that provided a common source of power for homes, shops, and industrial enterprises.

Electricity spawned a whole series of inventions. The invention of the lightbulb by the American Thomas Edison (1847–1931) and the Briton Joseph Swan (1828–1914) opened homes and cities to illumination by electric lights. A revolution in communications was fostered when Alexander Graham Bell (1847–1922) invented the telephone in 1876 and Guglielmo Marconi (1874–1937) sent the first radio waves across the Atlantic in 1901. Although most electricity was initially used for lighting, it was eventually put to use in transportation. The first electric railway was installed in Berlin in 1879. By the 1880s, streetcars and subways had appeared in major European cities and had begun to replace horse-drawn buses. Electricity also transformed the factory. Conveyor belts, cranes, machines, and machine tools could all be powered by electricity and located anywhere. In the First Industrial Revolution, coal had been the major source of energy. Countries without adequate coal supplies lagged behind in industrialization. Thanks to electricity, they could now enter the industrial age.

THE INTERNAL COMBUSTION ENGINE The development of the internal combustion engine had a similar effect. The first internal combustion engine, fired by gas and air, was produced in 1878. It proved unsuitable for widespread use as a source of power in transportation until the development of liquid fuels—petroleum and its distilled derivatives. An oil-fired engine was made in 1897, and by 1902, the Hamburg-Amerika Line had switched from coal to oil on its new ocean liners. By the end of the nineteenth century, some naval fleets had been converted to oil burners as well.

An Age of Progress. In the decades after 1871, the Second Industrial Revolution led many Europeans to believe that they were living in an age of progress when most human problems would be solved by scientific achievements. This illustration is taken from a special issue of the *Illustrated London News* celebrating the Diamond Jubilee of Queen Victoria in 1897. On the left are scenes from 1837, when Victoria came to the British throne; on the right are scenes from 1897. The vivid contrast underscored the magazine's conclusion: "The most striking . . . evidence of progress during the reign is the ever increasing speed which the discoveries of physical science have forced into everyday life. Steam and electricity have conquered time and space to a greater extent during the last sixty years than all the preceding six hundred years witnessed."

The development of the internal combustion engine gave rise to the automobile and the airplane. The invention of a light engine by Gottlieb Daimler (GUHT-leeb DYM-lur) in 1886 was the key to the development of the automobile. In 1900, world production stood at nine thousand cars; by 1906, Americans had overtaken the initial lead of the French. It was an American, Henry Ford (1863–1947), who revolutionized the car industry with the mass production of the Model T. By 1916, Ford's factories were producing 735,000 cars a year. Air transportation began with the Zeppelin (ZEP-puh-lin) airship in 1900. In 1903, at Kitty Hawk, North Carolina, Wilbur and Orville Wright made the first flight in a fixed-wing plane powered by a gasoline engine. It took World War I to stimulate the aircraft industry, however, and the first regular passenger air service was not established until 1919.

New Markets

The growth of industrial production depended on the development of markets for the sale of manufactured goods. After 1870, the best foreign markets were already heavily saturated, forcing Europeans to take a renewed look at their domestic markets. As Europeans were the richest consumers in the world, those markets offered abundant possibilities. The dramatic population increases

after 1870 (see "Population Growth" later in this chapter) were accompanied by a steady rise in national incomes. The leading industrialized nations, Britain and Germany, doubled or tripled their national incomes. Between 1850 and 1900, real wages increased by two-thirds in Britain and by one-third in Germany. As the prices of both food and manufactured goods declined due to lower transportation costs, Europeans could spend more on consumer products. Businesses soon perceived the value of using new techniques of mass marketing to sell the consumer goods made possible by the development of the steel and electrical industries. By bringing together a vast array of new products in one place, they created the department store (see the box on p. 707). The desire to own sewing machines, clocks, bicycles, electric lights, and typewriters rapidly created a new consumer ethic that became a crucial part of the modern economy (see "Mass Consumption" later in this chapter).

TARIFFS AND CARTELS Meanwhile, increased competition for foreign markets and the growing importance of domestic demand led to a reaction against free trade. To many industrial and political leaders, protective **tariffs** guaranteed domestic markets for the products of their own industries. That is why, after a decade of experimentation with free trade in the 1860s, Europeans returned to tariff protection.

The Department Store and the Beginnings of Mass Consumerism

Domestic markets were especially important for the sale of the goods being turned out by Europe's increasing number of industrial plants. Techniques of mass marketing were developed to encourage people to purchase the new consumer goods. The Parisians pioneered the department store, and this selection is taken from a contemporary's account of the growth of these stores in the French capital city.

✦ ✦ ✦

E. Lavasseur, *On Parisian Department Stores*

It was in the reign of Louis-Philippe that department stores for fashion goods and dresses, extending to material and other clothing, began to be distinguished. The type was already one of the notable developments of the Second Empire; it became one of the most important ones of the Third Republic. These stores have increased in number and several of them have become extremely large. Combining in their different departments all articles of clothing, toilet articles, furniture and many other ranges of goods, it is their special object so to combine all commodities as to attract and satisfy customers who will find conveniently together an assortment of a mass of articles corresponding to all their various needs. They attract customers by permanent display, by free entry into the shops, by periodic exhibitions, by special sales, by fixed prices, and by their ability to deliver the goods purchased to customers' homes, in Paris and to the provinces. Turning themselves into direct intermediaries between the producer and the consumer, even producing sometimes some of their articles in their own workshops, buying at lowest prices because of their large orders and because they are in a position to profit from bargains, working with large sums, and selling to most of their customers for cash only, they can transmit these benefits in lowered selling prices. They can even decide to sell at a loss, as an advertisement or to get rid of out-of-date fashions. Taking 5–6 percent on 100 million brings them in more than 20 percent would bring to a firm doing a turnover of 50,000 francs.

The success of these department stores is only possible thanks to the volume of their business and this volume needs considerable capital and a very large turnover. Now capital, having become abundant, is freely combined nowadays in large enterprises, although French capital has the reputation of being more wary of the risks of industry than of State or railway securities. On the other hand, the large urban agglomerations, the ease with which goods can be transported by the railways, the diffusion of some comforts to strata below the middle classes, have all favored these developments.

As example we may cite some figures relating to these stores, since they were brought to the notice of the public in the *Revue des Deux-Mondes*. . . .

Le Louvre, dating to the time of the extension of the rue de Rivoli under the Second Empire, did in 1893 a business of 120 million at a profit of 6.4 percent. *Le Bon Marché,* which was a small shop when Mr. Boucicaut entered it in 1852, already did a business of 20 million at the end of the Empire. During the republic its new buildings were erected; Mme. Boucicaut turned it by her will into a kind of cooperative society, with shares and an ingenious organization; turnover reached 150 million in 1893, leaving a profit of 5 percent. . . .

According to the tax records of 1891, these stores in Paris, numbering 12, employed 1,708 persons and were rated on their site values at 2,159,000 francs; the largest had then 542 employees. These same stores had, in 1901, 9,784 employees; one of them over 2,000 and another over 1,600; their site value has doubled (4,089,000 francs).

Q Did the invention of department stores respond to or create the new "consumer ethic" in industrialized societies? What was the new turn-of-the-century ethic? According to Lavasseur, what were the positive effects of department stores for Parisian society?

During this same period, **cartels** were being formed to decrease competition internally. In a cartel, independent enterprises worked together to control prices and fix production quotas, thereby restraining the kind of competition that led to reduced prices. Cartels were especially strong in Germany, where banks moved to protect their investments by eliminating the "anarchy of competition." German businesses established cartels in potash, coal, steel, and chemicals.

LARGER FACTORIES The formation of cartels was paralleled by a move toward ever-larger manufacturing plants, especially in the iron and steel, machinery, heavy electrical equipment, and chemical industries. Although evident in Britain, France, and Belgium, the trend was most pronounced in Germany. Between 1882 and 1907, the number of people working in German factories with more than one thousand employees rose from 205,000 to 879,000. This growth in the size of industrial plants led to pressure for greater efficiency in factory production at the same time that competition led to demands for greater economy. The result was a desire to streamline or rationalize production as much as possible. One way to accomplish this was by cutting labor costs through the mechanization of transport within plants, such as using electric cranes to move materials. Even more important, the development of precision tools enabled manufacturers to produce interchangeable parts, which in turn led to the creation of the assembly line for production. First used in the United States for small arms and clocks, the assembly line had moved to Europe by 1850. In the second half of the nineteenth century, it was used primarily in manufacturing nonmilitary goods, such as sewing machines, typewriters, bicycles, and eventually automobiles. Principles of scientific management were also introduced by 1900 to maximize workers' efficiency.

New Patterns in an Industrial Economy

The Second Industrial Revolution played a role in the emergence of basic economic patterns that have characterized much of modern European economic life. Although the period after 1871 has been described as an age of material prosperity, recessions and crises were still very much a part of economic life. Although some historians question the appropriateness of characterizing the period from 1873 to 1895 as a great **depression,** Europeans did experience a series of economic crises during those years. Prices, especially those of agricultural products, fell dramatically. Slumps in the business cycle reduced profits, although recession occurred at different times in different countries. France and Britain, for example, sank into depression in the 1880s while Germany and the United States were recovering from their depression of the 1870s. From 1895 until World War I, however, Europe overall experienced an economic boom and achieved a level of prosperity that encouraged people later to look back to that era as *la belle époque* (lah BEL ay-PUK)—a golden age in European civilization.

GERMAN INDUSTRIAL LEADERSHIP After 1870, Germany replaced Great Britain as the industrial leader of Europe. Within two decades, Germany's superiority was evident in new areas of manufacturing, such as organic chemicals and electrical equipment, and increasingly apparent in its ever-greater share of worldwide trade. Why had industrial leadership passed from Britain to Germany?

Britain's early lead in industrialization gave it established industrial plants and made it more difficult to shift to the new techniques of the Second Industrial Revolution. As later entrants to the industrial age, the Germans could build the latest and most efficient industrial plants. British entrepreneurs made the situation worse by their tendency to be suspicious of innovations and their reluctance to invest in new plants and industries. As one manufacturer remarked, "One wants to be thoroughly convinced of the superiority of a new method before condemning as useless a large plant that has hitherto done good service."[1] German managers, by contrast, were accustomed to change, and the formation of large cartels encouraged German banks to provide enormous sums for investment. Then, too, unlike the Germans, the British were not willing to encourage formal scientific and technical education.

After 1870, the relationship of science and technology grew closer. Newer fields of industrial activity, such as organic chemistry and electrical engineering, required more scientific knowledge than the commonsense tinkering employed by amateur inventors. Companies began to invest capital in laboratory equipment for their own research or hired scientific consultants for advice. Nowhere was the relationship between science and technology more apparent than in Germany. In 1899, German technical schools were allowed to award doctorate degrees, and by 1900, they were turning out three to four thousand graduates a year. Many of these graduates made their way into industrial firms.

EUROPEAN ECONOMIC ZONES The struggle for economic (and political) supremacy between Great Britain and Germany should not cause us to overlook the other great polarization of the age. By 1900, Europe was divided into two economic zones. Great Britain, Belgium, France, the Netherlands, Germany, the western part of the Austro-Hungarian Empire, and northern Italy constituted an advanced industrialized core that had a high standard of living, decent systems of transportation, and relatively healthy and educated populations (see Map 23.1). Another part of Europe, the backward and little industrialized area to the south and east, consisting of southern Italy, most of Austria-Hungary, Spain, Portugal, the Balkan kingdoms, and Russia, was still largely agricultural and relegated by the industrial countries to the function of providing food and raw materials. The presence of Romanian oil, Greek olive oil, and Serbian pigs and prunes in western Europe served as reminders of an economic division of Europe that continued well into the twentieth century.

The growth of an industrial economy also led to new patterns for European agriculture. An abundance of grain and lower transportation costs caused the prices of farm commodities to plummet. Some countries responded with tariff barriers against lower-priced foodstuffs. Where agricultural labor was scarce and hence expensive, as in Britain and Germany, landowners introduced machines for threshing and harvesting. The slump in grain prices also led some countries to specialize in other food products. Denmark, for example, exported eggs, butter, and cheese; sugar beets predominated in Bohemia and northern France; fruit in Mediterranean countries; and wine in Spain and Italy. This age also witnessed the introduction of chemical fertilizers. Large estates could make these adjustments easily, but individual small farmers could not afford them and formed farm cooperatives that provided capital for making improvements and purchasing equipment and fertilizer.

THE SPREAD OF INDUSTRIALIZATION After 1870, industrialization began to spread beyond western and central Europe and North America. Especially noticeable was its rapid development in Russia (see Chapter 24) and Japan. In Japan, the imperial government took the lead in promoting industry. The government financed industries,

Railroad development
— Lines completed by 1848
— Area of main railroad completed by 1870
— Other major lines

▲ Steel
◆ Engineering
⬬ Chemicals
■ Electrical industry

⛟ Low-grade coal
🛒 High-grade coal
⚒ Iron ore deposits
▮ Petroleum deposits

○ Oil production

Industrial concentration:
▫ Cities
▒ Areas

MAP 23.1   The Industrial Regions of Europe at the End of the Nineteenth Century. By the end of the nineteenth century, the Second Industrial Revolution—in steelmaking, electricity, petroleum, and chemicals—had spurred substantial economic growth and prosperity in western and central Europe; it also sparked economic and political competition between Great Britain and Germany.

Q *Look back at Map 20.2. What parts of Europe not industrialized in 1850 had become industrialized in the ensuing decades?*

built railroads, brought foreign experts to train Japanese employees in new industrial techniques, and instituted a universal educational system based on applied science. By the end of the nineteenth century, Japan had developed key industries in tea, silk, armaments, and shipbuilding. Workers for these industries came from the large number of people who had abandoned their farms due to severe hardships in the countryside and fled to the cities, where they provided an abundant source of cheap labor.

As in Europe during the early decades of the Industrial Revolution, workers toiled for long hours in the coal mines and textile mills, often under horrendous conditions. Reportedly, coal miners employed on a small island in Nagasaki harbor worked naked in temperatures up to 130 degrees Fahrenheit. If they tried to escape, they were shot.

A WORLD ECONOMY   The economic developments of the late nineteenth century, combined with the transportation revolution that saw the growth of marine transport and railroads, also fostered a true world economy. By 1900, Europeans were importing beef and wool from Argentina

A Textile Factory in Japan. The development of the factory forced workers to adjust to a new system of discipline in which they worked regular hours under close supervision. Shown here is one of the earliest industrial factories in Japan, the Tomioka silk factory, built in the 1870s. As can be seen by comparing this illustration to the one on p. 613, in Chapter 20, although women are doing the work in both factories, the managers are men.

and Australia, coffee from Brazil, nitrates from Chile, iron ore from Algeria, and sugar from Java. European capital was also invested abroad to develop railways, mines, electrical power plants, and banks. High rates of return, such as 11.3 percent on Latin American banking shares that were floated in London, provided plenty of incentive. Of course, foreign countries also provided markets for the surplus manufactured goods of Europe. With its capital, industries, and military might, Europe dominated the world economy by the end of the nineteenth century.

Women and Work: New Job Opportunities

The Second Industrial Revolution had an enormous impact on the position of women in the labor market. During the course of the nineteenth century, considerable controversy erupted over a woman's "right to work." Working-class organizations tended to reinforce the underlying ideology of domesticity: women should remain at home to bear and nurture children and should not be allowed in the industrial workforce. Working-class men argued that keeping women out of industrial work would ensure the moral and physical well-being of families. In reality, keeping women out of the industrial workforce simply made it easier to exploit them when they needed income to supplement their husbands' wages or to support their families when their husbands were unemployed. The desperate need to work at times forced women to do marginal work at home or labor as pieceworkers in sweatshops. "Sweating" referred to the subcontracting of piecework usually, but not exclusively, in the tailoring trades; it was done at home since it required few skills or equipment. Pieceworkers were poorly paid and worked long hours. The poorest-paid jobs for the cheapest goods were called "slop work." In this description of the

room of a London slopper, we see how precarious her position was:

> I then directed my steps to the neighborhood of Drury-lane, to see a poor woman who lived in an attic on one of the closest courts in that quarter. On the table was a quarter of an ounce of tea. Observing my eye to rest upon it, she told me it was all she took. "Sugar," she said, "I broke myself of long ago; I couldn't afford it. A cup of tea, a piece of bread, and an onion is generally all I have for my dinner, and sometimes I haven't even an onion, and then I sops my bread."[2]

Often excluded from factories and in need of income, many women had no choice but to work for the pitiful wages of the sweated industries.

WHITE-COLLAR JOBS After 1870, however, new job opportunities for women became available. Although the growth of heavy industry in the mining, metallurgy, engineering, chemicals, and electrical sectors meant fewer jobs for women in manufacturing, the development of larger industrial plants and the expansion of government services created a large number of service or white-collar jobs. The increased demand for white-collar workers at relatively low wages, coupled with a shortage of male workers, led employers to hire women. Big businesses and retail shops needed clerks, typists, secretaries, file clerks, and salesclerks. The expansion of government services created opportunities for women to be secretaries and telephone operators and to take jobs in health and social services. Compulsory education necessitated more teachers, and the development of modern hospital services opened the way for an increase in nurses.

Many of the new white-collar jobs were unexciting. The work was routine and, except for teaching and nursing, required few skills beyond basic literacy. Although there was little hope for advancement, these jobs had distinct

New Jobs for Women: The Telephone Exchange. The invention of the telephone in 1876 soon led to its widespread use. As is evident from this illustration of a telephone exchange in Paris in 1904, most of the telephone operators were women. This was but one of a number of new job opportunities for women created by the Second Industrial Revolution.

advantages for the daughters of the middle classes and especially the upward-aspiring working classes. For some middle-class women, the new jobs offered freedom from the domestic patterns expected of them. Nevertheless, because middle-class women did not receive an education comparable to that of men, the careers they could pursue were limited. Thus, they found it easier to fill the jobs at the lower end of middle-class occupations, such as teaching and civil service jobs, especially in the postal service.

Most of the new white-collar jobs, however, were filled by working-class women who saw them as an opportunity to escape from the "dirty" work of the lower-class world. Studies in France and Britain indicate that the increase in white-collar jobs did not lead to a rise in the size of the female labor force, but resulted only in a shift from industrial jobs to the white-collar sector of the economy.

PROSTITUTION   Despite the new job opportunities, many lower-class women were forced to become prostitutes to survive. The rural, working-class girls who flocked into the cities in search of new opportunities were often naive and vulnerable. Employment was unstable, and wages were low. No longer protected by family or village community and church, some girls faced only one grim alternative—prostitution. In Paris, London, and many other large cities with transient populations, thousands of prostitutes plied their trade. One journalist estimated that there were 60,000 prostitutes in London in 1885. Most prostitutes were active for only a short time, usually from their late teens through their early twenties. Many eventually rejoined the regular workforce or married when they could.

In most European countries, prostitution was licensed and regulated by government and municipal authorities. Although the British government provided minimal regulation of prostitution, it did attempt to enforce the Contagious Diseases Acts in the 1870s and 1880s by giving authorities the right to examine prostitutes for venereal disease. Prostitutes found to be infected were confined for some time to special institutions called lock hospitals,

where they were given moral instruction. But opposition to the Contagious Diseases Acts soon arose from middle-class female reformers. Their leader was Josephine Butler (1828–1906), who objected to laws that punished women but not men who suffered from venereal disease. Known as the "shrieking sisters" because they discussed sexual matters in public, Butler and her fellow reformers were successful in gaining the repeal of the acts in 1886.

Organizing the Working Classes

In the first half of the nineteenth century, many workers had formed trade unions that had functioned primarily as mutual aid societies (see Chapter 20). In return for a small weekly payment, benefits were provided to assist unemployed workers. In the late nineteenth century, the desire to improve their working and living conditions led many industrial workers to form political parties and labor unions, often based on the ideas of Karl Marx (see Chapter 22). One of the most important of the working-class or socialist parties was formed in Germany in 1875.

SOCIALIST PARTIES   Under the direction of its two Marxist leaders, Wilhelm Liebknecht (VIL-helm LEEP-knekht) (1826–1900) and August Bebel (ow-GOOST BAY-bul) (1840–1913), the German Social Democratic Party (SPD) espoused revolutionary Marxist rhetoric while organizing itself as a mass political party competing in elections for the Reichstag (the German parliament). Once in the Reichstag, SPD delegates worked to enact legislation to improve the condition of the working class. As August Bebel explained, "Pure negation would not be accepted by the voters. The masses demand that something should be done for today irrespective of what will happen on the morrow."[3] Despite government efforts to destroy it (see "Central and Eastern Europe: Persistence of the Old Order" later in this chapter), the SPD continued to grow. In 1890, it received 1.5 million votes and thirty-five seats in the Reichstag. When it received 4 million votes in the

"Proletarians of the World, Unite." To improve their working and living conditions, many industrial workers, inspired by the ideas of Karl Marx, joined working-class or socialist parties. Pictured here is a socialist-sponsored poster that proclaims in German the closing words of *The Communist Manifesto*: "Proletarians of the World, Unite!"

1912 elections, it became the largest single party in Germany.

Socialist parties also emerged in other European states, although none proved as successful as the German Social Democrats. France had a variety of socialist parties, including a Marxist one. The leader of French socialism, Jean Jaurès (ZHAHNH zhaw-RESS) (1859–1914), was an independent socialist who looked to the French revolutionary tradition rather than Marxism to justify revolutionary socialism. In 1905, the French socialist parties succeeded in unifying themselves into a single, mostly Marxist-oriented socialist party. Social democratic parties on the German model were founded in Belgium, Austria, Hungary, Bulgaria, Poland, Romania, and the Netherlands before 1900. The Marxist Social Democratic Labor Party had been organized in Russia by 1898.

As the socialist parties grew, agitation for an international organization that would strengthen their position against international capitalism also grew. In 1889, leaders of the various socialist parties formed the Second International, which was organized as a loose association of national groups. Although the Second International took some coordinated actions—May Day (May 1), for example, was made an international labor day to be marked by strikes and mass labor demonstrations—differences often wreaked havoc at the organization's congresses. Two issues proved particularly divisive: revisionism and nationalism.

EVOLUTIONARY SOCIALISM Some Marxists believed in a pure **Marxism** that accepted the imminent collapse of capitalism and the need for socialist ownership of the means of production. The guiding light of the German Social Democrats, August Bebel, confided to another socialist that "every night I go to sleep with the thought that the last hour of bourgeois society strikes soon." Earlier, Bebel had said, "I am convinced that the fulfillment of our aims is so close, that there are few in this hall who will not live to see the day."[4] But a severe challenge to this orthodox Marxist position arose in the form of **evolutionary socialism,** also known as **revisionism.**

Most prominent among the evolutionary socialists was Eduard Bernstein (AY-doo-art BAYRN-shtyn) (1850–1932), a member of the German Social Democratic Party who had spent years in exile in Britain, where he had been influenced by moderate English socialism and the British parliamentary system. In 1899, Bernstein challenged Marxist orthodoxy with his book *Evolutionary Socialism* in which he argued that some of Marx's ideas had turned out to be quite wrong (see the box on p. 713). The capitalist system had not broken down, said Bernstein. Contrary to Marx's assertion, the middle class was actually expanding, not declining. At the same time, the proletariat was not sinking further down; instead, its position was improving as workers experienced a higher standard of living. In the face of this reality, Bernstein discarded Marx's emphasis on class struggle and revolution. The workers, he asserted, must continue to organize in mass political parties and even work together with the other advanced elements in a nation to bring about change. With the extension of the right to vote, workers were in a better position than ever to achieve their aims through democratic channels. Evolution by democratic means, not revolution, would achieve the desired goal of socialism. German and French socialist leaders, as well as the Second International, condemned evolutionary socialism as heresy and opportunism. But many socialist parties, including the German Social Democrats, while spouting revolutionary slogans, followed Bernstein's revisionist, gradualist approach.

THE PROBLEM OF NATIONALISM A second divisive issue for international socialism was nationalism. Marx and Engels had said that "the working men have no country" and that "national differences and antagonisms between peoples are daily more and more vanishing, owing to the development of the bourgeoisie."[5] They proved drastically wrong. Congresses of the Second International passed resolutions in 1907 and 1910 advocating joint action by workers of different countries to avert war but provided no real

The Voice of Evolutionary Socialism: Eduard Bernstein

The German Marxist Eduard Bernstein was regarded as the foremost late-nineteenth-century theorist of Marxist revisionism. In his book *Evolutionary Socialism,* Bernstein argued that Marx had made some fundamental mistakes and that socialists needed to stress cooperation and evolution rather than class conflict and revolution.

Eduard Bernstein, *Evolutionary Socialism*

It has been maintained in a certain quarter that the practical deductions from my treatises would be the abandonment of the conquest of political power by the proletariat organized politically and economically. That is quite an arbitrary deduction, the accuracy of which I altogether deny.

I set myself against the notion that we have to expect shortly a collapse of the bourgeois economy, and that social democracy should be induced by the prospect of such an imminent, great, social catastrophe to adapt its tactics to that assumption. That I maintain most emphatically.

The adherents of this theory of a catastrophe base it especially on the conclusions of the *Communist Manifesto.* This is a mistake in every respect.

The theory which the *Communist Manifesto* sets forth of the evolution of modern society was correct as far as it characterized the general tendencies of that evolution. But it was mistaken in several special deductions, above all in the estimate of the time the evolution would take.... But it is evident that if social evolution takes a much greater period of time than was assumed, it must also take upon itself forms and lead to forms that were not foreseen and could not be foreseen then.

Social conditions have not developed to such an acute opposition of things and classes as is depicted in the *Manifesto.* It is not only useless, it is the greatest folly to attempt to conceal this from ourselves. The number of members of the possessing classes is today not smaller but larger. The enormous increase of social wealth is not accompanied by a decreasing number of large capitalists but by an increasing number of capitalists of all degrees.

The middle classes change their character but they do not disappear from the social scale....

In all advanced countries we see the privileges of the capitalist bourgeoisie yielding step by step to democratic organizations. Under the influence of this, and driven by the movement of the working classes which is daily becoming stronger, a social reaction has set in against the exploiting tendencies of capital, a counteraction which, although it still proceeds timidly and feebly, yet does exist, and is always drawing more departments of economic life under its influence. Factory legislation, the democratizing of local government, and the extension of its area of work, the freeing of trade unions and systems of cooperative trading from legal restrictions, the consideration of standard conditions of labor in the work undertaken by public authorities—all these characterize this phase of the evolution.

But the more the political organizations of modern nations are democratized the more the needs and opportunities of great political catastrophes are diminished.... But is the conquest of political power by the proletariat simply to be by a political catastrophe? Is it to be the appropriation and utilization of the power of the State by the proletariat exclusively against the whole non-proletarian world?...

No one has questioned the necessity for the working classes to gain the control of government. The point at issue is between the theory of a social cataclysm and the question whether, with the given social development in Germany and the present advanced state of its working classes in the towns and the country, a sudden catastrophe would be desirable in the interest of the social democracy. I have denied it and deny it again, because in my judgment a greater security for lasting success lies in a steady advance than in the possibilities offered by a catastrophic crash.

Q Based on this selection, how would you define evolutionary socialism? What broader forces in nineteenth-century European society came together to promote this type of political thinking?

---

machinery to implement the resolutions. In truth, socialist parties varied from country to country and remained tied to national concerns and issues. Socialist leaders always worried that in the end, national loyalties might outweigh class loyalties among the masses. When World War I came in 1914, not only the working-class masses but even many of their socialist party leaders supported the war efforts of their national governments. Nationalism had proved a much more powerful force than socialism.

THE ROLE OF TRADE UNIONS Workers also formed trade unions to improve their working conditions. Attempts to organize the workers did not come until after unions had won the right to strike in the 1870s. Strikes proved necessary to achieve the workers' goals. A walkout by female workers in the match industry in 1888 and by dockworkers in London the following year led to the establishment of trade union organizations for both groups. By 1900, 2 million workers were enrolled in British unions, and by the outbreak of World War I, this number had risen to between 3 million and 4 million, although this was still less than one-fifth of the total workforce.

Trade unions failed to develop as quickly on the Continent as they had in Britain. In France, the union movement was from the beginning closely tied to socialist ideology. As there were a number of French socialist parties, the socialist trade unions remained badly splintered. Not until 1895 did French unions create a national organization called the General Confederation of Labor. Its decentralization and failure to include some of the more important individual unions, however, kept it weak and ineffective.

German trade unions, also closely attached to political parties, were first formed in the 1860s. Although there were liberal trade unions comprising skilled artisans and Catholic or Christian trade unions, the largest German trade unions were those of the socialists. By 1899, even the latter had accepted the practice of collective bargaining with employers. As strikes and collective bargaining achieved successes, German workers were increasingly inclined to forgo revolution for gradual improvements. By 1914, its 3 million members made the German trade union movement the second largest in Europe, after Great Britain's. Almost 85 percent of these 3 million belonged to socialist unions. Trade unions in the rest of Europe had varying degrees of success, but by the beginning of World War I, they had made considerable progress in bettering both the living and the working conditions of the laboring classes.

THE ANARCHIST ALTERNATIVE Despite the revolutionary rhetoric, socialist parties and trade unions gradually became less radical in pursuing their goals. Indeed, this lack of revolutionary fervor drove some people from Marxist socialism into **anarchism,** a movement that was especially prominent in less industrialized and less democratic countries.

Initially, anarchism was not a violent movement. Early anarchists believed that people were inherently good but had been corrupted by the state and society. True freedom could be achieved only by abolishing the state and all existing social institutions. In the second half of the nineteenth century, however, anarchists in Spain, Portugal, Italy, and Russia began to advocate using radical means to accomplish this goal. The Russian Michael Bakunin (buh-KOON-yun) (1814–1876), for example, believed that small groups of well-trained, fanatical revolutionaries could perpetrate so much violence that the state and all its institutions would disintegrate. To revolutionary anarchists, that would usher in the anarchist golden age. The Russian anarchist Lev Aleshker wrote shortly before his execution:

> Slavery, poverty, weakness, and ignorance—the external fetters of man—will be broken. Man will be at the center of nature. The earth and its products will serve everyone dutifully. Weapons will cease to be a measure of strength and gold a measure of wealth; the strong will be those who are bold and daring in the conquest of nature, and riches will be the things that are useful. Such a world is called "Anarchy." It will have no castles, no place for masters and slaves. Life will be open to all. Everyone will take what he needs—this is the anarchist ideal. And when it comes about, men will live wisely and well. The masses must take part in the construction of this paradise on earth.[6]

After Bakunin's death in 1876, anarchist revolutionaries used assassination as their primary instrument of terror. The list of victims of anarchist assassins at the turn of the century included a Russian tsar (1881), a president of the French Republic (1894), the king of Italy (1900), and a president of the United States (1901). Despite anarchist hopes, these states did not collapse.

The Emergence of a Mass Society

 FOCUS QUESTIONS: What is a mass society, and what were its main characteristics? What role were women expected to play in society and family life in the latter half of the nineteenth century, and how closely did patterns of family life correspond to this ideal?

The new patterns of industrial production, mass consumption, and working-class organization that we identify with the Second Industrial Revolution were only one aspect of the new **mass society** that emerged in Europe after 1870. A larger and vastly improved urban environment, new patterns of social structure, gender issues, mass education, and mass leisure were also important features of European society.

Population Growth

The European population increased dramatically between 1850 and 1910, rising from 270 million to more than 460 million by 1910 (see Table 23.1). Between 1850 and

TABLE 23.1 European Populations, 1851–1911 (in thousands)

	1851	1881	1911
England and Wales	17,928	25,974	36,070
Scotland	2,889	3,736	4,761
Ireland	6,552	5,175	4,390
France	35,783	37,406	39,192
Germany	33,413	45,234	64,926
Belgium	4,530	5,520	7,424
Netherlands	3,309	4,013	5,858
Denmark	1,415	1,969	2,757
Norway	1,490	1,819	2,392
Sweden	3,471	4,169	5,522
Spain	15,455	16,622	19,927
Portugal	3,844	4,551	5,958
Italy	24,351	28,460	34,671
Switzerland	2,393	2,846	3,753
Austria	17,535	22,144	28,572
Hungary	18,192	15,739	20,886
Russia	68,500	97,700	160,700
Romania	—	4,600	7,000
Bulgaria	—	2,800	4,338
Greece	—	1,679	2,632
Serbia	—	1,700	2,912

SOURCE: Data from B. R. Mitchell, *European Historical Statistics, 1750–1970* (New York, 1975).

1880, the main cause of the population increase was a rising birthrate, at least in western Europe, but after 1880, a noticeable decline in death rates largely explains the increase in population. Although the causes of this decline have been debated, two major factors—medical discoveries and environmental conditions—stand out. Some historians have stressed the importance of developments in medical science. Smallpox vaccinations, for example, were compulsory in many European countries by the mid-1850s. More important were improvements in the urban environment in the second half of the nineteenth century that greatly reduced fatalities from such diseases as diarrhea, dysentery, typhoid fever, and cholera, which had been spread through contaminated water supplies and improper elimination of sewage. Improved nutrition also made a significant difference in the health of the population. The increase in agricultural productivity combined with improvements in transportation facilitated the shipment of food supplies from areas of surplus to regions with poor harvests. Better nutrition and food hygiene were especially instrumental in the decline in infant mortality by 1900. The pasteurization of milk reduced intestinal disorders that had been a major cause of infant deaths.

Emigration

Although growing agricultural and industrial prosperity supported an increase in the European population, it could not do so indefinitely, especially in areas that had little industrialization and severe rural overpopulation. Some of the excess labor from underdeveloped areas migrated to the industrial regions of Europe (see Map 23.2). By 1913, more than 400,000 Poles were working in the heavily industrialized Ruhr region of western Germany, and thousands of Italian laborers had migrated to France. The industrialized regions of Europe, however, were not able to absorb the entire surplus population of heavily agricultural regions like southern Italy, Spain, Hungary, and

Inhabitants per square mile

| | <20 | | 20–50 | | 50–100 | | 100+ |

MAP 23.2   Population Growth in Europe, 1820–1900. Europe's population increased steadily throughout the nineteenth century. Advances in medical science, hygiene, nutrition, living conditions, and standards of living help account for the population increase, even though emigration to the United States, South America, and other regions reduced the total growth numbers.

Q *Which regions experienced the greatest population growth between 1820 and 1900, and how can you account for this?*

View an animated version of this map or related maps on the CourseMate website.

TABLE 23.2 European Emigration, 1876–1910 (Average Annual Emigration to Non-European Countries per 100,000 Population)

	1876–1880	1881–1885	1886–1890	1891–1895	1896–1900	1901–1905	1906–1910
Europe	94	196	213	185	147	271	322
Ireland	650	1,422	1,322	988	759	743	662
Great Britain	102	174	162	119	88	127	172
Denmark	157	380	401	338	117	292	275
Norway	432	1,105	819	597	312	903	746
Sweden	301	705	759	587	249	496	347
Germany	108	379	207	163	47	50	44
Belgium	—	—	86	50	23	57	69
Netherlands	32	136	111	76	25	45	58
France	8	14	49	14	13	12	12
Spain	—	280	437	434	446	391	758
Portugal	258	356	423	609	417	464	694
Italy	396	542	754	842	974	1,706	1,938
Austria	48	90	114	182	182	355	469
Hungary	—	92	156	134	205	437	616
Russia	6	13	42	47	32	63	67

SOURCE: Robert Gildea, *Barricades and Borders: Europe, 1800–1914* (Oxford, 1987), p. 283.

Romania, where the land could not support the growing numbers of people. The booming economies of North America after 1898 and cheap shipping fares after 1900 led to mass emigration from southern and eastern Europe to North America at the beginning of the twentieth century. In 1880, about 500,000 people left Europe each year on average; between 1906 and 1910, annual departures increased to 1.3 million, many of them from southern and eastern Europe. Altogether, between 1846 and 1932, probably 60 million Europeans left Europe, half of them bound for the United States and most of the rest for Canada or Latin America (see Table 23.2).

It was not only economic motives that caused people to leave eastern Europe. Migrants from Austria and Hungary, for example, were not the dominant nationalities, the Germans and Magyars, but mostly their oppressed minorities, such as Poles, Slovaks, Serbs, Croats, Romanians, and Jews. Between 1880 and 1914, some 3.5 million Poles from Russia, Austria, and Germany went to the United States. Jews, who were severely persecuted, constituted 40 percent of the Russian emigrants to the United States between 1900 and 1913 and almost 12 percent of all emigrants to the United States during the first five years of the twentieth century.

Transformation of the Urban Environment

One of the most important consequences of industrialization and the population explosion of the nineteenth

© Bradford Art Galleries and Museums, UK/The Bridgeman Art Library

The Emigrants. In this painting from 1880, C. J. Staniland presented a sentimental image of the scene experienced by the tens of millions of Europeans who migrated to other parts of the world, especially the United States, Canada, and Latin America. In the painting, people are shown boarding a ship, saying farewell to family members and loved ones they might never see again. Ships were often crowded, making conditions uncomfortable during the journey.

century was urbanization. In the course of the nineteenth century, urban dwellers came to make up an ever-increasing percentage of the European population. In 1800, they constituted 40 percent of the population in Britain, 25 percent in France and Germany, and only 10 percent in eastern Europe. By 1914, urban inhabitants had increased to 80 percent of the population in Britain, 45 percent in France, 60 percent in Germany, and 30 percent in eastern Europe. The size of cities also expanded dramatically, especially in industrialized countries. In 1800, there were 21 European cities with populations over 100,000; by 1900, there were 147. Between 1800 and 1900, London's population grew from 960,000 to 6.5 million and Berlin's from 172,000 to 2.7 million.

Urban populations grew faster than the general population primarily because of the vast migration from rural areas to cities. People were driven from the countryside to the cities by sheer economic necessity—unemployment, land hunger, and physical want. Urban centers offered something positive as well, usually mass employment in factories and later in service trades and professions. But cities also grew faster in the second half of the nineteenth century because health and living conditions in them were improving.

IMPROVING LIVING CONDITIONS In the 1840s, a number of urban reformers, such as Edwin Chadwick in Britain (see Chapter 20) and Rudolf Virchow (ROO-dulf FEER-khoh) and Solomon Neumann (NOI-mahn) in Germany, had pointed to filthy living conditions as the primary cause of epidemic disease and urged sanitary reforms to correct the problem. Soon legislative acts created boards of health that brought governmental action to bear on public heath issues. Urban medical officers and building inspectors were authorized to inspect dwellings for public health hazards. New building regulations made it more difficult for private contractors to build shoddy housing. The Public Health Act of 1875 in Britain, for example, prohibited the construction of new buildings without running water and an internal drainage system. For the first time in Western history, the role of municipal governments had been expanded to include detailed regulations for the improvement of the living conditions of urban dwellers.

Essential to the public health of the modern European city was the ability to bring clean water into the city and to expel sewage from it. The accomplishment of those two tasks was a major engineering feat in the second half of the nineteenth century. The problem of fresh water was solved by a system of dams and reservoirs that stored the water and aqueducts and tunnels that carried it from the countryside to the city and into individual dwellings. Regular private baths became accessible to more people as gas heaters in the 1860s and later electric heaters made hot baths possible. The shower had appeared by the 1880s.

The treatment of wastewater was improved by building mammoth underground pipes that carried raw sewage far from the city for disposal. In the late 1860s, a number of German cities began to construct sewer systems. Frankfurt began its program after a lengthy public campaign enlivened by the slogan "From the toilet to the river in half an hour." London devised a system of five enormous sewers that discharged their loads 12 miles from the city, where the waste was chemically treated. Unfortunately, in many places, new underground sewers simply discharged their raw sewage into what soon became highly polluted lakes and rivers. Nevertheless, the development of pure water and sewerage systems dramatically improved the public health of European cities.

HOUSING NEEDS Middle-class reformers who denounced the unsanitary living conditions of the working classes also focused on their housing needs. Overcrowded, disease-ridden slums were viewed as dangerous not only to physical health but also to the political and moral health of the entire nation. V. A. Huber, the foremost early German housing reformer, wrote in 1861, "Certainly it would not be too much to say that the home is the communal embodiment of family life. Thus, the purity of the dwelling is almost as important for the family as is the cleanliness of the body for the individual."[7] To Huber, good housing was a prerequisite for a stable family life and hence a stable society.

Early efforts to attack the housing problem emphasized the middle-class, liberal belief in the efficacy of private enterprise. Reformers such as Huber believed that the construction of model dwellings renting at a reasonable price would force other private landlords to elevate their housing standards. A fine example of this approach was the work of Octavia Hill, granddaughter of a celebrated social reformer (see the box on p. 718). With the financial assistance of a friend, she rehabilitated some old dwellings and constructed new ones to create housing for 3,500 tenants.

As the number and size of cities continued to mushroom, by the 1880s governments came to the conclusion—reluctantly—that private enterprise could not solve the housing crisis. In 1890, a British law empowered local town councils to collect new taxes and construct cheap housing for the working classes. London and Liverpool were the first communities to take advantage of their new powers. Similar activity had been set in motion in Germany by 1900. Everywhere, however, these lukewarm measures failed to do much to meet the real housing needs of the working classes. In housing, as in so many other areas of life in the late nineteenth century, the liberal principle that the government that governs least governs best had simply proved untrue. More and more, governments were stepping into areas of activity that they would never have touched earlier.

The Housing Venture of Octavia Hill

Octavia Hill was a practical-minded British housing reformer who believed that workers and their families were entitled to happy homes. At the same time, she was convinced that the poor needed guidance and encouragement, not charity. In this selection, she describes her housing venture.

— ❈ —

Octavia Hill, *Homes of the London Poor*

About four years ago I was put in possession of three houses in one of the worst courts of Marylebone. Six other houses were bought subsequently. All were crowded with inmates.

The first thing to be done was to put them in decent tenantable order. The set last purchased was a row of cottages facing a bit of desolate ground, occupied with wretched, dilapidated cow-sheds, manure heaps, old timber, and rubbish of every description. The houses were in a most deplorable condition—the plaster was dropping from the walls; on one staircase a pail was placed to catch the rain that fell through the roof. All the staircases were perfectly dark; the banisters were gone, having been burnt as firewood by tenants. The grates, with large holes in them, were falling forward into the rooms. The wash-house, full of lumber belonging to the landlord, was locked up; thus, the inhabitants had to wash clothes, as well as to cook, eat and sleep in their small rooms. The dustbin, standing in the front part of the houses, was accessible to the whole neighborhood, and boys often dragged from it quantities of unseemly objects and spread them over the court. The state of the drainage was in keeping with everything else. The pavement of the back-yard was all broken up, and great puddles stood in it, so that the damp crept up the outer walls. . . .

As soon as I entered into possession, each family had an opportunity of doing better: those who would not pay, or who led clearly immoral lives, were ejected. The rooms they vacated were cleansed; the tenants who showed signs of improvement moved into them, and thus, in turn, an opportunity was obtained for having

each room distempered [painted] and papered. The drains were put in order, a large slate cistern was fixed, the wash-house was cleared of its lumber, and thrown open on stated days to each tenant in turn. The roof, the plaster, the woodwork were repaired; the staircase walls were distempered; new grates were fixed; the layers of paper and rag (black with age) were torn from the windows, and glass put in; out of 192 panes only eight were found unbroken. The yard and footpath were paved.

The rooms, as a rule, were re-let at the same prices at which they had been let before; but tenants with large families were counseled to take two rooms, and for these much less was charged than if let singly: this plan I continue to pursue. In-coming tenants are not allowed to take a decidedly insufficient quantity of room, and no subletting is permitted. . . .

The pecuniary result has been very satisfactory. Five percent has been paid on all the capital invested. A fund for the repayment of capital is accumulating. A liberal allowance has been made for repairs. . . .

My tenants are mostly of a class far below that of mechanics. They are, indeed, of the very poor. And yet, although the gifts they have received have been next to nothing, none of the families who have passed under my care during the whole four years have continued in what is called "distress," except such as have been unwilling to exert themselves. Those who will not exert the necessary self-control cannot avail themselves of the means of livelihood held out to them. But, for those who are willing, some small assistance in the form of work has, from time to time, been provided—not much, but sufficient to keep them from want or despair. ⌖

Q Did Octavia Hill's housing venture generate financial returns on her initial investment? What benefits did her tenants receive in turn? What feelings and beliefs about the lower classes are evident in Hill's account?

REDESIGNING THE CITIES Housing was but one area of urban reconstruction after 1870. As urban populations expanded in the nineteenth century, the older layout, confining the city to a compact area enclosed by defensive walls, seemed restrictive and utterly useless. In the second half of the nineteenth century, many of the old defensive walls—worthless anyway from a military standpoint—were pulled down, and the areas were converted into parks and boulevards. In Vienna, for example, the great boulevards of the Ringstrasse replaced the old medieval walls.

While the broad streets served a military purpose—the rapid deployment of troops to crush civil disturbances—they also offered magnificent views of the city hall, the university, and the parliament building, all powerful symbols of middle-class social values.

Like Vienna, many European urban centers were redesigned during the second half of the nineteenth century. The reconstruction of Paris after 1850 by Emperor Napoleon III was perhaps the most famous project and provided a model for other cities. The old middle-class populations to live in their own suburban neighborhoods far removed from their places of work. Cheap, modern transportation essentially separated home and work for many Europeans.

Social Structure of the Mass Society

Despite the improvements in living standards for many people in the last decades of the nineteenth century, wide disparities in wealth continued to exist. While the wealthiest members of the upper middle class were finding their way into the upper classes and the numbers of the middle classes were growing, most Europeans were still in the lower classes.

THE UPPER CLASSES At the top of European society stood a wealthy elite, constituting only 5 percent of the population but controlling between 30 and 40 percent of its wealth. In the course of the nineteenth century, aristocrats coalesced with the most successful industrialists, bankers, and merchants to form this new elite. Big business had produced this group of wealthy **plutocrats,** while aristocrats, whose income from landed estates had declined, invested in railway shares, public utilities, government bonds, and businesses, sometimes on their own estates. Gradually, the greatest fortunes shifted into the hands of the upper middle class. In Great Britain, for example, landed aristocrats constituted 73 percent of the country's millionaires at midcentury, while commercial and financial magnates made up 14 percent. By the period 1900–1914, landowners had declined to 27 percent.

Increasingly, aristocrats and plutocrats fused as the wealthy upper middle class purchased landed estates to join the aristocrats in the pleasures of country living and the aristocrats bought lavish town houses for part-time urban life. Common bonds were also forged when the sons of wealthy middle-class families were admitted to the elite schools dominated by the children of the aristocracy. At Oxford, the landed upper class made up 40 percent of the student body in 1870 but only 15 percent in 1910, while undergraduates from business families went from 7 to 21 percent during the same period. This educated elite, whether aristocratic or middle class in background, assumed leadership roles in government bureaucracies and military hierarchies. Marriage also served to unite the two groups. Daughters of tycoons acquired titles, while aristocratic heirs gained new sources of cash. Wealthy

Paris Transformed. These two photographs, both of L'avenue de l'Opéra, show the degree of destruction that was needed to create the grand boulevards and monuments of late-nineteenth-century Paris. The first photograph was taken in 1865, and the second is from the 1880s. Evident in the latter photograph are the new uniform buildings, gas street lamps, and broad boulevards that linked the city's great cultural sites, such as the Opéra, shown in the background, the most expensive building constructed during the Second Empire.

residential districts in the central city, many of them working-class slums, were demolished and replaced with town halls, government office buildings, retail stores including the new department stores, museums, cafés, and theaters, all of which provided for the shopping and recreational pleasures of the middle classes.

As cities expanded and entire groups of people were displaced from urban centers by reconstruction, city populations spilled over into the neighboring villages and countrysides, which were soon incorporated into the cities. The construction of streetcar and commuter train lines by the turn of the century enabled both working-class and

American heiresses were in special demand. When Consuelo Vanderbilt married the duke of Marlborough, the new duchess brought £2 million (approximately $10 million) to her husband.

THE MIDDLE CLASSES The middle classes consisted of a variety of groups. Below the upper middle class was a level that included such traditional groups as professionals in law, medicine, and the civil service as well as moderately well-to-do industrialists and merchants. The industrial expansion of the nineteenth century also added new groups to this segment of the middle class. These included business managers and new professionals, such as the engineers, architects, accountants, and chemists who formed professional associations as the symbols of their newfound importance. A lower middle class of small shopkeepers, traders, manufacturers, and prosperous peasants provided goods and services for the classes above them.

Standing between the lower middle class and the lower classes were new groups of white-collar workers who were the product of the Second Industrial Revolution. They were the traveling sales representatives, bookkeepers, bank tellers, telephone operators, department store salesclerks, and secretaries. Although largely propertyless and often paid little more than skilled laborers, these white-collar workers were often committed to middle-class ideals and optimistic about improving their status.

The moderately prosperous and successful middle classes shared a common lifestyle and values that dominated nineteenth-century society. The members of the middle class were especially active in preaching their worldview to their children and to the upper and lower classes of their society. This was particularly evident in Victorian Britain, often considered a model of middle-class society. It was the European middle classes who accepted and promulgated the importance of progress and science. They believed in hard work, which they viewed as the primary human good, open to everyone and guaranteed to have positive results. They were also regular churchgoers who believed in the good conduct associated with traditional Christian morality. The middle class was concerned with propriety, the right way of doing things, which gave rise to an incessant number of books aimed at the middle-class market with such titles as *The Habits of Good Society* and *Don't: A Manual of Mistakes and Improprieties More or Less Prevalent in Conduct and Speech.*

THE LOWER CLASSES Almost 80 percent of Europeans belonged to the lower classes. Many of them were landholding peasants, agricultural laborers, and sharecroppers, especially in eastern Europe. This was less true, however, in western and central Europe. About 10 percent of the British population worked in agriculture; in Germany, the figure was 25 percent. Many prosperous, landowning peasants shared the values of the middle class. Military conscription brought peasants into contact with the other groups of society, and state-run elementary schools forced the children of peasants to speak the national dialect and accept national loyalties.

The urban working class consisted of many different groups, including skilled artisans in such trades as cabinetmaking, printing, and jewelry making. Semiskilled laborers, who included such people as carpenters, bricklayers, and many factory workers, earned wages that were about two-thirds of those of highly skilled workers. At the bottom of the working-class hierarchy stood the largest group of workers, the unskilled laborers. They included day laborers, who worked irregularly for very low wages, and large numbers of domestic servants. One out of every seven employed persons in Great Britain in 1900 was a domestic servant. Most were women.

Urban workers did experience a real betterment in the material conditions of their lives after 1871. For one thing, urban improvements meant better living conditions. A rise in real wages, accompanied by a decline in many consumer costs, especially in the 1880s and 1890s, made it possible for workers to buy more than just food and housing. Workers' budgets now provided money for more clothes and even leisure at the same time that strikes and labor agitation were winning shorter (ten-hour) workdays and Saturday afternoons off.

"The Woman Question": The Role of Women

"The woman question" was the catchphrase used to refer to the debate over the role of women in society. In the nineteenth century, women remained legally inferior, economically dependent, and largely defined by family and household roles. Many women still aspired to the ideal of femininity popularized by writers and poets. Alfred, Lord Tennyson's poem *The Princess* expressed it well:

> Man for the field and woman for the hearth:
> Man for the sword and for the needle she:
> Man with the head and woman with the heart:
> Man to command and woman to obey;
> All else confusion.

Historians have pointed out that this traditional characterization of the sexes, based on gender-defined social roles, was elevated to the status of universal male and female attributes in the nineteenth century, due largely to the impact of the Industrial Revolution on the family. As the chief family wage earners, men worked outside the home, while women were left with the care of the family, for which they were paid nothing. Of course, the ideal did not always match reality, especially for the lower classes, where the need for supplemental income drove women to do sweatwork.

MARRIAGE AND DOMESTICITY Throughout most of the nineteenth century, marriage was viewed as the only honorable and available career for most women. Though the middle class glorified the ideal of domesticity (see the box on p. 721), for most women, marriage was a matter of

Advice to Women: Two Views

Industrialization had a strong impact on middle-class women as gender-based social roles became the norm. Men worked outside the home to support the family, while women provided for the needs of their children and husband at home. In the first selection, *Woman in Her Social and Domestic Character* (1842), Elizabeth Poole Sanford gives advice to middle-class women on their proper role and behavior.

Although a majority of women probably followed the nineteenth-century middle-class ideal of women as keepers of the household and nurturers of husband and children, an increasing number of women fought for the rights of women. The second selection is taken from the third act of Henrik Ibsen's 1879 play *A Doll's House,* in which the character Nora Helmer declares her independence from her husband's control.

Elizabeth Poole Sanford, *Woman in Her Social and Domestic Character*

The changes wrought by Time are many. It influences the opinions of men as familiarity does their feelings; it has a tendency to do away with superstition, and to reduce every thing to its real worth.

It is thus that the sentiment for woman has undergone a change. The romantic passion which once almost deified her is on the decline; and it is by intrinsic qualities that she must now inspire respect. She is no longer the queen of song and the star of chivalry. But if there is less of enthusiasm entertained for her, the sentiment is more rational, and, perhaps, equally sincere; for it is in relation to happiness that she is chiefly appreciated.

And in this respect it is, we must confess, that she is most useful and most important. Domestic life is the chief source of her influence; and the greatest debt society can owe to her is domestic comfort; for happiness is almost an element of virtue; and nothing conduces more to improve the character of men than domestic peace. A woman may make a man's home delightful, and may thus increase his motives for virtuous exertion. She may refine and tranquilize his mind,—may turn away his anger or allay his grief. Her smile may be the happy influence to gladden his heart, and to disperse the cloud that gathers on his brow. And in proportion to her endeavors to make those around her happy, she will be esteemed and loved. She will secure by her excellence that interest and that regard which she might formerly claim as the privilege of her sex, and will really merit the deference which was then conceded to her as a matter of course....

Perhaps one of the first secrets of her influence is adaptation to the tastes, and sympathy in the feelings, of those around her. This holds true in lesser as well as in graver points. It is in the former, indeed, that the absence of interest in a companion is frequently most disappointing. Where want of congeniality impairs domestic comfort, the fault is generally chargeable on the female side. It is for woman, not for man, to make the sacrifice, especially in indifferent matters. She must, in a certain degree, be plastic herself if she would mold others....

Nothing is so likely to conciliate the affections of the other sex as a feeling that woman looks to them for support and guidance. In proportion as men are themselves superior, they are accessible to this appeal. On the contrary, they never feel interested in one who seems disposed rather to offer than to ask assistance. There is, indeed, something unfeminine in independence. It is contrary to nature, and therefore it offends. We do not like to see a woman affecting tremors, but still less do we like to see her acting the amazon. A really sensible woman feels her dependence. She does what she can; but she is conscious of inferiority, and therefore grateful for support. She knows that she is the weaker vessel, and that as such she should receive honor. In this view, her weakness is an attraction, not a blemish.

In every thing, therefore, that women attempt, they should show their consciousness of dependence. If they are learners, let them evince a teachable spirit; if they give an opinion, let them do it in an unassuming manner. There is something so unpleasant in female self-sufficiency that it not unfrequently deters instead of persuading, and prevents the adoption of advice which the judgment even approves.

Henrik Ibsen, *A Doll's House*

NORA (*Pause*): Does anything strike you as we sit here?

HELMER: What should strike me?

NORA: We've been married eight years; does it not strike you that this is the first time we two, you and I, man and wife, have talked together seriously?

HELMER: Seriously? What do you mean, *seriously?*

NORA: For eight whole years, and more—ever since the day we first met—we have never exchanged one serious word about serious things....

HELMER: Why, my dearest Nora, what have you to do with serious things?

(continued)

NORA: There we have it! You have never understood me. I've had great injustice done to me, Torvald; first by Father, then by you.

HELMER: What! Your father *and* me? We, who have loved you more than all the world!

NORA (*Shaking her head*): You have never loved me. You just found it amusing to think you were in love with me.

HELMER: Nora! What a thing to say!

NORA: Yes, it's true, Torvald. When I was living at home with Father, he told me his opinions and mine were the same. If I had different opinions, I said nothing about them, because he would not have liked it. He used to call me his doll-child and played with me as I played with my dolls. Then I came to live in your house.

HELMER: What a way to speak of our marriage!

NORA (*Undisturbed*): I mean that I passed from Father's hands into yours. You arranged everything to your taste and I got the same tastes as you; or pretended to—I don't know which—both, perhaps; sometimes one, sometimes the other. When I look back on it now, I seem to have been living here like a beggar, on handouts. I lived by performing tricks for you, Torvald. But that was how you wanted it. You and Father have done me a great wrong. It is your fault that my life has come to naught.

HELMER: Why, Nora, how unreasonable and ungrateful! Haven't you been happy here?

NORA: No, never. I thought I was, but I never was.

HELMER: Not—not happy! . . .

NORA: I must stand quite alone if I am ever to know myself and my surroundings; so I cannot stay with you.

HELMER: Nora! Nora!

NORA: I am going at once. I daresay [my friend] Christina will take me in for tonight.

HELMER: You are mad! I shall not allow it! I forbid it!

NORA: It's no use your forbidding me anything now. I shall take with me only what belongs to me; from you I will accept nothing, either now or later.

HELMER: This is madness!

NORA: Tomorrow I shall go home—I mean to what was my home. It will be easier for me to find a job there.

HELMER: On, in your blind inexperience—

NORA: I must try to gain experience, Torvald.

HELMER: Forsake your home, your husband, your children! And you don't consider what the world will say.

NORA: I can't pay attention to that. I only know that I must do it.

HELMER: This is monstrous! Can you forsake your holiest duties?

NORA: What do you consider my holiest duties?

HELMER: Need I tell you that? Your duties to your husband and children.

NORA: I have other duties equally sacred.

HELMER: Impossible! What do you mean?

NORA: My duties toward myself.

HELMER: Before all else you are a wife and a mother.

NORA: That I no longer believe. Before all else I believe I am a human being just as much as you are—or at least that I should try to become one. I know that most people agree with you, Torvald, and that they say so in books. But I can no longer be satisfied with what most people say and what is in books. I must think things out for myself and try to get clear about them. ⤐

Q According to Elizabeth Sanford, what is the proper role of women? What forces in nineteenth-century European society merged to shape Sanford's understanding of "proper" gender roles? In Ibsen's play, what challenges does Nora Helmer make to Sanford's view of the proper role and behavior of wives? Why is her husband so shocked? Why did Ibsen title this play *A Doll's House*?

---

economic necessity. The lack of meaningful work and the lower wages paid to women made it difficult for single women to earn a living. Retiring to convents as in the past was no longer an option; many spinsters who could not find sufficiently remunerative work therefore elected to enter domestic service as live-in servants. Most women chose instead to marry, which was reflected in an increase in marriage rates and a decline in illegitimacy rates in the course of the nineteenth century.

BIRTHRATES AND BIRTH CONTROL Birthrates also dropped significantly at this time. A very important factor in the evolution of the modern family was the decline in the number of offspring born to the average woman. The change was not necessarily due to new technological products. Although the invention of vulcanized rubber in

the 1840s made possible the production of condoms and diaphragms, they were not widely used as effective contraceptive devices until World War I. Some historians maintain that the change in attitude that led parents to deliberately limit the number of offspring was more important than the method used. Although some historians attribute increased birth control to more widespread use of coitus interruptus, or male withdrawal before ejaculation, others have emphasized the ability of women to restrict family size through abortion and even infanticide or abandonment. That a change in attitude occurred was apparent in the emergence of a movement to increase awareness of birth control methods. Authorities prosecuted individuals who spread information about contraception for "depraving public morals" but were unable to stop them. In 1882 in Amsterdam, Dr. Aletta Jacob founded Europe's first birth control clinic. Initially, "family planning" was the suggestion of reformers who thought that the problem of poverty could be solved by reducing the number of children among the lower classes. In fact, the practice spread quickly among the propertied classes, rather than among the impoverished, a good reminder that considerable differences still remained between middle-class and working-class families.

THE MIDDLE-CLASS FAMILY The family was the central institution of middle-class life. Men provided the family income, while women focused on household and child care. The use of domestic servants in many middle-class homes, made possible by an abundant supply of cheap labor, reduced the amount of time middle-class women had to spend on household work. At the same time, by reducing the number of children in the family, mothers could devote more time to child care and domestic leisure. The idea that leisure should be used for constructive purposes supported and encouraged the cult of middle-class domesticity.

The middle-class family fostered an ideal of togetherness. The Victorians created the family Christmas with its yule log, Christmas tree, songs, and exchange of gifts. In the United States, Fourth of July celebrations changed from drunken revels to family picnics by the 1850s. The education of middle-class females in domestic crafts, singing, and piano playing prepared them for their function of providing a proper environment for home recreation.

The new domestic ideal had an impact on child raising and children's play. Late-eighteenth-century thought, beginning with Rousseau, had encouraged a new view of children as unique beings, not small adults, which had carried over into the nineteenth century. They were entitled to a long childhood involved in activities with other children their own age. The early environment in which they were raised, it was thought, would determine how they turned out. And mothers were seen as the most important force in protecting children from the harmful influences of the adult world. New children's games and toys, including mass-produced dolls for girls, appeared in middle-class homes. The middle-class emphasis on the functional value of knowledge was also evident in these games. One advice manual maintained that young children should learn checkers because it "calls forth the resources of the mind in the most gentle as well as the most successful manner."

Since the sons of the middle-class family were expected to follow careers like their father's, they were sent to schools where they were kept separate from the rest of society until the age of sixteen or seventeen. Sport was used in the schools to "toughen boys up," and their leisure activities centered around both national military concerns and character building. This combination was especially evident in the establishment of the Boy Scouts in Britain in 1908. Boy Scouts provided organized recreation for boys between the ages of twelve and eighteen; adventure was combined with the discipline of earning merit badges

and ranks in such a way as to instill ideals of patriotism, self-sacrifice, and masculinity.

The emphasis on manliness stemmed not only from military concerns but also from conceptions of masculinity formed during the late nineteenth century as the middle and upper classes looked for ways to control sexual licentiousness in the form of venereal disease or prostitution. Boy Scouts and *The Scout* magazine promoted an image of manliness with stories of youthful heroes who demonstrated their self-control by conquering the challenges of the wilderness. Thus, the Boy Scouts sought to reinforce Victorian and Edwardian codes of masculinity in an effort to counter the possible dangers that female domination of the home posed for male development. As one scout leader wrote, "The REAL Boy Scout is not a sissy. [He] adores his mother [but] is not hitched to [her] apron strings."

There was little organized recreational activity of this type for girls, although Robert Baden-Powell (BAD-un-POW-ul) (1857–1941), the founder of the Boy Scouts, did encourage his sister to establish a girls' division as an afterthought. Its goal is evident from Agnes Baden-Powell's comment that "you do not want to make tomboys of refined girls, yet you want to attract, and thus raise, the slum girl from the gutter. The main object is to give them all the ability to be better mothers and Guides to the next generation."[8] Despite her comment, most organizations of this kind were for middle-class children, although some reformers tried to establish boys' clubs for working-class youths to reform them.

The new ideal of the middle-class woman as nurturing mother and wife who "determined the atmosphere of the household" through her character, not her work, frequently did not correspond to reality. In France, Germany, and even mid-Victorian Britain, relatively few families could actually afford to hire a host of servants. More often, middle-class families had one servant, usually a young working-class or country girl not used to middle-class lifestyles. Women, then, were often forced to work quite hard to maintain the expected appearance of the well-ordered household. A German housekeeping manual makes this evident:

> It often happens that even high-ranking ladies help at home with housework, and particularly with kitchen chores, scrubbing, etc., so that, above all, the hands have good cause to become very rough, hard, and calloused. When these ladies appear in society, they are extremely upset at having such rough-looking hands. In order to perform the hardest and most ordinary chores . . . and, at the same time, to keep a soft hand like those fine ladies who have no heavier work to do than embroidering and sewing, always keep a piece of fresh bacon, rub your hands with it just before bedtime, and you will fully achieve your goal. You will, as a result, have the inconvenience of having to sleep with gloves on, in order not to soil the bed.[9]

Many middle-class wives, then, were caught in a no-win situation. Often, for the sake of the advancement of her

The Middle-Class Family

Nineteenth-century middle-class moralists considered the family the fundamental pillar of a healthy society. The family was a crucial institution in middle-class life, and togetherness constituted one of the important ideals of the middle-class family. The painting below by William P. Frith, titled *Many Happy Returns of the Day,* shows grandparents, parents, and children taking part in a family birthday celebration for a little girl. The servant at the left holds the presents for the little girl. New

games and toys also appeared for middle-class children. The illustration on the bottom right is taken from a book of games of 1889 and shows young girls playing a game called battledore and shuttlecock, which is described in the book as "a most convenient game because one solitary individual can find amusement as well as any number, provided there is a bat for each player. The object of the game is to keep the shuttlecock going as long as possible." The final illustration shows the cover of *The Scout,* a magazine of the scouting movement founded by Robert Baden-Powell. The cover shows one of the new scouts wearing his uniform and watching a ship at sea, an activity that could later have military value in time of war. ☞

© Harrogate Museums and Art Gallery, UK/The Bridgeman Art Library

No. 1. Vol. 1.   APRIL 18, 1908.   PRICE ONE PENNY.

THE SCOUT

FOUNDED BY
GEN. BADEN-POWELL

© The Art Archive/Bodleian Library (JJ Boy Scouts), Oxford, UK

BATTLEDORE & SHUTTLECOCK.

This is a most convenient game, because one solitary individual can find amusement as well as any number, provided there is a bat for each player. The object of the game is to keep the shuttlecock going as long as possible.

© The Art Archive/Greenaway Collection Keats House, London

husband's career, she was expected to maintain in public the image of the "idle" wife, freed from demeaning physical labor and able to pass her days in ornamental pursuits. In truth, it was frequently the middle-class woman who paid the price for this facade in a life of unpaid work, carefully managing the family budget and participating in housework that could never be done by only one servant girl. As one historian has argued, the reality of many middle-class women's lives was that "what appears at first glance to be idleness is revealed, on closer examination, to be difficult and tiresome work."

THE WORKING-CLASS FAMILY Hard work was, of course, standard fare for women in working-class families. Daughters in working-class families were expected to work until they married; even after marriage, they often did piecework at home to help support the family. For the children of the working classes, childhood was over by the age of nine or ten, when they became apprentices or were employed in odd jobs.

Between 1890 and 1914, however, family patterns among the working class began to change. High-paying jobs in heavy industry and improvements in the standard of living made it possible for working-class families to depend on the income of husbands and the wages of grown children. By the early twentieth century, some working-class mothers could afford to stay at home, following the pattern of middle-class women. At the same time, new consumer products, such as sewing machines, clocks, bicycles, and cast-iron stoves, spurred consumerism, focusing society on ever-higher levels of consumption.

The working classes also followed the middle classes in limiting the size of their families. Children began to be viewed as dependents rather than as potential wage earners as child labor laws and compulsory education moved children out of the workforce and into schools. Improvements in public health, as well as advances in medicine and a better diet, resulted in a decline in infant mortality rates for the lower classes, especially noticeable in the cities after 1890, and made it easier for working-class families to choose to have fewer children. At the same time, strikes and labor agitation led to laws that reduced work hours to ten per day by 1900 and eliminated work on Saturday afternoons, which enabled working-class parents to devote more attention to their children and develop deeper emotional ties with them. Even working-class fathers became involved in their children's lives. One observer in the French town of Belleville in the 1890s noted that "the workingman's love for his children borders on being an obsession."[10] Interest in educating children as a way to improve their future also grew.

Education in the Mass Society

Mass education was a product of the mass society of the late nineteenth century. Being "educated" in the early nineteenth century meant attending a secondary school or possibly even a university. Secondary schools emphasized a Classical education based on the study of Greek and Latin. Secondary and university education was primarily for the elite, the sons of government officials, nobles, or wealthier middle-class families. After 1850, secondary education was expanded as more middle-class families sought employment in public service and the professions or entry into elite scientific and technical schools.

At the beginning of the nineteenth century, European states showed little interest in primary education. Only in the German states was there a state-run system for it. In 1833, the French government created a system of state-run secular schools by instructing local government to establish an elementary school for both boys and girls. None of these primary schools required attendance, however, which tended to be irregular at best. In rural society, children were still expected to work in the fields. In industrializing countries like Britain and France, both employers and parents were eager to maintain the practice of child labor.

UNIVERSAL ELEMENTARY EDUCATION In the decades after 1870, the functions of the state were extended to include the development of mass education in state-run systems. Most Western governments began to offer at least primary education to both boys and girls between the ages of six and twelve. In most countries, it was not optional. Austria had established free, compulsory elementary education in 1869. In France, an 1882 law made primary education compulsory for all children between six and thirteen. Elementary education was made compulsory in Britain in 1880, but it was not until 1902 that an act of Parliament brought all elementary schools under county and town control. States also assumed responsibility for the quality of teachers by establishing teacher-training schools. By 1900, many European states, especially in northern and western Europe, were providing state-financed primary schools, salaried and trained teachers, and free, compulsory elementary education for the masses.

Why did European states make this commitment to mass education? Liberals believed that education was important to personal and social improvement and also sought, as in France, to supplant Catholic education with moral and civic training based on secular values. Even conservatives were attracted to mass education as a means of improving the quality of military recruits and training people in social discipline. In 1875, a German military journal stated, "We in Germany consider education to be one of the principal ways of promoting the strength of the nation and above all military strength."[11]

Another incentive for mass education came from industrialization. In the early Industrial Revolution, unskilled labor was sufficient to meet factory needs, but the new firms of the Second Industrial Revolution demanded skilled labor. Both boys and girls with an elementary education had new possibilities of jobs beyond their villages or small towns, including white-collar jobs in railways, subway stations, post offices, banking and shipping firms, teaching, and nursing. To industrialists, then, mass education furnished the trained workers they needed.

Nevertheless, the chief motive for mass education was political. For one thing, the expansion of voting rights necessitated a more educated electorate. Even more important, however, mass compulsory education instilled patriotism and nationalized the masses, providing an opportunity for even greater national integration. As people lost their ties to local regions and even to religion, nationalism supplied a new faith. The use of a single national language created greater national unity than loyalty to a ruler did.

A nation's motives for universal elementary education largely determined what was taught in its elementary schools. Indoctrination in national values took on great importance. At the core of the academic curriculum were reading, writing, arithmetic, national history (especially geared to a patriotic view), geography, literature, and some singing and drawing. The education of boys and girls varied, however. Where possible, the sexes were separated. Girls did less math and no science but concentrated on such domestic skills as sewing, washing, ironing, and cooking, all prerequisites for providing a good home for husband and children. Boys were taught some practical skills, such as carpentry, and even some military drill. Most of the elementary schools also inculcated the middle-class virtues of hard work, thrift, sobriety, cleanliness, and respect for the family. For most students, elementary education led to apprenticeship and a job.

FEMALE TEACHERS The development of compulsory elementary education created a demand for teachers, and most of them were female. In the United States, for example, women constituted two-thirds of all teachers by the 1880s. Many men viewed the teaching of children as an extension of women's "natural role" as nurturers of children. Moreover, females were paid lower salaries, in itself a considerable incentive for governments to encourage the establishment of teacher-training institutes for women. The first colleges for women were really teacher-training schools. In Britain, the women's colleges of Queen's and Bedford were established in the 1840s to provide teacher training for middle-class spinsters who needed to work. Barbara Bodichon (boh-di-SHOHNH) (1827–1891), a pioneer in the development of female education, established her own school where girls were trained for economic independence as well as domesticity. Not until the beginning of the twentieth century, however, were women permitted to enter the male-dominated universities. In France, 3 percent of university students in 1902 were women; by 1914, their number had increased to 10 percent of the total.

LITERACY AND NEWSPAPERS The most immediate result of mass education was an increase in literacy. Compulsory elementary education and the growth of literacy were directly related. In Germany, Great Britain, France, and the Scandinavian countries, adult illiteracy was virtually eliminated by 1900. Where there was less schooling, the story is very different. Adult illiteracy rates were 79 percent in Serbia, 78 percent in Romania, 72 percent in Bulgaria, and 79 percent in Russia. All of these countries had made only a minimal investment in compulsory mass education.

With the dramatic increase in literacy after 1871 came the rise of mass-circulation newspapers, such as the *Evening News* (1881) and *Daily Mail* (1896) in London, which sold millions of copies a day. Known as the "yellow press" in the United States, these newspapers shared some common characteristics. They were written in an easily understood

© Bettmann/CORBIS

A Women's College. Women were largely excluded from male-dominated universities before 1900. Consequently, women's desire for higher education led to the establishment of women's colleges, most of which were primarily teacher-training schools. This photograph shows female medical students dissecting cadavers in anatomy class at the Women's Medical College of Philadelphia, Pennsylvania.

style and tended toward the sensational. Unlike eighteenth-century newspapers, which were full of serious editorials and lengthy political analyses, these tabloids provided lurid details of crimes, jingoistic diatribes, gossip, and sports news. There were other forms of cheap literature as well. Specialty magazines, such as the *Family Herald* for the entire family, and women's magazines began in the 1860s. Pulp fiction for adults included the extremely popular westerns with their innumerable variations on conflicts between cowboys and Indians. Literature for the masses was but one feature of the new mass culture; another was the emergence of new forms of leisure.

Mass Leisure

In the preindustrial centuries, play or leisure activities had been closely connected to work patterns based on the seasonal or daily cycles typical of the life of peasants and artisans. The process of industrialization in the nineteenth century had an enormous impact on those traditional patterns. The factory imposed new work patterns that were determined by the rhythms of machines and clocks and removed work time completely from the family environment of farms and workshops. Work and leisure became opposites as leisure came to be viewed as what people did for fun when not on the job. In fact, the new leisure hours created by the industrial system—evening hours after work, weekends, and later a week or two in the summer—largely determined the contours of the new **mass leisure.**

New technology and business practices also determined the forms of leisure pursuits. New technology created novelties such as the Ferris wheel at amusement parks. The mechanized urban transportation systems of the 1880s meant that even the working classes were no longer dependent on neighborhood taverns but could make their way to athletic events, amusement parks, and dance halls. Likewise, railroads could take people to the beaches on weekends.

MUSIC AND DANCE HALLS Music and dance halls appeared in the second half of the nineteenth century. The first music hall in London was constructed in 1849 for a lower-class audience. As is evident from one Londoner's observation, music halls were primarily for males:

> [They were a] popular place of Saturday night resort with working men, as at them they can combine the drinking of the Saturday night glass and smoking of the Saturday night pipe, with the seeing and hearing of a variety of entertainments, ranging from magnificent ballets and marvelous scenic illusions to inferior tumbling, and from well-given operatic selections to the most idiotic of the so-called comic songs.[12]

By the 1880s, there were five hundred music halls in London. Promoters gradually made them more respectable and broadened their fare to entice both women and children to attend the programs. The new dance halls, which were all the rage by 1900, were more strictly oriented toward adults. Contemporaries were often shocked by the sight of young people engaged in sexually suggestive dancing.

MASS TOURISM The upper and middle classes had created the first market for tourism, but as wages increased and workers were given paid vacations, tourism became another form of mass leisure. Thomas Cook (1808–1892) was a British pioneer of mass tourism. Secretary to a British temperance group, Cook had been responsible for organizing a railroad trip to temperance gatherings in 1841. This experience led him to offer trips on a regular basis after he found that he could make substantial profits by renting special trains, lowering prices, and increasing the number of passengers. In 1867, he offered tours to Paris and by the 1880s to Switzerland. Of course, overseas tours were for the industrial and commercial middle classes, but soon, thanks to savings clubs, even British factory workers were able to take weekend excursions.

TEAM SPORTS Team sports had also developed into yet another form of mass leisure by the late nineteenth century. Sports were by no means a new activity. Unlike the old rural games, however, they were no longer chaotic and spontaneous activities but became strictly organized, with written rules and officials to enforce them. The rules were the products of organized athletic groups, such as the English Football Association (1863) and the American Bowling Congress (1895).

The new sports were not just for fun; like other forms of middle-class recreation, they were intended to provide training for people, especially adolescents. Not only could the participants develop individual skills, but they could also acquire a sense of teamwork useful for military service. These characteristics were already evident in the British public schools (which were really private boarding schools) in the 1850s and 1860s when such schools as Harrow, Uppingham, and Loretto placed organized sports at the center of the curriculum (see the box on p. 728). At Loretto, for example, education was supposed to instill "First—Character. Second—Physique. Third—Intelligence. Fourth—Manners. Fifth—Information."

The new team sports rapidly became professionalized. In Britain, soccer had its Football Association in 1863 and rugby its Rugby Football Union in 1871. In the United States, the first national association to recognize professional baseball players was formed in 1863. By 1900, the National League and American League had a monopoly over professional baseball. The development of urban transportation systems made possible the construction of stadiums where thousands could attend, making mass spectator sports a big business. In 1872, some 2,000 people watched the British Soccer Cup Final. By 1885, the crowd had increased to 10,000 and by 1901 to 100,000. Professional teams became objects of mass adulation by crowds of urbanites who compensated for their lost sense of identity in mass urban areas by developing these new loyalties. Spectator sports even reflected class differences.

The Fight Song: Sports in the English Public School

In the second half of the nineteenth century, organized sports were often at the center of the curriculum in English public schools. These sports were not just for leisure but were intended to instill character, strength, and teamwork. This "fight song" was written by H. B. Tristam for the rugby team at Loretto School.

❧❦❧

H. B. Tristam, "Going Strong"

Sing Football the grandest of sports in the world,
And you know it yourself if your pluck's never curled,
If you've gritted your teeth and gone hard to the last,
And sworn that you'll never let anyone past.

Chorus
Keeping close upon the ball—we drive it through
   them all,
And again we go rushing along, along, along;
O the tackle and the run, and the matches we
   have won,

From the start to the finish going strong, strong,
   strong, going strong!

If you live to be a hundred you'll never forget
How they hacked in the scrum, how you payed back
   the debt;
The joy of the swing when you tackled your man,
The lust of the fray when the battle began.

Long hence when you look with a quivering eye
On the little white tassel you value so high;
You'll think of the matches you've played in and won,
And you'll long for the days that are over and done. ❧

Q How would the singing of such songs and the virtues they express work to shape the boys' conceptions of proper male behavior, masculine values, and masculinity itself?

Upper-class soccer teams in Britain viewed working-class teams as vicious and prone to "money-grubbing, tricks, sensational displays, and utter rottenness."

The sports cult of the late nineteenth century was mostly male oriented. Many men believed that females were not particularly suited for "vigorous physical activity," although it was permissible for middle-class women to indulge in less active sports such as croquet and lawn tennis. Eventually, some athletics crept into women's colleges and girls' public schools in England.

© Rischgitz/Getty Images

© Rischgitz/Getty Images

Soccer Moments. Until 1863, football (soccer) in Britain was an aggressive sport with few set rules. One of the first things the new English Football Association did after it was established on October 26, 1863, was to set up fourteen rules of play. At the left, a sketch from a magazine called *The Graphic* shows a scene from an international soccer match in 1872. The two players with the ball have the rose of England on their shirts. At the right, another sketch from *The Graphic* shows the first match of the Ladies' Football Club in 1895.

Standardized forms of amusement drew mass audiences. Although some authorities argued that the new amusements were important for improving people, in truth, they served primarily to provide entertainment and distract people from the realities of their work lives. The new mass leisure also represented a significant change from earlier forms of popular culture. Festivals and fairs had been based on active and spontaneous community participation, whereas the new forms of mass leisure were businesses, standardized for largely passive mass audiences and organized to make profits.

Mass Consumption

Amusement parks, dance halls, organized tourist trips, and athletic events all offered new forms of leisure for masses of people, but they also quickly became part of the new mass consumption of the late nineteenth century. Earlier most people's purchases had been limited: some kitchen utensils, bedding, furniture, and a few select pieces of tailor-made clothing. Now middle- and upper-class Europeans were able to purchase and enjoy a wide variety of material goods. The new mass consumption was made possible by improvements in the standard of living, the factory system, population growth, expanded transportation systems, urbanization, and the modernization of retailing in which standardized merchandise was sold in large volumes.

When European cities were reconstructed in the late nineteenth century, space was allotted for department stores. Constructed of the new industrial materials—iron columns and plate-glass windows—department stores such as Paris's Le Bon Marché (luh BAHN mar-SHAY) offered consumers an endless variety of goods in large spaces; Le Bon Marché covered 52,000 square meters of surface space (see the box on p. 707). In 1860, its merchandise included shawls, cloaks, bedding, and fabrics; by the 1880s, its stock had expanded to include women's, men's, and children's clothing, accessories, furniture, rugs, umbrellas, toothbrushes, stationery, perfume, toys, shoes, and cutlery. Sales at Le Bon Marché in 1877 registered 73 million francs. Omnibuses carried people throughout Paris, enabling them to travel beyond their neighborhoods to shop at the new stores. Advertising in mass newspapers introduced Europeans to the new products, while department store catalogs enabled people living outside the cities to also purchase the new goods.

Although most advertisements were directed toward women, men also took part in the new consumer culture of the late nineteenth century. Not only did men consume goods such as alcohol and tobacco, but they were also the chief purchasers of ready-made clothing in the late nineteenth century. In the United States in 1890, men bought 71 percent of all ready-made clothing. As work and leisure were separated, men needed to expand their wardrobes to include both clothes for work outside the home and clothes to be worn for entertaining at home or other leisure activities. Men also consumed such goods as shaving soaps, aftershave lotions, hair dyes, and sporting goods.

The National State

 Focus Question: What general political trends were evident in the nations of western Europe in the last decades of the nineteenth century, and how did these trends differ from the policies pursued in Germany, Austria-Hungary, and Russia?

Within the major European states, considerable progress was made toward achieving such liberal practices as constitutions and parliaments, but it was largely in western European states that **mass politics** became a reality. Reforms encouraged the expansion of political democracy through voting rights for men and the creation of mass political parties. At the same time, however, these developments were strongly resisted in parts of Europe where the old political forces remained strong.

Western Europe: The Growth of Political Democracy

In general, parliamentary government was most firmly rooted in the western European states. Both Britain and France saw an expansion of the right to vote, but liberal reforms proved less successful in Spain and Italy.

REFORM IN BRITAIN By 1871, Great Britain had a functioning two-party parliamentary system, and the growth of political democracy became one of the preoccupations of British politics. Its cause was pushed along by the expansion of suffrage. Much advanced by the Reform Act of 1867 (see Chapter 22), the right to vote was further extended during the second ministry of William Gladstone (1880–1885) with the passage of the Reform Act of 1884. It gave the vote to all men who paid regular rents or taxes; by largely enfranchising agricultural workers, a group previously excluded, the act added another 2 million male voters to the electorate (see Table 22.1 on p. 688 in Chapter 22). Women were still denied the right to vote. The following year, the Redistribution Act eliminated historic boroughs and counties and established constituencies with approximately equal populations and one representative each. The payment of salaries to members of the House of Commons beginning in 1911 further democratized that institution by at least opening the door to people other than the wealthy. The British system of gradual reform through parliamentary institutions had become the way of British political life.

Gradual reform failed to solve the problem of Ireland, however. The Irish had long been subject to British rule, and the Act of Union of 1801 had united the English and Irish Parliaments. Like other unfree ethnic groups in Europe, the Irish developed a sense of national self-consciousness. They detested the absentee British landlords and their burdensome rents.

In 1870, William Gladstone attempted to alleviate Irish discontent by enacting limited land reform, but as Irish tenants continued to be evicted in the 1870s, the Irish began to make new demands. In 1879, a group called the Irish Land League, which advocated independence, called on Parliament to at least institute land reform. Charles Parnell (1846–1891), a leader of the Irish representatives in Parliament, called for **home rule,** which meant self-government by having a separate Parliament but not complete independence. Soon Irish peasants were responding to British inaction with terrorist acts. When the British government reacted with more force, Irish Catholics began to demand independence.

The Liberal leader William Gladstone, continuing to hope for a peaceful solution to the "Irish Question," introduced a home rule bill in 1886 that would have created an Irish Parliament without granting independence. But even this compromise was voted down in Parliament, especially by Conservative members who believed that concessions would only result in more violence. Gladstone tried again when he was prime minister in 1893 but experienced yet another defeat. The Irish Question remained unresolved.

THE THIRD REPUBLIC IN FRANCE The defeat of France by the Prussian army in 1870 brought the downfall of Louis Napoleon's Second Empire. French republicans initially set up a provisional government, but the victorious Otto von Bismarck intervened and forced the French to choose a government by universal male suffrage. The French people rejected the republicans and overwhelmingly favored the monarchists, who won 400 of the 630 seats in the new National Assembly. In response, on March 26, 1871, radical republicans formed an independent republican government in Paris known as the Commune.

But the National Assembly refused to give up its power and decided to crush the revolutionary Commune. When vicious fighting broke out in April, many working-class men and women stepped forth to defend the Commune. At first, women's activities were the traditional ones: caring for the wounded soldiers and feeding the troops. Gradually, however, women expanded their activities to include taking care of weapons, working as scouts, and even setting up their own fighting brigades. Louise Michel (mee-SHEL) (1830–1905), a schoolteacher, emerged as one of the leaders of the Paris Commune (see the box on p. 731). She proved tireless in forming committees for the defense of the revolutionary Commune.

All of these efforts were in vain, however. In the last week of May, government troops massacred thousands of the Commune's defenders. Estimates are that 20,000 were shot; another 10,000 (including Louise Michel) were shipped to the French penal colony of New Caledonia in the South Pacific. The brutal repression of the Commune bequeathed a legacy of hatred that continued to plague French politics for decades. The split between the middle and working classes, begun in the revolutionary hostilities of 1848–1849, had widened immensely. The harsh punishment of women who participated in the revolutionary activity also served to discourage any future efforts by working-class women to improve their conditions.

Although a majority of the members of the monarchist-dominated National Assembly wished to restore a monarchy to France, inability to agree on who should be king caused the monarchists to miss their opportunity and led in 1875 to an improvised constitution that established a republican form of government as the least divisive compromise. This constitution established a bicameral legislature with an upper house, the Senate, elected indirectly and a lower house, the Chamber of Deputies, chosen by universal male suffrage; a president, selected by the legislature for a term of seven years, served as executive of the government. The Constitution of 1875, intended only as a stopgap measure, solidified the republic—the Third Republic—which lasted sixty-five years. New elections in 1876 and 1877 strengthened the hands of the republicans who managed by 1879 to institute ministerial responsibility and establish the power of the Chamber of Deputies. The prime minister or premier and his ministers were now responsible not to the president but to the Chamber of Deputies.

Although the government's moderation gradually encouraged more and more middle-class and peasant support, the position of the Third Republic remained precarious because monarchists, Catholic clergy, and professional army officers were still its enemies.

A major crisis in the 1880s, however, actually served to strengthen the republican government. General Georges Boulanger (ZHORZH boo-lahnh-ZHAY) (1837–1891) was a popular military officer who attracted the public attention of all those discontented with the Third Republic: the monarchists, Bonapartists, aristocrats, and nationalists who favored a war of revenge against Germany. Boulanger appeared as the strong man on horseback, the savior of France. By 1889, just when his strength had grown to the point where many expected a coup d'état, he lost his nerve and fled France, a completely discredited man. In the long run, the Boulanger crisis served to rally support for the resilient republic.

SPAIN In Spain, a new constitution, drafted in 1875 under King Alfonso XII (1874–1885), established a parliamentary government dominated by two political groups, the Conservatives and the Liberals, whose members stemmed from the same small social group of great landowners allied with a few wealthy industrialists. Because suffrage was limited to the propertied classes, Liberals and Conservatives alternated in power but followed basically the same conservative policies. Spain's defeat in the Spanish-American War in 1898 and the loss of Cuba and the Philippines to the United States increased the discontent with the status quo. When a group of young intellectuals known as the Generation of 1898 called for political and social reforms, both Liberals and Conservatives attempted to enlarge the electorate and win the masses' support for their policies. The attempted reforms did little to allay the unrest, however, and the growth of industrialization in some areas resulted in more workers being attracted to the radical solutions of socialism and anarchism. When violence erupted in Barcelona in July 1909,

A Leader of the Paris Commune

Louise Michel was a schoolteacher in Paris who took an interest in radical ideas. She became active among revolutionary groups in Paris in 1870 and then emerged as a leader of the Paris Commune in 1871. Exiled to New Caledonia after the crushing of the Commune, in 1880 she was allowed to return to France, where she became a heroic figure among radical groups. Later, she spent three years in prison and then lived much of the time in England in self-imposed exile. In her memoirs, Michel discusses what happened on March 18, 1871, when the National Assembly sent troops to seize cannons that had been moved earlier to the hills of Montmartre. She also reflected on her activities in the Commune.

Louise Michel, *Memoirs*

Learning that the Versailles soldiers [troops of the National Assembly] were trying to seize the cannon, men and women of Montmartre swarmed up the Butte in a surprise maneuver. Those people who were climbing believed they would die, but they were prepared to pay the price.

The Butte of Montmartre was bathed in the first light of day, through which things were glimpsed as if they were hidden behind a thin veil of water. Gradually the crowd increased. The other districts of Paris, hearing of the events taking place on the Butte of Montmartre, came to our assistance.

The women of Paris covered the cannon with their bodies. When their officers ordered the soldiers to fire, the men refused. The same army that would be used to crush Paris two months later decided now that it did not want to be an accomplice of the reaction. They gave up their attempt to seize the cannon from the National Guard. They understood that the people were defending the Republic by defending the arms that the royalists and imperialists would have turned on Paris in agreement with the Prussians. When we had won our victory, I looked around and noticed my poor mother, who had followed me to the Butte of Montmartre, believing that I was going to die.

On this day, the eighteenth of March, the people awakened. If they had not, it would have been the triumph of some king; instead it was a triumph of the people. The eighteenth of March could have belonged to the allies of kings, or to foreigners, or to the people. It was the people's. . . .

During the entire time of the Commune, I only spent one night at my poor mother's. I never really went to bed during that time. I just napped a little whenever there was nothing better to do, and many other people lived the same way. Everybody who wanted deliverance gave himself totally to the cause. . . . During the Commune I went unhurt except for a bullet that grazed my wrist, although my hat was literally riddled with bullet holes.

Q What does this account from the memoirs of the Parisian feminist Louise Michel tell you about new opportunities for political involvement that were available to female and male residents of European capital cities during the late nineteenth century?

the military forces brutally suppressed the rebels. The revolt and its repression made clear that reform would not be easily accomplished because the Catholic Church, the large landowners, and the army remained tied to a conservative social order.

ITALY By 1870, Italy had emerged as a geographically united state with pretensions to great power status. Its internal weaknesses, however, gave that claim a particularly hollow ring. One Italian leader said after unification, "We have made Italy; now we must make Italians." But many Italians continued to put loyalty to their families, towns, and regions above their loyalty to the new state.

Sectional differences—a poverty-stricken south and an industrializing north—also weakened any sense of community. Most of the Italian leaders were northerners who treated southern Italians with contempt. The Catholic Church, which had lost control of the Papal States as a result of unification, even refused to accept the existence of the new state. Chronic turmoil between workers and industrialists undermined the social fabric. And few Italians felt empowered in the new Italy: only 2.5 percent of the people could vote for the legislative body. In 1882, the number was increased, but only to 10 percent. The Italian government was unable to deal effectively with these problems because of the extensive corruption among government officials and the lack of stability created by ever-changing government coalitions.

Central and Eastern Europe: Persistence of the Old Order

Germany, Austria-Hungary, and Russia pursued political policies that were quite different from those of the western European nations. The central European states (Germany and Austria-Hungary) had the trappings of parliamentary government, including legislative bodies and elections by universal male suffrage, but authoritarian forces, especially powerful monarchies and conservative social groups, remained strong. In eastern Europe, especially Russia, the old system of autocracy was barely touched by the winds of change.

GERMANY Despite unification, important divisions remained in German society that could not simply be papered over by the force of nationalism. These divisions were already evident in the new German constitution that provided for a federal system with a bicameral legislature. The Bundesrat, or upper house, represented the twenty-five states that made up Germany. Individual states, such as Bavaria and Prussia, kept their own kings, their own post offices, and even their own armies in peacetime. The lower house of the German parliament, the Reichstag, was elected on the basis of universal male suffrage, but it did not have ministerial responsibility. Ministers of government, the most important of which was the chancellor, were responsible not to the parliament but to the emperor. The emperor also commanded the armed forces and controlled foreign policy and internal administration. Though the creation of a parliament elected by universal male suffrage presented opportunities for the growth of a real political democracy, it failed to develop in Germany before World War I. The army and Bismarck were two major reasons why it did not.

The German (largely Prussian) army viewed itself as the defender of monarchy and aristocracy and sought to escape any control by the Reichstag by operating under a general staff responsible only to the emperor. Prussian military tradition was strong, and military officers took steps to ensure the loyalty of their subordinates to the emperor, which was easy as long as Junker landowners were officers. As the growth of the army made it necessary to turn to the middle class for officers, extreme care was taken to choose only sons "of honorable bourgeois families in whom the love for King and Fatherland, a warm heart for the soldier's calling, and Christian morality are planted and nurtured."

The policies of Otto von Bismarck, who served as chancellor of the new German state until 1890, often served to prevent the growth of more democratic institutions. At first, Bismarck worked with the liberals to achieve greater centralization of Germany through common codes of criminal and commercial law. The liberals also joined Bismarck in his attack on the Catholic Church, the so-called ***Kulturkampf*** (kool-TOOR-kahmf), or "struggle for civilization." Like Bismarck, middle-class liberals distrusted Catholic loyalty to the new Germany. Bismarck's strong-arm tactics against the Catholic clergy and Catholic institutions proved counterproductive, however, and Bismarck welcomed an opportunity in 1878 to abandon the attack on Catholicism by making an abrupt shift in policy.

Otto von Bismarck, Memoirs, excerpts (1898)

In 1878, Bismarck abandoned the liberals and began to persecute the socialists. When the Social Democratic Party elected twelve deputies to the Reichstag in 1877, Bismarck grew alarmed. He genuinely believed that the socialists' antinationalistic, anticapitalistic, and antimonarchical stance represented a danger to the empire. In 1878, Bismarck got parliament to pass a stringent antisocialist law that outlawed the Social Democratic Party and limited socialist meetings and publications, although socialist candidates were still permitted to run for the Reichstag. In addition to repressive measures, Bismarck also attempted to woo workers away from socialism by enacting social welfare legislation (see the box on p. 733). Between 1883 and 1889, the Reichstag passed laws that established sickness, accident, and disability benefits as well as old-age pensions financed by compulsory contributions from workers, employers, and the state. Bismarck's social security system was the most progressive the world had yet seen, although even his system left much to be desired, as the Social Democrats pointed out. A full pension, for example, was payable only at age seventy after forty-eight years of contributions. In the event of a male worker's death, no benefits were paid to his widow or children.

Both the repressive and the social welfare measures failed to stop the growth of socialism, however. The Social Democratic Party continued to grow. In his frustration, Bismarck planned still more repressive measures in 1890, but before he could carry them out, the new emperor, William II (1888–1918), eager to pursue his own policies, cashiered the aged chancellor.

Bismarck and William II. In 1890, Bismarck sought to undertake new repressive measures against the Social Democrats. Disagreeing with this policy, Emperor William II forced him to resign. This political cartoon shows William II reclining on a throne made of artillery and cannonballs and holding a doll labeled "socialism." Bismarck bids farewell as Germany, personified as a woman, looks on with grave concern.

Bismarck and the Welfare of the Workers

In his attempt to win workers away from socialism, Bismarck favored an extensive program of social welfare benefits, including old-age pensions and compensation for absence from work due to sickness, accident, or disability. This selection is taken from Bismarck's address to the Reichstag on March 10, 1884, in which he explained his motives for social welfare legislation.

⭑⭑⭑

Bismarck, Address to the Reichstag

The positive efforts began really only in the year... 1881... with the imperial message... in which His Majesty William I said: "Already in February of this year, we have expressed our conviction that the healing of social ills is not to be sought exclusively by means of repression of Social Democratic excesses, but equally in the positive promotion of the welfare of the workers."

In consequence of this, first of all the insurance law against accidents was submitted.... And it reads... "But those who have, through age or disability, become incapable of working have a confirmed claim on all for a higher degree of state care than could have been their share heretofore...."

The worker's real sore point is the insecurity of his existence. He is not always sure he will always have work. He is not sure he will always be healthy, and he foresees some day he will be old and incapable of work. But also if he falls into poverty as a result of long illness, he is completely helpless with his own powers, and society hitherto does not recognize relief, even when he has worked ever so faithfully and diligently before. But ordinary poor relief leaves much to be desired, especially in the great cities where it is extraordinarily much worse than in the country.... We read in Berlin newspapers of suicide because of difficulty in making both ends meet, of people who died from direct hunger and have hanged themselves because they have nothing to eat, of people who announce in the paper they were tossed out homeless and have no income.... For the worker it is always a fact that falling into poverty and onto poor relief in a great city is synonymous with misery, and this insecurity makes him hostile and mistrustful of society. That is humanly not unnatural, and as long as the state does not meet him halfway, just as long will this trust in the state's honesty be taken from him by accusations against the government, which he will find where he wills; always running back again to the socialist quacks... and, without great reflection, letting himself be promised things, which will not be fulfilled. On this account, I believe that accident insurance, with which we show the way,... will still work on the anxieties and ill-feeling of the working class. ⭢

Q What arguments did Bismarck advance for social welfare legislation? How did Bismarck benefit politically from these moves toward state protection of workers' interests? To what broader forces in nineteenth-century European social and political life was Bismarck responding when he formulated these policies?

AUSTRIA-HUNGARY After the creation of the Dual Monarchy of Austria-Hungary in 1867, the Austrian part received a constitution that established a parliamentary system with the principle of ministerial responsibility. But Emperor Francis Joseph (1848–1916) largely ignored ministerial responsibility and proceeded to personally appoint and dismiss his ministers and rule by decree when parliament was not in session.

The problem of the minorities continued to trouble the empire. The ethnic Germans, who made up only one-third of Austria's population, governed Austria but felt increasingly threatened by the Czechs, Poles, and other Slavic groups within the empire. The difficulties in dealing with this problem were especially evident from 1879 to 1893 when Count Edward von Taaffe (TAH-fuh) (1833–1895) served as prime minister. Taaffe attempted to "muddle through" by relying on a coalition of German conservatives, Czechs, and Poles to maintain a majority in parliament. But his concessions to national minorities, such as allowing the Slavic languages as well as German to be used in education and administration, antagonized the German-speaking Austrian bureaucracy and aristocracy, two of the basic pillars of the empire. Opposition to Taaffe's policies brought his downfall in 1893 but did not solve the **nationalities problem.** While the dissatisfied non-German groups demanded concessions, the ruling Austrian Germans resisted change.

What held the Austro-Hungarian Empire together was a combination of forces. Francis Joseph, the emperor, was one unifying factor. Although strongly anti-Hungarian, the cautious emperor made an effort to take a position above national differences. Loyalty to the Catholic Church also helped keep such national groups as Czechs, Slovaks, and Poles loyal to the Catholic Habsburg dynasty. Finally, although dominated by German-speaking officials, the large imperial bureaucracy served as a unifying force for the empire.

Unlike Austria, Hungary had a working parliamentary system, but it was controlled by the great Magyar landowners who dominated both the Hungarian peasantry and the other ethnic groups in Hungary. The Hungarians attempted to solve their nationalities problem by systematic Magyarization. The Magyar language was imposed on all schools and was the only language that could be used by government and military officials.

CHRONOLOGY National States of Europe, 1871–1894

Great Britain

Second ministry of William Gladstone	1880–1885
Reform Act	1884

France

Surrender of French provisional government to Germany	1871 (January 28)
Paris Commune	1871 (March–May)
Republican constitution (Third Republic)	1875
Boulanger is discredited	1889

Spain

King Alfonso XII	1874–1885
New constitution	1875

Germany

Bismarck as chancellor	1871–1890
Antisocialist law	1878
Social welfare legislation	1883–1889

Austria-Hungary

Emperor Francis Joseph	1848–1916
Count Edward von Taaffe as prime minister	1879–1893

Russia

Tsar Alexander III	1881–1894

RUSSIA In Russia, the government made no concession whatever to liberal and democratic reforms, eliminating altogether any possibility of a mass politics. The assassination of Alexander II in 1881 convinced his son and successor, Alexander III (1881–1894), that reform had been a mistake, and he quickly instituted what he said were "exceptional measures." The powers of the secret police were expanded. Advocates of constitutional monarchy and social reform, along with revolutionary groups, were persecuted. Entire districts of Russia were placed under martial law if the government suspected the inhabitants of treason. The powers of the zemstvos, created by the reforms of Alexander II, were sharply curtailed.

Alexander also pursued a radical Russification program of the numerous nationalities that made up the Russian Empire. Russians themselves constituted only 40 percent of the population, which did not stop the tsar from banning the use of all languages except Russian in schools. The policy of Russification served primarily to anger national groups and create new sources of opposition to tsarist policies.

When Alexander III died, his weak son and successor, Nicholas II (1894–1917), adopted his father's conviction that the absolute power of the tsars should be preserved: "I shall maintain the principle of autocracy just as firmly and unflinchingly as did my unforgettable father."[13] But conditions were changing, especially with the growth of industrialization, and the tsar's approach was not realistic in view of the new circumstances he faced.

CHAPTER SUMMARY

The Second Industrial Revolution helped create a new material prosperity that led Europeans to believe they had ushered in a new age of progress. In this second revolution, steel, chemicals, electricity, petroleum, and the internal combustion engine led the way to new industrial frontiers. Europe became divided into an industrialized north and a poorer south and east, while European manufactured goods and investment capital were exported abroad in exchange for raw materials, creating a true world economy. New jobs provided work opportunities for many women, although prostitution remained an avenue for survival for other women. Working-class socialist parties, such as Germany's Social Democratic Party, began working for change by forming trade unions and electing representatives to legislative bodies.

A major feature of this "new age of progress" was the emergence of a mass society. Better sanitation and improved diets led to a dramatic population increase, while emigration enabled Europe to avoid overcrowding. Class divisions continued to dictate styles of living, while industrialism reinforced traditional gender patterns: women stayed at home while men went out to work. Nevertheless, some women began to espouse birth control as an avenue for change. The lower classes benefited from the right to vote, a higher standard of living, and a modicum of education from new schools as most states assumed responsibility for mass compulsory education for children. New forms of mass transportation, combined with new work patterns, enabled large numbers of people to participate in new mass leisure activities, including weekend excursions to amusement parks and seaside resorts, dance halls, and sporting events. New patterns of mass consumption arose, encouraging people to accumulate more material possessions.

By 1871, the national state had become the focus of people's lives. Especially in western Europe, liberal and democratic reforms brought new possibilities for greater participation in the political process, although women were still largely excluded from political rights. After 1871, the national state also began to expand its functions beyond all previous activities by adopting social insurance measures to protect workers against accidents, illness, and old age, and by enacting public health and housing measures, designed to curb the worst ills of urban living.

This extension of state functions took place in an atmosphere of increased national loyalty. After 1871, Western national states increasingly sought to solidify the social order and win the active loyalty and support of their citizens by deliberately cultivating national feelings. Yet this policy contained potentially great dangers. As we shall see in the next chapter, nations had discovered once again that imperialistic adventures and military successes could arouse nationalistic passions, but they also found that nationalistic feelings could lead to intense international rivalries that made war almost inevitable.

CHAPTER TIMELINE

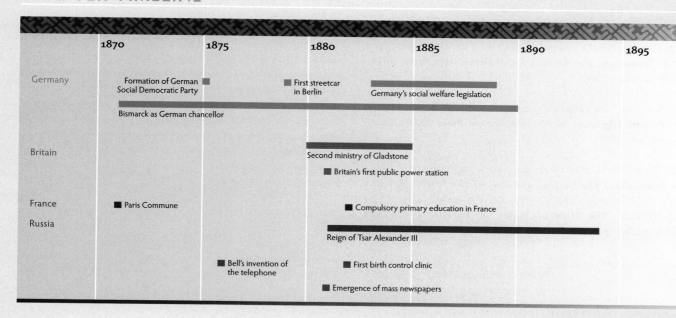

CHAPTER REVIEW

Upon Reflection

Q To what extent did the emergence and development of socialist parties and trade unions meet the needs of the working classes between 1871 and 1894?

Q How were the promises and problems of the new mass society reflected in education, leisure, and consumption?

Q Between 1871 and 1894, two major domestic political issues involved the achievement of liberal practices and the growth of political democracy. To what extent were these realized in Great Britain, France, Germany, Austria-Hungary, and Russia?

Key Terms

tariffs (p. 706)
cartels (p. 707)

depression (p. 708)
Marxism (p. 712)
evolutionary socialism (p. 712)
revisionism (p. 712)
anarchism (p. 714)
mass society (p. 714)
plutocrats (p. 719)
mass education (p. 725)
mass leisure (p. 727)
mass politics (p. 729)
home rule (p. 730)
Kulturkampf (p. 732)
nationalities problem (p. 733)

Suggestions for Further Reading

GENERAL WORKS In addition to the general works on the nineteenth century and individual European countries cited in

Chapters 21 and 22, a more specialized work on the subject matter of this chapter is available in **F. Gilbert** and **D. C. Large, *The End of the European Era, 1890 to the Present,*** 5th ed. (New York, 2002).

SECOND INDUSTRIAL REVOLUTION   The subject of the Second Industrial Revolution is well covered in **D. Landes, *The Unbound Prometheus,*** cited in Chapter 20. For a fundamental survey of European industrialization, see **A. S. Milward** and **S. B. Saul, *The Development of the Economies of Continental Europe, 1850–1914*** (Cambridge, Mass., 1977). The impact of the new technology on European thought is imaginatively discussed in **S. Kern, *The Culture of Time and Space, 1880–1918,*** rev. ed. (Cambridge, Mass., 2003).

SOCIALISM   For an introduction to international socialism, see **A. Lindemann, *A History of European Socialism*** (New Haven, Conn., 1983). On the emergence of German social democracy, see **W. L. Guttsman, *The German Social Democratic Party, 1875–1933*** (London, 1981).

MIGRATION   On European emigration, see **L. P. Moch, *Moving Europeans: Migration in Western Europe Since 1650*** (Bloomington, Ind., 1993).

SOCIAL CLASSES   An interesting work on aristocratic life is **D. Cannadine, *The Decline and Fall of the British Aristocracy*** (New Haven, Conn., 1990). On the middle classes, see **P. Pilbeam, *The Middle Classes in Europe, 1789–1914*** (Basingstoke, England, 1990). On the working classes, see **R. Magraw, *A History of the French Working Class*** (Cambridge, Mass., 1992).

WOMEN'S EXPERIENCES   There are good overviews of women's experiences in the nineteenth century in **B. G. Smith, *Changing Lives: Women in European History Since 1700,*** rev. ed. (Lexington, Mass., 2005). The world of women's work is examined in **L. A. Tilly** and **J. W. Scott, *Women, Work, and Family,*** rev. ed. (New York, 1987). Important studies of women include **M. J. Peterson, *Family, Love and Work in the Lives of Victorian Gentlewomen*** (Bloomington, Ind., 1989), and **B. Franzoi, *At the Very Least She Pays the Rent: Women and German Industrialization, 1871–1914*** (Westport, Conn., 1985). For a new perspective on domestic life, see **J. Flanders, *Inside the Victorian Home: A Portrait of Domestic Life in Victorian England*** (New York, 2004). Prostitution is discussed in **J. R. Walkowitz, *Prostitution and Victorian Society: Women, Class and the State*** (Cambridge, 1980).

MASS EDUCATION, LEISURE, AND CONSUMPTION   On various aspects of education, see **M. J. Maynes, *Schooling in Western Europe: A Social History*** (Albany, N.Y., 1985). A concise and well-presented survey of leisure patterns is **G. Cross, *A Social History of Leisure Since 1600*** (State College, Pa., 1990). On the new consumer culture, see **C. Breward, *The Hidden Consumer: Masculinities, Fashion and City Life 1860–1914*** (Manchester, 1999), and **G. Crossick, *Cathedrals of Consumption: The European Department Store*** (New York, 1999).

DOMESTIC POLITICS   The domestic politics of the period can be examined in the general works on individual countries listed in the bibliographies for Chapters 21 and 22. There are also specialized works on aspects of each country's history. On Britain, see **D. Read, *The Age of Urban Democracy: England, 1868–1914*** (New York, 1994). On the Paris Commune, see **D. A. Shafer, *The Paris Commune*** (New York, 2005), and **C. J. Eichner, *Surmounting the Barricades: Women in the Paris Commune*** (Bloomington, Ind., 2004). On Germany, see **W. J. Mommsen, *Imperial Germany, 1867–1918*** (New York, 1995).

Visit the CourseMate website at www.cengagebrain.com for additional study tools and review materials for this chapter.

CourseMate

1. Otto von Bismarck's skillful use of diplomacy in concert with war and aggression best exemplifies the nineteenth-century practice of

   (A) *Kristallnacht*.
   (B) balance of power.
   (C) *kunstreig*.
   (D) *realpolitik*.
   (E) *ostpolitik*.

2. Which of the following statements best describes European family life in the nineteenth century?

   (A) All marriages were arranged by the patriarch in order to enhance his financial stability.
   (B) All marriages were arranged by the matriarch in order to enhance her domestic status.
   (C) Formality and emotional distance were atypical behaviors for the nuclear family.
   (D) Parents sought to enhance their own well-being by raising good children.
   (E) The Industrial Revolution forced families into economic dependency on their extended family members.

3. Which of the following best describes the changes in social life in the nineteenth century?

   (A) A decrease in wars and conflicts between nations led to an increase in family sizes.
   (B) A natural rise in female fertility forced many families to become dependent on state welfare for economic survival.
   (C) Greater access to news and communication led to an increase in basic literacy.
   (D) A population boom crippled local markets and froze community economies.
   (E) Outbreaks of smallpox devastated the poor in large numbers.

4. Contributing greatly to the expansion of state economies in the nineteenth century, industrialists of the era were most often

   (A) members of the ruling nobility seeking to engage in modern politics.
   (B) civil servants looking to foster nationalist feelings and loyalty to the state.
   (C) members of the farming class making a transition into urban life.
   (D) members of the middle class who worked in a hierarchical class structure.
   (E) Chinese workers imported as labor needed to offset European emigration.

5. Which of the following best describes the social reforms in urban life during the Victorian Age?

   (A) They addressed problems that arose almost a century after industrialization had started.
   (B) They were unable to address the practice of prostitution.
   (C) They were quickly enacted and widely praised due to a lack of class division.
   (D) They were only possible because men supported many of the political causes of women, such as the right to vote.
   (E) They were unsuccessful in preventing the rise and growth of trade unions.

6. One of the major social costs of late-nineteenth-century urbanization was that

   (A) working women were forced to return to the household.
   (B) the nuclear family unit fractured, breaking up countless homes.
   (C) children were separated from their working parents as early childhood centers cared for them.
   (D) families were forced to neglect the care of their elders.
   (E) it facilitated frequent outbreaks of cholera.

7. Which of the following organizations was formed in the Victorian Age to encourage young males to be active and curious?

   (A) the Boy Scouts
   (B) the Young Men's Christian Association
   (C) the Boys Club
   (D) the British Science Clubs
   (E) the Levellers

8. Which of the following best describes the changes in family life between the seventeenth century and the late nineteenth century?

   (A) The number of children per family unit doubled.
   (B) Moral standards for women became more rigid.
   (C) Children become less of an economic asset to their parents.
   (D) The divorce rate fell after 1750.
   (E) Men married at an earlier age.

9. Europe's population growth in the late nineteenth century can be attributed primarily to

(A) a declining mortality rate.
(B) a decline in emigration to the New World.
(C) a trend toward larger families.
(D) declining marriage rates in western Europe.
(E) population growth rates that were higher in western Europe than in central Europe.

10. Which of the following was the central issue for nineteenth-century European advocates of women's rights?

(A) equal pay for equal work
(B) alimony and child support after a divorce
(C) the right to civil marriage ceremonies
(D) a woman's ability to decide whom and when to marry
(E) the right of women to control their own property

11. Which of the following is NOT true about family life in the late nineteenth century?

(A) Men controlled the family finances, and women mainly cared for the children.
(B) Families were smaller since children were no longer an earning asset for the parents.
(C) The men led the family in religious matters and made sure the family went to church.
(D) With the rise of mass production and consumerism, middle-class families were able to buy some of the "finer" things in life.
(E) Women gained access to new jobs as secondary school teachers, telephone operators, and skilled assistants in stores.

12. The concept of Zionism, fostered by Herzl, suggested that

(A) racism was a positive result of urbanized society and benefited the people.
(B) anti-Semitism was reemerging and a separate Jewish state was necessary.
(C) social Darwinism would help to create a new, stronger Europe.
(D) racial superiority could indeed be scientifically proved and that the Aryan race had been proved to be the strongest.
(E) nations should cooperate to commit to the growth of a Palestinian state.

13. By the 1890s, European socialism was largely

(A) Marxist in that most socialists believed a massive revolution would unfold and redefine world history.
(B) revisionist in that most socialists favored democratic reforms passed by parliaments.
(C) anarchist in that most socialists sought to remove all authority.
(D) syndicalist in that most socialists sought cooperatives as a form of national rule.
(E) dead in western Europe, but active in eastern Europe.

The Eiffel Tower at the World's Fair of 1900 in Paris

An Age of Modernity, Anxiety, and Imperialism, 1894–1914

CHAPTER OUTLINE AND FOCUS QUESTIONS

Toward the Modern Consciousness: Intellectual and Cultural Developments

Q What developments in science, intellectual affairs, and the arts in the late nineteenth and early twentieth centuries "opened the way to a modern consciousness," and how did this consciousness differ from earlier worldviews?

Politics: New Directions and New Uncertainties

Q What gains did women make in their movement for women's rights? How did a new right-wing politics affect the Jews in different parts of Europe? What political problems did Great Britain, Italy, France, Germany, Austria-Hungary, and Russia face between 1894 and 1914, and how did they solve them?

The New Imperialism

Q What were the causes of the new imperialism that took place after 1880, and what effects did European imperialism have on Africa and Asia?

International Rivalry and the Coming of War

Q What was the Bismarckian system of alliances, and how successful was it at keeping the peace? What issues lay behind the international crises that Europe faced in the late nineteenth and early twentieth centuries?

CRITICAL THINKING

Q What is the connection between the "new imperialism" of the late nineteenth century and the causes of World War I?

IN 1889, THE EIFFEL TOWER stood above Paris as a beacon of progress, a symbol of what technology and industrialization could accomplish. Constructed from iron to mark the entrance to the World's Fair, it was the tallest structure in the world, extending 1,000 feet above the city. Over a period of five months, 3.5 million visitors paid to ascend the tower and overlook the grounds teeming with throngs of people. Almost 175,000 people a day came to visit the fair's 60,000 exhibits, which included an Algerian bazaar, Swedish chalet, Indian palace, and Japanese garden. Guidebooks for the fair posited that a visitor would need ten to twenty days to see all of the displays. One awestruck visitor declared, "There is only one cry; this is the most grandiose, the most dazzling, the most marvelous spectacle ever seen."[1] For most in attendance, the modern era was indeed an age of progress that was providing higher standards of living, better cities, more goods to consume, and greater democratization.

The optimism found at the World's Fair and throughout Europe's cities was not unchallenged, however. Some were still struggling to achieve progress. Many workers continued to endure pitiful housing conditions and low wages, while many women fought for the right to vote. Beneath the apparent calm, tensions were also building, fueled by imperialist adventures, international rivalries, and cultural uncertainties. After 1880, Europeans engaged in a great race for colonies around the world. This competition for lands abroad greatly intensified existing antagonisms among European states.

Ultimately, Europeans proved incapable of finding constructive ways to cope with their international rivalries. The development of two large alliance systems—the Triple Alliance and the Triple Entente—may have helped preserve peace for a time, but eventually the alliances made it easier for the European nations to be drawn into World War I.

The cultural life of Europe in the decades before 1914 reflected similar dynamic tensions. The advent of mass education produced better-informed citizens but also made it easier for governments to stir up the masses by nationalistic appeals through the new mass journalism. At the same time, despite the appearance of progress, European philosophers, writers, and artists were creating modern cultural expressions that questioned traditional ideas and values and incited a crisis of confidence. Before 1914, many intellectuals had a sense of unease about the direction in which society was heading, accompanied by a feeling of imminent catastrophe. They proved remarkably prophetic.

Toward the Modern Consciousness: Intellectual and Cultural Developments

Q Focus Question: What developments in science, intellectual affairs, and the arts in the late nineteenth and early twentieth centuries "opened the way to a modern consciousness," and how did this consciousness differ from earlier worldviews?

Before 1914, most Europeans continued to believe in the values and ideals that had been generated by the Scientific Revolution and the Enlightenment. *Reason, science,* and *progress* were still important buzzwords in the European vocabulary. The ability of human beings to improve themselves and achieve a better society seemed to be well demonstrated by a rising standard of living, urban improvements, and mass education. Such products of modern technology as electric lights, phonographs, cinema, and automobiles reinforced the popular prestige of science and the belief in the ability of the human mind to comprehend the universe through the use of reason. Near the end of the nineteenth century, however, a dramatic transformation in the realm of ideas and culture challenged many of these assumptions. A new view of the physical universe, an appeal to the irrational, alternative views of human nature, and radically innovative forms of literary and artistic expression shattered old beliefs and opened the way to a modern consciousness. These new ideas called forth a sense of confusion and anxiety that would become even more pronounced after World War I.

Developments in the Sciences: The Emergence of a New Physics

Science was one of the chief pillars supporting the optimistic and rationalistic view of the world that many Westerners shared in the nineteenth century. Supposedly based on hard facts and cold reason, science offered a certainty of belief in the orderliness of nature that was comforting to many people for whom traditional religious beliefs no longer had much meaning. Many naively believed that the application of already known scientific laws would give humanity a complete understanding of the physical world and an accurate picture of reality. The new physics dramatically altered that perspective.

Throughout much of the nineteenth century, Westerners adhered to the mechanical conception of the universe postulated by the classical physics of Isaac Newton. In this perspective, the universe was viewed as a giant machine in which time, space, and matter were objective realities that existed independently of the people observing them. Matter was thought to be composed of indivisible solid material bodies called atoms.

These views were first seriously questioned at the end of the nineteenth century. The French scientist Marie Curie (kyoo-REE) (1867–1934) and her husband Pierre (1859–1906) discovered that the element radium gave off rays of radiation that apparently came from within the atom itself. Atoms were not simply hard, material bodies but small worlds containing such subatomic particles as electrons and protons that behaved in seemingly random and inexplicable fashion. Inquiry into the disintegrative process within atoms became a central theme of the new physics.

Building on this work, in 1900, a Berlin physicist, Max Planck (PLAHNK) (1858–1947), rejected the belief that a heated body radiates energy in a steady stream but maintained instead that energy is radiated discontinuously, in irregular packets that he called "quanta." The quantum theory raised fundamental questions about the subatomic realm of the atom. By 1900, the old view of atoms as the basic building blocks of the material world was being seriously questioned, and Newtonian physics was in trouble.

THE WORK OF EINSTEIN Albert Einstein (YN-styn *or* YN-shtyn) (1879–1955), a German-born patent officer working in Switzerland, pushed these theories of thermodynamics into new terrain. In 1905, Einstein published a paper titled "The Electro-Dynamics of Moving Bodies" that contained his special theory of relativity. According to **relativity theory,** space and time are not absolute but relative to the observer, and both are interwoven into what Einstein called a four-dimensional space-time continuum. Neither space nor time had an existence independent of human experience. As Einstein later explained simply to a journalist, "It was formerly believed that if all material things disappeared out of the universe, time and space would be left. According to the relativity theory,

AP Images

Marie Curie. Marie Curie was born in Warsaw, Poland, but studied at the University of Paris, where she received degrees in both physics and mathematics. She was the first woman to win two Nobel Prizes, one in 1903 in physics and another in 1911 in chemistry. She is shown here in her Paris laboratory in 1921. She died of leukemia, a result of her laboratory work with radioactivity.

however, time and space disappear together with the things."[2] Moreover, matter and energy reflected the relativity of time and space. Einstein concluded that matter was nothing but another form of energy. His epochal formula $E = mc^2$—each particle of matter is equivalent to its mass times the square of the velocity of light—was the key theory explaining the vast energies contained within the atom. It led to the atomic age.

Many scientists were unable to comprehend Einstein's ideas, but during a total eclipse of the sun in May 1919, scientists were able to demonstrate that light was deflected in the gravitational field of the sun, just as Einstein had predicted. This confirmed Einstein's general theory of relativity and opened the scientific and intellectual world to his ideas. The 1920s would become the "heroic age" of physics.

Toward a New Understanding of the Irrational

Intellectually, the decades before 1914 witnessed a combination of contradictory developments. Thanks to the influence of science, confidence in human reason and progress still remained a dominant thread. At the same time, however, a small group of intellectuals attacked the idea of optimistic progress, dethroned reason, and glorified the irrational.

NIETZSCHE Friedrich Nietzsche (FREED-rikh NEE-chuh or NEE-chee) (1844–1900) was one of the intellectuals who glorified the irrational. According to Nietzsche, Western bourgeois society was decadent and incapable of any real cultural creativity, primarily because of its excessive emphasis on the rational faculty at the expense of emotions, passions, and instincts. Reason, Nietzsche claimed, actually played little role in human life because humans were at the mercy of irrational life forces.

Nietzsche believed that Christianity should shoulder much of the blame for Western civilization's enfeeblement. The "slave morality" of Christianity, he believed, had obliterated the human impulse for life and had crushed the human will:

> I call Christianity the one great curse, the one enormous and innermost perversion. . . . I call it the one immortal blemish of mankind. . . . Christianity has taken the side of everything weak, base, ill-constituted, it has made an ideal out of opposition to the preservative instincts of strong life. . . . Christianity is called the religion of pity.—Pity stands in antithesis to the basic emotions which enhance the energy of the feeling of life: it has a depressive effect. One loses force when one pities.[3]

How, then, could Western society be renewed? First, said Nietzsche, one must recognize that "God is dead." Europeans had killed God, he said, and it was no longer possible to believe in some kind of cosmic order. Eliminating God and hence Christian morality had liberated human beings and made it possible to create a higher kind of being Nietzsche called the superman: "I teach you the Superman. Man is something that is to be surpassed."[4] Superior intellectuals must free themselves from the ordinary thinking of the masses, create their own values, and lead the masses. Nietzsche rejected and condemned political democracy, social reform, and universal suffrage.

BERGSON Another popular revolutionary against reason in the 1890s was Henri Bergson (AHN-ree BERG-son) (1859–1941), a French philosopher whose lectures at the University of Paris made him one of the most important influences in French thought in the early twentieth century. Bergson accepted rational, scientific thought as a practical instrument for providing useful knowledge but maintained that it was incapable of arriving at truth or ultimate reality. To him, reality was the "life force" that suffused all things; it could not be divided into analyzable parts. Reality was a whole that could only be grasped intuitively and experienced directly. When we analyze it, we have merely a description, no longer the reality we have experienced.

Sigmund Freud. Freud was one of the intellectual giants of the nineteenth and twentieth centuries. Born in Moravia, Freud began to study medicine at the University of Vienna in 1873. After entering private practice, he began to study patients suffering from psychosomatic symptoms. This led him to his belief that unconscious forces strongly determine human behavior. This idea formed the foundation for twentieth-century psychoanalysis.

SOREL Georges Sorel (ZHORZH soh-RELL) (1847–1922), a French political theorist, combined Bergson's and Nietzsche's ideas on the limits of rational thinking with his own passionate interest in **revolutionary socialism.** Sorel understood the political potential of the nonrational and advocated violent action as the only sure way to achieve the aims of socialism. To destroy capitalist society, he recommended the use of the **general strike,** envisioning it as a mythic image that had the power to inspire workers to take violent, heroic action against the capitalist order. Sorel also came to believe that the new socialist society would have to be governed by a small elite ruling body because the masses were incapable of ruling themselves.

Sigmund Freud and Psychoanalysis

Around the turn of the twentieth century, a Viennese doctor, Sigmund Freud (SIG-mund or ZIG-munt FROID)

(1856–1939), put forth a series of theories that undermined optimism about the rational nature of the human mind. Freud's thought, like the new physics and the irrationalism of Nietzsche, added to the uncertainties of the age. His major ideas were published in 1900 in *The Interpretation of Dreams,* which contained the basic foundation of what came to be known as **psychoanalysis.**

Sigmund Freud, *The Interpretation of Dreams,* excerpts (1900)

ROLE OF THE UNCONSCIOUS According to Freud, human behavior was strongly determined by the unconscious, by earlier experiences and inner forces of which people were largely oblivious. To explore the content of the unconscious, Freud relied not only on hypnosis but also on dreams, but the latter were dressed in an elaborate code that had to be deciphered if the content was to be properly understood.

But why did some experiences whose influence persisted in controlling an individual's life remain unconscious? According to Freud, the answer was repression (see the box on p. 741), a process by which unsettling experiences were blotted from conscious awareness but still continued to influence behavior because they had become part of the unconscious. To explain how repression worked, Freud elaborated an intricate theory of the inner life of human beings.

According to Freud, a human being's inner life was a battleground of three contending forces: the id, ego, and superego. The id was the center of unconscious drives and was ruled by what Freud termed the pleasure principle. As creatures of desire, human beings directed their energy toward pleasure and away from pain. The id contained all kinds of lustful drives and desires and crude appetites and impulses. The ego was the seat of reason and hence the coordinator of the inner life. It was governed by the reality principle. Although humans were dominated by the pleasure principle, a true pursuit of pleasure was not feasible. The reality principle meant that people rejected pleasure so that they might live together in society. The superego was the locus of conscience and represented the inhibitions and moral values that society in general and parents in particular imposed on people. The superego served to force the ego to curb the unsatisfactory drives of the id.

The human being was thus a battleground among id, ego, and superego. Ego and superego exerted restraining influences on the unconscious id and repressed or kept out of consciousness what they wanted to. The most important repressions, according to Freud, were sexual, and he went on to develop a theory of infantile sexual drives embodied in the Oedipus complex (Electra complex for females), or the infant's craving for exclusive possession of the parent of the opposite sex. Repression began in childhood, and psychoanalysis was accomplished through a dialogue between psychotherapist and patient in which the therapist probed deeply into memory in order to retrace the chain of repression all the way back to its

Freud and the Concept of Repression

Freud's psychoanalytical theories resulted from his attempt to understand the world of the unconscious. This excerpt is taken from a lecture given in 1909 in which Freud described how he arrived at his theory of the role of repression. Although Freud valued science and reason, his theories of the unconscious produced a new image of the human being as governed less by reason than by irrational forces.

‒‒‒ ✦❊❊ ✦ ‒‒‒

Sigmund Freud, *Five Lectures on Psychoanalysis*

I did not abandon [the technique of encouraging patients to reveal forgotten experiences], however, before the observations I made during my use of it afforded me decisive evidence. I found confirmation of the fact that the forgotten memories were not lost. They were in the patient's possession and were ready to emerge in association to what was still known by him; but there was some force that prevented them from becoming conscious and compelled them to remain unconscious. The existence of this force could be assumed with certainty, since one became aware of an effort corresponding to it if, in opposition to it, one tried to introduce the unconscious memories into the patient's consciousness. The force which was maintaining the pathological condition became apparent in the form of resistance on the part of the patient.

It was on this idea of resistance, then, that I based my view of the course of physical events in hysteria. In order to effect a recovery, it had proved necessary to remove these resistances. Starting out from the mechanism of cure, it now became possible to construct quite definite ideas of the origin of the illness. The same forces which, in the form of resistance, were now offering opposition to the forgotten material's being made conscious, must formerly have brought about the forgetting and must have pushed the pathogenic experiences in question out of consciousness. I gave the name of "repression" to this hypothetical process, and I considered that it was proved by the undeniable existence of resistance.

The further question could then be raised as to what these forces were and what the determinants were of the repression in which we now recognized the pathogenic mechanism of hysteria. A comparative study of the pathogenic situations which we had come to know through the cathartic procedure made it possible to answer this question. All these experiences had involved the emergence of a wishful impulse which was in sharp contrast to the subject's other wishes and which proved incompatible with the ethical and aesthetic standards of his personality. There had been a short conflict, and the end of this internal struggle was that the idea which had appeared before consciousness as the vehicle of this irreconcilable wish fell a victim to repression, was pushed out of consciousness with all its attached memories, and was forgotten. Thus, the incompatibility of the wish in question with the patient's ego was the motive for the repression; the subject's ethical and other standards were the repressing forces. An acceptance of the incompatible wishful impulse or a prolongation of the conflict would have produced a high degree of unpleasure; this unpleasure was avoided by means of repression, which was thus revealed as one of the devices serving to protect the mental personality. ⯈

Q According to Freud, how did he discover the existence of repression? What function does repression perform? What aspects of modern European society might have contributed to forcing individuals into repressive modes of thinking and acting?

childhood origins. By making the conscious mind aware of the unconscious and its repressed contents, the patient's psychic conflict was resolved.

Although many of Freud's ideas have been shown to be wrong in many details, he is still regarded as an important figure because of the impact his theories have had.

The Impact of Darwin

In the second half of the nineteenth century, scientific theories were sometimes wrongly applied to achieve other ends. The application of Darwin's principle of organic evolution to the social order came to be known as **social Darwinism.**

SOCIAL DARWINISM The most popular exponent of social Darwinism was the British philosopher Herbert Spencer (1820–1903). Using Darwin's terminology, Spencer argued that societies were organisms that evolved through time from a struggle with their environment. Progress came from "the struggle for survival," as the "fit"—the strong—advanced while the weak declined. As Spencer expressed it in 1851 in his book *Social Statics:*

Herbert Spencer, *Social Statics*, excerpt (1851)

Pervading all Nature we may see at work a stern discipline which is a little cruel that it may be very kind. . . . Meanwhile, the well-being of existing humanity and the unfolding of it into this ultimate perfection, are both secured by the same beneficial though severe discipline to which the animate creation at large is subject. It seems hard that an unskillfulness, which with all his efforts he cannot overcome, should entail hunger upon the artisan. It seems hard that a laborer, incapacitated by sickness from competing with his stronger fellows, should have to bear the resulting privations. It seems hard that widows and orphans should be left to struggle for life or death. Nevertheless, when regarded not separately but in connection with the interests of universal humanity, these harsh fatalities are seen to be full of beneficence—the same beneficence which brings to early graves the children of diseased parents, and singles out the intemperate and the debilitated as the victims of an epidemic.[5]

The state should not intervene in this natural process.

RACISM Darwin's ideas were also applied to human society in an even more radical way by rabid nationalists and racists. In their pursuit of national greatness, extreme nationalists argued that nations, too, were engaged in a "struggle for existence" in which only the fittest survived. The German general Friedrich von Bernhardi (FREED-rikh fun bayrn-HAR-dee) argued in 1907:

> War is a biological necessity of the first importance, a regulative element in the life of mankind which cannot be dispensed with, since without it an unhealthy development will follow, which excludes every advancement of the race, and therefore all real civilization. "War is the father of all things." The sages of antiquity long before Darwin recognized this.[6]

Numerous nationalist organizations preached the same doctrine as Bernhardi. The Nationalist Association of Italy, for example, founded in 1910, declared that "we must teach Italy the value of international struggle. But international struggle is war? Well, then, let there be war! And nationalism will arouse the will for a victorious war, . . . the only way to national redemption."[7]

Racism, too, was dramatically revived and strengthened by new biological arguments. Perhaps nowhere was the combination of extreme nationalism and racism more evident and more dangerous than in Germany. The concept of the *Volk* (FULK) (nation, people, or race) had been an underlying idea in German history since the beginning of the nineteenth century. One of the chief propagandists for German **volkish thought** at the turn of the twentieth century was Houston Stewart Chamberlain (1855–1927), an Englishman who became a German citizen. His book *The Foundations of the Nineteenth Century,* published in 1899, made a special impact on Germany. Modern-day Germans, according to Chamberlain, were the only pure successors of the "Aryans," who were portrayed as the true and original creators of Western culture. The Aryan (AR-ee-un) race, under German leadership, must be prepared to fight for Western civilization and save it from the destructive assaults of such lower races as Jews, Negroes, and Orientals. Increasingly, Jews were singled out by German volkish nationalists as the racial enemy in biological terms and as parasites who wanted to destroy the Aryan race.

The Attack on Christianity

The growth of scientific thinking as well as the forces of modernization presented new challenges to the Christian churches. Industrialization and urbanization had an especially adverse effect on religious institutions. The mass migration of people from the countryside to the city meant a change from the close-knit, traditional ties of the village in which the church had been a key force to new urban patterns of social life from which the churches were often excluded. The established Christian churches had a weak hold on workers.

The political movements of the late nineteenth century were also hostile to the established Christian churches. Beginning during the eighteenth-century Enlightenment and continuing well into the nineteenth century, European governments, especially in predominantly Catholic countries, had imposed controls over church courts, religious orders, and appointments of the clergy. But after the failure of the revolutions of 1848, governments were eager to use the churches' aid in reestablishing order and therefore relaxed these controls.

Eventually, however, the close union of state authorities with established churches produced a backlash in the form of **anticlericalism,** especially in the liberal nation-states of the late nineteenth century. As one example, in the 1880s, the French republican government substituted civic training for religious instruction in order to undermine the Catholic Church's control of education. In 1901, Catholic teaching orders were outlawed, and four years later, in 1905, church and state were completely separated.

Science became one of the chief threats to all the Christian churches and even to religion itself in the nineteenth century. Darwin's theory of evolution, accepted by ever-larger numbers of educated Europeans, seemed to contradict the doctrine of divine creation. By seeking to suppress Darwin's books and to forbid the teaching of the evolutionary hypothesis, the churches often caused even more educated people to reject established religions.

The scientific spirit also encouraged a number of biblical scholars to apply critical principles to the Bible, leading to the so-called higher criticism. One of its leading exponents was Ernst Renan (re-NAHNH) (1823–1892), a French Catholic scholar. In his *Life of Jesus,* Renan questioned the historical accuracy of the Bible and presented a radically different picture of Jesus. He saw Jesus not as the son of God but as a human being whose value lay in the example he provided by his life and teaching.

RESPONSE OF THE CHURCHES One response of the Christian churches to these attacks was the outright rejection of modern ideas and forces. Protestant fundamentalist sects were especially important in maintaining a literal interpretation of the Bible. The Catholic Church under Pope Pius IX (1846–1878) also took a rigid stand against modern ideas. In 1864, Pope Pius issued a papal encyclical called the *Syllabus of Errors* in which he stated that it is "an error to believe that the Roman Pontiff can and ought to reconcile himself to, and agree with, progress, liberalism, and modern civilization." He condemned nationalism, socialism, religious toleration, and freedom of speech and press.

Rejection of the new was not the churches' only response, however. A religious movement called Modernism included an attempt by the churches to reinterpret Christianity in the light of new developments. The modernists viewed the Bible as a book of useful moral ideas, encouraged Christians to become involved in social reforms, and insisted that the churches must provide a greater sense of community. The Catholic Church condemned Modernism in 1907 and had driven it underground by the beginning of World War I.

Yet another response of the Christian churches to modern ideas was compromise, an approach especially evident in the Catholic Church during the pontificate of Leo XIII (1878–1903). Pope Leo permitted the teaching of evolution as a hypothesis in Catholic schools and also responded to the challenges of modernization in the economic and social spheres. In his encyclical *De Rerum Novarum* (day RAYR-um noh-VAR-um), issued in 1891, he upheld the individual's right to private property but at the same time criticized "naked" capitalism for the poverty and degradation in which it had left the working classes. Much in socialism, he declared, was Christian in principle, but he condemned Marxist socialism for its materialistic and antireligious foundations. The pope recommended that Catholics form socialist parties and labor unions of their own to help the workers.

Pope Leo XIII, *De Rerum Novarum* (1891)

Other religious groups also made efforts to win support for Christianity among the working-class poor and to restore religious practice among the urban working classes. Sects of evangelical missionaries were especially successful; a prime example is the Salvation Army, founded in London in 1865 by William Booth, the army's first "general." The Salvation Army established food centers, shelters where the homeless could sleep, and "rescue homes" for women, but all these had a larger purpose, as Booth admitted: "It is primarily and mainly for the sake of saving the soul that I seek the salvation of the body."[8]

The Culture of Modernity: Literature

The revolution in physics and psychology was paralleled by a revolution in literature and the arts. Before 1914, writers and artists self-consciously rejected the traditional literary and artistic styles that had dominated European cultural life since the Renaissance. The changes that they produced have since been called **Modernism.**

NATURALISM Throughout much of the late nineteenth century, literature was dominated by Naturalism. Naturalists accepted the material world as real and felt that literature should be realistic. By addressing social problems, writers could contribute to an objective understanding of the world. Although Naturalism was a continuation of Realism, it lacked the underlying note of liberal optimism about people and society that had been prevalent in the 1850s. The Naturalists were pessimistic about Europe's future and often portrayed characters caught in the grip of forces beyond their control.

The novels of the French writer Émile Zola (ay-MEEL ZOH-lah) (1840–1902) provide a good example of Naturalism. Against a backdrop of the urban slums and coalfields of northern France, Zola showed how alcoholism and different environments affected people's lives. He had read Darwin's *Origin of Species* and had been impressed by its emphasis on the struggle for survival and the importance of environment and heredity. These themes were central to his *Rougon-Macquart,* a twenty-volume series of novels on the "natural and social history of a family." Zola maintained that the artist must analyze and dissect life as a biologist would a living organism. He said, "I have simply done on living bodies the work of analysis which surgeons perform on corpses."

The second half of the nineteenth century was a golden age for Russian literature. The nineteenth-century realistic novel reached its high point in the works of Leo Tolstoy (TOHL-stoy) (1828–1910) and Fyodor Dostoevsky (FYUD-ur dus-tuh-YEF-skee) (1821–1881). Tolstoy's greatest work was *War and Peace,* a lengthy novel played out against the historical background of Napoleon's invasion of Russia in 1812. It is realistic in its vivid descriptions of military life and character portrayal. Each person is delineated clearly and analyzed psychologically. Upon a great landscape, Tolstoy imposed a fatalistic view of history that ultimately proved irrelevant in the face of life's enduring values of human love and trust.

Dostoevsky combined narrative skill and acute psychological and moral observation with profound insights into human nature. He maintained that the major problem of his age was a loss of spiritual belief. Western people were attempting to gain salvation through the construction of a materialistic paradise built only by human reason and human will. Dostoevsky feared that the failure to incorporate spirit would result in total tyranny. His own life experiences led him to believe that only through suffering and faith could the human soul be purified, views that are evident in his best-known works, *Crime and Punishment* and *The Brothers Karamazov.*

SYMBOLISM At the turn of the century, a new group of writers, known as the Symbolists, reacted against Realism. Primarily interested in writing poetry, the Symbolists believed that an objective knowledge of the world was impossible. The external world was not real but only a collection of symbols that reflected the true reality of the individual human mind. Art, they believed, should function for its own sake instead of serving, criticizing, or seeking to understand society. In the works of such Symbolist poets as W. B. Yeats (YAYTS) and Rainer Maria Rilke (RY-nuh mah-REE-uh RILL-kuh), poetry ceased to be part of popular culture because only through a knowledge of the poet's personal language could one hope to understand what the poem was saying (see the box on p. 744).

Symbolist Poetry: Art for Art's Sake

Arthur Rimbaud (ar-TOOR ram-BOH) was one of Symbolism's leading practitioners in France. Although his verses seem to have little real meaning, they were not meant to describe the external world precisely but to enchant the mind. Art was not meant for the masses but only for "art's sake." Rimbaud wrote, "By the alchemy of the words, I noted the inexpressible. I fixed giddiness."

Arthur Rimbaud, *The Drunken Boat*

As I floated down impassable rivers,
I felt the boatmen no longer guiding me.
After them came redskins who with war cries
Nailed them naked to the painted poles.

I was oblivious to the crew,
I who bore Flemish wheat and English cotton.
When the racket was finished with my boatmen,
The waters let me drift my own free way.

In the tide's furious pounding,
I, the other winter, emptier than children's minds,
I sailed! And the unmoored peninsulas
Have not suffered more triumphant turmoils.

The tempest blessed my maritime watches.
Lighter than a cork I danced on the waves,
Those eternal rollers of victims,
Ten nights, without regretting the lantern-foolish eye!

Sweeter than the bite of sour apples to a child,
The green water seeped through my wooden hull,
Rinsed me of blue wine stains and vomit,
Broke apart grappling iron and rudder.

And then I bathed myself in the poetry
Of the star-sprayed milk-white sea,
Devouring the azure greens; where, pale
And ravished, a pensive drowned one sometimes floats;

Where, suddenly staining the blueness, frenzies
And slow rhythms in the blazing of day,

Stronger than alcohol, vaster than our lyres,
The russet bitterness of love ferments. . . .

I have dreamed of the green night bedazzled
    with snow,
A kiss climbing slowly to the eyes of the sea,
The flow of unforgettable sap,
And the yellow-blue waking of singing phosphorous!

Long months I have followed, like maddened cattle,
The surge assaulting the rocks
Without dreaming that the Virgin's luminous feet
Could force a muzzle on the panting ocean!

I have struck against the shores of incredible Floridas
Mixing panther-eyed flowers like human skins!
Rainbows stretched like bridle reins
Under the ocean's horizon, toward sea-green troops!

I have seen the fermenting of monstrous marshes,
Nets where a whole Leviathan rots in the reeds!
The waters collapsing in the middle of the calm,
And horizons plunging toward the abyss!

Glaciers, silver suns, waves of pearl, charcoal skies,
Hideous beaches at the bottom of brown gulfs
Where giant serpents devoured by vermin
Tumble from twisted trees with black perfumes!

I would have liked to show the children those
    dolphins
On the blue waves, those golden singing fish.
—The froth of flowers lulled my voyagings,
Ineffable winds gave me wings by the moment. . . . 🖙

Q After reading Rimbaud's poem, what do you think Symbolism is? What strikes you as the goals or ambitions of the Symbolists in this era of artistic innovation and challenge to older forms of expression?

Modernism in the Arts

Since the Renaissance, artists had tried to represent reality as accurately as possible, carefully applying brushstrokes and employing perspective to produce realistic portrayals of their subjects. By the late nineteenth century, however, artists were seeking new forms of expression.

IMPRESSIONISM The preamble to modern painting can be found in **Impressionism,** a movement that originated in France in the 1870s when a group of artists rejected the studios and museums and went out into the countryside to paint nature directly. Their subjects included figures from daily life, street scenes of Paris, and nature. Instead of adhering to the conventional modes of painting and subject matter, the Impressionists sought originality and distinction from past artworks. Camille Pissarro (kah-MEEL pee-SAH-roh) (1830–1903), one of Impressionism's founders, expressed what they sought:

Precise drawing is dry and hampers the impression of the whole, it destroys all sensations. Do not define too closely the outlines of things; it is the brushstroke of the right value and color which should produce the drawing. . . . Work at the same time upon sky, water, branches, ground, keeping

Claude Monet, *Impression, Sunrise.* Impressionists rejected "rules and principles" and sought to paint what they observed and felt in order "not to lose the first impression." Monet entered this painting, *Impression, Sunrise*, in the first Impressionist show in 1874. He sought to capture his impression of the fleeting moments of sunrise through the simple interplay of light, water, and atmosphere.

everything going on an equal basis and unceasingly rework until you have got it.... Don't proceed according to rules and principles, but paint what you observe and feel. Paint generously and unhesitatingly, for it is best not to lose the first impression.[9]

Impressionists like Pissarro sought to put into their paintings their impressions of the changing effects of light on objects in nature.

Pissarro's ideas are visibly portrayed in the work of Claude Monet (CLOHD moh-NEH) (1840–1926). He was especially enchanted with water and painted many pictures in which he attempted to capture the interplay of light, water, and atmosphere, especially evident in *Impression, Sunrise*. But the Impressionists did not just paint scenes from nature. Streets and cabarets, rivers, and busy boulevards—wherever people congregated for work and leisure—formed their subject matter.

Another important Impressionist painter was Berthe Morisot (BAYRT mor-ee-ZOH) (1841–1895), who broke with the practice of women being only amateur artists and became a professional painter. Her dedication to the new style of painting won her the disfavor of the traditional French academic artists. Morisot believed that women had a special vision, which was, as she said, "more delicate than that of men." Her special touch is evident in the lighter colors and flowing brushstrokes of *Young Girl by the Window*. Near the end of her life, Morisot lamented the refusal of men to take her work seriously: "I don't think there has ever been a man who treated a woman as an equal, and that's all I would have asked, for I know I'm worth as much as they."[10]

POST-IMPRESSIONISM By the 1880s, a new movement known as **Post-Impressionism** had emerged in France and soon spread to other European countries. Post-Impressionism retained the Impressionist emphasis on light and color but revolutionized it even further by paying more attention to structure and form. Post-Impressionists sought to use both color and line to express inner feelings and produce a personal statement of reality rather than an imitation of objects. Impressionist paintings had retained a sense of realism, but the Post-Impressionists shifted from objective reality to subjective reality and in so doing began to withdraw from the artist's traditional task of depicting the external world. Post-Impressionism was the real beginning of modern art.

Paul Cézanne (say-ZAHN) (1839–1906) was one of the most important Post-Impressionists. Initially, he was influenced by the Impressionists but soon rejected their work. In paintings, such as *Mont Sainte-Victoire*, Cézanne sought to express visually the underlying geometric structure and form of everything he painted. He accomplished this by pressing his wet brush directly onto the canvas, forming cubes of color on which he built the form of the mountain. His technique enabled him to break down forms to their basic components. As Cézanne explained to one young painter: "You must see in nature the cylinder, the sphere, and the cone."

Another famous Post-Impressionist was a tortured and tragic figure, Vincent van Gogh (van GOH *or* vahn GOK) (1853–1890). For van Gogh, art was a spiritual experience. He was especially interested in color and believed that it could act as its own form of language. Van Gogh maintained

Berthe Morisot, Young *Girl by the Window*. Berthe Morisot came from a wealthy French family that settled in Paris when she was seven. The first female painter to join the Impressionists, she developed her own unique Impressionist style. Her gentle colors and strong use of pastels are especially evident in *Young Girl by the Window*, painted in 1878. Many of her paintings focus on women and domestic scenes.

that artists should paint what they feel, which is evident in his *Starry Night*.

THE SEARCH FOR INDIVIDUAL EXPRESSION By the beginning of the twentieth century, the belief that the task of art was to represent "reality" had lost much of its meaning. By that time, psychology and the new physics had made it evident that many people were not sure what constituted reality anyway. Then, too, the development of photography gave artists another reason to reject visual realism. Invented in the 1830s, photography became popular and widespread after George Eastman produced the first Kodak camera for the mass market in 1888. What was the point of an artist doing what the camera did better? Unlike the camera, which could only mirror reality, artists could create reality. Individual consciousness became the source of meaning. Between 1905 and 1914, this search for individual expression produced a wide variety of schools of painting, all of which had their greatest impact after World War I.

Paul Cézanne, *Mont Sainte-Victoire*. Post-Impressionists sought above all to express their inner feelings and capture on canvas their own vision of reality. In *Mont Sainte-Victoire*, depicting a mountain near his home that he painted more than sixty times, Cézanne challenged traditional landscape painting by eliminating a single perspective and replacing it with subtle color that created the form of the mountain.

Vincent van Gogh, *The Starry Night*. The Dutch painter Vincent van Gogh was a major figure among the Post-Impressionists. His originality and power of expression made a strong impact on his artistic successors. In *The Starry Night,* painted in 1889, van Gogh's subjective vision was given full play as the dynamic swirling forms of the heavens above overwhelm the village below. The heavens seem alive with a mysterious spiritual force. Van Gogh painted this work in an asylum one year before he committed suicide.

In 1905, one of the most important figures in modern art was just beginning his career. Pablo Picasso (pi-KAH-soh) (1881–1973) was from Spain but settled in Paris in 1904. Picasso was extremely flexible and painted in a remarkable variety of styles. He was instrumental in the development of a new style called **Cubism** that used geometric designs as visual stimuli to re-create reality in the viewer's mind. Picasso's 1907 work *Les Demoiselles d'Avignon* (lay dem-wah-ZEL dah-vee-NYONH) has been called the first Cubist painting.

The modern artist's flight from "visual reality" reached a high point in 1910 with the beginning of **abstract painting.** Wassily Kandinsky (vus-YEEL-yee kan-DIN-skee) (1866–1944), a Russian who worked in Germany, was one of the founders of abstract painting. As is evident in his *Square with White Border,* Kandinsky sought to avoid representation altogether. He believed that art should speak directly to the soul. To do so, it must avoid any reference to visual reality and concentrate on color.

Modernism in Music

In the first half of the nineteenth century, the Romantics' attraction to exotic and primitive cultures had sparked a fascination with folk music, which became increasingly important as musicians began to look for ways to express their national identities. In the second half of the century, new flames of nationalistic spirit were fanned in both literary and musical circles.

GRIEG One example of this new nationalistic spirit may be found in the Scandinavian composer Edvard Grieg (ED-vart GREEG) (1843–1907), who remained a dedicated supporter of Norwegian nationalism throughout his life. Grieg's nationalism expressed itself in the lyric melodies found in the folk music of his homeland. Among his best-known works is the *Peer Gynt Suite* (1876), incidental music to a play by Henrik Ibsen. Grieg's music paved the way for the creation of a national music style in Norway.

The Struggle for the Right to Vote

Emmeline Pankhurst, with the help of her daughters, was the leader of the women's movement for the right to vote in Britain at the end of the nineteenth century and the beginning of the twentieth century. Believing that peaceful requests were achieving little from the members of Parliament, Pankhurst came to advocate more forceful methods, as is evident in this selection from *My Own Story,* her autobiography published in 1914. Although this confrontational approach was abandoned during World War I, the British government granted women the right to vote in 1918 at the end of the war.

━━ ⋙⋘ ━━

Emmeline Pankhurst, *My Own Story*

I had called upon women to join me in striking at the Government through the only thing that governments are really very much concerned about—property—and the response was immediate. Within a few days the newspapers rang with the story of the attack made on letter boxes in London, Liverpool, Birmingham, Bristol, and half a dozen other cities. In some cases the boxes, when opened by postmen, mysteriously burst into flame; in others the letters were destroyed by corrosive chemicals; in still others the addresses were rendered illegible by black fluids. Altogether it was estimated that over 5,000 letters were completely destroyed and many thousands more were delayed in transit.

It was with a deep sense of their gravity that these letter-burning protests were undertaken, but we felt that something drastic must be done in order to destroy the apathy of the men of England who view with indifference the suffering of women oppressed by unjust laws. As we pointed out, letters, precious though they may be, are less precious than human bodies and souls. . . . And so, in order to call attention to greater crimes against human beings, our letter burnings continued.

In only a few cases were the offenders apprehended, and one of the few women arrested was a helpless cripple, a woman who could move about only in a wheeled chair. She received a sentence of eight months in the first division, and, resolutely hunger striking, was forcibly fed with unusual brutality, the prison doctor deliberately breaking one of her teeth in order to insert a gag. In spite of her disabilities and her weakness the crippled girl persisted in her hunger strike and her resistance to prison rules, and within a short time had to be released. The excessive sentences of the other pillar box destroyers resolved themselves into very short terms because of the resistance of the prisoners, every one of whom adopted the hunger strike.

It was at this time, February, 1913, less than two years ago as I write these words, that militancy, as it is now generally understood by the public began—militancy in the sense of continued, destructive, guerrilla warfare against the Government through injury to private property. Some property had been destroyed before this time, but the attacks were sporadic, and were meant to be in the nature of a warning as to what might become a settled policy. Now we indeed lighted the torch, and we did it with the absolute conviction that no other course was open to us. We had tried every other measure, as I am sure that I have demonstrated to my readers, and our years of work and suffering and sacrifice had taught us that the Government would not yield to right and justice, what the majority of members of the House of Commons admitted was right and justice, but that the Government would, as other governments invariably do, yield to expediency. Now our task was to show the Government that it was expedient to yield to the women's just demands. In order to do that we had to make England and every department of English life insecure and unsafe. We had to make English law a failure and the courts farce comedy theatres; we had to discredit the Government and Parliament in the eyes of the world; we had to spoil English sports, hurt business, destroy valuable property, demoralize the world of society, shame the churches, upset the whole orderly conduct of life.

That is, we had to do as much of this guerrilla warfare as the people of England would tolerate. When they came to the point of saying to the Government: "Stop this, in the only way it can be stopped, by giving the women of England representation," then we should extinguish our torch. ⋈

 What methods did Emmeline Pankhurst advocate be used to achieve the right to vote for women? Why did she feel justified in using these methods? Do you think she was justified? Why or why not?

---

in front of the king's horse at the Epsom Derby horse race. **Suffragists** had one fundamental aim: the right of women to full citizenship in the nation-state.

Although few women elsewhere in Europe used the Pankhursts' confrontational methods, demands for women's rights were heard throughout Europe and the United States before World War I. Nevertheless, only in Finland, Norway, and some American states did women actually receive the right to vote before 1914. It would take the dramatic upheaval of World War I before male-dominated governments capitulated on this basic issue (see Chapter 25).

EFFORTS FOR PEACE Women reformers took on other issues besides suffrage. In many countries, women supported

The Struggle for the Right to Vote

For many feminists, the right to vote came to represent the key to other reforms that would benefit women. In Britain, suffragists attracted attention to their cause by unusual publicity stunts. The photograph at the left shows the arrest of a suffragist who had chained herself to the railings of Buckingham Palace in London. Below is a photo of Emily Davison throwing herself under the king's horse at the Epsom Derby horse race. Shortly before her sacrificial action, she had written, "The glorious and indomitable Spirit of Liberty has but one further penalty within its power, the surrender of life itself, the supreme consummation of sacrifice." The third illustration shows police preventing Emmeline Pankhurst and her two daughters from entering Buckingham Palace to present a petition to the king.

peace movements. Bertha von Suttner (ZOOT-nuh) (1843–1914) became the head of the Austrian Peace Society and protested against the growing arms race of the 1890s. Her novel *Lay Down Your Arms* became a best seller and brought her the Nobel Peace Prize in 1905. Lower-class women also took up the cause of peace. In 1911, a group of female workers marched in Vienna and demanded, "We want an end to armaments, to the means of murder and we want these millions to be spent on the needs of the people."[13]

THE NEW WOMAN Bertha von Suttner was but one example of the "new women" who were becoming more prominent at the turn of the century. These women renounced traditional feminine roles. Although some of them supported political ideologies such as socialism that flew in the face of the ruling classes, others simply sought new freedom outside the household and new roles other than those of wives and mothers.

Maria Montessori (mahn-tuh-SOR-ee) (1870–1952) was a good example of the "new woman." Breaking with tradition, she attended medical school at the University of Rome. Although often isolated by the male students, she persisted and in 1896 became the first Italian woman to receive a medical degree. Three years later, she undertook a lecture tour in Italy on the subject of the "new woman," whom she characterized as a woman who followed a rational, scientific perspective. In keeping with this ideal, Montessori put her medical background to work in a school for mentally handicapped children. She devised new teaching materials that enabled these children to read and write and became convinced, as she later wrote, "that similar methods applied to normal students would develop or set free their personality in a marvelous and surprising way." Subsequently, she established a system of childhood education based on natural and spontaneous activities in which students learned at their own pace. By the 1930s, hundreds of Montessori schools had been established in Europe and the United States. As a professional woman and an unwed mother, Montessori also embodied some of the freedoms of the "new woman."

Jews in the European Nation-State

Near the end of the nineteenth century, a revival of racism combined with extreme nationalism to produce a new right-wing politics aimed primarily at the Jews. Of course, anti-Semitism was not new to European civilization. Since the Middle Ages, Jews had been portrayed as the murderers of Jesus and subjected to mob violence; their rights had been restricted, and they had been physically separated from Christians in quarters known as ghettos.

In the nineteenth century, as a result of the ideals of the Enlightenment and the French Revolution, Jews were increasingly granted legal equality in many European countries. The French revolutionary decrees of 1790 and 1791 emancipated the Jews and admitted them to full citizenship. After the revolutions of 1848, emancipation

became a fact of life for Jews throughout western and central Europe. For many Jews, emancipation enabled them to leave the ghetto and become assimilated as hundreds of thousands of Jews entered what had been the closed worlds of parliaments and universities. In 1880, for example, Jews made up 10 percent of the population of the city of Vienna, Austria, but 39 percent of its medical students and 23 percent of its law students. A Jew could "leave his Jewishness behind," as the career of Benjamin Disraeli, who became prime minister of Great Britain, demonstrated. Many other Jews became successful bankers, lawyers, scientists, scholars, journalists, and stage performers.

ANTI-SEMITISM IN THE AUSTRIAN EMPIRE AND GERMANY These achievements represented only one side of the picture, however. In Austrian politics, for example, the Christian Socialists combined agitation for workers with a virulent **anti-Semitism.** They were most powerful in Vienna, where they were led by Karl Lueger (LOO-gur), mayor of Vienna from 1897 to 1910. Imperial Vienna at the turn of the century was a brilliant center of European culture, but it was also the home of an insidious German nationalism that blamed Jews for the corruption of German culture. It was in Vienna between 1907 and 1913 that Adolf Hitler later claimed to have found his worldview, one that was largely based on violent German nationalism and rabid anti-Semitism.

Germany, too, had its right-wing anti-Semitic parties, such as Adolf Stocker's Christian Social Workers. These parties used anti-Semitism to win the votes of traditional lower-middle-class groups who felt threatened by the new economic forces of the times. These German anti-Semitic parties were based on race. In medieval times, Jews could convert to Christianity and escape from their religion. To modern racial anti-Semites, Jews were racially stained; this could not be altered by conversion. One could not be both a German and a Jew. Hermann Ahlwardt (AHL-vart), an anti-Semitic member of the German Reichstag, made this clear in a speech to that body:

> The Jew is no German.... A Jew who was born in Germany does not thereby become a German; he is still a Jew. Therefore it is imperative that we realize that Jewish racial characteristics differ so greatly from ours that a common life of Jews and Germans under the same laws is quite impossible because the Germans will perish.[14]

After 1898, the political strength of the German anti-Semitic parties began to decline.

PERSECUTION OF JEWS IN EASTERN EUROPE The worst treatment of Jews in the last two decades of the nineteenth century and the first decade of the twentieth occurred in eastern Europe, where 72 percent of the entire world Jewish population lived. Russian Jews were admitted to secondary schools and universities only under a quota system and were forced to live in certain regions of the country. Persecutions and **pogroms** (organized massacres) were widespread. Between 1903 and 1906, pogroms took place in almost seven hundred Russian towns and villages, mostly in Ukraine. Hundreds of thousands of Jews decided to emigrate to escape the persecution. Between 1881 and 1899, an average of 23,000 Jews left Russia each year. Many of them went to the United States and Canada, although some (probably about 25,000) moved to Palestine, which soon became the focus for a Jewish nationalist movement called **Zionism.**

THE ZIONIST MOVEMENT The emancipation of the nineteenth century had presented vast opportunities for some Jews but dilemmas for others. Did emancipation mean full assimilation, and did assimilation mean the disruption of traditional Jewish life? Many Jews paid the price willingly, but others questioned its value and advocated a different

Palestine

answer, a return to Palestine. For many Jews, Palestine, the land of ancient Israel, had long been the land of their dreams. During the nineteenth century, as nationalist ideas spread and Italians, Poles, Irish, Greeks, and others sought national emancipation, so did the idea of national independence capture the imagination of some Jews. A key figure in the growth of political Zionism was Theodor Herzl (TAY-oh-dor HAYRT-sul) (1860–1904). In 1896, he published a book called *The Jewish State* (see the box on p. 754) in which he maintained that "the Jews who wish it will have their state." Financial support for the development of settlements in Palestine came from wealthy Jewish banking families who wanted a refuge in Palestine for persecuted Jews. Establishing settlements was difficult, though, because Palestine was then part of the Ottoman Empire and Ottoman authorities were opposed to Jewish immigration. In 1891, one Jewish essayist pointed to the problems this would create:

> We abroad are accustomed to believe that Erez Israel [the land of Israel] is almost totally desolate at present . . . but in reality it is not so. . . . Arabs, especially those in towns, see and understand our activities and aims in the country but keep quiet and pretend as if they did not know, . . . and they try to exploit us, too, and profit from the new guests while laughing at us in their hearts. But if the time comes and our people make such progress as to displace the people of the country . . . they will not lightly surrender the place.[15]

Despite the warnings, however, the First Zionist Congress, which met in Switzerland in 1897, proclaimed as its aim the creation of a "home in Palestine secured by public law" for the Jewish people. One thousand Jews migrated to Palestine in 1901, and the number rose to three thousand annually between 1904 and 1914; but on the eve of World War I, the Zionist dream remained just that.

The Transformation of Liberalism: Great Britain and Italy

In dealing with the problems created by the new mass politics, liberal governments often followed policies that undermined the basic tenets of liberalism. This was particularly true in Great Britain and Italy.

GREAT BRITAIN In Britain, the demands of the working-class movement caused Liberals to move away from their ideals. Liberals were forced to adopt significant social reforms due to the pressure of two new working-class organizations: trade unions and the Labour Party. Frustrated by the government's failure to enact social reform, trade unions began to advocate more radical change of the economic system, calling for "collective ownership and control over production, distribution, and exchange." This "new unionism" also led to the union organization of many steel factory workers and to new confrontations in the streets of London as British workers struck for a minimum wage and other benefits.

At the same time, a movement for laborers emerged among a group of intellectuals known as the Fabian Socialists who stressed the need for the workers to use their right to vote to capture the House of Commons and pass legislation that would benefit the laboring class. Neither the Fabian Socialists nor the British trade unions were Marxist. They did not advocate class struggle and revolution but instead favored evolution toward a socialist state by democratic means. In 1900, representatives of the trade unions and Fabian Socialists coalesced to form the Labour Party. Although the new party won only one seat in 1900, it managed to elect twenty-nine members to the House of Commons in 1906.

The Liberals, who gained control of the House of Commons in that year and held the government from 1906 to 1914, perceived that they would have to enact a program of social welfare or lose the support of the workers. The policy of reform was especially advanced by David Lloyd George (1863–1945), a brilliant orator from Wales who had been deeply moved by the misery of Welsh coal miners and served as chancellor of the Exchequer from 1908 to 1915. The Liberals abandoned the classic principles of *laissez-faire* and voted for a series of social reforms. The National Insurance Act of 1911 provided benefits for workers in case of sickness and unemployment, to be paid for by compulsory contributions from workers, employers, and the state. Additional legislation provided a small pension for retirees over seventy and compensation for workers injured on the job. To pay for the new program, Lloyd George increased the tax burden on the wealthy classes. Though both the benefits of the program and the tax increases were modest, they were the

The Voice of Zionism: Theodor Herzl and the Jewish State

The Austrian Jewish journalist Theodor Herzl wrote *The Jewish State* in the summer of 1895 in Paris while he was covering the Dreyfus case for his Vienna newspaper. During several weeks of feverish composition, he set out to analyze the fundamental causes of anti-Semitism and devise a solution to the "Jewish problem." In this selection, he discusses two of his major conclusions.

⊹ ⊱⊰ ⊹

Theodor Herzl, *The Jewish State*

I do not intend to arouse sympathetic emotions on our behalf. That would be a foolish, futile, and undignified proceeding. I shall content myself with putting the following questions to the Jews: Is it true that, in countries where we live in perceptible numbers, the position of Jewish lawyers, doctors, technicians, teachers, and employees of all descriptions becomes daily more intolerable? True, that the Jewish middle classes are seriously threatened? True, that the passions of the mob are incited against our wealthy people? True, that our poor endure greater sufferings than any other proletariat?

I think that this external pressure makes itself felt everywhere. In our economically upper classes it causes discomfort, in our middle classes continual and grave anxieties, in our lower classes absolute despair.

Everything tends, in fact, to one and the same conclusion, which is clearly enunciated in that classic Berlin phrase: "Juden raus!" (Out with the Jews!)

I shall now put the Jewish Question in the curtest possible form: Are we to "get out" now? And if so, to what place?

Or, may we yet remain? And if so, how long?

Let us first settle the point of staying where we are. Can we hope for better days, can we possess our souls in patience, can we wait in pious resignation till the princes and peoples of this earth are more mercifully disposed toward us? I say that we cannot hope for a change in the current of feeling. And why not? Were we as near to the hearts of princes as are their other subjects, even so they could not protect us. They would only feed popular hatred of Jews by showing us too much favor. By "too much," I really mean less than is claimed as a right by every ordinary citizen, or by every

race. The nations in whose midst Jews live are all, either covertly or openly, Anti-Semitic....

The whole plan is in its essence perfectly simple, as it must necessarily be if it is to come within the comprehension of all.

Let the sovereignty be granted us over a portion of the globe large enough to satisfy the rightful requirements of a nation; the rest we shall manage for ourselves.

The creation of a new State is neither ridiculous nor impossible. We have in our day witnessed the process in connection with nations which were not in the bulk of the middle class, but poorer, less educated, and consequently weaker than ourselves. The Governments of all countries scourged by Anti-Semitism will be keenly interested in assisting us to obtain the sovereignty we want....

Palestine is our ever-memorable historic home. The very name of Palestine would attract our people with a force of marvelous potency. Supposing his Majesty the Sultan were to give us Palestine, we could in return undertake to regulate the whole finances of Turkey. We should there form a portion of the rampart of Europe against Asia, an outpost of civilization as opposed to barbarism. We should as a neutral State remain in contact with all Europe, which would have to guarantee our existence. The sanctuaries of Christendom would be safeguarded by assigning to them an extra-territorial status such as is well known to the law of nations. We should form a guard of honor about these sanctuaries, answering for the fulfillment of this duty with our existence. This guard of honor would be the great symbol of the solution of the Jewish Question after eighteen centuries of Jewish suffering. ⊱

Q What forces in European society came together to intensify anti-Semitism in the late nineteenth century? What was the relationship between nationalism and Zionism at this time? Was Herzl's Zionism simply a reaction to Western anti-Semitism, or did other developments also contribute to his movement?

---

first hesitant steps toward the future British welfare state. Liberalism, which had been based on the principle that the government that governs least governs best, had been transformed.

In the effort to achieve social reform, Lloyd George was also forced to confront the power of the House of Lords. Composed of hereditary aristocrats, the House of Lords took a strong stance against Lloyd George's effort to pay for social reform measures by taxes, however modest, on

the wealthy. In 1911, the Liberals pushed through a law that restricted the ability of the House of Lords to impede legislation enacted by the House of Commons. After 1911, the House of Lords became largely a debating society.

The Liberals also tried to solve the Irish problem (see Chapter 23). Parliament finally granted home rule in 1914, but the explosive situation in Ireland itself created more problems. Irish Protestants in northern Ireland, especially in the province of Ulster, wanted no part of an

Irish Catholic state. The outbreak of World War I enabled the British government to sidestep the potentially explosive issue and to suspend Irish home rule for the duration of the war. Failure to deal decisively with the issue simply led to more problems later.

ITALY Liberals had even greater problems in Italy. A certain amount of stability was achieved from 1903 to 1914 when the liberal leader Giovanni Giolitti (joh-VAHN-nee joh-LEE-tee) served intermittently as prime minister. Giolitti was a master of using *trasformismo*, or **transformism,** a system in which old political groups were transformed into new government coalitions by political and economic bribery. In the long run, however, Giolitti's devious methods made Italian politics even more corrupt and unmanageable. When urban workers turned to violence to protest their living and working conditions, Giolitti tried to appease them with social welfare legislation and universal male suffrage in 1912. To strengthen his popularity, he also aroused nationalistic passions by conquering Libya. Despite his efforts, however, worker unrest continued, and in 1914 government troops had to be used to quell rioting workers.

France: Travails of the Third Republic

In the 1890s, the fragile Third Republic experienced yet another crisis, which was also evidence of the renewed anti-Semitism in Europe in the late nineteenth century. Early in 1895, Alfred Dreyfus (DRY-fuss), a Jew and a captain in the French general staff, was found guilty by a secret military court of selling army secrets and condemned to life imprisonment on Devil's Island. Evidence soon emerged that pointed to his innocence. Another officer, a Catholic aristocrat, was more obviously the traitor, but the army, a stronghold of aristocratic and Catholic officers, refused a new trial. Some right-wing journalists even used the case to push their own anti-Semitic views. Republic leaders, however, insisted on a new trial after a wave of intense public outrage. Although the new trial failed to set aside the guilty verdict, the government pardoned Dreyfus in 1899, and in 1906, he was finally fully exonerated.

The impact of the Dreyfus affair extended beyond France. It convinced Theodor Herzl, who covered the trial for a Viennese newspaper, that assimilation did not protect Jews from anti-Semitism. As a result, as we have seen, he came to advocate that Jews needed a country of their own, leading to the Zionist movement.

In France itself, the Dreyfus affair led to a change in government. Moderate republicans lost control to radical republicans who were determined to make greater progress toward a more democratic society by breaking the power of the Republic's enemies, especially the army and the Catholic Church. The army was purged of all high-ranking officers who had antirepublican reputations. Most of the Catholic religious orders that had controlled many French schools were forced to leave France. Moreover, church and state were officially separated in 1905, and

during the next two years, the government seized church property and stopped paying clerical salaries.

These changes ended the political threat from the right to the Third Republic, which by now commanded the loyalty of most French people. Nevertheless, problems remained. As a nation of small businessmen and farmers, the French lagged far behind Great Britain, Germany, and the United States in industrial activity. Moreover, a surge of industrialization after 1896 left the nation with the realization that little had been done to appease the discontent of the French working classes and their abysmal working conditions. Since only a quarter of the French wage earners worked in industry, there was little pressure for labor legislation from the French parliament. This made the use of strikes more appealing to the working classes. The brutal government repression of labor walkouts in 1911 only further alienated the working classes.

Growing Tensions in Germany

The new imperial Germany begun by Bismarck in 1871 continued as an "authoritarian, conservative, military-bureaucratic power state" during the reign of Emperor William II (1888–1918). Unstable and aggressive, the emperor was inclined to tactless remarks, as when he told the soldiers of a Berlin regiment that they must be prepared to shoot their fathers and mothers if he ordered them to do so. A small group of about twenty powerful men joined William in setting government policy.

By 1914, Germany had become the strongest military and industrial power on the Continent. New social configurations had emerged as more than 50 percent of German workers had jobs in industry while only 30 percent of the workforce was still in agriculture. Urban centers had mushroomed in number and size. The rapid changes in William's Germany helped produce a society torn between modernization and traditionalism.

The growth of industrialization led to even greater expansion for the Social Democratic Party. Despite the enactment of new welfare legislation to favor the working classes, William II was no more successful than Bismarck at slowing the growth of the Social Democrats. By 1912, it had become the largest single party in the Reichstag. At the same time, the party increasingly became less revolutionary and more revisionist in its outlook. Nevertheless, its growth frightened the middle and upper classes, who blamed labor for their own problems.

With the expansion of industry and cities came demands for more political participation and growing sentiment for reforms that would produce greater democratization. Conservative forces, especially the landowning nobility and representatives of heavy industry, two of the powerful ruling groups in Germany, tried to block it by supporting William II's activist foreign policy (see "New Directions and New Crises" later in this chapter). Expansionism, they believed, would divert people from further democratization.

The tensions in German society created by the conflict between modernization and traditionalism were also manifested in a new, radicalized, right-wing politics. A number of pressure groups arose to support nationalistic goals. Groups such as the Pan-German League stressed strong German nationalism and advocated imperialism as a tool to overcome social divisions and unite all classes. They were also anti-Semitic and denounced Jews as the destroyers of the national community.

Austria-Hungary: The Problem of the Nationalities

At the beginning of the 1890s, Austria-Hungary was still troubled by the problem of its numerous nationalities (see Chapter 23). The granting of universal male suffrage in 1907 served only to exacerbate the problem when nationalities that had played no role in the government now agitated in the parliament for autonomy. This led prime ministers after 1900 to ignore the parliament and rely increasingly on imperial emergency decrees to govern. Parliament itself became a bizarre forum in which, in the words of one incredulous observer, "about a score of men, all decently clad, were seated or standing, each at his little desk. Some made an infernal noise violently opening and shutting the lids of their desks. Others emitted a blaring sound from little toy trumpets; . . . still others beat snare drums."[16]

The threat the nationalities posed to the position of the dominant German minority in Austria also produced a backlash in the form of virulent German nationalism. As Austria industrialized in the 1870s and 1880s, two working-class parties came into existence, both strongly influenced by nationalism. The Social Democrats, although a Marxist party, supported the Austrian government, fearful that the autonomy of the different nationalities would hinder industrial development and prevent improvements for workers. Even more nationalistic, however, were the Christian Socialists, who, as we have seen, combined agitation for workers with a virulent anti-Semitism.

While subjugating their nationalities, the ruling Magyars in Hungary developed a movement for complete separation from Austria. In 1903, when they demanded that the Hungarian army be separated from the imperial army, Emperor Francis Joseph (as king of Hungary) responded quickly and forcefully. He threatened to impose universal male suffrage on Hungary, a move that would challenge Magyar domination of the minorities. Hungarian leaders fell into line, and the new Hungarian parliamentary leader, Count István Tisza (ISHT-vun TISS-ah), cooperated in maintaining the Dual Monarchy. Magyar rule in Hungary, he realized, was inextricably bound up with the Dual Monarchy; its death would only harm the rule of the Magyar landowning class.

Industrialization and Revolution in Imperial Russia

Starting in the 1890s, Russia experienced a massive surge of state-sponsored industrialism under the guiding hand of Sergei Witte (syir-GYAY VIT-uh) (1849–1915), the minister for finance from 1892 to 1903. Count Witte saw industrial growth as crucial to Russia's national strength. Believing that railroads were a powerful weapon in economic development, Witte pushed the government toward a program of massive railroad construction. By 1900, some 35,000 miles of railroads had been built, including large parts of the 5,000-mile trans-Siberian line between Moscow and Vladivostok, on the Pacific Ocean. Witte also encouraged a system of protective tariffs to help Russian industry and persuaded Tsar Nicholas II (1894–1917) that foreign capital was essential for rapid industrial development. Witte's program made possible the rapid growth of a modern steel and coal industry in Ukraine, making Russia by 1900 the fourth-largest producer of steel behind the United States, Germany, and Great Britain.

With industrialization came factories, an industrial working class, industrial suburbs around Saint Petersburg and Moscow, and the pitiful working and living conditions that accompanied the beginnings of industrialization everywhere. Socialist thought and socialist parties developed, although repression in Russia soon forced them to go underground and become revolutionary. The Marxist Social Democratic Party, for example, held its first congress in Minsk in 1898, but the arrest of its leaders caused the next one to be held in Brussels in 1903, attended by

Nicholas II. The last tsar of Russia hoped to preserve the traditional autocratic ways of his predecessors. In this photograph, Nicholas II and his wife, Alexandra, are shown around 1907 with their four daughters and son on holiday on the deck of a ship.

Bloody Sunday

On January 9, 1905, a massive procession of workers led by a Russian Orthodox priest loyal to the tsar, Father Gregory Gapon, carried pictures of the tsar and a petition to present to him at his imperial palace in Saint Petersburg. Although the tsar was not even there, government officials ordered troops to fire on the crowd. This account is by the leader of the procession, Father Gapon.

An Account of Bloody Sunday

We were not more than thirty yards from the soldiers, being separated from them only by the bridge over the Tarakanovskii Canal, which here marks the border of the city, when suddenly, without any warning and without a moment's delay, was heard the dry crack of many rifle-shots. I was informed later on that a bugle was blown, but we could not hear it above the singing, and even if we had heard it we should not have known what it meant.

Vasiliev, with whom I was walking hand in hand, suddenly left hold of my arm and sank upon the snow. One of the workmen who carried the banners fell also. Immediately one of the two police officers to whom I had referred shouted out, "What are you doing? How dare you fire upon the portrait of the Tsar?" This, of course, had no effect, and both he and the other officer were shot down—as I learned afterwards, one was killed and the other dangerously wounded.

I turned rapidly to the crowd and shouted to them to lie down, and I also stretched myself out upon the ground. As we lay thus another volley was fired, and another, and yet another, till it seemed as though the shooting was continuous. The crowd first kneeled and then lay flat down, hiding their heads from the rain of bullets, while the rear rows of the procession began to run away. The smoke of the fire lay before us like a thin cloud, and I felt it stiflingly in my throat. An old man named Lavrentiev, who was carrying the Tsar's portrait, had been one of the first victims. Another old man caught the portrait as it fell from his hands and carried it till he too was killed by the next volley. With his last gasp the old man said, "I may die, but I will see the Tsar." One of the banner-carriers had his arm broken by a bullet. A little boy of ten years, who was carrying a church lantern, fell pierced by a bullet, but still held the lantern tightly and tried to rise again, when another shot struck him down. Both the smiths who had guarded me were killed, as well as all those who were carrying the icons and banners; and all these emblems now lay scattered on the snow. . . .

Horror crept into my heart. The thought flashed through my mind, "And this is the work of our Little Father, the Tsar." Perhaps this anger saved me, for now I knew in very truth that a new chapter was opened in the book of the history of our people. I stood up, and a little group of workmen gathered round me again. Looking backward, I saw that our line, though still stretching away into the distance, was broken and that many of the people were fleeing. It was in vain that I called to them, and in a moment I stood there, the center of a few scores of men, trembling with indignation amid the broken ruins of our movement.

Q What may have led the troops to fire on the demonstrators? According to this selection, who was responsible for the shooting? Was the author justified in holding them responsible? Why or why not? What impact, if any, might the violence of 1905 have had on the events of 1917?

Russian émigrés. The Social Revolutionaries worked to overthrow the tsarist autocracy and establish peasant socialism. Having no other outlet for their opposition to the regime, they advocated political terrorism and attempted to assassinate government officials and members of the ruling dynasty. The growing opposition to the tsarist regime finally exploded into revolution in 1905.

THE REVOLUTION OF 1905 As had happened elsewhere in Europe in the nineteenth century, defeat in war led to political upheaval at home. Russia's territorial expansion to the south and east, especially its designs on northern Korea, led to a confrontation with Japan. Japan made a surprise attack on the Russian eastern fleet at Port Arthur on February 8, 1904. In turn, Russia sent its Baltic fleet halfway around the world to the East, only to be defeated by the new Japanese navy at Tsushima Strait off the coast of Japan. Much to the astonishment of many Europeans, who could not believe that an Asian state was militarily superior to a great European power, the Russians admitted defeat and sued for peace in 1905.

In the midst of the war, the growing discontent of increased numbers of Russians rapidly led to upheaval. A middle class of business and professional people longed for liberal institutions and a liberal political system. Nationalities were dissatisfied with their domination by an ethnic Russian population that constituted only 40 percent of the empire's total population. Peasants were still suffering from lack of land, and laborers felt oppressed by their working and living conditions in Russia's large cities. The breakdown of the transport system caused by the Russo-Japanese War led to food shortages in the major cities of Russia. As a result, on January 9, 1905, a massive procession of workers went to the Winter Palace in Saint Petersburg to present a petition of grievances to the tsar. Troops foolishly opened fire on the peaceful demonstration, killing hundreds and launching a revolution (see the box above). This "Bloody Sunday" incited workers to call strikes and form unions; meanwhile, zemstvos demanded parliamentary government, ethnic groups revolted, and peasants burned the houses of landowners. After a general strike in October 1905, the government capitulated. Nicholas II issued the October Manifesto, in which he granted civil liberties and agreed to create a legislative assembly known as the Duma (DOO-muh), elected directly by a broad franchise. This satisfied the middle-class moderates, who now supported the government's repression of a workers' uprising in Moscow at the end of 1905.

FAILURE OF THE REVOLUTION But real constitutional monarchy proved short-lived. Under Peter Stolypin (stuh-LIP-yin), who served as the tsar's chief adviser from late 1906 until his assassination in 1911, important agrarian reforms dissolved the village ownership of land and opened the door to private ownership by enterprising peasants. Nicholas II, however, was no friend of reform. Already by 1907, the tsar had curtailed the power of the Duma, and after Stolypin's murder, he fell back on the army and bureaucracy to rule Russia.

The Rise of the United States

Between 1860 and 1914, the United States made the shift from an agrarian to a mighty industrial nation. American heavy industry stood unchallenged in 1900. In that year, the Carnegie Steel Company alone produced more steel than Great Britain's entire steel industry. Industrialization also led to urbanization. While established cities, such as New York, Philadelphia, and Boston, grew even larger, other moderate-size cities, such as Pittsburgh, grew by leaps and bounds because of industrialization. Whereas 20 percent of Americans lived in cities in 1860, over 40 percent did in 1900. Four-fifths of the population growth in cities came from migration. Eight to 10 million Americans moved from rural areas into the cities, and 14 million foreigners came from abroad.

The United States had become the world's richest nation and greatest industrial power. Yet serious questions remained about the quality of American life. In 1890, the richest 9 percent of Americans owned an incredible 71 percent of all the wealth. Labor unrest over unsafe working conditions, strict work discipline, and periodic cycles of devastating unemployment led workers to organize. By the turn of the century, one national organization, the American Federation of Labor, emerged as labor's dominant voice. Its lack of real power, however, was reflected in its membership figures. In 1900, it included only 8.4 percent of the American industrial labor force.

During the so-called Progressive Era after 1900, an age of reform swept across the United States. State governments enacted economic and social legislation, such as laws that governed hours, wages, and working

CHRONOLOGY Politics, 1894–1914

Reign of Emperor William II	1888–1918
Reign of Tsar Nicholas II	1894–1917
Dreyfus affair in France	1895–1899
Theodor Herzl, *The Jewish State*	1896
Austrian Christian Socialists under Karl Lueger	1897–1910
First congress of Social Democratic Party in Russia	1898
Beginning of the Progressive Era in the United States	1900
Formation of Labour Party in Britain	1900
Pankhursts establish Women's Social and Political Union	1903
Ministries of Giovanni Giolitti in Italy	1903–1914
Russo-Japanese War	1904–1905
Revolution in Russia	1905
National Insurance Act in Britain	1911
Universal male suffrage in Italy	1912
Social Democratic Party becomes largest party in Germany	1912

conditions, especially for women and children. The realization that state laws were ineffective in dealing with nationwide problems, however, led to a Progressive movement at the national level. The Meat Inspection Act (1906) and Pure Food and Drug Act (1905) provided for a limited degree of federal regulation of corrupt industrial practices. The presidency of Woodrow Wilson (1913–1921) witnessed the enactment of a graduated federal income tax and the establishment of the Federal Reserve System, which permitted the federal government to play a role in important economic decisions formerly made by bankers. Like European nations, the United States was slowly adopting policies that extended the functions of the state.

The Growth of Canada

Canada faced problems of national unity at the end of the nineteenth century. In 1870, the Dominion of Canada had four provinces: Quebec, Ontario, Nova Scotia, and New Brunswick. With the addition of two more—Manitoba and British Columbia—the following year, Canada stretched from the Atlantic to the Pacific.

Real unity was difficult to achieve, however, because of the distrust between the English-speaking majority and the French-speaking Canadians, living primarily in Quebec. Wilfred Laurier (LOR-ee-ay) (1841–1919), who became the first French Canadian prime minister in 1896, was able to reconcile the two groups.

Canada, 1871

During his administration, industrialization boomed, especially the production of textiles, furniture, and railway equipment. Hundreds of thousands of immigrants, primarily from Europe, also flowed into Canada. Many settled on lands in the west, thus helping populate Canada's vast territories.

The New Imperialism

Q **FOCUS QUESTION:** What were the causes of the new imperialism that took place after 1880, and what effects did European imperialism have on Africa and Asia?

In the 1880s, European states embarked on an intense scramble for overseas territory. This **"new imperialism,"** as some have called it, led Europeans to carve up Asia and Africa. What explains the mad scramble for colonies after 1880?

Causes of the New Imperialism

The existence of competitive nation-states and growing nationalism after 1870 was undoubtedly a major determinant in the growth of the new imperialism. As European affairs grew tense, heightened competition spurred European states to acquire colonies abroad that provided ports and coaling stations for their navies. Great Britain, for example, often expanded into new regions not for economic reasons but to keep the French, Germans, or Russians from setting up bases that could harm British interests. Colonies were also a source of international prestige. Once the scramble for colonies began, failure to enter the race was perceived as a sign of weakness, totally unacceptable to an aspiring great power. As a British foreign minister wrote, "When I left the Foreign Office in 1880, nobody thought about Africa. When I returned to it in 1885, the nations of Europe were almost quarreling with each other as to the various portions of Africa which they should obtain."[17] Late-nineteenth-century imperialism was closely tied to nationalism.

Patriotic fervor was often used to arouse interest in imperialism. Schools used maps of colonial territories in teaching geography. Newspapers and magazines often featured soldiers' letters that made imperialism seem a heroic adventure on behalf of one's country. Volunteer groups, such as geographic societies and naval leagues, fostered enthusiasm for imperial adventures. Plays were even written to excite people about expansion abroad.

THE ROLE OF SOCIAL DARWINISM AND RACISM Imperialism was also tied to social Darwinism and racism. As noted earlier, social Darwinists believed that in the struggle between nations, the fit are victorious and survive. Superior races must dominate inferior races by military force to show how strong and virile they are. As British professor of mathematics Karl Pearson argued in

1900, "The path of progress is strewn with the wrecks of nations; traces are everywhere to be seen of the [slaughtered remains] of inferior races. . . . Yet these dead people are, in very truth, the stepping stones on which mankind has arisen to the higher intellectual and deeper emotional life of today."[18] Others were equally blunt. One Englishman wrote, "To the development of the White Man, the Black Man and the Yellow must ever remain inferior, and as the former raised itself higher and yet higher, so did these latter seem to shrink out of humanity and appear nearer and nearer to the brutes."[19]

RELIGIOUS MOTIVES Some Europeans took a more religious or humanitarian approach to imperialism, arguing that Europeans had a moral responsibility to civilize ignorant peoples. This notion of the "white man's burden" (see the box on p. 760) helped at least the more idealistic individuals rationalize imperialism in their own minds. One British official declared that the British Empire

The first step towards lightening

The White Man's Burden

is through teaching the virtues of cleanliness.

Pears' Soap

is a potent factor in brightening the dark corners of the earth as civilization advances, while amongst the cultured of all nations it holds the highest place—it is the ideal toilet soap.

© North Wind Picture Archives

Soap and the White Man's Burden. The concept of the "white man's burden" included the belief that the superiority of their civilization obligated Europeans to impose their practices on supposedly primitive nonwhites. This advertisement for Pears' Soap clearly communicates the Europeans' view of their responsibility toward other peoples.

Opposing >VIEWPOINTS

White Man's Burden Versus Black Man's Burden

One of the justifications for European imperialism was the notion that superior white peoples had a moral obligation to raise ignorant native peoples to a higher level of civilization. The British poet Rudyard Kipling (1865–1936) captured this notion in his poem *The White Man's Burden*. The Western attempt to justify imperialism on the basis of moral responsibility, evident in Kipling's poem, was often hypocritical. Edward Morel, a British journalist who spent time in the Congo, pointed out the destructive effects of Western imperialism on Africans in his book *The Black Man's Burden*.

＊＝＊＝＊

Rudyard Kipling, *The White Man's Burden*

Take up the White Man's burden—
Send forth the best ye breed—
Go bind your sons to exile
to serve your captives' needs;
To wait in heavy harness,
On fluttered folk and wild—
Your new-caught sullen peoples,
Half-devil and half-child.

Take up the White Man's burden—
In patience to abide,
To veil the threat of terror
And check the show of pride;
By open speech and simple,
An hundred times made plain
To seek another's profit,
And work another's gain.

Take up the White Man's burden—
The savage wars of peace—
Fill full the mouth of Famine
And bid the sickness cease;
And when your goal is nearest
The end for others sought,
Watch sloth and heathen Folly
Bring all your hopes to nought.

Take up the White Man's burden—
No tawdry rule of kings,
But toil of serf and sweeper—
The tale of common things.
The ports ye shall not enter,
The roads ye shall not tread,
Go mark them with your living,
And mark them with your dead.

Take up the White Man's burden—
And reap his old reward:

The blame of those ye better,
The hate of those ye guard—
The cry of hosts ye humour
(Ah, slowly!) toward the light—
"Why brought ye us from bondage,
Our loved Egyptian night?"

Take up the White Man's burden—
Ye dare not stoop to less—
Nor call too loud on Freedom
To cloak your weariness;
By all ye cry or whisper,
By all you leave or do,
The silent, sullen peoples
Shall weigh your gods and you.

Take up the White Man's burden—
Have done with childish days—
The lightly proferred laurel,
The easy, ungrudged praise.
Comes now, to search your manhood
Through all the thankless years,
Cold, edged with dear-bought wisdom,
The judgment of your peers!

Edward Morel, *The Black Man's Burden*

It is [the Africans] who carry the "Black man's burden." They have not withered away before the white man's occupation. Indeed . . . Africa has ultimately absorbed within itself every Caucasian and, for that matter, every Semitic invader, too. In hewing out for himself a fixed abode in Africa, the white man has massacred the African in heaps. The African has survived, and it is well for the white settlers that he has. . . .

What the partial occupation of his soil by the white man has failed to do; what the mapping out of European political "spheres of influence" has failed to do; what the Maxim [machine gun] and the rifle, the slave gang, labor in the bowels of the earth and the lash, have failed to do; what imported measles, smallpox and syphilis have failed to do; whatever the overseas slave trade failed to do; the power of modern capitalistic exploitation, assisted by modern engines of destruction, may yet succeed in accomplishing.

For from the evils of the latter, scientifically applied and enforced, there is no escape for the African. Its destructive effects are not spasmodic: they are permanent. In its permanence resides its fatal consequences. It kills not the body merely, but the soul. It breaks the spirit. It attacks the African at every turn, from every point of vantage.

(continued)

It wrecks his polity, uproots him from the land, invades his family life, destroys his natural pursuits and occupations, claims his whole time, enslaves him in his own home....

In Africa, especially in tropical Africa, which a capitalistic imperialism threatens and has, in part, already devastated, man is incapable of reacting against unnatural conditions. In those regions man is engaged in a perpetual struggle against disease and an exhausting climate, which tells heavily upon childbearing; and there is no scientific machinery for saving the weaker members of the community. The African of the tropics is capable of tremendous physical labors. But he cannot accommodate himself to the European system of monotonous, uninterrupted labor, with its long and regular hours, involving, moreover, as it frequently does, severance from natural surroundings and nostalgia, the condition of melancholy resulting from separation from home, a malady to which the African is specially prone. Climatic conditions forbid it. When the system is forced upon him, the tropical African droops and dies.

Nor is violent physical opposition to abuse and injustice henceforth possible for the African in any part of Africa. His chances of effective resistance have been steadily dwindling with the increasing perfectibility in the killing power of modern armament....

Thus the African is really helpless against the material gods of the white man, as embodied in the trinity of imperialism, capitalistic exploitation, and militarism....

To reduce all the varied and picturesque and stimulating episodes in savage life to a dull routine of endless toil for uncomprehended ends, to dislocate social ties and disrupt social institutions; to stifle nascent desires and crush mental development; to graft upon primitive passions the annihilating evils of scientific slavery, and the bestial imaginings of civilized man, unrestrained by convention or law; in fine, to kill the soul in a people—this is a crime which transcends physical murder.

Q What arguments did Kipling make to justify European expansion in Africa and Asia? How does the selection by Edward Morel challenge or undermine Kipling's beliefs?

"was under Providence, the greatest instrument for good that the world has seen." Thousands of Catholic and Protestant missionaries went abroad to seek converts to their faith. Nevertheless, the belief that the superiority of their civilization obligated them to impose modern industries and new medicines on supposedly primitive nonwhites was yet another form of racism.

THE ECONOMIC MOTIVE   Some historians have emphasized an economic motivation for imperialism. There was a great demand for natural resources and products not found in Western countries, such as rubber, oil, and tin. Instead of just trading for these products, European investors advocated direct control of the areas where the raw materials were found. The large surpluses of capital that bankers and industrialists were accumulating often encouraged them to seek higher rates of profit in underdeveloped areas. All of these factors combined to create an **economic imperialism** whereby European finance dominated the economic activity of a large part of the world. This economic imperialism, however, was not necessarily the same thing as colonial expansion. Businesses invested where it was most profitable, not necessarily where their own countries had colonial empires. For example, less than 10 percent of French foreign investments before 1914 went to French colonies; most of the rest went to Latin American and European countries. Even the British had more trade with Belgium than with all of Africa in the 1890s. It should also be remembered that much of the colonial territory that was acquired was mere wasteland from the perspective of industrialized Europe and cost more to administer than it produced economically. Only the search for national prestige could justify such losses.

Followers of Karl Marx were especially eager to argue that imperialism was economically motivated because they associated imperialism with the ultimate demise of the capitalist system. Marx had hinted at this argument, but it was one of his followers, the Russian V. I. Lenin (see Chapter 25), who in *Imperialism, the Highest Stage of World Capitalism* developed the idea that capitalism leads to imperialism. According to Lenin, as the capitalist system concentrates more wealth in ever-fewer hands, the possibility for investment at home is exhausted, and capitalists are forced to invest abroad, establish colonies, and exploit small, weak nations. In his view, then, the only cure for imperialism was the destruction of capitalism.

The Scramble for Africa

Europeans controlled relatively little of the African continent before 1880. Earlier, when their economic interests were more limited (in the case of Africa, primarily the slave trade), European states had generally been satisfied to deal with existing independent states rather than attempting to establish direct control over vast territories. For the most part, the Western presence in Africa had been limited to controlling the regional trade network and establishing a few footholds where the foreigners could carry on trade and missionary activity. During the last two decades of the nineteenth century, however, the quest for colonies became a scramble as all of the major European states engaged in a land grab.

SOUTH AFRICA During the Napoleonic wars, the British had established themselves in South Africa by taking control of Cape Town, originally founded by the Dutch. After the wars, the British encouraged settlers to come to what they called the Cape Colony. British policies disgusted the Boers (BOORS *or* BORS) or Afrikaners (ah-fri-KAH-nurz), as the descendants of the Dutch colonists were called, and led them in 1835 to migrate north on the Great Trek to the region between the Orange and Vaal rivers (later known as the Orange Free State) and north of the Vaal River (the Transvaal). Hostilities between the British and the Boers continued, however. In 1877, the British governor of the Cape Colony seized the Transvaal, but a Boer revolt led the British government to recognize Transvaal as the independent South African Republic. These struggles between the British and the Boers did not prevent either white group from massacring and subjugating the Zulu and Xhosa (KHOH-suh) peoples of the region.

The Struggle for South Africa

In the 1880s, British policy in South Africa was largely determined by Cecil Rhodes (1853–1902). Rhodes founded both diamond and gold companies that monopolized production of these precious commodities and enabled him to gain control of a territory north of Transvaal that he named Rhodesia after himself. Rhodes was a great champion of British expansion. He said once, "If there be a God, I think what he would like me to do is to paint as much of Africa British red as possible." One of his goals was to create a series of British colonies "from the Cape to Cairo," all linked by a railroad. His imperialist ambitions led to his downfall in 1896, however, when the British government forced him to resign as prime minister of the Cape Colony after he conspired to overthrow the Boer government of the South African Republic without British approval. Although the British government had hoped to avoid war with the Boers, it could not stop extremists on both sides from precipitating a conflict.

THE BOER WAR The Boer War began in 1899 and dragged on until 1902 as the Boers proved to be an effective opponent. Due to the Boers' use of guerrilla tactics, the British sustained high casualties and immense expenses in securing victory. Almost 450,000 British and imperial forces were needed to defeat 87,000 Boers at a cost of 22,000 British deaths. Mass newspapers in Britain reported on the high casualties, costs, and brutalities against Boer women and children, causing a public outcry

and arousing antiwar sentiment at home. Despite Britain's victory, the cost of the Boer War demonstrated that increased military and monetary investment would be needed to maintain the British Empire.

British policy toward the defeated Boers was remarkably conciliatory. Transvaal and the Orange Free State had representative governments by 1907, and in 1910, the Union of South Africa was created. Like Canada, Australia, and New Zealand, it became a fully self-governing dominion within the British Empire

PORTUGUESE AND FRENCH POSSESSIONS Before 1880, the only other European settlements in Africa had been made by the French and the Portuguese. The Portuguese had held on to their settlements in Angola on the west coast and Mozambique on the east coast. The French had started the conquest of Algeria in Muslim North Africa in 1830, although it was not until 1879 that French civilian rule was established there. The next year, 1880, the European scramble for possession of Africa began in earnest. By 1900, the French had added the huge area of French West Africa and Tunisia to their African empire. In 1912, they established a protectorate over much of Morocco; the rest was left to Spain.

OTHER BRITISH POSSESSIONS The British took an active interest in Egypt after the Suez Canal was opened by the French in 1869. Believing that the canal was their lifeline to India, the British sought to control the canal area. Egypt was a well-established state with an autonomous Muslim government, but that did not stop the British from landing an expeditionary force there in 1882. Although they claimed that their occupation was only temporary, they soon established a protectorate over Egypt. From Egypt, the British moved south into the Sudan and seized it after narrowly averting a war with France. Not to be outdone, Italy joined in the imperialist scramble. Their humiliating defeat by the Ethiopians in 1896 only led the Italians to try again in 1911, when they invaded and seized Ottoman Tripoli, which they renamed Libya.

BELGIUM AND CENTRAL AFRICA Central Africa was also added to the list of European colonies. Popular interest in the forbiddingly dense tropical jungles of Central Africa was first aroused in the 1860s and 1870s by explorers, such as the Scottish missionary David Livingstone and the British-American journalist Henry M. Stanley. But the real driving force for the colonization of Central Africa was King Leopold II (1865–1909) of Belgium, who rushed enthusiastically into the pursuit of empire in Africa: "To open to civilization," he said, "the only part of our globe where it has not yet penetrated, to pierce the darkness which envelops whole populations, is a crusade, if I may say so, a crusade worthy of this century of progress." Profit, however, was far more important to Leopold than progress; his treatment of the Africans was so brutal that even other Europeans condemned his actions. In 1876, Leopold created the International Association for the

CHRONOLOGY The New Imperialism: Africa

Great Trek of the Boers	1835
Opening of the Suez Canal	1869
Leopold of Belgium establishes settlements in the Congo	1876
British seizure of Transvaal	1877
French conquest of Algeria	1879
British expeditionary force in Egypt	1882
Ethiopians defeat the Italians	1896
Battle of Omdurman in the Sudan	1898
Boer War	1899–1902
Union of South Africa	1910
Italians seize Tripoli	1911
French protectorate over Morocco	1912

Exploration and Civilization of Central Africa and engaged Henry Stanley to establish Belgian settlements in the Congo. Alarmed by Leopold's actions, the French also moved into the territory north of the Congo River.

GERMAN POSSESSIONS Between 1884 and 1900, most of the rest of Africa was carved up by the European powers. Germany entered the ranks of the imperialist powers at this time. Initially, Bismarck had downplayed the significance of colonies, but as domestic political pressures for a German empire intensified, Bismarck became a political convert to colonialism. As he expressed it, "All this colonial business is a sham, but we need it for the elections." The Germans established colonies in South-West Africa, the Cameroons, Togoland, and Tanganyika.

IMPACT ON AFRICA By 1914, Britain, France, Germany, Belgium, Spain, and Portugal had carved up the entire African continent (see Map 24.1). Only Liberia, founded by emancipated American slaves, and Ethiopia remained free states. Despite the humanitarian rationalizations about the "white man's burden," Africa had been conquered by European states determined to create colonial empires (see the box on p. 760). Any peoples who dared to resist (with the exception of the Ethiopians, who defeated the Italians) were simply devastated by the superior military force of the Europeans. In 1898, Sudanese tribesmen attempted to defend their independence and stop a British expedition armed with the recently developed machine gun. In the ensuing Battle of Omdurman, the Sudanese were massacred. One observer noted, "It was not a battle but an execution. . . . The bodies were not in heaps—bodies hardly ever are; but they spread evenly over acres and acres. Some lay very composedly with their slippers placed under their heads for a last pillow; some knelt, cut short in the middle of a last prayer. Others were torn to pieces."[20] The battle casualties at Omdurman tell the story of the one-sided conflicts between Europeans and Africans: twenty-eight British deaths to 11,000 Sudanese. Military superiority was frequently accompanied by brutal treatment of blacks. Nor did Europeans hesitate to deceive the Africans to gain their way. One South African king, Lo Bengula, informed Queen Victoria about how he had been cheated:

> Some time ago a party of men came to my country, the principal one appearing to be a man called Rudd. They asked me for a place to dig for gold, and said they would give me certain things for the right to do so. I told them to bring what they could give and I would show them what I would give. A document was written and presented to me for signature. I asked what it contained, and was told that in it were my words and the words of those men. I put my hand to it. About three months afterwards I heard from other sources that I had given by that document the right to all the minerals of my country.[21]

Imperialism in Asia

Although Asia had been open to Western influence since the sixteenth century, not much of its immense territory had fallen under direct European control. The Dutch were established in the East Indies, the Spanish were in the Philippines, and the French and Portuguese had trading posts on the Indian coast. China, Japan, Korea, and Southeast Asia had largely managed to exclude Westerners. The British and the Russians, however, had acquired the most Asian territory.

THE BRITISH IN ASIA It was not until the explorations of Australia by Captain James Cook between 1768 and 1771 that Britain took an active interest in the East. The availability of land for grazing sheep and the discovery of gold in Australia led to an influx of settlers who slaughtered many of the indigenous inhabitants. In 1850, the British government granted the various Australian colonies virtually complete self-government, and fifty years later, on January 1, 1901, all the colonies were unified into the Commonwealth of Australia. Nearby New Zealand, which the British had declared a colony in 1840, was granted dominion status in 1907.

A private trading company known as the British East India Company had been responsible for subjugating much of India. In 1858, however, after a revolt of the sepoys, or Indian troops of the East India Company's army, had been crushed, the British Parliament transferred the company's powers directly to the government in London. In 1876, the title Empress of India was bestowed on Queen Victoria; Indians were now her colonial subjects.

THE RUSSIANS IN ASIA Russian expansion in Asia was a logical outgrowth of its traditional territorial aggrandizement. Russian explorers had penetrated the wilderness of Siberia in the seventeenth century and reached the Pacific coast in 1637. In the eighteenth century, Russians established a claim on Alaska, which they sold to the United States in 1867. Gradually, Russian settlers moved into cold and forbidding Siberia. Altogether, 7 million Russians settled in Siberia between 1800 and 1914, by which time 90 percent of the Siberian population was Slavic, not Asiatic.

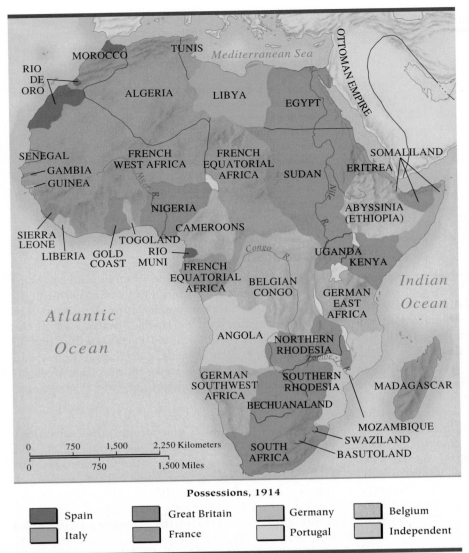

Possessions, 1914

- Spain
- Italy
- Great Britain
- France
- Germany
- Portugal
- Belgium
- Independent

MAP 24.1 Africa in 1914. The major European powers' rush to acquire colonies was motivated by a combination of factors: ports and fueling stations for navies, enhancement of international prestige, outlets for nationalist feelings, expression of social Darwinism, and a desire to "civilize" non-Europeans.

Q *Of the two countries with the largest amount of territory in Africa, which one's colonies were more geographically concentrated, and what could be the benefits of this?*

View an animated version of this map or related maps on the CourseMate website.

spheres of influence. Halted by the British in their expansion to the south, the Russians moved east in Asia. The Russian occupation of Manchuria and an attempt to move into Korea brought war with the new imperialist power, Japan. After losing the Russo-Japanese War in 1905, the Russians agreed to a Japanese protectorate in Korea, and their Asian expansion was brought to a temporary halt (see Map 24.2).

CHINA The thrust of imperialism after 1880 led Westerners to move into new areas of Asia hitherto largely free of Western influence. By the nineteenth century, the ruling Manchu dynasty of the Chinese Empire was showing signs of decline. In 1842, the British had obtained (through war) the island of Hong Kong and trading rights in a number of Chinese cities. Other Western nations soon rushed in to gain similar trading privileges. Chinese attempts to resist this foreign encroachment led to military defeats and new demands. Only rivalry among the great powers themselves prevented the complete dismemberment of the Chinese Empire. Instead, Britain, France, Germany, Russia, the United States, and Japan established spheres of influence and long-term leases of Chinese territory. In 1899, urged along by the American secretary of state, John Hay, they agreed to an "open door" policy in which one country would not restrict the commerce of the other countries in its sphere of influence.

JAPAN AND KOREA Japan avoided Western intrusion until 1853–1854, when American naval forces under Commodore Matthew Perry forced the Japanese to grant the United States trading and diplomatic privileges. Japan, however, managed to avoid China's fate. Korea had also largely excluded Westerners. The fate of Korea was determined by the struggle first between China and Japan in 1894–1895 and later between Japan and Russia in 1904–1905. Japan's victories gave it clear superiority, and in 1910, Japan formally annexed Korea.

SOUTHEAST ASIA In Southeast Asia, Britain established control over Burma (modern Myanmar) and the Malay States, and France played an active role in

The Russians also moved south, attracted by warmer climes and the crumbling Ottoman Empire. By 1830, the Russians had established control over the entire northern coast of the Black Sea and then pressed on into Central Asia, securing the trans-Caspian area by 1881 and Turkestan in 1885. These advances brought the Russians to the borders of Persia and Afghanistan, where the British also had interests because of their desire to protect their holdings in India. In 1907, the Russians and British agreed to make Afghanistan a buffer state between Russian Turkestan and British India and to divide Persia into two

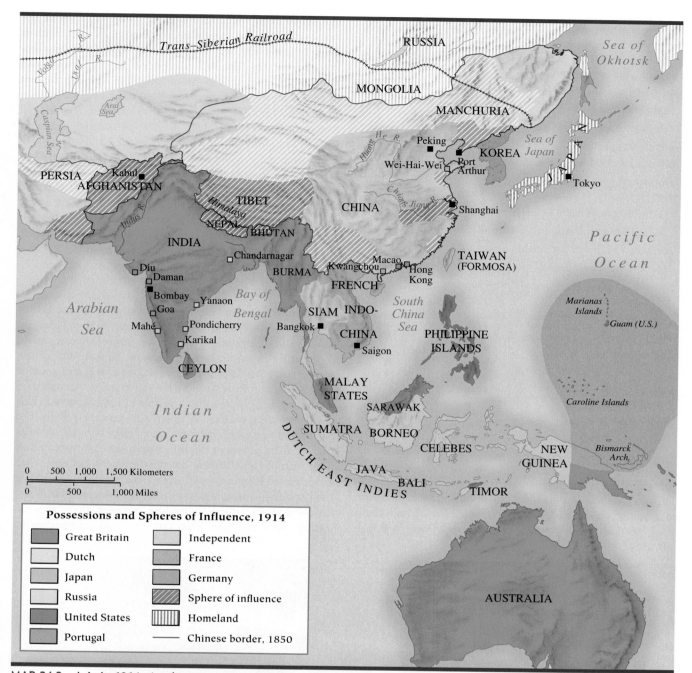

MAP 24.2 Asia in 1914. Asia became an important arena of international competition in the nineteenth and early twentieth centuries. Beset by economic stagnation and an inability to modernize, a weak China was unable to withstand the demands of the United States, European powers, and a Westernizing Japan. Britain, France, Russia, Japan, and the United States had direct or indirect control of nearly all of Asia by 1914.

Q *Why would both Russia and Japan covet Manchuria?*

Q *View an animated version of this map or related maps on the CourseMate website.*

subjugating Indochina. The city of Saigon was occupied in 1858, and four years later, Cochin China was taken. In the 1880s, the French extended "protection" over Cambodia, Annam, Tonkin, and Laos and organized them into the Union of French Indochina. Only Siam

(Thailand) remained free as a buffer state because of British-French rivalry.

AMERICAN IMPERIALISM   The Pacific islands were also the scene of great power competition and witnessed the

Britain obtains Hong Kong and trading rights from Chinese government	1842
Australian colonies receive self-government	1850
Mission of Commodore Perry to Japan	1853–1854
Rebellion of sepoys in India	1857–1858
French occupy Saigon	1858
Overthrow of the shogun in Japan	1867
Emperor Mutsuhito and the Meiji Restoration	1867–1912
Queen Victoria is made Empress of India	1876
Russians in Central Asia (trans-Caspian area)	1881
Formation of Indian National Congress	1883
Japanese defeat of China	1894–1895
Spanish-American War; United States annexes Philippines	1898
"Open door" policy in China	1899
Boxer Rebellion in China	1900–1901
Commonwealth of Australia	1901
Commonwealth of New Zealand	1907
Russian-British agreement over Afghanistan and Persia	1907
Japan annexes Korea	1910
Overthrow of Manchu dynasty in China	1912

entry of the United States onto the imperialist stage. The Samoan Islands became the first important American colony; the Hawaiian Islands were the next to fall. Soon after Americans had made Pearl Harbor into a naval station in 1887, American settlers gained control of the sugar industry on the islands. When Hawaiian natives tried to reassert their authority, the U.S. Marines were brought in to "protect" American lives. Hawaii was annexed by the United States in 1898 during the era of American nationalistic fervor generated by the Spanish-American War. The American defeat of Spain encouraged Americans to extend their empire by acquiring Puerto Rico, Guam, and the Philippine Islands. Although the Filipinos hoped for independence, the Americans refused to grant it. As President William McKinley said, the United States had the duty "to educate the Filipinos and uplift and Christianize them," a remarkable statement in view of the fact that most of them had been Roman Catholics for centuries. It took three years and 60,000 troops to pacify the Philippines and establish American control.

Responses to Imperialism

When Europeans imposed their culture on peoples they considered inferior, how did the conquered peoples respond? Initial attempts to expel the foreigners only led to devastating defeats at the hands of Westerners, whose industrial technology gave them modern weapons of war with which to crush the indigenous peoples. Accustomed to rule by small elites, most people simply accepted their new governors, making Western rule relatively easy. The conquered peoples subsequently adjusted to foreign rule in different ways. Traditionalists sought to maintain their cultural traditions, but modernizers believed that adoption of Western ways would enable them to reform their societies and eventually challenge Western rule. Most people probably stood somewhere between these two extremes. Four examples illustrate different approaches to

The French in Southeast Asia. In Saigon, the French created a new city plan with wide streets and constructed cultural and administrative buildings designed by Europeans, such as the Post Office building pictured here. The Post Office was designed by Gustave Eiffel, the architect who built the Eiffel Tower in Paris. Buildings such as the Post Office reflected France's increasing investment in its colonial holdings during the late nineteenth century.

the question of how indigenous peoples responded to foreign rule.

AFRICA By the beginning of the twentieth century, a new class of African leaders had emerged. Educated in colonial schools and some even in the West, they were the first generation of Africans to know a great deal about the West and to write in the language of their colonial masters. Although this "new class" admired Western culture and even disliked the ways of their own countries, many came to resent the foreigners and their arrogant contempt for colonial peoples. Westerners had exalted democracy, equality, and political freedom, but these values were not applied in the colonies. There were few democratic institutions, and colonial peoples could hold only lowly jobs in the colonial bureaucracy. Equally important, the economic prosperity of the West never extended to the colonies. To many Africans, colonialism meant the loss of their farmlands or terrible jobs on plantations or in sweatshops and factories run by foreigners.

Although middle-class Africans did not suffer to the extent that poor peasants or workers on plantations did, they too had complaints. They usually qualified only for menial jobs in the government or business. The purported superiority of the Europeans over the natives was also expressed in a variety of ways. Segregated clubs, schools, and churches were set up as more European officials brought their wives and began to raise families. Europeans also had a habit of addressing natives by their first names or calling an adult male "boy."

Such conditions led many of the new urban educated class to have very complicated feelings about their colonial masters and the civilization they represented. Though willing to admit the superiority of many aspects of Western culture, these new intellectuals fiercely hated colonial rule and were determined to assert their own nationality and cultural destiny. Out of this mixture of hopes and resentments emerged the first stirrings of modern nationalism in Africa. During the first quarter of the twentieth century, in colonial societies across Africa, educated native peoples began to organize political parties and movements seeking the end of foreign rule.

CHINA The humiliation of China by the Western powers led to much antiforeign violence, but the Westerners used this lawlessness as an excuse to extort further concessions from the Chinese. A major outburst of violence against foreigners occurred in the Boxer Rebellion in 1900–1901. "Boxers" was the popular name given to Chinese who belonged to a secret organization called the Society of Harmonious Fists, whose aim was to push the foreigners out of China. The Boxers murdered foreign missionaries, Chinese who had converted to Christianity, railroad workers, foreign businessmen, and even the German envoy to Beijing. Response to the killings was immediate and overwhelming. An allied army consisting of British, French, German, Russian, American, and Japanese troops attacked Beijing, restored order, and demanded more concessions from the

Chinese government. The imperial government was so weakened that the forces of the revolutionary leader Sun Yat-sen (1866–1925), who adopted a program of "nationalism, democracy, and socialism," overthrew the Manchu dynasty in 1912. The new Republic of China remained weak and ineffective, and China's travails were far from over.

JAPAN In the late 1850s and early 1860s, it looked as if Japan would follow China's fate and be carved up into spheres of influence by aggressive Western powers. A remarkably rapid transformation, however, produced a very different result. Before 1868, the shogun, a powerful hereditary military governor assisted by a warrior nobility known as the samurai, exercised real power in Japan. The emperor's functions had become primarily religious. After the shogun's concessions to the Western nations, antiforeign sentiment led to a samurai revolt in 1867 and the restoration of the emperor as the rightful head of the government. The new emperor was the astute, dynamic, young Mutsuhito (moo-tsoo-HEE-toh) (1867–1912), who called his reign the Meiji (MAY-jee) (Enlightened

The West and Japan. In their attempt to modernize, the Japanese absorbed and adopted Western methods. They were also influenced by Western culture as Western fashions became the rage in elite circles. Baseball was even imported from the United States. This painting shows Western-style stone houses in Tokyo and streets filled with people dressed in a variety of styles.

Government). The new leaders who controlled the emperor now inaugurated a remarkable transformation of Japan that has since been known as the Meiji Restoration.

Recognizing the obvious military and industrial superiority of the West, the new leaders decided to modernize Japan by absorbing and adopting Western methods. Thousands of young Japanese were sent abroad to receive Western educations, especially in the social and natural sciences. A German-style army and a British-style navy were established. The Japanese copied the industrial and financial methods of the United States and developed a modern commercial and industrial system. A highly centralized administrative system copied from the French replaced the old system. Initially, the Japanese adopted the French principles of social and legal equality, but by 1890, they had created a political system that was democratic in form but authoritarian in practice.

In imitating the West, Japan also developed a powerful military state. Universal military conscription was introduced in 1872, and a modern peacetime army of 240,000 was eventually established. The Japanese avidly pursued the Western imperialistic model. They defeated China in 1894–1895, annexed some Chinese territory, and established their own sphere of influence in China. After they had defeated the Russians in 1905, the Japanese made Korea a colony under harsh rule. The Japanese had proved that an Asian power could play the "white man's" imperialistic game and provided a potent example to peoples in other regions of Asia and Africa.

INDIA The British government had been in control of India since the mid-nineteenth century. After crushing a major revolt in 1858, the British ruled India directly. Under Parliament's supervision, a small group of British civil servants directed the affairs of India's almost 300 million people.

The British brought order to a society that had been divided by civil wars for some time and created a relatively honest and efficient government. They also brought Western technology—railroads, banks, mines, industry, medical knowledge, and hospitals. The British introduced Western-style secondary schools and colleges where the Indian upper and middle classes and professional classes were educated so that they could serve as trained subordinates in the government and army.

British legislation also affected the legal status of Indian women. In 1829, the British banned the practice of *sati*, which called for a widow to immolate herself on her husband's funeral pyre. Some scholars question how extensive the practice was, however, and suggest that the abolition of *sati* became central to Britain's image of itself as culturally superior. Female infanticide was also

Japanese Expansion

- Japan's possessions, 1875
- Territorial acquisitions, 1894–1914
- Spheres of Japanese influence, 1918

discouraged. Although women's position in Indian society was not significantly altered, the recognition of women by the law did afford some protection against these practices.

The Indian people paid a high price for the peace and stability brought by British rule. Due to population growth in the nineteenth century, extreme poverty was a way of life for most Indians; almost two-thirds of the population was malnourished in 1901. British industrialization brought little improvement for the masses. British manufactured goods destroyed local industries, and Indian wealth was used to pay British officials and a large army. The system of education served only the elite, upper-class Indians, and it was conducted only in the rulers' English language while 90 percent of the population remained illiterate. Even for the Indians who benefited the most from their Western educations, British rule was degrading. The best jobs and the best housing were reserved for Britons. Despite their education, the Indians were never considered equals of the British, whose racial attitudes were made quite clear by Lord Kitchener, one of Britain's foremost military commanders in India, when he said, "It is this consciousness of the inherent superiority of the European which has won for us India. However well educated and clever a native may be, and however brave he may prove himself, I believe that no rank we can bestow on him would cause him to be considered an equal of the British officer."[22] Such smug racial attitudes made it difficult for British rule, no matter how beneficent, ever to be ultimately accepted and led to the rise of an Indian nationalist movement. By 1883, when the Indian National Congress was formed, moderate, educated Indians were beginning to seek self-government. By 1919, in response to British violence and British insensitivity, Indians were demanding complete independence.

Results of the New Imperialism

By 1900, almost all the societies of Africa and Asia were either under full colonial rule or, as in the case of China and the Ottoman Empire, at a point of virtual collapse. Only a handful of states, such as Japan in East Asia, Thailand in Southeast Asia, Afghanistan and Persia in the Middle East, and mountainous Ethiopia in East Africa, managed to escape internal disintegration or subjection to colonial rule. For the most part, the exceptions were the result of good fortune rather than design. Thailand escaped subjugation primarily because officials in Britain and France found it more convenient to transform the country into a buffer state than to fight over it. Ethiopia and Afghanistan survived due to their remote location and mountainous terrain. Only Japan managed to avoid the common fate through a concerted strategy of political and economic reform. With the coming of imperialism, a global economy was finally established, and the domination of Western civilization over those of Africa and Asia appeared to be complete. At the same time, the competition for lands abroad also heightened the existing rivalries among European states.

International Rivalry and the Coming of War

Q **FOCUS QUESTIONS:** What was the Bismarckian system of alliances, and how successful was it at keeping the peace? What issues lay behind the international crises that Europe faced in the late nineteenth and early twentieth centuries?

Before 1914, Europeans had experienced almost fifty years of peace. There had been wars (including wars of conquest in the non-Western world), but none had involved the great powers. A series of crises had occurred that might easily have led to general war. One reason they did not is that until 1890, Bismarck of Germany exercised a restraining influence on the Europeans.

The Bismarckian System

Bismarck knew that the emergence of a unified Germany in 1871 had upset the balance of power established at Vienna in 1815. Fearing the French desire for revenge over their loss of Alsace-Lorraine in the Franco-Prussian War, Bismarck made an alliance first in 1873 and again in 1881 with the traditionally conservative powers Austria-Hungary and Russia. But the Three Emperors' League, as it was called, failed to work very well, primarily because of Russian-Austrian rivalry in the Balkans.

THE BALKANS: DECLINE OF OTTOMAN POWER The problem in the Balkans was a by-product of the disintegration of the Ottoman Empire. As subject peoples in the Balkans clamored for independence, corruption and inefficiency weakened the Ottoman government. Only the interference of the great European powers,

who were fearful of each other's designs on its territories, kept the Ottoman Empire alive. Complicating the situation was the rivalry between Russia and Austria, which both had designs on the Balkans. For Russia, the Balkans provided the shortest overland route to Constantinople and the Mediterranean. Austria viewed the Balkans as fertile ground for Austrian expansion. Although Germany had no real interests in the Balkans, Bismarck was fearful of the consequences of a war between Russia and Austria over the region and served as a restraining influence on both powers. Events in the Balkans, however, precipitated a new crisis.

In 1876, the Balkan states of Serbia and Montenegro declared war on the Ottoman Empire. Both were defeated, but Russia, with Austrian approval, attacked and defeated the Ottomans. By the Treaty of San Stefano in 1878, a large Bulgarian state, extending from the Danube in the north to the Aegean Sea in the south, was created. As Bulgaria was viewed as a Russian satellite, this Russian success caused the other great powers to call for a congress of European powers to discuss a revision of the treaty.

The Congress of Berlin, which met in the summer of 1878, was dominated by Bismarck. The congress effectively demolished the Treaty of San Stefano, much to Russia's humiliation. The new Bulgarian state was considerably reduced, and the rest of the territory was returned to Ottoman control. The three Balkan states of Serbia, Montenegro, and Romania, until then nominally under Ottoman control, were recognized as independent.

The other Balkan territories of Bosnia and Herzegovina were placed under Austrian protection; Austria could occupy but not annex them.

NEW ALLIANCES After the Congress of Berlin, the European powers sought new alliances to safeguard their security. Angered by the Germans' actions at the congress, the Russians terminated the Three Emperors' League in 1879. Bismarck then made an alliance with Austria in 1879 that was joined by Italy in 1882. The Triple Alliance of 1882 committed Germany, Austria, and Italy to support the existing political order while providing a defensive alliance against France or "two or more great powers not members of the alliance." At the same time,

The Balkans in 1878

The Emperor's Big Mouth

Emperor William II had the unfortunate tendency to stir up trouble by his often tactless public remarks. In this 1908 interview, for example, William intended to strengthen Germany's ties with Britain. His words had just the opposite effect and raised a storm of protest in both Britain and Germany.

Daily Telegraph Interview, October 28, 1908

His Majesty [William II] honored me with a long conversation, and spoke with impulsive and unusual frankness. "You English," he said, "are mad, mad, mad as March hares. What has come over you that you are so completely given over to suspicions quite unworthy of a great nation? What more can I do than I have done? I declared with all the emphasis at my command, in my speech at Guildhall, that my heart is set upon peace, and that it is one of my dearest wishes to live on the best of terms with England. Have I ever been false to my word? Falsehoods and prevarication are alien to my nature. My actions ought to speak for themselves, but you listen not to them but to those who misinterpret and distort them. That is a personal insult which I feel and resent. To be forever misjudged, to have my repeated offers of friendship weighed and scrutinized with jealous, mistrustful eyes, taxes my patience severely. I have said time after time that I am a friend of England, and your Press—or, at least, a considerable section of it—bids the people of England to refuse my proffered hand, and insinuates that the other holds a dagger. How can I convince a nation against its will?

"I repeat," continued his Majesty, "that I am a friend of England, but you make things difficult for me. My task is not of the easiest. The prevailing sentiment among large sections of the middle and lower classes of my own people is not friendly to England. I am, therefore, so to speak, in a minority in my own land, but it is a minority of the best elements as it is in England with

respect to Germany. That is another reason why I resent your refusal to accept my pledged word that I am the friend of England. I strive without ceasing to improve relations, and you retort that I am your arch-enemy. You make it hard for me. Why is it? . . .

"But, you will say, what of the German Navy? Surely, that is a menace to England! Against whom but England are my squadrons being prepared? If England is not in the minds of those Germans who are bent on creating a powerful fleet, why is Germany asked to consent to such new and heavy burdens of taxation? My answer is clear. Germany is a young and growing Empire. She has a worldwide commerce, which is rapidly expanding, and to which the legitimate ambition of patriotic Germans refuses to assign any bounds. Germany must have a powerful fleet to protect that commerce, and her manifold interests in even the most distant seas. She expects those interests to go on growing, and she must be able to champion them manfully in any quarter of the globe. Germany looks ahead. Her horizons stretch far away. She must be prepared for any eventualities in the Far East. Who can foresee what may take place in the Pacific in the days to come, days not so distant as some believe, but days, at any rate, for which all European Powers with Far Eastern interests ought steadily to prepare? Look at the accomplished rise of Japan; think of the possible national awakening of China; and then judge of the vast problems of the Pacific. Only those Powers which have great navies will be listened to with respect, when the future of the Pacific comes to be solved; and, if for that reason only, Germany must have a powerful fleet. It may even be that England herself will be glad that Germany has a fleet when they speak together on the same side in the great debates of the future."

Q What did William II mean to say? What did he actually say? What does this interview with William II reveal about the emperor's attitudes and character?

Bismarck sought to remain on friendly terms with the Russians and signed the Reinsurance Treaty with Russia in 1887, hoping to prevent a French-Russian alliance that would threaten Germany with the possibility of a two-front war. The Bismarckian system of alliances, geared to preserving peace and the status quo, had worked, but in 1890, Emperor William II dismissed Bismarck and began to chart a new direction for Germany's foreign policy.

New Directions and New Crises

Emperor William II embarked on an activist foreign policy dedicated to enhancing German power by finding, as he put it, Germany's rightful "place in the sun." One of his

changes in Bismarck's foreign policy was to drop the Reinsurance Treaty with Russia, which he viewed as being at odds with Germany's alliance with Austria. The ending of the alliance achieved what Bismarck had feared: it brought France and Russia together. Long isolated by Bismarck's policies, republican France leaped at the chance to draw closer to tsarist Russia, and in 1894, the two powers concluded a military alliance.

During the next ten years, German policies abroad caused the British to draw closer to France (see the box above). By 1907, a loose confederation of Great Britain, France, and Russia—known as the Triple Entente—stood opposed to the Triple Alliance of Germany, Austria-Hungary, and Italy. Europe was divided into two opposing camps that became more and more inflexible and unwilling to compromise. When the members of the two alliances became involved in a new series of crises between 1908 and 1913 over control of the remnants of the Ottoman Empire in the Balkans, the stage was set for World War I.

CRISES IN THE BALKANS, 1908–1913 The Bosnian Crisis of 1908–1909 initiated a chain of events that eventually spun out of control. Since 1878, Bosnia and Herzegovina had been under the protection of Austria, but in 1908, Austria took the drastic step of annexing these two Slavic-speaking territories. Serbia became outraged at this action because it dashed the Serbs' hopes of creating a large Serbian kingdom that would include most of the southern Slavs. This was why the Austrians had annexed Bosnia and Herzegovina. To the Austrians, a large Serbia would be a threat to the unity of the Austro-Hungarian Empire, with its large Slavic population. The Russians, as protectors of their fellow Slavs and desiring to increase their own authority in the Balkans, supported the Serbs and opposed the Austrian action. Backed by the Russians, the Serbs prepared for war against Austria. At this point,

William II intervened and demanded that the Russians accept Austria's annexation of Bosnia and Herzegovina or face war with Germany. Weakened from their defeat in the Russo-Japanese War in 1904–1905, the Russians backed down. Humiliated, they vowed revenge.

European attention returned to the Balkans in 1912 when Serbia, Bulgaria, Montenegro, and Greece organized the Balkan League and defeated the Ottomans in the First Balkan War. When the victorious allies were unable to agree on how to divide the conquered Ottoman provinces of Macedonia and Albania, the Second Balkan War erupted in 1913. Greece, Serbia, Romania, and the Ottoman Empire attacked and defeated Bulgaria. As a result, Bulgaria obtained only a small part of Macedonia, and most of the rest was divided between Serbia and Greece (see Map 24.3). Yet Serbia's aspirations remained unfulfilled. The two Balkan wars left the inhabitants embittered and created more tensions among the great powers.

One of Serbia's major ambitions had been to acquire Albanian territory that would give it a port on the Adriatic. At the London Conference, arranged by Austria at the end of the two Balkan wars, the Austrians had blocked

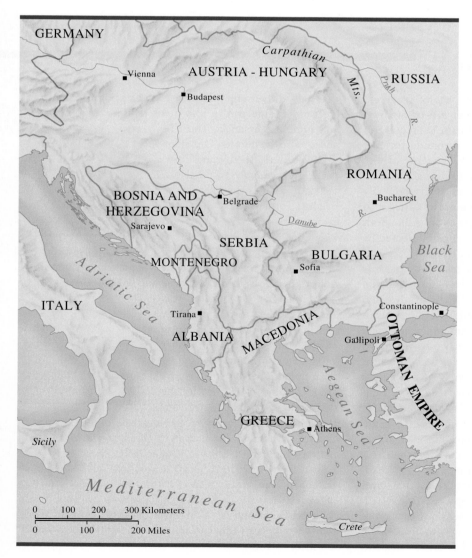

MAP 24.3   The Balkans in 1913. The First Balkan War (1912) liberated most of the region from Ottoman control; the Second Balkan War (1913) increased the size of Greece and Serbia at Bulgaria's expense. Russia supported the ambitions of fellow Slavs in Serbia, who sought to rule a large Slavic kingdom in the Balkans. Austria and its ally Germany opposed Serbia's ambitions.

Q *Look at the map on p. 769. What territories had the Ottomans lost by the end of 1913?*

CHRONOLOGY European Diplomacy

Three Emperors' League	1873
Serbia and Montenegro attack the Ottoman Empire	1876
Treaty of San Stefano	1878
Congress of Berlin	1878
Defensive alliance: Germany and Austria	1879
Triple Alliance: Germany, Austria, and Italy	1882
Reinsurance Treaty: Germany and Russia	1887
Military alliance: Russia and France	1894
Triple Entente: France, Britain, and Russia	1907
First Balkan War	1912
Second Balkan War	1913

supporters, the Russians were also upset by the turn of events in the region. A feeling had grown among Russian leaders that they could not back down again in the event of a confrontation with Austria or Germany in the Balkans. One Russian military journal even stated early in 1914, "We are preparing for a war in the west. The whole nation must accustom itself to the idea that we arm ourselves for a war of annihilation against the Germans."

Austria-Hungary had achieved another of its aims, but it was still convinced that Serbia was a mortal threat to its empire and must at some point be crushed. Meanwhile, the French and Russian governments renewed their alliance and promised each other that they would not back down at the next crisis. Britain drew closer to France. By the beginning of 1914, the two armed camps viewed each other with suspicion. An American in Europe observed, "The whole of Germany is charged with electricity. Everybody's nerves are tense. It only needs a spark to set the whole thing off." The German ambassador to France noted at the same time that "peace remains at the mercy of an accident." The European "age of progress" was about to come to an inglorious and bloody end.

Serbia's wishes by creating an independent Albania. The Germans, as Austrian allies, had supported this move. In their frustration, Serbian nationalists increasingly portrayed the Austrians as monsters who were keeping the Serbs from becoming a great nation. As Serbia's chief

CHAPTER SUMMARY

What many Europeans liked to call their "age of progress" in the decades before 1914 was also an era of anxiety. Driven by national rivalry, social Darwinism, religious and humanitarian concerns, and economic demands for raw materials and overseas investment, at the end of the nineteenth century Western nations began a renewed frenzy of imperialist expansion around the world. By 1914, European nations had carved up most of Africa into colonies and created spheres of influence in Asia. Both

China and Japan were also affected by Western imperialism. The opening of China to Western trade concessions ultimately led to a revolution and the overthrow of the Manchu dynasty. Japan adopted Western military, educational, and governmental ways, even becoming an imperialist power in its own right. At the same time, Western treatment of non-Western peoples as racial inferiors caused educated, non-Western elites in the colonies to initiate movements for national independence. Before these movements could be successful, however, the power that Europeans had achieved through their mass armies and technological superiority had to be weakened. The Europeans soon inadvertently accomplished this task by demolishing their own civilization on the battlegrounds of Europe in World War I.

This war was a result of the growing tensions that arose as a result of national rivalry. In competing with and fearing each other, the European nations formed defensive alliances

that helped maintain a balance of power but also led to the creation of large armies, enormous military establishments, and immense arsenals. The alliances also generated tensions that were unleashed when Europeans were unable to resolve a series of crises, especially in the Balkans, and rushed into the catastrophic carnage of World War I.

The cultural revolutions before 1914 had also produced anxiety and a crisis of confidence in European civilization. Albert Einstein showed that time and space were relative to the observer, that matter was simply another form of energy, and that the old Newtonian view of the universe was no longer valid. Sigmund Freud argued that human behavior was governed not by reason but by the unconscious, adding to the uncertainties of the age. Some intellectuals used the ideas of Charles Darwin to argue that in the struggle of race and nations the fittest survive. Collectively, these new ideas helped create a modern consciousness that questioned most Europeans' optimistic faith in reason, the rational structure of nature, and the certainty of progress. As we shall see in the next two chapters, the devastating experiences of World War I would turn this culture of uncertainty into a way of life after 1918.

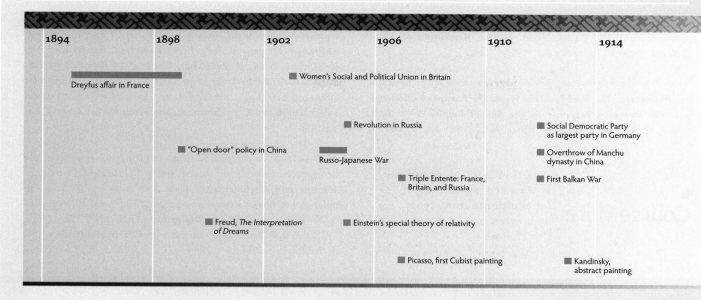

| 1894 | 1898 | 1902 | 1906 | 1910 | 1914 |

- Dreyfus affair in France
- Women's Social and Political Union in Britain
- Revolution in Russia
- Social Democratic Party as largest party in Germany
- "Open door" policy in China
- Russo-Japanese War
- Overthrow of Manchu dynasty in China
- Triple Entente: France, Britain, and Russia
- First Balkan War
- Freud, *The Interpretation of Dreams*
- Einstein's special theory of relativity
- Picasso, first Cubist painting
- Kandinsky, abstract painting

CHAPTER REVIEW

Upon Reflection

Q How is Modernism evident in literature and the arts between 1894 and 1914? How do these literary and artistic products reflect the political and social developments of the age?

Q One historian has written that the history of colonial expansion was "one of long-range schemes that appear almost accidental when viewed singly." Does the practice of imperialism in Africa and Asia substantiate this statement? Why or why not?

Q What might European diplomats have done between 1894 and 1914 to avoid war?

Key Terms

relativity theory (p. 738)
revolutionary socialism (p. 740)
general strike (p. 740)
psychoanalysis (p. 740)
social Darwinism (p. 741)
volkish thought (p. 742)
anticlericalism (p. 742)
Modernism (p. 743)
Impressionism (p. 744)
Post-Impressionism (p. 745)
Cubism (p. 747)
abstract painting (p. 747)
political democracy (p. 749)
suffragists (p. 750)
anti-Semitism (p. 752)
pogroms (p. 752)
Zionism (p. 753)

transformism (p. 755)
new imperialism (p. 759)
economic imperialism (p. 761)

Suggestions for Further Reading

INTELLECTUAL AND CULTURAL DEVELOPMENTS On Modernism, see **P. Gay, *Modernism: The Lure of Heresy*** (New York, 2007). Two well-regarded studies of Freud are **P. D. Kramer, *Sigmund Freud: Inventor of the Modern Mind*** (New York, 2006), and **P. Gay, *Freud: A Life for Our Time,*** rev. ed. (New York, 2006). Nietzsche is examined in **L. Spinks, *Friedrich Nietzsche*** (London, 2003). On Bergson, see **S. Guerlac, *Thinking in Time: An Introduction to Henri Bergson*** (Ithaca, N.Y., 2006). Very valuable on modern art are **M. Powell-Jones, *Impressionism*** (London, 1994); **G. Crepaldi, *The Impressionists*** (New York, 2002); **B. Denvir, *Post-Impressionism*** (New York, 1992); and **T. Parsons, *Post-Impressionism: The Rise of Modern Art*** (London, 1992).

POLITICS: NEW DIRECTIONS The rise of feminism is examined in **J. Rendall, *The Origins of Modern Feminism: Women in Britain, France and the United States*** (London, 1985). On the "new woman," see **M. L. Roberts, *Disruptive Acts: The New Woman in Fin-de-Siècle France*** (Chicago, 2002), and **A. Richardson** and **C. Willis, eds., *The New Woman in Fiction and Fact,*** rev. ed. (New York, 2007). The subject of modern anti-Semitism is covered in **A. S. Lindemann, *Esau's Tears: Modern Anti-Semitism and the Rise of the Jews*** (New York, 1997). European racism is analyzed in **N. MacMaster, *Racism in Europe, 1870–2000*** (New York, 2001). Anti-Semitism in France is the subject of **L. Derfler, *The Dreyfus Affair*** (Westport, Conn., 2002). On Theodor Herzl, see **J. Kornberg, *Theodor Herzl: From Assimilation to Zionism*** (Bloomington, Ind., 1993). The beginnings of the Labour Party are examined in **R. J. H. Stewart, *Origins of the British Labour Party*** (New York, 2003).

There are good introductions to the political world of William II's Germany in **T. A. Kohut, *Wilhelm II and the Germans: A Study in Leadership*** (New York, 1991), and **C. Clark, *Kaiser Wilhelm II*** (London, 2000). On Russia, see **A. Ascher, *Revolution of 1905: A Short History*** (Stanford, Calif., 2004).

THE NEW IMPERIALISM For broad perspectives on imperialism, see **P. Curtain, *The World and the West: The European Challenge and the Overseas Response in the Age of Empire*** (New York, 2000); **M. W. Doyle, *Empires*** (Ithaca, N.Y., 1986); and **P. Darby,** *Three Faces of Imperialism: British and American Approaches to Asia and Africa, 1870–1970* (New Haven, Conn., 1987). Different aspects of imperialism are covered in **A. Burton, *Burdens of History: British Feminists, Indian Women, and Imperial Culture, 1865–1915*** (Chapel Hill, N.C., 1994); **P. Levine, *Gender and Empire*** (Oxford, 2004); **N. Ferguson, *Empire: The Rise and Demise of the British World Order*** (New York, 2002), a broad survey that emphasizes how the British Empire gave rise to many aspects of the modern world; and **T. Pakhenham, *The Scramble for Africa*** (New York, 1991).

INTERNATIONAL RIVALRY Two fundamental works on the diplomatic history of the period are **W. L. Langer, *European Alliances and Alignments,*** 2nd ed. (New York, 1966), and ***The Diplomacy of Imperialism,*** 2nd ed. (New York, 1965). Also valuable are **N. Rich, *Great Power Diplomacy: 1814–1914*** (New York, 1991), and **C. J. Bartlett, *Peace, War and European Powers,*** rev. ed. (New York, 1996).

Visit the CourseMate website at www.cengagebrain.com for additional study tools and review materials for this chapter.

1. Sigmund Freud's work led him to propose that

    (A) individuals are helpless without guidance from a higher power.
    (B) individuals were made to be controlled by the rational thoughts in their minds.
    (C) human beings no longer need God's guidance and can find answers to life's questions within themselves.
    (D) sexual roles in society have little effect on humans' intentions.
    (E) medical intervention is necessary for mental health.

2. The suffragist movement

    (A) was a unified women's movement to win the right to vote in Great Britain.
    (B) limited its tactics to lobbying Parliament and holding peaceful rallies to bring attention to the plight of women.
    (C) was often feared by men, who thought the women's vote would lead Britain into political uncertainty.
    (D) was openly accepted by all women and received popular support from men as well.
    (E) was largely limited to Britain, as women on the Continent were not interested in extending the franchise.

3. Which of the following best describes the scientific achievements of Marie Curie, Max Planck, and Albert Einstein?

    (A) They successfully combined science and religion in their work.
    (B) Their theories, supported by Darwin, suggested the importance of limiting scientific practice to men.
    (C) Their theories fueled the concept that life was pointless and random.
    (D) They changed scientific thought about atoms and introduced the theory of relativity.
    (E) They won equal standing for women and their contributions to the field of science.

4. Some European Jews gained political freedoms by the end of the nineteenth century; at the same time,

    (A) their right to vote was won by the religious activist Theodore Herzl.
    (B) they found comfort living within Europe and outwardly refused the land given by the Balfour Declaration.
    (C) their political and social activism won additional freedoms by the beginning of the twentieth century.
    (D) many Jews in western Europe secured complete religious and political freedom.
    (E) their fellow Europeans remained generally anti-Semitic and sought a homeland for the Jews outside Europe.

5. The Dreyfus affair in France

    (A) highlighted the religious tensions still existing between Protestants and Catholics.
    (B) resulted in the complete separation of church and state.
    (C) was written about by Émile Zola, who supported the actions of the French government.
    (D) increased the power and stability of the Third Republic.
    (E) led to the creation of a new coalition government uniting the moderate and radical republicans.

6. The scramble for Africa resulted in

    (A) Great Britain claiming East and South Africa, France controlling western Africa, and other European states taking control of Central Africa.
    (B) America seeking new colonial holdings in the Middle East.
    (C) renewed attempts by European states to re-colonize South America.
    (D) the sub-Saharan African nations uniting against the imperialists.
    (E) a decrease in racism across the African continent.

7. Under David Lloyd George's leadership, Great Britain achieved all of the following EXCEPT

    (A) passage of the National Insurance Act of 1911.
    (B) a decrease in the tax burden on the wealthy.
    (C) passage of a grant of home rule to Ireland.
    (D) abandonment of the principle of *laissez-faire*.
    (E) rejection of Fabian socialism and Marxism.

8. Herbert Spencer's application of social Darwinism

    (A) helped many others accept the new theory of evolution.
    (B) was embraced by many in the countries colonized by Europe.
    (C) contributed to racist attitudes against non-Europeans.
    (D) was useful to those who instituted socialist governments.
    (E) was based on the concept of class struggle and the desire of the lower classes to rise up against their oppressors.

9. All of the following were true of Germany in 1914
EXCEPT

   (A) a Pan-German League had emerged within the
       state and had declared its anti-Semitism.
   (B) William II and Bismarck worked closely together as
       emperor and chancellor.
   (C) the Social Democratic Party was the largest
       political party in the Reichstag.
   (D) Germany led Europe in industrial output.
   (E) Germany had the strongest military on the
       Continent.

10. "I teach you the Superman. Man is something that is
    to be surpassed." This statement by Nietzsche is best
    characterized by the concept of

    (A) atheism.
    (B) rationalism.
    (C) progressivism.
    (D) existentialism.
    (E) voidism.

11. Which of the following best explains the emergence of
    the new imperialism?

    (A) European nations had a great need to extract
        raw resources from colonies in order to expand
        industrial production.
    (B) European nations had a burning desire to showcase
        their theater to the world and to secure their
        reputation as centers of high culture.
    (C) Europeans were largely racist and wanted to
        conquer all of the inferior races of the non-
        European world.
    (D) European nations wished to map the vast parts of
        the world that remained unexplored.
    (E) Industrialized nations needed new lands to
        produce weapons for a global war effort.

12. Each of the following contributed to the issuing of the
    October Manifesto EXCEPT

    (A) Russian failure in the Russo-Japanese War.
    (B) lack of political representation for the middle class.
    (C) the march on the Winter Palace on "Bloody
        Sunday."
    (D) an increase in wages for the middle class that
        angered the aristocrats.
    (E) oppressive working conditions in urban areas.

13. During the reign of Tsar Nicholas II, Sergei Witte was
    responsible for

    (A) uniting the socialists and Marxists.
    (B) increasing taxation on the working class.
    (C) Russia's invasion of Japan.
    (D) organizing the serfs against the tsar.
    (E) Russia's rapid industrialization and railroad
        construction.

14. The Impressionists and Post-Impressionists

    (A) both aimed to portray emotional experiences and
        have the viewer personally connect with their
        paintings.
    (B) both desired to give a realistic depiction of nature
        and the human form.
    (C) both began in France; however, the Post-
        Impressionists split from their predecessors in
        their desire to portray emotion more than reality.
    (D) opened the door for those not classically trained in
        art to excel in the field.
    (E) worked in reaction to what they saw as the ugliness
        of the industrial cities and the brutishness of
        human beings.

Canadian soldiers prepare for an attack at the Battle of the Somme.

The Beginning of the Twentieth-Century Crisis: War and Revolution

CHAPTER OUTLINE AND FOCUS QUESTIONS

The Road to World War I

Q What were the long-range and immediate causes of World War I?

The War

Q What did the belligerents expect at the beginning of World War I, and why did the course of the war turn out to be so different from their expectations? How did World War I affect the belligerents' governmental and political institutions, economic affairs, and social life?

War and Revolution

Q What were the causes of the Russian Revolution of 1917, and why did the Bolsheviks prevail in the civil war and gain control of Russia?

The Peace Settlement

Q What were the objectives of the chief participants at the Paris Peace Conference of 1919, and how closely did the final settlement reflect these objectives?

⌐ CRITICAL THINKING ══════════════

Q What was the relationship between World War I and the Russian Revolution?

ON JULY 1, 1916, British and French infantry forces attacked German defensive lines along a 25-mile front near the Somme River in France. Each soldier carried almost 70 pounds of equipment, making it "impossible to move much quicker than a slow walk." German machine guns soon opened fire: "We were able to see our comrades move forward in an attempt to cross No-Man's Land, only to be mown down like meadow grass," recalled one British soldier. "I felt sick at the sight of this carnage and remember weeping."[1] In one day, more than 21,000 British soldiers died. After six months of fighting, the British had advanced 5 miles; one million British, French, and German soldiers had been killed or wounded.

Philip Gibbs, an English war correspondent, described what he saw in the German trenches that the British forces overran: "Victory! . . . Some of the German dead were young boys, too young to be killed for old men's crimes, and others might have been old or young. One could not tell because they had no faces, and were just masses of raw flesh in rags of uniforms. Legs and arms lay separate without any bodies thereabout."[2]

World War I (1914–1918) was the defining event of the twentieth century. It devastated the prewar economic, social, and political order of Europe, and its uncertain outcome served to prepare the way for an even more destructive war. Overwhelmed by the size of its battles, the number of its casualties, and the extent of its impact on all facets of European life, contemporaries referred to it simply as the Great War.

The Great War was all the more disturbing to Europeans because it came after a period that many believed to have been an age of progress. There had been international crises before 1914, but somehow Europeans had managed to avoid serious and prolonged military confrontations. When smaller European states had gone to war, as in the Balkans in 1912 and 1913, the great European powers had shown the ability to keep the conflict localized. Material prosperity and a fervid belief in scientific and technological progress had convinced many people that Europe stood on the verge of creating the utopia that humans had dreamed of for centuries. The historian Arnold Toynbee expressed what the pre–World War I era had meant to his generation:

> [It was expected] that life throughout the World would become more rational, more humane, and more democratic and that, slowly, but surely, political democracy would produce greater social justice. We had also expected that the progress of science and technology would make mankind richer, and that this increasing wealth would gradually spread from a minority to a majority. We had expected that all this would happen peacefully. In fact we thought that mankind's course was set for an earthly paradise.[3]

After 1918, it was no longer possible to maintain naive illusions about the progress of Western civilization. As World War I was followed by the destructiveness of World War II and the mass murder machines of totalitarian regimes, it became all too apparent that instead of a utopia, European civilization had become a nightmare. The Great War resulted not only in great loss of life and property but also in the annihilation of one of the basic intellectual precepts on which Western civilization had been thought to have been founded—the belief in progress. A sense of hopelessness and despair soon replaced blind faith in progress. World War I and the revolutions it spawned can properly be seen as the first stage in the crisis of the twentieth century.

The Road to World War I

Q **Focus Question:** What were the long-range and immediate causes of World War I?

On June 28, 1914, the heir to the Austrian throne, Archduke Francis Ferdinand, was assassinated in the Bosnian city of Sarajevo. Although this event precipitated the confrontation between Austria and Serbia that led to World War I, war was not inevitable. Previous assassinations of European leaders had not led to war, and European statesmen had managed to localize such conflicts. Although the decisions that European statesmen made during this crisis were crucial in leading to war, there were also long-range underlying forces that were propelling Europeans toward armed conflict.

Nationalism

In the first half of the nineteenth century, liberals had maintained that the organization of European states along national lines would lead to a peaceful Europe based on a sense of international fraternity. They had been very wrong. The system of nation-states that had emerged in Europe in the second half of the nineteenth century led not to cooperation but to competition. Rivalries over colonial and commercial interests intensified during an era of frenzied imperialist expansion, and the division of Europe's great powers into two loose alliances (Germany, Austria, and Italy and France, Great Britain, and Russia) only added to the tensions (see Map 25.1). The series of crises that tested these alliances in the early years of the new century had taught European states a dangerous lesson. Governments that had exercised restraint in order to avoid war wound up being publicly humiliated, whereas those that went to the brink of war to maintain their national interests had often been praised for having preserved national honor. In either case, by 1914, the major European states had come to believe that their allies were important and that their security depended on supporting those allies, even when they took foolish risks.

Diplomacy based on brinkmanship was especially frightening in view of the nature of the European state system. Each nation-state regarded itself as sovereign, subject to no higher interest or authority. Each state was motivated by its own self-interest and success. As Emperor William II of Germany remarked, "In questions of honor and vital interests, you don't consult others." Such attitudes made war an ever-present possibility, particularly since most statesmen considered war an acceptable way to preserve the power of their national states. And within each state, there were circles of political and military leaders who thought that war was inevitable and provided an opportunity to achieve their goals. In Germany, there were those who advocated the creation of a German empire by acquiring parts of Russia and possibly even parts of Belgium and France. France wished to regain control of Alsace-Lorraine, which had been seized by the Germans in the Franco-Prussian War. Austria-Hungary sought to prevent Serbia from creating a large Serbian state at the expense of its own multinational empire. Britain sought to preserve its world empire, and Russia felt compelled to maintain its great power status by being a protector of its fellow Slavic peoples in the Balkans.

Internal Dissent

The growth of nationalism in the nineteenth century had yet another serious consequence. Not all ethnic groups had achieved the goal of nationhood. Slavic minorities in the Balkans and the Austrian Empire, for example, still dreamed of creating their own national states. So did the Irish in the British Empire and the Poles in the Russian Empire.

National aspirations, however, were not the only source of internal strife at the beginning of the twentieth century.

MAP 25.1 **Europe in 1914.** By 1914, two alliances dominated Europe: the Triple Entente of Britain, France, and Russia and the Triple Alliance of Germany, Austria-Hungary, and Italy. Russia sought to bolster fellow Slavs in Serbia, whereas Austria-Hungary was intent on increasing its power in the Balkans and thwarting Serbia's ambitions. Thus, the Balkans became the flash point for World War I.

Q *Which nonaligned nations were positioned between the two alliances?*

View an animated version of this map or related maps on the CourseMate website.

Socialist labor movements had grown more powerful and were increasingly inclined to use strikes, even violent ones, to achieve their goals. Some conservative leaders, alarmed at the increase in labor strife and class division, even feared that European nations were on the verge of revolution. Did these statesmen opt for war in 1914 because they believed that "prosecuting an active foreign policy," as one leader expressed it, would smother "internal troubles"? Some historians have argued that the desire to suppress internal disorder may have encouraged some leaders to take the plunge into war in 1914.

Militarism

The growth of large mass armies after 1900 not only heightened the existing tensions in Europe but made it inevitable that if war did come, it would be highly destructive. **Conscription** had been established as a regular practice in most Western countries before 1914 (the United States and Britain were major exceptions). European military machines had doubled in size between 1890 and 1914. With its 1.3 million men, the Russian army had grown to be the largest, but the French and Germans were not far behind with 900,000 each. The British, Italian, and Austrian armies numbered between 250,000 and 500,000 soldiers. Most European land armies were filled with peasants, since many young, urban working-class males were unable to pass the physical examinations required for military service.

Militarism, however, involved more than just large armies. As armies grew, so did the influence of military leaders, who drew up vast and complex plans for quickly mobilizing millions of men and enormous quantities of supplies in the event of war. Fearful that changes in these plans would create chaos in the armed forces, military leaders insisted that their plans could not be altered. In the crises during the summer of 1914, the generals' lack of flexibility forced European political leaders to make decisions for military instead of political reasons.

The Outbreak of War: The Summer of 1914

Militarism, nationalism, and the desire to stifle internal dissent may all have played a role in the coming of World War I, but the decisions made by European leaders in the summer of 1914 directly precipitated the conflict. It was another crisis in the Balkans that forced this predicament on European statesmen.

ANOTHER CRISIS IN THE BALKANS   As we have seen, states in southeastern Europe had struggled to free themselves from Ottoman rule in the course of the nineteenth and early twentieth centuries. But the rivalry between Austria-Hungary and Russia for domination of these new states created serious tensions in the region. The crises between 1908 and 1913 had only intensified the antagonisms.

By 1914, Serbia, supported by Russia, was determined to create a large, independent Slavic state in the Balkans, but Austria, which had its own Slavic minorities to contend with, was equally set on preventing that possibility. Many Europeans perceived the inherent dangers in this combination of Serbian ambition bolstered by Russian opposition to Austria and Austria's conviction that Serbia's success would mean the end of its empire. The British ambassador to Vienna wrote in 1913:

> Serbia will some day set Europe by the ears, and bring about a universal war on the Continent.... I cannot tell you how exasperated people are getting here at the continual worry which that little country causes to Austria under encouragement from Russia.... It will be lucky if Europe succeeds in avoiding war as a result of the present crisis. The next time a Serbian crisis arises,... I feel sure that Austria-Hungary will refuse to admit of any Russian interference in the dispute and that she will proceed to settle her differences with her little neighbor by herself.[4]

It was against this backdrop of mutual distrust and hatred between Austria-Hungary and Russia, on the one hand, and Austria-Hungary and Serbia, on the other, that the events of the summer of 1914 were played out.

ASSASSINATION OF FRANCIS FERDINAND   The assassination of the Austrian Archduke Francis Ferdinand and his wife, Sophia, on June 28, 1914, was carried out by a Bosnian activist who worked for the Black Hand, a Serbian terrorist organization dedicated to the creation of a pan-Slavic kingdom. Although the Austrian government did not know whether the Serbian government had been directly involved in the archduke's assassination, it saw an opportunity to "render Serbia impotent once and for all by a display of force," as the Austrian foreign minister put it. Fearful of Russian intervention on Serbia's behalf, Austrian leaders sought the backing of their German allies. Emperor William II and his chancellor, Theobald von Bethmann-Hollweg (TAY-oh-bahlt fun BET-mun-HOHL-vek), responded with the infamous "blank check," their assurance that Austria-Hungary could rely on Germany's "full support," even if "matters went to the length of a war between Austria-Hungary and Russia." Much historical debate has focused on this "blank check" extended to the Austrians. Did the Germans realize that an Austrian-Serbian war could lead to a wider war? If so, did they actually want one? Historians are still divided on the answers to these questions.

Led by Franz Conrad von Hötzendorf (FRAHNTS KON-raht fun HEHT-sen-dorf), chief of the Austro-Hungarian General Staff, who thought war with Serbia was both necessary and inevitable, Austrian leaders had already decided by July 14 to send Serbia an ultimatum that threatened war. But the Austrians decided to wait until the end of the official French state visit to Russia before issuing the ultimatum. On July 23, the day the French president left Russia, Austrian leaders issued their ultimatum to Serbia. Their demands were so extreme that Serbia had little choice but to reject some of them in order

CHRONOLOGY   The Road to World War I

	1914
Assassination of Archduke Francis Ferdinand	June 28
Austria's ultimatum to Serbia	July 23
Austria declares war on Serbia	July 28
Russia mobilizes	July 29
Germany's ultimatum to Russia	July 31
Germany declares war on Russia	August 1
Germany declares war on France	August 3
German troops invade Belgium	August 4
Great Britain declares war on Germany	August 4

to preserve its sovereignty. Austria then declared war on Serbia on July 28. Although Austria had hoped to keep the war limited to Serbia and Austria in order to ensure its success in the Balkans, these hopes soon vanished.

DECLARATIONS OF WAR   Still smarting from its humiliation in the Bosnian crisis of 1908, Russia was determined to support Serbia's cause. On July 28, Tsar Nicholas II ordered partial **mobilization** of the Russian army against Austria. At this point, the rigidity of the military war plans played havoc with diplomatic and political decisions. The Russian General Staff informed the tsar that their mobilization plans were based on a war against both Germany and Austria simultaneously. They could not execute partial mobilization without creating chaos in the army. Consequently, the Russian government ordered full mobilization of the Russian army on July 29, knowing that the Germans would consider this an act of war against them (see the box on p. 779). Germany responded to Russian mobilization with its own ultimatum that the Russians must halt their mobilization within twelve hours. When the Russians ignored it, Germany declared war on Russia on August 1.

At this stage of the conflict, German war plans determined whether France would become involved in the war. Under the guidance of General Alfred von Schlieffen (SHLEE-fun), chief of staff from 1891 to 1905, the German General Staff had devised a military plan based on the assumption of a two-front war with France and Russia, since the two powers had formed a

The Schlieffen Plan

"You Have to Bear the Responsibility for War or Peace"

After Austria declared war on Serbia on July 28, 1914, Russian support of Serbia and German support of Austria threatened to escalate the conflict in the Balkans into a wider war. As we can see in these last-minute telegrams between the Russians and the Germans, neither side was able to accept the other's line of reasoning.

━━━━━━ ━━━ ━━━━━━

Communications between Berlin and Saint Petersburg on the Eve of World War I

Emperor William II to Tsar Nicholas II, July 28, 10:45 P.M.

I have heard with the greatest anxiety of the impression which is caused by the action of Austria-Hungary against Servia [Serbia]. The inscrupulous agitation which has been going on for years in Servia, has led to the revolting crime of which Archduke Franz Ferdinand has become a victim. The spirit which made the Servians murder their own King and his consort still dominates that country. Doubtless You will agree with me that both of us, You as well as I, and all other sovereigns, have a common interest to insist that all those who are responsible for this horrible murder shall suffer their deserved punishment....

Your most sincere and devoted friend and cousin

(Signed)
Wilhelm

Tsar Nicholas II to Emperor William II, July 29, 1:00 P.M.

I am glad that You are back in Germany. In this serious moment I ask You earnestly to help me. An ignominious war has been declared against a weak country and in Russia the indignation which I full share is tremendous. I fear that very soon I shall be unable to resist the pressure exercised upon me and that I shall be forced to take measures which will lead to war. To prevent a calamity as a European war would be, I urge You in the name of our old friendship to do all in Your power to restrain Your ally from going too far.

(Signed)
Nicolas

Emperor William II to Tsar Nicholas II, July 29, 6:30 P.M.

I have received Your telegram and I share Your desire for the conservation of peace. However: I cannot—as I told You in my first telegram—consider the action of Austria-Hungary as an "ignominious war." Austria-Hungary knows from experience that the promises of Servia as long as they are merely on paper are entirely unreliable.... I believe that a direct understanding is possible and desirable between Your Government and Vienna, an understanding which I—as I have already telegraphed You—my Government endeavors to aid with all possible effort. Naturally military measures by Russia, which might be construed as a menace by Austria-Hungary, would accelerate a calamity which both of us desire to avoid and would undermine my position as mediator which—upon Your appeal to my friendship and aid—I willingly accepted.

(Signed)
Wilhelm

Emperor William II to Tsar Nicholas II, July 30, 1:00 A.M.

My Ambassador has instructions to direct the attention of Your Government to the dangers and serious consequences of a mobilization. I have told You the same in my last telegram. Austria-Hungary has mobilized only against Servia, and only a part of her army. If Russia, as seems to be the case, according to Your advice and that of Your Government, mobilizes against Austria-Hungary, the part of the mediator with which You have entrusted me in such friendly manner and which I have accepted upon Your express desire, is threatened if not made impossible. The entire weight of decision now rests upon Your shoulders, You have to bear the responsibility for war or peace.

(Signed)
Wilhelm

German Chancellor to German Ambassador at Saint Petersburg, July 31, URGENT

In spite of negotiations still pending and although we have up to this hour made no preparations for mobilization, Russia has mobilized her entire army and navy, hence also against us. On account of these Russian measures, we have been forced, for the safety of the country, to proclaim the threatening state of war, which does not yet imply mobilization. Mobilization, however, is bound to follow if Russia does not stop every measure of war against us and against Austria-Hungary within 12 hours, and notifies us definitely to this effect. Please to communicate this at once to M. Sasonof and wire hour of communication.

Q How do the telegrams exchanged between William II and Nicholas II reveal why the Europeans foolishly went to war in 1914? What do they tell us about the nature of the relationship between these two monarchs?

---

military alliance in 1894. The Schlieffen Plan called for a minimal troop deployment against Russia while most of the German army would make a rapid invasion of western France by way of neutral Belgium. After the planned quick defeat of the French, the German army expected to redeploy to the east against Russia. Under the Schlieffen Plan, Germany could not mobilize its troops solely against Russia and therefore declared war on France on August 3 after issuing an ultimatum to Belgium on August 2 demanding the right of German troops to pass through Belgian territory. On August 4, Great Britain declared war on Germany, officially over this violation of Belgian neutrality but in fact over the British desire to maintain world power. As one British diplomat argued, if Germany and Austria were to win the war, "what would be the position of a friendless England?" By August 4, all the great powers of Europe were at war. Through all the maneuvering of the last few days before the war, one fact stands out—all the great powers seemed willing to risk war. They were not disappointed.

The War

Q **FOCUS QUESTIONS:** What did the belligerents expect at the beginning of World War I, and why did the course of the war turn out to be so different from their expectations? How did World War I affect the belligerents' governmental and political institutions, economic affairs, and social life?

Before 1914, many political leaders had become convinced that war involved so many political and economic risks that it was not worth fighting. Others had believed that "rational" diplomats could control any situation and prevent the outbreak of war. At the beginning of August 1914, both of these prewar illusions were shattered, but the new illusions that replaced them soon proved to be equally foolish.

1914–1915: Illusions and Stalemate

Many Europeans went to war in 1914 with remarkable enthusiasm (see the box on p. 781). Government propaganda had been successful in stirring up national antagonisms before the war. Now, in August 1914, the urgent pleas of governments for defense against aggressors found many receptive ears in every belligerent nation. Middle-class crowds, often composed of young students, were especially enthusiastic, but workers in the cities and peasants in the countryside were considerably less eager for war. Once the war began, however, most people seemed genuinely convinced that their nation's cause was just. Even domestic differences were temporarily shelved in the midst of war fever. Socialists had long derided "imperialist war" as a blow against the common interests that united the working classes of all countries. Nationalism, however, proved more powerful than working-class solidarity in

The Excitement of War. World War I was greeted with incredible enthusiasm. Each of the major belligerents was convinced of the rightness of its cause. Everywhere in Europe, jubilant civilians sent their troops off to war with joyous fervor as is evident in the photograph at the top, showing French troops marching off to war. The photograph below shows a group of German soldiers marching off to battle with civilian support. The belief that the soldiers would be home by Christmas proved to be a pathetic illusion.

the summer of 1914 as socialist parties everywhere dropped plans for strikes and workers expressed their readiness to fight for their country. The German Social Democrats, for example, decided that it was imperative to "safeguard the culture and independence of our own country."

A new set of illusions fed the enthusiasm for war. Almost everyone in August 1914 believed that the war

The Excitement of War

The incredible outpouring of patriotic enthusiasm that greeted the declaration of war at the beginning of August 1914 demonstrated the power that nationalistic feeling had attained at the beginning of the twentieth century. Many Europeans seemingly believed that the war had given them a higher purpose, a renewed dedication to the greatness of their nations. These selections are taken from three sources: the autobiography of Stefan Zweig, an Austrian writer; the memoirs of Robert Graves, a British writer; and a letter by a German soldier, Walter Limmer, to his parents.

→→ ⊟⊹⊟ →→

Stefan Zweig, *The World of Yesterday*

The next morning I was in Austria. In every station placards had been put up announcing general mobilization. The trains were filled with fresh recruits, banners were flying, music sounded, and in Vienna I found the entire city in a tumult.... There were parades in the street, flags, ribbons, and music burst forth everywhere, young recruits were marching triumphantly, their faces lighting up at the cheering....

And to be truthful, I must acknowledge that there was a majestic, rapturous, and even seductive something in this first outbreak of the people from which one could escape only with difficulty. And in spite of all my hatred and aversion for war, I should not like to have missed the memory of those days. As never before, thousands and hundreds of thousands felt what they should have felt in peace time, that they belonged together. A city of two million, a country of nearly fifty million, in that hour felt that they were participating in world history, in a moment which would never recur, and that each one was called upon to cast his infinitesimal self into the glowing mass, there to be purified of all selfishness. All differences of class, rank, and language were flooded over at that moment by the rushing feeling of fraternity....

What did the great mass know of war in 1914, after nearly half a century of peace? They did not know war, they had hardly given it a thought. It had become legendary, and distance had made it seem romantic and heroic. They still saw it in the perspective of their school readers and of paintings in museums; brilliant cavalry attacks in glittering uniforms, the fatal shot always straight through the heart, the entire campaign a resounding march of victory—"We'll be home at Christmas," the recruits shouted laughingly to their mothers in August of 1914.... A rapid excursion into the romantic, a wild, manly adventure—that is how the war of 1914 was painted in the imagination of the simple man, and the younger people were honestly afraid that they might miss this most wonderful and exciting experience of their lives; that is why they hurried and thronged to the colors, and that is why they shouted and sang in the trains that carried them to the slaughter; wildly and feverishly the red wave of blood coursed through the veins of the entire nation.

Robert Graves, *Goodbye to All That*

I had just finished with Charterhouse and gone up to Harlech, when England declared war on Germany. A day or two later I decided to enlist. In the first place, though the papers predicted only a very short war—over by Christmas at the outside—I hoped that it might last long enough to delay my going to Oxford in October, which I dreaded. Nor did I work out the possibilities of getting actively engaged in the fighting, expecting garrison service at home, while the regular forces were away. In the second place, I was outraged to read of the Germans' cynical violation of Belgian neutrality. Though I discounted perhaps twenty per cent of the atrocity details as wartime exaggeration, that was not, of course, sufficient.

Walter Limmer, Letter to His Parents

In any case I mean to go into this business.... That is the simple duty of every one of us. And this feeling is universal among the soldiers, especially since the night when England's declaration of war was announced in the barracks. We none of us got to sleep till three o'clock in the morning, we were so full of excitement, fury, and enthusiasm. It is a joy to go to the Front with such comrades. We are bound to be victorious! Nothing else is possible in the face of such determination to win. ⊱

Q What do these excerpts reveal about the motivations of people to join and support World War I? Do the excerpts reveal anything about the power of nationalism in Europe in the early twentieth century?

would be over in a few weeks. People were reminded that the major battles in European wars since 1815 had in fact ended in a matter of weeks, conveniently overlooking the American Civil War (1861–1865), which was the true prototype for World War I. The illusion of a short war was also bolstered by another illusion, the belief that in an age of modern industry, war could not be conducted for more than a few months without destroying a nation's economy. Both the soldiers who exuberantly boarded the trains for the war front in August 1914 and the jubilant citizens who bombarded them with flowers when they departed believed that the warriors would be home by Christmas.

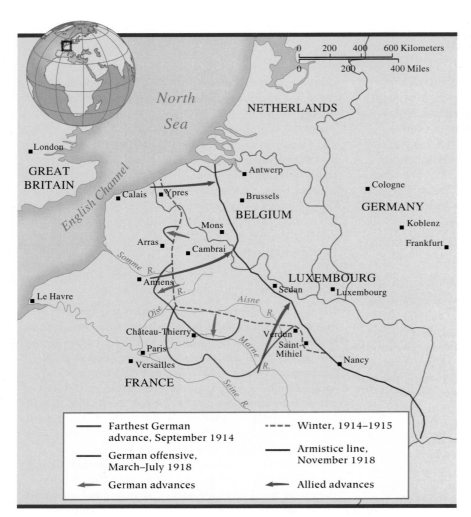

MAP 25.2 **The Western Front, 1914–1918.** The Western Front was the site of massive carnage: millions of soldiers died in offensives and counteroffensives as they moved battle lines a few miles at a time in France and Belgium from 1914 to 1917. Soldiers in the trenches were often surrounded by the rotting bodies of dead comrades.

Q *What is the approximate distance between the armistice line near Sedan and the closest approach of the Germans to Paris?*

View an animated version of this map or related maps on the CourseMate website.

Map legend:
- Farthest German advance, September 1914
- German offensive, March–July 1918
- German advances
- Winter, 1914–1915
- Armistice line, November 1918
- Allied advances

Then, too, war held a fatal attraction for many people. To some, war was an exhilarating release from humdrum bourgeois existence, from a "world grown old and cold and weary," as one poet wrote. To some, war meant a glorious adventure, as a young German student wrote to his parents: "My dear ones, be proud that you live in such a time and in such a nation and that you . . . have the privilege of sending those you love into so glorious a battle."[5] And finally, some believed that the war would have a redemptive effect, that millions would abandon their petty preoccupations with material life, ridding the nation of selfishness and sparking a national rebirth based on self-sacrifice, heroism, and nobility. All of these illusions about war died painful deaths on the battlefields of World War I.

WAR IN THE WEST German hopes for a quick end to the war rested on a military gamble. The Schlieffen Plan had called for the German army to proceed through Belgium into northern France with a vast encircling movement that would sweep around Paris and surround most of the French army. But the plan suffered a major defect from the beginning; it called for a strong right flank for the encircling of Paris, but German military leaders, concerned about a Russian invasion in the east, had moved forces from the right flank to strengthen the German army in the east.

On August 4, German troops crossed into Belgium. They encountered little resistance, but when they did, they responded with fierce measures, burning villages, killing civilians, and senselessly destroying a good part of the city of Louvain, including the university library.

By the first week of September, the Germans had reached the Marne River, only 20 miles from Paris. The Germans seemed on the verge of success but had underestimated the speed with which the British would be able to mobilize and put troops into battle in France. An unexpected counterattack by British and French forces under the French commander General Joseph Joffre (ZHUFF-ruh) stopped the Germans at the First Battle of the Marne (September 6–10) east of Paris (see Map 25.2). The German troops fell back, but the exhausted French army was unable to pursue its advantage. The war quickly turned into a stalemate as neither the Germans nor the French could dislodge the other from the trenches they had begun to dig for shelter. Two lines of trenches soon extended from the English Channel to the frontiers of Switzerland. The Western Front had become bogged down in **trench warfare,** which kept both sides in virtually the same positions for four years.

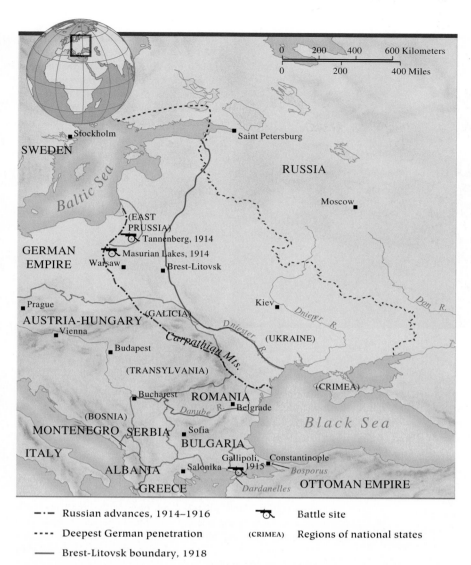

MAP 25.3 The Eastern Front, 1914–1918. Russia made early gains but then was pushed far back into its own territory by the German army. After the Bolsheviks seized power, they negotiated the Treaty of Brest-Litovsk, which extracted Russia from the war at the cost of substantial Russian territory (see Map 25.4).

Q *What is the approximate average distance between the farthest advances of Russia into Germany and the farthest advances of Germany into Russia?*

- –·– Russian advances, 1914–1916
- ---- Deepest German penetration
- —— Brest-Litovsk boundary, 1918
- ⚓ Battle site
- (CRIMEA) Regions of national states

WAR IN THE EAST In contrast to the west, the war in the east was marked by much more mobility, although the cost in lives was equally enormous. At the beginning of the war, the Russian army moved into eastern Germany but was decisively defeated at the Battles of Tannenberg on August 30 and the Masurian Lakes on September 15 (see Map 25.3). These battles established the military reputations of the commanding general, Paul von Hindenburg (POWL fun HIN-den-boork), and his chief of staff, General Erich Ludendorff (LOO-dun-dorf). The Russians were no longer a threat to German territory.

The Austrians, Germany's allies, fared less well initially. They had been defeated by the Russians in Galicia and thrown out of Serbia as well. To make matters worse, the Italians broke their alliance with the Germans and Austrians and entered the war on the Allied side by attacking Austria in May 1915. By this time, the Germans had come to the aid of the Austrians. A German-Austrian army defeated and routed the Russian army in Galicia and pushed the Russians back 300 miles into their own territory. Russian casualties stood at 2.5 million killed, captured, or wounded; the Russians had almost been knocked out of the war. Buoyed by their success, the Germans and Austrians, joined by the Bulgarians in September 1915, attacked and eliminated Serbia from the war.

1916–1917: The Great Slaughter

The successes in the east enabled the Germans to move back to the offensive in the west. The early trenches dug in 1914 had by now become elaborate systems of defense. Both lines of trenches were protected by barbed wire entanglements 3 to 5 feet high and 30 yards wide, concrete machine-gun nests, and mortar batteries, supported further back by heavy artillery. Troops lived in holes in the ground, separated from each other by a "no-man's land."

The unexpected development of trench warfare baffled military leaders, who had been trained to fight wars of

Impact of the Machine Gun. Trench warfare on the Western Front stymied military leaders, who had expected to fight a war based on movement and maneuver. Their efforts to effect a breakthrough by sending masses of men against enemy lines were the height of folly in view of the brutal efficiency of the machine gun. This photograph shows a group of German soldiers in their machine-gun nest.

movement and maneuver. But public outcries for action put them under heavy pressure. The only plan generals could devise was to attempt a breakthrough by throwing masses of men against enemy lines that had first been battered by artillery barrages. Once the decisive breakthrough had been achieved, they thought, they could then return to the war of movement that they knew best. Periodically, the high command on either side would order an offensive that would begin with an artillery barrage to flatten the enemy's barbed wire and leave the enemy in a state of shock. After "softening up" the enemy in this fashion, a mass of soldiers would climb out of their trenches with fixed bayonets and try to work their way toward the enemy trenches. The attacks rarely worked; the machine gun put hordes of men advancing unprotected across open fields at a severe disadvantage. In 1916 and 1917, millions of young men were killed in the search for the elusive breakthrough. In the German offensive at Verdun (ver-DUN) in 1916, the British campaigns on the Somme (SUM) in 1916 and at Ypres (EE-preh) in 1917, and the French attack in Champagne in 1917, the senselessness of trench warfare became all too obvious. In ten months at Verdun, 700,000 men lost their lives over a few square miles of terrain.

DAILY LIFE IN THE TRENCHES Warfare in the trenches of the Western Front produced unimaginable horrors (see the box on p. 786). Many participants commented on the cloud of confusion that covered the battlefields. When attacking soldiers entered "no-man's land," the noise, machine-gun fire, and exploding artillery shells often caused them to panic and lose their bearings; they went forward only because they were carried on by the momentum of the soldiers beside them. Rarely were battles as orderly

Private Donald Fraser, War Journal (1915–1916)

as they were portrayed on military maps and in civilian newspapers.

Battlefields were hellish landscapes of barbed wire, shell holes, mud, and injured and dying men (see the Film & History feature on p. 787). The introduction of poison gas in 1915 produced new forms of injuries, as one British writer described:

> I wish those people who write so glibly about this being a holy war could see a case of mustard gas . . . could see the poor things burnt and blistered all over with great mustard-colored suppurating blisters with blind eyes all sticky . . . and stuck together, and always fighting for breath, with voices a mere whisper, saying that their throats are closing and they know they will choke.[6]

Soldiers in the trenches also lived with the persistent presence of death. Since combat went on for months, they had to carry on in the midst of countless bodies of dead men or the remains of men dismembered by artillery barrages. Many soldiers remembered the stench of decomposing bodies and the swarms of rats that grew fat in the trenches.

Soldiers on the Western Front did not spend all of their time on the front line or in combat when they were on the front line. An infantryman spent one week out of every month in the front-line trenches, one week in the reserve lines, and the remaining two weeks somewhere behind the lines. Daily life in the trenches was predictable. Thirty minutes before sunrise, troops had to "stand to," ready to repel any attack. If no attack was forthcoming that day, the day's routine consisted of breakfast followed by inspection, sentry duty, restoration of the trenches, care of personal items, or whiling away the time as best they could. Soldiers often recalled the boredom of life in the dreary, lice-ridden, muddy or dusty trenches (see Images of Everyday Life on p. 788).

Victims of the Machine Gun. Masses of men weighed down with equipment and advancing slowly across open land made magnificent targets for opponents armed with machine guns. This photograph shows French soldiers moving across a rocky terrain, all open targets for their enemies manning the new weapons.

© Hulton Archive/Getty Images

At many places along the opposing lines of trenches, a "live and let live" system evolved based on the realization that neither side was going to drive out the other anyway. The "live and let live" system resulted in arrangements such as not shelling the latrines or attacking during breakfast. Some parties even worked out agreements to make noise before lesser raids so that the opposing soldiers could retreat to their bunkers.

On both sides, troops produced their own humorous magazines to help pass the time and fulfill the need to laugh in the midst of the daily madness. The British trench magazine, the *B.E.F. Times,* devoted one of its issues to defining military terms. A typical definition was "DUDS—These are of two kinds. A shell on impact failing to explode is called a dud. They are unhappily not as plentiful as the other kind, which often draws a big salary and explodes for no reason. These are plentiful away from the fighting areas."[7] Soldiers' songs also captured a mixture of the sentimental and the frivolous (see the box on p. 789).

The Widening of the War

As another response to the stalemate on the Western Front, both sides looked for new allies that might provide a winning advantage. The Ottoman Empire had already come into the war on Germany's side in the autumn of 1914. Russia, Great Britain, and France declared war on the Ottoman Empire in November. Although the forces of the British Empire attempted to open a Balkan front by landing forces at Gallipoli, southwest of Constantinople, in April 1915, the entry of Bulgaria into the war on the side of the Central Powers (as Germany, Austria-Hungary, and the Ottoman Empire were called) and a disastrous campaign at Gallipoli caused them to withdraw. The Italians, as we have seen, entered the war on the Allied side

after France and Britain promised to further their acquisition of Austrian territory. In the long run, however, Italian military incompetence forced the Allies to come to the assistance of Italy.

A GLOBAL CONFLICT Because the major European powers controlled colonial empires in other parts of the world, the war in Europe soon became a world war. In the Middle East, the British officer T. E. Lawrence (1888–1935), who came to be known as Lawrence of Arabia, incited Arab princes to revolt against their Ottoman overlords in 1916. In 1918, British forces from Egypt and Mesopotamia destroyed the rest of the Ottoman Empire in the Middle East. For their Middle East campaigns, the British mobilized forces from India, Australia, and New Zealand.

The Allies also took advantage of Germany's preoccupation in Europe and lack of naval strength to seize German colonies in Africa. But there too the war did not end quickly. The first British shots of World War I were actually fired in Africa when British African troops moved into the German colony of Togoland near the end of August 1914. But in East Africa, the German commander Colonel Paul von Lettow-Vorbeck (POWL fun LEH-toh-FOR-bek) managed to keep his African troops fighting one campaign after another for four years; he did not surrender until two weeks after the armistice ended the war in Europe.

In the battles in Africa, Allied governments drew mainly on African soldiers, but some states, especially France, also recruited African troops to fight in Europe. The French drafted more than 170,000 West African soldiers, many of whom fought in the trenches on the Western Front. African troops were also used as occupation forces in the German Rhineland at the end of the war. About 80,000 Africans were killed or injured in Europe,

The Reality of War: Trench Warfare

The romantic illusions about the excitement and adventure of war that filled the minds of so many young men who marched off to battle (see the box on p. 781) quickly disintegrated after a short time in the trenches on the Western Front. This description of trench warfare is taken from the most famous novel that emerged from World War I, Erich Maria Remarque's *All Quiet on the Western Front,* published in 1929. Remarque had fought in the trenches in France.

Erich Maria Remarque, *All Quiet on the Western Front*

We wake up in the middle of the night. The earth booms. Heavy fire is falling on us. We crouch into corners. We distinguish shells of every caliber.

Each man lays hold of his things and looks again every minute to reassure himself that they are still there. The dug-out heaves, the night roars and flashes. We look at each other in the momentary flashes of light, and with pale faces and pressed lips shake our heads.

Every man is aware of the heavy shells tearing down the parapet, rooting up the embankment and demolishing the upper layers of concrete. . . . Already by morning a few of the recruits are green and vomiting. They are too inexperienced. . . .

The bombardment does not diminish. It is falling in the rear too. As far as one can see it spouts fountains of mud and iron. A wide belt is being raked.

The attack does not come, but the bombardment continues. Slowly we become mute. Hardly a man speaks. We cannot make ourselves understood.

Our trench is almost gone. At many places it is only eighteen inches high, it is broken by holes, and craters, and mountains of earth. A shell lands square in front of our post. At once it is dark. We are buried and must dig ourselves out. . . .

Towards morning, while it is still dark, there is some excitement. Through the entrance rushes in a swarm of fleeing rats that try to storm the walls. Torches light up the confusion. Everyone yells and curses and slaughters. The madness and despair of many hours unloads itself in this outburst. Faces are distorted, arms strike out, the beasts scream; we just stop in time to avoid attacking one another. . . .

Suddenly it howls and flashes terrifically, the dug-out cracks in all its joints under a direct hit, fortunately only a light one that the concrete blocks are able to withstand. It rings metallically, the walls reel, rifles, helmets, earth, mud, and dust fly everywhere. Sulphur fumes pour in. . . . The recruit starts to rave again and two others follow suit. One jumps up and rushes out, we have trouble with the other two. I start after the one who escapes and wonder whether to shoot him in the leg—then it shrieks again, I fling myself down and when I stand up the wall of the trench is plastered with smoking splinters, lumps of flesh, and bits of uniform. I scramble back.

The first recruit seems actually to have gone insane. He butts his head against the wall like a goat. We must try tonight to take him to the rear. Meanwhile we bind him, but so that in case of attack he can be released.

Suddenly the nearer explosions cease. The shelling continues but it has lifted and falls behind us, our trench is free. We seize the hand-grenades, pitch them out in front of the dug-out and jump after them. The bombardment has stopped and a heavy barrage now falls behind us. The attack has come.

No one would believe that in this howling waste there could still be men; but steel helmets now appear on all sides out of the trench, and fifty yards from us a machine-gun is already in position and barking.

The wire-entanglements are torn to pieces. Yet they offer some obstacle. We see the storm-troops coming. Our artillery opens fire. Machine-guns rattle, rifles crack. The charge works its way across. Haie and Kropp begin with the hand-grenades. They throw as fast as they can, others pass them, the handles with the strings already pulled. Haie throws seventy-five yards, Kropp sixty, it has been measured, the distance is important. The enemy as they run cannot do much before they are within forty yards.

We recognize the distorted faces, the smooth helmets: they are French. They have already suffered heavily when they reach the remnants of the barbed-wire entanglements. A whole line has gone down before our machine-guns; then we have a lot of stoppages and they come nearer.

I see one of them, his face upturned, fall into a wire cradle. His body collapses, his hands remain suspended as though he were praying. Then his body drops clean away and only his hands with the stumps of his arms, shot off, now hang in the wire.

Q What does this excerpt from Erich Maria Remarque reveal about the realities of trench warfare? Would the surviving front-line victims of the war have been able to describe or explain their experiences there to those left behind on the home front? What effect would that have on postwar European society?

Paths of Glory, directed by Stanley Kubrick, is a powerful antiwar film made in 1957 and based on the novel with the same name by Humphrey Cobb. Set in France in 1916, the film deals with the time during World War I when the Western Front had become bogged down in brutal trench warfare. The novel was based loosely on a true story of five French soldiers who were executed for mutiny. In the film, General George Broulard (Adolphe Menjou) of the French General Staff suggests to his subordinate, General Mireau (George Macready), that he launch what would amount to a suicidal attack on the well-defended Ant Hill. Mireau refuses until Broulard mentions the possibility of a promotion, at which point Mireau abruptly changes his mind and accepts the challenge. He walks through the trenches preparing his men with the stock question: "Hello there soldier, are you ready to kill more Germans?" Mireau persuades Colonel Dax (Kirk Douglas) to mount the attack, despite Dax's protest that it will be a disaster. Dax proves to be right. None of the French soldiers reach the German lines, and one-third of the troops are not even able to leave their trenches because of enemy fire. To avoid blame for the failure, General Mireau accuses his men of cowardice, and three of them (one from each company, chosen in purely arbitrary fashion) are brought before a hastily arranged court-martial. Dax defends his men but to no avail. The decision has already been made, and the three men are shot in front of the assembled troops. As General Broulard cynically comments, "One way to maintain discipline is to shoot a man now and then." After the execution, when General Broulard offers Dax a promotion, Dax responds, "Would you like me to suggest what you can do with that promotion?" Replies Broulard, "You're an idealist; I pity you." But Dax has the last word: "I pity you for not seeing the wrongs you have done." The film ends with the troops being ordered back to the front.

The film realistically portrays the horrors of trench warfare in World War I—the senseless and suicidal attacks through no-man's land against well-entrenched machine-gun

Colonel Dax (Kirk Douglas) begins to lead his men out of the trenches to attack Ant Hill.

United Artists/The Kobal Collection

batteries. The film is also scathing in its portrayal of military leaders. The generals are shown drinking cognac in the palaces they requisitioned for their headquarters while the troops live in the mud and filth of the trenches. Both generals are portrayed as arrogant, ego-driven individuals who think nothing of the slaughter of their men in battle. The men condemned to die for cowardice are scapegoats sacrificed to cover up the mistakes of their superior officers who are determined to pursue "paths of glory" to advance themselves. The film's portrayal of the military executions was not accurate, however. The French army did not choose individuals at random for punishment, although it did execute some soldiers on charges of cowardice, as did the armies of the other belligerents.

This realistic indictment of war and the military elites offended some countries. French authorities saw it as an insult to the honor of the army and did not allow it to be shown in France until 1975. The military regime of Francisco Franco in Spain also banned the film for its antimilitary content. Kubrick himself went on to make two other antiwar films, capturing the Vietnam War in *Full Metal Jacket* and the Cold War in *Dr. Strangelove* (see the Film & History feature on p. 933). ▷

where they were often at a distinct disadvantage due to the unfamiliar terrain and climate.

Hundreds of thousands of Africans were also used for labor, especially for carrying supplies and building roads and bridges. In East Africa, both sides drafted African

laborers as carriers for their armies. More than 100,000 of these laborers died from disease and starvation caused by neglect.

The immediate impact of World War I in Africa was the extension of colonial rule since Germany's African

Life in the Trenches

The slaughter of millions of men in the trenches of World War I created unimaginable horrors for the participants. For the sake of survival, many soldiers learned to harden themselves against the stench of decomposing bodies and the sight of bodies horribly dismembered by artillery barrages, as is evident in the photograph at the top left. Life in the trenches could also be boring as soldiers whiled away the time as best they could when they were not fighting. Shown in the photograph at the top right is a group of German soldiers in their trench reading and writing letters during a lull in the fighting. The introduction of poison gas in 1915 led quickly to the use of protective gas masks. The bottom photograph shows Austrian soldiers in their trench demonstrating how to use the gas masks. ▷

The Songs of World War I

On the march, in bars, in trains, and even in the trenches, the soldiers of World War I spent time singing. The songs sung by soldiers of different nationalities varied considerably. "The Watch on the Rhine," a German favorite, focused on heroism and patriotism. British war songs often partook of black humor, as in "The Old Barbed Wire." An American favorite was the rousing "Over There," written by the professional songwriter George M. Cohan.

From "The Watch on the Rhine"

There sounds a call like thunder's roar,
Like the crash of swords, like the surge of waves.
To the Rhine, the Rhine, the German Rhine!
Who will the stream's defender be?
   Dear Fatherland, rest quietly
   Sure stands and true the Watch,
   The Watch on the Rhine.

To heaven he gazes.
Spirits of heroes look down.
He vows with proud battle-desire:
O Rhine! You will stay as German as my breast!
   Dear Fatherland, [etc.]

Even if my heart breaks in death,
You will never be French.
As you are rich in water
Germany is rich in hero's blood.
   Dear Fatherland, [etc.]

So long as a drop of blood still glows,
So long a hand the dagger can draw,
So long an arm the rifle can hold—
Never will an enemy touch your shore.
   Dear Fatherland, [etc.]

From "The Old Barbed Wire"

If you want to find the old battalion,
I know where they are,
I know where they are.
If you want to find a battalion,
I know where they are,
They're hanging on the old barbed wire.
I've seen 'em, I've seen 'em,
Hanging on the old barbed wire,
I've seen 'em,
Hanging on the old barbed wire.

George M. Cohan, "Over There"

Over There
Over There
Send the word
Send the word
Over There
That the Yanks are coming
The Yanks are coming,
The drums rum-tuming everywhere.
So prepare,
Say a prayer
Send the word
Send the word
To beware.
We'll be over.
We're coming over
And we won't come back
Till it's over
Over There.

Johnnie get your gun
Get your gun
Get your gun
Take it on the run
On the run
On the run
Hear them calling you and me
Every son of liberty
Hurry right away
No delay, go today
Make your Daddy glad
To have had such a lad
Tell your sweetheart not to pine
To be proud her boy's in line.

Q Based on their war songs, what ideas or themes do you think helped soldiers on all sides maintain the will to fight? How do you think the lyrics and performances of these songs worked to shape the psychology of the singers?

colonies were simply transferred to the winning powers, especially the British and the French. But the war also had unintended consequences for the Europeans. African soldiers who had gone to war for the Allies, especially those who left Africa and fought in Europe, became politically aware and began to advocate political and social equality.

As one African who had fought for the French said, "We were not fighting for the French, we were fighting for ourselves [to become] French citizens."[8] Moreover, educated African elites, who had aided their colonial overlords in enlisting local peoples to fight, did so in the belief that they would be rewarded with citizenship and new political

French African Troops. The French drafted more than 170,000 West African soldiers to fight in Europe. Shown here are some French African troops who fought in France on the Western front. The French army set up a photographic service to record aspects of the war.

possibilities after the war. When their hopes were frustrated, they soon became involved in anticolonial movements (see Chapter 26).

In East Asia and the Pacific, Japan joined the Allies on August 23, 1914, primarily to seize control of German territories in Asia. As one Japanese statesman declared, the war in Europe was "divine aid . . . for the development of the destiny of Japan."[9] The Japanese took possession of German territories in China, as well as the German-occupied islands in the Pacific. New Zealand and Australia quickly joined the Japanese in conquering the German-held parts of New Guinea.

ENTRY OF THE UNITED STATES   The United States tried to remain neutral in the Great War but found it more difficult to do so as the war dragged on. Although there was considerable sentiment for the British side in the conflict, the immediate cause of American involvement grew out of the naval conflict between Germany and Great Britain. Only once did the German and British naval forces engage in direct combat—at the Battle of Jutland on May 31, 1916, when the Germans won an inconclusive victory.

Britain used its superior naval power to maximum effect, however, by imposing a naval blockade on Germany. Germany retaliated with a counterblockade enforced by the use of unrestricted submarine warfare. At the beginning of 1915, the German government declared the area around the British Isles a war zone and threatened to torpedo any ship caught in it. Strong American protests over the German sinking of passenger liners, especially the British ship *Lusitania* on May 7, 1915, when more than one hundred Americans lost their lives, forced the German government to modify its policy of unrestricted submarine warfare starting in September 1915 and to briefly suspend unrestricted submarine warfare a year later.

In January 1917, however, eager to break the deadlock in the war, the Germans decided on another military gamble by returning to unrestricted submarine warfare. German naval officers convinced Emperor William II that the use of unrestricted submarine warfare could starve the British into submission within five months. When the emperor expressed concern about the Americans, he was told not to worry. The Americans, the chief of the German Naval Staff said, were "disorganized and undisciplined." The British would starve before the Americans could act. And even if the Americans did intervene, Admiral Holtzendorff (HOHLT-sen-dorf) assured the emperor, "I give your Majesty my word as an officer, that not one American will land on the Continent."

The return to unrestricted submarine warfare brought the United States into the war on April 6, 1917. Although American troops did not arrive in Europe in large numbers until the following year, the entry of the United States into the war in 1917 gave the Allied Powers a psychological boost when they needed it. The year 1917 was not a good one for them. Allied offensives on the Western Front were disastrously defeated. The Italian armies were smashed in October, and in November, the Bolshevik Revolution in Russia led to Russia's withdrawal from the war (see "The Russian Revolution" later in this chapter). The cause of the Central Powers looked favorable, although war weariness in the Ottoman Empire, Bulgaria, Austria-Hungary, and Germany was beginning to take its toll. The home front was rapidly becoming a cause for as much concern as the war front.

Woodrow Wilson, Proposal for declaration of war (1917)

A New Kind of Warfare

By the end of 1915, airplanes appeared on the battlefront. The planes were first used to spot the enemy's position, but soon they began to attack ground targets, especially enemy communications. Fights for control of the air occurred and increased over time. At first, pilots fired at each other with handheld pistols, but later machine guns were mounted on the noses of planes, which made the skies considerably more dangerous.

The Germans also used their giant airships—the zeppelins—to bomb London and eastern England. This caused little damage but frightened many people. Germany's enemies, however, soon found that zeppelins, which were filled with hydrogen gas, quickly became raging infernos when hit by antiaircraft guns.

TANKS Tanks were also introduced to the battlefields of Europe in 1916. The first tank—a British model—used caterpillar tracks, which enabled it to move across rough terrain. Armed with mounted guns, tanks could attack enemy machine-gun positions as well as enemy infantry. But the first tanks were not very effective, and it was not until 1918, with the introduction of the British Mark V model, that tanks had more powerful engines and greater maneuverability. They could now be used in large numbers, and coordinated with infantry and artillery, they became effective instruments in pushing back the retreating German army.

The tank came too late to have a great effect on the outcome of World War I, but the lesson was not lost on those who realized the tank's potential for creating a whole new kind of warfare. In World War II (see Chapter 27), lightning attacks that depended on tank columns and massive air power enabled armies to cut quickly across battle lines and encircle entire enemy armies. It was a far cry from the trench warfare of World War I.

The Home Front: The Impact of Total War

The prolongation of World War I made it a **total war** that affected the lives of all citizens, however remote they might be from the battlefields. World War I transformed the governments, economies, and societies of the European belligerents in fundamental ways. The need to organize masses of men and matériel for years of combat (Germany alone had 5.5 million men in active units in 1916) led to increased centralization of government powers, economic regimentation, and manipulation of public opinion to keep the war effort going.

TOTAL WAR: POLITICAL CENTRALIZATION AND ECONOMIC REGIMENTATION As we have seen, the outbreak of World War I was greeted with a rush of patriotism; even socialists went enthusiastically into the fray. As the war dragged on, governments realized, however, that more than patriotism would be needed. Since the war was expected to be short, little thought had been given to economic problems and long-term wartime needs. Governments had to respond quickly, however, when the war machines failed to achieve their knockout blows and made evergreater demands for men and matériel.

The extension of government power was a logical outgrowth of these needs. Most European countries had already devised some system of mass conscription or military draft. It was now carried to unprecedented heights as countries mobilized tens of millions of young men for that elusive breakthrough to victory. Even countries that traditionally relied on volunteers (Great Britain had the largest volunteer army in modern history—one million men—in 1914 and 1915) were forced to resort to conscription, especially to ensure that skilled workers did not enlist but remained in factories that were crucial to the production of munitions. In 1916, despite widespread resistance to this extension of government power, compulsory military service was introduced in Great Britain.

Throughout Europe, wartime governments expanded their powers over their economies. Free market capitalistic systems were temporarily shelved as governments experimented with price, wage, and rent controls, the rationing of food supplies and materials, the regulation of imports and exports, and the **nationalization** of transportation systems and industries. Some governments even moved toward compulsory employment. In effect, to mobilize the entire resources of their nations for the war effort, European nations had moved toward planned economies directed by government agencies. Under total war mobilization, the distinction between soldiers at war and civilians at home was narrowed. In the view of political leaders, all citizens constituted a national army dedicated to victory. As the American president, Woodrow Wilson (1856–1924), expressed it, the men and women "who remain to till the soil and man the factories are no less a part of the army than the men beneath the battle flags."

Not all European nations made the shift to total war equally well. Germany had the most success in developing a planned economy. At the beginning of the war, the government asked Walter Rathenau (VAHL-tuh RAH-tuh-now), head of the German General Electric Company, to use his business methods to organize the War Raw Materials Board, which would allocate strategic raw materials to produce the goods that were most needed. Rathenau made it possible for the German war machine to be effectively supplied. The Germans were much less successful with the rationing of food, however. Even before the war, Germany had to import about 20 percent of its food supply. The British blockade of Germany and a decline in farm labor made food shortages inevitable. Daily food rations in Germany were cut from 1,350 calories in 1916 to 1,000 by 1917, barely adequate for survival. As a result of a poor potato harvest in the winter of 1916–1917, turnips became the basic staple for the poor. An estimated 750,000 German civilians died of hunger during World War I.

The German war government was eventually consolidated under military authority. The two popular military heroes of the war, General Paul von Hindenburg, chief of the General Staff, and Erich Ludendorff, deputy chief of staff, came to control the government by 1916 and virtually became the military dictators of Germany. In 1916,

© Bettmann/CORBIS

The Wartime Leaders of Germany. Over the course of the war, the power of central governments was greatly enlarged in order to meet the demands of total war. In Germany, the two military heroes of the war, Paul von Hindenburg (left) and Erich Ludendorff (right), became virtual military dictators by 1916. The two are shown here with Emperor William II (center), whose power declined as the war dragged on.

Hindenburg and Ludendorff decreed a system of complete mobilization for total war. In the Auxiliary Service Law of December 2, 1916, they required all male noncombatants between the ages of seventeen and sixty to work only in jobs deemed crucial to the war effort.

Germany, of course, had an authoritarian political system before the war began. France and Britain did not, but even in those countries, the power of the central government was dramatically increased. At first, Great Britain tried to fight the war by continuing its liberal tradition of limited government interference in the economy. The pressure of circumstances, however, forced the British government to take a more active role in economic matters. The need to ensure adequate production of munitions led to the creation in July 1915 of the Ministry of Munitions under a dynamic leader, David Lloyd George. The Ministry of Munitions took numerous steps to ensure that private industry would produce war matériel at limited profits. It developed a vast bureaucracy of 65,000 clerks to oversee munitions plants. Beginning in 1915, it was given the power to take over plants manufacturing war goods that did not cooperate with the government. The British

government also rationed food supplies and imposed rent controls.

The French were less successful than the British and Germans in establishing a strong war government during much of the war. For one thing, the French faced a difficult obstacle in organizing a total war economy. German occupation of northeastern France cost the nation 75 percent of its coal production and almost 80 percent of its steelmaking capacity. Then, too, the relationship between civil and military authorities in France was extraordinarily strained. For the first three years of the war, military and civil authorities struggled over who would oversee the conduct of the war. Not until the end of 1917 did the French war government find a strong leader in Georges Clemenceau (ZHORZH kluh-mahn-SOH) (1841–1929). Declaring that "war is too important to be left to generals," Clemenceau established clear civilian control of a total war government.

The three other major belligerents—Russia, Austria-Hungary, and Italy—had much less success than Britain, Germany, and France in mobilizing for total war. The autocratic empires of Russia and Austria-Hungary had backward economies that proved incapable of turning out the quantity of war matériel needed to fight a modern war. The Russians, for example, conscripted millions of men but could arm only one-fourth of them. Unarmed Russian soldiers were sent into battle anyway and told to pick up rifles from their dead colleagues. With their numerous minorities, both the Russian and Austro-Hungarian empires found it difficult to achieve the kind of internal cohesion needed to fight a prolonged total war. Italy, too, lacked both the public enthusiasm and the industrial resources needed to wage a successful total war.

PUBLIC ORDER AND PUBLIC OPINION As the Great War dragged on and both casualties and privations worsened, internal dissatisfaction replaced the patriotic enthusiasm that had marked the early stages of the war. By 1916, there were numerous signs that civilian morale was beginning to crack under the pressure of total war.

The first two years of the war witnessed only a few scattered strikes, but thereafter strike activity increased dramatically. In 1916, 50,000 German workers carried out a three-day work stoppage in Berlin to protest the arrest of a radical socialist leader. In France and Britain, the number of strikes increased significantly. Even worse was the violence that erupted in Ireland when members of the Irish Republican Brotherhood and Citizens Army occupied government buildings in Dublin on Easter Sunday (April 24) in 1916. British forces crushed the Easter Rebellion and then condemned its leaders to death.

Internal opposition to the war came from two major sources in 1916 and 1917, liberals and socialists. Liberals in both Germany and Britain sponsored peace resolutions calling for a negotiated peace without any territorial acquisitions. They were largely ignored. Socialists in

Germany and Austria also called for negotiated settlements. By 1917, war morale had so deteriorated that more dramatic protests took place. Mutinies in the Italian and French armies were put down with difficulty. Czech leaders in the Austrian Empire openly called for an independent democratic Czech state. In April 1917, some 200,000 workers in Berlin went out on strike for a week to protest the reduction of bread rations. Only the threat of military force and prison brought them back to their jobs. Despite the strains, all of the belligerent countries except Russia survived the stresses of 1917 and fought on.

War governments also fought back against the growing opposition to the war. Authoritarian regimes, such as those of Germany, Russia, and Austria-Hungary, had always relied on force to subdue their populations. Under the pressures of the war, however, even parliamentary regimes resorted to an expansion of police powers to stifle internal dissent. At the very beginning of the war, the British Parliament passed the Defence of the Realm Act, which allowed the public authorities to arrest dissenters as traitors. The act was later extended to authorize public officials to censor newspapers by deleting objectionable material and even to suspend newspaper publication. In France, government authorities had initially been lenient about public opposition to the war. But by 1917, they began to fear that open opposition to the war might weaken the French will to fight. When Georges Clemenceau became premier near the end of 1917, the lenient French policies came to an end, and basic civil liberties were suppressed for the duration of the war. The editor of an antiwar newspaper was even executed on a charge of treason.

Wartime governments made active use of propaganda to arouse enthusiasm for the war. At the beginning, public officials needed to do little to achieve this goal. The British and French, for example, exaggerated German atrocities in Belgium and found that their citizens were only too willing to believe these accounts. But as the war dragged on and morale sagged, governments were forced to devise new techniques to stimulate declining enthusiasm. In one British recruiting poster, for example, a small daughter asked her father, "Daddy, what did you do in the Great War?" while her younger brother played with toy soldiers and cannons.

THE SOCIAL IMPACT OF TOTAL WAR Total war made a significant impact on European society, most visibly by bringing an end to unemployment. The withdrawal of millions of men from the labor market to fight, combined with the heightened demand for wartime products, led to jobs for everyone able to work.

The cause of labor also benefited from the war. The enthusiastic patriotism of workers was soon rewarded with a greater acceptance of trade unions. To ensure that labor problems would not disrupt production, war governments in Britain, France, and Germany not only sought union

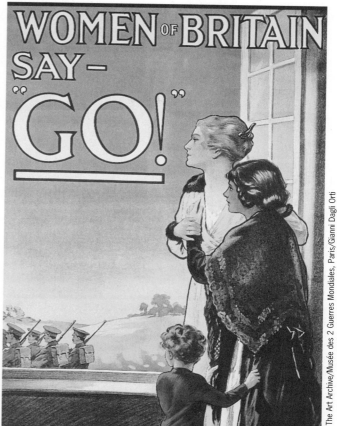

British Recruiting Poster. As the conflict persisted month after month, governments resorted to active propaganda campaigns to generate enthusiasm for the war. In this British recruiting poster, the government tried to pressure men into volunteering for military service. By 1916, the British were forced to adopt compulsory military service.

cooperation but also for the first time allowed trade unions to participate in making important government decisions on labor matters. In return, unions cooperated on wage limits and production schedules. Labor gained two benefits from this cooperation: it opened the way to the collective bargaining practices that became more widespread after World War I and increased the prestige of trade unions, enabling them to attract more members.

World War I also created new roles for women. With so many men off fighting at the front, women were called on to take over jobs and responsibilities that had not been open to them before. These included certain clerical jobs that only small numbers of women had held earlier. In Britain, for example, the number of women who worked in banking rose from 9,500 to almost 64,000 in the course of the war, while the number of women in commerce rose from a half million to almost one million. Overall, 1,345,000 women in Britain obtained new jobs or replaced men during the war. Women were also now employed in jobs that had been considered "beyond the capacity of women." These included such occupations as chimney sweeps, truck drivers, farm laborers, and,

Women Munition Workers in a British Factory. World War I created new opportunities for women. They were now employed in jobs that had earlier been considered beyond their capacity. As seen in the picture at the left, British women, dressed in caps and smocks, are making munitions in an armaments factory. As the recruitment poster at the right shows, the British government encouraged women to work in the munitions factories to aid the war effort. Women working in these factories were often nicknamed "munitionettes."

above all, factory workers in heavy industry (see the box on p. 795). In France, 684,000 women worked in armaments plants for the first time; in Britain, the figure was 920,000. Thirty-eight percent of the workers in the Krupp (KROOP) armaments works in Germany in 1918 were women.

Male resistance, however, often made it difficult for women to enter these new jobs, especially in heavy industry. One Englishwoman who worked in a munitions factory recalled her experience: "I could quite see it was hard on the men to have women coming into all their pet jobs and in some cases doing them a good deal better. I sympathized with the way they were torn between not wanting the women to undercut them, and yet hating them to earn as much."[10] While male workers expressed concern that the employment of females at lower wages would depress their own wages, women began to demand equal-pay legislation. The French government passed a law in July 1915 that established a minimum wage for women homeworkers in textiles, an industry that had grown dramatically because of the need for military uniforms. In 1917, the government decreed that men and women should receive equal rates for piecework. Despite the noticeable increase in women's wages that resulted from government regulations, women's industrial wages still were not equal to men's wages at the end of the war.

Even worse, women had achieved little real security about their place in the workforce. Both men and women

seemed to think that many of the new jobs for women were only temporary, an expectation quite evident in the British poem "War Girls," written in 1916:

> There's the girl who clips your ticket for the train,
> And the girl who speeds the lift from floor to floor,
> There's the girl who does a milk-round in the rain,
> And the girl who calls for orders at your door.
> Strong, sensible, and fit,
> They're out to show their grit,
> And tackle jobs with energy and knack.
> No longer caged and penned up,
> They're going to keep their end up
> Till the khaki soldier boys come marching back.[11]

At the end of the war, governments moved quickly to remove women from the jobs they had encouraged them to take earlier. By 1919, there were 650,000 unemployed women in Britain, and wages for women who were still employed were also lowered. The work benefits for women from World War I seemed to be short-lived.

Nevertheless, in some countries, the role played by women in the wartime economies did have a positive impact on the women's movement for social and political

Women in the Factories

During World War I, women were called on to assume new job responsibilities, including factory work. In this selection, Naomi Loughnan, a young, upper-middle-class woman, describes the experiences in a munitions plant that considerably broadened her perspective on life.

+ → ⊫⬦⫤ → +

Naomi Loughnan, "Munition Work"

We little thought when we first put on our overalls and caps and enlisted in the Munition Army how much more inspiring our life was to be than we had dared to hope. Though we munition workers sacrifice our ease we gain a life worth living. Our long days are filled with interest, and with the zest of doing work for our country in the grand cause of Freedom. As we handle the weapons of war we are learning great lessons of life. In the busy, noisy workshops we come face to face with every kind of class, and each one of these classes has something to learn from the others....

Engineering mankind is possessed of the unshakable opinion that no woman can have the mechanical sense. If one of us asks humbly why such and such an alteration is not made to prevent this or that drawback to a machine, she is told, with a superior smile, that a man has worked her machine before her for years, and that therefore if there were any improvement possible it would have been made. As long as we do exactly what we are told and do not attempt to use our brains, we give entire satisfaction, and are treated as nice, good children. Any swerving from the easy path prepared for us by our males arouses the most scathing contempt in their manly bosoms.... Women have, however, proved that their entry into the munition world has increased

the output. Employers who forget things personal in their patriotic desire for large results are enthusiastic over the success of women in the shops. But their workmen have to be handled with the utmost tenderness and caution lest they should actually imagine it was being suggested that women could do their work equally well, given equal conditions of training—at least where muscle is not the driving force....

The coming of the mixed classes of women into the factory is slowly but surely having an educative effect upon the men. "Language" is almost unconsciously becoming subdued. There are fiery exceptions who make our hair stand up on end under our close-fitting caps, but a sharp rebuke or a look of horror will often straighten out the most savage.... It is grievous to hear the girls also swearing and using disgusting language. Shoulder to shoulder with the children of the slums, the upper classes are having their eyes opened at last to the awful conditions among which their sisters have dwelt. Foul language, immorality, and many other evils are but the natural outcome of overcrowding and bitter poverty.... Sometimes disgust will overcome us, but we are learning with painful clarity that the fault is not theirs whose actions disgust us, but must be placed to the discredit of those other classes who have allowed the continued existence of conditions which generate the things from which we shrink appalled. ⇨

Q What did Naomi Loughnan learn about men and lower-class women while working in the munitions factory? What did she learn about herself? What can one conclude about the effects of total war on European women?

emancipation. The most obvious gain was the right to vote, given to women in Germany and Austria immediately after the war (in Britain already in January 1918). The Nineteenth Amendment to the U.S. Constitution gave women in the United States the right to vote in 1920. Contemporary media, however, tended to focus on the more noticeable yet in some ways more superficial social emancipation of upper- and middle-class women. In ever-larger numbers, these young women took jobs, had their own apartments, and showed their new independence by smoking in public and wearing shorter dresses, cosmetics, and boyish hairstyles.

In one sense, World War I had been a great social leveler. Death in battle did not distinguish between classes. Although all social classes suffered casualties in battle, two groups were especially hard-hit. Junior officers who led the charges across the "no-man's land" that separated the lines of trenches experienced death rates that were three times higher than regular casualty rates. Many of these junior

officers were members of the aristocracy (see the box on p. 796). The unskilled workers and peasants who made up the masses of soldiers mowed down by machine guns also suffered heavy casualties. The fortunate ones were the skilled laborers who gained exemptions from military service because they were needed at home to train workers in the war industries.

The burst of patriotic enthusiasm that marked the beginning of the war deceived many into believing that the war was creating a new sense of community that meant the end of the class conflict that had marked European society in the decades before the war. David Lloyd George, who became the British prime minister in 1916, wrote in September 1914 that "all classes, high and low, are shedding themselves of selfishness.... It is bringing a new outlook to all classes.... We can see for the first time the fundamental things that matter in life, and that have been obscured from our vision by the...growth of prosperity."[12] Lloyd George's optimistic opinion proved to be quite

War and the Family

John Mott was a captain in the British army. He came from an aristocratic family with a strong military tradition. He married Muriel Backhouse in 1907, and they had three sons before he was called up for service in World War I. These excerpts are taken from four of Mott's letters to his wife and a letter informing her of her husband's death during the Gallipoli campaign. The human experience of World War I was made up of millions of stories like that of John Mott and his family.

━━ ✠ ━━

One Family's War

1 July [1915]

My darling Childie,

I hope you got home safely. I have been promised that I shall know the ship we go on tomorrow. But it will be no good writing to Gibraltar as we should get there before the letter. Try Malta as that goes over land. If you get overdrawn go and see Cox. Goodbye Darling. Don't worry I shall come back alright.

Your devoted husband
John F. Mott

13 July

Mediterranean field force, Mudros
My darling Childie,

This island is very hot indeed but beastly windy. We have absolutely no news from the Front. Troops are pouring out now and I expect we shall be in it next week.

We have all gone through our little bout of diarrhea. I was not too bad and only had pains in my stomach otherwise I am very well indeed.

Everyone is standing the heat very well. The Brigadier has a tent but everybody else is out in the blazing sun.

31 July

My darling Childie,

I got more letters from you today dated 5th, 6th, 7th. I had no idea till I read the letter that they could do all that about writs. I would never have left things in such a muddle, I only hope you can get straight.

Yesterday I left here at 5:30 am to go to the trenches with the Brigadier. We had an awful day, and I am not at all keen to go into that lot at all events. We sailed over in a trawler and had a long walk in the open under shrapnel fire. It was not very pleasant. Then we got to the communications trenches and had a mile and a half of them to go up. When we got to the fire trenches the stink was awful. Arms and legs of Turks sticking out of the trench parapets and lying dead all round. In one place the bottom of the trench was made up by dead Turks, but this has been abandoned as the place was too poisonous.

Our battle ships have been shelling very heavily so there may be an attack on. I must write to my mother tonight. All my love and kisses for ever.

Your loving husband
John F. Mott

6 August

My darling Childie,

We are off today just as we stand up, with four days rations. I can't say where we are going but we shall see spots. I shall not get a chance to write again for a bit as we shall be on the move. I expect you have got a map of the place by now and perhaps you will hear where we have gone.

Very good to get away. All my love and kisses for ever.

Your loving husband
John F. Mott
Best love to all kids and baby

Pte A Thompson
6 Batt Y and L Red Cross Hospital

We landed on the 6th of Aug and took 2 hills and at daybreak on the 7th advanced across an open plain to the left of Salt Lake and got an awful shelling. We came to a small hill which was flat on top and it was about 2 hundred yards further on where the Capt was hit. They gave us it worse than ever when we got on there and I might have been happen 50 yds away when I saw the Capt and about 5 men fall badly hit. I could not say whether it was shrapnel or common shell but I think it was most probably shrapnel as they use that mostly. It was that thick that no one could get to the Capt at the time and I don't think he lived very long, well he could not the way they were hit and was afterwards buried when things had quietened down in the evening and a cross was put on his grave with an inscription and he got as good a burial as could be given out there. Well I think I have told you all I know about Capt Mott. I only wishe I could have given you better news, so I will close with Kind Regards.

Yours Obediently,
Pte Thompson ✐

Q What do these letters tell you about the ordinary officer's perspective on the war? How great do you think the gulf was between front line and home front? What does the tone of Private Thompson's final letter suggest about the ordinary soldier's experience of battle and the effects of such service on fighting men?

misguided, however. The Great War did not eliminate the class conflict that had characterized pre-1914 Europe, and this became increasingly apparent as the war dragged on.

The economic impact of the war was felt unevenly. One group of people who especially benefited were the owners of the large industries manufacturing the weapons of war. Despite public outrage, governments rarely limited the enormous profits made by the industrial barons. In fact, in the name of efficiency, wartime governments tended to favor large industries when scarce raw materials were allocated.

Small firms considered less essential to the war effort even had to shut down because of a lack of resources.

Inflation also caused inequities. The combination of full employment and high demand for scarce consumer goods caused prices to climb. Many skilled workers were able to earn wages that enabled them to keep up with inflation, but this was not true for unskilled workers or those in nonessential industries. Only in Great Britain did the wages of workers outstrip prices. Everywhere else in Europe, people experienced a loss of purchasing power.

Many middle-class people were hit especially hard by inflation. They included both those who lived on fixed incomes, such as retired people on pensions, and professional people, such as clerks, lesser civil servants, teachers, small shopkeepers, and members of the clergy, whose incomes remained stable at a time when prices were rising. By the end of the war, many of these people were actually doing less well economically than skilled workers. Their discontent would find expression after the war.

War and Revolution

 FOCUS QUESTION: What were the causes of the Russian Revolution of 1917, and why did the Bolsheviks prevail in the civil war and gain control of Russia?

By 1917, total war was creating serious domestic turmoil in all of the European belligerent states. Most countries were able to prop up their regimes and convince their people to continue the war for another year, but others were coming close to collapse. In Austria, for example, a government minister warned that "if the monarchs of the Central Powers cannot make peace in the coming months, it will be made for them by their peoples." Russia, however, was the only belligerent that actually experienced the kind of complete collapse in 1917 that others were predicting might happen throughout Europe. Out of Russia's collapse came the Russian Revolution, whose impact would be widely felt in Europe for decades to come.

The Russian Revolution

After the Revolution of 1905 had failed to bring any substantial changes to Russia, Tsar Nicholas II relied on the army and bureaucracy to uphold his regime. But World War I magnified Russia's problems and severely challenged the tsarist government. The tsar, possessed of a strong sense of moral duty to his country, was the only European monarch to take personal charge of the armed forces, despite a lack of training for such an awesome responsibility. Russian industry was unable to produce the weapons needed for the army. Ill-led and ill-armed, Russian armies suffered incredible losses. Between 1914 and 1916, 2 million soldiers were killed while another 4 to 6 million were wounded or captured.

The tsarist government was unprepared for the tasks that it faced in 1914. The surge of patriotic enthusiasm that greeted the outbreak of war was soon dissipated by a government that distrusted its own people. Although the middle classes and liberal aristocrats still hoped for a constitutional monarchy, they were sullen over the tsar's revocation of the political concessions made during the Revolution of 1905. Peasant discontent flourished as conditions worsened. The concentration of Russian industry in a few large cities made workers' frustrations all the more evident and dangerous. In the meantime, Nicholas was increasingly insulated from events by his wife, Alexandra.

This German-born princess was a well-educated woman who had fallen under the influence of Rasputin (rass-PYOO-tin), a Siberian peasant whom the tsarina regarded as a holy man because he alone seemed able to stop the bleeding of her hemophiliac son, Alexis. Rasputin's influence made him a power behind the throne, and he did not hesitate to interfere in government affairs. As the leadership at the top experienced a series of military and economic disasters, the middle class, aristocrats, peasants, soldiers, and workers grew more and more disenchanted with the tsarist regime. Even conservative aristocrats who supported the monarchy felt the need to do something to reverse the deteriorating situation. For a start, they assassinated Rasputin in December 1916. By then it was too late to save the monarchy, and its fall came quickly in the first weeks of March 1917.

THE MARCH REVOLUTION At the beginning of March, a series of strikes broke out in the capital city of Petrograd (formerly Saint Petersburg). Here the actions of working-class women helped change the course of Russian history. Weeks earlier, the government had introduced bread rationing in the city after the price of bread skyrocketed. Many of the women who stood in the lines waiting for bread were also factory workers who put in twelve-hour days. The number of women working in Petrograd factories had doubled since 1914. The Russian government had become aware of the volatile situation in the capital from police reports, one of which stated:

> Mothers of families, exhausted by endless standing in line at stores, distraught over their half-starving and sick children, are today perhaps closer to revolution than [the liberal opposition leaders] and of course they are a great deal more dangerous because they are the combustible material for which only a single spark is needed to burst into flame.[13]

On March 8, a day celebrated since 1910 as International Women's Day, about ten thousand women marched through Petrograd shouting "Peace and bread" and "Down with autocracy." Soon the women were joined by other workers, and together they called for a general strike that succeeded in shutting down all the factories in the city on March 10. The tsarina wrote to Nicholas at the battlefront that "this is a hooligan movement. If the weather were very cold they would all probably stay at home." Believing his wife, Nicholas told his military commanders, "I command you tomorrow to stop the disorders in the capital, which are unacceptable in the difficult time of war with

The Women's March in Petrograd. After the imposition of bread rationing in Petrograd, ten thousand women engaged in mass demonstrations and demanded "Peace and bread" for the families of soldiers. This photograph shows the women marching through the streets of Petrograd on March 8, 1917.

Germany and Austria."[14] The troops were ordered to disperse the crowds, shooting them if necessary. Initially, the troops cooperated, but soon significant numbers of the soldiers joined the demonstrators. The situation was now out of the tsar's control. The Duma, or legislature, which the tsar had tried to dissolve, met anyway and on March 12 declared that it was assuming governmental responsibility. It established a provisional government on March 15; the tsar abdicated the same day.

In just one week, the tsarist regime had fallen apart. Although no particular group had been responsible for the outburst, the moderate Constitutional Democrats were responsible for establishing the provisional government. They represented primarily a middle-class and liberal aristocratic minority. Their program consisted of a liberal agenda that included working toward a parliamentary democracy and passing reforms that provided universal suffrage, civil equality, and an eight-hour workday.

The provisional government also faced another authority, the **soviets,** or councils of workers' and soldiers' deputies. The soviet of Petrograd had been formed in March 1917; around the same time, soviets sprang up spontaneously in army units and towns. The soviets represented the more radical interests of the lower classes and were largely composed of socialists of various kinds. Among them was the Marxist Social Democratic Party, which had formed in 1898 but divided in 1903 into two factions known as the Mensheviks (MENS-shuh-viks) and the **Bolsheviks** (BOHL-shuh-viks). The Mensheviks wanted the Social Democrats to be a mass electoral socialist party based on a Western model. Like the Social Democrats of Germany, they were willing to cooperate temporarily in a parliamentary democracy while working toward the ultimate achievement of a socialist state.

The Bolsheviks were a small faction of Russian Social Democrats who had come under the leadership of Vladimir Ulianov, known to the world as V. I. Lenin (1870–1924). Born in 1870, Lenin received a legal education and became a lawyer. In 1887, he turned into a dedicated enemy of tsarist Russia when his older brother was executed for planning to assassinate the tsar. Lenin's search for a revolutionary faith led him to Marxism, and in 1894 he moved to Saint Petersburg, where he helped organize an illegal group known as the Union for the Liberation of the Working Class. Arrested for this activity, Lenin was shipped to Siberia. After his release, he chose to go into exile in Switzerland and eventually assumed the leadership of the Bolshevik wing of the Russian Social Democratic Party.

Under Lenin's direction, the Bolsheviks became a party dedicated to a violent revolution that would destroy the capitalist system. He believed that a "vanguard" of activists must form a small party of well-disciplined professional revolutionaries to accomplish the task. Between 1900 and 1917, Lenin spent most of his time in Switzerland. The outbreak of war in 1914 gave him hope that all of Europe was ripe for revolution, and when the provisional government was formed in March 1917, he believed that an opportunity for the Bolsheviks to seize power in Russia had come. A few weeks later, with the connivance of the German High Command, who hoped to

Lenin and Trotsky. V. I. Lenin and Leon Trotsky were important figures in the Bolsheviks' successful seizure of power in Russia. On the left, Lenin is seen addressing a rally in Moscow in 1917. On the right, Trotsky, who became commissar of war in the new regime, is shown haranguing his troops.

create disorder in Russia, Lenin, his wife, and a small group of his followers were shipped to Russia in a "sealed train" by way of Finland.

Lenin's arrival in Russia on April 3 opened a new stage in the Russian Revolution. In his "April Theses," issued on April 20, Lenin presented a blueprint for revolutionary action based on his own version of Marxist theory. According to Lenin, it was not necessary for Russia to experience a bourgeois revolution before it could move toward socialism, as orthodox Marxists had argued. Instead, Russia could move directly into socialism. In the April Theses, Lenin maintained that the soviets of soldiers, workers, and peasants were ready-made instruments of power. The Bolsheviks must work toward gaining control of these groups and then use them to overthrow the provisional government. At the same time, the Bolsheviks articulated the discontent and aspirations of the people, promising an end to the war, the redistribution of all land to the peasants, the transfer of factories and industries from capitalists to committees of workers, and the relegation of government power from the provisional government to the soviets. Three simple slogans summed up the Bolshevik program: "Peace, land, bread," "Worker control of production," and "All power to the soviets."

In late spring and early summer, while the Bolsheviks set about winning over the masses to their program and gaining a majority in the Petrograd and Moscow soviets, the provisional government struggled to gain control of Russia against almost overwhelming obstacles. Peasants began land reform by seizing property on their own in March. The military situation was also deteriorating. The Petrograd soviet had issued its Army Order No. 1 in March

to all Russian military forces, encouraging them to remove their officers and replace them with committees composed of "the elected representatives of the lower ranks" of the army. Army Order No. 1 led to the collapse of all discipline and created military chaos. When the provisional government attempted to initiate a new military offensive in July, the army simply dissolved as masses of peasant soldiers turned their backs on their officers and returned home to join their families in seizing land.

THE BOLSHEVIK REVOLUTION In July 1917, Lenin and the Bolsheviks were falsely accused of inciting an attempt to overthrow the provisional government, and Lenin was forced to flee to Finland. But the days of the provisional government were numbered. In July 1917, Alexander Kerensky (kuh-REN-skee), a moderate socialist, had become prime minister in the provisional government. In September, when General Lavr Kornilov (LAH-vur kor-NYEE-luff) attempted to march on Petrograd and seize power, Kerensky released Bolsheviks from prison and turned to the Petrograd soviet for help. Although General Kornilov's forces never reached Petrograd, Kerensky's action had strengthened the hands of the Petrograd soviet and had shown Lenin how weak the provisional government really was.

By the end of October, the Bolsheviks had achieved a slight majority in the Petrograd and Moscow soviets. The number of party members had also grown from 50,000 to 240,000. Reports of unrest abroad had convinced Lenin that "we are on the threshold of a world proletarian revolution," and he tried to persuade his fellow Bolsheviks that the time was ripe for the overthrow of the provisional government. Although he faced formidable opposition within the Bolshevik ranks, he managed to gain support for his policy. With Leon Trotsky (TRAHT-skee) (1877–1940), a fervid revolutionary, as chairman of the Petrograd soviet, the Bolsheviks were in a position to seize power in the name of the soviets. During the night of November 6, pro-soviet and pro-Bolshevik forces took control of Petrograd under the immensely popular slogan "All power to the soviets." The provisional government quickly collapsed with little bloodshed. The following night, the all-Russian congress of Soviets, representing local soviets from all over the country, affirmed the transfer of power. At the second session, on the night of November 8, Lenin announced the new Soviet government, the Council of People's Commissars, with himself as its head.

One immediate problem the Bolsheviks faced was the Constituent Assembly, which had been initiated by the provisional government and was scheduled to meet in January 1918. Elections to the assembly by universal suffrage had resulted in a defeat for the Bolsheviks, who had only 225 delegates compared to the 420 garnered by the Socialist Revolutionaries. But no matter. Lenin simply broke the Constituent Assembly by force. "To hand over power," he said, "to the Constituent Assembly would again be compromising with malignant bourgeoisie" (see the box on p. 801).

But the Bolsheviks (soon renamed the Communists) still had a long way to go. Lenin, ever the opportunist, realized the importance of winning mass support as quickly as possible by fulfilling Bolshevik promises. In his first law, issued on the new regime's first day in power, Lenin declared the land nationalized and turned it over to local rural land committees. In effect, this action merely ratified the peasants' seizure of the land and assured the Bolsheviks of peasant support, especially against any attempt by the old landlords to restore their power. Lenin also met the demands of urban workers by turning over control of the factories to committees of workers. To Lenin, however, this was merely a temporary expedient.

The new government also introduced a number of social changes. Alexandra Kollontai (kul-lun-TY) (1872–1952), who had become a supporter of revolutionary socialism while in exile in Switzerland, took the lead in pushing a Bolshevik program for women's rights and social welfare reforms. As minister of social welfare, she tried to provide health care for women and children by establishing "palaces for the protection of maternity and children." Between 1918 and 1920, the new regime enacted a series of reforms that made marriage a civil act, legalized divorce, decreed the equality of men and women, and permitted abortions. Kollontai was also instrumental in establishing a women's bureau, known as Zhenotdel (zhen-ut-DELL), within the Communist Party. This bureau sent men and women to all parts of the Russian Empire to explain the new social order. Members of Zhenotdel were especially eager to help women with matters of divorce and women's rights. In the eastern provinces, several Zhenotdel members were brutally murdered by angry males who objected to any kind of liberation for their wives and daughters. Much to Kollontai's disappointment, many of these Communist social reforms were later undone as the Communists came to face more pressing matters, including the survival of the new regime.

Lenin had also promised peace, and that, he realized, was not an easy task because of the humiliating losses of Russian territory that it would entail. There was no real choice, however. On March 3, 1918, the new Communist government signed the Treaty of Brest-Litovsk (BREST-li-TUFFSK) with Germany and gave up eastern Poland, Ukraine, Finland, and the Baltic provinces. To his critics, Lenin argued that it made no difference since the spread of socialist revolution throughout Europe would make the treaty largely irrelevant. In any case, he had promised peace to the Russian people, but real peace did not occur, for the country soon lapsed into civil war.

CIVIL WAR There was great opposition to the new Bolshevik regime, not only from groups loyal to the tsar but also from bourgeois and aristocratic liberals and anti-Leninist socialists, including Mensheviks and Socialist Revolutionaries. In addition, thousands of Allied troops were eventually sent to different parts of Russia in the hope of bringing Russia back into the Great War.

Between 1918 and 1921, the Bolshevik (Red) Army was forced to fight on many fronts (see Map 25.4). The first serious threat to the Bolsheviks came from Siberia, where a White (anti-Bolshevik) force under Admiral Alexander Kolchak (kul-CHAHK) pushed westward and advanced almost to the Volga River before being stopped. Attacks also came from the Ukrainians in the southeast and from the Baltic regions. In mid-1919, White forces under General Anton Denikin (ahn-TOHN dyin-YEE-kin), probably the most effective of the White generals, swept through Ukraine and advanced almost to Moscow. At one point in late 1919, three separate White armies seemed to be closing in on the Bolsheviks but were eventually pushed back. By 1920, the major White forces had been defeated, and Ukraine was retaken. The next year, the Communist regime regained control over the independent nationalist governments in the Caucasus: Georgia, Russian Armenia, and Azerbaijan.

The royal family was yet another victim of the civil war. After the tsar had abdicated, he, his wife, and their five children had been taken into custody. They were moved in August 1917 to Tobolsk in Siberia and in April 1918 to Ekaterinburg (i-kat-tuh-RIN-burk), a mining town in the Urals. On the night of July 16, members of the local soviet murdered the tsar and his family and burned their bodies in a nearby mine shaft.

How had Lenin and the Bolsheviks triumphed over what seemed at one time to be overwhelming forces? For one thing, the Red Army became a well-disciplined and formidable fighting force, thanks largely to the organizational genius of Leon Trotsky. As commissar of war, Trotsky reinstated the draft and even recruited and gave commands to former tsarist army officers. Trotsky insisted

Soldier and Peasant Voices

In 1917, Russia experienced a cataclysmic upheaval as two revolutions overthrew the tsarist regime and then the provisional government that replaced it. Peasants, workers, and soldiers poured out their thoughts and feelings on these events, some of them denouncing the Bolsheviks for betraying their socialist revolution. These selections are taken from two letters, the first from a soldier and the second from a peasant. Both are addressed to Bolshevik leaders.

Letter from a Soldier in Leningrad to Lenin, January 6, 1918

Bastard! What the hell are you doing? How long are you going to keep on degrading the Russian people? After all, it's because of you they killed the former minister...and so many other innocent victims. Because of you, they might kill even other former ministers belonging to the [Socialist Revolutionary] party because you call them counterrevolutionaries and even monarchists.... And you, you Bolshevik gang leader hired either by Nicholas II or by Wilhelm II, are waging this pogrom propaganda against men who may have done time with you in exile.

Scoundrel! A curse on you from the politically conscious Russian proletariat, the conscious ones and not the kind who are following you—that is, the Red Guards, the tally clerks, who, when they are called to military service, all hide at the factories and now are killing...practically their own father, the way the soldiers did in 1905 when they killed their own, or the way the police and gendarmes did in [1917]. That's who they're more like. They're not pursuing the ideas of socialism because they don't understand them (if they did they wouldn't act this way) but because they get paid a good salary both at the factory and in the Red Guards. But not all the workers are like that—there are very politically aware ones and the soldiers—again not all of them—are like that but only former policemen, constables, gendarmes and the very very ignorant ones who under the old regime tramped with hay on one foot and straw on the other because they couldn't tell their right foot from their left and they are pursuing not the ideas of socialism that you advocate but to be able to lie on their cots in the barracks and do absolutely nothing not even be asked to sweep the floor, which is already piled with several inches of filth. And so the entire proletariat of Russia is following you, by count fewer than are against you, but they are only physically or rather technically stronger than the majority, and that is what you're abusing when you disbanded the Constituent Assembly the way Nicholas II disbanded the Duma.

You point out that counterrevolutionaries gathered there. You lie, scoundrel, there wasn't a single counterrevolutionary and if there was then it was you, the Bolsheviks, which you proved by your actions when you encroached on the gains of the revolution: you are shutting down newspapers, even socialist ones, arresting socialists, committing violence and deceiving the people; you promised loads but did none of it.

Letter from a Peasant to the Bolshevik Leaders, January 10, 1918

TO YOU!

Rulers, plunderers, rapists, destroyers, usurpers, oppressors of Mother Russia, citizens Lenin, Trotsky, Uritsky, Zinoviev, Spiridonova, Antonov, Lunacharsky, Krylenko, and Co. [leaders of the Bolshevik party]:

Allow me to ask you how long you are going to go on degrading Russia's millions, its tormented and exhausted people. Instead of peace, you signed an armistice with the enemy, and this gave our opponent a painful advantage, and you declared war on Russia. You moved the troops you had tricked to the Russian-Russian front and started a fratricidal war. Your mercenary Red Guards are looting, murdering, and raping everywhere they go. A fire has consumed all our dear Mother Russia. Rail transport is idle, as are the plants and factories; the entire population has woken up to find itself in the most pathetic situation, without bread or kerosene or any of the other essentials, unclothed and unshod in unheated houses. In short: hungry and cold.... You have strangled the entire press, and freedom with it, you have wiped out the best freedom fighters, you have destroyed all Russia. Think it over, you butchers, you hirelings of the Kaiser [William II]. Isn't your turn about up, too? For all you are doing, we, politically aware Great Russians, are sending you butchers, you hirelings of the Kaiser, our curse. May you be damned, you accursed one, you bloodthirsty butchers, you hirelings of the Kaiser—don't think you're in the clear, because the Russian people will sober up and that will be the end of you. I'm writing in red ink to show that you are bloodthirsty.... I'm writing these curses, a Great Russian native of Orel Province, peasant of Mtsensk Uezd. ✑

Q What arguments do the writers of these letters use against Lenin and the Bolsheviks? Why do they feel so betrayed by the Bolsheviks?

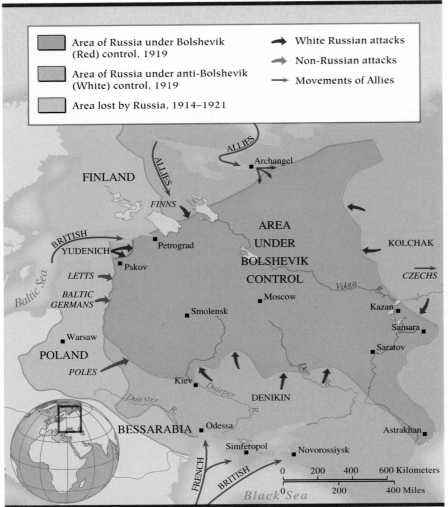

MAP 25.4   The Russian Revolution and Civil War. The Russian Civil War lasted from 1918 to 1921. A variety of disparate groups, including victorious powers from World War I, sought to either overthrow the Bolsheviks or seize Russian territory. Lack of cohesion among their enemies helped the Bolsheviks triumph, but at the cost of much hardship and bloodshed.

Q *How did the area under Bolshevik control make it easier for the Bolsheviks to defeat the White forces?*

of purpose. Inspired by their vision of a new socialist order, the Communists had the advantage of possessing the determination that comes from revolutionary fervor and revolutionary convictions.

The Communists also succeeded in translating their revolutionary faith into practical instruments of power. A policy of **war communism**, for example, was used to ensure regular supplies for the Red Army. War communism included the nationalization of banks and most industries, the forcible requisition of grain from peasants, and the centralization of state administration under Bolshevik control. Another Bolshevik instrument was "revolutionary terror." Although the old tsarist secret police had been abolished, a new Red secret police—known as the Cheka (CHEK-uh)—replaced it. The Red Terror instituted by the Cheka aimed at nothing less than the destruction of all opponents of the new regime. "Class enemies"—the bourgeoisie—were especially singled out, at least according to a Cheka officer: "The first questions you should put to the accused person are: To what class does he belong, what is his origin, what was his education, and what is his profession? These should determine the fate of the accused." In practice, however, the Cheka promulgated terror against members of all classes, including the proletariat, if they opposed the new regime. Thousands were executed. The Red Terror added an element of fear to the Bolshevik regime.

Finally, the intervention of foreign armies enabled the Communists to appeal to the powerful force of Russian patriotism. Although the Allied Powers had initially intervened in Russia to encourage the Russians to remain in the war, the end of the war on November 11, 1918, had made that purpose inconsequential. Nevertheless, Allied troops remained, and Allied countries did not hide their anti-Bolshevik feelings. At one point, British, American, French, and (in Siberia) Japanese forces were stationed on Russian soil. These forces rarely engaged in pitched battles, however, nor did they pursue a common strategy, although they did give material assistance to the anti-Bolsheviks. This intervention by the Allies enabled the Communist government to appeal to patriotic Russians to fight the attempts of foreigners to control their country. Allied interference was never substantial enough to make a military difference in the civil war, but it did serve indirectly to help the Bolshevik cause.

on rigid discipline; soldiers who deserted or refused to obey orders were summarily executed. The Red Army also had the advantage of interior lines of defense and was able to move its troops rapidly from one battlefront to the other.

The disunity of the anti-Communist forces seriously weakened their efforts. Political differences created distrust among the Whites and prevented them from cooperating effectively with each other. Some Whites, such as Admiral Kolchak, insisted on restoring the tsarist regime, but others understood that only a more liberal and democratic program had any chance of success. Since the White forces were forced to operate on the fringes of the Russian Empire, it was difficult enough to achieve military cooperation. Political differences made it virtually impossible.

The Whites' inability to agree on a common goal contrasted sharply with the Communists' single-minded sense

	1917
March of women in Petrograd	March 8
General strike in Petrograd	March 10
Establishment of provisional government	March 15
Tsar abdicates	March 15
Formation of Petrograd soviet	March
Lenin arrives in Russia	April 3
Lenin's "April Theses"	April 20
Failed attempt to overthrow provisional government	July
Bolsheviks gain majority in Petrograd soviet	October
Bolsheviks overthrow provisional government	November 6–7
	1918
Lenin disbands Constituent Assembly	January
Treaty of Brest-Litovsk	March 3
Civil war	1918–1921

By 1921, the Communists had succeeded in retaining control of Russia (though not without an enormous loss of life and destruction in the country; see Chapter 27). In the course of the civil war, the Bolshevik regime had also transformed Russia into a bureaucratically centralized state dominated by a single party. It was also a state that was largely hostile to the Allied Powers that had sought to assist the Bolsheviks' enemies in the civil war. To most historians, the Russian Revolution is unthinkable without the total war of World War I, for only the collapse of Russia made it possible for a radical minority like the Bolsheviks to seize the reins of power. In turn, the Russian Revolution had an impact on the course of World War I.

The Last Year of the War

For Germany, the withdrawal of the Russians from the war in March 1918 offered renewed hope for a favorable outcome. The victory over Russia persuaded Ludendorff and most German leaders to make one final military gamble—a grand offensive in the west to break the military stalemate. The German attack was launched in March and lasted into July. The German forces succeeded in advancing 40 miles to the Marne River, within 35 miles of Paris. But an Allied counterattack, led by the French General Ferdinand Foch (FAYR-dee-nawnh FUSH) and supported by the arrival of 140,000 fresh American troops, defeated the Germans at the Second Battle of the Marne on July 18. Ludendorff's gamble had failed. Having used up his reserves, Ludendorff knew that defeat was now inevitable. With the arrival of one million more American troops on the Continent, Allied forces began making a steady advance toward Germany.

On September 29, 1918, General Ludendorff informed German leaders that the war was lost. Unwilling to place

	1914
Battle of Tannenberg	August 26–30
First Battle of the Marne	September 6–10
Battle of Masurian Lakes	September 15
Russia, Great Britain, and France declare war on Ottoman Empire	November
	1915
Battle of Gallipoli begins	April 25
Italy declares war on Austria-Hungary	May 23
Entry of Bulgaria into the war	September
	1916
Battle of Verdun	February 21–December 18
Battle of Jutland	May 31
Somme offensive	July 1–November 19
	1917
Germany returns to unrestricted submarine warfare	January
United States enters the war	April 6
Champagne offensive	April 16–29
	1918
Last German offensive	March 21–July 18
Second Battle of the Marne	July 18
Allied counteroffensive	July 18–November 10
Armistice between Allies and Germany	November 11
	1919
Paris Peace Conference begins	January 18
Peace of Versailles	June 28

the burden of defeat on the army, Ludendorff demanded that the government sue for peace at once. When German officials discovered that the Allies were unwilling to make peace with the autocratic imperial government, they instituted reforms to set up a liberal government. But these reforms came too late for the exhausted and angry German people. On November 3, naval units in Kiel mutinied, and within days, councils of workers and soldiers, German versions of the Russian soviets, were forming throughout northern Germany and taking over the supervision of civilian and military administrations. William II capitulated to public pressure and left the country on November 9, while the socialists under Friedrich Ebert (FREED-rikh AY-bert) announced the establishment of a republic. Two days later, on November 11, 1918, an armistice agreed to by the new German government went into effect. The war was over, but the revolutionary forces set in motion by the war were not yet exhausted.

THE CASUALTIES OF THE WAR World War I devastated European civilization. Between 8 and 9 million soldiers died on the battlefields; another 22 million were wounded. Many of those who survived later died from war injuries or suffered the loss of arms or legs or other forms of mutilation. The birthrate in many European countries declined noticeably as a result of the death or maiming of so many young men. World War I also created a "lost generation" of war veterans who had become accustomed to violence and who would form the postwar bands of fighters who supported Mussolini and Hitler in their bids for power (see Chapter 27).

Nor did the killing affect only soldiers. Untold numbers of civilians died from war, civil war, or starvation. In 1915, using the excuse of a rebellion by the Armenian minority and their supposed collaboration with the Russians, the Turkish government began systematically to kill Armenian men and expel women and children. Within seven months, 600,000 Armenians had been killed, and 500,000 had been deported. Of the latter, 400,000 died while marching through the deserts and swamps of Syria and Iraq. By September 1915, as many as one million, and possibly more, Armenians were dead, the victims of **genocide.**

Revolutionary Upheavals in Germany and Austria-Hungary

Like Russia, Germany and Austria-Hungary experienced political revolution as a result of military defeat. In November 1918, when Germany began to disintegrate in a convulsion of mutinies and mass demonstrations (known as the November Revolution), only the Social Democrats were numerous and well organized enough to pick up the pieces. But the German socialists had divided into two groups during the war. A majority of the Social Democrats still favored parliamentary democracy as a gradual approach to social democracy and the elimination of the capitalist system. A minority of German socialists, however, disgusted with the Social Democrats' support of the war, had formed their own Independent Social Democratic Party in 1916. In 1918, the more radical members of the Independent Socialists favored an immediate social revolution carried out by the councils of soldiers, sailors, and workers. Led by Karl Liebknecht (LEEP-knekht) and Rosa Luxemburg (LOOK-sum-boork), these radical, left-wing socialists formed the German Communist Party in December 1918. In effect, two parallel governments were established in Germany: the parliamentary republic proclaimed by the majority Social Democrats and the revolutionary socialist republic declared by the radicals.

Unlike Russia's Bolsheviks, Germany's radicals failed to achieve control of the government. By ending the war on November 11, the moderate socialists had removed a major source of dissatisfaction. When the radical socialists (now known as Communists) attempted to seize power in Berlin in January 1919, Friedrich Ebert and the moderate socialists called on the regular army and groups of antirevolutionary volunteers known as Free Corps to crush the rebels. The victorious forces brutally murdered Liebknecht and Luxemburg. A similar attempt at Communist revolution in the city of Munich in southern Germany was also crushed by the Free Corps and the regular army. The German republic had been saved, but only because the moderate socialists had relied on the traditional army—in effect, the same conservatives who had dominated the old imperial regime. Moreover, this "second revolution" of January 1919, bloodily crushed by the republican government, created a deep fear of communism among the German middle classes. All too soon, this fear would be cleverly manipulated by a politician named Adolf Hitler.

Austria-Hungary, too, experienced disintegration and revolution. When it attacked Serbia in 1914, the imperial regime had tried to crush the nationalistic forces that it believed were destroying the empire. By 1918, those same nationalistic forces had brought the complete breakup of the Austro-Hungarian Empire. As war weariness took hold of the empire, ethnic minorities increasingly sought to achieve national independence. This desire was further encouraged by Allied war aims that included calls for the independence of the subject peoples. By the time the war ended, the Austro-Hungarian Empire had been replaced by the independent republics of Austria, Hungary, and Czechoslovakia and a new southern Slavic monarchical state that eventually came to be called Yugoslavia. Other regions clamored to join Italy, Romania, and a reconstituted Poland. Rivalries among the nations that succeeded Austria-Hungary would weaken eastern Europe for the next eighty years. Ethnic pride and national statehood proved far more important to these states than class differences. Only in Hungary was there an attempt at social revolution when Béla Kun (BAY-luh KOON) established a Communist state. It was crushed after a brief five-month existence.

The Peace Settlement

 FOCUS QUESTION: What were the objectives of the chief participants at the Paris Peace Conference of 1919, and how closely did the final settlement reflect these objectives?

In January 1919, the delegations of the victorious Allied nations gathered in Paris to conclude a final settlement of the Great War. By that time, the reasons for fighting World War I had been transformed from selfish national interests to idealistic principles. At the end of 1917, after they had taken over the Russian government, Lenin and the Bolsheviks had publicly revealed the contents of secret wartime treaties found in the archives of the Russian foreign ministry. The documents made it clear that European nations had gone to war primarily to achieve territorial gains. At the beginning of 1918, however, the American president, Woodrow Wilson, had attempted to shift the discussion of war aims from territorial gains to a higher ground.

Peace Aims

On January 8, 1918, President Wilson submitted to the U.S. Congress an outline known as the "Fourteen Points" that he believed justified the enormous military struggle as being fought for a moral cause. Later, Wilson spelled out additional steps for a truly just and lasting peace. Wilson's proposals included "open covenants of peace, openly arrived at" instead of secret diplomacy; the reduction of national armaments to a "point consistent with domestic safety"; and the **self-determination** of peoples so that "all well-defined national aspirations shall be accorded the utmost satisfaction." Wilson characterized World War I as a people's war waged against "absolutism and militarism," two scourges of liberty that could only be eliminated by creating democratic governments and a "general association of nations" that would guarantee the "political independence and territorial integrity to great and small states alike" (see the box on p. 806). As the spokesman for a new world order based on democracy and international cooperation, Wilson was enthusiastically cheered by many Europeans when he arrived in Europe for the peace conference. Wilson's rhetoric on self-determination was also heard by peoples in the colonial world and was influential in inspiring anticolonial nationalist movements in Africa, Asia, and the Middle East (see Chapter 26).

Wilson soon found, however, that other states at the Paris Peace Conference were guided by considerably more pragmatic motives. The secret treaties and agreements, for example, that had been made before the war could not be totally ignored, even if they did conflict with the principle of self-determination enunciated by Wilson. National interests also complicated the deliberations of the Paris Peace Conference. David Lloyd George, prime minister of Great Britain, had won a decisive electoral victory in December 1918 on a platform of making the Germans pay for this dreadful war.

France's approach to peace was primarily determined by considerations of national security. Georges Clemenceau, the feisty premier of France, believed that the French people had borne the brunt of German aggression and deserved revenge and security against future German aggression (see the box on p. 806). Clemenceau wanted a demilitarized Germany, vast German reparations to pay for the costs of the war, and a separate Rhineland as a buffer state between France and Germany—demands that Wilson viewed as vindictive and contrary to the principle of national self-determination.

Yet another consideration affected the negotiations at Paris: the fear that Bolshevik revolution would spread from Russia to other European countries. This concern led the Allies to enlarge and strengthen such eastern

The Big Four at Paris. Shown here are the Big Four at the Paris Peace Conference: David Lloyd George of Britain, Vittorio Orlando of Italy, Georges Clemenceau of France, and Woodrow Wilson of the United States. Although Italy was considered one of the Big Four powers, Britain, France, and the United States (the Big Three) made the major decisions at the peace conference.

European states as Poland, Czechoslovakia, and Romania at the expense of both Germany and Bolshevik Russia.

Although twenty-seven nations were represented at the Paris Peace Conference, the most important decisions were made by Wilson, Clemenceau, and Lloyd George. Italy was considered one of the so-called Big Four powers but played a much less important role than the other three countries. Germany, of course, was not invited to attend, and Russia could not because of civil war, although the Allies were also unwilling to negotiate with the Communist regime that was then fighting for power in Russia.

In view of the many conflicting demands at the conference table, it was inevitable that the Big Three would quarrel. Wilson was determined to create a "league of nations" to prevent future wars. Clemenceau and Lloyd George were equally determined to punish Germany. In the end, only compromise made it possible to achieve a peace settlement. On January 25, 1919, the conference adopted the principle of the League of Nations. The details of its structure were left for later sessions, and Wilson willingly agreed to make compromises on territorial arrangements to guarantee the establishment of the League, believing that a functioning League could later rectify bad arrangements. Clemenceau also compromised to obtain some guarantees for French security. He renounced France's desire for a separate Rhineland and instead accepted a defensive alliance with Great Britain and the United States. Both states pledged to help France if it was attacked by Germany.

Opposing >< VIEWPOINTS

Three Voices of Peacemaking

When the Allied powers met in Paris in January 1919, it soon became apparent that the victors had different opinions on the kind of peace they expected. The first selection is a series of excerpts from the speeches of Woodrow Wilson in which the American president presented his idealistic goals for a peace based on justice and reconciliation.

The French leader Georges Clemenceau had a vision of peacemaking quite different from that of Woodrow Wilson. The French sought revenge and security. In the selection from his book *Grandeur and Misery of Victory*, Clemenceau revealed his fundamental dislike and distrust of Germany.

Yet a third voice of peacemaking was heard in Paris in 1919, although not at the peace conference. W. E. B. Du Bois, an African American writer and activist, had organized the Pan-African Congress to meet in Paris during the sessions of the Paris Peace Conference. The goal of the Pan-African Congress was to present a series of resolutions that promoted the cause of Africans and people of African descent. As can be seen in the selection presented here, the resolutions did not call for immediate independence for African nations.

Woodrow Wilson, Speeches

May 26, 1917

We are fighting for the liberty, the self-government, and the undictated development of all peoples, and every feature of the settlement that concludes this war must be conceived and executed for that purpose. Wrongs must first be righted and then adequate safeguards must be created to prevent their being committed again. . . .

No people must be forced under sovereignty under which it does not wish to live. No territory must change hands except for the purpose of securing those who inhabit it a fair chance of life and liberty. No indemnities must be insisted on except those that constitute payment for manifest wrongs done. No readjustments of power must be made except such as will tend to secure the future peace of the world and the future welfare and happiness of its peoples.

And then the free peoples of the world must draw together in some common covenant, some genuine and practical cooperation that will in effect combine their force to secure peace and justice in the dealings of nations with one another.

April 6, 1918

We are ready, whenever the final reckoning is made, to be just to the German people, deal fairly with the German power, as with all others. There can be no difference between peoples in the final judgment, if it is indeed to be a righteous judgment. To propose anything but justice, even-handed and dispassionate justice, to Germany at any time, whatever the outcome of the war, would be to renounce and dishonor our own cause. For we ask nothing that we are not willing to accord.

January 3, 1919

Our task at Paris is to organize the friendship of the world, to see to it that all the moral forces that make for right and justice and liberty are united and are given a vital organization to which the peoples of the world will readily and gladly respond. In other words, our task is no less colossal than this, to set up a new international psychology, to have a new atmosphere.

Georges Clemenceau, *Grandeur and Misery of Victory*

War and peace, with their strong contrasts, alternate against a common background. For the catastrophe of 1914 the Germans are responsible. Only a professional liar would deny this. . . .

What after all is this war, prepared, undertaken, and waged by the German people, who flung aside every scruple of conscience to let it loose, hoping for a peace of enslavement under the yoke of a militarism, destructive of all human dignity? It is simply the continuance, the recrudescence, of those never-ending acts of violence by which the first savage tribes carried out their depredations with all the resources of barbarism. . . .

I have sometimes penetrated into the sacred cave of the Germanic cult, which is, as every one knows, the *Bierhaus* [beer hall]. A great aisle of massive humanity where there accumulate, amid the fumes of tobacco and beer, the popular rumblings of a nationalism upheld by the sonorous brasses blaring to the heavens the supreme voice of Germany, *Deutschland über alles! Germany above everything!* Men, women, and children, all petrified in reverence before the divine stoneware pot, brows furrowed with irrepressible power, eyes lost in a dream of infinity, mouths twisted by the intensity of willpower, drink in long draughts the celestial hope of vague expectations. These only remain to be realized presently when the chief marked out by Destiny shall have given the word. There you have the ultimate framework of an old but childish race.

(continued)

Pan-African Congress

Resolved

That the Allied and Associated Powers establish a code of law for the international protection of the natives of Africa....

The Negroes of the world demand that hereafter the natives of Africa and the peoples of African descent be governed according to the following principles:

1. The Land: the land and its natural resources shall be held in trust for the natives and at all times they shall have effective ownership of as much land as they can profitably develop....

3. Labor: slavery and corporal punishment shall be abolished and forced labor except in punishment for crime....

5. The State: the natives of Africa must have the right to participate in the government as fast as their development permits, in conformity with the principle that the government exists for the natives, and not the natives for the government.

Q How did the peacemaking aims of Wilson and Clemenceau differ? How did their different views affect the deliberations of the Paris Peace Conference and the nature of the final peace settlement? How and why did the views of the Pan-African Congress differ from those of Wilson and Clemenceau?

The Treaty of Versailles

The final peace settlement of Paris consisted of five separate treaties with the defeated nations—Germany, Austria, Hungary, Bulgaria, and the Ottoman Empire. The Treaty of Versailles with Germany, signed on June 28, 1919, was by far the most important. The Germans considered it a harsh peace, conveniently overlooking that the Treaty of Brest-Litovsk, which they had imposed on Bolshevik Russia, was even more severe. The Germans were particularly unhappy with Article 231, the so-called **War Guilt Clause,** which declared Germany (and Austria) responsible for starting the war and ordered Germany to pay **reparations** for all the damage to which the Allied governments and their people were subjected as a result of the war "imposed upon them by the aggression of Germany and her allies." Reparations were a logical consequence of the wartime promises that Allied leaders had made to their people that the Germans would pay for the war effort. The treaty did not establish the amount to be paid but left that to be determined later by a reparations commission (see Chapter 26).

Treaty of Versailles, excerpts (1919)

The military and territorial provisions of the treaty also rankled the Germans, although they were by no means as harsh as the Germans claimed. Germany had to reduce its army to 100,000 men, cut back its navy, and eliminate its air force. German territorial losses included the cession of Alsace and Lorraine to France and sections of Prussia to the new Polish state. German land west and as far as 30 miles east of the Rhine was established as a demilitarized zone and stripped of all armaments or fortifications to serve as a barrier to any future German military moves westward against France. Outraged by the "dictated peace," the new German government vowed to resist rather than accept the treaty, but it had no real alternative. Rejection meant a renewal of the war, and as the army pointed out, that was no longer practicable.

The Other Peace Treaties

The separate peace treaties made with the other Central Powers extensively redrew the map of eastern Europe. Many of these changes merely ratified what the war had already accomplished. The empires that had controlled eastern Europe for centuries had been destroyed or weakened, and a number of new states appeared on the map of Europe (see Map 25.5).

Both the German and Russian empires lost considerable territory in eastern Europe, and the Austro-Hungarian Empire disappeared altogether. New nation-states emerged from the lands of these three empires: Finland, Latvia, Estonia, Lithuania, Poland, Czechoslovakia, Austria, and Hungary. Territorial rearrangements were also made in the Balkans. Romania acquired additional lands from Russia, Hungary, and Bulgaria. Serbia formed the nucleus of the new state of Yugoslavia.

Although the Paris Peace Conference was supposedly guided by the principle of self-determination, the mixtures of peoples in eastern Europe made it impossible to draw boundaries along neat ethnic lines. Compromises had to be made, sometimes to satisfy the national interest of the victors. France, for example, had lost Russia as its major ally on Germany's eastern border and wanted to strengthen and expand Poland, Czechoslovakia, Yugoslavia, and Romania as much as possible so that those states could serve as barriers against Germany and Communist Russia. As a result of compromises, virtually every eastern European state was left with a minorities problem that could lead to future conflicts. Germans in Poland; Hungarians, Poles, and Germans in Czechoslovakia; and Serbs, Croats, Slovenes, Macedonians, and Albanians in Yugoslavia all became sources of later conflict.

The centuries-old Ottoman Empire was dismembered by the peace settlement after the war. To gain Arab support against the Ottomans during the war, the Allies had promised to recognize the independence of Arab states in

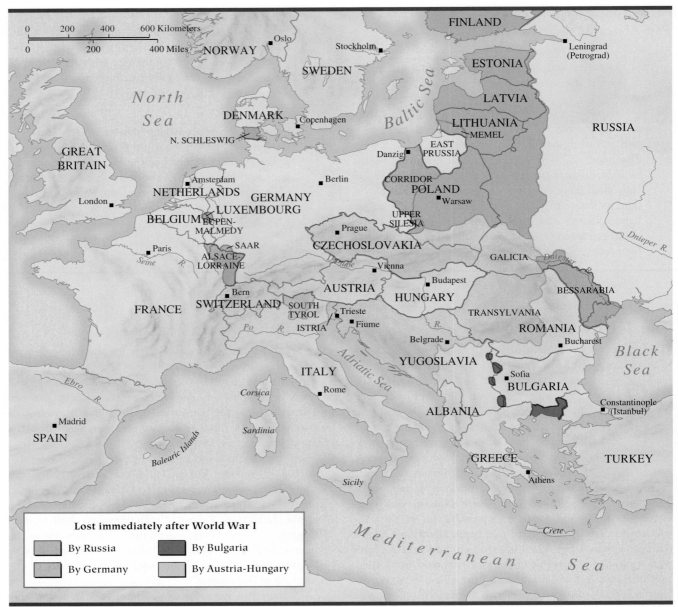

MAP 25.5 Europe in 1919. The victorious allies met to determine the shape and nature of postwar Europe. At the urging of U.S. President Woodrow Wilson, many nationalist aspirations of former imperial subjects were realized with the creation of several new countries from the prewar territory of Austria-Hungary, Germany, and Russia.

Q *What new countries emerged, and what countries gained territory when Austria-Hungary was dismembered?*

View an animated version of this map or related maps on the CourseMate website.

---

the Middle Eastern lands of the Ottoman Empire. But the imperialist habits of Europeans died hard. After the war, France took control of Lebanon and Syria, and Britain received Iraq and Palestine (see the map on p. 809). Officially, both acquisitions were called **mandates.** Since Woodrow Wilson had opposed the outright annexation of colonial territories by the Allies, the peace settlement had created a system of mandates whereby a nation officially administered a territory on behalf of the League of Nations. The system of mandates could not hide the fact that the principle of national self-determination at the Paris Peace Conference was largely for Europeans.

The peace settlement negotiated at Paris soon came under attack, not only by the defeated Central Powers but also by others who felt that the peacemakers had been shortsighted. Some people agreed, however, that the settlement was the best that could be achieved under the circumstances. They believed that self-determination had served reasonably well as a central organizing principle, and the establishment of the League of Nations gave some hope that future conflicts could be resolved peacefully. Yet within twenty years, Europe would again be engaged in deadly conflict. As some historians have suggested, perhaps a lack of enforcement, rather than the structure of the settlement, may account for the failure of the peace of 1919.

Successful enforcement of the peace necessitated the active involvement of its principal architects, especially in helping the new German state develop a peaceful and democratic republic. The failure of the U.S. Senate to ratify the Treaty of Versailles, however, meant that the United States never

Constantinople (Instanbul)
TURKEY
SYRIA
LEBANON Beirut · PERSIA
Mediterranean Sea · Damascus · Baghdad
PALESTINE · IRAQ
Jerusalem · TRANS-
Cairo · JORDAN · KUWAIT
EGYPT · SAUDI
0 250 500 750 Kilometers · ARABIA
0 250 500 Miles
Caspian Sea

The Middle East in 1919

joined the League of Nations. The Senate also rejected Wilson's defensive alliance with Great Britain and France. Already by the end of 1919, the United States was pursuing policies intended to limit its direct involvement in future European wars.

This retreat had dire consequences. American withdrawal from the defensive alliance with Britain and France led Britain to withdraw as well. By removing itself from European affairs, the United States forced France to stand alone facing its old enemy, leading the embittered nation to take strong actions against Germany that only intensified German resentment. By the end of 1919, it appeared that the peace established mere months earlier was already beginning to unravel.

CHAPTER SUMMARY

The assassination of Archduke Francis Ferdinand of Austria-Hungary in the Bosnian capital of Sarajevo in the summer of 1914 led within six weeks to a major war

among the major powers of Europe. The Germans drove the Russians back in the east, but a stalemate developed in the west, where trenches extending from the Swiss border to the English Channel were defended by barbed wire and machine guns. The Ottoman Empire joined Germany, and Italy became one of the Allies. After German submarine attacks, the United States entered the war in 1917, but even from the beginning of the war, battles also took place in the African colonies of the Great Powers as well as in the East, making this a truly global war.

Unprepared for war, Russia soon faltered and collapsed, leading to a revolution against the tsar. But the new provisional government in Russia also soon failed,

enabling the revolutionary Bolsheviks of V. I. Lenin to seize power. Lenin established a dictatorship and made a costly peace with Germany. After Russia's withdrawal from the war, Germany launched a massive attack in the west but had been

severely weakened by the war. In the fall of 1918, after American troops entered the conflict, the German government collapsed, leading to the armistice on November 11, 1918.

World War I was the defining event of the twentieth century. It shattered the liberal and rational assumptions of late-nineteenth and early-twentieth-century European society. The incredible destruction and the deaths of almost 10 million people undermined the whole idea of progress. New propaganda techniques had manipulated entire populations into sustaining their involvement in a meaningless slaughter.

World War I was a total war that required extensive mobilization of resources and populations. As a result, government centralization increased, as did the power of the state over the lives of its citizens. Civil liberties, such as freedom of the press, speech, assembly, and movement, were circumscribed in the name of national security. Governments' need to plan the production and distribution of goods and to ration consumer goods led to restrictions on economic freedom. Although the late nineteenth and early twentieth centuries had witnessed

the extension of government authority into such areas as mass education, social welfare legislation, and mass conscription, World War I made the practice of strong central authority a way of life.

Finally, World War I ended the age of European hegemony over world affairs. In 1917, the Russian Revolution had laid the foundation for the creation of a new Eurasian power, the Soviet Union, and the United States had entered the war. The waning of the European age was not evident to all, however, for it was clouded by American isolationism and the withdrawal of the Soviets from world affairs while they nurtured the growth of their own socialist system. These developments, though temporary, created a political vacuum in Europe that all too soon was filled by the revival of German power.

CHAPTER TIMELINE

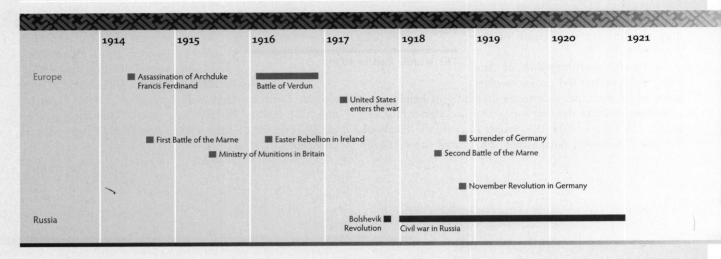

CHAPTER REVIEW

Upon Reflection

Q Which nation, if any, was most responsible for causing World War I? Why?

Q Why can 1917 be viewed as the year that witnessed the decisive turning point of the war?

Q How did Lenin and the Bolsheviks manage to seize and hold power despite their small numbers?

Key Terms

conscription (p. 777)
militarism (p. 777)
mobilization (p. 778)
trench warfare (p. 782)
total war (p. 791)
nationalization (p. 791)
soviets (p. 798)
Bolsheviks (p. 798)
war communism (p. 802)
genocide (p. 804)
self-determination (p. 805)
War Guilt Clause (p. 807)
reparations (p. 807)
mandates (p. 808)

Suggestions for Further Reading

GENERAL WORKS ON TWENTIETH-CENTURY EUROPE A number of general works on European history in the twentieth century provide a context for understanding both World War I and the Russian Revolution. Especially valuable is **N. Ferguson, *The War of the World: Twentieth-Century Conflict and the Descent of the West*** (New York, 2006). See also **R. Paxton, *Europe in the Twentieth Century,*** 4th ed. (New York, 2004), and **H. James, *Europe Reborn: A History, 1914–2000*** (London, 2003).

CAUSES OF WORLD WAR I The historical literature on the causes of World War I is enormous. Good starting points are **J. Joll** and **G. Martel, *The Origins of the First World War,*** 3rd ed. (London, 2006), and **A. Mombauer, *The Origins of the First World War: Controversies and Consensus*** (London, 2002). On the role of militarism, see **D. Hermann, *The Arming of Europe and the Making of the First World War*** (New York, 1997). On the events leading to war, see **D. Fromkin, *Europe's Last Summer: Who Started the Great War in 1914?*** (New York, 2004).

WORLD WAR I The best brief account of World War I is **H. Strachan, *The First World War*** (New York, 2003). Two additional accounts of World War I are **M. Gilbert, *The First World War*** (New York, 1994), and the lavishly illustrated book by **J. M. Winter, *The Experience of World War I*** (New York, 1989). There is an excellent collection of articles in **H. Strachan, *The Oxford Illustrated History of the First World War*** (New York, 1998). See also **S. Audoin-Rouzeau** and **A. Becker, *14–18: Understanding the Great War*** (New York, 2002). On the global nature of World War I, see **M. S. Neiberg, *Fighting the Great War: A Global History*** (Cambridge, Mass., 2005), and **J. H. Morrow Jr., *The Great War: An Imperial History*** (London, 2004). For an interesting perspective on World War I and the beginnings of the modern world, see **M. Eksteins, *Rites of Spring: The Great War and the Birth of the Modern Age*** (Boston, 1989). For a new interpretation, see **D. Stevenson, *Cataclysm: The First World War as Political Tragedy*** (New York, 2004).

WOMEN IN WORLD WAR I   On the role of women in World War I, see **S. Grayzel, *Women and the First World War*** (London, 2002), and **G. Braybon** and **P. Summerfield, *Women's Experiences in Two World Wars*** (London, 1987).

THE RUSSIAN REVOLUTION   A good introduction to the Russian Revolution can be found in **R. A. Wade, *The Russian Revolution, 1917,*** 2nd ed. (Cambridge, 2005), and **S. Fitzpatrick, *The Russian Revolution, 1917–1932,*** 2nd ed. (New York, 2001). For a study that puts the Russian Revolution into the context of World War I, see **P. Holquist, *Making War, Forging Revolution*** (Cambridge, Mass., 2002). On Lenin, see **R. Service, *Lenin: A Biography*** (Cambridge, Mass., 2000). On social reforms, see **W. Goldman, *Women, the State and Revolution*** (Cambridge, 1993). A comprehensive study of the Russian civil war is **W. B. Lincoln, *Red Victory: A History of the Russian Civil War*** (New York, 1989).

THE PEACE SETTLEMENT   On the Paris Peace Conference, see **M. MacMillan, *Paris 1919: Six Months That Changed the World*** (New York, 2002), and **E. Goldstein, *The First World War Peace Settlements*** (London, 2002). On the impact of Woodrow Wilson's ideas on the colonial world, see **E. Manela, *The Wilsonian Moment: Self-Determination and the International Origins of Anticolonial Nationalism*** (Oxford, 2007).

Visit the CourseMate website at www.cengagebrain.com for additional study tools and review materials for this chapter.

AP⁂ REVIEW QUESTIONS FOR CHAPTER 25

1. Which of the following alliances contributed the MOST to causing World War I?

   (A) France–United States
   (B) Germany-Italy
   (C) Serbia-Russia
   (D) Austria-Hungary–Ottoman Empire
   (E) Great Britain–Poland

2. Nationalism contributed to World War I by

   (A) suppressing negative attitudes toward minorities within newly created nation-states.
   (B) encouraging the rearmament of many nations to protect against their unruly masses.
   (C) generating the desire for self-rule and the willingness to take extreme measures to gain it.
   (D) creating a sense of identity within the new states of Western Europe as they sought greater control over colonized countries in Africa and Asia.
   (E) encouraging alliances between minorities across regions so they could gain political power throughout northern Europe.

3. Which of the following was NOT a new technology used in World War I?

   (A) airplanes
   (B) submarines
   (C) rifles
   (D) tanks
   (E) poison gas

4. Lenin's rallying cry of "Peace, Land and Bread" led to which of the following events?

   (A) Russia allied itself with the western powers in hopes that they would supply Russia with much-needed food and supplies.
   (B) Lenin successfully convinced the Russian people that he would guide them to a more prosperous time.
   (C) The Mensheviks retaliated against the Romanovs and won greater support from those hesitant to support the revolution.
   (D) Russia withdrew from World War I, dealing a huge blow to Germany and Austria-Hungary.
   (E) The Provisional government toppled the Bolshevik regime, as Lenin's slogan suggested that Russia might suffer psychological defeat by leaving the war.

5. Which of the following best describes the global scale of World War I?

   (A) People from India to Africa to China found themselves embroiled in the conflict.
   (B) Much of the fighting during the war took place in Japan and Africa instead of Europe.
   (C) People within colonized nations chose to fight on the side opposing their mother country.
   (D) Countless smaller wars broke out simultaneously throughout the world.
   (E) The United States acted as the official peacekeeper between Europe and the East.

6. All of the following contributed to World War I's high death toll EXCEPT

   (A) trench warfare.
   (B) following antiquated military strategy.
   (C) using modern weaponry.
   (D) a lack of sophisticated medical knowledge and resources.
   (E) decreasing global food production.

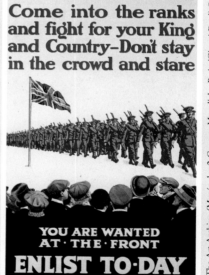

7. In the enlistment poster above, the British government was most likely appealing to

   (A) mothers and wives to encourage their sons and husbands to take part in the war.
   (B) unemployed and poor men who were seeking war employment.
   (C) educated professionals who were choosing not to enlist.
   (D) colonial subjects in the British Empire that were not taking part in the war.
   (E) Americans to help with the war and join the effort against the Central Powers.

8. The Russian Civil War resulted in

   (A) a cultural revival within the new Soviet state.
   (B) the establishment of a dictatorship led by the Mensheviks and supported by the United States and western Europe.
   (C) the formation of a republic dedicated to peace that held widespread popular support.
   (D) a Russian state under the direct leadership of a single-party regime.
   (E) the establishment of a new Duma and universal suffrage.

9. Which of the following was a legacy of World War I?

   (A) It tilted the balance of power from western Europe to Asia under China's leadership.
   (B) It sparked a new movement of nationalism that led to European decolonization.
   (C) Its embodiment of total war left entire nations devoid of a generation of men.
   (D) It instilled a collective fear of modernized warfare and a desire to reduce arms worldwide.
   (E) It created an effective peacekeeping body charged with establishing and maintaining world peace supported by a global military.

10. Which of the following was the spark that led to World War I?

   (A) the Serbian nationalist Gavrilo Princip's assassination of Archduke Francis Ferdinand
   (B) the United States' pursuit of unrestricted submarine warfare
   (C) the German invasions of Austria and Poland
   (D) the German invasion of Belgium in violation of Belgium's neutrality proclamation
   (E) the alliance of Austria-Hungary against Germany in response to the death of the Austrian leader

11. The Treaty of Versailles, signed in 1919,

   (A) created an amicable agreement among all the European states involved in World War I and established a peacekeeping body to eliminate further global tensions.
   (B) required Germany to accept the "war guilt" clause taking full responsibility for the war, and created new nations out of the broken Austro-Hungarian and Ottoman Empires.
   (C) successfully broke up the empires of central and eastern Europe and required western Europe to police the actions of the eastern countries.
   (D) signaled the emergence of the United States and Great Britain as world superpowers dedicated to maintaining global peace.
   (E) failed to give independence to many of the nations that fought for their autonomy during World War I.

12. Women were involved in World War I in all of the following ways EXCEPT

   (A) they worked in the factories in their home countries.
   (B) they served as nurses to help those injured during the conflict.
   (C) they were combatants in some countries, such as Russia.
   (D) they worked within government offices to support the war effort.
   (E) they led government agencies and held military commands.

13. Which of the following best describes the United States' contribution to World War I?

   (A) It remained neutral throughout the conflict, agreeing to help broker peace between the Allies and the Central Powers.
   (B) It provided weapons and supplies to both sides, becoming wealthier as a result.
   (C) It entered the war at about the same time that Russia left the war, continuing a unified assault against the Central Powers.
   (D) It sent troops at the beginning of the war and provided much-needed military leadership throughout the entire conflict.
   (E) It joined forces with Mexico in an attempt to retaliate against the Zimmermann Telegram issued by Germany.

14. *"Even if my heart breaks in death,*
   You will never be French.
   As you are rich in water
   Germany is rich in hero's blood.
   *   Dear Fatherland . . . ."*

   This song excerpt represents the concept of

   (A) militarism.
   (B) individualism.
   (C) nationalism.
   (D) volunteerism.
   (E) Marxism.

15. All of the following leaders played a part in World War I EXCEPT

   (A) Emperor William II of Germany.
   (B) President Woodrow Wilson of the United States.
   (C) Tsar Nicholas II of Russia.
   (D) Prime Minister Lloyd George of Great Britain.
   (E) Emperor Joseph II of Austria.

Woman with a soup bowl on her way to a soup kitchen in Germany in 1930

© Interfoto/Alamy

The Futile Search for Stability: Europe Between the Wars, 1919–1939

CHAPTER OUTLINE AND FOCUS QUESTIONS

An Uncertain Peace

Q What was the impact of World War I, and what problems did European countries face in the 1920s?

The Democratic States in the West

Q How did France, Great Britain, and the United States respond to the various crises, including the Great Depression, that they faced in the interwar years? How did World War I affect Europe's colonies in Asia and Africa?

The Authoritarian and Totalitarian States

Q Why did many European states experience a retreat from democracy in the interwar years? What are the characteristics of totalitarian states, and to what degree were these characteristics present in Fascist Italy, Nazi Germany, and Stalinist Russia?

The Expansion of Mass Culture and Mass Leisure

Q What new dimensions in mass culture and mass leisure emerged during the interwar years, and what role did these activities play in the totalitarian states?

Cultural and Intellectual Trends in the Interwar Years

Q What were the main cultural and intellectual trends in the interwar years?

CRITICAL THINKING

Q Why have some historians called the 1920s both an age of anxiety and a period of hope?

ONLY TWENTY YEARS after the Treaty of Versailles, Europeans were again at war. Yet in the 1920s, many people assumed that the world was about to enter a new era of international peace, economic growth, and political democracy. In all of these areas, the optimistic hopes of the 1920s failed to be realized. After 1919, most people wanted peace but were unsure how to maintain it. The League of Nations, conceived as a new instrument to provide for collective security, failed to work well. New treaties that renounced the use of war looked good on paper but had no means of enforcement. Then, too, virtually everyone favored disarmament, but few could agree on how to achieve it.

Europe faced serious economic and social hardships after World War I. The European economy did not begin to recover from the war until 1922, and even then it was beset by financial problems left over from the war and, most devastating of all, the severe depression that began at the end of 1929. The Great Depression brought misery to millions of people. Begging for food on the streets became widespread, especially when soup kitchens were unable to keep up with the demand. Larger and larger numbers of people were homeless and moved from place to place looking for work and shelter. In the United States, the homeless set up shantytowns they derisively named "Hoovervilles" after the U.S. president,

Herbert Hoover. Some of the destitute saw but one solution; as one unemployed person expressed it, "Today, when I am experiencing this for the first time, I think that I should prefer to do away with myself, to take gas, to jump into the river, or leap from some high place.... Would I really come to such a decision? I do not know. Animals die, plants wither, but men always go on living." Social unrest spread rapidly, and some unemployed staged hunger marches to get attention. In democratic countries, more and more people began to listen to and vote for radical voices calling for extreme measures.

According to Woodrow Wilson, World War I had been fought to make the world safe for democracy, and for a while after 1919, political democracy seemed well on its way. But hope soon faded as authoritarian regimes spread into Italy and Germany and across eastern Europe.

An Uncertain Peace

 FOCUS QUESTION: What was the impact of World War I, and what problems did European countries face in the 1920s?

Four years of devastating war had left many Europeans with a profound sense of despair and disillusionment. The Great War indicated to many people that something was dreadfully wrong with Western values. In *The Decline of the West,* the German writer Oswald Spengler (1880–1936) reflected this disillusionment when he emphasized the decadence of Western civilization and posited its collapse.

The Impact of World War I

The enormous suffering and the deaths of almost 10 million people shook traditional society to its foundations and undermined the whole idea of progress. New propaganda techniques had manipulated entire populations into maintaining their involvement in a senseless slaughter. How did Europeans deal with such losses? In France, for example, probably two-thirds of the population were in mourning over the deaths of these young people.

An immediate response was the erection of war memorials accompanied by ceremonies to honor the dead. Battlefields also became significant commemorative sites with memorial parks, large monuments, and massive cemeteries, including ossuaries or vaults where the bones of thousands of unidentified soldiers were interred. Virtually all belligerent countries adopted national ceremonies for the burial of an Unknown Soldier, a telling reminder of the brutality of World War I. Moreover, businesses, schools, universities, and other corporate bodies all set up their own war memorials.

It is impossible to calculate the social impact of the mourning for the lost soldiers. One French mother explained, "No matter how proud as Frenchwomen we poor mothers may be of our sons, we nevertheless carry wounds in our hearts that nothing can heal. It is strongly contrary to nature for our children to depart before us." Another Frenchman wrote, "Why should the old people remain alive, when the children who might have initiated the most beautiful era in French history march off to the sacrifice?"[1]

World War I created a lost generation of war veterans who had become accustomed to violence. In the course of the war, extreme violence and brutality became a way of life and a social reality. As one Frenchman recounted: "Not only did war make us dead, impotent or blind. In the midst of beautiful actions, of sacrifice and self-abnegation, it also awoke in us, ... ancient instincts of cruelty and barbarity. At times, I, who have never punched anyone, who loathes disorder and brutality, took pleasure in killing."[2] After the war, some veterans became pacifists, but for many veterans, the violence of the war became a starting point for the use of violence in the new political movements of the 1920s and 1930s (see "The Authoritarian and Totalitarian States" later in this chapter). These men were fiercely nationalistic and eager to restore the national interests they felt had been betrayed in the peace treaties.

The Search for Security

The peace treaties at the end of World War I had tried to fulfill the nineteenth-century dream of nationalism by redrawing boundaries and creating new states. Nevertheless, this peace settlement had left many nations unhappy. Conflicts over disputed border regions poisoned mutual relations in eastern Europe for years, and many Germans viewed the Peace of Versailles as a dictated peace and vowed to seek its revision.

U.S. President Woodrow Wilson had recognized that the peace treaties contained unwise provisions that could serve as new causes for conflicts and had put many of his hopes for the future in the League of Nations. Although the League had some success in guaranteeing protection for the rights of the many ethnic and religious minorities that remained in some of the newly formed states, the League was not particularly effective at maintaining the peace. The failure of the United States to join the League and the subsequent American determination to be less involved in European affairs undermined the League's effectiveness from the beginning. Moreover, the League's sole weapon for halting aggression was the imposition of economic sanctions such as trade embargoes and the severance of financial ties by League members. Such measures, however, failed to prevent League members from engaging in military action: Greece embarked on land-grabbing expeditions in Asia Minor, Italian naval forces bombed the Greek island of Corfu, and Japan seized Manchuria in 1931. The League's failure to reprimand its members for their acts of military aggression further undermined its credibility. Efforts to promote disarmament were also ineffective, despite provisions in both the League's covenant and the Treaty of Versailles. Although the League established a special commission to handle the task in 1926, it did not meet until 1932, and by that time Japan had already begun to rearm and Germany would soon do so.

The weakness of the League of Nations and the failure of the United States to honor its promise to form a defensive military alliance with France left the French feeling embittered and alone. Fear of German aggression led them to reject the possibility of disarmament. Before World War I, France's alliance with Russia had served to threaten Germany with the possibility of a two-front war. But Communist Russia was now a hostile power. To compensate, France built a network of alliances in eastern Europe with Poland and the members of the so-called Little Entente (Czechoslovakia, Romania, Yugoslavia). Although these alliances looked good on paper as a way to contain Germany and maintain the new status quo, they overlooked the fundamental military weaknesses of those nations. Poland and the Little Entente states were not substitutes for Russia.

THE FRENCH POLICY OF COERCION (1919–1924) Unable to secure military support through the League of Nations, France sought security between 1919 and 1924 by relying primarily on a strict enforcement of the Treaty of Versailles. This tough policy toward Germany began with the issue of reparations, the payments that the Germans were supposed to make to compensate for the "damage done to the civilian population of the Allied and Associated Powers and to their property," as the treaty asserted. In April 1921, the Allied Reparations Commission settled on a sum of 132 billion marks ($33 billion) for German reparations, payable in annual installments of 2.5 billion (gold) marks. Allied threats to occupy the Ruhr valley, Germany's chief industrial and mining center, led the new German republic to accept the reparations settlement and make its first payment in 1921. By the following year, however, facing financial problems, the German government announced that it was unable to pay any more. Outraged by what they considered Germany's violation of the peace settlement, the French government sent troops to occupy the Ruhr valley. If the Germans would not pay reparations, the French would collect reparations in kind by operating and using the Ruhr mines and factories.

Both Germany and France suffered from the French occupation of the Ruhr. The German government adopted a policy of passive resistance that was largely financed by printing more paper money, but this only intensified the inflationary pressures that had already appeared in Germany by the end of the war. The German mark soon became worthless. In 1914, a dollar was worth 4.2 marks; by November 1, 1923, the rate had reached 130 billion marks to the dollar, and by the end of November, it had snowballed to an incredible 4.2 trillion marks to the dollar.

The Little Entente

Economic disaster fueled political upheavals as Communists staged uprisings in October 1923, and Adolf Hitler's band of Nazis attempted to seize power in Munich in November (see "Hitler and Nazi Germany" later in this chapter). But the French were hardly victorious. Their gains from the occupation were not enough to offset the costs. Meanwhile, pressure from the United States and Great Britain forced the French to agree to a new conference of experts to reassess the reparations problem. By the time the conference did its work in 1924, both France and Germany were willing to pursue a more conciliatory approach toward each other.

The Hopeful Years (1924–1929)

The formation of new governments in both Great Britain and France opened the door to conciliatory approaches to

The Effects of Inflation. The inflationary pressures that had begun in Germany at the end of World War I intensified during the French occupation of the Ruhr. By the early 1920s, the value of the German mark had fallen precipitously. This photograph shows German children using bundles of worthless money as building blocks. The wads of money were cheaper than toys.

© Three Lions/Getty Images

Germany and the reparations problem. At the same time, a new German government led by Gustav Stresemann (GOOS-tahf SHTRAY-zuh-mahn) (1878–1929) ended the policy of passive resistance and committed Germany to carry out most of the provisions of the Treaty of Versailles while seeking a new settlement of the reparations question. At the same time, the German government stabilized the currency and ended the extreme inflation by issuing a new temporary currency, the Rentenmark, equal to 3 trillion old marks.

In August 1924, an international commission produced a new plan for reparations. Named the Dawes Plan after the American banker who chaired the commission, it reduced reparations and stabilized Germany's payments on the basis of its ability to pay. The Dawes Plan also granted an initial $200 million loan for German recovery, which opened the door to heavy American investments in Europe that helped usher in a new era of European prosperity between 1924 and 1929.

THE SPIRIT OF LOCARNO   With prosperity came new efforts at European diplomacy. A spirit of international cooperation was fostered by the foreign ministers of Germany and France, Gustav Stresemann and Aristide Briand (ah-ruh-STEED bree-AHNH) (1862–1932), who concluded the Treaty of Locarno in 1925. This guaranteed Germany's new western borders with France and Belgium. Although Germany's new eastern borders with Poland were conspicuously absent from the agreement, a clear indication that Germany did not accept those borders as permanent, the Locarno pact was viewed by many as the beginning of a new era of European peace. On the day after the pact was concluded, the headline in the *New York Times* ran "France and Germany Ban War Forever," and the *London Times* declared, "Peace at Last."[3]

Germany's entry into the League of Nations in March 1926 soon reinforced the new spirit of conciliation engendered at Locarno. Two years later, similar optimistic attitudes prevailed in the Kellogg-Briand pact, drafted by the American secretary of state Frank B. Kellogg and the French foreign minister Aristide Briand. Sixty-three nations eventually agreed to the pact, in which they pledged "to renounce war as an instrument of national policy." Nothing was said, however, about what would be done if anyone violated the treaty.

Kellogg-Briand
Pact (1928)

The spirit of Locarno was based on little real substance. Germany lacked the military power to alter its western borders even if it wanted to. And the issue of disarmament soon proved that even the spirit of Locarno could not induce nations to cut back on their weapons. The League of Nations Covenant had suggested the "reduction of national armaments to the lowest point consistent with national safety." Germany, of course, had been disarmed with the expectation that other states would do likewise. Numerous disarmament conferences, however, failed to achieve anything substantial as states proved unwilling to trust their security to anyone but their own military forces. When the world disarmament conference finally met in Geneva in 1932, the issue was already dead.

COEXISTENCE WITH SOVIET RUSSIA   One other hopeful sign in the years between 1924 and 1929 was the new coexistence of the West with Soviet Russia. By the beginning of 1924, Soviet hopes for Communist revolutions in Western states had largely dissipated. In turn, these states had realized by then that the Bolshevik regime could not be ousted. By 1924, Germany, Britain, France, and Italy, as well as several smaller European countries, had established full diplomatic relations with Soviet Russia. Nevertheless, Western powers remained highly suspicious of Soviet intentions.

The Great Depression

After World War I, most European states hoped to return to the liberal ideal of a market economy based on private enterprise and largely free of state intervention. But the war had vastly strengthened business cartels and labor unions, making some government regulation of these powerful organizations appear necessary. Then, too, the economic integration of Europe before 1914 that had been based on free trade was soon undermined by a wave of protectionism and trade barriers, and reparations and war debts had further damaged the postwar international economy. Consequently, the prosperity that did occur between 1924 and 1929 was uncommonly fragile, and the dream of returning to a self-regulating market economy was mere illusion. Then, to dash the dream altogether, along came the Great Depression.

CAUSES   Two factors played an important role in bringing on the Great Depression: a downturn in domestic economies and an international financial crisis caused by the collapse of the American stock market in 1929. Already in the mid-1920s, prices for agricultural goods were beginning to decline rapidly due to overproduction of basic commodities, such as wheat. During the war, farmers in Argentina, Australia, Canada, and the United States had expanded food production to meet the demands of the warring European nations. Following the war, production was not curtailed, in the expectation that Europe would not recover from the devastation of its fields and the loss of farmers. By 1927, however, European production returned to prewar levels, causing a sharp decline in commodity prices. Prices fell by 30 percent between 1924 and 1929. Moreover, in 1925, states in central and eastern Europe began to impose tariffs, closing their markets to other countries' goods. An increase in the use of oil and hydroelectricity led to a slump in the coal industry even before 1929.

Furthermore, much of Europe's prosperity between 1924 and 1929 had been built on American bank loans to Germany. Twenty-three billion new marks had been invested in German municipal bonds and German industries

The Great Depression: Bread Lines in Paris. The Great Depression devastated the European economy and had serious political repercussions. Because of its more balanced economy, France did not feel the effects of the depression as quickly as other European countries. By 1931, however, even France was experiencing lines of unemployed people at free-food centers.

since 1924. Already in 1928 and 1929, American investors had begun to pull money out of Germany in order to invest in the booming New York stock market. The crash of the American stock market in October 1929 led panicky American investors to withdraw even more of their funds from Germany and other European markets. The withdrawal of funds seriously weakened the banks of Germany and other central European states. The Credit-Anstalt, Vienna's most prestigious bank, collapsed on May 31, 1931. By that time, trade was slowing down, industrialists were cutting back production, and unemployment was increasing as the ripple effects of international bank failures had a devastating impact on domestic economies.

UNEMPLOYMENT Economic depression was by no means a new phenomenon in European history. But the depth of the economic downturn after 1929 fully justifies the "Great Depression" label. During 1932, the worst year of the depression, one British worker in four was unemployed, and 6 million Germans—40 percent of the German labor force—were out of work. Between 1929 and 1932, industrial production plummeted almost 50 percent in the United States and nearly as much in Germany. The unemployed and homeless filled the streets of cities throughout the advanced industrial countries (see the box on p. 817).

SOCIAL AND POLITICAL REPERCUSSIONS The economic crisis also had unexpected social repercussions. Women were often able to secure low-paying jobs as servants, housecleaners, or laundresses while many men remained unemployed, either begging on the streets or staying at home to do household tasks. Many unemployed men, resenting this reversal of traditional gender roles, were open to the shrill cries of demagogues with simple solutions to the economic crisis. High unemployment rates among young males often led them to join gangs that gathered in

parks or other public places, arousing fear among local residents.

Governments seemed powerless to deal with the crisis. The classical liberal remedy for depression, a deflationary policy of balanced budgets, which involved cutting costs by lowering wages and raising tariffs to exclude other countries' goods from home markets, only served to worsen the economic crisis and create even greater mass discontent. This in turn led to serious political repercussions. Increased government activity in the economy was one reaction, even in countries like the United States that had a strong *laissez-faire* tradition. Another effect was a renewed interest in Marxist doctrines, since Marx had predicted that capitalism would destroy itself through overproduction. Communism took on new popularity, especially among workers and intellectuals. Finally, the Great Depression increased the attractiveness of simplistic dictatorial solutions, especially from a new authoritarian movement known as **fascism.** Everywhere in Europe, democracy seemed on the defensive in the 1930s.

The Democratic States in the West

Q **FOCUS QUESTIONS:** How did France, Great Britain, and the United States respond to the various crises, including the Great Depression, that they faced in the interwar years? How did World War I affect Europe's colonies in Asia and Africa?

Woodrow Wilson proclaimed that World War I had been fought to make the world safe for democracy, and in 1919, there seemed to be some justification for that claim. Four major European states and a host of minor ones had functioning political democracies. In a number of nations,

The Great Depression: Unemployed and Homeless in Germany

In 1932, Germany had 6 million unemployed workers, many of them wandering aimlessly through the country, begging for food and seeking shelter in city lodging houses for the homeless. The Great Depression was an important factor in the rise to power of Adolf Hitler and the Nazis. This selection presents a description of the unemployed homeless in 1932.

Heinrich Hauser, "With Germany's Unemployed"

An almost unbroken chain of homeless men extends the whole length of the great Hamburg-Berlin highway.... All the highways in Germany over which I have traveled this year presented the same aspect....

Most of the hikers paid no attention to me. They walked separately or in small groups, with their eyes on the ground. And they had the queer, stumbling gait of barefooted people, for their shoes were slung over their shoulders. Some of them were guild members—carpenters ... milkmen ... and bricklayers ... —but they were in a minority. Far more numerous were those whom one could assign to no special profession or craft—unskilled young people, for the most part, who had been unable to find a place for themselves in any city or town in Germany, and who had never had a job and never expected to have one. There was something else that had never been seen before—whole families that had piled all their goods into baby carriages and wheelbarrows that they were pushing along as they plodded forward in dumb despair. It was a whole nation on the march.

I saw them—and this was the strongest impression that the year 1932 left with me—I saw them, gathered into groups of fifty or a hundred men, attacking fields of potatoes. I saw them digging up the potatoes and throwing them into sacks while the farmer who owned the field watched them in despair and the local policeman looked on gloomily from the distance. I saw them staggering toward the lights of the city as night fell, with their sacks on their backs. What did it remind me of? Of the War, of the worst periods of starvation in 1917 and 1918, but even then people paid for the potatoes....

I saw that the individual can know what is happening only by personal experience. I know what it is to be a tramp. I know what cold and hunger are.... But there are two things that I have only recently experienced—begging and spending the night in a municipal lodging house.

I entered the huge Berlin municipal lodging house in a northern quarter of the city....

Distribution of spoons, distribution of enameled-ware bowls with the words "Property of the City of Berlin" written on their sides. Then the meal itself. A big kettle is carried. Men with yellow smocks have brought it in and men with yellow smocks ladle out the food. These men, too, are homeless and they have been expressly picked by the establishment and given free food and lodging and a little pocket money in exchange for their work about the house.

Where have I seen this kind of food distribution before? In a prison that I once helped to guard in the winter of 1919 during the German civil war. There was the same hunger then, the same trembling, anxious expectation of rations. Now the men are standing in a long row, dressed in their plain nightshirts that reach to the ground, and the noise of their shuffling feet is like the noise of big wild animals walking up and down the stone floor of their cages before feeding time. The men lean far over the kettle so that the warm steam from the food envelops them and they hold out their bowls as if begging and whisper to the attendant, "Give me a real helping. Give me a little more." A piece of bread is handed out with every bowl.

My next recollection is sitting at a table in another room on a crowded bench that is like a seat in a fourth-class railway carriage. Hundreds of hungry mouths make an enormous noise eating their food. The men sit bent over their food like animals who feel that someone is going to take it away from them. They hold their bowl with their left arm part way around it, so that nobody can take it away, and they also protect it with their other elbow and with their head and mouth, while they move the spoon as fast as they can between their mouth and the bowl.

Q Why did Hauser compare the scene he describes from 1932 with conditions in the years 1917 and 1918? How did the growing misery of many ordinary Germans promote the rise of extremist political parties like the Nazis?

---

universal male suffrage had even been replaced by universal suffrage as male politicians rewarded women for their contributions to World War I by granting them the right to vote (except in Italy, France, and Spain, where women had to wait until the end of World War II). Women also began to enter political life as deputies to parliamentary bodies. In the new German republic, for example, almost 10 percent of the deputies elected to the Reichstag in 1919 were women, although the number dropped to 6 percent by 1926.

Great Britain

After World War I, Great Britain went through a period of painful readjustment and serious economic difficulties.

The Struggles of a Democracy: Unemployment and Slums in Great Britain

During the 1920s and 1930s, Britain struggled with a series of economic difficulties. Unemployment was widespread, especially after the onset of the Great Depression. Even after Britain began to recover in the late 1930s, many Britons still lived in wretched conditions. These selections reflect Britain's economic and social problems.

Men Without Work: A Report Made to the Pilgrim Trust, 1938

A week's notice may end half a lifetime's service, with no prospects, if he is elderly, but the dole, followed by a still further reduction in his means of livelihood when the old age pension comes. We take as an example a shoe laster from Leicester, who had worked thirty-seven years with one firm. "When I heard the new manager going through and saying: 'The whole of this side of this room, this room, and this room is to be stopped,' I knew it would be uphill work to get something." He went on to describe to us how he had not been able to bring himself to tell his wife the bad news when he got home, how she had noticed that something was wrong, how confident she had been that he would get work elsewhere, but how he had known that the chances were heavily against him. For months and indeed often for years such men go on looking for work, and the same is true of many casual laborers. There were in the sample old men who have not a remote chance of working again but yet make it a practice to stand every morning at six o'clock at the works gates in the hope that perhaps they may catch the foreman's eye.

George Orwell, "A Woman in the Slums"

As we moved slowly through the outskirts of the town we passed row after row of little grey slum houses.... At the back of one of the houses a young woman was kneeling on the stones, poking a stick up the leaden wastepipe which ran from the sink inside, and which I suppose was blocked.... She had a round pale face, the usual exhausted face of the slum girl who is twenty-five and looks forty, thanks to miscarriages and drudgery; and it wore, for the second in which I saw it, the most desolate, hopeless expression I have ever seen. It struck me then that we are mistaken when we say that "It isn't the same for them as it would be for us," and that people bred in the slums can imagine nothing but the slums. For what I saw in her face was not the ignorant suffering of an animal. She knew well enough what was happening to her—understood as well as I did how dreadful a destiny it was to be kneeling there in the bitter cold, on the slimy stones of a slum backyard, poking a stick up a foul drain-pipe.

Q What economic and social problems are described in these documents? What do these pieces tell you about the quality of life and politics in Great Britain during the interwar years?

During the war, Britain had lost many of its markets for industrial products, especially to the United States and Japan. The postwar decline of such staple industries as coal, steel, and textiles led to a rise in unemployment, which reached the 2 million mark in 1921. The continuing wartime coalition government led by Liberal David Lloyd George proved unable to change this situation.

By 1923, British politics experienced a major transformation when the Labour Party surged ahead of the Liberals as the second most powerful party in Britain after the Conservatives. In fact, after the elections of November 1923, a Labour-Liberal agreement enabled Ramsay MacDonald (1866–1937) to become the first Labour prime minister of Britain. Dependent on Liberal support, MacDonald rejected any extreme social or economic experimentation. His government lasted only ten months, however, as the Conservative Party's charge that his administration was friendly toward communism proved to be a highly successful campaign tactic.

Under the direction of Stanley Baldwin (1867–1947) as prime minister, the Conservatives guided Britain during an era of recovery from 1925 to 1929. This recovery, however, was relatively superficial. British exports in the 1920s never compensated for the overseas investments lost during the war, and unemployment remained at a startling 10 percent level. Coal miners were especially affected by the decline of the antiquated and inefficient British coal mines, which also suffered from a world glut of coal. Attempts by mine owners to lower coal miners' wages led to a national strike (the General Strike of 1926) by miners and sympathetic trade unions. A compromise settled the strike, but many miners refused to accept the settlement and were eventually forced back to work at lower wages for longer hours.

In 1929, just as the Great Depression was beginning, a second Labour government came into power, but its failure to solve the nation's economic problems caused it to fall in 1931. A National Government (a coalition of Liberals and Conservatives) claimed credit for bringing Britain out of the worst stages of the depression, primarily by using the traditional policies of balanced budgets and protective tariffs. By 1936, unemployment had dropped to 1.6 million after reaching a depression high of 3 million in 1932 (see the box above).

British politicians largely ignored the new ideas of a Cambridge economist, John Maynard Keynes (KAYNZ) (1883–1946), who published his *General Theory of Employment, Interest and Money* in 1936. He condemned the traditional view that in a free economy, depressions should be left to work themselves out. Instead, Keynes argued that unemployment stemmed not from overproduction but from a decline in demand and that demand could be increased by public works, financed, if necessary, through deficit spending to stimulate production.

France

After the defeat of Germany, France had become the strongest power on the European continent. Its greatest need was to rebuild the devastated areas of northern and eastern France. The conservative National Bloc government, led by Raymond Poincaré (ray-MOHNH pwanh-kah-RAY) (1860–1934), sought to use German reparations for this purpose, which resulted in Poincaré's hard-line policy toward Germany and the Ruhr invasion. When Poincaré's conservative government was forced to raise taxes in 1924 to pay for the cost of the Ruhr fiasco, his National Bloc was voted out of power and replaced by the so-called Cartel of the Left.

The Cartel of the Left was a coalition government formed by two French leftist parties, the Radicals and the Socialists. These parties shared a belief in antimilitarism, anticlericalism, and the importance of education. But despite their name, the Radicals were a democratic party of small property owners, whereas the Socialists were nominally committed to Marxist socialism. Although they cooperated to win elections, their differences on economic and financial issues made their efforts to solve France's financial problems between 1924 and 1926 largely futile. The failure of the Cartel of the Left led to the return of Raymond Poincaré, whose government from 1926 to 1929 stabilized the French economy during a period of relative prosperity.

France began to feel the full effects of the Great Depression in 1932, and that economic instability soon had political repercussions. During a nineteen-month period in 1932 and 1933, six different cabinets were formed as France faced political chaos. During the same time, French right-wing groups, adhering to policies similar to those of the Fascists in Italy and the Nazis in Germany, marched through French streets in numerous demonstrations. The riots of February 1934, fomented by a number of French right-wing leagues, frightened many into believing that the extremists intended to seize power. These fears began to drive the leftist parties together despite their other differences and led in 1936 to the formation of the Popular Front.

The first Popular Front government was formed in June 1936 and was a coalition of the Socialists and Radicals. The Socialist leader, Léon Blum (LAY-ohnh BLOOM) (1872–1950), served as prime minister. The Popular Front succeeded in initiating a program for workers that some have

called the French New Deal. It established the right of collective bargaining, a forty-hour workweek, two-week paid vacations, and minimum wages. The Popular Front's policies failed to solve the problems of the depression, however. By 1938, the French were experiencing a serious decline of confidence in their political system that left them unprepared to deal with their aggressive Nazi enemy to the east.

The Scandinavian States

The Scandinavian states were particularly successful in coping with the Great Depression. Socialist parties had grown steadily in the late nineteenth and early twentieth centuries and between the wars came to head the governments of Sweden, Denmark, Norway, and Finland. These Social Democratic governments encouraged the development of rural and industrial cooperative enterprises. Ninety percent of the Danish milk industry, for example, was organized on a cooperative basis by 1933. Privately owned and managed, Scandinavian cooperatives seemed to avoid the pitfalls of either Communist or purely capitalist economic systems.

Social Democratic governments also greatly expanded social services. Not only did Scandinavian governments increase old-age pensions and unemployment insurance, but they also provided such novel forms of assistance as subsidized housing, free prenatal care, maternity allowances, and annual paid vacations for workers. To achieve their social welfare states, the Scandinavian governments required high taxes and large bureaucracies, but these did not prevent both private and cooperative enterprises from prospering. Indeed, between 1900 and 1939, Sweden experienced a greater rise in real wages than any other European country.

The United States

After Germany, no Western nation was more affected by the Great Depression than the United States. By the end of 1932, industrial production was down almost 50 percent. By 1933, there were 15 million unemployed. Under these circumstances, the Democrat Franklin Delano Roosevelt (1882–1945) won the 1932 presidential election by a landslide.

Roosevelt and his advisers pursued a policy of active government intervention in the economy that came to be known as the New Deal. The first New Deal created a variety of agencies designed to bring relief, recovery, and reform. To support the nation's banks, the Federal Deposit Insurance Corporation was established; it insured the safety of bank deposits up to $5,000. The Federal Emergency Relief Administration provided funds to help states and local communities meet the needs of the destitute and the homeless. The Civilian Conservation Corps employed more than 2 million people on reforestation projects and federal road and conservation projects.

By 1935, it was becoming apparent that the initial efforts of Roosevelt's administration had produced only a

CHRONOLOGY The Democratic States

Great Britain

First Labour Party government	1924
Conservative Party government	1924–1929
General strike	1926
Second Labour Party government	1929–1931
Beginning of National Government coalition	1931

France

Cartel of the Left	1924–1926
Poincaré's government	1926–1929
Formation of the Popular Front	1936

United States

Election of Franklin D. Roosevelt	1932
Beginning of the New Deal	1933
Second New Deal	1935

slow recovery at best. As his policies came under more and more criticism by people who advocated more radical change, Roosevelt inaugurated new efforts that collectively became known as the Second New Deal. These included a stepped-up program of public works, such as the Works Progress Administration (WPA), established in 1935. This government organization employed between 2 and 3 million people who worked at building bridges, roads, post offices, and airports. The Roosevelt administration was also responsible for social legislation that launched the American welfare state. In 1935, the Social Security Act created a system of old-age pensions and unemployment insurance. The National Labor Relations Act of 1935 encouraged the rapid growth of labor unions.

The New Deal provided some social reform measures that perhaps averted the possibility of social revolution in the United States. It did not, however, solve the unemployment problems of the Great Depression. After partial recovery between 1933 and 1937, the economy experienced another downturn during the winter of 1937–1938. In May 1937, American unemployment still stood at 7 million; by the following year, it had increased to 11 million. Only World War II and the subsequent growth of armaments industries brought American workers back to full employment.

European States and the World: The Colonial Empires

World War I and the Great Depression also had an impact on Europe's colonial empires. Despite the war, the Allied nations had managed to keep their colonial empires intact. Great Britain and France had even added to their empires by dividing up many of Germany's colonial possessions and, as we have seen, taking control of large parts of the Middle East through a system of mandates.

Although Europe had emerged from World War I relatively intact, its political and social foundations and its self-confidence had been severely undermined. In Asia and Africa, a rising tide of unrest against European political domination began to emerge. That unrest took a variety of forms but was most notably displayed in increasing worker activism, rural protests, and a rising sense of national fervor. In areas of Asia and Africa, the discontent fostered by the war and later by the Great Depression led to movements for change.

THE MIDDLE EAST For the countries of the Middle East, the period between the two world wars was a time of transition. With the fall of the Ottoman and Persian empires, new modernizing regimes emerged in Turkey and Iran. A fiercely independent government was established in Saudi Arabia in 1932. Iraq, too, gained its independence from Britain in the same year. Elsewhere in the Middle East, European influence remained strong; the British and French maintained their mandates in Syria, Lebanon, Jordan, and Palestine.

Although Britain and France had made plans to divide up Ottoman territories in the Middle East, General Mustafa Kemal (MOOS-tah-fah kuh-MAHL) (1881–1938) led Turkish forces in creating a new republic of Turkey in 1923. Kemal wanted to modernize Turkey along Western lines. The trappings of a democratic system were put in place, although the new president did not tolerate opposition. In addition to introducing a state-run industrial system, Kemal also westernized Turkish culture. The Turkish language was now written using the Latin alphabet. Popular education was introduced, and old aristocratic titles were abolished. All Turkish citizens were forced to adopt family names, in the European style; Kemal himself adopted the name Atatürk (ah-tah-TIRK), meaning "Father Turk." Atatürk made Turkey a secular republic and broke the power of the Islamic religion. New laws gave women equal rights with men in all aspects of marriage and inheritance, and in 1934, women received the right to vote. Education and the professions were now open to citizens of both sexes. By and large, the Turkish republic was the product of Atatürk's determined efforts to use nationalism and Western ways to create a modern Turkish nation.

INDIA By the time of World War I, the Indian people had already begun to refer to Mohandas Gandhi (moh-HAHN-dus GAHN-dee) as India's "Great Soul," or Mahatma (mah-HAHT-muh). Gandhi (1869–1948) set up a movement based on nonviolent resistance whose aim was to force the British to improve the lot of the poor and grant independence to India. When the British tried to suppress Indian calls for independence, Gandhi called on his followers to follow a peaceful policy of **civil disobedience** by refusing to obey British regulations. Gandhi also began to manufacture his own clothes and dressed in a simple *dhoti* (DOH-tee) or loincloth made of coarse homespun cotton. He adopted the spinning wheel as a symbol of India's resistance to imports of British textiles.

Gandhi. Mahatma Gandhi, India's "Great Soul," became the spiritual leader of India's struggle for independence from British colonial rule. Unlike many other nationalist leaders, Gandhi rejected the materialistic culture of the West and urged his followers to return to the native traditions of the Indian village. To illustrate his point, as seen in this illustration, Gandhi dressed in the simple Indian *dhoti* rather than in the Western fashion favored by many of his colleagues.

Although the British resisted Gandhi's movement, in 1935 they granted India internal self-government to be implemented through a gradual program. Legislative councils at the local level were enlarged and given responsibility for education, local affairs, and public health, and Indian participation in government slowly increased. Responsibility for law and order, land revenue, and famine relief remained under the control of the British, however. Complete independence would have to wait until after World War II.

AFRICA Black Africans who fought in World War I in the armies of the British and the French hoped for independence after the war. As one newspaper in the Gold Coast put it, if African volunteers who fought on European battlefields were "good enough to fight and die in the Empire's cause, they were good enough to have a share in the government of their countries." This feeling was shared by many. The peace settlement after World War I turned out be a great disappointment. Germany was stripped of its African colonies, but they were awarded to the British and the French to administer as mandates for the League of Nations.

After World War I, Africans became more active politically. Africans who had fought in World War I had learned new ideas in the West about freedom and nationalism. Even in Africa itself, missionary schools had often taught their African pupils about liberty and equality. As more Africans became aware of the enormous gulf between Western ideals and practices, they decided to seek reform. As yet independence remained only a dream.

Protest took different forms. In Nigeria and South Africa, workers organized trade unions that tried to gain benefits for workers. But there were also incidents of violent protest. In British Nigeria in 1929, a group of women protested the high taxes that were levied on the goods they were selling in the markets. During the riot that ensued, women called for all white men to leave their country. The British ended the riot, killing fifty women in the process. Although colonial powers responded to these protest movements with force, they also began to make some reforms in the hope of satisfying indigenous peoples. The reforms, however, were too few and too late, and by the 1930s, an increasing number of African leaders were calling for independence, not reform.

The clearest calls came from a new generation of young African leaders who had been educated in Europe and the United States. Those who went to the United States were especially influenced by the pan-African ideas of W. E. B. Du Bois (doo-BOISS) (1868–1963) and Marcus Garvey (1887–1940). Du Bois, an African American educated at Harvard, was the leader of a movement that tried to make all Africans aware of their own cultural heritage. Garvey, a Jamaican who lived in Harlem in New York, also stressed the need for the unity of all Africans. Leaders and movements in individual African nations also appeared. In his book *Facing Mount Kenya*, Jomo Kenyatta (JOH-moh ken-YAHT-uh) (1894–1978) of Kenya, who had been educated in Great Britain, argued that British rule was destroying the traditional culture of the peoples of black Africa.

The Authoritarian and Totalitarian States

Q **FOCUS QUESTIONS:** Why did many European states experience a retreat from democracy in the interwar years? What are the characteristics of totalitarian states, and to what degree were these characteristics present in Fascist Italy, Nazi Germany, and Stalinist Russia?

The apparent triumph of liberal democracy in 1919 proved extremely short-lived. By 1939, only two major states (Great Britain and France) and several minor ones (the Low Countries, the Scandinavian states, Switzerland, and Czechoslovakia) remained democratic. What had happened to Woodrow Wilson's claim that World War I had been fought to make the world safe for democracy?

Actually, World War I turned out to have had the opposite effect.

The Retreat from Democracy

The postwar expansion of the electorate made mass politics a reality and seemed to enhance the spread of democracy in Europe. But the war itself had created conditions that led the new mass electorate to distrust democracy and move toward a more radicalized politics.

Many postwar societies were badly divided, especially along class lines. During the war, to maintain war production, governments had been forced to make concessions to trade unions and socialist parties, which strengthened the working class after the war. At the same time, the position of many middle-class people had declined as consumer industries had been curtailed during the war and war bonds, which had been purchased by the middle classes as their patriotic contribution to the war effort, sank in value and even became worthless in some countries.

Gender divisions also weakened social cohesion. After the war, as soldiers returned home, women were forced out of jobs they had taken during the war, jobs that many newly independent women wanted to retain. The loss of so many men during the war had also left many younger women with no marital prospects and widows with no choice but to find jobs in the labor force. At the same time, fears about a declining population because of the war led many male political leaders to encourage women to return to their traditional roles as wives and mothers. Many European countries outlawed abortions and curtailed the sale of birth control devices while providing increased welfare benefits to entice women to remain at home and bear children.

The Great Depression served to deepen social conflict. Larger and larger numbers of people felt victimized, first by the war, and now by socioeconomic conditions that seemed beyond their control. Postwar politics became more and more polarized as people reverted to the wartime practice of dividing into friends and enemies, downplaying compromise and emphasizing conflict. Moderate centrist parties that supported democracy soon found themselves with fewer and fewer allies as people became increasingly radicalized politically, supporting the extremes of left-wing communism or right-wing fascism. In the 1920s, Italy had become the first Fascist state while the Soviet Union moved toward a repressive **totalitarian state.** In the 1930s, a host of other European states adopted authoritarian structures of various kinds.

The dictatorial regimes between the wars assumed both old and new forms. Dictatorship was not a new phenomenon, but the modern totalitarian state was. The totalitarian regimes, whose best examples can be found in Stalinist Russia and Nazi Germany, extended the functions and power of the central state far beyond what they had been in the past. The immediate origins of totalitarianism can be found in the total warfare of World War I when governments, even in the democratic states, exercised controls over economic, political, and personal freedom in order to achieve victory.

The modern totalitarian state expected the active loyalty and commitment of citizens to the regime's goals. It used modern mass **propaganda** techniques and high-speed modern communications to conquer the minds and hearts of its subjects. The total state aimed to control not only the economic, political, and social aspects of life but the intellectual and cultural aspects as well. But that control also had a purpose: the active involvement of the masses in the achievement of the regime's goal, whether it be war, a socialist state, or a thousand-year Reich.

The modern totalitarian state was to be led by a single leader and a single party. It ruthlessly rejected the liberal ideal of limited government power and constitutional guarantees of individual freedoms. Indeed, individual freedom was to be subordinated to the collective will of the masses, organized and determined for them by a leader or leaders. Modern technology also gave total states unprecedented police controls to enforce their wishes on their subjects.

Totalitarianism is an abstract term, and no state followed all its theoretical implications. The fascist states—Italy and Nazi Germany—as well as Stalin's Soviet Union have all been labeled totalitarian, although their regimes exhibited significant differences and met with varying degrees of success. Totalitarianism transcended traditional political labels. Fascism in Italy and Nazism in Germany grew out of extreme rightist preoccupations with nationalism and, in the case of Germany, with racism. Communism in the Soviet Union emerged out of Marxist socialism, a radical leftist program. Thus, totalitarianism could and did exist in what were perceived as extreme right-wing and left-wing regimes. This fact helped bring about a new concept of the political spectrum in which the extremes were no longer seen as opposites on a linear scale but came to be viewed as similar to each other in at least some respects.

Fascist Italy

In the early 1920s, in the wake of economic turmoil, political disorder, and the general insecurity and fear stemming from World War I, Benito Mussolini burst onto the Italian scene with the first fascist movement in Europe.

IMPACT OF WORLD WAR I As a new European state after 1861, Italy faced a number of serious problems that were only magnified when it became a belligerent in World War I. An estimated 700,000 Italian soldiers died, and the treasury reckoned the cost of the war at 148 billion lire, twice the sum of all government expenditures between 1861 and 1913. Italy did gain some territory, namely, Trieste, and a new northern border that included the formerly Austrian South Tyrol area. Italy's demands for Fiume and Dalmatia on the Adriatic coast were rejected, however, which gave rise to the myth that Italy

Territory Gained by Italy

had been cheated of its just rewards by the other victors. The war created immense domestic confusion. Inflation undermined middle-class security. Demobilization of the troops created high unemployment and huge groups of dissatisfied veterans. The government proved unable to deal effectively with these problems.

THE BIRTH OF FASCISM Benito Mussolini (1883–1945) was an unruly and rebellious child who ultimately received a diploma as an elementary school teacher. After an unsuccessful stint as a teacher, Mussolini became a socialist and gradually became well known in Italian socialist circles. In 1912, he obtained the important position of editor of *Avanti* (Forward), the official socialist daily newspaper. After editorially switching his position from ardent neutrality, the socialist position, to intervention in World War I, he was expelled from the Socialist Party.

In 1919, Mussolini laid the foundations for a new political movement that came to be called fascism after the name of his group, the *Fascio di Combattimento* (FASH-ee-oh dee com-bat-ee-MEN-toh) (League of Combat). It received little attention in the elections of 1919, but political stalemate in Italy's parliamentary system and strong nationalist sentiment saved Mussolini and the Fascists.

The new parliament elected in November quickly proved incapable of governing Italy. Three major parties, the Socialists, Liberals, and Popolari (or Christian Democrats, a new Catholic party formed in January 1919), were unable to form an effective coalition. The Socialists, who had now become the largest party, spoke theoretically of the need for revolution, which alarmed conservatives, who quickly associated them with Bolsheviks or Communists. Thousands of industrial and agricultural strikes in 1919 and 1920 created a climate of class warfare and continual violence. Mussolini shifted quickly from leftist to rightist politics and began to gain support from middle-class industrialists fearful of working-class agitation and large landowners who objected to the agricultural strikes. Mussolini also perceived that Italians were angry over Italy's failure to receive more fruits of victory in the form of territorial acquisitions after World War I. He realized then that anticommunism, antistrike activity, and nationalist rhetoric combined with the use of brute force might help him obtain what he had been unable to achieve in free elections.

In 1920 and 1921, bands of armed Fascists called **squadristi** (skwah-DREES-tee) were formed and turned loose in attacks on Socialist offices and newspapers. Strikes by trade unionists and Socialist workers and peasant leagues were broken up by force. At the same time, Mussolini entered into a political alliance with the Liberals under Giovanni Giolitti, then the prime minister. No doubt, Giolitti and the Liberals believed that the Fascists could be used to crush socialism temporarily and then be dropped. In this game of mutual deceit, Mussolini soon proved to be the more skillful player. By allying with the government coalition, he gained respectability and a free hand for his violent *squadristi*. Mussolini's efforts were rewarded when the Fascists won thirty-five parliamentary seats, or 7 percent of the total, in the election of May 1921.

The use of violence was crucial to Mussolini's plans. By 1921, the black-shirted Fascist squads numbered 200,000 and had become a regular feature of Italian life. World War I veterans and students were especially attracted to the *squadristi* and relished the opportunity to use unrestrained violence. Administering large doses of castor oil to unwilling victims became one of their favorite tactics.

Mussolini and the Fascists believed that these terrorist tactics would eventually achieve political victory. They deliberately created conditions of disorder knowing that fascism would flourish in such an environment. The Fascists construed themselves as the party of order and drew the bulk of their support from the middle and upper classes; white-collar workers, professionals and civil servants, landowners, merchants and artisans, and students made up almost 60 percent of the membership of the Fascist Party. The middle-class fear of socialism, Communist revolution, and disorder made the Fascists attractive.

As the Italian political situation deteriorated further, Mussolini and the Fascists were emboldened to plan a march on Rome in order to seize power. In a speech in Naples to Fascist Blackshirts on October 24, 1922, Mussolini exclaimed, "Either we are allowed to govern, or we will seize power by marching on Rome" to "take by the throat the miserable political class that governs us."[4] Bold words, but in truth the planned march on Rome was a calculated bluff to frighten the government into giving them power. The bluff worked, and the government capitulated even before the march occurred. On October 29, 1922, King Victor Emmanuel III (1900–1946) made Mussolini prime minister of Italy. Twenty-four hours later, the Fascist Blackshirts were allowed to march into Rome in order to create the myth that they had gained power by an armed insurrection after a civil war.

MUSSOLINI AND THE ITALIAN FASCIST STATE Since the Fascists constituted but a small minority in parliament, the new prime minister was forced to move slowly. In the summer of 1923, Mussolini began to prepare for a national election that would consolidate the power of his Fascist government and give him a more secure base from which to govern. In July 1923, parliament enacted the Acerbo Law, which stipulated that any party winning at least 25 percent of the votes in the next national election would automatically be allotted two-thirds of the seats in

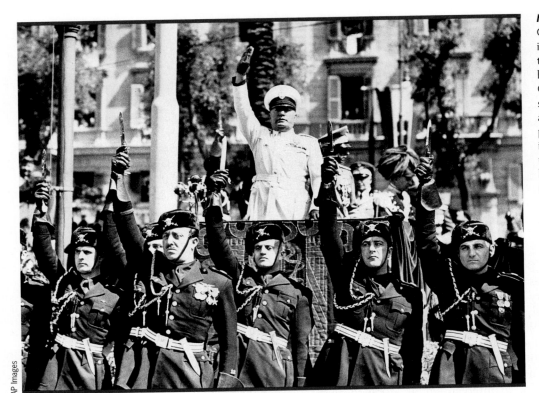

Mussolini, the Iron Duce.
One of Mussolini's favorite images of himself was that of the Iron Duce—the strong leader who is always right. Consequently, he was often seen in military-style uniforms and military poses. This photograph shows Mussolini in one of his numerous uniforms with his Blackshirt bodyguards giving the Fascist salute.

AP Images

parliament. The national elections that were subsequently held on April 6, 1924, resulted in an enormous victory for the Fascists. They won 65 percent of the votes and garnered 374 seats out of a total of 535 in parliament. Although the elections were conducted in an atmosphere of Fascist fraud, force, and intimidation, the size of the victory indicated the growing popularity of Mussolini and his Fascists.

By 1926, Mussolini had established his Fascist dictatorship. Press laws gave the government the right to suspend any publications that fostered disrespect for the Catholic Church, the monarchy, or the state. The prime minister was made "head of government" with the power to legislate by decree. A police law empowered the police to arrest and confine anybody for nonpolitical or political crimes without due process of law. The government was given the power to dissolve political and cultural associations. In 1926, all anti-Fascist parties were outlawed. A secret police, known as the OVRA, was also established. By the end of 1926, Mussolini ruled Italy as *Il Duce* (eel DOO-chay), the leader.

Mussolini conceived of the Fascist state as totalitarian: "Fascism is totalitarian, and the Fascist State, the synthesis and unity of all values, interprets, develops and gives strength to the whole life of the people"[5] (see the box on p. 825). Mussolini did try to create a police state, but police activities in Italy were never as repressive, efficient, or savage as those of Nazi Germany. Likewise, the Italian Fascists' attempt to exercise control over all forms of mass media, including newspapers, radio, and cinema, so that they could use propaganda as an instrument

to integrate the masses into the state, failed to achieve its major goals. Most commonly, Fascist propaganda was disseminated through simple slogans, such as "Mussolini is always right," plastered on walls all over Italy.

Mussolini and the Fascists also attempted to mold Italians into a single-minded community by pursuing a Fascist educational policy and developing Fascist organizations. Because the secondary schools maintained considerable freedom from Fascist control, the regime relied more and more on the activities of youth organizations, known as the Young Fascists, to indoctrinate the young people of the nation in Fascist ideals. By 1939, about 6.8 million children, teenagers, and young adults of both sexes, or 66 percent of the population between eight and eighteen, were enrolled in some kind of Fascist youth group. Activities for these groups included unpopular Saturday afternoon marching drills and calisthenics, seaside and mountain summer camps, and competitions. An underlying motif for all of these activities was the Fascist insistence on militarization. Beginning in the 1930s, all male groups were given some kind of premilitary exercises to develop discipline and provide training for war. Results were mixed. Italian teenagers, who liked neither military training nor routine discipline of any kind, simply refused to attend Fascist youth meetings on a regular basis.

The Fascist organizations hoped to create a new Italian—hardworking, physically fit, disciplined, intellectually sharp, and martially inclined. In practice, the Fascists largely reinforced traditional social attitudes in Italy, as is evident in their policies regarding women. The Fascists portrayed the family as the pillar of the state and women

The Voice of Italian Fascism

In 1932, an article on fascism appeared in the *Italian Encyclopedia.* Attributed to Mussolini, it was largely written by the philosopher Giovanni Gentile. Mussolini had always argued that fascism was based only on the need for action, not on doctrines, but after its success, he felt the need to summarize the basic political and social ideas of fascism. These excerpts are taken from that article.

·—·—▨◆▨—·—·

Benito Mussolini, "The Political and Social Doctrine of Fascism"

Above all, Fascism . . . believes neither in the possibility nor the utility of perpetual peace. It thus repudiates the doctrine of Pacifism—born of a renunciation of struggle and an act of cowardice in the face of sacrifice. War alone brings up to its highest tension all human energy and puts the stamp of nobility upon the peoples who have the courage to meet it. All other trials are substitutes, which never really put men into the position where they have to make the great decision—the alternative of life or death. Thus, a doctrine which is founded upon this harmful postulate of peace is hostile to Fascism. . . . Thus, the Fascist accepts life and loves it, knowing nothing of and despising suicide: he rather conceives of life as duty and struggle and conquest. . . .

Fascism is the complete opposite of Marxian socialism, the materialist conception of history; according to which the history of human civilization can be explained simply through the conflict of interests among the various social groups and by the change and development in the means and instruments of production. That the changes in the economic field have their importance no one can deny; but that these factors are sufficient to explain the history of humanity excluding all others is an absurd delusion. Fascism, now and always, believes in holiness and in heroism; that is to say, in actions influenced by no economic motive, direct or indirect. . . .

After Socialism, Fascism combats the whole complex system of democratic ideology, and repudiates it, whether in its theoretical premises or in its practical application. Fascism denies that the majority, by the simple fact that it is a majority, can direct human society; it denies that numbers alone can govern by means of a periodical consultation, and it affirms the immutable, beneficial, and fruitful inequality of mankind, which can never be permanently leveled through the mere operation of a mechanical process such as universal suffrage.

The foundation of Fascism is the conception of the State, its character, its duty and its aim. Fascism conceives of the State as an absolute, in comparison with which all individuals or groups are relative, only to be conceived of in their relation to the State. . . . The Fascist state organizes the nation, but leaves a sufficient margin of liberty to the individual; the latter is deprived of all useless and possibly harmful freedom, but retains what is essential; the deciding power in the question cannot be the individual, but the State alone. . . .

For Fascism, the growth of empire, that is to say the expansion of the nation, is an essential manifestation of vitality, and its opposite a sign of decadence. Peoples which are rising, or rising again after a period of decadence, are always imperialist; any renunciation is a sign of decay and of death. Fascism is the doctrine best adapted to represent the tendencies and the aspirations of a people, like the people of Italy, who are rising again after many centuries of abasement and foreign servitude. But Empire demands discipline, the coordination of all forces and a deeply felt sense of duty and sacrifice. ▧

Q In Mussolini's view, what were the basic principles of Italian Fascism? Why might such principles have appealed to a broad public in the aftermath of World War I?

---

as the basic foundation of the family. "Woman into the home" became the Fascist slogan. Women were to be homemakers and baby producers, "their natural and fundamental mission in life," according to Mussolini, who viewed population growth as an indicator of national strength. To Mussolini, female emancipation was "unfascist." Employment outside the home was an impediment distracting women from conception. "It forms an independence and consequent physical and moral habits contrary to child bearing."[6] A practical consideration also underlay the Fascist attitude toward women: eliminating women from the job market reduced male unemployment figures in the depression economy of the 1930s.

In the 1930s, the Fascists translated their attitude toward women into law with a series of enactments aimed at

encouraging larger families. Families with many offspring were offered supplementary pay, loans, prizes, and subsidies, and mothers of many children received gold medals. A national "Mother and Child" holiday was celebrated on December 24, with prizes awarded for fertility. Also in the 1930s, decrees were passed that set quotas on the employment of women, but they were not successful in accomplishing their goal.

Despite the instruments of repression, the use of propaganda, and the creation of numerous Fascist organizations, Mussolini failed to attain the degree of totalitarian control achieved in Hitler's Germany or Stalin's Soviet Union. Mussolini and the Fascist Party never really destroyed the old power structure. Some institutions, including the armed forces and the monarchy, were never

Creation of *Fascio di Combattimento*	1919
Squadristi violence	1920–1921
Fascists win thirty-five seats in Parliament	1921
Mussolini is made prime minister	1922
Acerbo Law	1923
Electoral victory for Fascists	1924
Establishment of Fascist dictatorship	1925–1926
Lateran Accords with Catholic Church	1929

absorbed into the Fascist state and managed to maintain their independence. Mussolini had boasted that he would help the workers and peasants, but instead he generally allied himself with the interests of the industrialists and large landowners at the expense of the lower classes.

Even more indicative of Mussolini's compromise with the traditional institutions of Italy was his attempt to gain the support of the Catholic Church. In the Lateran Accords of February 1929, Mussolini's regime recognized the sovereign independence of a small enclave of 109 acres within Rome, known as Vatican City, which had remained in the church's possession since the unification of Italy in 1870; in return, the papacy recognized the Italian state. The Lateran Accords also guaranteed the church a large grant of money and recognized Catholicism as the "sole religion of the state." In return, the Catholic Church urged Italians to support the Fascist regime.

In all areas of Italian life under Mussolini and the Fascists, there was a noticeable dichotomy between Fascist ideals and practice. The Italian Fascists promised much but delivered considerably less, and they were soon overshadowed by a much more powerful fascist movement to the north.

Hitler and Nazi Germany

In 1923, a small rightist party, known as the Nazis, led by an obscure Austrian rabble-rouser named Adolf Hitler, tried to seize power in southern Germany in conscious imitation of Mussolini's march on Rome in 1922. Although the attempt failed, Hitler and the Nazis achieved sudden national prominence. Within ten years, they had taken over complete power.

WEIMAR GERMANY After Germany's defeat in World War I, a German democratic state known as the Weimar (VY-mar) Republic had been established. Formed by a coalition of Social Democrats, the Catholic Center Party, and German Democrats, the fragmented republic had no outstanding political leader and proved to be unstable. In 1925, Paul von Hindenburg, the World War I military hero, was elected president. Hindenburg was a traditional military man, monarchist in sentiment, who at heart was not in favor of the republic. The young republic suffered

politically from attempted uprisings and attacks from both the left and the right.

Another of the republic's problems was its inability to change Germany's basic governmental structure. The government never really controlled the army, which operated as a state within a state. Other institutions maintained their independence as well. Hostile judges, teachers, and bureaucrats remained in office and used their positions to undermine democracy from within. At the same time, important groups of landed aristocrats and leaders of powerful business cartels refused to accept the overthrow of the imperial regime and remained hostile to the republic.

The Weimar Republic also faced serious economic difficulties. The runaway inflation of 1922 and 1923 had serious social repercussions. Widows, orphans, the retired elderly, army officers, teachers, civil servants, and others who lived on fixed incomes all watched their monthly stipends become worthless and their lifetime savings disappear. Their economic losses increasingly pushed the middle class to the rightist parties that were hostile to the republic. To make matters worse, after a period of prosperity from 1924 to 1929, Germany faced the Great Depression. Unemployment increased to nearly 4.4 million by December 1930. The depression paved the way for social discontent, fear, and extremist parties. The political, economic, and social problems of the Weimar Republic provided an environment in which Hitler and the Nazis were able to rise to power.

THE EMERGENCE OF ADOLF HITLER Born in 1889, Adolf Hitler was the son of an Austrian customs official. He was a total failure in secondary school and eventually made his way to Vienna to become an artist. Though he was rejected by the Vienna Academy of Fine Arts, Hitler stayed on in Vienna to live the bohemian lifestyle of an artist. In his autobiography, *Mein Kampf* (myn KAHMPF) (My Struggle), Hitler characterized his years in Vienna from 1908 to 1913 as an important formative period in his life: "In this period there took shape within me a world picture and a philosophy which became the granite foundation of all my acts. In addition to what I then created, I have had to learn little, and I have had to alter nothing."[7]

In Vienna, then, Hitler established the basic ideas of an ideology from which he never deviated for the rest of his life. At the core of Hitler's ideas was racism, especially anti-Semitism (see the box on p. 827). His hatred of the Jews lasted to the very end of his life. Hitler also became an extreme German nationalist who learned from the mass politics of Vienna how political parties could effectively use propaganda and terror. Finally, in his Viennese years, Hitler also came to a firm belief in the need for struggle, which he saw as the "granite foundation of the world."

In 1913, Hitler moved to Munich, still without purpose and with no real future in sight. World War I saved him: "Overpowered by stormy enthusiasm, I fell down on my knees and thanked Heaven from an overflowing heart for

Adolf Hitler's Hatred of the Jews

A believer in Aryan racial supremacy, Adolf Hitler viewed the Jews as the archenemies of the Aryans. He believed that the first task of a true Aryan state would be the elimination of the Jewish threat. This is why Hitler's political career both began and ended with a warning against the Jews. In this excerpt from his autobiography, *Mein Kampf,* Hitler describes how he came to be an anti-Semite when he lived in Vienna in his early twenties.

✦✦✦

Adolf Hitler, *Mein Kampf*

My views with regard to anti-Semitism thus succumbed to the passage of time, and this was my greatest transformation of all....

Once, as I was strolling through the Inner City [of Vienna], I suddenly encountered an apparition in a black caftan and black hair locks. Is this a Jew? was my first thought.

For, to be sure, they had not looked like that in Linz. I observed the man furtively and cautiously, but the longer I stared at this foreign face, scrutinizing feature for feature, the more my first question assumed a new form:

Is this a German?

As always in such cases, I now began to try to relieve my doubts by books. For a few pennies I bought the first anti-Semitic pamphlets of my life....

Yet I could no longer very well doubt that the objects of my study were not Germans of a special religion, but a people in themselves; for since I had begun to concern myself with this question and to take cognizance of the Jews, Vienna appeared to me in a different light than before. Wherever I went, I began to see Jews, and the more I saw, the more sharply they became distinguished in my eyes from the rest of humanity....

In a short time I was made more thoughtful than ever by my slowly rising insight into the type of activity carried on by the Jews in certain fields.

Was there any form of filth or profligacy, particularly in cultural life, without at least one Jew involved in it?...

Sometimes I stood there thunderstruck.

I didn't know what to be more amazed at: the agility of their tongues or their virtuosity at lying.

Gradually I began to hate them. ✑

Q What was Hitler's attitude toward the Jews? Why do you think such crazed views became acceptable (or at least tolerable) to large numbers of ordinary Germans in the aftermath of World War I?

---

granting me the good fortune of being permitted to live at this time."[8] As a dispatch runner on the Western Front, Hitler distinguished himself by his brave acts. At the end of the war, finding again that his life had no purpose or meaning, he returned to Munich and decided to enter politics and found, at last, his true profession.

THE RISE OF THE NAZIS Hitler joined the obscure German Workers' Party, one of a number of right-wing extreme nationalist parties in Munich. By the summer of 1921, Hitler had assumed total control of the party, which he renamed the National Socialist German Workers' Party, or Nazi for short (from the first two syllables of its German name). His idea was that the party's name would distinguish the Nazis from the socialist parties while gaining support from both working-class and nationalist circles. Hitler worked assiduously to develop the party into a mass political movement with flags, badges, uniforms, its own newspaper, and its own police force or militia known as the SA, the *Sturmabteilung* (SHTOORM-ap-ty-loonk), or Storm Troops. The SA was used to defend the party in meeting halls and to break up the meetings of other parties. Hitler's own oratorical skills were largely responsible for attracting an increasing number of followers. By 1923, the party had grown from its early hundreds into a membership of 55,000, plus another 15,000 in the SA.

When it appeared that the Weimar Republic was on the verge of collapse in the fall of 1923, the Nazis and other right-wing leaders in the south German state of Bavaria decided to march on Berlin to overthrow the Weimar government. When his fellow conspirators reneged, Hitler and the Nazis decided to act on their own by staging an armed uprising in Munich on November 8. The so-called Beer Hall Putsch was quickly crushed. Hitler was arrested, put on trial for treason, and sentenced to prison for five years, a lenient sentence indeed from sympathetic right-wing judges.

During his brief stay in prison, Hitler wrote *Mein Kampf,* an autobiographical account of his movement and its underlying ideology. Extreme German nationalism, virulent anti-Semitism, and vicious anticommunism are linked together by a social Darwinian theory of struggle that stresses the right of superior nations to **Lebensraum** (LAY-benz-rowm) (living space) through expansion and the right of superior individuals to secure authoritarian leadership over the masses. What is perhaps most remarkable about *Mein Kampf* is its elaboration of a series of ideas that directed Hitler's actions once he took power. That others refused to take Hitler and his ideas seriously was one of his greatest advantages.

HITLER'S NEW TACTICS The Beer Hall Putsch proved to be a major turning point in Hitler's career. Rather than

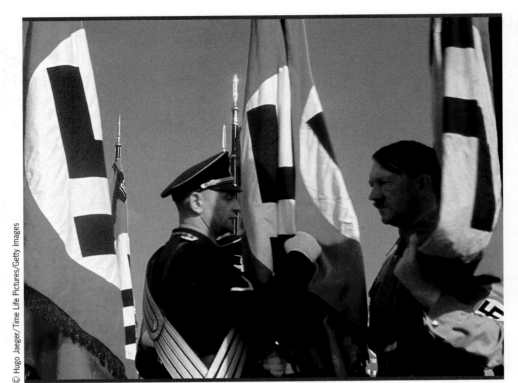

Hitler and the Blood Flag Ritual. In developing his mass political movement, Adolf Hitler used ritualistic ceremonies as a means of binding party members to his own person. Here Hitler is shown touching the "blood flag," which had supposedly been stained with the blood of Nazis killed during the Beer Hall Putsch, to an SS banner while the SS standard-bearer makes a "blood oath" of allegiance: "I vow to remain true to my Führer, Adolf Hitler. I bind myself to carry out all orders conscientiously and without reluctance. Standards and flags shall be sacred to me." The SS originated as Hitler's personal bodyguard and later became a secret police force and instrument of terror in the Nazi state.

discouraging him, his trial and imprisonment reinforced his faith in himself and in his mission. He now clearly understood the need for a change in tactics. If the Nazis could not overthrow the Weimar Republic by force, they would have to use constitutional means to gain power. This implied the formation of a mass political movement that would actively compete for votes with the other political parties.

After his release from prison, Hitler set about organizing the Nazi Party for the lawful takeover of power. His position on leadership in the party was quite clear. There was to be no discussion of ideas in the party, and the party was to follow the ***Führerprinzip*** (FYOOR-ur-prin-TSEEP), the leadership principle, which entailed nothing less than a single-minded party under one leader. As Hitler expressed it, "A good National Socialist is one who would let himself be killed for his Führer at any time."[9]

In the late 1920s, Hitler reorganized the Nazi Party on a regional basis and expanded it to all parts of Germany. By 1929, the Nazis had a national party organization. The party also grew from 27,000 members in 1925 to 178,000 by the end of 1929. Especially noticeable was the youthfulness of the regional, district, and branch leaders of the Nazi organization. Many were under thirty and were fiercely committed to Hitler because he gave them the kind of active politics they sought. Rather than democratic debate, they wanted brawls in beer halls, enthusiastic speeches, and comradeship in the building of a new Germany. One new young Nazi member expressed his excitement about the party:

> For me this was the start of a completely new life. There was only one thing in the world for me and that was service in the

movement. All my thoughts were centered on the movement. I could talk only politics. I was no longer aware of anything else. At the time I was a promising athlete; I was very keen on sport, and it was going to be my career. But I had to give this up too. My only interest was agitation and propaganda.[10]

Such youthful enthusiasm gave Nazism the aura of a "young man's movement" and a sense of dynamism that the other parties could not match.

By 1929, the Nazi Party had also made a significant shift in strategy. Between 1925 and 1927, Hitler and the Nazis had pursued an urban strategy geared toward winning workers from the socialists and Communists. But failure in the 1928 elections, when the Nazis gained only 2.6 percent of the vote and twelve seats in the Reichstag, convinced Hitler of the need for a change. By 1929, the party began to pursue middle-class and lower-middle-class votes in small towns and rural areas, especially in northern, central, and eastern Germany.

Germany's economic difficulties paved the way for the Nazis' rise to power. Unemployment rose dramatically, from 4.35 million in 1931 to 6 million by the winter of 1932. The economic and psychological impact of the Great Depression made the radical solutions offered by extremist parties appear more attractive. Already in the Reichstag elections of September 1930, the Nazis polled 18 percent of the vote and gained 107 seats in the Reichstag, making the Nazi Party one of the largest in Germany.

By 1930, Chancellor Heinrich Brüning (HYN-rikh BROO-ning) (1885–1970) had found it impossible to form a working parliamentary majority in the Reichstag and relied on the use of emergency decrees by President

Hindenburg to rule. In a real sense, then, parliamentary democracy was already dying in 1930, three years before Hitler destroyed it.

THE NAZI SEIZURE OF POWER Hitler's quest for power from late 1930 to early 1933 depended on the political maneuvering around President Hindenburg. Nevertheless, the elections from 1930 through 1932 were indirectly responsible for the Nazis' rise to power since they showed the importance of the Nazi Party. The party itself grew dramatically during this period, from 289,000 members in September 1930 to 800,000 by 1932. The SA also rose to 500,000 members.

The Nazis proved very effective in developing modern electioneering techniques. In their election campaigns, party members pitched their themes to the needs and fears of different social groups. But even as they were making blatant appeals to class interests, the Nazis were denouncing conflicts of interest and maintaining that they stood above classes and parties. Hitler, in particular, claimed to stand above all differences and promised to create a new Germany free of class differences and party infighting. His appeal to national pride, national honor, and traditional militarism struck chords of emotion in his listeners.

Elections, however, proved to have their limits. In the elections of July 1932, the Nazis won 230 seats, making them the largest party in the Reichstag. But four months later, in November, they declined to 196 seats. It became apparent to many Nazis that they would not gain power simply by the ballot box. Hitler saw clearly, however, that after 1930 the Reichstag was not all that important, since the government ruled by decree with the support of President Hindenburg. Increasingly, the right-wing elites of Germany—the industrial magnates, landed aristocrats, military establishment, and higher bureaucrats—came to see Hitler as the man who had the mass support to establish a right-wing, authoritarian regime that would save Germany and their privileged positions from a Communist takeover. These people almost certainly thought that they could control Hitler and, like many others, may well have underestimated his abilities. Under pressure from these elites, President Hindenburg agreed to allow Hitler to become chancellor (on January 30, 1933) and form a new government.

Within two months, Hitler had laid the foundations for the Nazis' complete control over Germany. One of Hitler's important cohorts, Hermann Göring (GUR-ing) (1893–1946), had been made minister of the interior and hence head of the police of the Prussian state, the largest of the federal states in Germany. He used his power to purge the police of non-Nazis and to establish an auxiliary police force composed of SA members. This action legitimized Nazi terror. On the day after a fire broke out in the Reichstag building (February 27), supposedly set by the Communists, Hitler was also able to convince President Hindenburg to issue a decree that gave the government emergency powers. It suspended all basic rights of citizens for the full duration of the emergency, thus enabling the Nazis to arrest and imprison anyone without redress.

The crowning step of Hitler's "legal seizure" of power came after the Nazis had gained 288 Reichstag seats in the elections of March 5, 1933. Since they still did not possess an absolute majority, on March 23 the Nazis sought the passage of an Enabling Act, which would empower the government to dispense with constitutional forms for four years while it issued laws that would deal with the country's problems. Since the act was to be an amendment to the Weimar constitution, the Nazis needed and obtained a two-thirds vote to pass it. Only the Social Democrats had the courage to oppose Hitler. The Enabling Act provided the legal basis for Hitler's subsequent acts. He no longer needed either the Reichstag or President Hindenburg. In effect, Hitler became a dictator appointed by the parliamentary body itself.

With their new source of power, the Nazis acted quickly to enforce *Gleichschaltung* (glykh-SHAHL-toonk), the co-ordination of all institutions under Nazi control. The civil service was purged of Jews and democratic elements, concentration camps were established for opponents of the new regime, the autonomy of the federal states was eliminated, trade unions were dissolved and swallowed up by the gigantic Labor Front, and all political parties except the Nazis were abolished. By the end of the summer of 1933, within seven months of being appointed chancellor, Hitler and the Nazis had established the foundations for a totalitarian state.

Why had this seizure of power been so quick and easy? The Nazis were not only ruthless in their use of force but ready to take control. The depression and the Weimar Republic's failure to resolve it had weakened what little faith the Germans had in their democratic state. But negative factors alone cannot explain the Nazi success. To many Germans, the Nazis offered a national awakening. "Germany awake," one of the many Nazi slogans, had a powerful appeal to a people psychologically crushed by their defeat in World War I. The Nazis presented a strong image of a dynamic new Germany that was above parties and above classes.

By the end of 1933, there were only two sources of potential danger to Hitler's authority: the armed forces and the SA within his own party. The SA, under the leadership of Ernst Röhm (RURM), openly criticized Hitler and spoke of the need for a "second revolution" and the replacement of the regular army by the SA. Neither the army nor Hitler favored such a possibility. Hitler solved both problems simultaneously on June 30, 1934, by having Röhm and a number of other SA leaders killed in return for the army's support in allowing Hitler to succeed Hindenburg when the president died. When Hindenburg died on August 2, 1934, the office of president was abolished, and Hitler became sole ruler of Germany. Public officials and soldiers were all required to take a personal oath of loyalty to Hitler as the "Führer of the German Reich and people." The Third Reich had begun.

Propaganda and Mass Meetings in Nazi Germany

Propaganda and mass rallies were two of the chief instruments that Hitler used to prepare the German people for the tasks he set before them. In the first selection, taken from a speech to a crowd at Nuremberg, Hitler describes the kind of mystical bond he hoped to create through his mass rallies. In the second excerpt, a Hamburg schoolteacher provides her impression of a Hitler rally.

Adolf Hitler, Speech at the Nuremberg Party Rally, 1936

Do we not feel once again in this hour the miracle that brought us together? Once you heard the voice of a man, and it struck deep into your hearts; it awakened you, and you followed this voice. Year after year you went after it, though him who had spoken you never even saw. You heard only a voice, and you followed it. When we meet each other here, the wonder of our coming together fills us all. Not everyone of you sees me, and I do not see everyone of you. But I feel you, and you feel me. It is the belief in our people that has made us small men great, that has made us poor men rich, that has made brave and courageous men out of us wavering, spiritless, timid folk; this belief made us see our road when we were astray; it joined us together into one whole! . . . You come, that . . . you may, once in a while, gain the feeling that now we are together; we are with him and he with us, and we are now Germany!

A Teacher's Impression of a Hitler Rally, 1932

The April sun shone hot like in summer and turned everything into a picture of gay expectation. There was immaculate order and discipline, although the police left the whole square to the stewards and stood on the sidelines. Nobody spoke of "Hitler," always just "the Führer," "the Führer says," "the Führer wants," and what he said and wanted seemed right and good. The hours passed, the sun shone, expectations rose. In the background, at the edge of the track there were columns of carriers like ammunition carriers. . . . Aeroplanes above us. Testing of the loudspeakers, buzzing of the cine-cameras. It was nearly 3 P.M. "The Führer is coming!" A ripple went through the crowds. Around the speaker's platform one could see hands raised in the Hitler salute. A speaker opened the meeting, abused the "system," nobody listened to him. A second speaker welcomed Hitler and made way for the man who had drawn 120,000 people of all classes and ages. There stood Hitler in a simple black coat and looked over the crowd, waiting—a forest of swastika pennants swished up, the jubilation of this moment was given vent in a roaring salute. Main theme: Out of parties shall grow a nation, the German nation. He censured the "system" ("I want to know what there is left to be ruined in this state!"). "On the way here Socialists confronted me with a poster, 'Turn back, Adolf Hitler.' Thirteen years ago I was a simple unknown soldier. I went my way. I never turned back. Nor shall I turn back now." Otherwise he made no personal attacks, nor any promises, vague or definite. His voice was hoarse after all his speaking during the previous days. When the speech was over, there was roaring enthusiasm and applause. Hitler saluted, gave his thanks, the Horst Wessel song sounded out across the course. Hitler was helped into his coat. Then he went.—How many look up to him with touching faith! as their helper, their savior, their deliverer from unbearable distress—to him who rescues the Prussian prince, the scholar, the clergyman, the farmer, the worker, the unemployed, who rescues them from the parties back into the nation.

Q In Hitler's view, what would mass meetings accomplish for his movement? How do mass rallies further the development of nationalism?

THE NAZI STATE (1933–1939) Having smashed the parliamentary state, Hitler now felt that the real task was at hand: to develop the "total state." Hitler's aims had not been simply power for power's sake or a tyranny based on personal ambition. He had larger ideological goals. The development of an Aryan racial state that would dominate Europe and possibly the world for generations to come required a massive movement in which the German people would be actively involved, not passively cowed by force. Hitler stated:

> We must develop organizations in which an individual's entire life can take place. Then every activity and every need of every individual will be regulated by the collectivity represented by the party. There is no longer any arbitrary will, there are no longer any free realms in which the individual belongs to himself. . . . The time of personal happiness is over.[11]

The Nazis pursued the creation of this totalitarian state in a variety of ways. Mass demonstrations and spectacles were employed to integrate the German nation into a collective fellowship and to mobilize it as an instrument for Hitler's policies. These mass demonstrations, especially the Nuremberg party rallies that were held every September and the Harvest Festivals celebrated at the Bückeberg (BOOK-uh-bayrk) near Hamelin every fall, combined the symbolism of a religious service with the merriment of a popular amusement. They had great appeal and usually evoked mass enthusiasm and excitement (see the box above).

The Nazi Mass Spectacle. Hitler and the Nazis made clever use of mass spectacles to rally the German people behind the Nazi regime. These mass demonstrations evoked intense enthusiasm, as is evident in this photograph of Hitler arriving at the Bückeberg near Hamelin for the Harvest Festival in 1937. Almost one million people were present for the celebration.

Labor Front could a worker obtain and retain a workbook. The Labor Front also sponsored activities to keep the workers happy (see "Mass Leisure" later in this chapter).

For those who needed coercion, the Nazi total state had its instruments of terror and repression. Especially important was the SS, the *Schutzstaffeln* (SHOOTS-shtah-fuhn), or Protection Squads. Originally created as Hitler's personal bodyguard, the SS, under the direction of Heinrich Himmler (1900–1945), came to control all of the regular and secret police forces. Himmler and the SS functioned on the basis of two principles: terror and ideology. Terror included the instruments of repression and murder: the secret police, criminal police, concentration camps, and later the execution squads and death camps for the exter-

Some features of the state apparatus of Hitler's total state seem contradictory. One usually thinks of Nazi Germany as having an all-powerful government that maintained absolute control and order. In truth, Nazi Germany was the scene of almost constant personal and institutional conflict, which resulted in administrative chaos. Incessant struggle characterized relationships within the party, within the state, and between party and state. By fostering rivalry within the party and between party and state, Hitler became the ultimate decision maker.

In the economic sphere, Hitler and the Nazis also established control, but industry was not nationalized, as the left wing of the Nazi Party wanted. Hitler felt that it was irrelevant who owned the means of production so long as the owners recognized their master. Although the regime pursued the use of public works projects and "pump-priming" grants to private construction firms to foster employment and end the depression, there is little doubt that rearmament did far more to solve the unemployment problem. Unemployment, which had stood at 6 million in 1932, dropped to 2.6 million in 1934 and less than 500,000 in 1937. The regime claimed full credit for solving Germany's economic woes, and the improved economy was an important factor in convincing many Germans to accept the new regime, despite its excesses.

The German Labor Front under Robert Ley regulated the world of labor. The Labor Front was a state-controlled union. To control all laborers, it used the workbook. Every salaried worker had to have one in order to hold a job. Only by submitting to the policies of the Nazi-controlled

mination of the Jews (see Chapter 27). For Himmler, the SS was a crusading order whose primary goal was to further the Aryan master race. SS members, who constituted a carefully chosen elite, were thoroughly indoctrinated in racial ideology.

Other institutions, such as the Catholic and Protestant churches, primary and secondary schools, and universities, were also brought under the control of the Nazi totalitarian state. Nazi professional organizations and leagues were formed for civil servants, teachers, women, farmers, doctors, and lawyers. Because the early indoctrination of the nation's youth would lay the foundation for a strong totalitarian state, youth organizations, the *Hitler Jugend* (HIT-luh YOO-gunt) (Hitler Youth) and its female counterpart, the *Bund Deutscher Mädel* (BOONT DOIT-chuh MAY-dul) (German Girls Association), were given special attention. The oath required of Hitler Youth members demonstrates the dedication expected of youth in the Nazi state: "In the presence of this blood banner, which represents our Führer, I swear to devote all my energies and my strength to the savior of our country, Adolf Hitler. I am willing and ready to give up my life for him, so help me God."

Women played a crucial role in the Aryan racial state as bearers of the children who would bring about the triumph of the Aryan race. To the Nazis, the differences between men and women were quite natural. Men were warriors and political leaders; women were destined to be wives and mothers. Motherhood was also exalted in an annual ceremony on August 12, Hitler's mother's birthday, when Hitler awarded the German Mother's Cross to a

Hitler as Munich politician	1919–1923
Beer Hall Putsch	1923
Nazis win 107 seats in Reichstag	1930 (September)
Hitler is made chancellor	1933 (January 30)
Reichstag fire	1933 (February 27)
Enabling Act	1933 (March 23)
Purge of the SA	1934 (June 30)
Hindenburg dies; Hitler as sole ruler	1934 (August 2)
Nuremberg laws	1935
Kristallnacht	1938 (November 9–10)

non-Aryans, especially Jewish parents or grandparents") from the legal profession, civil service, judgeships, the medical profession, teaching positions, cultural and entertainment enterprises, and the press.

In September 1935, the Nazis announced new racial laws at the annual party rally in Nuremberg. These "Nuremberg laws" excluded German Jews from German citizenship and forbade marriages and extramarital relations between Jews and German citizens. The Nuremberg laws essentially separated Jews from the Germans politically, socially, and legally and were the natural extension of Hitler's stress on the preservation of a pure Aryan race.

Nuremberg Laws: German Blood and Honor

Another considerably more violent phase of anti-Jewish activity took place in 1938 and 1939; it was initiated on November 9–10, 1938, the infamous *Kristallnacht* (kri-STAHL-nahkht), or Night of Shattered Glass. The assassination of a third secretary in the German embassy in Paris by a young Polish Jew became the excuse for a Nazi-led destructive rampage against the Jews in which synagogues were burned, seven thousand Jewish businesses were destroyed, and at least one hundred Jews were killed. Moreover, 30,000 Jewish males were rounded up and sent to concentration camps. *Kristallnacht* also led to further drastic steps. Jews were barred from all public buildings and prohibited from owning, managing, or working in any retail store. Finally, under the direction of the SS, Jews

select group of German mothers. Those with four children received a bronze cross, those with six a silver cross, and those with eight or more a gold cross.

Nazi ideas determined employment opportunities for women. The Nazis hoped to drive women out of heavy industry or other jobs that might hinder them from bearing healthy children, as well as certain professions, including university teaching, medicine, and law, which were considered inappropriate for women, especially married women. The Nazis encouraged women to pursue professional occupations that had direct practical application, such as social work and nursing. In addition to restrictive legislation against females, the Nazi regime pursued its campaign against working women with such poster slogans as "Get hold of pots and pans and broom and you'll sooner find a groom!" Nazi policy toward female workers remained inconsistent, however. Especially after the rearmament boom and increased conscription of males for military service resulted in a labor shortage, the government encouraged women to work, even in areas previously dominated by males.

The Nazi total state was intended to be an Aryan racial state. From its beginning, the Nazi Party reflected Hitler's strong anti-Semitic beliefs. Once in power, the Nazis translated anti-Semitic ideas into anti-Semitic policies. Already on April 1, 1933, the new Nazi government initiated a two-day boycott of Jewish businesses. A series of laws soon followed that excluded "non-Aryans" (defined as anyone "descended from

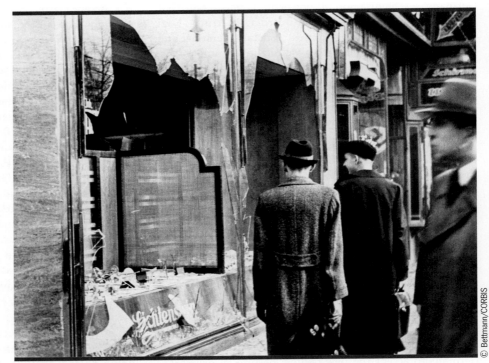

Anti-Semitism in Nazi Germany. At the core of Hitler's ideology was an intense anti-Semitism. Soon after seizing power, Hitler and the Nazis began to translate their anti-Semitic ideas into anti-Semitic policies. This photograph shows one example of Nazi action against the Jews as Germans are seen passing by the broken windows of a Jewish shop in Berlin the morning after *Kristallnacht*, the Night of Shattered Glass, when thousands of Jewish businesses were destroyed.

were encouraged to "emigrate from Germany." After the outbreak of World War II, the policy of emigration was replaced by a more gruesome one.

The Soviet Union

Yet another example of totalitarianism was to be found in the Soviet Union. The civil war in Russia had come to an end by the beginning of 1921. It had taken an enormous toll of life, but the Red Terror and the victories of the Red Army had guaranteed the survival of the Communist regime. During the civil war, Lenin had pursued a policy of "war communism." Under this policy of expedience, the government had nationalized transportation and communication facilities as well as banks, mines, factories, and businesses that employed more than ten workers. The government had also assumed the right to requisition food from the peasants, who often resisted fiercely, slaughtering their own animals and destroying their crops, though without much success. Hunger led to an untold number of deaths in the countryside. Added to this problem was drought, which caused a great famine between 1920 and 1922 that claimed as many as 5 million lives. Industrial collapse paralleled the agricultural disaster. By 1921, industrial output was at only 20 percent of its 1913 levels. Russia was exhausted. As Leon Trotsky observed, "The collapse of the productive forces surpassed anything of the kind that history had ever seen. The country, and the government with it, were at the very edge of the abyss."[12]

THE NEW ECONOMIC POLICY In March 1921, Lenin pulled Russia back from the abyss by establishing his **New Economic Policy** (NEP). The NEP was a modified version of the old capitalist system. Peasants were now allowed to sell their produce openly, and retail stores as well as small industries that employed fewer than twenty employees could now operate under private ownership; heavy industry, banking, and mines remained in the hands of the government. In 1922, Lenin and the Communists formally created a new state called the Union of Soviet Socialist Republics, known by its initials as the USSR and commonly called the Soviet Union. Already in that year, a revived market and good harvest had brought the famine to an end; Soviet agriculture climbed to 75 percent of its prewar level. Industry, especially state-owned heavy industry, fared less well and continued to stagnate. Only coal production had reached prewar levels by 1926. Overall, the NEP had saved the Soviet Union from complete economic disaster even though Lenin and other leading Communists intended it to be only a temporary, tactical retreat from the goals of communism.

In the meantime, Lenin and the Communists were strengthening their one-party state. The number of bureaucrats increased dramatically and soon constituted a new elite with the best jobs, food, and dwellings. Even Lenin issued warnings about the widening power of the bureaucracy that he had helped create.

THE STRUGGLE FOR POWER Between 1922 and 1924, Lenin suffered a series of strokes that finally led to his death on January 21, 1924. Although Communist control theoretically rested on a principle of collective leadership, Lenin had in fact provided one-man rule. His death inaugurated a struggle for power among the members of the Politburo, the institution that had become the leading organ of the party.

In 1924, the Politburo of seven members was severely divided over the future direction of the nation. The Left, led by Leon Trotsky, wanted to end the NEP and launch the Soviet Union on the path of rapid industrialization, primarily at the expense of the peasantry. This same group wanted to continue the revolution, believing that the survival of the Russian Revolution ultimately depended on the spread of communism abroad. Another group in the Politburo, called the Right, rejected the cause of world revolution and wanted instead to concentrate on constructing a socialist state. Believing that too rapid industrialization would worsen the living standards of the Soviet peasantry, this group also favored a continuation of Lenin's NEP.

These ideological divisions were underscored by an intense personal rivalry between Leon Trotsky and Joseph Stalin. Trotsky had been a key figure in the success of the Bolshevik Revolution and the Red Army. In 1924, he held the post of commissar of war and was the leading spokesman for the Left in the Politburo. Joseph Stalin (1879–1953) had joined the Bolsheviks in 1903 and had come to Lenin's attention after staging a daring bank robbery to obtain funds for the Bolshevik cause. Stalin, who was neither a dynamic speaker nor a forceful writer, was content to hold the dull bureaucratic job of party general secretary while other Politburo members held party positions that enabled them to display their brilliant oratorical abilities. He was a good organizer (his fellow Bolsheviks called him "Comrade Card-Index"), and the other members of the Politburo soon found that the position of party secretary was really the most important in the party hierarchy. The general secretary appointed the regional, district, city, and town party secretaries. In 1922, for example, Stalin had made some ten thousand appointments, many of them trusted followers whose holding of key positions proved valuable in the struggle for power. Although Stalin at first refused to support either the Left or the Right in the Politburo, he finally came to favor the goal of "socialism in one country" rather than world revolution.

Stalin used his post as party general secretary to gain complete control of the Communist Party. Trotsky was expelled from the party in 1927. Eventually, he made his way to Mexico, where he was murdered in 1940, no doubt on Stalin's orders. By 1929, Stalin had succeeded in eliminating the Old Bolsheviks of the revolutionary era from the Politburo and establishing a dictatorship so powerful that the Russian tsars of old would have been envious.

THE STALINIST ERA (1929–1939) The Stalinist era marked the beginning of an economic, social, and political revolution that was more sweeping in its results than the revolutions of 1917. Stalin made a significant shift in economic policy in 1928 when he launched his first five-year

Joseph Stalin, Industrialization of the Country (1928)

plan. Its real goal was nothing less than the transformation of the Soviet Union from an agricultural country into an industrial state virtually overnight. Instead of consumer goods, the first five-year plan emphasized maximum production of capital goods and armaments and succeeded in quadrupling the production of heavy machinery and doubling oil production. Between 1928 and 1937, during the first two five-year plans, steel production increased from 4 to 18 million tons per year, and hard coal output went from 36 to 128 million tons.

The social and political costs of industrialization were enormous. Little provision was made for absorbing the expanded labor force into the cities. Though the industrial labor force increased by millions between 1932 and 1940, total investment in housing actually declined after 1929; as a result, millions of workers and their families lived in pitiful conditions. Real wages in industry also declined by 43 percent between 1928 and 1940, and strict laws limited workers' freedom of movement. To inspire and pacify the workers, government propaganda stressed the need for sacrifice to create the new socialist state. Soviet labor policy stressed high levels of achievement, typified by the Stakhanov cult. Alexei Stakhanov (uh-LEK-say stuh-KHAH-nuf) was a coal miner who mined 102 tons of coal in one shift, exceeding the norm by 1,300 percent. He was held up as an example to others, even though his feat had been contrived for publicity purposes.

Rapid industrialization was accompanied by an equally rapid collectivization of agriculture. Stalin believed that the capital needed for industrial growth could be gained by creating agricultural surpluses through eliminating private farms and pushing people onto collective farms (see the box on p. 835). The first step was to eliminate the kulaks, or wealthy farmers, who were sent to the Siberian camps beginning in 1930. By eliminating private property, a Communist ideal would also be achieved.

By 1930, some 10 million peasant households had been collectivized; by 1934, the Soviet Union's 26 million family farms had been collectivized into 250,000 units. This was done at tremendous cost since Stalin did not hesitate to starve the peasants to force them to comply with the policy of collectivization, especially in Ukraine, where 2.9 million died. Stalin himself supposedly told Winston Churchill during World War II that 10 million peasants died during the artificially created famines of 1932 and 1933. The only concession Stalin made to the peasants was to allow each household to have one tiny, privately owned garden plot.

CHRONOLOGY The Soviet Union

New Economic Policy begins	1921
Death of Lenin	1924
Trotsky is expelled from the Communist Party	1927
First five-year plan begins	1928
Stalin's dictatorship is established	1929
Height of Stalin's purges	1936–1938

Stalin's program of rapid industrialization entailed additional costs as well. To achieve his goals, Stalin strengthened the party bureaucracy under his control. Those who resisted were sent into forced labor camps in Siberia. Stalin's desire for sole control of decision making also led to purges of the Old Bolsheviks. Between 1936 and 1938, the most prominent Old Bolsheviks were put on trial and condemned to death. During this same time, Stalin undertook a purge of army officers, diplomats, union officials, party members, intellectuals, and numerous ordinary citizens. One old woman was sent to Siberia for saying, "If people prayed, they would work better." Estimates are that 8 million Russians were arrested; millions died in Siberian forced labor camps. This gave Stalin the distinction of being one of the greatest mass murderers in human history. The Stalinist bloodbath made what some Western intellectuals had hailed as the "new civilization" much less attractive by the late 1930s.

Disturbed by a rapidly declining birthrate, Stalin also reversed much of the permissive social legislation of the early 1920s. Advocating complete equality of rights for

Stalin Signing a Death Warrant. Terror played an important role in the authoritarian system created by Joseph Stalin. Here Stalin is shown signing what is supposedly a death warrant in 1933. As the terror increased in the late 1930s, Stalin signed such orders every day.

© Time Life Pictures/Getty Images

The Formation of Collective Farms

Accompanying the rapid industrialization of the Soviet Union was the collectivization of agriculture, a feat that involved nothing less than transforming Russia's 26 million family farms into 250,000 collective farms (*kolkhozes*). This selection provides a firsthand account of how the process worked.

Max Belov, *The History of a Collective Farm*

General collectivization in our village was brought about in the following manner: Two representatives of the [Communist] Party arrived in the village. All the inhabitants were summoned by the ringing of the church bell to a meeting at which the policy of general collectivization was announced.... The upshot was that although the meeting lasted two days, from the viewpoint of the Party representatives nothing was accomplished.

After this setback the Party representatives divided the village into two sections and worked each one separately. Two more officials were sent to reinforce the first two. A meeting of our section of the village was held in a stable which had previously belonged to a kulak. The meeting dragged on until dark. Suddenly someone threw a brick at the lamp, and in the dark the peasants began to beat the Party representatives who jumped out the window and escaped from the village barely alive. The following day seven people were arrested. The militia was called in and stayed in the village until the peasants, realizing their helplessness, calmed down....

By the end of 1930 there were two kolkhozes in our village. Though at first these collectives embraced at most only 70 percent of the peasant households, in the months that followed they gradually absorbed more and more of them.

In these kolkhozes the great bulk of the land was held and worked communally, but each peasant household owned a house of some sort, a small plot of ground and perhaps some livestock. All the members of the kolkhoz were required to work on the kolkhoz a certain number of days each month; the rest of the time they were allowed to work on their own holdings. They derived their income partly from what they grew on their garden strips and partly from their work in the kolkhoz.

When the harvest was over, and after the farm had met its obligations to the state and to various special funds (for instance, seed, etc.) and had sold on the market whatever undesignated produce was left, the remaining produce and the farm's monetary income were divided among the kolkhoz members according to the number of "labor days" each one had contributed to the farm's work.... It was in 1930 that the kolkhoz members first received their portions out of the "communal kettle." After they had received their earnings, at the rate of 1 kilogram of grain and 55 kopecks per labor day, one of them remarked, "You will live, but you will be very, very thin."

In the spring of 1931 a tractor worked the fields of the kolkhoz for the first time. The tractor was "capable of plowing every kind of hard soil and virgin soil," as Party representatives told us at the meeting in celebration of its arrival. The peasants did not then know that these "steel horses" would carry away a good part of the harvest in return for their work....

By late 1932 more than 80 percent of the peasant households ... had been collectivized.... That year the peasants harvested a good crop and had hopes that the calculations would work out to their advantage and would help strengthen them economically. These hopes were in vain. The kolkhoz workers received only 200 grams of flour per labor day for the first half of the year; the remaining grain, including the seed fund, was taken by the government. The peasants were told that industrialization of the country, then in full swing, demanded grain and sacrifices from them.

Q What was the purpose of collectivizing Soviet agriculture? According to Belov, why did the peasants of his village assault the Communist Party representatives? What was the result of their protest?

women, the Communists had made divorce and abortion easy to obtain while also encouraging women to work outside the home and liberate themselves sexually. After Stalin came to power, the family was praised as a miniature collective in which parents were responsible for inculcating values of duty, discipline, and hard work. Abortion was outlawed, and divorced fathers who did not support their children were fined heavily. A new divorce law of June 1936 imposed fines for repeated divorces, and homosexuality was declared a criminal activity. The regime now praised motherhood and urged women to have large families as a patriotic duty. But by this time, many Soviet women worked in factories and spent many additional hours waiting in line to purchase increasingly scarce consumer goods. Despite the change in policy, no dramatic increase in the birthrate occurred.

The Stalinist era did witness some positive changes in the everyday lives of Soviet citizens. To create leaders for the new Communist society, Stalin began a program to enable workers, peasants, and young Communists to receive higher education, especially in engineering. There was also tremendous growth in part-time schools where large numbers of adults took courses to become literate so that they could advance to technical school or college. Increasing numbers of people saw education as the key to better jobs and upward mobility in Soviet society. One woman of peasant background recounted: "In Moscow I had a burning desire to study. Where or what wasn't important; I wanted to study." For what purpose? "We had a saying at work: 'Without that piece of paper [the diploma] you are an insect; with it, a human being.' My lack of higher education prevented me from getting decent wages."[13]

Authoritarianism in Eastern Europe

A number of other states in Europe were not totalitarian but did have conservative authoritarian governments. These states adopted some of the trappings of totalitarian states, especially wide police powers, but their greatest concern was not the creation of a mass movement aimed at the establishment of a new kind of society but rather the defense of the existing social order. Consequently, the **authoritarian state** tended to limit the participation of the masses and was content with passive obedience rather than active involvement in the goals of the regime. A number of states in eastern Europe adopted this kind of authoritarian government.

Nowhere had the map of Europe been more drastically altered by World War I than in eastern Europe. The new states of Austria, Poland, Czechoslovakia, and Yugoslavia adopted parliamentary systems, and the preexisting kingdoms of Romania and Bulgaria gained new parliamentary constitutions in 1920. Greece became a republic in 1924. Hungary's government was parliamentary in form but was controlled by its landed aristocrats. At the beginning of the 1920s, political democracy seemed well established, but almost everywhere in eastern Europe, parliamentary governments soon gave way to authoritarian regimes.

Eastern Europe After World War I

Several problems helped create this situation. Eastern European states had little tradition of liberalism or parliamentary politics and no substantial middle class to support them. Then, too, these states were largely rural and agrarian. Much of the land was still dominated by large landowners who feared the growth of agrarian peasant parties with their schemes for land redistribution. Ethnic conflicts also threatened to tear these countries apart. Fearful of land reform, Communist agrarian upheaval, and ethnic conflict, powerful landowners, the churches, and even some members of the small middle class looked to authoritarian governments to maintain the old system.

Already in the 1920s, some eastern European states began to move away from political democracy toward authoritarian structures. A military coup d'état established an authoritarian regime in Bulgaria in 1923. Poland established an authoritarian regime in 1926 when Marshal Joseph Pilsudski (peel-SOOT-skee) (1867–1935) created a military dictatorship. In Yugoslavia, King Alexander I (1921–1934) abolished the constitution and imposed a royal dictatorship in 1929. During the 1930s, all of the remaining parliamentary regimes except Czechoslovakia succumbed to authoritarianism. Eastern European states were increasingly attracted to the authoritarian examples of Fascist Italy and Nazi Germany.

Although Admiral Miklós Horthy (MIK-lohsh HOR-tee) (1868–1957) had ruled Hungary as "regent" since 1919, the appointment of Julius Gömbös (GUM-buhsh) (1886–1936) as prime minister in 1932 brought Hungary even closer to Italy and Germany. Romania witnessed the development of a strong fascist movement led by Corneliu Codreanu (kor-NELL-yoo kaw-dree-AH-noo) (1899–1938). Known as the Legion of the Archangel Michael, it possessed its own paramilitary squad called the Iron Guard. As Codreanu's fascist movement grew and became Romania's third largest political party, King Carol II (1930–1940) responded in 1938 by ending parliamentary rule, crushing the leadership of the legion, and imposing authoritarian rule. In Greece, General John Metaxas (muh-tahk-SAHSS) (1871–1941) imposed a dictatorship in 1936.

Only Czechoslovakia, with its substantial middle class, liberal tradition, and strong industrial base, maintained its political democracy. Thomas Masaryk (MAS-uh-rik) (1850–1937), an able and fair leader who served as president from 1918 to 1935, was able to maintain an uneasy but stable alliance of reformist socialists, agrarians, and Catholics.

Dictatorship in the Iberian Peninsula

Parliamentary regimes also failed to survive in both Spain and Portugal. Both countries were largely agrarian, illiterate, and dominated by powerful landlords and Catholic clergy.

Spain's parliamentary monarchy was unable to deal with the social tensions generated by the industrial boom and inflation that accompanied World War I. Supported by King Alfonso XIII (1886–1931), General Miguel Primo de Rivera (PREE-moh day ri-VAY-ruh) (1870–1930) led a successful military coup in September 1923 and created a personal dictatorship that lasted until 1930. But a faltering economy because of the Great Depression led to the collapse of Primo de Rivera's regime in January 1930 as well as to a widespread lack of support for the monarchy. Alfonso XIII left Spain in 1931, and a new Spanish republic was instituted, governed by a coalition of democrats and reformist socialists. Political turmoil ensued as control of the government passed from leftists to rightists until the Popular Front, an antifascist coalition composed of democrats, socialists, Communists, and other leftist

Opposing >< VIEWPOINTS

Spain Divided: The Poems of Two Brothers

During the Spanish Civil War, many families became divided as their members found themselves on opposite sides based on their political allegiances. Antonio Machado (1875–1939) was a Republican, but his older brother, Manuel (1874–1947), supported the Nationalists. Antonio, whose fame as a poet overshadowed that of his older brother, wrote an elegy, *The Crime Was in Granada*, for the poet Federico García Lorca, who was killed in Granada in 1936 by a Nationalist militia. Lorca's international fame and untimely death made him an early martyr for the Republican cause. For Antonio, Granada was "one of the stupidest cities in Spain.... Could Granada have defended its poet? I think so. It would have been easy for it to prove to the Fascist assassins that Lorca was politically innocuous and that the common people whom Federico loved and whose songs he collected were not precisely those who sing the Internationale" (the anthem of international socialism, sung by socialists and Communists). In contrast to Antonio's devotion to the Republican cause, Manuel's poem, *Francisco Franco*, evokes themes of the Nationalist cause: faith, military greatness, and traditional Spain.

Antonio Machado, *The Crime Was in Granada*

To Federico García Lorca

I: *The Crime*

He was seen, surrounded by rifles,
moving down a long street
and out to the country
in the chill before dawn, with the stars still out.
They killed Federico
at the first glint of daylight.

The band of assassins shrank from his glance.
They all closed their eyes,
muttering: "See if God helps you now!"
Federico fell,
lead in his stomach, blood on his face.
And Granada was the scene of the crime.
Think of it—poor Granada—his Granada.

Manuel Machado, *Francisco Franco*

Leader of the new Reconquest [the first was
    Christian Spain's conquest of Muslim
    Spain in the Middle Ages]
Lord of Spain, through him her faith renews,
knows triumph and smiles, and reaps
the harvest from the fields of conquest.

Knows triumph and smiles, his military skill
stands out in warlike glory,
sure and steadfast. And to make History
God wanted much more for him: genius.

Faith and love he inspires. Wherever he goes
the prestige of triumph follows
as the fatherland rises from his advance.

For a tomorrow that yesterday does not deny,
for a Spain evermore Spain,
the smile of Franco shines! ⇨

 In what ways does each brother's poem reflect the side he supported? What examples of political allegiance to either the Republicans or Nationalists are evident in these works? Why do you think two brothers would be on opposing sides in a civil war?

---

groups, took over in 1936. The Popular Front was unacceptable, however, to senior army officers. Led by General Francisco Franco (1892–1975), Spanish military forces revolted against the government and inaugurated a brutal and bloody civil war that lasted three years.

THE SPANISH CIVIL WAR The war split the country between left and right (see the box above). On the left were the Republicans who supported the Popular Front. They were concentrated in urban areas such as Madrid and Barcelona and favored modernization, workers' rights, the expansion of manufacturing, a civilian army, and secularization. On the right were the Nationalists who supported Franco's military coup, the monarchy, the military, an agrarian economy, and the Catholic Church.

The Spanish conflict was complicated by foreign intervention. In 1936, Great Britain, France, Germany, Italy, and the Soviet Union signed a Non-Intervention Agreement, declaring that they would not provide economic or military support for either side. Germany and Italy quickly rejected the agreement, however, and sent troops, weapons, and military advisers to assist Franco. Hitler used the Spanish Civil War as an opportunity to test the new weapons of his revived air force. The devastating air attack on Guernica on April 26, 1937, initiated a new level of brutally destructive warfare. Meanwhile, the British and French adhered to their position of nonintervention, so the Republicans turned to the Soviet Union for aid. The Soviets sent tanks, planes, and pilots. The Republicans also gained

The Destruction of Guernica. On April 26, 1937, the German Condor Legion dropped 100,000 tons of explosives in three hours on the small Basque town of Guernica, killing 1,654 people and wounding 889. The first illustration shows the ruins of Guernica after the German attack. The scene was also captured in Picasso's *Guernica* (1937), a large (11 by 25 feet) Cubist piece that portrays the horror and human destruction caused by mass bombings. The fragmented bodies include a woman holding her dead child, dismembered limbs, and terrified horses.

assistance from international brigades of volunteers, including the Abraham Lincoln Brigade from the United States.

Gradually, Franco's forces wore down the Popular Front, and after they captured Madrid on March 28, 1939, the Spanish Civil War finally came to an end. The war had been a brutal one. Probably 400,000 people died in the war, only one-fourth of them on the battlefield. Civilians died from air raids, disease, and bloody reprisals by both sides against their enemies and their supporters. Another 200,000 people were executed in the years following Franco's victory.

THE FRANCO REGIME General Franco soon established a dictatorship that lasted until his death in 1975. It was not a fascist government, although it was unlikely to oppose the Fascists in Italy or the Nazis in Germany. The fascist movement in Spain, known as the Falange (fuh-LANJ) and led by José Antonio Primo de Rivera, son of the former dictator, contributed little to Franco's success and played a minor role in the new regime. Franco's government, which favored large landowners, business, and the Catholic clergy, was yet another example of a traditional, conservative, authoritarian regime.

PORTUGAL In 1910, the Portuguese had overthrown their monarchy and established a republic. Severe inflation after World War I, however, undermined support for the republic and helped intensify political instability. In 1926, a group of army officers seized power, and by the early 1930s, the military junta's finance minister, Antonio Salazar (SAL-uh-zahr) (1889–1970), had become the strongman of the regime. Salazar controlled the Portuguese government for the next forty years.

Eastern Europe

Military coup d'état establishes authoritarian regime in Bulgaria	1923
Pilsudski creates military dictatorship in Poland	1926
Alexander I creates royal dictatorship in Yugoslavia	1929
Gömbös is made prime minister in Hungary	1932
Dictatorship of General Metaxas in Greece	1936
Carol II crushes Iron Guard and imposes authoritarian rule in Romania	1938

Spain

Dictatorship of Primo de Rivera	1923–1930
Creation of Spanish Republic	1931
Spanish Civil War	1936–1939
Dictatorship of Franco	1939–1975

The Expansion of Mass Culture and Mass Leisure

 FOCUS QUESTION: What new dimensions in mass culture and mass leisure emerged during the interwar years, and what role did these activities play in the totalitarian states?

The decade of the 1920s came to be known as the Roaring Twenties for the exuberance of its popular culture. Berlin, the capital of Germany, became the entertainment center of Europe with its theaters, cabarets, cinemas, and jazz clubs. The Roaring Twenties were especially known for dance crazes. People danced in clubs and dance halls, at home, and in the streets, doing the Charleston, the Bunny Hug, and a variety of other dances. Josephine Baker (1906–1975), an American singer and dancer, became especially well known in Europe, appearing at European clubs featuring American "Negro" jazz music. One critic said, "She dances for hours without the slightest trace of tiredness." She became a wonderful symbol of the popular "flapper," the unconventional and lively young woman of the 1920s.

So popular was jazz, a musical form that had originated with African American musicians in the United States, that the 1920s also were known as the Jazz Age. Admired for its improvised qualities and forceful rhythms, jazz spread throughout the Western world as King Oliver, Bix Beiderbecke (BIKS BY-der-bek), Jelly Roll Morton, and others wrote and played some of the greatest jazz music of the time.

Radio and Movies

A series of technological inventions in the late nineteenth century had prepared the way for a revolution in

The Charleston. Dancing became the rage during the Roaring Twenties, and the Charleston was the most popular and enduring dance of the decade. This photograph shows a couple dancing the Charleston in a scene from a London musical, *Just a Kiss,* performed in 1926.

mass communications. Especially important was Guglielmo Marconi's discovery of "wireless" radio waves. But it was not until June 16, 1920, that a radio broadcast (of a concert by soprano Nellie Melba from London) for a mass audience was attempted. Permanent broadcasting facilities were then constructed in the United States, Europe, and Japan during 1921 and 1922, and mass production of radios (receiving sets) also began. In 1926, when the British Broadcasting Corporation (BBC) was made into a public corporation, there were 2.2 million radios in Great Britain. By the end of the 1930s, there were 9 million.

The technical foundation for motion pictures had already been developed in the 1890s when short movies were produced as novelties for music halls. Shortly before World War I, full-length features, such as the Italian film *Quo Vadis* and the American film *Birth of a Nation,* were released, and it quickly became apparent that cinema was a new form of entertainment for the masses. By 1939, about 40 percent of adults in the more advanced industrial countries were attending the movies once a week. That figure increased to 60 percent by the end of World War II.

Mass forms of communication and entertainment were not new, but the increased size of audiences and the ability of radio and cinema, unlike the printed word, to provide an immediate shared experience added new dimensions to mass culture. Favorite film actors and actresses became stars who then became the focus of public adoration and scrutiny. Sensuous actresses such as Marlene Dietrich, whose appearance in the early sound film *The Blue Angel* catapulted her to fame, popularized new images of women's sexuality.

Of course, radio and movies could also be used for political purposes. Hitler had said that "without motor cars, sound films, and wireless, no victory of National Socialism." Radio seemed to offer great opportunities for reaching the masses, especially when it became apparent that the emotional harangues of a demagogue such as Hitler had just as much impact on people when heard on radio as in person. The Nazi regime encouraged radio listening by urging manufacturers to produce cheap radios that could be bought on the installment plan. The Nazis also erected loudspeaker pillars in the streets to encourage communal radio listening, especially to broadcasts of mass meetings.

Film, too, had propaganda potential, a possibility not lost on Joseph Goebbels (GUR-bulz) (1897–1945), the propaganda minister of Nazi Germany. Believing that film constituted one of the "most modern and scientific means of influencing the masses," Goebbels created a special film section in his Propaganda Ministry and encouraged the production of both documentaries and popular feature films that carried the Nazi message. *Triumph of the Will*, for example, was a documentary of the 1934 Nuremberg party rally that forcefully conveyed the power of National Socialism to viewers (see the Film & History feature on p. 841). Both Fascist Italy and Nazi Germany also controlled and exploited the content of newsreels shown in movie theaters.

Mass Leisure

Mass leisure activities had developed at the turn of the century, but new work patterns after World War I dramatically expanded the amount of free time available to take advantage of them. By 1920, the eight-hour day had become the norm for many office and factory workers in northern and western Europe.

SPORTS Professional sporting events for mass audiences became an especially important aspect of mass leisure. Attendance at association football (soccer) games increased dramatically, and the inauguration of the World Cup contest in 1930 added to the nationalistic rivalries that began to surround such mass sporting events. Increased attendance also made the 1920s and 1930s a great era of stadium building. For the 1936 Olympics, the Germans built a stadium in Berlin that seated 140,000 people.

TOURISM Travel opportunities also added new dimensions to mass leisure activities. The military use of aircraft during World War I spurred improvements in planes that made civilian air travel a reality. The first regular international airmail service began in 1919, and regular passenger service soon followed. Although air travel remained the preserve of the wealthy or the adventurous, trains, buses, and private cars made excursions to beaches or resorts more popular and more affordable. Beaches, such as the one at Brighton in England, were increasingly mobbed by crowds of people from all social classes, a clear reflection of the growth of democratic politics. In France, the Popular Front government passed legislation that provided paid vacations for all salaried employees or wage earners. Workers were granted a fifteen-day paid vacation in the summer, corresponding to school vacation. Whereas in Italy and Germany (see the next section) mass leisure activities were used to support state initiatives, in France paid vacations became a citizen's right.

Europeans living in the colonies of the European states also increasingly found opportunities for tourism. They flocked to colonial spas where they could find reminders of European culture and medicinal treatment. Hydrotherapy (treatment with mineral water) was employed to treat malaria and yellow fever, ailments that often afflicted Europeans living in the colonies, especially in Africa.

ORGANIZED MASS LEISURE IN ITALY AND GERMANY Mass leisure provided totalitarian regimes with new ways to control their populations. Mussolini's Italy created the *Dopolavoro* (duh-puh-LAH-vuh-roh) (Afterwork) as a vast national recreation agency. The *Dopolavoro* was responsible for establishing clubhouses with libraries, radios, and athletic facilities in virtually every town and village. In some places, they included auditoriums for plays and films, as well as travel agencies that arranged tours, cruises, and resort vacations on the Adriatic at reduced rates. *Dopolavoro* groups introduced many Italians to various facets of mass culture and mass leisure with activities such as band concerts, movies, choral groups, roller skating, and ballroom dancing. Essentially, the *Dopolavoro* enabled the Italian government to provide recreational activities and supervise them as well. By doing so, the state imposed new rules and regulations on previously spontaneous activities, thus breaking down old group solidarities and enabling these groups to be guided by the goals of the state.

The Nazi regime adopted a program similar to the *Dopolavoro* in its *Kraft durch Freude* (KRAHFT doorkh FROI-duh) (Strength Through Joy). The purpose of *Kraft durch Freude* was to coordinate the free time of the working class by offering a variety of leisure time activities, including concerts, operas, films, guided tours, and sporting events. Especially popular were inexpensive vacations, much like modern package tours, such as cruises to Scandinavia or the Mediterranean or, more likely for workers, short trips to various sites in Germany. Some 130,000 workers took cruises in 1938; 7 million took short trips.

Triumph of the Will (1934)

Probably the best-known films of Nazi Germany today are the documentaries, in particular those of Leni Riefenstahl. Riefenstahl was an actress who turned to directing in 1932. Adolf Hitler liked her work and invited her to make a film about the 1934 Nuremberg party rally. In filming this party day of unity—as it was called—Hitler was trying to demonstrate, in the wake of the purge of the SA on June 30, that the Nazi Party was strongly united behind its leader. Hitler provided the film's title, *Triumph des Willens* (*Triumph of the Will*).

Much of the film's success was due to careful preparation. Riefenstahl was assisted by a crew of 172 people. Good camera work was coordinated with the physical arrangements for the rally to produce a spectacle that was manipulated for cinematic purposes from beginning to end. As one critic remarked, "The Rally was planned not only as a spectacular mass meeting, but as a spectacular propaganda film." To add to the dramatic effect, Riefenstahl used a number of techniques, including moving cameras (one was even mounted on Hitler's Mercedes), telephoto lenses for unusual perspectives, aerial photographs, and music carefully synchronized with each scene. The result is an effective piece of propaganda aimed at conveying to viewers the power of National Socialism.

The movie begins with introductory titles that are almost religious in character:

> Twenty years after the outbreak of the World War,
> Sixteen years after the beginning of Germany's suffering,
> Nineteen months after the beginning of the rebirth of Germany,
> Adolf Hitler flew to Nuremberg to review his faithful followers.

The rest of the film is devoted to scenes from the six days of the party rally: the dramatic opening when Hitler is greeted with thunderous applause; the major speeches of party leaders; an outdoor rally of Labor Service men who perform pseudo-military drills with their shovels; a Hitler Youth rally in which Hitler tells thousands of German boys, "in you Germany will live"; military exercises; and massive ceremonies with thousands of parading SA and SS men.

A scene from *Triumph of the Will* showing one of the many mass rallies at Nuremberg.

NSDAP/The Kobal Collection

The film ends with Hitler's closing speech in which he reviews the struggle of the Nazi Party to take control of Germany. The screen fades to black as the crowd sings "The Horst Wessel Lied," a famous Nazi anthem.

Throughout the film, Hitler is shown in messianic terms—his descent from the clouds at the beginning, his motorcades through the streets with him standing like a god in an open car as thousands of people cheer, and his many appearances at the rally where he commands the complete adulation of the masses assembled before him. In his speeches, Hitler emphasized the power of the new German state: "It is our will that this state shall endure for a thousand years." He also stressed the need for unity: "We want to be one people, one nation, and with one leader." As Rudolf Hess, Hitler's deputy, summed up at the end of the film: "The Party is Hitler. Hitler is Germany just as Germany is Hitler."

Considerable controversy has surrounded the film. Riefenstahl was accused by many of using art to promote a murderous and morally corrupt regime. In Germany, under postwar denazification laws, the film can be shown only for educational purposes. Yet Riefenstahl always maintained, against all the evidence, that it was "a pure historical film." To a viewer today, however, the film is obviously a propaganda piece. The speeches seem tedious and the ideas simplistic, but to watch thousands of people responding the way they did is a terrible reminder of how Hitler used mass spectacles to achieve his goal of educating the German people to his new authoritarian state. ⇲

More and more, mass culture and mass leisure had the effect of increasing the homogeneity of national populations, a process that had begun in the nineteenth century with the development of the national state and mass politics. Local popular culture was increasingly replaced by national and even international culture as new forms of mass production and consumption brought similar styles of clothing and fashion to people throughout Europe.

Cultural and Intellectual Trends in the Interwar Years

 Focus Question: What were the main cultural and intellectual trends in the interwar years?

The artistic and intellectual innovations of the pre–World War I period, which had shocked many Europeans, had been the preserve primarily of a small group of avant-garde artists and intellectuals. In the 1920s and 1930s, they became more widespread as artists and intellectuals continued to work out the implications of the ideas developed before 1914. But what made the prewar avant-garde culture acceptable in the 1920s and the 1930s? Perhaps the most important factor was the impact of World War I.

To many people, the experiences of the war seemed to confirm the prewar avant-garde belief that human beings were violent and irrational animals who were incapable of creating a sane and rational world. The Great Depression of the late 1920s and early 1930s, as well as the growth of fascist movements based on violence and the degradation of individual rights, only added to the uncertainties generated by the Great War. The crisis of confidence in Western civilization ran deep and was well captured in the words of the French poet Paul Valéry (POHL vah-lay-REE) in the early 1920s:

> The storm has died away, and still we are restless, uneasy, as if the storm were about to break. Almost all the affairs of men remain in a terrible uncertainty. We think of what has disappeared, and we are almost destroyed by what has been destroyed; we do not know what will be born, and we fear the future.... Doubt and disorder are in us and with us. There is no thinking man, however shrewd or learned he may be, who can hope to dominate this anxiety, to escape from this impression of darkness.[14]

Political and economic uncertainties were paralleled by social insecurities. The war had served to break down many traditional middle-class attitudes, especially toward sexuality. In the 1920s, women's physical appearance changed dramatically. Short skirts, short hair, the use of cosmetics that were once thought to be the preserve of prostitutes, and the new practice of suntanning gave women a new image. This change in physical appearance, which stressed more exposure of a woman's body, was also accompanied by frank discussions of sexual matters. In England in 1918, Marie Stopes published *Married Love,* which emphasized

sexual pleasure in marriage and soon became a best seller. In 1926, the Dutch physician Theodore van de Velde (TAY-oh-dor vahn duh VELL-duh) published *Ideal Marriage: Its Physiology and Technique.* Translated into a number of languages, it became an international best seller. Van de Velde described female and male anatomy, discussed birth control techniques, and glorified sexual pleasure in marriage. New ideas on sexuality and birth control were also spread to the working classes by family planning clinics, such as those of Margaret Sanger in the United States and Marie Stopes in Britain.

Nightmares and New Visions: Art and Music

Uncertainty also pervaded the cultural and intellectual achievements of the interwar years. Postwar artistic trends were largely a working out of the implications of prewar developments. Abstract painting, for example, became ever more popular as many pioneering artists of the early twentieth century matured in the decades after the war. In addition, prewar fascination with the absurd and the unconscious contents of the mind seemed even more appropriate after the nightmare landscapes of World War I battlefronts. This gave rise to both the Dada movement and Surrealism, although it was German Expressionist artists who best captured directly the disturbingly destructive effects of World War I.

GERMAN EXPRESSIONISTS Although Expressionism as a movement began before World War I, the war itself had a devastating impact on a group of German Expressionist artists who focused on the suffering and shattered lives caused by the war. George Grosz (GROHS) (1893–1959), one of these artists, expressed his anger in this way: "Of course, there was a kind of mass enthusiasm at the start.... And then after a few years when everything bogged down, when we were defeated, when everything went to pieces, all that remained, at least of me and most of my friends, were disgust and horror."[15] Another German artist who gave visual expression to the horrors of World War I was Otto Dix (1891–1969), who had also served in the war and was well versed in its effects. In *The War,* he gave a graphic presentation of the devastating effects of the Great War.

THE DADA MOVEMENT **Dadaism** attempted to enshrine the purposelessness of life. Tristan Tzara (TRISS-tun TSAHR-rah) (1896–1945), a Romanian-French poet and one of the founders of Dadaism, expressed the Dadaist contempt for the Western tradition in a lecture in 1922: "The acts of life have no beginning or end. Everything happens in a completely idiotic way.... Like everything in life, Dada is useless." Revolted by the insanity of life, the Dadaists tried to give it expression by creating "anti-art." The 1918 Berlin Dada Manifesto maintained that "Dada is the international expression of our times, the great rebellion of artistic movements."

Otto Dix, _The War._ In _The War,_ Otto Dix used the traditional format of a triptych—a three-paneled painting usually used as an altarpiece—to demonstrate the devastating effects of World War I. In the left panel, soldiers march off to battle, while the results of the battlefield are shown in the center and right panels in the contorted and mutilated bodies riddled with bullets. The coffinlike bottom panel is filled with dead soldiers. Dix portrayed himself in the right panel as a ghostlike soldier towing a fellow soldier from battle.

In the hands of Hannah Höch (HEKH) (1889–1978), Dada became an instrument to comment on women's roles in the new mass culture. Höch was the only female member of the Berlin Dada Club, which featured the use of photomontage. Her work was part of the first Dada show in Berlin in 1920. In _Dada Dance,_ she seemed to criticize the "new woman" by making fun of the way women were inclined to follow new fashion styles. In other works, however, she created positive images of the modern woman and expressed a keen interest in new freedoms for women.

SURREALISM Perhaps more important as an artistic movement was **Surrealism,** which sought a reality beyond the material, sensible world and found it in the world of the unconscious through the portrayal of fantasies, dreams, or nightmares. Employing logic to portray

Hannah Höch, _Cut with the Kitchen Knife Dada Through the Last Weimar Beer Belly Cultural Epoch of Germany._ Hannah Höch, a prominent figure in the postwar Dada movement, used photomontage to create images that reflected on women's issues. In _Cut with the Kitchen Knife_ (1919), she combined pictures of German political leaders with sports stars, Dada artists, and scenes from urban life. One major theme emerged: the confrontation between the anti-Dada world of German political leaders and the Dada world of revolutionary ideals. Höch associated women with Dada and the new world.

Salvador Dalí, *The Persistence of Memory.* Surrealism was another important artistic movement between the wars. Influenced by the theories of Freudian psychology, Surrealists sought to reveal the world of the unconscious, or the "greater reality" that they believed existed beyond the world of physical appearances. As is evident in this 1931 painting, Salvador Dalí sought to portray the world of dreams by painting recognizable objects in unrecognizable relationships.

the illogical, the Surrealists created disturbing and evocative images. The Spaniard Salvador Dalí (dah-LEE *or* DAH-lee) (1904–1989) became the high priest of Surrealism and in his mature phase became a master of representational Surrealism. In *The Persistence of Memory,* Dalí portrayed recognizable objects divorced from their normal context. By placing these objects in unrecognizable relationships, Dalí created a disturbing world in which the irrational had become tangible, forcing viewers to question the rational.

FUNCTIONALISM IN MODERN ARCHITECTURE The move to **functionalism** in modern architecture also became more widespread in the 1920s and 1930s. First conceived near the end of the nineteenth century, functionalism meant that buildings, like the products of machines, should be "functional" or useful, fulfilling the purpose for which they were constructed. Art and engineering were to be unified, and all unnecessary ornamentation was to be stripped away. Functionalism was based on the architects' belief that art had a social function and could help create a new civilization.

The United States was a leader in these pioneering architectural designs. Unprecedented urban growth and the absence of restrictive architectural traditions allowed for new building methods, especially in the relatively "new city" of Chicago. The Chicago School of the 1890s, led by Louis H. Sullivan (1856–1924), used reinforced concrete, steel frames, and electric elevators to build skyscrapers virtually free of external ornamentation. One of Sullivan's most successful pupils was Frank Lloyd Wright (1867–1959), who became known for innovative designs in domestic architecture. Wright's private houses, built chiefly for wealthy patrons, featured geometric structures with long lines, overhanging roofs, and severe planes of brick and stone. The interiors were open spaces that included

cathedral ceilings and built-in furniture and lighting fixtures. Wright pioneered the modern American house.

Especially important in the spread of functionalism was the Bauhaus (BOW-howss) School of art, architecture, and design, founded in 1919 at Weimar, Germany, by the Berlin architect Walter Gropius (VAHL-tuh GROH-peeuss) (1883–1969). The Bauhaus teaching staff consisted of architects, artists, and designers who worked together to blend the study of fine arts (painting and sculpture) with the applied arts (printing, weaving, and furniture

Walter Gropius, The Bauhaus. Walter Gropius was one of Europe's pioneers in modern architecture. When the Bauhaus moved to Dessau in 1925, Gropius designed a building for its activities. His straightforward use of steel, reinforced concrete, and rows of windows reflects the move to functionalism in modern architecture.

making). Gropius urged his followers to foster a new union of arts and crafts to create the buildings and objects of the future. Gropius's own buildings were often unornamented steel boxes with walls of windows, reflecting his belief that the "sensibility of the artist must be combined with the knowledge of the technician to create new forms in architecture and design."

A POPULAR AUDIENCE Important to the development of artistic expression between the wars was the search for a new popular audience. To attract a wider audience, artists and musicians began to involve themselves in the new mass culture. The German Kurt Weill (VYL) (1900–1950), for example, had been a struggling composer of classical music before he turned to jazz rhythms and other popular musical idioms for the music for *The Threepenny Opera*. Some artists even regarded art as a means to transform society and located their studios in poor, working-class neighborhoods. Theater proved especially attractive as postwar artists sought to make an impact on popular audiences. The German director Erwin Piscator (AYR-vin PIS-kuh-tor) began his directing career by offering plays to workers on picket lines. Piscator hoped to reach workers by experimental drama with political messages. Like many other artists, however, he became frustrated by his failure to achieve a mass audience.

The postwar acceptance of modern art forms was by no means universal. Many traditionalists denounced what they considered degeneracy and decadence in the arts. Nowhere was this more evident than in the totalitarian states of Nazi Germany and the Soviet Union.

ART IN TOTALITARIAN REGIMES In the 1920s, Weimar Germany was one of the chief European centers for modern arts and sciences. Hitler and the Nazis rejected modern art as "degenerate" or "Jewish" art. In an address at the premiere of the Great German Art Exhibition in the newly opened House of German Art in July 1937, Hitler proclaimed, "The people regarded this art [modern art] as the outcome of an impudent and unashamed arrogance or of a simply shocking lack of skill; . . . these achievements—which might have been produced by untalented children of from eight to ten years old—could never be valued as an expression of our own times or of the German future."[16] Hitler and the Nazis believed that they had laid the foundation for a new and genuine German art, which would glorify the strong, the healthy, and the heroic—all supposedly attributes of the Aryan race. The new German art was actually the old nineteenth-century genre art with its emphasis on realistic scenes of everyday life.

So, too, was the art produced by the school of "socialist realism" in the Soviet Union. After the bold experimentalism of the 1920s, the Stalinist era imposed a stifling uniformity on artistic creativity. Like German painting, Soviet painting was expected to focus on a nineteenth-century pictorial style aimed at realistic presentation. Both the new German art and socialist realism were intended to inculcate social values useful to the ruling regimes.

A NEW STYLE IN MUSIC At the beginning of the twentieth century, a revolution in music parallel to the revolution in art had begun with the work of Igor Stravinsky (see Chapter 24). But Stravinsky still wrote music in a definite key. The Viennese composer Arnold Schönberg (AR-nawlt SHURN-bayrk) (1874–1951) began to experiment with a radically new style by creating musical pieces in which tonality is completely abandoned, a system that he called atonal music. Since the use of traditional forms was virtually impossible in atonal music, Schönberg created a new system of composition—twelve-tone composition—which used a scale of twelve notes independent of any tonal key. Resistance to modern music was even greater than to modern painting, and atonal music did not begin to win favor until after World War II.

The Search for the Unconscious in Literature

The interest in the unconscious, heightened by the impact of World War I and evident in Surrealism, was also apparent in the new literary techniques that emerged in the 1920s. One of its most visible manifestations was the "stream-of-consciousness" technique in which the writer presented an interior monologue, or a report of the innermost thoughts of each character. One example of this genre was written by the Irish exile James Joyce (1882–1941). His *Ulysses,* published in 1922, told the story of one day in the life of ordinary people in Dublin by following the flow of their inner dialogue. Disconnected ramblings and veiled allusions pervade Joyce's work.

Another famous writer who used her own stream-of-consciousness technique was Virginia Woolf (1882–1942). Woolf belonged to a group of intellectuals and artists, known as the Bloomsbury Circle, who sought to create new artistic and literary forms. In her novels *Mrs. Dalloway* and *Jacob's Room,* Woolf used the inner monologues of her main characters to reveal their world of existence. Woolf came to believe that for a woman to be a writer, she would need to have her own income to free herself from the expected roles of wife and mother.

The German writer Hermann Hesse (HESS-uh) (1877–1962) dealt with the unconscious in a different fashion. His novels reflected the influence of both Carl Jung's psychological theories and Eastern religions and focused among other things on the spiritual loneliness of modern human beings in a mechanized urban society. *Demian* was a psychoanalytic study of incest, and *Steppenwolf* mirrored the psychological confusion of modern existence. Hesse's novels made a large impact on German youth in the 1920s (see the box on p. 846). He won the Nobel Prize for Literature in 1946.

The Unconscious in Psychology: Carl Jung

The growing concern with the unconscious also led to greater popular interest in psychology. The full impact of

Hesse and the Unconscious

The novels of Hermann Hesse made a strong impact on young people, first in Germany in the 1920s and then in the United States in the 1960s after they had been translated into English. Many of these young people shared Hesse's fascination with the unconscious and his dislike of modern industrial civilization. This excerpt from *Demian* spoke directly to many of them.

Hermann Hesse, *Demian*

The following spring I was to leave the preparatory school and enter a university. I was still undecided, however, as to where and what I was to study. I had grown a thin mustache, I was a full-grown man, and yet I was completely helpless and without a goal in life. Only one thing was certain: the voice within me, the dream image. I felt the duty to follow this voice blindly wherever it might lead me. But it was difficult and each day I rebelled against it anew. Perhaps I was mad, as I thought at moments; perhaps I was not like other men? But I was able to do the same things the others did;

with a little effort and industry I could read Plato, was able to solve problems in trigonometry or follow a chemical analysis. There was only one thing I could not do: wrest the dark secret goal from myself and keep it before me as others did who knew exactly what they wanted to be—professors, lawyers, doctors, artists, however long this would take them and whatever difficulties and advantages this decision would bear in its wake. This I could not do. Perhaps I would become something similar, but how was I to know? Perhaps I would have to continue my search for years on end and would not become anything, and would not reach a goal. Perhaps I would reach this goal but it would turn out to be an evil, dangerous, horrible one.

I wanted only to try to live in accord with the promptings which came from my true self. Why was that so very difficult?

Q How does Hesse's interest in the unconscious appear in this excerpt? Why was a dislike of mechanized society particularly intense after World War I?

Sigmund Freud's thought was not felt until after World War I. The 1920s witnessed a worldwide acceptance of his ideas. Freudian terms, such as *unconscious, repression, id, ego,* and *Oedipus complex,* entered the common vocabulary. Popularization of Freud's ideas led to the widespread misconception that an uninhibited sex life was necessary for a healthy mental life. Despite such misconceptions, psychoanalysis did develop into a major profession, especially in the United States. But Freud's ideas did not go unchallenged, even by his own pupils. One of the most prominent challenges came from Carl Jung (YOONG).

A disciple of Freud, Carl Jung (1856–1961) came to believe that Freud's theories were too narrow and reflected Freud's own personal biases. Jung's study of dreams—his own and those of others—led him to diverge sharply from Freud. Whereas for Freud the unconscious was the seat of repressed desires or appetites, for Jung it was an opening to deep spiritual needs and ever-greater vistas for humans.

Jung viewed the unconscious as twofold: a "personal unconscious" and, at a deeper level, a "collective unconscious." The collective unconscious was the repository of memories that all human beings share and consisted of archetypes, mental forms or images that appear in dreams. The archetypes are common to all people and have a special energy that creates myths, religions, and philosophies. To Jung, the archetypes proved that mind was only in part personal or individual because their origin was buried so far in the past that they seemed to have no human source.

Their function was to bring the original mind of humans into a new, higher state of consciousness.

The "Heroic Age of Physics"

The prewar revolution in physics initiated by Max Planck and Albert Einstein continued in the interwar period. In fact, Ernest Rutherford (1871–1937), one of the physicists responsible for demonstrating that the atom could be split, dubbed the 1920s the "heroic age of physics." By the early 1940s, seven subatomic particles had been distinguished, and a sufficient understanding of the atom had been achieved to lay the foundations for the development of a sophisticated new explosive device, the atomic bomb.

The new picture of the universe that was unfolding continued to undermine the old scientific certainties of classical physics. Classical physics had rested on the fundamental belief that all phenomena could be predicted if they could be completely understood; thus, the weather could be accurately predicted if we knew everything about the wind, sun, and water. In 1927, the German physicist Werner Heisenberg (VAYR-nur HY-zun-bayrk) (1901–1976) upset this belief when he posited the **uncertainty principle.** In essence, Heisenberg argued that no one could determine the path of an electron because the very act of observing the electron with light affected the electron's location. The uncertainty principle was more than an explanation for the path of an electron, however; it was a new worldview. Heisenberg shattered confidence in predictability and dared to propose that uncertainty was at the root of all physical laws.

CHAPTER SUMMARY

The devastation wrought by World War I destroyed the liberal optimism of the prewar era. Yet many in the 1920s still hoped that the progress of Western civilization, so seemingly evident before 1914, could somehow be restored. These hopes proved largely unfounded. France, feeling vulnerable to another invasion, sought to weaken Germany by occupying the Ruhr when Germany failed to pay reparations but gained little from the occupation. European recovery, largely the result of American loans and investments, ended when the Great Depression began at the end of the 1920s.

The democratic states—Great Britain, France, the Scandinavian countries, and the United States—spent much of the 1930s trying to recover from the Great Depression. Totalitarian governments, which required the active commitment of their citizens, came to power in Italy, Germany, and the Soviet Union. Italian Fascism resulted from Italy's losses in World War I, economic problems, and incompetent politicians. Mussolini organized the Fascist movement in 1919 and by threatening to march on Rome was chosen as prime minister in 1922. Rival parties were outlawed, and Mussolini used repression and propaganda to create a Fascist state. Mussolini failed, however to attain the degree of totalitarian control achieved in Hitler's Germany. Heading the Nazi Party, Adolf Hitler became chancellor in 1933 and within six months had seized dictatorial control. Hitler rearmed Germany, abolished all other political parties and the labor unions, and created a police state under the direction of the SS. Jews were excluded from citizenship and beginning in 1938 with *Kristallnacht* were often persecuted and encouraged to leave Germany.

After assuming leadership of the Soviet Union, Joseph Stalin created his own version of a totalitarian state. Five-year plans were instituted to turn the Soviet Union into an industrial society, while opponents were sent to Siberia, sentenced to labor camps, or liquidated. With the exception of Czechoslovakia, authoritarian governments appeared in eastern Europe as well as in Portugal and Spain. In the Spanish Civil War, the fascist states aided Francisco Franco, and the Soviet Union backed the Popular Front.

The new authoritarian governments not only restricted individual freedoms and the rule of law but, especially in Germany and the Soviet Union, sought even greater control over the lives of their subjects in order to manipulate and guide them to achieve the goals of their regimes. For many people, despite the loss of personal freedom, these mass movements offered some sense of security in a world that seemed fraught with uncertainty, an uncertainty that was also evident in popular culture, the arts, literature, and even physics. But the seeming security of these mass movements gave rise to even great uncertainty as Europeans, after a brief twenty-year interlude of peace, again plunged into war.

CHAPTER TIMELINE

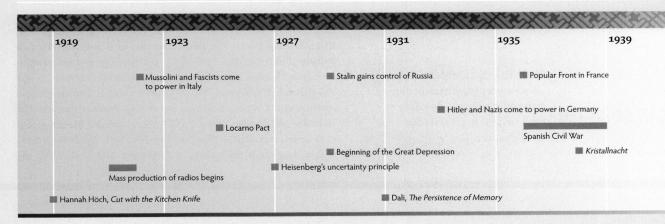

1919	1923	1927	1931	1935	1939
	Mussolini and Fascists come to power in Italy		Stalin gains control of Russia		Popular Front in France
				Hitler and Nazis come to power in Germany	
	Locarno Pact			Spanish Civil War	Kristallnacht
			Beginning of the Great Depression		
		Heisenberg's uncertainty principle			
Mass production of radios begins					
Hannah Höch, Cut with the Kitchen Knife			Dali, The Persistence of Memory		

Upon Reflection

Q What were the causes of the Great Depression, and how did European states respond to it?

Q What were Hitler's ideas, and how did he implement them once he and the Nazis had established the Nazi state in Germany?

Q How do the cultural and intellectual trends of the 1920s and 1930s reflect a crisis of confidence in Western civilization?

Key Terms

fascism (p. 816)
civil disobedience (p. 820)
totalitarian state (p. 822)
propaganda (p. 822)
squadristi (p. 823)
Lebensraum (p. 827)
Führerprinzip (p. 828)
New Economic Policy (p. 833)
authoritarian state (p. 836)
Dadaism (p. 842)
Surrealism (p. 843)
functionalism (p. 844)
uncertainty principle (p. 846)

Suggestions for Further Reading

GENERAL WORKS For a general introduction to the interwar period, see **M. Kitchen, *Europe Between the Wars: A Political History,*** 2nd ed. (London, 2006). On Europe in the 1930s, see **P. Brendon, *The Dark Valley*** (New York, 2002). On the Great Depression, see **C. P. Kindleberger, *The World in Depression, 1929–39,*** rev. ed. (Berkeley, Calif., 1986).

THE DEMOCRATIC STATES On Great Britain, see **R. Overy, *The Twilight Years: The Paradox of Britain Between the Wars*** (New York, 2009). France is covered in **A. P. Adamthwaite, *Grandeur and Misery: France's Bid for Power in Europe, 1914–1940*** (London, 1995).

FASCISM AND FASCIST ITALY For general studies of fascist movements, see **S. Payne, *A History of Fascism*** (Madison, Wis., 1996),

and **R. O. Paxton, *The Anatomy of Fascism*** (New York, 2004). The best biographies of Mussolini are **D. Mack Smith, *Mussolini*** (New York, 1982), and **R. J. B. Bosworth, *Mussolini*** (London, 2002). On Fascist Italy, see **R. J. B. Bosworth, *Mussolini's Italy: Life Under the Fascist Dictatorship*** (New York, 2006), and **V. de Grazia, *How Fascism Ruled Women: Italy, 1922–1945*** (Berkeley, Calif., 1993).

NAZI GERMANY On the Weimar Republic, see **P. Bookbinder, *Weimar Germany*** (New York, 1996). Two brief but sound surveys of Nazi Germany are **J. J. Spielvogel** and **D. Redles, *Hitler and Nazi Germany: A History,*** 6th ed. (Upper Saddle River, N.J., 2010), and **W. Benz, *A Concise History of the Third Reich,*** trans. **T. Dunlap** (Berkeley, Calif., 2006). A more detailed examination can be found in the three-volume history of Nazi Germany by **R. J. Evans: *The Coming of the Third Reich*** (New York, 2004), ***The Third Reich in Power: 1933–1939*** (New York, 2005), and ***The Third Reich at War*** (New York, 2009). The best biography of Hitler is **I. Kershaw, *Hitler, 1889–1936: Hubris*** (New York, 1999), and ***Hitler: Nemesis*** (New York, 2000). On women, see **C. Koonz, *Mothers in the Fatherland: Women, the Family, and Nazi Politics*** (New York, 1987). The Hitler Youth is examined in **M. Kater, *The Hitler Youth*** (Cambridge, Mass., 2004).

AUTHORITARIAN STATES Starting points for the study of eastern Europe are **J. Rothschild, *East Central Europe Between the Two World Wars,*** rev. ed. (New York, 1993), and **J. R. Lampe, *Balkans into Southeastern Europe: A Century of War and Transition*** (London, 2006). On the Spanish Civil War, see **F. J. R. Salvado, *The Spanish Civil War*** (New York, 2005).

THE STALINIST ERA The collectivization of agriculture in the Soviet Union is examined in **S. Fitzpatrick, *Stalin's Peasants: Resistance and Survival in the Russian Village After Collectivization*** (New York, 1995); industrialization is covered in **H. Kuromiya, *Stalin's Industrial Revolution: Politics and Workers, 1928–1932*** (New York, 1988). On Stalin, see **R. Service, *Stalin: A Biography*** (Cambridge, Mass., 2006). On everyday life in the Stalinist era, see **S. Fitzpatrick, *Everyday Stalinism*** (Oxford, 1999).

SOCIETY AND CULTURE The use of cinema for propaganda purposes is well examined in **D. Welch, *Propaganda and the German Cinema*** (New York, 1985). Gender issues are discussed in **S. K. Kent, *Making Peace: The Reconstruction of Gender in Interwar Britain*** (Princeton, N.J., 1993). On tourism, see **S. Baronowski, *Strength Through Joy: Consumerism and Mass Tourism in the Third Reich*** (Cambridge, 2001). On the cultural and intellectual environment of Weimar Germany, see **P. Gay, *Weimar Culture: The Outsider as Insider*** (New York, 1968), and **R. Metzger** and **C. Brandstetter, *Berlin: The Twenties*** (New York, 2007). For a study of Carl Jung, see **D. Bair, *Jung: A Biography*** (New York, 2003).

Visit the CourseMate website at www.cengagebrain.com for additional study tools and review materials for this chapter.

1. What development in Germany does this picture demonstrate?

© Three Lions/Getty Images

(A) Germany had overproduced currency, which allowed for an increase in capital wealth.

(B) Hyperinflation caused Germany's currency to be virtually valueless.

(C) Germany enjoyed great wealth after World War I, thanks to reparations paid by Austria.

(D) Germany experienced a great economic recovery under Hitler's leadership, which created new wealth throughout the nation.

(E) Germany's elite became wealthy from war profiteering, and money was like a toy to them.

2. The occupation of the Ruhr by France accomplished all of the following EXCEPT

(A) it showed the aggressiveness of France and its desire to penalize Germany.

(B) it allowed France to collect money and resources by controlling the mines and factories in the region.

(C) it won greater support for France from countries like the United States and Great Britain.

(D) it sparked further inflation within both France and Germany.

(E) it contributed to greater tensions between France and Germany.

3. The Locarno Treaty

(A) fostered new agreements within Europe; however, it failed to be backed by a strong military.

(B) ended German reparations and reestablished relations between France and Germany.

(C) brought about a lasting treaty to ban war on the Continent.

(D) established a peace between Soviet Russia and the rest of Europe.

(E) attempted to rectify the problems that led to World War I by creating new, less divisive national boundaries.

4. The first of Joseph Stalin's five-year plans was successful in that

(A) it kept in place elements of Lenin's New Economic Policy.

(B) it pushed for collectivization while still allowing for some privatization of the Soviet economy.

(C) it placed a greater emphasis on industrial output than on agrarian output.

(D) it brought about the first planned economy headed by the Communist Party.

(E) its systematic approach to equality met with little resistance from the peasant population.

5. "The acts of life have no beginning or end. Everything happens in a completely idiotic way." This quotation best represents which artistic movement?

(A) Surrealism

(B) Dadaism

(C) Expressionism

(D) Realism

(E) Cubism

6. The Kellogg-Briand pact

(A) was neither approved by nor agreed to by the United States.

(B) excluded Germany from the League of Nations.

(C) forged an alliance between the United States and France.

(D) asked nations to reduce their total tonnage of military weaponry.

(E) outlawed the use of war as an instrument of national policy.

7. Following World War I, the state of mind of most Western Europeans could be best described as

(A) positive, in that many Europeans saw the crisis of the war as nothing more than an expression of their subconscious that could be healed through therapy.

(B) a feeling of uncertainly and anxiety, as reflected in the new literary and artistic movements of the age.

(C) a rededication to religious and moral feeling.

(D) overwhelming greed and a desire to become wealthy entrepreneurs.

(E) a greater appreciation for diversity over universal conformity.

8. The Popular Front in Spain was more radical than the Popular Front in France for all of the following reasons EXCEPT

(A) it turned to the Soviet Union for military aid.

(B) it confiscated property from wealthy landowners.

(C) it promoted revolutionary movements and encouraged workers to strike.

(D) it publicly denounced the Catholic Church.

(E) both were led by passive leaders.

9. Which of the following best describes Europe in the 1920s?

(A) Like the United States, Europe experienced a new cultural and economic boom after the war that allowed for new growth in the private sector.

(B) Western Europe returned to its pre-war prosperity, while eastern Europe was plagued with inflation and high unemployment.

(C) Great Britain withdrew from Continental affairs, while the rest of Europe struggled to regain economic stability in the wake of the war's physical destruction.

(D) Europeans sought wider markets in the colonies for their finished goods.

(E) Europeans in their despair turned to the Catholic Church for solace.

10. After the end of the Weimar Republic, Adolf Hitler ruled Germany

(A) through a coalition government that allied the military leadership with leaders of various Nazi parties.

(B) as a totalitarian ruler who toppled Hindenburg's government through force and illegal means.

(C) as a dictator who led the state into a war-time economy that provided employment and economic stability for many.

(D) using a program similar to that of Italy, as Hitler and Mussolini often conferred on economic policies.

(E) differently than did Stalin in the Soviet Union, because Hitler sought to maintain a peaceful co-existence with those in the Reichstag who disagreed with him.

11. Which of the following best describes the economic policies of Great Britain and France?

(A) The two countries worked together to forge a new economic union following World War I.

(B) Great Britain followed a classical economic policy of shrinking the government, while France pursued a policy of deficit spending as espoused by Keynes.

(C) Their economies faltered, contributing to the rise in western Europe of strong totalitarian governments that promised economic relief.

(D) Both governments failed to create any significant economic recovery by the early 1930s.

(E) Great Britain insisted on the need to reduce taxes and expand social benefits, while France cut all benefits to those not working directly for the government.

12. Which of the following best describes the experience of women under totalitarian governments in Europe?

(A) They saw their rights expanded as dictators sought their help in improving the nation.

(B) They lost ground gained during World War I, as dictators instituted policies to limit their personal and political freedoms.

(C) Their responsibilities as mothers and wives became subservient to that of serving the state.

(D) They won the legal protection of equal pay for equal work.

(E) They were encouraged to have fewer children in order to help end the economic depression.

13. By the mid-1930s, all of the following states were under totalitarian control EXCEPT

(A) Italy.

(B) Germany.

(C) Yugoslavia.

(D) Spain.

(E) Czechoslovakia.

14. Which of the following best describes the cultural effect of the invention of the radio and silent movies?

(A) Both totalitarian and democratic states used these devices to entertain and influence their populations.

(B) Mass culture was no longer influenced by high art or literature.

(C) Political rallies and labor strikes occurred less frequently as people were pacified by the entertainment.

(D) Public education levels declined as fewer people were reading or writing.

(E) The horrors of modern society could no longer be hidden, so rulers were held to a higher public standard.

15. Which of the following best describes the experience of colonized countries after World War I?

(A) Most colonial empires came to an end in the 1920s as colonies were granted their independence.

(B) By participating in the war, colonized people came to feel greater patriotism toward their parent country and lost the desire to break away from the empire.

(C) Increasing worker activism and feelings of nationalism sparked unrest in many colonies.

(D) African countries lost interest in breaking away from Europe as they enjoyed the benefits they received from their mother countries.

(E) Gandhi became a leading activist in India, arguing that it should become an equal member of the British Empire.

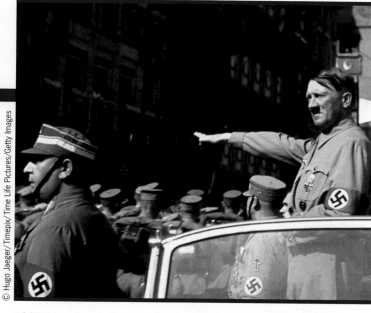

Adolf Hitler salutes soldiers marching in Nuremberg during the party rally in 1938.

CHAPTER 27

The Deepening of the European Crisis: World War II

CHAPTER OUTLINE AND FOCUS QUESTIONS

Prelude to War (1933–1939)

Q What were Hitler's foreign policy goals, and what steps did he take to achieve them between 1933 and 1939? How did Japan's policies lead to war in Asia?

The Course of World War II

Q What were the main events of World War II in Europe and in Asia, and why were the Allies ultimately victorious?

The New Order

Q How was the Nazi empire organized? What was the Holocaust, and what role did it play in Nazi policy?

The Home Front

Q What were conditions like on the home front for Japan and the major Western nations involved in World War II?

Aftermath of the War

Q What were the costs of World War II? How did the Allies' visions of postwar Europe differ, and how did these differences contribute to the emergence of the Cold War?

CRITICAL THINKING

Q What was the relationship between World War I and World War II, and how did the ways in which the wars were fought differ?

ON FEBRUARY 3, 1933, only four days after he had been appointed chancellor of Germany, Adolf Hitler met secretly with Germany's leading generals. He revealed to them his desire to remove the "cancer of democracy," create a new authoritarian leadership, and forge a new domestic unity. All Germans would need to realize that "only a struggle can save us and that everything else must be subordinated to this idea." Youth especially must be trained and their wills strengthened "to fight with all means." Since Germany's living space was too small for its people, Hitler said, Germany must rearm and prepare for "the conquest of new living space in the east and its ruthless Germanization." Even before he had consolidated his power, Hitler had a clear vision of his goals, and their implementation meant another European war. World War II was clearly Hitler's war. Although other countries may have helped make the war possible by not resisting Hitler's Germany earlier, it was Nazi Germany's actions that made World War II inevitable.

World War II was more than just Hitler's war, however. This chapter will focus on the European theater of war, but both European and American armies were also involved in fighting around the world. World War II consisted of two conflicts: one provoked by the ambitions of Germany in Europe, the other by the ambitions of Japan in Asia. By 1941, with the involvement of the United States in both wars, the two had merged into one global conflict.

Although World War I has been described as a total war, World War II was even more so and was fought on a scale unknown in history. Almost everyone in the warring countries was involved in one way or another: as soldiers; as workers in wartime industries; as ordinary citizens subject to invading armies, military occupation, or bombing raids; as refugees; or as victims of mass extermination. The world had never witnessed such widespread willful death and destruction.

Prelude to War (1933–1939)

Q FOCUS QUESTIONS: What were Hitler's foreign policy goals, and what steps did he take to achieve them between 1933 and 1939? How did Japan's policies lead to war in Asia?

Only twenty years after the "war to end all war," Europe plunged back into the nightmare of total war. The efforts at collective security in the 1920s—the League of Nations, the attempts at disarmament, the pacts and treaties—all proved meaningless in light of the growth of Nazi Germany and its deliberate scrapping of the postwar settlement in the 1930s. Still weary from the last war, France and Britain refused to accept the possibility of another war. The Soviet Union, treated as an outcast by the Western powers, had turned in on itself, and the United States had withdrawn into its traditional isolationism. The small successor states to Austria-Hungary were too weak to oppose Germany. Thus, the power vacuum in the heart of Europe encouraged a revived and militarized Germany to acquire the living space that Hitler claimed Germany needed for its rightful place in the world.

The Role of Hitler

World War II in Europe began in the mind of Adolf Hitler, who believed that only the Aryans were capable of building a great civilization. But to Hitler, the Germans, in his view the leading group of Aryans, were threatened from the east by a large mass of inferior peoples, the Slavs, who had learned to use German weapons and technology. Germany needed more land to support a larger population and be a great power. Hitler was a firm believer in the doctrine of *Lebensraum* (living space), espoused by Karl Haushofer (HOWSS-hoh-fuh), a professor of geography at the University of Munich. The doctrine of *Lebensraum* maintained that a nation's power depended on the amount and kind of land it occupied. Already in the 1920s, in the second volume of *Mein Kampf,* Hitler had indicated where a National Socialist regime would find this land: "And so we National Socialists . . . take up where we broke off six hundred years ago. We stop the endless German movement to the south and west, and turn our gaze toward the land in the east. . . . If we speak of soil in Europe today, we can primarily have in mind only Russia and her vassal border states."[1]

In Hitler's view, the Russian Revolution had created the conditions for Germany's acquisition of land to its east.

Imperial Russia had been strong only because of its German leadership. The seizure of power by the Bolsheviks (who, in Hitler's mind, were Jewish) had left Russia weak and vulnerable. Once it had been conquered, the land of Russia could be resettled by German peasants, and the Slavic population could be used as slave labor to build the Aryan racial state that would dominate Europe for the next thousand years. Hitler's conclusion was clear: Germany must prepare for its inevitable war with the Soviet Union. Hitler's ideas were by no means secret. He had spelled them out in *Mein Kampf,* a book readily available to anyone who wished to read it (see the box on p. 851).

Hitler and the Nazis were neither the first Europeans nor the first Germans to undertake European conquest and world power. A number of elite circles in Germany before World War I had argued that Germany needed to annex lands to its south, east, and west if it wished to compete with the large states and remain a great power. The defeat in World War I destroyed this dream of world power, but the traditional conservative elites in the German military and the Foreign Office supported Hitler's foreign policy until 1937, largely because it accorded with their own desires for German expansion. But, as they realized too late, Nazi policy went far beyond previous German goals. Hitler's desire to create an Aryan racial empire led to slave labor and even mass extermination on a scale that would have been incomprehensible to previous generations of Germans.

Although Hitler had defined his goals, he had no prearranged timetable for achieving them. During his rise to power, he had demonstrated the ability to be both ideologue and opportunist. After 1933, a combination of military and diplomatic situations, organizational chaos in the administration of Germany, and economic pressures, especially after 1936, caused Hitler periodically to take steps that seemed to contradict the foreign policy goals of *Mein Kampf.* But he always returned to his basic ideological plans for racial supremacy and empire. He was certain of one thing: only he had the ability to accomplish these goals, and his fears for his health pushed him to fulfill his mission as quickly as possible. His impatience would become a major cause of his own undoing.

The "Diplomatic Revolution" (1933–1936)

Between 1933 and 1936, Hitler and Nazi Germany achieved a "diplomatic revolution" in Europe. When Hitler became chancellor of Germany on January 30, 1933, Germany's position in Europe seemed weak. The Versailles treaty had created a demilitarized zone on Germany's western border that would allow the French to move into the heavily industrialized parts of Germany in the event of war. To Germany's east, the smaller states, such as Poland and Czechoslovakia, had defensive treaties with France. The Versailles treaty had also limited Germany's army to 100,000 troops with no air and limited naval forces.

Hitler's Foreign Policy Goals

Adolf Hitler was a firm believer in the geopolitical doctrine of *Lebensraum,* which advocated that nations must find sufficient living space to be strong. This idea was evident in *Mein Kampf,* but it was explained in even more detail in a treatise that Hitler wrote in 1928. It was not published in his lifetime.

Hitler's *Secret Book,* 1928

I have already dealt with Germany's various foreign policy possibilities in this book. Nevertheless I shall once more briefly present the possible foreign policy goals so that they may yield a basis for the critical examination of the relations of these individual foreign policy aims to those of other European states.

1. Germany can renounce setting a foreign policy goal altogether. This means that in reality she can decide for anything and need be committed to nothing at all.... [Hitler rejects this alternative.]
2. Germany desires to effect the sustenance of the German people by peaceful economic means, as up to now. Accordingly even in the future she will participate most decisively in world industry, export and trade.... From a folkish standpoint setting this foreign policy aim is calamitous, and it is madness from the point of view of power politics.
3. Germany establishes the restoration of the borders of the year 1914 as her foreign policy aim. This goal is insufficient from a national standpoint,

unsatisfactory from a military point of view, impossible from a folkish standpoint with its eye on the future, and mad from the viewpoint of its consequences....
4. Germany decides to go over to a clear, far-seeing territorial policy. Thereby she abandons all attempts at world-industry and world-trade and instead concentrates all her strength in order, through the allotment of sufficient living space for the next hundred years to our people, also to prescribe a path of life. Since this territory can be only in the East, the obligation to be a naval power also recedes into the background. Germany tries anew to champion her interests through the formation of a decisive power on land.

This aim is equally in keeping with the highest national as well as folkish requirements. It likewise presupposes great military power means for its execution, but does not necessarily bring Germany into conflict with all European great powers. As surely as France here will remain Germany's enemy, just as little does the nature of such a political aim contain a reason for England, and especially for Italy, to maintain the enmity of the World War. 🐍

Q According to Hitler, what were Germany's possible foreign policy goals? Which one did Hitler prefer? Why? What were the consequences of his decisions in this realm?

The Germans were not without advantages, however. Germany was the most populous European state after the Soviet Union and still possessed a great industrial capacity. Hitler was also well aware that Great Britain and France, dismayed by the costs and losses of World War I, wanted to avoid another war. Hitler knew that France posed a threat to an unarmed Germany, but he believed that if he could keep the French from acting against Germany in his first years, he could remove the restrictions imposed on Germany by Versailles and restore its strength.

Hitler's ability to rearm Germany and fulfill his expansionist policies depended initially on whether he could convince others that his intentions were peaceful. Posing as a man of peace in his public speeches, Hitler emphasized that Germany wished only to revise the unfair provisions of Versailles by peaceful means and achieve Germany's rightful place among the European states. During his first two years in office, Hitler pursued a prudent foreign policy without unnecessary risks. His dramatic action in October 1933, when he withdrew Germany from the Geneva Disarmament Conference and the League of Nations, was

done primarily for domestic political reasons, to give the Germans the feeling that their country was no longer dominated by other European states.

GERMAN REARMAMENT By the beginning of 1935, Hitler had become convinced that Germany could break some of the provisions of the Treaty of Versailles without serious British and French opposition. Hitler had come to believe, based on their responses to his early actions, that both states wanted to maintain the international status quo, but without using force. Consequently, he decided to announce publicly what had been going on secretly for sometime—Germany's military rearmament. On March 9, 1935, Hitler announced the creation of a new air force and, one week later, the introduction of a military draft that would expand Germany's army from 100,000 to 550,000 troops.

Hitler's unilateral repudiation of the disarmament clauses of the Versailles treaty brought a swift reaction as France, Great Britain, and Italy condemned Germany's action and warned against future aggressive steps. But nothing concrete was done. Even worse, Britain subsequently moved toward open acceptance of Germany's right to rearm when it agreed to the Anglo-German Naval Pact on June 18, 1935. This treaty allowed Germany to build a navy that would be 35 percent of the size of the British navy, with equality in submarines. The British were starting a policy of **appeasement,** based on the belief that if European states satisfied the reasonable demands of dissatisfied powers, the latter would be content, and stability and peace would be achieved in Europe. British appeasement was grounded in large part on Britain's desire to avoid another war, but it was also fostered by British statesmen who believed that Nazi Germany offered a powerful bulwark against Soviet communism.

OCCUPATION OF THE RHINELAND   On March 7, 1936, buoyed by his conviction that the Western democracies had no intention of using force to maintain all aspects of the Treaty of Versailles, Hitler sent German troops into the demilitarized Rhineland. According to the Versailles treaty, the French had the right to use force against any violation of the demilitarized Rhineland. But France would not act without British support, and the British viewed the occupation of German territory by German troops as another reasonable action by a dissatisfied power. The London *Times* noted that the Germans were only "going into their own back garden." The French and British response only reinforced Hitler's growing conviction that they were weak nations unwilling to use force to defend the old order. At the same time, since the German generals had opposed his plan, Hitler became even more convinced of his own superior abilities. Many Germans expressed fresh enthusiasm for a leader who was restoring German honor.

NEW ALLIANCES   Meanwhile, Hitler gained new allies. In October 1935, Benito Mussolini had committed Fascist Italy to imperial expansion by invading Ethiopia. Angered by French and British opposition to his invasion, Mussolini welcomed Hitler's support and began to draw closer to the German dictator he had once called a buffoon. The joint intervention of Germany and Italy on behalf of General Francisco Franco in the Spanish Civil War in 1936 also drew the two nations closer together. In October 1936, Mussolini and Hitler concluded an agreement that recognized their common political and economic interests, and one month later, Mussolini referred publicly to the new Rome-Berlin Axis. Also in November 1936, Germany and Japan (the rising military power in the East) concluded the Anti-Comintern Pact and agreed to maintain a common front against communism.

By the end of 1936, Hitler and Nazi Germany had achieved a "diplomatic revolution" in Europe. The Treaty of Versailles had been virtually scrapped, and Germany was once more a "world power," as Hitler proclaimed. Hitler had demonstrated a great deal of diplomatic skill in taking advantage of Europeans' burning desire for peace. He had used the tactic of peaceful revision as skillfully as he had used the tactic of legality in his pursuit of power in

Germany. By the end of 1936, Nazi power had increased enough that Hitler could initiate an even more daring foreign policy. As Hitler perceived, if the Western states were so afraid of war that they resisted its use when they were strong and Germany was weak, then they would be even more reluctant to do so now that Germany was strong. Although many Europeans still wanted to believe that Hitler desired peace, his moves had actually made war more possible.

The Path to War in Europe (1937–1939)

On November 5, 1937, at a secret conference with his military leaders in Berlin, Adolf Hitler revealed his future aims. Germany's ultimate goal, he assured his audience, must be the conquest of living space in the east. Although this might mean war with France and Great Britain, Germany had no alternative if the basic needs of the German people were to be met. First, however, Germany must deal with Austria and Czechoslovakia and secure its eastern and southern flanks.

ONGOING REARMAMENT   In the meantime, Hitler had continued Germany's rearmament at an ever-quickening pace. Expenditures on rearmament rose dramatically: in 1933, 1 billion Reichsmarks; in 1935, 5 billion; in 1937, 9.5 billion; and in 1939, 30 billion. Important to rearmament was the planning for a new type of warfare known as **Blitzkrieg** (BLITZ-kreeg), or "lightning war." Hitler and some of his military commanders wanted to avoid the trench warfare of World War I and conceived a lightning warfare that depended on mechanized columns and massive air power to cut quickly across battle lines and encircle and annihilate entire armies. Blitzkrieg meant the quick defeat of an enemy and also determined much of Hitler's rearmament program: the construction of a large air force—the Luftwaffe (LOOFT-vah-uh)—and immense numbers of tanks and armored trucks to carry infantry. The tanks, mechanized infantry, and mobile artillery formed the new strike forces called panzer divisions that, with air force support, would lead the Blitzkrieg attack (each **panzer division** consisted of about three hundred tanks with accompanying forces and supplies). At the same time, the number of men in the German armed services rose from 550,000 in 1935 to 4.5 million in 1939. Naval rearmament also proceeded after the Anglo-German Naval Pact of 1935.

UNION WITH AUSTRIA   By the end of 1937, Hitler was convinced that neither the French nor the British would provide much opposition to his plans. Neville Chamberlain (1869–1940), who had become prime minister of Britain in May 1937, was a strong advocate of appeasement and believed that the survival of the British Empire depended on an accommodation with Germany. Chamberlain had made it known to Hitler in November 1937 that he would not oppose changes in central Europe, provided that they were executed peacefully.

Hitler Arrives in Vienna. By threatening to invade Austria, Hitler forced the Austrian government to capitulate to his wishes. Austria was annexed to Germany. Shown here is the triumphal arrival of Hitler in Vienna on March 13, 1938. Sitting in the car beside Hitler is Arthur Seyss-Inquart, Hitler's new handpicked governor of Austria.

Hitler decided to move first on Austria. By threatening Austria with invasion, Hitler coerced the Austrian chancellor, Kurt von Schuschnigg (SHOOSH-nik) (1897–1977), into putting an Austrian Nazi in charge of the government. When German troops marched unopposed into Austria on March 12, 1938, they did so on the "legal basis" of the new Austrian chancellor's request for German troops to assist in establishing law and order. One day later, on March 13, after his triumphal return to his native land, Hitler formally annexed Austria to Germany. Great Britain's ready acknowledgment of Hitler's action and France's inability to respond due to a political crisis only increased the German dictator's contempt for Western weakness.

The annexation of Austria improved Germany's strategic position in central Europe and put Germany in position for Hitler's next objective, the destruction of Czechoslovakia (see Map 27.1). On May 30, 1938, Hitler had already told his generals that it was his "unalterable decision to smash Czechoslovakia by military action in the near future."[2] This goal might have seemed unrealistic since democratic Czechoslovakia was quite prepared to defend itself and was well supported by pacts with France and Soviet Russia. Nevertheless, Hitler believed that France and Britain would not use force to defend Czechoslovakia.

CZECHOSLOVAKIA In the meantime, Hitler had stepped up his demands on the Czechs. Initially, the Germans had asked for autonomy for the Sudetenland (soo-DAY-tun-land), the mountainous northwestern border area of Czechoslovakia that was home to 3 million ethnic Germans. As Hitler knew, the Sudetenland also contained Czechoslovakia's most important frontier defenses and considerable industrial resources as well. But on

September 15, 1938, Hitler demanded the cession of the Sudetenland to Germany and expressed his willingness to risk "world war" to achieve his objective. By that time, Hitler was convinced that France and Britain would not use force to defend Czechoslovakia. On paper, the Czech republic seemed well protected by a pact with France. Yet the French made it clear that they would act only if the British supported them. The British refused to do so, and on September 29, at the hastily arranged Munich Conference, the British, French, Germans, and Italians (neither the Czechs nor the Russians were invited) reached an agreement that essentially met all of Hitler's demands. German troops were allowed to occupy the Sudetenland as the Czechs, abandoned by their Western allies, stood by helplessly. The Munich Conference was the high point of Western appeasement of Hitler. When Chamberlain returned to England from Munich, he boasted that the Munich agreement meant "peace for our time." Hitler had promised Chamberlain that he had made his last demand; all other European problems could be settled by negotiation. Like many German politicians, Chamberlain had believed Hitler's assurances (see the box on p. 855).

In fact, Munich confirmed Hitler's perception that the Western democracies were weak and would not fight. Increasingly, Hitler was convinced of his own infallibility, and he had by no means been satisfied at Munich. Already at the end of October 1938, Hitler told his generals to prepare for the final liquidation of the Czechoslovakian state. Using the internal disorder that he had deliberately fostered as a pretext, Hitler occupied the Czech lands (Bohemia and Moravia) while the Slovaks, with Hitler's encouragement, declared their independence of the Czechs and became a puppet state (Slovakia) of Nazi

MAP 27.1 **Changes in Central Europe, 1936–1939.** Hitler's main objectives in the late 1930s were the reoccupation of the Rhineland, incorporation into a greater Germany of lands that contained German people (Austria and the Sudetenland), and the acquisition of *Lebensraum* (living space) in eastern Europe for the expansion of the German people.

Q *What aspects of Czechoslovakia's location would have made it difficult for France and Britain to come directly to its aid in 1938?*

View an animated version of this map or related maps on the CourseMate website.

Germany. On the evening of March 15, 1939, Hitler triumphantly declared in Prague that he would be known as the greatest German of them all.

POLAND At last, the Western states reacted vigorously to Hitler's threat. After all, the Czechs were not Germans crying for reunion with Germany. Hitler's naked aggression made clear that his promises were utterly worthless.

When Hitler began to demand the return to Germany of Danzig, which had been made a free city by the Treaty of Versailles to serve as a seaport for Poland, Britain recognized the danger and offered to protect Poland in the event of war. At the same time, both France and Britain, realizing that only the Soviet Union was powerful enough to help contain Nazi aggression, began political and military negotiations with Joseph Stalin and the Soviets.

Opposing >VIEWPOINTS

The Munich Conference: Two Views

At the Munich Conference, the leaders of France and Great Britain capitulated to Hitler's demands on Czechoslovakia. Although the British prime minister, Neville Chamberlain, defended his actions at Munich as necessary for peace, another British statesman, Winston Churchill, characterized the settlement at Munich as "a disaster of the first magnitude."

—————————

Winston Churchill, Speech to the House of Commons, October 5, 1938

I will begin by saying what everybody would like to ignore or forget but which must nevertheless be stated, namely, that we have sustained a total and unmitigated defeat, and that France has suffered even more than we have.... The utmost my right honorable Friend the Prime Minister ... has been able to gain for Czechoslovakia and in the matters which were in dispute has been that the German dictator, instead of snatching his victuals from the table, has been content to have them served to him course by course.... And I will say this, that I believe the Czechs, left to themselves and told they were going to get no help from the Western Powers, would have been able to make better terms than they have got....

We are in the presence of a disaster of the first magnitude which has befallen Great Britain and France. Do not let us blind ourselves to that....

And do not suppose that this is the end. This is only the beginning of the reckoning. This is only the first sip, the first foretaste of a bitter cup which will be proffered to us year by year unless by a supreme recovery of moral health and martial vigor, we arise again and take our stand for freedom as in the olden time.

Neville Chamberlain, Speech to the House of Commons, October 6, 1938

That is my answer to those who say that we should have told Germany weeks ago that, if her army crossed the border of Czechoslovakia, we should be at war with her. We had no treaty obligations and no legal obligations to Czechoslovakia.... When we were convinced, as we became convinced, that nothing any longer would keep the Sudetenland within the Czechoslovakian State, we urged the Czech Government as strongly as we could to agree to the cession of territory, and to agree promptly.... It was a hard decision for anyone who loved his country to take, but to accuse us of having by that advice betrayed the Czechoslovakian State is simply preposterous. What we did was to save her from annihilation and give her a chance of new life as a new State, which involves the loss of territory and fortifications, but may perhaps enable her to enjoy in the future and develop a national existence under a neutrality and security comparable to that which we see in Switzerland today. Therefore, I think the Government deserve the approval of this House for their conduct of affairs in this recent crisis which has saved Czechoslovakia from destruction and Europe from Armageddon.

Q. What were the opposing views of Churchill and Chamberlain on the Munich Conference? Why did they disagree so much? With whom do you agree? Why?

The West's distrust of Soviet communism, however, made an alliance unlikely.

Meanwhile, Hitler pressed on in the belief that the West would not really fight over Poland. He ordered his generals to prepare for the invasion of Poland on September 1, 1939. To preclude an alliance between the West and the Soviet Union, which would create the danger of a two-front war, Hitler, ever the opportunist, negotiated his own nonaggression pact with Stalin and shocked the world with its announcement on August 23, 1939. A secret protocol to the treaty created German and Soviet spheres of influence in eastern Europe: Finland, the Baltic states of Estonia and Latvia, and eastern Poland would go to the Soviet Union, while Germany would acquire western Poland. The treaty with the Soviet Union gave Hitler the freedom to attack Poland. He told his generals: "Now

Poland is in the position in which I wanted her.... I am only afraid that at the last moment some swine or other will yet submit to me a plan for mediation."[3] He need not have worried. On September 1, German forces invaded Poland; two days later, Britain and France declared war on Germany. Two weeks later, on September 17, Germany's newfound ally, the Soviet Union, sent its troops into eastern Poland. Europe was again at war.

The Path to War in Asia

The war in Asia arose from the ambitions of Japan, whose rise to the status of world power had been swift. Japan had defeated China in 1895 and Russia in 1905 and had taken over many of Germany's eastern and Pacific colonies in World War I. By 1933, the Japanese Empire and the Dutch East Indies. In 1935, Japan began to construct a modern naval fleet, and after 1936, the armed forces exercised much influence over the government.

JAPANESE GOALS IN EAST ASIA In September 1931, Japanese soldiers had seized Manchuria, an area of northeastern China that had natural resources Japan needed. Eventually, worldwide protests against the Japanese action led the League of Nations to condemn the Japanese seizure, which caused Japan to withdraw from the League. During the next several years, Japan consolidated its hold on Manchuria, which it renamed Manchukuo (man-CHOO-kwoh), and then began to expand its control in North China. By the mid-1930s, militant elements connected with the government and the armed forces were effectively in control of Japanese politics.

For the moment, the prime victim of Tokyo's militant strategy was China. When clashes between Chinese and Japanese troops broke out, the Chinese Nationalist leader, Chiang Kai-shek (CHANG ky-SHEK) (1887–1975), sought to appease Tokyo by granting Japan the authority to administer areas in North China. But as Japan moved steadily southward, popular protests in Chinese cities against Japanese aggression intensified. When Chinese and Japanese forces clashed at the Marco Polo Bridge, south of Beijing, in July 1937, China refused to apologize, and hostilities spread.

Japan had not planned to declare war on China, but neither side would compromise, and the 1937 incident eventually turned into a major conflict. The Japanese advanced up the Yangtze valley and seized the Chinese capital of Nanjing (nan-JING), raping and killing thousands of innocent civilians in the process. But Chiang Kai-shek refused to capitulate and moved his government upriver to Hankou (HAHN-kow). Japanese strategists had hoped to force Chiang to join a Japanese-dominated new order in East Asia, comprising Japan, Manchuria, and China. This aim was part of a larger plan to seize Soviet Siberia with its rich resources and create a new "Monroe Doctrine for Asia," in which Japan would guide its Asian neighbors on the path to development and prosperity.

During the late 1930s, Japan began to cooperate with Nazi Germany on the assumption that the two countries would ultimately launch a joint attack on the Soviet Union and divide up its resources between them. But when Germany surprised the world by signing a nonaggression pact with the Soviets in August 1939, Japanese strategists were compelled to reevaluate their long-term objectives. Japan was not strong enough to defeat the Soviet Union alone, so the Japanese began to shift their gaze southward

Hitler Declares War. Adolf Hitler believed that it was necessary for Germany to gain living space through conquest in the east. This policy meant war. Hitler's nonaggression pact with the Soviet Union on August 23, 1939, paved the way for his invasion of Poland on September 1. On that day, Hitler spoke to the German Reichstag and announced the outbreak of war.

included Korea, Formosa (Taiwan), Manchuria, and the Marshall, Caroline, and Mariana islands in the Pacific.

By the early 1930s, Japan was experiencing severe internal tensions. Its population had exploded from 30 million in 1870 to 80 million by 1937. Much of Japan's ability to feed its population and to pay for industrial raw materials depended on the manufacture of heavy industrial goods (especially ships) and textiles. But in the 1930s, Western nations established tariff barriers to protect their own economies from the effects of the depression. Japan was devastated, both economically and politically.

Although political power had been concentrated in the hands of the emperor and his cabinet, Japan had also experienced a slow growth of political democracy with universal male suffrage in 1924 and the emergence of mass political parties. The economic crises of the 1930s stifled this democratic growth. Right-wing patriotic societies allied themselves with the army and navy to push a program of expansion at the expense of China and the Soviet Union, while the navy hoped to make Japan self-sufficient in raw materials by conquering British Malaya

A Japanese Victory March in China. After consolidating its authority over Manchuria, Japan began to expand into northern China. Direct hostilities between Japanese and Chinese forces began in 1937. This photograph shows a Japanese victory march in Shanghai at the beginning of December 1937. By 1939, Japan had conquered most of eastern China.

CHRONOLOGY	Prelude to War, 1933–1939
Japan seizes Manchuria	September 1931
Hitler becomes chancellor	January 30, 1933
Hitler announces a German air force	March 9, 1935
Hitler announces military conscription	March 16, 1935
Anglo-German Naval Pact	June 18, 1935
Mussolini invades Ethiopia	October 1935
Hitler occupies demilitarized Rhineland	March 7, 1936
Mussolini and Hitler intervene in the Spanish Civil War	1936
Rome-Berlin Axis	October 1936
Anti-Comintern Pact (Japan and Germany)	November 1936
Japan invades China	1937
Germany annexes Austria	March 13, 1938
Munich Conference: Germany occupies Sudetenland	September 29, 1938
Germany occupies the rest of Czechoslovakia	March 1939
German-Soviet Nonaggression Pact	August 23, 1939
Germany invades Poland	September 1, 1939
Britain and France declare war on Germany	September 3, 1939
Soviet Union invades Poland	September 17, 1939

to the vast resources of Southeast Asia—the oil of the Dutch East Indies, the rubber and tin of Malaya, and the rice of Burma and Indochina.

A move southward, of course, would risk war with the European colonial powers, especially Britain and France, as well as with the other rising power in the Pacific, the United States. When the Japanese took military control of southern Vietnam in July 1941, the Americans responded by cutting off sales of vital scrap iron and oil to Japan. Japan's military leaders decided to preempt any further American response by attacking the American naval fleet in the Pacific.

The Course of World War II

Q **FOCUS QUESTION:** What were the main events of World War II in Europe and in Asia, and why were the Allies ultimately victorious?

Nine days before he attacked Poland, Hitler made clear to his generals what was expected of them: "When starting and waging a war it is not right that matters, but victory.

Close your hearts to pity. Act brutally. Eighty million people must obtain what is their right.... The wholesale destruction of Poland is the military objective. Speed is the main thing. Pursuit until complete annihilation."[4] Hitler's remarks set the tone for what became the most destructive war in human history.

Victory and Stalemate

Unleashing an early form of Blitzkrieg, or "lightning war," Hitler stunned Europe with the speed and efficiency of the German attack. Moving into Poland with about 1.5 million troops from two fronts, German forces used panzer divisions, or armored columns, supported by airplanes to break quickly through the Polish lines and encircle the outnumbered and poorly equipped Polish armies. The coordinated air and ground assaults included the use of Stuka dive bombers; as they descended from the skies, their sirens emitted a blood-curdling shriek, adding a frighteningly destructive element to the German attack. Regular infantry units, still on foot with their supplies drawn by horses, then marched in to hold the newly conquered territory. Soon afterward, Soviet military forces attacked eastern Poland. Within four weeks, Poland had surrendered. On September 28, 1939, Germany and the Soviet Union officially divided Poland between them.

HITLER'S ATTACK IN THE WEST Although Hitler's hopes of avoiding a war in the west were dashed when France and Britain declared war on September 3, he was confident that he could control the situation. Expecting another war of attrition and economic blockade, Britain and France refused to go on the offensive. Between 1930 and 1935, France had built a series of concrete and steel fortifications armed with heavy artillery—known as the Maginot (MA-zhi-noh) Line—along its border with Germany. Now France was quite happy to remain in its defensive shell.

After a winter of waiting (called the "phony war"), Hitler resumed the war on April 9, 1940, with another Blitzkrieg, this time against Denmark and Norway. The invasion of Norway was dramatic; the Nazis landed troops at key positions along the coast and dropped paratroopers into airfields and major cities. The British landed a force of almost 50,000 troops but were eventually driven out. Norway surrendered on June 9, and Germany's northern flank was now secure.

One month later, on May 10, the Germans launched their attack on the Netherlands, Belgium, and France. The Netherlands fell in five days. The Dutch city of Rotterdam was devastated by bombing and quickly became a symbol of ruthless Nazi destruction of civilian life. The German forces pushed into Belgium as if to move into France as they had done in World War I, but this was only a trick. The Germans now unleashed their main assault through Luxembourg and the Ardennes, a move that was completely unexpected by the French and British forces. German panzer divisions broke through the weak French defensive positions there, outflanking the Maginot Line, raced across northern France, and reached the English Channel on May 21, splitting the Allied armies. The main Belgian army surrendered on May 28, and the other British and French forces were trapped at Dunkirk. At this point Hitler stopped the advance of the German armored units and ordered the Luftwaffe (the German air force) to destroy the Allied army on the beaches of Dunkirk. The Luftwaffe was ineffective in bombing the Allied forces, however, and by the time Hitler ordered his armored units to advance again, the British had rebuilt their defenses sufficiently to allow for a gigantic evacuation of 350,000 French and British troops by a fleet of small ships. The "miracle of Dunkirk" saved a well-trained army to fight another day.

On June 5, the Germans launched another offensive into southern France. Five days later, Benito Mussolini, believing that the war was over and eager to grab some of the spoils, declared war on France and invaded from the south. Dazed by the speed of the German offensive, the French were never able to mount an adequate resistance and surrendered on June 22. German armies occupied about three-fifths of France while the French hero of World War I, Marshal Henri Pétain (AHN-ree pay-TANH) (1856–1951), established an authoritarian regime—known as Vichy (VISH-ee) France—over the remainder. The Allies regarded the Pétain government as a Nazi puppet state, and a French government-in-exile took up residence in Britain. Germany was now in control of western and central Europe, but Britain still had not been defeated.

THE PROBLEM OF BRITAIN The German victories in Denmark and Norway had led to a change of government in Britain. Growing dissatisfaction with the apostle of appeasement, Neville Chamberlain, led a member of his own party to say to the prime minister, "You have sat too long for any good you have been doing. Depart, I say, and let us have done with you. In the name of God go!"[5] Chamberlain resigned, and on May 10, 1940, Winston Churchill (1874–1965), a longtime advocate of a hard-line policy toward Nazi Germany, became prime minister. Churchill was confident that he could guide Britain to ultimate victory. "I thought I knew a great deal about it all," he later wrote, "and I was sure I should not fail." Churchill proved to be an inspiring leader who rallied the British people with stirring speeches. Hitler had hoped that the British could be persuaded to make peace so that he could fulfill his long-awaited opportunity to gain living space in the east. Led by the stubbornly determined Churchill, who believed there could be no compromise with Nazism, the British refused, and Hitler was forced to prepare for an invasion of Britain, a prospect that he faced with little confidence.

As Hitler realized, an amphibious invasion of Britain would be possible only if Germany gained control of the air. By August 1940, the Luftwaffe had launched a major offensive against British air and naval bases, harbors, communication centers, and war industries. The British fought back doggedly, supported by an effective radar system that gave them early warning of German attacks. Moreover, the Ultra intelligence operation, which had broken German military codes, gave the British air force information about the specific targets of German air attacks. Nevertheless, the British air force suffered critical losses by the end of August and was probably saved by Hitler's change of strategy. In September, in retaliation for a British attack on Berlin, Hitler ordered a shift from military targets to massive bombing of cities to break British morale. The British rebuilt their air strength quickly and were soon inflicting major losses on Luftwaffe bombers. By the end of September, Germany had lost the Battle of Britain, and the invasion of Britain had to be postponed.

At this point, Hitler pursued the possibility of a Mediterranean strategy, which would involve capturing Egypt and the Suez Canal and closing the Mediterranean to British ships, thereby shutting off Britain's supply of oil. Hitler's commitment to the Mediterranean was never wholehearted, however. His initial plan was to let the Italians, whose role was to secure the Balkan and Mediterranean flanks, defeat the British in North Africa, but this strategy failed when the British routed the Italian army. Although Hitler then sent German troops to the North African theater of war, his primary concern lay elsewhere: he had already reached the decision to fulfill his lifetime obsession with the acquisition of living space in the east.

INVASION OF THE SOVIET UNION Already at the end of July 1940, Hitler had told his army leaders to begin preparations for the invasion of the Soviet Union. Although he had no desire for a two-front war, Hitler became convinced that Britain was remaining in the war only because it expected Soviet support. If the Soviet Union were smashed, Britain's last hope would be eliminated. Moreover, Hitler had convinced himself that the Soviet Union, with its Jewish-Bolshevik leadership and a pitiful army, could be defeated quickly and decisively. Although the invasion of the Soviet Union was scheduled for spring 1941, the attack was delayed because of problems in the Balkans.

Hitler had already obtained the political cooperation of Hungary, Bulgaria, and Romania. Mussolini, however, who liked to think of the Balkans as being within the Italian sphere of influence, became considerably upset over Germany's gains in southeastern Europe. To ensure the extension of Italian influence in that region, Mussolini launched an attack on Greece on October 28, 1940. But the Italians were militarily unprepared, and their invasion was quickly stopped. Hitler was furious because the disastrous invasion of Greece exposed his southern flank to British air bases in Greece. To secure his Balkan flank, Hitler first invaded Yugoslavia on April 6, 1941. After its surrender on April 17, he smashed Greece in six days. Now reassured, Hitler turned to the east and invaded the Soviet Union, believing that the Soviets could still be decisively defeated before winter set in.

On June 22, 1941, Nazi Germany launched its attack on the Soviet Union, by far the largest invasion the Germans had yet attempted. The German force consisted of 180 divisions, including 20 panzer divisions, 8,000 tanks, and 3,200 airplanes. German troops were stretched out along an 1,800-mile front (see Map 27.2). The Soviets had 160 infantry divisions but were able to mobilize another 300 divisions out of reserves within half a year. Hitler had badly miscalculated the Soviets' potential power.

The German troops advanced rapidly, capturing 2 million Soviet soldiers. By November, one German army group had swept through Ukraine while a second was besieging Leningrad; a third approached within 25 miles of Moscow, the Soviet capital. But despite their successes, the Germans had failed to achieve their primary objective. They did not eliminate the Soviet army, nor did the Soviet state collapse in a few months, as Hitler thought it would.

An early winter and unexpected Soviet resistance brought the German advance to a halt. Armor and transport vehicles stalled in temperatures of 30 below zero. Hitler's commanders wished to withdraw and regroup for the following spring, but Hitler refused. Fearing the disintegration of his lines, he insisted that there would be no retreat. A Soviet counterattack in December 1941 by an army supposedly exhausted by Nazi victories came as an ominous ending to the year. Although the Germans managed to hold on and reestablish their lines, a war diary kept by a member of Panzer Group Three described their desperate situation: "Discipline is breaking down. More

German Troops in the Soviet Union. At first, the German attack on the Soviet Union was enormously successful, leading one German general to remark in his diary: "It is probably no overstatement to say that the Russian campaign has been won in the space of two weeks." This picture shows German troops firing on Soviet positions.

and more soldiers are heading west on foot without weapons. . . . The road is under constant air attack. Those killed by bombs are no longer being buried. All the hangers-on (cargo troops, Luftwaffe, supply trains) are pouring to the rear in full flight."[6] By December 1941, another of Hitler's decisions—the declaration of war on the United States—had probably made his defeat inevitable and turned another European conflict into a global war.

The War in Asia

On December 7, 1941, Japanese carrier-based aircraft attacked the United States naval base at Pearl Harbor in the Hawaiian Islands. The same day, other units launched additional assaults on the Philippines and began advancing toward the British colony of Malaya. The next day, the United States declared war on Japan. Three days later, Hitler declared war on the United States, although he was by no means required to do so by his loose alliance with Japan. This action enabled President Franklin D. Roosevelt to overcome strong American isolationist sentiment and bring the United States into the European conflict.

Shortly after the American entry into the war, Japanese forces invaded the Dutch East Indies and

MAP 27.2 World War II in Europe and North Africa. With its fast and effective military, Germany quickly overwhelmed much of western Europe. Hitler had overestimated his country's capabilities, however, and underestimated those of his foes. By late 1942, his invasion of the Soviet Union was failing, and the United States had become a major factor in the war. The Allies successfully invaded Italy in 1943 and France in 1944.

Q *Which countries were neutral, and how did geography help make their neutrality an option?*

View an animated version of this map or related maps on the CourseMate website.

occupied a number of islands in the Pacific Ocean (see Map 27.3). In some cases, as on the Bataan peninsula and the island of Corregidor in the Philippines, resistance was fierce, but by the spring of 1942, almost all of Southeast Asia and much of the western Pacific had fallen into Japanese hands. Tokyo declared the creation of the Great East Asia Co-Prosperity Sphere, encompassing the entire region under Japanese tutelage, and announced its intention to liberate the colonial areas of Southeast Asia from Western colonial rule. For the moment, however, Japan needed the resources of the region

for its war machine and placed the countries under its rule on a wartime basis.

Japanese leaders had hoped that their lightning strike at American bases would destroy the U.S. Pacific Fleet and persuade the Roosevelt administration to accept Japanese domination of the Pacific. The American people, in the eyes of Japanese leaders, had been made soft by material indulgence. But Tokyo had miscalculated. The attack on Pearl Harbor galvanized American opinion and won broad support for Roosevelt's war policy. The United States now joined with European nations and Nationalist China in a

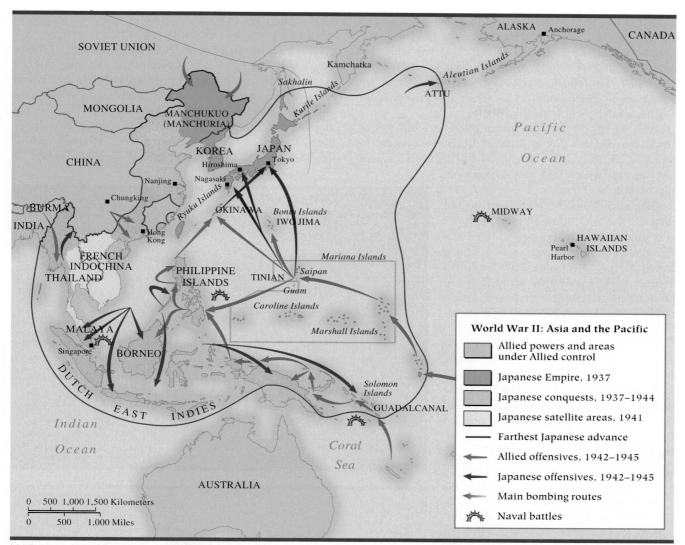

MAP 27.3 World War II in Asia and the Pacific. In 1937, Japan invaded northern China, beginning its effort to create a "Great East Asia Co-Prosperity Sphere." Further expansion caused the United States to end iron and oil sales to Japan. Deciding that war with the United States was inevitable, Japan engineered a surprise attack on Pearl Harbor.

Q *Why was control of the islands in the western Pacific of great importance both to the Japanese and to the Allies?*

View an animated version of this map or related maps on the CourseMate website.

combined effort to defeat Japan and bring to an end its hegemony in the Pacific.

The Turning Point of the War (1942–1943)

The entry of the United States into the war created a coalition (the Grand Alliance) that ultimately defeated the Axis powers (Germany, Italy, Japan). Nevertheless, the three major Allies—Britain, the United States, and the Soviet Union—had to overcome mutual suspicions before they could operate as an effective alliance. Two factors aided that process. First, Hitler's declaration of war on the United States made it easier for the Americans to accept the British and Soviet contention

that the defeat of Germany should be the first priority of the United States. For that reason, the United States increased the quantity of trucks, planes, and other arms that it sent to the British and Soviets. Also important to the alliance was the tacit agreement of the three chief Allies to stress military operations while ignoring political differences and larger strategic issues concerning any postwar settlement. At the beginning of 1943, the Allies agreed to fight until the Axis powers surrendered unconditionally. Although this principle of **unconditional surrender** might have discouraged dissident Germans and Japanese from overthrowing their governments in order to arrange a negotiated peace, it also had the effect of cementing the Grand Alliance by making it nearly impossible for Hitler to divide his foes.

Defeat was far from Hitler's mind at the beginning of 1942, however. As Japanese forces advanced into Southeast Asia and the Pacific after crippling the American naval fleet at Pearl Harbor, Hitler and his European allies continued the war in Europe against Britain and the Soviet Union. Until the fall of 1942, it appeared that the Germans might still prevail on the battlefield.

After the British defeat of Italian troops in North Africa, Hitler sent General Erwin Rommel (RAHM-ul), whom he described as "the most daring general of armored forces in the German army," with the German Afrika Korps to Libya in February 1941. Leading a combined force of Germans and Italians, Rommel attacked on March 30 and by the end of May had reached the Egyptian frontier, where he was finally forced to halt. Reinforcements in North Africa in 1942 enabled the Afrika Korps to break though the British defenses in Egypt, capture Tobruk in June, and begin an advance toward Alexandria.

The Germans were also continuing their success in the Battle of the North Atlantic as their submarines continued to attack Allied ships carrying supplies to Great Britain. In the spring of 1942, a renewed German offensive in the Soviet Union led to the capture of the entire Crimea, causing Hitler to boast in August 1942:

> As the next step, we are going to advance south of the Caucasus and then help the rebels in Iran and Iraq against the English. Another thrust will be directed along the Caspian Sea toward Afghanistan and India. Then the English will run out of oil. In two years we'll be on the borders of India. Twenty to thirty elite German divisions will do. Then the British Empire will collapse.[7]

But this would be Hitler's last optimistic outburst. By the fall of 1942, the war had turned against the Germans.

In North Africa, British forces had stopped Rommel's troops at El Alamein in the summer of 1942 and then forced them back across the desert. In November 1942, British and American forces invaded French North Africa and forced the German and Italian troops to surrender in May 1943. By that time, new detection devices had enabled the Allies to destroy increasing numbers of German submarines in the shipping war in the Atlantic.

BATTLE OF STALINGRAD   On the Eastern Front, the turning point of the war occurred at Stalingrad. After the capture of the Crimea, Hitler's generals wanted him to concentrate on the Caucasus and its oil fields, but Hitler decided that Stalingrad, a major industrial center on the Volga, should be taken first.

The German advance on Stalingrad encountered fierce resistance, but Hitler was determined to capture the city named after the Soviet dictator. Stalin had issued a war order called "Not a Step Back." Although the Germans destroyed much of the city, the Soviet troops used the bombed-out buildings and factories as well-fortified defensive positions. A deadly and brutal street-by-street conflict evolved during September, October, and November, in

The Battle of Stalingrad. The Battle of Stalingrad was a major turning point on the Eastern Front. Shown in the first illustration is a German infantry platoon in the ruins of a tractor factory they had captured in the northern part of Stalingrad. This victory took place on October 15, 1942, at a time when Hitler still believed he was winning the battle for Stalingrad. That belief was soon dashed as a Soviet counteroffensive in November led to a total defeat for the Germans. The second illustration shows thousands of captured soldiers being marched across frozen Soviet soil to prison camps. The soldiers in white fur hats are Romanian. Fewer than 6,000 captured soldiers survived to go home; the remainder—almost 85,000 prisoners—died in captivity.

A German Soldier at Stalingrad

The Soviet victory at Stalingrad was a major turning point in World War II. This excerpt comes from the diary of a German soldier who fought and died in the Battle of Stalingrad. His dreams of victory and a return home with medals were soon dashed by the realities of Soviet resistance.

Diary of a German Soldier

Today, after we'd had a bath, the company commander told us that if our future operations are as successful, we'll soon reach the Volga, take Stalingrad and then the war will inevitably soon be over. Perhaps we'll be home by Christmas.

July 29. The company commander says the Russian troops are completely broken, and cannot hold out any longer. To reach the Volga and take Stalingrad is not so difficult for us. The Führer knows where the Russians' weak point is. Victory is not far away....

August 10. The Führer's orders were read out to us. He expects victory of us. We are all convinced that they can't stop us.

August 12. This morning outstanding soldiers were presented with decorations.... Will I really go back to Elsa without a decoration? I believe that for Stalingrad the Führer will decorate even me....

September 4. We are being sent northward along the front toward Stalingrad. We marched all night and by dawn had reached Voroponovo Station. We can already see the smoking town. It's a happy thought that the end of the war is getting nearer. That's what everyone is saying....

September 8. Two days of non-stop fighting. The Russians are defending themselves with insane stubbornness. Our regiment has lost many men....

September 16. Our battalion, plus tanks, is attacking the [grain storage] elevator, from which smoke is pouring—the grain in it is burning, the Russians seem to have set light to it themselves. Barbarism. The battalion is suffering heavy losses....

October 10. The Russians are so close to us that our planes cannot bomb them. We are preparing for a decisive attack. The Führer has ordered the whole of Stalingrad to be taken as rapidly as possible....

October 22. Our regiment has failed to break into the factory. We have lost many men; every time you move you have to jump over bodies....

November 10. A letter from Elsa today. Everyone expects us home for Christmas. In Germany everyone believes we already hold Stalingrad. How wrong they are. If they could only see what Stalingrad has done to our army....

November 21. The Russians have gone over to the offensive along the whole front. Fierce fighting is going on. So, there it is—the Volga, victory and soon home to our families! We shall obviously be seeing them next in the other world.

November 29. We are encircled. It was announced this morning that the Führer has said: "The army can trust me to do everything necessary to ensure supplies and rapidly break the encirclement."

December 3. We are on hunger rations and waiting for the rescue that the Führer promised....

December 14. Everybody is racked with hunger. Frozen potatoes are the best meal, but to get them out of the ice-covered ground under fire from Russian bullets is not so easy....

December 26. The horses have already been eaten. I would eat a cat; they say its meat is also tasty. The soldiers look like corpses or lunatics, looking for something to put in their mouths. They no longer take cover from Russian shells; they haven't the strength to walk, run away and hide. A curse on this war!

Q What did this soldier believe about the Führer? Why? What was the source of his information? Why is the battle for Stalingrad considered a major turning point in World War II?

which both sides took severe losses. On November 8, Hitler announced that the German Sixth Army had taken Stalingrad, but in fact, on November 19 and 20, the Soviets attacked German positions north and south of Stalingrad, and by November 23 they had surrounded the German forces. Hitler commanded General Friedrich Paulus to stand firm with his Sixth Army and forbade attempts to break out of the encirclement. Winter privations and Soviet attacks, however, forced the Germans to surrender on February 2, 1943 (see the box above). The entire German Sixth Army of 300,000 men was lost. By February 1943, German forces in the Soviet Union were back to their positions of June 1942. By the spring of 1943, even Hitler knew that the Germans would not defeat the Soviet Union.

BATTLE OF MIDWAY The tide of battle in Asia also turned dramatically in 1942. In the Battle of the Coral Sea on May 7–8, 1942, American naval forces stopped the Japanese advance and temporarily relieved Australia of the threat of invasion. On June 4, at the Battle of Midway Island, American planes destroyed all four of the attacking Japanese aircraft carriers and established American naval superiority in the Pacific. The victory came at a high cost; about two-fifths of the American planes were shot down in the encounter. By the fall of 1942, Allied forces were beginning to gather for offensive operations in three areas: from bases in north Burma and India into the rest of Burma; in the Solomon Islands and on New Guinea, with forces under the direction of American general

Douglas MacArthur moving toward the Philippines; and across the Pacific where combined U.S. Army, Marine, and Navy forces would mount attacks against Japanese-held islands. After a series of bitter engagements in the waters off the Solomon Islands from August to November 1942, Japanese fortunes began to fade.

The Last Years of the War

By the beginning of 1943, the tide of battle had turned against Germany, Italy, and Japan, but it would take a long time to achieve the goal of unconditional surrender of the three Axis powers. After the Axis forces had surrendered in Tunisia on May 13, 1943, the Allies crossed the Mediterranean and carried the war to Italy, an area that Winston Churchill had called the "soft underbelly" of Europe. After taking Sicily, Allied troops began the invasion of mainland Italy in September. In the meantime, after the ouster and arrest of Benito Mussolini, a new Italian government offered to surrender to Allied forces. But Mussolini was liberated by the Germans in a daring raid and then set up as the head of a puppet German state in northern Italy while German troops moved in and occupied much of Italy. The new defensive lines established by the Germans in the hills south of Rome were so effective that the Allied advance up the Italian peninsula was a painstaking affair accompanied by heavy casualties. Rome did not fall to the Allies until June 4, 1944. By that time, the Italian war had assumed a secondary role anyway as the Allies opened their long-awaited "second front" in western Europe two days later.

ALLIED ADVANCES IN THE WEST   Since the autumn of 1943, the Allies had been planning a cross-channel invasion of France from Britain. A series of Allied deceptions managed to trick the Germans into believing that the invasion would come on the flat plains of northern France.

Instead, the Allies, under the direction of the American general, Dwight D. Eisenhower (1890–1969), landed five assault divisions on the Normandy beaches on June 6 in history's greatest amphibious invasion. Three airborne divisions were also sent to secure the flanks of the areas where the troops went ashore. Putting 150,000 troops ashore in one day required the support of more than 7,000 naval ships. An initially indecisive German response enabled the Allied forces to establish a beachhead. Within three months, they had landed 2 million men and a half-million vehicles that pushed inland and broke through the German defensive lines.

After the breakout, Allied troops moved south and east and liberated Paris by the end of August. Supply problems as well as a last-minute, desperate (and unsuccessful) offensive by German troops in the Battle of the Bulge slowed the Allied advance. Nevertheless, by March 1945, Allied armies had crossed the Rhine River and advanced further into Germany. At the end of April, Allied forces in northern Germany moved toward the Elbe River, where they finally linked up with the Soviets.

SOVIET OFFENSIVE IN THE EAST   The Soviets had come a long way since the Battle of Stalingrad in 1943. In the summer of 1943, Hitler's generals had urged him to build an "east wall" based on river barriers to halt the Soviets. Instead, Hitler gambled on taking the offensive by making use of newly developed heavy tanks. German forces were soundly defeated by the Soviets at the Battle of Kursk (KOORSK) (July 5–12), the greatest tank battle of World War II. The Germans lost eighteen of their best panzer divisions. Soviet forces now began a relentless advance westward. The Soviets had reoccupied Ukraine by the end of 1943 and lifted the siege of Leningrad and moved into the Baltic states by the beginning of 1944. Advancing along a northern front, Soviet troops occupied Warsaw in January 1945 and entered Berlin in April. Meanwhile,

National Archives (111-C-273), Washington, DC

Crossing the Rhine. After landing at Normandy, Allied forces liberated France and prepared to move into Germany. Makeshift bridges enabled the Allies to cross the Rhine in some areas and advance deeper into Germany. Units of the U.S. Seventh Army of General Patch are shown here crossing the Rhine at Worms on a pontoon bridge constructed by battalions of engineers alongside the ruins of the old bridge.

Germany and the Soviet Union divide Poland	September 1939
Blitzkrieg against Denmark and Norway	April 1940
Blitzkrieg against Belgium, Netherlands, and France	May 1940
Churchill becomes British prime minister	May 10, 1940
France surrenders	June 22, 1940
Battle of Britain	Summer 1940
Nazi seizure of Yugoslavia and Greece	April 1941
Germany invades the Soviet Union	June 22, 1941
Japanese attack on Pearl Harbor	December 7, 1941
Battle of the Coral Sea	May 7–8, 1942
Battle of Midway Island	June 4, 1942
Allied invasion of North Africa	November 1942
Soviets win Battle of Stalingrad	February 2, 1943
Axis forces surrender in North Africa	May 13, 1943
Battle of Kursk	July 5–12, 1943
Invasion of mainland Italy	September 1943
Allied invasion of France	June 6, 1944
Hitler commits suicide	April 30, 1945
Germany surrenders	May 7, 1945
Atomic bomb dropped on Hiroshima	August 6, 1945
Japan surrenders	August 14, 1945

Soviet troops swept along a southern front through Hungary, Romania, and Bulgaria.

In January 1945, Adolf Hitler had moved into a bunker 55 feet under Berlin to direct the final stages of the war. Hitler continued to arrange his armies on worn-out battle maps as if it still made a difference. In his final political testament, Hitler, consistent to the end in his rabid anti-Semitism, blamed the Jews for the war: "Above all I charge the leaders of the nation and those under them to scrupulous observance of the laws of race and to merciless opposition to the universal poisoner of all peoples, international Jewry."[8] Hitler committed suicide on April 30, two days after Mussolini had been shot by partisan Italian forces. On May 7, German commanders surrendered. The war in Europe was over.

DEFEAT OF JAPAN The war in Asia continued. Beginning in 1943, American forces had gone on the offensive and advanced their way, slowly at times, across the Pacific. American forces took an increasing toll of enemy resources, especially at sea and in the air. When President Harry Truman (Roosevelt had died on April 12, 1945) and his advisers became convinced that American troops might suffer heavy casualties in the invasion of the Japanese homeland, they made the decision to drop the newly developed atomic bomb on Hiroshima (hee-roh-SHEE-muh)

and Nagasaki (nah-gah-SAH-kee). The Japanese surrendered unconditionally on August 14. World War II was finally over.

The New Order

 FOCUS QUESTIONS: How was the Nazi empire organized? What was the Holocaust, and what role did it play in Nazi policy?

The initial victories of the Germans and the Japanese gave them the opportunity to create new orders in Europe and Asia. Although both countries presented positive images of these new orders for publicity purposes, in practice both followed policies of ruthless domination of their subject peoples.

The Nazi Empire

After the German victories in Europe, Nazi propagandists created glowing images of a new European order based on "equal chances" for all nations and an integrated economic community. This was not Hitler's conception of a European New Order. He saw the Europe he had conquered simply as subject to German domination. Only the Germans, he once said, "can really organize Europe."

The Nazi empire stretched across continental Europe from the English Channel in the west to the outskirts of Moscow in the east. In no way was this empire organized systematically or governed efficiently. Some states—Spain, Portugal, Switzerland, Sweden, and Turkey—remained neutral and outside the empire. Germany's allies—Italy, Romania, Bulgaria, Hungary, and Finland—kept their independence but found themselves increasingly restricted by the Germans as the war progressed. The remainder of Europe was largely organized in one of two ways. Some areas, such as western Poland, were directly annexed by Nazi Germany and made into German provinces. Most of occupied Europe was administered by German military or civilian officials, combined with varying degrees of indirect control from collaborationist regimes. Competing lines of authority by different offices in occupied Europe made German occupation inefficient.

Racial considerations played an important role in how conquered peoples were treated in the **Nazi New Order.** German civil administrations were established in Norway, Denmark, and the Netherlands because the Nazis considered their peoples Aryan, racially akin to the Germans and hence worthy of more lenient treatment. "Inferior" Latin peoples, such as the occupied French, were given military administrations. By 1943, however, as Nazi losses continued to multiply, all the occupied territories of northern and western Europe were ruthlessly exploited for material goods and workers for Germany's war needs.

PLANS FOR AN ARYAN RACIAL EMPIRE Because the conquered lands in the east contained the living space for

Hitler's Plans for a New Order in the East

Hitler's nightly monologues to his postdinner guests, which were recorded by the Führer's private secretary, Martin Bormann, reveal much about the New Order he wished to create. On the evening of October 17, 1941, he expressed his views on what the Germans would do with their newly conquered territories in the east.

✦━❖❖❖━✦

Hitler's Secret Conversations, October 17, 1941

In comparison with the beauties accumulated in Central Germany, the new territories in the East seem to us like a desert.... This Russian desert, we shall populate it.... We'll take away its character of an Asiatic steppe, we'll Europeanize it. With this object, we have undertaken the construction of roads that will lead to the southernmost point of the Crimea and to the Caucasus. These roads will be studded along their whole length with German towns, and around these towns our colonists will settle.

As for the two or three million men whom we need to accomplish this task, we'll find them quicker than we think. They'll come from Germany, Scandinavia, the Western countries and America. I shall no longer be here to see all that, but in twenty years the Ukraine will already be a home for twenty million inhabitants besides the natives. In three hundred years, the country will be one of the loveliest gardens in the world.

As for the natives, we'll have to screen them carefully. The Jew, that destroyer, we shall drive out.... We shan't settle in the Russian towns, and we'll let them fall to pieces without intervening. And, above all, no remorse on this subject! We're not going to play at children's nurses; we're absolutely without obligations as far as these people are concerned. To struggle against the hovels, chase away the fleas, provide German teachers, bring out newspapers—very little of that for us! We'll confine ourselves, perhaps, to setting up a radio transmitter, under our control. For the rest, let them know just enough to understand our highway signs, so that they won't get themselves run over by our vehicles.... There's only one duty: to Germanize this country by the immigration of Germans, and to look upon the natives as Redskins. If these people had defeated us, Heaven have mercy! But we don't hate them. That sentiment is unknown to us. We are guided only by reason....

All those who have the feeling for Europe can join in our work.

In this business I shall go straight ahead, cold-bloodedly. What they may think about me, at this juncture, is to me a matter of complete indifference. I don't see why a German who eats a piece of bread should torment himself with the idea that the soil that produces this bread has been won by the sword. ✑

Q What new order did Hitler envision in the east? What would its achievement have meant for the peoples of eastern Europe?

German expansion and were populated in Nazi eyes by racially inferior Slavic peoples, Nazi administration there was considerably more ruthless. Hitler's racial ideology and his plans for an Aryan racial empire were so important to him that he and the Nazis began to implement their racial program soon after the conquest of Poland. Heinrich Himmler, a strong believer in Nazi racial ideology and the leader of the SS, was put in charge of German resettlement plans in the east. Himmler's task was to evacuate the inferior Slavic peoples and replace them with Germans, a policy first applied to the new German provinces created from the lands of western Poland. One million Poles were uprooted and dumped in southern Poland. Hundreds of thousands of ethnic Germans (descendants of Germans who had migrated years earlier from Germany to various parts of southern and eastern Europe) were encouraged to colonize the designated areas in Poland. By 1942, 2 million ethnic Germans had been settled in Poland.

The invasion of the Soviet Union inflated Nazi visions of German colonization in the east. Hitler spoke to his intimate circle of a colossal project of social engineering after the war, in which Poles, Ukrainians, and Soviets would become slave labor and German peasants would settle on the abandoned lands and Germanize them (see the box above). Nazis involved in this kind of planning were well aware of the human costs. Himmler told a gathering of SS officers that although the destruction of 30 million Slavs was a prerequisite for German plans in the east, "whether nations live in prosperity or starve to death interests me only insofar as we need them as slaves for our culture. Otherwise it is of no interest."[9]

ECONOMIC EXPLOITATION Economically, the Nazi New Order meant the ruthless exploitation of conquered Europe's resources. In eastern Europe, economic exploitation was direct and severe. The Germans seized raw materials, machines, and food, leaving only enough to maintain local peoples at a bare subsistence level. Although the Germans adopted legal formalities in their economic exploitation of western Europe, military supplies and important raw materials were taken outright. As Nazi policies created drastic shortages of food, clothing, and shelter, many Europeans suffered severely.

USE OF FOREIGN WORKERS Labor shortages in Germany led to a policy of ruthless mobilization of foreign labor for Germany. After the invasion of the Soviet Union, the 4 million Soviet prisoners of war captured by the Germans became a major source of heavy labor, but it was wasted by allowing 3 million of them to die from neglect. In 1942, a special office was created to recruit labor for German farms and industries. By the summer of 1944, 7 million foreign workers were laboring in Germany and constituted 20 percent of Germany's labor force. At the same time, another 7 million workers were supplying forced labor in their own countries on farms, in industries, and even in military camps. Forced labor often proved counterproductive, however, because it created economic chaos in occupied countries and disrupted industrial production that could have helped Germany. Even worse for the Germans, the brutal character of Germany's recruitment policies often caused more and more people to resist the Nazi occupation forces.

Resistance Movements

German policies toward conquered peoples quickly led to the emergence of resistance movements throughout Europe, especially in the east, where brutality toward the native peoples produced a strong reaction. In Ukraine and the Baltic states, for example, the Germans were initially hailed as liberators from Communist rule, but Hitler's policies of treating Slavic peoples as subhumans only drove those peoples to support and join guerrilla forces.

RESISTANCE MOVEMENTS IN NAZI-OCCUPIED EUROPE Resistance movements were formed throughout Europe. Active resisters committed acts of sabotage against German installations, assassinated German officials, disseminated anti-German newspapers, wrote anti-German sentiments on walls, and spied on German military positions for the Allies. Some anti-Nazi groups from occupied countries, such as the Free French movement under Charles de Gaulle (SHAHRL duh GOHL), created governments-in-exile in London. In some countries, resistance groups even grew strong enough to take on the Germans in pitched battles. In Yugoslavia, for example, Josip Broz (yaw-SEEP BRAWZ), known as Tito (1892–1980), led a band of guerrillas against German occupation forces. By 1944, his partisan army numbered 250,000, including 100,000 women.

After the invasion of the Soviet Union in 1941, Communists throughout Europe assumed leadership roles in underground resistance movements. This sometimes led to conflict with other local resistance groups who feared the postwar consequences of Communist power. Charles de Gaulle's Free French movement, for example, thwarted the attempt of French Communists to dominate the major French resistance groups.

Women, too, joined resistance movements in large numbers throughout Nazi-occupied Europe. Women served as message carriers, planted bombs in Nazi headquarters, assassinated Nazi officers, published and distributed anti-German underground newspapers, spied on German military movements and positions, and used shopping baskets to carry weapons, medicines, and money to help their causes. In Norway, women smuggled Jews into neutral Sweden. In Greece, wives dressed their husbands as women to save them when the Nazis sought to stop acts of sabotage by vicious reprisals in which all the males of a village were executed.

RESISTANCE IN GERMANY Germany had its resistance movements, too, although the increased control of the SS over everyday life made resistance both dangerous and ineffectual. The White Rose movement involved an attempt by a small group of students and one professor at the University of Munich to distribute pamphlets denouncing the Nazi regime as lawless, criminal, and godless. Its members were caught, arrested, and promptly executed. Likewise, Communist resistance groups were mostly crushed by the Gestapo (the secret police).

Only one plot against Hitler and the Nazi regime came remotely close to success. It was the work primarily of a group of military officers and conservative politicians who were appalled at Hitler's warmongering and sickened by the wartime atrocities he had encouraged. One of their number, Colonel Count Claus von Stauffenberg (KLOWSS fun SHTOW-fen-berk) (1907–1944), believed that only the elimination of Hitler would bring the overthrow of the Nazi regime. On July 20, 1944, a bomb planted by Stauffenberg in Hitler's East Prussian headquarters exploded, but it failed to kill the dictator. The plot was then quickly uncovered and crushed. Five thousand people were executed, and Hitler remained in control of Germany.

The Holocaust

There was no more terrifying aspect of the Nazi New Order than the deliberate attempt to exterminate the Jewish people of Europe. Racial struggle was a key element in Hitler's ideology and meant to him a clearly defined conflict of opposites: the Aryans, creators of human cultural development, against the Jews, parasites who were trying to destroy the Aryans. At a meeting of the Nazi Party in 1922, Hitler proclaimed, "There can be no compromise—there are only two possibilities: either victory of the Aryan or annihilation of the Aryan and the victory of the Jew."[10] Although Hitler later toned down his anti-Semitic message when his party sought mass electoral victories, anti-Semitism was a recurring theme in Nazism and resulted in a wave of legislative acts against the Jews between 1933 and 1939 (see Chapter 26).

EARLY NAZI POLICY By the beginning of 1939, Nazi policy focused on promoting the "emigration" of German Jews from Germany. At the same time, Hitler had given ominous warnings about the future of European Jewry. When he addressed the German Reichstag on January 30, 1939, he stated:

> I have often been a prophet in life and was generally laughed at. During my struggle for power, the Jews primarily received with laughter my prophecies that I would someday assume the leadership of the state and thereby of the entire Volk and then, among many other things, achieve a solution of the Jewish problem.... Today I will be a prophet again: if international finance Jewry within Europe and abroad should succeed once more in plunging the peoples into a world war, then the consequence will be not the Bolshevization of the world and therewith a victory of Jewry, but on the contrary, the destruction of the Jewish race in Europe.[11]

At the time, emigration was still the favored policy. Once the war began in September 1939, the so-called Jewish problem took on new dimensions. For a while, there was discussion of the Madagascar Plan, which aspired to the mass shipment of Jews to the island of Madagascar, off the eastern coast of Africa. When war contingencies made this plan impracticable, an even more drastic policy was conceived (see the Film & History feature on p. 869).

THE SS AND THE *EINSATZGRUPPEN* Heinrich Himmler and the SS organization closely shared Adolf Hitler's racial ideology. The SS was given responsibility for what the Nazis called their **Final Solution** to the Jewish problem—the annihilation of the Jewish people. Reinhard Heydrich (RYN-hart HY-drikh) (1904–1942), head of the SS's Security Service, was given administrative responsibility for the Final Solution. After the defeat of Poland, Heydrich ordered the special strike forces—***Einsatzgruppen*** (YN-zahtz-groop-un)—that he had created to round up all Polish Jews and concentrate them in ghettos established in a number of Polish cities.

In June 1941, the *Einsatzgruppen* were given new responsibilities as mobile killing units. These SS death squads followed the regular army's advance into the Soviet Union. Their job was to round up Jews in their villages and execute and bury them in mass graves, often giant pits dug by the victims themselves before they were shot. The leader of one of these death squads described the mode of operation:

> The unit selected for this task would enter a village or city and order the prominent Jewish citizens to call together all Jews for the purpose of resettlement. They were requested to hand over their valuables to the leaders of the unit, and shortly before the execution to surrender their outer clothing. The men, women, and children were led to a place of execution which in most cases was located next to a more deeply excavated anti-tank ditch. Then they were shot, kneeling or standing, and the corpses thrown into the ditch.[12]

Library of Congress (2391, f.401), Washington, DC

The Holocaust: Activities of the *Einsatzgruppen*. The activities of the mobile killing units known as the *Einsatzgruppen* were the first stage in the mass killings of the Holocaust. This picture shows the execution of a Jew by a member of one of these SS killing squads. Onlookers include members of the German army, the German Labor Service, and even Hitler Youth. When it became apparent that this method of killing was inefficient, it was replaced by the death camps.

Such regular killing created morale problems among the SS executioners. During a visit to Minsk in the Soviet Union, SS leader Himmler tried to build morale by pointing out that "he would not like it if Germans did such a thing gladly. But their conscience was in no way impaired, for they were soldiers who had to carry out every order unconditionally. He alone had responsibility before God and Hitler for everything that was happening, ... and he was acting from a deep understanding of the necessity for this operation."[13]

THE DEATH CAMPS Although it has been estimated that as many as one million Jews were killed by the *Einsatzgruppen,* this approach to solving the Jewish problem was soon perceived as inadequate. Instead, the Nazis opted for the systematic annihilation of the European Jewish population in specially built death camps. The plan was simple. Jews from countries occupied by Germany (or sympathetic to Germany) would be rounded up, packed like cattle into freight trains, and shipped to Poland, where six extermination centers were built for

Europa, Europa (1990)

Directed by Agnieszka Holland, *Europa, Europa* (known as *Hitlerjunge Salomon* [Hitler Youth Salomon] in Germany) is a harrowing story of one Jewish boy's escape from the horrors of Nazi persecution. It is based on the memoirs of Salomon Perel, a German Jew of Polish background who survived by pretending to be a pure Aryan. The film begins in 1938 during *Kristallnacht* when the family of Solly (a nickname for Salomon Perel) is attacked in their hometown of Peine, Germany. Solly's sister is killed, and the family moves back to Poland. When the Nazis invade Poland, Solly (Marco Hofschneider) and his brother are sent east, but the brothers become separated and Solly is placed in a Soviet orphanage in Grodno in the eastern part of Poland occupied by the Soviets.

For two years Solly becomes a dedicated Communist youth, but when the Germans invade in 1941, he falls into their hands and quickly assumes a new identity in order to survive. He becomes Josef "Jupp" Peters, supposedly the son of German parents from Latvia. Fluent in both Russian and German, Solly/Jupp becomes a translator for the German forces. After an unintended act of bravado, he is rewarded by being sent to a Hitler Youth school where he lives in fear of being exposed as a Jew because of his circumcised penis. He manages to survive the downfall of Nazi Germany and at the end of the war makes his way with his brother, who has also survived, to Palestine. Throughout much of the movie, Solly/Jupp lives in constant fear that his true identity as a Jew will be recognized, but his luck, charm, and resourcefulness enable him to survive a series of extraordinary events.

Although there is no way of knowing if each detail of this movie is historically accurate (and a few are absurdly inaccurate, such as a bombing run by a plane that was not developed until after the war), overall the story has the ring of truth. The fanaticism of both the Soviet and the Nazi officials who indoctrinate young people seems real. The scene in the Hitler Youth school on how to identify a Jew is realistic, even when it is made ironic by the instructor's choice of Solly/Jupp to demonstrate the characteristics of a true Aryan. The movie also realistically portrays the fearful world in which Jews had to live under the Nazis before the war and the horrible conditions of the Jewish ghettos in Polish cities during the war. The film

Salomon Perel/Josef Peters (Marco Hofschneider) as a Hitler Youth member.

shows how people had to fight for their survival in a world of ideological madness, when Jews were killed simply for being Jews. The attitudes of the German soldiers also seem real. Many are shown following orders and killing Jews based on the beliefs in which they have been indoctrinated. But the movie also portrays some German soldiers whose humanity did not allow them to kill Jews. One homosexual soldier discovers that Solly/Jupp is a Jew when he tries—unsuccessfully—to have sex with him. The soldier then becomes the boy's protector until he himself is killed in battle.

Many movies have been made about the horrible experiences of Jews during World War II, but this one is quite different from most of them. It might never have been made except for the fact that Salomon Perel, who was told by his brother not to tell his story because no one would believe it, was inspired to write his memoirs after a 1985 reunion with his former Hitler Youth group leader. This passionate and intelligent film is ultimately a result of that encounter.

---

this purpose (see Map 27.4). The largest and most infamous was Auschwitz-Birkenau (OWSH-vitz-BEER-kuh-now). Technical assistance for the construction of the camps was provided by experts from the T-4 program, which had been responsible for the extermination of 80,000 alleged racially unfit mental and physical defectives in Germany between 1938 and 1941. Based on their experiences, medical technicians chose Zyklon B (the commercial name for hydrogen cyanide) as the most effective gas for quickly killing large numbers of people in gas chambers designed to look like shower rooms to facilitate the cooperation of the victims. After gassing, the corpses would be burned in specially built crematoria.

To inform party and state officials of the general procedures for the Final Solution, a conference was held at

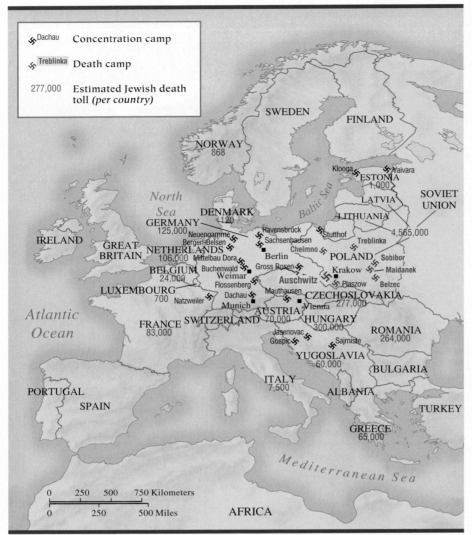

MAP 27.4 The Holocaust. Hitler used the fiction of the Aryan race, to which Germans supposedly belonged, to help radicalize the German people and justify his hatred of Jews. Hitler's "Final Solution" to the "Jewish problem" was the mass execution of Europe's Jews in death camps.

Q *Which region lost the largest number of Jews in the camps, and what helps explain this?*

Map legend:

Dachau — Concentration camp

Treblinka — Death camp

277,000 — Estimated Jewish death toll *(per country)*

elimination of the ghettos in Poland, by the summer of 1942, Jews were also being shipped from France, Belgium, and the Netherlands. In 1943, there were shipments of Jews from the capital cities of Berlin, Vienna, and Prague and from Greece, southern France, Italy, and Denmark. Even as the Allies were making important advances in 1944, Jews were being shipped from Greece and Hungary. These shipments depended on the cooperation of Germany's Transport Ministry, and despite desperate military needs, the Final Solution had priority in using railroad cars for the transportation of Jews to the death camps. Even the military argument that Jews could be used to produce armaments was overridden by the demands of extermination.

A harrowing experience awaited the Jews when they arrived at one of the six death camps. Rudolf Höss (HESS), commandant at Auschwitz-Birkenau, described it:

> We had two SS doctors on duty at Auschwitz to examine the incoming transports of prisoners. The prisoners would be marched by one of the doctors who would make spot decisions as they walked by. Those who were fit for work were sent into the camp. Others were sent immediately to the extermination plants. Children of tender years were invariably exterminated since by reason of their youth they were unable to work. . . . At Auschwitz we endeavored to fool the victims into thinking that they were to go through a delousing process. Of course, frequently they realized our true intentions and we sometimes had riots and difficulties due to that fact.[14]

About 30 percent of the arrivals at Auschwitz were sent to a labor camp; the remainder went to the gas chambers (see the box on p. 872). After they had been gassed, the bodies were burned in the crematoria. The victims' goods and even their bodies were used for economic gain. Female hair was cut off, collected, and turned into mattresses or cloth. Some inmates were also subjected to cruel and painful "medical" experiments. The Germans killed between 5 and 6 million Jews, more than 3 million of them in the death camps. Virtually 90 percent of the Jewish populations of Poland, the Baltic

Wannsee (VAHN-zay), outside Berlin, on January 20, 1942. Reinhard Heydrich outlined the steps that would now be taken to "solve the Jewish question." He explained how "in the course of the practical implementation of the final solution Europe is to be combed through from west to east" for Jews, who would then be brought "group by group, into so-called transit ghettos, to be transported from there farther to the east." The conference then worked out all of the bureaucratic details so that party and state officials would cooperate fully in the final elimination of the Jews.

By the spring of 1942, the death camps were in operation. Although initial priority was given to the

Wannsee Conference, "The Final Solution" (1942)

The Holocaust: The Extermination Camp at Auschwitz. After his initial successes in the east, Hitler set in motion the machinery for the physical annihilation of Europe's Jews. Shown here is a group of Hungarian Jews arriving at Auschwitz. Hungarian Jews were not rounded up and shipped to the death camps until 1944, at the time when the Allies were making significant advances in the war. In fact, between May 2 and July 9, 1944, more than 430,000 Hungarian Jews were deported to Auschwitz.

countries, and Germany were exterminated. Overall, the Holocaust was responsible for the death of nearly two out of every three European Jews.

THE OTHER HOLOCAUST The Nazis were also responsible for the deliberate death by shooting, starvation, or overwork of at least another 9 to 10 million people. Because the Nazis also considered the Gypsies of Europe (like the Jews) a race containing alien blood, they were systematically rounded up for extermination. About 40 percent of Europe's one million Gypsies were killed in the death camps. The leading elements of the "subhuman" Slavic peoples—the clergy, intelligentsia, civil leaders, judges, and lawyers—were arrested and deliberately killed. Probably, an additional 4 million Poles, Ukrainians, and Belorussians lost their lives as slave laborers for Nazi Germany, and at least 3 to 4 million Soviet prisoners of war were killed in captivity. The Nazis also singled out homosexuals for persecution, and thousands lost their lives in concentration camps.

The New Order in Asia

Once Japan's takeover was completed, Japanese war policy in the occupied areas in Asia became essentially defensive, as Japan hoped to use its new possessions to meet its needs for raw materials, such as tin, oil, and rubber, as well as to serve as an outlet for Japanese manufactured goods. To provide a structure for the arrangement, Japanese leaders set up the Great East Asia Co-Prosperity Sphere as a self-sufficient community designed to provide mutual benefits to the occupied areas and the home country.

The Japanese conquest of Southeast Asia had been accomplished under the slogan "Asia for the Asians." Japanese officials in occupied territories quickly promised that independent government would be established under Japanese tutelage. Such governments were eventually established in Burma, the Dutch East Indies, Vietnam, and the Philippines.

In fact, however, real power rested with Japanese military authorities in each territory, and the local Japanese military command was directly subordinated to the army general staff in Tokyo. The economic resources of the colonies were exploited for the benefit of the Japanese war machine, while natives were recruited to serve in local military units or were conscripted to work on public works projects. In some cases, the people living in the occupied areas were subjected to severe hardships.

The Holocaust: The Camp Commandant and the Camp Victims

The systematic annihilation of millions of men, women, and children in extermination camps makes the Holocaust one of the most horrifying events in history. The first document is taken from an account by Rudolf Höss, commandant of the extermination camp at Auschwitz-Birkenau. In the second document, a French doctor explains what happened to the victims at one of the crematoria described by Höss.

⊣⊢⊨⊟⊨⊢⊢

Commandant Höss Describes the Equipment

The two large crematoria, Nos. I and II, were built during the winter of 1942–43.... They each ... could cremate c. 2,000 corpses within twenty-four hours.... Crematoria I and II both had underground undressing and gassing rooms which could be completely ventilated. The corpses were brought up to the ovens on the floor above by lift. The gas chambers could hold c. 3,000 people.

The firm of Topf had calculated that the two smaller crematoria, III and IV, would each be able to cremate 1,500 corpses within twenty-four hours. However, owing to the wartime shortage of materials, the builders were obliged to economize and so the undressing rooms and gassing rooms were built above ground and the ovens were of a less solid construction. But it soon became apparent that the flimsy construction of these two four-retort ovens was not up to the demands made on it. No. III ceased operating altogether after a short time and later was no longer used. No. IV had to be repeatedly shut down since after a short period in operation of 4–6 weeks, the ovens and chimneys had burnt out.

The victims of the gassing were mainly burnt in pits behind crematorium IV.

The largest number of people gassed and cremated within twenty-four hours was somewhat over 9,000.

A French Doctor Describes the Victims

It is mid-day, when a long line of women, children, and old people enter the yard. The senior official in charge ... climbs on a bench to tell them that they are going to have a bath and that afterward they will get a drink of hot coffee. They all undress in the yard.... The doors are opened and an indescribable jostling begins. The first people to enter the gas chamber begin to draw back. They sense the death which awaits them. The SS men put an end to this pushing and shoving with blows from their rifle butts beating the heads of the horrified women who are desperately hugging their children. The massive oak double doors are shut. For two endless minutes one can hear banging on the walls and screams which are no longer human. And then—not a sound. Five minutes later the doors are opened. The corpses, squashed together and distorted, fall out like a waterfall.... The bodies which are still warm pass through the hands of the hairdresser who cuts their hair and the dentist who pulls out their gold teeth.... One more transport has just been processed through No. IV crematorium.

Q What equipment does Höss describe? What process does the French doctor describe? It there any sympathy for the victims in either account? Why or why not? How could such a horrifying process have been allowed to occur?

Like German soldiers in occupied Europe, Japanese military forces often had little respect for the lives of their subject peoples. In their conquest of Nanjing, China, in 1937, Japanese soldiers had spent several days killing, raping, and looting. Almost 800,000 Koreans were sent overseas, most of them as forced laborers, to Japan. Tens of thousands of Korean women were forced to serve as "comfort women" (prostitutes) for Japanese troops. In construction projects to help their war effort, the Japanese also made extensive use of labor forces composed of both prisoners of war and local peoples. In building the Burma-Thailand railway in 1943, for example, the Japanese used 61,000 Australian, British, and Dutch prisoners of war and almost 300,000 workers from Burma, Malaya, Thailand, and the Dutch East Indies. By the time the railway was completed, 12,000 Allied prisoners of war and 90,000 native workers had died from the inadequate diet and appalling working conditions in an unhealthy climate.

The Home Front

Q FOCUS QUESTION: What were conditions like on the home front for Japan and the major Western nations involved in World War II?

World War II was even more of a total war than World War I. Fighting was much more widespread and covered most of the globe. Economic mobilization was more extensive; so too was the mobilization of women. The number of civilians killed was far higher; almost 20 million died as a result of bombing raids, mass extermination policies, and attacks by invading armies.

The Mobilization of Peoples

The home fronts of the major belligerents varied considerably, based on national circumstances.

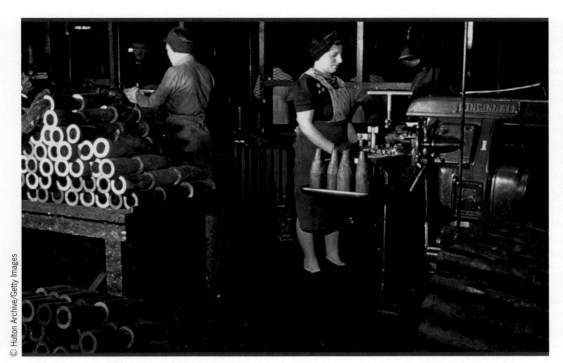

Women in the Factories. Although only the Soviet Union used women in combat positions, the number of women working in industry increased dramatically in most belligerent countries. British women are shown here in a British munitions factory during World War II, probably in 1943.

GREAT BRITAIN The British mobilized their resources more thoroughly than their allies or even Germany. By the summer of 1944, fully 55 percent of the British people were in the armed forces or civilian "war work." The British were especially determined to make use of women. Most women under forty years of age were called on to do war work of some kind. By 1944, women held almost 50 percent of the civil service positions, and the number of women in agriculture doubled as "land girls" performed agricultural labor usually undertaken by men.

The government encouraged the "Dig for Victory" campaign to increase food production. Fields normally reserved for athletic events were turned over to citizens to plant gardens in "Grow Your Own Food" campaigns. Even with 1.4 million new gardens in 1943, Britain still faced a shortage of food as German submarines continued to sink hundreds of British merchant vessels. Food rationing, with its weekly allotments of bacon, sugar, fats, and eggs, intensified during the war as the British became accustomed to a diet dominated by bread and potatoes. For many British people, hours after work were spent in such wartime activities as "Dig for Victory," the Civil Defence, or the Home Guard. The Home Guard had been founded in 1940 to fight off German invaders. Even elderly people were expected to help manufacture airplane parts in their homes.

During the war, the British placed much emphasis on a planned economy. In 1942, the government created a ministry for fuel and power to control the coal industry and a ministry for production to oversee supplies for the armed forces. Although controls and bureaucratic "red tape" became unpopular, especially with businesspeople, most British citizens seemed to accept that total war required unusual governmental interference in people's lives. The British did make substantial gains in manufacturing

war matériel. Tank production quadrupled between 1940 and 1942, and the production of aircraft grew from 8,000 in 1939 to 26,000 in 1943 and 1944.

THE SOVIET UNION World War II had an enormous impact on the Soviet Union. Known to the Soviets as the Great Patriotic War, the German-Soviet war witnessed the greatest land battles in history as well as incredible ruthlessness. To Nazi Germany, it was a war of oppression and annihilation that called for merciless measures. Two out of every five persons killed in World War II were Soviet citizens.

The shift to a war footing necessitated only limited administrative changes in the Soviet Union. As the central authority, the dictator Joseph Stalin simply created a system of "supercentralization," by which he directed military and political affairs. All civil and military organizations were subjected to the control of the Communist Party and the Soviet police.

The initial defeats of the Soviet Union led to drastic emergency mobilization measures that affected the civilian population. Leningrad, for example, experienced nine hundred days of siege, during which its inhabitants became so desperate for food that they ate dogs, cats, and mice. As the German army made its rapid advance into Soviet territory, the factories in the western part of the Soviet Union were dismantled and shipped to the interior—to the Urals, western Siberia, and the Volga region. Machines were placed on the bare ground, and walls went up around them as workers began their work. The Kharkov Tank Factory produced its first twenty-five T-34 tanks only ten weeks after the plant had been rebuilt.

This widespread military, industrial, and economic mobilization created yet another industrial revolution for the Soviet Union. Stalin labeled it a "battle of machines," and the Soviets won, producing 78,000 tanks and 98,000 artillery pieces. Fifty-five percent of Soviet national income went for war matériel, compared to 15 percent in 1940. As a result of the emphasis on military goods, Soviet citizens experienced incredible shortages of both food and housing. Civilian food consumption fell by 40 percent during the war; in the Volga area, the Urals, and Siberia, workers lived in dugouts or dilapidated barracks.

Soviet women played a major role in the war effort. Women and girls worked in factories, mines, and railroads. Women constituted between 26 and 35 percent of the laborers in mines and 48 percent in the oil industry. Overall, the number of women working in industry increased almost 60 percent. Soviet women were also expected to dig antitank ditches and work as air-raid wardens. In addition, the Soviet Union was the only country in World War II to use women as combatants. Soviet women served as snipers and also as aircrews in bomber squadrons. The female pilots who helped defeat the Germans at Stalingrad were known as the "Night Witches."

Soviet peasants were asked to bear enormous burdens. Not only did the peasants furnish 60 percent of the military forces, but at the same time, they were expected to feed the Red Army and the Soviet people under very trying conditions. The German occupation in the early months of the war resulted in the loss of 47 percent of the country's grain-producing regions. Although new land was opened in the Urals, Siberia, and Soviet Asia, a shortage of labor and equipment hindered the effort to expand agricultural production. Because farm tractors and trucks were requisitioned to carry guns for the military, women and children were literally harnessed to do the plowing, and everywhere peasants worked long hours on collective farms for no pay. In 1943, the Soviet harvest was only 60 percent of its 1940 figure, a shortfall that meant extreme hardship for many people.

Total mobilization produced victory for the Soviet Union. Stalin and the Communist Party had quickly realized after the start of the German invasion that the Soviet people would not fight for Communist ideology but would do battle to preserve "Mother Russia." Government propaganda played on patriotic feelings. In a speech on the anniversary of the Bolshevik Revolution in November 1941, Stalin rallied the Soviet people by speaking of the country's past heroes, including the famous tsars of imperial Russia.

THE UNITED STATES The home front in the United States was quite different from those of its two chief wartime allies, largely because the United States faced no threat of war in its own territory. Although the economy and labor force were slow to mobilize, eventually the United States became the arsenal of the Allied powers, producing the military equipment they needed. The mobilization of the United States also had a great impact on American social and economic developments.

The immediate impact of mobilization was a dramatic expansion of the American economy, which ultimately brought an end to the Great Depression. Old factories were converted from peacetime goods to war goods, and many new factories were built. Massive amounts of government money also financed new industries, such as chemicals and electronics. A new government Office of Scientific Research and Development provided funds for contracts with universities and scientists to create such new products as rocket engines. The Manhattan Project for the development of an atomic bomb, which employed 130,000 people and cost $2 billion, involved the cooperation of scientists, defense contractors, and the federal government.

American industry supplied not only the U.S. armed forces but also the other Allies with the huge quantities of tanks, trucks, jeeps, and airplanes needed to win the war. During the war years, gross national product (GNP) rose by 15 percent a year. During the high point of war production in the United States in November 1943, the nation was constructing six ships a day and $6 billion worth of other military equipment a month. The production of airplanes increased from 6,000 in 1939 to more than 96,000 in 1944.

Industrial mobilization led to an increased government role in the economy. The federal bureaucracy grew dramatically with the establishment of a War Production Board, which allocated resources and managed production; a War Labor Board, which settled labor disputes; and an Office of Price Administration, which controlled prices and rationed scarce goods, such as gasoline, rubber, and meat.

The mobilization of the American economy also caused social problems. The construction of new factories created boomtowns where thousands came to work but then faced a shortage of houses, health facilities, and schools. The dramatic expansion of small towns into large cities often brought a breakdown in traditional social mores, especially evident in the increase in teenage prostitution. Economic mobilization also led to a widespread movement of people, which in turn created new social tensions. Sixteen million men and women were enrolled in the military, and another 16 million, mostly wives and sweethearts of the servicemen or workers looking for jobs, also relocated. More than one million African Americans migrated from the rural South to the industrial cities of the North and West, looking for jobs in industry. The presence of African Americans in areas where they had not lived before led to racial tensions and sometimes even racial riots. In Detroit in June 1943, white mobs roamed the streets attacking African Americans. Many of the one million African Americans who enlisted in the military, only to be segregated in their own battle units, were angered by the way they were treated. Some became militant and prepared to fight for their civil rights.

Japanese Americans were treated even more shabbily. On the West Coast, 110,000 Japanese Americans, 65 percent of whom had been born in the United States, were removed to camps encircled by barbed wire and required to take loyalty oaths. Although public officials claimed that this policy was necessary for security reasons, no similar treatment of German Americans or Italian Americans ever took place. The racism inherent in this treatment of Japanese Americans was evident when the California governor, Culbert Olson, said, "You know, when I look out at a group of Americans of German or Italian descent, I can tell whether they're loyal or not. I can tell how they think and even perhaps what they are thinking. But it is impossible for me to do this with inscrutable orientals, and particularly the Japanese."[15]

GERMANY   In August 1914, Germans had enthusiastically cheered their soldiers marching off to war. In September 1939, the streets were quiet. Many Germans were apathetic or, even worse for the Nazi regime, had a foreboding of disaster. Hitler was very aware of the importance of the home front. He believed that the collapse of the home front in World War I had caused Germany's defeat, and in his determination to avoid a repetition of that experience, he adopted economic policies that may indeed have cost Germany the war.

To maintain the morale of the home front during the first two years of the war, Hitler refused to convert production from consumer goods to armaments. Blitzkrieg allowed the Germans to win quick victories, after which they could plunder the food and raw materials of conquered countries in order to avoid diverting resources away from the civilian economy. After the German defeats on the Soviet front and the American entry into the war, the economic situation changed. Early in 1942, Hitler finally ordered a massive increase in armaments production and the size of the army. Hitler's personal architect, Albert Speer (SHPAYR), was made minister for armaments and munitions in 1942. By eliminating waste and rationalizing procedures, Speer was able to triple the production of armaments between 1942 and 1943 despite the intense Allied air raids. Speer's urgent plea for a total mobilization of resources for the war effort went unheeded, however. Hitler, fearful of civilian morale problems that would undermine the home front, refused any dramatic cuts in the production of consumer goods. A total mobilization of the economy was not implemented until 1944, when schools, theaters, and cafés were closed and Speer was finally permitted to use all remaining resources for the production of a few basic military items. By that time, it was in vain. Total war mobilization was too little and too late in July 1944 to save Germany from defeat.

The war produced a reversal in Nazi attitudes toward women. Nazi resistance to female employment declined as the war progressed and more and more men were called up for military service. Nazi magazines now proclaimed, "We see the woman as the eternal mother of our people, but also as the working and fighting comrade of the man."[16] But the number of women working in industry, agriculture, commerce, and domestic service increased only slightly. The total number of employed women in September 1944 was 14.9 million, compared to 14.6 in May 1939. Many women, especially those of the middle class, resisted regular employment, particularly in factories. Even the introduction of labor conscription for women in January 1943 failed to achieve much as women found ingenious ways to avoid the regulations.

JAPAN   Wartime Japan was a highly mobilized society. To guarantee its control over all national resources, the government set up a planning board to control prices, wages, the utilization of labor, and the allocation of resources. Traditional habits of obedience and hierarchy, buttressed by the concept of imperial divinity, were emphasized to encourage citizens to sacrifice their resources, and sometimes their lives, for the national cause. Especially important was the code of *bushido* (BOO-shee-doh), or the way of the warrior, the old code of morality of the samurai, who had played a prominent military role in medieval and early modern Japanese history. The code of *bushido* was revived during the nationalistic fervor of the 1930s. Based on an ideal of loyalty and service, the code emphasized the obligation to honor and defend emperor, country, and family and to sacrifice one's life if one failed in this sacred mission. The system culminated in the final years of the war when young Japanese were encouraged to volunteer en masse to serve as pilots in suicide missions—known as *kamikaze* (kah-mi-KAH-zay) ("divine wind")—against U.S. warships.

Women's rights, too, were to be sacrificed to the greater national cause. Already by 1937, Japanese women were being exhorted to fulfill their patriotic duty by bearing more children and by espousing the slogans of the Greater Japanese Women's Association. Nevertheless, Japan was extremely reluctant to mobilize women on behalf of the war effort. General Hideki Tojo (hee-DEK-ee TOH-joh), prime minister from 1941 to 1944, opposed female employment, arguing that "the weakening of the family system would be the weakening of the nation.... We are able to do our duties only because we have wives and mothers at home."[17] Female employment increased during the war, but only in areas where women traditionally had worked, such as the textile industry and farming. Instead of using women to meet labor shortages, the Japanese government brought in Korean and Chinese laborers.

Front-Line Civilians: The Bombing of Cities

Bombing was used in World War II in a variety of ways: against nonhuman military targets, against enemy troops, and against civilian populations. The use of bombs made World War II as devastating for civilians as for front-line soldiers (see the box on p. 876). A small number of bombing raids in the last year of World War I had given rise to the argument, first expressed by the Italian general Giulio Douhet (JOOL-yoh doo-AY) and then widely accepted,

The Bombing of Civilians

The home front became a battle front when civilian populations became the targets of mass bombing raids. Many people believed that mass bombing could effectively weaken the morale of the civilian population and shorten the war. Rarely did it achieve its goal. In these selections, British, German, and Japanese civilians relate their experiences during bombing raids.

＋·≡✦≡·＋

London, 1940

Early last evening, the noise was terrible. My husband and Mr. P. were trying to play chess in the kitchen. I was playing draughts with Kenneth in the cupboard.... Presently I heard a stifled voice "Mummy! I don't know what's become of my glasses." "I should think they are tied up in my wool." My knitting had disappeared and wool seemed to be everywhere! We heard a whistle, a bang which shook the house, and an explosion.... Well, we straightened out, decided draughts and chess were no use under the circumstances, and waited for a lull so we could have a pot of tea.

Hamburg, 1943

As the many fires broke through the roofs of the burning buildings, a column of heated air rose more than two and a half miles high and one and a half miles in diameter.... This column was turbulent, and it was fed from its base by in-rushing cooler ground-surface air. One and one half miles from the fires this draught increased the wind velocity from eleven to thirty-three miles per hour. At the edge of the area the velocities must have been appreciably greater, as trees three feet in diameter were uprooted. In a short time the temperature reached ignition point for all combustibles, and the entire area was ablaze. In such fires complete burn-out occurred; that is, no trace of combustible material remained, and only after two days were the areas cool enough to approach.

Hiroshima, August 6, 1945

I heard the airplane; I looked up at the sky, it was a sunny day, the sky was blue.... Then I saw something drop—and pow!—a big explosion knocked me down. Then I was unconscious—I don't know for how long. Then I was conscious but I couldn't see anything.... Then I see people moving away and I just follow them. It is not light like it was before, it is more like evening. I look around; houses are all flat!... I follow the people to the river. I couldn't hear anything, my ears are blocked up. I am thinking a bomb has dropped!... I didn't know my hands were burned, nor my face.... My eyes were swollen and felt closed up. ✈

Q What common elements do you find in these three different descriptions of bombing raids? What effect did aerial bombing have on the nature of modern warfare?

---

that the public outcry generated by the bombing of civilian populations would be an effective way to coerce governments into making peace. Consequently, European air forces began to develop long-range bombers in the 1930s.

LUFTWAFFE ATTACKS The first sustained use of civilian bombing contradicted Douhet's theory. Beginning in early September 1940, the German Luftwaffe subjected London and many other British cities and towns to nightly air raids, making the Blitz (as the British called the German air raids) a national experience. Londoners took the first heavy blows and set the standard for the rest of the British population by refusing to panic. One British woman expressed well what many others apparently felt:

> It was a beautiful summer night, so warm it was incredible, and made more beautiful than ever by the red glow from the East, where the docks were burning. We stood and stared for a minute, and I tried to fix the scene in my mind, because one day this will be history, and I shall be one of those who actually saw it. I wasn't frightened any more.[18]

But London morale was helped by the fact that German raids were widely scattered over a very large city. Smaller communities were more directly affected by the devastation. On November 14, 1940, for example, the Luftwaffe destroyed hundreds of shops and 100 acres of the city center of Coventry. The destruction of smaller cities did produce morale problems as wild rumors of heavy casualties spread quickly in these communities. Nevertheless, morale was soon restored. In any case, war production in these areas seems to have been little affected by the raids.

THE BOMBING OF GERMANY The British failed to learn from their own experience, however, and soon proceeded to bomb German cities. Churchill and his advisers believed that destroying German communities would break civilian morale and bring victory. Major bombing raids began in 1942 under the direction of Arthur Harris, the wartime leader of the British air force's Bomber Command, which was rearmed with four-engine heavy bombers capable of taking the war into the center of occupied Europe. On May 31, 1942, Cologne became the first German city to be subjected to an attack by one thousand bombers.

With the entry of the Americans into the war, the bombing strategy changed. American planes flew daytime missions aimed at the precision bombing of transportation facilities and war industries, while the British Bomber Command continued nighttime saturation bombing of all German cities with populations over 100,000. Bombing raids added an element of terror to circumstances already made difficult by growing shortages of food, clothing, and fuel. Germans especially feared the incendiary bombs, which created firestorms that swept destructive paths through the cities. Four raids on Hamburg in August 1943 produced temperatures of 1,800 degrees Fahrenheit, obliterated half the city's buildings, and killed thousands of civilians. The ferocious bombing of Dresden from February 13 to 15, 1945, created a firestorm that may have killed as many as 35,000 inhabitants and refugees (see Images of Everyday Life on p. 878). Even some Allied leaders began to criticize what they saw as the unnecessary terror bombing of German cities. Urban dwellers became accustomed to living in air-raid shelters, usually cellars in businesses or houses. Occupants of shelters could be crushed to death, however, if the shelters were hit directly or die by suffocation from the effects of high-explosive bombs. Not until 1943 did Nazi leaders begin to evacuate women and children to rural areas. But evacuation created its own problems since people in country villages were often hostile to the urban newcomers.

Germany suffered enormously from the Allied bombing raids. Millions of buildings were destroyed, and possibly half a million civilians died in the raids. Nevertheless, it is highly unlikely that Allied bombing sapped the morale of the German people. Instead, Germans, whether pro-Nazi or anti-Nazi, fought on stubbornly, often driven simply by a desire to live. Nor did the bombing destroy Germany's industrial capacity. The Allied Strategic Bombing survey revealed that the production of war matériel actually increased between 1942 and 1944. Even in 1944 and 1945, Allied raids cut German production of armaments by only 7 percent. Nevertheless, the widespread destruction of transportation systems and fuel supplies made it extremely difficult for the new matériel to reach the German military. Because of strong German air defenses, air raids were also costly for the Allies. Nearly 40,000 Allied planes were destroyed, and 160,000 airmen lost their lives.

The destruction of German cities from the air did accomplish one major goal. There would be no stab-in-the-back myth after World War II as there had been after World War I. The loss of the war could not be blamed on the collapse of the home front. Many Germans understood that the home front had been a battlefront, and they had fought on their front just as the soldiers had on theirs.

THE BOMBING OF JAPAN: THE ATOMIC BOMB The bombing of civilians eventually reached a new level with the dropping of the first atomic bomb on Japan. Fearful of German attempts to create a superbomb through the use of uranium, the American government pursued a dual strategy. While sabotaging German efforts, the United States and Britain recruited scientists, including many who had fled from Germany, to develop an atomic bomb. Working under the direction of J. Robert Oppenheimer at a secret laboratory in Los Alamos, New Mexico, Allied scientists built and tested the first atomic bomb by the summer of 1945. A new era in warfare was about to begin.

Japan was especially vulnerable to air raids because its air force had been virtually destroyed in the course of the war, and its crowded cities were built of flimsy materials. Attacks on Japanese cities by the new American B-29 Superfortresses, the biggest bombers of the war, had begun on November 24, 1944. By the summer of 1945, many of Japan's factories had been destroyed, along with one-fourth of its dwellings. After the Japanese government decreed the mobilization of all people between the ages of thirteen and sixty into a "people's volunteer corps," President Truman and his advisers feared that Japanese fanaticism might mean heavy American casualties. This concern led them to drop the atomic bomb on Hiroshima (August 6) and Nagasaki (August 9). The destruction was incredible. Of 76,000 buildings near the hypocenter of the explosion in Hiroshima, 70,000 were flattened; 140,000 of the city's 400,000 inhabitants died by the end of 1945. By the end of 1950, another 50,000 had perished from the effects of radiation.

Aftermath of the War

 FOCUS QUESTIONS: What were the costs of World War II? How did the Allies' visions of postwar Europe differ, and how did these differences contribute to the emergence of the Cold War?

World War II was the most destructive war in history. Much had been at stake. Nazi Germany followed a world-view based on racial extermination and the enslavement of millions in order to create an Aryan racial empire. The Japanese, fueled by extreme nationalist ideals, also pursued dreams of empire in Asia that led to mass murder and untold devastation. Fighting the Axis powers in World War II required the mobilization of millions of ordinary men and women in the Allied countries who rose to the occasion and struggled to preserve a different way of life. As Winston Churchill once put it, "War is horrible, but slavery is worse."

The Costs of World War II

The costs of World War II were enormous. At least 21 million soldiers died. Civilian deaths were even greater and are now estimated at around 40 million, of whom more than 28 million were Russian and Chinese. The Soviet Union experienced the greatest losses: 10 million soldiers and 19 million civilians. In 1945, millions of people around the world faced starvation; in Europe, 100 million people depended on food relief of some kind.

Millions of people had also been uprooted by the war and became "displaced persons." Europe alone may have had 30 million displaced persons, many of whom found it hard to return home. After the war, millions of Germans were

The Impact of Total War

World War II was a total war for civilians as political leaders came to see the bombing of civilians as a legitimate way to attempt to demoralize the population and end the war. The results of this policy are evident in these three scenes of life between 1941 and 1945. In the first photograph (top left), a group of refugees walk past a bombed tenement building, where 800 people died and 800 more were injured during a German bombing raid in March 1941 on Clydebank near Glasgow in Scotland. Only 7 of the city's 12,000 houses were left undamaged; 35,000 of the 47,000 inhabitants became homeless overnight. The raid on Clydebank was Scotland's only severe bombing experience. The city was attacked because of its proximity to nearby shipyards that were refitting ships to serve in the war. The second photograph (bottom left) shows the devastation in Dresden, Germany, as a result of British and American bombing raids on February 13 and 14, 1945. An area of 2.5 square miles in the city was destroyed, and as many as 35,000 people died. The most devastating destruction of civilians came near the end of World War II when the United States dropped atomic bombs on the Japanese cities of Hiroshima and Nagasaki. The panoramic view of Hiroshima after the bombing in the third photograph shows the incredible devastation produced by the atomic bomb.

© Keystone/Getty Images

© Bettmann/CORBIS

© J. R. Eyerman/Time Life Pictures/Getty Images

expelled from the Sudetenland in Czechoslovakia, and millions more were ejected from former eastern German territories that were turned over to Poland, all of which seemed reasonable to people who had suffered so much at the hands of the Germans. In Asia, millions of Japanese were returned from the former Japanese empire to Japan, while thousands of Korean forced laborers returned to Korea.

Everywhere cities lay in ruins. In Europe, physical devastation was especially bad in eastern and southeastern Europe as well as in the cities of western and central Europe. In Asia, China had experienced extensive devastation from eight years of conflict. So too had the Philippines, while large parts of the major cities in Japan had been destroyed in air raids. At the same time, millions of tons of shipping were now underneath the seas; factories, farms, transportation systems, bridges, and dams were in ruins. The total monetary cost of the war has been estimated at $4 trillion. The economies of most belligerents, with the exception of the United States, were left drained and on the brink of disaster.

The Allied War Conferences

The total victory of the Allies in World War II was succeeded not by true peace but by a new conflict known as the **Cold War** that dominated European and world politics for more than forty years. The Cold War stemmed from military, political, and ideological differences, especially between the Soviet Union and the United States, that became apparent at the Allied war conferences held in the last years of the war. Although Allied leaders were mostly preoccupied with how to end the war, they also were strongly motivated by differing and often conflicting visions of postwar Europe.

THE CONFERENCE AT TEHRAN Stalin, Roosevelt, and Churchill, the leaders of the Big Three of the Grand Alliance, met at Tehran (the capital of Iran) in November 1943 to decide the future course of the war. Their major tactical decision concerned the final assault on Germany, and after much debate, they decided on an American-British invasion of the Continent through France, which they scheduled for the spring of 1944. The acceptance of this plan had important consequences. It meant that Soviet and British-American forces would meet in defeated Germany along a north-south dividing line and that, most likely, eastern Europe would be liberated by Soviet forces. The Allies also agreed to a partition of postwar Germany, but differences over questions like the frontiers of Poland were carefully set aside. Roosevelt was pleased with the accord with Stalin. Harry Hopkins, one of Roosevelt's advisers at the conference, remarked:

Tehran Conference (1943)

> We really believed in our hearts that this was the dawn of the new day. . . . We were absolutely certain that we had won the first great victory of the peace—and by "we," I mean all of us, the whole civilized human race. The Russians had proved that they could be reasonable and far-seeing and there wasn't any doubt in the minds of the President or any of us that we could live with them and get along with them peacefully for as far into the future as any of us could imagine.[19]

THE YALTA CONFERENCE By the time of the conference at Yalta in Ukraine in February 1945, the defeat of Germany was a foregone conclusion. The Western powers, which had earlier believed that the Soviets were in a weak position, were now faced with the reality of 11 million Red Army soldiers taking possession of eastern and much of central Europe. Stalin was still operating under the notion of spheres of influence. He was deeply suspicious of the Western powers and desired a buffer to protect the Soviet Union from possible future Western aggression. At the same time, however, Stalin was eager to obtain economically important resources and strategic military positions. Roosevelt by this time was moving away from the notion of spheres of influence to the ideal of self-determination. He called for "the end of the system of unilateral action, exclusive alliances, and spheres of influence." The Grand Alliance approved the "Declaration on Liberated Europe." This was a pledge to assist liberated European nations in the creation of "democratic institutions of their own choice." Liberated countries were to hold free elections to determine their political systems.

Yalta Conference (1945)

At Yalta, Roosevelt sought Soviet military help against Japan. The atomic bomb was not yet assured, and American military planners feared the possible loss of many men in amphibious assaults on the Japanese home islands. Roosevelt therefore agreed to Stalin's price for military assistance against Japan: possession of Sakhalin and the Kurile Islands as well as two warm-water ports and railroad rights in Manchuria.

The creation of the United Nations was a major American concern at Yalta. Roosevelt hoped to ensure the participation of the Big Three powers in a postwar international organization before difficult issues divided them into hostile camps. After a number of compromises, both Churchill and Stalin accepted Roosevelt's plans for a United Nations organization and set the first meeting for San Francisco in April 1945.

The issues of Germany and eastern Europe were treated less decisively. The Big Three reaffirmed that Germany must surrender unconditionally and created four occupation zones. Churchill, over the objections of the Soviets and Americans, insisted that the French be given one occupation zone, carved out of the British and American zones. German reparations were set at $20 billion. A compromise was also worked out with regard to Poland. It was agreed that a provisional government would be established with members of both the Lublin Poles, who were Polish Communists living in exile in the Soviet

The Victorious Allied Leaders at Yalta. Even before World War II ended, the leaders of the Big Three of the Grand Alliance, Churchill, Roosevelt, and Stalin (seated, left to right), met in wartime conferences to plan the final assault on Germany and negotiate the outlines of the postwar settlement. At the Yalta meeting (February 5–11, 1945), the three leaders concentrated on postwar issues. The American president, who died two months later, was already a worn-out man at Yalta.

Union, and the London Poles, who were non-Communists exiled in Britain. Stalin also agreed to free elections in the future to determine a new government. But the issue of free elections in eastern Europe caused a serious rift between the Soviets and the Americans. The principle was that eastern European governments would be freely elected, but they were also supposed to be pro-Soviet. As Churchill expressed it, "The Poles will have their future in their own hands, with the single limitation that they must honestly follow in harmony with their allies, a policy friendly to Russia."[20] This attempt to reconcile two irreconcilable goals was doomed to failure, as soon became evident at the next conference of the Big Three powers.

INTENSIFYING DIFFERENCES   Even before the conference at Potsdam (PAHTS-dam) took place in July 1945, Western relations with the Soviets were deteriorating rapidly. The Grand Alliance had been one of necessity in which disagreements had been subordinated to the pragmatic concerns of the war. The Allied powers' only common aim was the defeat of Nazism. Once this aim had all but been accomplished, the many differences that troubled East-West relations came to the surface. Each side committed acts that the other viewed as unbecoming of "allies."

From the perspective of the Soviets, the United States' termination of Lend-Lease aid before the war was over and its failure to respond to the Soviet request for a $6 billion loan for reconstruction exposed the Western desire to keep the Soviet state weak. On the American side, the Soviet Union's failure to fulfill its Yalta pledge on the "Declaration on Liberated Europe" as applied to eastern Europe set a dangerous precedent. This was evident in Romania as early as February 1945, when the Soviets engineered a coup and installed a new government under the Communist Petra Groza (PET-ruh GRO-zhuh), called the "Little Stalin." One month later, the Soviets sabotaged

the Polish settlement by arresting the London Poles and their sympathizers and installing the Soviet-backed Lublin Poles in power. To the Americans, the Soviets seemed to be asserting control of eastern European countries under puppet Communist regimes (see Map 27.5).

THE POTSDAM CONFERENCE   The Potsdam Conference of July 1945 consequently began under a cloud of mistrust. Roosevelt had died on April 12 and had been succeeded by Harry Truman. During the conference, Truman received word that the atomic bomb had been successfully tested. Some historians have argued that this knowledge resulted in Truman's stiffened resolve against the Soviets. Whatever the reasons, there was a new coldness in the relations between the Soviets and Americans. At Potsdam, Truman demanded free elections throughout eastern Europe. Stalin responded, "A freely elected government in any of these East European countries would be anti-Soviet, and that we cannot allow."[21] After a bitterly fought and devastating war, Stalin sought absolute military security. To him, it could be gained only by the presence of Communist states in eastern Europe. Free elections might result in governments hostile to the Soviets. By the middle of 1945, only an invasion by Western forces could undo developments in eastern Europe, and after the world's most destructive conflict had ended, few people favored such a policy.

Emergence of the Cold War

The Soviets did not view their actions as dangerous expansionism but as legitimate security maneuvers. Was it not the West that had attacked the East? When Stalin sought help against the Nazis in the 1930s, had not the West turned a deaf ear? But there was little sympathy in the West for Soviet fears and even less trust in Stalin. When the American secretary of state, James Byrnes,

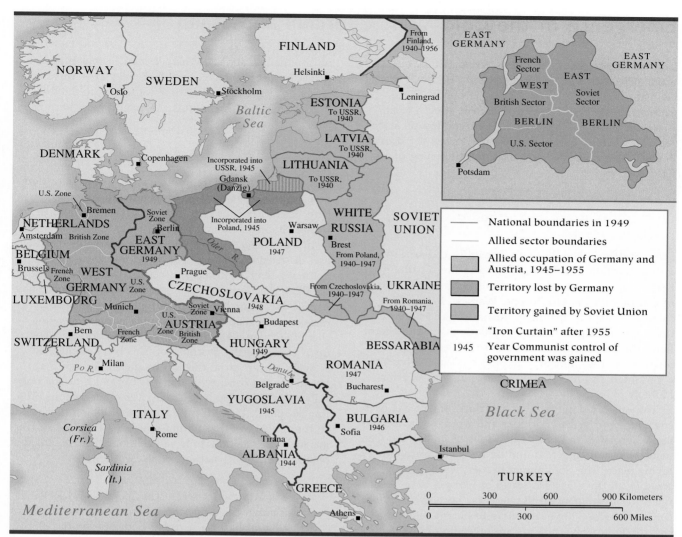

MAP 27.5   Territorial Changes After World War II. In the last months of World War II, the Red Army occupied much of eastern Europe. Stalin sought pro-Soviet satellite states in the region as a buffer against future invasions from western Europe, whereas Britain and the United States wanted democratically elected governments. Soviet military control of the territory settled the question.

Q *Which country gained the greatest territory at the expense of Germany?*

proposed a twenty-five-year disarmament of Germany, the Soviet Union rejected it. In the West, many saw this as proof of Stalin's plans to expand in central Europe and create a Communist East German state. When Byrnes responded by announcing that American troops would be needed in Europe for an indefinite time and made moves that foreshadowed the creation of an independent West Germany, the Soviets saw this as a direct threat to Soviet security in Europe.

As the war slowly receded into the past, the reality of conflicting ideologies had reappeared. Many in the West interpreted Soviet policy as part of a worldwide Communist conspiracy. The Soviets, for their part, viewed Western, especially American, policy as nothing less than global capitalist expansionism or, in Leninist terms, economic imperialism. Vyacheslav Molotov (vyich-chiss-SLAHF MAHL-uh-tawf), the Russian foreign minister, referred to the Americans as "insatiable imperialists" and "warmongering groups of adventurers."[22] In March 1946, in a speech to an American audience, former British prime minister Winston Churchill declared that "an iron curtain" had "descended across the continent," dividing Germany and Europe into two hostile camps. Stalin branded Churchill's speech a "call to war with the Soviet Union" (see the box on p. 882). Only months after the world's most devastating conflict had ended, the world seemed once again bitterly divided. Would the twentieth-century crisis of Western civilization never end?

Emergence of the Cold War: Churchill and Stalin

Less than a year after the end of World War II, the major Allies that had fought together to destroy Hitler's Germany had divided into two hostile camps. These excerpts, taken from Winston Churchill's speech to an American audience on March 5, 1946, and Joseph Stalin's reply to Churchill only nine days later, reveal the divisions in the Western world that marked the beginning of the Cold War.

Churchill's Speech at Fulton, Missouri, March 5, 1946

From Stettin in the Baltic to Trieste in the Adriatic, an iron curtain has descended across the continent. Behind that line lie all the capitals of the ancient states of central and eastern Europe. Warsaw, Berlin, Prague, Vienna, Budapest, Belgrade, Bucharest, and Sofia, all these famous cities and the populations around them lie in the Soviet sphere and all are subject, in one form or another, not only to Soviet influence but to a very high and increasing measure of control from Moscow. . . .

The Russian-dominated Polish Government has been encouraged to make enormous and wrongful inroads upon Germany, and mass expulsions of millions of Germans on a scale grievous and undreamed of are now taking place. The Communist parties, which were very small in all these eastern states of Europe, have been raised to preeminence and power far beyond their numbers and are seeking everywhere to obtain totalitarian control. Police governments are prevailing in nearly every case, and so far, except in Czechoslovakia, there is no true democracy. . . . Whatever conclusions may be drawn from these facts—and facts they are—this is certainly not the liberated Europe we fought to build up. Nor is it one which contains the essentials of permanent peace.

Stalin's Reply to Churchill, March 14, 1946

In substance, Mr. Churchill now stands in the position of a firebrand of war. And Mr. Churchill is not alone here. He has friends not only in England but also in the United States of America.

In this respect, one is reminded remarkably of Hitler and his friends. Hitler began to set war loose by announcing his racial theory, declaring that only people speaking the German language represent a fully valuable nation. Mr. Churchill begins to set war loose, also by a racial theory, maintaining that only nations speaking the English language are fully valuable nations, called upon to decide the destinies of the entire world.

The German racial theory brought Hitler and his friends to the conclusion that the Germans, as the only fully valuable nation, must rule over other nations. The English racial theory brings Mr. Churchill and his friends to the conclusion that nations speaking the English language, being the only fully valuable nations, should rule over the remaining nations of the world.

Q What do the statements of Churchill and Stalin tell us about the origins and rhetoric of the Cold War? Why might it be said that both sides in this global conflict persistently misunderstood the other?

CHAPTER SUMMARY

Between 1933 and 1939, Europeans watched as Adolf Hitler rebuilt Germany into a great military power. For Hitler, military power was an absolute prerequisite for the creation of a German racial empire that would dominate Europe and the world for generations to come. During that same period, the nation of Japan fell under the influence of military leaders who conspired with right-wing forces to push a program of expansion at the expense of China and the Soviet Union as well as territories in Southeast Asia. The ambitions of Germany in Europe and those of Japan in Asia led to a global conflict that became the most devastating war in human history.

The Axis nations, Germany, Italy, and Japan, proved victorious during the first two years of the war, which began after the German invasion of Poland on September 1, 1939. By 1942, the war had begun to turn in favor of the Allies, an alliance of Great Britain, the Soviet Union, and the United States. The Japanese advance was ended at the naval battles of the Coral Sea and Midway in 1942. In February 1943, the Soviets won the Battle of Stalingrad and began to push westward. By mid-1943, Germany and Italy had been driven out of North Africa; in June 1944, Rome fell to the Allies, and an Allied invasion force landed in

Normandy in France. After the Soviets linked up with British and American forces in April 1945, Hitler committed suicide, and the war in Europe came to an end. After atomic bombs were dropped on Hiroshima and Nagasaki in August 1945, the war in Asia also ended.

During its domination of Europe, the Nazi empire brought death and destruction to many, especially Jews, minorities, and others that the Nazis considered racially inferior peoples. The Japanese New Order in Asia, while claiming to promote a policy of "Asia for the Asians" also brought economic exploitation, severe hardships, and often death for the subject peoples under Japanese control. All sides bombed civilian populations, making World War II as devastating for civilians as for front-line soldiers.

If Hitler had been successful, the Nazi New Order, built on authoritarianism, racial extermination, and the brutal oppression of peoples, would have a meant a triumph of barbarism and the end of freedom and equality, which, however imperfectly realized, had become important ideals in Western civilization.

The Nazis lost, but only after tremendous sacrifices and costs. Much of European civilization lay in ruins, and the old Europe had disappeared forever. Europeans, who been accustomed to dominating the world at the beginning of the twentieth century, now watched helplessly at mid-century as the two new superpowers created by the two world wars took control of their destinies. Even before the last battles had been fought, the United States and the Soviet Union had arrived at different visions of the postwar European world. No sooner had the war ended than their differences gave rise to a new and potentially even more devastating conflict known as the Cold War.

CHAPTER TIMELINE

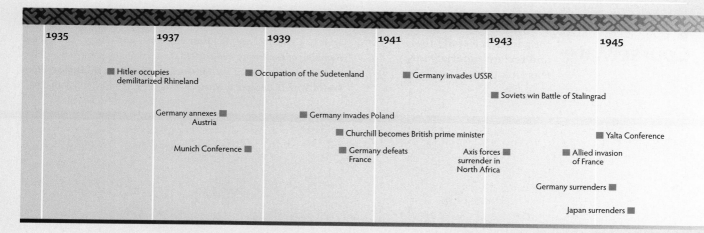

1935   1937   1939   1941   1943   1945

- Hitler occupies demilitarized Rhineland
- Occupation of the Sudetenland
- Germany invades USSR
- Soviets win Battle of Stalingrad
- Germany annexes Austria
- Germany invades Poland
- Churchill becomes British prime minister
- Yalta Conference
- Munich Conference
- Germany defeats France
- Axis forces surrender in North Africa
- Allied invasion of France
- Germany surrenders
- Japan surrenders

CHAPTER REVIEW

Upon Reflection

Q How do you account for the early successes of the Germans from 1939 through 1941?

Q How did the Nazis attempt to establish a New Order in Europe after their military victories, and what were the results of their efforts?

Q How did the attempt to arrive at a peace settlement after World War II lead to the beginnings of a new conflict known as the Cold War?

Key Terms

appeasement (p. 852)
Blitzkrieg (p. 852)
panzer division (p. 852)
unconditional surrender (p. 861)
Nazi New Order (p. 865)

Final Solution (p. 868)
Einsatzgruppen (p. 868)
Cold War (p. 879)

Suggestions for Further Reading

PRELUDE TO WAR On the causes of World War II, see **A. J. Crozier, *Causes of the Second World War*** (Oxford, 1997). On the origins of the war in the Pacific, see **A. Iriye, *The Origins of the Second World War in Asia and the Pacific*** (London, 1987). The basic study of Germany's prewar foreign policy can be found in **G. Weinberg, *The Foreign Policy of Hitler's Germany: Diplomatic Revolution in Europe, 1933–36*** (Chicago, 1970), and ***The Foreign Policy of Hitler's Germany: Starting World War II, 1937–1939*** (Chicago, 1980).

GENERAL WORKS General works on World War II include the comprehensive work by **G. Weinberg, *A World at Arms: A Global History of World War II,*** 2nd ed. (Cambridge, 2005), and

J. Campbell, *The Experience of World War II* (New York, 1989). On Hitler's attack on Poland, see **A. B. Rossino, *Hitler Strikes Poland: Blitzkrieg, Ideology, and Atrocity*** (Lawrence, Kans., 2003). The Eastern Front is covered in **O. Bartov, *The Eastern Front, 1941–45: German Troops and the Barbarisation of Warfare*** (London, 1986). For a good military history of World War II, see **W. Murray** and **A. Millett, *A War to Be Won: Fighting the Second World War*** (Cambridge, Mass., 2000). On the impact of the war on civilians, see **J. Bourke, *The Second World War: A People's History*** (Oxford, 2003).

THE NEW ORDER   A standard work on the German New Order in Russia is **A. Dallin, *German Rule in Russia, 1941–1945,*** rev. ed. (London, 1985). On Poland, see **P. T. Rutherford, *Prelude to the Final Solution: The Nazi Program for Deporting Ethnic Poles, 1939–1941*** (Lawrence, Kans., 2007). A fundamental study on resistance in Germany is **H. Mommsen, *Alternatives to Hitler: German Resistance Under the Third Reich,*** trans. **A. McGeoch** (Princeton, N.J., 2003).

Visit the CourseMate website at www.cengagebrain.com for additional study tools and review materials for this chapter.

THE HOLOCAUST   The best studies of the Holocaust include **R. Hilberg, *The Destruction of the European Jews,*** rev. ed., 3 vols. (New York, 1985); **S. Friedländer, *The Years of Extermination: Nazi Germany and the Jews, 1939–1945*** (New York, 2007); and **L. Yahil, *The Holocaust*** (Oxford, 1990). Other Nazi atrocities are examined in **R. C. Lukas, *Forgotten Holocaust: The Poles Under German Occupation, 1939–44,*** 2nd ed. (Lexington, Ky., 2001).

THE HOME FRONT   General studies on the impact of total war include **J. Costello, *Love, Sex and War: Changing Values, 1939–1945*** (London, 1985); **P. Summerfield, *Women Workers in the Second World War: Production and Patriarchy in Conflict*** (London, 1984); and **M. R. Marrus, *The Unwanted: European Refugees in the Twentieth Century*** (New York, 1985). On the home front in Germany, see **M. Kitchen, *Nazi Germany at War*** (New York, 1995), and **J. Stephenson, *The Nazi Organisation of Women*** (London, 1981). On the home front in Britain, see **S. Rose, *Which People's War? National Identity and Citizenship in Britain, 1939–1945*** (Oxford, 2003). The Soviet Union during the war is examined in **M. Harrison** and **J. Barber, *The Soviet Home Front 1941–1945*** (London, 1991).

THE BOMBING CAMPAIGNS   On the Allied bombing campaign against Germany, see **R. Hansen, *Fire and Fury: The Allied Bombing of Germany, 1942–1945*** (London, 2008). On the use of the atomic bomb in Japan, see **M. Gordin, *Five Days in August: How World War II Became a Nuclear War*** (Princeton, N.J., 2006).

AP* REVIEW QUESTIONS FOR CHAPTER 27

1. During the 1930s, the Jews of Germany

   (A) were effective in their efforts to prevent Nazi policies from taking effect.
   (B) looked to Britain and other western nations to intervene on their behalf.
   (C) believed that their plight could not get any worse and so became good citizens who followed the laws of the German government.
   (D) initiated a program known as "Zionism" in which many emigrated to the Middle East.
   (E) appealed successfully to the German government for relief against their persecution.

2. The turning point for the Allies during World War II came when Germany invaded

   (A) the Soviet Union.
   (B) Yugoslavia.
   (C) France.
   (D) Britain.
   (E) Italy.

3. When the invading Nazi army was turned back by the Russian winter and counterattacks from the Soviet army, Hitler

   (A) made irrational tactical decisions without consulting his generals.
   (B) heeded the warnings of his commanders by withdrawing the army until winter ended.
   (C) established a new alliance with the Soviet Union.
   (D) declared war on England, redirecting the Luftwaffe toward the British Isles.
   (E) surrendered on all fronts, bringing an end to World War II.

4. The Soviet Union

   (A) emerged from World War II with few casualties and only minor damage to its infrastructure.
   (B) suffered the greatest number of casualties among all warring states.
   (C) primarily used female combat troops after male units were depleted.
   (D) withdrew from World War II after the outbreak of the Bolshevik revolution.
   (E) allied with Japan in the infamous Tokyo-Moscow Pact.

5. As a neutral nation prior to 1941, the United States supported the Allies through the

   (A) Smoot-Hawley tariff.
   (B) Open Door Policy.
   (C) Lend-Lease Act.
   (D) Marshall Plan.
   (E) Berlin Airlift.

6. Stalin and Hitler

   (A) had similar political goals as they both supported totalitarian government and communism.
   (B) allied their countries with Japan throughout the course of World War II.
   (C) faced the attack and invasion of their countries by the Allied forces.
   (D) worked together secretly in the mutual division of Poland.
   (E) invaded North Africa in league with Mussolini at the start of the war.

7. During the war,

   (A) the Allied leaders met several times to solidify their common goals and confer on how best to end the war.
   (B) the Allied leaders allowed Russia to take the lead in peace talks as that country was on better terms with Germany and Japan.
   (C) the Allied leaders agreed that dropping an atomic bomb on Japan would be the most efficient way to end the war.
   (D) the leaders of the United States and Great Britain secretly met several times with Hitler to avoid angering the Soviet Union.
   (E) the Allied leaders decided that each country should determine its own policies, including when to end the war.

8. The U.S. involvement in World War II included all of the following areas EXCEPT

   (A) the Pacific.
   (B) the European Eastern Front.
   (C) the European Western Front.
   (D) the North African Front.
   (E) the beaches of Normandy.

9. Which of the following statements best explains the surrender of Japan in 1945?

   (A) The Japanese army was easily defeated whenever it met the Allied forces.
   (B) The bombings of Hiroshima and Nagasaki convinced the Japanese to end the war.
   (C) The sudden illness and death of Hirohito left the country without a leader.
   (D) A massive combined attack by the British, Soviet, and American forces crippled Japan.
   (E) Massive suicide attacks by Japanese pilots left the Japanese Empire defenseless.

10. After the end of World War II,

   (A) the world momentarily sought peace and a way to prevent future conflict.
   (B) the ideological divisions between the Allies, suppressed during the war, reemerged.
   (C) the United States and Great Britain retreated into isolationism on global issues.
   (D) most world leaders were leery of agreeing to military alliances for fear of being dragged into another armed conflict.
   (E) the world slipped back into an economic depression.

11. Following the end of World War II, the Soviet Union occupied all of the following regions EXCEPT

   (A) Estonia.
   (B) Latvia.
   (C) Lithuania.
   (D) Poland.
   (E) Yugoslavia.

12. In a speech at Westminster College in Fulton, Missouri, Winston Churchill said that "an 'iron curtain' has descended across the continent." This statement meant that

   (A) Europe was physically divided by a wall that separated the democratic West from the Communist East.
   (B) America should seek out political radicals and expel them from the country as they were dangerous and volatile.
   (C) Europe was ideologically divided and the two halves were allowed little interaction.
   (D) Japan and Germany would now be forever divided and prohibited from allying together.
   (E) Europeans were divided over the morality of using nuclear weapons to end wars.

13. Under Hitler's leadership,

   (A) Germany instituted the "final solution," resulting in the death of millions of Jews.
   (B) non-Jewish minorities such as Gypsies and Slavic peoples were sent to work camps, but were not killed.
   (C) German aircraft dropped two nuclear weapons in eastern Europe.
   (D) Germany's air attacks on London forced Britain's surrender.
   (E) the Nazis and their Soviet allies were able to dominate the course of the war.

14. Which of the following statements was true of occupied France?

   (A) Charles de Gaulle led the French Resistance against the Nazis.
   (B) French citizens willingly accepted the rule of the Germans.
   (C) the Vichy government achieved complete control over the actions of the people.
   (D) Jews were safe from Nazi attack.
   (E) the British led a variety of failed invasions leading up to D-Day.

Survivors cooking in the ruins of Nuremberg, Germany, at the end of World War II

Cold War and a New Western World, 1945–1965

CHAPTER OUTLINE
AND FOCUS QUESTIONS

Development of the Cold War

Q Why were the United States and the Soviet Union suspicious of each other after World War II, and what events between 1945 and 1949 heightened the tensions between the two nations? How and why did the Cold War become a global affair after 1949?

Europe and the World: Decolonization

Q Why and how did the European colonies in Africa, the Middle East, and Asia gain independence between 1945 and 1965?

Recovery and Renewal in Europe

Q What were the main developments in the Soviet Union, Eastern Europe, and Western Europe between 1945 and 1965?

The United States and Canada: A New Era

Q What were the main political developments in North America between 1945 and 1965?

Postwar Society and Culture in the Western World

Q What major changes occurred in Western society and culture between 1945 and 1965?

⌐ CRITICAL THINKING ⌐

Q What were the similarities and differences in the political, social, and economic history of Eastern Europe and Western Europe between 1945 and 1965?

THE END OF WORLD WAR II in Europe had been met with great joy. One visitor to Moscow reported, "I looked out of the window [at 2 A.M.], almost everywhere there were lights in the window—people were staying awake. Everyone embraced everyone else, someone sobbed aloud." But after the victory parades and celebrations, Europeans awoke to a devastating realization: their civilization was in ruins. Some wondered if Europe would ever regain its former prosperity and importance. Winston Churchill wrote, "What is Europe now? A rubble heap, a charnel house, a breeding ground of pestilence and hate." There was ample reason for his pessimism. Almost 40 million people (soldiers and civilians) had been killed during the preceding six years. Massive air raids and artillery bombardments had reduced many of the great cities of Europe to heaps of rubble. The Polish capital of Warsaw had been almost completely obliterated. An American general described Berlin: "Wherever we looked we saw desolation. It was like a city of the dead."

Suffering and shock were visible in every face. Dead bodies still remained in canals and lakes and were being dug out from under bomb debris. Millions of Europeans faced starvation as grain harvests were only half of what they had been in 1939. Millions were also homeless. In the parts of the Soviet Union that had been occupied by the Germans, almost 25 million people were without homes. The destruction of bridges, roads, and railroads had left transportation systems paralyzed. Untold millions of people had been uprooted by the war; now they became "displaced persons," trying to find food and then their way home. Eleven million prisoners of war had to be returned to their native countries while 15 million Germans and Eastern Europeans were driven out of countries where they were no longer wanted. Yet despite the chaos, Europe was soon on the road to a remarkable recovery. Already by 1950, Europe's industrial and agricultural output was 30 percent above prewar levels.

World War II had cost Europe more than physical destruction, however. European supremacy in world affairs had also been destroyed. After 1945, the colonial empires of the European nations disintegrated, and Europe's place in the world changed radically. As the Cold War conflict between the world's two superpowers—the United States and the Soviet Union—intensified, the European nations were divided into two armed camps dependent on one or the other of these two major powers. The United States and the Soviet Union, whose rivalry raised the specter of nuclear war, seemed to hold the survival of Europe and the world in their hands.

Development of the Cold War

Q FOCUS QUESTIONS: Why were the United States and the Soviet Union suspicious of each other after World War II, and what events between 1945 and 1949 heightened the tensions between the two nations? How and why did the Cold War become a global affair after 1949?

Even before World War II had ended, the two major Allied powers—the United States and the Soviet Union—had begun to disagree on the nature of the postwar European world. Unity had been maintained during the war because of the urgent need to defeat the Axis powers, but once they were defeated, the differences between the Americans and Soviets again surged to the front.

Confrontation of the Superpowers

Considerable historical debate has been waged about who was responsible for starting the Cold War. Both the United States and the Soviet Union took steps at the end of World War II that were unwise or might have been avoided. Both nations, however, were working within a framework conditioned by the past. Ultimately, the rivalry between the two superpowers stemmed from their different historical perspectives and their irreconcilable political ambitions. Intense competition for political and military supremacy had long been a regular feature of Western civilization. The United States and the Soviet Union were the heirs of that European tradition of power politics, and it should not surprise us that two such different systems would seek to extend their way of life to the rest of the world. Because of its need to feel secure on its western border, the Soviet Union was not prepared to give up the

advantages it had gained in Eastern Europe from Germany's defeat. But neither were American leaders willing to give up the power and prestige the United States had gained throughout the world. Suspicious of each other's motives, the United States and the Soviet Union soon raised their mutual fears to a level of intense competition (see the box on p. 887). In recent years, some historians have emphasized Soviet responsibility, especially in view of new evidence from previously closed Soviet archives that indicates that Joseph Stalin had even been willing to go to war to spread communism to all of Europe. Regardless of who was responsible, however, a number of events between 1945 and 1949 embroiled the Soviet Union and the United States in continual conflict.

DISAGREEMENT OVER EASTERN EUROPE   Eastern Europe was the first area of disagreement. The United States and Great Britain had championed self-determination and democratic freedom for the liberated nations of Eastern Europe. Stalin, however, fearful that the Eastern European nations would return to traditional anti-Soviet attitudes if they were permitted free elections, opposed the West's plans. Having liberated Eastern Europe from the Nazis, the Red Army proceeded to install pro-Soviet governing regimes in Poland, Romania, Bulgaria, and Hungary. These pro-Soviet governments satisfied Stalin's desire for a buffer zone against the West, but the local populations and their sympathizers in the West saw the regimes as an expansion of Stalin's empire. Only another war could change this situation, and few people wanted another armed conflict.

THE TRUMAN DOCTRINE   A civil war in Greece provided another arena for confrontation between the superpowers. In 1946, the Communist People's Liberation Army and the anti-Communist forces supported by the British were fighting each other for control of Greece. Great Britain had initially assumed primary responsibility for promoting postwar reconstruction in the eastern Mediterranean, but in 1947 ongoing postwar economic problems caused the British to withdraw from the active role they had been playing in both Greece and Turkey. President Harry Truman of the United States, alarmed by British weakness and the possibility of Soviet expansion into the eastern Mediterranean, responded with the **Truman Doctrine** (see the box on p. 888). The Truman Doctrine said, in essence, that the United States would provide financial aid to countries that claimed they were threatened by Communist expansion. If the Soviets were not stopped in Greece, the United States would have to face the spread of communism throughout the free world. As Dean Acheson, the American secretary of state, explained, "Like apples in a barrel infected by disease, the corruption of Greece would infect Iran and all the East . . . likewise Africa . . . Italy . . . France. . . . Not since Rome and Carthage had there been such a polarization of power on this earth."[1] In March 1947, Truman requested $400 million in economic and military aid for Greece and Turkey from the U.S. Congress.

Who Started the Cold War? American and Soviet Perspectives

Although the United States and the Soviet Union had cooperated during World War II to defeat the Germans and Japanese, differences began to appear as soon as victory became certain. The year 1946 was an especially important turning point in the relationship between the two new superpowers. George Kennan, an American diplomat regarded as an expert on Soviet affairs, was asked to write an analysis of one of Stalin's speeches. His U.S. Foreign Service dispatch, which came to be known as the Long Telegram, was sent to U.S. embassies, U.S. State Department officials, and military leaders. The Long Telegram gave a strong view of Soviet intentions. A response to Kennan's position was written by Nikolai Novikov, a former Soviet ambassador to the United States. His response was read by Vyacheslav Molotov, the Soviet foreign minister, but historians are not sure if Stalin or other officials also read it and were influenced by it.

⟶ ⊰✛⊱ ⟵

George Kennan, The Long Telegram, February 1946

At the bottom of [the Soviet] neurotic view of world affairs is a traditional and instinctive Russian sense of insecurity. Originally, this was the insecurity of a peaceful agricultural people trying to live on a vast exposed plain in the neighborhood of fierce nomadic peoples. To this was added, as Russia came into contact with the economically advanced West, the fear of more competent, more powerful, more highly organized societies. . . . For this reason they have always feared foreign penetration, feared direct contact between the Western world and their own. . . . And they have learned to seek security only in patient but deadly struggle for total destruction of rival power, never in compacts and compromises with it. . . .

In summary, we have here a political force committed fanatically to the belief that with the United State there can be no permanent modus vivendi, that it is desirable and necessary the internal harmony of our society be disrupted, our traditional way of life be destroyed, the international authority of our state be broken, if Soviet power is to be secure. . . . In addition it has an elaborate and far-flung apparatus for exertion of its influence in other countries, an apparatus of amazing flexibility and versatility, managed by people whose experience and skill in underground methods are presumably without parallel in history. Finally, it is seemingly inaccessible to considerations of reality in its basic reactions. . . . This is admittedly not a pleasant picture. . . . But I would like to record my conviction that the problem is within our power to solve—and that without recourse to any

general conflict. . . . I think we may approach calmly and with good heart the problem of how to deal with Russia . . . [but] we must have the courage and self-confidence to cling to our own methods and conceptions of human society. After all, the greatest danger that can befall us in coping with this problem of Soviet communism is that we shall allow ourselves to become like those with whom we are coping.

Nikolai Novikov, Telegram, September 27, 1946

One of the stages in the achievement of dominance over the world by the United States is its understanding with England concerning the partial division of the world on the basis of mutual concessions. The basic lines of the secret agreement between the United States and England regarding the division of the world consist, as shown by facts, in their agreement on the inclusion of Japan and China in the sphere of influence of the United States in the Far East. . . . The American policy in China is striving for the complete economic and political submission of China to the control of American monopolistic capital. . . .

Obvious indications of the U.S. effort to establish world dominance are also to be found in the increase in military potential in peacetime and in the establishment of a large number of naval and air bases both in the United States and beyond its borders. . . .

Careful note should be taken of the fact that the preparation by the United States for a future war is being conducted with the prospect of war against the Soviet Union, which in the eyes of American imperialists is the main obstacle in the path of the United States to world domination. This is indicated by facts such as the tactical training of the American army for war with the Soviet Union as the future opponent, the placing of American strategic bases in regions from which it is possible to launch strikes on Soviet territory, intensified training and strengthening of Arctic regions as close approaches to the USSR, and attempts to prepare Germany and Japan to use those countries in a war against the USSR. ✈

Q In Kennan's view, what was the Soviet policy after World War II? What did he believe determined that policy, and how did he think the United States should respond? In Novikov's view, what was the goal of U.S. foreign policy, and how did he believe the Americans planned to achieve it? Why was it so difficult to find a common ground between the two positions?

The Truman Doctrine

By 1947, the battle lines had been clearly drawn in the Cold War. This selection is taken from a speech by President Harry Truman to the U.S. Congress in which he justified his request for aid to Greece and Turkey. Truman expressed the urgent need to contain the expansion of communism.

⊷ ⊰≡⊱ ⊶

President Harry Truman, Address to Congress, March 12, 1947

The peoples of a number of countries of the world have recently had totalitarian regimes forced upon them against their will. The Government of the United States has made frequent protests against coercion and intimidation, in violation of the Yalta agreement, in Poland, Romania, and Bulgaria. I must also state that in a number of other countries there have been similar developments.

At the present moment in world history nearly every nation must choose between alternative ways of life. The choice is too often not a free one.

One way of life is based upon the will of the majority, and is distinguished by free institutions, representative government, free elections, guaranties of individual liberty, freedom of speech and religion, and freedom from political oppression.

The second way of life is based upon the will of a minority forcibly imposed upon the majority. It relies upon terror and oppression, a controlled press and radio, fixed elections, and the suppression of personal freedoms.

I believe that it must be the policy of the United States to support free peoples who are resisting attempted subjugation by armed minorities or by outside pressures.

I believe that we must assist free people to work out their own destinies in their own way.

I believe that our help should be primarily through economic and financial aid which is essential to economic stability and orderly political processes.... I therefore ask the Congress for assistance to Greece and Turkey in the amount of $400 million. ⊷

Q How did President Truman defend his request for aid to Greece and Turkey? Did this decision play a role in intensifying the Cold War? Why or why not?

THE MARSHALL PLAN The proclamation of the Truman Doctrine was followed in June 1947 by the European Recovery Program, better known as the **Marshall Plan.** Intended to rebuild prosperity and stability, this program included $13 billion for the economic recovery of war-torn Europe. Underlying it was the belief that Communist aggression fed off economic turmoil. General George C. Marshall had noted in a commencement speech at Harvard, "Our policy is not directed against any country or doctrine but against hunger, poverty, desperation and chaos."[2]

George C. Marshall, The Marshall Plan (1947)

Nevertheless, the Marshall Plan, which did not include the Soviet Union, helped speed up the division of Europe into two competing blocs. According to the Soviet view, the Marshall Plan aimed at the "construction of a bloc of states bound by obligations to the USA, and to guarantee the American loans in return for the relinquishing by the European states of their economic and later also their political independence."[3] Some scholars believe that the Marshall Plan encouraged Stalin to push for even greater control of Eastern Europe to safeguard Soviet interests.

THE AMERICAN POLICY OF CONTAINMENT By 1947, the split in Europe between East and West had become a fact of life (see the Film & History feature on p. 889). At the end of World War II, the United States had favored a quick end to its commitments in Europe. But American fears of Soviet aims caused the United States to play an increasingly important role in European affairs. In an article in *Foreign Affairs* in July 1947, George Kennan, a well-known American diplomat with much knowledge of Soviet affairs, advocated a policy of **containment** against further aggressive Soviet moves. Kennan favored the "adroit and vigilant application of counter-force at a series of constantly shifting geographical and political points, corresponding to the shifts and maneuvers of Soviet policy." After the Soviet blockade of Berlin in 1948, containment of the Soviet Union became formal American policy.

CONTENTION OVER GERMANY The fate of Germany also became a source of heated contention between East and West. Besides **denazification** and the partitioning of Germany (and Berlin) into four occupied zones, the Allied powers had agreed on little else with regard to the conquered nation. The Soviets, hardest hit by the war, took reparations from Germany in the form of booty. The technology-starved Soviets dismantled and removed to the Soviet Union 380 factories from the western zones of Berlin before transferring their control to the Western powers. By the summer of 1946, two hundred chemical, paper, and textile factories in the Soviets' East German zone had likewise been shipped to the Soviet Union. At the same time, the German Communist Party was reestablished under the control of Walter Ulbricht (VAHL-tuh OOL-brikkt) (1893–1973) and was soon in charge of the political reconstruction of the Soviet zone in eastern Germany.

The Third Man (1949)

Directed by Sir Carol Reed, *The Third Man* is a classic thriller set in post–World War II Vienna. It is based on a novel by Graham Greene, who also wrote the screenplay for the movie. When he arrives in Vienna, Holly Martins (Joseph Cotten), an out-of-work American writer of pulp-fiction Westerns, learns that his old school friend Harry Lime (Orson Welles), who had offered him a job in Vienna, has recently died in a traffic accident. But the circumstances surrounding Lime's death are suspicious. With the help of Lime's girlfriend, Anna Schmidt (Alida Valli), Martins sets out to determine what really happened. Eventually, he finds that Lime did not really die but has gone underground in the Russian sector of Vienna to avoid capture by the British Major Calloway (Trevor Howard). British authorities have ascertained that Lime has been active in the black market, as

Harry Lime (Orson Welles) tries to avoid capture.

London Films/The Kobal Collection

are many people in postwar Vienna. Lime, however, has been involved in the heinous sale of watered-down penicillin that has led to pain and death for many children. When Lime and Martins finally meet, Lime justifies his activities with the cynical words:

> Don't be so gloomy. After all it's not that awful. Like the fella says, in Italy for 30 years under the Borgias they had warfare, terror, murder, and bloodshed, but they produced Michelangelo, Leonardo da Vinci, and the Renaissance. In Switzerland they had brotherly love—they had 500 years of democracy and peace, and what did that produce? The cuckoo clock.

Martins agrees to help the British authorities track down Lime, who tries without success to escape through the massive sewers underneath the cobblestone streets of Vienna.

The Third Man is a thriller, but it also gives viewers a picture of the bleakness of postwar Europe. Carol Reed had worked for a British wartime documentary group and insisted that the movie be shot completely on location in Vienna, where piles of rubble and bomb craters still remained alongside architectural masterpieces. The movie

accurately reflects the different perspectives of the Americans and Europeans at the end of World War II. The United States was beginning to experience an economic boom, and most Americans had a great deal of hope for the future. Europeans, in contrast, were world-weary and disillusioned. Many lived, as in Vienna, in a joyless world, reflected in the words of Anna Schmidt when Martins asks her about Lime's untimely death: "I don't know anything anymore, except that I want to be dead, too."

The Third Man also reflected the uncertainties and paranoia associated with the emerging Cold War in Europe. Bombed-out Vienna was divided into four zones, each with its group of suspicious officials from the four powers—the United States, Britain, France, and the Soviet Union. The inner city was jointly administered by the four powers. As the authorities spar over the details of governing Vienna, Holly Martins is never quite sure who he can trust in this new world of confused loyalties. In the film, the Russians are trying to take Anna Schmidt back to her native Czechoslovakia, a clear indication of the growing Soviet power in Eastern Europe. And Major Calloway is obviously suspicious of his Russian counterparts. Vienna itself is a forlorn city where black marketers control the economy and the underground sewer system serves as a route for travel between the closed sectors of the city.

At the same time, the British, French, and Americans gradually began to merge their zones economically and by February 1948 were making plans for the unification of these three western sections of Germany and the formal creation of a West German federal government. The Soviets responded with a blockade of West Berlin that allowed neither trucks nor trains to enter the three western zones of Berlin. The Soviets hoped to secure economic control of all Berlin and force the Western powers to halt the creation of a separate West German state.

The Western powers faced a dilemma. Direct military confrontation seemed dangerous, and no one wished to risk World War III. Therefore, an attempt to break through the blockade with tanks and trucks was ruled out. But how could the 2.5 million people in the three western zones of Berlin be kept alive when the whole city was inside the Soviet zone? The solution was the Berlin Air Lift.

It was an enormous task. Western Allied air forces worked around the clock for almost a year to supply the city of Berlin with foodstuffs as well as the coal, oil, and gasoline needed to heat the city's dwellings and run its power stations, sewer plants, and factories. At the peak, 13,000 tons of supplies were being flown to Berlin daily. Altogether the Western powers shipped 2.3 million tons of food on 277,500 flights. Seventy-three Allied airmen lost their lives due to accidents. The Soviets, also not wanting war, did not interfere and finally lifted the blockade in May 1949. The blockade of Berlin had severely increased tensions between the United States and the Soviet Union and brought about the separation of Germany into two states. At the end of May, a constitution was drafted for a Federal Republic of Germany (West Germany). Konrad Adenauer (AD-uh-now-ur) (1876–1967) was elected as the new German chancellor in September 1949. A month later, the separate German Democratic Republic was established in East Germany. Berlin remained a divided city and the source of much contention between East and West.

→ Air Lift routes

NETHERLANDS
Hamburg
Hanover
Braunschweig
British Zone
BELGIUM
Frankfurt
LUXEMBOURG
French Zone
SWITZERLAND
POLAND
Berlin
Soviet Zone
CZECHOSLOVAKIA
American Zone
AUSTRIA

0   200   400 Kilometers
0   100   200 Miles

The Berlin Air Lift

NEW MILITARY ALLIANCES The Soviet Union also detonated its first atomic bomb in 1949, and all too soon, both superpowers were involved in an escalating arms race that resulted in the construction of ever more destructive nuclear weapons. Soon the search for security took the form of **mutual deterrence,** the belief that an arsenal of nuclear weapons prevented war by assuring that if one nation launched its nuclear weapons in a preemptive first strike, the other nation would still be able to respond and devastate the attacker. Therefore, the assumption was that neither side would risk using the massive arsenals that had been assembled.

The search for security in the uncertain atmosphere of the Cold War also led to the formation of military alliances. The North Atlantic Treaty Organization (**NATO**) was formed in April 1949 when Belgium, Britain, Denmark, France, Iceland, Italy, Luxembourg, the Netherlands, Norway, and Portugal signed a treaty with the United States and Canada. All the powers agreed to provide mutual assistance if any one of them was attacked. A few years later West Germany, Greece, and Turkey joined NATO.

The North Atlantic Treaty (NATO) (1949)

The Eastern European states soon followed suit. In 1949, they formed the Council for Mutual Economic Assistance (COMECON) for economic cooperation. Then in 1955, Albania, Bulgaria, Czechoslovakia, East Germany, Hungary, Poland, Romania, and the Soviet Union organized a formal military alliance in the **Warsaw Pact.** As had

© Bettmann/CORBIS

The Berlin Air Lift. During the Berlin Air Lift, the United States and its Western allies flew 13,000 tons of supplies daily to Berlin and thus were able to break the Soviet land blockade of the city. In this photograph, residents of West Berlin watch an American plane arrive with supplies for the city.

United States/NATO

Symbol	Description
⭿	Missile bases: NATO
⚔	Troops: U.S.
✈	Nuclear bombers: U.S.
⚓	Naval port: U.S.
⛴	Fleet: U.S.
⚓	Nuclear missile submarine: U.S.

Soviet/Warsaw Pact

Symbol	Description
⭿	Missile bases: Warsaw Pact
⚔	Troops: Soviet
✈	Nuclear bombers: Soviet
⚓	Naval port: Soviet
⛴	Fleet: Soviet
⚓	Nuclear missile submarine: Soviet

NATO member

NATO ally

Warsaw Pact member

MAP 28.1 **The New European Alliance Systems in the 1950s and 1960s.** With the United States as its leader, NATO was formed in 1949 to counter the perceived military threat of the Soviet Union and its Eastern European satellites, which formally created the Warsaw Pact in 1955. Soviet and American troops, each backed by nuclear weapons, directly faced each other, heightening Cold War tensions.

Q *Which NATO countries shared a border with one or more Warsaw Pact countries?*

▶ *View an animated version of this map or related maps on the CourseMate website.*

happened so many times before, Europe was divided into hostile alliance systems (see Map 28.1).

Globalization of the Cold War

The Cold War soon spread from Europe to the rest of the world. In 1949, the victory of the Chinese Communists in the Chinese civil war brought a new Communist regime and intensified American fears about the spread of communism. Shortly thereafter, the Korean War turned the Cold War into a worldwide struggle, eventually leading to a system of military alliances around the globe.

THE KOREAN WAR The removal of Korea from Japanese control had been one of the stated objectives of the Allies in World War II, and on the eve of the Japanese surrender in August 1945, the Soviet Union and the United States agreed to divide the country into two separate occupation zones at the 38th parallel. They originally planned to hold national elections after the restoration of peace to reunify

Korea under an independent government. But as U.S.-Soviet relations deteriorated, two separate governments emerged in Korea, a Communist one in the north (Democratic People's Republic of Korea or North Korea) and an anti-Communist one (Republic of Korea or South Korea) in the south.

Tensions between the two governments ran high along the dividing line, and on June 25, 1950, with the apparent approval of Joseph Stalin, North Korean troops invaded South Korea. The Americans, seeing this as yet another example of Communist aggression and expansion, gained the support of the United Nations and intervened by sending American troops to turn back the invasion. By September, United Nations forces (mostly Americans and South Koreans) under the command of General Douglas MacArthur marched northward across the 38th parallel with the aim of unifying Korea under a single non-Communist government. But Mao Zedong (mow zee-DAHNG) (1893–1976), the leader of Communist China, sent Chinese forces into the fray and forced MacArthur's troops back to South Korea.

The Korean War

To many Americans, the Chinese intervention in Korea was clear evidence that China intended to promote communism throughout Asia. In fact, China's decision to enter the war was probably motivated in large part by the fear that hostile U.S. forces might be stationed on the Chinese frontier. When two more years of fighting failed to produce a conclusive victory, an armistice was finally signed in 1953. The boundary line between North and South Korea remained roughly at the 38th parallel. To many Americans, the policy of containing communism had succeeded in Asia, just as it had earlier in Europe, though at the cost of losing more than 33,000 men in the war. The Chinese invasion also hardened Western attitudes against the new Chinese government and led to China's isolation from the major capitalist powers for two decades. As a result, China was forced to rely almost entirely on the Soviet Union, with which it had signed a pact of friendship and cooperation in early 1950.

THE FIRST VIETNAM WAR   A struggle began in French Indochina after World War II, when the Indochinese Communist Party led by Ho Chi Minh (HOH CHEE MIN) (1890–1969) formed a multiparty nationalist alliance called the Vietminh Front and seized power in northern and central Vietnam. When the negotiations between Ho's government and the returning French collapsed, war broke out in December 1946.

For three years, the Vietminh gradually increased in size and effectiveness. What had begun as an anticolonial struggle by Ho Chi Minh's Vietminh Front against the French soon became entangled in the Cold War as both the United States and the new Communist government in China began to intervene in the conflict in the early 1950s. China began to provide military assistance to the Vietminh to protect its own borders from hostile forces. The Americans supported the French but pressured the French government to prepare for an eventual transition to a non-Communist government in Vietnam.

At the Geneva Conference in 1954, with the French public tired of fighting the "dirty war" in Indochina, the French agreed to a peace settlement with Ho Chi Minh's Vietminh. Vietnam was temporarily divided into a northern Communist half (known as the Democratic Republic of Vietnam) and a non-Communist southern half based in Saigon (known eventually as the Republic of Vietnam). Elections were to be held in two years to create a unified government.

ESCALATION OF THE COLD WAR   The Korean and Vietnamese experiences seemed to confirm American fears of Communist expansion and reinforced American determination to contain Soviet power. In the mid-1950s, the administration of President Dwight D. Eisenhower (1890–1969) adopted a policy of massive retaliation, which advocated the full use of American nuclear bombs to counteract even a Soviet ground attack in Europe, although there was no evidence that Stalin ever planned such an attack. Meanwhile, American military alliances were extended around the world. Eisenhower claimed, "The freedom we cherish and defend in Europe and in the Americas is no different from the freedom that is imperiled in Asia." The Central Treaty Organization (CENTO) of Great Britain, Iran, Iraq, Pakistan, Turkey, and the United States was intended to prevent the Soviet Union from expanding at the expense of its southern neighbors. In addition, Australia, Britain, France, New Zealand, Pakistan, the Philippines, Thailand, and the United States formed the Southeast Asia Treaty Organization (SEATO). By the mid-1950s, the United States found itself allied militarily with forty-two states around the world.

Despite the escalation of the Cold War, hopes for a new era of peaceful coexistence also appeared. The death of Stalin in 1953 caused some people in the West to think that the new Soviet leadership might be more flexible in its policies. But this optimism proved premature. A summit conference at Geneva in 1955 between President Eisenhower and Nikolai Bulganin (nyik-uh-LY bool-GAN-yin), then leader of the Soviet government, produced no real benefits. A year later, all talk of **rapprochement** (ra-prohsh-MAHN) between East and West temporarily ceased when the Soviet Union used its armed forces to crush Hungary's attempt to assert its independence from Soviet control.

ANOTHER BERLIN CRISIS A crisis over Berlin also added to the tension in the late 1950s. In August 1957, the Soviet Union had launched its first intercontinental ballistic missile (ICBM) and, shortly thereafter, *Sputnik I*, the first space satellite. Fueled by partisan political debate, fears of a "missile gap" between the United States and the Soviet Union seized the American public. Nikita Khrushchev (nuh-KEE-tuh KHROOSH-chawf) (1894–1971), the new leader of the Soviet Union, attempted to take advantage of the American frenzy over missiles to solve the problem of West Berlin. Khrushchev had said that Berlin was like "the testicles of the West: every time I want to make the West scream, I squeeze on Berlin."[4] West Berlin had remained a "Western island" of prosperity in the midst of the relatively poverty-stricken East Germany. Many East Germans also managed to escape East Germany by fleeing through West Berlin.

In November 1958, Khrushchev announced that unless the West removed its forces from West Berlin within six months, he would turn over control of the access routes to Berlin to the East Germans. Unwilling to accept an ultimatum that would have abandoned West Berlin to the Communists, Eisenhower and the West stood firm, and Khrushchev eventually backed down.

The crisis was revived when John F. Kennedy (1917–1963) became the American president. During a summit meeting in Vienna in June 1961, Khrushchev threatened Kennedy with another six-month ultimatum over West Berlin. Kennedy left Vienna convinced of the need to deal firmly with the Soviet Union, and Khrushchev was forced once again to back off. Frustrated, Khrushchev conspired with Walter Ulbricht, the East German leader, to build a wall around West Berlin to cut off the flow of refugees to the West. On August 13, 1961, East German workers under military supervision began the construction of the Berlin Wall. Within a few months, more than 100 miles of wall, topped by numerous watchtowers, surrounded West Berlin. Since access from West Germany into West Berlin was still permitted, the Americans acquiesced and accepted the wall's existence. The Berlin Wall became a powerful symbol of a divided Europe. And Khrushchev, determined to achieve some foreign policy success, soon embarked on an even more dangerous venture in Cuba.

THE CUBAN MISSILE CRISIS The Cold War confrontation between the United States and the Soviet Union reached frightening levels during the Cuban Missile Crisis. In 1959, a left-wing revolutionary named Fidel Castro (fee-DELL KASS-troh) (b. 1927) had overthrown the Cuban dictator Fulgencio Batista (FULL-jen-see-oh bah-TEES-tuh) and established a Soviet-supported totalitarian regime. In 1961, an American-supported attempt to invade Cuba via the Bay of Pigs and overthrow Castro's regime ended in utter failure. The next year, in 1962, the Soviet

CHRONOLOGY The Cold War to 1962	
Truman Doctrine	1947
European Recovery Program (Marshall Plan)	1947
Berlin blockade	1948–1949
Communists win civil war in China	1949
Soviet Union explodes first atomic bomb	1949
Formation of NATO	1949
Formation of COMECON	1949
Korean War	1950–1953
End of First Vietnam War	1954
Formation of Warsaw Pact	1955
Berlin Crisis	1958
Vienna summit	1961
Cuban Missile Crisis	1962

Union decided to station nuclear missiles in Cuba. The United States was not prepared to allow nuclear weapons within such close striking distance of the American mainland, even though it had placed nuclear weapons in Turkey within easy range of the Soviet Union. Khrushchev was quick to point out that "your rockets are in Turkey. You are worried by Cuba . . . because it is 90 miles from the American coast. But Turkey is next to us."[5] When U.S. intelligence discovered that a Soviet fleet carrying missiles was heading to Cuba, President Kennedy decided to blockade Cuba and prevent the fleet from reaching its destination. This approach to the problem had the benefit of delaying confrontation and giving each side time to find a peaceful solution (see the box on p. 894). Khrushchev agreed to turn back the fleet if Kennedy pledged not to invade Cuba. In a conciliatory letter to Kennedy, Khrushchev wrote:

> We and you ought not to pull on the ends of the rope in which you have tied the knot of war, because the more the two of us pull, the tighter that knot will be tied. And a moment may come when that knot will be tied too tight that even he who tied it will not have the strength to untie it. . . . Let us not only relax the forces pulling on the ends of the rope, let us take measures to untie that knot. We are ready for this.[6]

The Cuban Missile Crisis brought the world frighteningly close to nuclear war. Indeed, in 1992, a high-ranking Soviet officer revealed that short-range rockets armed with nuclear devices would have been used against American troops if the United States had invaded Cuba, an option that President Kennedy fortunately had rejected. The intense feeling that the world might have been annihilated in a few days had a profound influence on both sides. A hotline communication system between Moscow and Washington was installed in 1963 to expedite rapid communication between the two superpowers in a time of crisis. In the same year, the two

The Cuban Missile Crisis from Khrushchev's Perspective

The Cuban Missile Crisis was one of the sobering experiences of the Cold War. It led the two superpowers to seek new ways to lessen the tensions between them. This version of the events is taken from the memoirs of Nikita Khrushchev.

◆─━◆━━◆

Nikita Khrushchev, *Khrushchev Remembers*

I will explain what the Caribbean crisis of October 1962, was all about.... At the time that Fidel Castro led his revolution to victory and entered Havana with his troops, we had no idea what political course his regime would follow.... All the while the Americans had been watching Castro closely. At first they thought that the capitalist underpinnings of the Cuban economy would remain intact. So by the time Castro announced that he was going to put Cuba on the road toward Socialism, the Americans had already missed their chance to do any thing about it by simply exerting their influence: there were no longer any forces left which could be organized to fight on America's behalf in Cuba. That left only one alternative—invasion! ...

After Castro's crushing victory over the counterrevolutionaries we intensified our military aid to Cuba.... We were sure that the Americans would never reconcile themselves to the existence of Castro's Cuba. They feared, as much as we hoped, that a Socialist Cuba might become a magnet that would attract other Latin American countries to Socialism.... It was clear to me that we might very well lose Cuba if we didn't take some decisive steps in her defense.... We had to think up some way of confronting America with more than words. We had to establish a tangible and effective deterrent to American interference in the Caribbean. But what exactly? The logical answer was missiles. We knew that American missiles were aimed against us in Turkey and Italy, to say nothing of West Germany.... My thinking went like this: if we installed the missiles

secretly and then if the United States discovered the missiles were there after they were already poised and ready to strike, the Americans would think twice before trying to liquidate our installations by military means.... I want to make one thing absolutely clear: when we put our ballistic missiles in Cuba we had no desire to start a war. On the contrary, our principal aim was only to deter America from starting a war....

President Kennedy issued an ultimatum, demanding that we remove our missiles and bombers from Cuba.... We sent the Americans a note saying that we agreed to remove our missiles and bombers on the condition that the President give us his assurance that there would be no invasion of Cuba by the forces of the United States or anybody else. Finally Kennedy gave in and agreed to make a statement giving us such an assurance.... It had been, to say the least, an interesting and challenging situation. The two most powerful nations of the world had been squared off against each other, each with its finger on the button. You'd have thought that war was inevitable. But both sides showed that if the desire to avoid war is strong enough, even the most pressing dispute can be solved by compromise. And a compromise over Cuba was indeed found. The episode ended in a triumph of common sense.... It was a great victory for us, though, that we had been able to extract from Kennedy a promise that neither America nor any of her allies would invade Cuba.... The Caribbean crisis was a triumph of Soviet foreign policy and a personal triumph in my own career as a statesman and as a member of the collective leadership. We achieved, I would say, a spectacular success without having to fire a single shot! ⇛

Q According to his memoirs, why did Khrushchev decide to install missiles in Cuba? Why did he later agree to remove them? What did each side "lose" and what did each side "win" in the Cuban Missile Crisis?

---

powers agreed to ban nuclear tests in the atmosphere, a step that served to lessen the tensions between the two nations.

Europe and the World: Decolonization

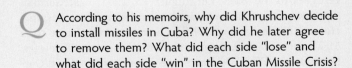

Q FOCUS QUESTION: Why and how did the European colonies in Africa, the Middle East, and Asia gain independence between 1945 and 1965?

As we saw in Chapter 26, movements for independence had begun in earnest in Africa and Asia in the years between the wars. After World War II, these movements

grew even louder. The ongoing subjugation of peoples by colonial powers seemed at odds with the goals the Allies had pursued in overthrowing the repressive regimes of Germany, Italy, and Japan. Then, too, indigenous peoples everywhere took up the call for national self-determination and expressed their determination to fight for independence.

The ending of the European colonial empires did not come easy, however. In 1941, Winston Churchill had said, "I have not become His Majesty's Chief Minister in order to preside over the liquidation of the British Empire." Britain and France in particular seemed reluctant to let go of their colonies, but for a variety of reasons both eventually gave in to the obvious: the days of empire were over.

During the war, the Japanese had already humiliated the Western states by overrunning their colonial empires. In addition, colonial soldiers who had fought on behalf of the Allies were well aware that Allied war aims included the principle of self-determination for the peoples of the world. Equally important to the process of **decolonization** after the war, the power of the European states had been destroyed by the exhaustive struggles of World War II. The greatest colonial empire builder, Great Britain, no longer had the energy or the wealth to maintain its colonial empire. Given the combination of circumstances, a rush of decolonization swept the world. Between 1947 and 1962, virtually every colony achieved independence and attained statehood. Although some colonial powers willingly relinquished their control, others had to be driven out by national wars of liberation. Decolonization was a difficult and even bitter process, but it created a new world as the non-Western states ended the long era of Western domination.

Africa: The Struggle for Independence

After World War II, Europeans reluctantly realized that colonial rule in Africa would have to come to an end, but little had been done to prepare Africans for self-rule. Political organizations that had been formed by Africans before the war to gain their rights became formal political parties with independence as their goal. In the Gold Coast, Kwame Nkrumah (KWAH-may en-KROO-muh) (1909–1972) formed the Convention People's Party, the first African political party in black Africa. In the late 1940s, Jomo Kenyatta (JOH-moh ken-YAHT-uh) (1894–1978) founded the Kenya African National Union, which focused on economic issues but also sought self-rule for Kenya.

For the most part, these political activities were nonviolent and were led by Western-educated African intellectuals. Their constituents were primarily merchants, urban professionals, and members of labor unions. But the demand for independence was not restricted to the cities. In Kenya, for example, the widely publicized Mau Mau movement among the Kikuyu (ki-KOO-yuh) peoples used terrorism to demand *uhuru* (oo-HOO-roo) (Swahili for "freedom") from the British. Mau Mau terrorism alarmed the European population and convinced the British in 1959 to promise eventual independence.

A similar process was occurring in Egypt, which had been a protectorate of Great Britain since the 1880s. In 1918, a formal political party called the Wafd (WAHFT) was organized to promote Egyptian independence. Although Egypt gained its formal independence in 1922, it still remained under British control. Egyptian intellectuals, however, were opposed as much to the Egyptian monarchy as to the British, and in 1952, an army coup overthrew King Farouk and set up an independent republic.

In North Africa, the French, who were simply not strong enough to maintain control of their far-flung colonial empire, granted full independence to Morocco and Tunisia in 1956 (see Map 28.2). Since Algeria was home to 2 million French settlers, however, France chose to retain its dominion

Algerian Independence. Although the French wanted to retain control of their Algerian colony, a bloody war of liberation finally led to Algeria's freedom. This photograph shows Algerians celebrating the announcement of independence on July 3, 1962.

there. But a group of Algerian nationalists organized the National Liberation Front (FLN) and in 1954 initiated a guerrilla war to liberate their homeland (see the box on p. 897). The French people became so divided over this war that their leader, Charles de Gaulle, accepted the inevitable and granted Algerian independence in 1962.

In areas such as South Africa, where the political system was dominated by European settlers, the transition to independence was more complicated. In South Africa, political activity by local blacks began with the formation of the African National Congress (ANC) in 1912. At first, it was a group of intellectuals whose goal was to gain economic and political reforms, including full equality for educated Africans, within the framework of the existing system. The ANC's efforts, however, met with little success. At the same time, by the 1950s, South African whites were strengthening the laws separating whites and blacks, creating a system of racial segregation in South Africa known as **apartheid.** When blacks demonstrated against the apartheid laws, the white government brutally repressed the demonstrators. After the arrest of Nelson Mandela (b. 1918), the ANC

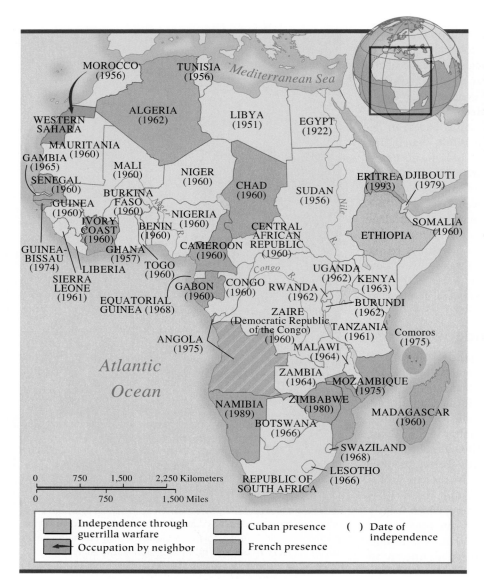

MAP 28.2 Decolonization in Africa. By the late 1950s, Britain and France had decided to allow independence for most of their African colonies, although France fought hard before relinquishing Algeria. Most of the new states had difficulty promoting economic growth and dealing with internal ethnic animosities.

Q *What is a significant characteristic shared by a majority of the countries that gained independence from 1975 onward?*

leader, in 1962, members of the ANC called for armed resistance to the white government.

When both the British and the French decided to let go of their colonial empires, most black African nations achieved their independence in the late 1950s and 1960s. The Gold Coast, now renamed Ghana and under the guidance of Kwame Nkrumah, was first in 1957. Nigeria, the Belgian Congo (renamed Zaire), Kenya, Tanganyika (later, when joined with Zanzibar, renamed Tanzania), and others soon followed. Seventeen new African nations emerged in 1960. Another eleven followed between 1961 and 1965. By the late 1960s, only parts of southern Africa and the Portuguese possessions of Mozambique and Angola remained under European rule. After a series of brutal guerrilla wars, the Portuguese finally gave up their colonies in the 1970s.

Conflict in the Middle East

Although Turkey, Iran, Saudi Arabia, and Iraq had become independent states between the two world wars, the end of World War II led to the emergence of other independent states in the Middle East. Jordan, Syria, and Lebanon, all European mandates before the war, became independent (see Map 28.3). Sympathy for the idea of Arab unity led to the formation of the Arab League in 1945, but different points of view among its members prevented it from achieving anything of substance.

THE QUESTION OF PALESTINE The one issue on which all Muslim states in the area could agree was the question of Palestine. As tensions between Jews and Arabs intensified in that mandate during the 1930s, the British reduced Jewish immigration into the area and firmly rejected Jewish proposals for an independent state in Palestine. The Zionists, who wanted Palestine as a home for Jews, were not to be denied, however. Many people had been shocked at the end of World War II when they learned about the Holocaust, and sympathy for the Jewish cause grew dramatically. As a result, the Zionists turned for support to the United States, and in March 1948, the Truman administration approved the concept of an

Frantz Fanon and the Wretched of the Earth

Born on the island of Martinique, Frantz Fanon (1925–1961) studied psychiatry in France. His work as head of a psychiatric hospital in Algeria led him to favor violence as a necessary instrument to overthrow Western imperialism, which to Fanon was itself rooted in violence. *The Wretched of the Earth,* published in 1961, provided an argument for national liberation movements in the Third World. In the last part of the book, Fanon discussed the problem of mental disorders that arose from Algeria's war of national liberation.

＊＊＊

The Wretched of the Earth: Colonial War and Mental Disorders, Series B

We have here brought together certain cases or groups of cases in which the event giving rise to the illness is in the first place the atmosphere of total war which reigns in Algeria.

Case No. 1: The murder by two young Algerians, thirteen and fourteen years old respectively, of their European playmate.

We had been asked to give expert medical advice in a legal matter. Two young Algerians thirteen and fourteen years old, pupils in a secondary school, were accused of having killed one of their European schoolmates. They admitted having done it. The crime was reconstructed, and photos were added to the record. Here one of the children could be seen holding the victim while the other struck at him with a knife. The little defendants did not go back on their declarations. We had long conversations with them. We here reproduce the most characteristic of their remarks:

The boy fourteen years old:

This young defendant was in marked contrast to his school fellow. He was already almost a man, and an adult in his muscular control, his appearance, and the content of his replies. He did not deny having killed either. Why had he killed? He did not reply to the question but asked me had I ever seen a European in prison. Had there ever been a European arrested and sent to prison after the murder of an Algerian? I replied that in fact I had never seen any Europeans in prison.

"And yet there are Algerians killed every day, aren't there?"

"Yes."

"So why are only Algerians found in the prisons? Can you explain that to me?"

"No. But tell me why you killed this boy who was your friend."

"I'll tell you why. You've heard tell of the Rivet business?" [Rivet was a village near Algiers where in 1956 the French militia dragged forty men from their own beds and afterward murdered them.]

"Yes."

"Two of my family were killed then. At home, they said that the French had sworn to kill us all, one after the other. And did they arrest a single Frenchman for all those Algerians who were killed?"

"I don't know."

"Well, nobody at all was arrested. I wanted to take to the mountains, but I was too young. So [my friend] and I said we'd kill a European."

"Why?"

"In your opinion, what should we have done?"

"I don't know. But you are a child and what is happening concerns grown-up people."

"But they kill children too."

"That is no reason for killing your friend."

"Well, kill him I did. Now you can do what you like."

"Had your friend done anything to harm you?"

"Not a thing."

"Well?"

"Well, there you are."

Q What does this selection tell you about some of the fundamental characteristics of European colonial regimes? What broader forces, perhaps liberated or focused by World War II, could have contributed to the uprisings and to the crimes the colonized committed against the colonizers in the postwar period?

---

independent Jewish state in Palestine, even though Jews comprised only about one-third of the local population. When a United Nations resolution divided Palestine into a Jewish state and an Arab state, the Jews in Palestine acted. On May 14, 1948, they proclaimed the state of Israel.

Its Arab neighbors saw the new state as a betrayal of the Palestinian people, 90 percent of whom were Muslim. Outraged at the lack of Western support for Muslim interests in the area, several Arab countries invaded the new Jewish state. The invasion failed, but both sides remained bitter. The Arab states refused to recognize the existence of Israel.

NASSER AND PAN-ARABISM In Egypt, a new leader arose who would play an important role in the Arab world and the Arab-Israeli conflict. Colonel Gamal Abdel Nasser (juh-MAHL ahb-DOOL NAH-sur) (1918–1970) seized control of the Egyptian government in 1954 and two years later nationalized the Suez Canal Company, which had been under British and French administration. Seeing a threat to their route to the Indian Ocean, the British and

MAP 28.3 **Decolonization in the Middle East.** Under the control of the Ottoman Empire prior to World War I, much of the Middle East was ruled directly or indirectly by the British and French after the war. Britain, the main colonial power, granted independence to most of its holdings in the first years after World War II, although it did maintain control of small states in the Persian Gulf and Arabian Sea region until 1971.

Q *Which countries are major oil producers?*

View an animated version of this map or related maps on the CourseMate website.

French launched a joint attack on Egypt to protect their investment. They were joined by Israel, whose leaders had grown exasperated at sporadic Arab commando raids on Israeli territory and now decided to strike back. But the Eisenhower administration in the United States, concerned that the attack smacked of a revival of colonialism, joined with the Soviet Union, its Cold War enemy, and supported Nasser. Together, they brought about the withdrawal of foreign forces from Egypt and of Israeli troops from the Sinai peninsula.

Nasser emerged from the conflict as a powerful leader and now began to promote Pan-Arabism, or Arab unity. In March 1958, Egypt formally united with Syria in the United Arab Republic (UAR), and Nasser was named president of the new state. Egypt and Syria hoped that the union would eventually include all Arab states, but many other Arab leaders were suspicious of Pan-Arabism. Oil-rich Arab states such as Iraq and Saudi Arabia feared that they would be asked to share their vast oil revenues with the poorer states of the Middle East. In 1961, Nasser's plans and the UAR came to an end when military leaders seized control of Syria and withdrew it from its union with Egypt.

THE ARAB-ISRAELI DISPUTE The breakup of the UAR did not end the dream of Pan-Arabism. At a meeting of Arab leaders held in Jerusalem in 1964, Egypt took the lead in forming the Palestine Liberation Organization (PLO) to represent the interests of the Palestinians. The PLO believed that only the Palestinian peoples (and not Jewish immigrants from abroad) had the right to form a state in Palestine. A guerrilla movement called al-Fatah (al-FAH-tuh), led by the PLO political leader Yasir Arafat (yah-SEER ah-ruh-FAHT) (1929–2004), began to launch terrorist attacks on Israeli territory.

During the 1960s, the dispute between Israel and other states in the Middle East intensified. Essentially alone except for the sympathy of the United States and a few Western European countries, Israel adopted a policy of immediate retaliation against any hostile act by the PLO and its Arab neighbors. By the spring of 1967, Nasser in Egypt had stepped up his military activities and imposed a blockade against Israeli shipping through the Gulf of Aqaba. Learning that an attack was imminent, on June 5, 1967, Israel launched preemptive air strikes against Egypt and several of its Arab neighbors. Israeli warplanes bombed seventeen Egyptian airfields and wiped out most of the Egyptian air force. Israeli armies then broke the blockade at the head of the Gulf of Aqaba and occupied the Sinai peninsula. Other Israeli forces seized Jordanian territory on the West Bank of the Jordan River, occupied all of Jerusalem (formerly divided between Israel and Jordan), and attacked Syrian military positions in the Golan Heights area along the Israeli-Syrian border. In this brief Six-Day War, as it is called, Israel devastated Nasser's forces and tripled the size of its territory. The new Israel aroused even more bitter hatred among the Arabs. Furthermore, another million Palestinians now lived inside Israel's new borders, most of them on the West Bank.

Asia: Nationalism and Communism

In Asia, the United States initiated the process of decolonization in 1946 when it granted independence to the Philippines (see Map 28.4). Britain soon followed suit with India. But ethnic and religious differences made the process both difficult and violent.

At the end of World War II, the British negotiated with both the Indian National Congress, which was mostly Hindu, and the Muslim League. British India's Muslims and Hindus were bitterly divided and unwilling to accept a single Indian state. Britain soon realized that British India would have to be divided into two countries, one Hindu (India) and one Muslim (Pakistan). Pakistan would actually consist of two regions separated by more than 1,000 miles.

Among Congress leaders, only Mahatma Gandhi objected to the division of India. A Muslim woman, critical of his opposition to partition, asked him, "If two brothers were living together in the same house and wanted to separate and live in two different houses, would you object?" "Ah," Gandhi replied, "if only we could separate

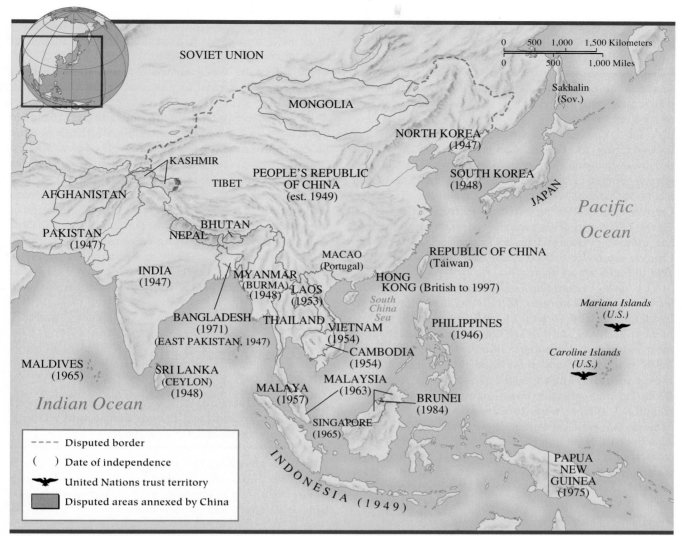

MAP 28.4 Decolonization in Asia. Britain and the United States facilitated relatively peaceful transitions to independence for their possessions in Asia. France fought hard to hold Indochina but left after major military defeats. Cold War tensions in Asia led to both the Korean War and the Vietnam War.

Q *What two neighboring countries' presence helps explain why Korea has had difficulty maintaining complete independence throughout much of its history?*

as two brothers. But we will not. It will be an orgy of blood. We shall tear ourselves asunder in the womb of the mother who bears us."[7]

On August 15, 1947, India and Pakistan became independent. But Gandhi had been right. The flight of millions of Hindus and Muslims across the new borders led to violence, and more than a million people were killed—including Gandhi, who was assassinated on January 30, 1948, by a Hindu militant. India's new beginning had not been easy.

Jawaharlal Nehru, Speech on the Granting of Indian Independence (1947)

Other areas of Asia also achieved independence. In 1948, Britain granted independence to Ceylon (modern Sri Lanka) and Burma (modern Myanmar). When the Dutch failed to reestablish control over the Dutch East Indies, Indonesia emerged as

an independent nation in 1949. The French effort to remain in Indochina led to a bloody struggle with the Vietminh, led by Ho Chi Minh, the Communist and nationalist leader of the Vietnamese. After their defeat in 1954, the French granted independence to Laos and Cambodia, and Vietnam was temporarily divided in anticipation of elections in 1956 that would decide its fate. But the elections were never held, and the division of Vietnam under Communist and pro-Western regimes eventually led to the Second Vietnam War (see Chapter 29).

CHINA UNDER COMMUNISM At the end of World War II, two Chinese governments existed side by side. The Nationalist government of Chiang Kai-shek, based in southern and central China, was supported by the Americans. The Communists, under the leadership of Mao Zedong, had built a strong base in North China. Their People's Liberation Army included nearly one million troops.

When efforts to form a coalition government in 1946 failed, full-scale war between the Nationalists and the Communists broke out. In the countryside, millions of peasants were attracted to the Communists by promises of land, and many joined Mao's army. By 1948, the People's Liberation Army had surrounded Beijing. The following spring, the Communists crossed the Yangtze and occupied Shanghai. During the next few months, Chiang's government and 2 million of his followers fled to the island of Taiwan, off the coast of mainland China. On October 1, 1949, Mao mounted the rostrum of the Gate of Heavenly Peace in Beijing and made a victory statement to the thousands gathered in the square before him. The Chinese people have stood up, he said, and no one will be able to humiliate us again.

The newly victorious Communist Party, under the leadership of its chairman, Mao, had a long-term goal of building a socialist society. In 1955, the Chinese government collectivized all private farmland and nationalized most industry and commerce. When the collective farms failed to increase food production, Mao began a more radical program, known as the Great Leap Forward, in 1958. Existing collective farms, normally the size of the traditional village, were combined into vast "people's communes," each containing more than 30,000 people. Mao hoped this program would mobilize the people for a massive effort to speed up economic growth and reach the final stage of communism—the classless society—before the end of the twentieth century. But the Great Leap Forward was a disaster. Bad weather and peasant hatred of the new system combined to drive food production downward. Despite his failures, Mao was not yet ready to abandon his dream of a totally classless society, and in 1966 he launched China on a new forced march toward communism (see Chapter 29).

Decolonization and Cold War Rivalries

The process of decolonization also became embroiled in Cold War politics. As independent nations emerged in Asia and Africa, they often found themselves caught in the rivalry between the United States and the Soviet Union. In Vietnam, for example, the division of the country in 1954 left the northern half under the Communist leader Ho Chi Minh supported by the Soviet Union. Meanwhile, South Vietnam was kept afloat by American financial and military aid. The Second Vietnam War resulted from the American perception that it needed to keep communism from expanding, while Ho Chi Minh saw the struggle between North and South as an attempt to overthrow Western colonial masters (the Americans had simply replaced the French) and achieve self-determination for the Vietnamese people.

Many new nations tried to stay neutral in the Cold War. Under the leadership of Jawaharlal Nehru (juh-WAH-hur-lahl NAY-roo) (1889–1964), for example, India took a neutral stance in the Cold War and sought to provide leadership to all newly independent nations in Asia and Africa. India's neutrality put it at odds with the United States, which during the 1950s was trying to mobilize all nations against what it viewed as the menace of international communism.

Often, however, new nations found it difficult to remain nonaligned. In Indonesia, for example, which achieved its independence from the Dutch in 1949, President Sukarno (soo-KAHR-noh) (1901–1970), who was highly suspicious of the West, nationalized foreign-owned enterprises and sought economic aid from China and the Soviet Union while relying for domestic support on the Indonesian Communist Party. The army and conservative Muslims resented Sukarno's increasing reliance on the Communists, overthrew him in 1965, and established a military government under General Suharto (soo-HAHR-toh) (1921–2008), who quickly restored good relations with the West.

Recovery and Renewal in Europe

Q **FOCUS QUESTION:** What were the main developments in the Soviet Union, Eastern Europe, and Western Europe between 1945 and 1965?

Just a few years after the defeat of Germany and Italy in World War II, economic revival brought renewed growth to European society, although major differences remained between Western and Eastern Europe.

The Soviet Union: From Stalin to Khrushchev

World War II had devastated the Soviet Union. To create a new industrial base, Stalin returned to the method that he had used in the 1930s—the acquisition of development capital from Soviet labor. Working hard for little pay, poor housing, and precious few consumer goods, Soviet laborers were expected to produce goods for export with little in return for themselves. The incoming capital from abroad could then be used to purchase machinery and Western technology. The loss of millions of men in the war meant that much of this tremendous workload fell upon Soviet women. Almost 40 percent of heavy manual labor was performed by women.

Economic recovery in the Soviet Union was nothing less than spectacular. By 1947, industrial production had attained prewar levels; three years later, it had surpassed them by 40 percent. New power plants, canals, and giant factories were built, and new industries and oil fields were established in Siberia and Soviet Central Asia.

STALIN'S POLICIES Although Stalin's economic policy was successful in promoting growth in heavy industry,

Khrushchev Denounces Stalin

Three years after the death of Stalin, the new Soviet premier, Nikita Khrushchev, addressed the Twentieth Congress of the Communist Party and denounced the former Soviet dictator for his crimes. This denunciation was the beginning of a policy of de-Stalinization.

Nikita Khrushchev, Address to the Twentieth Party Congress, February 1956

Comrades, . . . quite a lot has been said about the cult of the individual and about its harmful consequences. . . . The cult of the person of Stalin . . . became at a certain specific stage the source of a whole series of exceedingly serious and grave perversions of Party principles, of Party democracy, of revolutionary legality.

Stalin absolutely did not tolerate collegiality in leadership and in work and . . . practiced brutal violence, not only toward everything which opposed him, but also toward that which seemed to his capricious and despotic character, contrary to his concepts.

Stalin abandoned the method of ideological struggle for that of administrative violence, mass repressions and terror. . . . Arbitrary behavior by one person encouraged and permitted arbitrariness in others. Mass arrests and deportations of many thousands of people, execution without trial and without normal investigation created conditions of insecurity, fear and even desperation.

Stalin showed in a whole series of cases his intolerance, his brutality and his abuse of power. . . . He often chose the path of repression and annihilation, not only against actual enemies, but also against individuals who had not committed any crimes against the Party and the Soviet government. . . .

Many Party, Soviet and economic activists who were branded in 1937–8 as "enemies" were actually never enemies, spies, wreckers and so on, but were always honest communists; they were only so stigmatized, and often, no longer able to bear barbaric tortures, they charged themselves (at the order of the investigative judges-falsifiers) with all kinds of grave and unlikely crimes.

This was the result of the abuse of power by Stalin, who began to use mass terror against the Party cadres. . . . Stalin put the Party and the NKVD [the secret police] up to the use of mass terror when the exploiting classes had been liquidated in our country and when there were no serious reasons for the use of extraordinary mass terror. The terror was directed . . . against the honest workers of the Party and the Soviet state. . . .

Stalin was a very distrustful man, sickly suspicious. . . . Everywhere and in everything he saw "enemies," "two-facers" and "spies." Possessing unlimited power, he indulged in great willfulness and choked a person morally and physically. A situation was created where one could not express one's own will. When Stalin said that one or another would be arrested, it was necessary to accept on faith that he was an "enemy of the people." What proofs were offered? The confession of the arrested. . . . How is it possible that a person confesses to crimes that he had not committed? Only in one way—because of application of physical methods of pressuring him, tortures, bringing him to a state of unconsciousness, deprivation of his judgment, taking away of his human dignity.

 According to Khrushchev, what were Stalin's crimes? What purposes, political and historical, do you think Khrushchev intended his denunciation of Stalin to serve?

---

primarily for the benefit of the military, consumer goods were scarce. The development of thermonuclear weapons in 1953, MIG fighters from 1950 to 1953, and the first space satellite (*Sputnik*) in 1957 may have elevated the Soviet state's reputation as a world power abroad, but domestically, the Soviet people were shortchanged. Heavy industry grew at a rate three times that of personal consumption. Moreover, the housing shortage was acute. A British military attaché in Moscow reported that "all houses, practically without exception, show lights from every window after dark. This seems to indicate that every room is both a living room by day and a bedroom by night. There is no place in overcrowded Moscow for the luxury of eating and sleeping in separate rooms."[8]

When World War II ended in 1945, Stalin had been in power for more than fifteen years. During that time, he had removed all opposition to his rule. Although he was the undisputed master of the Soviet Union, Stalin's morbid suspicions fueled the constantly increasing repression that was a characteristic of his regime. In 1946, the government decreed that all literary and scientific works must conform to the political needs of the state. Along with this anti-intellectual campaign came political terror. A new series of purges seemed imminent in 1953 when a number of Jewish doctors were implicated in a spurious plot to kill high-level party officials. Only Stalin's death on March 5, 1953, prevented more bloodletting.

KHRUSHCHEV'S RULE A new collective leadership succeeded Stalin until Nikita Khrushchev emerged as the chief Soviet policy maker. Khrushchev had been responsible for ending the system of forced-labor camps, a regular feature of Soviet life under Stalin. At the Twentieth Congress of the Communist Party in 1956, Khrushchev condemned Stalin for his "administrative violence, mass repression, and terror" (see the box above).

© Ralph Crane/Time Life Pictures/Getty Images

Khrushchev's Visit to Yugoslavia. The leadership of Nikita Khrushchev appeared for a while to open the door to more flexible Soviet policies. In 1955, he visited Yugoslavia in an attempt to improve relations with a Communist state that had deviated from Soviet policies. Khrushchev is shown here making a conciliatory speech with Marshal Tito, the leader of Yugoslavia, looking on.

Khrushchev's personality also did not endear him to the higher Soviet officials, who frowned at his tendency to crack jokes and play the clown. Nor were the higher members of the Party bureaucracy pleased when Khrushchev tried to curb their privileges. Foreign policy failures caused additional damage to Khrushchev's reputation among his colleagues. His rash plan to place missiles in Cuba was the final straw. While he was on vacation in 1964, a special meeting of the Soviet Politburo voted him out of office (because of "deteriorating health") and forced him into retirement. Although a group of leaders succeeded him, real power came into the hands of Leonid Brezhnev (lee-oh-NYEET BREZH-neff) (1906–1982), the "trusted" supporter of Khrushchev who had engineered his downfall.

Once in power, Khrushchev took steps to undo some of the worst features of Stalin's repressive regime. A certain degree of intellectual freedom was now permitted; Khrushchev said that "readers should be given the chance to make their own judgments" regarding the acceptability of controversial literature and that "police measures shouldn't be used."[9] In 1962, he allowed Alexander Solzhenitsyn (sohl-zhuh-NEET-sin) to publish his novel *A Day in the Life of Ivan Denisovich,* a grim portrayal of the horrors of the forced-labor camps. Most important, Khrushchev extended the process of **de-Stalinization** by reducing the powers of the secret police and closing some of the Siberian prison camps. Khrushchev's revelations about Stalin at the Twentieth Congress caused turmoil in Communist ranks everywhere, however, and encouraged a spirit of rebellion in Soviet satellite countries in Eastern Europe. Soviet troops reacted by crushing an uprising in Hungary in 1956, and Khrushchev and the Soviet leaders, fearful of further undermining the basic foundations of the regime, downplayed their de-Stalinization campaign.

Economically, Khrushchev tried to place more emphasis on light industry and consumer goods. Attempts to increase agricultural output by growing corn and cultivating vast lands east of the Ural Mountains proved less successful and damaged Khrushchev's reputation within the Party. These failures, combined with increased military spending, hurt the Soviet economy. The industrial growth rate, which had soared in the early 1950s, now declined dramatically from 13 percent in 1953 to 7.5 percent in 1964.

Eastern Europe: Behind the Iron Curtain

At the end of World War II, Soviet military forces remained in all the lands they had liberated from the Nazis in Eastern Europe and the Balkans except for Greece, Albania, and Yugoslavia. All of the occupied states came to be part of the Soviet sphere of influence and, after 1945, experienced similar political developments. Between 1945 and 1947, one-party Communist governments became firmly entrenched in East Germany, Bulgaria, Romania, Poland, and Hungary. In Czechoslovakia, which had some tradition of democratic institutions, the Communists did not achieve their goals until 1948 when all other parties were dissolved and Klement Gottwald (GUT-vald) (1896–1953), the leader of the Communists, became the new president of Czechoslovakia.

ALBANIA AND YUGOSLAVIA Albania and Yugoslavia were exceptions to this progression of Soviet dominance in Eastern Europe. Both had had strong Communist resistance movements during the war, and in both countries, the Communist Party simply took over power when the war ended. In Albania, local Communists established a rigidly Stalinist regime that grew increasingly independent of the Soviet Union.

In Yugoslavia, Josip Broz Tito, leader of the Communist resistance movement, seemed to be a loyal Stalinist. After the war, however, he moved toward the establishment of an independent Communist state in Yugoslavia. Stalin hoped to take control of Yugoslavia, just as he had done in other Eastern European countries, but Tito refused to capitulate to Stalin's demands and gained the support of the people by portraying the struggle as one of Yugoslav national freedom. In 1958, the Yugoslav party congress asserted that Yugoslav Communists did not see themselves as deviating from communism, only Stalinism. They considered their way closer to the Marxist-Leninist ideal. This included a more decentralized economic and political system in which workers could manage themselves and local communes could exercise some political power.

Between 1948 and Stalin's death in 1953, the Eastern European satellite states followed a policy of **Stalinization.** They instituted Soviet-type five-year plans with emphasis on heavy industry rather than consumer goods. They began to collectivize agriculture. They eliminated all non-Communist parties and established the institutions of repression—secret police and military forces. But communism—a foreign import—had not developed deep roots among the peoples of Eastern Europe. Moreover, Soviet economic exploitation of Eastern Europe resulted in harsh living conditions for most people.

1956: UPHEAVAL IN EASTERN EUROPE After Stalin's death, many Eastern European states began to pursue a new, more nationalistically oriented course as the new Soviet leaders, including Khrushchev, interfered less in the internal affairs of their satellites. But in the late 1950s, the Soviet Union also made it clear, particularly in Poland and Hungary, that it would not allow its Eastern European satellites to become independent of Soviet control.

In 1956, after the circulation of Khrushchev's denunciation of Stalin, protests—especially by workers—erupted in Poland. In response, the Polish Communist Party adopted a series of reforms in October 1956 and elected Wladyslaw Gomulka (vlah-DIS-lahf goh-MOOL-kuh) (1905–1982) as first secretary. Gomulka declared that Poland had the right to follow its own socialist path. Fearful of Soviet armed response, however, the Poles compromised. Poland pledged to remain loyal to the Warsaw Pact, and the Soviets agreed to allow Poland to follow its own path to socialism.

The developments in Poland in 1956 inspired national Communists in Hungary to seek the same kinds of reforms and independence. Intense debates eventually resulted in the ouster of the ruling Stalinist and the selection of Imry Nagy (IM-ray NAHJ) (1896–1958) as the new Hungarian leader. Internal dissent, however, was not directed simply against the Soviets but against communism in general, which was viewed as a creation of the Soviets, not the Hungarians. The Stalinist secret police had also bred much terror and hatred. This dissatisfaction, combined with economic difficulties, created a situation ripe for revolt. To quell the rising rebellion, Nagy declared Hungary a free nation on November 1, 1956. He promised free elections, and the mood of the country made it clear that this could mean the end of Communist rule in Hungary. But Khrushchev was in no position at home to allow a member of the Communist flock to fly the coop. Just three days after Nagy's declaration, the Red Army invaded the capital city of Budapest (see the box on p. 904). The Soviets reestablished control over the

(see the box on p. 904)

CHRONOLOGY   The Soviet Union and Satellite States in Eastern Europe

Death of Stalin	1953
Khrushchev's denunciation of Stalin	1956
Attempt at reforms in Poland	1956
Hungarian revolt is crushed	1956
Berlin Wall is built	1961
Brezhnev replaces Khrushchev	1964

country, and János Kádár (YAH-nush KAH-dahr) (1912–1989), a reform-minded cabinet minister, replaced Nagy and worked with the Soviets to quash the revolt. By collaborating with the Soviet invaders, Kádár saved many of Nagy's economic reforms. The developments in Poland and Hungary in 1956 discouraged any similar upheavals elsewhere in Eastern Europe.

Western Europe: The Revival of Democracy and the Economy

All the countries of Western Europe faced similar kinds of problems at the end of World War II. They needed to rebuild their economies, re-create their democratic institutions, and contend with the growth of Communist parties.

The important role that Communists had played in the resistance movements against the Nazis gained them a new respectability and strength once the war was over. Communist parties did well in elections in Italy and France in 1946 and 1947, but Communist success was short-lived. After the hardening of the divisions in the Cold War, their advocacy of Soviet policies hurt the Communist parties at home, and support began to dwindle. Only in France and Italy, where social inequities remained their focus, did Communist parties retain significant support—about 25 percent of the vote.

As part of their electoral strategy, Communist parties had often joined forces with other left-wing parties, such as the Social Democrats. Socialist parties had also fared well immediately after the war as the desire to overthrow the old order led to the abandonment of conservative politics. But support for the socialists soon waned. In France, for example, socialists won 23 percent of the vote in 1945 but 18 percent in 1946 and only 12.6 percent in 1962. The Cold War also hurt the cause of socialism. Socialist parties had originally been formed in the late nineteenth century as Marxist parties, and their identification with Communist parties in postwar coalitions cost them dearly. In the late 1950s, many socialist parties on the Continent perceived the need to eliminate their old doctrinal emphasis on class struggle and began to call for social justice and liberty. Although they advocated economic and social planning, they no longer demanded the elimination of the capitalist system.

Soviet Repression in Eastern Europe: Hungary, 1956

Developments in Poland in 1956 inspired the Communist leaders of Hungary to begin to remove their country from Soviet control. But there were limits to Khrushchev's tolerance, and he sent Soviet troops to crush Hungary's movement for independence. The first selection is a statement by the Soviet government justifying the use of Soviet troops; the second is a brief and tragic final statement from Imry Nagy, the Hungarian leader.

＊ ＝＊＝ ＊

Statement of the Soviet Government, October 30, 1956

The Soviet Government regards it as indispensable to make a statement in connection with the events in Hungary.

The course of the events has shown that the working people of Hungary, who have achieved great progress on the basis of their people's democratic order, correctly raise the question of the necessity of eliminating serious shortcomings in the field of economic building, the further raising of the material well-being of the population, and the struggle against bureaucratic excesses in the state apparatus.

However, this just and progressive movement of the working people was soon joined by forces of black reaction and counterrevolution, which are trying to take advantage of the discontent of part of the working people to undermine the foundations of the people's democratic order in Hungary and to restore the old landlord and capitalist order.

The Soviet Government and all the Soviet people deeply regret that the development of events in Hungary has led to bloodshed. On the request of the Hungarian People's Government the Soviet Government consented to the entry into Budapest of the Soviet Army units to assist the Hungarian People's Army and the Hungarian authorities to establish order in the town.

The Last Message of Imry Nagy, November 4, 1956

This fight is the fight for freedom by the Hungarian people against the Russian intervention, and it is possible that I shall only be able to stay at my post for one or two hours. The whole world will see how the Russian armed forces, contrary to all treaties and conventions, are crushing the resistance of the Hungarian people. They will also see how they are kidnapping the Prime Minister of a country which is a Member of the United Nations, taking him from the capital, and therefore it cannot be doubted at all that this is the most brutal form of intervention. I should like in these last moments to ask the leaders of the revolution, if they can, to leave the country. I ask that all that I have said in my broadcast, and what we have agreed on with the revolutionary leaders during meetings in Parliament, should be put in a memorandum, and the leaders should turn to all the peoples of the world for help and explain that today it is Hungary and tomorrow, or the day after tomorrow, it will be the turn of other countries because the imperialism of Moscow does not know borders, and is only trying to play for time. ⌦

Q Based on this selection, what was the Soviet Union's policy toward its Eastern European satellite states in the 1950s? Compare this policy with Soviet policy in Eastern Europe in the late 1980s (see Chapter 29). What impact did the change in policy have on Eastern Europe?

By 1950, moderate political parties had made a remarkable comeback in Western Europe. Especially important was the rise of Christian Democratic parties. The new Christian Democrats were not connected to the prewar church-based parties that had been advocates of church interests and had crusaded against both liberal and socialist causes. The new Christian Democrats were sincerely interested in democracy and in significant economic reforms. They were especially strong in Italy and Germany.

Western European countries recovered relatively rapidly from the devastation of World War II. The Marshall Plan played a significant role in this process. Between 1947 and 1950, European countries received $9.4 billion to be used for new equipment and raw materials. By 1950, industrial output in Europe was 30 percent above prewar levels. Between 1947 and 1950, steel production alone expanded by 70 percent. And this economic recovery continued well into the 1950s and 1960s. Those years were a time of dramatic economic growth and prosperity in Western Europe, which experienced virtually full employment.

FRANCE: THE DOMINATION OF DE GAULLE The history of France for nearly a quarter century after the war was dominated by one man—Charles de Gaulle (1890–1970)—who possessed an unshakable faith that he had a historic mission to reestablish the greatness of the French nation. During the war, de Gaulle had assumed leadership of some resistance groups and played an important role in ensuring the establishment of a French provisional government after the war. The declaration of the Fourth Republic, with a return to a parliamentary system based on parties that de Gaulle considered weak, led him to

Charles de Gaulle. As president, Charles de Gaulle sought to revive the greatness of the French nation. He is shown here dressed in his military uniform during a formal state ceremony on a visit to Quebec, Canada, in July 1967.

command. With an eye toward achieving the status of a world power, de Gaulle invested heavily in the nuclear arms race. France exploded its first nuclear bomb in 1960. Despite his successes, de Gaulle did not really achieve his ambitious goals of world power. Although his successors maintained that France was the "third nuclear power" after the United States and the Soviet Union, in truth France was too small for such global ambitions.

Although the cost of the nuclear program increased the defense budget, de Gaulle did not neglect the French economy. Economic decision making was centralized. Between 1958 and 1968, the French gross national product increased by 5.5 percent annually, faster than the U.S. economy was growing. By the end of de Gaulle's era, France was a major industrial producer and exporter, particularly in such areas as automobiles and armaments. Nevertheless, problems remained. The **nationalization** (government ownership) of traditional industries, such as coal, steel, and railroads, led to large government deficits. The cost of living increased faster than in the rest of Europe. Consumer prices were 45 percent higher in 1968 than they had been ten years earlier.

Increased dissatisfaction with the inability of de Gaulle's government to deal with these problems soon led to more violent action. In May 1968, a series of student protests, followed by a general strike by the labor unions, shook the government. Although de Gaulle managed to restore order, the events of May 1968 seriously undermined the French people's respect for their aloof and imperious president. Tired and discouraged, de Gaulle resigned from office in April 1969 and died within a year.

withdraw from politics. Eventually, he formed the French Popular Movement, a decidedly rightist organization. It blamed the parties for France's political mess and called for a stronger presidency, a goal that de Gaulle finally achieved in 1958.

The fragile political stability of the Fourth Republic had been badly shaken by the Algerian crisis. The French army had suffered defeat in Indochina in 1954 and was determined to resist Algerian demands for independence. But a strong antiwar movement among French intellectuals and church leaders led to bitter divisions that opened the door to the possibility of civil war in France. The panic-stricken leaders of the Fourth Republic offered to let de Gaulle take over the government and revise the constitution.

In 1958, de Gaulle immediately drafted a new constitution for the Fifth Republic that greatly enhanced the power of the president, who would now have the right to choose the prime minister, dissolve parliament, and supervise both defense and foreign policy. As the new president, de Gaulle sought to return France to the position of a great power. He believed that playing a pivotal role in the Cold War might enhance France's stature. For that reason, he pulled France out of the NATO high

WEST GERMANY: A RECONCEIVED NATION Already by the end of 1945, the Western powers occupying Germany (the United States, Britain, and France) had allowed the reemergence of political parties in their zones. Three major parties came forth: the Social Democrats (SPD), the Christian Democrats (CDU), and the Free Democrats (FDP). Over the next three years, the occupation forces gradually allowed the political parties to play greater roles in their zones.

As a result of the pressures of the Cold War, the unification of the three Western zones into the Federal Republic of Germany became a reality in 1949. Konrad Adenauer, the leader of the CDU who served as chancellor from 1949 to 1963, became the "founding hero" of the Federal Republic. Adenauer sought respect for West Germany by cooperating with the United States and the other Western European nations. He was especially desirous of reconciliation with France, Germany's longtime enemy. The beginning of the Korean War in June 1950 had unexpected repercussions for West Germany. The fear that South Korea might fall to the Communist forces of the north led many Germans and Westerners to worry about the security of West Germany and led to calls for the rearmament of West Germany. Although many people, concerned about a revival of German militarism, condemned this proposal, Cold War tensions were decisive. West Germany rearmed in 1955 and became a member of NATO.

Adenauer's chancellorship saw the resurrection of the West German economy, often referred to as the "economic miracle." It was largely guided by the minister of finance, Ludwig Erhard (LOOD-vik AYR-hart) (1897–1977), who pursued a policy of a new currency, free markets, low taxes, and elimination of controls, which, combined with American financial aid, led to rapid economic growth. Although West Germany had only 75 percent of the population and 52 percent of the territory of prewar Germany, by 1955 the West German gross national product exceeded that of prewar Germany. Real wages doubled between 1950 and 1965 even though work hours were cut by 20 percent. Unemployment fell from 8 percent in 1950 to 0.4 percent in 1965. To maintain its economic expansion, West Germany even imported hundreds of thousands of **guest workers,** primarily from Italy, Spain, Greece, Turkey, and Yugoslavia.

Throughout its postwar existence, West Germany was troubled by its Nazi past. The surviving major Nazi leaders had been tried and condemned as war criminals at war crimes trials held in Nuremberg in 1945 and 1946. As part of the denazification of Germany, the victorious Allies continued war crimes trials of lesser officials, but these diminished as the Cold War brought about a shift in attitudes. By 1950, German courts had begun to take over the war crimes trials, and the German legal machine persisted in prosecuting cases.

Adenauer resigned in 1963, after fourteen years of firmly guiding West Germany through its postwar recovery. Adenauer had wanted no grand experimentation at home or abroad; he was content to give Germany time to regain its equilibrium. Ludwig Erhard succeeded Adenauer and largely continued his policies. But an economic downturn in the mid-1960s opened the door to the rise of the Social Democrats, and in 1969, they became the leading party.

GREAT BRITAIN: THE WELFARE STATE The end of World War II left Britain with massive economic problems. In elections held immediately after the war, the Labour Party overwhelmingly defeated Churchill's Conservative Party. The Labour Party had promised far-reaching reforms, particularly in the area of social welfare, and in a country with a tremendous shortage of consumer goods and housing, its platform was quite appealing. The new Labour government, with Clement Attlee (1883–1967) as prime minister, proceeded to enact reforms that created a modern **welfare state.**

The establishment of the British welfare state began with the nationalization of the Bank of England, the coal and steel industries, public transportation, and public utilities, such as electricity and gas. In the area of social welfare, the new government enacted the National Insurance Act and the National Health Service Act in 1946.

The British Welfare State: Free Milk at School. The creation of the welfare state was a prominent social development in postwar Europe. The desire to improve the health of children led to welfare programs that provided free food for young people. Pictured here are boys at a grammar school in England during a free milk break.

The insurance act established a comprehensive **social security** program and nationalized medical insurance, thereby enabling the state to subsidize the unemployed, the sick, and the aged. The health act created a system of **socialized medicine** that required doctors and dentists to work with state hospitals, although private practices could be maintained. This measure was especially costly for the state, but within a few years, 90 percent of medical practitioners were participating. The British welfare state became the model for most European states after the war.

The cost of building a welfare state at home forced the British to reduce expenses abroad. This meant the dismantling of the British Empire and the reduction of military aid to such countries as Greece and Turkey. It was not a belief in the morality of self-determination but economic necessity that brought an end to the British Empire.

Continuing economic problems, however, brought the Conservatives back into power from 1951 to 1964. Although they favored private enterprise, the Conservatives accepted the welfare state and even extended it when they undertook an ambitious construction program to improve British housing. Although the British economy had recovered from the war, it had done so at a slower rate than other European countries. Moreover, the slow rate of recovery masked a long-term economic decline caused by a variety of factors. The demands of British trade unions for wages that rose faster than productivity were a problem in the late 1950s and 1960s. The unwillingness of the British to invest in modern industrial machinery and to adopt new methods also did not help. Underlying the immediate problems, however, was a deeper issue. As a result of World War II, Britain had lost much of its prewar revenues from abroad but was left with a burden of debt from its many international commitments. Britain was no longer a world power.

ITALY: WEAK COALITION GOVERNMENT After the war, Italy faced a period of heavy reconstruction. Only Germany had sustained more physical destruction. The monarchy was abolished when 54 percent of Italian voters rejected the royal house, and in June 1946, Italy became a democratic republic.

In the first postwar parliamentary elections, held in April 1948, the Christian Democrats, still allied with the Catholic Church, emerged as the leading political party. Alcide de Gasperi (ahl-SEE-day day GAHSS-pe-ree) (1881–1954) served as prime minister from 1948 to 1953, an unusually long span of time for an Italian government. Like pre-Fascist governments, postwar Italian coalitions, largely dominated by the Christian Democrats, were famous for their instability and short lives. Although the Italian Communist Party was one of Italy's three largest parties, it was largely excluded from all of these government coalitions. It did, however, manage to gain power in a number of provinces and municipalities in the 1960s. The Christian Democrats were able to maintain control by keeping the support of the upper and middle classes and the southern peasantry.

Italy, too, experienced an "economic miracle" after the war, although it was far less publicized than Germany's. The Marshall Plan helped stabilize the postwar Italian economy. Especially during the late 1950s and early 1960s, Italy made rapid strides in economic growth. The production of electrical appliances, cars, and office machinery made the most significant leap. As in other Western welfare states, the Italian economy combined private enterprise with government management, particularly of heavy industry. In 1965, for example, the government controlled 60 percent of Italy's steel production. The major economic problem continued to be the backwardness of southern Italy, a region that possessed 36 percent of the total population but generated only 25 percent of the national income. In the 1960s, millions of Italians from the south migrated to the more prosperous north.

Western Europe: The Move Toward Unity

As we have seen, the divisions created by the Cold War led the nations of Western Europe to form the North Atlantic Treaty Organization in 1949. But military unity was not the only kind of unity fostered in Europe after 1945. The destructiveness of two world wars caused many thoughtful Europeans to consider the need for some form of European unity. National feeling was still too powerful,

CHRONOLOGY Western Europe After the War

Welfare state emerges in Great Britain	1946
Italy becomes a democratic republic	1946
Alcide de Gasperi becomes prime minister of Italy	1948
Konrad Adenauer becomes chancellor of West Germany	1949
Formation of European Coal and Steel Community	1951
West Germany joins NATO	1955
Suez Crisis	1956
Formation of EURATOM	1957
Formation of European Economic Community (Common Market)	1957
Charles de Gaulle assumes power in France	1958
Erhard becomes chancellor of Germany	1963

however, for European nations to give up their political sovereignty. Consequently, the desire for a sense of solidarity was forced to focus primarily on the economic arena, not the political one.

In 1951, France, West Germany, the Benelux countries (Belgium, Netherlands, and Luxembourg), and Italy formed the European Coal and Steel Community (ECSC). Its purpose was to create a common market for coal and steel products among the six nations by eliminating tariffs and other trade barriers. The success of the ECSC encouraged its members to proceed further, and in 1957 they created the European Atomic Energy Community (EURATOM) to further European research on the peaceful uses of nuclear energy.

In the same year, these six nations signed the Rome Treaty, which created the European Economic Community (EEC), also known as the Common Market. The EEC eliminated customs barriers for the six member nations and created a large free-trade area protected from the rest of the world by a common external tariff. By promoting free trade, the EEC also encouraged cooperation and standardization in many aspects of the six nations' economies. All the member nations benefited economically. With a total population of 165 million, the EEC became the world's largest exporter and purchaser of raw materials. Only the United States surpassed the EEC in steel production.

European Economic Community, 1957

The United States and Canada: A New Era

Q **Focus Question**: What were the main political developments in North America between 1945 and 1965?

At the end of World War II, the United States was one of the world's two superpowers. As the Cold War with the Soviet Union intensified, the United States worked hard to prevent the spread of communism throughout the world. American domestic political life after 1945 was played out against a background of American military power abroad.

American Politics and Society in the 1950s

Between 1945 and 1970, the ideals of Franklin Roosevelt's New Deal largely determined the patterns of American domestic politics. The New Deal had brought basic changes to American society, including a dramatic increase in the role and power of the federal government, the rise of organized labor as a significant force in the economy and politics, the beginning of a welfare state, and a grudging realization of the need to deal fairly with the concerns of minorities.

The New Deal tradition was bolstered by the election of three Democratic presidents—Harry Truman in 1948, John Kennedy in 1960, and Lyndon Johnson in 1964. Even the election of a Republican president, Dwight Eisenhower, in 1952 and 1956 did not change the basic direction of American politics. As Eisenhower stated, "Should any political party attempt to abolish Social Security and eliminate labor laws and farm programs, you would not hear of that party again in our political history."

The economic boom after World War II fueled confidence in the American way of life. A shortage of consumer goods during the war had left Americans with both extra income and a pent-up desire to buy these goods after the war. Then, too, the growth of labor unions brought higher wages that enabled more and more workers to buy consumer goods. Between 1945 and 1973, real wages grew 3 percent a year on average, the most prolonged advance in American history.

Prosperity was not the only characteristic of the early 1950s. Cold War confrontations abroad had repercussions at home. The takeover of China by Mao Zedong's Communist forces in 1949 and Communist North Korea's invasion of South Korea in 1950 led to a fear that Communists had infiltrated the United States. President Truman's attorney general warned that Communists "are everywhere—in factories, offices, butcher stores, on street corners, in private businesses. And each carried in himself the germ of death for society." A demagogic senator from Wisconsin, Joseph R. McCarthy, helped intensify the "Red Scare" with his exposés of supposed Communists in high government positions. McCarthy went too far when he attacked alleged "Communist conspirators" in the U.S. Army and was censured by Congress in 1954. Very quickly, his anti-Communist crusade came to an end.

Decade of Upheaval: America in the 1960s

During the 1960s, the United States experienced a period of upheaval that brought to the fore problems that had been glossed over in the 1950s. The 1960s began on a youthful and optimistic note. At age forty-three, John F. Kennedy became the youngest elected president in the history of the United States. His own administration, cut short by an assassin's bullet on November 22, 1963, focused primarily on foreign affairs. Kennedy's successor, Lyndon B. Johnson (1908–1973), who won a new term as president in a landslide in 1964, used his stunning mandate to pursue what he called the Great Society, heir to the welfare state first begun in the New Deal. Johnson's programs included health care for the elderly, a "war on poverty" to be fought with food stamps and the new Job Corps, the new Department of Housing and Urban Development to deal with the problems of the cities, and federal assistance for education.

CIVIL RIGHTS MOVEMENT Johnson's other domestic passion was equal rights for African Americans. The civil rights movement had its beginnings in 1954 when the U.S. Supreme Court took the dramatic step of striking down the practice of racially segregating public schools. An eloquent Baptist minister named Martin Luther King Jr. (1929–1968) became the leader of a growing movement for racial equality, and by the early 1960s, a number of groups, including King's Southern Christian Leadership Conference (SCLC), were organizing sit-ins and demonstrations across the South to end racial segregation. In August 1963, King led the March on Washington for Jobs and Freedom to dramatize African Americans' desire for equal rights and opportunities. This march and King's impassioned plea for racial equality had an electrifying effect on the American people.

President Johnson took up the cause of civil rights. As a result of his initiative, Congress passed the Civil Rights Act of 1964, which created the machinery to end segregation and discrimination in the workplace and all public places. A voting rights act the following year made it easier for blacks to vote in southern states. But laws alone could not guarantee the Great Society, and Johnson soon faced bitter social unrest, both from African Americans and from the burgeoning movement opposing the Vietnam War.

In the North and the West, African Americans had had voting rights for many years, but local patterns of segregation led to higher unemployment rates for blacks than for whites and left African Americans segregated in huge urban ghettos. In these ghettos, the call for action by radical black leaders, such as Malcom X (1925–1965) of

The Civil Rights Movement. In the early 1960s, Martin Luther King Jr. and his Southern Christian Leadership Conference organized a variety of activities to pursue the goal of racial equality. He is shown here with his wife Coretta (right) and Rosa Parks and Ralph Abernathy (far left) leading a march against racial discrimination in 1965.

the Black Muslims, attracted more attention than the nonviolent appeals of Martin Luther King. Malcom X's advice was straightforward: "If someone puts a hand on you, send him to the cemetery."

In the summer of 1965, race riots broke out in the Watts district of Los Angeles. Thirty-four people died and more than one thousand buildings were destroyed. Cleveland, San Francisco, Chicago, Newark, and Detroit likewise exploded in the summers of 1966 and 1967. After the assassination of Martin Luther King in 1968, more than one hundred cities experienced riots. The combination of riots and extremist comments by radical black leaders led to a "white backlash" and a severe division of the American population.

The Development of Canada

Canada experienced many of the same developments as the United States in the postwar years. For twenty-five years after World War II, prosperous Canada set out on a new path of industrial development. Canada had always had a strong export economy based on its abundant natural resources. Now it also developed electronic, aircraft, nuclear, and chemical engineering industries on a large scale. Much of the Canadian growth, however, was financed by capital from the United States, which led to American ownership of Canadian businesses. Although many Canadians welcomed the economic growth, others feared American economic domination.

Canadians also worried about playing a secondary role politically and militarily to their neighboring superpower. Canada agreed to join NATO in 1949 and even sent military forces to fight in Korea the following year. At the same time, to avoid subordination to the United States, Canada actively supported the United Nations. Nevertheless, concerns about

the United States did not keep Canada from maintaining a special relationship with its southern neighbor. The North American Air Defense Command (NORAD), formed in 1957, maintained close cooperation between the air forces of the two countries for the defense of North America against Soviet bombers.

After 1945, the Liberal Party continued to dominate Canadian politics until 1957, when John Diefenbaker (1895–1979) achieved a Conservative Party victory. But major economic problems returned the Liberals to power, and under Lester Pearson (1897–1972), they created Canada's welfare state by enacting a national social security system (the Canada Pension Plan) and a national health insurance program.

Postwar Society and Culture in the Western World

 FOCUS QUESTION: What major changes occurred in Western society and culture between 1945 and 1965?

During the postwar era, Western society and culture witnessed remarkably rapid change. Computers, television, jet planes, contraceptive devices, and new surgical techniques all dramatically and quickly altered the pace and nature of human life. The rapid changes in postwar society, fueled by scientific advances and rapid economic growth, led many to view it as a new society.

The Structure of European Society

The structure of European society was altered after 1945. Especially noticeable were the changes in the middle class.

Such traditional middle-class groups as businesspeople and professionals in law, medicine, and the universities were greatly augmented by a new group of managers and technicians as large companies and government agencies employed increasing numbers of white-collar supervisory and administrative personnel. In both Eastern and Western Europe, the new managers and experts were very much alike. Everywhere their positions depended on specialized knowledge acquired from some form of higher education. Everywhere they focused on the effective administration of their organizations. Because their positions usually depended on their skills, they took steps to ensure that their own children would be educated.

A SOCIETY OF CONSUMERS Changes also occurred among the traditional lower classes. Especially noticeable was the dramatic shift of people from rural to urban areas. The number of people working in agriculture declined dramatically, yet the size of the industrial labor force remained the same. In West Germany, industrial workers made up 48 percent of the labor force throughout the 1950s and 1960s. Thereafter, the number of industrial workers began to dwindle as white-collar and service jobs increased. At the same time, a substantial increase in their real wages enabled the working classes to aspire to the consumption patterns of the middle class, leading to what some observers have called the **consumer society.** Buying on the installment plan, introduced in the 1920s, became widespread in the 1950s and gave workers a chance to imitate the middle class by buying such products as televisions, washing machines, refrigerators, vacuum cleaners, and stereos. Shopping for everyday commodities, such as food products, also became easier and cheaper with the introduction of supermarkets (see Images of Everyday Life on p. 911). But the most visible symbol of mass consumerism was the automobile. Before World War II, cars were reserved mostly for the European upper classes. In 1948, there were 5 million cars in all of Europe, but by 1957, the number had tripled. By the 1960s, there were almost 45 million cars.

MASS LEISURE Rising incomes, combined with shorter working hours, created an even greater market for mass leisure activities. Between 1900 and 1960, the workweek was reduced from sixty hours to a little more than forty hours, and the number of paid holidays increased. In the 1960s, German and Italian workers received between thirty-two and thirty-five paid holidays a year. All aspects of popular culture—music, sports, media—became commercialized and offered opportunities for leisure activities, including concerts, sporting events, and television viewing.

Another visible symbol of mass leisure was the growth of mass tourism. Before World War II, mostly the upper and middle classes traveled for pleasure. After the war, the combination of more vacation time, increased prosperity, and the flexibility provided by package tours with their lower rates and less expensive lodgings enabled millions to expand their travel possibilities. By the mid-1960s, 100 million tourists were crossing European boundaries each year.

Creation of the Welfare State

One of the most noticeable social developments in postwar Europe was the creation of the welfare state. In one sense, the welfare state represented another extension of the power of the state over the lives of its citizens, a process that had increased dramatically as a result of two world wars. Yet the goal of the welfare state was to make it possible for people to live better and more meaningful lives. Advocates of the welfare state believed that by eliminating poverty and homelessness, providing medical services for all, ensuring dignity for older people, and extending educational opportunities for all who wanted them, the state would satisfy people's material needs and thereby free them to achieve happiness.

Social welfare schemes were not new to Europe. Beginning in the late nineteenth century, some states had provided for the welfare of the working class by instituting old-age pensions, medical insurance, and unemployment compensation. But these efforts were piecemeal and were by no means based on a general belief that society had a responsibility to care for all of its citizens.

The new postwar social legislation greatly extended earlier benefits and created new ones as well. Of course, social welfare benefits differed considerably from country to country in quantity and quality as well as in how they were paid for and managed. Nevertheless, there were some common trends. In many countries, already existing benefits for sickness, accidents, unemployment, and old age were simply extended to cover more people and provide larger payments. Men were generally eligible for old-age pensions at age sixty-five and women at sixty.

Affordable health care for all people was another goal of the welfare state, although the methods of achieving this goal varied. In some countries, medical care was free to all people with some kind of insurance, but in others, people had to contribute toward the cost of their medical care. The amount ranged from 10 to 25 percent of the total cost.

Another feature of welfare states was the use of **family allowances,** which were instituted in some countries to provide a minimum level of material care for children. Most family allowance programs provided a fixed amount per child. Family allowances were also conceived in large part as a way to increase the population after the decline suffered during the war. The French, for example, increased the amount of aid for each new child after the first one.

Welfare states also sought to remove class barriers to opportunity by expanding the number of universities and providing scholarship aid to allow everyone to attend these institutions of higher learning. Overall, European states moved toward free tuition or modest fees for university attendance. These policies did not always achieve their goals, however. In the early 1960s, most students in

IMAGES OF EVERYDAY LIFE

The Rise of the Supermarket

For more than a decade after World War II, many food supplies were still scarce in Europe. Consequently, food was much more expensive in Europe than in the United States. For American consumers, the introduction of standardized foodstuffs and self-service supermarkets had led to lower prices for basic staples, leaving families more money to spend on refrigerators, televisions, and automobiles. In the 1950s, an average working family in Europe spent about 50 percent of its budget on food, twice as much as a typical American family spent. In the mid-1950s, however, supermarkets began to open in major European cities. The first illustration shows

German shoppers looking at bins of produce at a new supermarket in Frankfurt in 1954. These early supermarkets were not an immediate success. Few Europeans had refrigerators or automobiles, so storing and transporting large food purchases was difficult. Moreover, because most Europeans purchased their food from small vendors in their neighborhoods, there had never been a system of mass distribution or brand-name goods. In time, however, as more women entered the workforce, both women and men began to appreciate the convenience of shopping at a supermarket, as shown in the second photograph of a newly opened supermarket in Maidenhead, England. The third illustration shows shoppers looking at wrapped packages of meat in refrigerated cases, a new phenomenon of the times. As families moved to the suburbs and acquired automobiles, supermarkets became more accessible. Between 1956 and 1961, the number of self-service supermarkets increased dramatically, rising from 1,380 to 30,680 in West Germany, from 603 to 2,700 in France, and from 3,000 to 9,000 in Britain. During the 1960s, the supermarket became a fixture in Western European cities. ▷

Western European universities still came from privileged backgrounds. In Britain, 25 percent of university students came from working-class backgrounds; in France, the figure was only 17.6 percent.

The welfare state dramatically increased the amount of money states expended on social services. In 1967, such spending constituted 17 percent of the gross national product of the major European countries; by the 1980s, it absorbed 40 to 50 percent. To some critics, these figures proved that the welfare state had produced a new generation of citizens overly dependent on the state. But most people favored the benefits, and most leaders were well aware that it was political suicide to advocate curtailing or seriously lowering those benefits.

GENDER ISSUES IN THE WELFARE STATE Gender issues also influenced the form that the welfare state took in different countries. One general question dominated the debate: Should women be recognized in a special category as mothers, or should they be regarded as individuals? William Beveridge, the economist who drafted the report that formed the basis for the British welfare state, said that women had "vital work to do in ensuring the adequate continuance of the British race." "During marriage," he said, "most women will not be gainfully employed. The small minority of women who undertake paid employment or other gainful employment or other gainful occupations after marriage require special treatment differing from that of single women."[10] Accordingly, the British welfare system was based on the belief that women should stay home with their children: women received subsidies for children, but married women who worked were given few or no benefits. Employers were also encouraged to pay women lower wages to discourage them from joining the workforce. Thus, the British welfare system encouraged the dependence of wives on their husbands. So did the West German system. The West German government passed laws that discouraged women from working. In keeping its women at home, West Germany sought to differentiate itself from neighboring Communist countries in Eastern Europe and the Soviet Union, where women were encouraged to work outside the home. At the same time, to help working women raise families, Communist governments also provided day-care facilities, as well as family subsidies and maternity benefits.

France sought to maintain the individual rights of women in its welfare system. The French government recognized women as equal to men and thus as entitled to the same welfare benefits as men for working outside the home. At the same time, wanting to encourage population growth, the government provided incentives for women to stay home and bear children as well as day-care and after-school programs to assist working mothers.

Women in the Postwar Western World

Despite their enormous contributions to the war effort, women were removed from the workforce at the end of World War II to provide jobs for the soldiers returning home. After the horrors of war, people seemed willing for a while to return to traditional family practices. Female participation in the workforce declined, and birthrates began to rise, creating a "baby boom." This increase in the birthrate did not last, however, and birthrates, and thus the size of families, began to decline by the end of the 1950s. Largely responsible for this decline was the widespread practice of birth control. Invented in the nineteenth century, the condom was already in wide use, but the development in the 1960s of oral contraceptives, known as birth control pills or simply "the pill," provided a reliable means of birth control that quickly spread to all Western countries.

WOMEN IN THE WORKFORCE The trend toward smaller families no doubt contributed to the change in the character of women's employment in both Europe and the United States as women experienced considerably more years when they were not involved in rearing children. The most important development was the increased number of married women in the workforce. At the beginning of the twentieth century, even working-class wives tended to stay at home if they could afford to do so. In the postwar period, this was no longer the case. In the United States, for example, in 1900, married women made up about 15 percent of the female labor force; by 1970, their number had increased to 62 percent. The percentage of married women in the female labor force in Sweden increased from 47 to 66 percent between 1963 and 1975. Figures for the Soviet Union and its satellites were even higher. In 1970, fully 92.5 percent of all women in the Soviet Union held jobs, compared to around 50 percent in France and West Germany.

But the increased number of women in the workforce did not change some old patterns. Working-class women in particular still earned salaries lower than those of men for equal work. In the 1960s, women earned only 60 percent of men's wages in Britain, 50 percent in France, and 63 percent in West Germany. In addition, women still tended to enter traditionally female jobs. As one Swedish female guidance counselor remarked in 1975, "Every girl now thinks in terms of a job. This is progress. They want children, but they don't pin their hopes on marriage. They don't intend to be housewives for some future husband. But there has been no change in their vocational choices."[11] Many European women also still faced the double burden of earning income on the one hand and raising a family and maintaining the household on the other.

SUFFRAGE AND THE SEARCH FOR LIBERATION The participation of women in the two world wars helped them achieve one of the major aims of the nineteenth-century women's movement—the right to vote. Already after World War I, many governments acknowledged the contributions of women to the war effort by granting them suffrage. Sweden, Great Britain, Germany, Poland,

The Voice of the Women's Liberation Movement

Simone de Beauvoir was an important figure in the emergence of the postwar women's liberation movement. This excerpt is taken from her influential book *The Second Sex,* in which she argued that women have been forced into a position subordinate to men.

━━ ✠⚎✠ ━━

Simone de Beauvoir, *The Second Sex*

Now, woman has always been man's dependent, if not his slave; the two sexes have never shared the world in equality. And even today woman is heavily handicapped, though her situation is beginning to change. Almost nowhere is her legal status the same as man's and frequently it is much to her disadvantage. Even when her rights are legally recognized in the abstract, long-standing custom prevents their full expression in the mores. In the economic sphere men and women can almost be said to make up two castes; other things being equal, the former hold the better jobs, get higher wages, and have more opportunity for success than their new competitors. In industry and politics men have a great many more positions and they monopolize the most important posts. In addition to all this they enjoy a traditional prestige that the education of children tends in every way to support, for the present enshrines the past—and in the past all history has been made by men. At the present time, when women are beginning to take part in the affairs of the world, it is still a world that belongs to men—they have no doubt of it at all and women have scarcely any. To decline to be the Other, to refuse to be a party to a deal—this would be for women to renounce all the advantages conferred upon them by their alliance with the superior caste. Man-the-sovereign will provide woman-the-liege with material protection and will undertake the moral justification of her existence; thus she can evade at once both economic risk and the metaphysical risk of a liberty in which ends and aims must be contrived without assistance. Indeed, along with the ethical urge of each individual to affirm his subjective existence, there is also the temptation to forgo liberty and become a thing. This is an inauspicious road, for he who takes it—passive, lost, ruined—becomes henceforth the creature of another's will, frustrated in his transcendence and deprived of every value. But it is an easy road; on it one avoids the strain involved in undertaking an authentic existence. When man makes of woman the *Other* he may, then, expect her to manifest deep-seated tendencies toward complicity. Thus woman may fail to lay claim to the status of subject because she lacks definite resources, because she feels the necessary bond that ties her to man regardless of reciprocity, and because she is often very well pleased with her role as the *Other.*

Now, what peculiarly signalizes the situation of woman is that she—a free and autonomous being like all human creatures—nevertheless finds herself living in a world where men compel her to assume the status of the Other. ✒

Q What factors or values do you think informed de Beauvoir's implicit call for a new history of women? Why was she outraged by the neglect of women in the Western historical consciousness?

Hungary, Austria, and Czechoslovakia did so in 1918, followed by the United States in 1920. Women in France and Italy did not obtain the right to vote until 1945. After World War II, European women tended to fall back into the traditional roles expected of them, and little was heard of feminist concerns.

A women's liberation movement would arise in the late 1960s (see Chapter 29), but much of the theoretical foundation for the emergence of the postwar women's liberation movement was evident in the earlier work of Simone de Beauvoir (see-MUHN duh boh-VWAR) (1908–1986). Born into a Catholic middle-class family and educated at the Sorbonne in Paris, she supported herself as a teacher and later as a novelist and writer. She maintained a lifelong relationship (but not marriage) with Jean-Paul Sartre (ZHAHNH-POHL SAR-truh). Her involvement in the existentialist movement, the leading intellectual movement of the time (see "The Philosophical Dilemma: Existentialism" later in this chapter), led to her involvement in political causes. De Beauvoir believed that she lived a "liberated" life for a twentieth-century European woman, but for all her freedom, she still came to perceive that as a woman she faced limits that men did not. In 1949, she published her highly influential work *The Second Sex,* in which she argued that as a result of male-dominated societies, women had been defined by their differences from men and consequently received second-class status: "What peculiarly signalizes the situation of woman is that she—a free and autonomous being like all human creatures—nevertheless finds herself living in a world where men compel her to assume the status of the Other."[12] De Beauvoir took an active role in the French women's movement of the 1970s, and her book was a major influence on both sides of the Atlantic (see the box above).

Postwar Art and Literature

Many artists and writers struggled to understand the horrors of World War II. The German philosopher Theodor Adorno believed that "to write poetry after Auschwitz is barbaric."

© 2010 Artists Rights Society (ARS), New York/ADAGP, Paris. On Loan to the Hamburg Kunsthalle, Hamburg//The Bridgeman Art Library

Jean Dubuffet, *Portrait of Jean Paulhan.* In 1947, Jean Dubuffet exhibited more than seventy portraits of his friends and colleagues at the Galerie René Drouin in Paris. The subjects of Dubuffet's portraits included both Nazi sympathizers and fighters against the German occupation. Jean Paulhan, the subject of this portrait, was a well-known critic and writer. Paulhan, who promoted Dubuffet's work, had led an underground movement to resist Nazi propaganda during World War II.

ART Jean Dubuffet (ZHAHNH doo-buh-FAY) (1901–1985) was a French artist who adopted an intentionally raw style of art to depict the atrocities wrought by global conflict and genocide. Dubuffet consciously rejected notions of beauty to capture the effects of war. Borrowing from the art of children and the psychologically distressed, Dubuffet developed *Art Brut* (AR BROOT), a gritty style that suggested no formal training. He created numerous portraits that caricatured Nazi sympathizers and members of the French resistance alike.

Although Dubuffet remained in Paris during the war years, many artists and writers, particularly the Surrealists, fled to the United States to avoid persecution for their revolutionary ideas. Following the war, the United States dominated the art world, much as it did the world of popular culture (see "The Americanization of the World" later in this chapter). New York City replaced Paris as the artistic center of the West. The Guggenheim Museum,

the Museum of Modern Art, and the Whitney Museum of Modern Art, together with New York's numerous art galleries, promoted modern art and helped determine artistic tastes throughout much of the world. One of the styles that became synonymous with the emergence of the New York art scene was **Abstract Expressionism.**

Dubbed "action painting" by one critic, Abstract Expressionism was energetic and spontaneous, qualities evident in the enormous canvases of Jackson Pollock (1912–1956). In such works as *Lavender Mist* (1950), paint seems to explode, enveloping the viewer with emotion and movement. Pollock's swirling forms and seemingly chaotic patterns broke all conventions of form and structure. His drip paintings, with their total abstraction, were extremely influential with other artists, and he eventually became a celebrity. Inspired by Native American sand painters, Pollock painted with the canvas on the floor. He explained, "On the floor I am more at ease. I feel nearer, more a part of the painting, since this way I can walk around in, work from four sides and be literally *in* the painting. When I am in the painting, I am not aware of what I am doing. There is pure harmony."

The 1950s and early 1960s saw the emergence of **Pop Art,** which took images of popular culture and transformed them into works of fine art. Several British art students, known as the Independent Group, incorporated science fiction and American advertising techniques into their exhibitions. "This Is Tomorrow," an exhibit held in 1956 at the Whitechapel Gallery in London, was the group's crowning achievement. It featured environments inspired by advertisements as well as mural-sized reproductions of movie characters like Robby the Robot.

Andy Warhol (1930–1987), who began as an advertising illustrator, became the most famous of the American Pop artists. Warhol adapted images from commercial art, such as Campbell's soup cans, and photographs of celebrities such as Marilyn Monroe. Derived from mass culture, these works were mass-produced and deliberately "of the moment," expressing the fleeting whims of popular culture. The detached style of Warhol's silk-screened prints put Pop Art at odds with the aggressive, painterly techniques of the Abstract Expressionists.

LITERATURE The most significant new trend in postwar literature was called the "Theater of the Absurd." This new convention in drama began in France in the 1950s, although its most famous proponent was the Irishman Samuel Beckett (1906–1990), who lived in France. In Beckett's *Waiting for Godot* (1952), the action on stage is not realistic. Two men wait incessantly for the appearance of someone, with whom they may or may not have an appointment. No background information on the two men is provided. During the course of the play, nothing seems

914 ❖ **CHAPTER 28** Cold War and a New Western World, 1945–1965

Jackson Pollock Painting. After World War II, Abstract Expressionism moved to the center of the artistic mainstream. One of its best-known practitioners was the American Jackson Pollock, who achieved his ideal of total abstraction in his drip paintings. He is shown here at work in his Long Island studio. Pollock found it easier to cover his large canvases with spontaneous patterns of color when he put them on the floor.

to be happening. The audience is never told if what they are watching is real or not. Unlike traditional theater, suspense is maintained not by having the audience wonder what is going to happen next but by having them ask, what is happening now?

The Theater of the Absurd reflected its time. The postwar period was a time of disillusionment with ideological beliefs in politics or religion. A sense of the world's meaninglessness underscored the desolate worldview of absurdist drama and literature. This can be seen in the novel *The Tin Drum* (1959) by Günter Grass (b. 1927), which reflected postwar Germany's preoccupation with the seeming incomprehensibility of Nazi Germany.

The Philosophical Dilemma: Existentialism

The sense of meaninglessness that inspired the Theater of the Absurd also underscored the philosophy of

existentialism. It was born largely of the desperation caused by two world wars and the breakdown of traditional values. Existentialism reflected the anxieties of the twentieth century and became especially well known after World War II through the works of two Frenchmen, Jean-Paul Sartre (1905–1980) and Albert Camus (ahl-BAYR ka-MOO) (1913–1960).

The central point of the existentialism of Sartre and Camus was the absence of God in the universe. The death of God, though tragic, meant that humans had no preordained destiny and were utterly alone in the universe, with no future and no hope. As Camus expressed it:

> A world that can be explained even with bad reasons is a familiar world. But, on the other hand, in a universe suddenly divested of illusions and lights, man feels an alien, a stranger. His exile is without remedy since he is deprived of the memory of a lost home or the hope of a promised land. This divorce between man and his life, the actor and his setting, is properly the feeling of absurdity.[13]

According to Camus, then, the world was absurd and without meaning; humans, too, are without meaning and purpose. Reduced to despair and depression, humans have but one source of hope—themselves.

Though the world might be absurd, Camus argued, it could not be absurd unless people judged it to be so. People are unique in the world, and their kind of being is quite different from that of all others. In the words of Sartre, human "existence precedes essence." Humans are beings who first exist and then define themselves. They determine what they will be. According to Sartre, "Man is nothing else but what he makes of himself. Such is the first principle of existentialism." People, then, must take full responsibility for what they are. They create their values and give their lives meaning. And this can only be done by their involvement in life. Only through one's acts can one determine one's values.

Existentialism, therefore, involved an ethics of action, of involvement in life. But people could not define themselves without their involvement with others. Thus, existentialism's ethical message was just as important as its philosophy of being. Essentially, the message of existentialism was one of authenticity. Individuals true to themselves refused to be depersonalized by their society. As one author noted, "Existentialism is the struggle to discover the human person in a depersonalized age."

The Attempt to Revive Religion

Existentialism was one response to the despair generated by the apparent collapse of civilized values in the twentieth century. The attempt to revive religion was another. Ever since the Enlightenment of the eighteenth century, Christianity and religion had been on the defensive. But a number of religious thinkers and leaders attempted to bring new life to Christianity in the twentieth century.

One expression of this religious revival was the attempt by the Protestant theologian Karl Barth (BAHRT)

(1886–1968) to infuse traditional Christian teachings with new life. In his numerous writings, Barth attempted to reinterpret the religious insights of the Reformation era for the modern world. To Barth, the sinful and hence imperfect nature of human beings meant that humans could know religious truth not through reason but only through the grace of God.

In the Catholic Church, an attempt at religious renewal also came from a charismatic pope. Pope John XXIII (1881–1963) reigned as pope for only a short time (1958–1963) but sparked a dramatic revival of Catholicism when he summoned the twenty-first ecumenical council of the Catholic Church. Known as Vatican II, the council liberalized a number of Catholic practices. For example, the liturgy of the Mass, the central feature of Catholic worship, was now to be spoken in the vernacular, not in Latin. New avenues of communication with other Christian faiths were also opened for the first time since the Reformation.

But these attempts to redefine Christianity were not necessarily successful at rekindling people's faith. Although many churches experienced an upswing in involvement in the late 1940s and early 1950s, no doubt as a response to the war, by the late 1950s and 1960s, attendance was declining at European churches. Even in Italy, regular attendance by members of the Catholic Church fell from 69 percent in 1956 to 48 percent in 1968.

The Explosion of Popular Culture

Since World War II, popular culture has played an increasingly important role in helping Western people define themselves. The history of popular culture is also the history of the economic system that supports it, for this system manufactures, distributes, and sells the images that people consume as popular culture. As popular culture and its economic support system have become increasingly intertwined, industries of leisure have emerged. As one historian of popular culture has argued, "Industrial societies turn the provision of leisure into a commercial activity, in which their citizens are sold entertainment, recreation, pleasure, and appearance as commodities that differ from the goods at the drugstore only in the way they are used."[14] Thus, modern popular culture is inextricably tied to the mass consumer society in which it has emerged.

THE AMERICANIZATION OF THE WORLD The United States has been the most influential force in shaping popular culture in the West and, to a lesser degree, the rest of the world. Through movies, music, advertising, and television, the United States has spread its particular form of consumerism and the American dream to millions around the world. Already in 1923, the New York *Morning Post* noted that "the film is to America what the flag was once to Britain. By its means Uncle Sam may hope some day . . . to Americanize the world."[15] In movies, television, and popular music, the impact of American popular culture on the Western world is pervasive.

Motion pictures were the primary vehicle for the diffusion of American popular culture in the years immediately following the war, and they continued to dominate both European and American markets in the next decades (40 percent of Hollywood's income in the 1960s came from the European market). Nevertheless, the existence of a profitable art-house circuit in America and Europe enabled European filmmakers to make films whose themes and avant-garde methods were quite different from those

The Beatles. Although rock-and-roll originated in the United States, it inspired musical groups around the world. This was certainly true of Britain's Beatles, who caused a sensation among young people when they came to the United States in the 1960s. Here the Beatles are shown during a performance on *The Ed Sullivan Show*.

AP Images

of Hollywood. Italy and Sweden, for example, developed a tradition of "national cinema" that reflected "specific cultural traits in a mode in which they could be successfully exported." The 1957 film *The Seventh Seal*, by the Swedish director Ingmar Bergman (1918–2007), was a good example of the successful European art film. Bergman's films caused him to be viewed as "an artist of comparable stature to a novelist or playwright." So too were François Truffaut (frahnh-SWAH troo-FOH) (1932–1984) in France and Federico Fellini (1920–1993) in Italy; such directors gloried in experimenting with subject matter and technique and produced films dealing with more complex and daring themes than Hollywood would attempt.

Although developed in the 1930s, television did not become readily available until the late 1940s. By 1954, there were 32 million sets in the United States as television became the centerpiece of middle-class life. In the 1960s, as television spread around the world, American networks unloaded their products on Europe and the Third World at extraordinarily low prices. For instance, the British Broadcasting Corporation (BBC) could buy American programs for one-tenth the cost per viewer of producing its own. Only the establishment of quota systems prevented American television from completely inundating these countries.

The United States has dominated popular music since the end of World War II. Jazz, blues, rhythm and blues, and rock-and-roll have been by far the most popular music forms in the Western world—and much of the non-Western world—during this time. All of them originated in the United States, and all are rooted in African American musical innovations. These forms later spread around the globe, inspiring local artists who then transformed the music in their own way. Often these transformed models then returned to the United States to inspire American artists. This was certainly the case with rock-and-roll. Through the 1950s, American artists such as Chuck Berry, Little Richard, and Elvis Presley inspired the Beatles and other British performers, who then led an "invasion" of the United States in the 1960s, creating a sensation and in part sparking new rockers in America. Rock music itself developed in the 1950s. In 1952, white disc jockeys began playing rhythm and blues and traditional blues music performed by African Americans to young white audiences. The music was popular with this audience, and record companies began recording watered-down white "cover" versions of this music. It was not until performers such as Elvis Presley mixed white "folkabilly" with rhythm and blues that rock-and-roll became popular with the larger white audience.

CHAPTER SUMMARY

At the end of a devastating world war, a new kind of conflict erupted in the Western world as two of the victors, the United States and the Soviet Union, emerged as superpowers and began to argue over the political organization of a Europe liberated

from Nazi Germany. Europeans, whether they wanted to or not, were forced to become supporters of one side or the other. The Western world was soon divided between supporters of a capitalistic West and adherents of a Communist East. In 1949, the North Atlantic Treaty Organization (NATO) was created by the United States, Canada, and ten nations of Western Europe as a defensive alliance against Soviet aggression. In 1955, the Soviet Union formed a military alliance with seven Eastern European states, and Europe was once again divided into hostile alliance systems.

Western Europe emerged as a new community in the 1950s and the 1960s and staged a remarkable economic recovery. While the Western European economy boomed, Eastern Europe seemed to stagnate under the control of the Soviet Union. The economic integration of the Western European nations began in 1951 with the European Coal and Steel Community and continued in 1957

with the formation of the European Economic Community, also known as the Common Market. Eastern European states had made their own efforts at economic cooperation when they formed the Council for Mutual Economic Assistance in 1949. Regardless of their economic differences, however, both Western and Eastern Europeans were well aware that their future still depended on the conflict between the two superpowers.

A new European society also emerged after World War II. White-collar workers increased in number, and installment plan buying helped create a consumer society. Rising incomes, combined with shorter working hours, created an ever-greater market for mass leisure activities. The welfare state provided both pensions and health care. Birth control led to smaller families, and more women joined the workforce.

In addition to the Cold War conflict, the postwar era was also characterized by decolonization. After World War II, the colonial empires of the European states were largely dissolved, and the liberated territories of Africa, Asia, and the Middle East emerged as sovereign states. All too soon, these newly independent nations often found themselves caught in the Cold War rivalry between the United States and the Soviet Union. After the United States fought in Korea to prevent the spread of communism, the ideological division that had begun in Europe quickly spread to the rest of the world.

CHAPTER TIMELINE

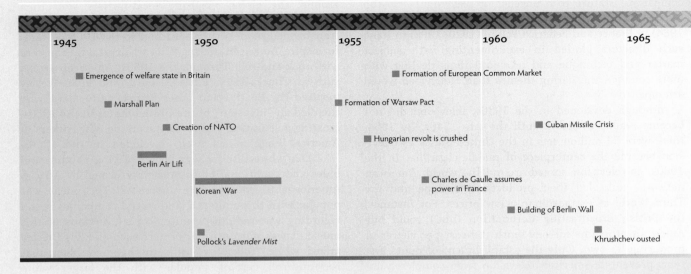

| 1945 | 1950 | 1955 | 1960 | 1965 |

- ■ Emergence of welfare state in Britain
- ■ Marshall Plan
- ■ Creation of NATO
- ▬ Berlin Air Lift
- ▬ Korean War
- ■ Pollock's *Lavender Mist*
- ■ Formation of European Common Market
- ■ Formation of Warsaw Pact
- ■ Hungarian revolt is crushed
- ■ Charles de Gaulle assumes power in France
- ■ Cuban Missile Crisis
- ■ Building of Berlin Wall
- ■ Khrushchev ousted

CHAPTER REVIEW

Upon Reflection

Q What were the major turning points in the development of the Cold War through 1965?

Q How did Soviet policies affect the history of Eastern Europe between 1945 and 1965?

Q What role did popular culture play in the Western world between 1945 and 1965?

Key Terms

Truman Doctrine (p. 886)
Marshall Plan (p. 888)
containment (p. 888)
denazification (p. 888)
mutual deterrence (p. 890)
NATO (p. 890)
Warsaw Pact (p. 890)
rapprochement (p. 892)
decolonization (p. 895)
apartheid (p. 895)
de-Stalinization (p. 902)
Stalinization (p. 903)
nationalization (p. 905)
guest workers (p. 906)
welfare state (p. 906)
social security (p. 906)
socialized medicine (p. 906)
consumer society (p. 910)

family allowances (p. 910)
Abstract Expressionism (p. 914)
Pop Art (p. 914)
existentialism (p. 915)

Suggestions for Further Reading

GENERAL WORKS   For a well-written survey on Europe since 1945, see **T. Judt, *Postwar: A History of Europe Since 1945*** (New York, 2005). See also **W. I. Hitchcock, *The Struggle for Europe: The Turbulent History of a Divided Continent, 1945–2002*** (New York, 2003).

COLD WAR   There is a detailed literature on the Cold War. A good account is **J. L. Gaddis, *The Cold War: A New History*** (New York, 2005). See also **J. W. Langdon, *A Hard and Bitter Peace: A Global History of the Cold War*** (Englewood Cliffs, N.J., 1995). On the Berlin Wall and the Cold War in Germany, see **F. Taylor, *The Berlin Wall: A World Divided, 1961–1989*** (New York, 2006). On the Cuban Missile Crisis, see **D. Munton** and **D. A. Welch, *The Real Thirteen Days: A Concise History of the Cuban Missile Crisis*** (Oxford, 2006).

DECOLONIZATION   On decolonization after World War II, see **R. F. Betts, *Decolonization*,** 2nd ed. (London, 2004). To put the subject into a broader context, see **D. Newsom, *Imperial Mantle: The United States, Decolonization and the Third World*** (Bloomington, Ind., 2001).

SOVIET UNION AND EASTERN EUROPE   On the Khrushchev years, see **W. Taubman, *Khrushchev: The Man and His Era***

(New York, 2004). For a general study of the Soviet satellites in Eastern Europe, see **J. Rothschild, *Return to Diversity: A Political History of East Central Europe Since World War II,*** 3rd ed. (New York, 1999), and **M. Pittaway, *Brief Histories: Eastern Europe 1945–2000*** (London, 2003).

POSTWAR WESTERN EUROPE   The rebuilding of postwar Europe is examined in **D. W. Ellwood, *Rebuilding Europe: Western Europe, America, and Postwar Reconstruction*** (London, 1992). On the building of common institutions in Western Europe, see **S. Henig, *The Uniting of Europe: From Discord to Concord*** (London, 1997). For a survey of West Germany, see **H. A. Turner, *Germany from Partition to Reunification*** (New Haven, Conn., 1992). France under de Gaulle is examined in **J. Jackson, *Charles de Gaulle*** (London, 2003). On Britain, see **K. O. Morgan, *The People's Peace: British History, 1945–1990*** (Oxford, 1992). On Italy, see **P. Ginsborg, *A History of Contemporary Italy: Society and Politics, 1943–1988*** (New York, 1990).

POSTWAR SOCIETY AND CULTURE   On the welfare state, see **A. de Swann, *In Care of the State: Health Care, Education, and Welfare in Europe and the United States in the Modern Era*** (New York, 1988). On women and the welfare state, see **R. Cleave et al., *Gender and the Welfare State*** (New York, 2003), and **D. Sainsbury, ed., *Gendering Welfare States*** (London, 1994). On Simone de Beauvoir, see **T. Keefe, *Simone de Beauvoir*** (New York, 1998). A classic work on existentialism is **W. Barrett, *Irrational Man*** (Garden City, N.Y., 1962), but see also **T. Flynn, *Existentialism: A Very Short History,*** 5th ed. (Oxford, 2006). On the arts, see **A. Marwick, *Arts in the West Since 1945*** (Oxford, 2002), and **D. Anfam, *Abstract Expressionism*** (New York, 1990). An excellent survey of twentieth-century popular culture is **R. Maltby, ed., *Passing Parade: A History of Popular Culture in the Twentieth Century*** (Oxford, 1989).

Visit the CourseMate website at www.cengagebrain.com for additional study tools and review materials for this chapter.

AP* REVIEW QUESTIONS FOR CHAPTER 28

1. By 1945, the United States

   (A) was the world's greatest power.
   (B) was recovering from large losses of population within its cities.
   (C) had the world's fastest growing economy.
   (D) operated as a powerful actor in a uni-polar world.
   (E) had shaped most political and economic policies in areas such as Asia, Latin America, and Africa.

2. Which of the following countries did NOT take part in the Marshall Plan?

   (A) France
   (B) Sweden
   (C) Poland
   (D) Austria
   (E) West Germany

3. Which of the following statements most accurately describes the period of economic reconstruction after World War II?

   (A) Most of Europe continued to follow economic policies in place prior to 1939.
   (B) Europe lagged behind the United States in economic growth.
   (C) Trade was limited primarily to domestic development in most European nations.
   (D) The impact of the global depression was minimal due to global war and its consequences.
   (E) A new balance of power took hold in the economic sphere, just as one had ruled in the political sphere prior to the war.

4. Which of the following economists promoted the theory of spending and stimulus by the government in order to expand the economy?

   (A) John Maynard Keynes
   (B) Adam Smith
   (C) Milton Friedman
   (D) John Bloom
   (E) Jeremy Bentham

5. By the end of 1948, Eastern Bloc nations

   (A) reaped great financial reward from being allies with the Soviet Union.
   (B) struggled to maintain their economic autonomy in relation to the Soviet Union.
   (C) made very little progress economically.
   (D) devised arrangements that brought about centrally planned economies.
   (E) cooperated politically with the Soviets, but not economically.

6. The year that saw the greatest unrest among European students was

   (A) 1956.
   (B) 1960.
   (C) 1962.
   (D) 1968.
   (E) 1973.

7. Which of the following statements is true of Betty Friedan?

   (A) She argued that women should find their own sexual identity.
   (B) She argued that men force women to live a cloistered life.
   (C) She initiated the women's rights movement of the 1960s.
   (D) She found that most women struggled from crises of identity.
   (E) She was highly critical of the causes championed by the National Organization for Women (NOW).

8. Which of the following European nations took the lead in the "propagation of the sexual revolution"?

   (A) France
   (B) England
   (C) Sweden
   (D) West Germany
   (E) Italy

9. Which of the following best explains the extended period of peace between the United States and Soviet Union in the 1970s?

   (A) Both powers eased the tensions between them as part of a general policy of "détente."
   (B) The two powers pursued economic alliances and collaborated in economic development.
   (C) The election of Ronald Regan as president of the United States forced the Soviet rulers to engage in a highly intense arms race.
   (D) Leaders from both powers saw little reason to limit their power and so refused to make any nuclear arms treaties.
   (E) The decolonization of African and Asian states distracted the two powers by forcing them to deal with armed rebellions.

10. *"Don't stand in the doorway,*
Don't block up the hall.
For he that gets hurt
Will be he who has stalled.
There's a battle outside
And it is ragin',
It'll soon shake your windows
And rattle your walls.
For the times they are a-changin'."

The above lyrics by Bob Dylan most likely describe

(A) the widening cultural gap experienced by elderly citizens.
(B) the frustration felt by women over their inability to earn real wages.
(C) the frustration felt by musicians over the misuse of their music.
(D) the rebellious mood of many young people.
(E) the sense of pride and patriotism felt by men returning home from the Vietnam War.

11. Following World War II, many European women

(A) earned the same pay as men for the same kind of work.
(B) chose to remain in the home to serve as domestic workers.
(C) earned approximately two-thirds the earned income of men for the same work.
(D) were elevated to managerial positions.
(E) focused on bringing wider awareness of the social ills of consumerism.

12. The policy of containment

(A) fostered a general acceptance of the division of the world between Communist governments and democratic ones.
(B) withered after the creation of the United Nations, which rendered the policy unnecessary.
(C) caused further conflict as each great power wanted to limit the growth of the other.
(D) was devised by the Soviet Union in reaction to the growing power of China.
(E) successfully stopped the spread of communism throughout the world.

13. The Berlin Airlift

(A) ultimately led to the liberation of East Berlin by the United States.
(B) ultimately resulted in Khrushchev's erection of the Berlin Wall.
(C) was a failure for the United States as it was unable to get supplies to the people of Berlin.
(D) showed the world that the Soviet Union was weaker than it was previously thought to be.
(E) was instituted by the Soviet Union in order to isolate East Germany.

14. European decolonization sparked conflict in all of the following areas EXCEPT

(A) Vietnam.
(B) Korea.
(C) Algeria.
(D) India.
(E) Israel.

The barricades go up in Paris in May 1968.

Protest and Stagnation: The Western World, 1965–1985

CHAPTER OUTLINE AND FOCUS QUESTIONS

A Culture of Protest

Q What were the goals of the revolt in sexual mores, the youth protests and student revolts, the feminist movement, and the antiwar protests? To what extent were their goals achieved?

A Divided Western World

Q What were the major political developments in the Soviet Union, Eastern Europe, Western Europe, and the United States between 1965 and 1985?

The Cold War: The Move to Détente

Q What were the main events in the Cold War between 1965 and 1985, and how important was the role of détente in those events?

Society and Culture in the Western World

Q What were the major social and cultural developments in the Western world between 1965 and 1985?

⌐ CRITICAL THINKING ══════════════

Q What are the similarities and differences between the feminist movement of the nineteenth century and the post–World War II feminist movement?

BETWEEN 1945 AND 1965, Europe not only overcame the devastating effects of World War II but actually experienced an economic recovery that seemed nothing less than miraculous to many people. Economic growth and virtually full employment continued so long that the first post–World War II recession in 1973 came as a shock to Western Europe.

In 1968, Europe had experienced a different kind of shock. May 1968 is now remembered as a historic month because of events in Paris, where a student revolt occurred. It erupted at the University of Nanterre outside Paris but soon spread to the Sorbonne, the main campus of the University of Paris, where about five hundred students gathered for demonstrations and demanded a greater voice in the administration of the university. The authorities decided to react with force and arrested a number of the demonstrators, although as one police officer said, "To tell the truth, we were not enthusiastic about it if we could avoid it, knowing too well, from experience, that our interventions created more problems than they solved." Indeed, students fought back, prying up paving stones from the streets to use as weapons. On May 3, eighty policemen and about three hundred students were hurt; almost six hundred were arrested. Demonstrations then spread to other universities, which served to embolden the students in Paris. On the night of May 10, barricades, formed by overturning cars, went up in the streets of Paris. When police moved in to tear down the barricades, violence ensued. One eyewitness recounted: "A young girl came rushing out into the street practically naked and was manhandled from one cop to another; then beaten like the other wounded students." Students expanded the scale of their protests by inviting workers to support them. Half of France's workforce went on strike in May 1968. After de Gaulle's government instituted a hefty wage hike, the workers returned to work, and the police repressed the remaining student protesters.

The year 1968 saw widespread student protests around the world, and for a brief moment, students and radicals everywhere believed the time had come for a complete renovation of society and government. But the moment passed, and the Western world was left with the new order created in the twenty years after World War II. In Eastern Europe, the crushing of Czechoslovakia in 1968 by Soviet troops left Eastern Europeans with little choice but to remain as Soviet satellites. In Western Europe, democracies continued to evolve. But everywhere, resignation and stagnation seemed to prevail as the new order established in the Western world during the twenty years after World War II appeared to have become permanent: a prosperous, capitalistic West and an impoverished Communist East.

A Culture of Protest

Q **Focus Questions:** What were the goals of the revolt in sexual mores, the youth protests and student revolts, the feminist movement, and the antiwar protests? To what extent were their goals achieved?

In the late 1960s, the Western world was rocked by a variety of protest movements relating to sexual mores, education, and women's rights as well as a strong antiwar movement against the Second Vietnam War (see "The Second Vietnam War" later in this chapter). Although many of the dreams of the protesters were not immediately realized, the forces they set in motion helped to transform Western society.

A Revolt in Sexual Mores

The **permissive society** was a label used by critics to describe the new society of postwar Europe. World War I had opened the first significant crack in the rigid code of manners and morals of the nineteenth century. The 1920s had witnessed experimentation with drugs, the appearance of pornography, and a new sexual freedom (police in Berlin, for example, issued cards that permitted female and male homosexual prostitutes to practice their trade). But these indications of a new attitude appeared mostly in major cities and touched only small numbers of people. After World War II, changes in manners and morals were far more extensive and far more noticeable.

Sweden took the lead in the propagation of the so-called sexual revolution of the 1960s. Sex education in the schools and the decriminalization of homosexuality were

but two aspects of Sweden's liberal legislation. The rest of Europe and the United States soon followed Sweden's example. A gay rights movement emerged in California in 1969 and had spread to France, Italy, and Britain by 1970.

The introduction of the birth control pill, which became widely available by the mid-1960s, gave people more freedom in sexual behavior. Meanwhile, sexually explicit movies, plays, and books broke new ground in the treatment of once-hidden subjects. Cities like Amsterdam, which allowed open prostitution and the public sale of pornography, attracted thousands of curious tourists.

The new standards were evident in the breakdown of the traditional family. Divorce rates increased dramatically, especially in the 1960s, and premarital and extramarital sexual experiences also rose substantially. A survey in the Netherlands in 1968 revealed that 78 percent of men and 86 percent of women had engaged in extramarital sex. The appearance of *Playboy* magazine in the 1950s had also already added a new dimension to the sexual revolution for adult males. Along with photographs of nude women, *Playboy* offered well-written articles on various aspects of masculinity. *Playboy*'s message was clear: men were encouraged to seek sexual gratification outside marriage.

Youth Protest and Student Revolt

The decade of the 1960s also saw the emergence of a drug culture, especially among young people. For most college and university students, marijuana was the recreational drug of choice. For young people more interested in mind expansion into higher levels of consciousness, Timothy Leary, who had done psychedelic research at Harvard on the effects of LSD (lysergic acid diethylamide), became the high priest of hallucinogenic experiences.

New attitudes toward sex and the use of drugs were only two manifestations of a growing youth movement in the 1960s that questioned authority and fostered rebellion against the older generation (see Images of Everyday Life on p. 922). Spurred on by the Second Vietnam War and a growing political consciousness, the youth rebellion became a youth protest movement by the second half of the 1960s (see the box on p. 923).

Before World War II, higher education had largely remained the preserve of Europe's wealthier classes. After the war, European states began to foster greater equality of opportunity in higher education by reducing or eliminating fees, and universities experienced an influx of students from the middle and lower classes. Enrollments grew dramatically; in France, 4.5 percent of young people attended a university in 1950. By 1965, the figure had increased to 14.5 percent.

But there were problems. Classrooms with too many students, professors who paid little attention to their students, and administrators who acted in an authoritarian fashion led to student resentment. In addition, despite changes in the curriculum, students often felt that the universities were not providing an education relevant

Youth Culture in the 1960s

Protest was an integral part of the growing youth movement in the 1960s. Young people questioned authority and fostered rebellion in an attempt to change the social thinking of an older generation. The photograph at the bottom left shows a group of young protesters facing the bayonets of the National Guardsmen who had been called in by Governor Ronald Reagan to restore order on the Berkeley campus of the University of California during an antiwar rally. The "love-in" at the top left shows another facet of the youth movement. In the 1960s, a number of outdoor public festivals for young people combined music, drugs, and sex. Flamboyant dress, face painting, free-form dancing, and drugs were vital ingredients in creating an atmosphere dedicated to "love and peace." A popular slogan was "Make Love, Not War." Shown here are dozens of hippies dancing around a decorated bus at a "love-in" during the Summer of Love, 1967. Many young people were excited about creating a new culture based on love and community. In the photograph at the bottom right, a member of the Diggers, a communal group in San Francisco, is shown feeding a flower child. ▷

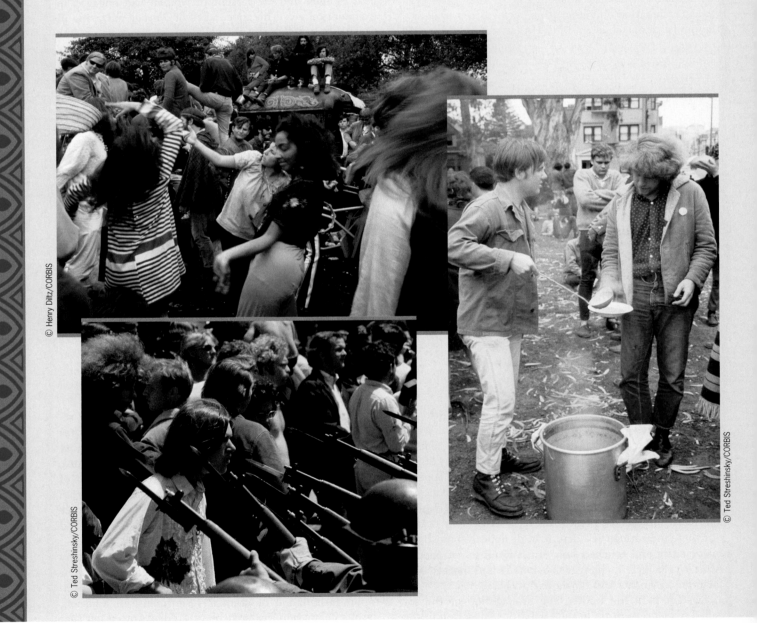

© Henry Diltz/CORBIS

© Ted Streshinsky/CORBIS

© Ted Streshinsky/CORBIS

"The Times They Are A-Changin'": The Music of Youthful Protest

In the 1960s, the lyrics of rock and folk music reflected the rebellious mood of many young people. Bob Dylan (b. 1941) expressed the feelings of the younger generation. His song "The Times They Are A-Changin'," released in 1964, has been called an "anthem for the protest movement."

Bob Dylan, "The Times They Are A-Changin'"

Come gather round people
Wherever you roam
And admit that the waters
Around you have grown
And accept it that soon
You'll be drenched to the bone
If your time to you
Is worth savin'
Then you better start swimmin'
Or you'll sink like a stone
For the times they are a-changin'

Come writers and critics
Who prophesize with your pen
And keep your eyes wide
The chance won't come again
And don't speak too soon
For the wheel's still in spin
And there's no tellin' who
That it's namin'
For the loser now
Will be later to win
For the times they are a-changin'

Come senators, congressmen
please heed the call
Don't stand in the doorway
Don't block up the hall

For he that gets hurt
Will be he who has stalled
There's a battle outside
And it is ragin'
It'll soon shake your windows
And rattle your walls
For the times they are a-changin'

Come mothers and fathers
Throughout the land
And don't criticize
What you can't understand
Your sons and your daughters
Are beyond your command
Your old road
Is rapidly agin'
Please get out of the new one
If you can't lend your hand
For the times they are a-changin'

The line it is drawn
The curse it is cast
The slow one now
Will later be fast
As the present now
Will later be past
The order is
Rapidly fadin'
And the first one now
Will later be last
For the times they are a-changin'

Q What caused the student campus revolts of the 1960s? What and whom does Dylan identify in this song as the problem?

---

to the realities of the modern age. This discontent led to an outburst of student revolts in the late 1960s (see the box on p. 924). In part, these protests were an extension of the spontaneous disruptions in American universities in the mid-1960s, which were often sparked by student opposition to the Second Vietnam War. Perhaps the most famous student revolt occurred in France in 1968, as we saw in the introduction to this chapter.

The French revolt spurred student protests elsewhere in Europe, although none of them succeeded in becoming mass movements. In West Berlin, university students led a protest against Axel Springer, leader of Germany's largest newspaper establishment. Many German students were motivated by a desire to destroy what they considered to be the corrupt old order and were especially influenced by the ideas of the German American social philosopher Herbert Marcuse (mar-KOO-zuh) (1898–1979). In *One-Dimensional Man*, published in 1964, Marcuse argued that capitalism had undermined the dissatisfaction of the oppressed masses by encouraging the consumption of material things. He proposed that a small cadre of unindoctrinated students could liberate the masses from the control of the capitalist ruling class. But the German students' attempt at revolutionary violence backfired as angry Berliners supported police repression of the students.

The student protest movement reached its high point in 1968, although scattered incidents lasted into the early 1970s. There were several reasons for the student

1968: The Year of Student Revolts

The outburst of student upheavals in the late 1960s reached its high point in 1968. These two very different selections illustrate some of the issues that prompted university students to occupy campus buildings and demand reforms.

⬥━━◼◆◼━━⬥

A Student Manifesto in Search of a Real and Human Educational Alternative, University of British Columbia, June 1968

Today we as students are witnessing a deepening crisis within our society. We are intensely aware, in a way perhaps not possible for the older generation, that humanity stands on the edge of a new era. Because we are young, we have insights into the present and visions of the future that our parents do not have. Tasks of an immense gravity wait solution in our generation. We have inherited these tasks from our parents. We do not blame them so much for that . . . but we do blame them for being unwilling to admit that there are problems or for saying that it is we who have visited these problems on ourselves because of our perversity, ungratefulness and unwillingness to listen to "reason."

 Much of the burden of solving the problems of the new era rests on the university. We have been taught to look to it for leadership. While we know that part of the reason for the university is to render direct services to the community, we are alarmed at its servility to industry and government as to what and how it teaches. We are scandalized that the university fails to realize its role in renewing and vivifying those intellectual and moral energies necessary to create a new society—one in which a sense of personal dignity and human community can be preserved.

Student Inscriptions on the Walls of Paris, May and June 1968

The dream is the reality.
May 1968. World revolution is the order of the day.
I decree a state of permanent happiness.
To be free in 1968 is to take part.
Take the trip every day of your life.
Make love, not war.
No exams.
The mind travels farther than the heart but it doesn't
 go as far.
Run, comrade, the old are behind you!
Don't make a revolution in the image of your
 confused and hide-bound university.
Exam = servility, social promotion, hierarchic society.
Love each other.
SEX. It's good, said Mao, but not too often.
Alcohol kills. Take LSD.
Are you consumers or participants?
Professors, you are as old as your culture; your
 modernism is only the modernization of the
 police.
Live in the present.
Revolution, I love you.
Long live direct democracy!

Q Based on these selections, what do you believe were the key problems or causes that motivated the student protesters of this era? Did the student revolts resolve any of the issues raised, or are their complaints still relevant today?

---

radicalism. Some students were genuinely motivated by the desire to reform the university. Others were protesting the Second Vietnam War, which they viewed as a product of Western imperialism. They also attacked other aspects of Western society, such as its materialism, and expressed concern about becoming cogs in the large and impersonal bureaucratic jungles of the modern world. For many students, the calls for democratic decision making within the universities were a reflection of their deeper concerns about the direction of Western society. Although the student revolts fizzled out in the 1970s, the larger issues they raised were increasingly revived in the 1990s.

The Feminist Movement

By the late 1960s, women began to assert their rights and speak as feminists. Along with the student upheavals of the late 1960s came renewed interest in **feminism,** or the women's liberation movement, as it was now called. Increasingly, women protested that the acquisition of political and legal equality had not brought true equality with men:

> We are economically oppressed: in jobs we do full work for half pay, in the home we do unpaid work full time. We are commercially exploited by advertisement, television, and the press; legally, we often have only the status of children. We are brought up to feel inadequate, educated to narrower horizons than men. This is our specific oppression as women. It is as women that we are, therefore, organizing.[1]

These were the words of a British Women's Liberation Workshop in 1969.

 An important contributor to the growth of the women's movement in the 1960s was Betty Friedan (free-DAN) (1921–2006). A journalist and the mother of three children,

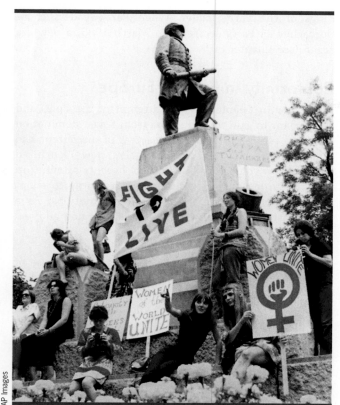

AP Images

Women's Liberation Movement. In the late 1960s, as women began once again to assert their rights, a revived women's liberation movement emerged. Feminists in the movement maintained that women themselves must alter the conditions of their lives. During this women's liberation rally, some women climbed the statue of Admiral Farragut in Washington, D.C., to exhibit their signs.

Antiwar Protests

One of the major issues that mobilized youthful European protesters was the U.S. war in Vietnam, which they viewed as an act of aggression and imperialism. In 1968, demonstrations broke out in universities in Italy, France, and Britain. In London, 30,000 demonstrators took to the streets protesting America's war in Vietnam. But student protests in Europe also backfired in that they provoked a reaction from people who favored order over the lawlessness of privileged young people. As Pier Paolo Pasolini, an Italian poet and intellectual, wrote: "Now all the journalists of the world are licking your arses . . . but not me, my dears. You have the faces of spoiled brats, and I hate you, like I hate your fathers. . . . When yesterday at Valle Giulia [in Rome] you beat up the police, I sympathized with the police because they are the sons of the poor."[3]

Antiwar protests also divided the American people after President Lyndon Johnson sent American troops to war in Vietnam. As the war dragged on and a military draft continued, protests escalated. Teach-ins, sit-ins, and the occupation of buildings at universities alternated with more radical demonstrations that led to violence. The killing of four student protesters at Kent State University in 1970 by the Ohio National Guard caused a reaction, and the antiwar movement began to decline. By that time, however, antiwar demonstrations had worn down the willingness of many Americans to continue the war. The combination of antiwar demonstrations and ghetto riots in the cities also heightened the appeal of a call for "law and order," used by Richard Nixon, the Republican presidential candidate in 1968.

A Divided Western World

 FOCUS QUESTION: What were the major political developments in the Soviet Union, Eastern Europe, Western Europe, and the United States between 1965 and 1985?

Between 1945 and 1965, economic recovery had brought renewed growth to Europe. Nevertheless, the political divisions between Western and Eastern Europe remained; so did disparities in prosperity.

Stagnation in the Soviet Union

Between 1964 and 1982, significant change in the Soviet Union seemed highly unlikely. The man in charge, Leonid Brezhnev (1906–1982), lived by the slogan "No experimentation." Brezhnev had entered the ranks of the Party leadership under Stalin and, after the overthrow of Khrushchev in 1964, had become head of both the Communist Party and the state. He was optimistic, yet reluctant to reform. Overall, the Brezhnev years were relatively calm, although the **Brezhnev Doctrine**—the

Friedan grew increasingly uneasy with her attempt to fulfill the traditional role of the "ideal housewife and mother." In 1963, she published *The Feminine Mystique,* in which she analyzed the problems of middle-class American women in the 1950s and argued that women were being denied equality with men. She wrote, "The problem that has no name—which is simply the fact that American women are kept from growing to their full human capacities—is taking a far greater toll on the physical and mental health of our country than any known disease."[2]

The Feminine Mystique became a best seller and propelled Friedan into a newfound celebrity. In 1966, she founded the National Organization for Women (NOW), whose stated goal was to take "action to bring women into full participation in the mainstream of American society *now,* exercising all the privileges and responsibilities thereof in truly equal partnership with men." Friedan's voice was also prominent in calling for the addition to the U.S. Constitution of an amendment guaranteeing equal rights for women.

National Organization for Women, Statement of Purpose (1966)

right of the Soviet Union to intervene if socialism was threatened in another socialist state—became an article of faith and led to the use of Soviet troops in Czechoslovakia in 1968.

THE BREZHNEV YEARS Brezhnev benefited from the more relaxed atmosphere associated with **détente** (day-TAHNT) (see "The Cold War: The Move to Détente" later in this chapter). The Soviets had reached a rough parity with the United States in nuclear arms and enjoyed a sense of external security that seemed to allow for a relaxation of authoritarian rule. The regime permitted more access to Western styles of music, dress, and art, although dissenters were still punished. Andrei Sakharov (ahn-DRAY SAH-kuh-rawf) (1921–1989), for example, who had played an important role in the development of the Soviet hydrogen bomb, was placed under house arrest for his defense of human rights.

In his economic policies, Brezhnev continued to emphasize heavy industry. Overall industrial growth declined, although the Soviet production of iron, steel, coal, and cement surpassed that of the United States. Two problems bedeviled the Soviet economy. The government's insistence on vigorous central planning led to a huge, complex bureaucracy that discouraged efficiency and reduced productivity. Moreover, the Soviet system, based on guaranteed employment and a lack of incentives, bred apathy, complacency, absenteeism, and drunkenness. Agricultural problems added to Soviet economic woes. Bad harvests in the mid-1970s, caused by a series of droughts, heavy rains, and early frosts, forced the Soviet government to buy grain from the West, particularly the United States. To their chagrin, the Soviets were increasingly dependent on capitalist countries.

By the 1970s, the Soviet Union had developed a ruling system that depended on patronage as a major avenue of advancement. Those who aspired to rise in the Communist Party and the state bureaucracy needed the support of successful Party leaders. At the same time, Party and state leaders—as well as leaders of the army and the secret police (KGB)—were granted awards and material privileges. Brezhnev was unwilling to tamper with the Party leadership and state bureaucracy despite the inefficiency and corruption that the system encouraged.

By 1980, the Soviet Union was ailing. A declining economy, a rise in infant mortality rates, a dramatic surge in alcoholism, and a deterioration in working conditions all gave impetus to a decline in morale and a growing perception that the system was foundering. Within the Party, a small group of reformers emerged who understood the real condition of the Soviet Union. One member of this group was Yuri Andropov (YOOR-ee ahn-DRAHP-awf) (1914–1985), head of the KGB and successor to Brezhnev after the latter's death in November 1982. But Andropov was already old and in poor health when he came to power, and he was unable to make any substantive changes. His most significant move may have been his support for a young reformer, Mikhail Gorbachev (meek-HAYL GOR-buh-chof) (b. 1931), who was climbing the rungs of the Party ladder. When Party leaders chose Gorbachev as Party secretary in March 1985, a new era began (see Chapter 30).

Conformity in Eastern Europe

As we saw in Chapter 28, the attempt of the Poles and Hungarians to gain their freedom from Soviet domination had been repressed in 1956. This year of discontent had consequences, however. Soviet leaders now recognized that Moscow could maintain control over its satellites in Eastern Europe only by granting them leeway to adopt domestic policies appropriate to local conditions. As a result, Eastern European Communist leaders now adopted reform programs to make socialism more acceptable to their subject populations.

In Poland, continued worker unrest led to the rise of the independent labor movement called Solidarity. Led by Lech Walesa (LEK vah-WENT-sah) (b. 1943), Solidarity represented 10 million of Poland's 35 million people. With the support of the workers, many intellectuals, and the Catholic Church, Solidarity was able to win a series of concessions. The Polish government seemed powerless to stop the flow of concessions until December 1981, when it arrested Walesa and other Solidarity leaders, outlawed the union, and imposed military rule.

The government of János Kádár in Hungary enacted the most far-reaching reforms in Eastern Europe. In the early 1960s, Kádár legalized small private enterprises, such as retail stores, restaurants, and artisan shops. His economic reforms were termed "Communism with a capitalist facelift." Under his leadership, Hungary moved slowly away from its strict adherence to Soviet dominance and even established fairly friendly relations with the West.

THE PRAGUE SPRING Czechoslovakia did not share in the thaw of the mid-1950s and remained under the rule of Antonin Novotny (AHN-toh-nyeen noh-VAHT-nee) (1904–1975), who had been placed in power by Stalin himself. By the late 1960s, however, Novotny had alienated many members of his own party and was particularly resented by Czechoslovakia's writers, such as the playwright Vaclav Havel (VAHT-slahf HAH-vul) (b. 1936). A writers' rebellion late in 1967, in fact, led to Novotny's resignation. In January 1968, Alexander Dubček (DOOB-chek) (1921–1992) was elected first secretary of the Communist Party and soon introduced a number of reforms, including freedom of speech and the press, freedom to travel abroad, and a relaxation of secret police activities. Dubček hoped to create "communism with a human face." A period of euphoria erupted that came to be known as the "Prague Spring" (see the box on p. 928).

It proved short-lived. The euphoria had led many to call for more far-reaching reforms, including neutrality and withdrawal from the Soviet bloc. To forestall the spreading of this "spring" fever, the Red Army invaded Czechoslovakia in August 1968 and crushed the reform movement.

Gustáv Husák (goo-STAHV HOO-sahk) (1913–1991), a committed nonreformist, replaced Dubček, abolished his reforms, and reestablished the old order.

Repression in East Germany and Romania

Elsewhere in Eastern Europe, Stalinist policies continued to hold sway. In the early 1950s, the ruling Communist government in East Germany, led by Walter Ulbricht, had consolidated its position and become a faithful Soviet satellite. Industry was nationalized and agriculture collectivized. After a workers' revolt in 1953 was crushed by Soviet tanks, a steady flight of East Germans to West Germany ensued, primarily through the divided city of Berlin. This exodus of mostly skilled laborers created economic problems and led the East German government in 1961 to build the infamous Berlin Wall separating West from East Berlin, as well as equally fearsome barriers along the entire border with West Germany.

After building the wall, East Germany succeeded in developing the strongest economy among the Soviet Union's Eastern European satellites. In 1971, Ulbricht was succeeded by Erich Honecker (HOH-nek-uh) (1912–1992), a party hard-liner who made use of the Stasi (SHTAH-see), the secret police, to rule with an iron fist for the next eighteen years. By 1989, there was one Stasi officer for every 165 people in East Germany. Prosperity (by 1980, East Germany had the tenth-largest economy in the world) and repression were the two mainstays of East Germany's stability.

Repression was also an important part of Romania's postwar history. By 1948, with Soviet assistance, the Communist People's Democratic Front had assumed complete power in Romania. In 1965, leadership of the

CHRONOLOGY The Soviet Bloc

Era of Brezhnev	1964–1982
Rule of Ceauşescu in Romania	1965–1989
Prague Spring	1968
Honecker succeeds Ulbricht in East Germany	1971
Emergence of Solidarity in Poland	1980
Gorbachev comes to power in the Soviet Union	1985

Communist government passed into the hands of Nicolae Ceauşescu (nee-koh-LY chow-SHES-koo) (1918–1989), who with his wife, Elena, established a rigid and dictatorial regime. Ceauşescu ruled Romania with an iron grip, using a secret police force—the Securitate—as his personal weapon against dissent.

Western Europe: The Winds of Change

After two decades of incredible economic growth, Europe experienced severe economic recessions in 1973–1974 and 1979–1983. Both inflation and unemployment rose dramatically. A substantial increase in the price of oil in 1973 was a major cause for the first downturn. But other factors were present as well. A worldwide recession had led to a decline in demand for European goods, and in Europe itself, the reconstruction of many European cities after their devastation in World War II had largely been completed. The economies of the Western European states recovered in the course of the 1980s, although problems remained.

WEST GERMANY After the Adenauer era, West German voters moved politically from the center-right politics of

Soviet Invasion of Czechoslovakia, 1968. The attempt of Alexander Dubček, the new first secretary of the Communist Party in Czechoslovakia, to liberalize Communist rule in that country failed when Soviet troops invaded and crushed the reform movement. This photograph, taken on August 21, shows young Czechs standing on an overturned truck and bravely holding Czechoslovakian flags while other Prague residents surround a Soviet tank carrying wary Soviet troops.

AP Images/Libor Hajsky/CTK

Opposing ⊰VIEWPOINTS

Czechoslovakia, 1968: Two Faces of Communism

In the summer of 1968, a serious rupture began to appear in the Soviet-dominated Communist world. Under the guidance of Alexander Dubček, Czechoslovakia appeared poised to take a path that deviated from Soviet Communist ideals. The first selection is taken from a manifesto written by a group of Czech Communist intellectuals in June 1968. The manifesto became the symbol of the "Prague Spring." The second selection is taken from a letter written in July to the Communist Party of Czechoslovakia by Soviet leader Leonid Brezhnev to justify intervention in Czechoslovakia. In August military forces of several Soviet bloc nations entered Czechoslovakia and imposed a new government. The move was justified by the principle that came to be known as the Brezhnev Doctrine.

Two Thousand Words Manifesto

The first threat to our national life was from the war. Then came other evil days and events that endangered the nation's spiritual well being and character. Most of the nation welcomed the socialist program with high hopes. But it fell into the hands of the wrong people. . . .

After enjoying great popular confidence immediately after the war, the communist party by degrees bartered this confidence away for office, until it had all the offices and nothing else. We feel we must say this, it is familiar to those of us who are communists and who are as disappointed as the rest at the way things turned out. The leaders' mistaken policies transformed a political party and an alliance based on ideas into an organization for exerting power, one that proved highly attractive to power-hungry individuals eager to wield authority. . . . The influx of members such as these affected the character and behavior of the party, whose internal arrangements made it impossible, short of scandalous incidents, for honest members to gain influence and adapt it continuously to modern conditions. Many communists fought against this decline, but they did not manage to prevent what ensued.

We all bear responsibility for the present state of affairs. But those among us who are communists bear more than others, and those who acted as components or instruments of unchecked power bear the greatest responsibility of all. The power they wielded was that of a self-willed group spreading out through the party apparatus into every district and community. It was this apparatus that decided what might and might not be done. . . .

Since the beginning of this year we have been experiencing a regenerative process of democratization.

It started inside the communist party, that much we must admit, even those communists among us who no longer had hopes that anything good could emerge from that quarter know this. It must also be added, of course, that the process could have started nowhere else. For after twenty years the communists were the only ones able to conduct some sort of political activity. It was only the opposition inside the communist party that had the privilege to voice antagonistic views. The effort and initiative now displayed by democratically minded communists are only then a partial repayment of the debt owed by the entire party to the non-communists whom it had kept down in an unequal position. . . .

In this moment of hope, albeit hope still threatened, we appeal to you. It took several months before many of us believed it was safe to speak up; many of us still do not think it is safe. But speak up we did exposing ourselves to the extent that we have no choice but to complete our plan to humanize the regime. If we did not, the old forces would exact cruel revenge. We appeal above all to those who so far have waited on the sidelines. The time now approaching will decide events for years to come.

A Letter to Czechoslovakia

To the Central Committee of the Communist Party of Czechoslovakia

Warsaw, July 15, 1968

Dear comrades!

On behalf of the Central Committees of the Communist and Workers' Parties of Bulgaria, Hungary, the German Democratic Republic, Poland, and the Soviet Union, we address ourselves to you with this letter, prompted by a feeling of sincere friendship based on the principles of Marxism-Leninism and proletarian internationalism and by the concern of our common affairs for strengthening the positions of socialism and the security of the socialist community of nations.

The development of events in your country evokes in us deep anxiety. It is our firm conviction that the offensive of the reactionary forces, backed by imperialists, against your Party and the foundations of the social system in the Czechoslovak Socialist Republic, threatens to push your country off the road of socialism and that consequently it jeopardizes the interests of the entire socialist system. . . .

We neither had nor have any intention of interfering in such affairs as are strictly the internal business of your Party and your state, nor of violating the

(continued)

(Opposing Viewpoints continued)

principles of respect, independence, and equality in the relations among the Communist Parties and socialist countries. . . .

At the same time we cannot agree to have hostile forces push your country from the road of socialism and create a threat of severing Czechoslovakia from the socialist community. . . . This is the common cause of our countries, which have joined in the Warsaw Treaty to ensure independence, peace, and security in Europe, and to set up an insurmountable barrier against aggression and revenge. . . . We shall never agree to have imperialism, using peaceful or nonpeaceful methods, making a gap from the inside or from the outside in the socialist system, and changing in imperialism's favor the correlation of forces in Europe. . . .

That is why we believe that a decisive rebuff of the anticommunist forces, and decisive efforts for the preservation of the socialist system in Czechoslovakia are not only your task but ours as well. . . .

We express the conviction that the Communist Party of Czechoslovakia, conscious of its responsibility, will take the necessary steps to block the path of reaction. In this struggle you can count on the solidarity and all-round assistance of the fraternal socialist countries. ⇨

Q What Communist ideals are expressed in the manifesto? How do those ideals differ from those expressed by Leonid Brezhnev? How do you explain the differences?

---

the Christian Democrats to center-left politics, and in 1969, the Social Democrats became the leading party. By forming a ruling coalition with the small Free Democratic Party (FPD), the Social Democrats remained in power until 1982. The first Social Democratic chancellor was Willy Brandt (VIL-ee BRAHNT) (1913–1992). Brandt was especially successful with his "opening toward the east"—known as *Ostpolitik* (OHST-paw-li-teek)—for which he received the Nobel Peace Prize in 1972. On March 19, 1971, Brandt met with Walter Ulbricht, the leader of East Germany, and worked out the details of a treaty that was signed in 1972. This agreement did not establish full diplomatic relations with East Germany but did call for "good neighborly" relations. As a result, it led to greater cultural, personal, and economic contacts between West and East Germany. Despite this success, the discovery of an East German spy among Brandt's advisers caused his resignation in 1974.

His successor, Helmut Schmidt (HEL-moot SHMIT) (b. 1918), was more of a technocrat than a reform-minded socialist and concentrated primarily on the economic problems largely brought about by high oil prices between 1973 and 1975. Schmidt was successful in eliminating a deficit of 10 billion marks in three years. In 1982, when the coalition of Schmidt's Social Democrats with the Free Democrats fell apart over the reduction of social welfare expenditures, the Free Democrats joined with the Christian Democratic Union of Helmut Kohl (HEL-moot KOHL) (b. 1930) to form a new government.

GREAT BRITAIN: THATCHER AND THATCHERISM

Between 1964 and 1979, the Conservative and Labour Parties alternated in power. Neither could solve the problem of fighting between Catholics and Protestants in Northern Ireland. Violence increased as the Irish Republican Army

(IRA) staged a series of dramatic terrorist acts in response to the suspension of Northern Ireland's parliament in 1972 and the establishment of direct rule by London. Nor was either party able to deal with Britain's ailing economy. Failure to modernize made British industry less and less competitive. Moreover, Britain was hampered by frequent labor strikes, many of them caused by conflicts between rival labor unions.

In 1979, after Britain's economic problems had seemed to worsen during five years under a Labour government, the Conservatives returned to power under Margaret Thatcher (b. 1925). She became the first woman to serve as prime minister in British history (see the box on p. 930). Thatcher

Margaret Thatcher. Great Britain's first female prime minister, Margaret Thatcher was a strong leader who dominated British politics in the 1980s. Thatcher is shown here shaking hands with Soviet leader Mikhail Gorbachev in 1984.

© Peter Jordan/Time Life Pictures/Getty Images

Margaret Thatcher: Entering a Man's World

In 1979, Margaret Thatcher became the first woman to serve as Britain's prime minister and went on to be its longest-serving prime minister as well. In this excerpt from her autobiography, Thatcher describes how she was interviewed by Conservative Party officials when they first considered her as a possible candidate for Parliament as a representative from Dartford. Thatcher ran for Parliament for the first time in 1950; she lost but increased the Conservative vote total in the district by 50 percent over the previous election.

⟶ ⟩⟨ ⟵

Margaret Thatcher, *The Path to Power*

And they did [consider her]. I was invited to have lunch with John Miller and his wife, Phee, and the Dartford Woman's Chairman, Mrs. Fletcher, on the Saturday on Llandudno Pier. Presumably, and in spite of any reservations about the suitability of a woman candidate for their seat, they liked what they saw. I certainly got on well with them. The Millers were to become close friends and I quickly developed a healthy respect for the dignified Mrs. Fletcher. After lunch we walked back along the pier to the Conference Hall in good time for a place to hear Winston Churchill give the Party Leader's speech. It was the first we had seen of him that week, because in those days the Leader did not attend the Conference itself, appearing only at a final rally on the Saturday. Foreign affairs naturally dominated his speech—it was the time of the Berlin blockade and the Western air lift—and his message was somber, telling us that only American nuclear weapons stood between Europe and communist tyranny and warning of "what seems a remorselessly approaching third world war."

I did not hear from Dartford until December, when I was asked to attend an interview at Palace Chambers, Bridge Street—then housing Conservative Central Office—not far from Parliament itself. With a large number of other hopefuls I turned up on the evening of Thursday 30 December for my first Selection Committee.

Very few outside the political arena know just how nerve-racking such occasions are. The interviewee who is not nervous and tense is very likely to perform badly: for, as any chemist will tell you, the adrenaline needs to flow if one is to perform at one's best. I was lucky in that at Dartford there were some friendly faces around the table, and it has to be said that on such occasions there are advantages as well as disadvantages to being a young woman making her way in the political world.

I found myself short-listed, and was asked to go to Dartford itself for a further interview. Finally, I was invited to the Bull Hotel in Dartford on Monday 31 January 1949 to address the Association's Executive Committee of about fifty people. As one of five would-be candidates, I had to give a fifteen-minute speech and answer questions for a further ten minutes.

It was the questions which were more likely to cause me trouble. There was a good deal of suspicion of woman candidates, particularly in what was regarded as a tough industrial seat like Dartford. This was quite definitely a man's world into which not just angels feared to tread. There was, of course, little hope of winning it for the Conservatives, though this is never a point that the prospective candidate even in a Labour seat as safe as Ebbw Vale would be advised to make. The Labour majority was an all but unscalable 20,000. But perhaps this unspoken fact turned to my favour. Why not take the risk of adopting the young Margaret Roberts? There was not much to lose, and some good publicity for the Party to gain.

The most reliable sign that a political occasion has gone well is that you have enjoyed it. I enjoyed that evening at Dartford, and the outcome justified my confidence. I was selected. 🖙

Q In this account, is Margaret Thatcher's being a woman more important to her or to others? Why would this disparity exist?

---

pledged to lower taxes, reduce government bureaucracy, limit social welfare, restrict union power, and end inflation. The "Iron Lady," as she was called, did break the power of the labor unions. Although she did not eliminate the basic components of the social welfare system, she did use austerity measures to control inflation. "Thatcherism," as her economic policy was termed, improved the British economic situation, but at a price. The south of England, for example, prospered, but the old industrial areas of the Midlands and north declined and were beset by high unemployment, poverty, and sporadic violence. Cutbacks in education seriously undermined the quality of British education, long regarded as among the world's finest.

In the area of foreign policy, Thatcher, like Ronald Reagan in the United States, took a hard-line approach toward communism. She oversaw a large military buildup aimed at replacing older technology and reestablishing Britain as a world police officer. In 1982, when Argentina attempted to take control of the Falkland Islands (one of Britain's few remaining colonial outposts; known to Argentines as the Malvinas) 300 miles off its coast, the British successfully rebuffed the Argentines, although at considerable economic cost and the loss of 255 lives. The Falklands War, however, did generate popular support for Thatcher, as many in Britain reveled in memories of the nation's glorious imperial past. In truth, however, in a world dominated by two superpowers—the United States and the Soviet Union—Britain was no longer a world power.

UNCERTAINTIES IN FRANCE The worsening of France's economic situation in the 1970s brought a shift to the left politically. By 1981, the Socialists had become the dominant party in the National Assembly, and the Socialist leader, François Mitterrand (frahnh-SWAH MEE-tayr-rahnh) (1916–1995), was elected president. His first concern was with France's economic difficulties. In 1982, Mitterrand froze prices and wages in the hope of reducing the huge budget deficit and high inflation. He also passed a number of liberal measures to aid workers: an increased minimum wage, expanded social benefits, a mandatory fifth week of paid vacation for salaried workers, a thirty-nine-hour workweek, and higher taxes for the rich. Mitterrand's administrative reforms included both centralization (nationalization of banks and industry) and decentralization (granting local governments greater powers). The party's victory had convinced the Socialists that they could enact some of their more radical reforms. Consequently, the government nationalized the steel industry, major banks, the space and electronics industries, and important insurance firms.

The Socialist policies largely failed, however, and within three years, a decline in support for the Socialists caused the Mitterrand government to turn portions of the economy back over to private enterprise. Some economic improvement in the late 1980s enabled Mitterrand to win a second seven-year term in the 1988 presidential elections.

CONFUSION IN ITALY In the 1970s and 1980s, Italy continued to practice the politics of coalitions that had characterized much of its history. Italy witnessed the installation of its fiftieth postwar government in 1991, and its new prime minister, Giulio Andreotti (JOOL-yoh ahn-dray-AH-tee), had already served six times in that office. Italian governments continued to consist of coalitions mostly led by the Christian Democrats.

In the 1980s, even the Communists had been included briefly in the government. The Italian Communists had become advocates of **Eurocommunism,** basically an attempt to broaden communism's support by dropping its Marxist ideology. Although its popularity declined in the 1980s, the Communist Party still garnered 26 percent of the vote in 1987. The Communists also won a number of local elections and took charge of municipal governments in several cities, including Rome and Naples, for a brief time.

In the 1970s, Italy suffered from a severe economic recession. The Italian economy, which depended on imported oil as its chief source of energy, was especially vulnerable to the steep increase in oil prices in 1973. Parallel to the economic problems was a host of political and social problems: student unrest, mass strikes, and terrorist attacks. In 1978, a former prime minister, Aldo Moro, was kidnapped and killed by the Red Brigades, a terrorist

CHRONOLOGY Western Europe, 1965–1985

Willy Brandt becomes chancellor of West Germany	1969
Helmut Schmidt becomes chancellor of West Germany	1974
Margaret Thatcher becomes prime minister of Britain	1979
François Mitterrand becomes president of France	1981
Falklands War	1982
Helmut Kohl becomes chancellor of West Germany	1982

organization. Then, too, there was the all-pervasive and corrupting influence of the Mafia, which had always been an important factor in southern Italy but spread to northern Italy as well in the 1980s. Italy survived the crises of the 1970s and in the 1980s began to experience remarkable economic growth. But severe problems remained.

THE EUROPEAN COMMUNITY After 1970, Western European states continued to pursue the goal of integrating their economies. Beginning with six states in 1957, the European Economic Community expanded in 1973 when Great Britain, Ireland, and Denmark joined what its members now renamed the European Community (EC). Greece joined in 1981, followed by Spain and Portugal in 1986. The economic integration of the members of the EC led to cooperative efforts in international and political affairs as well. The foreign ministers of the twelve members consulted frequently and provided a common front in negotiations on important issues.

The United States: Turmoil and Tranquillity

With the election of Richard Nixon (1913–1994) as president in 1968, American politics made a shift to the right. Nixon ended American involvement in Vietnam by 1973 by gradually withdrawing American troops. Politically, he pursued a "southern strategy," carefully calculating that "law and order" issues and a slowdown in racial desegregation would appeal to southern whites. The South, which had once been a Democratic stronghold, began to form a new allegiance to the Republican Party. The Republican strategy also gained support among white Democrats in northern cities, where court-mandated busing to achieve racial integration had led to a backlash among whites.

As president, Nixon was paranoid about conspiracies and began to use illegal methods to gather intelligence on his political opponents. One of the president's advisers explained that their intention was to "use the available federal machinery to screw our political enemies." Nixon's zeal led to the Watergate scandal—the attempted bugging of Democratic National Headquarters, located in the Watergate apartment and hotel complex in Washington, D.C. Although Nixon repeatedly lied to the American public about his involvement in the affair, secret tapes of his own conversations in the White House revealed the truth. On August 9, 1974, Nixon resigned the presidency rather than face possible impeachment and then trial by the U.S. Congress.

ECONOMIC PROBLEMS After Watergate, American domestic politics focused on economic issues. Vice President Gerald Ford (1913–2006) became president when Nixon resigned, only to lose in the 1976 election to the former governor of Georgia, Jimmy Carter (b. 1924). Both Ford and Carter faced severe economic problems. The period from 1973 to the mid-1980s was one of economic stagnation, which came to be known as **stagflation**—a combination of high inflation and high unemployment. In part, the economic downturn stemmed from a dramatic change in oil prices. Oil was considered a cheap and abundant source of energy in the 1950s, and Americans had grown dependent on imported oil from the Middle East. But an oil embargo and price increases by the Organization of Petroleum Exporting Countries (OPEC) as a result of the Arab-Israeli War in 1973 quadrupled oil prices. Additional price hikes increased oil prices twenty-fold by the end of the 1970s, encouraging inflationary tendencies throughout the economy.

By 1980, the Carter administration faced two devastating problems. High inflation and a noticeable decline in average weekly earnings were causing a drop in American living standards. At the same time, a crisis abroad had erupted when fifty-three Americans were taken hostage by the Iranian government of Ayatollah Khomeini (khoh-MAY-nee). Carter's inability to gain the release of the hostages led to perceptions at home that he was a weak president. His overwhelming loss to Ronald Reagan (1911–2004) in the election of 1980 enabled the chief exponent of right-wing Republican policies to assume the presidency and initiate a new political order.

THE REAGAN REVOLUTION The Reagan Revolution, as it has been called, consisted of a number of new policies. Reversing decades of increased spending on social welfare, Reagan cut back on the welfare state by reducing spending on food stamps, school lunch programs, and job programs. At the same time, his administration fostered the largest peacetime military buildup in American history. Total federal spending rose from $631 billion in 1981 to more than $1 trillion by 1986. But instead of raising taxes to pay for the new expenditures, which far outweighed the budget cuts in social areas, Reagan convinced Congress to rely on "supply-side economics." Massive tax cuts would supposedly stimulate rapid economic growth and produce new revenues. Much of the tax cut went to the wealthy. Reagan's policies seemed to work in the short run as the United States experienced an economic upturn that lasted until the end of the 1980s. The spending policies of the Reagan administration, however, also produced record government deficits, which loomed as an obstacle to long-term growth. In 1980, the total government debt was around $930 billion. By 1988, the total debt had almost tripled, reaching $2.6 trillion.

Canada

In 1963, during a major economic recession, the Liberals had been returned to power in Canada. The most prominent Liberal government was that of Pierre Trudeau (PYAYR troo-DOH) (1919–2000), who came to power in 1968. Although French Canadian in background, Trudeau was dedicated to Canada's federal union, and in 1968, his government passed the Official Languages Act that allowed both English and French to be used in the federal civil service. Although Trudeau's government vigorously pushed an industrialization program, high inflation and Trudeau's efforts to impose the will of the federal government on the powerful provincial governments alienated voters and weakened his government. Economic recession in the early 1980s brought Brian Mulroney (b. 1939), leader of the Progressive Conservative Party, to power in 1984.

The Cold War: The Move to Détente

 FOCUS QUESTION: What were the main events in the Cold War between 1965 and 1985, and how important was the role of détente in those events?

The Cuban Missile Crisis led to the lessening of tensions between the United States and the Soviet Union (see the Film & History feature on p. 933). But within another year the United States had been drawn into a new confrontation that had an important impact on the Cold War—the Second Vietnam War.

The Second Vietnam War

After Vietnamese forces had defeated their French colonial masters in 1954, Vietnam had been divided. A strongly nationalistic regime in the north under Ho Chi Minh received Soviet aid, while American sponsors worked to establish a pro-Western regime in South Vietnam. President John F. Kennedy maintained Eisenhower's policy of providing military and financial aid to the regime of Ngo Dinh Diem (GOH din DYEM) (1901–1963), the autocratic ruler of South Vietnam. But the Kennedy administration grew increasingly disenchanted with the Diem regime, which was corrupt and seemed incapable of gaining support from the people. From the American point of view, this lack of support simply undermined the ability of the South Vietnamese government to deal with the Vietcong, the South Vietnamese Communist guerrillas backed by the North Vietnamese. In November 1963, the U.S. government supported a military coup that overthrew the Diem regime.

The new military government seemed even less able to govern the country, and by early 1965, the Vietcong, their ranks now swelled by military units infiltrating from North Vietnam, were on the verge of seizing control of the entire

Dr. Strangelove, Or: How I Learned to Stop Worrying and Love the Bomb (1964)

In 1964, director Stanley Kubrick released *Dr. Strangelove, Or: How I Learned to Stop Worrying and Love the Bomb,* a black comedy about the Cold War and nuclear weapons. The film begins when a general in the U.S. Air Force, Jack D. Ripper (Sterling Hayden), orders a nuclear attack on the Soviet Union because he believes that Communists are secretly poisoning American drinking water with fluoride. The situation becomes critical when efforts to call off Ripper's air strike fail. The Soviet Union, in an attempt to deter such an attack, has created the "Doomsday Device," a computerized defense system that will destroy the earth if triggered. This system is irreversible, so unless Ripper's men are stopped, the entire planet will be consumed by nuclear holocaust.

Numerous communications lapses occur throughout the film, as it satirizes the leadership protocol each nation has implemented to oversee its nuclear arsenal. The president of the United States (Peter Sellers) and the Soviet premier lack the means to fully prevent the pending nuclear war. Meanwhile, the mysterious Dr. Strangelove (also played by Peter Sellers), a German physicist and adviser to the president, suggests how accidents and misunderstandings could easily cause the destruction of our planet.

Even Dr. Strangelove's plan to repopulate the planet fails, as he relies on Nazi ideals and prejudices to select those who will survive.

Kubrick based the film on Peter George's 1958 novel *Red Alert,* a thriller about accidental nuclear war. Written at a time when more than 34,000 nuclear weapons existed, the film pokes fun at military and political leaders and the posturing that resulted from the Cold War arms race. Although it is a parody, *Dr. Strangelove* accurately portrayed American paranoia and policies during the Cold War. Senator Joseph McCarthy and the House Un-American Activities Committee (HUAC) sought out anyone who might be conspiring against America or promoting Communist ideals, and the threat of nuclear attack prompted the creation of numerous bomb shelters and contingency plans. Schoolchildren were trained to hide under their desks in the event of a disaster, and a telephone hotline connected Moscow and Washington, D.C., to ensure communications between the two superpowers.

The military showdown in *Dr. Strangelove* paralleled actual events, in particular the Cuban Missile Crisis of 1962. In the film, General Turgidson (George C. Scott) suggests that a preemptive nuclear strike would catch the Soviets by surprise. "We would therefore prevail," declares Turgidson, "and suffer only modest and acceptable civilian casualties from their remaining force which would be badly damaged and uncoordinated." Turgidson believed that "acceptable" casualties would number

General Turgidson (George C. Scott) with the president (Peter Sellers).

Dr. Strangelove (Peter Sellers).

(continued)

no more than 10 to 20 million killed, an irreverent jab at President Kennedy's advisers, who in 1962 recommended attacking Cuba despite the threat of nuclear missiles. The Doomsday Device of *Dr. Strangelove* also mocked the superpowers' attempts at deterrence. Nikita Khrushchev claimed that by placing missiles in Cuba, the Soviets would deter the United States from starting war,

and the fictional Doomsday Device was intended to produce a similar effect. As Dr. Strangelove explained, "Deterrence is the art of producing in the mind of the enemy . . . the fear to attack." Hailed by one film critic as "arguably the best political satire of the century," *Dr. Strangelove* evoked the fear and anxiety of the Cold War.

The Vietnam War

country. In desperation, President Lyndon Johnson decided to launch bombing raids on the north and to send U.S. combat troops to South Vietnam to prevent a total defeat of the anti-Communist government in Saigon and keep the Communist regime of the north from uniting the entire country under its control. Although nationalism played a powerful role in this conflict, American policy makers saw it in terms of a **domino theory** concerning the spread of communism. If the Communists succeeded in Vietnam, so the argument went, all the other countries in Asia freeing themselves from colonial domination would fall, like dominoes, to communism.

Despite their massive superiority in equipment and firepower, U.S. forces failed to prevail over the persistence of the North Vietnamese and especially the Vietcong. These guerrilla forces were extremely effective against American troops. Natives of Vietnam, they were able to live off the land, disappear among the people, and attack when least expected. Many South Vietnamese villagers were so opposed to their own government that they sheltered and supported the Vietcong.

The growing number of American troops sent to Vietnam soon produced a persistent antiwar movement in the United States, especially among college students of draft age. As described earlier, a similar movement also arose in Europe. Although Europeans had generally acquiesced in American leadership of the Cold War, some Europeans recognized the need for Europe to play its own role in foreign affairs. Under President Charles de Gaulle, France grew especially critical of U.S. involvement in Vietnam. De Gaulle believed that the Vietnamese should be allowed to live in their own unified country and in 1965 called the United States "the greatest danger in the world today to peace." After President Johnson escalated the American

war effort, antiwar protests broke out all over France in 1966 and 1967 and soon spread throughout Europe.

The mounting destruction and increasing brutalization of the war, brought into American homes every evening on television, also turned American public opinion against the war. Finally, in 1973, President Richard Nixon reached an agreement with North Vietnam that allowed the United States to withdraw its forces. Within two years,

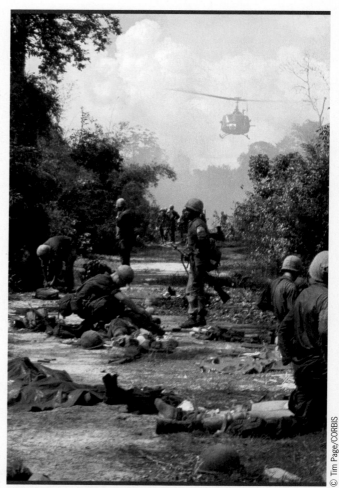

The Second Vietnam War. Between 1965 and 1973, U.S. troops fought against Vietcong guerrillas and North Vietnamese regular forces until they were finally withdrawn as a result of the Paris Agreement reached in January 1973. Shown here are U.S. troops after a Vietcong attack. The helicopter that is arriving would soon remove the American wounded from the battlefield.

Vietnam had been forcibly reunited by Communist armies from the North.

Despite the success of the North Vietnamese Communists, the domino theory proved unfounded. A noisy rupture between Communist China and the Soviet Union put an end to the idea of a monolithic communism directed by Moscow. Under President Nixon, American relations with China were resumed. New nations in Southeast Asia also managed to avoid Communist governments. Above all, Vietnam helped show the limitations of American power. By the end of the Second Vietnam War, a new era in American-Soviet relations, known as détente, had begun to emerge.

China and the Cold War

The Johnson administration had sent U.S. combat troops to South Vietnam in 1965 in an effort to prevent the expansion of communism in Southeast Asia. The primary concern of the United States, however, was not the Soviet Union but Communist China. By the mid-1960s, U.S. officials viewed the Soviet Union as an essentially conservative power, more concerned with protecting its vast empire than with expanding its borders. Mao Zedong's attempt to create a totally classless society had received much attention, and, despite his failures with the Great Leap Forward (see Chapter 28), he now launched China on an even more dramatic forced march toward communism.

THE GREAT PROLETARIAN CULTURAL REVOLUTION Mao was convinced that only an atmosphere of constant revolutionary fervor could enable the Chinese to overcome the past and achieve the final stage of communism. Accordingly, in 1966 he unleashed the Red Guards, revolutionary units composed of unhappy Communist Party members and discontented young people who were urged to take to the streets to cleanse Chinese society of impure elements guilty of taking the capitalist road. Schools, universities, factories, and even government ministries were all subject to the scrutiny of the Red Guards. This so-called Great Proletarian Cultural Revolution (literally, the Chinese name translates as "great revolution to create a proletarian culture") lasted for ten years, from 1966 to 1976. Red Guards set out across the nation to eliminate the "four olds"—old ideas, old culture, old customs, and old habits (see the box on p. 936). They destroyed temples, books written by foreigners, and jazz records. They tore down street signs and replaced them with ones carrying revolutionary names. Destruction of property was matched by vicious attacks on individuals who had supposedly deviated from Mao's thought. Those accused were humiliated at public meetings where they were forced to

The Great Proletarian Cultural Revolution. The Cultural Revolution, which began in 1966, was a massive effort by Mao Zedong and his radical supporters to eliminate rival elements within the Chinese Communist Party and achieve the final stage of communism—a classless society. Shown here in front of a picture of Chairman Mao Zedong is a group of Chinese children in uniform holding Mao's *Little Red Book* (a collection of Mao's thoughts that became a sort of bible for Chinese Communists) during the Cultural Revolution in 1968.

© Hulton Archive/Getty Images

admit their "crimes." Many were brutally beaten, often to death.

Mao found, however, that it was not easy to maintain a constant mood of revolutionary enthusiasm. Key groups, including Party members, urban professionals, and many military officers, did not share Mao's desire for "permanent revolution." People began to turn against the movement, and in September 1976, when Mao died, a group of practical-minded reformers seized power from the radicals and adopted a more rational approach to China's problems.

U.S.-CHINA RELATIONS For years U.S. policy toward Communist China was determined by American fears of Communist expansion in Asia. Already in 1950, the Truman administration had adopted a new national policy that implied that the United States would take whatever steps were necessary to stem expansion of communism in the region, a policy that Truman invoked when he sent troops to Korea in 1950 (see "The Korean War" in Chapter 28). The Second Vietnam War raised additional concerns about Communist China's intentions.

The Fury of the Red Guards

In 1966, Mao Zedong unleashed the fury of the Red Guards on all levels of society, exposing anti-Maoist elements, suspected "capitalists," and those identified with the previous ruling class. In this excerpt, Nien Cheng, the widow of an official of Chiang Kai-shek's regime, describes a visit by Red Guards to her home during the height of the Cultural Revolution.

* ＊ *

Nien Cheng, *Life and Death in Shanghai*

Suddenly the doorbell began to ring incessantly. At the same time, there was furious pounding of many fists on my front gate, accompanied by the confused sound of hysterical voices shouting slogans. The cacophony told me that the time of waiting was over and that I must face the threat of the Red Guards and the destruction of my home....

Outside, the sound of voices became louder. "Open the gate! Open the gate! Are you all dead? Why don't you open the gate?" Someone was swearing and kicking the wooden gate. The horn of the truck was blasting too....

I stood up to put the book on the shelf. A copy of the Constitution of the People's Republic caught my eye. Taking it in my hand and picking up the bunch of keys I had ready on my desk, I went downstairs.

At the same moment, the Red Guards pushed open the front door and entered the house. There were thirty or forty senior high school students, aged between fifteen and twenty, led by two men and one woman much older.

The leading Red Guard, a gangling youth with angry eyes, stepped forward and said to me, "We are the Red Guards. We have come to take revolutionary action against you!"

Though I knew it was futile, I held up the copy of the Constitution, and said calmly, "It's against the Constitution of the People's Republic of China to enter a private house without a search warrant."

The young man snatched the document out of my hand and threw it on the floor. With his eyes blazing, he said, "The Constitution is abolished. It was a document written by the Revisionists within the Communist Party. We recognize only the teachings of our Great Leader Chairman Mao."...

Another young man used a stick to smash the mirror hanging over the blackwood chest facing the front door.

Mounting the stairs, I was astonished to see several Red Guards taking pieces of my porcelain collection out of their padded boxes. One young man had arranged a set of four Kangxi wine cups in a row on the floor and was stepping on them. I was just in time to hear the crunch of delicate porcelain under the sole of his shoe. The sound pierced my heart. Impulsively I leapt forward and caught his leg just as he raised his foot to crush the next cup. He toppled. We fell in a heap together.... The other Red Guards dropped what they were doing and gathered around us, shouting at me angrily for interfering in their revolutionary activities.

The young man whose revolutionary work of destruction I had interrupted said angrily, "You shut up! These things belong to the old culture. They are useless toys of the feudal emperors and the modern capitalist class and have no significance to us, the proletarian class. They cannot be compared to the cameras and binoculars, which are useful for our struggle in time of war. Our Great Leader Chairman Mao taught us, 'If we destroy, we cannot establish.' The old culture must be destroyed to make way for the new socialist culture."

Q What were the tactics of the Red Guards? To what degree did they succeed in remaking the character of the Chinese people?

President Richard Nixon, however, opened a new door in American relations when he visited China and met with Mao Zedong in 1972. Despite Nixon's reputation as a devout anti-Communist, the visit was a success as the two leaders agreed to put aside their most bitter differences in an effort to reduce tensions in Asia. During the 1970s, Chinese-American relations continued to improve. In 1979, diplomatic ties were established between the two countries, and by the end of the 1970s, China and the United States had forged a "strategic relationship" in which they would cooperate against the threat of Soviet intervention in Asia.

The Practice of Détente

By the 1970s, American-Soviet relations had entered a new phase known as détente, marked by a reduction of tensions between the two superpowers. An appropriate symbol of détente was the Antiballistic Missile Treaty, signed in 1972, in which the two nations agreed to limit their systems for launching antiballistic missiles (ABMs). The U.S. objective in pursuing the treaty was to make it unlikely that either superpower could win a nuclear exchange by launching a preemptive strike against the other. U.S. officials believed that a policy of "equivalence," in which there was a roughly equal power balance on each side, was the best way to avoid a nuclear confrontation.

In 1975, the Helsinki Accords provided yet another example of reduced tensions between the superpowers. Signed by the United States, Canada, and all European nations, these accords recognized all borders that had been established in Europe since the end of World War II, thereby acknowledging the Soviet sphere of influence in Eastern Europe. The Helsinki Accords also committed the signatory powers to recognize and protect the human rights of their citizens.

The Limits of Détente

This protection of human rights became one of the major foreign policy goals of the next American president, Jimmy Carter. Although hopes ran high for the continuation of détente, the Soviet invasion of Afghanistan in 1979, undertaken to restore a pro-Soviet regime, hardened relations between the United States and the Soviet Union. President Carter canceled American participation in the 1980 Olympic Games in Moscow and placed an embargo on the shipment of American grain to the Soviet Union.

The early administration of President Ronald Reagan witnessed a return to the harsh rhetoric, if not all of the harsh practices, of the Cold War. Calling the Soviet Union an "evil empire," Reagan began a military buildup that stimulated a renewed arms race. In 1982, the Reagan administration introduced the nuclear-tipped cruise missile, whose ability to fly at low altitudes made it difficult to detect. President Reagan also became an ardent proponent of the Strategic Defense Initiative (SDI), nicknamed "Star Wars." Its purpose was to create a space shield that could destroy incoming missiles.

By providing military support to the anti-Soviet insurgents in Afghanistan, the Reagan administration helped maintain a Vietnam-like war in Afghanistan that would embed the Soviet Union in its own quagmire. Like the Second Vietnam War, the conflict in Afghanistan resulted in heavy casualties and demonstrated that the influence of a superpower was limited in the face of strong nationalist, guerrilla-type opposition.

Society and Culture in the Western World

 Focus Question: What were the major social and cultural developments in the Western world between 1965 and 1985?

Dramatic social and cultural developments accompanied political and economic changes after 1965. Scientific and technological achievements revolutionized people's lives, while at the same time environmental problems were becoming increasingly apparent. Intellectually and culturally, the Western world after 1965 was notable for its diversity and innovation. New directions led some observers to speak of a Postmodern cultural world.

The World of Science and Technology

Before World War II, theoretical science and technology were largely separated. Pure science was the domain of university professors who were far removed from the practical technological concerns of technicians and engineers. But during World War II, university scientists were recruited to work for their governments and develop new weapons and practical instruments of war. In 1940, British physicists played a crucial role in the development of an improved radar system that helped defeat the German air force in the Battle of Britain. German scientists created self-propelled rockets and jet airplanes to keep Hitler's hopes alive for a miraculous turnaround in the war. The computer, too, was a wartime creation. The British mathematician Alan Turing designed a primitive computer to assist British intelligence in breaking the secret codes of German ciphering machines. The most famous product of wartime scientific research was the atomic bomb, created by a team of American and European scientists under the guidance of the American physicist J. Robert Oppenheimer. Obviously, most wartime devices were created for destructive purposes, but merely to mention computers and jet airplanes demonstrates that they could easily be adapted for peacetime uses.

The sponsorship of research by governments and the military during World War II created a new scientific model. Science had become very complex, and only large organizations with teams of scientists, huge laboratories, and complex equipment could undertake such large-scale projects. Such facilities were so expensive that they could only be provided by governments and large corporations.

There was no more stunning example of how the new scientific establishment operated than the space race of the 1960s. The announcement by the Soviets in 1957 that they had sent the first space satellite, *Sputnik,* into orbit around the earth caused the United States to launch a gigantic project to land a manned spacecraft on the moon within a decade. Massive government funds financed the scientific research and technological advances that attained this goal in 1969, an achievement that was greeted by some with great expectations for the future of humanity. One *New York Times* editorialist wrote:

> It will take years, decades, perhaps centuries, for man to colonize even the moon, but that is the end inherent in Armstrong's first step on extraterrestrial soil. Serious and hard-headed scientists envision, even in the not remote future, lunar communities capable of growing into domed cities subsisting on hydroponically grown food, of developing the moon's resources, and eventually of acquiring a breathable atmosphere and a soil capable of being farmed. What with the dire threats of population explosion at best and nuclear explosion at worst, the human race, as Sir Bernard Lovell warns, may find itself sometime in the 21st century "having to consider how best to insure the survival of the species."[4]

THE COMPUTER The alliance of science and technology has led to an accelerated rate of change that has become a fact of life in Western society. One product of this alliance—the computer—may be the most revolutionary of all the technological inventions of the twentieth century.

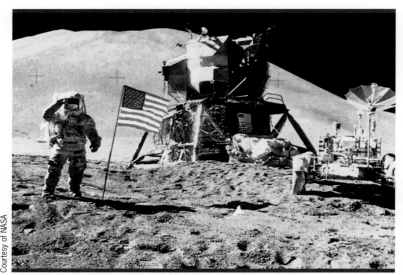

On the Moon. The first landing on the moon in 1969 was one of the great technological achievements of the twentieth century. This photograph shows astronaut James Irwin shortly after he raised the American flag during a moonwalk in 1971. The lunar module and lunar rover are also visible in the picture.

Early computers, which required thousands of vacuum tubes to function, were large and took up considerable space. An important figure in the development of the early computer was Grace Hopper (1906–1992), a career Navy officer. Hopper was instrumental in inventing COBOL, a computer language that enabled computers to respond to words as well as numbers.

The development of the transistor and then the silicon chip produced a revolutionary new approach to computers. In 1971, the invention of the microprocessor, a machine that combines the equivalent of thousands of transistors on a single, tiny silicon chip, opened the road for the development of the personal computer.

NEW CONCEPTION OF THE UNIVERSE After World War II, a number of physicists continued to explore the implications of Einstein's revolution in physics and raised fundamental questions about the nature of reality. To some physicists, quantum and relativity theory described the universe as a complicated web of relations in which there were no isolated building blocks. Thus, the universe was not a "collection of physical objects" but a complicated web of relations between "various parts of a unified whole." Moreover, this web of relations that is the universe also included the human observer. Human beings could not be objective observers of objects detached from themselves because the very act of observation made them participants in the process. These speculations implied that the old Newtonian conception of the universe as a machine was an outdated tool for understanding the nature of the universe.

DANGERS OF SCIENCE AND TECHNOLOGY Despite the marvels that were produced by the alliance of science and technology, some people came to question the underlying assumption of this alliance—that scientific knowledge gave human beings the ability to manipulate the environment for their benefit. They maintained that some technological advances had far-reaching side effects damaging to the environment. For example, the chemical fertilizers that were touted for producing larger crops wreaked havoc with the ecological balance of streams, rivers, and woodlands. *Small Is Beautiful,* written by the British economist E. F. Schumacher (1911–1977), was a fundamental critique of the dangers of the new science and technology (see the box on p. 939). The proliferation of fouled beaches and dying forests and lakes made environmentalism one of the important issues of the late twentieth century.

The Environment and the Green Movements

By the 1970s, serious ecological problems had become all too apparent. Air pollution, produced by nitrogen oxide and sulfur dioxide emissions from motor vehicles, power plants, and industrial factories, was causing respiratory illnesses and having corrosive effects on buildings and monuments. Many rivers, lakes, and seas had become so polluted that they posed serious health risks. Dying forests and disappearing wildlife alarmed more and more people. A nuclear power disaster at Chernobyl in the Ukrainian Soviet Socialist Republic in 1986 made Europeans even more aware of potential environmental hazards. The opening of Eastern Europe after the revolutions of 1989 (see Chapter 30) brought to the world's attention the incredible environmental destruction of that region caused by unfettered industrial pollution. Environmental concerns forced the major political parties in Europe to advocate new regulations for the protection of the environment.

Growing ecological awareness also gave rise to the Green movements and Green parties that emerged throughout Europe in the 1970s. The origins of these movements were by no means uniform. Some came from the antinuclear movement; others arose out of such causes as women's liberation and concerns for foreign workers. Most started at the local level and then gradually expanded to include activities at the national level, where they became formally organized as political parties. Green parties competed successfully in Sweden, Austria, and Switzerland. Most visible was the Green Party in Germany, which was officially organized in 1979 and by 1987 had elected forty-two delegates to the West German parliament.

Although the Green movements and parties have played an important role in making people aware of ecological problems, they have not replaced the traditional political parties, as some political analysts in the mid-1980s forecast. For one thing, the coalitions that made up the Greens found it difficult to agree on all issues and tended to splinter into different cliques.

Courtesy of NASA

The Limits of Modern Technology

Although science and technology have produced an amazing array of achievements in the postwar world, some voices have been raised in criticism of their sometimes destructive aspects. In 1975, in his book *Small Is Beautiful,* the British economist E. F. Schumacher examined the effects modern industrial technology has had on the earth's resources.

E. F. Schumacher, *Small Is Beautiful*

Is it not evident that our current methods of production are already eating into the very substance of industrial man? To many people this is not at all evident. Now that we have solved the problem of production, they say, have we ever had it so good? Are we not better fed, better clothed, and better housed than ever before—and better educated? Of course we are: most, but by no means all, of us: in the rich countries. But this is not what I mean by "substance." The substance of man cannot be measured by Gross National Product. Perhaps it cannot be measured at all, except for certain symptoms of loss. However, this is not the place to go into the statistics of these symptoms, such as crime, drug addiction, vandalism, mental breakdown, rebellion, and so forth. Statistics never prove anything.

I started by saying that one of the most fateful errors of our age is the belief that the problem of production has been solved. This illusion, I suggested, is mainly due to our inability to recognize that the modern industrial system, with all its intellectual sophistication, consumes the very basis on which it has been erected. To use the language of the economist, it lives on irreplaceable capital which it cheerfully treats as income. I specified three categories of such capital: fossil fuels, the tolerance margins of nature, and the human substance. Even if some readers should refuse to accept all three parts of my argument, I suggest that any one of them suffices to make my case.

And what is my case? Simply that our most important task is to get off our present collision course. And who is there to tackle such a task? I think *every* one of us.... To talk about the future is useful only if it leads to action *now.* And what can we do *now,* while we are still in the position of "never having had it so good"? To say the least ... we must thoroughly understand the problem and begin to see the possibility of evolving a new life-style, with new methods of production and new patterns of consumption: a life-style designed for permanence. To give only three preliminary examples: in agriculture and horticulture, we can interest ourselves in the perfection of production methods which are biologically sound, build up soil fertility, and produce health, beauty and permanence. Productivity will then look after itself. In industry, we can interest ourselves in the evolution of small-scale technology, relatively nonviolent technology, "technology with a human face," so that people have a chance to enjoy themselves while they are working, instead of working solely for their pay packet and hoping, usually forlornly, for enjoyment solely during their leisure time.

Q What was Schumacher's critique of modern technology? To what extent has this critique been substantiated by developments since 1975?

Moreover, traditional political parties co-opted the environmental issues of the Greens. More and more European governments began to sponsor projects to safeguard the environment and clean up the worst sources of pollution.

Postmodern Thought

The term *Postmodern* covers a variety of artistic and intellectual styles and ways of thinking that have been prominent since the 1970s. In the broadest sense, **Postmodernism** rejects the modern Western belief in an objective truth and instead focuses on the relative nature of reality and knowledge. Human knowledge is defined by a number of factors that must be constantly revised and tested by human experiences.

While existentialism wrestled with notions of meaning and existence, a group of French philosophers in the 1960s attempted to understand how meaning and knowledge operate through the study of language and signs. In the early twentieth century, the Swiss language scholar Ferdinand de Saussure (fayr-di-nawh duh SOH-SOOR) (1857–1913) gave birth to structuralism by asserting that the very nature of signs is arbitrary and that language is a human construct. And though the external world has existed for ages, de Saussure believed that humans possessed no capacity for knowledge until language was devised. Language employs signs to denote meaning and, according to de Saussure, possesses two components: the *signifier,* the expression of a concept, and the *signified,* its meaning. For de Saussure, meaning seeks expression in language, although the reliance on language for knowledge suggested that such meaning is learned rather than preexisting.

Jacques Derrida (ZHAHK DEH-ree-duh) (1930–2004) drew on the ideas of de Saussure to demonstrate how dependent Western culture is on binary oppositions. In Western thought, one set of oppositions is generally favored over the other (in the case of de Saussure, speech was favored over writing), but Derrida showed that the privileged depends on the inferior. Rather than reversing the opposition and claiming that writing surpasses speech, for example, Derrida showed that spelling often altered pronunciation. This indebtedness to written language demonstrates that oral speech is not superior. **Poststructuralism,** or **deconstruction,** which Derrida formulated, believes that culture is created and can therefore be analyzed in a variety of ways, according to the manner in which people create their own meaning. Hence, there is no fixed truth or universal meaning.

Michel Foucault (mih-SHELL foo-KOH) (1926–1984) likewise drew upon de Saussure and Derrida to explore relationships of power. Believing that "power is exercised, rather than possessed," Foucault argued that the diffusion of power and oppression marks all relationships. For example, any act of teaching entails components of assertion and submission, as the student adopts the ideas of the one in power. Therefore, all norms are culturally produced and entail some degree of power struggle. In establishing laws of conduct, society not only creates ideal behavior from those who conform, but it also invents a subclass of individuals who do not conform. In *The History of Sexuality,* Foucault suggested that homosexuality was produced by cultures attempting to define and limit homosexual acts. Yet in seeking to control and delineate homosexuality, those in power established the grounds on which it could be defined and practiced. As such, power ultimately requires resistance for it to exist; otherwise, it loses all meaning.

Trends in Art, Literature, and Music

Beginning in the 1960s and continuing well into the 1980s, styles emerged that some have referred to as "Postmodern." Postmodernism tends to move away from the futurism or "cutting-edge" qualities of Modernism. Instead it favors "tradition," whether that means using earlier styles of painting or elevating traditional crafts to the level of fine art. Weavers, potters, glassmakers, metalsmiths, and furniture makers have gained respect as artists. Postmodern artists and architects frequently blur the distinction between the arts, creating works that include elements of film, performance, popular culture, sculpture, and architecture.

ART In the 1960s and 1970s, artists often rejected the notion of object-based artworks. Instead, performances and installations that were either too fleeting or too large to appear in the traditional context of a museum were produced. Allen Kaprow (1927–2006) suggested that "happenings," works of art rooted in performance, grew out of Jackson Pollock's process of action painting. Rather

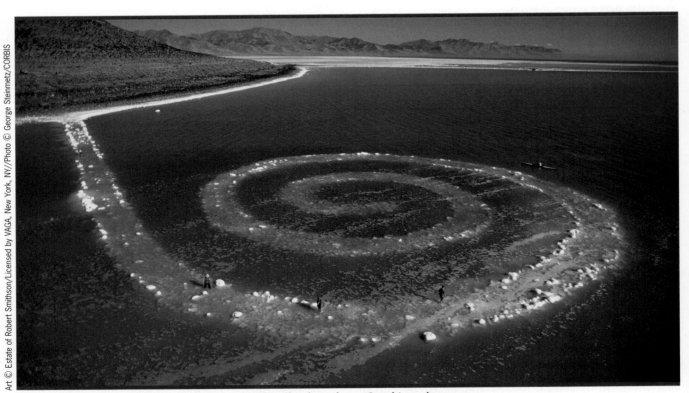

Art © Estate of Robert Smithson/Licensed by VAGA, New York, NY//Photo © George Steinmetz/CORBIS

Robert Smithson, *Spiral Jetty.* Built on an abandoned industrial site, *Spiral Jetty* disappears and reappears according to the rise and fall of the Great Salt Lake's water level. As seen in this 2002 photograph, the surface has become encrusted in salt as drought has lowered the lake level. Robert Smithson filmed the construction of *Spiral Jetty,* carefully noting the various geological formations included in his creation. Earthworks like *Spiral Jetty* increased in number as the welfare of the world's ecosystems became a growing concern in the 1960s and 1970s.

than producing abstract paintings, however, Kaprow created events that were not scripted but chance occurrences. These "happenings" often included audience participation. Kaprow's emphasis on the relationship of art to its surroundings was continued in the "land art" of the early 1970s. In one such example, *Spiral Jetty* (1970), Robert Smithson (1938–1973) used a bulldozer to move more than 6,000 tons of earth into a 1,500-foot-long corkscrew in Utah's Great Salt Lake. Responding to the founding of the Environmental Protection Agency as well as to the cycles of nature, Smithson's artwork resembled a science-fiction wasteland while challenging notions of traditional fine art.

Postmodernism's eclectic mixing of past tradition with Modernist innovation became increasingly evident in architecture. Robert Venturi (b. 1925) argued that architects should look as much to the commercial strips of Las Vegas as to the historical styles of the past for inspiration. Venturi advocated an architecture of "complexity and contradiction" as appropriate for the diversity of experiences offered by contemporary life. One example is provided by Charles Moore (1929–1993). His *Piazza d'Italia* (1976–1980) in New Orleans is an outdoor plaza that combines Roman columns with stainless steel and neon lights. This blending of modern-day materials with historical reference distinguished the Postmodern architecture of the late 1970s and 1980s from the Modernist glass box.

Another Postmodern response to Modernism can be seen in a return to Realism in the arts, a movement called Photorealism. Some Photorealists paint or sculpt with such minute attention to detail that their paintings appear to be photographs and their sculptures living human beings. Their subjects are often ordinary individuals, stuck in ordinary lives, demonstrating the Postmodern emphasis on low culture and the commonplace rather than the ambitious nature of high art. These works were often pessimistic or cynical.

LITERATURE Postmodernism was also evident in literature. In the Western world, the best examples were found in Latin America, in a literary style called "magic realism," and in central and Eastern Europe. Magic realism combined realistic events with dreamlike or fantastic backgrounds. One of the finest examples of magic realism can be found in the novel *One Hundred Years of Solitude,* by Gabriel García Márquez (mar-KEZ) (b. 1928), who won the Nobel Prize for Literature in 1982. The novel is the story of the fictional town of Macondo as seen by several generations of the Buendias, its founding family. The author slips back and forth between fact and fantasy. Villagers are not surprised when a local priest rises into the air and floats. Yet, when wandering Gypsies introduce these villagers to magnets, telescopes, and magnifying glasses, the villagers are dumbfounded by what they see as magic. According to the author, fantasy and fact depend on one's point of view.

The European center of Postmodernism is well represented by the work of the Czech writer Milan Kundera (MEE-lahn koon-DAYR-uh) (b. 1929). Like the magic realists of Latin America, Kundera also blended fantasy with realism. Unlike the magic realists, Kundera used fantasy to examine moral issues and remained optimistic about the human condition. Indeed, in his novel, *The Unbearable Lightness of Being* (1984), Kundera does not despair because of the political repression in his native Czechoslovakia that

Charles Moore, *Piazza d'Italia.* Dedicated to the Italian communities of New Orleans, *Piazza d'Italia* includes a schematic map of Italy on its pavement. The architect, Charles Moore, combined elements from Italy's rich cultural past, such as Roman columns and Renaissance Baroque colonnades, with modern materials like neon lighting and stainless steel to create an eclectic Postmodern plaza.

he so aptly describes but allows his characters to use love as a way to a better life. The human spirit can be lessened but not destroyed.

MUSIC Like modern art, modern music has focused on variety and radical experimentation. Also like modern art, modern classical music witnessed a continuation of pre-war developments. Some composers, the neoclassicists, remained closely tied to nineteenth-century Romantic music, although they occasionally incorporated some twentieth-century developments, such as atonality and dissonance. Their style was strongly reminiscent of Stravinsky (see Chapter 24).

The major musical trend since the war, however, has been serialism. Inspired mostly by the twelve-tone music of Schönberg (see Chapter 26), serialism is a compositional procedure in which an order of succession is set for specific values: pitch (for tones of the tempered scale), loudness (for dynamic levels), and units of time (for rhythm). By predetermining the order of succession, the composer restricts his or her intuitive freedom as the work to some extent creates itself. Nevertheless, the mechanism the composer initially establishes could generate unanticipated musical events, thereby creating new and exciting compositions. Serialist composition diminishes the role of intuition and emotion in favor of intellect and mathematical precision. The first recognized serialist was the Frenchman Olivier Messiaen (oh-lee-VYAY meh-SYANH) (1908–1992). Significantly, Messiaen was influenced by, among other things, Indian and Greek music, plainchant, folk music, and birdsongs. Most critics have respected serialism, although the public has been largely indifferent, if not hostile, to it.

An offshoot of serialism that has won popular support, but not the same critical favor, is minimalism. Like serialism, this style uses repeated patterns and series and steady pulsation with gradual changes occurring over time. But whereas serialism is often atonal, minimalism is usually tonal and more harmonic. Perhaps the most successful minimalist composer is Philip Glass (b. 1937), who demonstrated in *Einstein on the Beach* that minimalist music could be adapted to full-scale opera. Like other modern American composers, Glass found no contradiction in moving between the worlds of classical music and popular music. His *Koyaanisqatsi* (koh-YAH-niss-kaht-si) was used as background music to a documentary film on the disintegrative forces in Western society.

Popular Culture: Image and Globalization

The period from 1967 to 1973 was probably the true golden age of rock. During this brief period, much experimentation in rock music took place, as it did in society in general. Straightfoward rock-and-roll competed with a new hybrid blues rock, created in part by British performers such as the Rolling Stones, who were in turn inspired by African American blues artists. Many musicians also experimented with non-Western musical sounds, such as Indian sitars. Some of the popular music of the 1960s also focused on social issues. It was against the Vietnam War and materialism and promoted "peace and love" as alternatives to the prevailing "establishment" culture.

The same migration of a musical form from the United States to Britain and back to the United States that characterized the golden age of rock also occurred when the early punk movement in New York spread to Britain in the mid-1970s after failing to make an immediate impact in the United States. The more influential British punk movement of 1976–1979 was also fueled by an economic crisis that had resulted in large numbers of unemployed and undereducated young people. Punk was not simply a proletarian movement, however. Many of its supporters, performers, and promoters were British art school graduates who applied avant-garde experimentation to the movement. Punk rockers such as Britain's Sex Pistols rejected most social conventions and preached anarchy and rebellion. They often wore tattered clothes and pins in their cheeks, symbolizing their rejection of a materialistic and degenerate culture. Pure punk was short-lived, partly because its intense energy quickly burned out (as did many of its performers) and partly because, as ex-punk Mick Hucknall said, "the biggest mistake of the punks was that they rejected music." Offshoots of punk proliferated through the 1980s, however, especially in Eastern Europe, with groups named Crisis, Sewage, and Dead Organism.

The introduction of the video music channel MTV in the early 1980s radically changed the music scene by making image as important as sound in selling records. Artists like Michael Jackson became superstars by treating the music video as an art form. Jackson's videos often were short films with elaborate staging and special effects set to music. Technological advances became prevalent in the music of the 1980s with the advent of the synthesizer, an electronic piano that produced computerized sounds. Some performers replaced ensembles of guitar, bass, and drums with synthesizers, creating a futuristic and manufactured sound.

Paralleling the rise of the music video was the emergence of rap or hip-hop. Developed in New York City in the late 1970s and early 1980s, rap combined rhymed lyrics with disco beats and turntable manipulations. One scholar noted that hip-hop "also encompassed break dancing, graffiti art, and new styles of language and fashion." Early rap groups like Public Enemy and Grandmaster Flash and the Furious Five instilled social commentaries into their songs, using the popularity of hip-hop to raise awareness about social conditions in American cities (see the box on p. 943).

THE GROWTH OF MASS SPORTS Sports became a major product of both popular culture and the leisure industry. The development of satellite television and various electronic breakthroughs helped make sports a global

Grandmaster Flash and the Furious Five: "The Message"

In the 1982 hit single "The Message," Grandmaster Flash and the Furious Five added depth to rap music. No longer novelty or dance music, hip-hop began tackling serious social issues like the harsh realities of ghetto life. More and more rappers began to use music as a means of social protest and commentary. "The Message" tells of a boy who shunned education in favor of a flashy but criminal lifestyle. The story has a tragic ending when the young man dies in prison, as the chorus equates life in the ghetto to a jungle.

—————— ✦✥✦ ——————

"The Message"

> A child is born, with no state of mind
> Blind to the ways of mankind
> God is smiling on you but he's frowning too
> Cause only God knows what you'll go through
> You'll grow in the ghetto, living second rate
> And your eyes will sing a song of deep hate
> The places you play and where you stay
> Looks like one great big alleyway
> You'll admire all the number book takers
> Thugs, pimps, pushers and the big money makers
> Driving big cars, spending twenties and tens
> And you wanna grow up to be just like them
> Smugglers, scramblers, burglars, gamblers

> Pickpockets, peddlers and even pan-handlers
> You say I'm cool, I'm no fool
> But then you wind up dropping out of high school
> Now you're unemployed, all null 'n' void
> Walking around like you're Pretty Boy Floyd
> Turned stickup kid, look what you done did
> Got send up for an eight year bid
> Now you man is took and you're a Maytag
> Spend the next two years as an undercover fag
> Being used and abused, and served like hell
> Till one day you was found hung dead in a cell
> It was plain to see that your life was lost
> You was cold and your body swung back and forth
> But now your eyes sing the sad sad song
> Of how you lived so fast and died so young

> It's like a jungle sometimes, it makes me wonder
> How I keep from goin' under

Q What differences and similarities do you see between the lyrics of "The Message" and those of Bob Dylan's "The Times They Are A-Changin'" on p. 923, and what do they tell you about the differences and similarities between the decades of the 1960s and the 1980s?

---

phenomenon. The Olympic Games could now be broadcast around the globe from anywhere in the world. Sports were a cheap form of entertainment since fans did not have to leave their homes to enjoy athletic competitions. In fact, some sports organizations initially resisted television, fearing that it would hurt ticket sales. Soon, however, the tremendous revenues possible from television contracts overcame this hesitation. As sports television revenue escalated, many sports came to receive the bulk of their yearly revenue from television contracts. The Olympics, for example, are now funded primarily by American television. These contracts are paid for by advertising sponsors, mostly for products to be consumed while watching the sport: beer, soda, and snack foods.

Sports became big politics as well as big business. Football (soccer) remained the dominant world sport and more than ever became a vehicle for nationalist sentiment and expression. The World Cup is the most watched event on television. Although the sport can be a positive outlet for national and local pride, all too often it has been marred by violence as nationalistic energies have overcome rational behavior.

The most telling example of the potent mix of politics and sport continued to be the Olympic Games. When the Soviets entered Olympic competition in 1952, the Olympics began to take on Cold War implications and became

known as the "war without weapons." The Soviets saw the Olympics as a way to stimulate nationalist spirit, as well as to promote the Communist system as the best path for social progress. The Soviets led the Olympics in terms of total medals won between 1956 and 1988. The nature of the Olympics, with their daily medal count by nation and elaborate ceremonies and rituals such as the playing of the national anthem of the winning athletes and the parade of nations, virtually ensured the politicization of the games originally intended to foster international cooperation through friendly competition.

The political nature of the games found expression in other ways as well. In 1956, six nations withdrew from the games to protest the Soviet crushing of the Hungarian uprising. In 1972, twenty-seven African nations threatened to pull out of the Munich Olympics because of apartheid in South Africa. Also at the Munich Games, the Palestinian terrorist group Black September seized eleven Israeli athletes as hostages, all of whom died in a confrontation at an airport. The United States led a boycott of the 1980 Moscow Games to protest the Soviet invasion of Afghanistan, and the Soviets responded by boycotting the Los Angeles Games in 1984.

As sports assumed a prominent position in the social life of the world, the pressures and rewards to not just compete but win intensified. Fueled by advertising endorsements, the scientific study of sport led to aerodynamic helmets for cyclists, skintight bodysuits for skiers and swimmers, and improved nutritional practices in all sports. Such technological advances, however, also increased the manner in which athletes might break the rules. From steroids to blood doping, some have used medical supplements to illegally enhance their conditioning. Mandatory drug testing for athletes competing in many events including the Olympics, Tour de France, and World Cup attempts to level the playing field and avoid repercussions such as occurred when reports of steroid abuse prompted a governmental investigation of Major League Baseball.

POPULAR CULTURE: INCREASINGLY GLOBAL Media critic and theorist Marshall McLuhan (1911–1980) predicted in the 1960s that advances in mass communications technology, such as satellites and electronics, would eventually lead to a shrinking of the world, a lessening of cultural distinctions, and a breaking down of cultural barriers, all of which would in time transform the world into a single "global village." McLuhan was optimistic about these developments, and his ideas became quite popular at the time. Many critics have since argued that McLuhan was too utopian about the benefits of technological progress and maintain that the mass media created by these technological breakthroughs are still controlled by a small number of multinational corporations that "colonize the rest of the world, sometimes benignly, sometimes not." They argue that this has allowed Western popular culture to disrupt the traditional cultures of less developed countries and inculcate new patterns of behavior as well as new desires and new dissatisfactions. Cultural contacts, however, often move in two directions. While the world has been "Americanized" to a great extent, formerly unfamiliar ways of life and styles of music have also come into the world of the West (see Chapter 30).

CHAPTER SUMMARY

The late 1960s experienced a rash of protest movements. A revolt in sexual mores was the result of the so-called sexual revolution of the 1960s, which was encouraged by the birth control pill as well as sexually explicit movies, plays, and books. A growing youth movement in the 1960s

questioned authority and fostered rebellion against the older generation. Numerous groups of students and radicals protested the war in Vietnam and unsatisfactory university conditions. Women actively sought equality of rights with men. The women's movement gained momentum in the 1970s and 1980s, but the student upheavals were not a "turning point in the history of postwar Europe," as some people thought at the time, especially in 1968, when the student protest movement reached its height. In the 1970s and 1980s, student rebels became middle-class professionals, and revolutionary politics remained mostly a memory.

In the 1970s, the Cold War took a new direction known as détente as the Soviet Union and the United States moved, if ever fitfully, toward a lessening of tensions. With the Antiballistic Missile Treaty in 1972, the United States and the Soviet Union believed that they had reached a balance, or "equivalence," that would assure peace. The early 1980s, however, saw renewed tensions between the superpowers. The Soviet invasion of Afghanistan in 1979 and the introduction of the cruise missile and "Star Wars" by the American president Ronald Reagan brought a decline in détente. But as we shall see in the next chapter, a dramatic shift in Soviet leadership would soon bring an unexpected end to the Cold War.

Between 1965 and 1985, the Western world remained divided between a prosperous capitalistic and democratic West and a stagnant, politically repressed Eastern Europe. After two decades of incredible economic growth, Western European states experienced severe economic recessions in 1973–1974 and 1979–1983, although their economies largely recovered in the course of the 1980s. In Eastern Europe, Soviet leaders continued to exercise control over their satellite states

while recognizing the need to provide some leeway in adopting domestic policies appropriate to local conditions.

Dramatic social and cultural developments accompanied political and economic changes after 1965. Scientific and technological developments, especially the rapid advance of the personal computer, began to revolutionize people's lives, while ecological problems became increasingly apparent and led to the Green movements and Green parties that emerged throughout Europe in the 1970s. Intellectu-

ally and culturally, the Western world after 1965 was notable for its diversity and innovation. New directions led some observers to speak of a Postmodern world in both literature and the arts.

CHAPTER TIMELINE

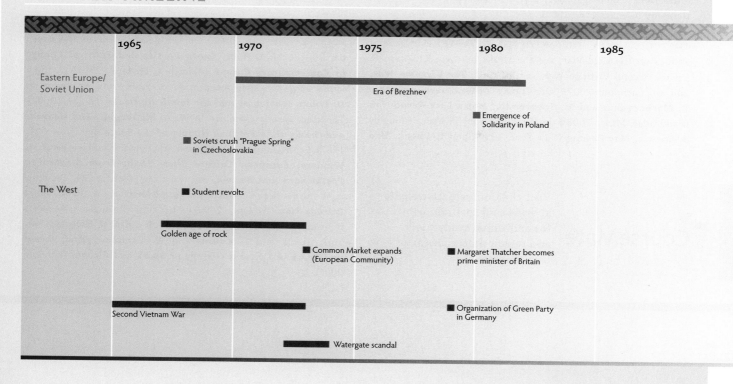

	1965	1970	1975	1980	1985

Eastern Europe/Soviet Union

Era of Brezhnev

■ Emergence of Solidarity in Poland

■ Soviets crush "Prague Spring" in Czechoslovakia

The West

■ Student revolts

Golden age of rock

■ Common Market expands (European Community)

■ Margaret Thatcher becomes prime minister of Britain

Second Vietnam War

■ Organization of Green Party in Germany

Watergate scandal

CHAPTER REVIEW

Upon Reflection

Q What were the major turning points in the Cold War between 1965 and 1985?

Q What were the major successes and failures of the Western European democracies between 1965 and 1985, and how did Soviet policies affect the Eastern European states during the same time period?

Q What role did popular culture play in the Western world between 1965 and 1985?

Key Terms

permissive society (p. 921)
feminism (p. 924)
Brezhnev Doctrine (p. 925)
détente (p. 926)
Eurocommunism (p. 931)
stagflation (p. 932)
domino theory (p. 934)
Postmodernism (p. 939)
poststructuralism (deconstruction) (p. 940)

Suggestions for Further Reading

GENERAL WORKS For a well-written survey on Europe between 1965 and 1985, see **T. Judt, _Postwar: A History of Europe Since_**

_1945_ (New York, 2005). Additional general surveys of contemporary European history are listed in Chapter 28.

A CULTURE OF PROTEST On the sexual revolution of the 1960s, see **D. Allyn, _Make Love, Not War: The Sexual Revolution—An Unfettered History_** (New York, 2000). On the turbulent 1960s, see **A. Marwick, _The Sixties: Social and Cultural Transformation in Britain, France, Italy, and the United States_** (Oxford, 1999), and **T. H. Anderson, _The Sixties_** (London, 1998). On the women's liberation movement, see **C. Duchen, _Women's Rights and Women's Lives in France, 1944–1968_** (New York, 1994); **D. Meyer, _The Rise of Women in America, Russia, Sweden, and Italy,_** 2nd ed. (Middletown, Conn., 1989); and **K. C. Berkeley, _The Women's Liberation Movement in America_** (Westport, Conn., 1999).

SOVIET UNION AND EASTERN EUROPE On the Brezhnev era in the Soviet Union, see **E. Bacon, ed., _Brezhnev Remembered_** (New York, 2003). On events in Eastern Europe, see the surveys listed in Chapter 28. On the Czech upheaval in 1968, see **K. Williams, _The Prague Spring and Its Aftermath: Czechoslovak Politics, 1968–1970_** (Cambridge, 1997).

WESTERN EUROPE For general works on Western Europe and individual countries, see the works cited in Chapter 28. More specific works dealing with the period 1965–1985 include **E. J. Evans, _Thatcher and Thatcherism_** (New York, 1997); **D. S. Bell, _François_**

Mitterrand (Cambridge, 2005); and **R. J. Dalton, *Politics in West Germany*** (Glenview, Ill., 1989).

THE COLD WAR: THE MOVE TO DÉTENTE For general studies on the Cold War, see the works listed in Chapter 28. On the Second Vietnam War, see **M. Hall, *The Vietnam War,*** 2nd ed. (London, 2007). On China's cultural revolution, see **R. MacFarquhar** and **M. Schoenhals, *Mao's Last Revolution*** (Cambridge, Mass., 2006); the brief biography of Mao Zedong by **J. Spence, *Mao Zedong*** (New York, 1999); and **T. Cheek, *Mao***

Zedong and China's Revolutions: A Brief History (Boston, 2002).

SOCIETY AND CULTURE On the development of the Green parties, see **M. O'Neill, *Green Parties and Political Change in Contemporary Europe*** (Aldershot, England, 1997). A physicist's view of a new conception of reality can be found in **D. Bohm, *Wholeness and the Implicate Order*** (London, 2002). The space race is examined in **W. A. McDougall, *The Heavens and the Earth: A Political History of the Space Age*** (New York, 1987). For a general view of postwar thought and culture, see **J. A. Winders, *European Culture Since 1848: From Modern to Postmodern and Beyond,*** rev. ed. (New York, 2001). On Postmodernism, see **C. Butler, *Postmodernism: A Very Short Introduction*** (Oxford, 2002). The cultural impact of sports is examined in **R. Mandell, *Sport: A Cultural History*** (New York, 1999), and **T. Collins** and **W. Vamplew, *Mud, Sweat and Beers: A Cultural History of Sport and Alcohol*** (London, 2002).

Visit the CourseMate website at www.cengagebrain.com for additional study tools and review materials for this chapter.

1. During the presidency of Ronald Reagan,

    (A) relations between the United States and Iran became less contentious.
    (B) the United States declined in world leadership as the European Union emerged.
    (C) the nuclear arms race was renewed as Cold War tensions increased.
    (D) the United States and Great Britain experienced a fundamental ideological separation, as the two countries were unable to agree on international policy.
    (E) fighting in Afghanistan resulted in a victory for the Soviet Union and a defeat for American forces.

2. All of the following were causes for student revolts in France EXCEPT

    (A) the educational system had deteriorated and could no longer meet the needs of the growing student population.
    (B) growing opposition to warfare in places like Vietnam.
    (C) there was a widespread feeling of disillusionment as many felt that ordered society—and possibly the world—would cease to exist.
    (D) the rise of a materialist, consumer society in France, driven by capitalist desires.
    (E) the involvement of France in Western alliances such as NATO.

3. The Brezhnev Doctrine

    (A) allowed Western European nations to provide economic relief and military support to those behind the Iron Curtain.
    (B) provided a rationale for the Soviet Union to invade regions in the Middle East.
    (C) caused greater tension by suggesting that the Soviet Union held carte blanche over Eastern Europe.
    (D) stated that the Soviet Union and the United States would begin to decrease their stockpiles of nuclear warheads.
    (E) opened trade and peace negotiations between the Soviet Union and Communist China.

4. In the 1980s, the Soviet Union experienced

    (A) political chaos as no strong single party or leader emerged.
    (B) economic resurgence as military production powered a flourishing economy.
    (C) declining morale and an economic slump as the costs of being a superpower began to weigh heavily on the country.
    (D) a cultural revolution in which Soviet artists and writers were celebrated throughout the world.
    (E) a continued era of prosperity and power as the Soviet Union increased its holdings through a number of successful invasions in the Middle East.

5. Which of the following best describes European popular culture in the late twentieth century?

    (A) There were new experiments in rock music, and artistic images and attitudes had greater influence on society.
    (B) The wide variety of artistic venues meant that few iconic artists with mass appeal emerged.
    (C) Music was largely limited to traditional pop rock, leading to shared experiences across the Continent.
    (D) Sports and entertainment withered as the economic crisis forced many to give up such luxuries.
    (E) Popular media such as radio and newspapers had a large influence on the masses.

6. In regard to the Cold War, détente provided

    (A) a time of increased tensions as it spurred militarization and globalization.
    (B) a decade of relaxed tension between the Republic of China and the Soviet Union.
    (C) a period of relaxation in which democratic and Communist powers worked to reduce nuclear arms.
    (D) an opportunity for the United States to seize Soviet territories in the Middle East.
    (E) a means by which other Western powers could participate in the nuclear arms race.

7. Within Poland, leaders such as Lech Walesa

    (A) forged a political alliance between Poland and Yugoslavia in order to subvert the Soviet Union.
    (B) organized a movement that would bolster the stability of the Communist Party.
    (C) took advantage of a political vacuum created by the lack of Communist Party leadership.
    (D) organized Solidarity, a grassroots labor movement dedicated to ending oppressive Communist rule.
    (E) seized power over the Communist Party in order to increase Poland's standing with the Soviet Union.

8. The process of decolonization

    (A) was largely peaceful as European powers transferred power to their colonies.
    (B) was instituted to increase European dominance over Asia.
    (C) often contributed to an increase in conflict as Cold War tensions played out in newly independent lands.
    (D) allowed the United States to become less involved in world affairs.
    (E) led to détente and a reduction in nuclear arms.

9. The Prague Spring of 1968 and the Hungarian uprising of 1956

   (A) led to further intervention by the Soviet Union in Eastern Bloc countries.
   (B) won greater political and intellectual freedoms that continued throughout the 1960s and 1970s.
   (C) expanded the greater social freedoms set forth in samizdat publications.
   (D) were anticipated and spurred on by dissidents within the Soviet Union who hoped to usurp Soviet power.
   (E) witnessed mass executions of thousands within both countries as Khrushchev reasserted Soviet authority.

10. In the decades following World War II, women experienced

   (A) the destruction of the glass ceiling as equal pay for equal work was finally realized.
   (B) legal repression as government agencies advocated that the number of women in the workforce be reduced.
   (C) a sexual revolution and increased involvement in politics.
   (D) widespread social pressure to remain out of the workforce after marriage.
   (E) political gender equality including the institution of mandatory military service for both sexes.

11. Which of the following best describes the changes to European family life by the 1980s?

   (A) Most children attended and graduated from both secondary and postsecondary schools.
   (B) Many families were single-parent families, and family size dramatically declined.
   (C) Large families became the new norm as women were encouraged to stay at home to care for children.
   (D) Young adults living in cities married quickly and started families.
   (E) Consumerism and materialism lost their influence over the career decisions of many young adults.

12. Margaret Thatcher, known as the "Iron Lady," engaged in all of the following EXCEPT

   (A) the privatization of such national industries as the airlines.
   (B) a reduction in the power of labor unions.
   (C) an attempt to reduce inflation.
   (D) an increase in resources for the British educational system.
   (E) a hard-line approach to Communists and a military buildup.

13. What was the primary rationale for the creation of the European Union?

   (A) to create new agricultural tariffs to promote the buying of European crops
   (B) to create an economic community that would link European nations together and make war less attractive to all those involved
   (C) to combine the economies of Eastern and Western Europe into a single unit
   (D) to combine political and economic legislation within Western Europe
   (E) to continue a previous agreement that allowed Great Britain and Germany to combine their economic goals

14. Josip Broz Tito, dictator of Yugoslavia, accomplished all of the following EXCEPT

   (A) he formed political and economic alliances between his country and the Soviet Union.
   (B) he kept Yugoslavia Communist and yet separate from the Warsaw Pact.
   (C) he instituted a period of relative peace and prosperity in Yugoslavia as the rest of Eastern Europe suffered greatly.
   (D) he forged political ties with Western European nations like Great Britain.
   (E) he formed a single, cohesive nation made up of diverse ethnic minorities.

CHAPTER

With clenched fist, Boris Yeltsin speaks out against an attempted right-wing coup.

After the Fall: The Western World in a Global Age (Since 1985)

CHAPTER OUTLINE AND FOCUS QUESTIONS

Toward a New Western Order

Q What reforms did Gorbachev institute in the Soviet Union, and what role did he play in the demise of the Soviet Union? What are the major political developments in Eastern Europe, Western Europe, and North America since 1985?

After the Cold War: New World Order or Age of Terrorism?

Q How and why did the Cold War end? What are the main issues in the struggle with terrorism?

New Directions and New Problems in Western Society

Q What are the major developments in the women's movement since 1985, and what problems have immigrants created for European society?

Western Culture Today

Q What major Western cultural trends have emerged since 1985?

The Digital Age

Q What is the Digital Age, and what are its products, results, and dangers?

Toward a Global Civilization: New Challenges and Hopes

Q What is globalization, and what are some of its important aspects in the twenty-first century?

CRITICAL THINKING

Q In what ways were the major social, economic, and political developments in the second half of the twentieth century similar to those in the first half of the century? In what ways were they different?

BY 1985, AFTER FOUR DECADES of the Cold War, Westerners had become accustomed to a new division of Europe between West and East that seemed to be permanent. A prosperous Western Europe allied with the United States stood opposed to a still-struggling Eastern Europe that remained largely subject to the Soviet Union. The division of Germany symbolized the new order, which seemed so well established. Yet within a few years, a revolutionary upheaval in the Soviet Union and Eastern Europe brought an end to the Cold War and to the division of postwar Europe. Even the Soviet Union ceased to exist as a nation.

On August 19, 1991, a group of Soviet leaders opposed to reform arrested Mikhail Gorbachev, the president of the Soviet Union, and tried to seize control of the government. Hundreds of thousands of Russians, led by Boris Yeltsin, poured into the streets of Moscow and Leningrad to resist the attempted coup. Some army units, sent out to enforce the wishes of the rebels, defected to Yeltsin's side, and within days, the rebels were forced to surrender. This failed attempt to seize power had unexpected results as Russia and many of the other Soviet republics declared their independence. By the end of 1991, the Soviet Union—one of the largest empires in world history—had come to an end, and a new era of cooperation between the successor states in the old Soviet Union and the nations of the West had begun.

As the world adjusted to the transformation from Cold War to post–Cold War sensibilities, other changes shaped the Western outlook. The demographic face of European countries changed as massive numbers of immigrants created more ethnically diverse populations. New artistic and intellectual currents, the continued advance of science and technology, the emergence of a Digital Age, the surge of the women's liberation movement—all spoke of a vibrant, ever-changing world. At the same time, a devastating terrorist attack on the World Trade Center in New York City and the Pentagon outside Washington, D.C., in 2001 made the Western world vividly aware of its vulnerability to international terrorism. But most important of all, Western nations, like all nations on the planet, have become aware of the political and economic interdependence of the world's nations and the global nature of our twenty-first-century problems.

Toward a New Western Order

Q **Focus Questions:** What reforms did Gorbachev institute in the Soviet Union, and what role did he play in the demise of the Soviet Union? What are the major political developments in Eastern Europe, Western Europe, and North America since 1985?

Between 1945 and 1985, a new political order following the devastation of World War II had seemingly left the Western world divided permanently between a prosperous, capitalistic West and an impoverished, Communist East. But in the late 1980s and early 1990s, the Soviet Union and its Eastern European satellite states underwent a revolutionary upheaval that dramatically altered the European landscape (see Map 30.1) and left many Europeans with both new hopes and new fears.

The Revolutionary Era in the Soviet Union

By 1980, it was becoming apparent to a small number of reformers in the Communist Party that the Soviet Union was seriously ailing. When one of these young reformers, Mikhail Gorbachev, was chosen as Party secretary in March 1985, a new era began in the Soviet Union.

THE GORBACHEV ERA Born into a peasant family in 1931, Mikhail Gorbachev combined farm work with school and received the Order of the Red Banner for his agricultural efforts. This award and his good school record enabled him to study law at the University of Moscow.

After receiving his law degree in 1955, he returned to his native southern Russia, where he eventually became first secretary of the Party in the city of Stavropol (he had joined the Party in 1952) and then first secretary of the regional Party committee. In 1978, Gorbachev was made a member of the Party's Central Committee in Moscow. Two years later, he became a full member of the ruling Politburo and secretary of the Central Committee. In March 1985, Party leaders elected him general secretary of the Party, and he became the new leader of the Soviet Union.

Educated during the years of reform under Khrushchev, Gorbachev seemed intent on taking earlier reforms to their logical conclusions. He had said to his wife on achieving power, "We cannot go on living like this."[1] By the 1980s, Soviet economic problems were obvious. Rigid, centralized planning had led to mismanagement and stifled innovation. Although the Soviets still excelled in space exploration, they had fallen behind the West in high technology, especially in the development and production of computers for private and public use. Most noticeable to the Soviet people was the decline in the standard of living. In February 1986, at the Twenty-Seventh Congress of the Communist Party, Gorbachev made clear the need for changes in Soviet society: "The practical actions of the Party and state agencies lag behind the demands of the times and of life itself. . . . Problems grow faster than they are solved. Sluggishness, ossification in the forms, and methods of management decrease the dynamism of work. . . . Stagnation begins to show up in the life of society."[2] Thus, from the start, Gorbachev preached the need for radical reforms.

The cornerstone of Gorbachev's radical reforms was **perestroika** (per-uh-STROI-kuh), or "restructuring" (see the box on p. 950). At first, this meant only a reordering of economic policy as Gorbachev called for the beginning of a market economy with limited free enterprise and some private property. Gorbachev soon perceived, however, that in the Soviet system, the economic sphere was intimately tied to the social and political spheres. Attempting to reform the economy without political or social reform would be doomed to failure. One of the most important instruments of *perestroika* was **glasnost** (GLAHZ-nohst), or "openness." Soviet citizens and officials were encouraged to discuss openly the strengths and weaknesses of the Soviet Union. *Pravda* (PRAHV-duh), the official newspaper of the Communist Party, began to include reports of official corruption, sloppy factory work, and protests against government policy. The arts also benefited from the new policy. Previously banned works were now published, and music based on Western styles, such as jazz and rock, began to be performed openly.

Political reforms were equally revolutionary. At the Communist Party conference in 1988, Gorbachev called for the creation of a new Soviet parliament, the Congress of People's Deputies, whose members were to be chosen in competitive elections. It convened in 1989, the first such meeting in Russia since 1918. Early in 1990, Gorbachev legalized the formation of other political parties and

MAP 30.1   The New Europe. The combination of an inefficient economy and high military spending had led to stagnation in the Soviet Union by the early 1980s. Mikhail Gorbachev came to power in 1985, unleashing political, economic, and nationalist forces that led to independence for the former Soviet republics and also for Eastern Europe.

 Compare this map with Map 28.1. What new countries had emerged by the early twenty-first century?

 View an animated version of this map or related maps on the CourseMate website.

struck Article 6, which had guaranteed the "leading role" of the Communist Party, from the Soviet constitution. At the same time, Gorbachev attempted to consolidate his power by creating a new state presidency. The new position was a consequence of the separation of the state from the Communist Party. Hitherto, the position of first secretary of the Party had been the most important post in the Soviet Union, but as the Communist Party became less closely associated with the state, the powers of this office diminished correspondingly. In March 1990, Gorbachev became the Soviet Union's first president.

One of Gorbachev's most serious problems stemmed from the nature of the nation he led. The Union of Soviet Socialist Republics was a truly multiethnic country, containing 92 nationalities and 112 recognized languages. Previously, the iron hand of the Communist Party, centered in Moscow, had kept a lid on the centuries-old ethnic tensions that had periodically erupted. As Gorbachev released this iron grip, tensions resurfaced, a by-product of *glasnost* that Gorbachev had not anticipated.

Ethnic groups took advantage of the new openness to protest what they perceived as ethnically motivated slights. When violence erupted, the Soviet army, in disrepair since its ill-fated decade-long foray into Afghanistan, had difficulty controlling the situation.

The years 1988 to 1990 also witnessed the appearance of nationalist movements in the republics that made up the Soviet Union. Many were motivated by ethnic concerns, with calls for sovereignty and independence from the Russian-based rule centered in Moscow. These movements sprang up first in Georgia in late 1988 and then in Latvia (LAT-vee-uh), Estonia (ess-TOH-nee-uh), Moldova (mohl-DOH-vuh), Uzbekistan (ooz-BEK-i-stan), Azerbaijan (az-ur-by-JAHN), and Lithuania (li-thuh-WAY-nee-uh). On March 11, 1990, the Lithuanian Supreme Council proclaimed Lithuania an independent state.

THE END OF THE SOVIET UNION   During 1990 and 1991, Gorbachev struggled to deal with Lithuania and the other problems unleashed by his reforms. On the one

Gorbachev and *Perestroika*

After assuming the leadership of the Soviet Union in 1985, Mikhail Gorbachev worked to liberalize and restructure the country. His policies opened the door to rapid changes in Eastern Europe and in Soviet-American relations at the end of the 1980s. In his book *Perestroika,* Gorbachev explained some of his "New Thinking."

Mikhail Gorbachev, *Perestroika*

The fundamental principle of the new political outlook is very simple: *nuclear war cannot be a means of achieving political, economic, ideological or any other goals.* This conclusion is truly revolutionary, for it means discarding the traditional notions of war and peace. It is the political function of war that has always been a justification for war, a "rational" explanation. Nuclear war is senseless; it is irrational. There would be neither winners nor losers in a global nuclear conflict: world Civilization would inevitably perish. . . .

But military technology has developed to such an extent that even a non-nuclear war would now be comparable with a nuclear war in its destructive effect. That is why it is logical to include in our category of nuclear wars this "variant" of an armed clash between major powers as well.

Thereby, an altogether different situation has emerged. A way of thinking and a way of acting, based on the use of force in world politics, have formed over centuries, even millennia. It seems they have taken root as something unshakable. Today, they have lost all reasonable grounds. . . . For the first time in history, basing international politics on moral and ethical norms that are common to all humankind, as well as humanizing interstate relations, has become a vital requirement. . . .

There is a great thirst for mutual understanding and mutual communication in the world. It is felt among politicians, it is gaining momentum among the intelligentsia, representatives of culture, and the public at large. And if the Russian word "perestroika" has easily entered the international lexicon, this is due to more than just interest in what is going on in the Soviet Union. Now the whole world needs restructuring, i.e., progressive development, a fundamental change.

People feel this and understand this. They have to find their bearings, to understand the problems besetting mankind, to realize how they should live in the future. The restructuring is a must for a world overflowing with nuclear weapons; for a world ridden with serious economic and ecological problems; for a world laden with poverty, backwardness and disease; for a human race now facing the urgent need of ensuring its own survival.

We are all students, and our teacher is life and time. I believe that more and more people will come to realize that through RESTRUCTURING in the broad sense of the word, the integrity of the world will be enhanced. Having earned good marks from our main teacher—life—we shall enter the twenty-first century well prepared and sure that there will be further progress.

Q How revolutionary was Gorbachev's rejection of nuclear war? What impact did this idea of restructuring have on communism and the Soviet Union's ability to reform itself?

---

hand, he tried to appease conservatives who complained about the growing disorder within the Soviet Union. On the other hand, he tried to accommodate the liberal forces, especially those in the Soviet republics, who increasingly favored a new kind of decentralized Soviet federation. In particular, Gorbachev labored to cooperate more closely with Boris Yeltsin (YELT-sun) (1931–2007), who had been elected president of the Russian Republic in June 1991.

By 1991, the conservative leaders of the traditional Soviet institutions—the army, government, KGB, and military industries—had grown increasingly worried about the impending dissolution of the Soviet Union and its impact on their own fortunes. On August 19, 1991, a group of these discontented rightists arrested Gorbachev and attempted to seize power. Gorbachev's unwillingness to work with the conspirators and the brave resistance in Moscow of Yeltsin and thousands of Russians who had grown accustomed to their new liberties caused the coup to disintegrate rapidly. The actions of these right-wing plotters, however, served to accelerate the very process they had hoped to stop—the disintegration of the Soviet Union.

Despite desperate pleas by Gorbachev, the Soviet republics soon moved for complete independence. Ukraine voted for independence on December 1, 1991, and a week later, the leaders of Russia, Ukraine, and Belarus (bell-uh-ROOSS) announced that the Soviet Union had "ceased to exist" and would be replaced by the new and voluntary Commonwealth of Independent States. Gorbachev resigned on December 25, 1991, and turned over his responsibilities as commander in chief to Boris Yeltsin, the president of Russia. By the end of 1991, one of the largest empires in world history had evaporated, and a new era had begun in its lands.

THE NEW RUSSIA A new power struggle soon ensued within Russia, by far the largest of the former Soviet republics. Yeltsin was committed to introducing a free market economy as quickly as possible, but the transition was not easy. Economic hardships and social disarray, made worse

Yeltsin Resists a Right-Wing Coup.
In August 1991, the attempt of right-wing plotters to overthrow Mikhail Gorbachev and seize power in the Soviet Union was thwarted by the efforts of Boris Yeltsin, president of the Russian Republic, and his supporters. Yeltsin (holding papers) is shown here atop a tank in front of the Russian parliament building in Moscow, urging the Russian people to resist the conspirators.

by a dramatic rise in the activities of organized crime mobs, led increasing numbers of Russians to support both former Communists and hard-line nationalists who tried to place new limits on Yeltsin's powers. Yeltsin fought back and pushed ahead with plans for a new Russian constitution that would abolish the Congress of People's Deputies, create a two-chamber parliament, and establish a strong presidency. A hard-line parliamentary minority resisted and in early October 1993 took the offensive, urging their supporters to take over government offices. Yeltsin responded by ordering military forces to storm the parliament building and arrest his hard-line opponents. Yeltsin used his victory to consolidate his power in parliamentary elections held in December.

During the mid-1990s, Yeltsin sought to implement reforms that would set Russia on a firm course toward a pluralistic political system and a market economy. But the new post-Communist Russia remained as fragile as ever. Growing economic inequality and rampant corruption aroused widespread criticism and shook the confidence of the Russian people in the superiority of the capitalist system over the one that had existed under Communist rule. A nagging war in the Caucasus—where the Muslim people of Chechnya (CHECH-nee-uh) sought national independence from Russia—drained the government's budget and exposed the decrepit state of the once vaunted Red Army. Yeltsin won reelection as president in 1996, although his precarious health raised serious questions about his ability to govern.

THE PUTIN ERA At the end of 1999, Yeltsin suddenly resigned and was replaced by Vladimir Putin (POO-tin) (b. 1952), a former member of the KGB. Putin vowed to strengthen the role of the central government in managing

the affairs of state. During the succeeding months, the parliament approved his proposal to centralize power in the hands of the federal government in Moscow.

The new president also vowed to return the breakaway state of Chechnya to Russian authority and to adopt a more assertive role in international affairs. Fighting in Chechnya continued throughout 2000, nearly reducing the republic's capital city of Grozny to ruins. In July 2001, Putin launched reforms, which included the unrestricted sale and purchase of land and tax cuts aimed at boosting economic growth and budget revenues. Although Russia soon experienced a budget surplus and a growing economy, serious problems remained.

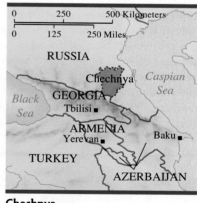

Chechnya

Putin attempted to deal with the chronic problems in Russian society by centralizing his control over the system and by silencing critics—notably in the Russian media. Although he was criticized in the West for these moves, many Russians expressed sympathy with Putin's attempts to restore a sense of pride and discipline in Russian society.

In 2008, Dmitry Medvedev (di-MEE-tree mehd-VYEH-dehf) (b. 1965) became president of Russia when Putin could not run for reelection under Russia's constitution. Instead, Putin became prime minister, and the two men have since shared power.

Eastern Europe: The Revolutions of 1989 and the Collapse of the Communist Order

Stalin's postwar order had imposed Communist regimes throughout Eastern Europe. The process of sovietization seemed so complete that few people believed that the new order could be undone. But discontent with their Soviet-style regimes always simmered beneath the surface of these satellite states, and after Mikhail Gorbachev made it clear that his government would not intervene militarily, the Communist regimes fell quickly in the revolutions of 1989.

THE FALL Martial law had not solved Poland's problems after it had been imposed in 1981, and in 1988, new demonstrations led the Polish regime to agree to free parliamentary elections—the first free elections in Eastern Europe in forty years. Bowing to the inevitable, the military regime allowed the newly elected Solidarity coalition to form a new government, thus ending forty-five years of Communist rule. The Soviet Union, in line with Gorbachev's new policy of nonintervention, also took no action to reverse the verdict in Poland. In December 1990, Lech Walesa, the head of Solidarity, was chosen as the new Polish president.

In Hungary, the economy had sagged by the late 1980s, and in 1989, the Communist regime, aware of growing dissatisfaction, began to undertake reforms. But they came too late as new political parties called for Hungary to become a democratic republic. After elections in March 1990, a new coalition government was formed that committed Hungary to democratic government.

Czechoslovakia, too, found a peaceful way to a new political system. Government attempts to suppress mass demonstrations in Prague and other cities in 1988 and 1989 only led to more and larger demonstrations. In December 1989, as demonstrations continued, the Communist government, lacking any real support, collapsed. President Gustáv Husák resigned and at the end of December was replaced by Vaclav Havel, a longtime dissident playwright who had played an important role in bringing the Communist government down. Havel set out on a goodwill tour to various Western countries where he proved to be an eloquent spokesman for Czech democracy and a new order in Europe (see the box on p. 953).

Czechoslovakia's revolutionary path was considerably less violent than Romania's, where opposition grew as the dictator Nicolae Ceaușescu rejected the reforms in Eastern Europe promoted by Gorbachev. Ceaușescu's extreme measures to reduce Romania's external debt led to economic difficulties. Although he was successful in reducing foreign debt, the sharp drop in living standards that resulted from those hardship measures angered many Romanians. A small incident became the spark that ignited heretofore suppressed flames of discontent. The ruthless crushing of a demonstration in Timisoara in December 1989 led to other mass demonstrations. After the dictator was booed at a mass rally on December 21, the army refused to support any more repression. Ceaușescu and his wife were captured on December 22 and tried and executed on Christmas Day. Leadership now passed into the hands of the hastily formed National Salvation Front.

AFTER THE FALL The fall of Communist governments in Eastern Europe during the revolutions of 1989 brought a wave of euphoria to Europe. The new structures meant an end to a postwar European order that had been imposed on unwilling peoples by the victorious forces of the Soviet Union. In 1989 and 1990, new governments throughout Eastern Europe worked diligently to scrap the remnants of the old system and introduce the democratic procedures and market systems they believed would revitalize their scarred lands. But this process proved to be neither simple nor easy.

Most Eastern European countries had little or even no experience with democratic systems. Then, too, ethnic divisions, which had troubled these areas before World

A Romanian Revolutionary. The revolt against Communist rule in Eastern Europe in 1989 came last to Romania. It was also more violent as the government at first tried to stem the revolt by massacring demonstrators. This picture shows a young Romanian rebel waving the national flag with the Communist emblem cut out of the center. He is on a balcony overlooking the tanks, soldiers, and citizens filling Palace Square in Bucharest.

© Peter Turnley/CORBIS

Vaclav Havel: The Call for a New Politics

In attempting to deal with the world's problems, some European leaders have pointed to the need for a new perspective, especially a moral one, if people are to live in a sane world. These two excerpts are taken from speeches by Vaclav Havel, who was elected president of Czechoslovakia at the end of 1989. The first is from his inaugural address as president on January 1, 1990; the second is from a speech given to the U.S. Congress.

⊷ ⊰◈⊱ ⊷

Vaclav Havel, Address to the People of Czechoslovakia, January 1, 1990

But all this is still not the main problem [the environmental devastation of the country by its Communist leaders]. The worst thing is that we live in a contaminated moral environment. We fell morally ill because we became used to saying something different from what we thought. We learned not to believe in anything, to ignore each other, to care only about ourselves. Concepts such as love, friendship, compassion, humility, or forgiveness lost their depth and dimensions, and for many of us they represented only psychological peculiarities, or they resembled gone-astray greetings from ancients, a little ridiculous in the era of computers and spaceships. Only a few of us were able to cry out loud that the powers that be should not be all-powerful, and that special farms, which produce ecologically pure and top-quality food just for them should send their produce to schools, children's homes and hospitals if our agriculture was unable to offer them to all. The previous regime—armed with its arrogant and intolerant ideology—reduced man to a force of production and nature to a tool of production. In this it attacked both their very substance and their mutual relationship. It reduced gifted and autonomous people, skillfully working in their own country, to nuts and bolts of some monstrously huge, noisy, and stinking machine, whose real meaning is not clear to anyone.

Vaclav Havel, Speech to Congress, February 21, 1990

For this reason, the salvation of this human world lies nowhere else than in the human heart, in the human power to reflect, in human meekness and in human responsibility.

Without a global revolution in the sphere of human consciousness, nothing will change for the better in the sphere of our being as humans, and the catastrophe toward which this world is headed—be it ecological, social, demographic or a general breakdown of civilization—will be unavoidable....

We are still a long way from that "family of man." In fact, we seem to be receding from the ideal rather than growing closer to it. Interests of all kinds—personal, selfish, state, nation, group, and if you like, company interests—still considerably outweigh genuinely common and global interests. We are still under the sway of the destructive and vain belief that man is the pinnacle of creation and not just a part of it and that therefore everything is permitted....

In other words, we still don't know how to put morality ahead of politics, science and economics. We are still incapable of understanding that the only genuine backbone of all our actions, if they are to be moral, is responsibility.

Responsibility to something higher than my family, my country, my company, my success—responsibility to the order of being where all our actions are indelibly recorded and where and only where they will be properly judged.

The interpreter or mediator between us and this higher authority is what is traditionally referred to as human conscience. ▷

Q How different is Havel's view of politics from the views of mainstream politicians? What broader forces working in modern European society do you believe shaped Havel's thinking? How can Havel's view of our common humanity and responsibility to conscience help revitalize Western civilization?

War II and had been forcibly submerged under Communist rule, reemerged with a vengeance. Finally, the rapid conversion to market economies also proved painful. The adoption of "shock-therapy" austerity measures produced much suffering. Unemployment, for example, climbed to over 13 percent in Poland in 1992.

Nevertheless, by the beginning of the twenty-first century, many of these states, especially Poland and the Czech Republic, were making a successful transition to both free markets and democracy. In Poland, Aleksander Kwaśniewski (kwahsh-NYEF-skee) (b. 1954), although a former Communist, was elected president in November 1995 and pushed Poland toward an increasingly prosperous free market economy. His successor, Lech Kaczyński (LEK kuh-ZIN-skee) (1949–2010), emphasized the need to combine modernization with tradition. In July 2010, Bronislaw Komorowski (b. 1952) was elected president to succeed Kaczyński, who had died in a plane crash in April. In Czechoslovakia, the shift to non-Communist rule was complicated by old problems, especially ethnic issues. Czechs and Slovaks disagreed over the makeup of the new state but were able to agree to a peaceful division of the country. On January 1, 1993, Czechoslovakia split into the Czech Republic and Slovakia. Vaclav Havel was elected the first president of the new Czech Republic. In Romania, the current president, Traian Băsescu (tri-YAHN buh-SES-koo) (b. 1951), leads a country that is just beginning to show economic growth and the rise of a middle class.

The revival of the post–Cold War Eastern European states is evident in their desire to join both NATO and the European Union (EU), the two major Cold War institutions of Western European unity. In 1997, Poland, the Czech Republic, and Hungary became full members of NATO. In 2004, ten nations—including Hungary, Poland, the Czech Republic, Slovenia, Estonia, Latvia, and Lithuania—joined the EU, and Romania and Bulgaria joined in 2007.

Yet not all are convinced that inclusion in European integration is a good thing. Eastern Europeans fear that their countries will be dominated by investment from their prosperous neighbors, while their counterparts in Western Europe are concerned about a possible influx of low-wage workers from the new member countries. The global financial crisis that began in 2008 also added to the economic problems of Eastern European countries.

The Reunification of Germany

Perhaps the most dramatic events took place in East Germany, where a persistent economic slump and the ongoing oppressiveness of the regime of Erich Honecker led to a flight of refugees and mass demonstrations against the regime in the summer and fall of 1989. After more than half a million people flooded the streets of East Berlin on November 4, shouting, "The wall must go!" the German Communist government soon capitulated to popular pressure and on November 9 opened the entire border with the West. Hundreds of thousands of Germans swarmed across the border, mostly to visit and return. The Berlin Wall, long a symbol of the Cold War, became the site of massive celebrations as thousands of people used sledgehammers to tear it down. By December, new political parties had emerged, and on March 18, 1990, in East Germany's first free elections ever, the Christian Democrats won almost 50 percent of the vote.

The Christian Democrats supported rapid monetary unification, and on July 1, 1990, the economies of West and East Germany were united, with the West German deutsche mark becoming the official currency of the two countries. And after months of political negotiations between West and East German officials as well as the original four postwar occupying powers (the United States, Great Britain, France, and the Soviet Union), political reunification was achieved on October 3, 1990. What had seemed almost impossible at the beginning of 1989 had become a reality by the end of 1990.

The Disintegration of Yugoslavia

From its beginning in 1919, Yugoslavia had been an artificial creation. The peace treaties at the end of World War I combined Serbs, Croats, and Slovenes into a new south Slav state called Yugoslavia (known until 1929 as the Kingdom of the Serbs, Croats, and Slovenes). After World War II, the dictatorial Marshal Tito had managed to hold the six republics and two autonomous provinces that constituted Yugoslavia together. After his death in 1980, no strong leader emerged, and his responsibilities passed

And the Wall Came Tumbling Down. The Berlin Wall, long a symbol of Europe's Cold War divisions, became the site of massive celebrations after the East German government opened its border with the West. The activities included spontaneous acts of demolition as Germans used sledgehammers and crowbars to tear down parts of the wall. In this photograph, a demonstrator pounds away at the Berlin Wall as East German border guards observe from above.

to a collective state presidency and the League of Communists of Yugoslavia. At the end of the 1980s, Yugoslavia was caught up in the reform movements sweeping through Eastern Europe. The League of Communists collapsed, and new parties quickly emerged.

The Yugoslav political scene was complicated by the development of separatist movements. In 1990, the republics of Slovenia, Croatia, Bosnia-Herzegovina, and Macedonia began to lobby for a new federal structure of Yugoslavia that would fulfill their separatist desires. Slobodan Milošević (sluh-BOH-dahn mi-LOH-suh-vich) (1941–2006), who had become the leader of the Serbian Communist Party in 1987 and had managed to stay in power by emphasizing his Serbian nationalism, rejected these efforts. He asserted that these republics could be independent only if new border arrangements were made to accommodate the Serb minorities in those republics who did not want to live outside the boundaries of a Greater Serbian state. Serbs constituted 11.6 percent of Croatia's population and 32 percent of Bosnia-Herzegovina's in 1991.

	1989
Collapse of Communist government in Czechoslovakia	December
Collapse of East German government	December
Execution of Ceauşescu in Romania	December 25
	1990
Lithuania declares independence	March 11
East German elections—victory of Christian Democrats	March 18
Reunification of Germany	October 3
Walesa becomes president of Poland	December
	1991
Yeltsin becomes president of Russia	June
Slovenia and Croatia declare independence	June
Right-wing coup in the Soviet Union	August 19
Dissolution of the Soviet Union	December

After negotiations among the six republics failed, Slovenia and Croatia declared their independence in June 1991. Milošević's government sent the Yugoslavian army, which it controlled, into Slovenia, without much success. In September 1991, it began a full assault against Croatia. Increasingly, the Yugoslavian army was becoming the Serbian army, while Serbian irregular forces played a growing role in military operations. Before a cease-fire was arranged, the Serbian forces had captured one-third of Croatia's territory in brutal and destructive fighting.

THE WAR IN BOSNIA   The recognition of independent Bosnia-Herzegovina, Slovenia, and Croatia by many European states and the United States early in 1992 did not stop the Serbs from turning their guns on Bosnia. By mid-1993, Serbian forces had acquired 70 percent of Bosnian territory (see the box on p. 956). The Serbian policy of **"ethnic cleansing"**—killing or forcibly removing Bosnian Muslims from their lands—revived memories of Nazi atrocities during World War II. This account by one Muslim survivor from the town of Srebrenica (sreb-bruh-NEET-suh) is eerily reminiscent of the activities of the Nazi *Einsatzgruppen* (see Chapter 27):

> When the truck stopped, they told us to get off in groups of five. We immediately heard shooting next to the trucks.... About ten Serbs with automatic rifles told us to lie down on the ground face first. As we were getting down, they started to shoot, and I fell into a pile of corpses. I felt hot liquid running down my face. I realized that I was only grazed. As they continued to shoot more groups, I kept on squeezing myself in between dead bodies.[3]

Almost 8,000 men and boys were killed in the Serbian massacre at Srebrenica. Nevertheless, despite worldwide outrage, European governments failed to take a decisive and forceful stand against these Serbian activities. By 1995,

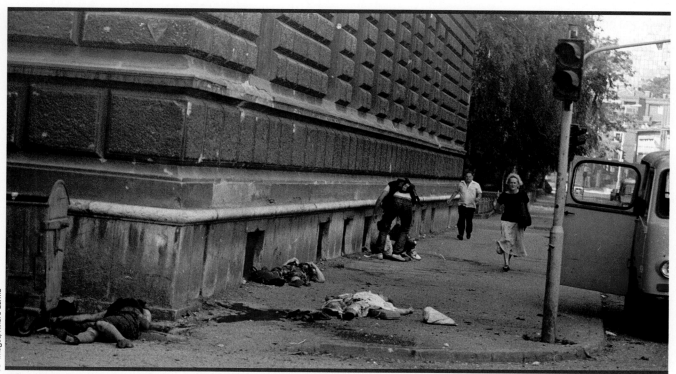

The War in Bosnia. By mid-1993, irregular Serb forces had overrun much of Bosnia-Herzegovina amid scenes of untold suffering. This photograph shows a woman running past the bodies of victims of a mortar attack on Sarajevo on August 21, 1992. Three mortar rounds landed, killing at least three people.

A Child's Account of the Shelling of Sarajevo

When Bosnia declared its independence in March 1992, Serbian army units and groups of Bosnian Serbs went on the offensive and began to shell the capital city of Sarajevo. One of its residents was Zlata Filipovic, the ten-year-old daughter of a middle-class lawyer. Zlata was a fan of MTV and pizza, but when the Serbs began to shell Sarajevo from the hills above the city, her life changed dramatically, as is apparent in this excerpt from her diary.

⚬ ⚬ ⚬

Zlata Filipovic, *Zlata's Diary, A Child's Life in Sarajevo*

April 3, 1992: Daddy came back . . . all upset. He says there are terrible crowds at the train and bus stations. People are leaving Sarajevo.

April 4, 1992: There aren't many people in the streets. I guess it's fear of the stories about Sarajevo being bombed. But there's no bombing. . . .

April 5, 1992: I'm trying hard to concentrate so I can do my homework (reading), but I simply can't. Something is going on in town. You can hear gunfire from the hills.

April 6, 1992: Now they're shooting from the Holiday Inn, killing people in front of the parliament. . . . Maybe we'll go to the cellar . . .

April 9, 1992: I'm not going to school. All the schools in Sarajevo are closed. . . .

April 14, 1992: People are leaving Sarajevo. The airport, train and bus stations are packed. . . .

April 18, 1992: There's shooting, shells are falling. This really is WAR. Mommy and Daddy are worried, they sit up late at night, talking. They're wondering what to do, but it's hard to know. . . . Mommy can't make up her mind—she's constantly in tears. She tries to hide it from me, but I see everything.

April 21, 1992: It's horrible in Sarajevo today. Shells falling, people and children getting killed, shooting. We will probably spend the night in the cellar.

April 26, 1992: We spent Thursday night with the Bobars again. The next day we had no electricity. We had no bread, so for the first time in her life Mommy baked some.

April 28, 1992: SNIFFLE! Everybody has gone. I'm left with no friends.

April 29, 1992: I'd write to you much more about the war if only I could. But I simply don't want to remember all these horrible things. ⬭

Q How do you think Zlata Filipovic was able to deal with the new conditions in her life?

---

some 250,000 Bosnians (mostly civilians) had been killed, and 2 million others were left homeless.

Renewed offensives by mostly Muslim Bosnian government army forces and by the Croatian army regained considerable territory that had been lost to Serbian forces. Air strikes by NATO bombers, strongly advocated by U.S. President Bill Clinton, were launched in retaliation for Serb attacks on civilians and weakened the Serb military positions. All sides were now encouraged by the United States to end the war and met in Dayton, Ohio, in November 1995 for negotiations. A formal peace treaty was signed in Paris on December 14 that split Bosnia into a loose union of a Serb republic (with 49 percent of the land) and a Muslim-Croat federation (with 51 percent of the land). NATO agreed to send a force of 60,000 troops (20,000 American troops made up the largest single contingent) that would monitor the frontier between the new political entities (see Map 30.2).

THE WAR IN KOSOVO Peace in Bosnia, however, did not bring peace to the remnants of Yugoslavia. A new war erupted in 1999 over Kosovo, which had been made an autonomous province within Yugoslavia in 1974. Kosovo's inhabitants were mainly ethnic Albanians who were allowed to keep their Albanian language. But Kosovo also had a Serbian minority who considered Kosovo sacred territory because it contained the site where Serbian forces had been defeated by the Ottoman Turks in the fourteenth century in a battle that became a defining moment in Serbian history (see Chapter 12).

In 1989, Yugoslav president Milošević, who had become an ardent Serbian nationalist, stripped Kosovo of its autonomous status and outlawed any official use of the Albanian language. In 1993, some groups of ethnic Albanians founded the Kosovo Liberation Army (KLA) and began a campaign against Serbian rule in Kosovo. When Serb forces began to massacre ethnic Albanians in an effort to crush the KLA, the United States and its NATO allies sought to arrange a settlement. After months of negotiations, the Kosovo Albanians agreed to a peace plan that would have given the ethnic Albanians in Kosovo broad autonomy for a three-year interim period. When Milošević refused to sign the agreement, the United States and its NATO allies began a bombing campaign that forced the Yugoslavian government into compliance.

THE AFTERMATH Since 1991, Yugoslavia had been embroiled in an appalling and destructive war, largely caused by the policies of Slobodan Milošević. By 2000, the Serbian people had finally tired of the violence and in the fall elections ousted Milošević from power. The new Serbian government under Vojislav Koštunica (VOH-yee-slav kuh-STOO-nit-suh) (b. 1944) moved quickly to cooperate with the international community and begin rebuilding the Serbian economy. On June 28, 2001, the Serbian government agreed to allow Milošević to be put on trial by an

MAP 30.2 The Lands of the Former Yugoslavia, 1995. By 1991, resurgent nationalism and the European independence wave overcame the forces that held Yugoslavia together. Declarations of independence by Slovenia, Croatia, and Bosnia-Herzegovina led to war with the Serbian-dominated rump Yugoslavia of Slobodan Milošević.

Q *What aspects of Slovenia's location help explain why its war of liberation was briefer and less bloody than others in the former Yugoslavia?*

international tribunal for crimes against humanity for his ethnic cleansing policies throughout Yugoslavia's disintegration. He died in prison in 2006 before his trial could be completed.

The fate of Bosnia and Kosovo has not yet been finally determined. Some 30,000 NATO troops remain in Bosnia, trying to keep the peace between the Serb republic and the Muslim-Croat federation. More than thirty international organizations are at work rebuilding schools, roads, and sewers, but only the presence of NATO troops keeps old hatreds from erupting again.

In Kosovo, NATO military forces were brought in to maintain an uneasy peace, while United Nations officials worked to create democratic institutions and the European Union provided funds for rebuilding the region's infrastructure. These efforts are ongoing but are made difficult by the festering hatred between Kosovo Albanians and the remaining Serbs.

The last political vestiges of Yugoslavia ceased to exist in 2004 when the Koštunica government officially renamed the truncated country Serbia and Montenegro. Two years later, Montenegrins voted in favor of independence, and in 2008, Kosovo declared its independence as well. Thus ninety years after Yugoslavia was cobbled together, all six of its constituent republics (Slovenia, Croatia, Bosnia-Herzegovina, Serbia, Macedonia, and Montenegro) were once again independent nations, and a new one (Kosovo) had been born.

Western Europe and the Search for Unity

With the revolutions of 1989, Western Europe was faced with new political possibilities and challenges. Germany was once again united, delighting the Germans but frightening their neighbors. At the same time, new opportunities for thinking of all of Europe as a political entity also emerged. Eastern Europe was no longer cut off from Western Europe by the Iron Curtain of the Cold War.

GERMANY RESTORED With the end of the Cold War, West Germany faced a new challenge. Chancellor Helmut Kohl had benefited greatly from an economic boom in the mid-1980s. Gradually, however, discontent with the Christian Democrats increased, and by 1988, their political prospects seemed diminished. But unexpectedly, the 1989 revolution in East Germany led to the reunification of the two Germanies, leaving the new Germany, with its 79 million people, the leading power in Europe. Reunification, which was accomplished during Kohl's administration and owed much to his efforts, brought rich political dividends to the Christian Democrats. In the first all-German federal election in 1990, Kohl's Christian Democrats won 44 percent of the vote, while their coalition partners, the Free Democrats, received 11 percent.

But the excitement over reunification soon dissipated as new problems arose. All too soon, the realization set in that

The Lives of Others (2006)

Directed by Florian Henckel von Donnersmarck, *The Lives of Others,* which won the Academy Award for Best Foreign Film, is a German film (*Das Leben der Anderen*) that brilliantly re-creates the depressing debilitation of East German society under its Communist regime, and especially the Stasi, the secret police. Georg Dreyman (Sebastian Koch) is a successful playwright in the German Democratic Republic (East Germany). Although he is a dedicated socialist who has not offended the authorities, they try to determine whether he is completely loyal by wiretapping his apartment, where he lives with his girlfriend, Christa-Maria Sieland (Martina Gedeck), an actress in some of Dreyman's plays. Captain Gerd Wiesler (Ulrich Mühe) of the Stasi takes charge of the spying operation. He is the epitome of the perfect functionary——a cold, calculating, dedicated professional who is convinced he is building a better society and is only too eager to fight the "enemies of socialism." But in the course of listening to the everyday details of Dreyman's life, Wiesler begins to develop a conscience and becomes sympathetic to the writer. After a close friend of Dreyman's commits suicide, Dreyman turns against the Communist regime and writes an article on the alarming number of suicides in East German society for *Der Spiegel,* a West German magazine. Lieutenant Colonel Grubitz (Ulrich Tukur), Wiesler's boss, suspects that Dreyman is the author. His girlfriend is brought in for questioning and provides some damning information about Dreyman's involvement. Horrified by what she has done, she commits suicide, but Wiesler, who is now determined to save Dreyman, fudges his reports and protects him from being arrested. Wiesler's boss suspects what Wiesler has done and demotes him. The film ends after the fall of the Berlin Wall when the new German government opens the Stasi files. When Dreyman reads his file, he realizes how Wiesler saved him and writes a book dedicated to him.

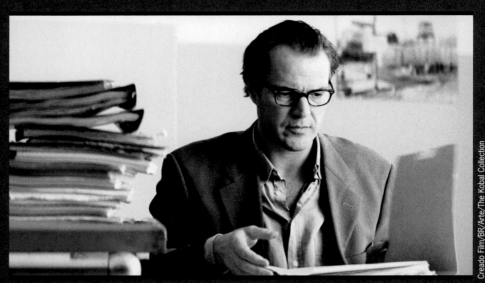

Georg Dreyman (Sebastian Koch) examines his Stasi files.

The film brilliantly depicts the stifling atmosphere of East Germany under Communist rule. The Stasi had about 90,000 employees but also recruited a network of hundreds of thousands of informers who submitted secret reports on their friends, family, bosses, and coworkers. Some volunteered the information, but as the film makes clear, others were bribed or blackmailed into working with the authorities. As the movie demonstrates, the Stasi were experts at wiretapping dwellings and compiling detailed written reports about what they heard, including conversations, arguments, jokes, and even sexual activities. Ironically, Ulrich Mühe, who plays Captain Wiesler in the film, was an East German who himself had been spied on by the Stasi.

The Lives of Others has been praised by East Germans for accurately depicting the drab environment of their country and the role of the Stasi in fostering a society riddled by secrecy, fear, and the abuse of power. The dangers of governments that monitor their citizens are apparent and quite relevant in an age of Patriot Acts designed to fight terrorism. The police state is revealed for what it is, a soulless and hollow world with no redeeming features or values. ⯈

the revitalization of eastern Germany would take far more money than was originally thought, and Kohl's government was soon forced to face the politically undesirable task of raising taxes substantially. Moreover, the virtual collapse of the economy in eastern Germany led to extremely high levels of unemployment and severe discontent. One reason for the problem was the government's decision to establish a 1:1 ratio between the East and West German marks. This policy raised salaries for East German workers, but it increased labor costs and caused many companies to hire workers abroad.

East Germans were also haunted by another memory from their recent past. The opening of the files of the secret police (the Stasi) showed that millions of East Germans had spied on their neighbors and colleagues, and even their spouses and parents, during the Communist era (see the Film & History feature above). A few senior Stasi officials were put on trial for their past actions, but many Germans preferred simply to close the door on an unhappy period in their lives.

As the century neared its close, then, Germans struggled to cope with the challenge of building a new, united nation. To reduce the debt incurred because of economic reconstruction in the east, the government threatened to cut back on many of the social benefits West Germans had long been accustomed to receiving. This in turn sharpened resentments that were already beginning to emerge between western and eastern Germany.

In 1998, voters took out their frustrations at the ballot box. Helmut Kohl's conservative coalition was defeated in new elections, and a new prime minister, Social Democrat Gerhard Schröder (GAYR-hahrt SHRUR-duh) (b. 1944), came into office. But Schröder had little success at solving Germany's economic woes, and as a result of elections in 2005, Angela Merkel (b. 1954), leader of the Christian Democrats, became the first female chancellor in German history. Merkel pursued health care reform and new energy policies at home while taking a leading role in the affairs of the European Union. After new elections in 2009, she began a second term as Germany's chancellor and in 2010 led EU nations in attempting a financial bailout of Greece's deteriorating economy.

POST-THATCHER BRITAIN While Margaret Thatcher dominated British politics in the 1980s, the Labour Party, beset by divisions between its moderate and radical wings, offered little effective opposition. Only in 1990 did Labour's fortunes seem to revive when Thatcher's government attempted to replace local property taxes with a flat-rate tax payable by every adult to a local authority. Though Thatcher maintained that this would make local government more responsive to its electors, many argued that this was nothing more than a poll tax that would enable the rich to pay the same rate as the poor. In 1990, after antitax riots broke out, Thatcher's once remarkable popularity fell to an all-time low. At the end of November, a revolt within her own party caused Thatcher to resign as Britain's longest-serving prime minister. She was replaced by John Major, whose Conservative Party won a narrow victory in the general elections held in April 1992. His government, however, failed to capture the imagination of most Britons. In new elections on May 1, 1997, the Labour Party won a landslide victory. The new prime minister, Tony Blair (b. 1953), was a moderate whose youthful energy immediately instilled new vigor into the political scene. Adopting centrist policies reminiscent of those followed by President Bill Clinton in the United States (see "The United States: Move to the Center" later in this chapter), his party dominated the political arena into the new century. Blair was one of the prominent leaders in forming an international coalition against terrorism after the terrorist attack on the United States in 2001. Three years later, however, his support of the U.S. war in Iraq, when a majority of Britons opposed it, caused his popularity to plummet, although the failure of the

Conservative Party to field a popular candidate kept him in power until the summer of 2007, when he stepped down and allowed the new Labour leader Gordon Brown (b. 1951) to become prime minister. Elections held in early May 2010 were inconclusive: the Conservatives won the largest number of seats in Parliament but were twenty short of a majority. When Brown resigned a few days after the elections, Conservative David Cameron (b. 1966) became prime minister on the basis of a coalition with the Liberal Democrats.

FRANCE: A MOVE TO THE RIGHT Although François Mitterrand was able to win a second term as president in 1988, France's economic decline continued. In 1993, French unemployment stood at 10.6 percent, and in the elections in March of that year, the Socialists won only 28 percent of the vote as a coalition of conservative parties gained 80 percent of the seats in the National Assembly. The move to the right in France was strengthened when the conservative mayor of Paris, Jacques Chirac (ZHAHK shee-RAK) (b. 1932), was elected president in 1995 and reelected in 2002.

By 1995, resentment against foreign-born residents had become a growing political reality. Spurred by rising rates of unemployment and large numbers of immigrants from North Africa (often identified in the public mind with terrorist actions committed by militant groups based in the Middle East), many French voters advocated restrictions on all new immigration. Chirac himself pursued a plan of sending illegal immigrants back to their home countries. He said, "France cannot accept all of the wretched of the earth" (see the box on p. 897).

In the fall of 2005, however, antiforeign sentiment provoked a backlash of its own, as young Muslims in the crowded suburbs of Paris rioted against dismal living conditions and the lack of employment opportunities for foreign residents in France. After the riots subsided, government officials promised to adopt measures to respond to the complaints, but tensions between the Muslim community and the remainder of the French population have become a chronic source of social unrest throughout the country—an unrest that Nicolas Sarkozy (b. 1955), elected as president in 2007, promised to address but without much success. In 2009, unemployment among those under 25 was almost 22 percent, but in the suburbs that are home to many Muslims, youth joblessness exceeded 50 percent.

CORRUPTION IN ITALY Corruption has continued to trouble Italian politics. In 1993, hundreds of politicians and business leaders were under investigation for their involvement in a widespread scheme to use political bribes to secure public contracts. Public disgust with political corruption became so intense that in April 1996, Italian voters took the unusual step of giving control of the government to a center-left coalition that included the Communists. In recent years, Silvio Berlusconi (SEEL-vee-oh bayr-loo-SKOH-nee), owner of a media empire, has

First all-German federal election	1990
Victory of Conservative Party under John Major in Britain	1992
Conservative victory in France	1993
Creation of European Union	1994
Jacques Chirac becomes president of France	1995
Election of Tony Blair in Britain	1997
Gerhard Schröder becomes chancellor of Germany	1998
Reelection of Chirac	2002
Angela Merkel becomes chancellor of Germany	2005
Romano Prodi becomes prime minister of Italy	2006
Election of Nicolas Sarkozy in France	2007
Reelection of Merkel	2009
David Cameron becomes prime minister of Britain	2010

dominated Italian politics, even though he became a politician primarily in order to protect his own business interests. Although he lost to Socialist Romano Prodi (b. 1939) in a close election in 2006, Berlusconi again became prime minister after new elections in 2008.

The Unification of Europe

With the addition of Austria, Finland, and Sweden in 1995, the European Community (EC) had grown to fifteen members. The EC was primarily an economic union, not a political one. By 2000, it contained 370 million people and constituted the world's largest single trading entity, transacting one-fourth of the world's commerce. In 1986, the EC had created the Single Europe Act, which had opened the door by 1992 to a truly united internal market, thereby eliminating all barriers to the exchange of people, goods, services, and capital. This was followed by a proposal for a monetary union and a common currency. The Treaty on European Union (also called the Maastricht Treaty after the city in the Netherlands where the agreement was reached) represented an attempt to create a true economic and monetary union of all EC members. On January 1, 1994, the EC renamed itself the European Union (EU). One of its first goals was to introduce a common currency, called the euro, adopted by twelve EU nations early in 1999. On June 1, 1999, a European Central Bank was created, and by January 2010, the euro had officially replaced sixteen national currencies. The euro serves approximately 327 million people and has become the world's second largest reserve currency after the U.S. dollar.

A major crisis for the euro emerged in 2010, when Greece's burgeoning public debt threatened the bankruptcy of that country as well as financial difficulties for many European banks. To avoid financial disaster, other EU members, led by Germany, labored to put together a financial rescue plan. Whether it will succeed and prevent the decline of the euro, as many Europeans fear, was not yet clear by August.

GOALS In addition to having a single internal market for its members and a common currency, the European Union also established a common agricultural policy, under which subsidies are provided to farmers to enable them to sell their goods competitively on the world market. The policy also provides aid to the EU's poorest regions as well as subsidies for job training, education, and modernization. The end of national passports gave millions of Europeans greater flexibility in travel.

The EU has been less successful in setting common foreign policy goals, primarily because individual nations still see foreign policy as a national prerogative and are reluctant to give it up to an overriding institution. Although EU foreign ministers meet periodically, they usually do not draw up a uniform policy. Nevertheless, the EU did create a military force of 60,000, to be used chiefly for humanitarian and peacekeeping purposes. Indeed, the focus of the EU is on peaceful conflict resolution, not making war.

In 2009, the EU ratified the Lisbon Treaty, which created a full-time presidential post and a new voting system that reflects the size of each country's population. It also provided more power for the European Parliament in an effort to promote the EU's foreign policy goals.

PROBLEMS As successful as the European Union has been, problems still exist. Europeans are often divided on the EU. Some oppose it because the official representatives of the EU are not democratically accountable to the people. Moreover, many Europeans do not regard themselves as "Europeans" but remain committed to a national identity. Despite these problems, a majority—although not a large one—of the members remain committed to the EU. In a poll taken in the fall of 2001, some 54 percent of Europeans said that membership in the EU was a "good thing."

TOWARD A UNITED EUROPE At the beginning of the twenty-first century, the EU has established a new goal: to incorporate into the union the states of eastern and southeastern Europe. Many of these states are considerably poorer than the older members, which raised the possibility that adding these nations might weaken the EU itself. To lessen the danger, EU members established a set of qualifications that focus on demonstrating a commitment both to market capitalism and to democracy, including not only the rule of law but also respect for minorities and human rights. Hence, joining the EU might well add to the stability of these nations and make possible the dream of a united Europe. In May 2004, the EU took the plunge and added ten new members: Cyprus, the Czech Republic, Estonia, Hungary, Latvia, Lithuania, Malta, Poland, Slovakia, and Slovenia. Their addition enlarged the population of the EU to 455 million people.

MAP 30.3   European Union, 2007. Beginning in 1967 as the European Economic Community, also known as the Common Market, the union of European states seeking to integrate their economies has gradually grown from six members to twenty-seven in 2007. By 2002, the European Union had achieved two major goals—the creation of a single internal market and a common currency—although it has been less successful at working toward common political and foreign policy goals.

Q   *What additional nations do you think will eventually join the European Union?*

In January 2007, the EU expanded again as Bulgaria and Romania joined the union (see Map 30.3).

The United States: Move to the Center

After twelve years of Republican administrations, the Democratic Party captured the U.S. presidency in the elections in November 1992. The inability of George H. W. Bush (b. 1924), Ronald Reagan's successor, to deal with the deficit problem, as well as an economic downturn, enabled Democrat Bill Clinton (b. 1946) to become president. The new president was a southerner who claimed to be a "new Democrat"—one who favored fiscal responsibility and a more conservative social agenda—a clear indication that the rightward drift in American politics had not been reversed by his victory. During his first term in office, Clinton reduced the budget deficit and signed a bill turning the welfare program back to the states while pushing measures to provide job opportunities for those Americans removed from the welfare rolls.

By seizing the center of the American political agenda, Clinton was able to win reelection in 1996, although the Republican Party now held a majority in both houses of Congress.

Clinton's political fortunes were helped considerably by a lengthy economic revival. At the same time, a steady reduction in the annual government budget deficit strengthened confidence in the performance of the national economy. Much of Clinton's second term, however, was overshadowed by charges of presidential misconduct stemming from the president's affair with a White House intern. After a bitter partisan struggle, the U.S. Senate acquitted the president on two articles of impeachment brought by the House of Representatives. But Clinton's problems helped the Republican candidate, George W. Bush (b. 1946), win the presidential election in 2000. Although Bush lost the popular vote to Al Gore, he narrowly won the electoral vote after a highly controversial victory in the state of Florida decided ultimately by the U.S. Supreme Court.

The first four years of Bush's administration were largely occupied with the war on terrorism and the U.S.-led war on Iraq. The Department of Homeland Security was established after the 2001 terrorist assaults to help protect the United States from future terrorist acts. At the same time, Bush pushed tax cuts through Congress that mainly favored the wealthy and helped produce record deficits reminiscent of the Reagan years. Environmentalists were especially disturbed by the Bush administration's efforts to weaken environmental laws and impose regulations to benefit American corporations. In November 2004, after a highly negative political campaign, Bush was narrowly elected to a second term. From 2005 to 2007, Bush's popularity plummeted drastically as discontent grew over the Iraq War and financial corruption in the Republican Party, as well as the administration's poor handling of relief efforts after Hurricane Katrina.

The many failures of the Bush administration led to the lowest approval ratings for a modern president and opened the door for a dramatic change in American politics. The new and often inspiring voice of Barack Obama (b. 1961), who campaigned on a platform of change "we can believe in" and ending the war in Iraq, resulted in an overwhelming Democratic victory in the elections of 2008. The Democrats were also aided by the dramatic collapse of the American financial system in the fall of 2008. Obama moved quickly in 2009 to deal with the worst economic recession since the Great Depression. At the same time, Obama emphasized the need to deal with the health care crisis, global warming, the decline in the educational system, and failed economic policies.

Contemporary Canada

The government of Brian Mulroney, who came to power in 1984, sought greater privatization of Canada's state-run corporations and negotiated a free trade agreement with the United States. Bitterly resented by many Canadians, the agreement cost Mulroney's government much of its popularity. In 1993, the ruling Conservatives were overwhelmingly defeated, and the Liberal leader, Jean Chrétien (ZHAHNH kray-TEN) (b. 1934), became prime minister. Chrétien's conservative fiscal policies, combined with strong economic growth, enabled his government to have a budgetary surplus by the late 1990s and led to another Liberal victory in the elections of 1997. Charges of widespread financial corruption in the government, however, led to a Conservative victory early in 2006, and Stephen Harper (b. 1959) became the new prime minister.

Mulroney's government had been unable to settle the ongoing crisis over the French-speaking province of Quebec. In the late 1960s, the Parti Québécois (par-TEE kay-bek-KWA), headed by René Lévesque (ruh-NAY luh-VEK), ran on a platform of Quebec's secession from the Canadian union. To pursue their dream of separation, some underground separatist groups even resorted to

Quebec

terrorist bombings. In 1976, the Parti Québécois won Quebec's provincial elections and in 1980 called for a referendum that would enable the provincial government to negotiate Quebec's independence from the rest of Canada. Quebec voters narrowly rejected the plan in 1995, however, and debate over the province's status continues to divide Canada.

After the Cold War: New World Order or Age of Terrorism?

 Focus Questions: How and why did the Cold War end? What are the main issues in the struggle with terrorism?

Even before the collapse of the Soviet Union, there had been tantalizing signs of a thaw in the Cold War. China and the United States had decided in 1979 to establish mutual diplomatic relations, a consequence of Beijing's decision to focus on domestic reform and stop supporting wars of national liberation in Asia. Six years later, the ascent of Mikhail Gorbachev to leadership, culminating in the demise of the Soviet Union in 1991, brought a final end to almost half a century of bitter rivalry between the world's two superpowers.

The End of the Cold War

The accession of Mikhail Gorbachev to power in the Soviet Union in 1985 eventually brought a dramatic end to the Cold War. Gorbachev was willing to rethink many of the fundamental assumptions underlying Soviet foreign policy, and his "New Thinking," as it was called, opened the door to a series of stunning changes. For one, Gorbachev initiated a plan for arms limitation that led in 1987 to an agreement with the United States to eliminate intermediate-range nuclear weapons (the INF Treaty). Both sides had incentives to dampen the expensive arms race. Gorbachev hoped to make extensive economic and internal reforms, and the United States had serious deficit problems. During the Reagan years, the United States had moved from being a creditor nation to being the world's biggest debtor nation. By 1990, both countries were becoming aware that their large military budgets made it difficult for them to solve their serious social problems.

The years 1989 and 1990 were a crucial period in the ending of the Cold War. As described earlier, the postwar settlements came unstuck as a mostly peaceful revolutionary

Reagan and Gorbachev. The willingness of Mikhail Gorbachev and Ronald Reagan to dampen the arms race was a significant factor in ending the Cold War confrontation between the United States and the Soviet Union. Reagan and Gorbachev are shown here standing before Saint Basil's Cathedral during Reagan's visit to Moscow in 1988.

corner of the Arabian peninsula at the head of the Persian Gulf. The Iraqi invasion of Kuwait sparked an international outcry, and an international force led by the United States liberated Kuwait and destroyed a substantial part of Iraq's armed forces in the early months of 1991.

The Gulf War was the first important military conflict in the post–Cold War period. Although Gorbachev tried to persuade Iraq to withdraw its forces from Kuwait before the war began, overall the Soviets played a minor role in the crisis and supported the American action. By the end of 1991, the Soviet Union had disintegrated, making any renewal of global rivalry between the superpowers impossible and leaving the United States as the world's leading military power. With the end of superpower rivalry and the collapse of the Soviet Union in 1991, attention focused on the new post–Cold War era. Many observers were optimistic. U.S. president George H. W. Bush looked forward to a new era of peace and international cooperation that he called the "New World Order." Others predicted the beginning of a new "American century," characterized by the victory of liberal democratic values and free market capitalism.

But the voices of optimism began to fade as it became clear that forces were now being released that had long been held in check by the ideological rigidities of the Cold War. The age of conflict that had long characterized the twentieth century was not at an end but was simply beginning to take a different form.

This was soon apparent around the world. In Southeast Asia, even before the end of the Cold War, former allies in China, Vietnam, and Cambodia turned on each other in a conflict that joined territorial ambitions with deep-seated historical suspicions based on the memory of past conflicts. The pattern was repeated elsewhere: in Africa, where several nations erupted into civil war during the late 1980s and 1990s; in the Balkans, where Yugoslavia broke apart in a bitter conflict not yet completely resolved; and in the Middle East, where disputes in Palestine and the Persian Gulf have grown in strength and erupted into open war.

upheaval swept through Eastern Europe. Gorbachev's policy of allowing greater autonomy for the Communist regimes of Eastern Europe meant that the Soviet Union would no longer militarily support Communist governments that faced internal revolt. The unwillingness of the Soviet regime to use force to maintain the status quo, as it had in Hungary in 1956 and in Czechoslovakia in 1968, opened the door to the overthrow of the Communist regimes. The reunification of Germany on October 3, 1990, marked the end of one of the most prominent legacies of the Cold War.

The Persian Gulf War provided the first major opportunity for testing the new relationship between the United States and the Soviet Union in the post–Cold War era. In early August 1990, Iraqi military forces suddenly occupied the small neighboring country of Kuwait, in the northeastern

An Age of Terrorism?

Acts of terror by individuals and groups opposed to governments have become a frightening aspect of modern Western society and indeed of all the world. In 1996, President Clinton called terrorism "the enemy of our generation," and since the end of Cold War, it has often seemed as though terrorism has replaced communism as the West's number one enemy.

Already during the late 1970s and 1980s, concern about terrorism was often at the top of foreign policy agendas in the United States and many European countries. Small bands of terrorists used assassination; indiscriminate killing of civilians, especially by bombing; the taking of hostages; and the hijacking of airplanes to draw attention to their demands or to destabilize governments in the hope of achieving their political goals. Terrorist acts garnered considerable media attention. When Palestinian terrorists kidnapped and killed eleven Israeli athletes at the Munich Olympic Games in 1972, hundreds of millions of people watched the drama unfold on television.

Motivations for terrorist acts varied considerably. Left- and right-wing terrorist groups flourished in the late 1970s and early 1980s. Left-wing groups, such as the Baader-Meinhof (BAH-durr-MYN-huff) gang (also known as the Red Army Faction) in Germany and the Red Brigades in Italy, consisted chiefly of affluent middle-class young people who denounced the injustices of capitalism and supported acts of revolutionary terrorism in an attempt to bring down the system. Right-wing terrorist groups, such as the New Order in Italy and the Charles Martel Club in France, used bombings to foment disorder and bring about authoritarian regimes. These groups received little or no public support, and authorities were able to crush them fairly quickly.

But terrorist acts also stemmed from militant nationalists who wished to create separatist states. Because they received considerable support from local populations sympathetic to their cause, these terrorist groups could maintain their activities over a long period of time. Most prominent was the Irish Republican Army (IRA), which resorted to vicious attacks against the ruling government and innocent civilians in Northern Ireland. Over a period of twenty years, IRA terrorists were responsible for the deaths of two thousand people in Northern Ireland; three-fourths of the victims were civilians.

Although left- and right-wing terrorist activities declined in Europe in the 1980s, international terrorism remained commonplace. Angered over the loss of their territory to Israel in 1967, some militant Palestinians responded with a policy of terrorist attacks against Israel's supporters. Palestinian terrorists operated throughout European countries, attacking both Europeans and American tourists; vacationers at airports in Rome and Vienna were massacred by Palestinian terrorists in 1985. State-sponsored terrorism was often an integral part of international terrorism. Militant governments, especially in Iran, Libya, and Syria, assisted terrorist organizations that made attacks on Europeans and Americans. On December 21, 1988, Pan American flight 103 from Frankfurt to New York exploded over Lockerbie, Scotland, killing all 258 passengers and crew members. A massive investigation finally revealed that the bomb responsible for the explosion had been planted by two Libyan terrorists who were connected to terrorist groups based in Iran and Syria.

Terrorist Attack on the United States

One of the most destructive acts of terrorism occurred on September 11, 2001, in the United States. Four groups of terrorists hijacked four commercial jet airplanes after takeoff from Boston, Newark, and Washington, D.C. The hijackers flew two of the airplanes directly into the towers of the World Trade Center in New York City, causing these buildings, as well as a number of surrounding buildings, to collapse. A third hijacked plane slammed into the Pentagon near Washington, D.C. The fourth plane, believed to be headed for Washington, crashed instead in an isolated area of Pennsylvania, apparently as the result of an attempt by a group of heroic passengers to overcome the hijackers. In total, nearly three thousand people were killed, including everyone aboard the four airliners.

These coordinated acts of terror were carried out by hijackers connected to an international terrorist organization known as al-Qaeda ("the Base"), run by Osama bin Laden (b. 1957). A native of Saudi Arabia, bin Laden used an inherited fortune to set up terrorist training camps in Afghanistan, under the protection of the nation's militant fundamentalist Islamic rulers known as the Taliban. Bin Laden was also suspected of directing earlier terrorist attacks against the United States, including the bombing of two U.S. embassies in Africa in 1998 and an attack on a naval ship, the U.S.S. *Cole,* in 2000.

WAR IN AFGHANISTAN U.S. president George W. Bush vowed to wage a lengthy war on terrorism and worked to create a coalition of nations to assist in ridding the world of al-Qaeda and other terrorist groups. In October 2001, United States and NATO air forces began bombing Taliban-controlled command centers, airfields, and al-Qaeda hiding places in Afghanistan. On the ground, Afghan forces opposed to the Taliban, assisted by U.S. special forces, pushed the Taliban out of the capital city of Kabul and seized control of nearly all of the country by the end of November. A multiethnic government was installed but faced problems as a result of renewed Taliban activity after the United States began to focus much of its military attention on the war in Iraq. In 2009, President Obama decided to deal with the deteriorating situation by promising to send an additional 30,000 U.S. troops to Afghanistan.

WAR IN IRAQ In 2002, President George W. Bush, charging that Iraqi dictator Saddam Hussein (1937–2006) had not only provided support to bin Laden's terrorist organization but also sought to develop weapons of mass destruction, threatened to invade Iraq and remove him from power. Both claims were widely doubted by other member states at the United Nations. As a result, the United States was forced to attack Iraq with little world support. Moreover, the plan to attack upset many Arab leaders and fanned anti-American sentiment throughout the Muslim world.

In March 2003, a largely American-led army invaded Iraq. The Iraqi army was quickly defeated, and in the months that followed, occupation forces sought to restore stability to the country while setting forth plans to lay the foundations of a future democratic society. But although

Terrorist Attack on the World Trade Center in New York City. On September 11, 2001, hijackers flew two commercial jetliners into the twin towers of the World Trade Center. Shown at the left are the two towers in the New York skyline before the attack. The middle picture shows the second of the two jetliners about to hit one of the towers while smoke billows from the site of the first attack. In the scene below, firefighters are making their way through what was left of the 110-story towers after the collapse.

Saddam Hussein was later captured by U.S. troops, Saddam's supporters, foreign terrorists, and Islamic militants continued to battle the American-led forces.

American efforts focused on training an Iraqi military force capable of defeating the insurgents and establishing an Iraqi government that could hold free elections and create a democracy. Establishing a new government was difficult, however, because of the differences among the three major groups in Iraqi society: Shi'ite Muslims, Sunni Muslims, and ethnic Kurds. Although a new Iraqi government came into being, it has been unable to establish a unified state. By 2006, violence had increased dramatically and Iraq seemed to be descending into a widespread civil war, especially between the Shi'ites, who control southern Iraq, and the Sunnis, who control central Iraq. An increase in American troops in 2007 helped stabilize conditions within a year. The U.S. and Iraqi governments then agreed to a complete withdrawal of American troops by 2011, a goal that President Obama affirmed after taking office.

The West and Islam

One of the major sources of terrorist activity against the West, especially the United States, has come from some parts of the Muslim world. No doubt, the ongoing Israeli-Palestinian conflict, in which the United States has steadfastly supported Israel, helped give rise to anti-Western and especially anti-U.S. feeling among many Muslims. In 1979, a revolution in Iran that led to the overthrow of the shah and the creation of a new Islamic government led by Ayatollah Khomeini, also fed anti-Western sentiment. In the eyes of the ayatollah and his followers, the United States was the "great Satan," the powerful protector of Israel, and the enemy of Muslim peoples everywhere. Furthermore, the United States was blamed for the corruption of Iranian society under the shah.

The involvement of the United States in the liberation of Kuwait in the Persian Gulf War in 1991 also had unexpected consequences in the relationship of Islam and the West. During that war, U.S. forces were stationed in Saudi Arabia, the location of many sacred Islamic sites. The presence of American forces was considered an affront to Islam by anti-Western Islamic groups, especially that of Osama bin Laden and his followers. These anti-Western attitudes came to be shared by a number of radical Islamic groups, as is evident in the 2003 bombing in Madrid and the 2005 bombing on subway trains in London.

The U.S. attack on Iraq in 2003 has further inflamed some Islamic groups against the West. Although there was no evidence of a relationship between al-Qaeda terrorists and the regime of Saddam Hussein, this claim was one of the excuses used by the United States to launch a preemptive war against Iraq. Although many Iraqis welcomed the overthrow of Saddam, the deaths of innocent civilians and the torturing of prisoners by American soldiers in prisons in Iraq served to deepen anti-American sentiment in the Muslim world.

New Directions and New Problems in Western Society

 Focus Question: What are the major developments in the women's movement since 1985, and what problems have immigrants created for European society?

Dramatic social developments have accompanied political and economic changes since 1985. New opportunities for women have emerged, and a reinvigorated women's movement has sought to bring new meaning to the principle of equality with men. New problems for Western society have also arisen with a growing reaction against foreign workers and immigrants.

Transformation in Women's Lives

It is estimated that parents need to average 2.1 children to ensure a natural replacement of a country's population. In many European countries, the population stopped growing in the 1960s, and the trend has continued since then. By the 1990s, birthrates were down drastically; among the nations of the European Union, the average number of children per mother was 1.4. Spain's rate of 1.15 was among the lowest in the world in 2002.

At the same time, the number of women in the workforce continued to rise. In Britain, for example, women made up 44 percent of the labor force in 1990, up from 32 percent in 1970. Moreover, women were entering new employment areas. Greater access to universities and professional schools enabled women to take jobs in law, medicine, government, business, and education. In the Soviet Union, about 70 percent of doctors and teachers were women. Nevertheless, economic inequality still often prevailed; women received lower wages than men for comparable work and found fewer opportunities for advancement to management positions.

THE WOMEN'S MOVEMENT Feminists in the women's liberation movement came to believe that women themselves must transform the fundamental conditions of their lives. They did so in a variety of ways. First, they formed numerous "consciousness-raising" groups to heighten awareness of women's issues. Women got together to share

their personal experiences and become aware of the many ways that male dominance affected their lives. This consciousness-raising helped many women become activists.

Women also sought and gained a measure of control over their own bodies by insisting that they had a right to both contraception and abortion. In the 1960s and 1970s, hundreds of thousands of European women worked, often successfully, to repeal the laws that outlawed contraception and abortion. In 1968, a French law permitted the sale of contraceptive devices, and in the 1970s, French feminists began to call for the legalization of abortion. One group of 343 prominent French women even signed a manifesto declaring that they had had abortions. In 1979, abortion became legal in France. Even in Catholic countries, where the church remained adamantly opposed to abortion, legislation allowing contraception and abortion was passed in the 1970s and 1980s.

As more women became activists, they also became involved in new issues. In the 1980s and 1990s, women faculty in universities concentrated on developing new cultural attitudes through the new academic field of women's studies. Courses in women's studies, which stressed the role and contributions of women in history, mushroomed in both American and European colleges and universities.

Other women began to try to affect the political environment by allying with the antinuclear movement. In 1982, a group of women protested American nuclear missiles in Britain by chaining themselves to the fence of an American military base. Thousands more joined in creating a peace camp around the military compound. Enthusiasm ran high; one participant said: "I'll never forget that feeling; it'll live with me forever.... We walked round, and we clasped hands.... It was for women; it was for peace; it was for the world."[4]

Some women joined the ecological movement. As one German writer who was concerned with environmental issues said, it is women "who must give birth to children, willingly or unwillingly, in this polluted world of ours." Especially prominent were the female members of the Green Party in Germany (see "The Environment and the Green Movements" in Chapter 29), which supported environmental issues and elected forty-two delegates to the West German parliament in 1987. Among the delegates was Petra Kelly (b. 1947), one of the founders of the German Green Party and a tireless campaigner for the preservation of the environment as well as human rights and equality.

Women in the West have also reached out through international conferences to work with women from the rest of the world in changing the conditions of their lives. Between 1975 and 1995, the United Nations held conferences in Mexico City, Copenhagen, Nairobi, and Beijing. These meetings made clear that women from Western and non-Western countries had different priorities. Whereas women from Western countries spoke about political, economic, cultural, and sexual rights, women from developing countries in Latin America, Africa, and Asia focused on bringing an end to the violence, hunger, and disease

An Antinuclear Protest. Women were active participants in the antinuclear movement of the 1980s. Shown here are some of the ten thousand antinuclear protesters who linked hands to form a human chain around the 9-mile perimeter of the U.S. Air Force base at Greenham Common, England, on December 13, 1982. They were protesting the planned siting of ninety-six U.S. cruise missiles at the base.

that haunt their lives. Despite these differences, the meetings were an indication of how women in both developed and developing nations were organizing to make people aware of women's issues.

Guest Workers and Immigrants

As the economies of the Western European countries revived in the 1950s and 1960s, a severe labor shortage encouraged them to rely on foreign workers. Government and businesses actively recruited so-called **guest workers** to staff essential jobs. Scores of Turks and eastern and southern Europeans came to Germany, North Africans to France, and people from the Caribbean, India, and Pakistan to Great Britain. Overall, there were probably 15 million guest workers in Europe in the 1980s. They constituted 17 percent of the labor force in Switzerland and 10 percent in Germany.

Although these workers had been recruited for economic reasons, they often found themselves unwelcome socially and politically. Many foreign workers complained that they received lower wages and inferior social benefits. Moreover, their concentration in certain cities or certain sections of cities often created tensions with the local native populations. Foreign workers, many of them nonwhites, constituted almost one-fifth of the population in the German cities of Frankfurt, Munich, and Stuttgart. Having become settled in their new countries, many wanted to stay, even after the end of the postwar boom in the early 1970s led to mass unemployment. Moreover, as guest workers settled permanently in their host countries, additional family members migrated to join them. Although they had little success in getting guest workers already there to leave, some European countries passed legislation or took other measures to restrict new immigration.

In 1991, thousands of Albanians fled their homeland after its Communist government began to fall apart, but when they arrived in Italy, the Italian authorities forcibly evicted them and sent them back to Albania.

In the 1980s, there was an influx of other refugees, especially to West Germany, which had liberal immigration laws that permitted people seeking asylum for political persecution to enter the country. During the 1970s and 1980s, West Germany absorbed more than a million refugees from Eastern Europe and East Germany. In 1986 alone, 200,000 political refugees from Pakistan, Bangladesh, and Sri Lanka entered the country. Other parts of Europe saw a similar influx of foreigners. Between 1992 and 2002, London and the southeast region of England witnessed an increase of 700,000 new foreigners, primarily from Yugoslavia, Southeast Asia, the Middle East, and Africa. A survey in 1998 found that English was not the first language of one-third of inner-city children in London.

The arrival of so many foreigners strained not only the social services of European countries but also the patience of many native residents who opposed making their countries ethnically diverse. Antiforeign sentiment, especially in a time of growing unemployment, increased and was encouraged by new right-wing political parties that catered to people's complaints. Thus, the National Front in France, organized by Jean-Marie Le Pen (b. 1928), and the Republican Party in Germany, led by Franz Schönhuber (1923–2005), a former SS officer, advocated restricting all new immigration and limiting the assimilation of settled immigrants. Although these parties had only limited success in elections, even that modest accomplishment encouraged traditional conservative and even moderately conservative parties to adopt more nationalistic policies. Occasionally, an antiforeign party was quite successful. Jorg Haider (YORG HY-dur) (1950–2008), whose Freedom

Party received 27 percent of the vote in 1999, cushioned his rejection of foreigners by appealing to Austrian nationalism and attacking the European Union: "We Austrians should answer not to the European Union, not to Maastricht, not to some international idea or other, but to this our Homeland."[5] Even more frightening than the growth of these right-wing political parties were the organized campaigns of violence in the early 1990s, especially against African and Asian immigrants, by radical, right-wing groups.

Even nations that have been especially tolerant in opening their borders to immigrants and seekers of asylum are changing their policies. In the Netherlands, 19 percent of the people have a foreign background, representing almost 180 nationalities. In 2004, however, the Dutch government passed tough new immigration laws, including a requirement that newcomers pass a Dutch language and culture test before being admitted to the Netherlands.

Sometimes these policies have been aimed at religious practices. One of the effects of the influx of foreigners into Europe has been a dramatic increase in the Muslim population. Although Christians still constitute a majority (though many no longer practice their faith), the number of Muslims has mushroomed in France, Britain, Belgium, the Netherlands, and Germany. It has been estimated that at least 15 million Muslims were living in European Union nations in the first decade of the twenty-first century. In some nations, concern that Muslim immigration will result in an erosion of national values has led to attempts to restrict the display of Islamic symbols. In a referendum held in November 2009, for example, 57.5 percent of the voters in Switzerland approved a measure prohibiting the construction of minarets, the prayer towers of mosques.

In 2004, France enacted a law prohibiting female students from wearing a headscarf (*hijab*) to school. Article 1 stated: "In public elementary, middle and high schools, the wearing of signs or clothing which conspicuously manifest students' religious affiliations is prohibited." The law further clarified "conspicuous" to mean "a large cross, a veil, or a skullcap."[6] Small religious symbols, such as small crosses or medallions, were not included. Critics of this law argue that it will exacerbate ethnic and religious tensions in France, while supporters maintain that it upholds the traditions of secularism and equality for women in France (see the box on p. 969).

Western Culture Today

Q **FOCUS QUESTION:** What major Western cultural trends have emerged since 1985?

Western culture has expanded to most parts of the world, although some societies see it as a challenge to their own culture and national identity. At the same time, other societies are also strongly influencing Western cultural expressions, making recent Western culture a reflection of the evolving global response to the rapid changes in human society today.

Varieties of Religious Life

Despite the attempt to revive religion after World War II, church attendance in Europe and the United States declined dramatically in the 1960s and 1970s as a result of growing secular attitudes. Yet even though the numbers of regular churchgoers in established Protestant and Catholic churches continued to decline, the number of fundamentalist churches and churchgoers has been growing, especially in the United States.

Fundamentalism was originally a movement within Protestantism that arose early in the twentieth century. Its goal was to maintain a strict traditional interpretation of the Bible and the Christian faith, especially in opposition to the theory of Darwinian evolution and secularism. In the 1980s and 1990s, fundamentalists became involved in a struggle against so-called secular humanism, godless communism, legalized abortion, and homosexuality. Especially in the United States, fundamentalists organized politically to elect candidates who supported their views. This so-called Christian right played an influential role in electing both Ronald Reagan and George W. Bush to the presidency.

THE GROWTH OF ISLAM Fundamentalism, however, is not unique to Protestantism. In Islam, the term *fundamentalism* is used to refer to a return to traditional Islamic values, especially in opposition to a perceived weakening of moral values due to the corrupting influence of Western ideas and practices. After the Iranian Revolution of 1979, the term was also applied to militant Islamic movements, such as the Taliban in Afghanistan, who favored militant action against Western influence.

Despite the wariness of Islamic radicalism in the aftermath of the September 11, 2001 terrorist attacks on the United States, Islam is growing in both Europe and the United States, thanks primarily to the migration of people from Muslim countries. As Muslim communities became established in France, Germany, Britain, Italy, and Spain during the 1980s and 1990s, they built mosques for religious worship and religious education. In the United States, the states of California and New York each have more than two hundred mosques.

POPE JOHN PAUL II Although changes have also occurred in the Catholic Church, much of its history in the 1980s and 1990s was dominated by the charismatic Pope John Paul II (1920–2005). Karol Wojtyla (KAH-rul voy-TEE-wah), who had been the archbishop of Krakow in Poland before his elevation to the papacy in 1978, was the first non-Italian to be elected pope since the sixteenth century. Although he alienated a number of people by reasserting traditional Catholic teaching on such issues as birth control, women in the priesthood, and clerical celibacy, John Paul's numerous travels around the world helped strengthen the Catholic Church throughout the

Islam and the West: Secularism in France

The banning of headscarves in schools in 2004 was preceded by a debate on the secular state in France. Secularism in France extends beyond the separation of church and state: while recognizing the right to religious expression, French law dictates that religious expression must remain in the private sphere and cannot enter the public realm. Before the law banning headscarves was enacted, President Jacques Chirac set up a committee (called the Stasi Commission after its chair, Bernard Stasi) to interview school, religious, and political leaders on whether students should be allowed to wear headscarves in schools. The commission decided in favor of prohibiting all conspicuous religious symbols in schools.

The first selection below is taken from a speech by President Chirac, who favored the ban. The second selection is taken from interviews with French Muslim women, many of them from the Maghreb (the Arabic term for Northwest Africa, chiefly Morocco, Algeria, and Tunisia). Many of these women questioned how the law protects their individual rights and freedom of religious expression.

French President Jacques Chirac on Secularism in French Society

The debate on the principle of secularism goes to the very heart of our values. It concerns our national cohesion, our ability to live together, our ability to unite on what is essential. . . . Many young people of immigrant origin, whose first language is French, and who are in most cases of French nationality, succeed and feel at ease in a society which is theirs. This kind of success must also be made possible by breaking the wall of silence and indifference which surrounds the reality of discrimination today. I know about the feeling of being misunderstood, of helplessness, sometimes even of revolt, among young French people of immigrant origin whose job applications are rejected because of the way their names sound, and who are too often confronted with discrimination in the fields of access to housing or even simply of access to leisure facilities. . . . All of France's children, whatever their history, whatever their origin, whatever their beliefs, are the daughters and sons of the republic. They have to be recognized as such, in law but above all in reality. By ensuring respect for this requirement, by reforming our integration policy, by our ability to bring equal opportunities to life, we shall bring national cohesion to life again. We shall also do so by bringing to life the principle of secularism, which is a pillar of our constitution. It expresses our

wish to live together in respect, dialogue and tolerance. Secularism guarantees freedom of conscience. It protects the freedom to believe or not to believe. . . . We also need to reaffirm secularism in schools, because schools must be preserved absolutely. . . .

There is of course no question of turning schools into a place of uniformity, of anonymity, where religious life or belonging would be banned. It is a question of enabling teachers and head teachers, who are today in the front-line and confronted with real difficulties, to carry out their mission serenely with the affirmation of a clear rule. Until recently, as a result of a reasonable custom which was respected spontaneously, nobody ever doubted that pupils, who are naturally free to live their faith, should nevertheless not arrive in schools, secondary schools or A-level colleges, in religious clothes. It is not a question of inventing new rules or of shifting the boundaries of secularism. It is a question of expressing, with respect but clearly and firmly, a rule which has been part of our customs and practices for a very long time. I have consulted, I have studied the report of the Stasi Commission, I have examined the arguments put forward by the National Assembly committee [on secularism], by political parties, by religious authorities, by major representatives of major currents of thought. In all conscience, it is my view that the wearing of clothes or of symbols which conspicuously demonstrate religious affiliations must be banned in state schools.

North African Women in France Respond to the Headscarf Ban

Labiba (Thirty-Five-Year-Old Algerian)

I don't feel that they should interfere in the private life of people in the respect that we're in a secular country; France shouldn't take a position toward one religion to the detriment of another. . . . I think that in a secular school, we should all be secular, otherwise we need to have religious school and then everyone is free to wear what he wants.

Nour (Thirty-Four-Year-Old Algerian)

Honestly, you know the secular school, it doesn't miss celebrating Easter, and when they celebrate Easter, it doesn't bother me. My daughter comes home with painted Easter eggs and everything; it's pretty; it's cute. There are classes that are over 80 percent Maghrebin in the suburbs, and they celebrate Easter, they celebrate Christmas, you see? And that's not a problem for the secular school. And I don't find that fair.

(continued)

I find that when it's Ramadan, they should talk about Ramadan. Honestly, me, it wouldn't be a problem. On the contrary, someone who comes into class . . . with a veil, that would pose a question actually, that we could discuss in class, to know why this person wears the veil. So why punish them, amputate them from that part of their culture without discussing it? Why is it so upsetting to have someone in class who wears a veil, when we could make it a subject of discussion on all religions? Getting stuck on the veil hides the question. They make such a big deal out of it, the poor girls, they take them out of school; people turn them into extraterrestrials. In the end we turn them into people who will have problems in their identities, in their culture and everything. . . . For a country that is home to so many cultures, there's no excuse.

Isma (Thirty-Six-Year-Old Algerian)

The girls who veil in France, especially the high school and junior high students, it's first of all a question of identity, because these girls are born in France to foreign parents. . . . At a given time an adolescent want to affirm himself, to show that he's someone, that he's an individual, so he thinks, I'd say, he thinks that it's by his clothes that he shows that he comes from somewhere, that he's from someone. So then, I think you should let them do it, and afterwards, by themselves, people come back to who they really are.

Q What were the perspectives of the French president and the French Muslim women who were interviewed? How do they differ? Do you think there might be a way to reconcile the opposing positions? Why or why not?

---

non-Western world. A strong believer in social justice, John Paul was a powerful figure in reminding Europeans of their spiritual heritage and the need to temper the pursuit of materialism with spiritual concerns. He also condemned nuclear weapons and constantly reminded

leaders and laity of their obligations to prevent war (see the box on p. 971).

Art and Music in the Age of Commerce: The 1980s and 1990s

Throughout the 1980s and 1990s, the art and music industries increasingly adopted the techniques of marketing and advertising. With large sums of money invested in artists and musicians, pressure mounted to achieve critical and commercial success. Negotiating the distinction between art and popular culture was essential since many equated merit with sales or economic value.

THE VISUAL ARTS In the art world, Neo-Expressionism reached its zenith in the mid-1980s. The economic boom and free spending of the Reagan years contributed to a thriving art scene in the United States. Neo-Expressionist artists like Anselm Kiefer (AN-selm KEEF-uhr) and Jean-Michel Basquiat (ZHAHN-mee-SHELL BAHS-kwee-aht) (1960–1988) became increasingly popular as the art market soared.

Born in Germany in 1945, Kiefer combines aspects of Abstract Expressionism, collage, and German Expressionism to create works that are stark and haunting. His works in the 1980s became a meditation on German

Anselm Kiefer, *Athanor.* In 2007, Kiefer painted a monumental work (30 feet by 15 feet) on the wall of a stairwell in the Louvre Museum in Paris. This textured painting is named after the athanor, a furnace that alchemists used in their efforts to transform base metals into gold. The painting shows a nude man on his back connected by a beam of light extending from his stomach to the heavens above. According to Kiefer, the man is not dead, but "in the universe." At the bottom of the painting, Kiefer poured liquid lead onto a layer of soil from the area where he lives in southern France; higher up in the painting are silver and then gold, symbolizing the stages of the alchemical process.

Pope John Paul II: An Appeal for Peace

Pope John Paul II became the spiritual leader of the Catholic Church in 1978. He made numerous trips to all parts of the globe, addressing a variety of spiritual and social issues. He made a point of speaking directly to as many lay groups as possible, often focusing on one of his chief themes, the desire for peace.

—— ✠ ——

Pope John Paul II, *Speeches*

Today peace has become, throughout the world, a preoccupation not only for those responsible for the destiny of nations but even more so for broad sections of the population and innumerable individuals who generously and tenaciously dedicate themselves to creating an outlook of peace and to establishing genuine peace between peoples and nations. This is comforting. But there is no hiding the fact that in spite of the efforts of all men and women of good will, there are still serious threats to peace in the world. Some of these threats take the form of divisions within various nations; others stem from deep-rooted and acute tensions between opposing nations and blocs within the world community. In reality, the confrontations that we witness today are distinguished from those of past history by certain new characteristics. In the first place they are worldwide: even a local conflict is often an expression of tensions originating elsewhere in the world. In the same way, it often happens that a conflict has profound effects far from where it broke out. Another characteristic is totality: present day tensions mobilize all the forces of the nations involved; moreover, selfish monopolization and even hostility are to be found today as much in the way economic life is run and in the technological application of science as in the way that the mass media or military resources are utilized. . . .

Elsewhere, fear of a precarious peace, military and political imperatives, and economic and commercial interests lead to the establishment of arms stockpiles or to the sale of weapons capable of appalling destruction. The arms race, then, prevails over the great tasks of peace, which ought to unite peoples in new solidarity; it fosters sporadic but murderous conflicts and builds up the gravest threats. It is true that at first sight the cause of peace seems to be handicapped to a crippling extent.

But we must reach peace. Peace, as I said earlier, is threatened when uncertainty, doubt, and suspicion reign, and violence makes good use of this. Do we really want peace? Then we must dig deep within ourselves, and going beyond the divisions we find within us and between us, we must find the areas in which we can strengthen our conviction that human beings' basic driving forces and the recognition of their real nature carry them toward openness to others, mutual respect, community, and peace. The course of this laborious search for the objective and universal truth about humanity, and the result of the search, will develop men and women of peace and dialogue, people who draw both strength and humility from a truth that they realize they must serve and not make use of for partisan interests. ⌲

 What lessons did Pope John Paul II seek to teach here, and what do these lessons tell you about the objectives of institutionalized religion in modern times?

---

history, especially the horrors of Nazism. Kiefer hoped that a portrayal of Germany's atrocities in such works as *Departure from Egypt* and *Nigredo* could free Germans from their past and bring some good out of evil.

Another example of Neo-Expressionism can be seen in the work of Basquiat. The son of Haitian and Puerto Rican immigrants, Basquiat first made his name as a graffiti artist in New York City and became an overnight success during the 1980s art market boom.

While some critics dismissed Basquiat's paintings as a fad, other artists were criticized for employing controversy to market their art. Moreover, artists whose works were deemed to be inappropriate also had to contend with censorship. Andres Serrano and Robert Mapplethorpe became the focal point of debate in the mid-1980s because they received financial aid from a U.S. government agency, the National Endowment for the Arts (NEA). Mapplethorpe was known for his portraits of male nudes that often featured homoerotic imagery, while Serrano created photographs of objects submerged in bodily fluids, including a crucifix immersed in urine. As a result of the controversy, the U.S. Congress reduced the budget of the NEA for supporting indecency.

MUSIC As artists and musicians became increasingly disenchanted with the excesses of the Reagan era, they also began to question the consumerism that had seemingly homogenized popular culture. The emergence of "grunge" music in the early 1990s reflected this attitude, as rock bands like Nirvana, Sonic Youth, and Pearl Jam rejected the materialism of the previous decade. Employing distortion and amplified feedback in their music, grunge artists often sang of disillusion and angst. Rather than conforming to the mass-produced norms of the fashion industry, these musicians typically wore ripped jeans and weathered flannel attire to protest the excesses of capitalism.

Hip-hop continued to gain popularity following the success of Grandmaster Flash and the Furious Five

Jean-Michel Basquiat, *Self Portrait*, 1986. In his paintings, Basquiat combined Abstract Expressionist brushwork with the popular culture of urban life. He dabbled with hip-hop and included references to comic book characters, jazz musicians, and sports heroes in his work.

(see Chapter 29). In the early 1990s, rappers like Dr. Dre and Snoop Doggy Dogg created "gangsta rap," an offshoot of hip-hop with raw lyrics praising violence, drugs, and promiscuous sex. By the late 1990s, teen and preteen consumers had steered the music industry back to pop music, generating millions of dollars of sales in the process. Many pop acts became successful as music turned away from grunge and gangsta rap. Instead, musicians and audiences favored the lighthearted music that made Ricky Martin and Britney Spears famous. Drawing from rhythm and blues, Latin music, and hip-hop, these artists used catchy dance beats and extravagant music videos to market their work.

The Digital Age

Q FOCUS QUESTION: What is the Digital Age, and what are its products, results, and dangers?

Since the invention of the microprocessor in 1971, the capabilities of computers have continued to grow, resulting in today's "Information" or "Digital Age." Beginning in the 1980s, computer companies like Apple and Microsoft competed to create more powerful computers. By the 1990s, the booming technology industry had made Microsoft founder Bill Gates the richest man in the world. Much of this success was due to several innovations within computers that made them essential devices for communication, information, and entertainment.

The Technological World

The advent of electronic mail, or e-mail, in the mid-1990s transformed the way that people communicate. As the capacity of computers to transmit data increased, e-mail messages could carry document and image attachments, making them a workable and speedier alternative to "snail mail," as conventional postal mail came to be called. Perhaps even more transformative was the Internet, a network of smaller, interlinking Web pages with sites devoted to news, commerce, entertainment, and academic scholarship. At first, Web sites were limited to text-based documents, but as computer processors became more powerful, video and music were added.

As Web capabilities increased, new forms of communication began to emerge with Twitter, a communications platform that allows people to send instant updates from their cell phones to their friends; Facebook, a social networking site; and YouTube, an Internet video site that now is even used for President Obama's weekly radio addresses. By the early 2000s, the Internet had become a part of everyday life for the Western world. These new forms of communication have allowed for greater access to information and people in a short period. Nevertheless, some have argued that communication by means of the computer results in a lack of social interaction. Others question the accuracy of much of the information available on the Web.

Advances in telecommunications led to cellular or mobile phones. Though cellular phones existed in the 1970s and 1980s, it was not until the digital components of these devices were reduced in size in the 1990s that cell phones became truly portable. Cell phones have since become enormously important, and not just for communication. Indeed, many nations have become financially dependent on their sales for economic growth. For example, the Nokia Corporation of Finland is largely responsible for the country's fiscal stability. Sales of Nokia phones, more than $25 billion annually, nearly equal the total Finnish budget. The ubiquity of cell phones and their ability to transfer data electronically have made text messaging a global communications craze. Text and instant messaging have revolutionized written language, as shorthand script has replaced complete sentences for the purposes of relaying brief messages.

In 2001, Apple Computer Company introduced the iPod. This pocket-sized digital music player has since revolutionized the music industry, as downloading music from the Internet has surpassed the purchasing of albums from record stores. In fact, album sales declined by nearly 25 percent from 2000 to 2006, while digital-single sales have risen 2,930 percent in the past four years. In April 2007, Apple sold its 100 millionth iPod, an indication of the iPod's status as a worldwide cultural phenomenon.

Music and Art in the Digital Age

Whereas the iPod altered the way in which we listen to, store, and access music, innovations in digital technology have changed the sound and production of music. In the late-1990s, musicians such as Moby and Fatboy Slim became internationally famous for creating music layered with synthesizers, distorted guitars, and simulated drum beats. These artists sampled earlier soul music to create albums and film scores.

Many visual artists have also adopted digital effects in producing artworks that fuse photography, sculpture, and cinema. Bill Viola (b. 1951) was one of the first artists to exclusively employ video in his exhibits. By projecting films in a gallery space, Viola created powerful sensory experiences. Using allusions to rebirth and mysticism, he evoked mystical sensations, contrasting light, sound, and focus with techniques of slow motion and editing.

VIDEO GAMES   While record sales have struggled worldwide, the video game industry has skyrocketed. In 2007, it was projected that global sales of video games would outnumber those of the music industry. With faster data processors fueling enhanced graphics in such video game consoles as the PlayStation 3 and Xbox 360, higher levels of realism have been developed. Despite the popularity of video games, many questions have arisen about their role in childhood obesity as well as neurological disorders. In June 2007, the American Medical Association heard testimony concerning video game addiction. Though video game manufacturers reject the claim, some psychologists fear that learning disabilities and dependency can result from excessive gaming.

FILM: FANTASY AND EPICS   The films, video games, and literature of the late 1990s and early 2000s made fantasy and historical epics internationally popular. The successful adaptation of the *Lord of the Rings* trilogy and Harry Potter series indicated the manner in which mythology, magic, and medieval fantasies appeal to contemporary sensibilities. At the heart of these epic motion pictures, *Troy* and *Gladiator* included, is a mythical struggle between good and evil that is governed by a moral sense of right and wrong, love, and companionship. Yet these romanticized tales also featured non-Western cultures as Japanese animé and martial arts films increased in worldwide popularity. The computer animation and digitized special effects of these movies reflect the impact of computers on the film industry as it too enters the Digital Age.

Reality in the Digital Age

Advances in communication and information during the Digital Age have led many to believe that world cultures are becoming increasingly interdependent and homogenized. Many contemporary artists have questioned the effects of the computer age on identity and material reality. According to some, the era of virtual reality, or what one French intellectual has termed "hyperreality," has displaced cultural uniqueness and bodily presence.

THE BODY AND IDENTITY IN CONTEMPORARY ART   By focusing on bodily experience and cultural norms, contemporary artists have attempted to restore that which has been lost in the Digital Age. Kiki Smith (b. 1954), an American artist born in Germany, creates sculptures of the human body that often focus on anatomical processes. These works, commonly made of wax or plaster, question the politics surrounding the body, including AIDS and domestic abuse, while reconnecting to bodily experiences.

Contemporary artists also continue to explore the interaction between the Western and non-Western world, particularly with the **multiculturalism** generated by global migrations (see "The Social Challenges of Globalization" later in this chapter). For example, the art of Yinka Shonibare (YEEN-kuh SHOW-nih-bar-eh) (b. 1962), who was born in London, raised in Nigeria, and now resides in England, creates works that investigate the notion of hybrid identity. This is evident in his work, *How to Blow Up Two Heads at Once (Gentlemen)*, which depicts European Victorian figures dressed in Dutch wax cloth.

Two-channel video and sound installation, continuous loop 16 feet × 27 feet 6 inches × 57 feet (4.9 × 8.4 × 17.4 m) Solomon R. Guggenheim Museum (2000.61), New York. Gift, The Bohen Foundation, 2000. Photograph by Sally Ritts © The Solomon R. Guggenheim Foundation, New York

Bill Viola, *The Crossing*, 1996. In this video piece, Viola projected two films on each side of a 16-foot-high screen. On one side, a man is inundated with water, while on the other side, he is consumed by flames. The events occur in slow motion and, when experienced in conjunction with the sound of the deluge and/or flames, evoke feelings of spiritual regeneration.

Yinka Shonibare, *How to Blow Up Two Heads at Once (Gentlemen)*. In *How to Blow Up Two Heads at Once (Gentlemen)*, Yinka Shonibare humorously re-creates a nineteenth-century European duel in which two headless figures wearing Victorian costumes are simultaneously aiming guns at each other's heads. His choice of Victorian figures and costume reflect his interest in the history of Britain's colonial endeavors. The Dutch wax cloth used for the costumes symbolizes the complexity of modern African identity in Europe. The cloth was produced in the Netherlands and Britain and then sold in West Africa during the nineteenth century.

MULTICULTURALISM IN LITERATURE The interaction of East and West has also preoccupied numerous authors since the late-1990s. Jhumpa Lahiri (JOOM-puh luh-HEER-ee) (b. 1967) has received international attention for writings that explore contemporary Indian life. Lahiri won the Pulitzer Prize for her collection of stories, *Interpreter of Maladies* (1999), while her first novel, *The Namesake* (2003), chronicled the lives of Indian immigrants in the United States. Both works examine generation gaps, particularly the alienation and unique synthesis that can accompany cross-cultural exchange. The success of Lahiri's work and other novels such as Arthur Golden's *Memoirs of a Geisha* (1997) indicates how, in the Digital Age, Western peoples remain interested in other cultures and traditions. This emergence of a global culture has become part of the new globalism at the beginning of the twenty-first century.

Toward a Global Civilization: New Challenges and Hopes

Q **FOCUS QUESTION:** What is globalization, and what are some of its important aspects in the twenty-first century?

Multiculturalism in literature reminds us that more and more people are becoming aware of the political, economic, and social interdependence of the world's nations and the global nature of our contemporary problems. We are coming to understand that destructive forces generated in one part of the world soon affect the entire world. Smokestack pollution in one nation can produce acid rain in another. Oil spills and dumping of wastes in the ocean have an impact on the shores of many nations. As crises of food, water, energy, and natural resources proliferate, one nation's solutions often become other nations' problems. The new globalism includes the recognition that the challenges that seem to threaten human existence today are global. In October 2001, in response to the terrorist attacks of September 11, British prime minister Tony Blair said, "We are realizing how fragile are our frontiers in the face of the world's new challenges. Today, conflict rarely stays within national boundaries."

As we saw in the discussion of the Digital Age, an important part of global awareness is the technological dimension. The growth of new technology has made possible levels of world communication that simply did not exist before. At the same time that Osama bin Laden and al-Qaeda were denouncing the forces of modernization, they were doing so by using advanced telecommunication systems that have only recently been developed. The technology revolution has tied peoples and nations closely together and contributed to **globalization,** the term that is frequently used today to describe the process by which peoples and nations have become more interdependent. Economically, globalization has taken the form of a **global economy.**

The Earth. For many people in the West, as in the rest of the world, the view of the earth from outer space fostered an important sense of global unity. The American astronaut Russell Schweickart wrote, "From where you see it, the thing is a whole, and it is so beautiful." In a similar reaction, Yuri Gagarin, the first Soviet cosmonaut, remarked, "What strikes me, is not only the beauty of the continents . . . but their closeness to one another . . . their essential unity."

The Global Economy

Especially since the 1970s, the world has developed a global economy in which the production, distribution, and sale of goods are accomplished on a worldwide scale. Several international institutions have contributed to the rise of the global economy. Soon after the end of World War II, the United States and other nations established the World Bank and the International Monetary Fund (IMF). The World Bank is a group of five international organizations, largely controlled by developed countries, which provides grants, loans, and advice for economic development to developing countries. The goal of the IMF, which was also founded in 1945, is to oversee the global financial system by supervising exchange rates and offering financial and technical assistance to developing nations. Today, 186 countries are members of the IMF. Critics have argued that both the World Bank and the IMF push inappropriate Western economic practices on non-Western nations that only aggravate the poverty and debt of developing nations.

Another reflection of the new global economic order is the **multinational corporation** or **transnational corporation** (a company that has divisions in more than two countries). Prominent examples of multinational corporations include Siemens, General Electric, ExxonMobil, Mitsubishi, and the Sony Corporation. These companies are among the 200 largest multinational corporations, which are responsible for more than half of the world's industrial production. In 2000, 142 of the leading 200 multinational corporations were headquartered in three countries—the United States, Japan, and Germany. In addition, these super corporations dominate much of the world's investment capital, technology, and markets. A recent comparison of corporate sales and national gross domestic product disclosed that only 49 of the world's largest economies are nations; the remaining 51 are corporations. For this reason, some observers believe that economic globalization is more appropriately labeled "corporate globalization."

Another important component of economic globalization is free trade. In 1947, talks led to the General Agreement on Tariffs and Trade (GATT), a global trade organization that was replaced in 1995 by the World Trade Organization (WTO). Made up of more than 150 member nations, the WTO arranges trade agreements and settles trade disputes. Yet many critics charge that the WTO has ignored environmental and health concerns, harmed small and developing countries, and created an ever-growing gap between rich and poor nations.

THE END OF EXCESS The global economy experienced worldwide financial troubles beginning in 2007, following the collapse of the U.S. housing market. Spurred by low interest rates in the early 2000s, easily available mortgages drove up housing values in the United States. In response, investment banks began selling financial investments called collateralized debt obligations (CDOs), which were based on bundles of mortgages. Banks in New York sold CDOs to banks in Europe and elsewhere, spreading the wealth and the risk of investment. Many of the mortgages used as investments had been subprime—issued to borrowers with low credit ratings and a high likehood of default. As the low introductory rates on the mortgages expired beginning in 2006, default rates increased, and all asset securities began to lose their value. By September 2008, a number of large financial institutions, insurance and mortgage companies, investment firms, and banks were approaching or had fallen into bankruptcy. The rapid collapse of CDO values and falling housing prices caused a precipitous decline in the U.S. stock market as stocks lost almost $8 trillion in value from mid-September to November.

Ultimately, the crash of the U.S. housing market led to a worldwide recession. As the American economy slowed, trade decreased worldwide because American consumers, who had been consuming because of higher home values, could no longer afford to do so. Production in Asia decreased, and prices of commodities fell, including the price of oil, which had an impact on Middle Eastern countries and Russia as well.

The United States responded to the financial crisis with an emergency program to recapitalize financial institutions and a stimulus package to support growth and reduce unemployment. Europe faced less severe problems than the United States, although European banks with exposure to subprime investments required government assistance to recapitalize. In Eastern Europe, economies that had recently adopted free market institutions experienced a drastic devaluation of their currencies as investors fled to the stronger dollar and euro. Moreover, the euro crisis in 2010 brought even more concern about the danger of another severe economic recession in Europe. Although governmental measures prevented a systemic failure of the world financial system, high unemployment and weak consumption will probably plague Western nations for several years to come, as people pay off their debts from the previous era of excess.

Globalization and the Environmental Crisis

Taking a global perspective at the beginning of the twenty-first century has led many people to realize that everywhere on the planet human beings are interdependent in regard to the air they breathe, the water they drink, the food they consume, and the climate that affects their lives. At the same time, however, human activities are creating environmental challenges that threaten the very foundation of human existence on earth, especially evident in the Gulf of Mexico oil spill in 2010—the worst oil spill in U.S. history (see the box on p. 977).

One problem is population growth. As of May 2010, the world population was estimated at more than 6.8 billion people, only twenty-two years after passing the 5 billion mark. At its current rate of growth, the world population could reach 12.8 billion by 2050, according to the United Nations' long-range population projections. The result has been an increased demand for food and other resources that has put great pressure on the earth's ecosystems. At the same time, the failure to grow enough food for more and more people has created a severe problem as an estimated 1 billion people worldwide today suffer from hunger. Every year, more than 8 million people die of hunger, many of them young children.

Another problem is the pattern of consumption, as the wealthy nations of the Northern Hemisphere consume vast quantities of the planet's natural resources. The United States, with just 6 percent of the planet's people, consumes 30 to 40 percent of its resources. The spread of these consumption patterns to other parts of the world raises serious questions about the ability of the planet to sustain itself and its population.

Yet another threat to the environment is **global warming,** which has the potential to create a global crisis. Virtually all of the world's scientists agree that the **greenhouse effect,** the warming of the earth because of the buildup of carbon dioxide in the atmosphere, is contributing to devastating droughts and storms, the melting of the polar ice caps, and rising sea levels that could inundate coastal regions in the second half of the twenty-first century. Also alarming is the potential loss of biodiversity. Seven out of ten biologists believe that the planet is now experiencing an alarming extinction of both plant and animal species.

The Social Challenges of Globalization

Since 1945, tens of millions of people have migrated from one part of the world to another. These migrations have occurred for many reasons. Persecution for political reasons caused many people from Pakistan, Bangladesh, Sri Lanka, and Eastern Europe to seek refuge in Western European countries, while brutal civil wars in Asia, Africa, the Middle East, and Europe led millions of refugees to seek safety in neighboring countries. Most people who have migrated, however, have done so to find jobs. Latin Americans seeking a better life have migrated to the United States, while guest workers from Turkey, southern and eastern Europe, North Africa, India, and Pakistan have migrated to more prosperous Western European lands. In 2005, nearly 200 million people, about 3 percent of the world's population, lived outside the country where they were born.

As discussed earlier, the migration of millions of people has created a social backlash in many countries. Foreign workers have often become scapegoats when countries face economic problems. Political parties in France and Norway have called for the removal of blacks and Arabs in order to protect the ethnic purity of their nations, while in Asian countries, there is animosity against other Asian ethnic groups. The problem of foreigners has also led to a more general attack on globalization itself as being responsible for a host of social ills that are undermining national sovereignty.

Another challenge of globalization is the wide gap between rich and poor nations. The rich nations, or **developed nations,** are located mainly in the Northern Hemisphere. They include countries such as the United States, Canada, Germany, and Japan, which have well-organized industrial and agricultural systems, advanced technologies, and effective educational systems. The poor nations, or **developing nations,** are located mainly in the Southern Hemisphere. They include many nations in Africa, Asia, and Latin America, which often have primarily agricultural economies with little technology. A serious problem in many developing nations is the explosive population growth, which has led to severe food shortages often caused by poor soil but also by economic factors. Growing crops for export to developed countries, for example, may lead to enormous profits for large landowners but leaves many small farmers with little land on which to grow food.

Civil wars have also created food shortages. War not only disrupts normal farming operations, but warring groups try to limit access to food to destroy their enemies. In the Sudan, 1.3 million people starved when combatants of a civil war in the 1980s prevented food from reaching them. As unrest continued during the early 2000s in

A Warning to Humanity

As human threats to the environment grew, world scientists began to organize and respond to the crisis. One such group, founded in 1969, was the Union of Concerned Scientists, a nonprofit organization of professional scientists and private citizens, now with more than 200,000 members. In November 1992, the Union of Concerned Scientists published an appeal from 1,700 of the world's leading scientists. The first selection is taken from this "Warning to Humanity."

Earlier, in 1988, in response to the threat of global warming, the United Nations established an Intergovernmental Panel on Climate Change (IPCC) to study the most up-to-date scientific information on global warming and climate change. In 2007, more than 2,500 scientists from more than 130 countries contributed to the group's most recent report, "Climate Change 2007: The Fourth Assessment Report." The second selection is taken from the Web page that summarizes the basic findings of the 2007 report.

—◁◆▷—

World Scientists' Warning to Humanity, 1992

Human beings and the natural world are on a collision course. Human activities inflict harsh and often irreversible damage on the environment and on critical resources. If not checked, many of our current practices put at serious risk the future that we wish for human society and the plant and animal kingdoms, and may so alter the living world that it will be unable to sustain life in the manner that we know. Fundamental changes are urgent if we are to avoid the collision our present course will bring about. The environment is suffering critical stress:

The Atmosphere
Stratospheric ozone depletion threatens us with enhanced ultraviolet radiation at the earth's surface, which can be damaging or lethal to many life forms. Air pollution near ground level, and acid precipitation, are already causing widespread injury to humans, forests, and crops.

Water Resources
Heedless exploitation of depletable ground water supplies endangers food production and other essential human systems. Heavy demands on the world's surface waters have resulted in serious shortages in some 80 countries, containing 40% of the world's population. Pollution of rivers, lakes, and ground water further limits the supply.

Oceans
Destructive pressure on the oceans is severe, particularly in the coastal regions which produce most of the world's food fish. The total marine catch is now at or above the estimated maximum sustainable yield. Some fisheries have already shown signs of collapse.

Soil
Loss of soil productivity, which is causing extensive land abandonment, is a widespread by-product of current practices in agriculture and animal husbandry. Since 1945, 11% of the earth's vegetated surface has been degraded—an area larger than India and China combined—and per capita food production in many parts of the world is decreasing.

Forests
Tropical rain forests, as well as tropical and temperate dry forests, are being destroyed rapidly. At present rates, some critical forest types will be gone in a few years, and most of the tropical rain forest will be gone before the end of the next century. With them will go large numbers of plant and animal species.

Living Species
The irreversible loss of species, which by 2100 may reach one-third of all species now living, is especially serious. We are losing the potential they hold for providing medicinal and other benefits, and the contribution that genetic diversity of life forms gives to the robustness of the world's biological systems and to the astonishing beauty of the earth itself.

Much of this damage is irreversible on a scale of centuries, or permanent. Other processes appear to pose additional threats. Increasing levels of gases in the atmosphere from human activities, including carbon dioxide released from fossil fuel burning and from deforestation, may alter climate on a global scale.

Warning
We the undersigned, senior members of the world's scientific community, hereby warn all humanity of what lies ahead. A great change in our stewardship of the earth and the life on it is required, if vast human misery is to be avoided and our global home on this planet is not to be irretrievably mutilated.

Findings of the IPCC Fourth Assessment Report, 2007

Human Responsibility for Climate Change
The report finds that it is "very likely" that emissions of heat-trapping gases from human activities have caused "most of the observed increase in globally averaged temperatures since the mid-20th century." Evidence that human activities are the major cause of recent climate change is even stronger than in prior assessments.

(continued)

(continued)

Warming Is Unequivocal

The report concludes that it is "unequivocal" that Earth's climate is warming, "as is now evident from observations of increases in global average air and ocean temperatures, widespread melting of snow and ice, and rising global mean sea level." The report also confirms that the current atmospheric concentration of carbon dioxide and methane, two important heat-trapping gases, "exceeds by far the natural range over the last 650,000 years." Since the dawn of the industrial era, concentrations of both gases have increased at a rate that is "very likely to have been unprecedented in more than 10,000 years."

Additional IPCC Findings on Recent Climate Change

Rising Temperatures

- Eleven of the last 12 years rank among the 12 hottest years on record (since 1850, when sufficient worldwide temperature measurements began).
- Over the last 50 years, "cold days, cold nights, and frost have become less frequent, while hot days, hot nights, and heat waves have become more frequent."

Increasingly Severe Weather (storms, precipitation, drought)

- The intensity of tropical cyclones (hurricanes) in the North Atlantic has increased over the past 30 years, which correlates with increases in tropical sea surface temperatures.
- Storms with heavy precipitation have increased in frequency over most land areas. Between 1900 and 2005, long-term trends show significantly increased precipitation in eastern parts of North and South America, northern Europe, and northern and central Asia.
- Between 1900 and 2005, the Sahel (the boundary zone between the Sahara desert and more fertile regions of Africa to the south), the Mediterranean, southern Africa, and parts of southern Asia have become drier, adding stress to water resources in these regions.
- Droughts have become longer and more intense, and have affected larger areas since the 1970s, especially in the tropics and subtropics. ☞

Q What problems and challenges do these two reports present? What do these two reports have in common? How do they differ?

Darfur, families were forced to leave their farms. As a result, an estimated 70,000 people starved by mid-2004.

New Global Movements and New Hopes

As the heirs of Western civilization have become aware that the problems humans face are not just national but global, they have responded to this challenge in different ways. One approach has been to develop grassroots social movements, including environmental, women's and men's liberation, human potential, appropriate-technology, and nonviolence movements. "Think globally, act locally" is frequently the slogan of these grassroots groups. Related to the emergence of these social movements is the growth of nongovernmental organizations (NGOs). According to one analyst, NGOs are an important instrument in the cultivation of global perspectives: "Since NGOs by definition are identified with interests that transcend national boundaries, we expect all NGOs to define problems in global terms, to take account of human interests and needs as they are found in all parts of the planet."[7] NGOs are often represented at the United Nations and include professional, business, and cooperative organizations; foundations; religious, peace, and disarmament groups; youth and women's organizations; environmental and human rights groups; and research institutes. The number of international NGOs increased from 176 in 1910 to 37,000 in 2000.

And yet hopes for global approaches to global problems have also been hindered by political, ethnic, and religious disputes. Pollution of the Rhine River by factories along its banks provokes angry disputes among European nations, and the United States and Canada have argued about the effects of acid rain on Canadian forests. The collapse of the Soviet Union and its satellite system seemed to provide an enormous boost to the potential for international cooperation on global issues, but it has had almost the opposite effect. The bloody conflict in the former Yugoslavia indicates the dangers inherent in the rise of nationalist sentiment among various ethnic and religious groups in Eastern Europe. The widening gap between the wealthy nations in the Northern Hemisphere and the poor, developing nations in the Southern Hemisphere threatens global economic stability. Many conflicts begin with regional issues and then develop into international concerns. International terrorist groups seek to wreak havoc around the world.

Thus, even as the world becomes more global in culture and interdependent in its mutual relations, centrifugal forces are still at work attempting to redefine the political, cultural, and ethnic ways in which the world is divided. Such efforts are often disruptive and can sometimes work against measures to enhance our human destiny.

Many lessons can be learned from the history of Western civilization, but one of them is especially clear. Lack of involvement in the affairs of one's society can lead to a sense of powerlessness. In an age that is often crisis-laden and chaotic, an understanding of our Western heritage and its lessons can be instrumental in helping us create new models for the future. For we are all creators of history, and the future of Western and indeed world civilization depends on us.

CHAPTER SUMMARY

When Mikhail Gorbachev came to power in the Soviet Union in 1985, he proposed radical reforms in both the economy and Soviet government. With these reforms, the pressure for more drastic change began to mount. In 1989, a wave of revolution swept through Eastern Europe as Communist regimes were overthrown and a new, mostly democratic order emerged, although serious divisions remained, especially in Yugoslavia. In 1991, the attempt of reactionary forces to undo the reforms of Gorbachev led instead to the complete disintegration of the Soviet Union and the emergence of a new Russia. The Cold War, which had begun at the end of World War II and had led to a Europe divided along ideological lines, was finally over.

Although many people were optimistic about a new world order after the collapse of communism, uncertainties still prevailed. Germany was successfully reunited, and the European Union became even stronger with the adoption of a common currency in the euro. Yugoslavia, however, disintegrated into warring states that eventually all became independent, and ethnic groups that had once been forced to live under distinct national banners began rebelling to form autonomous states. Although some were successful, others, such as the Chechnyans, were brutally repressed.

While the so-called new world order was fitfully developing, other challenges emerged. The arrival of many

foreigners, especially in Western Europe, not only strained the social services of European countries but also led to antiforeign sentiment and right-wing political parties that encouraged it. Environmental abuses led to growing threats not only to Europeans but also all humans. Terrorism, especially that carried out by some parts of the Muslim world, emerged as a threat to many Western states. Since the end of World War II, terrorism seemed to have replaced communism as the number one enemy of the West.

As the beginning of the twenty-first century, a major realization has been the recognition that the problems afflicting the Western world have also become global problems. The nation-state, whose history dominated the nineteenth and twentieth centuries and which still plays an important role in contemporary affairs, nevertheless appears to be an outmoded structure if humankind is to resolve its many challenges. Nations and peoples have become more interdependent, and many Westerners recognize that a global perspective must also now become a part of the Western tradition.

CHAPTER TIMELINE

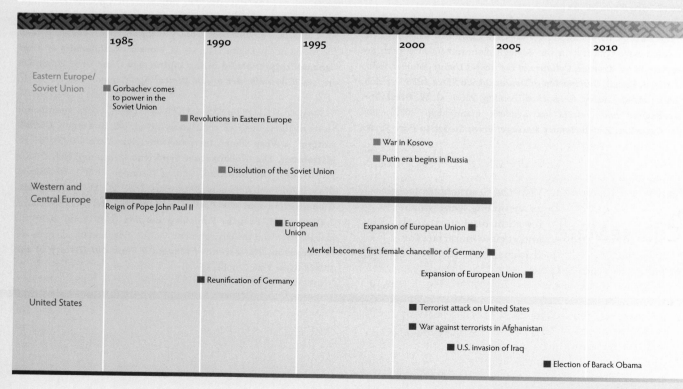

CHAPTER REVIEW

Upon Reflection

Q What roles did Mikhail Gorbachev and Ronald Reagan play in bringing an end to the Cold War? Which played a more important role? Why?

Q What directions did Eastern European nations take after they became free from Soviet control? Why did they react as they did?

Q What is globalization, and how does it relate to the technological and social concerns of our age?

Key Terms

perestroika (p. 948)
glasnost (p. 948)
ethnic cleansing (p. 955)
guest workers (p. 967)
multiculturalism (p. 973)
globalization (p. 974)
global economy (p. 974)
multinational corporation
    (transnational corporation) (p. 975)
global warming (p. 976)
greenhouse effect (p. 976)
developed nations (p. 976)
developing nations (p. 976)

Suggestions for Further Reading

GENERAL WORKS For a well-written survey on Europe from 1985 to 2004, see **T. Judt, *Postwar: A History of Europe Since 1945*** (New York, 2005).

TOWARD A NEW WESTERN ORDER Different aspects of the revolutionary upheaval in the Soviet Union and its aftermath are covered in **M. Kramer, *Collapse of the Soviet Union*** (Boulder, Colo., 2007); **S. Lovell, *Destination in Doubt: Russia Since 1989*** (London, 2006); **M. McCauley, *Gorbachev*** (London, 2000); **G. W. Breslauer, *Gorbachev and Yeltsin as Leaders*** (Cambridge, 2002); and **M. Garcelon, *Revolutionary Passage: From Soviet to Post-Soviet***

Russia, 1985–2000 (Philadelphia, 2005). On Eastern Europe, see **G. Stokes, *The Walls Came Tumbling Down: The Collapse of Communism in Eastern Europe*** (Oxford, 1993), and **P. Kenney, *The Burden of Freedom: Eastern Europe Since 1989*** (London, 2006). For general works on Western Europe and individual countries, see the works cited in Chapters 28 and 29. On the recent history of these countries, see **P. O'Dochartaigh, *Germany Since 1945*** (New York, 2004); **B. Thomaneck** and **J. K. Thomaneck, *Division and Reunification of Germany*** (London, 2000); and **M. Temple, *Blair*** (London, 2006), on the era of Tony Blair in Britain.

AFTER THE COLD WAR On the end of the Cold War, see **S. Dockrill, *The End of the Cold War Era*** (London, 2005), and **J. L. Gaddis, *The Cold War: A New History*** (New York, 2005). On terrorism, see **W. Laqueur, *History of Terrorism*** (New York, 2001); **C. E. Simonsen** and **J. R. Spendlove, *Terrorism Today: The Past, The Players, The Future,*** 3rd ed. (Upper Saddle River, N.J., 2006); and **T. R. Mockaitis, *The "New" Terrorism: Myth and Reality*** (New York, 2006).

NEW DIRECTIONS AND NEW PROBLEMS IN WESTERN SOCIETY The changing role of women is examined in **C. Duchen, *Feminism in France*** (London, 1986); **R. Rosen, *The World Split Open: How the Modern Women's Movement Changed America*** (New York, 2001); and **J. W. Scott, *The Politics of the Veil*** (Princeton, N.J., 2009). The problems of guest workers and immigrants are examined in **W. Laqueur, *The Last Days of Europe: Epitaph for an Old Continent*** (New York, 2007), and **R. Chin, *Guest Worker Question in Germany*** (Cambridge, 2007).

THE DIGITAL AGE For a comprehensive examination of the Digital Age, see **M. Castells, *The Information Age,*** 3 vols. (Oxford, 1996–1998). On the role of the Internet in our global age, see **M. Castells, *The Internet Galaxy*** (Oxford, 2001). On the role of the media in the Digital Age, see **R. Dominick, *Dynamics of Mass Communication: Media in the Digital Age*** (New York, 2006). On art, see **B. Wands, *Art of the Digital Age*** (London, 2007).

TOWARD A GLOBAL CIVILIZATION Useful books on different facets of the new global civilization include **M. B. Steger, *Globalization: A Very Short Introduction*** (New York, 2003); **J. H. Mittelman, *The Globalization Syndrome*** (Princeton, N.J., 2000); **M. Waters, *Globalization,*** 2nd ed. (London, 2001); **R. Gilpin, *Global Political Economy*** (Princeton, N.J., 2001); **A. Hoogvelt, *Globalization and the Postcolonial World,*** 2nd ed. (Baltimore, 2001); and **H. French, *Vanishing Borders*** (New York, 2000) on globalization and the environment. On the global financial crisis, see **N. Ferguson, *The Ascent of Money: A Financial History of the World*** (New York, 2008). ✄

CourseMate

Visit the CourseMate website at www.cengagebrain.com for additional study tools and review materials for this chapter.

1. Following its inception in 1919, the state of Yugoslavia could best be described as

   (A) an empire ruled by the former dynastic family known as the Habsburgs.
   (B) an artificial state comprised of multiethnic regions from the former Habsburg Empire.
   (C) an expansionistic state seeking to institute imperial rule in the Balkan region.
   (D) a democratic nation that sought to expand democracy within the Balkans.
   (E) a tribal state torn by decades of civil conflict between factions that sought political progress and others that held more conservative positions.

2. Slobodan Milošević, a Serbian nationalist, rejected the efforts

   (A) of ethnic minorities to separate from Yugoslavia.
   (B) of the Communist Party in Yugoslavia to maintain power.
   (C) of the United Nations to allow Serb minorities to live in separatist regions.
   (D) of long-serving bureaucrats to establish a stronger Yugoslavian state.
   (E) of the Communist Party to enhance his status as a nationalist leader.

3. The Serbian policy toward Bosnian Muslims is best defined as a process of

   (A) religious tolerance.
   (B) political autonomy.
   (C) growing radicalism.
   (D) *de jure* segregation.
   (E) ethnic cleansing.

4. The Kosovo Liberation Army (KLA)

   (A) fought to end Serbian rule in Kosovo.
   (B) was a collectivist organization seeking to expand Communist power in Yugoslavia.
   (C) was responsible for the death of a million ethnic Albanians.
   (D) desired a return of the Ottoman Empire and adherence to the Ottoman borders that divided the Balkans.
   (E) was a terrorist organization responsible for keeping Slobodan Milošević in power.

5. The "opening toward the east," instituted by Willy Brandt of West Germany, is also known as

   (A) *Realpolitik.*
   (B) *Politika.*
   (C) *Oslobodenje.*
   (D) *Politique.*
   (E) *Ostpolitik.*

6. The Russian Republic

   (A) was plagued by economic woes and divisive politics as it shifted from a Communist state to a capitalist economy.
   (B) joined NATO in order to form western alliances.
   (C) was able to compete in a global economy thanks to its superpower status.
   (D) was able to transfer to capitalism relatively easily, as the country had never fully implemented communism.
   (E) enjoyed tremendous stability following the presidency of Mikhail Gorbachev.

7. The European Union was created by the

   (A) Treaty of Utrecht.
   (B) Treaty of Versailles.
   (C) Treaty of Paris.
   (D) Maastricht Treaty.
   (E) Treaty of London.

8. Which of the following was a result of the Arab-Israeli conflict of 1973?

   (A) It signaled an end to détente between the United States and the Soviet Union.
   (B) Ronald Reagan was elected as president of the United States.
   (C) The Organization of Petroleum Exporting Countries imposed an oil embargo.
   (D) The nations involved in the fighting experienced an increase in economic opportunities.
   (E) Most global currencies experienced significant growth in value.

9. The Gulf War of 1991 most notably signaled

   (A) the declining influence of the Soviet Union as a major actor in global politics.
   (B) the growing military weakness of NATO.
   (C) an increase in bipolarity between the Soviet Union and the United States.
   (D) a new beginning to the Cold War.
   (E) the insignificance of the Middle East to global politics.

10. Al-Qaeda, the terrorist organization operated by Osama bin Laden, was instrumental in all of the following events EXCEPT

(A) an attack on a U.S. naval ship in 2000.
(B) the bombings of two American embassies in Africa.
(C) the hijacking of four passenger planes that were used as instruments of destruction.
(D) the creation of a global terrorist network dedicated to jihadist belief.
(E) the 1972 killing of eleven Jewish athletes at the Munich Olympic Games.

11. The Helsinki Accords

(A) were established by the United Nations to affirm that human rights should be upheld in every country.
(B) were a series of treaties designed to end nuclear proliferation.
(C) were economic policies put in place to halt the expansion of communism.
(D) were instituted to help African nations and others in the Third World.
(E) were instrumental in maintaining global peace throughout the Cold War.

12. Western European nations in the twenty-first century have often instituted new social policies aimed at migrant black Africans and Arabs

(A) to offset the high cost of providing basic services for those immigrants.
(B) after years of civil unrest and colonial tension over *de jure* segregation.
(C) as a means of enforcing cultural protectionism for Protestant and Catholic churches.
(D) to answer widespread concern over an increase in diseases.
(E) as nativist political organizations have risen to challenge immigration laws.

13. Which of the following best explains the decrease in warfare between developed nations?

(A) They have shared interests in seeking to expand their political borders.
(B) They each fear that another nation might consider using nuclear weapons.
(C) They are often tied together by a global economy.
(D) They all covet the prestige of winning a Nobel Peace Prize.
(E) They fear the damaging impact war might have on the world's environment.

14. Abstract Expressionist art most often represents

(A) rituals of joy and celebration for European ethnic communities.
(B) the horrors of violence and conflict that have shattered any sense of progress.
(C) the haunting, Gothic appeal of the atrocities of the twenty-first century.
(D) a reconstruction of the morality of political society.
(E) the evils of capitalism and its messages of greed and materialism.

15. At the end of the twentieth century, all of the following Eastern Bloc countries experienced a relatively peaceful rebellion against their Communist regimes EXCEPT

(A) Czechoslovakia.
(B) Poland.
(C) Romania.
(D) East Germany.
(E) Hungary.

GLOSSARY

abbess   the head of a convent or monastery for women.

abbot   the head of a monastery.

absolutism   a form of government in which the sovereign power or ultimate authority rested in the hands of a monarch who claimed to rule by divine right and was therefore responsible only to God.

Abstract Expressionism   a post–World War II artistic movement that broke with all conventions of form and structure in favor of total abstraction.

abstract painting   an artistic movement that developed early in the twentieth century in which artists focused on color to avoid any references to visual reality.

aediles   Roman officials who supervised the public games and the grain supply of the city of Rome.

agricultural revolution   the application of new agricultural techniques that allowed for a large increase in productivity in the eighteenth century.

Agricultural (Neolithic) Revolution   *see* Neolithic Revolution.

anarchism   a political theory that holds that all governments and existing social institutions are unnecessary and advocates a society based on voluntary cooperation.

anticlericalism   opposition to the power of the clergy, especially in political affairs.

anti-Semitism   hostility toward or discrimination against Jews.

apartheid   the system of racial segregation practiced in the Republic of South Africa until the 1990s, which involved political, legal, and economic discrimination against nonwhites.

appeasement   the policy, followed by the European nations in the 1930s, of accepting Hitler's annexation of Austria and Czechoslovakia in the belief that meeting his demands would assure peace and stability.

Arianism   a Christian heresy that taught that Jesus was inferior to God. Though condemned by the Council of Nicaea in 325, Arianism was adopted by many of the Germanic peoples who entered the Roman Empire over the next centuries.

aristocracy   a class of hereditary nobility in medieval Europe; a warrior class who shared a distinctive lifestyle based on the institution of knighthood, although there were social divisions within the group based on extremes of wealth.

audiencias   advisory groups to viceroys in Spanish America.

Ausgleich   the "Compromise" of 1867 that created the Dual Monarchy of Austria-Hungary. Austria and Hungary each had its own capital, constitution, and legislative assembly but were united under one monarch.

authoritarian state   a state that has a dictatorial government and some other trappings of a totalitarian state but does not demand that the masses be actively involved in the regime's goals as totalitarian states do.

auxiliaries   troops enlisted from the subject peoples of the Roman Empire to supplement the regular legions composed of Roman citizens.

balance of power   a distribution of power among several states such that no single nation can dominate or interfere with the interests of another.

Baroque   an artistic movement of the seventeenth century in Europe that used dramatic effects to arouse the emotions and reflected the search for power that was a large part of the seventeenth-century ethos.

benefice   in the Christian church, a position, such as a bishopric, that consisted of both a sacred office and the right of the holder to the annual revenues from the position.

bicameral legislature   a legislature with two houses.

Black Death   the outbreak of plague (mostly bubonic) in the mid-fourteenth century that killed from 25 to 50 percent of Europe's population.

Blitzkrieg   "lightning war." A war conducted with great speed and force, as in Germany's advance at the beginning of World War II.

Bolsheviks   a small faction of the Russian Social Democratic Party who were led by Lenin and dedicated to violent revolution; they seized power in Russia in 1917 and were subsequently renamed the Communists.

bourgeoisie (burghers)   inhabitants (merchants and artisans) of boroughs and burghs (towns).

boyars   the Russian nobility.

Brezhnev Doctrine   the doctrine, enunciated by Leonid Brezhnev, that the Soviet Union had a right to intervene if socialism was threatened in another socialist state; used to justify moving Soviet troops into Czechoslovakia in 1968.

Burschenschaften   student societies in the German states dedicated to fostering the goal of a free, united Germany.

caliph   the secular leader of the Islamic community.

capital   material wealth used or available for use in the production of more wealth.

cartel   a combination of independent commercial enterprises that work together to control prices and limit competition.

Cartesian dualism   Descartes's principle of the separation of mind and matter (and mind and body) that enabled scientists to view matter as something separate from themselves that could be investigated by reason.

celibacy   complete abstinence from sexual activity. Many early Christians viewed celibacy as the surest way to holiness.

centuriate assembly   the chief popular assembly of the Roman Republic. It passed laws and elected the chief magistrates.

chansons de geste   a form of vernacular literature in the High Middle Ages that consisted of heroic epics focusing on the deeds of warriors.

chivalry   the ideal of civilized behavior that emerged among the nobility in the eleventh and twelfth centuries under the influence of the church; a code of ethics knights were expected to uphold.

cholera   a serious and often deadly disease commonly spread by contaminated water; a major problem in nineteenth-century European cities before sewerage systems were installed.

Christian (northern) humanism   an intellectual movement in northern Europe in the late fifteenth and early sixteenth centuries that combined the interest in the classics of the Italian Renaissance with an interest in the sources of early Christianity, including the New Testament and the writings of the church fathers.

civic humanism   an intellectual movement of the Italian Renaissance that saw Cicero, who was both an intellectual and a statesman, as the ideal and held that humanists should be involved in government and use their rhetorical training in the service of the state.

civil disobedience   a policy of peaceful protest against laws or government policies in order to achieve political change.

civilization a complex culture in which large numbers of humans share a variety of common elements, including cities; religious, political, military, and social structures; writing; and significant artistic and intellectual activity.

civil rights the basic rights of citizens, including equality before the law, freedom of speech and press, and freedom from arbitrary arrest.

Cold War the ideological conflict between the Soviet Union and the United States after World War II.

collective farms large farms created in the Soviet Union by Stalin by combining many small holdings into large farms worked by the peasants under government supervision.

coloni free tenant farmers who worked as sharecroppers on the large estates of the Roman Empire (singular: *colonus*).

Columbian Exchange the reciprocal importation and exportation of plants and animals between Europe and the Americas.

commercial capitalism beginning in the Middle Ages, an economic system in which people invested in trade and goods in order to make profits.

common law law common to the entire kingdom of England; imposed by the king's courts beginning in the twelfth century to replace the customary law used in county and feudal courts that varied from place to place.

commune in medieval Europe, an association of townspeople bound together by a sworn oath for the purpose of obtaining basic liberties from the lord of the territory in which the town was located; also, the self-governing town after receiving its liberties.

conciliarism a movement in fourteenth- and fifteenth-century Europe that held that final authority in spiritual matters resided with a general church council, not the pope; it emerged in response to the Avignon papacy and the Great Schism and was used to justify the summoning of the Council of Constance (1414–1418).

condottieri leaders of bands of mercenary soldiers in Renaissance Italy who sold their services to the highest bidder.

confession one of the seven sacraments of the Catholic Church; it provided for the forgiveness of one's sins.

conquistadors "conquerors." Leaders in the Spanish conquests in the Americas, especially Mexico and Peru, in the sixteenth century.

conscription a military draft.

conservatism an ideology based on tradition and social stability that favored the maintenance of established institutions, organized religion, and obedience to authority and resisted change, especially abrupt change.

consuls the chief executive officers of the Roman Republic. Two were chosen annually to administer the government and lead the army in battle.

consumer society Western society that emerged after World War II as the working classes adopted the consumption patterns of the middle class and payment plans, credit cards, and easy credit made consumer goods such as appliances and automobiles affordable.

containment a policy adopted by the United States in the Cold War. Its goal was to use whatever means, short of all-out war, to limit Soviet expansion.

Continental System Napoleon's effort to bar British goods from the Continent in the hope of weakening Britain's economy and destroying its capacity to wage war.

cosmopolitan the quality of being sophisticated and having wide international experience.

cottage industry a system of textile manufacturing in which spinners and weavers worked at home in their cottages using raw materials supplied to them by capitalist entrepreneurs.

council of the plebs a council only for plebeians. After 287 B.C.E., however, its resolutions were binding on all Romans.

Crusade in the Middle Ages, a military campaign in defense of Christendom.

Cubism an artistic style developed at the beginning of the twentieth century, especially by Pablo Picasso, that used geometric designs to re-create reality in the viewer's mind.

cultural relativism the belief that no culture is superior to another because culture is a matter of custom, not reason, and derives its meaning from the group holding it.

cuneiform "wedge-shaped." A system of writing developed by the Sumerians that consisted of wedge-shaped impressions made by a reed stylus on clay tablets.

curiales city councilors in Roman cities who played an important role in governing the vast Roman Empire.

Dadaism an artistic movement in the 1920s and 1930s begun by artists who were revolted by the senseless slaughter of World War I and used their "anti-art" to express contempt for the Western tradition.

de-Christianization a policy, adopted in the radical phase of the French Revolution, aimed at creating a secular society by eliminating Christian forms and institutions from French society.

decolonization the process of becoming free of colonial status and achieving statehood; it occurred in most of the world's colonies between 1947 and 1962.

deconstruction (poststructuralism) a system of thought, formulated by Jacques Derrida, that holds that culture is created in a variety of ways, according to the manner in which people create their own meaning. Hence, there is no fixed truth or universal meaning.

deism belief in God as the creator of the universe who, after setting it in motion, ceased to have any direct involvement in it and allowed it to run according to its own natural laws.

demesne the part of a manor retained under the direct control of the lord and worked by the serfs as part of their labor services.

denazification after World War II, the Allied policy of rooting out any traces of Nazism in German society by bringing prominent Nazis to trial for war crimes and purging any known Nazis from political office.

depression a very severe, protracted economic downturn with high levels of unemployment.

de-Stalinization the policy of denouncing and undoing the most repressive aspects of Stalin's regime; begun by Nikita Khrushchev in 1956.

détente the relaxation of tension between the Soviet Union and the United States that occurred in the 1970s.

developed nations a term used to refer to rich nations, primarily in the Northern Hemisphere, that have well-organized industrial and agricultural systems, advanced technologies, and effective educational systems.

developing nations a term used to refer to poor nations, mainly in the Southern Hemisphere, that are primarily farming nations with little technology and serious population problems.

dialectic logic, one of the seven liberal arts that made up the medieval curriculum. In Marxist thought, the process by which all change occurs through the clash of antagonistic elements.

Diaspora the scattering of Jews throughout the ancient world after the Babylonian captivity in the sixth century B.C.E.

dictator in the Roman Republic, an official granted unlimited power to run the state for a short period of time, usually six months, during an emergency.

diocese the area under the jurisdiction of a Christian bishop; based originally on Roman administrative districts.

divination the practice of seeking to foretell future events by interpreting divine signs, which could appear in various forms, such as in entrails of animals, in patterns in smoke, or in dreams.

divine-right monarchy a monarchy based on the belief that monarchs receive their power directly from God and are responsible to no one except God.

domino theory the belief that if the Communists succeeded in Vietnam, other countries in Southeast and East Asia would also fall (like dominoes) to communism; cited as a justification for the U.S. intervention in Vietnam.

Donatism a Christian heresy that argued that the sacraments of the church were not valid if administered by an immoral priest.

dualism the belief that the universe is dominated by two opposing forces, one good and the other evil.

dynastic state a state in which the maintenance and expansion of the interests of the ruling family is the primary consideration.

economic imperialism the process in which banks and corporations from developed nations invest in underdeveloped regions and establish a major presence there in the hope of making high profits; not necessarily the same as colonial expansion in that businesses invest where they can make a profit, which may not be in their own nation's colonies.

economic liberalism the idea that government should not interfere in the workings of the economy.

Einsatzgruppen in Nazi Germany, special strike forces in the SS that played an important role in rounding up and killing Jews.

empiricism the practice of relying on observation and experiment.

encomienda in Spanish America, a form of economic and social organization in which a Spaniard was given a royal grant that enabled the holder of the grant to collect tribute from the Indians and use them as laborers.

enlightened absolutism an absolute monarchy in which the ruler follows the principles of the Enlightenment by introducing reforms for the improvement of society, allowing freedom of speech and the press, permitting religious toleration, expanding education, and ruling in accordance with the laws.

Enlightenment an eighteenth-century intellectual movement, led by the philosophes, that stressed the application of reason and the scientific method to all aspects of life.

entrepreneur one who organizes, operates, and assumes the risk in a business venture in the expectation of making a profit.

Epicureanism a philosophy founded by Epicurus in the fourth century B.C.E. that taught that happiness (freedom from emotional turmoil) could be achieved through the pursuit of pleasure (intellectual rather than sensual pleasure).

equestrians a group of extremely wealthy men in the late Roman Republic who were effectively barred from high office but sought political power commensurate with their wealth; called equestrians because many had gotten their start as cavalry officers (*equites*).

estates (orders) the traditional tripartite division of European society based on heredity and quality rather than wealth or economic standing, first established in the Middle Ages and continuing into the eighteenth century; traditionally consisted of those who pray (the clergy), those who fight (the nobility), and those who work (all the rest).

ethnic cleansing the policy of killing or forcibly removing people of another ethnic group; used by the Serbs against Bosnian Muslims in the 1990s.

Eucharist a Christian sacrament in which consecrated bread and wine are consumed in celebration of Jesus's Last Supper; also called the Lord's Supper or communion.

Eurocommunism a form of communism that dropped its Marxist ideology. It was especially favored in Italy.

evolutionary socialism a socialist doctrine espoused by Eduard Bernstein who argued that socialists should stress cooperation and evolution to attain power by democratic means rather than by conflict and revolution.

exchequer the permanent royal treasury of England. It emerged during the reign of King Henry II in the twelfth century.

excommunication in the Catholic Church, a censure depriving a person of the right to receive the sacraments of the church.

existentialism a philosophical movement that arose after World War II that emphasized the meaninglessness of life, born of the desperation caused by two world wars.

family allowances one aspect of the welfare state whereby the state provides a minimum level of material assistance for children.

fascism an ideology or movement that exalts the nation above the individual and calls for a centralized government with a dictatorial leader, economic and social regimentation, and forcible suppression of opposition; in particular, the ideology of Mussolini's Fascist regime in Italy.

federates German troops enlisted in groups to fight as allies for the Romans.

feminism the belief in the social, political, and economic equality of the sexes; also, organized activity to advance women's rights.

fief a landed estate granted to a vassal in exchange for military services.

Final Solution the attempted physical extermination of the Jewish people by the Nazis during World War II.

Five Pillars of Islam the major tenets of the Muslim faith: belief in Allah and Muhammad as his Prophet; standard prayer five times a day and public prayer on Friday; observance of the holy month of Ramadan by fasting from dawn to sunset; making a pilgrimage (the *hajj*) to Mecca in one's lifetime if possible; and giving alms to the poor.

folk culture the traditional arts and crafts, literature, music, and other customs of the people; something that people make, as opposed to modern popular culture, which is something people buy.

free trade the unrestricted international exchange of goods with low or no tariffs.

Führerprinzip in Nazi Germany, a leadership principle based on the belief in a single-minded party (the Nazis) under one leader (Hitler).

functionalism the idea that the function of an object should determine its design and materials.

general strike a strike by all or most workers in an economy; espoused by Georges Sorel as the heroic action that could be used to inspire the workers to destroy capitalist society.

genocide the deliberate extermination of a people.

gentry well-to-do English landowners below the level of the nobility. They played an important role in the English Civil War of the seventeenth century.

geocentric conception the belief that the earth was at the center of the universe and that the sun and other celestial objects revolved around the earth.

Girondins a faction in the National Convention during the French Revolution that favored keeping the king alive; so-called because their leaders came from the Gironde in southwestern France.

glasnost "openness." Mikhail Gorbachev's policy of encouraging Soviet citizens to openly discuss the strengths and weaknesses of the Soviet Union.

global economy an interdependent economy in which the production, distribution, and sale of goods are accomplished on a worldwide scale.

globalization a term referring to the trend by which peoples and nations have become more interdependent; often used to refer to the development of a global economy and culture.

global warming the increase in the temperature of the earth's atmosphere caused by the greenhouse effect.

good emperors the five emperors who ruled from 96 to 180 (Nerva, Trajan, Hadrian, Antoninus Pius, and Marcus Aurelius), a period of peace and prosperity for the Roman Empire.

Gothic a term used to describe the art and especially architecture of Europe in the twelfth, thirteenth, and fourteenth centuries.

Gothic literature a form of literature used by Romantics to emphasize the bizarre and unusual, especially evident in horror stories.

Great Schism the crisis in the late medieval church when there were first two and then three popes; ended by the Council of Constance (1414–1418).

greenhouse effect   the warming of the earth caused by the buildup of carbon dioxide in the atmosphere as a result of human activity.

guest workers   foreign workers working temporarily in European countries.

guild   an association of people with common interests and concerns, especially people working in the same craft. In medieval Europe, guilds came to control much of the production process and to restrict entry into various trades.

gymnasium   in Classical Greece, a place for athletics; in the Hellenistic Age, a secondary school with a curriculum centered on music, physical exercise, and literature.

heliocentric conception   the belief that the sun, not the earth, is at the center of the universe.

Hellenistic   literally, "imitating the Greeks"; the era after the death of Alexander the Great when Greek culture spread into the Near East and blended with the culture of that region.

helots   serfs in ancient Sparta who were permanently bound to the land that they worked for their Spartan masters.

heresy   the holding of religious doctrines different from the official teachings of the church.

Hermeticism   an intellectual movement beginning in the fifteenth century that taught that divinity is embodied in all aspects of nature; it included works on alchemy and magic as well as theology and philosophy. The tradition continued into the seventeenth century and influenced many of the leading figures of the Scientific Revolution.

hetairai   highly sophisticated courtesans in ancient Athens who offered intellectual and musical entertainment as well as sex.

hieroglyphics   a pictorial system of writing used in ancient Egypt.

high culture   the literary and artistic culture of the educated and wealthy ruling classes.

Holocaust   the mass slaughter of European Jews by the Nazis during World War II.

home rule   in the United Kingdom, self-government by having a separate parliament but not complete independence.

hoplites   heavily armed infantry soldiers in ancient Greece who entered battle in a phalanx formation.

Huguenots   French Calvinists.

humanism   an intellectual movement in Renaissance Italy based on the study of the Greek and Roman classics.

iconoclasm   a movement against the use of icons (pictures of sacred figures) in the eighth-century Byzantine Empire

iconoclast   a member of an eighth-century Byzantine movement against the use of icons, which was condemned as idolatry.

ideology   a political philosophy such as conservatism or liberalism.

imperium   in the Roman Republic, the right to command troops that belonged to the chief executive officers (consuls and praetors); a military commander was known as an *imperator*. In the Roman Empire, the title *imperator* (emperor) came to be used for the ruler.

Impressionism   an artistic movement that originated in France in the 1870s. Impressionists sought to capture their impressions of the changing effects of light on objects in nature.

individualism   emphasis on and interest in the unique traits of each person.

indulgence   in Christian theology, the remission of part or all of the temporal punishment in purgatory due to sin; granted for charitable contributions and other good deeds. Indulgences became a regular practice of the Christian church in the High Middle Ages, and their abuse was instrumental in sparking Luther's reform movement in the sixteenth century.

infanticide   the practice of killing infants.

inflation   a sustained rise in the price level.

intendants   royal officials in seventeenth-century France who were sent into the provinces to execute the orders of the central government.

interdict   in the Catholic Church, a censure by which a region or country is deprived of receiving the sacraments.

intervention, principle of   the idea, after the Congress of Vienna, that the great powers of Europe had the right to send armies into countries experiencing revolution to restore legitimate monarchs to their thrones.

isolationism   a foreign policy in which a nation refrains from making alliances or engaging actively in international affairs.

Janissaries   an elite core of eight thousand troops personally loyal to the sultan of the Ottoman Empire.

jihad   "striving in the way of the Lord." In Islam, the attempt to achieve personal betterment, although it can also mean fair, defensive fighting to preserve one's life and one's faith.

joint-stock company   a company or association that raises capital by selling shares to individuals who receive dividends on their investment while a board of directors runs the company.

joint-stock investment bank   a bank created by selling shares of stock to investors. Such banks potentially have access to much more capital than private banks owned by one or a few individuals.

justification   the primary doctrine of the Protestant Reformation, teaching that humans are saved not through good works but by the grace of God, bestowed freely through the sacrifice of Jesus.

Kulturkampf   "culture conflict." The name given to Bismarck's attack on the Catholic Church in Germany, which has come to refer to conflict between church and state anywhere.

laissez-faire   "let (them) do (as they please)." An economic doctrine that holds that an economy is best served when the government does not interfere but allows the economy to self-regulate according to the forces of supply and demand.

latifundia   large landed estates in the Roman Empire (singular: *latifundium*).

lay investiture   the practice in which someone other than a member of the clergy chose a bishop and invested him with the symbols of both his temporal office and his spiritual office; led to the Investiture Controversy, which was ended by compromise in the Concordat of Worms in 1122.

Lebensraum   "living space." The doctrine, adopted by Hitler, that a nation's power depends on the amount of land it occupies; thus, a nation must expand to be strong.

legitimacy, principle of   the idea that after the Napoleonic wars, peace could best be reestablished in Europe by restoring legitimate monarchs who would preserve traditional institutions; guided Metternich at the Congress of Vienna.

Leninism   Lenin's revision of Marxism that held that Russia need not experience a bourgeois revolution before it could move toward socialism.

liberal arts   the seven areas of study that formed the basis of education in medieval and early modern Europe. Following Boethius and other late Roman authors, they consisted of grammar, rhetoric, and dialectic or logic (the *trivium*) and arithmetic, geometry, astronomy, and music (the *quadrivium*).

liberalism   an ideology based on the belief that people should be as free from restraint as possible. Economic liberalism is the idea that the government should not interfere in the workings of the economy. Political liberalism is the idea that there should be restraints on the exercise of power so that people can enjoy basic civil rights in a constitutional state with a representative assembly.

limited monarchy (constitutional monarchy)   a system of government in which the monarch is limited by a representative assembly and by the duty to rule in accordance with the laws of the land.

major domus   the chief officer of the king's household in the Frankish kingdom.

mandates   a system established after World War I whereby a nation officially administered a territory (mandate) on behalf of the

League of Nations. Thus, France administered Lebanon and Syria as mandates, and Britain administered Iraq and Palestine.

Mannerism   a sixteenth-century artistic movement in Europe that deliberately broke down the High Renaissance principles of balance, harmony, and moderation.

manor   an agricultural estate operated by a lord and worked by peasants who performed labor services and paid various rents and fees to the lord in exchange for protection and sustenance.

Marshall Plan   the European Recovery Program, under which the United States provided financial aid to European countries to help them rebuild after World War II.

Marxism   the political, economic, and social theories of Karl Marx, which included the idea that history is the story of class struggle and that ultimately the proletariat will overthrow the bourgeoisie and establish a dictatorship en route to a classless society.

mass education   a state-run educational system, usually free and compulsory, that aims to ensure that all children in society have at least a basic education.

mass leisure   forms of leisure that appeal to large numbers of people in a society, including the working classes; emerged at the end of the nineteenth century to provide workers with amusements after work and on weekends; used during the twentieth century by totalitarian states to control their populations.

mass politics   a political order characterized by mass political parties and universal male and (eventually) female suffrage.

mass society   a society in which the concerns of the majority—the lower classes—play a prominent role; characterized by extension of voting rights, an improved standard of living for the lower classes, and mass education.

materialism   the belief that everything mental, spiritual, or ideal is an outgrowth of physical forces and that truth is found in concrete material existence, not through feeling or intuition.

mercantilism   an economic theory that held that a nation's prosperity depended on its supply of gold and silver and that the total volume of trade is unchangeable; its adherents therefore advocated that the government play an active role in the economy by encouraging exports and discouraging imports, especially through the use of tariffs.

Mesolithic Age   the period from 10,000 to 7000 B.C.E., characterized by a gradual transition from a food-gathering and hunting economy to a food-producing economy.

Mesopotamia   the valley between the Tigris and Euphrates rivers.

metics   resident foreigners in ancient Athens who were not permitted full rights of citizenship but did receive the protection of the laws.

Middle Passage   the journey of slaves from Africa to the Americas as the middle leg of the triangular trade.

militarism   a policy of aggressive military preparedness; in particular, the large armies based on mass conscription and complex, inflexible plans for mobilization that most European nations had before World War I.

millenarianism   the belief that the end of the world is at hand and the kingdom of God is about to be established on earth.

ministerial responsibility   a tenet of nineteenth-century liberalism that held that ministers of the monarch should be responsible to the legislative assembly rather than to the monarch.

mir   a peasant village commune in Russia.

mobilization   the organization of troops and supplies for service in time of war.

Modern Devotion   a movement founded by Gerard Groote in the fourteenth century, aimed at a practical mysticism based on leading lives serving the needs of fellow human beings.

Modernism   the artistic and literary styles that emerged in the decades before 1914 as artists rebelled against traditional efforts to portray reality as accurately as possible (leading to Impressionism and Cubism) and writers explored new forms.

monasticism   a movement that began in early Christianity whose purpose was to create communities of men and women who practiced a communal life dedicated to God as a moral example to the world around them.

monk   a man who chooses to live a communal life divorced from the world in order to dedicate himself totally to the will of God.

monogamy   the practice of being married to one person at a time.

monotheism   the doctrine or belief that there is only one God.

Mountain   a faction in the National Convention during the French Revolution that represented the interests of the city of Paris and favored the execution of the king.

multiculturalism   a term referring to the connection of several cultural or ethnic groups within a society.

multinational corporation   a company with divisions in more than two countries.

mutual deterrence   the belief that nuclear war could best be prevented if both the United States and the Soviet Union had sufficient nuclear weapons so that even if one nation launched a preemptive first strike, the other could respond and devastate the attacker.

mystery religions   religions that involve initiation into secret rites that promise intense emotional involvement with spiritual forces and a greater chance of individual immortality.

mysticism   the immediate experience of oneness with God.

nationalism   a sense of national consciousness based on awareness of being part of a community—a "nation"—that has common institutions, traditions, language, and customs and that becomes the focus of the individual's primary political loyalty.

nationalities problem   the dilemma faced by the Austro-Hungarian Empire in trying to unite a wide variety of ethnic groups (Austrians, Hungarians, Poles, Croats, Czechs, Serbs, Slovaks, and Slovenes, among others) in an era when nationalism and calls for self-determination were coming to the fore.

nationalization   the process of converting a business or industry from private ownership to government control and ownership.

nation in arms   the people's army raised by universal mobilization to repel the foreign enemies of the French Revolution.

nation-state   a form of political organization in which a relatively homogeneous people inhabits a sovereign state, as opposed to a state containing people of several nationalities.

NATO   the North Atlantic Treaty Organization, a military alliance formed in 1949 in which the signatories (Belgium, Canada, Denmark, France, Great Britain, Iceland, Italy, Luxembourg, the Netherlands, Norway, Portugal, and the United States) agreed to provide mutual assistance if any one of them was attacked; later expanded to include other nations.

natural laws   a body of laws or specific principles held to be derived from nature and binding on all human societies even in the absence of written laws governing such matters.

natural rights   certain inalienable rights to which all people are entitled, including the right to life, liberty, and property; freedom of speech and religion; and equality before the law.

natural selection   Darwin's idea that organisms that are most adaptable to their environment survive and pass on the variations that enabled them to survive, while less adaptable organisms become extinct; "survival of the fittest."

Nazi New Order   the Nazis' plan for their conquered territories; it included the extermination of Jews and others considered inferior, ruthless exploitation of resources, German colonization in the east, and the use of Poles, Russians, and Ukrainians as slave labor.

Neoclassicism   a late-eighteenth-century artistic movement that emerged in France. It sought to recapture the dignity and simplicity of the Classical style of ancient Greece and Rome.

Neolithic Revolution   the shift from hunting animals and gathering plants for sustenance to producing food by systematic agriculture that occurred gradually between 10,000 and 4000 B.C.E. (the Neolithic or "New Stone" Age).

Neoplatonism   a revival of Platonic philosophy in the third century C.E., associated with Plotinus; a similar revival in the Italian

Renaissance, associated with Marsilio Ficino, who attempted to synthesize Christianity and Platonism.

nepotism the appointment of family members to important political positions; derived from the regular appointment of nephews (Latin, *nepos*) by Renaissance popes.

New Economic Policy a modified version of the old capitalist system introduced in the Soviet Union by Lenin in 1921 to revive the economy after the ravages of the civil war and war communism.

new imperialism the revival of imperialism after 1880 in which European nations established colonies throughout much of Asia and Africa.

new monarchies the governments of France, England, and Spain at the end of the fifteenth century, whose rulers succeeded in re-establishing or extending centralized royal authority, suppressing the nobility, controlling the church, and insisting on the loyalty of all peoples living in their territories.

nobiles "nobles." The small group of families from both patrician and plebeian origins who produced most of the men who were elected to office in the late Roman Republic.

nominalist a member of a school of thought in medieval Europe that, following Aristotle, held that only individual objects are real and that universals are only names created by humans.

nuclear family a family group consisting only of a father, a mother, and one or more children.

nuns women who withdrew from the world and joined a religious community; the female equivalent of monks.

old order (old regime) the political and social system of France in the eighteenth century before the Revolution.

oligarchy rule by a few.

optimates "best men." Aristocratic leaders in the late Roman Republic who generally came from senatorial families and wished to retain their oligarchical privileges.

orders *see* estates.

organic evolution Darwin's principle that all plants and animals have evolved over a long period of time from earlier and simpler forms of life.

Paleolithic Age the period of human history when humans used simple stone tools (c. 2,500,000–10,000 B.C.E.).

pantheism a doctrine that equates God with the universe and all that is in it.

panzer division in the German army under Hitler, a strike force of about three hundred tanks and accompanying forces and supplies.

papal curia the administrative staff of the Catholic Church, composed of cardinals who assist the pope in running the church.

parlements provincial law courts in France.

pasteurization a process developed by Louis Pasteur for heating a product to destroy the microorganisms that might cause spoilage.

paterfamilias the dominant male in a Roman family whose powers over his wife and children were theoretically unlimited, though they were sometimes circumvented in practice.

patriarchal family a family in which the husband dominates his wife and children.

patriarchy a society in which the father is supreme in the clan or family; more generally, a society dominated by men.

patricians great landowners who became the ruling class in the Roman Republic.

patronage the practice of awarding titles and making appointments to government and other positions to gain political support.

Pax Romana "Roman peace." A term used to refer to the stability and prosperity that Roman rule brought to the Mediterranean world and much of western Europe during the first and second centuries C.E.

Pentateuch the first five books of the Hebrew Bible (Genesis, Exodus, Leviticus, Numbers, and Deuteronomy).

perestroika "restructuring." A term applied to Mikhail Gorbachev's economic, political, and social reforms in the Soviet Union.

perioikoi in ancient Sparta, free inhabitants but not citizens who were required to pay taxes and perform military service.

permissive society a term applied to Western society after World War II to reflect the new sexual freedom and the emergence of a drug culture.

Petrine supremacy the doctrine that the bishop of Rome (the pope), as the successor of Saint Peter (traditionally considered the first bishop of Rome), should hold a preeminent position in the church.

phalanstery a self-sustaining cooperative community, as advocated by Charles Fourier in the early nineteenth century.

phalanx a rectangular formation of tightly massed infantry soldiers.

philosophes intellectuals of the eighteenth-century Enlightenment who believed in applying a spirit of rational criticism to all things, including religion and politics, and who focused on improving and enjoying this world, rather than on the afterlife.

Pietism a movement that arose in Germany in the seventeenth century whose goal was to foster a personal experience of God as the focus of true religious experience.

pig iron a type of iron produced by smelting iron ore with coke; of lower quality than wrought iron.

plebeians the class of Roman citizens that included nonpatrician landowners, craftspeople, merchants, and small farmers in the Roman Republic. Their struggle for equal rights with the patricians dominated much of the Republic's history.

plebiscita laws passed by the council of the plebs.

pluralism the practice of holding several church offices simultaneously; a problem of the late medieval church.

plutocrats members of the wealthy elite.

pogroms organized massacres of Jews.

polis an ancient Greek city-state encompassing both an urban area and its surrounding countryside; a small but autonomous political unit where all major political and social activities were carried out centrally.

political democracy a form of government characterized by universal suffrage and mass political parties.

politiques a group who emerged during the French Wars of Religion in the sixteenth century, placed politics above religion, and believed that no religious truth was worth the ravages of civil war.

polytheism belief in or worship of more than one god.

Pop Art an artistic movement of the 1950s and 1960s in which artists took images of popular culture and transformed them into works of fine art. Andy Warhol's painting of Campbell's soup cans is one example.

popular culture as opposed to high culture, the unofficial written and unwritten culture of the masses, much of which was traditionally passed down orally and centered on public and group activities such as festivals. In the modern age, the term refers to the entertainment, recreation, and pleasures that people purchase as part of the mass consumer society.

populares "favoring the people." Aristocratic leaders in the late Roman Republic who tended to use the people's assemblies in an effort to break the stranglehold of the *nobiles* on political offices.

popular sovereignty the doctrine that government is created by and subject to the will of the people, who are the source of all political power.

populism a political philosophy or movement that supports the rights and power of ordinary people in their struggle against the privileged elite.

portolani charts of landmasses and coastlines made by navigators and mathematicians in the thirteenth and fourteenth centuries.

Post-Impressionism   an artistic movement that began in France in the 1880s. Post-Impressionists sought to use color and line to express inner feelings and produce a personal statement of reality.

Postmodernism   a term used to cover a variety of artistic and intellectual styles and ways of thinking prominent since the 1970s.

praetor   a Roman executive official responsible for the administration of the law.

praetorian guard   the military unit that served as the personal bodyguard of the Roman emperors.

predestination   the belief, associated with Calvinism, that God, as a consequence of his foreknowledge of all events, has predetermined those who will be saved (the elect) and those who will be damned.

prefect   during the reign of Napoleon, an official appointed by the central government to oversee all aspects of a local government.

price revolution   the dramatic rise in prices (inflation) that occurred throughout Europe in the sixteenth and early seventeenth centuries.

primogeniture   an inheritance practice in which the eldest son receives all or the largest share of the parents' estate.

principate   the form of government established by Augustus for the Roman Empire; it continued the constitutional forms of the Republic and consisted of the *princeps* ("first citizen") and the senate, although the *princeps* was clearly the dominant partner.

procurator   the head of the Holy Synod, the chief decision-making body for the Russian Orthodox Church.

proletariat   the industrial working class. In Marxism, the class that will ultimately overthrow the bourgeoisie.

propaganda   a program of distorted information put out by an organization or government to spread its policy, cause, or doctrine.

psychoanalysis   a method developed by Sigmund Freud to resolve a patient's psychic conflict.

purgatory   defined by the Catholic Church as the place where souls went after death to be purged of punishment for sins committed in life.

Puritans   English Protestants inspired by Calvinist theology who wished to remove all traces of Catholicism from the Church of England.

quadrivium   arithmetic, geometry, astronomy, and music; four of the seven liberal arts (the others made up the *trivium*) that formed the basis of medieval and early modern education.

quaestors   Roman officials responsible for the administration of financial affairs.

querelles des femmes   "arguments about women." A centuries-old debate about the nature of women that continued during the Scientific Revolution as those who argued for the inferiority of women found additional support in the new anatomy and medicine.

rapprochement   the rebuilding of harmonious relations between nations.

rationalism   a system of thought based on the belief that human reason and experience are the chief sources of knowledge.

Realism   a nineteenth-century school of painting that emphasized the everyday life of ordinary people, depicted with photographic accuracy.

realist   a subscriber to the medieval European school of thought that held, following Plato, that the individual objects we perceive are not real but merely manifestations of universal ideas existing in the mind of God.

Realpolitik   "politics of reality." Politics based on practical concerns rather than theory or ethics.

reason of state   the principle that a nation should act on the basis of its long-term interests and not merely to further the dynastic interests of its ruling family.

Reconquista   in Spain, the reconquest of Muslim lands by Christian rulers and their armies.

relativity theory   Einstein's theory that, among other things, (1) space and time are not absolute but are relative to the observer and interwoven into a four-dimensional space-time continuum and (2) matter is a form of energy ($E = mc^2$).

relics   the bones of Christian saints or objects intimately associated with saints that were considered worthy of veneration.

Renaissance   the "rebirth" of Classical culture that occurred in Italy between c. 1350 and c. 1550; also, the earlier revivals of Classical culture that occurred under Charlemagne and in the twelfth century.

rentier   a person who lives on income from property and is not personally involved in its operation.

reparations   payments made by a defeated nation after a war to compensate another nation for damage sustained as a result of the war; required from Germany after World War I.

revisionism   a socialist doctrine that rejected Marx's emphasis on class struggle and revolution and argued instead that workers should work through political parties to bring about gradual change.

revolution   a fundamental change in the political and social organization of a state.

revolutionary socialism   a socialist doctrine that violent action was the only way to achieve the goals of socialism.

rhetoric   the art of persuasive speaking; in the Middle Ages, one of the seven liberal arts.

risorgimento   a movement in Italy in the nineteenth century aimed at the creation of a united Italian republic.

Rococo   an eighteenth-century artistic movement that emphasized grace, gentility, lightness, and charm.

Romanesque   a term used to describe the art and especially architecture of Europe in the eleventh and twelfth centuries.

Romanization   the process by which Roman culture and institutions were spread to the provinces; often accomplished through the Roman army as colonies of veterans were established wherever the legions were stationed throughout the empire.

Romanticism   a nineteenth-century intellectual and artistic movement that rejected the emphasis on reason of the Enlightenment. Instead, Romantics stressed the importance of intuition, feeling, emotion, and imagination as sources of knowing.

sacraments   rites considered imperative for a Christian's salvation. By the thirteenth century, these consisted of the Eucharist or Lord's Supper, baptism, marriage, penance, extreme unction, holy orders, and confirmation of children; Protestant reformers of the sixteenth century generally recognized only two—baptism and communion (the Lord's Supper).

salons   gatherings of philosophes and other notables to discuss the ideas of the Enlightenment; so called from the elegant drawing rooms (salons) where they met.

sans-culottes   "without breeches." The common people, who did not wear the fine clothes of the upper classes and played an important role in the radical phase of the French Revolution.

satrap   a governor with both civil and military duties in the ancient Persian Empire, which was divided into satrapies, or provinces, each administered by a satrap.

scholasticism   the philosophical and theological system of the medieval schools, which emphasized rigorous analysis of contradictory authorities; often used to try to reconcile faith and reason.

scientific method   a method of seeking knowledge through inductive principles, using experiments and observations to develop generalizations.

Scientific Revolution   the transition from the medieval world-view to a largely secular, rational, and materialistic perspective that began in the seventeenth century and was popularized in the eighteenth.

scriptoria   writing rooms for the copying of manuscripts in medieval monasteries.

scutage   in the fourteenth century, a money payment for military service that replaced the obligation of military service in the lord-vassal relationship.

secularism   the process of becoming more concerned with material, worldly, temporal things and less with spiritual and religious things; a characteristic of the Italian Renaissance.

self-determination   the doctrine that the people of a given territory or a particular nationality should have the right to determine their own government and political future.

senate   the leading council of the Roman Republic; composed of about three hundred men (senators) who served for life and dominated much of the political life of the Republic.

separation of powers   a doctrine enunciated by Montesquieu in the eighteenth century that separate executive, legislative, and judicial powers serve to limit and control each other.

serf   a peasant who is bound to the land and obliged to provide labor services and pay various rents and fees to the lord; considered unfree but not a slave because serfs could not be bought and sold.

skepticism   a doubtful or questioning attitude, especially about religion.

social Darwinism   the application of Darwin's principle of organic evolution to the social order; led to the belief that progress comes from the struggle for survival as the fittest advance and the weak decline.

socialism   an ideology that calls for collective or government ownership of the means of production and the distribution of goods.

socialized medicine   health services for all citizens provided by government assistance.

social security   government programs that provide social welfare measures such as old-age pensions and sickness, accident, and disability insurance.

Socratic method   a form of teaching that uses a question-and-answer format to enable students to reach conclusions by using their own reasoning.

Sophists   wandering scholars and professional teachers in ancient Greece who stressed the importance of rhetoric and tended toward skepticism and relativism.

soviets   councils of workers' and soldiers' deputies formed throughout Russia in 1917 that played an important role in the Bolshevik Revolution.

sphere of influence   a territory or region over which an outside nation exercises political or economic influence.

squadristi   in Italy in the 1920s, bands of armed Fascists used to create disorder by attacking Socialist offices and newspapers.

stagflation   a combination of high inflation and high unemployment that was prevalent in the United States and elsewhere from 1973 to the mid-1980s.

Stalinization   the adoption by Eastern European Communist countries of features of the economic, political, and military policies implemented by Stalin in the Soviet Union.

Stoicism   a philosophy founded by Zeno in the fourth century B.C.E. that taught that happiness could be obtained by accepting one's lot and living in harmony with the will of God, thereby achieving inner peace.

subinfeudation   the practice whereby a lord's greatest vassals subdivided their fiefs and had vassals of their own, who in turn subdivided their fiefs, and so on down to simple knights, whose fiefs were too small to subdivide.

suffrage   the right to vote.

suffragists   advocates of extending the right to vote to women.

sultan   "holder of power." A title taken by Turkish leaders who took command of the Abbasid Empire in 1055.

surplus value   in Marxism, the difference between a product's real value and the wages of the worker who produced the product.

Surrealism   an artistic movement that arose between World War I and World War II. Surrealists portrayed recognizable objects in unrecognizable relationships in order to reveal the world of the unconscious.

syncretism   the combining of different forms of belief or practice, as, for example, when two gods are regarded as different forms of the same underlying divine force and are fused together.

tariffs   duties (taxes) imposed on imported goods, usually to raise revenue and to discourage imports and protect domestic industries.

tetrarchy   rule by four; the system of government established by Diocletian (284–305) in which the Roman Empire was divided into two parts, each ruled by an "Augustus" assisted by a "Caesar."

theocracy   a government ruled by a divine authority.

Third Estate   one of the traditional tripartite divisions (orders) of European society based on heredity and quality rather than wealth or economic standing, first established in the Middle Ages and continuing into the eighteenth century; consisted of all who were not members of the clergy or nobility (the first two estates).

three-field system   in medieval agriculture, the practice of dividing the arable land into three fields so that one could lie fallow while the others were planted in winter grains and spring crops.

tithe   a portion of one's harvest or income, paid by medieval peasants to the village church.

Torah   the body of law in Hebrew Scripture, contained in the Pentateuch (the first five books of the Hebrew Bible).

totalitarian state   a state characterized by government control over all aspects of economic, social, political, cultural, and intellectual life, the subordination of the individual to the state, and insistence that the masses be actively involved in the regime's goals.

total war   warfare in which all of a nation's resources, including civilians at home as well as soldiers in the field, are mobilized for the war effort.

trade union   an association of workers in the same trade, formed to help members secure better wages, benefits, and working conditions.

transformism   the theory that societies evolve gradually.

transnational corporation   another term for "a multinational corporation," or a company with divisions in more than two countries.

transubstantiation   a doctrine of the Roman Catholic Church that during the Eucharist, the substance of the bread and wine is miraculously transformed into the body and blood of Jesus.

trench warfare   warfare in which the opposing forces attack and counterattack from a relatively permanent system of trenches protected by barbed wire; a characteristic of World War I.

triangular trade   a pattern of trade in early modern Europe that connected Europe, Africa, and the Americas in an Atlantic economy.

tribunes of the plebs   beginning in 494 B.C.E., Roman officials who were given the power to protect plebeians against arrest by patrician magistrates.

trivium   grammar, rhetoric, and dialectic or logic; three of the seven liberal arts (the others made up the *quadrivium*) that were the basis of medieval and early modern education.

Truman Doctrine   the doctrine, enunciated by Harry Truman in 1947, that the United States would provide economic aid to countries that said they were threatened by Communist expansion.

tyrant   in an ancient Greek *polis* (or an Italian city-state during the Renaissance), a ruler who came to power in an unconstitutional way and ruled without being subject to the law.

ultraroyalists   in nineteenth-century France, a group of aristocrats who sought to return to a monarchical system dominated by a landed aristocracy and the Catholic Church.

uncertainty principle   a principle in quantum mechanics, posited by Heisenberg, that holds that one cannot determine the path of an electron because the very act of observing the electron would affect its location.

unconditional surrender   complete, unqualified surrender of a belligerent nation.

utopian socialists   intellectuals and theorists in the early nineteenth century who favored equality in social and economic conditions and wished to replace private property and competition with collective ownership and cooperation.

vassalage   the granting of a fief, or landed estate, in exchange for providing military services to the lord and fulfilling certain other obligations such as appearing at the lord's court when summoned and making a payment on the knighting of the lord's eldest son.

vernacular   the everyday language of a region, as distinguished from a language used for special purposes. For example, in medieval Paris, French was the vernacular, but Latin was used for academic writing and for classes at the University of Paris.

viceroy   the administrative head of the provinces of New Spain and Peru in the Americas.

volkish **thought**   the belief that German culture is superior and that the German people have a universal mission to save Western civilization from "inferior" races.

war communism   Lenin's policy of nationalizing industrial and other facilities and requisitioning the peasants' produce during the civil war in Russia.

war guilt clause   the clause in the Treaty of Versailles that declared that Germany (with Austria) was responsible for starting World War I and ordered Germany to pay reparations for the damage the Allies had suffered as a result of the war.

Warsaw Pact   a military alliance, formed in 1955, in which Albania, Bulgaria, Czechoslovakia, East Germany, Hungary, Poland, Romania, and the Soviet Union agreed to provide mutual assistance.

welfare state   a sociopolitical system in which the government assumes primary responsibility for the social welfare of its citizens by providing such things as social security, unemployment benefits, and health care.

wergeld   "money for a man." In early Germanic law, a person's value in monetary terms, paid by a wrongdoer to the family of the person who had been injured or killed.

world-machine   Newton's conception of the universe as one huge, regulated, and uniform machine that operated according to natural laws in absolute time, space, and motion.

wrought iron   a high-quality iron first produced during the eighteenth century in Britain; manufactured by puddling, a process developed by Henry Cort that involved using coke to burn away the impurities in pig iron.

zemstvos   local assemblies established in Russia in 1864 by Tsar Alexander II.

ziggurat   a massive stepped tower on which a temple dedicated to the chief god or goddess of a Sumerian city was built.

Zionism   an international movement that called for the establishment of a Jewish state or a refuge for Jews in Palestine.

Zollverein   the customs union of all the German states except Austria, formed by Prussia in 1834.

Zoroastrianism   a religion founded by the Persian Zoroaster in the seventh century B.C.E., characterized by worship of a supreme god, Ahuramazda, who represents the good against the evil spirit, identified as Ahriman.

CHAPTER NOTES

CHAPTER 11

1. Quoted in H. S. Lucas, "The Great European Famine of 1315, 1316, and 1317," *Speculum* 5 (1930): 359.
2. Quoted in Christos S. Bartsocas, "Two Fourteenth-Century Descriptions of the 'Black Death,'" *Journal of the History of Medicine* (October 1966): 395.
3. Quoted in David Herlihy, *The Black Death and the Transformation of the West,* ed. Samuel K. Cohn Jr. (Cambridge, Mass., 1997), p. 9.
4. Quoted in Rosemary Horrox, ed., *The Black Death* (Manchester, England, 1994), pp. 18–19.
5. Giovanni Boccaccio, *Decameron,* trans. Frances Winwar (New York, 1955), p. xxv.
6. Ibid., p. xxvi.
7. Jean Froissart, *Chronicles,* ed. and trans. Geoffrey Brereton (Harmondsworth, England, 1968), p. 111.
8. Quoted in James B. Ross and Mary M. McLaughlin, *The Portable Medieval Reader* (New York, 1949), pp. 218–219.
9. Quoted in Barbara W. Tuchman, *A Distant Mirror* (New York, 1978), p. 175.
10. Froissart, *Chronicles,* p. 212.
11. Ibid., p. 89.
12. Oliver J. Thatcher and Edgar H. McNeal, eds., *A Source Book for Medieval History* (New York, 1905), p. 288.
13. Quoted in D. S. Chambers, *The Imperial Age of Venice, 1380–1580* (London, 1970), p. 30.
14. Quoted in Robert Coogan, *Babylon on the Rhône: A Translation of Letters by Dante, Petrarch, and Catherine of Siena* (Washington, D.C., 1983), p. 115.
15. Quoted in Caroline Walker Bynum, *Holy Feast and Holy Fast: The Religious Significance of Food to Medieval Women* (Berkeley, Calif., 1987), p. 180.
16. Dante Alighieri, *Divine Comedy,* trans. Dorothy Sayers (New York, 1962), "Paradise," canto 33, line 145.
17. Petrarch, *Sonnets and Songs,* trans. Anna Maria Armi (New York, 1968), no. 74, p. 127.
18. Quoted in Millard Meiss, *Painting in Florence and Siena After the Black Death* (Princeton, N.J., 1951), p. 161.
19. Geoffrey Chaucer, *The Canterbury Tales,* in *The Portable Chaucer,* ed. Theodore Morrison (New York, 1949), p. 67.
20. Christine de Pizan, *The Book of the City of Ladies,* trans. E. Jeffrey Richards (New York, 1982), pp. 83–84.
21. Quoted in Susan Mosher Stuard, "The Dominion of Gender, or How Women Fared in the High Middle Ages," in Renate Bridenthal, Claudia Koonz, and Susan Stuard, eds., *Becoming Visible: Women in European History,* 3rd ed. (Boston, 1998), p. 147.
22. Quoted in David Herlihy, "Medieval Children," in Bede K. Lackner and Kenneth R. Philp, eds., *Essays on Medieval Civilization* (Austin, Tex., 1978), p. 121.
23. Quoted in Jean Gimpel, *The Medieval Machine* (New York, 1976), p. 168.

CHAPTER 12

1. Quoted in Jacob Burckhardt, *The Civilization of the Renaissance in Italy,* trans. S. G. C. Middlemore (London, 1960), p. 81.
2. Baldassare Castiglione, *The Book of the Courtier,* trans. Charles S. Singleton (Garden City, N.Y., 1959), pp. 288–289.
3. Quoted in De Lamar Jensen, *Renaissance Europe* (Lexington, Mass., 1981), p. 94.
4. Quoted in Iris Origo, "The Domestic Enemy: The Eastern Slaves in Tuscany in the Fourteenth and Fifteenth Centuries," *Speculum* 30 (1955): 333.
5. Quoted in Gene Brucker, ed., *Two Memoirs of Renaissance Florence* (New York, 1967), p. 132.
6. Quoted in Margaret L. King, *Women of the Renaissance* (Chicago, 1991), p. 3.
7. Quoted in Gene Brucker, ed., *The Society of Renaissance Florence* (New York, 1971), p. 190.
8. Quoted in Garrett Mattingly, *Renaissance Diplomacy* (Baltimore, 1964), p. 42.
9. Ibid., p. 95.
10. Niccolò Machiavelli, *The Prince,* trans. David Wootton (Indianapolis, 1995), p. 48.
11. Ibid., p. 55.
12. Ibid., p. 27.
13. Petrarch, "Epistle to Posterity," *Letters from Petrarch,* trans. Morris Bishop (Bloomington, Ind., 1966), pp. 6–7.
14. Quoted in Frances Yates, *Giordano Bruno and the Hermetic Tradition* (Chicago, 1964), p. 211.
15. Giovanni Pico della Mirandola, *Oration on the Dignity of Man,* in E. Cassirer, P. O. Kristeller, and J. H. Randall Jr., eds., *The Renaissance Philosophy of Man* (Chicago, 1948), p. 225.
16. Ibid., pp. 247, 249.
17. Quoted in W. H. Woodward, *Vittorino da Feltre and Other Humanist Educators* (Cambridge, 1897), p. 102.
18. Quoted in Iris Origo, *The Light of the Past* (New York, 1959), p. 136.
19. Quoted in Elizabeth G. Holt, ed., *A Documentary History of Art* (Garden City, N.Y., 1957), vol. 1, p. 286.
20. Quoted in Rosa M. Letts, *The Cambridge Introduction to Art: The Renaissance* (Cambridge, 1981), p. 86.
21. Quoted in Johan Huizinga, *The Waning of the Middle Ages* (Garden City, N.Y., 1956), p. 265.

CHAPTER 13

1. Desiderius Erasmus, *The Paraclesis,* in John Olin, ed., *Christian Humanism and the Reformation: Selected Writings of Erasmus,* 3rd ed. (New York, 1987), p. 101.
2. Thomas More, *Utopia,* trans. Paul Turner (Harmondsworth, England, 1965), p. 76.
3. Quoted in Alister E. McGrath, *Reformation Thought: An Introduction* (Oxford, 1988), p. 72.
4. Quoted in Gordon Rupp, *Luther's Progress to the Diet of Worms* (New York, 1964), p. 82.

5. Martin Luther, *On the Freedom of a Christian Man,* quoted in E. G. Rupp and Benjamin Drewery, eds., *Martin Luther* (New York, 1970), p. 50.

6. Quoted in Roland Bainton, *Here I Stand: A Life of Martin Luther* (New York, 1950), p. 144.

7. Quoted in De Lamar Jensen, *Reformation Europe* (Lexington, Mass., 1981), p. 83.

8. Quoted in Lee Palmer Wandel, *Voracious Idols and Violent Hands: Iconoclasm in Reformation Zürich, Strasbourg, and Basel* (New York, 1995), p. 81.

9. Quoted in A. G. Dickens and Dorothy Carr, eds., *The Reformation in England to the Accession of Elizabeth I* (New York, 1968), p. 72.

10. Quoted in Lewis W. Spitz, *The Renaissance and Reformation Movements* (Chicago, 1971), p. 414.

11. John Calvin, *Institutes of the Christian Religion,* trans. John Allen (Philadelphia, 1936), vol. 1, p. 220.

12. Ibid., vol. 1, p. 228; vol. 2, p. 181.

13. Quoted in Roland Bainton, *Women of the Reformation in Germany and Italy* (Minneapolis, 1971), p. 154.

14. Quoted in Bonnie S. Anderson and Judith P. Zinsser, *A History of Their Own: Women in Europe from Prehistory to the Present* (New York, 1988), vol. 1, p. 259.

15. Quoted in John A. Phillips, *Eve: The History of an Idea* (New York, 1984), p. 105.

16. Quoted in John O'Malley, *The First Jesuits* (Cambridge, Mass., 1993), p. 76.

17. Quoted in R. J. Knecht, *The French Wars of Religion, 1559–1598,* 2nd ed. (New York, 1996), p. 47.

18. Quoted in Mack P. Holt, *The French Wars of Religion, 1562–1629* (Cambridge, 1995), p. 86.

19. Quoted in Garrett Mattingly, *The Armada* (Boston, 1959), pp. 216–217.

20. Quoted in Theodore Schieder, *Handbuch der Europäischen Geschichte* (Stuttgart, 1979), vol. 3, p. 579.

CHAPTER 14

1. Quoted in J. R. Hale, *Renaissance Exploration* (New York, 1968), p. 32.

2. Quoted in J. H. Parry, *The Age of Reconnaissance: Discovery, Exploration, and Settlement, 1450 to 1650* (New York, 1963), p. 33.

3. Quoted in Richard B. Reed, "The Expansion of Europe," in Richard De Molen, ed., *The Meaning of the Renaissance and Reformation* (Boston, 1974), p. 308.

4. Quoted in K. N. Chaudhuri, *Trade and Civilization in the Indian Ocean: An Economic History from the Rise of Islam to 1750* (Cambridge, 1985), p. 65.

5. Quoted in Ian Cameron, *Explorers and Exploration* (New York, 1991), p. 42.

6. Bernal Díaz, *The Conquest of New Spain* (New York, 1963), pp. 405–406.

7. Quoted in J. H. Parry and Robert G. Keith, eds., *New Iberian World,* vol. 2 (New York, 1984), pp. 309–310.

8. Quoted in J. H. Elliott, *Empires of the Atlantic World* (New Haven, Conn., 2006), p. 125.

9. Quoted in A. Andrea and J. H. Overfield, *The Human Record: Sources of Global History,* 3rd ed. (Boston, 1998), p. 460.

10. Quoted in Basil Davidson, *Africa in History: Themes and Outlines,* rev. ed. (New York, 1991), p. 198.

11. Quoted in Cameron, *Explorers and Exploration,* p. 42.

12. Quoted in Louis J. Gallagher, ed. and trans., *China in the Sixteenth Century: The Journals of Matthew Ricci* (New York, 1953), p. 154.

13. Quoted in G. V. Scammell, *The First Imperial Age: European Overseas Expansion, c. 1400–1715* (London, 1989), p. 62.

14. Miguel Leon-Portilla, ed., *The Broken Spears: The Aztec Account of the Conquest of Mexico* (Boston, 1969), p. 51.

CHAPTER 15

1. Quoted in Joseph Klaits, *Servants of Satan: The Age of the Witch Hunts* (Bloomington, Ind., 1985), p. 68.

2. Quoted in Peter H. Wilson, *The Thirty Years War: Europe's Tragedy* (Cambridge, Mass., 2009), p. 783.

3. Quoted in John B. Wolf, *Louis XIV* (New York, 1968), p. 134.

4. Quoted in James B. Collins, *The State in Early Modern France* (Cambridge, 1995), p. 130.

5. Quoted in Wolf, *Louis XIV,* p. 618.

6. Quoted in D. H. Pennington, *Europe in the Seventeenth Century,* 2nd ed. (New York, 1989), p. 494.

7. Quoted in J. H. Elliot, *Imperial Spain, 1469–1716* (New York, 1963), p. 306.

8. Quoted in B. H. Sumner, *Peter the Great and the Emergence of Russia* (New York, 1962), p. 122.

9. Quoted in Simon Schama, *A History of Britain,* vol. 2, *The Wars of the British, 1603–1776* (New York, 2001), pp. 182, 185.

CHAPTER 16

1. Quoted in Alan G. R. Smith, *Science and Society in the Sixteenth and Seventeenth Centuries* (London, 1972), p. 59.

2. Edward MacCurdy, *The Notebooks of Leonardo da Vinci* (London, 1948), vol. 1, p. 634.

3. Ibid., p. 636.

4. Frances Yates, *Giordano Bruno and the Hermetic Tradition* (New York, 1964), p. 448.

5. Ibid., p. 450.

6. Quoted in Smith, *Science and Society,* p. 97.

7. Logan P. Smith, *Life and Letters of Sir Henry Wotton* (Oxford, 1907), vol. 1, pp. 486–487.

8. Quoted in John H. Randall, *The Making of the Modern Mind* (Boston, 1926), p. 234.

9. Quoted in Smith, *Science and Society,* p. 124.

10. Quoted in Betty J. Dobbs, *The Foundations of Newton's Alchemy* (Cambridge, 1975), pp. 13–14.

11. Jolande Jacobi, ed., *Paracelsus: Selected Writings* (New York, 1965), pp. 5–6.

12. Ibid., p. 21.

13. Quoted in Londa Schiebinger, *The Mind Has No Sex? Women in the Origins of Modern Science* (Cambridge, Mass., 1989), pp. 52–53.

14. Ibid., p. 85.

15. Quoted in Phyllis Stock, *Better than Rubies: A History of Women's Education* (New York, 1978), p. 16.

16. René Descartes, *Philosophical Writings,* ed. and trans. Norman K. Smith (New York, 1958), p. 95.

17. Ibid., pp. 118–119.

18. Francis Bacon, *The Great Instauration,* trans. Jerry Weinberger (Arlington Heights, Ill., 1989), pp. 2, 8, 16, 21.

19. Descartes, *Discourse on Method,* in *Philosophical Writings,* p. 75.

20. Margaret C. Jacob, *The Cultural Meaning of the Scientific Revolution* (New York, 1988), p. 73.

21. Stillman Drake, ed. and trans., *Discoveries and Opinions of Galileo* (New York, 1957), p. 182.

22. Benedict de Spinoza, *Ethics,* trans. R. H. M. Elwes (New York, 1955), pp. 75–76.

23. Ibid., p. 76.

24. Spinoza, *Letters,* quoted in Randall, *The Making of the Modern Mind,* p. 247.
25. Blaise Pascal, *Pensées,* trans. J. M. Cohen (Harmondsworth, England, 1961), p. 100.
26. Ibid., pp. 31, 52–53, 164, 165.

CHAPTER 17

1. Quoted in Paul Hazard, *The European Mind, 1680–1715* (New York, 1963), pp. 304–305.
2. Quoted in Dorinda Outram, *The Enlightenment* (Cambridge, 1995), p. 67.
3. Quoted in Hazard, *The European Mind,* p. 12.
4. John Locke, *An Essay Concerning Human Understanding* (New York, 1964), pp. 89–90.
5. Baron Paul d'Holbach, *Common Sense,* as quoted in Frank E. Manuel, ed., *The Enlightenment* (Englewood Cliffs, N.J., 1965), p. 62.
6. Jean-Jacques Rousseau, *A Discourse on Inequality,* trans. Maurice Cranston (Harmondsworth, England, 1984), p. 109.
7. Jean-Jacques Rousseau, *The Social Contract,* trans. Maurice Cranston (Harmondsworth, England, 1968), p. 141.
8. Mary Astell, *A Serious Proposal to the Ladies,* in Moira Ferguson, ed., *First Feminists: British Women Writers, 1578–1799* (Bloomington, Ind., 1985), p. 190.
9. Mary Astell, *Some Reflections upon Marriage,* in ibid., p. 193.
10. Kenneth Clark, *Civilization* (New York, 1969), p. 231.
11. Voltaire, *The Age of Louis XIV,* trans. Martyn P. Pollack (New York, 1961), p. 1.
12. Cesare Beccaria, *An Essay on Crimes and Punishments,* trans. E. D. Ingraham (Philadelphia, 1819), pp. 59–60.
13. Quoted in René Sand, *The Advance to Social Medicine* (London, 1952), pp. 86–87.
14. Quoted in Peter Burke, *Popular Culture in Early Modern Europe* (New York, 1978), p. 179.
15. Quoted in ibid., p. 186.
16. Quoted in C. A. Macartney, *The Habsburg and Hohenzollern Dynasties in the Seventeenth and Eighteenth Centuries* (New York, 1970), p. 157.

CHAPTER 18

1. Frederick II, *Forms of Government,* in Eugen Weber, *The Western Tradition* (Lexington, Mass., 1972), pp. 538, 544.
2. Quoted in Reinhold A. Dorwart, *The Administrative Reforms of Frederick William I of Prussia* (Cambridge, Mass., 1953), p. 36.
3. Quoted in Sidney B. Fay, *The Rise of Brandenburg-Prussia to 1786,* rev. Klaus Epstein (New York, 1964), p. 92.
4. Quoted in Hans Rosenberg, *Bureaucracy, Aristocracy, and Autocracy: The Prussian Experience, 1660–1815* (Cambridge, Mass., 1958), p. 40.
5. Quoted in Fernand Braudel, *Civilization and Capitalism* (London, 1981–1984), vol. 3, p. 378.
6. Quoted in ibid., p. 245.
7. Quoted in Witold Rybczynski, *Home: A Short History of an Idea* (New York, 1986), p. 105.
8. Quoted in Jonathan Dewald, *The European Nobility, 1400–1800* (Cambridge, 1996), pp. 91–92.
9. Quoted in Peter Gay, *Age of Enlightenment* (New York, 1966), p. 87.
10. Quoted in Paul Hazard, *The European Mind, 1680–1715* (Cleveland, Ohio, 1963), pp. 6–7.
11. Igor Vinogradoff, "Russian Missions to London, 1711–1789: Further Extracts from the Cottrell Papers," *Oxford Slavonic Papers,* New Series (1982), 15:76.

12. Quoted in Jeffrey Kaplow, *The Names of Kings: The Parisian Laboring Poor in the Eighteenth Century* (New York, 1972), p. 134.

CHAPTER 19

1. Quoted in R. R. Palmer, *The Age of the Democratic Revolutions* (Princeton, N.J., 1959), vol. 1, p. 239.
2. Quoted in ibid., p. 242.
3. Quoted in O. J. Hufton, "Toward an Understanding of the Poor of Eighteenth-Century France," in J. F. Bosher, ed., *French Government and Society, 1500–1850* (London, 1973), p. 152.
4. Arthur Young, *Travels in France During the Years 1787, 1788, and 1789* (Cambridge, 1929), p. 23.
5. Quoted in D. M. G. Sutherland, *France, 1789–1815: Revolution and Counter-Revolution* (New York, 1986), p. 74.
6. Quoted in William Doyle, *The Oxford History of the French Revolution* (Oxford, 1989), p. 156.
7. Quoted in ibid., p. 184.
8. Quoted in J. Hardman, ed., *French Revolution Documents* (Oxford, 1973), vol. 2, p. 23.
9. Quoted in W. Scott, *Terror and Repression in Revolutionary Marseilles* (London, 1973), p. 84.
10. Quoted in H. Morse Stephens, *The Principal Speeches of the Statesmen and Orators of the French Revolution* (Oxford, 1892), vol. 2, p. 189.
11. Quoted in Leo Gershoy, *The Era of the French Revolution* (Princeton, N.J., 1957), p. 157.
12. Quoted in J. M. Thompson, ed., *French Revolution Documents* (Oxford, 1933), pp. 258–259.
13. Quoted in Doyle, *Oxford History of the French Revolution,* p. 254.
14. Quoted in R. R. Palmer, *Twelve Who Ruled* (New York, 1965), p. 75.
15. Quoted in Darline Gay Levy, Harriet Branson Applewhite, and Mary Durham Johnson, eds., *Women in Revolutionary Paris, 1789–1795* (Urbana, Ill., 1979), p. 132.
16. Ibid., pp. 219–220.
17. Quoted in Elizabeth G. Sledziewski, "The French Revolution as the Turning Point," in Geneviève Fraisse and Michelle Perrot, eds., *A History of Women in the West* (Cambridge, 1993), vol. 4, p. 39.
18. Quoted in François Furet and Mona Ozouf, *A Critical Dictionary of the French Revolution,* trans. Arthur Goldhammer (Cambridge, Mass., 1989), p. 545.
19. Quoted in J. Christopher Herold, ed., *The Mind of Napoleon* (New York, 1955), p. 43.
20. Quoted in Felix Markham, *Napoleon* (New York, 1963), pp. 92–93.
21. Quoted in Doyle, *Oxford History of the French Revolution,* p. 381.
22. Quoted in Herold, ed., *The Mind of Napoleon,* pp. 74–75.
23. Quoted in Steven Englund, *Napoleon: A Political Life* (New York, 2004), p. 285.

CHAPTER 20

1. Quoted in W. Gordon Rimmer, *Marshall's of Leeds, Flax-Spinners, 1788–1886* (Cambridge, 1960), p. 40.
2. Daniel Defoe, *A Plan of the English Commerce* (Oxford, 1928), pp. 76–77.
3. Quoted in Albert Tucker, *A History of English Civilization* (New York, 1972), p. 583.
4. Quotations are from Lara Kriegel, *Grand Designs: Labor, Empire, and the Museum in Victorian Culture* (Durham, N.C., 2007), p. 120.

5. Quoted in E. Royston Pike, *Human Documents of the Industrial Revolution in Britain* (London, 1966), p. 320.

6. Ibid., p. 314.

7. Ibid., p. 343.

8. Ibid., p. 315.

9. Charles Dickens, *The Old Curiosity Shop* (New York, 2000), p. 340.

10. Quoted in A. J. Donajgrodzi, ed., *Social Control in Nineteenth-Century Britain* (London, 1977), p. 141.

11. Quoted in Pike, *Human Documents,* pp. 343–344.

12. Quoted in Eric J. Evans, *The Forging of the Modern State: Early Industrial Britain, 1783–1870* (London, 1983), p. 113.

13. Henry Mayhew, *London Labour and the London Poor* (London, 1851), vol.1, pp. 342–343.

14. Quoted in Pike, *Human Documents,* pp. 60–61.

15. Quoted in Evans, *Forging of the Modern State,* p. 124.

CHAPTER 21

1. Quoted in Charles Breunig, *The Age of Revolution and Reaction, 1789–1850* (New York, 1970), p. 119.

2. Quoted in M. S. Anderson, *The Ascendancy of Europe, 1815–1914,* 2nd ed. (London, 1985), p. 1.

3. Quotations from Burke can be found in Peter Viereck, *Conservatism* (Princeton, N.J., 1956), pp. 27, 114.

4. Quoted in René Albrecht-Carrié, *The Concert of Europe* (New York, 1968), p. 48.

5. Quoted in M. C. Eakin, *The History of Latin America: Collision of Cultures* (New York, 2007), p. 188.

6. Quoted in G. de Berthier de Sauvigny, *Metternich and His Times* (London, 1962), p. 105.

7. Quoted in S. Joan Moon, "Feminism and Socialism: The Utopian Synthesis of Flora Tristan," in Marilyn J. Boxer and Jean H. Quataert, eds., *Socialist Women* (New York, 1978), p. 38.

8. Quoted in Stanley Z. Pech, *The Czech Revolution of 1848* (Chapel Hill, N.C., 1969), p. 82.

9. Quoted in Clive Emsley, *Policing and Its Context, 1750–1870* (New York, 1984), p. 58.

10. Quoted in Clive Emsley, *Crime and Society in England, 1750–1900* (London, 1987), p. 173.

11. Quoted in Emsley, *Policing and Its Context,* p. 66.

12. Quoted in ibid., p. 102.

13. Quoted in Emsley, *Crime and Society in England,* p. 226.

14. William Wordsworth, "The Tables Turned," *Poems of Wordsworth,* ed. Matthew Arnold (London, 1963), p. 138.

15. William Wordsworth, *The Prelude* (Harmondsworth, England, 1971), p. 109.

16. Quoted in H. G. Schenk, *The Mind of the European Romantics* (Garden City, N.Y., 1969), p. 205.

17. Quoted in Siegbert Prawer, ed., *The Romantic Period in Germany* (London, 1970), p. 285.

18. Quoted in John B. Halsted, ed., *Romanticism* (New York, 1969), p. 156.

CHAPTER 22

1. Quoted in James F. McMillan, *Napoleon III* (New York, 1991), p. 37.

2. Quoted in Robert Gildea, *Barricades and Borders: Europe, 1800–1914,* 2nd ed. (Oxford, 1996), p. 170.

3. Quoted in Otto Pflanze, *Bismarck and the Development of Germany: The Period of Unification, 1815–1871* (Princeton, N.J., 1963), p. 60.

4. Louis L. Snyder, ed., *Documents of German History* (New Brunswick, N.J., 1958), p. 202.

5. Quoted in Pflanze, *Bismarck and the Development of Germany,* p. 327.

6. Quoted in György Szabad, *Hungarian Political Trends Between the Revolution and the Compromise, 1849–1867* (Budapest, 1977), p. 163.

7. Quoted in Rondo Cameron, "Crédit Mobilier and the Economic Development of Europe," *Journal of Political Economy* 61 (1953): 470.

8. Karl Marx and Friedrich Engels, *The Communist Manifesto* (Harmondsworth, England, 1967), p. 79.

9. Ibid., pp. 79, 81, 82.

10. Charles Darwin, *On the Origin of Species* (New York, 1872), vol. 1, pp. 77, 79.

11. Quoted in Albert Lyons and R. Joseph Petrucelli, *Medicine: An Illustrated History* (New York, 1978), p. 569.

CHAPTER 23

1. Quoted in David Landes, *The Unbound Prometheus: Technological Change and Industrial Development in Western Europe from 1750 to the Present* (Cambridge, 1969), p. 353.

2. Quoted in Barbara Franzoi, ". . . With the Wolf Always at the Door: Women's Work in Domestic Industry in Britain and Germany," in Marilyn J. Boxer and Jean H. Quataert, eds., *Connecting Spheres: Women in the Western World, 1500 to the Present* (New York, 1987), p. 151.

3. Quoted in W. L. Guttsman, *The German Social Democratic Party, 1875–1933* (London, 1981), p. 63.

4. Quoted in Leslie Derfler, *Socialism Since Marx: A Century of the European Left* (New York, 1973), p. 58.

5. Karl Marx and Friedrich Engels, *The Communist Manifesto* (Harmondsworth, England, 1967), p. 102.

6. Quoted in Paul Avrich, *The Russian Anarchists* (Princeton, N.J., 1971), p. 67.

7. Quoted in Nicholas Bullock and James Read, *The Movement for Housing Reform in Germany and France, 1840–1914* (Cambridge, 1985), p. 42.

8. Quoted in Gary Cross, *A Social History of Leisure Since 1600* (State College, Pa., 1990), pp. 116, 119.

9. Quoted in Sibylle Meyer, "The Tiresome Work of Conspicuous Leisure: On the Domestic Duties of the Wives of Civil Servants in the German Empire (1871–1918)," in Boxer and Quataert, *Connecting Spheres,* p. 161.

10. Quoted in Lenard R. Berlanstein, *The Working People of Paris, 1871–1914* (Baltimore, 1984), p. 141.

11. Quoted in Robert Gildea, *Barricades and Borders: Europe, 1800–1914,* 2nd ed. (Oxford, 1996), pp. 240–241.

12. Quoted in Cross, *Social History of Leisure,* p. 130.

13. Quoted in Shmuel Galai, *The Liberation Movement in Russia, 1900–1905* (Cambridge, 1973), p. 26.

CHAPTER 24

1. Quoted in Charles Rearick, *Pleasures of the Belle Époque: Entertainment and Festivity in Turn-of-the-Century France* (New Haven, Conn., 1985), p. 120.

2. Quoted in Arthur E. E. McKenzie, *The Major Achievements of Science* (New York, 1960), vol. 1, p. 310.

3. Friedrich Nietzsche, *Twilight of the Idols and the Anti-Christ,* trans. R. J. Hollingdale (New York, 1972), pp. 117–118.

4. Friedrich Nietzsche, *Thus Spake Zarathustra,* in *The Philosophy of Nietzsche* (New York, 1954), p. 6.

5. Herbert Spencer, *Social Statics* (New York, 1896), pp. 146, 150.

6. Friedrich von Bernhardi, *Germany and the Next War,* trans. Allen H. Powles (New York, 1914), pp. 18–19.

7. Quoted in Edward R. Tannenbaum, *1900: The Generation Before the Great War* (Garden City, N.Y., 1976), p. 337.

8. William Booth, *In Darkest England and the Way Out* (London, 1890), p. 45.

9. Quoted in John Rewald, *The History of Impressionism* (New York, 1961), pp. 456–458.

10. Quoted in Anne Higonnet, *Berthe Morisot's Images of Women* (Cambridge, Mass., 1992), p. 19.

11. Quoted in Craig Wright, *Listening to Music* (Saint Paul, Minn., 1992), p. 327.

12. Quoted in Catherine M. Prelinger, "Prelude to Consciousness: Amalie Sieveking and the Female Association for the Care of the Poor and the Sick," in John C. Fout, ed., *German Women in the Nineteenth Century: A Social History* (New York, 1984), p. 119.

13. Quoted in Bonnie G. Smith, *Changing Lives: Women in European History Since 1700* (Lexington, Mass., 1989), p. 379.

14. Quoted in Paul Massing, *Rehearsal for Destruction: A Study of Political Anti-Semitism in Imperial Germany* (New York, 1949), p. 147.

15. Quoted in Abba Eban, *Heritage: Civilization and the Jews* (New York, 1984), p. 249.

16. Quoted in John Merriman, *A History of Modern Europe* (New York, 1996), p. 953.

17. Quoted in ibid., p. 965.

18. Karl Pearson, *National Life from the Standpoint of Science* (London, 1905), p. 184.

19. Quoted in John Ellis, *The Social History of the Machine Gun* (New York, 1975), p. 80.

20. Quoted in ibid., p. 86.

21. Quoted in Louis L. Snyder, ed., *The Imperialism Reader* (Princeton, N.J., 1962), p. 220.

22. Quoted in K. M. Panikkar, *Asia and Western Dominance* (London, 1959), p. 116.

CHAPTER 25

1. Martin Gilbert, *The First World War: A Complete History* (New York, 1994), p. 259.

2. Quoted in ibid., p. 264.

3. Arnold Toynbee, *Surviving the Future* (New York, 1971), pp. 106–107.

4. Quoted in Joachim Remak, "1914—The Third Balkan War: Origins Reconsidered," *Journal of Modern History* 43 (1971): 364–365.

5. Quoted in Robert G. L. Waite, *Vanguard of Nazism* (New York, 1969), p. 22.

6. Quoted in J. M. Winter, *The Experience of World War I* (New York, 1989), p. 142.

7. Quoted in ibid., p. 137.

8. Quoted in Hew Strachan, *The First World War* (New York, 2004), pp. 94–95.

9. Quoted in ibid., p. 72.

10. Quoted in Gail Braybon, *Women Workers in the First World War: The British Experience* (London, 1981), p. 79.

11. Quoted in Catherine W. Reilly, ed., *Scars upon My Heart: Women's Poetry and Verse of the First World War* (London, 1981), p. 90.

12. Quoted in Robert Paxton, *Europe in the Twentieth Century,* 2nd ed. (New York, 1985), p. 110.

13. Quoted in William M. Mandel, *Soviet Women* (Garden City, N.Y., 1975), p. 43.

14. Quoted in Mark D. Steinberg, *Voices of Revolution, 1917* (New Haven, Conn., 2001), p. 55.

CHAPTER 26

1. Quoted in Stéphane Audoin-Rouzeau and Annette Becker, *14–18: Understanding the Great War,* trans. Catherine Temerson (New York, 2002), pp. 212–213.

2. Quoted in ibid., p. 41.

3. Quoted in Robert Paxton, *Europe in the Twentieth Century,* 2nd ed. (New York, 1985), p. 237.

4. Quoted in Denis Mack Smith, *Mussolini* (New York, 1982), p. 51.

5. Benito Mussolini, "The Doctrine of Fascism," in Adrian Lyttleton, ed., *Italian Fascisms from Pareto to Gentile* (London, 1973), p. 42.

6. Quoted in Alexander De Grand, "Women Under Italian Fascism," *Historical Journal* 19 (1976): 958–959.

7. Adolf Hitler, *Mein Kampf,* trans. Ralph Manheim (Boston, 1943), p. 22.

8. Ibid., p. 161.

9. Quoted in Joachim Fest, *Hitler,* trans. Richard Winston and Clara Winston (New York, 1974), p. 241.

10. Quoted in Jeremy Noakes and Geoffrey Pridham, eds., *Nazism, 1919–1945* (Exeter, England, 1983), vol. 1, pp. 50–51.

11. Quoted in Jackson J. Spielvogel and David Redles, *Hitler and Nazi Germany: A History,* 6th ed. (Upper Saddle River, N.J., 2010), p. 83.

12. Irving Howe, ed., *The Basic Writings of Trotsky* (London, 1963), p. 162.

13. Quoted in Sheila Fitzpatrick, *Everyday Stalinism. Ordinary Life in Extraordinary Times: Soviet Russia in the 1930s* (New York, 1999), p. 87.

14. Paul Valéry, *Variety,* trans. Malcolm Cowley (New York, 1927), pp. 27–28.

15. Quoted in Matthis Eberle, *World War I and the Weimar Artists: Dix, Grosz, Beckmann, Schlemmer* (New Haven, Conn., 1985), p. 54.

16. Norman H. Baynes, ed., *The Speeches of Adolf Hitler, 1922–1939* (Oxford, 1942), vol. 1, p. 591.

CHAPTER 27

1. Adolf Hitler, *Mein Kampf,* trans. Ralph Manheim (Boston, 1971), p. 654.

2. *Documents on German Foreign Policy* (London, 1956), ser. D, vol. 2, p. 358.

3. Ibid., vol. 7, p. 204.

4. Quoted in Norman Rich, *Hitler's War Aims* (New York, 1973), vol. 1, p. 129.

5. Quoted in Williamson Murray and Allan Millett, *A War to Be Won: Fighting the Second World War* (Cambridge, Mass., 2000), p. 66.

6. Quoted in ibid., p. 137.

7. Albert Speer, *Spandau,* trans. Richard Winston and Clara Winston (New York, 1976), p. 50.

8. *Nazi Conspiracy and Aggression* (Washington, D.C., 1946), vol. 6, p. 262.

9. International Military Tribunal, *Trial of the Major War Criminals* (Nuremberg, 1947–1949), vol. 22, p. 480.

10. Adolf Hitler, *My New Order,* ed. Raoul de Roussy de Sales (New York, 1941), pp. 21–22.

11. Quoted in Lucy Dawidowicz, *The War Against the Jews* (New York, 1975), p. 106.

12. *Nazi Conspiracy and Aggression,* vol. 5, pp. 341–342.

13. Quoted in Raul Hilberg, *The Destruction of the European Jews*, rev. ed. (New York, 1985), vol. 1, pp. 332–333.
14. *Nazi Conspiracy and Aggression*, vol. 6, p. 789.
15. Quoted in John Campbell, *The Experience of World War II* (New York, 1989), p. 170.
16. Quoted in Claudia Koonz, "Mothers in the Fatherland: Women in Nazi Germany," in Renate Bridenthal and Claudia Koonz, eds., *Becoming Visible: Women in European History* (Boston, 1977), p. 466.
17. Quoted in Campbell, *The Experience of World War II*, p. 143.
18. Quoted in ibid., p. 177.
19. Quoted in Robert E. Sherwood, *Roosevelt and Hopkins: An Intimate History* (New York, 1948), p. 870.
20. Quoted in Norman Graebner, *Cold War Diplomacy, 1945–1960* (Princeton, N.J., 1962), p. 117.
21. Quoted in ibid., p. 117.
22. Quoted in Wilfried Loth, *The Division of the World, 1941–1955* (New York, 1988), p. 81.

CHAPTER 28

1. Quoted in Joseph M. Jones, *The Fifteen Weeks (February 21–June 5, 1947)*, 2nd ed. (New York, 1964), pp. 140–141.
2. Quoted in Walter Laqueur, *Europe in Our Time* (New York, 1992), p. 111.
3. Quoted in Wilfried Loth, *The Division of the World, 1941–1955* (New York, 1988), pp. 160–161.
4. Quoted in William I. Hitchcock, *The Struggle for Europe: The Turbulent History of a Divided Continent, 1945–2002* (New York, 2003), p. 215.
5. Quoted in Peter Lane, *Europe Since 1945: An Introduction* (Totowa, N.J., 1985), p. 248.
6. Quoted in Robert F. Kennedy, *Thirteen Days: A Memoir of the Cuban Missile Crisis* (New York, 1969), pp. 89–90.
7. Quoted in Larry Collins and Dominique Lapierre, *Freedom at Midnight* (New York, 1975), p. 252.
8. R. Hilton, *Military Attaché in Moscow* (London, 1949), p. 41.
9. Nikita Khrushchev, *Khrushchev Remembers*, trans. Strobe Talbott (Boston, 1970), p. 77.

10. Quoted in Bonnie G. Smith, *Changing Lives: Women in European History Since 1700* (Lexington, Mass., 1989), p. 513.
11. Quoted in Hilda Scott, *Sweden's "Right to Be Human": Sex-Role Equality—The Goal and the Reality* (London, 1982), p. 125.
12. Simone de Beauvoir, *The Second Sex*, trans. H. M. Parshley (New York, 1961), p. xxviii.
13. Quoted in Henry Grosshans, *The Search for Modern Europe* (Boston, 1970), p. 421.
14. Richard Maltby, ed., *Passing Parade: A History of Popular Culture in the Twentieth Century* (Oxford, 1989), p. 8.
15. Quoted in ibid., p. 11.

CHAPTER 29

1. Quoted in Marsha Rowe et al., *Spare Rib Reader* (Harmondsworth, England, 1982), p. 574.
2. Betty Friedan, *The Feminine Mystique* (New York, 1963), p. 10.
3. Quoted in Tony Judt, *Postwar: A History of Europe Since 1945* (New York, 2005), p. 390.
4. "To Walk the Moon," *New York Times*, July 20, 1969.

CHAPTER 30

1. Quoted in Tony Judt, *Postwar: A History of Europe Since 1945* (New York, 2005), p. 585.
2. Mikhail Gorbachev, "Report to the 27th Party Congress," February 25, 1986, in *Current Soviet Policies* 9 (1986): 10.
3. Quoted in William I. Hitchcock, *The Struggle for Europe: The Turbulent History of a Divided Continent, 1945–2002* (New York, 2003), pp. 399–400.
4. Quoted in Renate Bridenthal, "Women in the New Europe," in Renate Bridenthal, Susan Mosher Stuard, and Merry E. Weisner, eds., *Becoming Visible: Women in European History*, 3rd ed. (Boston, 1998), pp. 564–565.
5. Quoted in Judt, *Postwar Europe*, p. 743.
6. Quoted in Joan W. Scott, *The Politics of the Veil* (Princeton, N.J., 2009), p. 1.
7. Elise Boulding, *Women in the Twentieth-Century World* (New York, 1977), pp. 186–187.

INDEX

Italicized page numbers show the locations of illustrations and maps.

Abernathy, Ralph, *909*
Abolition of slavery, 429
Abortion, 835, 966
Abraham Lincoln Brigade, 838
Absolutism, 640, 645, 683, 734; in central Europe, 462–464, 547–550; in eastern Europe, 464–466, 550–552; enlightened, 543, 551, 554; limits of, 469–470; in Ottoman Empire, 468–469; philosophes on, 518–519; in Russia, 464–466; in Sweden, 467; in western Europe, 446–447, 454–462. *See also* Enlightened absolutism
Abstract Expressionism, 914, *915*
Abstract painting, 747, *748*, 842
Acerbo Law (Italy), 823–824
Acheson, Dean, 886
Acid rain, 978
Act of Supremacy (England), 393, 407
Act of Uniformity (England), 407
Act of Union (1801), 729
Adams, John, 518, *577*
Addison, Joseph, 532
Address to Congress, March 12, 1947 (Truman), 888
Address to the Nobility of the German Nation (Luther), 382
Address to the People of Czechoslovakia (Havel), 953
Address to the Reichstag (Bismarck), 732
Address to the Twentieth Party Congress (Khrushchev), 901
Adenauer, Konrad, 890, 905, 906
Adimari, Fiammetta, 345
Administration. *See* Government
Adoration of the Magi (Dürer), 365, *366*
Adorno, Theodor, 913
Adrianople: Treaty of, 643
Advertising, 729
Aegean region, 769
Affonso of Congo (Bakongo), 428
Afghanistan, 768; Russia and, 764; Soviet Union and, 937, 943, 949; war on terrorism in, 964
Africa: civil wars in, 963; decolonization in, 895–896, *896*; imperialism in, 761–763, 767; in 1914, *764*; Paris Peace Conference and, 806, 807; Portugal and, 416–417; slaves and, 345, 416, 426–429, 437; slave trade and, 564; U.S. embassies attacked in, 964; World War I and, 785–790, *790*, 821. *See also* specific locations
African Americans, 688, 874, 908–909, 917
African National Congress (ANC), 895, 896
Afrika Korps, 862
Afrikaners (Boers), 762
Against the Robbing and Murdering Hordes of Peasants (Luther), 385
Age of Louis XIV, The (Voltaire), 530
Agincourt, Battle of, 317
Agricultural revolution, 561–562, 608
Agriculture: Columbian Exchange and, 440–441; in 18th century, 558; EU and, 960; industrial economy and, 708; in Middle Ages, 307; population growth and, 715; in 16th century, 442–443; in Soviet Union, 833, 834, 926; World War II and, 873, 874, 910. *See also* Land
Ahlwardt, Hermann, 752
Air force: in World War II, 853, 858, 863, 875–877

Airplanes, 706, 790–791, 840
Air pollution, 624, 938
Aix-la-Chapelle: congress at, 640; treaty of, 555
Akbar (Mughal Empire), 432
Alaska, 763
Albania and Albanians, 771, 772, 890, 902; Communist Party and, 902; in Italy, 967; in Kosovo, 956
Albany, New York, 436
Albert (England), *615*, *688*
Alberti, Leon Battista, 341, 346
Albuquerque, Afonso de, 417, 418–419
Alchemy, 489
Alcohol: in 18th century, 534–535; factory workers and, 613; in Soviet Union, 926
Aleshker, Lev, 714
Alexander I (Russia), 646
Alexander I (Yugoslavia), 836
Alexander II (Russia), 675, 683, 684, 685, 686, 734
Alexander III (Russia), 685, 734
Alexander V (Pope), 328
Alexander VI (Pope), 352, 372
Alexandra (Russia), *756*, 797
Alexandria, Egypt, 862
Alexis (Russia), 797
Al-Fatah, 898
Alfonso XII (Spain), 730
Alfonso XIII (Spain), 836
Algeria, 656, 762, 895, *895*, 905
Alliances: of Bismarck, 769–770; during Cold War, 890–891, *891*, 892; after Congress of Berlin, 770–771; Hanseatic League as, 342–343, *343*; in Italy, 349; after Napoleonic wars, 637; of Nazi Germany, 852; in Seven Years' War, 555; World War I and, 776, 805, 809, 814; World War II and, 862. *See also* specific alliances
Allied Reparations Commission, 814
Allies: World War I, 783, 785, 790, 800, 802, 803, 805, 807; World War II, 862, 863, 864, 877, 879–880
All Quiet on the Western Front (Remarque), 786
Al-Qaeda, 964, 966, 974
Alsace, 451, 460, 681, 807
Alsace-Lorraine, Germany and, 769
Alva, duke of, 405, 406
Amadeus (movie), 531
Amalgamated Society of Engineers, 632
Amazon region, 424
Amendments to Constitution (U.S.), 578
America(s): crops from, 558; European empires in, 435–436; horses in, 437; naming of, 420; plantation economy in, 564; voyages to, *413*, 413–414; and War of the Austrian Succession, 555. *See also* New World
American Federation of Labor, 758
American Indians. *See* Indians (Native Americans)
Americanization, of culture, 916–917, 944
American Medical Association: on video games, 973
American Philosophical Society, 526
American Revolution, 575–578, 640
American system, 618
Amish, 392
Amsterdam, 442, 471, 562–563, 921
Amusement parks, 704
Anabaptists, 390–392, 396, 405
Anarchism, 714
Anatomy, 500, 503

Andersen, Hans Christian, 662
Andes Mountains, 424, 641, *641*
Andreotti, Giulio, 931
Andropov, Yuri, 926
Anesthesia, 534, 696, 697
Angkor kingdom (Cambodia), 430
Anglican Church. *See* Church of England
Anglo-Dutch trade wars, 441
Anglo-German Naval Pact (1935), 852
Angola, 762, 896
Animals: in Columbian Exchange, 440
Anjou, France, 366
Anjou family, in Naples, 324
Annam, 765
Anne (England), 477, 545
Anne of Austria, 455
Anne of Cleves, 393
Annotations (Erasmus), 378
Antiballistic missiles (ABMs), 936
Antiballistic Missile Treaty (1972), 936
Anticlericalism, 742
Anti-Comintern Pact, 852
Anti-Corn Law League, 654
Antinuclear movement, women in, 966, *967*
Anti-Semitism: in Austria, 752; Dreyfus affair and, 755; in Germany, 752, 831, *832*, 832–833; of Hitler, 826, 827, 865, 867. *See also* Jews and Judaism
Antiseptic principle, 696
Antiwar protests: in Second Vietnam War, 908, 923, 924, 925, 934
Antwerp, 442
Apartheid, 895, 943
Appeasement: Japan and, 856; Nazi Germany and, 852, 853
Apple Computer Company, 972
Apprentices: in 18th century, 570; pauper, 629
"April Theses" (Lenin), 799
Aqaba, Gulf of, 898
Aqueducts, 421
Arab-Israeli disputes: in 1948, 897; in 1967, 898; in 1973, 932
Arab League, 896
Arabs and Arab world, 417; Israel and, 897, 898; World War I and, 785, 807–808. *See also* Islam; Middle East
Aragon: house of, 324
Archimedes and Archimedian screw, 488
Architecture: of country houses, 567; functionalism in, *844*, 844–845; in Italian Renaissance, 360, *360*; neo-Gothic, 662, *663*; Postmodernism in, 941, *941*; Rococo, 527
Arena Chapel, Padua, *333*
Argentina, 640, 641, 642, 939
Aristocracy. *See* Nobility
Aristotle, 488; on motion, 490, 496–497
Arkwright, Richard, 564, 609, 610
Armada (Spain), 409–410
Armed forces. *See* Military; Navy; Wars and warfare
Armenian people: genocide of, 804
Armistice, after World War I, 803
Arms and armaments. *See* Weapons
Arms race: in Cold War, 890; of 1890s, 752
Arouet, François-Marie. *See* Voltaire
Art(s): artists, society, and, 363–364; Baroque, 480, *481*; Black Death and, 332–333; body and identity in, 973; Classicism in, 481; Dadaism in, 842–843, *843*; digital effects

in, 973; in Enlightenment, 513–514, 526–531; Mannerism in, 479–480; Modernism in, 744–749; multiculturalism and, 973, *974*; Neoclassicism in, 527–528; Neo-Expressionism in, *970*, 970–971, *972*; Photorealism in, 941; Postmodernism in, 940–941; postwar, 913–915; Realism in, 698–700; in Renaissance, 358–366; Rococo style in, 527; Romanticism in, 664–665; Soviet, 948; Surrealism in, 843–844, *844*; totalitarian regimes and, 845. *See also* specific arts and artists

Art Brut, 914

Articles of Confederation, 576

Artisans, 627

Artois, 462; count of, 644

Aryan racial empire, Hitler and, 850, 865–866

"Aryans," racist concept of, 742, 827

Ascent of Mount Ventoux, The (Petrarch), 354

Ashkenazic Jews, 537

Asia: decolonization in, 898–900, *899*; European involvement in, 429–435, *430*; imperialism in, 763–765, *765*, 767–768; Mongols in, 307–308; in 1914, *765*; Portugal and, 429–430, 437; prelude to World War II in, 855–957; trade with, 564; water route to, 413–414; World War I in, 790; World War II in, 859–861, *861*, 865. *See also* Southeast Asia; specific locations

Asia Minor: Greece and, 813; Ottoman Turks from, 370

Asiento, 436

Assemblies: in Russia, 685. *See also* Parliament

Assembly line, 708

Assignats (paper money), 586, 587, 597

Assimilation: of Jews, 538, 752, 755

Associated Shipwrights Society, *632*

Astell, Mary, 524

Astrolabe, 415

Astrology, 309, 355, 489

Astronomy: Scientific Revolution and, 489–497; women in, 502

Atahualpa (Inca), 424

Atatürk. *See* Kemal, Mustafa

Athanor (Kiefer), *970*

Atheism, 522

Atlantic Ocean region: seaboard states in, 544–547; slave trade in, 426–429; winds in, 415; World War II in, 862

Atomic bomb, 846, 865, 877, 890, 938

Atonal music, 845, 942

Attlee, Clement, 906

Auburn Prison, New York, 662

Audiencias, 425

Augsburg: Diet of, 388; Peace of, *387*, 388, 449

Augustinians, 380

Auschwitz-Birkenau, 869, 870, *871*

Ausgleich (Compromise) of 1867, 682

Australia, 515, 661, 763, 785, 892

Austria, 369, 601, 644, 675, 804, 836, 960; antiforeign sentiment in, 967–968; Balkans and, 769, 771–772, 777–778; economy of, 682; France and, 587; Germany and, 656, 678, 852–853; Hitler in, 853, *853*; infanticide and, 560; Italy and, 464, 553, 640, 644, 657, 676; Jews in, 537, 538, 752; military in, 557; music in, 529; Napoleon and, 597; nationalities in, 657, 716; Ottomans and, 370, 388; Poland and, 552, 637; Quadruple Alliance and, 637, 640; religious toleration in, 537; revolts in, 454; Rococo in, *527*; in Triple Alliance, 769; and War of the Austrian Succession, 554–555; after War of the Spanish Succession, 461; World War I and, 776, 778, 792, 807. *See also* Austrian Netherlands; World War II

Austria-Hungary, 771, 772; alliances of, 769; as dual monarchy, 682–683; ethnic groups in, 682–683, *684*, 733; Serbia and, 771–772, 778; World War I and, 778, 779, 804, 807

Austrian Empire, *463*, 463–464, 636, 644, 650, 673; education in, 535; in 18th century, 549–550; as multinational state, 646; nationalities in, 657; revolution of 1848 in, 656–657, *657*. *See also* Austria; Austria-Hungary

Austrian Netherlands, 463, *463*, 555, 587, *591*, 638, 652. *See also* Belgium; Spanish Netherlands

Austro-Prussian War (1866), 678, 681, 682

Authoritarian conservatism, 640

Authoritarianism: in Iberian peninsula, 836–838; of Napoleon III, 671–673; World War I and, 792, 793, 821–838

Authoritarian states: in eastern Europe, 836

Autobiography (Shibuzawa Eiichi), 626

Autocracy: in Austria, 682; in Russia, 646–647

Automobiles, 706, 738, 910

Auxiliary Service Law (Germany, 1916), 792

Avanti (Forward), 823

Avignon, *327*; pope at, 326–327, 328

"Awakening," in Protestantism, 667

Axial rudder, 415

Axis powers (World War II), 861, 864

Ayacucho, battle at, 642

Azerbaijan, nationalism in, 949

Aztec people, 421–423, *422*

Baader-Meinhof gang (Germany), 964

Babeuf, Gracchus, 597

Babur (Mughal Empire), 432

Baby boom, 912

Babylonian Captivity of the Church (Luther), 382

Bach, Alexander von, 682

Bach, Johann Sebastian, 528, 529

Bacon, Francis, 505–506

Bacon, John, and family, *560*

Baden-Powell, Robert and Agnes, 723

Bahamas, 420

Baines, Edward, 609

Baker, Josephine, 839

Bakongo, 416

Bakunin, Michael, 714

Balaklava, Battle of, 675

Balance of power, 554; Bismarck and, 769; after Crimean War, 675; in Italy, 349, 350; after Napoleonic wars, 638–639

Balboa, Vasco Nuñez de, 420

Baldwin, Stanley, 818

Balkan League, 771

Balkan region: by 1830, *643*; in 1913, *771*; crises in (1908–1913), 771–772, 776; crises in (1914), 777–778; in late 19th century, 769; Ottoman Empire in, 370, 468, *769*; World War I and, 807; World War II and, 859. *See also* specific locations

Ball, John, 314

Baltic region: Denmark and, 450–451; Jews of, 870; Russia and, 466, *467*, 551; in Thirty Years' War, *450*, 450–451

Banking, 564, 707; in Amsterdam, 442, 471; commercial capitalism and, 442; in England, 608; Fugger and, 442, *443*; Great Depression and, 815–816; Medici and, 343; in U.S., 975–976

Banknotes, 562

Bank of England, 562

Baptism, 386, 392

Baptists, 538

Bar (French province), 366

Barbados, 435

Barclay family, 627

Baroque arts, 480, *481*; music as, 528–529

Barth, Karl, 915–916

Barton, Clara, 749

Baseball, 727, 767

Basecu, Traian, 953

Basel, 390

Basilicas: of Saint Peter, 363, 372–373

Basquiat, Jean-Michel, 970, 971, *972*

Bastille, fall of, 574, *574*, 582, 583

Bataan peninsula, 860

Batavia (Jakarta), 429, *430*

Batista, Fulgencio, 893

Battle of Britain, 858, 938

Battles. *See* specific battles and wars

Bauhaus, 844–845

Bavaria and Bavarians, 323, 451, 732

Bayle, Pierre, 515

Bay of Pigs invasion, 893

Beatles, *916*, 917

Bebel, August, 711, 712

Beccaria, Cesare, 533

Beckett, Samuel, 914

Beer Hall Putsch, 827

Beethoven, Ludwig van, 666

Beggars, 570

Beijing, 433

Belarus, independence of, 950

Belgian Congo. *See* Zaire

Belgioioso, Cristina, 657

Belgium, 405, 890, 907; Central Africa and, 762–763; Dutch Republic and, 652; industrialization in, 618; World War I and, 780, 782; World War II and, 638, 858. *See also* Austrian Netherlands; Low Countries

Belgrade, 468

Bell, Alexander Graham, 705

Belle époque, la, 708

Belov, Max, 835

Benedict (Saint) and Benedictine monasticism, 399

Benelux countries, 907

Bengal, 432, *556*

Benin, 429, 437

Bergman, Ingmar, 917

Bergson, Henri, 739

Berlin, 839, 864, 885, 890; blockade of, 888, 889–890; police in, 661

Berlin Academy, 502

Berlin Air Lift, 890, *890*

Berlin Wall, 893, 927, 954, *954*

Berlioz, Hector, 666–667

Berlusconi, Silvio, 959–960

Bermuda, 435

Bern, 390

Bernhardi, Friedrich von, 742

Bernini, Gian Lorenzo, 480, *481*

Bernstein, Eduard, 712, 713

Bessarabia, 674, 675

Bethmann-Hollweg, Theobald von, 778

Beveridge, William, 912

Bible: of Gutenberg, 358; Luther and, 381, 386; Modernist view of, 742. *See also* New Testament

Bicameral legislature: in France, 644, 730; in United States, 578

Big Four, after World War I, 805, *805*

Big Three, after World War I, 805

Big Three (Grand Alliance), World War II and, 879

Bill of Rights: in England, 477, 478; in United States, 578, 647

Bin Laden, Osama, 964, 965, 974

Birmingham, England, 623

Birth control, 722–723, 842, 966; in 18th century, 561; pill and, 921

Birthrate: baby boom and, 912; decline in, 966; in 18th century, 561; in late 1800s, 715, 722; in Middle Ages, 307; population growth and, 621; after World War I, 804

Bishop's Palace (Residenz), 527

Bismarck, Otto von, 671, 672–673, 679–682, 755; alliance system of, 769–770; as chancellor, 732, 733; colonies and, 763; France and, 730; Franco-Prussian War and, 681–683; William II (Germany) and, *732*

Black Death, 306, 312–315; art and, 332–333; Asian trade and, 307–308; burials from, *308*, 311–312; in Europe, 308–312; Jews and, 311, 312; medicine after, 335–336; spread of, *310*. *See also* Plague

Black Hand (Serbian organization), 778
Black Hole of Calcutta, 432
Black Holes of Worsley, 630
Black Man's Burden, The (Morel), 760–761
Black Prince. *See* Edward (Black Prince, England)
Blacks: slave trade and, 429. *See also* Africa;
    African Americans
Black Sea region, 552, *674, 675,* 764
Black September (Palestinian terrorists), 943
Blackshirts (Italy), 823
Blackwell, Elizabeth, 697
Blair, Tony, 959, 974
Blanc, Louis, 650–651, 655
Blenheim, battle at, 461
Blitz, 876
Blitzkrieg, 852, 857, 858, 875
Blockade(s): of Berlin, 888, 889–890; of Cuba,
    893; against Israel, 898; in World War I,
    790, 791
Blood circulation: Harvey on, 500–501
"Bloody Sunday" (Russia), 757
Blues (music), 917
Blum, Léon, 819
Board of Trade (Britain), 436
Bobbies (British police), 659–661, *662*
Boccaccio, Giovanni, 309, 311, 331
Bodichon, Barbara, 726
Bodin, Jean, 454
Boers, in South Africa, 426, 762
Boer War, 762
Bohemia, 369; Austria and, 657; Hussites in, 371;
    Ottomans and, 370
Bohemian phase, of Thirty Years' War, 449–450
Boigne, Comtesse de, 545
Boleyn, Anne, 392, 393, 407
Bolívar, Simón, 640, 641, *641,* 642
Bolivia, 642
Bologna: papacy and, 348; poverty in, 570;
    university in, 335
Bolshevik Revolution (1917), 790, 799–800
Bolsheviks, 798, 799, 800, 801, 833. *See also* Red
    Army; Soviet Union
Bombs and bombings. *See* Atomic bomb
Bonaparte, Jerome, 601. *See also* Napoleon I
    Bonaparte (France)
Boniface VIII (Pope), 326, *326,* 327, 328
Book of Common Prayer, 393, 407, 473
Book of the City of Ladies, The (Christine de Pizan),
    332
Book of the Courtier, The (Castiglione), 344
Books: Index of Forbidden Books and, 402; for
    middle class, 720; printing and, 358. *See also*
    Literature
Booth, William, 743
Borders: Helsinki Accords and, 936–937; Locarno
    Treaty and, 815. *See also* Frontiers
Borgia family: Alexander VI (Pope) and, 372;
    Cesare, 352, 372
Bormann, Martin, 866
Borodino, battle at, 603
Bosnia, 769, 957; war in, *955,* 955–956
Bosnia-Herzegovina, 954, 955, *955,* 957. *See also*
    Herzegovina
Bosnian Crisis (1908–1909), 771
Bosnian Serbs, 956
Bossuet, Jacques, 454
Bosworth Field, battle at, 367
Botticelli, Sandro, *346, 359, 359*
Boulanger, Georges, 730
Boulton, Matthew, *610*
Boundaries. *See* Borders; Frontiers
Bourbon dynasty, 460; Habsburgs and, 555; in
    Italy, 553; restoration of, 604, 637, 640,
    644; in Spain, 460–461, 553, 644; Thirty
    Years' War and, 449
Bourdonnaye, M. de la, 571
Bourgeois(ie), 580, 625, 692
Bourgeois monarchy, in France, 652
Boxer Rebellion (China), 767
Boyars (Russia), 464
Boys: in middle class, 723

Boy Scouts, 723
Brahe, Tycho, 491, *493*
Bramante, Donato, 363, *363*
Brancacci Chapel, 358, *359*
Brandenburg, 451, 460, *462,* 549
Brandenburg-Prussia, 461, *462,* 462–463, 558
Brandt, Willy, 929
Brazil, 426, 435, 436, 642
Bremen, 451
Brest-Litovsk, Treaty of, *783,* 800, 807
Breteuil, baron de, 551
Brétigny, Peace of, 316
Brezhnev, Leonid, 902, 925, 926, 928–929
Brezhnev Doctrine, 925–926, 928
Briand, Aristide, 815
Bright, John, 654
Britain. *See* England (Britain)
Britain, Battle of, 858, 938
British: use of term, 544
British Bomber Command, 876, 877
British Broadcasting Corporation (BBC), 839
British Columbia, 758
British East India Company, 432, 433, *556,* 763
British Empire, 556–557, 620, 906
British Soccer Cup Final, 727
British Women's Liberation Workshop, 924
Brothels, 334
Brothers Karamazov, The (Dostoevsky), 743
Brothers of the Common Life, 329, 377
Brown, Gordon, 959
Broz, Josip. *See* Tito (Josip Broz)
Bruges, 342
Brunel, I. K., *613*
Brunelleschi, Filippo, 360, *360, 361*
Bruni, Leonardo, 354, 355, 357
Brüning, Heinrich, 828
Bruno, Giordano, 355
Bubonic plague. *See* Black Death; Plague
Bucer, Martin, 390
Budget: deficits in U.S., 932, 961, 962
Bulganin, Nikolai, 892
Bulgaria, 769, 771, 807, 836, 890, 961;
    authoritarianism in, 836; communism in,
    886, 902; Ottomans in, 370; in World War I,
    783, 785; in World War II, 859, 865
Bulge, Battle of the, 864
Bullion, 443
Bundesrat, 681
Burckhardt, Jacob, 341
Bureaucracy: in Austria, 549; in Austria-Hungary,
    733; in 18th century, 547; in France, 600;
    military, 453; in Prussia, 548, 566; in
    Russia, 646; Soviet, 833, 834, 926; in U.S.,
    874; in World War I Britain, 792
Burghers, 344, 547. *See also* Bourgeois(ie)
Burgundy, duke of, 317, 323
Burgundy and Burgundians, 323, 366
Burke, Edmund, 639
Burma (Myanmar), 429, 430, 764, 857, 863, 899
Burma-Thailand railway, 872
Burschenschaften, 645–646
Bush, George H. W., 961, 963
Bush, George W., 961, 962, 964
Bushido code, 875
Business: government and, 608–609. *See also*
    Commercial capitalism; Industry
Business cycle, slumps in, 708
Bute (Lord), 545
Butler, Josephine, 711
Byrnes, James, 880–881
Byron, George Gordon (Lord), 664, *666*
Byzantine Empire: Ottoman conquest of, 370;
    plague in, 308. *See also* Eastern Orthodoxy

Cabinet system: in Britain, 545
Cabot, John, 420
Cabral, Pedro, 420
Caffa: plague and, 308
Cahiers de doléances, 581
Calais, 316, 319, 393

Calas, Jean, Voltaire and, 519
Calcutta, 432, 557
Calendar: of Maya, 421; in revolutionary France,
    594–595
Calicut, 430
California: missions in, 437
Calonne, Charles de, 580–581
Calvin, John, and Calvinism, 394–395, *395,* 396,
    397; in 18th century, 536; Huguenots and,
    402–404; in Netherlands, 395, 405, 408,
    471; Puritans and, 408, 473
Cambodia, 430, 765, 899
Cameron, David, 959
Cameroons, 763
Camus, Albert, 915
Canada, 689–690, 890; Dominion of, 690, 758;
    in 1871, *758;* England and, 545; European
    migration to, 716; France and, 436; French
    and Indian War and, 556–557; since 1970s,
    962; World War I and, 758–759; World
    War II and, 909
Candide (Voltaire), 520
Cane sugar. *See* Sugar plantations
Cannons, 319, 337
Canterbury Tales (Chaucer), 331–332
Canton, China, 433
Cantons: in Switzerland, *389*
Cape Colony, 762
Cape of Good Hope, 420, 426
Capetian dynasty, 315
Capital (financial), 608, 619, 708
Capitalism: commercial, 432, 442–443, 564;
    cottage industry and, 563; imperialism and,
    761; socialism and, 650; Sorel on, 740
Capital punishment, 661
Capuchins, 399
Caraffa, Gian Pietro, 401, 402
Caravan trade, 308
Carbonari, 644
Cardinals (church), 327–328
Caribbean region, 420, 426, 435, *435*
Carinthia, 463
Carlstadt, Andreas, 384
Carlyle, Thomas, 662
Carmelite nuns, 399
Carnegie Steel Company, 758
Carniola, 463
Carnival (festival), 534, *535*
Carol II (Romania), 836
Caroline Islands, 856
Cars. *See* Automobiles
Cartel of the Left (France), 819
Cartels, 707
Carter, Jimmy, 932, 937
Cartesian dualism, 504–505
Cartier, Jacques, 436
Cartwright, Edmund, 610
Castiglione, Baldassare, 344
Castile, 553
Castro, Fidel, 893
Casualties: of Holocaust, 868, *870,* 870–871; in
    Spanish Civil War, 838; in U.S. Civil War,
    688; of war in Bosnia, 956
Catalonia, 454
Catherine II the Great (Russia), 542, *542,* 543,
    550–552, 554
Catherine de' Medici, 403
Catherine of Aragon (England), 392, 393
Catherine of Siena, 327, 329
Catholic Center Party (Germany), 826
Catholic Church: anticlericalism and, 742; in Asia,
    430; in Austria, 549; Chaucer on, 332; in
    colonies, 437–438; Council of Trent and,
    402; crime problem and, 661; decline of,
    326–330; in 18th century, 536, *537,* 538; in
    England, 392–394, 473, 474, 477; Erasmus
    and, 377–378, 379; exploration and, 415;
    by 1560, *399;* in France, 644, 755; French
    Revolution and, 586, 592–595, 596; Galileo
    and, 491; in Germany, 732, 831; Great
    Schism in, 327–328; Habsburgs and,

386–387; in Hungary, 369; Indian conversions by, 425; in Italy, 731, 824, 826; in Japan, 435; Luther and, 381–383; Napoleon and, 599–600; Peace of Augsburg and, *387*; in Poland, 926; in Portugal, 553; Reformation and, 379–380; religious renewal in, 916; in Renaissance, 370–373; Romantic movement and, 667; in Spain, 368–369, 404–405, 461, 553; in Switzerland, 390; *Syllabus of Errors* and, 742–743. *See also* Catholic Reformation; Christianity; Missions and missionaries; Papacy; Pope; Protestant Reformation

Catholic League, of German states, 449, 451

Catholic Reformation, 398–402, 464

Cattle: in Americas, 437

Caucasus region, 800, 951

Cavalier Parliament, 476

Cavalry: English, 316

Cavendish, Margaret, 501–502, *502*

Cavour, Camillo de, 676–677

Ceausescu, Nicolae and Elena, 927, 952

Cecil, William, 408

Celibacy, 386

Cell phones, 972

Censorship: in arts, 971; in Enlightenment, 516; in Russia, 646; in World War I, 793

CENTO, 892

Central Africa, 416; imperialism in, 762–763. *See also* Africa

Central America, 421, 437; independence of, 642. *See also* Latin America; specific locations

Central Asia, 307, 308, 432, 764. *See also* Asia

Central Europe: absolutism in, 462–464; Calvinism in, 395; Jews in, 538; in late 1800s, 731, 732–733; power of, 547; repression in, 644–646; revolutions of 1848 in, 656–657. *See also* World War I; World War II

Centralization: in European states, 543, 554; in France, 600, 931; in Russia, 951; in World War I, 791–792

Central planning, of Soviet economy, 926

Central Powers (World War I), 785, 790; peace treaties with, 807–809

Central Treaty Organization. *See* CENTO

Ceremonies: Protestant, 398

Cereta, Laura, 356, 357

Ceylon. *See* Sri Lanka (Ceylon)

Cézanne, Paul, 745, *746*

Chacabuco, Battle of, 641, *641*

Chadwick, Edwin, 625, 717

Chamberlain, Houston Stewart, 742

Chamberlain, Neville, 852, 853, 858

Chamber of Deputies (France), 644, 652, 730

Chamber of Peers (France), 625, 644

Champagne region: battle in, 784

Chancellor: in Germany, 732

Charity, 329, 571

Charles I (England), 473–474

Charles II (England), 474–477, 507

Charles II (Spain), 460

Charles III (Spain), 553

Charles V (France), 316, 323

Charles V (Holy Roman Empire), 369, *387*, 388, *388*, 464; Aztecs and, 423; Henry VIII and, 392–393; Italy and, 350; Lutheranism and, 382, 386–387; Ottoman Empire and, 388

Charles VI (Austria), 554–555

Charles VI (France), 317, 323

Charles VII (France), 318, 366

Charles VIII (France), 350

Charles IX (France), 403

Charles X (France), 644, 651–652

Charles X (Sweden), 467

Charles XI (Sweden), 467

Charles XII (Sweden), 466, 467–468, 554

Charles Albert (Piedmont), 657, 676

Charles Martel Club (France), 964

Charles the Bold (Burgundy), 366, 369

Charleston (dance), 839, *839*

Charlotte (wife of Philip of Orléans), 459

Charter of the Nobility (Russia), 552

Chartism, 632–633

Chateaubriand, François-René de, 667

Châtelet, marquise du, 519

Chaucer, Geoffrey, 331–332

Chechnya, 951, *951*

Cheka, 802

Chemical fertilizers, 708, 938

Chemical industry, 705

Chemistry, 501, 694

Cheng, Nien, 936

Chennai, India. *See* Madras

Chernobyl, nuclear power disaster at, 938

Chiang Kai-shek, 856, 899

Chicago School of architecture (1890s), 844

Childbirth: in Renaissance, 346

Childe Harold's Pilgrimage (Byron), 664

Child labor, 614, 619, 628–629, 630, 633, 725

Children: in 18th century, 559–560; in Holocaust, 870, *871*; in Middle Ages, 334, 336, *336*; middle class, 723, 724, *724*; in 19th century, 631, 723; in Renaissance Italy, 345–346; as workers, 561; in working class, 725. *See also* Child labor

Chile, 424, 641, *641*, 642

China: civil war in, 899–890; communism in, 891, 900, 935; Cultural Revolution in, 935, 936; England and, 433; Europeans and, 432–435, 437; gunpowder and, 319; imperialism in, 764, 767; Japan and, 764, 855, 856, *857*; Jesuits in, 401, 438–439; Korean War and, 892; Portugal and, 419, 432; Republic of, 767; Russia and, 433; Soviet Union and, 892; U.S. relations with, 935–936

Chirac, Jacques, 959, 970

Chloroform, 696

Chocolate, 440, 441

Cholera, in cities, 625, 696

Cholula people, *422*

Chrétien, Jean, 962

Christian II (Denmark), 389

Christian III (Denmark), 389

Christian IV (Denmark), 450, 451, 466

Christian V (Denmark), 467

Christian VII (Denmark), 554

Christian, Frederick, 515

Christian church. *See* Christianity

Christian Democratic Union (West Germany), 929

Christian Democrats, 904; in East Germany, 954; in Germany, 957, 959; in Italy, 823, 907, 931; in West Germany, 823, 929, 957

Christian humanism, 377–379

Christianity, 742; Indians and, 420; response to attacks on, 742–743; revival of, 667; science and, 508–510; skepticism about, 515. *See also* Missions and missionaries; specific groups

Christian Socialists (Austria), 756

Christian Social Workers (Germany), 752

Christina (Sweden), 467

Christine de Pizan, 332, *332*; on Joan of Arc, 319, 322

Chronicles (Froissart), 314, 317

Chrysoloras, Manuel, 355

Church(es): in 18th century, 536–539; Nazi, 831; Protestant, 386. *See also* Church and state; De-Christianization; Religion

Church and state: Catholic Church and, 326; in 18th century, 536; in France, 755; separation of, 392, 647

Churchill, John, duke of Marlborough, 461

Churchill, Winston, 834, 877, 894; iron curtain speech of, 881, 882; World War II and, 858, 864, 885; Yalta conference and, 879, 880, *880*

Church of England, 393, 473, 536

Ciompi revolt, 315, 325

Circumnavigation of earth: by Magellan, *413*, 413–414, 420

Cities and towns: in 14th century, 334; in 18th century, 569–571; in 19th century, 622–625; in British colonies, 436; in French Revolution, 589, *589*; industrialization and, 618; redesign of, 718–719; in Renaissance, 344–345; revolts in, 314–315; trade and, 564–565; transformation of, 716–719; World War II bombings of, 875–877, *878*. *See also* City-states; Villages; specific locations

Citizens and citizenship: in France, 586; Jews and, 752

City-states: German, 323–324; Italian, 324–325, 348–349; in Renaissance Italy, 347–352

Civic humanism, 352–354

Civil Code (Napoleon), 600, 644

Civil Constitution of the Clergy (France), 586, 587

Civil disobedience, Gandhi and, 820

Civilian Conservation Corps, 819

Civilians: in World War I, 804; in World War II, 872–877, 878

Civilization: globalization of, 974–978; of Mesoamerica, 420–422. *See also* Culture(s)

Civilization of the Renaissance in Italy, The (Burckhardt), 341

Civil liberties: in World War I, 793

Civil Rights Act (1964), 908

Civil rights movement (U.S.), 908–909, *909*

Civil service: in France, 600; in Prussia, 548. *See also* Bureaucracy

Civil war(s): American Revolution as, 575; in England, 367–368, 473–476; food shortages from, 976–978; in France, 317. *See also* specific locations

Clarendon, Lord (Edward Hyde), 475

Classes: drinking habits of, 535; in 18th century, 565–571; in Enlightenment, 524–525; industrial middle class as, 625–627; industrial workers as, 627–631; in Prussia, 548; revolts and, 313; in welfare states, 910–912; World War I and, 795–796, 822. *See also* Social orders

Classical economics, 647

Classical learning: in 18th century, 532; in Renaissance, 352–355

Classicism: in arts, 481; Romanticism and, 662, 664, 666. *See also* Art(s); Neoclassicism

Clemenceau, Georges, 792, 793, 805, *805*, 806

Clement V (Pope), 326

Clement VI (Pope), 311

Clement VII (Pope), 387, 392

Clement XIV (Pope), 536

Clergy: conciliar movement and, 328; corruption of, 380; in 18th century, 536, 566; English, 393; as French First Estate, 578–579; French Revolution and, 586, 587, 590; marriage and, 382, 386, 393; Protestant, 538; as social estate, 312; in Spain, 368; taxation of, 326. *See also* Pope

Climate: change in, 977

"Climate Change 2007:...", 977–978

Clinton, Bill, 956, 959, 961, 963

Clive, Robert, 432, 556, *556*, 557

Clock, invention of, 337

Cloth industry, 314

Clothing: of Japanese elite, 767; ready-made, 729

Clydebank (Scotland): bombing of, *878*

Coal and coal industry, 756; industrialization and, 610, 611; working conditions in, 628, *628*

Coal Mines Act (England, 1842), *628*, 633

Cobb, Humphrey, 787

Cobbett, William, 607

Cobden, Richard, 654

COBOL, 938

Cochin China, 765

Code Napoléon. *See* Civil Code (Napoleon)

Codes of law. *See* Law codes

Codreanu, Corneliu, 836

Coffeehouses, 441, 526, 532, *532*

Cohan, George M., 789

Coitus interruptus, 561

Coke, 611, 618
Coke, Thomas, 569
Colbert, Jean-Baptiste, 458, *506*
Cold War, 879, 880–881, 882, *891*, 903; decolonization and, 900; détente in, 926, 935, 936–937; end of, 962–963; escalation of, 892–893; films on, 889, 933–934; globalization of, 891–894; Olympic Games and, 937, 943; superpowers in, 886–891; transition to post-Cold War, 948; U.S. and Soviet viewpoints on, 887
Cole (ship), terrorist attack on, 964
Collateralized debt obligations (CDOs), 975
Collective bargaining, 714
Collective security, after World War I, 812, 850
Collectivization: in China, 900; in eastern Europe, 903; in Soviet Union, 834, 835
Colleges. *See* Universities and colleges
Colloquy: of Marburg, 390, 391; of Regensburg, 401
Cologne: bombing of, 876
Colombia, 424, 641, 642
Colonies and colonization: in Africa, 761–763, 767; British, 435, 436, 556–557, 763; Dutch, 436; end of colonial empires, 894–895; European population and, 558; French, 435, 436, 556–557; globalization and, 443; impact on colonizers, 441; India as, 432; industrialization in, 620; Latin America and, 436, *642*, 643; mercantilist theory on, 564; missionaries and, 437–439; new imperialism and, 759; Spanish, 420–425; U.S. imperialism and, 766; World War I and, 785–790, 820–821. *See also* Decolonization; Imperialism; New imperialism
Colonna, Oddone, 328
Columbian Exchange, *440*, 440–441
Columbus, Christopher, 414, 415, 419–420, *420*, 421
Combination Acts (Britain), 631, 632
COMECON, 890
"Comfort women," 872
"Commentaries of the Great Afonso de Albuquerque, The," 419
Commerce: in Amsterdam, 471; Dutch, *430*; in England, 608; Jews in, 538. *See also* Mercantilism; Trade
Commercial capitalism, 432, 442–443, 564
Committee of Public Safety, 589, 590–591, 593, 595
Common Market. *See* European Economic Community (EEC, Common Market)
Common people: in French Revolution, 582–586; science and, 507
Commonwealth: in England, 478–479
Commonwealth of Australia, 763
Commonwealth of Independent States, 950. *See also* Russia
Commune (France, 1871), 730, 731. *See also* Paris Commune
Communication(s): in Digital Age, 972; globalization and, 974; revolution in, 705, 839–840
Communist League, 692
Communist Manifesto, The (Marx and Engels), 691, 692, 693, 713
Communist Party. *See* Communists and communism; specific locations
Communist People's Democratic Front (Romania), 927
Communist People's Liberation Army (Greece), 886
Communists and communism: domino theory and, 934; in eastern Europe, 902–903, 952; Eurocommunism and, 931; Nazis and, 867; Soviets and, 822, 833–836; in western Europe, 903. *See also* Marx, Karl, and Marxism
Compass, 415
Composers. *See* Music
Computers, 937–938, 948, 972, 973

Comte, Auguste, 698
Concentration camps, 831, 832, *870*
Concerning Character (Vergerio), 355
Concert of Europe, 640–643, 675
Conciliarism, 328, 553
Concordat, Napoleon and (1801), 599–600
Conditions of the Working Class in England, The (Engels), 691–692
Condorcet, Marie-Jean de, 522
Condottieri, 324, 347–348, 349
Confederate States of America, 688
Confederation of the Rhine, 601, 638
Confession, Luther and, 380
Congo, 428, 763. *See also* Zaire
Congress (U.S.), 578, 658
Congress of Berlin (1878), 769
Congress of Vienna (1815), 636, *636*, *637*, 637–639, *638*, 644, 652, 675
Conquistadors (Spain), 415, 420
Conscription: in Japan, 768; in Nazi Germany, 832, 851, 875; World War I and, 777, 791
Conservatism, 670, 755; in 1840s, 654; after Napoleonic wars, 636, 637–647
Conservative Party: in Canada, 909, 962; in England, 686, 687, 818, 906, 929, 959
Conservatives, in Spain, 730
Consistory, in Geneva, 395
Conspiracy of Equals, 597
Constable, John, 665
Constables (Britain), 660
Constance, Council of, 371–372
Constantine (Russia), 646
Constantinople (Istanbul), 468–469; siege and capture of (1453), 370
Constituent Assembly: in Russia, 800
Constituent assembly: in Austrian Empire, *656*
Constitution(s): in Austrian Empire, *656*; in England, 474; in France, 586–587, 596, 598–599, 652, 656, 730, 905; of Frankfurt Assembly, 656; German divisions and, 449; in Germany, 732; in Prussia, 678–679; in Russia, 951; Soviet, 949; in United States, 657–658; in West Germany, 890
Constitutional Democrats (Russia), 798
Constitutional monarchy: in Belgium, 652; in England, 477; in France, 586, 652; in Russia, 758
Consul (France), 600
Consumer goods, 643, 706, 901
Consumer society, 910
Consumption: in Industrial Revolution, 631; mass, 729; patterns of, 976
Contagious Diseases Acts (England), 711
Containment, 888, 892
Contarini, Gasparo, 401
Continental Army, 575
Continental Europe: industrialization in, 616–618; urban areas in, 623
Continental System, of Napoleon, 601–602, 603
Contraception. *See* Birth control
Convention People's Party (Gold Coast), 895
Conversation in the Park (Gainsborough), *568*
Conversion. *See* Missions and missionaries
Cook, James, 515, 763
Cook, Thomas, 727
Copernicus, Nicolaus, 489, 490–491, *491*, 492
Coral Sea, Battle of, 863
Corfu, 813
Corn, 437, 558, 561
Corn Law (England), 644, 654
Cornwallis, Charles, 575
Coronation, of Napoleon, 599
Corporations: multinational (transnational), 975
Corpus Hermeticum, 355
Corregidor, 860
Cort, Henry, 611
Cortes (Spain), 368, 644
Cortés, Hernán, 415, 422, 423
Corvinus, Matthias (Hungary), 369
Cosimo II (Florence). *See* Medici family

Cosmology, 489; of Newton, 499; Ptolemaic-Aristotelian, 491, 492, *493*, 497
Cosmopolitan movement, 516, 569
Cossacks, 552
Costa, Angelo, *570*
Costa Rica, 642
Cottage industry, 563, *564*, 618
Cotton industry: in Britain, 608, 610–611; on Continent, 618, 690; India and, 563–564; in U.S. South, 688; working conditions in, 628. *See also* Textiles and textile industry
Council for Mutual Economic Assistance. *See* COMECON
Council of Elders, 596
Council of 500 (France), 596
Council of People's Commissars (Soviet Union), 800
Council of Ten (Florence), 351
Council of Troubles (Council of Blood, Netherlands), 405–406
Councils (Christian): of Constance, 371–372; of Pisa, 328; of Trent, 401, 402
Counter-Reformation. *See* Catholic Reformation
Country houses, 567–569, *570*
Countryside: aristocratic lifestyle in, 567
Coup d'état: against Farouk, 895; by Napoleon, 597, 598; in Soviet Union, 947, 950, *951*
Courbet, Gustave, 698, *699*
Court (of law): in France, 455
Court (royal): in France, 446–447, 458–459, 545; lifestyles in, 567
Courtiers, Castiglione on, 344
Court of Star Chamber (England), 367
Coventry, bombing of, 875
Craftspeople, 627
Cranmer, Thomas, 393
Creation, The (Haydn), 529
Creation of Adam (Michelangelo), *340*, 363
Crécy, Battle of, 316
Credit, 562
Credit-Anstalt, 816
"Cremation of the Strasbourg Jews, The" (Königshofen), 312
Crime: in Austria, 549; in 18th century, 533; police forces and, 659–661; poverty and, 661; property, 658; in Russia, 951. *See also* Punishment
Crimea, 862
Crimean War, 673–675, *675*, 683, 749
Crime Was in Granada, The (Antonio Machado), 837
Croatia, 463, 954, 955, 957
Croats, 657, 954
Crompton, Samuel, 610
Cromwell, Oliver, 473–474, *474*, 475
Cromwell, Thomas, 393
Crop(s): in Americas, 437, 440; in 18th century, 561; fertilization of, 708. *See also* Agriculture
Crossbow, 315
Crossing, The (Viola), 972, *973*
Cruz, Juana Inés de la, 437
Crystal Palace Exhibition, 614–616, *615*
Cuba, 420, 730, 893
Cuban Missile Crisis, 893–894, 932
Cubism, 747, *748*, 838
Cultural relativism, 516
Cultural Revolution (China), 935, *935*, 936
Culture(s): Americanization of, 916–917, 944; drug, 921; in Enlightenment, 526–536; in 14th century, 330–333; high culture (18th century), 531–533; imperialism and, 766–768; since 1985, 968–972; Romanticism and, 662–667; youth, *922*. *See also* Art(s); Civilization; Nationalism; Popular culture; Renaissance
Curie, Marie, 738, *739*
Curie, Pierre, 738
Currency, 562, 960
Customs union, *Zollverein* as, 678
Cut with the Kitchen Knife... (Höch), 843

Cuzco, 423

Cyprus, 405, 960

Czechoslovakia, 804, 805, 807, 814, 836, 890; communism and, 902, 953; democracy in, 836, 952; German occupation of, 853–854; "Prague Spring" in, 926–927, 928; Soviet invasion of, 921, 926–927, 927, 928, 963

Czech people, 657, 733; Holy Roman Empire and, 369

Czech Republic, 953; in EU, 954, 960; in NATO, 954

Dada Dance (Höch), 843

Dadaism, 842–843, 843

Da Gama, Vasco, 416–417, 418, 418

Dahomey, 437

Daily Mail, 726

Daimler, Gottlieb, 706

Dali, Salvador, 844, 844

Dance: ballet, 749; in Roaring Twenties, 839

Dance halls, 727

Danish phase, of Thirty Years' War, 450–451

Danish War (1864), 680–681

Dante Alighieri, 330, 331

Danube River region, 690, 769

Danzig, 854

Dardanelles, 674

Darfur: starvation in, 978

Dark Ages: in Europe, 357

Darwin, Charles, 694–695, 741–742, 743

Das Kapital (Marx), 692

Dati, Gregorio, 346

Datini, Francesco, 345

Dauphin (France), 318

David (Donatello), 360, 360

David (Michelangelo), 363, 363

David, Jacques-Louis, 527–528, 529, 582, 599

Davison, Emily, 749–750, 751

Dawes Plan, 815

Day-care programs, 912

Day in the Life of Ivan Denisovich, A (Solzhenitsyn), 902

Dayton, Ohio, peace negotiations in, 956

Death camps, 831, 868–871, 869, 871, 872

Death of Sardanapalus, The (Delacroix), 665, 666

Death penalty, 533, 549

Death rates, 715; from Black Death, 308; decline in, 558, 621; in 18th century, 570; of infants, 560; from Middle Passage, 427; of Renaissance babies, 346

Debelleyme, Louis-Maurice, 659

Debt: concept of national, 562; in France, 580

Debussy, Claude, 748

Decameron (Boccaccio), 309, 311, 331

Decembrist Revolt (Russia, 1825), 646

Decentralization, in France, 931

De-Christianization: in French Revolution, 592–595

Declaration of Independence (U.S.), 543, 575, 577, 577, 578; French Revolution and, 585

Declaration of Indulgence, 476

Declaration of Pillnitz, 587

Declaration of the Rights of Man and the Citizen (France), 578, 584–585, 591, 647

Declaration of the Rights of Woman and the Female Citizen (Gouges), 584–585

"Declaration on Liberated Europe," 879, 880

Decline and Fall of the Roman Empire (Gibbon), 530–531

Decline of the West, The (Spengler), 813

Decolonization, 894–900, 896, 898

Deconstruction, 940

Decree on Serfs (Catherine the Great), 551

Deduction, 506

Defence of the Realm Act (England), 793

Defender of the Peace (Marsiglio of Padua), 328

Defense of the Liberal Instruction of Women (Cereta), 357

Deffand, marquise du, 526

Defoe, Daniel, 609

De Gaulle, Charles, 867, 895, 904–905, 905, 934

De Hooch, Pieter, 472, 472

Deism, 519, 538, 664

Delacroix, Eugène, 665, 666

Della Francesca, Piero, 349, 361

Démar, Claire, 651

De Meaux, Geoffrey, 309

Demian (Hesse), 845, 846

Democracy: in eastern Europe, 836; Locke and, 479; political, 749; in United States, 658; in western Europe, 903–907; after World War I, 816–818, 819, 821, 822

Democratic Party (U.S.), 688, 931, 961, 962

Demoiselles d'Avignon, Les (Picasso), 747, 748

Denazification, 888, 906

Denikin, Anton, 800

Denmark, 466–467, 890, 931; in 18th century, 554; Hansa and, 342; Russia and, 466; Scandinavian unification under, 389; upheavals in, 454; World War II in, 858. *See also* Scandinavia

Department stores, 706, 707, 729

Departure from Egypt (Kiefer), 971

Depressions, 631; of 1846, 654–655; of 1857–1858, 690; of 1873–1895, 708. *See also* Great Depression

De Rerum Novarum (Leo XIII), 743

Derrida, Jacques, 939–940

De Saussure, Ferdinand, 939

Descartes, René, 504, 504–505, 506

Descent of Man, The (Darwin), 694, 695

Despotism: in France, 600–601

De-Stalinization, 901, 902

Détente, 926, 935, 936–937

Developed and developing nations, 976

Diaghilev, Sergei, 749

Dialogue on the Two Chief World Systems… (Galileo), 495

"Diary of a Citizen," on slave trade, 428

Dias, Bartholomeu, 416

Díaz, Bernal, 422

Dickens, Charles, 623, 698, 700

Dictators and dictatorships, 822, 836–838. *See also* Totalitarianism; specific countries and individuals

Diderot, Denis, 519, 521, 523, 524, 534, 538; *Encyclopedia* of, 516, 519–520, 526; in Russia, 542

Diefenbaker, John, 909

Diet (food): in 18th century, 558; peasant, 566

Diet (legislative body): in Austria, 549; of Germanic Confederation, 645, 646, 680; in Poland, 369, 470; in Sweden, 554

Diet of Augsburg, 388

Diet of Worms, 376, 376

Diggers, 508

Digital Age, 948, 972–974

Diplomacy: in 18th century, 554; modern system of, 350–351; in Renaissance Italy, 348, 351–352; revolution in, 850–852; Seven Years' War and, 555; World War I and, 776, 815; World War II conferences and, 879–880. *See also* Alliances

Directory (France), 596–597

Disarmament conference (1932), 814, 815

Discourse on Method (Descartes), 504, 506

Discourse on the Origins of the Inequality of Mankind (Rousseau), 522–523

Discoveries. *See* Exploration

Disease, 694; decrease in, 715, 717; in 18th century, 558; European in New World, 422; in industrial cities, 623, 625; medical advances and, 499–501; Paracelsus on, 500; population growth and, 621; among prostitutes, 711; among slaves, 427. *See also* Medicine

Displaced persons, after World War II, 877–879, 885–886

Disraeli, Benjamin, 686–687, 752

Dissent. *See* Protest(s); Revolts and rebellions

Dissenters (England), 477

Diversity. *See* Minorities; Nationalities

Divine Comedy (Dante), 330, 331

Divine-right monarchy, 454, 646

Divinity: Heretics and, 355; humanists and, 357

Divorce, 749; in France, 600; in Soviet Union, 835; after World War II, 921

Dix, Otto, 842, 843

Doctors. *See* Physicians

Doge (Venice), 325

Doll's House, A (Ibsen), 771–772

Domesticity: Dutch, 472, 472; in late 1800s, 710, 720–722

Domestic system, 563

Dominican Republic, 420

Dominicans, 380, 399, 424–425, 437

Dominion of Canada. *See* Canada

Domino theory, 934, 935

Donatello, Donato di, 360, 360

Don Giovanni (Mozart), 529

Dopolavoro (Italy), 840

Doré, Gustave, 624, 624

Dostoevsky, Fyodor, 743

Douhet, Giulio, 875

Dowry: in Renaissance, 345

Draft (military). *See* Conscription

Drake, Francis, 408

Drama: in Elizabethan England, 483; in France, 484; popular, 845; in Spain, 484; Theater of the Absurd and, 914–915

Dresden, bombing of, 877, 878

Dreyfus, Alfred, 755

Dreyfus affair (France), 754, 755

Drinking. *See* Alcohol

Drogheda, battle at, 475

Dr. Strangelove… (movie), 933–934

Drug culture, 921

Drugs: Paracelsus and, 500; Romantics' experiments with, 664; sports and, 944

Drunken Boat, The (Rimbaud), 744

Dual Monarchy (Austria-Hungary), 682–683, 756. *See also* Austria-Hungary

Dubcek, Alexander, 926, 927

Dubois, François, 404

Du Bois, W. E. B., 806, 821

Dubuffet, Jean, 914, 914

Dufay, Guillaume, 365

Duke and Duchess of Urbino (Piero della Francesca), 349

Duma (Russia), 758, 798

Dunkirk, 858

Duomo (Florence), 360, 360

Dürer, Albrecht, 365, 366, 488

Dutch: Anabaptism and, 392; in Asia, 429, 430; domestic life of, 472, 472; economy of, 443; France and, 460; independence from Spain, 462; in India, 432; in Indonesia, 429, 437; in Japan, 435; North American colonies of, 436; painting of, 481–483, 482; slave trade and, 429; in South Africa, 426, 762; trade and, 442. *See also* Dutch Republic; Netherlands

Dutch East India Company, 426, 430, 442

Dutch East Indies, 763, 856, 857, 859, 899

Dutch Republic, 406, 638; Belgian revolt against, 652; British industry and, 609; decline of, 547; exploration by, 414; finance in, 562–563; France and, 460; golden age of, 470–471; Huguenots in, 457; Thirty Years' War and, 450; upheavals in, 454

Dutch West India Company, 436

Duties of Man, The (Mazzini), 657

Dylan, Bob, 923

Eakins, Thomas, 696

Earth, 975; circumnavigation of, 413, 413–414, 420. *See also* Planets; Universe

East Africa, 417, 785, 787

East Asia. *See* Asia

Eastern Europe: Allied war conferences and, 879–880; authoritarianism in, 836;

Calvinism in, 395; classes in, 566; after communism, 952–957; de-Stalinization and, 902; environment in, 938; in EU, 954, 960–961; immigrants from, 967; industrialization in, 619; Jews in, 311, 752–753; in late 1800s, 731, 733; migration from, 715–716; monarchies in, 369; NATO and, 954; plague in, 308; Poland-Lithuania in, 470; recession in (2008–), 976; revolutions of 1989 and, 952–954, 963; Soviets and, 886, 902, 921, 926–927, 947; Stalinization in, 903; Warsaw Pact in, 890–891, *891*; women in, 807; after World War I, 807, *836*. See also World War I; World War II

Eastern Front: in World War I, 783, *783*

Eastern Orthodoxy: in 18th century, *537*; Ottoman Empire and, 643; Russia and, 552

Easter Rebellion (Ireland), 792

East Germany, 881, 888, 890; communism in, 888, 902, 927; economy in, 927, 954; secret police in, 958–959. See also Germany; West Germany

East India Company. See British East India Company; Dutch East India Company

Eastman, George, 746

East Prussia, 462

Ebert, Friedrich, 803, 804

Ecclesiastical Ordinances, 395

Eck, Johann, 381

Eckhart (Meister), 329

Ecology, 938, 966. See also Environment

Economic imperialism, 761

Economic liberalism, 522, 647, 654

Economics: discipline of, 521–522; supply-side, 932

Economy: in 16th century, 442; in 17th century, 447; in 18th century, 558, 561–565; in 1970s and 1980s, 927; Black Death and, 312–313; in Brandenburg-Prussia, 463; EEC and, 907, 931; expansion and, 414–415, 440–441, 442–443; in France, 455, 458, 544, 580–581, 587, 591; global, 709–710, 954, 962, 974, 975–976; Great Depression and, 815–816; industrial, 708–710; Industrial Revolution and, 608; new imperialism and, 761; in Renaissance, 341–342; in Russia, 466; of Third Estate, 579–580; after Thirty Years' War, 452; trade and, 564; World War I and, 791, 796–797, 812; World War II and, 873, 874, 875. See also Mercantilism; Trade

Ecstasy of Saint Theresa, The (Bernini), 480, *481*

Ecuador, 424, 641

Edict of Fontainebleau, 457

Edict of Nantes, 404, 457

Edict of Restitution, 451

Edict of Worms, 383

Edison, Thomas, 705

Education: in 18th century, 532; elite, 719; in England, 687; in Fascist Italy, 824; in Germany, 708, 831; in India, 768; Luther on, 398; mass, 725–727; in Middle Ages, 334; Montessori, 752; primary, 535–536, 725–726; in Renaissance, 355–357; Rousseau on, 523; secondary schools and, 334, *398*, 725; in Soviet Union, 835–836; in welfare state, 910–912; for women, 356, 357, 397, 749, 966; after World War II, 921–923. See also Schools; Universities and colleges

Education Act (England, 1870), 687

Education of a Christian Prince (Erasmus), 353

Edward (Black Prince, England), 316, 317

Edward II (England), 315

Edward III (England), 315, 321

Edward VI (England), 393, 407

Ego, 740, 846

Egypt: Britain and, 762; independence in, 895; Israel and, 898; Napoleon and, 598; Nasser

and Pan-Arabism in, 897–898; Suez Canal and, 897–898; in World War I, 785

Eiffel, Gustave, 766

Eiffel Tower, 737, *737*

Eight-hour workday, 633

Einsatzgruppen, 868, *868*, 955

Einstein, Albert, 738–739, 846

Einstein on the Beach (Glass), 942

Eisenhower, Dwight D., 864, 892, 908

El Alamein, 862

Elba: Napoleon at, 604, 638

Elbe River region, 864

Elections. See Voting and voting rights

Elector of Saxony, 383

Electors, in Germany, 323–324

Electra complex, 740

Electricity, 694, 705

Electric light, 705, 738

"Electro-Dynamics of Moving Bodies, The" (Einstein), 738

Elegances of the Italian Language, The (Valla), 355

Elementary schools, 725–726

El Greco, *479*, 480

Elites, 719; in cities and towns, *570*; in Germany, 829, 850; as industrial entrepreneurs, 627; in Latin America, 640; science and, 507. See also Classes; Nobility

Elizabeth (movie), 409

Elizabeth (Russia), 556

Elizabeth I (England), 393, 405, *407*, 407–410, 483

El Salvador, 642

E-mail, 972

Emancipation: of Jews, 752, 753; of serfs, in Russia, 684–685, 686

Emancipation Proclamation (Lincoln), 686, 689

Embargo: on Soviet Union, 937

Emigrant, The (Staniland), *716*

Emigration, 715–716; European between 1876–1910, *716*; of Irish, 621; from Nazi Germany, 833, 867–868. See also Immigration

Émile (Rousseau), 523, 525, 559

Empires. See Imperialism; Seven Years' War; specific empires

Empiricism, 506

Employment. See Labor; Unemployment; Workers

Enabling Act (Germany), 829

Enclosure acts (England), 561–562

Encomienda system, 424, 425

Encyclopedia (Diderot), 516, 519–520, 526

Energy (power), 705–706

Engels, Friedrich, 691–692, 693

Engine: internal combustion, 705–706; steam, *610*, 610–611, 618, 690, 694

Engineering: Inca, 424

England (Britain), 931; agriculture in, 561–562, *562*; Allied war conferences and, 879–880; American colonies of, 436, 545; American Revolution and, 575, *576*; appeasement policy of, 852; Black Death in, 308; Canada and, 689–690; China and, 433; cities in, 622–623; civil wars in, 367–369, 473–476; conservatism in, 643–644; Crimean War and, 674–675; decolonization and, 895, 896, 898, 899; economy in, 685, 818, 906–907, 930; exploration by, 414; factory acts in, 630–631; Falklands War and, 930; financing in, 562–563; foreign policy of, 408–409; in 14th century, 312; France and, 315, 601–602; French American possessions to, 461; Glorious Revolution in, 477; government of, 608–609; Great Depression in, 818–819; Greece and, 643; Huguenots in, 457; Hundred Years' War and, 315–319; immigrants in, 967; imperialism of, 429, 762, 763, 764, *764*, *765*, 768; imports of, 443; India and, 432, 441, 763, 764, 768, 820–821, 898; Industrial Revolution in, 564, 608–616, *612*; Ireland and, 474, 475, 729–730, 754–755; Latin America and, 642,

643; liberalism in, 753–755; Lollardy in, 370; magazines in, 532; Middle East and, 785; military alliances of, 892; monarchy in, 477, 544–546; Monroe Doctrine and, 643; Napoleon and, 598, 601–602; in NATO, 890; navy of, 461, 601–602, 643; since 1980s, 959; at Paris Peace Conference, 805; Peasants' Revolt (1381) in, 313–314; police in, 659–661, *662*; population of, 558, 621; Protestant revivalism in, 538–539; Quadruple Alliance and, 637, 640; reform in, 652–654, 729–730; religion in, 392–394, 407–408; restoration in, 476–477; sciences in, 497; in Second Industrial Revolution, 708; in Seven Years' War, 555–557; in South Africa, 762; Southeast Asia trade and, 429; Spanish Armada and, 409–410; Suez crisis and, 897–898; suffragists in, 749–750, *751*; textile industry in, 690; Thirty Years' War and, 450; trade unions in, 631, 713; transportation in, 611–612; Triple Entente and, 770; in United Kingdom, 544; Victorian Age in, 685–688; after War of the Spanish Succession, 461; welfare state in, 906; women in, 793–794, 912; World War I and, 792, 808, 817–818; World War II and, 873. See also Stuart dynasty; Tudor dynasty; World War I; World War II

English Football Association, 727, *728*

English Royal Society. See Royal Society (England)

Enlightened absolutism, 543, 551, 554

Enlightenment, 441, 513–514, *517*, 647; American Revolution and, 578; arts in, 526–531; culture and society in, 526–536; families and, 559–560; Jews and Muslims in, 538; later period in, 522; philosophes in, 513, 516–524; politics and, 542–543; revolutions and, 578; science in, 514–515, *515*; social status and, 565–566; travel literature in, 515–516; women in, 523–524. See also Scientific Revolution

Entertainment: in amusement parks, 704; in Middle Ages, 336, *336*; in 1920s, 839–840

Entrepreneurs, 343, 705; industrial, 608, 609, 625–627

Environment, 938–939, 962; Enlightenment view of, 516; globalization and crisis in, 976, 977–978. See also Climate; Pollution

Environmental Protection Agency, 941

Epicycles: of planetary bodies, 489–490

Epidemics, 621, 717. See also Disease

Equality: in France, 595, 600, 644; in Soviet Union, 835; of women, 524, 651, 924

Equal rights amendment (U.S.), 924

Erasmus, Desiderius, 353, 377–378, *378*, 379, 380

Erhard, Ludwig, 906

Eroica symphony (Beethoven), 666

Essay Concerning Human Understanding (Locke), 516

Essay on the Principles of Population (Malthus), 647

Estates (political): in Denmark, 467

Estates (social orders), 312, 344; in France, 578–580, *579*; in Renaissance, 344–345

Estates-General: in France, 321–323, 366, 581

Este family (Ferrara), 349; Isabella d', 349, 350

Estonia, 466, 807, 949, 954, 960

Ether, in surgery, 697

Ethics Demonstrated in the Geometrical Manner (Spinoza), 509

Ethiopia, 762, 763, 768, 852

Ethnic cleansing, by Serbs, 955

Ethnic groups. See Ethnic cleansing; Minorities; Nationalities; specific groups

EU. See European Union (EU)

Eucharist, 329

Eurasia, Mongols and, 306, 307–308

Euripides, 355, 484

Euro, 960, 976

Eurocommunism, 931

Europa, Europa (movie), 869

Europe: in 15th century, *367*; in 1763, *547*; in 1871, *683*; in 1914, *777*; in 1919, *808*; alliances in (1950s–1960s), *891*; American empires of, 435–436; American Revolution and, 578; in Asia, 429–435, *430*; Black Death in, 308–312; changes in central (1936–1939), *854*; coalition against French Revolution, 589; after Congress of Vienna (1815), *638*; Continental industrialization in, 616–618, *617*; economic zones in, 708; English industrialization in, 608–616; industry and, 563–565, *709*; New Europe (1980s), *949*; population in 17th century, 447; religious populations in 18th century, *537*; Renaissance monarchies in, 366–370; in Seven Years' War, 555–556, *557*; southeastern, *371*; state system and, 543; trade within, 564; unification of, 960–961, *961*; after World War II, 885–886, 909–913
European Atomic Energy Community (EURATOM), 907
European Central Bank, 960
European Coal and Steel Community (ECSC), 907
European Community (EC), 931, 959. *See also* European Union (EU)
European Economic Community (EEC, Common Market), 907, *907*, 931
European Parliament, 960
European Recovery Program. *See* Marshall Plan
European Union (EU), 954, *961*; bailout of Greece, 959, 960; eastern European states in, 960–961; identity and, 960; Muslims in, 968
Evangelicalism, 661, 743; of Lutheranism, 384; of Zwingli, 384
Evolution, Darwin on, 694–695, 968
Evolutionary socialism, 712, 713
Evolutionary Socialism (Bernstein), 712, 713
Exchange Bank of Amsterdam, 471
Executions: in 18th century, 533
Existentialism, 913, 915, 939
Expansion, 414–415; of Amsterdam, 471; economy and, 440–441, 442–443; during French Revolution, *591*; Hitler and, 850; impact of European, 437–441; by Russia, 466, *467*, 552; by Venice, 325. *See also* Colonies and colonization; Exploration; Imperialism; New Imperialism
Exploration: in 15th and 16th centuries, *417*; of New World, 419–425; Portuguese, 416–419; of space, 937, *938*; Spanish, 419–425. *See also* Colonies and colonization
Exports, 443; from Latin America, 643
Expressionism: German, 842
Extermination camps. *See* Death camps

Fabian Socialists, 753
Facebook, 972
Facing Mount Kenya (Kenyatta), 821
Factories: capitalism and, 691; child labor in, 629; discipline in, 613–614; electricity and, 705; growth of, 707–708; industrialization and, 607, 610, 612–614, *613*; labor in, 612–614, *613*, 619, 628–629; in Russia, 756; in United States, 874; women in, 794, *794*, 795, 873, *873*; working conditions in, 627–631
Factory acts: in England, 630–631, 633
Fairy tales, 662
Faith. *See* Justification by faith alone
Falange, 838
Falklands War, 930
"Fall of the House of Usher, The" (Poe), 663
Families: chapels of, 329; economy and, 561; in 18th century, 558–561, *560*; as factory workers, 619, 630; in Italy, 345–347, 824–825; in medieval society, 334; middle-class, 723–725; in permissive society, 921; Protestantism and, 396–397; in Soviet Union, 835; in welfare state, 910, 912;

working-class, 725; in World War I, 796; after World War II, 921. *See also* Children
Family allowances, 910
Family of Henry VIII, The, *394*
Family planning, 723
Famine, 566; disappearance of, 621; in Ireland, 621, 622; in Middle Ages, 307; in Soviet Union, 833, 834
Fanon, Frantz, 897
Fantasy literature: expansion and, 414
Faraday, Michael, 694
Farm cooperatives, 561, 708
Farms and farming. *See* Agriculture; Crop(s)
Farouk (Egypt), 895
Fascio di Combattimento (League of Combat), 823
Fascism, 816; in Italy, 822–826; in Romania, 836; in Spain, 838. *See also* Nazi Germany
Fatah. *See* Al-Fatah
Fawcett, Millicent, 749
Fedele, Cassandra, 356
Federalists (U.S.), 658
Federal Republic of Germany. *See* West Germany
Federal Reserve System, 758
Fellini, Federico, 917
Female Association for the Care of the Poor and Sick, 749
Female Medical College of Pennsylvania, 697
Female Spectator, The (periodical), 532
Feminine Mystique, The (Friedan), 925
Feminism, 524, 651, 924. *See also* Women; Women's liberation movement; Women's rights
Ferdinand, duke of Modena, *549*
Ferdinand I (Austria), 657
Ferdinand I (Holy Roman Empire), 388
Ferdinand I (Naples and Sicily), 640
Ferdinand II (Holy Roman Empire), 450, 451
Ferdinand VII (Spain), 640, 644
Ferdinand of Aragon, *368*, 368–369
Ferrara, 348, 349
Festivals: in 18th century, 534, *535*
Fichte, Johann Gottlieb, 602–603
Ficino, Marsilio, 355
Fiction writing, 529–530
Fielden, Joshua, 625
Fielding, Henry, 530
Filipinos. *See* Philippines
Filipovic, Zlata, 956
Films. *See* Movies
Final Solution, 868, 869, 870
Finances. *See* Economy
Finland, 470, 750, 807, 960, 972
Firearms: Japan and, 433; in Thirty Years' War, 452. *See also* Weapons
Firebird, The (Stravinsky), 749
Firestorms, in World War II, 877
Fireworks Music (Handel), 529
First Balkan War, 771, *771*
First Battle of the Marne, 782
First Estate: in European society, 344; in France, 578–579, 581; Swedish nobility as, 467
First International, 692
First World War. *See* World War I
First Zionist Congress, 753
Five Lectures on Psychoanalysis (Freud), 741
Five-year plans: in Soviet Union, 834
Flagellants, 311, *311*
Flanders: arts in, 364–365; Hansa and, 342
Flanders Fleet, of Venice, 341–342
"Flappers," 839
Flaubert, Gustav, 698
Flemish language, 406
Fleury (Cardinal), 544
Florence, 464; arts in, 359–360; *ciompi* revolt in, 315; as city-state, 325; Macchiavelli in, 351–352; Medici in, 343; Republic of, 324, 348; woolen industry in, 314
Fluyt (ship), 471
Foch, Ferdinand, 803
Fontenelle, Bernard de, 514

Food: in 18th century, 561; in 19th century, 623; population growth and, 976; Renaissance banquet and, 342; shortages of, 976–978; supermarkets and, 911; World War II and, 873, 874. *See also* Diet (food); Famine
Food and drug act: in England, 623
Football (soccer), 727, 728, *728*, 943
Forced labor camps, Soviet, 834, 901, 902
Ford, Gerald, 932
Ford, Henry, 706
Foreign affairs: in French Revolution, 587, 589
Foreign workers: for Nazi Germany, 867
Formosa (Taiwan), 856, 900
Fort William. *See* Calcutta
Foucault, Michel, 940
Foundations of the Nineteenth Century, The (Chamberlain), 742
Foundling homes, 560
Fourier, Charles, 650, 651
Fourteen Points, 805
Fourth Republic (France), 904–905
France: abolition of monarchy in, 588; absolutism in, 454–461; administrative restructuring of, 586–587; African colonies of, 762, 763; Algerian independence and, 895, 905; alliances of, 892; American colonies of, 435, 436, 461; American Revolution and, 575; Black Death in, 308; bourgeoisie in, 580; bureaucracy in, 600; Calvinism in, 395; Canada and, 436, 689; civil war in, 317; Classicism in arts and, 481; Communist Party in, 903; in Concert of Europe, 640; constitutions in, 586–587, 596, 598–599; Crimean War and, 674–675; decolonization and, 895, 896, 899; drama in, 484; in early 15th century, *318*; economy in, 455, 458, 580–581, 587, 673, 819, 905, 931, 959; England and, 315, 609; Estates-General in, 321–323, 366, 581; foreign policy of, 455; Germany and, 852, 853; Greece and, 643; Hundred Years' War and, 315–319; imperialism of, 762; India and, 432, 441; Indochina and, 764–765, 892, 899, 905; industrialization in, 618, 755; Italy and, 676–677; *Jacquerie* in, 313, *313*, 314; Jesuits and, 536; learned societies in, 506; Mexico and, 623; in mid-14th century, *318*; military in, 557; monarchs in, *315*, 321, 366, 455, 456, 580, 581; Muslims in, 959, 968, 969–970; in Naples, 350; Napoleonic, 597–603; after Napoleonic wars, 638–639; National Assembly in, 581–582; NATO and, 890, 905; in 1970s and 1980s, 931; since 1980s, 959; nobility in, 366, 455, 456, 580, 581; old regime in, 574, 578–580; papacy and, 387; at Paris Peace Conference, 805; peasants in, 313, *313*, 314, 582–585; police in, 659; population of, 558, 578; poverty in, 571, 580; religion in, 394, 454, 536; republics in, 588, 656, 707, 730, 755; restoration in, 604, 644; revolts in, 313, *313*, 314, 454, 730, 731; revolutionary army in, 589, 590; revolution of 1830 in, *651*, 651–652, 653; revolution of 1848 in, 654–656; salons in, 526; sciences and, 497; Second Empire in, 671–675; secularism in, 968, 969–970; in 17th century, 451; in Seven Years' War, 555–557; socialist parties in, 712; Spain and, 349, 460, 462, 644; student revolt in, 920–921, 923; Suez crisis and, 897–898; trade unions in, 713–714; Triple Entente and, 770; Vichy government in, 858; Vietnam and, 892, 899; War of the Austrian Succession and, 555; Wars of Religion in, 402; witchcraft trial in, 448; women in, 584–586, 591–592, 600, 794, 912; World War I and, 792, 808, 813, 814, 819. *See also* French Revolution; Government; Huguenots; Monarchs and monarchies; World War I; World War II
Franche-Comté, 369, 460

Francis I (Austrian Empire), 636
Francis I (France), 350, 387, 394
Franciscans, 380, 437
Francisco Franco (Manuel Machado), 837
Francis Ferdinand (Austria), 776, 778
Francis Joseph I (Austria), 657, 682, 733, 756
Francis of Assisi (Saint), 399
Franco, Francisco, 837, 838
Franco-Prussian War, 678, 681–682, 769
Franco-Swedish phase, of Thirty Years' War, 451
Frankenstein (Mary Shelley), 664
Frankfurt Assembly, 656
Franklin, Benjamin, 518, *577*
Frederick I (Denmark), 389
Frederick I (Prussia), 463
Frederick II the Great (Prussia), 543, 548, *549*,
      550, 554, 555, 556
Frederick III (Holy Roman Empire), 369
Frederick IV (Palatinate), 449
Frederick V (Elector of Palatinate), 449
Frederick the Wise (Saxony), 380
Frederick William (Great Elector), 462
Frederick William I (Prussia), 548, 550
Frederick William II (Prussia), 587
Frederick William III (Prussia), 645
Frederick William IV (Prussia), 656, 679
Free Corps (Germany), 804
Free Democratic Party (West Germany), 929, 957
Freedom(s): political liberalism and, 647, 648;
      in Prussia, 548; in Sweden, 548; in United
      States, 578. *See also* Liberty; Rights
Freedom Party (Austria), 967–968
Free French movement, 867
Free market economies, 950, 953
Freemasons. *See* Masons
Free trade, 706, 962, 975
French and Indian War, 556–557
French Canadians, 436, 932
French Empire: of Napoleon I, 601–603;
      Napoleon III and, 671–675
French Popular Movement, 905
French Revolution, 542, 574–575, 578–597, 605,
      637; Burke on, 639; European concerns
      about, 587–588; expansion during, *591*;
      radical revolution in, 587–595; Republic
      of Virtue in, 591, 595; slavery abolished
      during, 429. *See also* Reign of Terror
French Royal Academy of Sciences. *See* Royal
      Academy of Sciences (France)
Frescoes, *359*
Freud, Sigmund, *740*, 740–741, 846
Friars, 424–425
Friedan, Betty, 924–925
Friedrich, Caspar David, 664, *664*
Friends of the Blacks, 595
Frith, William P., *724*
Froissart, Jean, 314, 316, 317
Fronde, 455
Frontiers: of Russia, *553. See also* Borders
Fugger, Jacob, 442, *443*
Führerprinzip, 828
Functionalism, in architecture, *844*, 844–845
Fundamentalism (religious), 742, 964, 968

Gabelle (French tax), 323
Gagern, Heinrich von, 645
Gainsborough, Thomas, *568*
Galen (physician), 488, 500
Galicia, 552, 682, 783
Galilei, Galileo, 488, 489, 493–497, 507
Gallipoli campaign, 785, 796
Games: in 19th century, *724*, 724
Gamond, Zoé Gatti de, 651
Gandhi, Mohandas (Mahatma), 820, *821*,
      898–899
Gapon, Gregory, 757
García Márquez, Gabriel, 941
Garibaldi, Giuseppe, 677, *677*, 678
Garret, Elizabeth, 697
Garvey, Marcus, 821

Gascony, 315, 316
Gasperi, Alcide de, 907
Gas warfare, in World War I, 784, *788*
Gates, Bill, 972
Gaudry, Suzanne: trial of, 448
Gay rights movement, 921
Gays and lesbians. *See* Homosexuals and
      homosexuality
Geiler, Johannes, 380
Gender issues: Enlightenment, 523–524; in
      medieval society, 334; Scientific Revolution
      and, 502–504; in welfare state, 912; after
      World War I, 822. *See also* Men; Women
General Agreement on Tariffs and Trade (GATT),
      975
General Confederation of Labor (France), 714
General Directory (Prussia), 548
General strike: in England, 1926, 818; in France,
      905; Sorel on, 740
General Theory of Employment, Interest, and Money
      (Keynes), 819
General War Commissariat (Prussia), 462
Generation of 1898 (Spain), 730
Geneva, 395, 892
Geneva Conference (1954), 892
Geneva Disarmament Conference (1933), 851
Genevan Academy, 398
Genghis Khan, 432
Genius of Christianity (Chateaubriand), 667
Genoa, 308, 553
Genocide: against Armenians, 804. *See also*
      Holocaust
Gentile, Giovanni, 825
Gentileschi, Artemisia, 480, *481*
Gentry: in England, 473, 544; in Russia, 552
Gentz, Friedrich von (Germany), *637*
Geocentric conception of universe, 489
Geoffrin, Marie-Thérèse de, 513, 526
Geography (Ptolemy), 415, *416*
George I (England), 545, 567
George II (England), 567
George III (England), 434, 545, 546, 567
Georgia, nationalist movement in, 949
Georgian style houses, 567
Géricault, Theodore, *641*
German Democratic Republic. *See* East Germany
German Empire, *670*, *680*, 682
German Federal Republic. *See* West Germany
German Girls Association, 831
Germanic Confederation, 638, 644–645, 656, 678
German Workers' Party. *See* National Socialist
      German Workers' Party
Germany: absolutist states in, 462–463; African
      imperialism by, 763; alliances of, 769;
      Allied war conferences and, 879–880;
      anti-Semitism in, 752; Black Death in,
      308; Catholic Church in, 451; colonies
      of, 763, 785, 820, 821; Communist Party
      in, 804; denazification and partitioning
      of, 888–890; economy in, 814, 826, 828,
      954, 958, 959; electors in, 323; emigration
      from, 621; French coercion policy and, 814;
      Great Depression in, 817, 826; Hanseatic
      League and, *343*; Huguenots in, 457;
      illegitimacy in, 561; industrialization in,
      618, 755; industrial leadership in, 708;
      Jews of, 311, 871; in late 1800s, 732;
      Lutheranism in, 381–387; monarchy in,
      323–324; nationalism in, 602–603, 645–
      646; occupation zones in, 879; Paris Peace
      Conference and, 805; Peasants' War in, 385–
      386; Pietism in, 538; Poland and, *553*; police
      force in, 661; politics in, 386–387, 388–389;
      railroads in, 611; Reformation in, 384–385;
      religion in, 386–387, 449; reparations
      and, 807, 814, 888; reunification of, 954,
      957–959, 963; revolution of 1848 in, 656;
      Rococo in, *527*; after Thirty Years' War, 451,
      453; trade unions in, 714; in Triple Alliance,
      769; unification of, *649*, 656, *670*, 671,
      678–682, *680*; Versailles Treaty and, 807,

850; World War I and, 791–792, 804. *See
      also* Berlin; Nazi Germany; Prussia; Weimar
      Republic; World War II
Germ theory, 694, 695
Gestapo, 867
Ghana, independence of, 896
Ghent, 314
Ghettos: for Jews, 752, 867
Ghirlandaio, Ridolfo, *420*
Giangaleazzo Visconti, 324
Gibbon, Edward, 530–531
Gibbs, Philip, 775
Gibraltar, 461
Gigas, Herman, 309–310
Gin, 534
Giolitti, Giovanni, 755, 823
Giotto, 332, *333*, 358
Giovanni Arnolfini and His Bride (Van Eyck), 365,
      365
Giovanni di Dondi, 337
Girondins, 588
Gladstone, William, 687–688, 729, 730
Glasnost, 948
Glass, Philip, 942
Gleaners, The (Millet), 698, *699*
Gleichschaltung, 829
Global economy, 709–710, 769, 974, 975–976;
      financial crisis and (2008–), 954, 962,
      975–976
Globalization: of Cold War, 891–894;
      environmental crisis and, 976, 977–978;
      expansion and, 443; social challenges of,
      976–978; use of term, 974
Global warming, 962, 976, 977–978
Globe theater, 483
Glorious Revolution (England), 477
Goa, Portugal and, 417
Goebbels, Joseph, 840
Goethe, Johann Wolfgang von, 662
"Going Strong" (Tristam), 728
Golan Heights, 898
Gold: in Africa, 416; in South Africa, 762;
      Spanish, 404; for trade, 443
Gold Coast, 416, 895, 896. *See also* Ghana
Golden, Arthur, 974
Golden age: of Dutch Republic, 470–471
"Golden Speech, The" (Elizabeth I), 408
Gömbös, Julius, 836
Gomez, Franco, *641*
Gomulka, Wladyslaw, 903
Gonfalionere (Florence), 325
Gonzaga family (Mantua), 349, 356; Francesco,
      349; Gian Francesco I, 355
Goodbye to All That (Graves), 781
Gorbachev, Mikhail, 926, *929*, 947, 948–949, 950,
      952; end of Cold War and, 962, *963*
Gore, Al, 961
Gorée, Senegal: slave trade in, *427*
Göring, Hermann, 829
Gothic architecture, 662, *663*
Gothic literature, 662–664
Gottwald, Klement, 902
Gouges, Olympe de, 584–585, 589
Government: of Austrian Empire, 464, 549–550;
      of Catholic states, 536; Christianity and,
      742; economic involvement by, 647; of
      France, 456–457, 544, 586–587, 600; in
      Great Depression, 816; of Inca Empire, 424;
      industrialization and, 608–609, 616–617,
      690; industrial reform and, 633; of Italian
      city-states, 324–325; mass society and,
      705; Montesquieu on, 517–518; nobility in,
      566; Ottoman, 468–469; of Poland, 470; of
      Prussia, 462; of Russia, 465–466; scientific
      research funding by, 937; of Spain, 461–
      462; of Spanish America, 425; of United
      States, 576–578; World War I and, 791–793.
      See also Monarchs and monarchies; specific
      countries
Government bonds, 562
Goya, Francisco, *603*

Grammar schools, 334
Granada, 369
Grand Alliance (World War II), 861, 880. *See also* Allies, World War II; Big Three
Grand Army (Napoleon), *602*, 603
Grand Duchy of Warsaw, 601
Grand Empire (Napoleon), 601–602, *602*
Grandeur and Misery of Victory (Clemenceau), 806
Grandi (nobility), 325
Grandmaster Flash and the Furious Five, 942, 943, 971–972
Grand National Consolidated Trades Union, 632
Grand tour, 569
Grand viziers (Ottoman), 469
Grant, Ulysses S., 689
Grass, Günther, 915
Grassroots social movements, 978
Graves, Robert, 781
Gravitation, Newton on, 499
Gray, Thomas, 534, 569
Great Britain. *See* England (Britain)
Great council (Venice), 325
Great Council of barons, 321
Great Depression, *812*, 812–813, 815–816, *816*, 818–819, 819–820
Great East Asia Co-Prosperity Sphere, 860, *861*, 871
Greater Japanese Women's Association, 875
Great Exhibition (1851), 614–616, *615*
Great Famine: in Ireland, 621, 622
Great German Art Exhibition, 845
Great Instauration, The (Bacon), 505–506
Great Lakes region, 556, 557
Great Leap Forward, 900
Great Northern War, 466
Great Patriotic War, 873
Great Proletarian Cultural Revolution, 935, *935*, 936
"Great Retreat," by Napoleon, 603
Great Schism (Catholic Church), 327–328, 372
Great Society, 908
Great Trek (South Africa), 762, *762*
Great Wall (China), 433
Great War. *See* World War I
Great War for Empire, 556
Greco-Roman culture: Renaissance and, 341, *348*
Greece, 813, 836, 931; authoritarianism in, 836; Balkan wars and, 771; civil war in, 886; Classical, 354–355; EU bailout of, 959, 960; independence of, 643, 674; NATO and, 890; revolt in, 643; World War II in, 859
Greek Orthodoxy. *See* Eastern Orthodoxy
Greene, Graham, 889
Greenhouse effect, 976
Green movements and parties, 938–939, 966
Greenwich, England: Royal Observatory at, 507, *507*
Gregory XI (Pope), 327
Grieg, Edvard, 747
Grimm brothers, 662
Grimmelshausen, Jakob von, 453
Groote, Gerard, 329
Gropius, Walter, *844*, 844–845
Gros, Antoine-Jean (Baron), *598*
Gross Clinic, The (Eakins), *696*
Grossdeutsch state, 656
Grosz, George, 842
Groza, Petra, 880
Grozny (Chechnya), 951
Grunge music, 971
Guadeloupe, 435
Guam, 766
Guatemala, 422, 642
Guernica, 837, *838*
Guernica (Picasso), *838*
Guest workers, 906, 967
Guggenheim Museum, 914
Guicciardini, Francesco, 358
Guilds: in 18th century, 570; industrialization and, 616; Renaissance artists and, 363–364
Guillotine, *588*, 590

Guindorf, Reine, 651
Guise family (France), 403
Guizot, François, 652, 655
Gulf of Aqaba, 898
Gulf of Mexico, 422, 976
Gulf War. *See* Persian Gulf War
Gunpowder, 319, 337
Gustavus III (Sweden), 554
Gustavus Adolphus (Sweden), 451, 467
Gustavus Vasa. *See* Vasa, Gustavus
Gutenberg, Johannes, 358
Guzman, Gaspar de. *See* Olivares (Count)
Gymnasium, 398
Gypsies, in death camps, 871

Habsburg dynasty, 350, 369, *386*, 460, *463*, 464, 644, 646, 657, 682; Bourbon dynasty and, 555; economy and, 442; in 18th century, *547*, 549–550; Thirty Years' War and, 449, 451; and War of the Austrian Succession, 554–555
Habsburg-Valois Wars, 387
Haider, Jorg, 967–968
Haiti, 420, 421, 435–436, 595
Hall of Mirrors (Versailles), *458*, *670*, 671, 682
Hamburg, 451, 876, 877
Hamilton, Alexander, 518, 658
Hancock, John, *577*
Handbook of the Christian Knight (Erasmus), 377
Handel, George Frederick, 528–529
Hankou, Chiang Kai-shek in, 856
Hanover, 681
Hanoverian dynasty (England), 545, 567
Hanseatic League (Hansa), 342–343, *343*
Hardenberg, Karl August von, 603, *637*, 645
Hargreaves, James, 610
Harlem, 436
Harper, Stephen, 962
Harpers Ferry arsenal, 618
Harris, Arthur, 876
Harvey, William, 500–501
Hauser, Heinrich, 817
Haushofer, Karl, 850
Haussmann (Baron), Paris and, 673
Havel, Vaclav, 926, 952, 953
Hawaii, 766
Haydn, Franz Joseph, 529, 666
Headscarves (hijabs): in France, 968, 969–970
Healing. *See* Medicine
Health and health care, 910, 962; improvements in, 715; revolution in, 695–698. *See also* Medicine
Hegel, Georg Wilhelm Friedrich, 691
Heisenberg, Werner, 846
Heliocentric conception of universe, 490, *491*, *492*
Helsinki Accords (1975), 936–937
Henrietta Marie (England), 473
Henry II (France), 388, 402, *404*
Henry III (England), 315
Henry III (France), 403
Henry IV (England), 321
Henry V (England), 317
Henry VI (England), 319
Henry VII (England), 367–368, 420
Henry VIII (England), 378, 379, 392–393, *394*, 407
Henry of Navarre, 403–404
Henry the Navigator (Portugal), 415, 416, *417*
Herculaneum, 569
Heresy: in England, 393–394; in Renaissance, 370–371
Hermeticism, 355, 489, 491, 499, 508
Herzegovina, 769, 771. *See also* Bosnia-Herzegovina
Herzen, Alexander, 685
Herzl, Theodor, 753, 754, 755
Hesse, Hermann, 845, 846
Hesse-Cassel, 681
Hevelius, Johannes, *493*

Heydrich, Reinhard, 868, 870
Hierarchies (social): in Prussia, 548
High culture: of 18th century, 531–533
High Renaissance, artistic, 361–365
Hijabs. *See* Headscarves (hijabs)
Hill, Octavia, 717, 718
Himmler, Heinrich, 831, 866, 868
Hindenburg, Paul von, 783, 791–792, *792*, 826, 829
Hindus, in India, 430, 898–899
Hip-hop music, 942, 943, 971–972
Hippies, 922
Hippolytus (Euripides), 484
Hirado, 435
Hiroshima, bombing of, 865, 876, 877, *878*
Hispaniola, 420, 421, 424, 595
Historical and Critical Dictionary (Bayle), 515
History and historians: Enlightenment writing and, 530–531; humanism and, 357–358; Romantic interest in, 662
History of a Collective Farm, The (Belov), 835
History of Italy (Guicciardini), 358
History of Sexuality, The (Foucault), 940
History of the Cotton Manufacture in Great Britain, The (Baines), 609
History of the Florentine People (Bruni), 357
History of the Rebellion and Civil Wars in England, The (Clarendon), 475–476
History of Tom Jones, The... (Fielding), 530
Hitler, Adolf, 804, 826–829, *828*, *849*; anti-Semitism of, 752, 827, 865, 867; appeasement of, 852, 853; assassination attempt on, 867; "diplomatic revolution" and, 850–852; goals of, 830, 849, 851; home front and, 875; radio and movie use by, 840, 841; Spanish Civil War and, 837; suicide of, 865; in Vienna, 826, 853; war declaration by, *856*. *See also* Holocaust; Nazi Germany; World War II
Hitler Youth, 831
Hobbes, Thomas, 478–479
Höch, Hannah, 843, *843*
Ho Chi Minh, 892, 899, 900
Hoffman, E. T. A., 666
Hohenstaufen dynasty, 323
Hohenzollern dynasty, 462, 681
Holbach, Paul d' (Baron), 522, 532
Holbein, Ambrosius, 398
Holbein, Hans, the Younger, 378
Holidays, 723, 910
Holland. *See* Dutch; Netherlands
Holocaust, 867–871, *868*, *870*, *871*, 872, 896
Holstein, 680
Holtzendorff, Admiral, 790
Holy Land. *See* Jerusalem
Holy League, 403
Holy Office. *See* Roman Inquisition
Holy Roman Empire, *387*; Bohemia in, 369; Catholic Church and, 328; divisions in, 449; in 18th century, *547*; France and, 387, 460; German city-states and, 323–324; Habsburgs and, 369, *386*; independence of states in, 451; sovereign states in, 644; Thirty Years' War and, 449, 451
Home front: in World War I, 790, 791–797; in World War II, 872–877
Home Guard (Britain), 873
Homeland Security, Office of, 962
Homelessness: in Great Depression, 812, 816, 817; after World War II, 885–886
Home rule, for Ireland, 730, 754–755
Homes of the London Poor (Hill), 718
Homosexuals and homosexuality: Foucault on, 940; Nazis and, 871; Soviet, 835; after World War II, 921
Hondius, Henricus, *441*
Honduras, 642
Honecker, Erich, 927
Hong Kong, 764
Hoover, Herbert, 813
"Hoovervilles," 812

Hopkins, Harry, 879
Hopper, Grace, 938
Horses, 437
Horthy, Miklós, 836
Hospitals, 334, 534, 696; unwanted children at, 560
Höss, Rudolf, on death camps, 870
Hôtel-Dieu, 534
Hot-line communication system, 893
Hötzendorf, Franz Conrad von, 778
Households: industrial, 630
House of Commons (England), 321, 473, *544*, 544–546, 643, 652, 729, 753
House of Lords (England), 321, 544, 754
House of Medici. *See* Medici family
House of Representatives (U.S.), 961
Housing: in Amsterdam, 471; architecture of, 567; in cities, 624, 625; in late 1800s, 717; in Soviet Union, 901; in United States, 975; of workers, 623, 717, 718
Howard, Catherine, 393
How to Blow Up Two Heads at Once (Gentlemen) (Shonibare), 973, *974*
Huayna Inca, 423
Huber, V. A., 717
Hubertusburg, Peace of, 556
Hucknall, Mick, 942
Hudson, Henry, 436
Hudson's Bay Territory, 461
Huguenots, 402–404, *404*, 454, 457–458, 536
Humanism, 341, 352; Christian, 377–380; education and, 355–357; history and, 357–358; Luther and, 384–385; in Renaissance Italy, 352–355; sciences and, 488; secular, 968
Human rights, 937
Human sacrifice: in Benin, 429
Hume, David, 521, 526
Hundred Years' War, 315–319
Hungarians, in Austrian Empire, 646, 657
Hungary, 369, 836, 890; Austria and, 463, 682–683, 756; communism in, 886, 902; democracy in, 952; in EU, 954, 960; Jews of, *871*; Magyars in, 756; migrants from, 716; in NATO, 954; Ottomans and, 370, 388, 468, 469; reforms in, 926; revolts in, 454, 657, 902, 903; Roman Catholicism in, 369; Soviets and, 893, 903, 904, 963; World War I and, 804, 807; World War II and, 859, 865. *See also* Austria-Hungary
Hunt, Harriet, 697
Hurricane Katrina, 962
Hus, John, and Hussites, 371, 381
Husák, Gustáv, 927, 952
Hussite wars, 369, 371
Hyde, Edward (first earl of Clarendon), 475
Hydroelectric power, 705
Hygiene, 696, 715

Iberian peninsula, *368*, 368–369. *See also* Portugal; Spain
Ibsen, Henrik, 721–722, 747
Ice age: "little," 307, 447
Iceland, 890
Id, 740, 846
Ideal Marriage... (van de Velde), 842
Ideology, 647–651
Ignatius of Loyola. *See* Loyola, Ignatius of
Ignorant Philosopher, The (Voltaire), 520
Illegal immigrants: in France, 959
Illegitimacy, 561
Illiteracy, 726, 768
Illness. *See* Disease; Medicine
Imitation of Christ, The (Thomas à Kempis), 380
Immigration: to Canada, 759; to cities, 570; in France, 959; from Ireland, 621; of Jews, 753; in post-Cold War Europe, 967–968; United States and, 619, 758. *See also* Emigration

"Imperial Edict to the King of England, An" (Qianlong), 434
Imperialism: economic, 761; in 19th century, 441. *See also* New imperialism
Imperialism, the Highest Stage of World Capitalism (Lenin), 761
Imports, 443, 709–710
Impression, Sunrise (Monet), 745, *745*
Impressionism, 744–745, *745, 746*, 748
Inca Empire, 423–424, *424*
Income, national, 706
Independents: Puritans as, 473
Independent Social Democratic Party (Germany), 804
Index of Forbidden Books, 402, 464
India: Britain and, 763, 764; cotton from, 563–564; Dutch and, 432; England and, 432, 441, 545, 557; France and, 432, 441; Gandhi in, 820; goods from, 616; independence for, 898–899; industrialization and, 620; Jesuits in, 401; Mughal Empire in, 430–432; Napoleon and, 598; new imperialism in, 763, 768; Portugal and, 416–417, 432; in Seven Years' War, 555, 556; and War of the Austrian Succession, 555; World War I and, 785, 821
Indian National Congress, 768, 898
Indian Ocean region, 429
Indians (Native Americans): conversion of, 425; in French and Indian War, 556–557; in Latin American society, 437; Spanish treatment of, 424; use of term, 420
Individualism, 352, 360, 662
Indochina: Communist Party in, 892; France and, 892, 899, 905; Japanese occupation of, 857. *See also* Cambodia; Laos; Vietnam
Indonesia, 429, 437, 899; Communist Party in, 900
Induction, 506
Indulgences, 380, 381, 382
Industrial economy, 708–710
Industrialization, 616–620, 708–711, 742; of Continental Europe, 616–618, *617*, 690–691; factories and, 607, 610, 612–614; Latin America and, 643; Marxism and, 691–692; mass education and, 725–726; middle class and, 625–627; in nonindustrialized world, 619–620; poor people and, 624, *624*; Romantics and, 664; in Soviet Union, 834; and technology, 610–616; in United States, 618–619; urban reformers and, 623–625. *See also* Entrepreneurs; Industrial Revolution
Industrial Revolution, 607–608, 637; in England, 564, 608–616, *612*, 643, 652; Second, 704, 705–711; social impact of, 621–633; spread of, 616–620; transportation revolution and, 611–612. *See also* Industrialization
Industry: entrepreneurial class in, 625–627; European, 563–565; land and, 627; mechanized, 565; population in, 621; prosperity and, 705–714; in Renaissance, 343, 358; Spanish, 404; trade and, 564–565; in World War I, 796–797; in World War II, 873–874
Inertia, 497
Infanticide, 768; in 18th century, 560
Infant mortality, 307, 715, 926
Infection, Lister and, 696
Inflation, 797, 814, *814*, 815, 826, 927, 932; in 16th century, 442. *See also* Economy
"Information Age," 972
INF Treaty, 962
Inquisition, 464; Galileo and, 488, 494–495; Roman, 401, 494–495; Spanish, 368, 425
Installment plan, 910
Institutes of the Christian Religion (Calvin), 394
Institutional church, in 18th century, 536–538
Instruction (Catherine the Great), 550
Instrument of Government (England), 474

Intellectual thought: Chinese influence on, 441; interwar, 845–846; on irrational, 739–740; Postmodernism and, 939–940; Poststructuralism and, 940; pre-World War I sciences and, 738–739; in Renaissance Italy, 352–358; women and, 523–524. *See also* Enlightenment; Humanism; Philosophy; Renaissance; Scientific Revolution
Intendants, 454, 553, 571
Interchangeable parts, 618, 708
Intercontinental ballistic missile, 893
Internal combustion engine, 705–706
International Monetary Fund (IMF), 975
Internationals, Marx and, 692
International tribunal for crimes against humanity, 957
International women's conferences, 966–967
International Women's Day, 797
International Working Men's Association, 692
Internet, 972
Internment: of Japanese Americans, 874–875
Interpretation of Dreams, The (Freud), 740
Interpreter of Maladies (Lahiri), 974
Intervention principle, 640, 643, 644
Inventions: electric, 705; in 14th century, 336–337. *See also* specific inventions
Investment: foreign, 710; industrialization and, 616; new imperialism and, 761; after World War I, 815
iPod, 972
Iran, 820, 892, 896, 964; revolution in, 965; U.S. hostages in, 932. *See also* Persia
Iraq, 808, 820, 892, 896, 898; invasion of Kuwait by, 963; United States and, 966. *See also* Mesopotamia
Iraq War (2003–), 959, 962, 964–965, 966
Ireland, 931; England and, 474, 475, 729–730, 754–755; Great Famine in, 621; potato in, 561; in World War I, 792. *See also* Northern Ireland
Irish Land League, 730
Irish Republican Army (IRA), 929, 964
Irish Republican Brotherhood..., 792
Iron and iron industry, 705; in Britain, 690; on Continent, 618, 690; industrialization and, 611
Iron curtain speech (Churchill), 881, 882
Iron Guard (Romania), 836
"Iron law of wages" (Ricardo), 647
Irrationality, 739–740
Irwin, James, *938*
Isabella (Capetian family), 315
Isabella II (Spain), 681
Isabella of Castile, *368*, 368–369, 420, 424
Islam: fundamentalism in, 964, 968; in U.S. and Europe, 968; West and, 965–966, 967. *See also* Muslims
Israel, 897, 898, 943, 964, 965. *See also* Arab-Israeli disputes
Istanbul. *See* Constantinople (Istanbul)
Isthmus of Panama, 420
Italy, 807, 813, 890; Austria and, 463, 464, 553, 644, 657; Black Death in, 308; city-states in, 324–325, *325*, 348–349; Communist Party in, 903, 907, 931, 959; economy in, 907, 931; in 1815, *644*; Ethiopia and, 762, 852; fascism in, 823–826; France and, 350, *591*, 597, 601; Germany and, 323; Holy Roman Empire and, 387; intellectual thought in, 352–358; liberalism in, 753, 755; Libya and, 755; mannerism in, 479–480; Napoleon and, 598; national cinema of, 917; nationalism in, 659; in 1970s and 1980s, 931; at Paris Peace Conference, 805; Renaissance in, 341–366, *348*; revolts in, 640, 652, 657; slaves in, 345; Spain and, 350, 464; states in, 347–352, 553; in Triple Alliance, 769; unification of, *649*, 657, *676*, 676–678; warfare in, 349–350; World War I and, 783, 785, 792, 822–823, *823*; after

World War II, 907. *See also* Renaissance; Rome; World War I; World War II
Ivan III (Russia), 369
Ivan IV the Terrible (Russia), 464
Ivanhoe (Scott), 662

Jackson, Andrew, 658
Jacob, Aletta, 722–723
Jacobins, 587, 588, 596, 597
Jacob's Room (Woolf), 845
Jacquerie, 313, *313*, 314
Jadwiga (Poland), 470
Jagiello dynasty (Poland), 470
Jahn, Friedrich Ludwig, 645–646
Jakarta. *See* Batavia (Jakarta)
Jamaica, 435
James I (England), 472–473
James II (England), 476–477, 478
Jamestown, 436
Janissaries, 469
Japan: Anti-Comintern Pact and, 852; atomic bombing of, 865, 877, 879; Catholic Church in, 435; China and, 764, 855, 856, *857*; Empire of, 855–856; Europeans and, 433–435, *434*, 437; expansion by, 768, *768*, 813, 856–857; Great East Asia Co-Prosperity Sphere of, 860, *861*, 871; imperialism and, 764, 767–768; industrialization in, 708–709; Jesuits in, 401, 439; military influence in, 856; modernization of, 768; Nazi Germany and, 856; Russo-Japanese War and, 757, 764; textile factory in, *710*; war policy in Asia, 871–872; West and, 764, 767; World War I and, 790; World War II and, 790. *See also* World War II
Japanese Americans, internment of, 874–875
Jaurès, Jean, 712
Java, 429
Jazz, 839, 917
Jeanne d'Albret, 403
Jefferson, Thomas, 518, 575, 577, *577*, 658
Jerrold, Blanchard, 624, *624*
Jerusalem, 898
Jesuits, 399–401, 437–439, 464, 536
Jewish State, The (Herzl), 753, 754
Jews and Judaism, 312; in eastern Europe, 311, 752–753; migration by, 716; Nazis and, 829, 831, *832*, 832–833; plague and, 311; in Spain, 368–369; toleration and, 537–538; Zionism and, 753, 754. *See also* Anti-Semitism; Holocaust; Israel (modern)
Jex-Blake, Sophia, 697
Joanna (Spain), 369
Joan of Arc, 318–319, *319*, 320, 322
Joan of Arc (movie), 320
Joffre, Joseph, 782
John II (France), 316, 323
John XXIII (pope), 916
John of Leiden, 392
John Paul II (pope), 968–970, 971
Johnson, Lyndon B., 908, 925, 934
Johnson, Samuel, 530, 535, 569
Joint-stock company, 432, 442, 564
Joint-stock investment banks, 690
Jollain, Nicolas-René, the Elder, *446*
Jordan, 820, 896
Joseph II (Austria), 537, 538, 543, *549*, 549–550, 554
Josephine de Beauharnais (France), 597, *599*
Journal des Savants, 507
Journalism: mass, 738. *See also* Newspapers
Journal of the Reverend John Wesley, The, 539
Joyce, James, 845
Judaism. *See* Jews and Judaism
Judith Beheading Holofernes (Gentileschi), 480, *481*
Julius II (Pope), 340, 363, 372
July Ordinances (France), 651–652
July Revolution (France, 1830), *651*, 651–652
Jung, Carl, 845–846

Junkers, 462, 548, 732
Justification by faith alone, 381, 382, 386
Jutland, Battle of, 790

Kaczynski, Lech, 953
Kádár, János, 903, 926
Kamikaze, 875
Kandinsky, Wassily, 747, *748*
Kangxi (China), 433
Kansas-Nebraska Act (U.S., 1854), 688
Kant, Immanuel, 514
Kaprow, Allen, 940–941
Karelia, 466
Karlowitz, Treaty of, 463
Karlsbad Decrees, 646
Kaunitz, Wenzel von, 555
Kay-Shuttleworth, James, 623–624
Kellogg-Briand pact, 815
Kelly, Petra, 966
Kemal, Mustafa (Atatürk), 820
Kennan, George, 887, 888
Kennedy, John F., 893, 908, 932
Kent State University, protesters at, 925
Kenya, 821, 895, 896
Kenya African National Union, 895
Kenyatta, Jomo, 821, 895
Kepler, Johannes, 491–493, *493*, 494
Kerensky, Alexander, 799
Keynes, John Maynard, 498–499, 819
KGB, 926
Khanbaliq. *See* Beijing
Kharkov Tank Factory, 873
Khomeini, Ayatollah, 932, 965
Khrushchev, Nikita, 893, 894, 901–902, *902*, 903, 925
Khrushchev Remembers (Khrushchev), 894
Kiefer, Anselm, *970*, 970–971
Kiel mutiny, 803
Kikuyu people, Mau Mau movement of, 895
King, Coretta, *909*
King, Martin Luther, Jr., 908, 909, *909*
Kingdom of Naples, 324, 348, 350
Kingdom of the Two Sicilies, 644, 677
Kings and kingdoms. *See* Monarchs and monarchies
Kipling, Rudyard, 760
Kirch, Gottfried, 502
Kitchener (Lord), 768
Kivshenko, Alexei, *685*
Kleindeutsch state, 656
Knighton, Henry, 306, 312
Knights: in Hundred Years' War, 315–316
Knox, John, 395
Kohl, Helmut, 957, 958, 959
Kolchak, Alexander, 800, 802
Kollontai, Alexandra, 800
Königgrätz (Sadowa), battle at, 681
Königshofen, Jacob von, 312
Korea, 764, 856, 872
Korean War, 891–892, *892*, 905, 909
Kornilov, Lavr, 799
Kosciuszko, Thaddeus, 552
Kosovo, 957; Battle of (1389), 370; war in, 956
Kosovo Albanians, 956
Kosovo Liberation Army (KLA), 956
Kossuth, Louis, 657, 683
Kostunica, Yojislav, 956, 957
Koyaanisqatsi (Glass), 942
Kraft durch Freude (Strength Through Joy), 840
Kristallnacht, 832, *832*
Kuchuk-Kainarji, Treaty of, 552
Kulaks, 834
Kulturkampf, 732
Kun, Béla, 804
Kundera, Milan, 941–942
Kurds: in Iraq, 965
Kurile Islands, 879
Kuwait, 963, 965

Kwasniewski, Aleksander, 953
Kyushu, 435, 439

Labor: in 14th century, 312; in 18th century, 570; Black Death and, 306–307; census in Britain, 627; in factories, 612–614, *613*, 618; of foreign workers, 967; in Japan, 709; in Japanese occupied territories, 872; May Day and, 712; migration of, 715–716; in Russia, 756; as social estate, 312; in Soviet Union, 834, 926; in United States, 619; walkouts by, 713; women as, 793–794, 795, 873, *873*, 874, 875, 912; World War I and, 787, 792, 793–794, 795. *See also* Labor unions; Slavery; Trade unions; Workers; Working class
Labor camps (Holocaust), 870
Labor Front (Germany), 831
Labor movements, Solidarity as, 926
Labor unions: in England, 929. *See also* Strikes; Trade unions
Labour Party (England), 753, 818, 906, 929, 959
La Bruyère, Jean de, 504
Lafayette, marquis de, 578, 582
Lahiri, Jhumpa, 974
Laibach: congress at, 640
Laissez-faire doctrine, 522, 554, 596, 647, 753, 816
Lake Texcoco, 421
Lamentation (Giotto), *333*
Lampi, Johann, *542*
Land: in 18th century, 561; European conquerors and, 439–440; in High Middle Ages, 307; industry and, 627; in Ireland, 729–730. *See also* Agriculture
Land and Freedom (Russia), 685
Landed estates, 719
Landing of Marie de' Medici at Marseilles, The (Rubens), *480*
Landlords: in 14th century, 312–313
Language(s): in Canada, 758; in 19th century Europe, 649; in Soviet Union, 949
Laocoön (El Greco), *479*
Laos, 765, 899
Las Casas, Bartolomé de, 425
Last Conquest of Ireland, The (Mitchel), 622
Last Supper, The (Leonardo da Vinci), *361*, 362
Lateen sails, 415
Lateran Accords (1929), 826
Later Middle Ages, 306–340. *See also* Middle Ages
Latin America: in early 19th century, *642*; European colonies in, 436, 437; independence and, 595, 641–642; Monroe Doctrine and, 642–643; revolts in, 640–643. *See also* Colonies and colonization; specific locations
Latin Christianity. *See* Catholic Church
Latin language: in Renaissance, 355
La Tour, Maurice-Quentin de, *519*, *523*
Latvia, 807, 949, 954, 960
Laud, William, 473
Launay, marquis de, 574, 582
Laurier, Wilfred, 758–759
Lavasseur, E., 707
Lavender Mist (Pollock), 914
Lavoisier, Antoine and Marie-Anne, 501
Law(s). *See* Law codes; Scientific laws; specific laws
Law, John, 562
Law codes: Napoleonic, 600; in Sweden, 554
Law of 14 Frimaire, 595
Law of the General Maximum, 591
Lawrence, T. E. (Lawrence of Arabia), 785
Lay Down Your Arms (Suttner), 752
Lay piety, in 14th century, 329
Lazar (Serbia), 370
League of Communists of Yugoslavia, 954
League of Nations: Germany and, 815, 851; Japan and, 856; mandates and, 808
Learning. *See* Education; Intellectual thought

Leary, Timothy, 921
Lebanon, 808, 820, 896
Lebensraum, 827, 850, 851, *854*
Lee, Robert E., 689
Leeds Woolen Workers' Petition, The, 565
Legal issues. *See* Law codes
Legion of the Archangel Michael (Romania), 836
Legislative Assembly (France), 586, 587, 588, 596
Legislative Corps (France), 671–673
Legitimacy principle, Metternich and, 637–638
Leibniz, Gottfried, 502
Leiden, University of, 534
Leipzig Debate, 381
Leisure, 704, 727–729, 840–842, 910
Lend-Lease, 880
Lenin, V. I., 761, 798–800, *799*, 804, 833
Leningrad, 859, 864, 865
Leo X (Pope), *372*, 373, 381
Leo XIII (Pope), 743
Leonardo da Vinci, 358, *361*, 361–362, 364, 488, 489
Leopold II (Belgium), 761–763
Leopold II (Holy Roman Emperor), *549*, 587
Leopold of Hohenzollern-Sigmaringen, 681
Leopold of Saxe-Coburg, 652
Lepanto, Battle of, 405, 468
Le Pen, Jean-Marie, 967
Lerma, duke of (Spain), 461
Lesbians. *See* Homosexuals and homosexuality
Lesseps, Ferdinand de, *691*
Lesueur brothers, *590*
"Letter from a Peasant to the Bolshevik Leaders," 801
"Letter from a Soldier in Leningrad to Lenin," 801
Letters: of Isabella d'Este, 350; between Louis XIV Lee and King of Tonkin, 431
"Letter to His Father" (Gagern), 645
"Letter to Paolo Foscarini" (Bellarmine), 496–497
"Letter to Raphael Sanchez, Treasurer to the King and Queen of Spain" (Columbus), 421
"Letter to the Grand Duchess Christina" (Galileo), 496
Lettow-Vorbeck, Paul von, 785
Levellers, 474, 508
Lévesque, René, 962
Leviathan (Hobbes), 478
Ley, Robert, 831
Leyster, Judith, 481, *482*
Liberal arts, 355–356
Liberal Democrats (England), 959
Liberalization, in France, 673
Liberal Party: in Canada, 909, 932, 962; in England, 686, 687–688, 753–755, 818; in Italy, 823
Liberals and liberalism, 636–637, 644, 647–649, 670; economic, 522, 647, 654; nationalism and, 650, 681; political, 647–649; in Spain, 730; in World War I, 792
Liberia, 763
Liberty: Locke on, 479; Mill on, 648
Libya: Italy and, 755; terrorism and, 964; Tripoli as, 762
Liebknecht, Karl, 804
Liebknecht, Wilhelm, 711
Life and Death in Shanghai (Cheng), 936
Life of Jesus (Renan), 742
Life on the Mississippi (Twain), 620
Lifestyle, 621, 738, 948; in 14th century, 333–337; in 18th century, 565–571; of 19th-century workers, 631; in Amsterdam, 471; aristocratic, *568*, 568–569; Black Death and, 312–315; Columbian Exchange and, 441; in country houses, 567–569, *570*; of Dutch, 472, *472*; grand tour and, 569; improvements in, 717; in Industrial Revolution, 623; in Italian Renaissance, 343–345; of Louis XIV (France), 455, 458–459; of middle class, 720; of nobility, 566–569; in Russia, 464; of urban poor, 624, *624*; in World War I trenches, 784–785, 786, *788*

Lima, Pizarro in, 424
Limited monarchies, 447, 470
Limmer, Walter, letter to his parents, 781
Limoges: sack of, 317
Lincoln, Abraham, 686, 688, 689
Linen Cupboard, The (de Hooch), 472, *472*
Lisbon Treaty, 960
List, Friedrich, 617
Lister, Joseph, 696
Liszt, Franz, 700–701
Literacy, 398, 535–536, 726–727
Literature: Elizabethan, 483; in England, 483; feminist, 924; in France, 484; Gothic, 662–664; Modernism in, 743; multiculturalism in, 974; Naturalism in, 743; novels and, 529–530; Postmodernism in, 941–942; Realism in, 698; Romantic, 662–664; in Soviet Union, 901, 902; in Spain, 484; Symbolism in, 743, 744; travel, 515–516; unconscious in, 845, 846; vernacular, 330–332; after World War I, 914–915. *See also* specific works and writers
Lithuania, 470, 807, 949, 954, 960
Little Entente, 814, *814*
"Little ice age," 307, 447
Little Pretty Pocket-Book, 560
Little Red Book (Mao Zedong), 935
Little Richard, 917
"Live and let live" system: in trench warfare, 785
Liverpool-Manchester railroad, 611, 612
Lives of Others, The (movie), 958
Livestock, 561
Livingston, Robert, *577*
Livingstone, David, 762
Livonia, 466
Li Zicheng (China), 433
Lloyd George, David, 753, 754, 792, 795, 805, *805*, 818
Lo Bengula, 763
Locarno Treaty, 815
Locke, John, 478, 479, 516, 577
Lockerbie, Scotland, 964
Locomotives, 611
Lodi, Peace of, 349
Lollardy, 370
Lombardy, 324, 638, 644, 657, 676
London: Blitz of, 876; finance in, 563; living conditions of, 624, *624*; police in, 660, *661*; terrorism in, 965
London: A Pilgrimage (Jerrold), 624
London Conference, after Balkan wars, 771–772
London Mechanics' Institute, 661
London School of Medicine for Women, 697
London Working Men's Association, 632
Longbow, 316
Long Parliament, 473
Long Telegram, The (Kennan), 887
Looms, 564
Lope de Vega, Félix, 484
Lorca, Federico García, 837
Lord Protector (England), 474
Lords, 566. *See also* Nobility
Lord's Supper, 386, 392, 395. *See also* Eucharist
Lorraine, 460, 681, 807. *See also* Alsace-Lorraine
"Lost generation," 804, 813
Loughnan, Naomi, 795
Louis XI ("Spider" king, France), 366
Louis XIII (France), 451, 454, *455*
Louis XIV (France), 446, *446*, 459, 542, 544; absolutism of, 454, 455–461; letters to king of Tonkin, 431; parlements and, 580; religious minorities and, 536; Royal Academy of Sciences and, 508; Versailles court of, 455, 458–459, 567; wars of, 459–461, *460*
Louis XVI (France), 544, 545; execution of, 588, *588*; French Revolution and, 574, 587; National Assembly and, 582
Louis XVIII (France), 604, 637, 644
Louisbourg, 555, 556
Louis of Hungary, 388

Louis-Philippe (France), *651*, 652, 655
Louvois, marquis de (François-Michel Le Tellier), 460, 466
"Love-in," *922*
Low Countries, 308, 369, 616. *See also* Belgium; Netherlands
Lower Austria, 463
Lower classes, 454, 559, 661, 720, 910. *See also* Classes
Loyalists: in American Revolution, 575
Loyola, Ignatius of (Saint), 400, *401*
LSD, 921
Lübeck, *343*, 451
Luddites, 632
Ludendorff, Erich, 783, 791–792, *792*, 803
Ludlow, Edmund, 475
Lueger, Karl, 752
Luftwaffe, 852, 858, 876
Lusitania (ship), 790
Lussault, Françoise, 403
Luther (movie), 383
Luther, Martin, *376*, 376–377, 380–383, 646; on education, 398; marriage of, 396; Peasants' War and, 385–386; Zwingli and, 390, 391
Lutheranism, 383–386; in 18th century, 536; in Netherlands, 405; in Scandinavia, 389; spread of, 384–386
Luther Versus the Pope, 384
Lützen, Battle of, 451
Luxembourg, 369, 406, 858, 890, 907
Luxemburg, Rosa, 804
Luxury goods, 458, 631
Lyons, 589, 590

Maastricht Treaty, 960
MacArthur, Douglas, 864, 892
Macartney (Lord), China trade and, 433, 434
Macaulay, Thomas Babington, 653
MacDonald, Ramsay, 818
Macedonia, 771, 954, 957
Machado, Antonio, 837
Machado, Manuel, 837
Machiavelli, Niccolò, *351*, 351–352, 353
Machine gun, 763, 784, *784*, *785*, 791
Machinery, 616, 618, 708
Madagascar Plan, 868
Madame Bovary (Flaubert), 698
Madison, James, 518, 658
Madras (Chennai), 432, 555
Madrid: terrorism in, 965
Madrigals, 365–366
Magellan, Ferdinand, *413*, 413–414, 420, 429
Magenta, battle at, 677
Maghreb, 969
Magi, 355
Magic, 489, 491
Magic Flute, The (Mozart), 529
"Magic realism," 941
Maginot Line, 858
Magyar language (Hungary), 733
Magyars, 682, 733, 756
Maine, France, 366
Maistre, Joseph de, 639–640
Maize. *See* Corn
Major, John, 959
Malacca, 401, 418–419, 429
Malaya, 856, 857
Malay States, 764
Malay world, 429, 430
Malcolm X, 908–909
Mallarmé, Stéphane, 748
Malnutrition, 307
Malta, 960
Malthus, Thomas, 647, 694
Man and Woman Gazing at the Moon (Friedrich), 664, *664*
Manchester, demonstration in (1819), 644
Manchu dynasty (China), 433, 764, 766

Manchukuo, 856
Manchuria, 433, 764, 813, 856, 879
Mandates, 808, 820, 896
Mandela, Nelson, 895–896
Manhattan Project, 874
Mannerism, 479–480
Mantua, 349, 355, 356, 463
Manufacturing: on Continent, 618; in France, 458; industrialization and, 563; in World War II, 873. *See also* Industry
Many Happy Returns of the Day (Frith), *724*
Mao Zedong, 892, 899–900, 935, 936
Mapplethorpe, Robert, 971
Maps, 415, *416*, 441, *441*
Marburg Colloquy, 390, 391
Marcel, Étienne, 323
March on Washington, 908
March Revolution (Russia), 797–799
Marconi, Guglielmo, 705, 839
Marcuse, Herbert, 923
Mariana Islands, 856
Maria Theresa (Austria), 549, *549*, 555
Marie Antoinette (France), 544, *549*, 589
Marie Antoinette (movie), 546
Marijuana, 921
Markets: for British products, 609–610; in 18th century, *570*; industrial production and, 706–708; transportation and, 611
Marlborough, duke of (Charles Spencer-Churchill), 720
Marlborough, duke of (John Churchill), 461
Marne: First Battle of, 782; Second Battle of, 803
Marriage: age at, 561; in aristocracy, 719–720; arranged, 559; clerical, 393; in 18th century, 560–561; Habsburg dynastic, 369; in late 1800s, 720–722; Luther on, 382, 386; in Middle Ages, 334; Protestantism and, 396–397; in Renaissance Italy, 345, 346
Marriage of Figaro, The (Mozart), 529
Married Love (Stopes), 842
"Marseillaise," 587
Marseilles, 589, 590
Marshall, George C., 888
Marshall, John, 608, 658
Marshall Islands, 856
Marshall Plan, 888, 904, 907
Marsiglio of Padua, 328
Martin V (Pope), 328
Martinique, 435
Martyrdom of Saint Sebastian, The (Pollaiuolo), 358–359
Marx, Karl, and Marxism, 650, *691*, 691–692, 693, 711, 712, 799
Marxist Social Democratic Labor Party (Russia), 712
Mary, queen of Scots, 407–408, 472
Mary (Burgundy), marriage of, 369
Mary I (England), 393–394, 407
Mary II (England), 477, 478
Masaccio, 358, *359*
Masaryk, Thomas, 836
Masons, 526
Mass (Catholic Church), 916
Massachusetts, 436, 619
Mass consumerism, 707, 910
Mass culture, expansion of, 838–842, 845
Mass education, 725–727, 738
Massive retaliation policy, 892
Mass leisure, 704, 727–729, 840–842, 910
Mass media, Fascist control of, 824
Mass meetings, in Nazi Germany, 830, *831*
Mass politics, in late 1800s, 729–731
Mass society, 704–705, 714–729
Mass tourism, growth of, 727, 910
Mästlin, Michael, 491
Masurian Lakes, Battle of, 783
Materialism, 522, 694, 924, 971
Mathematical Principles of Natural Philosophy (Newton). *See Principia* (Newton)
Mathematics: Scientific Revolution and, 489, 497–498

Mau Mau movement, 895
Maurice (Saint), 345
Maximilian (Bavaria), 449, 450
Maximilian I (Holy Roman Empire), 369, 386
Maximilian of Austria, in Mexico, 673
Maya, *421*, 422
May Day, 712
Mazarin, Jules (Cardinal), 455
Mazzini, Giuseppe, 657, 659, 677
McCarthy, Joseph R., 908
McKinley, William, 766
McLuhan, Marshall, 944
Meat Inspection Act (U.S.), 758
Mechanics: motion and, 494–495
Mechanization, 565, 632
Mechanized looms, 690
Media, 921. *See also* Mass media
Medical schools, 335, *696*, 696–698
Medici family, 343, 345; Catherine de', 403; Church of San Lorenzo and, 360; Cosimo de', 348, 355; Cosimo II, 494; Lorenzo the Magnificent, 348, 359, 373
Medicine: in 14th century, 334–335; in 18th century, 533–534; death rate decline and, 715; in Middle Ages, 334–336, *337*; scientific basis for, 695; in Scientific Revolution, 499–501; socialized (Great Britain), 906; women in, 752. *See also* Disease; Health and health care
Medieval Europe. *See* Middle Ages
Mediterranean region: in 18th century, 553–554
Medvedev, Dmitry, 951
Mehmet II (Ottomans), 370
Meiji restoration (Japan), 768
Mein Kampf (Hitler), 826, 827, 850
Melanchthon, Philip, 384–385, 398
Melchiorites, 392
Memoirs (Comtesse de Boigne), 545
Memoirs (Ludlow), 475
Memoirs (Metternich), 639
Memoirs (Michel), 731
Memoirs (Saint-Simon), 459
Memoirs of a Geisha (Golden), 974
Memoirs of the Dauphin (Louis XIV), 456
Men, 728; roles of, 334
Mendeleyev, Dmitri, 694
Mennonites, 392
Mensheviks, 798, 800
Men Without Work (Pilgrim Trust report), 818
Mercantilism, 436, 443, 466, 522, 564–565
Mercator, Gerardus, 441
Mercator projection, 441
Mercenaries, 321, 324, 558
Merchant fleets, 564
Merchant marine: British, 609
Merchants: in Amsterdam, 471; in Asia, 430, 435; mercantilism and, 443; in Renaissance, 341–342; slave trade and, 428. *See also* Commerce; Trade
Merchant ships, 426
Merian, Maria Sibylla, 502
Merkel, Angela, 959
Mesoamerica, 420–422
Mesopotamia, 785
"Message, The" (Grandmaster Flash...), 943
Messenger, The: ..., 320–321
Messiaen, Olivier, 942
Messiah (Handel), 529
Mestizos, 437
Metallurgy, 442, 690
Metals, 611. *See also* Gold; Silver
Metamorphosis of the Insects of Surinam (Merian), 502
Metaxas, John, 836
Methodism, 539, 614, 667
Metternich, Klemens von, 637, *637*, 638, 639, 640, 644, 645, 646, 652, 657
Metz, 451
Mexico, 421; France and, 673; population of, 424; Spanish conquests in, 420–423
Michael Romanov, 464

Michel, Louise, 730, 731
Michelangelo, *340*, 340–341, 361, 362–363, *363*, 364
Microprocessor, 938
Middle Ages, 306–337; entertainment in, 336, *336*. *See also* Plague
Middle class(es): in Africa, 767; British, 643, 652, 654; French, 580, 590, 652, 655; industrial, 625–627, *626*, 647; in Industrial Revolution, 631; in late 1800s, 719, 720; Prussian, 548; World War I and, 797; World War II and, 909–910
Middle East: decolonization in, 896–898, *898*; in 1919, *809*; oil from, 932; World War I and, 785, 808, 820. *See also* Arabs and Arab world; specific locations
Middle Passage, 426–427
Midway, Battle of, 863–864
Midwives, 335, 503
MIG fighters, 901
"Mighty Fortress Is Our God, A" (Luther), 384
Migration: of Jews, 753; in Middle Ages, 307; reasons for, 976; social backlash from, 976; in U.S. (World War II), 874. *See also* Emigration; Immigration
Milan, 461; Austria and, 463; duchy of, 324–325, 347–348, 464, 553
Militarism: Prussian, 548; before World War I, 777
Military: in 18th century, 557–558; of EU, 960; Fascist Italy and, 824; in France, 589, 590, *590*, 597–598, 600, 603, 755; in Germany, 732, 755, 829, 852; in Hundred Years' War, 315–316; Japanese, 433–435, 768, 871–872; leadership of, 777; nobility and, 566; in Prussia, 462, 548–549, 679; Russian, 465, 466, 797, 799; in Spain, 462; after Thirty Years' War, 452–453; in United States, 874; before World War I, 777. *See also* Mercenaries; Navy; specific battles and wars
Milk, pasteurization of, 715
Mill, John Stuart, 647–649
Millenarianism, of Melchiorites, 392
Millet, Jean-François, 698–700, *699*
Milligen, J. G., 592
Mills, 608, 628, 629
Milosevic, Slobodan, 954, 956–957
Minerals, 343, 608
Mines and mining, 343, 628, *628*, 629, 630, 643, 709, 818
Ming dynasty (China), 432–433
Minimalism, in music, 942
Ministerial responsibility, 644, 647, 652
Minorities: in Austria-Hungary, 682–683, *684*, 733, 756, 804; as industrial leaders, 627; religious (18th century), 536–538; revolutions of 1848 and, 657; in Russia, 734; World War I and, 776, 807. *See also* Nationalities; specific groups
Mir (village commune), 684
Miracles: humanist historians on, 357
Missile gap, 893
Missiles, 893
Mission, The (movie), 439
Missions and missionaries: in Asia, 430; in colonies, 437–439; imperialism and, 761; in Japan, 435; Jesuit, 401; Methodist, 667
Mitchel, John, 622
Mitterrand, François, 931, 959
Mobility (social): in United States, 619
Mobilization, 777; in World War I, 778–780, 791–792; in World War II, 872–877
Moctezuma (Aztecs), 422
Model T Ford, 706
Modern Devotion, 329
Modernism (arts), 743, 744–749; Postmodernism and, 940, 941
Modernism (religious movement), 743
Mohács, Battle of, 388
Moldavia, 643, 674, 675, 949
Molière, Jean-Baptiste, 484

Molotov, Vyacheslav, 881, 887
Moluccas (Spice Islands), 401, 413, 418, 419, 429, 442
Monarchists, in France, 656, 730
Monarchs and monarchies: Austrian, 464; divine right and, 454; in Dutch Republic, 471; in eastern Europe, 369; in England, *315*, 367–368, 471–479, 544–546; in 14th century, 319–321; in France, 315, *315*, 323, 349, 366, 544, 580–581, 588, 604; in Germany, 323–324; Holy Roman Empire and, 369; limited, 470; Maistre on, 640; in Poland, 470; in Renaissance, 366–370; in 17th century, 446–447; in Spain, 349, 368–369; in Sweden, 467–468. *See also* Absolutism; Limited monarchies
Monet, Claude, 745, *745*
Money. *See also* Currency; Inflation
Money payments, as scutage, 319
Mongolia, 432
Mongols, 306, 307–308, 319, 369
Monism. *See* Pantheism
Monopolies: in England, 408
Monroe, James, 642
Monroe Doctrine, 642–643
"Monroe Doctrine for Asia," 856
Montcalm, Louis-Joseph, 557
Montecino, Antón, 424
Montefeltro family (Urbino), 349
Montenegro, 769, 771, 957
Montesquieu, baron de (Charles de Secondat), 517–518, 524, 526
Montessori, Maria, 752
Montgelas, Maximilian von, 637
Montpellier, 335
Mont Sainte-Victoire (Cézanne), 745, *746*
Moon, U.S. landing on, *938*
Moore, Charles, 941, *941*
Moravia, 392
More, Hannah, 536
More, Thomas, 378–379, 393
Morel, Edward, 760–761
Morisot, Berthe, 745, *746*
Moro, Aldo, 931
Morocco, 762, 895
Mortality. *See* Death rates
Mortgages: subprime, 975, 976
Moscow, 464, 603, 859
Mother, The (de Hooch), 472, *472*
Mothers, 346, 723, 725. *See also* Families; Women
Motion, 490, 492, 495–497, 499
Mott, John, World War I letters from, 796
Mountain, the (France), 588
Movable type, 358
Movies, 738, 839, 840, 916–917, 973
Mozambique, 762, 896
Mozart family: Leopold, Nannerl, and, *530*; Wolfgang Amadeus, 529, *530*, 531, 666
Mrs. Dalloway (Woolf), 845
Mughal Empire, 430–432, *432*
Mühlberg, Battle of, 388, *388*
Mulattoes, 437
Mule, in cotton industry, 610
Mulroney, Brian, 932, 962
Multiculturalism, 973, 974, *974*
Multinational (transnational) corporation, 975
Multinational states: Austria as, 646, 682; nationalism and, 649–650
Multiracial society, in Latin America, 437
Mumbai (Bombay), 417
Munich: Hitler in, 814, 827; terrorism at Olympic Games in, 943, 964
Munich Conference (1938), 853
Munitions factories: women in, 794, *794*, 795
"Munitions Work" (Loughnan), 795
Münster, Anabaptists in, 392
Müntzer, Thomas, 385
Murad (Ottoman Turks), 370
Museums: of Modern Art, 914
Music: American influence on, 917; atonal, 845, 942; current, 942, 943, 971–972; digital

technology for, 973; in Enlightenment, 528–529; Impressionist, 748; jazz, 839; Modernism in, 747–749; in Renaissance, 365–366; Romanticism in, 665–667, 700–701; World War I songs, 785, 789; youth protest, 923
Music video, 942
Muslim Bosnians, 956
Muslim-Croat federation: in former Yugoslavia, 956, 957
Muslim League, 898
Muslims, 643; in 18th century, *537*; Enlightenment and, 538; in EU nations, 968; in France, 959; in India, 430, 898–899; in North Africa, 762; Palestine, Israel, and, 897; in Spain, 368–369; terrorism and, 965–966; trade and, 307. *See also* Islam
Mussolini, Benito, 823–826, 852, 858, 859, 864, 865
Mutsuhito (Japan), 767–768
Mutual deterrence, 890
Myanmar. *See* Burma (Myanmar)
My Own Story (Emmeline Pankhurst), 750
Mysticism, 329

Nagasaki, *434*, 435, 865, 877, 878
Nagy, Imry, 903, 904
Nanjing, Japanese seizure of, 856, 872
Nanterre, University of, 920
Nantes, in French Revolution, 582
Naples, 461, 640, 644, 677; Austria and, 463; kingdom of, 324, 348, 350, 553; market square in, *570*; revolt in, 454
Napoleon I Bonaparte (France), 575, 596, 597–603, *598*, 641, *671*, 671–675; Civil Code of, 600, 644; Congress of Vienna and, 638; defeat of, 603–605; Grand Empire of, 601–603, *602*
Napoleon II (France), 671
Napoleon III (France), 656, 676–677, 681, 718, 730
Napoleonic wars, 636, 637–639, 646, 762
Narva, Battle of, 466
Naseby, battle at, 475
Nasser, Gamal Abdel, 897, 898
National Assembly (France), 581–582, 586, 587, 656, 671, 730, 931, 959
National Bloc (France), 819
National Convention (France), 588–589, 590, 593, 594
National debt, 562
National Endowment for the Arts (NEA), 971
National Front (France), 967
National Government (England), 818
National Guard (France), 582, 587
National Insurance Act (1911), 753
Nationalism, 602, 636–637, 644, *649*, 649–650, 670; in Africa, 767; in Austria, 646, 657; in former Yugoslavia, 956, *957*, 978; German, 602–603, 645–646, 678, 756; in Greece, 643; of Hitler, 826; in India, 768; in Italy, 644, 677; liberalism and, 650; Napoleon and, 602–603; in Prussia, 603; revolutions of 1830 and, 652; in Soviet Union, 949; Spanish, 602; terrorism and, 964; in United States, 658–659, 766; World War I and, 776–777, 780
Nationalist Chinese, 856, 899–900
Nationalists (Spain), 837
Nationalities: revolutions of 1848 and, 657; in Soviet Union, 949. *See also* Minorities
Nationalities problem (Austria-Hungary), 733, 756
Nationalization: in Britain, 906; in China, 900; of churches, 536, 586; in France, 905, 931; in Russia, 802; in World War I, 791
National Liberation Front (Algeria), 895
National liberation movements, 897
National Organization for Women, 924

National Socialist German Workers' Party, 827. *See also* Nazi Germany; Nazi Party
National System of Political Economy (List), 617
National workshops (France), 655, 656
Nation building, 670, 682–690
Nation in arms: in France, 589
Native Americans. *See* Indians
Native peoples: Christianization of, 437. *See also* Decolonization; Indians (Native Americans)
NATO, 890, *891*, 905, 907, 909; Afghanistan and, 964; in former Yugoslavia, 954, 956, 957
Nattier, Jean Marc, *464*
Naturalism, in literature, 743
Natural law, 514; of economics, 521–522; natural rights and, 543
Natural philosophers, 488, 499
Natural rights, 543, 584–585
Natural selection, 694
Nature: Romanticism and, 664, 665
Navarre, 402
Navigational aids, 489; astrolabe, 415; compass, 415
Navy: British, 461, 601–602, 643; French, 601–602; Japanese, 757; Russian, 465, 757; in 17th century, 453. *See also* Armada (Spain); Merchant marine; Military
Nazi Germany, 822, 831, 845; alliances of, 852; anti-Semitism in, 831, *832*, 832–833; empire of, 865–867; Japan and, 856; mass meetings in, 830, *831*; propaganda in, 830, 866; rearmament of, 831, 851–852; resistance to, 867; Rhineland and, 852; Soviet nonaggression pact and, 855, 856; women in, 831–832, 831–832, 875. *See also* Germany; Holocaust; World War II
Nazi New Order, 865, 866
Nazi Party, 827, 828, 829
Nehru, Jawaharlal, 900
Neoclassicism, 527–528, *529*, 942
Neo-Expressionism, *970*, 970–971, *972*
Neo-Gothic architecture, 662, *663*
Neoplatonism, 355, 364
Nepotism, 372
Netherlands, 638, 890, 907; Calvinism in, 395, 405, 408; in 18th century, 553; France and, 601; immigration laws of, 968; sciences and, 497; World War II in, 858. *See also* Austrian Netherlands; Dutch; Dutch Republic; Low Countries; Spanish Netherlands
Neumann, Balthasar, 527, *528*
Neumann, Solomon, 717
New Brunswick, 758
New Caledonia, 730, 731
New Cicero, The (Bruni), 354
New Deal, 819–820, 908
New Economic Policy (NEP), 833
New England: exploration of, 420
New Europe (1980s), *949*
Newfoundland, 461
New France, 689. *See also* Canada
New German School, music and, 700–701
New Guinea, 790, 863
New imperialism, 759–761, 766–769; in Africa, 761–763, *764*, 767; in Asia, 763–765, *765*, 767–768; by United States, 765–766. *See also* Imperialism
New Jerusalem, John of Leiden and, 392
New Lanark, Scotland, *650*
New Model Army (England), 473, 508
New monarchies, in Renaissance, 366–370
New Netherland, 436
New Order: in Asia, 871–872; Italian terrorist group as, 964; Nazi, 865, 866
New Spain, 425
Newspapers, 532, 726–727
New Testament, 384. *See also* Bible
"New Thinking," 962
Newton, Isaac, 489, 497–499, *498*, 738
"New woman," 752, 843
New World, 413–426; England and, 408; European diseases in, 422; exploration

of, 419–425; Monroe Doctrine and, 643; Portugal and, 413–414, 420; Spain and, 404, 408, 419–425; voyages to, *413*, 413–414, 419

"New World Order," 963

New York, 436, 914; September 11, 2001, terrorist attack on, 948, 964, *965*

New Zealand, 515, 763, 785, 892

Ngo Dinh Diem, 932

NGOs. *See* Nongovernmental organizations

Nicaragua, 642

Nice, 677

Nicholas I (Russia), *646*, 646–647, 654, 657, 675

Nicholas II (Russia), 734, 756, *756*, 758, 779; capture and murder of, 800; World War I and, 778, 797

Nigeria, 821, 896

Nightingale, Florence, 675, *675*, 749

Nigredo (Kiefer), 971

Nimwegen, peace at, 460

Niña (ship), 420

Nineteenth Amendment (U.S.), 795

Ninety-Five Theses (Luther), 381, 382, 646

Nixon, Richard, 925, 931–932, 934, 936

Nkrumah, Kwame, 895, 896

Nobility: absolutism and, 470; in Denmark, 467; in 18th century, 566–569; in England, 544, 643; as entrepreneurs, 627; in 14th century, 312–313, 319–320; in France, 366, 455, 456, 578, 580, 581, 587, 590, 600, 601; grand tour and, 569; in Poland, 470; in Prussia, 462–463, 548; in Renaissance, 344; in Russia, 464, 466, 552; in Scandinavia, 554; as social estate, 312; in Spain, 461; in Sweden, 467

"Noble savage" idea, 515

Nocturnal Spectator (Restif de la Bretonne), 533

Nogarola, Isotta, 356

Nongovernmental organizations, 978

Nonindustrial world, 619–620

Non-Intervention Agreement, 837

Nonviolent resistance, Gandhi and, 820

Nördlingen, Battle of, 451

Normandy, 317, 319, 864

North Africa: decolonization in, 895; France and, 762; immigrants from, 959; Ottomans and, 388; World War II in, 858, *859*, 862

North America: British in, 436, 441, 555; Dutch in, 436; European migration to, 716; French in, 436, 441, 555; 1700–1803, *576*; in Seven Years' War, 555–557; Spain and, 436; in War of the Spanish Succession, 461

North American Air Defense Command (NORAD), 909

North Atlantic, Battle of, 862

North Atlantic Treaty Organization. *See* NATO

Northern Europe: artistic Renaissance in, 364–366; governments in, 466–468; sciences in, 497

Northern Hemisphere, 976, 978

Northern Ireland, 929, 964. *See also* Ireland

Northern Renaissance humanism, 377–379

Northern Union (Russia), 646

Northern War: Denmark in, 466

North German Confederation, 681, 682

North Korea. *See* Korea; Korean War

North Vietnam. *See* Vietnam; Vietnam War

Norway, 747, 750, 890; Hansa and, 342; Scandinavian unification and, 389; World War II in, 858. *See also* Scandinavia

Notre-Dame Cathedral (Paris): as Temple of Reason, 594

Novalis, Friedrich, 664

Nova Scotia, 461, 758

Novels, 529–530, 662. *See also* Literature

November Revolution (Germany), 804

Novikov, Nikolai, 887

Novotny, Antonin, 926

Nuclear power disaster, at Chernobyl, 938

Nuclear weapons, 901; arms race and, 890, 905; ban on atmospheric testing, 894; limitation

on, 962; massive retaliation policy and, 892; missiles in Cuba, 893

Nuns, 399, 437

Nuremberg, 323, *885*; Lutheranism in, 384; war crime trials at, 906

Nuremberg laws, 832

Nursing, 675, *675*, 710, 749

Nutrition, 440–441, 715

Nystadt, Peace of, 466

Oath of the Horatii (David), 527–528, *529*

Obama, Barack, 962, 964, *965*

Observations upon Experimental Philosophy... (Cavendish), 501

Observatories, 507, *507*

Occult: Hermetic writings and, 355

Occupation zones: in Germany, 879, 888–890, 905; in Korea, 891

October Manifesto (Russia), 758

Oedipus complex, 740, 846

Official Languages Act (1968), 932

Ohio River region, 556, 557

Oil and oil industry, 705, 898, 927, 932

Oil embargo, 932

Oil spill: in Gulf of Mexico (2010), 976

"Old Barbed Wire, The" (song), 789

Old Bolsheviks, 833, 834

Old Curiosity Shop, The (Dickens), 700

Old order: in France, 580, 601

Old regime (France), 574, 578–580, 587

Old Testament. *See* Bible

Olivares (Count), 461, 462

Olson, Culbert, 875

Olympic Games, 944; in Berlin (1936), 840; global broadcast of, 943; in Los Angeles (1984), 943; in Moscow (1980), 937, 943; in Munich (1972), 943, 964; of 1956, 943

Omdurman, Battle of, 763

On Anatomical Procedures (Galen), 500

On Crimes and Punishments (Beccaria), 533

One-Dimensional Man (Marcuse), 923

One Hundred Years of Solitude (Garcia Márquez), 941

Onesti, Nastagio degli, *346*

On Liberty (Mill), 648

On Parisian Department Stores (Lavasseur), 707

Ontario, 689, 758

On the Fabric of the Human Body (Vesalius), 500

On the Family (Alberti), 346

On the Freedom of a Christian Man (Luther), 382

On the Motion of the Heart and Blood (Harvey), 500

On the Origin of Species by Means of Natural Selection (Darwin), 694, 743

On the Revolutions of the Heavenly Spheres (Copernicus), 490, *491*, 492

On the Subjection of Women (Mill and Taylor), 648–649

OPEC. *See* Organization of Petroleum Exporting Countries

Open door policy, in China, 765

Open-field system, 561

Opera, 529, 701

Oppenheimer, J. Robert, 877, 938

Orange, house of, 471, 547. *See also* William and Mary (England)

Orange Free State, 762

Oration on the Dignity of Man (Pico della Mirandola), 355, 356

Oratory of Divine Love, 380

Orbits, of planets, 490, 499

Ordered society, 658–662

Order of Preachers. *See* Dominicans

Orders of Friars Minor. *See* Franciscans

Organic evolution, 694

Organization of Petroleum Exporting Countries (OPEC), 932

Organization of Work, The (Blanc), 650

Orlando, Vittorio, *805*

Orléans, 317

Orléans, duke of, 317, 544

Orthodox Christianity. *See* Eastern Orthodoxy

Orwell, George, 818

Ostpolitik, 929

Ottoman Empire, *371*, 468–469; Balkan wars and, 771; Charles V and, 388; Crimean War and, 674–675; decline of, 673–674, *674*, 769, *769*, 807–808; Greek revolt and, 643; Middle East and, *898*; Palestine in, 753; regimes after, 819; Russian expansion and, 552, 643, 764; in 16th and 17th centuries, *469*; in World War I, 785

Ottoman Turks, 370, 418, 804. *See also* Ottoman Empire

Overpopulation, 647

Overseas trade, 442, 443, 564–565

"Over There" (song), 789

Owen, Robert, 632, 650, *650*

Oxenstierna, Axel, 467

Oxford University (England), 335

Pachakuti (Inca), 423

Pacification of Ghent, 406

Pacific Ocean region: American imperialism in, 765–766; Balboa in, 420; World War I in, 790; World War II in, 859–861, *861*, 863–864, 865

Padua: medical school in, 335

Painting: abstract, 747, 842; Baroque, 480, *480*; Cubist, 747, *748*; German Expressionist, 842; of Giotto, 332; Impressionist, 744–745, *745*, *746*; Mannerist, *479*, 479–480; Modernist, 744–747; Post-Impressionist, 745–746, *746*, 747; Realist, 481–483, *482*, 698–700; Romanticist, 664–665; Surrealist, 843–844, *844*

Pakistan, 892, 898

Palatinate, 449, 450

Paleologus dynasty, 370

Palestine, 674, *753*; Jewish state in, 896–897; after World War I, 808, 820; Zionism and, 753. *See also* Arab-Israeli disputes; Israel

Palestine Liberation Organization, 898

Palestinian terrorists, 964

Palladio, Andrea, 567

Palmerston, Lord (Henry John Temple), 686

Pamela: or, Virtue Rewarded (Richardson), 530

Pan-African Congress, 806, 807

Panama: Isthmus of, 420

Pan American flight 103, 964

Pan-Arabism, 898

Pan-German League, 756

Pankhurst family: Christabel, 749; Emmeline, 749, 750, *751*; Sylvia, 749

Pantheism, 355, 509, 664

Panzer division, 852, 853, 859

Papacy: at Avignon, 326–327, 328; in Catholic Reformation, 401–402; church-state struggle and, 326; decline in, 328–329, 536; France and, 387; Italy and, 464; Reformation and, 387; in Renaissance, *372*, 372–373; supremacy of, 327. *See also* Pope; specific popes

Papal bulls, 326, 400

Papal States, 348, 644; in 14th century, 327; Italy and, 464, 677; after unification, 731

Paper, 337

Paper money, 562, 586

Paracelsus, 500, 508

Paraguay, 642

Paris: in Enlightenment, 513; fall of Bastille in, 574, *574*, 582, 583; foundling homes in, 560; French Revolution and, 574, 582, 587, 588; Fronde in, 455; medical school in, 335; reconstruction of, 673, 718–719, *719*; revolution of 1848 in, 655; student revolt in (1968), *920*, 920–921, 924; in World War II, 864

Paris, Treaty of: of 1763, 556, 689; of 1783, 575; of 1856, 675; ending war in Bosnia, 956

Paris Agreement (1973), *934*

Paris Commune: in 1871, 730, 731; in French
    Revolution, 588, 592, 595
Paris Peace Conference, 804–807
Parks, Rosa, *909*
Parlement of Paris, 455, 581
Parlements (France), 457, 580
Parliament: in Austria-Hungary, 756; in Germany,
    679, 680; in Prussia, 681; in Sweden, 467.
    See also Parliament (England)
Parliament (England), 368, 472–473, 643, 644,
    663; Cavalier Parliament and, 476–477;
    English civil war and, 473–476; monarchy
    and, 477, 544–546; reform of, 729;
    structure of, 321
Parma, duke of, 409
Parnell, Charles, 730
Parr, Catherine, 393
Parti Québécois (Canada), 962
Partitions: of Germany, 888, 889; of India, 898–
    899; of Poland, *462*, 549, 552, *553*
Party of Movement (France), 652
Party of Resistance (France), 652
Pascal, Blaise, *509*, 509–510
Pasolini, Pier Paolo, 925
Pasteur, Louis, 694, 695–696
Pasteurization, 695, 715
Paths of Glory (novel and film), 787
Path to Power, The (Thatcher), 930
Patriarchies (family): in 18th century, 558–559
Patricians, 344
Patriotism, 781, 797, 802
Patriots: in American Revolution, 575; in Dutch
    Republic, 547; women in France as, *593*
Patronage: in England, 545; of scientists, 508
Paul III (Pope), 401, *401*, 402
Paul IV (Pope), 402
Paulus, Friedrich, 863
Pauper apprentices, 629
Peace: John Paul II on, 971; after Napoleonic
    wars, 636, 637–639; women's efforts for,
    750–752; World War I and, 792–793,
    804–809, 812, 813–816
"Peace for our time," 853
Peaceful coexistence, 892
Peace of Augsburg, *387*, 388, 449
Peace of Lodi, 349
Peace of the Pyrenees, 451, 462
Peace of Utrecht, 461
Peace of Westphalia, 451–452
Pearl Harbor, Hawaii, 766, 859, 860
Pearl Jam, 971
Pearson, Karl, 759
Pearson, Lester, 909
Peasants, 566; in 14th century, 312–314, *313*; in
    16th century, 442–443; in 18th century,
    569; diet of, 566; in England, 313–314; in
    France, 313, *313*, 314, 582–585, 587; in
    Germany, 453; in Japan, 435; landless, 621;
    literacy and, 535; in Poland, 369; potato
    and, 561; in Prussia, 548; in Renaissance,
    344–345; revolts by, 313–314, 454; in
    Russia, 552, 683–685, 757, 758, 799, 802;
    in Soviet Union, 833, 834; as Third Estate,
    579–580. *See also* Serfs and serfdom
Peasants' Revolt (England, 1381), 313–314
Peasants' War, 385–386, 392
Peel, Robert, 630, 654, 660, *661*
Peer Gynt Suite (Grieg), 747
Penny, Edward, *556*
Pensées (Pascal), 509, *509*, 510
Pentagon, terrorist attack on, 948, 964
Pentonville (Britain), 662
People's Charter, 632, 633
People's Liberation Army (China), 900
People's Will, 685
Perel, Salomon, 869
Perestroika, 948, 950
Perestroika (Gorbachev), 950
Periodicals: in 18th century, 532. *See also*
    Magazines; Newspapers
Periodic law, 694

Permanent Committee (Paris), 582
Permissive society, 921
Perry, Matthew, 764
Persia: Russia and, 764
Persian Gulf War, 963
Persian Letters (Montesquieu), 517
Persistence of Memory, The (Dali), 844, *844*
Peru, 423–424, 425, 641, 642
Pétain, Henri, 858
Peter III (Russia), 550, 556
Peterloo Massacre (1819), 644
Peter the Great (Russia), *464*, 464–466, *467*
Petite Roquette (France), 662
Petition of Right (England), 473
Petrarch, 330–331, 352, 354
Petrograd soviet, 798, 799
Petrushka (Stravinsky), 749
Phalanstery, 650
Phèdre (Racine), 484
Philip, Landgrave of Hesse, 390
Philip II (Spain), 393, 404, *405*, 461, 464;
    Elizabeth I (England) and, *405*, 408–409;
    French Wars of Religion and, 403; revolt of
    Netherlands and, 405–406; Spanish power
    under, *406*
Philip III (Spain), 461
Philip IV (the Fair, France), 315, 326, 327
Philip IV (Spain), 461–462
Philip V (Spain), 460–461, *461*, 553
Philip VI (France), 315, 323
Philip of Burgundy, marriage of, 369
Philip of Orléans, 459
Philippines, 413–414, 420, 730, 763, 766, 859,
    864, 892, 898
Philosophes, 513, 516–526; on enlightened
    rulers, 543; French Revolution and, 580; as
    historians, 530–531
Philosophical Transactions (Royal Society), 507
Philosophic Letters on the English (Voltaire), 518,
    519
Philosophy: existentialism as, 913, 915
"Phony war" (World War II), 858
Photography, 746
Photorealism, 941
Physicians: in 14th century, 334–335; in 18th
    century, 534; women as, 697–698. *See also*
    Medicine
Physics, 694, 738–739, 846
Physiocrats, 521–522
Piazza d'Italia (Moore), 941, *941*
Picasso, Pablo, 747, *748*, *838*
Pico della Mirandola, Giovanni, 355, 356
Piedmont, 638, 640, 644, 657, 676, 677
Pietism, 538–539, 667
Pig iron, 611
Pilsudski, Joseph, 836
Pinta (ship), 420
Piranesi, Giovanni Battista, 569
Pirates, 406, 441
Pisa: Council of, 328
Piscator, Erwin, 845
Pissarro, Camille, 744–745
Pitt, William: the Elder, 545, 554, 556; the
    Younger, *544*, 546
Pius VII (Pope), 599
Pius IX (Pope), 657, 742–743
Pizarro, Francisco, Inca and, 424
Plague, 306, 307–308. *See also* Black Death
Plains of Abraham, 557
Planck, Max, 738, 846
Planetary motion, 490, 492, 496–497
Planets, 489, 490
Planned economies, 791, 873
Plantation economy, 564
Plantations, 426, 435, 595
Plants: in Columbian Exchange, 440. *See also*
    Agriculture; Crop(s)
Plassey, Battle of, 432, *556*, 557
Plato, 355, 488
Platonic Academy (Florence), 364
Platonic thought, Neoplatonism and, 355

PLO. *See* Palestine Liberation Organization
Pluralism, 379
Plurality of Worlds (Fontenelle), 514
Plutocrats, 719
Pocket boroughs (England), 545, 643
Poe, Edgar Allan, 662–664
Poem of Joan of Arc, The (Christine de Pizan), 322
Poets and poetry: Romantic, 633, 664; on Spanish
    Civil War, 837; Symbolists and, 743, 744.
    See also Literature
Pogroms, 311, 537, 752–753
Poincaré, Raymond, 819
Poison gas, in World War I, 784, *788*
Poitiers: battle at (1356), 316, 323
Poland, 890; Anabaptists in, 392;
    authoritarianism in, 836; communism and,
    886, 902, 903, 953; death camps in, 805,
    814, 868–869, *870*; in EU, 954, 960; Jesuits
    in, 401; Jews in, 311, 870; monarchy in,
    369, 470; after Napoleonic wars, 637–638;
    in NATO, 954; Nazis and, 854–855, 857,
    865, 866; Ottomans and, 370; partitions
    of, *462*, 549, 552, *553*; protests in, 903;
    revolt in, 652, 681; Russia and, 466, 552;
    Solidarity in, 926, 952; Soviets and, 880,
    903; uprising in (1830), 652; after World
    War I, 807, 836; World War II and, 879–880
Poland-Lithuania, 470
Police forces, 659–661, *661*. *See also* Secret police
Politburo (Soviet Union), 833, 902, 948
"Political and Social Doctrine of Fascism, The"
    (Mussolini), 825
Political democracy, 749. *See also* Democracy
Political liberalism, 647–649
Political parties. *See* specific countries and parties
Political Treatise, A (Spinoza), 503
Politics: in 14th century, 319–325; between
    1894 and 1914, 749–759; in Africa, 821; of
    Anabaptists, 392; Enlightenment and, 542–
    543; French Wars of Religion and, 403–404;
    in Germany, 386–387, 388–389; in Great
    Depression, 816; in Italy, 823; religion and,
    451; slave trade and, 429; violence in, 595
Politics Drawn from the Very Words of Holy Scripture
    (Bossuet), 454
Politiques, 403
Pollaiuolo, Antonio, 358
Pollock, Jackson, 914, *915*, 940
Poll tax: in England, 313, 314
Pollution, 624, 717, 938, 974, 978
Polo, Marco, 414, 432
Poltava, Battle of, 466, 554
Pombal, marquis of, 553
Pompadour, Madame de, 544
Pompeii, 569
Pontiff. *See* Pope
Poor Law (England, 1834), 631, 654
Poor Law Commission (Britain), 623
Poor people. *See* Poverty
Pop Art, 914
Pope: Luther and, *384*; Napoleon and, 599–600;
    Philip IV (France) and, 326. *See also* Papacy;
    specific popes
Popolari (Christian Democrats), 823
Popolo grasso (industrial class), 325
Popolo minuto, 325
Popular culture: in 18th century, 531, 534–536;
    globalization of, 944; homogeneity of,
    842; postwar, 910, 916–917, 942–943; and
    religion, 398
Popular Front: in France, 819, 840; in Spain,
    836–837, 838
Popular religion: in 18th century, 538–539; in
    Middle Ages, 328–340
Popular sovereignty, 688
Population: in 17th century, 447; in 18th century,
    558; of Amsterdam, 471; Black Death and,
    308–311; in cities, 618, 622–623, 717;
    in Europe, *714*, 966; famine and, 307; in
    France, 578; growth of, 442, 706, 714–715,
    715, 976; in Industrial Revolution, 621;

in Ireland, 621; Jews in, 752; in Latin
America, 424–425; Malthus on, 647, 694;
in Prussia, 548; Ricardo on, 647
Populism, in Russia, 685
Pornography, 921
Port Arthur, Russo-Japanese War and, 757
Portolani (charts), 415
Portrait of Jean Paulhan (Dubuffet), *914*
Portraiture: in Renaissance, 360
Portugal, 890, 931; Africa and, 762, 896; Americas
and, 435; Asia and, 429–430, 437; Brazil
and, 642; China and, 419, 432; dictatorship
in, 838; in 18th century, 553; empire of,
416–419; expansion by, 414, 416–419;
imperialism of, 762; India and, 432; Japan
and, 433, *434*; Jesuits and, 536; Latin
America and, 436, 640, 641; New World
and, 413–414, 420; slavery and, 345, 416,
426; Spain and, 454; sphere of influence
of, 420
Portuguese Empire, 419, 429–430, 553
Post-Impressionism, 745–746, *746*, *747*
Postmodernism, 939–942
Poststructuralism (deconstruction), 940
Potatoes, 440, 558, 561, 566, 621
Potsdam Conference, 880
Pottery works: child labor in, 629
Poussin, Nicholas, 481
Poverty: in cities, 570–571; crime and, 661; in
18th century, 570–571; in France, 571, 580;
in India, 768; of peasants, 566, 621; urban,
623–625, *624*
Power (energy). *See* Energy (power)
Power loom, 610, 618
Pragmatic Sanction, 555
Prague, 449, 853
"Prague Spring," 926–927, *928–929*
Praise of Folly, The (Erasmus), 378, 379
Pravda, 948
Predestination, Calvin on, 394–395
Prefects (France), 600
Prelude to the Afternoon of a Faun (Debussy), 748
Presbyterians, 473–474
Presbyters, 473
President (U.S.), 576–577
Prester John, magical kingdom of, 414
Preventive medicine, 696
Price revolution, 442
Primary education, 535–536, 725
Primavera (Botticelli), 359, *359*
Primitivism: in music, 749
Primo de Rivera, José Antonio (Spain), 838
Primo de Rivera, Miguel (Spain), 836
Primogeniture, 560
Prince, The (Machiavelli), *351*, 351–352, 353
Princess, The (Tennyson), 720
Principia (Newton), 497, 499
Principle of intervention, 640, 643, 644
Principle of legitimacy, 637–638
Principles of Political Economy (Ricardo), 647
Printing, 358, 530
Prisoners of war, 427, *862*, 867, 871, 872,
886, 966
Prisons, reform of, 533, 661–662
Private schools: Protestant, 398
Proclamation to the French Troops in Italy
(Napoleon I), 598
Proclamation to the People (Napoleon III, 1851),
672
Procurator (Russia), 466
Prodi, Romano, 959
Production: in Britain, 609–610; industrial,
607–608, 631
Products, in late 1800s, 705–706
Professionalism: in policing, 660
Professions: medicine as, 696; middle class, 720;
in Nazi Germany, 831, 832; women and,
749, 966
Progress: in late 1800s, 704, 705, *706*; before
World War I, 737, 738
Progressive Conservative Party (Canada), 932

Progressive Era (United States), 758
Progress of the Human Mind, The (Condorcet),
522
Proletariat, 692; Bernstein on, 712; industrial,
691
Prometheus Unbound (Shelley), 664
Propaganda: in Fascist Italy, 824, 825; in Nazi
Germany, 830; radio, movies, and, 840; in
Soviet Union, 874; totalitarianism and, 822;
World War I and, 780, 793, *793*
Property rights: for women, 749
Prosperity. *See* Economy
Prostitution: "comfort women" and, 872; in 14th
century, 334; grand tour and, 569; lower-
class women in, 711; in Renaissance Italy,
347; after World War II, 921
Protective tariffs, 617
Protectorates, 762, 764
Protest(s): in Africa, 821; in Poland, 903; against
Vietnam War, 908, 923, 924, 925
Protestantism, 661; by 1560, 399; in 18th
century, 536, *537*; church organization in,
386; education and, 397–398, 535–536;
fundamentalism in, 742, 968; Peace of
Augsburg and, *387*, 388; Pietism and, 538;
Puritans and, 473; revivalism in, 538–539;
Romantic movement and, 667; spread
of, 389–396; women and, 397. *See also*
Huguenots
Protestant Reformation, 383–398
Protestant Union, 449
Provence, France, 366
Provisional government: in France, 655, 730; in
Russia, 798, 799, 801
Prussia, 462, *462*, 565, 601, 644, 645; Austria
and, 681; Dutch Republic and, 547; in 18th
century, *547*, 548–549; Franco-Prussian
War and, 681–682; Frankfurt Assembly
in, 656; German unification and, 678–682,
732; Italy and, 677, 678; military in, 557;
Napoleon and, 603, 638; nobility in, 566;
Poland and, 552, 637, 807; population
of, 558; Quadruple Alliance and, 637,
640; in Seven Years' War, 555. *See also*
Brandenburg-Prussia; Silesia
Psychoanalysis, 740, 741, 846
Ptolemaic-Aristotelian cosmology, 491, 492, *493*,
497, 499
Ptolemaic universe, 489, 492–493, 497
Ptolemy, Claudius, 415, *416*, *441*, 488
Public credit, 562
Public education. *See* Education
Public health, 335–336, 625, 696, 717
Public Health Act (Britain), 625, 717
Public order, in World War I, 792–793
Public schools, 398, 727, 728, 908
Public works, 820
Publishing, 532. *See also* Books; Printing
Puddling, in iron industry, 611
Puerto Rico, 766
Pugachev, Emelyan, 552
Punishment: in Austria, 549; in 18th century,
533; for Paris Commune, 730
Punk movement, 942
Pure Food and Drug Act (U.S.), 758
Purgatory, 329
Purges, in Soviet Union, 834
Puritans, 408, 473, 477, 508, 538
Putin, Vladimir, 951
Putting-out system, 563
Pym, John, 473
Pyramids: Mayan, 421

Qianlong (China), 433, 434
Qing Empire (China), 433, *433*
Quadruple Alliance, 637, 640
Quakers, 429, 538, 627
Quantum theory, 738
Quebec, 436, 689, 758, 962, *962*
Querelles des femmes, 502

Quesnay, François, 521–522
Quetzalcoatl (god), 422

Race and racism: in Germany, 742, 831, 832,
865; of Hitler, 850, 866; in India, 768; new
imperialism and, 759
Race riots, in United States, 909
Racine, Jean-Baptiste, 484, 518
Radar system, 937
Radcliffe, William, 625–627
Radiation, 738
Radical Reformation, 390–392
Radicals and radicalism, 804, 819, 924; in French
Revolution, 587–595
Radio, 839, 840
Railroads, *611*, 611–612, 690, 704; electric, 705;
in Russia, 756; in United States, 618
*Rain, Steam, and Speed—The Great Western
Railway* (Turner), *665*
Ramadan, 970
Ranters, 508
Raphael, 362, *362*, *372*, 373
Rap music, 942, 943, 972
Rapprochement, Cold War and, 892
Rasputin, 797
Rastatt, Peace of, 461
Rathenau, Walter, 791
Rationalism, 505. *See also* Reason
Rationing: in World War I, 791, 792; in World
War II, 873
Raw materials, 436, 643
Reaction: in French Revolution, 596
Reading, 532. *See also* Literacy
Reagan, Ronald, *922*, 930, 932, 937, 961, 962, *963*
Realism, 693, 743; in Dutch painting, 481–483,
482; in French painting, 698–700, *699*; in
literature, 698, 700; in medieval painting,
332; in Renaissance painting, 358–359
Realpolitik, 670, 672–673, 679
Realschule (Germany), 532
Real wages, 706, 720
Rearmament, of Germany, 831, 851–852,
905–906
Reason: in Enlightenment, 514, 516; before
World War I, 738, 739. *See also* Irrationality;
Rationalism
Reason of state, 554
Rebellions. *See* Revolts and rebellions
Recessions: in 17th century, 447; in 1866–1867,
690; in later 19th century, 708; in 1973–
1974, 920, 927; in 1979–1983, 927; in
2008–, 954, 962, 975–976
Red Army, 800–802, 874, 886, 903
Red Brigades (Italy), 931, 964
Red Guards (China), 935, 936
Redistribution Act (England), 729
Red Scare, 908
Red Shirts, 677, 678
Red Terror (Russia), 802, 833
Reflections on the Revolution in France (Burke), 639
Reform Acts (England): of 1832, 652, 653, 654,
685, *688*; of 1867, 686–687, *688*, 729; of
1884, *688*, 729
Reform and reformers: in Austria, 549–550;
of Catholic Church, 371–372; Christian
humanism and, 377–380; in cities, 717–
719; crime and, 661; in Denmark, 554; in
eastern Europe, 926; in England, 652–654,
686–688, 729–731, 753–755; in France,
323, 580; in Germany, 755, 803; industrial,
623–625, 633; Napoleonic, 599–601;
prison, 661–662; in Prussia, 603, 645; in
Russia, 466, 550–552, 683–685, 951; in
Soviet Union, 948–949; in Sweden, 554;
in United States, 758; urban, 717. *See also*
Reformation
Reformation, 376–377. *See also* Catholic
Reformation; Protestant Reformation
Reformed churches, 386, 536
Refugees, 457–458, 967

Regency: in England, 393
Regensburg Colloquy, 401
Reichsrat (Austria), 682
Reichstag (Germany), 382, 681, 711, 732, 828, 829
Reign of Terror (French Revolution), 589–590, 592, 593, 596
Reinsurance Treaty, 770
Relativism. *See* Cultural relativism
Relativity theory, 738–739
Relics (Catholic Church), 380
Religion: crime problem and, 661; in eastern Europe, 369; in 18th century, 536–539; in England, 392–394, 407, 473; expansion and, 415; in France, 394, 454, 457–458; fundamentalism in, 742, 964, 968; in Germany, 386–387, 388–389, 451; new imperialism and, 759–761; politics and, 451; popular culture and, 398; postwar revival of, 915–916; in Romantic age, 667; science and, 508–510, 742; skepticism about, 515; Thirty Years' War and, 449; Voltaire on, 519; Wars of, 402–404; witchcraft craze and, 447. *See also* Popular religion; Reformation; specific groups
Religious orders, 380, 399, 571
Religious toleration, 647; in 18th century, 536–538; by Joseph II (Austria), 537, 538, 549; Voltaire on, 519
Rém, Nicholas, 449
Remarque, Erich Maria, 786
Rembrandt van Rijn, 481–483, *482*
Reminiscences (Schurz), 653–654
Renaissance, 340–341; arts in, 358–366; Catholic Church in, 370–373; education in, 355–357; in Italy, 341–366, *348*, 352–358; magic in, 489; music in, 365–366; in northern Europe, 364–365; papacy in, *372*, 372–373; printing in, 358; social orders in, 344; state in, 366–370
Renan, Ernst, 742
Reparations: Dawes Plan and, 815; after World War I, 807, 814; after World War II, 879, 888
Report of Sadler's Committee (1832), 629
Report of the Children's Employment Commission (Great Britain), 628
Report on the Condition of the Labouring Population of Great Britain (Chadwick), 625
"Reports of the Genevan Consistory," 396
Representative assembly, 647
Repression: political and military, 644–646; psychological, 740, 741, 846
Republican Party (Germany), 967
Republican Party (U.S.), 658, 688, 931, 961, 962
Republicans: in France, 655–656, 755; in Spain, 837–838
Republic of Virtue, in France, 591, 595
Research, 693–694, 708, 938
Resettlement plans, of Nazi Germany, 866
Resistance movements, against Nazis, 867
Resources, 343, 608, 866
Restif de la Bretonne, Nicolas, 533
Restoration: in England, 476–477; in France, 604, 644; in Italy, 640; in Spain, 640, 644
Reunification, of Germany, 954, 957–959, 963
Revisionism, 712, 713
Revivalism, Protestant, 538–539
Revolts and rebellions: in cities, 314–315; in England, 473; in France, 313, *313*, 314, 315, 455, *589*; in Greece, 643; in Hungary, 657, 903, 904; in Italy, 640, 657; in Japan, 435; Luther and, 381–383; in Russia, 464, 465, 552; in Saint Domingue, 595, *595*; in Spain, 640, 644, 730–731; student, 920–921, 923–924; Thirty Years' War and, 454. *See also* specific events
Revolution(s), 574–575, 578; American, 575–578; in eastern Europe (1989), 952–954, 963; 1830–1850, *651*, 651–652, 654–657, *655*; of 1848–1849, 654–657, *655*, 682, 692; in

England, 478–479; in France, 578–597, 605; sexual, 921. *See also* Revolts and rebellions; specific locations
Revolutionaries, anarchist, 714
Revolutionary civil guard (Austrian Empire), *656*
Revolutionary socialism, 740
Revolutionary terrorism, 802, 964
Revolutionary Tribunal, The (Milligen), 592
Revolution Settlement (England), 477
Rhineland, 785, 807, 852, *854*
Rhine River region, 638, 690, 864, *864*
Rhodes, 388
Rhodes, Cecil, 762
Rhodesia, 762
Rhythm and blues, 917
Ricardo, David, 647
Ricci, Matteo, 401, 438
Richard II (England), 314, 321
Richard II (Shakespeare), 483
Richard III (England), 367
Richardson, Samuel, 530
Richelieu (Cardinal), 451, 454, *455*
Riefenstahl, Leni, 841
Rights: in France, 600; Locke on, 479; natural, 543
Riksdag (Sweden), 467
Rilke, Rainer Maria, 743
Rimbaud, Arthur, 744
Ring of the Nibelung, The (Wagner), 701
Riots: in Britain, 959; by Muslims in France, 959; race riots in United States, 874
Risorgimento, 657, 659
Rite of Spring, The (Stravinsky), 749
Rivals, The (Sheridan), 559
Roads and highways: Inca, 424; in Industrial Revolution, 611, 618
Roaring Twenties, 839
Robespierre, Maximilien, 589, 593, 594, 595, *596*
Robins, Thomas, *613*
Rochefoucauld-Liancourt, duc de la, 574
Rock-and-roll, *916*, 917, 942
Rocket (railroad engine), 611–612
Rococo style, 527
Rocroi, Battle of, 451, 462
Roman Catholic Church. *See* Catholic Church
Romania, 769, 805, 807, 814, 836, 890, 961; communism and, 880, 886, 902, 927, 953; revolt in, 952, *952*; in World War II, 859, 865
Roman Inquisition, 401, 494–495
Romanov dynasty, 464, 638
Romanticism, 523, 662–667, 698; in music, 665–667, 700–701; in poetry, 633; Rousseau and, 523
Rome (city): Italian annexation of, 678; sack of (1527), 350, 387; in World War II, 864
Rome, Treaty of (1951), 907
Rome-Berlin Axis, 852
Rommel, Erwin, 862
Roosevelt, Franklin D., 859, 865; at Allied war conferences, 879, *880*; Great Depression and, 819–820
Rossbach, Battle of, 556
Rossi, Luigi de', *372*
Rotten boroughs (England), 643, 652
Rouen, revolt in (1382), 314
Rougon-Macquart (Zola), 743
Rousseau, Jean-Jacques, 522–523, *523*, 524, 525, 559, 723
Royal Academy of Sciences (France), 502, 506, 507, 508, 514, *515*
Royal Albert Bridge, *613*
Royal College of Physicians (England), 534
Royal College of Surgeons (England), 534
Royal Council (Britain), 436
Royal council (France), 456
Royalists: in England, 474, 475–476
Royal Observatory, at Greenwich, England, 507, *507*
Royal Society (England), 502, 505, 506–507

Rubens, Peter Paul, 480, *480*
Rucellai family, 345
Rudder, 415
Rudolf II (Holy Roman Empire), 492
Rugby Football Union (England), 727
Ruhr region, 715, 814
"Rules of Reasoning in Philosophy" (Newton), 498
Rump Parliament, 474
Rural areas, 621, 758, 910
Russell, W. H., *675*
Russia: alliances of, 769; Asian expansion by, 763–764; Balkans and, 769, 771, 772, 777–778; China and, 433; civil war in, 800–803, *803*, 833; Communist Party in, 800; Crimean War and, 674–675; economy in, 466, 950, 951; in 18th century, 550–552; Enlightenment in, 542–543; German Reinsurance Treaty with, 770; government of, 465–466; industrialization in, 619–620, 708, 756–757; Jews and, 311, 753; in late 1800s, 734; literature in, 743; military in, 465, 466, 557; Mongols in, 369; Napoleon and, 601, 603; after Napoleonic wars, 646–647; Ottoman Empire and, 643, 674, 675; Peter the Great and, 464–466, *467*; Poland and, 466, 552, 637, 638, 652; population of, 558; under Putin, 951; Quadruple Alliance and, 637, 640; revolts in, 454, 464, 465, 552; socialist party in, 712; Triple Entente and, 770; West and, 466; women in, 466, 797, 800; World War I and, 792, 807. *See also* Commonwealth of Independent States; Soviet Union; World War I; World War II
Russian Empire, 673–674
Russian Orthodox Church, 464, 466. *See also* Eastern Orthodoxy
Russian Republic, 950
Russian Revolutions: Bolshevik Revolution (1917), 790, 799–800, 850; of March, 1917, 797–799; of 1905, 757–758, 797
Russian-Turkish war, 643
Russo-Japanese War, 757, 764, 771, 855
Ryswick, Treaty of, 460

SA. *See* Storm Troops (SA)
Sabotage, in World War II, 867
Sacraments: Calvin on, 395; Luther on, 382, 386
Sacrifices: in Benin, 429
Saddam Hussein, 964, 965, 966
Saigon, 765, *766*, 892
Sailors and sailing, 415; Portuguese, 419
Saint Bartholomew's Day Massacre, 403, *404*
Saint-Domingue, 435–436, 595. *See also* Haiti
Saint Helena, Napoleon on, 604
Saint-Just, Louis, 591
Saint Lawrence River region, 436, 555, 556
St. Peter's Basilica (Rome), 363, 372
St. Petersburg, Russia, 466, *467*, 757, 797, *798*; in 18th century, 569; foundling home in, 560
Saint Peter's Fields, Manchester, 644
"Saints," Anabaptists as, 392
Saint-Simon, comte de (socialist), 651
Saint-Simon, duc de (Louis de Rouvroy), 446–447, 459
Saint Vincent de Paul: religious order of, 571
Sakhalin Island, 879
Sakharov, Andrei, 926
Salazar, Antonio, 838
Salerno, medical school in, 335
Salons, 526
Salt, Titus, 622
Saltaire, England, *622*
Salvation: Calvin on, 394–395; charity for, 329; Luther and, 381, 382, 386; before Reformation, 379–380
Salvation Army, 743
Samoan Islands, 766
Samurai (Japan), 767, 875
Samurai revolt (1867), 767
Sanford, Elizabeth Poole, 721

Sanger, Margaret, 842
Sanitation: in cities, 570, 623, 624, *624*, 625, 717; in 14th century, 335–336
San Lorenzo, Church of, 360, *361*
San Martín, José de, 640, *641*, 641–642
Sans-culottes, 588
San Stefano, Treaty of, 769
Santa María (ship), 420
Santa Maria del Carmine, Florence, *359*
Santi di Tito, *351*
Santo Domingo, 424–425
Sarajevo, 776; shelling of, *955*, 956
Sardinia, 553, 638, 644, 676; Austria and, 463
Sarkozy, Nicolas, 959
Sartre, Jean-Paul, 913, 915
Sati, 768
Saudi Arabia, 820, 896, 898, 964, 965
Savoy, 644, 677; house of, 644, 677
Saxony, 323, 638
Scandinavia: Black Death in, 308; in 18th century, 554; Great Depression in, 819; Lutheranism in, 386, 389
Schleswig, 680
Schleswig-Holstein, 681
Schlieffen, Alfred von, 778
Schlieffen Plan, 778, 778–780, 782
Schmalkaldic League, 388
Schmidt, Helmut, 929
Scholarship. *See* Intellectual thought
Scholasticism, 355
Schönberg, Arnold, 845, 942
Schönborn prince-bishop (Würzburg): palace of, 527
Schönhuber, Franz, 967
School of Athens (Raphael), 362, *362*
Schools: in 18th century, 532, 535–536; for girls, 397; humanist, 355–357; Jesuit, 401; medical, 335; in Middle Ages, 334; monastic, 437; Protestant, 397–398, *398*. *See also* Education; Universities and colleges
Schröder, Gerhard, 959
Schumacher, E. F., 938, 939
Schurz, Carl, 653–654
Schuschnigg, Kurt von, 853
Schutzmannschaft (German police), 661
Schwartz, Matthaus, *443*
Schweickart, Russell, *975*
Science, 901; agriculture and, 561; in Enlightenment, 514–515, *515*; in nineteenth century, 693–694; religion and, 508–510, 742; Romantics and, 664; society and, 507–508, 698; technology and, 708, 938; women in, 501–504; before World War I, 738–739; since World War II, 937–938, *938*. *See also* Medicine; Scientific Revolution
Science of man: Diderot on, 521
Scientific laws: of Kepler, 492–493; of Newton, 499
Scientific management, 707
Scientific method, 505–506, 694
Scientific research, 693–694
Scientific Revolution, 441, 487–489, 693; medicine in, 499–501
Scientific societies, 502, 505, *506*, 506–507
Scotland: Calvinism in, 395; England and, 474; Knox in, 395; Mary, queen of Scots, in, 407–408; Presbyterian Church in, 473; in United Kingdom, 544
Scott, Walter, 662
Scout, The, 723, 724, *724*
Scripture, 386. *See also* Catholic Church; Protestantism; Theology
Sculpture: Baroque, 480, *481*; in Italian Renaissance, 360, *360*
Scutage, 319
Sea Beggars, 406
Sea routes: in Renaissance, 341–342
Seasons, The (Haydn), 529
SEATO, 892
Secondary education, 725
Secondary schools, 334, *398*

Second Balkan War, 771, *771*
Second Battle of the Marne, 803
Second Continental Congress, 575, 577, *577*
Second Empire (France), 671–675, 730
Second Estate: in European society, 344; in France, 579, 581
Second German Empire, 682
Second Industrial Revolution, 704, 705–711, 725
Second International, 712
Second Republic (France), 656
Second Vietnam War, 899, 900, 921, 931, 932–935, *934*; protests against, 908, 923, 924
Second World War. *See* World War II
Secret Book (Hitler), 851
Secret police: in East Germany, 927, 958–959; in Italy, 824; in Nazi Germany, 867; in Romania, 927; in Russia, 646, 734, 802; in Soviet Union, 902, 926
Secret societies: in Enlightenment, 526; in Italy, 644; in Russia, 646
Sectionalism, in Italy, 731
Secular humanism, 968
Secularism, 352, 446, 487, 694, 820, 968; France and, 968, 969–970
Sedan, battle at, 681
Seed drills, 561, *562*
Segregation: in colonies, 767; in United States, 908
Ségur Law, 579
Seibertz, Engelbert, *637*
Sejm (Polish diet), 369, 470
Select Society of Edinburgh, Scotland, 526
Self-determination, 649; for eastern Europe, 886; World War I and, 805, 807, 808, 809; after World War II, 895
Self-Help (Smiles), 626
Self-interest: as economic principle, 522
Self-Portrait (Basquiat), *972*
Seljuk Turks, 370
Senate in Venice, 325
Senate (France), 730
Separation of church and state, 392, 647
Separation of powers, Montesquieu on, 518
Separatist movement(s): in Quebec, 962; in Yugoslavia, 954
Sephardic Jews, 537–538
Sepoys, 763
September 11, 2001, terrorist attacks, 948, 959, 962, 964, *965*, 968
Serbia, 370, 769, 771, 772, 776, 957; World War I and, 778, 783, 807
Serbs, 657, 954, 955, 956
Serfs and serfdom: in Austria, 682; in eastern Europe, 566; in Prussia, 548, 645; in Russia, 552, 683–685, 686; in 16th century, 442–443. *See also* Peasants
Serialism, in music, 942
Serious Proposal to the Ladies, A (Astell), 524
Serrano, Andres, 971
Servants, 720, 723; as urban workers, 627; women as, 630
Sevastopol, 675
Seven Years' War, 545, *555*, 555–557, *576*; French Canada and, 436; India and, 432; Prussia in, 548
Sewage and sewer systems, 570, 715, 717
Sex and sexuality: Diderot on, 521; Freud on, 740; in marriage, 396; prostitution in 19th century, 711; in Renaissance Italy, 346–347; VD and, 711; after World War I, 842; after World War II, 921. *See also* Gender
Sexual revolution, 921
Seymour, Jane, 393
Seyss-Inquart, Arthur, *853*
Sforza family (Milan), 347–348; Battista, 349; Ludovico, 350
Shakespeare, William, 483
Shelley, Mary, 664
Shelley, Percy Bysshe, 664
Sheridan, Richard, 559
Sherman, Roger, *577*

Shibuzawa Eiichi, 626
Shi'ite Muslims, 965
Shikoku, 439
Ship money (English tax), 473
Ships and shipping, 442; Dutch *fluyt*, 471; in 18th century, 558; exploration and, 415; Napoleon and, 601–602; Portuguese, 419; slave trade and, 426–427; trade and, 564, 690; in World War II, 862. *See also* Navy; Steamboats
Shogun (Japan), 433, 767
Shonibare, Yinka, 973, *974*
Siam. *See* Thailand (Siam)
Siberia, 763, 834, 902
Sicily, 348, 644, 677, 864; Aragon rulers in, 324; Bourbons in, 553; revolts in, 454, 657
Siege warfare: in 18th century, 558
Sieveking, Amalie, 749
Sieyès, Abbé, 581
Sigismund (Holy Roman Empire), 328, 371
Sigismund III (Sweden and Poland), 470
Signing of the Declaration, The (Trumbull), 577
Signoria (Florence), 325
Signorini, Giovanni, *535*
Silesia: Prussia and, 548
Silesia, *462*, 555, 556
Silicon chip, 938
Silk Road, 307, 308
Silver: Spanish, 404, 405; for trade, 443
Simons, Menno, 392
Simplicius Simplicissimus (Grimmelshausen), 453
Sinai peninsula, 898
Single Europe Act (1986), 960
Sisters of Charity, 571
Sisters of the Common Life, 329
Sistine Chapel, Michelangelo and, *340*, 340–341, 362–363
Six Day War (1967), 898
Sixtus IV (Pope), 372
Skepticism, 514–515, 543
Skilled workers: mass education for, 725–726; in World War I, 795
Skyscrapers, 844
Slater, Samuel, 618
Slave labor: of Japanese, 872; of Nazi Germany, 866, 871
Slavery: African, 345, 416, 426–429; in French Revolution, 595; in Haiti, 435–436; in Renaissance, 345; in United States, 429, 686, 688–689, *690*
Slave trade, 426–429, *427*, 437, 564; in Latin America, 436
Slavic peoples, 683, 771; in eastern Europe, 369; Nazis and, 850, 866, 871; World War I and, 778
"Slop work," 710
Slovakia, 853, 953, 960
Slovenes, 657, 954
Slovenia, 463, 954, 955, 957, 960
Slums, in England, *624*, 818
Small Is Beautiful (Schumacher), 938, 939
Smallpox: Aztecs and, 422; Inca and, 424; vaccinations for, 715
Smiles, Samuel, 626
Smith, Adam, 521, 522
Smith, Kiki, 973
Smithson, Robert, *940*, 941
Soccer. *See* Football (soccer)
Social classes. *See* Classes
Social contract: Rousseau on, 522–523
Social Contract, The (Rousseau), 523, 524
Social Darwinism, 741–742, 827; imperialism and, 759
Social Democrats: in Austria, 756; Communist parties and, 903; in Germany, 711–712, 732, 755, 780, 804, 826, 829, 905, 906, 929; in Russia, 756–757, 798; in Scandinavia, 819
Socialism, 650–651; Bismarck and, 732; in France, 712, 819; Marx and, 691–692; Marxist, 743, 819, 822; revolutionary, 712, 713, 740; in

Russia, 756–757; in western Europe, 903; World War I and, 777, 780, 792–793
Socialist Party, 711–712; in France, 931, 959; in Italy, 823
Socialist realism, in Soviet Union, 845
Socialist Revolutionaries (Russia), 800
Socialized medicine, in Great Britain, 906
Social networking, 972
Social orders: in France, 578–580
Social Revolutionaries (Russia), 757
Social sciences: in Enlightenment, 521
Social security: in Canada, 909; in Germany, 732; in Great Britain, 906; in United States, 820
Social services: foreigner workers and, 967; spending on, 912
Social Statics (Spencer), 741–742
Social welfare: in England, 753–754; in Germany, 732, 733; in Italy, 755; in Scandinavia, 819; in U.S., 961. *See also* Welfare state
Society. *See* Lifestyle; Mass society
Society for Revolutionary Republican Women, 592
Society for the Diffusion of Useful Knowledge in the Field of Natural Sciences, Technical Science, and Political Economy, 661
Society of Friends. *See* Quakers
Society of Harmonious Fists (China), 767
Society of Jesus. *See* Jesuits
Society of Thirty, 578, 581
Sociology, Comte and, 698
Solar system. *See* Universe
Soldiers. *See* Military
Solferino, battle at, 677
Solidarity movement, 926, 952
Solomon Islands, in World War II, 863, 864
Solzhenitsyn, Alexander, 902
Some Reflections upon Marriage (Astell), 524
Somme, Battle of, 775, 775, 784
Songs: in Renaissance, 365; of World War I, 785, 789
Son of Heaven: Chinese emperor as, 432
Sophia (Austria), 778
Sophocles, 355
Sorel, Georges, 740
Sorrows of the Young Werther, The (Goethe), 662
Soup kitchens, during Great Depression, 812, 812
South Africa, 426, 762, 762, 821, 943; independence and, 895–896
South America: Spain and, 420, 435. *See also* Latin America; specific locations
Southeast Asia: Dutch in, 442; Japanese expansionism and, 857, 871; new imperialism in, 764–765, 766; in 1700, 429; wars in, 963; western involvement in, 429–430, 430; World War II in, 860
Southeast Asia Treaty Organization. *See* SEATO
Southern Christian Leadership Conference (SCLC), 908
Southern Europe: guest workers from, 967
Southern Hemisphere: developing nations in, 976, 978
"Southern strategy" (Nixon), 931
South Korea. *See* Korea; Korean War
South Vietnam. *See* Vietnam; Vietnam War
South-West Africa, 763
Soviets, in Russia, 798, 799
Soviet Union, 949; Afghanistan and, 937, 943, 949; Allied war conferences and, 879–880; attempted coup in, 947, 950, 951; under Brezhnev, 925–926; coexistence with, 815; Communist Party in, 926, 948–949; de-Stalinization in, 901, 902; eastern Europe and, 903, 904; economy in, 833, 900–901, 902, 926, 948; end of, 947–948, 949–950, 963, 978; German invasion of, 859, 859, 861, 862–861; under Gorbachev, 926, 948–949, 950, 962; Hitler and, 850; home front (World War II), 873–874; industry in, 833, 900, 902, 926; multiethnicity of, 949; Nazi nonaggression pact with, 855, 856; Persian Gulf War and,

963; political and military supremacy and, 886; purges in, 834; reforms in, 948–949; socialist realism in, 845; under Stalin, 833–836; Suez crisis and, 898; totalitarianism in, 822; United States and, 880; Warsaw Pact and, 890, 891; women in, 834–835, 900, 912. *See also* Cold War; Commonwealth of Independent States; Russia; World War II
Space exploration, 937, 938, 948
Space race, 937
Spain, 406, 931; African possession of, 762; in Americas, 435, 436; in Asia, 429; Aztecs and, 422–423; Black Death in, 308; Bourbons in, 644; Catholic Church in, 368–369, 404–405, 461, 553; decline of, 461–462; dictatorship in, 836, 838; in 18th century, 553; exploration by, 414, 419–425; France and, 349, 460, 462, 601; French and Indian War and, 557; government of, 461–462; Habsburg emperors and, 386; Inca Empire and, 424; Italy and, 350, 464; Jesuits and, 536; Jews expelled from, 368–369; in late 1800s, 730–731; Latin America and, 436, 640, 641; Muslims in, 368–369; Napoleon and, 602, 603; Netherlands and, 405–406, 553; New World and, 404; Ottoman Turks and, 468; Popular Front in, 836–837; population of, 558; revolts and, 454, 640, 644, 730–731; slavery and, 345, 426; Southeast Asia and, 429; sphere of influence of, 420; Thirty Years' War and, 449, 461–462; unification of, 368, 368–369; War of the Spanish Succession and, 460–461. *See also* Spanish Civil War
Spanish-American War, 730, 766
Spanish Armada, 409–410
Spanish Civil War, 837–838
Spanish Empire, 424–425
Spanish Inquisition, 368, 425
Spanish Netherlands, 460, 461, 462, 463, 471
Spectator (periodical), 532
Spectator sports, 727–728
Speculation: in France, 597
Speech at the Nuremberg Party Rally (Hitler, 1936), 830
Speech on Revolutionary Government (Robespierre), 593
Speech to Congress (Havel), 953
Speech to the German Reichstag (Bismarck, 1888), 672–673
Speech to the Prussian Reichstag (Bismarck, 1862), 672
Speer, Albert, 875
Spencer, Herbert, 741–742
Spengler, Lazarus, 384
Spengler, Oswald, 813
Speransky, Michael, 646
Spheres of influence: in China, 764; in eastern Europe, 855, 902, 937; of women, 503
Spice Islands. *See* Moluccas (Spice Islands)
Spices and spice trade, 430; Dutch and, 429; Portugal and, 417, 418–419, 429
Spinning frame, 609
Spinning jenny, 610
Spinoza, Benedict de, 503, 508–509
Spiral Jetty (Smithson), 940, 941
Spirit of the Laws, The (Montesquieu), 517–518
Spiritual Exercises (Loyola), 400
Spirituality: in 14th century, 329
Sports: for children, 723; growth of, 942–944; mass leisure and, 840; team, 727–728
Springer, Alex, 923
Sputnik I, 893, 901, 937
Squadristi, 823
Square with White Border (Kandinsky), 747, 748
Srebrenica, massacre at, 955
Sri Lanka (Ceylon), 418, 429, 899
SS (Nazi Germany). *See* Einsatzgruppen
Stadholder, 471, 547
Staël, Germaine de, 600
Stagflation, 932

Stakhanov, Alexei, 834
Stakhanov cult, 834
Stalin, Joseph, 833–836, 834, 854, 855, 873, 874; at Allied war conferences, 879, 880, 880; and Churchill's iron curtain speech, 881, 882; eastern Europe and, 886; economic policy of, 900–901; Korean War and, 892; Yugoslavia and, 902
Stalingrad, Battle of, 862, 862–863, 864
Stalinization, 903
Standard of living. *See* Lifestyle
Standing army, 453, 557
Staniland, C. J., 716
Stanley, Henry M., 762, 763
Starry Messenger, The (Galileo), 493, 495
Starry Night, The (van Gogh), 746, 747
Starvation, 976, 978
Stasi (East Germany), 927, 958–959
Stasi Committee (France), 969
State (nation): centralization of, 543; in 18th century, 543–554; in late 1800s, 705; in Renaissance, 366–370. *See also* Church and state; Government
Staten Island, 436
State of nature: Hobbes on, 478
States General (Netherlands), 471
State-sponsored terrorism, 964
State system (Europe), 543
Status. *See* Classes
Statute of Laborers (England), 312–313
Stauffenberg, Claus von, 867
Steamboats, 618, 619, 620
Steam engine, 610, 610–611, 618, 690, 694
Steam locomotive, 611
Steele, Richard, 532
Steel industry, 705, 756, 758, 904
Stein, Heinrich von, 603, 645
Stephenson, George, 611–612, 690
Steppenwolf (Hesse), 845
Stocker, Adolf, 752
Stock exchanges, 564
Stock market, 815, 816, 975
Stolypin, Peter, 758
Stonebreakers, The (Courbet), 698, 699
Stopes, Marie, 842
Storm Troops (SA), 827, 829
Strait of Magellan, 413
Strasbourg, 460; killing and cremation of Jews in, 312
Strategic Defense Initiative (SDI, Star Wars), 937
"Strategic relationship" (U.S.-China), 936
Stravinsky, Igor, 749, 845, 942
Streetcars, 705, 719
Streltsy rebellion, Peter the Great and, 465
Stresemann, Gustav, 815
Strikes (labor): in England, 818, 929; in France, 755, 905, 921; general, 740, 905; in Italy, 823; trade unions and, 713, 714; in World War I, 792
Strozzi family: Alessandra, 346, 347; Filippo, 347; marriage negotiations and, 345
Structuralism, 939
Struensee, John Frederick, 554
Strutt, Jedediah, 630
Stuart dynasty (England), 476, 545
Student Manifesto in Search of a Real and Human Educational Alternative, A, 924
Student protests, 905, 920–921, 923–924
Students: as Austrian revolutionaries, 656; in welfare state universities, 910–912. *See also* Universities and colleges
Student societies (German), 645–646
Styria, 463
Submarines, 790, 862
Suburbs, 719
Subways, 705
Sudan, 762, 763, 976
Sudetenland, cession to Germany, 853
Suez Canal, 691, 762, 897–898
Suffrage. *See* Voting and voting rights
Suffragists, 749–750, 751

Sugar and sugar industry, 766
Sugar plantations, 426, 435, *435*
Suharto (Indonesia), 900
Sukarno (Indonesia), 900
Suleiman I the Magnificent (Ottoman Empire), 388, 468
Sullivan, Louis H., 844
Sumatra, 429
Summit conferences: in Geneva (1955), 892; in Vienna (1961), 893
Sunni Muslims, 965
Sun Yat-sen (China), 767
Supercentralization system, of Stalin, 873
Superego, 740
Supermarkets, 910, 911, *911*
Superpowers, 886–891. *See also* Cold War; Soviet Union; United States
Supplement to the Voyage of Bougainville (Diderot), 521
Supply-side economics, 932
Supreme Court (U.S.), 658, 908, 961
Surat, India, 432
Surgeons and surgery, 335, 533, 696, 697
Surrealism, 843–844, *844*, 845
Survival of the fittest, 694
Suttner, Bertha von, 752
Swan, Joseph, 705
Sweatshops, 710
Sweden, 467–468, 960; Hansa and, 342; Lutheranism in, 389; national cinema of, 917; Poland and, 470; religion in, 554; Scandinavian unification and, 389; in 17th century, *468*; sexual revolution in, 921; upheavals in, 454; women in, 912. *See also* Scandinavia
Swedish Lutheran National Church, 389
Swedish phase, of Thirty Years' War, 451
Sweet potato, 437
Swiss Brethren, 392
Swiss Republic: France and, 601
Switzerland, *389*, 389–390, 394–395
Syllabus of Errors (Pius IX), 742–743
Symbolism, in literature, 743, 744, 748
Symphonic poem (Liszt), 701
Syndics of the Cloth Guild (Rembrandt), *482*
Syria, 808, 820, 896; terrorism and, 964; in United Arab Republic, 898
System of Nature (Holbach), 522
System of Positive Philosophy (Comte), 698

Taaffe, Edward von, 733
Table of Ranks (Russia), 465–466
Tabula rasa, Locke on, 516
Tahiti, 515
Taille (French tax), 323, 579
Taiwan. *See* Formosa (Taiwan)
Taliban, 964, 968
Talleyrand Perigord (Charles-Maurice de), *637*
Tamerlane, 432
Tanganyika, 763, 896. *See also* Tanzania
Tanks, 791, 852, 864
Tannenberg, Battle of, 783
Tanzania, 896
Tariffs, 443, 458, 554, 617, 644, 690, 706, 708, 756
Tartuffe (Molière), 484
Taverns, 534–535
Taxation: of American colonies, 575; armies and, 558; in Austria, 549; British, in India, 432; in England, 313, 473, 474, 477, 753, 754, 959; in France, 323, 326, 587, 600; in Germany, 958; in Russia, 552; in United States, 758, 932, 962
Taylor, Harriet, 648
Tea, 441
Teaching, 710, 725, 726
Team sports, 727–728
Tears of the Indians, The (Las Casas), 425
Technology: on Continent, 616, 618; dangers of, 938, 939; in Digital Age, 972–973;

industrial, 610–616, 693, 939; in metallurgy, 442; revolution in, 974; science and, 708; Scientific Revolution and, 488, 507; in United States, 618; since World War II, 937–938, *938*
Tehran conference, 879
Telecommunications, 972, 974
Telegraph, 705
Telephone, 705
Telescope, 493, *493*
Tempietto (Bramante), 363, *363*
Temple of Reason, Notre-Dame as, 594
Temuchin. *See* Genghis Khan
Ten Hours Act (1847), 633
Tennis Court Oath, 581, *582*
Tennyson, Alfred (Lord), 720
Tenochtitlán, 421, 422, 423
Teresa of Avila (Saint), 399
Terror, the. *See* Reign of Terror
Terrorism, 964; by Black Hand, 778; forms of, 964; international, 964; by Irish Republican Army, 929; in Italy, 823; by Mau Mau movement, 895; at Munich Olympics, 943; from Muslim world, 965–966; in Nazi Germany, 831; since 1970s, 963–964; by Quebec separatists, 962; September 11, 2001, attacks on U.S., 948, 959, 962, 964, *965*, 968
Test Act (England), 477
Testelin, Henri, *506*
Tetzel, Johann, 382
Texas: missions in, 437
Textbooks, medical, *337*
Textiles and textile industry, 343, *564*, 690, *710*; in Britain, 608, 610; child labor in, 628–629; on Continent, 618; India and, 563–564; in United States, 618. *See also* Industrial Revolution
Thackeray, William, 698
Thailand (Siam), 429, 430, 765, 768, 892
Thatcher, Margaret, *929*, 929–931, 959
Theater. *See* Drama
"Theater of the Absurd," 914–915
Theatines, 399
Theology: conciliarism and, 328; in 14th century, 329–330; Hermetic writings and, 355; Luther and, 380; of Zwingli, 389–390
Thermidorean Reaction, 596
Thermodynamics, 694
Thermonuclear weapons, 901
Thiers, Adolphe, 652, 655
Third Estate: in European society, 344–345
Third Estate (France), 323, *579*, 579–581; as National Assembly, 581–582, *582*. *See also* Peasants
Third Man, The (movie), 889
Third of May 1808, The (Goya), *603*
Third Reich, 829
Third Republic (France), 707, 730, 755
Thirty-Nine Articles, 407
Thirty Years' War, 449–454, *450*, *452*, 461–462, 466, 467
"This is Tomorrow" exhibit, 914
Thomas (apostle): community in India and, 414
Thomas à Kempis, 380
Three Emperors' League, 769
Threepenny Opera, The (Weill), 845
Throne of Saint Peter (Bernini), 480
Thucydides, 355
Tilly (Count), 451
Time, clocks and, 337
Time of Troubles (Russia), 464
"Times They Are A-Changin,' The" (Dylan), 923
Tin Drum, The (Grass), 915
Tisza, Istvàn, 756
Tithes, 587
Titian, *387*, *405*
Tito (Josip Broz), 867, *902*, 902–903, 954
Tlaxcala, 422
Togoland, 763, 785

Tojo, Hideki, 875
Tokugawa Ieyasu (Japan), 433, 435, 437
Toleration. *See* Religious toleration
Toleration Act (England, 1689), 477
Toleration Patent (Austria), 537
Tolstoy, Leo, 743
Tonkin, 765; letters of Louis XIV to king of, 431
Tools, 704, 708
Topa Inca, 423
Tordesillas, Treaty of, 420
Tories (England), 477, 643–644, 654, 686
Torture, 533, 548
Totalitarianism, 821–838, 845
Totalitarian state, 822
Total war: World War I as, 791–797, 822; World War II as, 849–850, 878
Toul, 451
Tour de France, 944
Tourism, 569, 727, 840, 910
Tournai, Belgium: plague deaths in, *308*
Toussaint L'Ouverture, 595
Towns. *See* Cities and towns; Villages
Townspeople, 569–571
Toynbee, Arnold, 776
Trade: in Amsterdam, 471; with China, 433; commercial capitalism and, 442; in 18th century, 564; in England, 608; EU and, 960; French, 458; globalization and, 443; imperialism and, 761; with India, 432; mercantile empires and, 564–565; in Middle Ages, 306, 314–315; overseas, 442, 443; plague and, 307–308; in Renaissance, 342–343; treaties in 1860s, 690; triangular, 426; worldwide, 418. *See also* Mercantilism; Slave trade
Trade unions, 631–632, *632*, 711, 713–714; in Africa, 821; in Britain, 753, 818, 906; working conditions and, 691; in World War I, 793. *See also* Labor unions
Trading companies: British East India Company, 432, 433, *556*, 763; Dutch East India Company, 426; Dutch West India Company, 436
Trading empires: of Portugal, 419
Trading posts: European, 430
Trafalgar, Battle of, 601
Traini, Francisco, 333, *333*
Trains. *See* Railroads
Transformism, 755
Transistor, 938
Transnational corporation, 975
Transportation: in cities, 719; internal combustion engine and, 705–706; mass leisure and, 727; in United States, 618–619. *See also* Airplanes; Automobiles; Railroads
Transportation revolution, 611–612, 618, 709
Trans-Siberian Railroad, 756
Transubstantiation, Luther on, 386
Transvaal, 762
Transylvania, 463
Travel, 515–516, 569, 840
Travels (Cook), 515
Travels (Polo), 414
Travels during the Years 1787, 1788, and 1789...in the Kingdom of France (Young), 563
Travels of John Mandeville, The, 414
Treason Act (England), 393
Treaties. *See* specific treaties
Treatise on Human Nature (Hume), 521
Treaty on European Union. *See* Maastricht Treaty
Trench warfare, in World War I, 775, 782, *782*, 783–785, 786, *788*
Trent, Council of, 401, 402
Trevithick, Richard, 611
"Trial of Suzanne Gaudry, The," 448
Trials: Nuremberg war crime trials, 906; for witchcraft, 447, 448
Triangular trade, 426
Tribute Money (Masaccio), *359*
Triennial Act (England), 473

Trieste, 822
Triple Alliance, 460, 738, 769
Triple Entente, 738, 770
Tripoli: as Libya, 762
Tristam, H. B., 728
Tristan, Flora, 651
Triumph of Death, The (Traini), 333, *333*
Triumph of the Will, The (movie), 840, 841
Troppau: congress at, 640
Trotsky, Leon, *799*, 800–802, 833
Troyes, Treaty of, 317
Trudeau, Pierre, 932
Truffaut, François, 917
Truman, Harry, 886, 888, 896, 908, 935;
    atomic bomb and, 865, 877; at Potsdam
    Conference, 880
Truman Doctrine, 886, 888
Trumbull, John, 577
Tsar (Russia), 646, 734
Tudor dynasty (England), 367, *394*
Tull, Jethro, 561, *562*
Tunisia, 762, 864, 895
Turing, Alan, 938
Turkestan, 764
Turkey, 886, 892, 896; missiles in, 893; NATO
    and, 890; after World War I, 820
Turks, 405, 552, 643. *See also* Ottoman Empire;
    Ottoman Turks
Turner, J. M. W., 664–665, *665*
Turnpikes, 611
Twain, Mark, 620
Twentieth Congress of the Communist Party,
    Khrushchev at, 901, 902
Twenty-Seventh Congress of the Communist
    Party, 948
Twitter, 972
Two Treatises of Government (Locke), 479
Two Women Teach a Child to Walk (de Hooch), 472, *472*
Tyler, Wat, 314
Tyrol, 463
Tzara, Tristan, 842

UAR. *See* United Arab Republic (UAR)
Uccello, Paolo, 358
Ukraine, 756, 800, 834, 938; anti-Jewish pogroms
    in, 753; independence of, 950; World War II
    in, 859, 864
Ulbricht, Walter, 888, 893, 927, 929
Ulianov, Vladimir. *See* Lenin, V. I.
Ultra-Catholics, 403
Ultra intelligence operation, 858
Ultraroyalists (France), 644
Ulysses (Joyce), 845
Unam Sanctam (Boniface VIII), 326
Unbearable Lightness of Being, The (Kundera),
    941–942
Uncertainty principle, 846
Unconscious, 740–741, 845–846
Unemployment, 631; after end of communism,
    953; in Great Depression, 813, 816, 817,
    818, 820, 828; Keynes on, 819. *See also*
    Economy
Unicameral legislature: in France, 656
Unification: of Europe, 960–961, *961*; of
    Germany, *649*, 656, *670*, 671, 678–682, *680*;
    of Italy, *649*, 657, *676*, 676–678; of Spain,
    368, 368–369
Union of Arras, 406
Union of Concerned Scientists, 977
Union of French Indochina, 765
Union of Kalmar, 389
Union of South Africa, 762
Union of Soviet Socialist Republics (USSR).
    See Soviet Union
Union of Utrecht, 406
Unions. *See* Labor unions; Trade unions
United Arab Republic (UAR), 898
United Kingdom, 544. *See also* England (Britain)
United Nations, 879, 896; Canada and, 909;
    Intergovernmental Panel on Climate

Change of, 977–978; Korean War and, 892;
    in Kosovo, 957; NGOs at, 978; women's
    conferences by, 966–967
United Netherlands. *See* Dutch Republic
United Provinces. *See* Dutch Republic
United States: in 1950s, 908; since 1990s, 961–
    962; Allied war conferences and, 879–880;
    antiwar protests in, 925; architecture
    in, 844; China and, 935–936; civil rights
    movement in, 908–909; Civil War in,
    688–689, *689*, 749, 781; containment policy
    of, 888, 892; creation of, 576–578; cultural
    influence of, 916–917; decolonization
    by, 898; economy in, 688, 908, 932,
    961, 962; European migration to, 716;
    fundamentalism in, 968; Great Depression
    in, 812–813, 819–820; housing market
    in, 975; imperialism of, 764, 765–766;
    industrialization of, 618–619, 758; Japan
    and, 764, 857; Japanese Americans
    during World War II, 874–875; Latin
    America and, 642–643; medicine in, 697;
    military alliances of, 892; national unity
    in, 657–658; NATO and, 890, *891*; Neo-
    Expressionism in, 970–971; Persian Gulf
    War and, 963; postwar in, 914; prison
    systems in, 662; Progressive Era in, 758;
    Second Vietnam War and, 900, 932–935;
    slavery and, 429, 686, 688–689, *690*;
    terrorism against, 948, 959, 962, 964, *965*;
    Versailles Treaty and, 809, 813; World War
    II and, 874–874. *See also* Cold War; World
    War I; World War II
Universal law of gravitation, 499
Universe: geocentric view of, 489; heliocentric view
    of, *490*, *491*; Kepler on, 491–493; medieval
    conception of, *490*; Scientific Revolution and,
    489–490. *See also* Astronomy
Universities and colleges: antiwar protests at,
    925; *Burschenschaften* in, 645–646; in 18th
    century, 532; in Soviet Union, 835–836;
    student revolts at, 920–921, 923–924; in
    welfare states, 910–912; women and, 726,
    726, 966. *See also* Education; Students
University of Leiden, 534
Upper Austria, 463
Upper classes: birth control in, 561; in 18th
    century, 535, *560*; families in, 559; in
    late 1800s, 719–720; lifestyle of, 567;
    Renaissance artists and, 364. *See also* Classes
Upper Italy, kingdom of, 676–677
Urban VI (Pope), 328
Urban areas: in 14th century, 334; in 18th
    century, 569–571; in 19th century, 622–
    625; in Renaissance, 341; transformation
    of, 716–719. *See also* Cities and towns;
    Ghettos
Urbanization, 621, 717, 742, 758
Urbino, 348, 349, 361
Ursulines, 399
Uruguay, 642
USSR. *See* Soviet Union
Utopia (More), 378
Utopian socialists, 650–651
Utrecht: Treaty (Peace) of (1713), 436, 461, 553
Uzbekistan, 949

Vacations, mass leisure and, 727, 840
Vaccinations, 696, 715
Valéry, Paul, 842
Valla, Lorenzo, 355
Valley of Mexico, 421. *See also* Mexico
Valois dynasty (France), 315, 350, 387, 402, 403
Values, 614
Vanderbilt, Consuelo, 720
Van de Velde, Theodore, 842
Van Eyck, Jan, 364–365, *365*
Van Gogh, Vincent, 745–746, *747*
Vanity Fair... (Thackeray), 698
Vasa, Gustavus, 389

Vasari, Giorgio, 341, 364
Vassals and vassalage, 315
Vassy, Huguenot massacre at, 403
Vatican II, 916
Vatican Palace, 362
VD. *See* Venereal disease (VD)
Vendée, department of, 589, 590
Venereal disease (VD), 711
Venetia, 638, 644, 657, 677–678, 681
Venezuela, 640, 641, 642
Venice, 464; in 18th century, 553; printing in,
    358; republic of, 324, 325, 347, 657; trade
    and, 341–342
Venturi, Robert, 941
Veracruz, Cortés in, 422
Verdun, 451; battle at, 784
Vergerio, Pietro Paolo, 355
Vernacular languages: literature in, 330–332;
    in Renaissance, 355
Verona: congress at, 640
Versailles, *457*, *458*; architecture and, 527;
    lifestyle at, 455, 458–459; Treaty of, 807,
    813, 814, 815, 850, 851, 852, 854; women's
    march to, 585–586, *586*
Vesalius, Andreas, 500, 503
Vespucci, Amerigo, 420
Veterans, 813
Viceroy, 425
Vichy France, 858
Victor Emmanuel II (Italy), 676, 677
Victor Emmanuel III (Italy), 823
Victoria (England), 615, *615*, 654, 685–686, 687,
    706, 763
Victorian England, 685–688, *689*, 720, 723
Video: in art, 973, *973*
Video games, 973
Vienna: Congress of, 636, *636*; Jews in, 752;
    Ottomans and, 388, 468, 469; re-design of,
    718; revolution of 1848 in, 657
Vierzehnheiligen, church of, 527, *528*
Vietcong, 932, 934
Vietminh, 892, 893
Vietnam, 429, 430, 433, 857, 892, 899, 900
Vietnam War: First, 892, 899; protests against,
    908, 923, 924, 925; Second, 899, 900, 921,
    923, 924, 931, 932–935, *934*
Villages, 566
Vindication of the Rights of Woman
    (Wollstonecraft), 524, 525–526
Viola, Bill, 973, *973*
Violence: anarchists and, 714; in domestic
    politics, 595; in Russia, 685
Virchow, Rudolf, 717
Virginia: Jamestown in, 436
Visconti family, 324, 347; Filippo Maria, 346
Vittorino da Feltre, school of, 355–356
Vodka, 534
Voilquin, Suzanne, 651
Volga River region, 552
Volkish thought, 742
Volkschulen (Austrian Empire), 535
Voltaire (François-Marie Arouet), 455, 518–519,
    519, 520, 526; on gender equality, 523–524;
    on writing of history, 530
Von Bora, Katherina, 386
Voting and voting rights: in Austria-Hungary,
    756; in England, 474, 545, 643, 652, 653,
    687, *688*, 729; in France, 652, 656, 671; in
    Italy, 731, 755; political liberalism and, 647;
    revolutions of 1848 and, 657; in Spain, 730;
    in United States, 658, 908; women and,
    729, 749–750, *751*, 795, 912–913
Voyages of exploration, *413*, 413–414, 416–420,
    419–420
Vulgate: Erasmus and, 378

Wafd (Egyptian political party), 895
Wages, 706; industrialization and, 631; iron law
    of, 647; price revolution and, 442; women
    vs. men, 912; for workers, 720

Wagner, Richard, 701
Waiting for Godot (Beckett), 914–915
Walesa, Lech, 926, 952
Wallachia, 370, 468, 643, 674, 675
Walled cities, 718
Wallenstein, Albrecht von, 450–451
Walnut Street Prison, Philadelphia, 662
Walpole, Robert, 545
Walsingham, Francis, 408
Wannsee: conference at, 870
Wappers, Gustave, *651*
War, The (Dix), 842, *843*
War and Peace (Tolstoy), 743
War communism, in Russia, 802, 833
War crime trials, after World War II, 906
War for Independence. *See* American Revolution
"War Girls" (poem), 794
War Guilt Clause, 807
Warhol, Andy, 914
"Warning to Humanity," 977
War of 1812, 658
War of the Austrian Succession, 548, 554–555, 556
War of the League of Augsburg, 460
War of the Spanish Succession, 460–461, 463
War of the Three Henries (France), 403
War on terrorism, 962, 964
Wars and warfare: Blitzkrieg, 852, 857; over colonies, 441; Dutch and, 471; in 18th century, 554–558, 557–558; guerrilla, 762, 867, 895; in Italy, 349–350; of Louis XIV, *460*, 460–461; in Middle East, 963; renunciation of, 812, 815; slave trade and, 429; after Thirty Years' War, 452–453, 454; trench warfare, 775, 782, *782*, 783–785, 786, *788*. *See also* specific battles and wars
Warsaw, 638, 885
Warsaw Pact, 890, *891*, 903
Warships, 453
Wars of Religion, 402–404
Wars of the Roses (England), 321
Wartburg Castle: assembly at (1817), 646; Luther at, 383
Washington, D. C.: terrorist attack on, 948, 964
Washington, George, 575, 578
Wastewater treatment, 717
"Watch on the Rhine, The" (song), 789
Water: clean, 717; for drinking, 570, 625
Water frame, 564, 610
Watergate scandal, 931–932
Waterloo, battle at, 604
Water pollution, 624
Watt, James, *610*
Watteau, Antoine, 527, *527*
Wealth: Catholic Church and, 536; in England, 754; industrial, 631; in late 1800s, 719–720; Physiocrats on, 522; in U.S., 932, 962
Wealth gap: globalization and, 976, 978; industrialization and, 758; in United States, 619
Wealth of Nations, The (Smith), 522
Weapons: in African trade, 437; in Hundred Years' War, 316, 319; Portuguese, 419; in Thirty Years' War, 452; in World War I, 784, *784*, *785*, 788, 790–791; in World War II, 852, 857, 862, 864. *See also* Atomic bomb; Nuclear weapons
Weapons of mass destruction, 964
Weather. *See* Climate
Weaving: in Industrial Revolution, 610
Web, 972
Weddings, in Renaissance, *346*
Weill, Kurt, 845
Weimar Republic, 826, 827, 828–829, 845
Welfare state, 910–912; in Canada, 909; in Great Britain, 754, 906, *906*; in Scandinavia, 819; in U.S., 820, 932. *See also* Social welfare
Wellington, duke of, 604
Wesley, John, *538*, 539
West, the. *See* Western civilization
West Africa, 416, 429, 437, 762, 785, *790*

West Bank (Jordan River), 898
West Berlin, 893, 923. *See also* Berlin
Western civilization: colonial populations and, 766–767; globalization and, 974–978; Southeast Asia and, 429–430; World War I and, 776
Western Europe: in 1970s and 1980s, 927–931; since 1985, 957–961; absolutism in, 446–447, 454–462; democracy in, 729–731, 903–907; prosperity in, 947; Russia and, 464, 465; unity in, 907, *907*, 960–961. *See also* World War I; World War II
Western Front, in World War I, 782, *782*, 784
Westernization: of Russia, 466; of Turkey, 820
West Germany, 881, 889, 890, 927–929; economy in, 906, 954; guest workers and immigrants in, 967; NATO and, 890; women in, 912; working class in, 910; after World War II, 905–906. *See also* East Germany
West Indies, 427, 435, 436, 595
Westphalia, 392, 638; Peace of, 451–452, 462, 471
West Prussia, 552
Wet nurses, 559
"What is the Third Estate?" (Sieyès), 581
Wheat: price of, 442
Whewell, William, 616
Whigs (Britain), 643, 652, 653, 686
Whitechapel Gallery, 914
White-collar workers, 710–711, 720
White forces, in Russia, 800, 802, *802*
"White man's burden," 759, *759*, 763
White Man's Burden, The (Kipling), 760
White Mountain, Battle of, 450
White Rose movement, 867
Whitney Museum of Modern Art, 914
William I (Belgium), 638
William I (Germany), 671, 679, 681, 682
William II (Germany), 755, 771, 778, 779, 803; Bismarck and, 732, *732*; nationalism of, 776; submarine warfare and, 790
William III (Orange), 471, 477, 478
William and Mary (England), 477, 478
William of Nassau. *See* William of Orange (the Silent)
William of Occam, 329–330
William of Orange (the Silent), 470
Wilson, Richard, *568*
Wilson, Woodrow, 758, 791, 804, 813; mandate system and, 808; at Paris Peace Conference, 805, *805*, 806; on World War I, 816
Windischgrätz, Alfred, 657
Winds, knowledge of, 415
Winkelmann, Maria, 502
Winter Palace (Russia), 757
Witchcraft, 447–449
"With Germany's Unemployed" (Hauser), 817
Witte, Sergei, 756
Wittenberg, Luther in, 381
Wives: middle-class, 723–725. *See also* Families; Women
Wolfe, James, 557
Wollstonecraft, Mary, 524, 525
Wolsey, Thomas (Cardinal), 392, 393
Woman in Her Social and Domestic Character (Sanford), 721
"Woman in the Slums, A" (Orwell), 818
Women, 334; in antinuclear movement, 966, *967*; as British prime minister, 929–931, 959; as Chartists, 632; Christine de Pizan on, 332; debates on nature of, 502–504; education and, 356, 357, 397, 535, 726, *726*; in Enlightenment, 523–524, 525–526; in factories, 630, 794, *794*, 795; feminism and, 924; in France, 584–586, 591–592, 600; headscarves (hijabs) and, 968, 969–970; in India, 768; Italian Fascists and, 824–825; in Italian Renaissance, 349; in late 1800s, 720–725; magazines for, 532; medical schools and, 697–698; missionary nunneries and, 437; in movies, 840;

mysticism of, 329; "new woman" and, 752, 843; Paris Commune and, 730; in postwar world, 912–913, 923–924; Protestant, 397; in Renaissance Italy, 345–346; Rousseau on, 523; in Russia, 466; salons and, 526; in sciences, 501–504; as servants, 627, 630; as socialists, 651; as teachers, 726; voting by, 795; in welfare state, 912; witchcraft and, 449; as workers, 561, 628, 710–711, 873, *873*, 874, 875, 912, 966; World War I and, 793–795, *794*, 842; World War II and, 867, 873, *873*, 874, 875. *See also* Birth control; Sex and sexuality; Women's rights
Women's liberation movement, 912–913, 924–925, *925*, 966–967
Women's march, to Versailles, 585–586, *586*
Women's rights, 650; in France, 912; in Japan, 875; Mill on, 648–649; movements for, 749–752, 794–795, 966–967
Women's Social and Political Union (England), 749
Women's studies, 966
Women's suffrage movement, 749–750, *751*
Woolen industry, 314, 343, 565
Woolf, Virginia, 845
Wordsworth, William, 633
Workday, 633, 725
Workers: children as, 561; in 18th century, 570; in factories, 607, 612–614; in French Revolution, 590; guest workers, 906; industrialization and, 564–565, 612–614, *613*, 618, 631–633; lifestyle of, 631; Luddites and, 632; as social class, 627–631; women as, 561, 607. *See also* Labor; Labor unions; Trade unions; Working class(es)
Worker's Union (Tristan), 651
Workhouses, 631, 654
Working class(es), 711–714; factory conditions and, 627–631; families of, 725; in France, 652, 655, 656, 730, 755; industrial, 627–631, 910; lifestyle of, 623; Marx, Engels, and, 692; in Renaissance, 344; in Russia, 756; urban, 719, 720. *See also* Workers
Workplace, 334, 631. *See also* Industrialization
Workweek: after World War II, 910
World Bank, 975
World Cup, 840, 943, 944
World economy, 709–710
World-machine: of Newton, 499
World of Yesterday, The (Zweig), 781
"World Scientists' Warning to Humanity," 977
World's Fair (Paris), 737
World Trade Center, terrorist attack on, 948, 964, *965*
World Trade Organization (WTO), 975
Worldview: scientific, 488
World War I, 775–809, 776–780, 813; in 1914–1915, 780–783; in 1916–1917, 783–785; in 1918, 803; Balkan region and, 769, 769–770, 771, 771–772; Eastern Front in, 783, *783*; enthusiasm for, *780*, 780–782; as global conflict, 785–790; home front in, 790, 791–797; international rivalry before, 769–772, 776; mobilization in, 778–780, 791–792; peace settlement after, 804–809; Russia and, *553*, 790, 797–800; social impact of, 793–797; treaties for, 804, 807–809, 812, 813, 815; trench warfare in, 775, 782, *782*, 783–785, 786, *788*; United States in, 790, 803; Western Front in, 782, *782*, 784
World War II, 852–857, 857–879; in 1942–1943, 861–864; in 1943–1945, 864–865; Allied war conferences in, 879–880; in Asia, 859–861, *861*, 865; atomic bomb in, 865, 877; bombing of civilians during, 858, 875–877, *878*; Cold War and, 879, 880–882; in Europe, 857–859, *860*, 861–863, 864–865, 885; as global conflict, 849; Holocaust during, 867–871, *872*; home front in, 872–877; in North Africa, 858, *860*, 862;

in Pacific, 859–861, *861*, 863–864, 865; Pearl Harbor attack and, 859, 860; territorial changes after, *881*
Wretched of the Earth, The (Fanon), 897
Wright, Frances, 650
Wright, Frank Lloyd, 844
Wright, Wilbur and Orville, 706
Writing: of history, 530–531
Wrought iron, 611
Wyclif, John, 370–371

Xavier, Francis (Saint), 401
Xhosa peoples, 762
Ximenes, Cardinal (Spain), 368, 380

Yalta conference, 879–880, *880*
Yeats, W. B., 743

Yellow press, 726–727
Yeltsin, Boris, 947, *947*, 950–951, *951*
Yorktown, battle at, 575
Young, Arthur, 563
Young Girl by the Window (Morisot), 745, 746
Young Italy movement, 657, 659, 677
Young people, 831, *922*
Young Victoria, The (movie), 687
Youth movement (1960s), 921–923, *922. See also* Student protests
YouTube, 972
Ypres, battle at, 784
Yucatán peninsula, 421
Yugoslavia, 804, 807, 814, 836; communism and Tito in, *902*, 902–903; Communist Party in, 902–903; disintegration of, 954–957, *957*, 963; resistance movement in, 867; World War II in, 859

Zaire, independence of, 896
Zaire (Congo) River, 416
Zalata's Diary, A Child's Life in Sarajevo (Filipovic), 956
Zanzibar. *See* Tanzania
Zasulich, Vera, 685
Zell, Katherine, 397
Zemsky Sobor (national assembly), 464
Zemstvos (assemblies), 685, 734, 758
Zeppelin airship, 706, 791
Zinzendorf, Nikolaus von (Count), 538
Zionism, 753, 754, 896
Zola, Émile, 743
Zollverein (customs union), 678
Zulu peoples, 762
Zürich, Protestants in, 389–390, 392
Zweig, Stefan, 781
Zwingli, Ulrich, 389–390, *390*, 391
Zyklon B (hydrogen cyanide), 869

Document-Based Questions (DBQs)

DBQ 1   Gender Role Expectations During the Renaissance (Chapter 12)   A–3

DBQ 2   Attitudes Toward Women During the Reformation (Chapter 13)   A–7

DBQ 3   Motives and Impact of Exploration (Chapter 14)   A–11

DBQ 4   Impact of the Thirty Years' War (Chapter 15)   A–15

DBQ 5   Reactions of Protestants and Catholics to the Scientific Revolution (Chapter 16)   A–20

DBQ 6   Enlightenment Thinkers and Their Impact on European Rulers (Chapters 17 and 18)   A–23

DBQ 7   Grievances of the French Third Estate (Chapter 19)   A–27

DBQ 8   Effects of the Industrial Revolution in England (Chapter 20)   A–31

DBQ 9   Concepts of Nationalism (Chapters 21 and 22)   A–36

DBQ 10   Rise of Mass Consumerism in Western Europe (Chapter 23)   A–41

DBQ 11   Struggles of English Women to Gain the Vote (Chapter 24)   A–44

DBQ 12   Uses of Propaganda During World War I (Chapter 25)   A–49

DBQ 13   Responses to the Crises of the Early Twentieth Century (Chapters 26 and 27)   A–54

DBQ 14   Soviet Perceptions of the West During the Cold War (Chapters 28 and 29)   A–58

DBQ 15   Arguments For and Against the Creation of a Unified Europe (Chapter 30)   A–61

INTRODUCTION

Think of a document-based question (DBQ) as a mini-research paper or a mini-investigation. It is a chance to show that you, like a professional historian or detective, can read the documents, question your sources, understand the backgrounds and motivations, and produce a good case or interpretation. In the words of the AP European History course description book, a DBQ tests your ability "to formulate and support an answer from documentary evidence."* It *does not* test your historical recall: the multiple-choice questions and the free-response essays do that. The DBQ is a test of your document-reading and analytical skills.

That last point is worth repeating: the DBQ is a test of your skills. It is scored or graded with a list of skills: when the AP reader sees a skill demonstrated, the reader gives you a point. Your essay can receive a maximum of 9 points when it is scored by an AP reader. Your classroom teacher may use a different system of grading, but she or he will be looking to see if you demonstrate the same skills.

This section is designed to be used in conjunction with chapters in *Western Civilization* and to give you practice on three of the most crucial and difficult skills: figuring out exactly what the question is asking you to do, writing an acceptable thesis statement, and analyzing a document for its content and point of view. The DBQs in this section mirror the format of the AP European History exam and feature nine to twelve documents each. Each question is designed to be completed in 60 minutes; this time includes a 15-minute mandatory reading period. In addition to completing the three tasks just mentioned, in your answer you need to reference all the documents and suggest an additional type of document that would support your thesis.

When working with documents, try the following three-step process:

---

1. Plot Summary: What is this document's basic subject matter and content? What is its date? Does it relate to some other important events in the same time period?

---

2. Point of View (POV):
   a. The first question is, "Who produced it?" What is his or her gender, age, ethnicity, social status, religion, or intellectual beliefs?
   b. The second question is, "Who was the intended audience?" Was it written privately, written to be read or heard by others (who?), an official document for a ruler to read, a commissioned painting, or some other type of document?
   c. The third question, as any good detective knows, would be "Why?" What is the *motivation* of the writer or producer of the document, based on what you can surmise about him or her?
   d. When you put the answers to these questions together, you get the POV: why *this* person would be producing *this* piece of information at *this* time. Then you can evaluate how much you "trust" the information in the document or determine what you think was *really* going on. It is useful to consider the tone or vocabulary of the document, just as you would in analyzing a piece of literature. It will sometimes convey the intent or the point of view of the author (anger, disdain, admiration, etc.).

---

3. Analysis: Now that you know the basic information and the POV of the author, how does this document help you to *answer the question that is being asked*?

2010 Course Description for AP European History (College Entrance Examination Board, NY, 2009), p. 21. Available online at www.apcentral.collegeboard.com.

DBQ 1: Gender Role Expectations During the Renaissance (Chapter 12)

Question: Identify and analyze the assumptions about the proper roles of men and women during the Renaissance.

Document 1

Source: Christine de Pizan, Italian-born noblewoman, *The Treasure of the City of Ladies,* 1405.

All wives of artisans should be very painstaking and diligent if they wish to have the necessities of life. They should encourage their husbands or their workmen to get to work early in the morning and work until late. . . . It is said that three things drive a man from his home: a quarrelsome wife, a smoking fireplace, and a leaking roof. She too ought to stay at home gladly and not go off every day traipsing hither and yon gossiping with neighbors and visiting her chums to find out what everyone is doing.

Document 2

Source: Leonardo Bruni, humanist, historian, and chancellor of Florence, in a letter to Battista Malatesta, 1405.

Why exhaust a woman with the . . . difficulties of rhetorical art, when she will never see the forum? . . . For if a woman throws her arms around while speaking, or if she increases the volume of her speech with greater forcefulness, she will appear threateningly insane and requiring restraint. These matters belong to men, as war, or battles, and also contests and public controversies.

Document 3

Source: Leon Battista Alberti, Italian painter, author, and priest, *On the Family,* c. 1430.

Men are by nature a more elevated mind than women. . . . The character of men is stronger than that of women; the female is tamer and gentler in disposition than the male, less powerful. . . . Women . . . are almost all timid by nature, soft, slow.

Document 4

Source: Jan van Eyck, Flemish artist, *Giovanni Arnolfini and His Bride,* 1434.

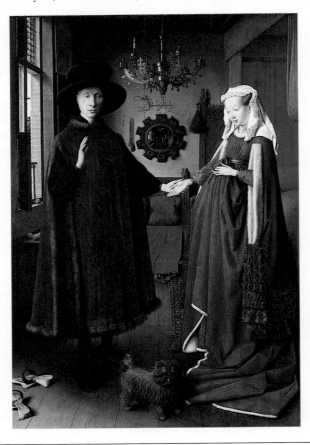

National Gallery, London//© Erich Lessing/Art Resource, NY

Document 5

Source: Alessandra Strozzi, letter to her son Filippo in Naples, 1464.

Concerning the matter of a wife [for you] it appears to me that if Francesco di Messer Tanagli wishes to give his daughter that would be a fine marriage. . . . Francesco Tanagli has a good reputation, and he has held office, not the highest, but still he has been in office. You may ask: "Why should he give her to someone in exile?" There are three reasons. First, there aren't many young men of good family who have both virtue and property. Second, she has only a small dowry, 1,000 florins, which is the dowry of an artisan [although not a small sum, either—senior officials in the government bureaucracy earned 300 florins a year]. . . . Third, I believe he will give her away, because he has a large family and he will need help to settle them.

Document 6

Source: Laura Cereta, Italian Renaissance humanist and feminist, letter to Sigismondo de Bucci, her father's attorney, 1486.

I still don't have any time that is unoccupied; not even to catch my breath; it is as though I am being pulled in two different directions—by meeting my father's demands and, at the same time, the needs of my husband. . . . I have no free time at all to spend on my books unless I work productively during the nights and sleep very little.

Document 7

Source: Giovanni Pico della Mirandola, Italian Renaissance humanist,
Oration on the Dignity of Man, 1486.

[God] therefore took man as a creature of indeterminate nature, and assigning him a place in the middle of the world, addressed him thus: "Neither a fixed abode nor a form that is yours alone nor any function peculiar to yourself have we given you, Adam, to the end that according to your longing and according to your judgment you may have and possess what abode, what form, and what functions you yourself desire."

Document 8

Source: Baldassare Castiglione, Italian humanist, *The Book of the Courtier*, 1496.

Thus, I would have our Courtier born of a noble and genteel family; because it is far less becoming for one of low birth to fail to do virtuous things than for one of noble birth, who, should he stray from the path of his forebears, stains the family name, and not only fails to achieve anything but loses what has already been achieved already. . . . She must avoid an error into which I have seen many women fall, which is to gossip and eagerly listen to evil spoken of other women. For those women who, when they hear of the unchaste ways of other women, bristle and pretend that the thing is incredible and that a woman so immodest is a monster, [and] in making so much of the fault give cause to think that they might be guilty of it themselves.

Document 9

Source: Michelangelo, Italian Renaissance painter, *Creation of Adam*, c. 1508.

Sistine Chapel, Vatican Palace, Vatican State//© Erich Lessing/Art

Document 10

Source: Niccolò Machiavelli, Italian humanist, *The Prince,* 1513.

A prince ought also to show himself a patron of ability, and to honor the proficient in every art. At the same time he should encourage his citizens to practice their callings peaceably, both in commerce and agriculture. . . . Further, a prince should entertain the people with festivals and spectacles at convenient seasons of the year. And as every city has its trade groups and societies, he ought to hold such bodies in esteem. He should visit with them sometimes, and show himself an example of courtesy and liberality. In all this, however, he should always maintain the majesty of his rank, for this he must never debase in any way.

Document 11

Source: Louise Labé, French poet, dedicatory preface written to a friend, c. 1556.

Since a time has come, Mademoiselle, when the severe laws of men no longer prevent women from applying themselves to the sciences and other disciplines, it seems to me that those of us who can should use this long craved freedom to study and let men see how greatly they wronged us when depriving us of its honor and advantage. And if any woman becomes so proficient as to be able to write down her thoughts, let her do so and not despise the honor but rather flaunt it instead of fine clothes, necklaces, and rings. For these may be considered ours only by use, whereas the honor of being educated is ours entirely.

DBQ 2: Attitudes Toward Women During the Reformation (Chapter 13)

Question: Analyze the views toward women during the time of the Reformation.

Document 1

Source: Thomas More, English Renaissance humanist and Catholic,
from his selected letters, c. 1501–1535.

To put virtue in the first place among goods, learning in the second; and in [women's] studies to esteem most whatever may teach them piety towards God, charity to all and modesty and Christian humility in themselves. . . . Let her understand that such conduct delights me more than all the learning in the world. Though I prefer learning joined with virtue to all the treasures of kings, yet renown for learning, if you take away moral probity, brings nothing else but notorious and noteworthy infamy, especially in woman.

Document 2

Source: Martin Luther, *Exhortation to the Knights of the Teutonic Order That They Lay Aside False Chastity and Assume the True Chastity of Wedlock,* 1523.

Whatever the husband has, this the wife has and possesses in its entirety. Their partnership involves not only their means but children, food, bed, and dwelling: their purposes, too, are the same. The result is that the husband differs from the wife in no other respect than in sex; otherwise the woman is altogether [as] man. . . . If the wife is honorable, virtuous, and pious, she shares in all the cares, endeavors, duties, and functions of her husband.

Document 3

Source: Katherine Zell, wife of an Anabaptist preacher, 1527.

Ever since I was ten years old I have been a student and a sort of church mother, much given to attending sermons. I have loved and frequented the company of learned men, and I conversed much with them, not about dancing, masquerades, and worldly pleasures but about the kingdom of God.

Document 4

Source: Peter Riedemann, Anabaptist missionary, *Confessions of Faith,* 1547.

We say, first, that since woman was taken from man, and not man from woman, man hath lordship but woman weakness, humility, and submission, therefore she should be under the yoke of man and obedient to him, even as the woman was commanded by God when he said to her, the man shall be thy Lord.

Document 5

Source: John Calvin, *11th Sermon on Job,* 1554–1555.

Men are preferred to females in the human race. We know that God constituted man as the head and gave him a dignity and preeminence above that of the woman. . . . It is true that the image of God is imprinted on all; but still woman is inferior to man.

Document 6

Source: Marcus Gheeraerts the Younger, *Queen Elizabeth I ("The Ditchley Portrait"),* Elizabeth Tudor I, queen of England and head of the Church of England, c. 1592.

Kingston Lacy Estate, Dorset, UK//© National Trust/Art Resource, NY

Document 7

Source: Jeanne d'Albret, mother of Henry IV, future king of France, pronounces her faith in an edict responding to the pope, 1561.

I am not planting a new [Calvinism] but restoring an old one. . . . I have forced no one with death, imprisonment or condemnation. . . . Your feeble arguments do not dent my tough skull. I am serving God and He knows how to sustain His cause. . . . How much good did it do my husband to defend Rome? . . . You have abandoned the holy walk of my mother for the humors of Rome. . . . If I err, I may be excused as a woman for my ignorance, but yours, as a cardinal, is shameful. I follow Beza*, Calvin and others only in so far they follow scripture.

*Theodore Beza was a follower and the successor of John Calvin.

Document 8

Source: Thirty-Nine Articles of the Church of England, 1563.

XXXII. Of the Marriage of Priests.

Bishops, Priests, and Deacons, are not commanded by God's Law, either to vow the estate of single life, or to abstain from marriage: therefore it is lawful for them, as for all other Christian men, to marry at their own discretion, as they shall judge the same to serve better to godliness.

Document 9

Source: Marie de Gournay, French writer and admirer of Michel de Montaigne, *The Equality of Men and Women*, 1622.

Suppose we believed that the Scriptures indeed order woman to submit to the authority of man because she cannot think as well as he can, see here the absurdity that would follow: Woman would be worthy of having been made in the likeness of the Creator, worthy of taking part in the holy Eucharist, of sharing the mysteries of the Redemption, Paradise, worthy of the vision, even the possession, of God, but not the status and privileges of men.

Document 10

Source: Margaret Fell Fox, founder of the Religious Society of Friends [Quakers], and preacher and missionary, *Women's Preaching Justified*, 1666.

Thus much may prove, that the Church of Christ is represented as a woman, and those that speak against this woman's speaking, speak against the Church of Christ, and the seed of the woman, which seed is Christ; that is to say, those that speak against the power of the Lord, and the spirit of the Lord speaking in a woman, simply by reason of her sex, or because she is a woman, not regarding the seed and spirit and power that speaks in her, such speak against Christ and his church, and are of the seed of the serpent, wherein lodgeth enmity.

Document 11

Source: Johannes Vermeer, Dutch Baroque painter, *The Milkmaid*, 1658.

© Image Asset Management Ltd./SuperStock

DBQ 3: Motives and Impact of Exploration (Chapter 14)

Question: Examine the attitudes of European explorers toward Native Americans, and assess the impact that exploration had on the "New World."

Document 1

Source: Pope Nicholas V, from Papal Bull *Romanus Pontifex*, written to King Alfonso V of Portugal concerning Portugal's rights of trade and colonization during the Age of Discovery, 1455.

We weighing all and singular the premises with due meditation, and noting that since we had formerly by other letters of ours granted among other things free and ample faculty to the aforesaid King Alfonso—to invade, search out, capture, vanquish, and subdue all Saracens and pagans whatsoever, and other enemies of Christ wheresoever placed, and the kingdoms, dukedoms, principalities, dominions, possessions, and all movable and immovable goods whatsoever held and possessed by them and to reduce their persons to perpetual slavery, and to apply and appropriate to himself and his successors the kingdoms, dukedoms, counties, principalities, dominions, possessions, and goods, and to convert them to his and their use and profit—by having secured the said faculty, the said King Alfonso, or, by his authority, the aforesaid *infant* [prince], justly and lawfully has acquired and possessed, and doth possess, these islands, lands, harbors, and seas, and they do of right belong and pertain to the said King Alfonso and his successors.

Document 2

Source: Christopher Columbus, journal extracts, written during his exploration of the area now known as the Bahamas, 1492.

Tomorrow morning before we depart, I intend to land and see what can be found in the neighborhood. Here is no village, but farther within the island is one, where our Indians inform us we shall find the king, and that he has much gold. I shall penetrate so far as to reach the village and see or speak with the king, who, as they tell us, governs all these islands, and goes dressed, with a great deal of gold about him. I do not, however, give much credit to these accounts, as I understand the natives but imperfectly, and perceive them to be so poor that a trifling quantity of gold appears to them a great amount. This island appears to me to be a separate one from that of Saomete [modern Crooked Island], and I even think there may be others between them. I am not solicitous to examine particularly everything here, which indeed could not be done in fifty years, because my desire is to make all possible discoveries, and return to your Highnesses, if it please our Lord, in April. But in truth, should I meet with gold or spices in great quantity, I shall remain till I collect as much as possible, and for this purpose I am proceeding solely in quest of them.

Document 3

Source: Antonio de Montesinos, Dominican friar, *The Sermon,* criticizing the Spanish colonists who had enslaved the people of the Caribbean, 1511.

On what authority have you waged a detestable war against these people, who dwelt quietly and peacefully on their own land? Why do you keep them so oppressed and weary, not giving them enough to eat, not taking care of them in their illness? For with the excessive work you demand of them they fall ill and die, or rather you kill them with your desire to extract and acquire gold every day. And what care do you take that they should be instructed in religion? Are these not men? Have they not rational souls? Are you not bound to love them as you love yourself?

Document 4

Source: Fernando de Alva Ixtlilxóchitl, whose father was one of the native allies of Cortés, 1520.

On the day that Tenochtitlán was taken, the Spaniards committed some of the most brutal acts ever inflicted upon the unfortunate people of this land. The cries of the helpless women and children were heart-rending. The Tlaxcaltecas and the other enemies of the Aztecs revenged themselves pitilessly for old offenses and robbed them of everything they could find. Only Prince Ixtlilxóchitl of Texcoco, ally of Cortés, felt compassion for the Aztecs, because they were of his own homeland. He kept his followers from maltreating the women and children as cruelly as did Cortés and the Spaniards. . . . The anguish and bewilderment of our foes was pitiful to see. The warriors gathered on the rooftops and stared at the ruins of their city in a dazed silence, and the women and children and old men were all weeping.

Document 5

Source: Aztec depiction of the stages of the smallpox epidemic that struck soon after the Spanish had fled, c. 1520.

Biblioteca Laurenziana, Florence//© Art Resource, NY

Document 6

Source: King Ferdinand and his daughter Juana of Spain, to be communicated to the Taino/Arawak (Native Americans) of Hispaniola, c. 1520.

The late Pope gave these islands and mainland of the ocean and the contents hereof to the above-mentioned King and Queen. . . . Therefore, we request that you . . . recognize the Church and its highest priest, the Pope, as rulers of the universe, and in their name the King and Queen of Spain as rulers of this land, allowing the religious fathers to preach our holy Faith to you. You own compliance as a duty to the King . . . . [We] shall not compel you to baptism unless you, informed of the Truth, wish to convert to our holy Catholic Faith as almost all your neighbors have done in other islands, in exchange for which Their Highnesses bestow many privileges and exemptions upon you.

    Should you fail to comply, or delay maliciously in so doing, we assure you that with the help of God we shall use force against you, declaring war upon you from all sides and with all possible means, and we shall bind you to the yoke of the Church and of Their Highnesses; we shall enslave your persons, wives and sons, sell you or dispose of you as the King sees fit; we shall seize your possessions and harm you as much as we can as disobedient and resisting vassals.

Document 7

Source: Pedro de Cieza de León, Spanish historian, *The Discovery and Conquest of Peru*, 1537.

There were five Indian men on board and two boys with three women, who became prisoners on the ship. Using signs [the Spaniards] asked them where they were from and what land lay ahead; and with the same signs they responded that they were natives of Tumbes, which was the truth. They showed them spun wool and raw wool that came from sheep, which they described through gesturing, and they said there were so many of them that they covered the fields. They often named Wayna Capac and Cuzco, where there was much gold and silver. They said so much about this and other things that the Christians who were on the ship thought they mocked them because the Indians always lie about many things they relate. But these [Indians] told the truth about everything. Bartolomé Ruiz, the pilot, treated them well, pleased to be bringing such people of good reason and who wore clothes so that Pizarro could question them.

Document 8

Source: Michel de Montaigne, French Renaissance essayist, *On Cannibals*, 1580.

I do not find that there is anything barbaric or savage about this nation [the "New World"], according to what I've been told, unless we are to call barbarism whatever differs from our own customs. Indeed, we seem to have no other standard of truth and reason than the opinions and customs of our own country. There at home is always the perfect religion, the perfect legal system—the perfect and most accomplished way of doing everything. These people are wild in the same sense that fruits are, produced by nature, alone, in her ordinary way.

Document 9

Source: Antonio Herra, Spanish painter, *Friendly Indians*, depicting Columbus's arrival in the "New World," seventeenth century.

DBQ 4: Impact of the Thirty Years' War (Chapter 15)

**Question: Examine the causes of the Thirty Years'
War and evaluate its impact on Europe.**

Historical Background: In the year 1555, Spanish Habsburg ruler and Holy Roman Emperor Charles V called a meeting at Augsburg to negotiate the Peace of Augsburg, which officially ended religious tension and conflict primarily within the Holy Roman Empire. This truce sought to establish legal boundaries by giving official recognition to Lutherans. Furthermore, it permitted local German princes to determine the official religion in their territories.

Document 1

Source: Catholic song, "Poor Winter King," Reflections of a Catholic upon Protestant King Frederick V, the "Winter King" of Bohemia, c. 1618.

Oh, shame on you, poor Winter King!
What's this that you have done?
Is't not a very naughty thing
To snatch the kaiser's crown?
Now you will have to stay away
Alike from Rhine and Prague,
And more than that—shame and dismay
Your days and nights will plague.

Dear Fritz, good fellow, oh, come now,
Give up, give up the crown!
To hell, to meet your just reward,
Full soon you will go down.

Document 2

Source: John Rushworth, English historian, description of the opening of the Thirty Years' War, 1618.

Whilst Spain and England were thus closing, the fire brake out in Germany between the states and princes Protestant and the house of Austria. These commotions, involved and drew along the affairs of most Christian princes, especially of the two potent kings now in treaty. The Catholic cause and the lot of the house of Austria engaged the king of Spain, who was the strongest branch of that stock. King James [James I of England] must needs be drawn in, both by common and particular interest: the religion which he professed and the state of his son-in-law, the elector palatine, who became the principal part of those wars and the most unfortunate.

Document 3

Source: Matthäus Merian the Elder, Swiss engraver, *The Second Defenestration of Prague*, depicting Protestants throwing imperial officials out of a castle window in Prague, 1618.

Kunstbibliothek, Staatliche Museen, Berlin//© Bildarchiv Preussischer Kulturbesitz/Art Resource, NY

Document 4

Source: Gustavus Adolphus, king of Sweden, in a speech to the representatives assembled at Stockholm, 1630.

I call on the all-powerful God to witness, by whose providence we are here assembled, that it is not by my own wish, or from any love of war, that I undertake this campaign. On the contrary, I have been now for several years goaded into it by the imperial party, not only through the reception accorded to our emissary to Lübeck, but also by the action of their general in aiding with his army our enemies, the Poles, to our great detriment. We have been urged, moreover, by our harassed brother-in-law [the elector of Branden-burg] to undertake this war, the chief object of which is to free our oppressed brothers in the faith from the clutches of the pope, which, God helping us, we hope to do.

Document 5

Source: Francisco de Quevedo, Spanish politician, nobleman, and writer, *Death-Warnings*, c. 1630.

I saw the ramparts of my native land
One time so strong, now dropping decay,
Their strength destroyed by this new age's way
That has worn out and rotted what was grand.
I went into the fields; there I could see
The sun drink up the waters newly thawed;
And on the hills the moaning cattle pawed,
Their miseries robbed the light of day for me.

I went into my house; I saw how spotted,
Decaying things made that old home their prize;
My withered walking-staff had come to bend.
I felt the age had won; my sword was rotted;
And there was nothing on which to set my eyes
That was not a reminder of the end.

Document 6

Source: Otto von Guericke, burgomeister of Magdeburg, *The Destruction of Magdeburg*, 1631.

Thus it came about that the city and all its inhabitants fell into the hands of the enemy. . . . It was only when everything had been brought forth and there was nothing left to give that the real trouble commenced. Then, what with blows and threats of shooting, stabbing, and hanging, the poor people were so terrified that if they had had anything left they would have brought it forth if it had been buried in the earth or hidden away in a thousand castles. In this frenzied rage, the great and splendid city that had stood like a fair princess in the land was now, in its hour of direst need and unutterable distress and woe, given over to the flames, and thousands of innocent men, women, and children, in the midst of a horrible din of heart-rending shrieks and cries, were tortured and put to death in so cruel and shameful a manner that no words would suffice to describe, nor no tears to bewail it.

Document 7

Source: Charles Vion de Dalibray, French poet, *Convivial Sonnet*, c. 1640.

I'm not going to expose my paunch to danger; neither Armand [Cardinal Richelieu] nor the king know me;
I want to find out just how long a coward like me can live without being a soldier or a captain.

I'd just die if in the middle of some battlefield, my drinking arm were mangled; so don't tell me that I'm as
likely to die at the dinner table in my pots, as where courage would lead me.

Don't tell me that in the heat of battle I could become immortal by a noble death—I still won't rush out to a
skirmish.

I want to die all in one piece, without glory or distinction, And—believe me, dear Clindor—if some orifice kills
me, it won't be the mouth of a cannon.

Document 8

Source: The Treaty of Westphalia, 1648.

That those of the Confession of Augsburg, and particularly the Inhabitants of Oppenheim, shall be put in possession again of their Churches, and Ecclesiastical Estates, as they were in the Year 1624, as also that all others of the said Confession of Augsburg, who shall demand it, shall have the free Exercise of their Religion, as well in public Churches at the appointed Hours, as in private in their own Houses, or in others chosen for this purpose by their Ministers, or by those of their Neighbors, preaching the Word of God.

Document 9

Source: Pope Innocent X, denouncing all articles in the treaties of Westphalia that relate to religious matters, 1648.

Accordingly it is not without deep pain that we have learned that by several articles in the peace concluded at Osnabrück, August 6, 1648 . . . great prejudice has been done to the Catholic religion . . . since by various articles in one of these treaties of peace the ecclesiastical possessions which the heretics formerly seized are abandoned to them and to their successors, and the heretics, called those of the Augsburg Confession, are permitted the free exercise of their heresy in various districts. They are promised places in which they may build temples for their worship and are admitted with the Catholics to public offices and positions.

Document 10

Source: Map of Europe, 1648.

Document 11

Source: Andreas Gryphius, German lyrical poet, *Tears of the Fatherland*, c. 1650.

We are now completely—no, more than completely—devastated! Troops of thugs, blaring trumpets, swords soaked in blood, and thundering cannons have consumed all the fruits of sweat and diligence and industry.

Towers burning, churches overturned, city halls cowering in fright, strong men shattered, maidens violated, and wherever we look, fire, plague, and death pierce our heart and soul. Fresh blood runs continually through trench and town; three times in the last six years, our stream's flow has almost stopped—clogged solid with corpses.

But I can barely talk about what's more troubling than death, more dismal than plague and arson and famine: that all hope of heaven has been snatched from so many souls.

DBQ 5: Reactions of Protestants and Catholics to the Scientific Revolution (Chapter 16)

Question: Analyze the attitudes and reactions of Protestants and Catholics toward the Scientific Revolution.

Document 1

Source: Sixteenth-century illustration of the universe with the earth at the center and Heaven beyond the outermost circle.

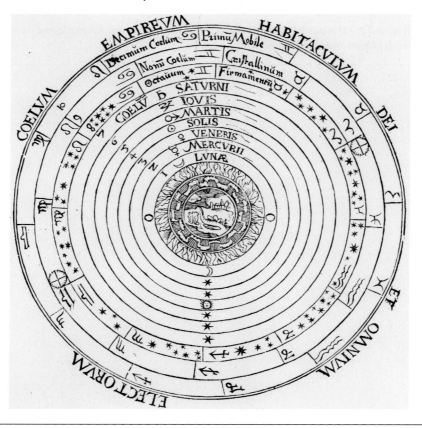

© Image Select/Art Resource, NY

Document 2

Source: Nicolaus Copernicus, Dedication of *On the Revolutions of the Heavenly Spheres* to Pope Paul III, published posthumously, 1543.

I CAN easily conceive, most Holy Father, that as soon as some people learn that in this book which I have written concerning the revolutions of the heavenly bodies, I ascribe certain motions to the Earth, they will cry out at once that I and my theory should be rejected.

Document 3

Source: Martin Luther, in reference to new scientific findings, 1539.

People gave ear to an upstart astrologer who strove to show that the earth revolves, not the heavens or the firmament, the sun and the moon. Whoever wishes to appear clever must devise some new system, which of all systems is the very best. This fool wishes to reverse the entire science of astronomy; but sacred Scripture tells us that Joshua commanded the sun to stand still, and not the earth [Joshua 10:13].

Document 4

Source: John Calvin, *Commentary on Genesis—Volume 1*, 1554.

Nevertheless, this study is not to be reprobated, nor this science to be condemned, because some frantic persons are wont boldly to reject whatever is unknown to them. For astronomy is not only pleasant, but also very useful to be known: it cannot be denied that this art unfolds the admirable wisdom of God. Wherefore, as ingenious men are to be honored who have expended useful labor on this subject, so they who have leisure and capacity ought not to neglect this kind of exercise.

Document 5

Source: Giordano Bruno, ex-Dominican monk, philosopher, and writer on mathematics and science, *On Cause, Principle, and Unity*, 1584.

This entire globe, this star, not being subject to death and dissolution and annihilation being impossible anywhere in Nature, from time to time renews itself by changing and altering all its parts. There is no absolute up or down, as Aristotle taught; no absolute position in space; but the position of a body is relative to that of other bodies. Everywhere there is incessant relative change in position throughout the universe, and the observer is always at the center of things.

Document 6

Source: Cardinal Robert Bellarmine, letter to Father Paolo Foscarini, 1615.

[A]s you know, the Council [of Trent] prohibits expounding the Scriptures contrary to the common agreement of the holy Fathers . . . and . . . you would find that all agree in explaining literally (*ad litteram*) that the sun is in the heavens and moves swiftly around the earth, and that the earth is far from the heavens and stands immobile in the center of the universe.

Document 7

Source: Pope Paul V, *Decree of General Congregation of the Index*, 1616.

Since it has come to the knowledge of this Holy Congregation that the false Pythagorean doctrine, altogether opposed to the Divine Scripture, of the mobility of the earth, and the immobility of the sun, which Nicolas Copernicus, in his work *De revolutionibus orbium caelestium*, and Didacus a Stunica in his *Commentary on Job*, teach, is being promulgated and accepted by many, as may be seen from a printed letter of a certain Carmelite Father [Foscarini], . . . therefore, lest this opinion insinuate itself further to the damage of Catholic truth, this Congregation has decreed that the said books, Copernicus *De revolutionibus orbium*, and Stunica *On Job*, be suspended till they are corrected, but that the book of Foscarini the Carmelite be altogether prohibited and condemned, and all other books that teach the same thing.

Document 8

Source: Pope Alexander VII, *Index of Prohibited Books*, 1664.

Forbidding all writings which affirm the motion of the earth . . . and condemning, all books teaching the movement of the earth and the stability of the sun. . . . [S]igned by the reigning Pope which, by virtue of his infallibility as a divinely guided teacher in matters of faith and morals.

Document 9

Source: Johannes Vermeer, Dutch painter and member of the Dutch Reformed Church, known to utilize a camera obscura*, *The Astronomer*, 1668.

Louvre, Paris/© Giraudon/The Bridgeman Art Library

*A camera obscura allowed the viewer to project an image on a screen.

DBQ 6: Enlightenment Thinkers and Their Impact on European Rulers (Chapters 17 and 18)

Question: Assess the extent to which Enlightenment philosophy influenced European rulers in the eighteenth century.

Document 1

Source: The Enlightenment in Europe.

Document 2

Source: John Locke, English, *Two Treatises on Government,* 1690.

A state also of equality, wherein all the power and jurisdiction is reciprocal, no one having more than another; there being nothing more evident, than that creatures of the same species and rank, promiscuously born to all the same advantages of nature, and the use of the same faculties, should also be equal one amongst another without subordination or subjection, unless the lord and master of them all should, by any manifest declaration of his will, set one above another, and confer on him, by an evident and clear appointment, an undoubted right to dominion and sovereignty.

Document 3

Source: Baron de Montesquieu, French, *The Spirit of the Laws,* 1748.

In every government there are three sorts of power; the legislative; the executive, in respect to things dependent on the law of nations; and the judicial, in regard to things that depend on the civil law. . . . When the legislative and executive powers are united in the same person, or in the same body of magistrates, there can be no liberty; because apprehensions may arise, lest the same monarch or senate should enact tyrannical laws, to execute them in a tyrannical manner.

Document 4

Source: David Hume, Scottish, *Of the Dignity or Meanness of Human Nature,* 1752.

In forming our notions of human nature, we are apt to make a comparison between men and animals. . . . Certainly this comparison is favorable to mankind. On the one hand, we see a creature, whose thoughts are not limited by any narrow bounds. . . . On the other hand, we are presented with a creature the very reverse of this; limited in its observations and reasonings to a few sensible objects which surround it.

Document 5

Source: Jean-Jacques Rousseau, *French, The Social Contract,* 1762.

To renounce liberty is to renounce being a man, to surrender the rights of humanity and even its duties. For him who renounces everything no indemnity is possible. Such a renunciation is incompatible with man's nature; to remove all liberty from his will is to remove all morality from his acts. Finally, it is an empty and contradictory convention that sets up, on the one side, absolute authority, and, on the other, unlimited obedience. Is it not clear that we can be under no obligation to a person from whom we have the right to exact everything?

Document 6

Source: Catherine II, empress of Russia, Decree on Serfs, 1767.

The Governing Senate . . . has deemed it necessary to make known . . . that the landlords' serfs and peasants . . . owe their landlords proper submission and absolute obedience in all matters, according to the laws . . . which provide that all persons who dare to incite serfs and peasants to disobey their landlords shall be arrested and taken to the nearest government office, there to be punished forthwith as disturbers of the public tranquility, according to the laws and without leniency. And should it so happen that even after the publication of the present decree of Her Imperial Majesty any serfs and peasants should cease to give the proper obedience to their landlords . . . and should make bold to submit unlawful petitions complaining of their landlords, and especially to petition Her Imperial Majesty personally, then both those who make the complaints and those who write up the petitions shall be punished by the knout and forthwith deported to Nerchinsk to penal servitude for life.

Document 7

Source: Voltaire, French, *Lettres philosophiques,* 1778.

No one is exempted in this country [England] from paying certain taxes because he is a nobleman or a priest. All duties and taxes are settled by the House of Commons, whose power is greater than that of the Peers, though inferior to it in dignity. The spiritual as well as temporal Lords have the liberty to reject a Money Bill brought in by the Commons; but they are not allowed to alter anything in it, and must either pass or throw it out without restriction. When the Bill has passed the Lords and is signed by the king, then the whole nation pays, every man in proportion to his revenue or estate, not according to his title, which would be absurd. There is no such thing as an arbitrary subsidy or poll-tax, but a real tax on the lands, of all which an estimate was made in the reign of the famous King William III.

Document 8

Source: Frederick II, king of Prussia, *Essay on Forms of Government and Testament Politique,* 1770.

Rulers should always remind themselves that they are men like the least of their subjects. The sovereign is the foremost judge, general, financier, and minister of his country, not merely for the sake of his prestige. Therefore, he should perform with care the duties connected with these offices. He is merely the principal servant of the State. Hence, he must act with honesty, wisdom, and complete disinterestedness in such a way that he can render an account of his stewardship to the citizens at any moment. . . . However, we have too many Jews in the towns. They are needed on the Polish border because in these areas Hebrews alone perform trade. As soon as you get away from the frontier, the Jews become a disadvantage, they form cliques, they deal in contraband and get up to all manner of rascally tricks which are detrimental to Christian burghers and merchants.

Document 9

Source: Joseph II, Holy Roman Emperor, The Serfdom Patent, 1781.

Patent of November 1, 1781, *in re* Manorial Lords and Subjects. The servile status of subjects is herewith abolished completely and the following dispositions enacted:

1. Any subject is entitled to marry, subject to previous notification and acquisition of a certificate, to be delivered free of charge.
2. He may, provided he observes the regulations governing conscription for military service, leave his present manor and settle or take service on another within the Province; but if he wishes to establish himself as a peasant cultivator or cottager on another manor, he must ask for a leaving certificate, which must also be issued him free of charge, to be shown to the new manorial authority.
3. A subject is free to learn any handicraft, trade, etc., and seek his livelihood where he will. For this no leaving permit is necessary.
4. Subjects are no longer required to perform domestic service for their lords, except orphans, who may be required to do such service for a period not exceeding three years.
5. No services shall be imposed on or required of subjects beyond the robot* and payments in kind and cash attaching to their holdings. Subjects are bound to render obedience to their lords in virtue of the existing laws.

*The robot was three days of unpaid labor a week, although many serfs worked every day except Sunday.

Document 10

Source: Satirical Depiction of the Closing of Monasteries as Decreed by Joseph II in the Year 1781, c. 1783.

Wien Museum Karlsplatz, Vienna//© Erich Lessing/Art Resource, NY

DBQ 7: Grievances of the French Third Estate (Chapter 19)

Question: Evaluate the grievances of the Third Estate prior to the French Revolution of 1789, and analyze the extent to which they were addressed during the course of the revolution to 1792.

Document 1

Source: Arthur Young, an Englishman, written while traveling through France, *Travels During the Years 1787, 1788 and 1789.*

The abuses attending the levy of taxes were heavy and universal. . . . The rolls of the *taille*, capitation, *vingtièmes**, and other taxes, were distributed among districts, parishes, and individuals, at the pleasure of the intendant, who could exempt, change, add, or diminish at pleasure. Such an enormous power, constantly acting, and from which no man was free, must, in the nature of things, degenerate in many cases into absolute tyranny. . . . Instances, and even gross ones, have been reported to me in many parts of the kingdom, that made me shudder at the oppression to which [people have been subjected] by the undue favors granted to such crooked influence. But, without recurring to such cases, what must have been the state of the poor people paying heavy taxes, from which the nobility and clergy were exempted?

*The *taille* was a tax levied on the value of a peasant's land or wealth; capitation referred to a head or poll tax paid for each person; and the *vingtième* was a tax on income that was paid chiefly by peasants.

Document 2

Source: French political cartoon, 1789.

© Bettmann/CORBIS

Document 3

Source: *Cahier* of the parish of Aix-en-Provence, one of the *cahiers de doléances* (lists of grievances) that were drawn up by each estate and presented to the Estates General, 1789.

Sire, it is with the heaviest pain that we see huge pensions granted to vile and scheming courtiers. . . . Significant remunerations are tied to jobs without duties.

If only you knew, Sire, how much sweat, how many tears soak the money going into your treasury. Without doubt, your kindness will be more on its guard against people's indiscreet requests who consume in one day the fruits of taxes from thousands of your poor subjects.

We cannot hide, Sire, that the nobility consumes the major part of State income. Indeed, it is this order of citizens, to whom we probably give the most merit, that furnishes the crown officers, the governors, the commanders, the quartermasters, and all the people who have honorable positions. A noble man, who knows how to dance well, ride a horse well, and handle a sword, thinks he deserves everything, and, nonetheless, he pretends that he does not owe anything to the State.

Document 4

Source: Declaration of the Rights of Man and the Citizen, 1789.

Consequently, the National Assembly recognizes and declares, in the presence and under the auspices of the Supreme Being, the following rights of man and citizen:

1. Men are born and remain free and equal in rights; social distinctions can be established only for the common benefit.
2. The aim of every political association is the conservation of the natural and imprescriptible rights of man; these rights are liberty, property, security, and resistance to oppression.
3. The source of all sovereignty is located in essence in the nation; no body, no individual can exercise authority which does not emanate from it expressly.
4. Liberty consists in being able to do anything that does not harm another person. Thus the exercise of the natural rights of each man has no limits except those which assure to the other members of society the enjoyment of these same rights; these limits can be determined only by law.

Document 5

Source: Olympe de Gouges, Declaration of the Rights of Woman and the Female Citizen, 1791.

Mothers, daughters, sisters and representatives of the nation demand to be constituted into a national assembly. Believing that ignorance, omission, or scorn for the rights of woman are the only causes of public misfortunes and of the corruption of governments, the women have resolved to set forth in a solemn declaration the natural, inalienable, and sacred rights of woman in order that this declaration, constantly exposed before all the members of the society, will ceaselessly remind them of their rights and duties.

Document 6

Source: Abbé Emmanuel Sieyès, French clergyman, deputy to Estates General,
What Is the Third Estate?, 1789.

Who is bold enough to maintain that the Third Estate does not contain within itself everything needful to constitute a complete nation? It is like a strong and robust man with one arm still in chains. If the privileged order were removed, the nation would not be something less but something more. What then is the Third Estate? All; but an "all" that is fettered and oppressed. What would it be without the privileged order? It would be all; but free and flourishing. Nothing will go well without the Third Estate; everything would go considerably better without the two others. . . . What is a nation? A body of associates living under *common* laws and represented by the same *legislative assembly*, etc. . . . Because of these special rights, the nobility does not belong to the common order. . . . Thus its private rights make it a people apart in the great nation.

Document 7

Source: Jacques-Louis David, *Tennis Court Oath*, 1789.

Musée de la Ville de Paris, Musée Carnavalet, Paris/© Giraudon/The Bridgeman Art Library

Document 8

Source: A Parisian newspaper account of the fall of the Bastille, 1789.

Meanwhile, they get ready to march; they leave amidst an enormous crowd; the applause, the outbursts of joy, the insults, the oaths hurled at the treacherous prisoners of war; everything is confused; cries of vengeance and of pleasure issue from every heart; the conquerors, glorious and covered in honor, carry their arms and the spoils of the conquered, the flags of victory, the militia mingling with the soldiers of the fatherland, the victory laurels offered them from every side, all this created a frightening and splendid spectacle. On arriving at the square, the people, anxious to avenge themselves, allowed neither De Launay nor the other officers to reach the place of trial; they seized them from the hands of their conquerors, and trampled them underfoot one after the other. De Launay was struck by a thousand blows, his head was cut off and hoisted on the end of a pike with blood streaming down all sides. . . . This glorious day must amaze our enemies, and finally usher in for us the triumph of justice and liberty. In the evening, there were celebrations.

Document 9

Source: The Decree Abolishing the Feudal System, August 11, 1789.

ARTICLE I. The National Assembly hereby completely abolishes the feudal system. It decrees that, among the existing rights and dues . . . all those originating in or representing real or personal serfdom shall be abolished without indemnification. All other dues are declared redeemable, the terms and mode of redemption to be fixed by the National Assembly. Those of the said dues which are not extinguished by this decree shall continue to be collected until indemnification shall take place.

Document 10

Source: Petition of Women of the Third Estate to the King, 1789.

We prefer, Sire, to place our cause at your feet; not wishing to obtain anything except from your heart, we address our complaints and confide our miseries to it.

The women of the Third Estate are almost all born without fortune; their education is very neglected or very defective. . . . If nature has refused them beauty, they get married without dowry to unfortunate artisans, lead aimless, difficult lives stuck away in the provinces, and give birth to children they are incapable of raising. If, on the contrary, they are born pretty, without culture, without principles, without any idea of morals, they become the prey of the first seducer, commit a first sin, come to Paris to bury their shame, end by losing it altogether, and die victims of licentious ways. . . .

To prevent so many ills, Sire, we ask that men not be allowed, under any pretext, to exercise trades that are the prerogative of women.

Document 11

Source: The Women's March to Versailles, 1789.

Depart des Heroines de Paris pour Versailles le 5 Octobre 1789.

Musée de la Ville de Paris, Musée Carnavalet, Paris //© Réunion des Musées Nationaux/Art Resource, NY

DBQ 8: Effects of the Industrial Revolution in England (Chapter 20)

Question: Analyze the arguments over the effects of the Industrial Revolution in England.

Document 1

Source: William Blake, English Romantic poet and painter, "And did those feet in ancient time," originally published in the preface to *Milton: A Poem*, c. 1804–1808.

And did those feet in ancient time.
Walk upon England's mountains green:
And was the holy Lamb of God,
On England's pleasant pastures seen!

And did the Countenance Divine,
Shine forth upon our clouded hills?
And was Jerusalem builded here,
Among these dark Satanic Mills?

Bring me my Bow of burning gold;
Bring me my Arrows of desire:
Bring me my Spear: O clouds unfold!
Bring me my Chariot of fire!

I will not cease from Mental Fight,
Nor shall my Sword sleep in my hand:
Till we have built Jerusalem,
In England's green & pleasant Land.

Document 2

Source: David Ricardo, British economist, *On the Principles of Political Economy and Taxation*, 1817.

The friends of humanity cannot but wish that in all countries the labouring classes should have a taste for comforts and enjoyments, and that they should be stimulated by all legal means in their exertions to produce them. There cannot be a better security against a superabundant population. In those countries where the labouring classes have the fewest wants, and are contented with the cheapest food, the people are exposed to the greatest vicissitudes and miseries. They have no place of refuge from calamity.

Document 3

Source: Joshua Drake, British, giving testimony to the Sadler Committee on the conditions of factories, 1832.

[Examiner] Supposing there was a law passed to limit the hours of labour to eight hours a day, or something of that sort, of course you are aware that a manufacturer could not afford to pay them the same wages?

[Drake] No, I do not suppose that they would, but at the same time I would rather have it, and I believe that it would bring me into employ; and if I lost *5d.* a day from my children's work, and I got half-a-crown myself, it would be better.

Document 4

Source: Excerpts from the Factory Act of 1833, as outlined by Parliament.

[N]o person under the age of eighteen shall be employed in any such mill . . . more than twelve hours in . . . one day, nor more than sixty-nine hours in . . . one week. . . . There shall be allowed . . . not less than one and a half hours for meals. It shall not be lawful . . . to employ in any factory . . . as aforesaid, except in mills for the manufacture of silk, any child who shall not have completed his or her ninth year. It shall not be lawful for any person to employ . . . in any factory . . . as aforesaid for longer than forty-eight hours in one week, nor for longer than nine hours in one day, any child who shall not have completed his or her eleventh year.

Document 5

Source: Andrew Ure, Scottish consulting chemist, *The Philosophy of Manufactures*, 1835.

Improvements in machinery have a three-fold bearing:

1st. They make it possible to fabricate some articles which, but for them, could not be fabricated at all.

2nd. They enable an operative to turn out a greater quantity of work than he could before—time, labour, and quality of work remaining constant.

3rd. They effect a substitution of labour comparatively unskilled, for that which is more skilled.

Document 6

Source: Edward Baines, English, *History of the Cotton Manufacture in Great Britain*, 1835.

In comparing the advantages of England for manufactures with those of other countries, we can by no means overlook the excellent commercial position of the country—intermediate between the north and south of Europe; and its insular situation, which, combined with the commands of the seas, secures our territory from invasion or annoyance. . . . In no country have these blessings been enjoyed in so high a degree, or for so long a continuance, as in England.

Document 7

Source: *Cottonopolis*, engraving by Edward Goodall, original title *Manchester, from Kersal Moor*, 1840.

© Pictorial Press Ltd/Alamy

Document 8

Source: Edwin Chadwick, British social reformer, *The Poor Law Commissioners on an Inquiry into the Sanitary Conditions of the Labouring Population of Great Britain*, 1842.

That for the protection of the labouring classes and of the ratepayers against inefficiency and waste in all new structural arrangements for the protection of the public health, and to ensure public confidence that the expenditure will be beneficial, securities should be taken that all new local public works are devised and conducted by responsible officers qualified by the possession of the science and skill of civil engineers.

Document 9

Source: Karl Marx, German socialist philosopher, *Economic and Philosophic Manuscripts*, 1844.

The worker becomes all the poorer the more wealth he produces, the more his production increases in power and in range. The worker becomes an ever cheaper commodity the more commodities he creates.

Document 10

Source: Friedrich Engels, German socialist philospher, *The Condition of the Working Class in England in 1844.*

The south bank of the Irk is here very steep and between fifteen and thirty feet high. On this declivitous hillside there are planted three rows of houses, of which the lowest rise directly out of the river, while the front walls of the highest stand on the crest of the hill of the hill in Long Millgate. . . . The background is furnished by old barrack-like factory buildings. . . . Enough! The whole side of the Irk is built in this way, a planless, knotted chaos of houses, more or less on the verge of uninhabitableness, whose unclean interiors fully correspond with their filthy external surroundings.

Document 11

Source: The Crystal Palace, which consisted of an iron and glass framework, was the center for the Great Industrial Exhibition in London, 1851.

© Guildhall Library, City of London, UK/The Bridgeman Art Library

Document 12

Source: Gustave Doré, French artist, *Dudley Street, Seven Dials,* from *London: A Pilgrimage,* 1872.

Bibliothèque des Arts Decoratifs, Paris//© Archives Charmet/The Bridgeman Art Library

DBQ 9: Concepts of Nationalism (Chapters 21 and 22)

Question: Analyze the arguments on which the modern idea of a nation-state is based.

Document 1

Source: Johann Gottfried von Herder, *Materials for the Philosophy of the History of Mankind*, 1784.

Nature brings forth families; the most natural state therefore is also one people, with a national character of its own. For thousands of years this character preserves itself within the people and, if the native princes concern themselves with it, it can be cultivated in the most natural way: for a people is as much a plant of nature as is a family, except that it has more branches. Nothing therefore seems more contradictory to the true end of governments than the endless expansion of states, the wild confusion of races and nations under one scepter. An empire made up of a hundred peoples and 120 provinces which have been forced together is a monstrosity, not a state-body. . . . No greater injury can be inflicted on a nation than to be robbed of her national character, the peculiarity of her spirit and her language. Reflect on this and you will perceive our irreparable loss.

Document 2

Source: Eugène Delacroix, French artist, *Liberty Leading the People*, 1830.

Document 3

Source: Thomas Davis, *Lament for the Death of Eoghan Ruadh O'Neill*, 1842. Davis founded an Irish nationalist newspaper and opposed the Act of Union in 1802 that created the United Kingdom.

O'Neill supported the Irish against an English invasion led by Oliver Cromwell in the seventeenth century.

"Did they dare, did they dare, to slay Eoghan Ruadh O'Neill?
Yes, they slew with poison him they feared to meet with steel.
May God wither up their hearts! May their blood cease to flow,
May they walk in living death, who poisoned Eoghan Ruadh.

Though it break my heart to hear, say again the bitter words.
From Derry, against Cromwell, he marched to measure swords:
But the weapon of the Sassanach met him on his way.
And he died at Cloch Uachtar, upon St. Leonard's day."

Document 4

Source: Georg Friedrich List, German, *National System of Political Economy*, 1840.

The civilization, political education and power of nations, depend chiefly on their economical condition and reciprocally; the more advanced their economy, the more civilized and powerful will be the nation, the more rapidly will its civilization and power increase, and the more will its economical culture be developed.

Document 5

Source: Female workers' petition to the French government, 1848.

Sirs,

The women workers exercising the trade of rabbit fur cutters for the hat industry, all diligent and mothers of families . . . find it impossible to earn a livelihood. For fifteen years, ten thousand foreign workers have arrived to bring misery to trade, which once flourished but which now is almost extinct. For these reasons, the petitioners . . . beg the provisional government . . . to restore their livelihood.

Document 6

Source: Bozena Nemcova, Czech nationalist female writer, *Granny*, 1855.

The Sibyl* foretold that great misery would come on the Czech lands, that there would be wars and famine and plague. But the worst of all would be when father wouldn't understand son, or son father, or brother brother, and when neither word nor bond would be worth anything. That would be the worst of all, she said, and then the Czech earth would be scattered under the hooves of horses.

* A Sibyl is a female prophet or fortuneteller.

Document 7

Source: "Right Leg in the Boot at Last," a wood engraving from the British satirical magazine *Punch*, depicting Giuseppe Garibaldi, an Italian republican nationalist, helping King Victor Emmanuel II put on the "boot" of Italy, 1860.

RIGHT LEG IN THE BOOT AT LAST.

GARIBALDI. "IF IT WON'T GO ON, SIRE, TRY A LITTLE MORE POWDER."

Bibliothèque Nationale, Paris/© Giraudon/The Bridgeman Art Library International

Document 8

Source: Anna Mozzoni, Italian feminist, *Women and Her Social Relations*, 1864.

The revision of the Civil Code by the Italian Parliament has placed in my mind the following arguments: woman, excluded by worn out customs from the councils of state, has always submitted to the law without participating in the making of it, has always contributed her resources and work to the public good and always without reward. . . . I begin with the principles that all rights and all duties have as their foundation and rationale to serve as the force which gives the conscience its legitimacy. . . . Humanity and the nation, civilization and morality, need women on their side.

Document 9

Source: The Unification of Germany, 1871.

◼	Prussia, 1862
◼	United in 1866–1867 with Prussia as North German Confederation
◼	South German Confederation
◻	Annexed in 1871 after Franco-Prussian War

Document 10

Source: Victor Emmanuel II, king of Italy, address to parliament, 1871.

Senators and Deputies, gentlemen:

The work to which we consecrated our life is accomplished. After long trials of expansion Italy is restored to herself and to Rome. Here, where our people, after centuries of separation, find themselves for the fist time solemnly reunited in the person of their representatives; here where we recognize the fatherland of our dreams, everything speaks to us of greatness; but at the same time it all reminds us of our duties. The joy that we experience must not let us forget them. . . .

We have proclaimed the separation of church and state. Having recognized the absolute independence of the spiritual authority, we are convinced that Rome, the capital of Italy, will continue to be the peaceful and respected seat of the Pontificate.

Document 11

Source: Otto von Bismarck, German chancellor, speech to the Reichstag, 1888.

If we Germans wish to wage a war with the full effect of our national strength, it must be a war which is approved by all who take part in it, all who sacrifice anything for it; in short, the whole nation. It must be a national war, a war carried on with the enthusiasm of 1870, when we were foully attacked.

Document 12

Source: Konstantin Pobedonostsev, Russian, expresses his thoughts about Count Sergei Witte's interest in Russia's westernization, memoirs, 1898.

This universal aspiration for a share in government has no constant limitations, and seeks no definite issue, but incessantly extends. . . . Forever extending its base, the new democracy now aspires to universal suffrage—a fatal error, and one of the most remarkable in the history of mankind.

DBQ 10: Rise of Mass Consumerism in Western Europe (Chapter 23)

Question: Evaluate the causes of and reactions to increased consumerism in western Europe in the nineteenth and twentieth centuries.

Document 1

Source: Sophie von la Roche, German writer, thoughts on London's fashionable shops, c. 1780s.

Behind great glass windows all absolutely one can think of is neatly, attractively displayed, and in such abundance of choice as almost to make one greedy.

Document 2

Source: Karl Marx, German socialist philosopher, "The Alienation of Labor," from *Economic and Philosophic Manuscripts of 1844.*

[W]e have shown that the laborer sinks to the level of a commodity and indeed becomes the most miserable commodity possible, that the misery of the laborer stands in an inverse relationship to the power and size of his production, that the natural result of competition is the accumulation of capital in a few hands, which is the most frightening type of monopoly . . . and the entire society must fall into two classes: those with property and those propertyless souls who labor.

Document 3

Source: Queen Victoria, queen of England, diary entry on the opening of the Great 1851 Exhibition, London.

This day is one of the greatest and most glorious days of our lives, with which to my pride and joy the name of my dearly beloved Albert is forever associated! . . . The Park presented a wonderful spectacle, crowds streaming through it—carriages and troops passing, quite like the Coronation and for me the same anxiety. . . .
I never saw Hyde Park look as it did, being filled with crowds as far as the eye could reach. A little rain fell, just as we started; but before we neared the Crystal Palace, the sun shone and gleamed upon the gigantic edifice, upon which the flags of every nation were flying. . . . In a few seconds we proceeded, Albert leading me, having Vicky at his hand and Bertie holding mine. The sight as we came to the centre where the steps and chair (on which I did not sit) was placed, facing the beautiful crystal fountain was magic and impressive. The tremendous cheering, the joy expressed in every face, the vastness of the building, with all its decorations and exhibits, the sound of the organ (with 200 instruments and 600 voices, which seemed nothing) and my beloved husband, the creator of this great "Peace Festival" uniting the industry and art of all nations of the earth, all this, was indeed moving, and a day to live forever.

Document 4

Source: Le Bon Marché, Paris, one of the first department stores in Europe, 1867.

Bibliothèque des Arts Decoratifs, Paris/© Archives Charmet/The Bridgeman Art Library International

Document 5

Source: Henrietta Thornhill, British, personal diary entries, 1876.

Mrs. Halsted and I had a shopping excursion. We trained & omnibussed & cabbed it to the stores. . . .
[We] went off to Victoria shopping [in the] stores. . . . We had a time of it . . . I went out about 11:30. . . .
Walked up Regent Street. Walked to the end of the shops. Came down St James' Park to Victoria. In fact
walked to Vauxhall . . . could not find what I wanted.

Document 6

Source: Gustav Stresemann, German, writing in an academic journal about department stores, c. 1900.

The elegant wives from west Berlin or from Charlottenberg are to be found in the crowds, just as the wives
of the artisans or workers from North and the East, who at all times when they attend Wertheim put on
their best clothes.

Document 7

Source: E. Suchsland, German, academic and public speaker, 1905.

These great bazaars and chain stores lure the customer into buying and stealing those masses of goods
which are so enticingly arranged; they have made many a vain and over-dressed woman a thief.

Document 8

Source: Émile Levasseur, French economist, *On Parisian Department Stores,* 1907.

These stores have increased in number and several of them have become extremely large. Combining in their different departments all articles of clothing, toilet articles, furniture and many other ranges of goods, it is their special object so to combine all commodities as to attract and satisfy customers who will find conveniently together an assortment of a mass of articles corresponding to all their various needs. They attract customers by permanent display, by free entry into the shops, by periodic exhibitions, by special sales, by fixed prices, and by their ability to deliver the goods purchased to customers' homes, in Paris and to the provinces. Turning themselves into direct intermediaries between the producer and the consumer, even producing sometimes some of their articles in their own workshops, buying at lowest prices because of their large orders and because they are in a position to profit from bargains, working with large sums, and selling to most of their customers for cash only, they can transmit these benefits in lowered selling prices.

Document 9

Source: Leo Colze, German writer, 1908.

At every spot where department store palaces have emerged, an exceedingly lively commerce has developed as a matter of course. Wisely cognizant of [the inherent potential of] the growing commercial traffic, specialty shops of all kinds have arisen, thereby disproving the old wives' tale that department stores have a destructive impact on such shops. With their modern facades, they incorporate, in both form and substance, the best elements of the department stores. . . . Small shopkeepers and firms that feel themselves too weak or insufficiently enterprising to keep up with the great department stores have left the area. New world class firms have taken their place, causing little harm to a local populace understandably long wont to demand the best. Here one breathes the air of a world class city.

Document 10

Source: Fashion plate showing Londoners walking in front of Harrods Department Store, London, 1909.

DBQ 11: Struggles of English Women to Gain the Vote (Chapter 24)

Question: Examine the various means that English women used in their attempt to gain political rights during the late nineteenth and early twentieth centuries, and evaluate the resistance that they faced.

Document 1

Source: Anti-Corn Law Circular, 1841.

The women of Manchester have set a noble example to their sisters throughout the country. They have already obtained more than 50,000 signatures to the memorial adopted at the Corn Exchange. The ladies of Bolton, Wigan, and Stockport are engaged in canvassing their respective towns.

Document 2

Source: John Stuart Mill, *The Subjection of Women*, 1869.

The general opinion of men is supposed to be, that the natural vocation of a woman is that of a wife and mother. I say, is supposed to be, because, judging from acts—from the whole of the present constitution of society—one might infer that their opinion was the direct contrary. They might be supposed to think that the alleged natural vocation of women was of all things the most repugnant to their nature; insomuch that if they are free to do anything else—if any other means of living, or occupation of their time and faculties, is open, which has any chance of appearing desirable to them—there will not be enough of them who will be willing to accept the condition said to be natural to them. If this is the real opinion of men in general, it would be well that it should be spoken out. I should like to hear somebody openly enunciating the doctrine (it is already implied in much that is written on the subject) —"It is necessary to society that women should marry and produce children. They will not do so unless they are compelled. Therefore it is necessary to compel them."

Document 3

Source: This Is the House That Man Built, London postcard, c. 1900.

© Mary Evans Picture Library/The Image Works

Document 4

Source: Edith Milner, letter to the editor of the London newspaper *The Times*, 1906.

Sir, I think the moment has come when the gentlewomen of England should protest against the proceedings of women to whom the prefix would be neither appropriate nor probably to their liking. I feel that I am voicing the sentiments of many hundreds of thousands when I say that I am satisfied with my present position, and of my almost unlimited power of usefulness, that I have no need of a solitary vote, and should not use it if I had it. The sexes are necessary to each other—"each has what the other lacks" as Ruskin so truly said; and I find that, when women undertake the duties for which men are constitutionally more fitted, if they perform them well they are still less fitted in some ways for those duties, while work which only women can perform is left undone.

Document 5

Source: Viscount Helmsley, speaking in the House of Commons, 1912.

[T]he way in which certain types of women, easily recognised, have acted in the last year or two, especially in the last few weeks, lends a great deal of colour to the argument that the mental equilibrium of the female sex is not as stable as the mental equilibrium of the male sex. . . . It seems to me that this House should remember that if the vote is given to women those who will take the greatest part in politics will not be the quiet, retiring, constitutional women . . . but those very militant women who have brought so much disgrace and discredit upon their sex. It would introduce a disastrous element into our public life. . . . One feels that it is not cricket for women to use force. . . . It is little short of nauseating and disgusting to the whole sex.

Document 6

Source: Suffragist protest after the failure of the Franchise Reform Bill, as described in the London newspaper *The Times*, 1913.

Nothing quite like it had been seen before in the precincts of Parliament. For six long, violent, sometimes brutal, hours there raged in Parliament Square what can only be described as a battle between the police and not the unemployed, the homeless or the destitute but middle- and upper-class women of all ages.

Document 7

Source: A suffragist being force-fed in prison after going on a hunger strike, 1912.

Document 8

Source: Emmeline Pankhurst, founder of the Women's Social and Political Union,
Why We Are Militant, 1913.

I know that in your minds there are questions like these; you are saying, "Woman Suffrage is sure to come . . . how is it that these militant women are using violence and upsetting the business arrangements of the country in their undue impatience to attain their end?" Let me try to explain to you the situation. Although we have a so-called democracy, and so-called representative government there, England is the most conservative country on earth. . . . If you had passed your life in England as I have, you would know that there are certain words which certainly, during the last two generations, certainly till about ten years ago, aroused a feeling of horror and fear in the minds of the mass of the people. The word revolution, for instance, was identified in England with all kind of horrible ideas. The idea of change, the idea of unsettling the established order of things was repugnant. . . . I believed, as many women still in England believe, that women could get their way in some mysterious manner, by purely peaceful methods. We have been so accustomed, we women, to accept one standard for men and another standard for women, that we have even applied that variation of standard to the injury of our political welfare. Having had better opportunities of education, and having had some training in politics, having in political life come so near to the "superior" being as to see that he was not altogether such a fount of wisdom as they had supposed, that he had his human weaknesses as we had, the twentieth century women began to say to themselves, "Is it not time, since our methods have failed and the men's have succeeded, that we should take a leaf out of their political book?"

Document 9

Source: Millicent Fawcett, president of the National Union of Women's Suffrage Societies, attacks Pankhurst's militants in their weekly periodical, *Common Cause,* 1913.

Every sincere suffragist shares the indignation which inspires the militant societies. But their means are disastrously ill adapted to attain the end. Our problem is, and has always been, to win, to arouse and to organise public opinion. It is today on our side. . . . What the militants apparently propose to do is to make war deliberately upon the public, to injure, alarm, and exasperate where we need countenance and support. The only consequence will be once more to make the suffrage movement unpopular, and to convince the Government that so far as the electors are concerned it may safely leave our grievances unredressed.

Document 10

Source: Derby Day, 1914, England. Suffragist Emily Davison, wearing a suffrage banner, commits suicide by throwing herself in front of the king's horse.

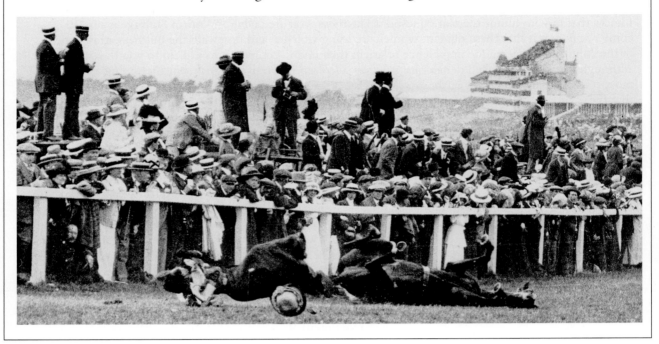

© Arthur Barrett/Getty Images

Document 11

Source: Lord Curzon, president of the National League for Opposing Women's Suffrage, in a speech in the Albert Hall, 1914.

The Anti-Suffrage cause stands in a stronger position at the present moment in all parts of the United Kingdom than it has done at any time during the past twenty years. This has been due, perhaps, in the main to the errors of our opponents, for which in passing let me give them a hearty vote of thanks. . . . I think we may say that the cause of the women's vote is absolutely dead in the present House of Commons.

DBQ 12: Uses of Propaganda During World War I (Chapter 25)

Question: Analyze the uses to which government propaganda was put in World War I.

Document 1

Source: Defense of the Realm Act, Great Britain, 1914.

1) His Majesty in Council has power during the continuance of the present war to issue regulations for securing the public safety and the defense of the realm . . . and may authorize the trial . . . and punishment of persons committing offenses . . . against any of the provisions of such regulations designed—

(a) to prevent persons communicating with the enemy or obtaining information for that purpose or any purpose calculated to jeopardize the success of the operations of any of his Majesty's forces or the forces of his Allies, or to assist the enemy; or . . .

(c) to prevent the spread of false reports or reports likely to cause disaffection to his Majesty or to interfere with the success of his Majesty's forces by land or sea or to prejudice his Majesty's relations with foreign powers.

Document 2

Source: Emperor William II of Germany, public speech, 1914.

A momentous hour has struck for Germany. Envious rivals everywhere force us to legitimate defense. The sword has been forced into our hand. I hope that, if my endeavours up to the very last moment should not succeed in bringing the adversaries to reason and in preserving peace, we may wield the sword, with God's help, so that we may sheathe it again with honor. War would demand enormous sacrifices from the German people, but we would show the enemy what it means to attack Germany. And so I commend you to God. Go now into the churches, kneel before God and implore His help for our brave army.

Document 3

Source: "Truth About Germany," a letter sent to the *New York Times* from a German citizen, 1914.

Try to realize, every one of you, what we are going through! Only a few weeks ago all of us were peacefully following our several vocations. The peasant was gathering in this summer's plentiful crop, the factory hand was working with accustomed vigor. Not one human being among us dreamed of war. We are a nation that wishes to lead a quiet and industrious life. This need hardly be stated to you Americans. You, of all others, know the temper of the German who lives within your gates. Our love of peace is so strong that it is not regarded by us in the light of a virtue; we simply know it to be an inborn and integral portion of ourselves. Since the foundation of the German Empire in the year 1871, we, living in the centre of Europe, have given an example of tranquility and peace, never once seeking to profit by any momentary difficulties of our neighbors. Our commercial extension, our financial rise in the world, is far removed from any love of adventure, it is the fruit of painstaking and plodding labor. We are not credited with this temper, because we are insufficiently known. Our situation and our way of thinking are not easily grasped.

Document 4

Source: George Coppard, British, *With a Machine Gun to Cambrai*, diary account of his war experiences from 1914 to 1916.

I feel I must mention a piece of psychological propaganda, put about by some War Office person, which brought poor comfort to Tommies. The story swept the world and, being gullible, we in the trenches were taken in by it for a while. With slight variations it indicated that the German war industry was in a bad way, and was short of fats for making glycerin. To overcome the shortage a vast secret factory had been erected in the Black Forest, to which the bodies of dead British soldiers were dispatched. The bodies, wired together in bundles, were pitch forked on to conveyor belts and moved into the factory for conversion into fats. War artists got busy, and dreadful scenes were depicted and published in Britain.

Document 5

Source: French war poster, "Sow Potatoes for the Soldiers and for France," 1915.

Document 6

Source: British recruiting poster, 1916.

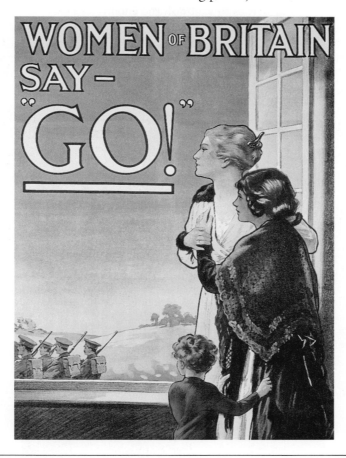

Document 7

Source: Russian war poster, "Whosoever subscribes to war bonds at 5.5% is helping our heroes to vanquish the enemy," 1916.

© The Art Archive/Musée des 2 Guerres Mondiales, Paris/Gianni Dagli Orti

Document 8

Source: British leaflet that was dropped into German trenches, 1917.

They tell you that you are fighting for the Fatherland. Have you ever thought why you are fighting? . . . They promise you victory and peace. You poor fools! It was promised your comrades for more than three years. They have indeed found peace, deep in the grave, but victory did not come! . . . An army of ten million is being prepared; soon it will come into battle. Have you thought of that, Michel*?

*Michel was the name often used to personify the national character of the German people.

Document 9

Source: Paul Nash, British war artist, complaining about what he could not draw, 1917.

I am not allowed to put dead men into my pictures because apparently they don't exist.

Document 10

Source: Vladimir Lenin, Russian revolutionary, "The *April Theses*,"
published in the newspaper *Pravda*, 1917.

[I]t is necessary . . . to explain the inseparable connection existing between capital and the imperialist war, and to prove that without overthrowing capital *it is impossible* to end the war by a truly democratic peace, a peace not imposed by violence.

　The most widespread propaganda of this view in the army on active service must be organized. . . .

　Abolition of the police, the army and the bureaucracy [i.e., the standing army to be replaced by the arming of the whole people].

　The salaries of all officials, all of whom are to be elected and to be subject to recall at any time, not to exceed the average wage of a competent worker.

　6. In the agrarian program the most important part to be assigned to the Soviets of Agricultural Labourers' Deputies.

　Confiscation of all landed estates.

　Nationalization of *all* lands in the country, the disposal of the land to be put in the charge of the local Soviets of Agricultural Labourers' and Peasants' Deputies. The organization of separate Soviets of Deputies of Poor Peasants. The creation of model farms on each of the large estates . . . under the control of the Soviets of Agricultural Labourers' Deputies and for the public account.

　7. The immediate amalgamation of all banks in the country into a single national bank, and the institution of control over it by the Soviets of Workers' Deputies.

　8. It is not our *immediate* task to "introduce" socialism, but only to bring social production and distribution of products at once under the *control* of the Soviets of Workers' Deputies.

Document 11

Source: Erich Ludendorff, chief aide to German Chancellor Paul von Hindenburg, 1917.

The war has demonstrated the paramount power of images and of film as means of enlightenment and influence. Unfortunately our enemies have used the advantages that they enjoy in that area so thoroughly that they have caused us great damage. . . . For the war to be concluded successfully, it is absolutely imperative that film be employed with the greatest force in all places where German influence is still possible.

DBQ 13: Responses to the Crises of the Early Twentieth Century (Chapters 26 and 27)

Question: Explain and analyze the responses to the crises of the early twentieth century.

Document 1

Source: Casualties of World War I, 1918.

COUNTRY	MILITARY DEATHS (ALL CAUSES)	MILITARY WOUNDED
Britain	722,785	1,662,625
France	1,322,100	4,266,000
Belgium	45,500	78, 624
Italy	680,000	947,000
Russia	1,850,000	4,950,000
United States	213,799	234,300
Germany	1,808,555	4,248,158
Austria-Hungary	1,496,200	3,620,000
Turkey	600,000	1,565,000
Bulgaria	101,224	155,026

Document 2

Source: Treaty of Versailles, Article 231, 1919.

The Allied and Associated Governments affirm, and Germany accepts, the responsibility of Germany and her allies for causing all the loss and damage to which the Allied and Associated Governments and their nationals have been subjected as a consequence of the war imposed upon them by the aggression of Germany and her allies.

Document 3

Source: Estimated German Unemployment, 1900–1940.

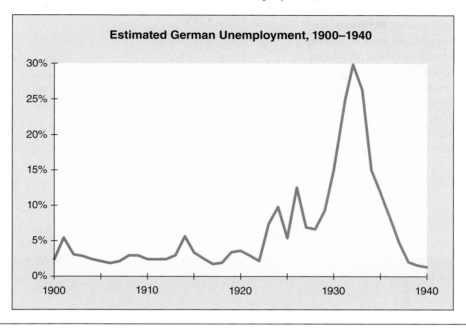

Author's estimate of German Unemployment, 1900–1940

Document 4

Source: Oswald Spengler, German philosopher and historian, *The Decline of the West*, 1922.

The idealist of the early democracy regarded popular education as enlightenment pure and simple—but it is precisely this that smooths the path for the coming Caesars of the world. The last century [the nineteenth] was the winter of the West, the victory of materialism and skepticism, of socialism, parliamentarianism, and money. But in this century blood and instinct will regain their rights against the power of money and intellect. The era of individualism, liberalism and democracy, of humanitarianism and freedom, is nearing its end. The masses will accept with resignation the victory of the *Caesars*, the strong men, and will obey them. Life will descend to a level of general uniformity, a new kind of primitivism, and the world will be better for it.

Document 5

Source: John Maynard Keynes, British economist, *The Economic Consequences of the Peace*, 1920.

This chapter must be one of pessimism. The Treaty includes no provisions for the economic rehabilitation of Europe—nothing to make the defeated Central Empires into good neighbors, nothing to stabilize the new States of Europe, nothing to reclaim Russia; nor does it promote in any way a compact of economic solidarity amongst the Allies themselves; no arrangement was reached at Paris for restoring the disordered finances of France and Italy, or to adjust the systems of the Old World and the New.

Document 6

Source: T. S. Eliot, British poet, *The Waste Land*, 1922.

In this decayed hole among the mountains
In the faint moonlight, the grass is singing
Over the tumbled graves, about the chapel
There is the empty chapel, only the wind's home.
It has no windows, and the door swings,
Dry bones can harm no one.
Only a cock stood on the rooftree
Co co rico co co rico
In a flash of lightning. Then a damp gust
Bringing rain

Document 7

Source: Salvador Dalí, Spanish artist, *The Persistence of Memory*, 1931.

Document 8

Source: Benito Mussolini, Italian Fascist leader, article written for the *Italian Encyclopedia* on "The Political and Social Doctrine of Fascism," 1932.

The foundation of Fascism is the conception of the State, its character, its duty, and its aim. Fascism conceives of the State as an absolute, in comparison with which all individuals or groups are relative, only to be conceived of in their relation to the State. The conception of the Liberal State is not that of a directing force, guiding the play and development, both material and spiritual, of a collective body, but merely a force limited to the function of recording results: on the other hand, the Fascist State is itself conscious and has itself a will and a personality—thus it may be called the "ethic" State.

Document 9

Source: Karl Barth, Swiss Protestant theologian who lived in Germany until expelled in 1935, *Theological Declaration of Barmen, 1933.*

In view of the errors of the "German Christians" of the present Reich Church government which are devastating the Church and also therefore breaking up the unity of the German Evangelical Church, we confess the following evangelical truths: . . . .

5. "Fear God. Honor the emperor." (1 Peter 2:17.)

Scripture tells us that, in the as yet unredeemed world in which the Church also exists, the State has by divine appointment the task of providing for justice and peace. [It fulfills this task] by means of the threat and exercise of force, according to the measure of human judgment and human ability. The Church acknowledges the benefit of this divine appointment in gratitude and reverence before him. It calls to mind the Kingdom of God, God's commandment and righteousness, and thereby the responsibility both of rulers and of the ruled. It trusts and obeys the power of the Word by which God upholds all things.

We reject the false doctrine, as though the State, over and beyond its special commission, should and could become the single and totalitarian order of human life, thus fulfilling the Church's vocation as well.

We reject the false doctrine, as though the Church, over and beyond its special commission, should and could appropriate the characteristics, the tasks, and the dignity of the State, thus itself becoming an organ of the State.

Document 10

Source: Pablo Picasso, Spanish-born artist, *Guernica,* 1937.

DBQ 14: Soviet Perceptions of the West During the Cold War (Chapters 28 and 29)

Question: Evaluate the perception of the West and its impact on citizens of the Soviet Union during the Cold War.

Document 1

Source: Oleg Kalugin, Russian, describing his travels outside the Soviet Union, 1958.

As we walked through the airport [in Copenhagen], I was to experience a feeling I would have countless times on future trips abroad: the shock of leaving the gray, monochrome world of the Soviet Union and landing in a place virtually exploding with colors and sights. We spent a few hours in the Danish capital, overwhelmed by the almost clinical cleanliness, the beautiful shop windows, the sea of lights. . . .

For the first few weeks, I walked ceaselessly around Manhattan, overwhelmed by its power and beauty and bustle. I visited scores of neighborhoods and all the major museums. I saw ball games and went to the Metropolitan Opera. I rode buses and subways for hours, and saw more than one hundred films. I went to a strip club in Greenwich Village, shelling out $40 for a drink with one of the dancers. I even won election to the Columbia University Student Council, undoubtedly the first KGB officer—and, I suppose, the last—to serve on that body.

Document 2

Source: Donald Kendall, American executive, chairman and chief executive officer of PepsiCo (1971–1986), speaking of Nikita Khrushchev's experience at the American National Exhibition in Moscow, 1959.

After sampling both [the Pepsi brought from the United States and the Pepsi made in Russia], he [Khrushchev] turned to the trailing throng of dignitaries and reporters and advised: "Drink the Pepsi-Cola made in Moscow. It's much better than the Pepsi made in the U.S." Before moving on, he would drink at least a half-dozen cups of Pepsi. He even handed some out to others. That meeting of East and West intrigued the news reporters and photographers nearby. The next day, foreign newspapers carried a picture of the cola-quaffing leader with a caption inspired by our advertising theme ("Be Sociable, Have a Pepsi") at the time: "Khrushchev learns to be sociable."

Document 3

Source: The Great Kitchen Debate, U.S. Vice President Richard Nixon and Soviet Premier Nikita Khrushchev, Moscow, 1959.

AP Images

Document 4

Source: Galina Ulanova, Russian ballerina, star of the Bolshoi Ballet, describing her thoughts after her first visit to the United States, 1959.

America was for us simply another planet. We knew so little about the outside world, and we were just amazed by the scale of the country. All those huge stores five and six floors high, with all these clothes on sale, and entire apartments on display—we just didn't have anything like that.

Document 5

Source: *Pravda* newspaper article, commenting on the American National Exhibition in Moscow, 1959.

"Where is the technology? Where are the achievements of American science?" the visitors asked the guides. The chilled Pepsi-Cola that is served to the visitors certainly cannot satisfy their thirst for knowledge about U.S. technical achievements. The visitor has an uncomfortable sense of disillusionment.

Document 6

Source: Vasily Aksyonov, Russian, writing about *dzhaz* (jazz), a Western import that Soviet conservatives tried to outlaw but eventually came to accept, 1960s.

Why did we love it so? Perhaps for the same reason the Communists (and the Nazis before them) hated it. For its refusal to be pinned down, its improvisatory nature. Living as we did in a totalitarian society, we needed relief from the strictures of our minutely controlled everyday lives, of the five-year plans, of historical materialism. In Eastern Europe, jazz became more than music; it took on an ideology or, rather an anti-ideology. Jazz was a rendezvous with freedom.

Document 7

Source: Pavel Palazchenko, Russian, Mikhail Gorbachev's future English-language interpreter, speaking of the Beatles and rock and roll, 1960s.

I am sure that the impact of the Beatles on the generation of young Soviets in the 1960s will one day be the object of studies. We knew their songs by heart. . . . In the dusky years of the Brezhnev regime they were not only a source of musical relief. They helped us create a world of our own, a world different from the dull and senseless ideological liturgy that increasingly reminded one of Stalinism. . . . [T]he Beatles were our quiet way of rejecting "the system" while conforming to most of its demands.

Document 8

Source: Sergei Boukhonine, Ukrainian, describing his childhood in Ukraine in the 1980s, "Blue Jeans, Boomboxes, and Rock-n-Roll."

When I was a college student, we put our money together and bought vinyl discs (LPs) on the black market. We then copied them to tapes and cassettes; then we traded our LPs for new ones. Ultimately, one disc could generate hundreds or thousands of copies. . . . Soviet consumer electronics were always so much behind the times! . . . For the Soviet people, boomboxes were another example of how glorious the West was—all the best, sleekest, and loudest came from there after all! One of the happiest days of my life was when my parents finally got me a foreign boombox in 1986.

Document 9

Source: Coca-Cola Company press release, 1986.

The Coca-Cola Company and officials of the Soviet Ministry of Foreign Trade announced today that a new, long-term trade agreement has been signed for a major expansion of The Coca-Cola Company's business in the Soviet Union. The company's activities in the U.S.S.R. began in 1979 with the bottling of Fanta orange in Moscow, Kiev, Tallin and other cities. Coca-Cola has been sold in the Soviet Union through shops which serve tourists and the international community since 1985. This business now will be expanded to include the bottling of Coca-Cola in the U.S.S.R. and the sale of Coca-Cola and Fanta to Soviet consumers.

Document 10

Source: Opening of McDonald's in Pushkin Square, Moscow, Soviet Union, 1990.

© Reuters/CORBIS

DBQ 15: Arguments For and Against the Creation of a Unified Europe (Chapter 30)

Question: Analyze the reasons for the changes and continuities in the arguments for and against the creation of a unified Europe.

Historical Background

Maps showing the progressive unification of Europe from the European Economic Community in 1958 to the present European Union.

After map and data © 2010 The Press and Information Office of the Federal Government of Germany

Document 1

Source: Jean Monnet, conceiver of the idea of the European Community, speaking to the National Liberation Committee in France, 1948.

There will be no peace in Europe if the States rebuild themselves on the basis of national sovereignty, with its implications of prestige politics and economic protection. . . . . The countries of Europe are not strong enough individually to be able to guarantee prosperity and social development for their peoples. The States of Europe must therefore form a federation or a European entity that would make them into a common economic unit.

Document 2

Source: Robert Schuman, French foreign minister, The Schuman Declaration, May 9, 1950.

Europe will not be made all at once, or according to a single plan. It will be built through concrete achievements which first create a *de facto* solidarity. The coming together of the nations of Europe requires the elimination of the age-old opposition of France and Germany. Any action taken must in the first place concern these two countries. With this aim in view, the French Government proposes that action be taken immediately on one limited but decisive point. It proposes that Franco-German production of coal and steel as a whole be placed under a common High Authority, within the framework of an organization open to the participation of the other countries of Europe.

The pooling of coal and steel production should immediately provide for the setting up of common foundations for economic development as a first step in the federation of Europe, and will change the destinies of those regions which have long been devoted to the manufacture of munitions of war, of which they have been the most constant victims.

Document 3

Source: Konrad Adenauer, chancellor of the Federal Republic of Germany (West Germany), 1952.

After the smashing of the totalitarian idols and after the sufferings of the war, the German people were left standing on the edge of an abyss. The catastrophe made the German people realize that in the past, peace had again and again been wrecked on the rocks of an exaggerated nationalism. This led to recognition that our existence, as well as that of all the other European nations, could be preserved only within a community transcending national frontiers.

Inspired by this conception, the Federal Republic has co-operated most readily in the preparation of two treaties. . . . I am referring to the treaty on the European coal and steel community and to the treaty on the European defense community.

Document 4

Source: Nikita Khrushchev, Soviet premier, article written for *The Kommunist,* 1962.

The Common Market provides tremendous benefits to the capitalist monopolies. . . . Small countries are becoming more and more dependent on their imperialist allies, and the aggressive forces are trying to exploit the Common Market for the strengthening of NATO and the pursuit of the armament race.

Document 5

Source: Campaign leaflets published during the referendum on whether Great Britain should become a member of the European Economic Community, 1975.

Why You Should Vote Yes

It makes good sense for our jobs and prosperity. It makes good sense for world peace. It makes good sense for the Commonwealth. It makes good sense for our children's future. Being in does not in itself solve our problems. No one pretends it could. It doesn't guarantee us a prosperous future. Only our own efforts will do that. But it offers the best framework for success, the best protection for our standard of living, the best foundation for greater prosperity. All the original six members have found that. They have done well—much better than we have—over the past 15 years. . . .

Why You Should Vote No

Your food, your jobs, our trade. We cannot afford to remain in the Common Market because: it must mean still higher food prices. Before we joined, we could buy our food at the lowest cost from the most efficient producers in the world. Since we joined, we are no longer allowed to buy all our food where it suits us best. Your jobs are at risk. If we stay in the Common Market, a British Government can no longer prevent the drift of industry southwards and increasingly to the Continent. The Common Market's dear food policy is designed to prop up inefficient farmers on the Continent by keeping food prices high. We are being forced to tax imported Commonwealth goods. The real aim of the Market is, of course, to become one single country in which Britain would be reduced to a mere province.

Document 6

Source: Margaret Thatcher, British prime minister, in a speech reacting to the Single European Act, 1988.

To try to suppress nationhood and concentrate power at the centre of a European conglomerate would be highly damaging. . . . [W]e certainly do not need new regulations which raise the cost of employment and make Europe's labour market less flexible and less competitive with overseas suppliers. . . . And certainly we in Britain would fight attempts to introduce collectivism and corporatism at the European level—although what people wish to do in their own countries is a matter for them.

Document 7

Source: Maastricht Treaty, 1992.

Article 2 (ex Article B). The Union shall set itself the following objectives:

to promote economic and social progress and a high level of employment and to achieve balanced and sustainable development, in particular through the creation of an area without internal frontiers, through the strengthening of economic and social cohesion and through the establishment of economic and monetary union, ultimately including a single currency in accordance with the provisions of this Treaty;

to assert its identity on the international scene, in particular through the implementation of a common foreign and security policy including the progressive framing of a common defence policy.

Document 8

Source: European Union in 2004, countries using the euro currency noted in orange; those not using the euro noted in green.

© European Union, 2010

Document 9

Source: Leon of Rotterdam, the Netherlands, a window cleaner who did not want his last name revealed, 2003.

There are too many people coming here who don't want to work. Before long there will be more foreigners than Dutch people, and Dutch people won't be the boss of their own country. That's why this has to be stopped.

Document 10

Source: Geert Wilders, member of the Dutch parliament, 2004.

Turkey is an Islamic country and so such doesn't belong in the EU. The flow [of Turks] is already too big. . . . There is a big problem with the integration of immigrants already in Holland. They top the list in terms of criminality, unemployment, welfare payments, and domestic violence. . . . Let us concentrate on solving the problems with the immigrants already here properly.

Document 11

Source: Yuri Andrukhovyh, Ukrainian writer, 2006.

In December 2004, in that miraculous moment between the completion of our Orange Revolution and the repeated round of presidential elections, I was offered the opportunity to address the members of the European Parliament in Strasbourg. The essence of my speech was a plea to the parliament and the European community at large to help a certain cursed country save itself. I told them roughly what I was hoping to hear: that Europe was waiting for us, that it couldn't do without us, that Europe would not be able to realize itself fully without Ukraine. Now it is finally clear that I was asking for too much.

CREDITS

DBQ 1

1: Christine de Pisan, *Treasure of the City of Ladies.* Translated by Sarah Lawson. Penguin Classics. 1985. The Western Heritage. Seventh edition. Page 325.   **2:** *The Humanism of Leonardo Bruni, Selected Texts,* trans. and intro. Gordon Griffiths, James Hankins, and David Thompson (Binghamton: Medieval and Renaissance Texts and Studies, 1987), 240–51.   **3:** Margaret Ann Franklin, *Boccaccio's Heroines: Power and Virtue in Renaissance Society.* Page 80. Ashgate Publishing. 2006. **5:** From *The Society of Renaissance Florence,* edited by Gene Brucker. Copyright © 1971 by Gene Brucker.   **6:** Barbara K. Gold, Paul Allen Miller, and Charles Platter. *Sex and Gender in Medieval and Renaissance Texts: The Latin Tradition* (State University of New York Press, 1997), 176.   **7:** From *The Renaissance Philosophy of Man* by Ernst Cassirer, Paul Kristeller, and John Randall, Jr. Copyright © 1948 by University of Chicago Press.   **8:** James Brophy, Steven Epstein, Cat Nilan, John Robertson, and Thomas Max Safley. *Perspectives from the Past,* Vol. 2. Norton Publishing. 2002. **10:** From *The Prince* by Niccolò Machiavelli, translated by W. K. Marriott. J. M. Dent and Co., London, E. P. Dutton, New York, 1908.   **11:** Vicki Leon, *Uppity Women of Medieval Times* (Red Wheel/Weiser, 1997), p. 108.

DBQ 2

1: Thomas More's Feminism: To Reform or Re-Form, by Judith P. Jones and Sherianne Sellers Seibel. *Albion: A Quarterly Journal Concerned with British Studies.* 1978. The North American Conference on British Studies.   **2:** Martin Luther. Exhortation to the Knights of the Teutonic Order That They Lay Aside False Chastity and Assume the True Chastity of Wedlock. 1523. Witherspoon Lecture: A Revolutionary Theology on Sex: Martin Luther on Sex, Marriage, and Family. July 2, 2004. Family Research Council.   **3:** From *Not in God's Image: Women in History from the Greeks to Victorians* by Julia O'Faolain and Lauro Martines. Copyright © 1973 by Julia O'Faolain and Lauro Martines.   **4:** Wes Harrison. *The Sixteenth Century Journal.* The Role of Women in Anabaptist Thought and Practice: The Hutterite Experience of the Sixteenth and Seventeenth Centuries. 1992. *The Sixteenth Century Journal.*   **5:** Cky J. Carrigan. Calvin on Gender Equality. 1991. On Truth, A Ministry of Dr. Cky J. Carrigan.   **7:** C. Warren Hollister, see page 117 sources: "Marguerite of Navarre, Jeanne d'Albret, and French Reform," in *The West Transformed.* Published by Harcourt Brace. Fort Worth, 2000.   **8:** *The Book of Common Prayer of the Episcopal Church in the United States of America* (1979).   **9:** Katharina M. Wilson and Frank J. Warnke (eds.), *Women Writers of the Seventeenth Century* (Athens: University of Georgia Press, 1989). **10:** *Renaissance Woman: A Sourcebook: Constructions of Femininity in England.* Edited by Kate Aughterson. 1995. Routledge.

DBQ 3

1: *European Treaties Bearing on the History of the United States and Its Dependencies to 1648,* Frances Gardiner Davenport, editor, Carnegie Institution of Washington, 1917, Washington, D.C., at pp. 20–26.   **2:** www.fordham.edu/halsall/source/columbus1.html **3:** "The Spanish Struggle for Justice in the Conquest of America" by Lewis Hanke © 1949, Little Brown and Company.   **4:** *Broken Spears: The Aztec Account of the Conquest of Mexico,* by Miguel León-Portilla, Beacon Press, 1992, p. 122. **6:** HISTORY OF THE INDIES by Bartolome De Las Casas. Harper Torchbooks, NY, 1971, pp. 192–93 (Book Three, section 57).   **7:** *The Discovery and Conquest of Peru: Chronicles of the New World Encounter,* by Pedro de Cieza de León, eds. Alexandra Parma Cook and Noble David Cook. Duke University Press, 1998, pp. 75–76.   **8:** Paul Brians, et al. *Reading About the World,* Vol. 2, 3rd edition, Harcourt Brace College Publishing, ISBN 0-15-512826-4.

DBQ 4

1: *Readings in European History,* James Harvey Robinson, ed. and trans., Vol. 2 (Boston: Ginn and Company, 1906), p. 204. **2:** *Readings in European History,* James Harvey Robinson, ed. and trans., Vol. 2 (Boston: Ginn and Company, 1906), p. 201. **4:** *Readings in European History,* James Harvey Robinson, ed. and trans., Vol. 2 (Boston: Ginn and Company, 1906), p. 207. **5:** *Hispanic Anthology: Poems Translated from the Spanish by English and North American Poets,* collected and arranged by Thomas Walsh. G. P. Putnam's Sons, New York, 1920. **6:** *Readings in European History,* James Harvey Robinson, ed. and trans., Vol. 2 (Boston: Ginn and Company, 1906), pp. 211–212.   **7:** *Dalibray, Le Pailleur, and the "New Astronomy" in French Seventeenth-Century Poetry,* by Beverly S. Ridgely © 1956 University of Pennsylvania Press.   **8:** The Treaty of Westphalia, 1648.   **9:** *Readings in European History,* James Harvey. Robinson, ed. and trans., Vol. 2 (Boston: Ginn and Company, 1906), pp. 214–215.   **11:** *Sonnets of Andreas Gryphius: Use of the Poetic Word in the Seventeenth Century,* Marvin S. Schindler, University Press of Florida; 1ST edition (March 1989).

DBQ 5

2: Prefaces and Prologues. Vol. XXXIX. The Harvard Classics. New York: P. F. Collier & Son, 1909–14; Bartleby.com, 2001. www.bartleby.com/39/   **3:** Thomas Kuhn, *The Copernican*

Revolution, Cambridge, Massachusetts, Harvard University Press, 1957, p. 191. **4:** John Calvin, *Commentary on Genesis—Volume I*, Grand Rapids, MI: Christian Classics Ethereal Library, 1996, p. 41. **5:** Michael White, *The Pope and the Heretic: The True Story of Giordano Bruno, the Man Who Dared to Defy the Roman Inquisition*, HarperCollins, 2003. Page 72. **6:** Robert Bellarmine, Letter to Paolo Foscarini, 1615. From *Galileo, Science, and the Church*, by Jerome J. Langford (New York: Desclee, 1966). **7:** Samuel Smith, *The Claims of Rome*, London: Oxford University. 1897, p. 65. **8:** Pope Alexander VII, Index of Prohibited Books, 1664.

DBQ 6

2: John Locke. *Two Treatises on Government.* www.fordham.edu/halsall/mod/1690locke-sel.html **3:** Baron de Montesquieu. *The Spirit of the Laws.* vol. 1, trans. Thomas Nugent. London: J. Nourse. 1777, pp. 221–237. **4:** David Hume, *Essays: Moral, Political and Literary*, ed. Eugene F. Miller. Indianapolis: Liberty Fund. 1985, pp. 80–86. **5:** Jean-Jacques Rousseau. *The Social Contract*, trans. Maurice Cranston (Penguin Classics; Modern Reprint edition, 1968), p. 55. **6:** *A Source Book for Russian History*, G. Vernadsky trans. (New Haven: Yale University Press, 1972), Vol. 2, pp. 453–454. **7:** *French and English Philosophers: Descartes, Rousseau, Voltaire, Hobbes: With Introduction, Notes, and Illustrations.* New York: P. F. Collier, © 1910. Series: The Harvard Classics. Vol. 34. **8:** Fordham. *The Foundations of Germany.* J. Ellis Barker trans. New York: E. P. Dutton. 1916. pp. 22–23. **9:** C. A. Macartney, ed. *The Habsburg and Hohenzollern Dynasties in the Seventeenth and Eighteenth Centuries. Documentary History of Western Civilization.* New York, Evanston, and London: Harper & Row. 1970, p. 177. Introduction, editorial notes, chronology, translations by the editor; and compilation copyright © 1970 by C. A. Macartney.

DBQ 7

1: Arthur Young, *Travels During the Years 1787, 1788 and 1789* (London: Printed for W. Richardson, 1792), pp. 533–540. **2:** Pierre Goubert and Michel Denis, *1789: Les Français ont la parole* (Paris: Juillard, 1964), 72–73. **3:** Declaration of the Rights of Man and the Citizen. From *The French Revolution* by Paul H. Beik. Copyright © 1970 by Paul H. Beik. **5:** From *Women in Revolutionary Paris, 1789–1795: Selected Documents Translated with Notes and Commentary.* Translated with notes and commentary by Darline Gay Levy, Harriet Branson Applewhite, and Mary Durham Johnson. Copyright 1979 by the Board of Trustees of the University of Illinois. **6:** From Emmanuel Joseph Sieyès, *What Is the Third Estate?* Trans. M. Blondel (1964), Praeger and Phaidon Press Limited. **8:** From *The Press in the French Revolution: A Selection of Documents Taken from the Press of the Revolution for the Years 1789–1794*, J. Gilchrist and W. J. Murray, eds. (London: Ginn, 1971). **10:** From *Women in Revolutionary Paris, 1789–1795: Selected Documents Translated with Notes and Commentary.* Translated with notes and commentary by Darline Gay Levy, Harriet Branson Applewhite, and Mary Durham Johnson. Copyright 1979 by the Board of Trustees of the University of Illinois. Pp. 18–19.

DBQ 8

1: William Blake, *Blake's Selected Poems.* Selected by David Erdman and Virginia Erdman. Courier Dover Publications, 1995,

page 68. **2:** David Ricardo and F. W. Kolthammer, *The Principles of Political Economy and Taxation.* Courier Dover Publications, 2004, page 57. **3:** Charles Wing, *Evils of the Factory System: Demonstrated by Parliamentary Evidence.* Routledge, 1967, p. 41. **4:** *Statutes of the Realm, 3 & 4 William IV*, c. 103 (William IV of the United Kingdom, 1765–1837). **5:** Andrew Ure, *The Philosophy of Manufactures*, Charles Knight: London, p. 30. **6:** Edward Baines, *History of the Cotton Manufacture in Great Britain*, Oxford University, H. Fisher, R. Fisher, and P. Jackson, 1835, p. 88. **8:** Edwin Chadwick and Michael Walter Flinn, *Report on the sanitary condition of the labouring population of Gt. Britain.* University Press, 1965, p. 23. **9:** James M. Brophy. *Perspectives from the Past.* Page 472. Norton Publishing 2002. **10:** Friedrich Engels and Florence Kelley, *The Condition of the Working Class in England in 1844*, S. Sonnenschein & Co., 1892, pp. 48, 50–51.

DBQ 9

1: Rachel Gibbons, *Exploring History, 1400–1900: An Anthology of Primary Sources*, Manchester University Press, 2006, p. 373. **3:** Colum, Padraic, ed. *Anthology of Irish Verse.* New York: Boni and Liveright, 1922, p. 223. **4:** Georg Friedrich List, *National System of Political Economy*, translated by G. A. Matile, Oxford University, 1856, p. 72. **5:** Bonnie Smith, *Changing Lives: Women in European History since 1700.* Published by D. C Heath and Company, 1989, p. 240. **6:** Bonnie Smith, *Changing Lives: Women in European History since 1700.* Published by D. C Heath and Company, 1989, p. 225. **8:** Bonnie Smith, *Changing Lives: Women in European History since 1700.* Published by D. C Heath and Company, 1989, p. 257. **10:** James Harvey Robinson and Charles Austin Beard, *Readings in Modern European History: Europe since the Congress of Vienna*, Boston: Ginn and Company, 1909, p. 134. **11:** Ellery Stowell, *The Diplomacy of the War of 1914*, Boston: Houghton Mifflin Company, 1915, p. 536. **12:** Edward Hodgetts, *The Court of Russia in the Nineteenth Century*, Volume 2, Publisher: Methuen, 1908, p. 243.

DBQ 10

1: Pamela Horn, *Behind the Counter* (Sutton, 2006), p. xx. **2:** Karl Marx, *Economic and Philosophic Manuscripts of 1844*, Progress Publishers, Moscow 1959. **3:** Christopher Hibbert, *Queen Victoria in Her Letters and Journals: A Selection*, Viking, 1985, p. 84. **5:** Henrietta Thornhill's diary entry for 14/01/1876, Lambeth archives, IV/81/13; Henrietta Thornhill's diary entry for 22/01/1876, Lambeth archives, IV/81/13; Henrietta Thornhill's diary entry for 06/06/1876, Lambeth archives, IV/81/13; Henrietta Thornhill's diary entry for 10/05/1879, Lambeth archives, IV/81/16. **6:** Coles, "Department stores as retail innovations in Germany: a historical-geographical perspective on the period 1870 to 1914," p. 797. **7:** Uwe Spiekermann, "Theft and thieves in German department stores, 1895–1930: a discourse on morality, crime and gender," in Crossick and Jaumain, *Cathedrals of Consumption: The European Department Store, 1850–1939*, p. 140. **8:** From *Documents of European Economic History*, Vol. I by Sidney Pollard and Colin Holmes. Copyright © Sidney Pollard and Colin Holmes, Palgrave Macmillan. **9:** Leo Colze, *Berliner Warenhäuser* [Berlin Department Stores]. Leipzig and Berlin, 1908, pp. 9–13.

DBQ 11

1: Helen Blackburn, *Women's Suffrage,* Williams & Norgate, 1902, p. 16.   **2:** John Stuart Mill, *The Subjection of Women,* New York: D. Appleton Co. 1869, pp. 48–52, 71–82, 177.   **4:** Constance Rover, *Women's Suffrage and Party Politics in Britain, 1866–1914,* Routledge & K. Paul, 1967, p. 173.   **5:** *Official Reports 5th Series Parliamentary Debates: Commons,* Vol. xxxvi (March 25–April 12, 1912), cols 615–732.   **6:** David Morgan. *Suffragists and Liberals: The Politics of Woman Suffrage in England.* Totowa: Rowman and Littlefield. 1975, p. 71.   **8:** Jane Marcus, *Women's Source Library,* Volume VIII: *Suffrage and the Pankhursts,* Routledge, 2002, pp. 153, 155.   **9:** www.history-ontheweb.co.uk/noticeboard/pdf_111_sourcesvotesforwomen.pdf   **11:** William Simpson, *Twentieth-Century British History,* Routledge, 2005, p. 93.

DBQ 12

1: *British Ruling Cases: From Courts of Great Britain, Canada, Ireland, Australia and Other Divisions of the British Empire,* extensively annotated, volume VII, The Lawyers Co-operative Publishing Company: Rochester, NY, 1918, pp. 727–728.   **2:** *The Times Documentary History of the War,* Volume II, Hodder and Stoughton: London, 1916, pp. 477–478.   **3:** *The New York Times Current History: The European War,* Volume I, The New York Times Company, 1917, p. 245.   **4:** George Coppard, *With a Machine Gun to Cambrai: The Tale of a Young Tommy in Kitchener's Army 1914–1918,* H.M.S.O., 1969, pp. 114–115.   **8:** Ian Cawood and David McKinnon-Bell, *The First World War,* Routledge, 2001, pp. 37–38.   **9:** Phillip Knightley, *The First Casualty: The War Correspondent as Hero and Myth-Maker from the Crimea to Iraq.* Johns Hopkins University Press, 2004, p. 105.   **10:** *A Documentary History of Communism in Russia.* Edited by Robert V. Daniels, University Press of New England, 1993, pp. 43–44.

DBQ 13

1: Spencer C. Tucker, ed., *The Encyclopedia of World War I,* ABC-CLIO, 2005, p. 273.   **2:** *Current History: A Monthly Magazine of The New York Times,* Volume X, April 1919–September 1919. The New York Times Company: New York City, 1919, p. 325.   **4:** Oswald Spengler, *The Decline of the West,* 2 vols., trans. Charles Francis Atkinson (New York: Alfred A. Knopf, 1922).   **5:** John Maynard Keynes, *The Economic Consequences of the Peace,* Harcourt, Brace and Howe: New York, 1920, p. 226.   **6:** T .S. Eliot, *The Waste Land, and Other Poems,* Houghton Mifflin Harcourt, 1962, pp. 44–45.   **8:** Raymond Phineas Stearns, *Pageant of Europe: Sources and Selections from the Renaissance to the Present Day,* Harcourt, Brace, 1947, p. 793.   **9:** *The Church's Confession Under Hitler* by Arthur C. Cochrane. Philadelphia: Westminster Press, 1962, pp. 237–242.

DBQ 14

1: Yale Richmond, *Cultural Exchange and the Cold War: Raising the Iron Curtain,* The Pennsylvania State University Press, 2004, pp. 32–33.   **2:** www.pepsico.com/Global-Sites/Russia/Donald_Kendall_Experience.html   **4:** Yale Richmond, *Cultural Exchange and the Cold War: Raising the Iron Curtain,* The Pennsylvania State University Press, 2004, p. 124.   **5:** *The Current Digest of the Soviet Press,* Volume 11, by the Joint Committee on Slavic Studies, American Council of Learned Societies, Social Science Research Council (U.S.), American Association for the Advancement of Slavic Studies, 1959, p. 7.   **6:** Yale Richmond, *Cultural Exchange and the Cold War: Raising the Iron Curtain,* The Pennsylvania State University Press, 2004, p. 206.   **7:** Pavel Palazchenko, *My Years with Gorbachev and Shevardnadze,* The Pennsylvania State University Press, 1997, p. 3.   **8:** www.lewrockwell.com/orig7/boukhonine3.html; written July 20, 2006.   **9:** COPYRIGHT 2009 PR Newswire Association LLC.

DBQ 15

1: Jerome R. Corsi, *The Late Great USA: The Coming Merger with Mexico and Canada,* Midpoint Trade Books Inc., 2007, pp. 2–3.   **2:** Europe—A Fresh Start: The Schuman Declaration, 1950–90, Office for Official Publications of the European Communities, 1990, p. 44.   **3:** *International Affairs,* Volume 28, The Royal Institute of International Affairs, 1952, p. 158.   **4:** *Soviet Studies,* Vol. 19, No. 3 (Jan. 1968), pp. 373–386. Published by Taylor & Francis, Ltd.   **5:** David Butler and Uwe W. Kitzinger, *The 1975 Referendum,* Macmillan, 1976, p. 291.   **6:** Ronald Tiersky, *Euro-skepticism: A Reader,* Rowman & Littlefield, 2001, pp. 106, 109.   **7:** John Ashley Soames Grenville, and Bernard Wasserstein, *The Major International Treaties of the Twentieth Century: A History and Guide with Texts,* Volume 1, 3rd edition, Taylor & Francis US, 2001, p. 563.   **9 and 10:** http://ec.europa.eu/publications/booklets/eu_documentation/05/txt_en.pdf   **11:** Yuri Andrukhovyh's acceptance speech for 2006's Leipzig Book Prize, posted online 19 APR 2006 http://neveryetmelted.com/2006/04/19/ukraine-and-the-european-union/